Webster's Concise Reference Library

Webster's
Concise
Reference
Library

Created in Cooperation
with the Editors of
MERRIAM-WEBSTER

SMITHMARK
REFERENCE

This edition published in 1996 by
SMITHMARK Publishers
a division of U.S. Media Holdings, Inc.
16 East 32nd Street
New York, NY 10016

SMITHMARK books are available for bulk purchase for sales promotion and premium use.
For details write or call the manager of special sales,
SMITHMARK Publishers,
16 East 32nd Street, New York, NY 10016.

Library of Congress Cataloging-in-Publication Data available on request.

Printed in the United States of America
10 9 8 7 6 5 4 3 2 1

Contents

Webster's Concise Dictionary

Preface

Webster's Concise Dictionary is a reference to those words which form the very core of the English vocabulary. This dictionary is one of the smallest of the family of dictionaries published by Merriam-Webster. It is intended to serve as a quick reference, especially for questions of spelling, pronunciation, and hyphenation of the most common words in everyday use.

This dictionary shares many details of presentation with the more comprehensive members of the Merriam-Webster family, such as *Merriam-Webster's Collegiate Dictionary, Tenth Edition*. However, conciseness of presentation necessarily requires special treatment of entries, and this book has a number of special features uniquely its own. Users need to be familiar with the following major features of this dictionary.

Main entries follow one another in alphabetical order. Centered periods within the entries show points at which a hyphen may be put when the word is broken at the end of a line.

Homographs (words spelled the same but having different meanings) are run in to a single main entry whey they are closely related. Second and succeeding homographs are represented by a swung dash. Homographs of distinctly different origin are given separate entries with preceding raised numerals.

Variant spellings that are quite common appear at the main entry following a comma (as **judg•ment, judge•ment**) and following other boldface entry words, such as inflected forms and run-entries.

Inflected forms of nouns, verbs, adjectives, and adverbs are shown when they are irregular as when requiring the dropping of a final *e* or changing a final *y* to *i* before the suffix (as **waged; waging** at **wage**) or when the form of the base word itself changes (as **rode...; rid•den** at **ride**) — or when there might be doubt about their spellings as (pl. **egos** at **ego**). They are given either in full (as **bet•ter; best** at **good**) or cut back to a convenient point of division (as **-ut•ed; ut•ing** at **dis•tri•bute**). Common variants of inflected forms are shown even if they are regular (as **burst** or **burst•ed** at **burst**). When the inflected forms of a verb involve no irregularity except the coupling of a

final consonant, the double consonant is shown instead of full or cutback inflected forms (as *vb*-**-gg-** at **lug**). A variant or inflect form whose alphabetical place is distant from the main entry is entered at its own place with a cross-reference in small capital letters to the main entry (as **hung** *past of* HANG).

Several other kinds of entries are also found in this dictionary. A **run-in entry** is a term related to a main entry that appears within a definition (as **small intestine** at **in•tes•tine**). It is set off by parentheses. Derivative words, made up usually of the main entry and a common word element, such as a suffix, are shown as **undefined run-on entries** following all definitions of a main entry. These are set off by a dash (as **—gar•den•er** at **gar•den**). The meaning of an undefined run-on entry can be inferred from the meaning of the main entry where it appears and that of the added word element, shown elsewhere in the book. A **run-on phrase** is a group of two or more words having the main entry as a major element and having a special meaning of its own (as **in force** at **force** or **look after** at look). Run-on phrases are always defined.

Lists of undefined words formed by the additon of a common English prefix to a word entered in the dictionary and having meanings that can be inferred from the meaning of the root word and that of the prefix will be found at entries for the following prefixes: *anti-, bi-, co-, counter-, extra-, hyper-, in-, inter-, mini-, multi-, non-, over-, post-, pre-, re-, self-, sub-, super-, un-,* and *vice-.*

Pronunciation information is either given explicitly or implied for every entry in the dictionary. Where the pronunciation is not indicated at a particular entry, or is indicated in a cutback form, the full pronunciation is to be inferred from an earlier indicated pronunciation.

The grammatical function of entry words is indicated by an italic **functional label** (as *vb, n,* or *prefix*).

Hyphens that are a fixed part of hyphenated compounds such as *self-conscious* are converted to a special "double hyphen" when the compound appears in lightface type and that hyphen comes at the end of a line in this dictionary. This indi-

cates to you that the hyphen is to be retained when the word is not at the end of a line. Fixed hyphens in boldface entry words are shown as short boldface dashes. which are a bit larger than ordinary hyphens. These short dashes or long hyphens in boldface words are retained at the end of a line in this dictionary.

Guide words are used at the top of pages to indicate the range of entries on those pages. In choosing guide words for a page, we select the alphabetically first and last spelled-out boldface words or phrases on that page. This means that any boldface entry—main entry, variant spelling, inflected form, run-in or run-on entry—can be used as a guide word. Please keep this in mind if the word used as a guide word does not happen to be the first or last main entry on the page. The guide words themselves are in alphabetical order throughout the book, so occasionally it has been necessary to modify this rule. When the alphabetically last entry on one page would come later than the alphabetically first entry on the following page, a different word is chosen as a guide word. On pages that contain a substantial number of undefined words following a prefix entry, that prefix may be used as the first or last guide word.

All **abbreviations** are used in this book are listed, along with a number of other common abbreviations, in a special section immediately following the dictionary proper.

A

^{1}a \ˈā\ *n, pl* **a's** *or* **as** \ˈāz\ : 1st letter of the alphabet
^{2}a \ə, ˈā\ *indefinite article* : one or some—used to indicate an unspecified or unidentified individual
aard•vark \ˈärd͵värk\ *n* : ant-eating African mammal
aback \əˈbak\ *adv* : by surprise
aba•cus \ˈabəkəs\ *n, pl* **aba•ci** \ˈabə͵sī, -͵kē\ *or* **aba•cus•es** : calculating instrument using rows of beads
abaft \əˈbaft\ *adv* : toward or at the stern
ab•a•lo•ne \͵abəˈlōnē\ *n* : large edible shellfish
^{1}aban•don \əˈbandən\ *vb* : give up without intent to reclaim —**aban•don•ment** *n*
^{2}abandon *n* : thorough yielding to impulses
aban•doned \əˈbandənd\ *adj* : morally unrestrained
abase \əˈbās\ *vb* **abased; abas•ing** : lower in dignity —**abase•ment** *n*
abash \əˈbash\ *vb* : embarrass —**abash•ment** *n*
abate \əˈbāt\ *vb* **abat•ed; abat•ing** : decrease or lessen
abate•ment \əˈbātmənt\ *n* : tax reduction
ab•at•toir \ˈabə͵twär\ *n* : slaughterhouse
ab•bess \ˈabəs\ *n* : head of a convent
ab•bey \ˈabē\ *n, pl* **-beys** : monastery or convent
ab•bot \ˈabət\ *n* : head of a monastery
ab•bre•vi•ate \əˈbrēvē͵āt\ *vb* **-at•ed; -at•ing** : shorten —**ab•bre•vi•a•tion** \ə͵brēvēˈāshən\ *n*
ab•di•cate \ˈabdi͵kāt\ *vb* **-cat•ed; -cating** : renounce —**ab•di•ca•tion** \͵abdiˈkāshən\ *n*
ab•do•men \ˈabdəmən, abˈdōmən\ *n* **1** : body area between chest and pelvis **2** : hindmost part of an insect —**abdom•i•nal** \abˈdämənᵊl\ *adj* —**abdom•i•nal•ly** *adv*
ab•duct \abˈdəkt\ *vb* : kidnap —**ab•duc•tion** \-ˈdəkshən\ *n* —**ab•duc•tor** \-tər\ *n*
abed \əˈbed\ *adv or adj* : in bed
ab•er•ra•tion \͵abəˈrāshən\ *n* : deviation or distortion —**ab•er•rant** \aˈberənt\ *adj*
abet \əˈbet\ *vb* **-tt-** : incite or encourage —**abet•tor, abet•ter** \-ər\ *n*
abey•ance \əˈbāəns\ *n* : state of inactivity
ab•hor \əbˈhȯr, ab-\ *vb* **-rr-** : hate —**ab•hor•rence** \-əns\ *n* —**ab•hor•rent** \-ənt\ *adj*
abide \əˈbīd\ *vb* **abode** \-ˈbōd\ *or* **abid•ed; abid•ing** **1** : endure **2** : remain, last, or reside
ab•ject \ˈab͵jekt, abˈ-\ *adj* : low in spirit or hope —**ab•jec•tion** \abˈjekshən\ *n* —**ab•ject•ly** *adv* —**ab•ject•ness** *n*
ab•jure \abˈju̇r\ *vb* **1** : renounce **2** : abstain from —**ab•ju•ra•tion** \͵abjəˈrāshən\ *n*
ablaze \əˈblāz\ *adj or adv* : on fire
able \ˈābəl\ *adj* **abler** \-blər\; **ablest** \-bləst\ **1** : having sufficient power, skill, or resources **2** : skilled or efficient —**abil•i•ty** \əˈbilətē\ *n* —**ably** \ˈāblē\ *adv*
-able, -ible \əbəl\ *adj suffix* **1** : capable of, fit for, or worthy of **2** : tending, given, or liable to
ab•lu•tion \əˈblüshən, aˈblü-\ *n* : washing of one's body
ab•ne•gate \ˈabni͵gāt\ *vb* **-gat•ed; -gating** **1** : relinquish **2** : renounce —**ab•ne•ga•tion** \͵abniˈgāshən\ *n*
ab•nor•mal \abˈnȯrməl\ *adj* : deviating from the normal or average —**ab•nor•mal•i•ty** \͵abnərˈmalətē, -nȯr-\ *n* —**ab•nor•mal•ly** *adv*
aboard \əˈbōrd\ *adv* : on, onto, or within a car, ship, or aircraft ~ *prep* : on or within
abode \əˈbōd\ *n* : residence
abol•ish \əˈbälish\ *vb* : do away with —**ab•o•li•tion** \͵abəˈlishən\ *n*
abom•i•na•ble \əˈbämənəbəl\ *adj* : thoroughly unpleasant or revolting
abom•i•nate \əˈbämə͵nāt\ *vb* **-nat•ed; -nat•ing** : hate —**abom•i•na•tion** \ə͵bäməˈnāshən\ *n*
ab•orig•i•nal \͵abəˈrijənəl\ *adj* **1** : original **2** : primitive
ab•orig•i•ne \-ˈrijənē\ *n* : original inhabitant
abort \əˈbȯrt\ *vb* : terminate prematurely —**abor•tive** \-ˈbȯrtiv\ *adj*
abor•tion \əˈbȯrshən\ *n* : spontaneous or induced termination of pregnancy
abound \əˈbau̇nd\ *vb* : be plentiful
about \əˈbau̇t\ *adv* : around ~ *prep* **1** : on every side of **2** : on the verge of **3** : having as a subject
above \əˈbəv\ *adv* : in or to a higher place ~ *prep* **1** : in or to a higher place than **2** : more than
above•board *adv or adj* : without deception
abrade \əˈbrād\ *vb* **abrad•ed; abrading** : wear away by rubbing —**abrasion** \-ˈbrāzhən\ *n*
abra•sive \əˈbrāsiv\ *n* : substance for grinding, smoothing, or polishing ~ *adj* **1** : tending to abrade **2** : causing irritation —**abra•sive•ly** *adv* —**abra•sive•ness** *n*
abreast \əˈbrest\ *adv or adj* **1** : side by side **2** : up to a standard or level
abridge \əˈbrij\ *vb* **abridged; abridging** : shorten or condense —**abridgment, abridge•ment** *n*
abroad \əˈbrȯd\ *adv or adj* **1** : over a wide area **2** : outside one's country
ab•ro•gate \ˈabrəgāt\ *vb* **-gat•ed; -gating** : annul or revoke —**ab•ro•ga•tion** \͵abrəˈgāshən\ *n*
abrupt \əˈbrəpt\ *adj* **1** : sudden **2** : so quick as to seem rude —**abrupt•ly** *adv*
ab•scess \ˈab͵ses\ *n* : collection of pus surrounded by inflamed tissue —**abscessed** \-͵sest\ *adj*
ab•scond \abˈskänd\ *vb* : run away and hide
ab•sent \ˈabsənt\ *adj* : not present ~ **absent** \abˈsent\ *vb* : keep oneself away —**ab•sence** \ˈabsəns\ *n* —**ab•sen•tee** \͵absənˈtē\ *n*
ab•sent•mind•ed \͵absəntˈmīndəd\ *adj* : unaware of one's surroundings or action —**ab•sent•mind•ed•ly** *adv* —**ab•sent•mind•ed•ness** *n*
ab•so•lute \ˈabsə͵lüt, ͵absəˈ-\ *adj* **1** : pure **2** : free from restriction **3** : definite —**ab•so•lute•ly** *adv*
ab•so•lu•tion \͵absəˈlüshən\ *n* : remission of sins
ab•solve \əbˈzälv, -ˈsälv\ *vb* **-solved; -solving** : set free of the consequences of guilt
ab•sorb \əbˈsȯrb, -ˈzȯrb\ *vb* **1** : suck up or take in as a sponge does **2** : engage (one's attention) —**ab•sor•ben•cy** \-ˈsȯrbənsē, -ˈzȯr-\ *n* —**ab•sor•bent** \-bənt\ *adj or n* —**ab•sorb•ing** *adj* —**ab•sorb•ing•ly** *adv*
ab•sorp•tion \əbˈsȯrpshən, -ˈzȯrp-\ *n* : process of absorbing —**ab•sorp•tive** \-tiv\ *adj*
ab•stain \əbˈstān\ *vb* : refrain from doing something —**ab•stain•er** *n* —**absten•tion** \-ˈstenchən\ *n* —**ab•sti•nence** \ˈabstənəns\ *n*
ab•ste•mi•ous \abˈstēmēəs\ *adj* : sparing in use of food or drink —**ab•ste•mi•ous•ly** *adv* —**ab•ste•mi•ous•ness** *n*
ab•stract \abˈstrakt, ˈab͵-\ *adj* **1** : expressing a quality apart from an object **2** : not representing something specific ~ \ˈab͵-\ *n* : summary ~ \abˈ-, ˈab͵-\ *vb* **1** : remove or separate **2** : make an abstract of —**ab•stract•ly** *adv* —**ab•stract•ness** *n*
ab•strac•tion \abˈstrakshən\ *n* **1** : act of abstracting **2** : abstract idea or work of art
ab•struse \əbˈstrüs, ab-\ *adj* : hard to understand —**ab•struse•ly** *adv* —**abstruse•ness** *n*
ab•surd \əbˈsərd, -ˈzərd\ *adj* : ridiculous or unreasonable —**ab•sur•di•ty** \-ətē\ *n* —**ab•surd•ly** *adv*
abun•dant \əˈbəndənt\ *adj* : more than enough —**abun•dance** \-dəns\ *n* —**abun•dant•ly** *adv*
abuse \əˈbyüz\ *vb* **abused; abus•ing** **1** : misuse **2** : mistreat **3** : attack with words ~ \-ˈbyüs\ *n* **1** : corrupt practice **2** : improper use **3** : mistreatment **4** : coarse and insulting speech —**abus•er** *n* —**abu•sive** \-ˈbyüsiv\ *adj* —**abu•sive•ly** *adv* —**abu•sive•ness** *n*
abut \əˈbət\ *vb* **-tt-** : touch along a border —**abut•ter** *n*
abut•ment \əˈbətmənt\ *n* : part of a bridge that supports weight
abys•mal \əˈbizməl\ *adj* **1** : immeasurably deep **2** : wretched —**abys•mal•ly** *adv*
abyss \əˈbis\ *n* : immeasurably deep gulf
-ac \͵ak\ *n suffix* : one affected with
aca•cia \əˈkāshə\ *n* : leguminous tree or shrub
ac•a•dem•ic \͵akəˈdemik\ *adj* **1** : relating to schools or colleges **2** : theoretical —**academic** *n* —**ac•a•dem•i•cal•ly** \-iklē\ *adv*
acad•e•my \əˈkadəmē\ *n, pl* **-mies** **1** : private high school **2** : society of scholars or artists
acan•thus \əˈkanthəs\ *n, pl* **acanthus** **1** : prickly Mediterranean herb **2** : ornament representing acanthus leaves
ac•cede \akˈsēd\ *vb* **-ced•ed; -ced•ing** **1** : become a party to an agreement **2** : express approval **3** : enter upon an office
ac•cel•er•ate \ikˈselə͵rāt, ak-\ *vb* **-at•ed; -at•ing** **1** : bring about earlier **2** : speed up —**ac•cel•er•a•tion** \-͵seləˈrāshən\ *n*
ac•cel•er•a•tor \ikˈselə͵rātər, ak-\ *n* : pedal for controlling the speed of a motor vehicle
ac•cent \ˈak͵sent\ *n* **1** : distinctive manner of pronunciation **2** : prominence given to one syllable of a word **3** : mark (as ´, `, ˆ) over a vowel in writing or printing to indicate pronunciation ~ \ˈak͵-, akˈ-\ *vb* : emphasize —**ac•cen•tu•al** \akˈsenchəwəl\ *adj*
ac•cen•tu•ate \akˈsenchə͵wāt\ *vb* **-at•ed; -at•ing** : stress or show off by a contrast —**ac•cen•tu•a•tion** \-͵senchəˈwāshən\ *n*
ac•cept \ikˈsept, ak-\ *vb* **1** : receive willingly **2** : agree to —**ac•cept•abil•i•ty** \ik͵septəˈbilətē, ak-\ *n* —**ac•cept•able** \-ˈseptəbəl\ *adj* —**ac•cep•tance** \-ˈseptəns\ *n*
ac•cess \ˈak͵ses\ *n* : capability or way of approaching —**ac•ces•si•bil•i•ty** \ik͵sesəˈbilətē, ak-\ *n* —**ac•ces•si•ble** \-ˈsesəbəl\ *adj*
ac•ces•sion \ikˈseshən, ak-\ *n* **1** : something added **2** : act of taking office
ac•ces•so•ry \ikˈsesərē, ak-\ *n, pl* **-ries** **1** : nonessential addition **2** : one guilty of aiding a criminal —**accessory** *adj*
ac•ci•dent \ˈaksədənt\ *n* **1** : event occurring by chance or unintentionally **2** : chance —**ac•ci•den•tal** \͵aksəˈdentᵊl\ *adj* —**ac•ci•den•tal•ly** *adv*
ac•claim \əˈklām\ *vb or n* : praise
ac•cla•ma•tion \͵akləˈmāshən\ *n* **1** : eager applause **2** : unanimous vote
ac•cli•mate \ˈaklə͵māt, əˈklīmət\ *vb* **-mat•ed; -mat•ing** : acclimatize —**ac•cli•ma•tion** \͵akləˈmāshən, -͵klī-\ *n*
ac•cli•ma•tize \əˈklīmə͵tīz\ *vb* **-tized; -tiz•ing** : accustom to a new climate or situation —**ac•cli•ma•ti•za•tion** \-͵klīmətəˈzāshən\ *n*
ac•co•lade \ˈakə͵lād\ *n* : expression of praise
ac•com•mo•date \əˈkämə͵dāt\ *vb* **-dated; -dat•ing** **1** : adapt **2** : provide with something needed **3** : hold without crowding
ac•com•mo•da•tion \ə͵käməˈdāshən\ *n* **1** : quarters —usu. pl. **2** : act of accommodating
ac•com•pa•ny \əˈkəmpənē\ *vb* **-nied; -ny•ing** **1** : go or occur with **2** : play supporting music —**ac•com•pa•ni•ment** \-nəmənt\ *n* —**ac•com•pa•nist** \-nist\ *n*
ac•com•plice \əˈkämpləs, -ˈkəm-\ *n* : associate in crime
ac•com•plish \əˈkämplish, -ˈkəm-\ *vb* : do, fulfill, or bring about —**ac•com•plished** *adj* —**ac•com•plish•er** *n* —**ac•com•plish•ment** *n*
ac•cord \əˈkȯrd\ *vb* **1** : grant **2** : agree ~ *n* **1** : agreement **2** : willingness to act —**ac•cor•dance** \-ˈkȯrdᵊns\ *n* —**ac•cor•dant** \-ᵊnt\ *adj*
ac•cord•ing•ly \əˈkȯrdiŋlē\ *adv* : consequently
according to *prep* **1** : in conformity with **2** : as stated by
ac•cor•di•on \əˈkȯrdēən\ *n* : keyboard instrument with a bellows and reeds ~ *adj* : folding like an accordion bellows —**ac•cor•di•on•ist** \-nist\ *n*
ac•cost \əˈkȯst\ *vb* : approach and speak to esp. aggressively
ac•count \əˈkau̇nt\ *n* **1** : statement of business transactions **2** : credit arrangement with a vendor **3** : report **4** : worth **5** : sum deposited in a bank ~ *vb* : give an explanation
ac•count•able \əˈkau̇ntəbəl\ *adj* : responsible —**ac•count•abil•i•ty** \-͵kau̇ntəˈbilətē\ *n*
ac•coun•tant \əˈkau̇ntᵊnt\ *n* : one skilled in accounting —**ac•coun•tan•cy** \-ᵊnsē\ *n*
ac•count•ing \əˈkau̇ntiŋ\ *n* : financial record keeping
ac•cou•tre, ac•cou•ter \əˈkütər\ *vb* **-tred** *or* **-tered; -tring** *or* **-ter•ing** \-ˈkütəriŋ, -ˈkütriŋ\ : equip
ac•cou•tre•ment, ac•cou•ter•ment \əˈkütrəmənt, -ˈkütər-\ *n* **1** : accessory item —usu. pl. **2** : identifying characteristic
ac•cred•it \əˈkredət\ *vb* **1** : approve officially **2** : attribute —**ac•cred•i•ta•tion** \-͵kredəˈtāshən\ *n*
ac•crue \əˈkrü\ *vb* **-crued; -cru•ing** : be added by periodic growth —**ac•cru•al** \-əl\ *n*
ac•cu•mu•late \əˈkyümyə͵lāt\ *vb* **-lated; -lat•ing** : collect or pile up —**ac•cu•mu•la•tion** \-͵kyümyəˈlāshən\ *n* —**ac•cu•mu•la•tor** \-ˈkyümyə͵lātər\ *n*
ac•cu•rate \ˈakyərət\ *adj* : free from error —**ac•cu•ra•cy** \-rəsē\ *n* —**ac•cu•rate•ly** *adv* —**ac•cu•rate•ness** *n*
ac•cursed \əˈkərst, -ˈkərsəd\, **ac•curst** \əˈkərst\ *adj* **1** : being under a curse **2** : damnable
ac•cuse \əˈkyüz\ *vb* **-cused; -cus•ing** : charge with an offense —**ac•cu•sa•tion** \͵akyəˈzāshən\ *n* —**ac•cus•er** *n*
ac•cused \əˈkyüzd\ *n, pl* **-cused** : defendant in a criminal case
ac•cus•tom \əˈkəstəm\ *vb* : make familiar through use or experience
ace \ˈās\ *n* : one that excels
acer•bic \əˈsərbik, a-\ *adj* : sour or biting in temper, mood, or tone
acet•amin•o•phen \ə͵sētəˈminəfən\ *n* : pain reliever
ac•e•tate \ˈasə͵tāt\ *n* : fabric or plastic derived from acetic acid
ace•tic acid \əˈsētik-\ *n* : acid found in vinegar
acet•y•lene \əˈsetᵊlən, -ᵊl͵ēn\ *n* : colorless gas used as a fuel in welding
ache \ˈāk\ *vb* **ached; ach•ing** **1** : suffer a dull persistent pain **2** : yearn —**ache** *n*
achieve \əˈchēv\ *vb* **achieved; achieving** : gain by work or effort —**achieve•ment** *n* —**achiev•er** *n*
ac•id \ˈasəd\ *adj* **1** : sour or biting to the taste **2** : sharp in manner **3** : of or relating to an acid ~ *n* : sour water-soluble chemical compound that reacts with a base to form a salt —**acid•ic** \əˈsidik\ *adj* —**acid•i•fy** \əˈsidə͵fī\ *vb* —**acid•i•ty** \-ətē\ *n* —**acid•ly** *adv*
ac•knowl•edge \ikˈnälij, ak-\ *vb* **-edged; -edg•ing** **1** : admit as true **2** : admit the authority of **3** : express thanks for —**ac•knowl•edg•ment** *n*
ac•me \ˈakmē\ *n* : highest point
ac•ne \ˈaknē\ *n* : skin disorder marked esp. by pimples
ac•o•lyte \ˈakə͵līt\ *n* : assistant to a member of clergy in a religious service
acorn \ˈā͵kȯrn, -kərn\ *n* : nut of the oak
acous•tic \əˈküstik\ *adj* : relating to hearing

or sound —acous•ti•cal \-stikəl\ adj —acous•ti•cal•ly \-klē\ adv
acous•tics \ə'küstiks\ n sing or pl 1 : science of sound 2 : qualities in a room that affect how sound is heard
ac•quaint \ə'kwānt\ vb 1 : inform 2 : make familiar
ac•quain•tance \ə'kwāntᵊns\ n 1 : personal knowledge 2 : person with whom one is acquainted —ac•quain•tance•ship n
ac•qui•esce \,akwē'es\ vb -esced; -esc•ing : consent or submit —ac•qui•es•cence \-'esᵊns\ n —ac•qui•es•cent \-ᵊnt\ adj —ac•qui•es•cent•ly adv
ac•quire \ə'kwīr\ vb -quired; -quir•ing : gain
ac•qui•si•tion \,akwə'zishən\ n : a gaining or something gained —acqui•si•tive \ə'kwizətiv\ adj
ac•quit \ə'kwit\ vb -tt- 1 : pronounce not guilty 2 : conduct (oneself) usu. well —ac•quit•tal \-ᵊl\ n
acre \'ākər\ n 1 pl : lands 2 : 4840 square yards
acre•age \'ākərij\ n : area in acres
ac•rid \'akrəd\ adj : sharp and biting —ac•rid•i•ty \a'kridətē, ə-\ n —ac•rid•ly adv —ac•rid•ness n
ac•ri•mo•ny \'akrə,mōnē\ n, pl -nies : harshness of language or feeling —ac•ri•mo•ni•ous \,akrə'mōnēəs\ adj —ac•ri•mo•ni•ous•ly adv
ac•ro•bat \'akrə,bat\ n : performer of tumbling feats —ac•ro•bat•ic \,akrə'batik\ adj
across \ə'krȯs\ adv : to or on the opposite side ~ prep 1 : to or on the opposite side of 2 : on so as to cross
acryl•ic \ə'krilik\ n 1 : plastic used for molded parts or in paints 2 : synthetic textile fiber
act \'akt\ n 1 : thing done 2 : law 3 : main division of a play ~ vb 1 : perform in a play 2 : conduct oneself 3 : operate 4 : produce an effect
ac•tion \'akshən\ n 1 : legal proceeding 2 : manner or method of performing 3 : activity 4 : thing done over a period of time or in stages 5 : combat 6 : events of a literary plot 7 : operating mechanism
ac•ti•vate \'aktə,vāt\ vb -vat•ed; -vat•ing : make active or reactive —ac•ti•va•tion \,aktə'vāshən\ n
ac•tive \'aktiv\ adj 1 : causing action or change 2 : lively, vigorous, or energetic 3 : erupting or likely to erupt 4 : now in operation —active n —ac•tive•ly adv
ac•tiv•i•ty \ak'tivətē\ n, pl -ties 1 : quality or state of being active 2 : what one is actively doing
ac•tor \'aktər\ n : one that acts
ac•tress \'aktrəs\ n : woman who acts in plays
ac•tu•al \'akchəwəl\ adj : really existing —ac•tu•al•i•ty \,akchə'walətē\ n —ac•tu•al•iza•tion \,akchəwələ'zāshən\ n —ac•tu•al•ize \'akchəwə,līz\ vb —ac•tu•al•ly adv
ac•tu•ary \'akchə,werē\ n, pl -ar•ies : one who calculates insurance risks and premiums —ac•tu•ar•i•al \,akchə'werēəl\ adj
ac•tu•ate \'akchə,wāt\ vb -at•ed; -at•ing : put into action —ac•tu•a•tor \-,wātər\ n
acu•men \ə'kyümən\ n : mental keenness
acu•punc•ture \'akyu̇,pəŋkchər\ n : treatment by puncturing the body with needles —acu•punc•tur•ist \,akyu̇'pəŋkchərist\ n
acute \ə'kyüt\ adj acut•er; acut•est 1 : sharp 2 : containing less than 90 degrees 3 : mentally alert 4 : severe —acute•ly adv —acute•ness n
ad \'ad\ n : advertisement
ad•age \'adij\ n : old familiar saying
ad•a•mant \'adəmənt, -,mant\ adj : insistent —ad•a•mant•ly adv
adapt \ə'dapt\ vb : adjust to be suitable for a new use or condition —adapt•abil•i•ty \ə,daptə'bilətē\ n —adapt•able adj —ad•ap•ta•tion \,ad,ap'tāshən, -əp-\ n —adapt•er n —adap•tive \ə'daptiv\ adj
add \'ad\ vb 1 : join to something else so as to increase in amount 2 : say further 3 : find a sum —ad•di•tion \ə'dishən\ n
ad•der \'adər\ n 1 : poisonous European snake 2 : No. American snake
ad•dict \'adikt\ n : one who is psychologically or physiologically dependent (as on a drug) ~ \ə'dikt\ vb : cause to become an addict —ad•dic•tion \ə'dikshən\ n —ad•dic•tive \-'diktiv\ adj
ad•di•tion•al \ə'dishənəl\ adj : existing as a result of adding —ad•di•tion•al•ly adv
ad•di•tive \'adətiv\ n : substance added to another
ad•dle \'adᵊl\ vb -dled; -dling : confuse
ad•dress \ə'dres\ vb 1 : direct one's remarks to 2 : mark an address on ~ \ə'dres, 'ad,res\ n 1 : formal speech 2 : place where a person may be reached or mail may be delivered
ad•duce \ə'düs, -'dyüs\ vb -duced; -duc•ing : offer as proof
ad•e•noid \'ad,nȯid, -ᵊnȯid\ n : enlarged tissue near the opening of the nose into the throat —usu. pl. —adenoid, ad•e•noi•dal \-əl\ adj
adept \ə'dept\ adj : highly skilled —adept•ly adv —adept•ness n
ad•e•quate \'adikwət\ adj : good or plentiful enough —ad•e•qua•cy \-kwəsē\ n —ad•e•quate•ly adv
ad•here \ad'hir, əd-\ vb -hered; -her•ing 1 : remain loyal 2 : stick fast —ad•her•ence \-'hirəns\ n —ad•her•ent \-ənt\ adj or n
ad•he•sion \ad'hēzhən, əd-\ n : act or state of adhering
ad•he•sive \-'hēsiv, -ziv\ adj : tending to adhere ~ n : adhesive substance
adieu \ə'dü, -dyü\ n, pl adieus or adieux \-'düz,-'dyüz\ : farewell
ad•ja•cent \ə'jāsᵊnt\ adj : situated near or next
ad•jec•tive \'ajiktiv\ n : word that serves as a modifier of a noun —ad•jec•ti•val \,ajik'tīvəl\ adj —ad•jec•ti•val•ly adv
ad•join \ə'jȯin\ vb : be next to
ad•journ \ə'jərn\ vb : end a meeting —ad•journ•ment n
ad•judge \ə'jəj\ vb -judged; -judg•ing 1 : think or pronounce to be 2 : award by judicial decision
ad•ju•di•cate \ə'jüdi,kāt\ vb -cat•ed; -cat•ing : settle judicially —ad•ju•di•ca•tion \ə,jüdi'kāshən\ n
ad•junct \'aj,əŋkt\ n : something joined or added but not essential
ad•just \ə'jəst\ vb : fix, adapt, or set right —ad•just•able adj —ad•just•er, ad•jus•tor \ə'jəstər\ n —ad•just•ment \-mənt\ n
ad•ju•tant \'ajətənt\ n : aide esp. to a commanding officer
ad–lib \'ad'lib\ vb -bb- : speak without preparation —ad–lib n or adj
ad•min•is•ter \əd'minəstər\ vb 1 : manage 2 : give out esp. in doses —ad•min•is•tra•ble \-strəbəl\ adj —ad•min•is•trant \-strənt\ n
ad•min•is•tra•tion \əd,minə'strāshən, ad-\ n 1 : process of managing 2 : persons responsible for managing —ad•min•is•tra•tive \əd'minə,strātiv\ adj —ad•min•is•tra•tive•ly adv
ad•min•is•tra•tor \əd'minə,strātər\ n : one that manages
ad•mi•ra•ble \'admərəbəl\ adj : worthy of admiration —ad•mi•ra•bly \-blē\ adv
ad•mi•ral \'admərəl\ n : commissioned officer in the navy ranking next below a fleet admiral
ad•mire \əd'mīr\ vb -mired; -mir•ing : have high regard for —ad•mi•ra•tion \,admə'rāshən\ n —ad•mir•er n —ad•mir•ing•ly adv
ad•mis•si•ble \əd'misəbəl\ adj : that can be permitted —ad•mis•si•bil•i•ty \-,misə'bilətē\ n
ad•mis•sion \əd'mishən\ n 1 : act of admitting 2 : admittance or a fee paid for this 3 : acknowledgment of a fact
ad•mit \əd'mit\ vb -tt- 1 : allow to enter 2 : permit 3 : recognize as genuine —ad•mit•ted•ly adv
ad•mit•tance \əd'mitᵊns\ n : permission to enter
ad•mix•ture \ad'mikschər\ n 1 : thing added in mixing 2 : mixture
ad•mon•ish \ad'mänish\ vb : rebuke —ad•mon•ish•ment \-mənt\ n —ad•mo•ni•tion \,admə'nishən\ n —ad•mon•i•to•ry \ad'mänə,tōrē\ adj
ado \ə'dü\ n 1 : fuss 2 : trouble
ado•be \ə'dōbē\ n : sun-dried building brick
ad•o•les•cence \,adᵊl'esᵊns\ n : period of growth between childhood and maturity —ad•o•les•cent \-ᵊnt\ adj or n
adopt \ə'däpt\ vb 1 : take (a child of other parents) as one's own child 2 : take up and practice as one's own —adop•tion \-'däpshən\ n
adore \ə'dōr\ vb adored; ador•ing 1 : worship 2 : be extremely fond of —ador•able adj —ador•ably adv —ad•o•ra•tion \,adə'rāshən\ n
adorn \ə'dȯrn\ vb : decorate with ornaments —adorn•ment n
adrift \ə'drift\ adv or adj 1 : afloat without motive power or moorings 2 : without guidance or purpose
adroit \ə'drȯit\ adj : dexterous or shrewd —adroit•ly adv —adroit•ness n
adult \ə'dəlt, 'ad,əlt\ adj : fully developed and mature ~ n : grown-up person —adult•hood n
adul•ter•ate \ə'dəltə,rāt\ vb -at•ed; -ating : make impure by mixture —adul•ter•a•tion \-,dəltə'rāshən\ n
adul•tery \ə'dəltərē\ n, pl -ter•ies : sexual unfaithfulness of a married person —adul•ter•er \-tərər\ n —adul•ter•ess \-tərəs\ n —adul•ter•ous \-tərəs\ adj
ad•vance \əd'vans\ vb -vanced; -vancing 1 : bring or move forward 2 : promote 3 : lend ~ n 1 : forward movement 2 : improvement 3 : offer ~ adj : being ahead of time —advance•ment n
ad•van•tage \əd'vantij\ n 1 : superiority of position 2 : benefit or gain —ad•van•ta•geous \,ad,van'tājəs, -vən-\ adj —ad•van•ta•geous•ly adv
ad•vent \'ad,vent\ n 1 cap : period before Christmas 2 : a coming into being or use
ad•ven•ti•tious \,advən'tishəs\ adj : accidental —ad•ven•ti•tious•ly adv
ad•ven•ture \əd'venchər\ n 1 : risky undertaking 2 : exciting experience —ad•ven•tur•er \-chərər\ n —ad•ven•ture•some \-chərsəm\ adj —ad•ven•tur•ous \-chərəs\ adj
ad•verb \'ad,vərb\ n : word that modifies a verb, an adjective, or another adverb —ad•ver•bi•al \ad'vərbēəl\ adj —ad•ver•bi•al•ly adv
ad•ver•sary \'advər,serē\ n, pl -sar•ies : enemy or rival —adversary adj
ad•verse \ad'vərs, 'ad-,\ adj : opposing or unfavorable —ad•verse•ly adv
ad•ver•si•ty \ad'vərsətē\ n, pl -ties : hard times
ad•vert \ad'vərt\ vb : refer
ad•ver•tise \'advər,tīz\ vb -tised; -tis•ing : call public attention to —ad•ver•tise•ment \,advər'tīzmənt, əd'vərtəzmənt\ n —ad•ver•tis•er n
ad•ver•tis•ing \'advər,tīziŋ\ n : business of preparing advertisements
ad•vice \əd'vīs\ n : recommendation with regard to a course of action
ad•vis•able \əd'vīzəbəl\ adj : wise or prudent —ad•vis•abil•i•ty \-,vīzə'bilətē\ n
ad•vise \əd'vīz\ vb -vised; -vis•ing : give advice to —ad•vis•er, ad•vis•or \-'vīzər\ n
ad•vise•ment \əd'vīzmənt\ n : careful consideration
ad•vi•so•ry \əd'vīzərē\ adj : having power to advise
ad•vo•cate \'advəkət, -,kāt\ n : one who argues or pleads for a cause or proposal ~ \-,kāt\ vb -cat•ed; -cat•ing : recommend —ad•vo•ca•cy \-vəkəsē\ n
adze \'adz\ n : tool for shaping wood
ae•gis \'ējəs\ n : protection or sponsorship
ae•on \'ēən, 'ē,än\ n : indefinitely long time
aer•ate \'ar,āt\ vb -at•ed; -at•ing : supply or impregnate with air —aer•a•tion \ar'āshən\ n —aer•a•tor \'ar,ātər\ n
ae•ri•al \'arēəl\ adj : inhabiting, occurring in, or done in the air ~ n : antenna
ae•rie \'arē, 'irē\ n : eagle's nest
aer•o•bic \ar'ōbik\ adj : using or needing oxygen
aer•o•bics \-biks\ n sing or pl : exercises that produce a marked increase in respiration and heart rate
aero•dy•nam•ics \,arōdī'namiks\ n : science of bodies in motion in a gas —aero•dy•nam•ic \-ik\ adj —aero•dy•nam•i•cal•ly \-iklē\ adv
aero•nau•tics \,arə'nȯtiks\ n : science dealing with aircraft —aero•nau•ti•cal \-ikəl\ adj
aero•sol \'arə,säl, -,sȯl\ n 1 : liquid or solid particles suspended in a gas 2 : substance sprayed as an aerosol
aero•space \'arō,spās\ n : earth's atmosphere and the space beyond —aero•space adj
aes•thet•ic \es'thetik\ adj : relating to beauty —aes•thet•i•cal•ly \-iklē\ adv
aes•thet•ics \-'thetiks\ n : branch of philosophy dealing with beauty
afar \ə'fär\ adv : from, at, or to a great distance —afar n
af•fa•ble \'afəbəl\ adj : easy to talk to —af•fa•bil•i•ty \,afə'bilətē\ n —af•fa•bly \'afəblē\ adv
af•fair \ə'far\ n : something that relates to or involves one
[1]**af•fect** \ə'fekt, a-\ vb : assume for effect —af•fec•ta•tion \,af,ek'tāshən\ n
[2]**affect** vb : produce an effect on
af•fect•ed \ə'fektəd, a-\ adj 1 : pretending to some trait 2 : artificially assumed to impress —af•fect•ed•ly adv
af•fect•ing \ə'fektiŋ, a-\ adj : arousing pity or sorrow —af•fect•ing•ly adv
af•fec•tion \ə'fekshən\ n : kind or loving feeling —af•fec•tion•ate \-shənət\ adj —af•fec•tion•ate•ly adv
af•fi•da•vit \,afə'dāvət\ n : sworn statement
af•fil•i•ate \ə'filē,āt\ vb -at•ed; -at•ing : become a member or branch —af•fil•i•ate \-ēət\ n —af•fil•i•a•tion \-,filē'āshən\ n
af•fin•i•ty \ə'finətē\ n, pl -ties : close attraction or relationship
af•firm \ə'fərm\ vb : assert positively —af•fir•ma•tion \,afər'māshən\ n
af•fir•ma•tive \ə'fərmətiv\ adj : asserting the truth or existence of something ~ n : statement of affirmation or agreement
af•fix \ə'fiks\ vb : attach
af•flict \ə'flikt\ vb : cause pain and distress to —af•flic•tion \-'flikshən\ n
af•flu•ence \'af,lüəns; a'flü-, ə-\ n : wealth —af•flu•ent \-ənt\ adj
af•ford \ə'fōrd\ vb 1 : manage to bear the cost of 2 : provide
af•fray \ə'frā\ n : fight
af•front \ə'frənt\ vb or n : insult
af•ghan \'af,gan, -gən\ n : crocheted or knitted blanket
afire \ə'fīr\ adj or adv : being on fire
aflame \ə'flām\ adj or adv : flaming
afloat \ə'flōt\ adj or adv : floating
afoot \ə'fu̇t\ adv or adj 1 : on foot 2 : in progress
afore•said \ə'fōr,sed\ adj : said or named before
afraid \ə'frād, South also ə'fred\ adj : filled with fear
afresh \ə'fresh\ adv : anew
aft \'aft\ adv : to or toward the stern or tail
af•ter \'aftər\ adv : at a later time ~ prep 1 : behind in place or time 2 : in pursuit of ~ conj : following the time when ~ adj 1 : later 2 : located toward the back
af•ter•life \'aftər,līf\ n : existence after death
af•ter•math \-,math\ n : results
af•ter•noon \,aftər'nün\ n : time between noon and evening
af•ter•thought n : later thought
af•ter•ward \'aftərwərd\, **af•ter•wards** \-wərdz\ adv : at a later time
again \ə'gen, -'gin\ adv 1 : once more 2 : on the other hand 3 : in addition
against \ə'genst\ prep 1 : directly opposite to 2 : in opposition to 3 : so as to touch or strike
agape \ə'gāp, -'gap\ adj or adv : having the mouth open in astonishment
ag•ate \'agət\ n : quartz with bands or masses of various colors
age \'āj\ n 1 : length of time of life or existence 2 : particular time in life (as majority or the latter part) 3 : quality of being old 4 : long time 5 : period in history ~ vb : become old or mature
-age \ij\ n suffix 1 : aggregate 2 : action or process 3 : result of 4 : rate of 5 : place of 6 : state or rank 7 : fee
aged adj 1 \'ājəd\ : old 2 \'ājd\ : allowed to mature
age•less \'ājləs\ adj : eternal
agen•cy \'ājənsē\ n, pl -cies 1 : one through which something is accomplished 2 : office or function of an agent 3 : government administrative division
agen•da \ə'jendə\ n : list of things to be done
agent \'ājənt\ n 1 : means 2 : person acting or doing business for another
ag•gran•dize \ə'gran,dīz, 'agrən-\ vb -dized; -diz•ing : make great or greater —ag•gran•dize•ment \ə'grandəzmənt, -,dīz-; ,agrən'dīz-\ n
ag•gra•vate \'agrə,vāt\ vb -vat•ed; -vating 1 : make more severe 2 : irritate —ag•gra•va•tion \,agrə'vāshən\ n
ag•gre•gate \'agrigət\ adj : formed into a mass ~ \-,gāt\ vb -gat•ed; -gat•ing : collect into a mass ~ \-gət\ n 1 : mass 2 : whole amount
ag•gres•sion \ə'greshən\ n 1 : unprovoked attack 2 : hostile behavior —ag•gres•sor \-'gresər\ n
ag•gres•sive \ə'gresiv\ adj 1 : easily provoked to fight 2 : hard working and enterprising —ag•gres•sive•ly adv —ag•gres•sive•ness n
ag•grieve \ə'grēv\ vb -grieved; -grieving 1 : cause grief to 2 : inflict injury on
aghast \ə'gast\ adj : struck with amazement or horror
ag•ile \'ajəl\ adj : able to move quickly and easily —agil•i•ty \ə'jilətē\ n
ag•i•tate \'ajə,tāt\ vb -tat•ed; -tat•ing 1 : shake or stir back and forth 2 : excite or trouble the mind of 3 : try to arouse public feeling —ag•i•ta•tion \,ajə'tāshən\ n —ag•i•ta•tor \'ajə,tātər\ n
ag•nos•tic \ag'nästik, əg-\ n : one who doubts the existence of God
ago \ə'gō\ adj or adv : earlier than the present
agog \ə'gäg\ adj : full of excitement
ag•o•nize \'agə,nīz\ vb -nized; -niz•ing : suffer mental agony —ag•o•niz•ing•ly adv
ag•o•ny \'agənē\ n, pl -nies : extreme pain or mental distress
agrar•i•an \ə'grerēən\ adj : relating to land ownership or farming interests —agrarian n —agrar•i•an•ism n
agree \ə'grē\ vb agreed; agree•ing 1 : be of the same opinion 2 : express willingness 3 : get along together 4 : be similar 5 : be appropriate, suitable, or healthful
agree•able \-əbəl\ adj 1 : pleasing 2 : willing to give approval —agreeable•ness n —agree•ably adv
agree•ment \-mənt\ n 1 : harmony of opinion or purpose 2 : mutual understanding or arrangement
ag•ri•cul•ture \'agri,kəlchər\ n : farming —ag•ri•cul•tur•al \,agri'kəlchərəl\ adj —ag•ri•cul•tur•ist \-rist\, ag•ri•cul•tur•al•ist \-rəlist\ n
aground \ə'graund\ adv or adj : on or onto the bottom or shore
ague \'āgyü\ n 1 : fever with recurrent chills and sweating 2 : malaria
ahead \ə'hed\ adv or adj 1 : in or toward

the front **2 :** into or for the future **3 :** in a more advantageous position

ahead of *prep* **1 :** in front or advance of **2 :** in excess of

ahoy \ə'hȯi\ *interj* —used in hailing

aid \'ād\ *vb* **:** provide help or support ~ *n* **:** help

aide \'ād\ *n* **:** helper

AIDS \'ādz\ *n* **:** serious disease of the human immune system

ail \'āl\ *vb* **1 :** trouble **2 :** be ill

ai•le•ron \'ālə,rän\ *n* **:** movable part of an airplane wing

ail•ment \'ālmənt\ *n* **:** bodily disorder

aim \'ām\ *vb* **1 :** point or direct (as a weapon) **2 :** direct one's efforts ~ *n* **1 :** an aiming or the direction of aiming **2 :** object or purpose **—aim•less** *adj* **—aim•less•ly** *adv* **—aim•less•ness** *n*

air \'ar\ *n* **1 :** mixture of gases surrounding the earth **2 :** melody **3 :** outward appearance **4 :** artificial manner **5 :** compressed air **6 :** travel by or use of aircraft **7 :** medium of transmission of radio waves ~ *vb* **1 :** expose to the air **2 :** broadcast **—air•borne** \-,bōrn\ *adj*

air–condition *vb* **:** equip with an apparatus **(air conditioner)** for filtering and cooling the air

air•craft *n, pl* **aircraft :** craft that flies

Aire•dale terrier \'ar,dāl-\ *n* **:** large terrier with a hard wiry coat

air•field *n* **:** airport or its landing field

air force *n* **:** military organization for conducting warfare by air

air•lift *n* **:** a transporting of esp. emergency supplies by aircraft **—airlift** *vb*

air•line *n* **:** air transportation system **—air•lin•er** *n*

air•mail *n* **:** system of transporting mail by airplane **—airmail** *vb*

air•man \-mən\ *n* **1 :** aviator **2 :** enlisted man in the air force in one of the 3 ranks below sergeant **3 :** enlisted man in the air force ranking just below airman first class

airman basic *n* **:** enlisted man of the lowest rank in the air force

airman first class *n* **:** enlisted man in the air force ranking just below sergeant

air•plane *n* **:** fixed-wing aircraft heavier than air

air•port *n* **:** place for landing aircraft and usu. for receiving passengers

air•ship *n* **:** powered lighter-than-air aircraft

air•strip *n* **:** airfield runway

air•tight *adj* **:** tightly sealed to prevent flow of air

air•waves \'ar,wāvz\ *n pl* **:** medium of transmission of radio waves

airy \'arē\ *adj* **air•i•er; -est 1 :** delicate **2 :** breezy

aisle \'īl\ *n* **:** passage between sections of seats

ajar \ə'jär\ *adj or adv* **:** partly open

akim•bo \ə'kimbō\ *adj or adv* **:** having the hand on the hip and the elbow turned outward

akin \ə'kin\ *adj* **1 :** related by blood **2 :** similar in kind

-al \əl\ *adj suffix* **:** of, relating to, or characterized by

al•a•bas•ter \'alə,bastər\ *n* **:** white or translucent mineral

alac•ri•ty \ə'lakrətē\ *n* **:** cheerful readiness

alarm \ə'lärm\ *n* **1 :** warning signal or device **2 :** fear at sudden danger ~ *vb* **1 :** warn **2 :** frighten

alas \ə'las\ *interj* —used to express unhappiness, pity, or concern

al•ba•tross \'albə,trȯs, -,träs\ *n, pl* **-tross** *or* **-trosses :** large seabird

al•be•it \ȯl'bēət, al-\ *conj* **:** even though

al•bi•no \al'bīnō\ *n, pl* **-nos :** person or animal with abnormally white skin **—al•bi•nism** \'albə,nizəm\ *n*

al•bum \'albəm\ *n* **1 :** book for displaying a collection (as of photographs) **2 :** collection of recordings

al•bu•men \al'byümən\ *n* **1 :** white of an egg **2 :** albumin

al•bu•min \-mən\ *n* **:** protein found in blood, milk, egg white, and tissues

al•che•my \'alkəmē\ *n* **:** medieval chemistry **—al•che•mist** \'alkəmist\ *n*

al•co•hol \'alkə,hȯl\ *n* **1 :** intoxicating agent in liquor **2 :** liquor **—alcoholic** *adj*

al•co•hol•ic \,alkə'hȯlik, -'häl-\ *n* **:** person affected with alcoholism

al•co•hol•ism \'alkə,hȯl,izəm\ *n* **:** addiction to alcoholic beverages

al•cove \'al,kōv\ *n* **:** recess in a room or wall

al•der•man \'ȯldərmən\ *n* **:** city official

ale \'āl\ *n* **:** beerlike beverage **—alehouse** *n*

alert \ə'lərt\ *adj* **1 :** watchful **2 :** quick to perceive and act ~ *n* **:** alarm ~ *vb* **:** warn **—alert•ly** *adv* **—alert•ness** *n*

ale•wife *n* **:** fish of the herring family

al•fal•fa \al'falfə\ *n* **:** cloverlike forage plant

al•ga \'algə\ *n, pl* **-gae** \'al,jē\ **:** any of a group of lower plants that includes seaweed **—al•gal** \-gəl\ *adj*

al•ge•bra \'aljəbrə\ *n* **:** branch of mathematics using symbols **—al•ge•bra•ic** \,aljə'brāik\ *adj* **—al•ge•bra•i•cal•ly** \-'brāəklē\ *adv*

alias \'ālēəs, 'ālyəs\ *adv* **:** otherwise called ~ *n* **:** assumed name

al•i•bi \'alə,bī\ *n* **1 :** defense of having been elsewhere when a crime was committed **2 :** justification ~ *vb* **-bied; -bi•ing :** offer an excuse

alien \'ālēən, 'ālyən\ *adj* **:** foreign ~ *n* **1 :** foreign-born resident **2 :** extraterrestrial

alien•ate \'ālēə,nāt, 'ālyə-\ *vb* **-at•ed; -at•ing :** cause to be no longer friendly **—alien•ation** \,ālēə'nāshən, ,ālyə-\ *n*

alight \ə'līt\ *vb* **:** dismount

align \ə'līn\ *vb* **:** bring into line **—align•er** *n* **—align•ment** *n*

alike \ə'līk\ *adj* **:** identical or very similar ~ *adv* **:** equally

al•i•men•ta•ry \,alə'mentərē\ *adj* **:** relating to or functioning in nutrition

al•i•mo•ny \'alə,mōnē\ *n, pl* **-nies :** money paid to a separated or divorced spouse

alive \ə'līv\ *adj* **1 :** having life **2 :** lively or animated

al•ka•li \'alkə,lī\ *n, pl* **-lies** *or* **-lis :** strong chemical base **—al•ka•line** \-kələn, -,līn\ *adj* **—al•ka•lin•i•ty** \,alkə'linətē\ *n*

all \'ȯl\ *adj* **1 :** the whole of **2 :** greatest possible **3 :** every one of ~ *adv* **1 :** wholly **2 :** so much **3 :** for each side ~ *pron* **1 :** whole number or amount **2 :** everything or everyone

Al•lah \'älə, 'al-\ *n* **:** God of Islam

all–around *adj* **:** versatile

al•lay \ə'lā\ *vb* **1 :** alleviate **2 :** calm

al•lege \ə'lej\ *vb* **-leged; -leg•ing :** assert without proof **—al•le•ga•tion** \,ali'gāshən\ *n* **—al•leg•ed•ly** \ə'lejədlē\ *adv*

al•le•giance \ə'lējəns\ *n* **:** loyalty

al•le•go•ry \'alə,gōrē\ *n, pl* **-ries :** story in which figures and actions are symbols of general truths **—al•le•gor•i•cal** \,alə'gȯrikəl\ *adj*

al•le•lu•ia \,alə'lüyə\ *interj* **:** hallelujah

al•ler•gen \'alərjən\ *n* **:** something that causes allergy **—al•ler•gen•ic** \,alər'jenik\ *adj*

al•ler•gy \'alərjē\ *n, pl* **-gies :** abnormal reaction to a substance **—al•ler•gic** \ə'lərjik\ *adj* **—al•ler•gist** \'alərjist\ *n*

al•le•vi•ate \ə'lēvē,āt\ *vb* **-at•ed; -at•ing :** relieve or lessen **—al•le•vi•a•tion** \ə,lēvē'āshən\ *n*

al•ley \'alē\ *n, pl* **-leys 1 :** place for bowling **2 :** narrow passage between buildings

al•li•ance \ə'līəns\ *n* **:** association

al•li•ga•tor \'alə,gātər\ *n* **:** large aquatic reptile related to the crocodiles

al•lit•er•a•tion \ə,litə'rāshən\ *n* **:** repetition of initial sounds of words **—al•lit•er•a•tive** \-'litə,rātiv\ *adj*

al•lo•cate \'alə,kāt\ *vb* **-cat•ed; -cat•ing :** assign **—al•lo•ca•tion** \,alə'kāshən\ *n*

al•lot \ə'lät\ *vb* **-tt- :** distribute as a share **—al•lot•ment** *n*

al•low \ə'lau̇\ *vb* **1 :** admit or concede **2 :** permit **—al•low•able** *adj*

al•low•ance \-əns\ *n* **1 :** allotted share **2 :** money given regularly for expenses

al•loy \'al,ȯi\ *n* **:** metals melted together **—al•loy** \ə'lȯi\ *vb*

all right *adv or adj* **1 :** satisfactorily **2 :** yes **3 :** certainly

all•spice \'ȯlspīs\ *n* **:** berry of a West Indian tree made into a spice

al•lude \ə'lüd\ *vb* **-lud•ed; -lud•ing :** refer indirectly **—al•lu•sion** \-'lüzhən\ *n* **—al•lu•sive** \-'lüsiv\ *adj* **—al•lu•sive•ly** *adv* **—al•lu•sive•ness** *n*

al•lure \ə'lu̇r\ *vb* **-lured; -lur•ing :** entice ~ *n* **:** attractive power

al•ly \ə'lī, 'al,ī\ *vb* **-lied; -ly•ing :** enter into an alliance **—al•ly** \'al,ī, ə'lī\ *n*

-al•ly \əlē\ *adv suffix* **:** -ly

al•ma•nac \'ȯlmə,nak, 'al-\ *n* **:** annual information book

al•mighty \ȯl'mītē\ *adj* **:** having absolute power

al•mond \'ämənd, 'am-, 'alm-, 'älm-\ *n* **:** tree with nutlike fruit kernels

al•most \'ȯl,mōst, ȯl'-\ *adv* **:** very nearly

alms \'ämz, 'älmz, 'almz\ *n, pl* **alms :** charitable gift

aloft \ə'lȯft\ *adv* **:** high in the air

alo•ha \ä'lōhä\ *interj* —used to greet or bid farewell

alone \ə'lōn\ *adj* **1 :** separated from others **2 :** not including anyone or anything else **—alone** *adv*

along \ə'lȯŋ\ *prep* **1 :** in line with the direction of **2 :** at a point on or during ~ *adv* **1 :** forward **2 :** as a companion **3 :** all the time

along•side *adv or prep* **:** along or by the side

alongside of *prep* **:** alongside

aloof \ə'lüf\ *adj* **:** indifferent and reserved **—aloof•ness** *n*

aloud \ə'lau̇d\ *adv* **:** so as to be heard

al•paca \al'pakə\ *n* **1 :** So. American mammal related to the llama **2 :** alpaca wool or cloth made of this

al•pha•bet \'alfə,bet, -bət\ *n* **:** ordered set of letters of a language **—al•pha•bet•i•cal** \,alfə'betikəl\, **al•pha•bet•ic** \-'betik\ *adj* **—al•pha•bet•i•cal•ly** \-klē\ *adv*

al•pha•bet•ize \'alfəbə,tīz\ *vb* **-ized; -iz•ing :** arrange in alphabetical order **—al•pha•bet•iz•er** *n*

al•ready \ȯl'redē\ *adv* **:** by a given time

al•so \'ȯlsō\ *adv* **:** in addition

al•tar \'ȯltər\ *n* **:** structure for rituals

al•ter \'ȯltər\ *vb* **:** make different **—alter•a•tion** \,ȯltə'rāshən\ *n*

al•ter•ca•tion \,ȯltər'kāshən\ *n* **:** dispute

al•ter•nate \'ȯltərnət, 'al-\ *adj* **1 :** arranged or succeeding by turns **2 :** every other ~ \-,nāt\ *vb* **-nat•ed; -nat•ing :** occur or cause to occur by turns ~ \-nət\ *n* **:** substitute **—al•ter•nate•ly** *adv* **—al•ter•na•tion** \,ȯltər'nāshən, ,al-\ *n*

alternating current *n* **:** electric current that regularly reverses direction

al•ter•na•tive \ȯl'tərnətiv, al-\ *adj* **:** offering a choice **—alternative** *n*

al•ter•na•tor \'ȯltər,nātər, 'al-\ *n* **:** alternating-current generator

al•though \ȯl'thō\ *conj* **:** even though

al•tim•e•ter \al'timətər, 'altə,mētər\ *n* **:** instrument for measuring altitude

al•ti•tude \'altə,tüd, -,tyüd\ *n* **1 :** distance up from the ground **2 :** angular distance above the horizon

al•to \'altō\ *n, pl* **-tos :** lower female choral voice

al•to•geth•er \,ȯltə'gethər\ *adv* **1 :** wholly **2 :** on the whole

al•tru•ism \'altru̇,izəm\ *n* **:** concern for others **—al•tru•ist** \-ist\ *n* **—al•tru•is•tic** \,altru̇'istik\ *adj* **—al•tru•is•ti•cal•ly** \-tiklē\ *adv*

al•um \'aləm\ *n* **:** crystalline compound containing aluminum

alu•mi•num \ə'lümənəm\ *n* **:** silver-white malleable ductile light metallic element

alum•na \ə'ləmnə\ *n, pl* **-nae** \-,nē\ **:** woman graduate

alum•nus \ə'ləmnəs\ *n, pl* **-ni** \-,nī\ **:** graduate

al•ways \'ȯlwēz, -wāz\ *adv* **1 :** at all times **2 :** forever

am *pres 1st sing of* BE

amal•gam \ə'malgəm\ *n* **1 :** mercury alloy **2 :** mixture

amal•gam•ate \ə'malgə,māt\ *vb* **-at•ed; -at•ing :** unite **—amal•ga•ma•tion** \-,malgə'māshən\ *n*

am•a•ryl•lis \,amə'riləs\ *n* **:** bulbous herb with clusters of large colored flowers like lilies

amass \ə'mas\ *vb* **:** gather

am•a•teur \'amə,tər, -,tu̇r, -,tyu̇r, -,chu̇r, -chər\ *n* **1 :** person who does something for pleasure rather than for pay **2 :** person who is not expert **—am•a•teur•ish** \,amə'tərish, -'tu̇r-, -'tyu̇r-\ *adj* **—ama•teur•ism** \'amə,tər,izəm, -,tu̇r-, -,tyu̇r-, -,chu̇r-, -chər-\ *n*

am•a•to•ry \'amə,tōrē\ *adj* **:** of or expressing sexual love

amaze \ə'māz\ *vb* **amazed; amaz•ing :** fill with wonder **—amaze•ment** *n* **—amaz•ing•ly** *adv*

am•a•zon \'amə,zän, -zən\ *n* **:** tall strong woman **—am•a•zo•ni•an** \,amə'zōnēən\ *adj*

am•bas•sa•dor \am'basədər\ *n* **:** representative esp. of a government **—am•bas•sa•do•ri•al** \-,basə'dōrēəl\ *adj* **—am•bas•sa•dor•ship** *n*

am•ber \'ambər\ *n* **:** yellowish fossil resin or its color

am•ber•gris \'ambər,gris, -,grēs\ *n* **:** waxy substance from certain whales used in making perfumes

am•bi•dex•trous \,ambi'dekstrəs\ *adj* **:** equally skilled with both hands **—am•bi•dex•trous•ly** *adv*

am•bi•ence, am•bi•ance \'ambēəns, 'ämbē,äns\ *n* **:** pervading atmosphere

am•big•u•ous \am'bigyəwəs\ *adj* **:** having more than one interpretation **—am•bi•gu•i•ty** \,ambə'gyüətē\ *n*

am•bi•tion \am'bishən\ *n* **:** eager desire for success or power **—am•bi•tious** \shəs\ *adj* **—am•bi•tious•ly** *adv*

am•biv•a•lence \am'bivələns\ *n* **:** simultaneous attraction and repulsion **—am•biv•a•lent** \-lənt\ *adj*

am•ble \'ambəl\ *vb* **-bled; -bling :** go at a leisurely gait **—amble** *n*

am•bu•lance \'ambyələns\ *n* **:** vehicle for carrying injured or sick persons

am•bu•la•to•ry \'ambyələ,tōrē\ *adj* **1 :** relating to or adapted to walking **2 :** able to walk about

am•bush \'am,bu̇sh\ *n* **:** trap by which a surprise attack is made from a place of hiding **—ambush** *vb*

ame•lio•rate \ə'mēlyə,rāt\ *vb* **-rat•ed; -rat•ing :** make or grow better **—ame•lio•ra•tion** \-,mēlyə'rāshən\ *n*

amen \'ā'men, 'ä-\ *interj* —used for affirmation esp. at the end of prayers

ame•na•ble \ə'mēnəbəl, -'men-\ *adj* **:** ready to yield or be influenced

amend \ə'mend\ *vb* **1 :** improve **2 :** alter in writing

amend•ment \-mənt\ *n* **:** change made in a formal document (as a law)

amends \ə'mendz\ *n sing or pl* **:** compensation for injury or loss

ame•ni•ty \ə'menətē, -'mē-\ *n, pl* **-ties 1 :** agreeableness **2** *pl* **:** social conventions **3 :** something serving to comfort or accommodate

am•e•thyst \'aməthəst\ *n* **:** purple gemstone

ami•a•ble \'āmēəbəl\ *adj* **:** easy to get along with **—ami•a•bil•i•ty** \,āmēə'bilətē\ *n* **—ami•a•bly** \'āmēəblē\ *adv*

am•i•ca•ble \'amikəbəl\ *adj* **:** friendly **—am•i•ca•bly** \-blē\ *adv*

amid \ə'mid\, **amidst** \-'midst\ *prep* **:** in or into the middle of

amino acid \ə'mēnō-\ *n* **:** nitrogen-containing acid

amiss \ə'mis\ *adv* **:** in the wrong way ~ *adj* **:** wrong

am•me•ter \'am,ētər\ *n* **:** instrument for measuring electric current

am•mo•nia \ə'mōnyə\ *n* **1 :** colorless gaseous compound of nitrogen and hydrogen **2 :** solution of ammonia in water

am•mu•ni•tion \,amyə'nishən\ *n* **1 :** projectiles fired from guns **2 :** explosive items used in war

am•ne•sia \am'nēzhə\ *n* **:** sudden loss of memory **—am•ne•si•ac** \-zē,ak, -zhē-\, **am•ne•sic** \-zik, -sik\ *adj or n*

am•nes•ty \'amnəstē\ *n, pl* **-ties :** a pardon for a group **—amnesty** *vb*

amoe•ba \ə'mēbə\ *n, pl* **-bas** *or* **-bae** \-,bē\ **:** tiny one-celled animal that occurs esp. in water **—amoe•bic** \-bik\ *adj*

amok \ə'mək, -'mäk\ *adv* **:** in a violent or uncontrolled way

among \ə'məŋ\ *prep* **1 :** in or through **2 :** in the number or class of **3 :** in shares to each of

am•o•rous \'amərəs\ *adj* **1 :** inclined to love **2 :** being in love **3 :** indicative of love **—am•o•rous•ly** *adv* **—am•o•rous•ness** *n*

amor•phous \ə'mȯrfəs\ *adj* **:** shapeless

am•or•tize \'amər,tīz, ə'mȯr-\ *vb* **-tized; -tiz•ing :** get rid of (as a debt) gradually with periodic payments **—amor•ti•za•tion** \,amərtə'zāshən, ə,mȯrt-\ *n*

amount \ə'mau̇nt\ *vb* **1 :** be equivalent **2 :** reach a total ~ *n* **:** total number or quantity

amour \ə'mu̇r, ä-, a-\ *n* **1 :** love affair **2 :** lover

am•pere \'am,pir\ *n* **:** unit of electric current

am•per•sand \'ampər,sand\ *n* **:** character & used for the word *and*

am•phib•i•ous \am'fibēəs\ *adj* **1 :** able to live both on land and in water **2 :** adapted for both land and water **—am•phib•i•an** \-ən\ *n*

am•phi•the•ater \'amfə,thēətər\ *n* **:** oval or circular structure with rising tiers of seats around an arena

am•ple \'ampəl\ *adj* **-pler** \-plər\; **-plest** \-pləst\ **1 :** large **2 :** sufficient **—amply** \-plē\ *adv*

am•pli•fy \'amplə,fī\ *vb* **-fied; -fy•ing :** make louder, stronger, or more thorough **—am•pli•fi•ca•tion** \,ampləfə'kāshən\ *n* **—am•pli•fi•er** \'amplə,fīər\ *n*

am•pli•tude \-,tüd, -,tyüd\ *n* **1 :** fullness **2 :** extent of a vibratory movement

am•pu•tate \'ampyə,tāt\ *vb* **-tat•ed; -tating :** cut off (a body part) **—am•pu•ta•tion** \,ampyə'tāshən\ *n* **—am•pu•tee** \,ampyə'tē\ *n*

amuck \ə'mək\ *var of* AMOK

am•u•let \'amyələt\ *n* **:** ornament worn as a charm against evil

amuse \ə'myüz\ *vb* **amused; amus•ing 1 :** engage the attention of in an interesting and pleasant way **2 :** make laugh **—amuse•ment** *n*

an \ən, 'an\ *indefinite article* **:** a —used before words beginning with a vowel sound

-an \ən\, **-ian** \ēən\, **-ean** \ēən\ *n suffix* **1 :** one that belongs to **2 :** one skilled in ~ *adj suffix* **1 :** of or belonging to **2 :** characteristic of or resembling

anach•ro•nism \ə'nakrə,nizəm\ *n* **:** one that is chronologically out of place **—anach•ro•nis•tic** \ə,nakrə'nistik\ *adj*

an•a•con•da \,anə'kändə\ *n* **:** large So. American snake

ana•gram \'anə,gram\ *n* **:** word or phrase made by transposing the letters of another word or phrase

anal \'ānᵊl\ *adj* **:** relating to the anus

an•al•ge•sic \,anᵊl'jēzik, -sik\ *n* **:** pain reliever

anal•o•gy \ə'naləjē\ *n, pl* **-gies 1 :** similarity between unlike things **2 :** example of something similar **—an•a•log•i•cal** \,anᵊl'äjikəl\ *adj* **—an•a•log•i•cal•ly** \-iklē\ *adv* **—anal•o•gous** \ə'naləgəs\ *adj*

anal•y•sis \ə'naləsəs\ *n, pl* **-y•ses** \-,sēz\ **1 :** examination of a thing to determine its parts **2 :** psychoanalysis **—an•a•lyst** \'anᵊlist\ *n* **—an•a•lyt•ic** \,anᵊl'itik\, **an•a•lyt•i•cal** \-ikəl\ *adj* **—an•a•lyt•i•cal•ly** \-iklē\ *adv*

an•a•lyze \'anᵊl,īz\ *vb* **-lyzed; -lyz•ing :** make an analysis of

an•ar•chism \'anər,kizəm, -,när-\ *n* : theory that all government is undesirable —**an•ar•chist** \-kist\ *n or adj* —**an•ar•chis•tic** \,anər'kistik\ *adj*
an•ar•chy \'anərkē, -,när-\ *n* : lack of government or order —**an•ar•chic** \a'närkik\ *adj* —**an•ar•chi•cal•ly** \-iklē\ *adv*
anath•e•ma \ə'nathəmə\ *n* **1** : solemn curse **2** : person or thing accursed or intensely disliked
anat•o•my \ə'natəmē\ *n, pl* **-mies** : science dealing with the structure of organisms —**an•a•tom•ic** \,anə'tämik\, **an•a•tom•i•cal** \-ikəl\ *adj* —**an•a•tom•i•cal•ly** *adv* —**anat•o•mist** \ə'natəmist\ *n*
-ance \əns\ *n suffix* **1** : action or process **2** : quality or state **3** : amount or degree
an•ces•tor \'an,sestər\ *n* : one from whom an individual is descended
an•ces•tress \-trəs\ *n* : female ancestor
an•ces•try \-trē\ *n* **1** : line of descent **2** : ancestors —**an•ces•tral** \an'sestrəl\ *adj*
an•chor \'aŋkər\ *n* : heavy device that catches in the sea bottom to hold a ship in place ~ *vb* : hold or become held in place by or as if by an anchor —**an•chor•age** \-kərij\ *n*
an•chor•man \'aŋkər,man\ *n* : news broadcast coordinator
an•cho•vy \'an,chōvē, an'chō-\ *n, pl* **-vies** *or* **-vy** : small herringlike fish
an•cient \'ānshənt\ *adj* **1** : having existed for many years **2** : belonging to times long past —**ancient** *n*
-ancy \ənsē\ *n suffix* : quality or state
and \ənd, 'and\ *conj* —used to indicate connection or addition
and•iron \'an,dīərn\ *n* : one of 2 metal supports for wood in a fireplace
an•drog•y•nous \an'dräjənəs\ *adj* **1** : having characteristics of both male and female **2** : suitable for either sex
an•ec•dote \'anik,dōt\ *n* : brief story —**an•ec•dot•al** \,anik'dōtᵊl\ *adj*
ane•mia \ə'nēmēə\ *n* : blood deficiency —**ane•mic** \ə'nēmik\ *adj*
anem•o•ne \ə'nemənē\ *n* : small herb with showy usu. white flowers
an•es•the•sia \,anəs'thēzhə\ *n* : loss of bodily sensation
an•es•thet•ic \,anəs'thetik\ *n* : agent that produces anesthesia —**anesthetic** *adj* —**anes•the•tist** \ə'nesthətist\ *n* —**anes•the•tize** \-thə,tīz\ *vb*
anew \ə'nü, -'nyü\ *adv* : over again
an•gel \'ānjəl\ *n* : spiritual being superior to humans —**an•gel•ic** \an'jelik\, **an•gel•i•cal** \-ikəl\ *adj* —**an•gel•i•cal•ly** *adv*
an•ger \'aŋgər\ *n* : strong feeling of displeasure ~ *vb* : make angry
an•gi•na \an'jīnə\ *n* : painful disorder of heart muscles —**an•gi•nal** \an'jīnᵊl\ *adj*
[1]an•gle \'aŋgəl\ *n* **1** : figure formed by the meeting of 2 lines in a point **2** : sharp corner **3** : point of view ~ *vb* **-gled; -gling** : turn or direct at an angle
[2]angle *vb* **an•gled; an•gling** : fish with a hook and line —**an•gler** \-glər\ *n* —**an•gle•worm** *n* —**an•gling** *n*
an•go•ra \aŋ'gōrə, an-\ *n* : yarn or cloth made from the hair of an Angora goat or rabbit
an•gry \'aŋgrē\ *adj* **-gri•er; -est** : feeling or showing anger —**an•gri•ly** \-grəlē\ *adv*
an•guish \'aŋgwish\ *n* : extreme pain or distress of mind —**an•guished** \-gwisht\ *adj*
an•gu•lar \'aŋgyələr\ *adj* **1** : having many or sharp angles **2** : thin and bony —**an•gu•lar•i•ty** \,aŋgyə'larətē\ *n*
an•i•mal \'anəməl\ *n* **1** : living being capable of feeling and voluntary motion **2** : lower animal as distinguished from humans
an•i•mate \'anəmət\ *adj* : having life ~ \-,māt\ *vb* **-mat•ed; -mat•ing 1** : give life or vigor to **2** : make appear to move —**an•i•mat•ed** *adj*
an•i•ma•tion \,anə'māshən\ *n* **1** : liveliness **2** : animated cartoon
an•i•mos•i•ty \,anə'mäsətē\ *n, pl* **-ties** : resentment
an•i•mus \'anəməs\ *n* : deep-seated hostility
an•ise \'anəs\ *n* : herb related to the carrot with aromatic seeds (**ani•seed** \-,sēd\) used in flavoring
an•kle \'aŋkəl\ *n* : joint or region between the foot and the leg —**an•kle•bone** *n*
an•nals \'anᵊlz\ *n pl* : chronological record of history —**an•nal•ist** \-ᵊlist\ *n*
an•neal \ə'nēl\ *vb* **1** : make less brittle by heating and then cooling **2** : strengthen or toughen
an•nex \ə'neks, 'an,eks\ *vb* : assume political control over (a territory) ~ \'an,eks, -iks\ *n* : added building —**an•nex•a•tion** \,an,ek'sāshən\ *n*
an•ni•hi•late \ə'nīə,lāt\ *vb* **-lat•ed; -lating** : destroy —**an•ni•hi•la•tion** \-,nīə'lāshən\ *n*
an•ni•ver•sa•ry \,anə'vərsərē\ *n, pl* **-ries** : annual return of the date of a notable event or its celebration
an•no•tate \'anə,tāt\ *vb* **-tat•ed; -tat•ing** : furnish with notes —**an•no•ta•tion** \,anə'tāshən\ *n* —**an•no•ta•tor** \'anə,tātər\ *n*
an•nounce \ə'nau̇ns\ *vb* **-nounced; -nouncing** : make known publicly —**an•nounce•ment** *n* —**an•nounc•er** *n*
an•noy \ə'nȯi\ *vb* : disturb or irritate —**an•noy•ance** \-əns\ *n* —**an•noy•ing•ly** \-'nȯiiŋlē\ *adv*
an•nu•al \'anyəwəl\ *adj* **1** : occurring once a year **2** : living only one year —**annual** *n* —**an•nu•al•ly** *adv*
an•nu•i•ty \ə'nüətē, -'nyü-\ *n, pl* **-ties** : amount payable annually or the right to such a payment
an•nul \ə'nəl\ *vb* **-ll-** : make legally void —**an•nul•ment** *n*
an•ode \'an,ōd\ *n* **1** : positive electrode **2** : negative battery terminal —**an•od•ic** \a'nädik\ *adj*
anoint \ə'nȯint\ *vb* : apply oil to as a rite —**anoint•ment** *n*
anom•a•ly \ə'näməlē\ *n, pl* **-lies** : something abnormal or unusual —**anom•a•lous** \ə'näməlәs\ *adj*
anon•y•mous \ə'nänəməs\ *adj* : of unknown origin —**an•o•nym•i•ty** \,anə'nimətē\ *n* —**anon•y•mous•ly** *adv*
an•oth•er \ə'nəthər\ *adj* **1** : any or some other **2** : one more ~ *pron* **1** : one more **2** : one different
an•swer \'ansər\ *n* **1** : something spoken or written in reply to a question **2** : solution to a problem ~ *vb* **1** : reply to **2** : be responsible **3** : be adequate —**an•swer•er** *n*
an•swer•able \-rəbəl\ *adj* : responsible
ant \'ant\ *n* : small social insect —**ant•hill** *n*
-ant \ənt\ *n suffix* **1** : one that performs or causes an action **2** : thing that is acted upon ~ *adj suffix* **1** : performing an action or being in a condition **2** : causing an action or process
an•tag•o•nism \an'tagə,nizəm\ *n* : active opposition or hostility —**an•tag•o•nist** \-ənist\ *n* —**an•tag•o•nis•tic** \-,tagə'nistik\ *adj*
an•tag•o•nize \an'tagə,nīz\ *vb* **-nized; -nizing** : cause to be hostile
ant•arc•tic \ant'ärktik, -'ärtik\ *adj* : relating to the region near the south pole
antarctic circle *n* : circle parallel to the equator approximately 23°27′ from the south pole
an•te•bel•lum \,anti'beləm\ *adj* : existing before the U.S. Civil War
an•te•ced•ent \,antə'sēdᵊnt\ *n* : one that comes before —**antecedent** *adj*
an•te•lope \'antᵊl,ōp\ *n, pl* **-lope** *or* **-lopes** : deerlike mammal related to the ox
an•ten•na \an'tenə\ *n, pl* **-nae** \-,nē\ *or* **-nas 1** : one of the long slender paired sensory organs on the head of an arthropod **2** *pl* **-nas** : metallic device for sending or receiving radio waves
an•te•ri•or \an'tirēər\ *adj* : located before in place or time
an•them \'anthəm\ *n* : song or hymn of praise or gladness
an•ther \'anthər\ *n* : part of a seed plant that contains pollen
an•thol•o•gy \an'thäləjē\ *n, pl* **-gies** : literary collection
an•thra•cite \'anthrə,sīt\ *n* : hard coal
an•thro•poid \'anthrə,pȯid\ *n* : large ape —**anthropoid** *adj*
an•thro•pol•o•gy \,anthrə'päləjē\ *n* : science dealing with humans —**an•thro•po•log•i•cal** \-pə'läjikəl\ *adj* —**an•thro•pol•o•gist** \-'päləjist\ *n*
anti- \,antē, -,tī\, **ant-, anth-** *prefix* **1** : opposite in kind, position, or action **2** : opposing or hostile toward **3** : defending against **4** : curing or treating

antiabortion
antiacademic
antiadministration
antiaggression
antiaircraft
antialien
antiapartheid
antiaristocratic
antiart
antiauthoritarian
antiauthority
antibacterial
antibias
antiblack
antibourgeois
antiboycott
antibureaucratic
antiburglar
antiburglary
antibusiness
anticancer
anticapitalism
anticapitalist
anti-Catholic
anticensorship
anti-Christian
anti-Christianity
antichurch
anticigarette
anticlerical
anticollision
anticolonial
anticommunism
anticommunist
anticonservation
anticonservationist
anticonsumer
anticonventional
anticorrosion
anticorrosive
anticorruption
anticrime
anticruelty
anticult
anticultural
antidandruff
antidemocratic
antidiscrimination
antidrug
antidumping
antiestablishment
antievolution
antievolutionary
antifamily
antifascism
antifascist
antifatigue
antifemale
antifeminine
antifeminism
antifeminist
antifertility
antiforeign
antiforeigner
antifraud
antigambling
antiglare
antigovernment
antiguerrilla
antigun
antihijack
antihomosexual
antihuman
antihumanism
antihumanistic
antihunting
anti-imperialism
anti-imperialist
anti-inflation
anti-inflationary
anti-institutional
anti-integration
anti-intellectual
anti-intellectualism
antijamming
anti-Jewish
antilabor
antiliberal
antiliberalism
antilitter
antilittering
antilynching
antimale
antimanagement
antimaterialism
antimaterialist
antimicrobial
antimilitarism
antimilitarist
antimilitary
antimiscegenation
antimonopolist
antimonopoly
antimosquito
antinoise
antiobesity
antiobscenity
antipapal
antipersonnel
antipolice
antipollution
antipornographic
antipornography
antipoverty
antiprofiteering
antiprogressive
antiprostitution
antirabies
antiracketeering
antiradical
antirape
antirealism
antirecession
antireform
antireligious
antirevolutionary
antiriot
antiromantic
antirust
antisegregation
antisex
antisexist
antisexual
antishoplifting
antislavery
antismoking
antismuggling
antismut
antispending
antistrike
antistudent
antisubmarine
antisubversion
antisubversive
antisuicide
antitank
antitax
antitechnological
antitechnology
antiterrorism
antiterrorist
antitheft
antitobacco
antitotalitarian
antitoxin
antitraditional
antitrust
antituberculosis
antitumor
antityphoid
antiulcer
antiunemployment
antiunion
antiuniversity
antiurban
antiviolence
antiviral
antivivisection
antiwar
anti-West
anti-Western
antiwhite
antiwoman

an•ti•bi•ot•ic \,antēbī'ätik, -bē-\ *n* : substance that inhibits harmful microorganisms —**antibiotic** *adj*
an•ti•body \'anti,bädē\ *n* : bodily substance that counteracts the effects of a foreign substance or organism
an•tic \'antik\ *n* : playful act ~ *adj* : playful
an•tic•i•pate \an'tisə,pāt\ *vb* **-pat•ed; -pat•ing 1** : be prepared for **2** : look forward to —**an•tic•i•pa•tion** \-,tisə'pāshən\ *n* —**an•tic•i•pa•to•ry** \-'tisəpə,tōrē\ *adj*
an•ti•cli•max \,antē'klī,maks\ *n* : something strikingly less important than what has preceded it —**an•ti•cli•mac•tic** \-klī'maktik\ *adj*
an•ti•dote \'anti,dōt\ *n* : remedy for poison
an•ti•freeze \'anti,frēz\ *n* : substance to prevent a liquid from freezing
an•ti•mo•ny \'antə,mōnē\ *n* : brittle white metallic chemical element
an•tip•a•thy \an'tipəthē\ *n, pl* **-thies** : strong dislike
an•ti•quar•i•an \,antə'kwerēən\ *adj* : relating to antiquities or old books —**antiquarian** *n* —**an•ti•quar•i•an•ism** *n*
an•ti•quary \'antə,kwerē\ *n, pl* **-quaries** : one who collects or studies antiquities
an•ti•quat•ed \'antə,kwātəd\ *adj* : out-of-date
an•tique \an'tēk\ *adj* : very old or out-of-date —**antique** *n*
an•tiq•ui•ty \an'tikwətē\ *n, pl* **-ties 1** : ancient times **2** *pl* : relics of ancient times
an•ti•sep•tic \,antə'septik\ *adj* : killing or checking the growth of germs —**antiseptic** *n* —**an•ti•sep•ti•cal•ly** \-tiklē\ *adv*
an•tith•e•sis \an'tithəsəs\ *n, pl* **-e•ses** \-,sēz\ : direct opposite
ant•ler \'antlər\ *n* : solid branched horn of a deer —**ant•lered** \-lərd\ *adj*
ant•onym \'antə,nim\ *n* : word of opposite meaning
anus \'ānəs\ *n* : the rear opening of the alimentary canal
an•vil \'anvəl\ *n* : heavy iron block on which metal is shaped
anx•i•ety \aŋ'zīətē\ *n, pl* **-eties** : uneasiness usu. over an expected misfortune
anx•ious \'aŋkshəs\ *adj* **1** : uneasy **2** : earnestly wishing —**anx•ious•ly** *adv*
any \'enē\ *adj* **1** : one chosen at random **2** : of whatever number or quantity ~ *pron* **1** : any one or ones **2** : any amount ~ *adv* : to any extent or degree
any•body \-bədē, -,bäd-\ *pron* : anyone
any•how \-,hau̇\ *adv* **1** : in any way **2** : nevertheless
any•more \,enē'mōr\ *adv* : at the present time
any•one \-'enē,wən\ *pron* : any person
any•place *adv* : anywhere
any•thing *pron* : any thing whatever
any•time *adv* : at any time whatever
any•way *adv* : anyhow
any•where *adv* : in or to any place
aor•ta \ā'ȯrtə\ *n, pl* **-tas** *or* **-tae** \-ē\ : main artery from the heart —**aor•tic** \ā'ȯrtik\ *adj*
apart \ə'pärt\ *adv* **1** : separately in place or time **2** : aside **3** : to pieces
apart•heid \ə'pär,tāt, -,tīt\ *n* : racial segregation
apart•ment \ə'pärtmənt\ *n* : set of usu. rented rooms
ap•a•thy \'apəthē\ *n* : lack of emotion or interest —**ap•a•thet•ic** \,apə'thetik\ *adj* —**ap•a•thet•i•cal•ly** \-iklē\ *adv*
ape \'āp\ *n* : large tailless primate ~ *vb* **aped; ap•ing** : imitate
ap•er•ture \'apər,chu̇r, -chər\ *n* : opening
apex \'ā,peks\ *n, pl* **apex•es** *or* **api•ces** \'āpə,sēz, 'apə-\ : highest point
aphid \'āfid, 'a-\ *n* : small insect that sucks plant juices
aph•o•rism \'afə,rizəm\ *n* : short saying stating a general truth —**aph•o•ris•tic** \,afə'ristik\ *adj*
aph•ro•di•si•ac \,afrə'dēzē,ak, -'diz-\ *n* : substance that excites sexual desire
api•a•rist \'āpēərist\ *n* : beekeeper —**api•ary** \-pē,erē\ *n*
apiece \ə'pēs\ *adv* : for each one
aplen•ty \ə'plentē\ *adj* : plentiful or abundant
aplomb \ə'pläm, -'pləm\ *n* : complete calmness or self-assurance
apoc•a•lypse \ə'päkə,lips\ *n* : writing prophesying a cataclysm in which evil forces are destroyed —**apoc•a•lyp•tic** \-,päkə'liptik\ *adj*
apoc•ry•pha \ə'päkrəfə\ *n* : writings of dubious authenticity —**apoc•ry•phal** \-fəl\ *adj*
apol•o•get•ic \ə,pälə'jetik\ *adj* : expressing apology —**apol•o•get•i•cal•ly** \-iklē\ *adv*
apol•o•gize \ə'pälə,jīz\ *vb* **-gized; -gizing** : make an apology —**apol•o•gist** \-jist\ *n*
apol•o•gy \ə'päləjē\ *n, pl* **-gies 1** : formal justification **2** : expression of regret for a wrong
ap•o•plexy \'apə,pleksē\ *n* : sudden loss of consciousness caused by rupture or obstruction of an artery of the brain —**ap•o•plec•tic** \,apə'plektik\ *adj*
apos•ta•sy \ə'pästəsē\ *n, pl* **-sies** : abandonment of a former loyalty —**apos•tate** \ə'päs,tāt\ *adj or n*
apos•tle \ə'päsəl\ *n* : disciple or advocate —**apos•tle•ship** *n* —**ap•os•tol•ic** \,apə'stälik\ *adj*
apos•tro•phe \ə'pästrə,fē\ *n* : punctuation mark ' to indicate the possessive case or the omission of a letter or figure
apoth•e•cary \ə'päthə,kerē\ *n, pl* **-caries** : druggist
ap•pall \ə'pȯl\ *vb* : fill with horror or dismay
ap•pa•ra•tus \,apə'ratəs, -'rāt-\ *n, pl* **-tus•es** *or* **-tus 1** : equipment **2** : complex machine or device
ap•par•el \ə'parəl\ *n* : clothing
ap•par•ent \ə'parənt\ *adj* **1** : visible **2** : obvious **3** : seeming —**ap•par•ent•ly** *adv*
ap•pa•ri•tion \,apə'rishən\ *n* : ghost
ap•peal \ə'pēl\ *vb* **1** : try to have a court case reheard **2** : ask earnestly **3** : have an attraction —**appeal** *n*
ap•pear \ə'pir\ *vb* **1** : become visible or evident **2** : come into the presence of someone **3** : seem
ap•pear•ance \ə'pirəns\ *n* **1** : act of appearing **2** : outward aspect
ap•pease \ə'pēz\ *vb* **-peased; -peas•ing** : pacify with concessions —**ap•pease•ment** *n*
ap•pel•late \ə'pelət\ *adj* : having power to review decisions
ap•pend \ə'pend\ *vb* : attach
ap•pend•age \ə'pendij\ *n* : something attached
ap•pen•dec•to•my \,apən'dektəmē\ *n, pl* **-mies** : surgical removal of the appendix
ap•pen•di•ci•tis \ə,pendə'sītəs\ *n* : inflammation of the appendix
ap•pen•dix \ə'pendiks\ *n, pl* **-dix•es** *or* **-di•ces** \-də,sēz\ **1** : supplementary matter **2** : narrow closed tube extending from lower right intestine
ap•pe•tite \'apə,tīt\ *n* **1** : natural desire esp. for food **2** : preference
ap•pe•tiz•er \-,tīzər\ *n* : food or drink to stimulate the appetite
ap•pe•tiz•ing \-ziŋ\ *adj* : tempting to the appetite —**ap•pe•tiz•ing•ly** *adv*

ap•plaud \ə'plȯd\ *vb* **:** show approval esp. by clapping
ap•plause \ə'plȯz\ *n* **:** a clapping in approval
ap•ple \'apəl\ *n* **:** rounded fruit with firm white flesh
ap•ple•jack \-ˌjak\ *n* **:** brandy made from cider
ap•pli•ance \ə'plīəns\ *n* **:** household machine or device
ap•pli•ca•ble \'aplikəbəl, ə'plikə-\ *adj* **:** capable of being applied **—ap•pli•ca•bil•i•ty** \ˌaplikə'bilətē, əˌplikə-\ *n*
ap•pli•cant \'aplikənt\ *n* **:** one who applies
ap•pli•ca•tion \ˌaplə'kāshən\ *n* **1 :** act of applying or thing applied **2 :** constant attention **3 :** request
ap•pli•ca•tor \'apləˌkātər\ *n* **:** device for applying a substance
ap•pli•qué \ˌaplə'kā\ *n* **:** cut-out fabric decoration **—appliqué** *vb*
ap•ply \ə'plī\ *vb* **-plied; -ply•ing 1 :** place in contact **2 :** put to practical use **3 :** devote (one's) attention or efforts to something **4 :** submit a request **5 :** have reference or a connection
ap•point \ə'pȯint\ *vb* **1 :** set or assign officially **2 :** equip or furnish **—ap•poin•tee** \əˌpȯin'tē, ˌa-\ *n*
ap•point•ment \ə'pȯintmənt\ *n* **1 :** act of appointing **2 :** nonelective political job **3 :** arrangement for a meeting
ap•por•tion \ə'pōrshən\ *vb* **:** distribute proportionately **—ap•por•tion•ment** *n*
ap•po•site \'apəzət\ *adj* **:** suitable **—ap•po•site•ly** *adv* **—ap•po•site•ness** *n*
ap•praise \ə'prāz\ *vb* **-praised; -prais•ing :** set value on **—ap•prais•al** \-'prāzəl\ *n* **—ap•prais•er** *n*
ap•pre•cia•ble \ə'prēshəbəl\ *adj* **:** considerable **—ap•pre•cia•bly** \-blē\ *adv*
ap•pre•ci•ate \ə'prēshēˌāt\ *vb* **-at•ed; -at•ing 1 :** value justly **2 :** be grateful for **3 :** increase in value **—ap•pre•cia•tion** \-ˌprēshē'āshən\ *n*
ap•pre•cia•tive \ə'prēshətiv, -shēˌāt-\ *adj* **:** showing appreciation
ap•pre•hend \ˌapri'hend\ *vb* **1 :** arrest **2 :** look forward to in dread **3 :** understand **—ap•pre•hen•sion** \-'henchən\ *n*
ap•pre•hen•sive \-'hensiv\ *adj* **:** fearful **—ap•pre•hen•sive•ly** *adv* **—ap•pre•hen•sive•ness** *n*
ap•pren•tice \ə'prentəs\ *n* **:** person learning a craft ~ *vb* **-ticed; -tic•ing :** employ or work as an apprentice **—ap•pren•tice•ship** *n*
ap•prise \ə'prīz\ *vb* **-prised; -pris•ing :** inform
ap•proach \ə'prōch\ *vb* **1 :** move nearer or be close to **2 :** make initial advances or efforts toward **—approach** *n* **—ap•proach•able** *adj*
ap•pro•ba•tion \ˌaprə'bāshən\ *n* **:** approval
ap•pro•pri•ate \ə'prōprēˌāt\ *vb* **-at•ed; -at•ing 1 :** take possession of **2 :** set apart for a particular use ~ \-prēət\ *adj* **:** suitable **—ap•pro•pri•ate•ly** *adv* **—ap•pro•pri•ate•ness** *n* **—ap•pro•pria•tion** \əˌprōprē'āshən\ *n*
ap•prov•al \ə'prüvəl\ *n* **:** act of approving
ap•prove \ə'prüv\ *vb* **-proved; -prov•ing :** accept as satisfactory
ap•prox•i•mate \ə'präksəmət\ *adj* **:** nearly correct or exact ~ \-ˌmāt\ *vb* **-mat•ed; -mat•ing :** come near **—ap•prox•i•mate•ly** *adv* **—ap•prox•i•ma•tion** \-ˌpräksə'māshən\ *n*
ap•pur•te•nance \ə'pərtᵊnəns\ *n* **:** accessory **—ap•pur•te•nant** \-'pərt- ᵊnənt\ *adj*
apri•cot \'aprəˌkät, 'ā-\ *n* **:** peachlike fruit
April \'āprəl\ *n* **:** 4th month of the year having 30 days
apron \'āprən\ *n* **:** protective garment
ap•ro•pos \ˌaprə'pō, 'aprəˌpō\ *adv* **:** suitably ~ *adj* **:** being to the point
apropos of *prep* **:** with regard to
apt \'apt\ *adj* **1:** suitable **2 :** likely **3 :** quick to learn **—apt•ly** *adv* **—aptness** *n*
ap•ti•tude \'aptəˌtüd, -ˌtyüd\ *n* **1 :** capacity for learning **2 :** natural ability
aqua \'akwə, 'äk-\ *n* **:** light greenish blue color
aquar•i•um \ə'kwarēəm\ *n, pl* **-i•ums** *or* **-ia** \-ēə\ **:** glass container for aquatic animals and plants
aquat•ic \ə'kwätik, -'kwat-\ *adj* **:** of or relating to water **—aquatic** *n*
aq•ue•duct \'akwəˌdəkt\ *n* **:** conduit for carrying running water
aq•ui•line \'akwəˌlīn, -lən\ *adj* **:** curved like an eagle's beak
-ar \ər\ *adj suffix* **1 :** of, relating to, or being **2 :** resembling
ar•a•besque \ˌarə'besk\ *n* **:** intricate design
ar•a•ble \'arəbəl\ *adj* **:** fit for crops
ar•bi•ter \'ärbətər\ *n* **:** final authority
ar•bi•trary \'ärbəˌtrerē\ *adj* **1 :** selected at random **2 :** autocratic **—ar•bi•trari•ly** \ˌärbə'trerəlē\ *adv* **—ar•bi•trari•ness** \'ärbəˌtrerēnəs\ *n*
ar•bi•trate \'ärbəˌtrāt\ *vb* **-trat•ed; -trat•ing :** settle a dispute as arbitrator **—ar•bi•tra•tion** \ˌärbə'trāshən\ *n*
ar•bi•tra•tor \'ärbəˌtrātər\ *n* **:** one chosen to settle a dispute
ar•bor \'ärbər\ *n* **:** shelter under branches or vines
ar•bo•re•al \är'bōrēəl\ *adj* **:** living in trees
arc \'ärk\ *n* **1 :** part of a circle **2 :** bright sustained electrical discharge ~ *vb* **arced** \'ärkt\; **arc•ing** \'ärkiŋ\ **:** form an arc
ar•cade \är'kād\ *n* **:** arched passageway between shops
ar•cane \är'kān\ *adj* **:** mysterious or secret
[1]arch \'ärch\ *n* **:** curved structure spanning an opening ~ *vb* **:** cover with or form into an arch
[2]arch *adj* **1 :** chief —usu. in combination **2 :** mischievous **—arch•ly** *adv* **—arch•ness** *n*
ar•chae•ol•o•gy, ar•che•ol•o•gy \ˌärkē'äləjē\ *n* **:** study of past human life **—ar•chae•o•log•i•cal** \-kēə'läjikəl\ *adj* **—ar•chae•ol•o•gist** \-kē'äləjist\ *n*
ar•cha•ic \är'kāik\ *adj* **:** belonging to an earlier time **—ar•cha•i•cal•ly** \-iklē\ *adv*
arch•an•gel \'ärkˌānjəl\ *n* **:** angel of high rank
arch•bish•op \ärch'bishəp\ *n* **:** chief bishop **—arch•bish•op•ric** \-əˌprik\ *n*
arch•di•o•cese \-'dīəsəs, -ˌsēz, -ˌsēs\ *n* **:** diocese of an archbishop
ar•chery \'ärchərē\ *n* **:** shooting with bow and arrows **—ar•cher** \-chər\ *n*
ar•che•type \'ärkiˌtīp\ *n* **:** original pattern or model
ar•chi•pel•a•go \ˌärkə'peləˌgō, ˌärchə-\ *n, pl* **-goes** *or* **-gos :** group of islands
ar•chi•tect \'ärkəˌtekt\ *n* **:** building designer
ar•chi•tec•ture \'ärkəˌtekchər\ *n* **1 :** building design **2 :** style of building **3 :** manner of organizing elements **—ar•chi•tec•tur•al** \ˌärkə'tekchərəl, -'tekshrəl\ *adj* **—ar•chi•tec•tur•al•ly** *adv*
ar•chives \'ärˌkīvz\ *n pl* **:** public records or their storage place **—ar•chi•vist** \'ärkəvist, -ˌkī-\ *n*
arch•way *n* **:** passageway under an arch
arc•tic \'ärktik, 'ärt-\ *adj* **1 :** relating to the region near the north pole **2 :** frigid
arctic circle *n* **:** circle parallel to the equator approximately 23°27′ from the north pole
-ard \ərd\ *n suffix* **:** one that is
ar•dent \'ärdᵊnt\ *adj* **:** characterized by warmth of feeling **—ar•dent•ly** *adv*
ar•dor \'ärdər\ *n* **:** warmth of feeling
ar•du•ous \'ärjəwəs\ *adj* **:** difficult **—ar•du•ous•ly** *adv* **—ar•du•ous•ness** *n*
are *pres 2d sing or pres pl of* BE
ar•ea \'arēə\ *n* **1 :** space for something **2 :** amount of surface included **3 :** region **4 :** range covered by a thing or concept
area code *n* **:** 3-digit area-identifying telephone number
are•na \ə'rēnə\ *n* **1 :** enclosed exhibition area **2 :** sphere of activity
ar•gon \'ärˌgän\ *n* **:** colorless odorless gaseous chemical element
ar•got \'ärgət, -ˌgō\ *n* **:** special language (as of the underworld)
argu•able \'ärgyəwəbəl\ *adj* **:** open to dispute
ar•gue \'ärgyü\ *vb* **-gued; -gu•ing 1 :** give reasons for or against something **2 :** disagree in words
ar•gu•ment \'ärgyəmənt\ *n* **1 :** reasons given to persuade **2 :** dispute with words
ar•gu•men•ta•tive \ˌärgyə'mentətiv\ *adj* **:** inclined to argue
ar•gyle \'ärˌgīl\ *n* **:** colorful diamond pattern in knitting
aria \'ärēə\ *n* **:** opera solo
ar•id \'arəd\ *adj* **:** very dry **—arid•i•ty** \ə'ridətē\ *n*
arise \ə'rīz\ *vb* **arose** \-'rōz\; **aris•en** \-'rizᵊn\; **aris•ing** \-'rīziŋ\ **1 :** get up **2 :** originate
ar•is•toc•ra•cy \ˌarə'stäkrəsē\ *n, pl* **-cies :** upper class **—aris•to•crat** \ə'ristəˌkrat\ *n* **—aris•to•crat•ic** \əˌristə'kratik\ *adj*
arith•me•tic \ə'rithməˌtik\ *n* **:** mathematics that deals with numbers **—ar•ith•met•ic** \ˌarith'metik\, **ar•ith•met•i•cal** \-ikəl\ *adj*
ark \'ärk\ *n* **:** big boat
[1]arm \'ärm\ *n* **1 :** upper limb **2 :** branch **—armed** \'ärmd\ *adj* **—arm•less** *adj*
[2]arm *vb* **:** furnish with weapons ~ *n* **1 :** weapon **2 :** branch of the military forces **3** *pl* **:** family's heraldic designs
ar•ma•da \är'mädə, -'mād-\ *n* **:** naval fleet
ar•ma•dil•lo \ˌärmə'dilō\ *n, pl* **-los :** burrowing mammal covered with bony plates
ar•ma•ment \'ärməmənt\ *n* **:** military arms and equipment
ar•ma•ture \'ärməˌchu̇r, -chər\ *n* **:** rotating part of an electric generator or motor
armed forces *n pl* **:** military
ar•mi•stice \'ärməstəs\ *n* **:** truce
ar•mor \'ärmər\ *n* **:** protective covering **—ar•mored** \-mərd\ *adj*
ar•mory \'ärmərē\ *n, pl* **-mor•ies :** factory or storehouse for arms
arm•pit *n* **:** hollow under the junction of the arm and shoulder
ar•my \'ärmē\ *n, pl* **-mies 1 :** body of men organized for war esp. on land **2 :** great number
aro•ma \ə'rōmə\ *n* **:** usu. pleasing odor **—ar•o•mat•ic** \ˌarə'matik\ *adj*
around \ə'rau̇nd\ *adv* **1 :** in or along a circuit **2 :** on all sides **3 :** near **4 :** in an opposite direction ~ *prep* **1 :** surrounding **2 :** along the circuit of **3 :** to or on the other side of **4 :** near
arouse \ə'rau̇z\ *vb* **aroused; arous•ing 1 :** awaken from sleep **2 :** stir up **—arous•al** \-'rau̇zəl\ *n*
ar•raign \ə'rān\ *vb* **1 :** call before a court to answer to an indictment **2 :** accuse **—ar•raign•ment** *n*
ar•range \ə'rānj\ *vb* **-ranged; -rang•ing 1 :** put in order **2 :** settle or agree on **3 :** adapt (a musical composition) for voices or instruments **—ar•range•ment** *n* **—ar•rang•er** *n*
ar•ray \ə'rā\ *vb* **1 :** arrange in order **2 :** dress esp. splendidly ~ *n* **1 :** arrangement **2 :** rich clothing **3 :** imposing group
ar•rears \ə'rirz\ *n pl* **:** state of being behind in paying debts
ar•rest \ə'rest\ *vb* **1 :** stop **2 :** take into legal custody **—arrest** *n*
ar•rive \ə'rīv\ *vb* **-rived; -riv•ing 1 :** reach a destination, point, or stage **2 :** come near in time **—ar•riv•al** \-əl\ *n*
ar•ro•gant \'arəgənt\ *adj* **:** showing an offensive sense of superiority **—ar•ro•gance** \-gəns\ *n* **—ar•ro•gant•ly** *adv*
ar•ro•gate \-ˌgāt\ *vb* **-gat•ed; -gat•ing :** to claim without justification
ar•row \'arō\ *n* **:** slender missile shot from a bow **—ar•row•head** *n*
ar•royo \ə'ròiō, -ə\ *n, pl* **-royos 1 :** watercourse **2 :** gully
ar•se•nal \'ärsᵊnəl\ *n* **1 :** place where arms are made or stored **2 :** store
ar•se•nic \'ärsᵊnik\ *n* **:** solid grayish poisonous chemical element
ar•son \'ärsᵊn\ *n* **:** willful or malicious burning of property **—ar•son•ist** \-ist\ *n*
art \'ärt\ *n* **1 :** skill **2 :** branch of learning **3 :** creation of things of beauty or works so produced **4 :** ingenuity
ar•te•rio•scle•ro•sis \ärˌtirēōsklə'rōsəs\ *n* **:** hardening of the arteries **—ar•te•rio•scle•rot•ic** \-'rätik\ *adj or n*
ar•tery \'ärtərē\ *n, pl* **-ter•ies 1 :** tubular vessel carrying blood from the heart **2 :** thoroughfare **—ar•te•ri•al** \är'tirēəl\ *adj*
art•ful \-fəl\ *adj* **1 :** ingenious **2 :** crafty **—art•ful•ly** *adv* **—art•ful•ness** *n*
ar•thri•tis \är'thrītəs\ *n, pl* **-ti•des** \-'thritəˌdēz\ **:** inflammation of the joints **—ar•thrit•ic** \-'thritik\ *adj or n*
ar•thro•pod \'ärthrəˌpäd\ *n* **:** invertebrate animal (as an insect or crab) with segmented body and jointed limbs **—arthropod** *adj*
ar•ti•choke \'ärtəˌchōk\ *n* **:** tall thistlelike herb or its edible flower head
ar•ti•cle \'ärtikəl\ *n* **1 :** distinct part of a written document **2 :** nonfictional published piece of writing **3 :** word (as *an, the*) used to limit a noun **4 :** item or piece
ar•tic•u•late \är'tikyələt\ *adj* **:** able to speak effectively ~ \-ˌlāt\ *vb* **-lated; -lat•ing 1 :** utter distinctly **2 :** unite by joints **—ar•tic•u•late•ly** *adv* **—ar•tic•u•late•ness** *n* **—ar•tic•u•la•tion** \-ˌtikyə'lāshən\ *n*
ar•ti•fact \'ärtəˌfakt\ *n* **:** object of esp. prehistoric human workmanship
ar•ti•fice \'ärtəfəs\ *n* **1 :** trick or trickery **2 :** ingenious device or ingenuity
ar•ti•fi•cial \ˌärtə'fishəl\ *adj* **1 :** man-made **2 :** not genuine **—ar•ti•fi•ci•al•i•ty** \-ˌfishē'alətē\ *n* **—ar•ti•fi•cial•ly** *adv* **—ar•ti•fi•cial•ness** *n*
ar•til•lery \är'tilərē\ *n, pl* **-ler•ies :** large caliber firearms
ar•ti•san \'ärtəzən, -sən\ *n* **:** skilled craftsman
art•ist \'ärtist\ *n* **:** one who creates art **—ar•tis•tic** \är'tistik\ *adj* **—ar•tis•ti•cal•ly** \-iklē\ *adv* **—art•ist•ry** \'ärtəstrē\ *n*
art•less \'ärtləs\ *adj* **:** sincere or natural **—art•less•ly** *adv* **—art•less•ness** *n*
arty \'ärtē\ *adj* **art•i•er; -est :** pretentiously artistic **—art•i•ly** \'ärtᵊlē\ *adv* **—art•i•ness** *n*
-ary \ˌerē\ *adj suffix* **:** of, relating to, or connected with
as \əz, ˌaz\ *adv* **1 :** to the same degree **2 :** for example ~ *conj* **1 :** in the same way or degree as **2 :** while **3 :** because **4 :** though ~ *pron* —used after *same* or *such* ~ *prep* **:** in the capacity of
as•bes•tos \as'bestəs, az-\ *n* **:** fibrous incombustible mineral
as•cend \ə'send\ *vb* **:** move upward **—as•cen•sion** \-'senchən\ *n*
as•cen•dan•cy \ə'sendənsē\ *n* **:** domination
as•cen•dant \ə'sendənt\ *n* **:** dominant position ~ *adj* **1 :** moving upward **2 :** dominant
as•cent \ə'sent\ *n* **1 :** act of moving upward **2 :** degree of upward slope
as•cer•tain \ˌasər'tān\ *vb* **:** determine **—as•cer•tain•able** *adj*
as•cet•ic \ə'setik\ *adj* **:** self-denying **—ascetic** *n* **—as•cet•i•cism** \-'setə- ˌsizəm\ *n*
as•cribe \ə'skrīb\ *vb* **-cribed; -crib•ing :** attribute **—as•crib•able** *adj* **—ascrip•tion** \-'skripshən\ *n*
asep•tic \ā'septik\ *adj* **:** free of disease germs
[1]ash \'ash\ *n* **:** tree related to the olives
[2]ash *n* **:** matter left when something is burned **—ash•tray** *n*
ashamed \ə'shāmd\ *adj* **:** feeling shame **—asham•ed•ly** \-'shāmədlē\ *adv*
ash•en \'ashən\ *adj* **:** deadly pale
ashore \ə'shōr\ *adv* **:** on or to the shore
aside \ə'sīd\ *adv* **1 :** toward the side **2 :** out of the way
aside from *prep* **1 :** besides **2 :** except for
as•i•nine \'asᵊnˌīn\ *adj* **:** foolish **—as•i•nin•i•ty** \ˌasᵊn'inətē\ *n*
ask \'ask\ *vb* **1 :** call on for an answer or help **2 :** utter (a question or request) **3 :** invite
askance \ə'skans\ *adv* **1 :** with a side glance **2 :** with mistrust
askew \ə'skyü\ *adv or adj* **:** out of line
asleep \ə'slēp\ *adv or adj* **1 :** sleeping **2 :** numbed **3 :** inactive
as long as *conj* **1 :** on condition that **2 :** because
as of *prep* **:** from the time of
as•par•a•gus \ə'sparəgəs\ *n* **:** tall herb related to the lilies or its edible stalks
as•pect \'asˌpekt\ *n* **1 :** way something looks to the eye or mind **2 :** phase
as•pen \'aspən\ *n* **:** poplar
as•per•i•ty \a'sperətē, ə-\ *n, pl* **-ties 1 :** roughness **2 :** harshness
as•per•sion \ə'spərzhən\ *n* **:** remark that hurts someone's reputation
as•phalt \'asˌfȯlt\ *n* **:** dark tarlike substance used in paving
as•phyx•ia \as'fiksēə\ *n* **:** lack of oxygen causing unconsciousness
as•phyx•i•ate \-sēˌāt\ *vb* **-at•ed; -at•ing :** suffocate **—as•phyx•i•a•tion** \-ˌfiksē'āshən\ *n*
as•pi•ra•tion \ˌaspə'rāshən\ *n* **:** strong desire to achieve a goal
as•pire \ə'spīr\ *vb* **-pired; -pir•ing :** have an ambition **—as•pir•ant** \'aspərənt, ə'spīrənt\ *n*
as•pi•rin \'asprən\ *n, pl* **aspirin** *or* **aspirins :** pain reliever
ass \'as\ *n* **1 :** long-eared animal related to the horse **2 :** stupid person
as•sail \ə'sāl\ *vb* **:** attack violently **—as•sail•able** *adj* **—as•sail•ant** *n*
as•sas•si•nate \ə'sasᵊnˌāt\ *vb* **-nat•ed; -nat•ing :** murder esp. for political reasons **—as•sas•sin** \-'sasᵊn\ *n* **—as•sas•si•na•tion** \-ˌsasᵊn'āshən\ *n*
as•sault \ə'sȯlt\ *n or vb* **:** attack
as•say \'asˌā, a'sā\ *n* **:** analysis (as of an ore) to determine quality or properties **—as•say** \a'sā, 'asˌā\ *vb*
as•sem•ble \ə'sembəl\ *vb* **-bled; -bling 1 :** collect into one place **2 :** fit together the parts of
as•sem•bly \-blē\ *n, pl* **-blies 1 :** meeting **2** *cap* **:** legislative body **3 :** a fitting together of parts
as•sem•bly•man \-mən\ *n* **:** member of a legislative assembly
as•sem•bly•wom•an \-ˌwu̇-mən\ *n* **:** woman who is a member of a legislative assembly
as•sent \ə'sent\ *vb or n* **:** consent
as•sert \ə'sərt\ *vb* **1 :** declare **2 :** defend **—as•ser•tion** \-'sərshən\ *n* **—as•sert•ive** \-'sərtiv\ *adj* **—as•sert•ive•ness** *n*
as•sess \ə'ses\ *vb* **1 :** impose (as a tax) **2 :** evaluate for taxation **—as•sess•ment** *n* **—as•ses•sor** \-ər\ *n*
as•set \'asˌet\ *n* **1** *pl* **:** individually owned property **2 :** advantage or resource
as•sid•u•ous \ə'sijəwəs\ *adj* **:** diligent **—as•si•du•i•ty** \ˌasə'düətē, -'dyü-\ *n* **—as•sid•u•ous•ly** *adv* **—as•sid•u•ous•ness** *n*
as•sign \ə'sīn\ *vb* **1 :** transfer to another **2 :** appoint to a duty **3 :** designate as a task **4 :** attribute **—assign•able** *adj* **—as•sign•ment** *n*
as•sim•i•late \ə'siməˌlāt\ *vb* **-lat•ed; -lat•ing 1 :** absorb as nourishment **2 :** understand **—as•sim•i•la•tion** \-ˌsimə'lāshən\ *n*
as•sist \ə'sist\ *vb* **:** help **—assist** *n* **—assis•tance** \-'sistəns\ *n* **—as•sis•tant** \-tənt\ *n*
as•so•ci•ate \ə'sōshēˌāt, -sē-\ *vb* **-at•ed; -at•ing 1 :** join in companionship or partnership **2 :** connect in thought **—as•so•ci•ate** \-shēət, -sēət\ *n* **—as•so•ci•a•tion** \-ˌsōshē'āshən, -sē-\ *n*
as soon as *conj* **:** when
as•sort•ed \ə'sȯrtəd\ *adj* **:** consisting of various kinds
as•sort•ment \-mənt\ *n* **:** assorted collection
as•suage \ə'swāj\ *vb* **-suaged; -suag•ing :** ease or satisfy
as•sume \ə'süm\ *vb* **-sumed; -sum•ing 1 :** take upon oneself **2 :** pretend to have or be **3 :** take as true
as•sump•tion \ə'səmpshən\ *n* **:** something assumed
as•sure \ə'shu̇r\ *vb* **-sured; -sur•ing 1 :** give confidence or conviction to **2 :** guarantee **—as•sur•ance** \-əns\ *n*
as•ter \'astər\ *n* **:** herb with daisylike flowers

as•ter•isk \'astə,risk\ *n* : a character * used as a reference mark or as an indication of omission of words

astern \ə'stərn\ *adv or adj* **1** : behind **2** : at or toward the stern

as•ter•oid \'astə,rȯid\ *n* : small planet between Mars and Jupiter

asth•ma \'azmə\ *n* : disorder marked by difficulty in breathing **—asth•mat•ic** \az'matik\ *adj or n*

astig•ma•tism \ə'stigmə,tizəm\ *n* : visual defect **—as•tig•mat•ic** \,astig'matik\ *adj*

as to *prep* **1** : concerning **2** : according to

as•ton•ish \ə'stänish\ *vb* : amaze **—as•ton•ish•ing•ly** *adv* **—as•ton•ish•ment** *n*

as•tound \ə'stau̇nd\ *vb* : fill with confused wonder **—as•tound•ing•ly** *adv*

astrad•dle \ə'stradᵊl\ *adv or prep* : so as to straddle

as•tral \'astrəl\ *adj* : relating to or coming from the stars

astray \ə'strā\ *adv or adj* : off the right path

astride \ə'strīd\ *adv* : with legs apart or one on each side ~ *prep* : with one leg on each side of

as•trin•gent \ə'strinjənt\ *adj* : causing shrinking or puckering of tissues **—as•trin•gen•cy** \-jənsē\ *n* **—astringent** *n*

as•trol•o•gy \ə'sträləjē\ *n* : prediction of events by the stars **—as•trol•o•ger** \-əjər\ *n* **—as•tro•log•i•cal** \,astrə'läjikəl\ *adj*

as•tro•naut \'astrə,nȯt\ *n* : space traveler

as•tro•nau•tics \,astrə'nȯtiks\ *n* : construction and operation of spacecraft **—as•tro•nau•tic** \-ik\, **as•tro•nau•ti•cal** \-ikəl\ *adj*

as•tro•nom•i•cal \,astrə'nämikəl\ *adj* **1** : relating to astronomy **2** : extremely large

as•tron•o•my \ə'stränəmē\ *n, pl* **-mies** : study of the celestial bodies **—as•tron•o•mer** \-əmər\ *n*

as•tute \ə'stüt, -'styüt\ *adj* : shrewd **—as•tute•ly** *adv* **—as•tute•ness** *n*

asun•der \ə'səndər\ *adv or adj* **1** : into separate pieces **2** : separated

asy•lum \ə'sīləm\ *n* **1** : refuge **2** : institution for care esp. of the insane

asym•met•ri•cal \,āsə'metrikəl\, **asym•met•ric** \-trik\ *adj* : not symmetrical **—asym•me•try** \,ā'simətrē\ *n*

at \ət, 'at\ *prep* **1** —used to indicate a point in time or space **2** —used to indicate a goal **3** —used to indicate condition, means, cause, or manner

at all *adv* : without restriction or under any circumstances

ate *past of* EAT

-ate \ət, ,āt\ *n suffix* **1** : office or rank **2** : group of persons holding an office or rank ~ *adj suffix* **1** : brought into or being in a state **2** : marked by having

athe•ist \'āthēist\ *n* : one who denies the existence of God **—athe•ism** \-,izəm\ *n* **—athe•is•tic** \,āthē'istik\ *adj*

ath•ero•scle•ro•sis \,athərōsklə'rōsəs\ *n* : arteriosclerosis with deposition of fatty substances in the arteries **—ath•ero•scle•rot•ic** \-'rätik\ *adj*

ath•lete \'ath,lēt\ *n* : one trained to compete in athletics

ath•let•ics \ath'letiks\ *n sing or pl* : exercises and games requiring physical skill **—ath•let•ic** \-ik\ *adj*

-a•tion \'āshən\ *n suffix* : action or process

-a•tive \,ātiv, ətiv\ *adj suffix* **1** : of, relating to, or connected with **2** : tending to

atlas \'atləs\ *n* : book of maps

at•mo•sphere \'atmə,sfir\ *n* **1** : mass of air surrounding the earth **2** : surrounding influence **—at•mo•spher•ic** \,atmə'sfirik, -'sfer-\ *adj* **—at•mo•spher•i•cal•ly** \-iklē\ *adv*

atoll \'a,tȯl, 'ā-, -,täl\ *n* : ring-shaped coral island

at•om \'atəm\ *n* **1** : tiny bit **2** : smallest particle of a chemical element that can exist alone or in combination

atom•ic \ə'tämik\ *adj* **1** : relating to atoms **2** : nuclear

atomic bomb *n* : bomb utilizing the energy released by splitting the atom

at•om•iz•er \'atə,mīzər\ *n* : device for dispersing a liquid as a very fine spray

atone \ə'tōn\ *vb* **atoned; aton•ing** : make amends **—atone•ment** *n*

atop \ə'täp\ *prep* : on top of ~ *adv or adj* : on, to, or at the top

atri•um \'ātrēəm\ *n, pl* **atria** \-trēə\ *or* **atri•ums** **1** : open central room or court **2** : heart chamber that receives blood from the veins

atro•cious \ə'trōshəs\ *adj* : appalling or abominable **—atro•cious•ly** *adv* **—atro•cious•ness** *n*

atroc•i•ty \ə'träsətē\ *n, pl* **-ties** : savage act

at•ro•phy \'atrəfē\ *n, pl* **-phies** : wasting away of a bodily part or tissue **—at•ro•phy** *vb*

at•ro•pine \'atrə,pēn\ *n* : drug used esp. to relieve spasms

at•tach \ə'tach\ *vb* **1** : seize legally **2** : bind by personalities **3** : join **—attach•ment** *n*

at•ta•ché \,atə'shā, ,a,ta-, ə,ta-\ *n* : technical expert on a diplomatic staff

at•tack \ə'tak\ *vb* **1** : try to hurt or destroy with violence or words **2** : set to work on ~ *n* **1** : act of attacking **2** : fit of sickness

at•tain \ə'tān\ *vb* **1** : achieve or accomplish **2** : reach **—at•tain•abil•i•ty** \ə,tānə'bilətē\ *n* **—at•tain•able** *adj* **—at•tain•ment** *n*

at•tempt \ə'tempt\ *vb* : make an effort toward **—attempt** *n*

at•tend \ə'tend\ *vb* **1** : handle or provide for the care of something **2** : accompany **3** : be present at **4** : pay attention **—at•ten•dance** \-'tendəns\ *n* **—at•ten•dant** \-dənt\ *adj or n*

at•ten•tion \ə'tenchən\ *n* **1** : concentration of the mind on something **2** : notice or awareness **—at•ten•tive** \-'tentiv\ *adj* **—at•ten•tive•ly** *adv* **—at•ten•tive•ness** *n*

at•ten•u•ate \ə'tenyə,wāt\ *vb* **-at•ed; -at•ing** **1** : make or become thin **2** : weaken **—at•ten•u•a•tion** \-,tenyə'wāshən\ *n*

at•test \ə'test\ *vb* : certify or bear witness **—at•tes•ta•tion** \,a,tes'tāshən\ *n*

at•tic \'atik\ *n* : space just below the roof

at•tire \ə'tīr\ *vb* **-tired; -tir•ing** : dress **—attire** *n*

at•ti•tude \'atə,tüd, -,tyüd\ *n* **1** : posture or relative position **2** : feeling, opinion, or mood

at•tor•ney \ə'tərnē\ *n, pl* **-neys** : legal agent

at•tract \ə'trakt\ *vb* **1** : draw to oneself **2** : have emotional or aesthetic appeal for **—at•trac•tion** \-'trakshən\ *n* **—at•trac•tive** \-'traktiv\ *adj* **—at•trac•tive•ly** *adv* **—at•trac•tive•ness** *n*

at•tri•bute \'atrə,byüt\ *n* : inherent characteristic ~ \ə'tribyət\ *vb* **-trib•ut•ed; -trib•ut•ing** **1** : regard as having a specific cause or origin **2** : regard as a characteristic **—at•trib•ut•able** *adj* **—at•tri•bu•tion** \,atrə'byüshən\ *n*

at•tune \ə'tün, -'tyün\ *vb* : bring into harmony

au•burn \'ȯbərn\ *adj* : reddish brown

auc•tion \'ȯkshən\ *n* : public sale of property to the highest bidder **—auction** *vb* **—auc•tion•eer** \,ȯkshə'nir\ *n*

au•dac•i•ty \ȯ'dasətē\ *n* : boldness or insolence **—au•da•cious** \ȯ'dāshəs\ *adj*

au•di•ble \'ȯdəbəl\ *adj* : capable of being heard **—au•di•bly** \-blē\ *adv*

au•di•ence \'ȯdēəns\ *n* **1** : formal interview **2** : group of listeners or spectators

au•dio \'ȯdē,ō\ *adj* : relating to sound or its reproduction ~ *n* : television sound

au•dio•vi•su•al \,ȯdēō'vizhəwəl\ *adj* : relating to both hearing and sight

au•dit \'ȯdət\ *vb* : examine financial accounts **—audit** *n* **—au•di•tor** \'ȯdətər\ *n*

au•di•tion \ȯ'dishən\ *n* : tryout performance **—audition** *vb*

au•di•to•ri•um \,ȯdə'tōrēəm\ *n, pl* **-riums** *or* **-ria** \-rēə\ : room or building used for public performances

au•di•to•ry \'ȯdə,tōrē\ *adj* : relating to hearing

au•ger \'ȯgər\ *n* : tool for boring

aug•ment \ȯg'ment\ *vb* : enlarge or increase **—aug•men•ta•tion** \,ȯgmən'tāshən\ *n*

au•gur \'ȯgər\ *n* : prophet ~ *vb* : predict **—au•gu•ry** \'ȯgyərē, -gər-\ *n*

au•gust \ȯ'gəst\ *adj* : majestic

Au•gust \'ȯgəst\ *n* : 8th month of the year having 31 days

auk \'ȯk\ *n* : stocky diving seabird

aunt \'ant, 'ȧnt\ *n* **1** : sister of one's father or mother **2** : wife of one's uncle

au•ra \'ȯrə\ *n* **1** : distinctive atmosphere **2** : luminous radiation

au•ral \'ȯrəl\ *adj* : relating to the ear or to hearing

au•ri•cle \'ȯrikəl\ *n* : atrium or ear-shaped pouch in the atrium of the heart

au•ro•ra bo•re•al•is \ə'rōrə,bōrē'aləs\ *n* : display of light in the night sky of northern latitudes

aus•pic•es \'ȯspəsəz, -,sēz\ *n pl* : patronage and protection

aus•pi•cious \ȯ'spishəs\ *adj* : favorable

aus•tere \ȯ'stir\ *adj* : severe **—aus•tere•ly** *adv* **—aus•ter•i•ty** \ȯ'sterətē\ *n*

au•then•tic \ə'thentik, ȯ-\ *adj* : genuine **—au•then•ti•cal•ly** \-iklē\ *adv* **—au•then•tic•i•ty** \,ȯ,then'tisətē\ *n*

au•then•ti•cate \ə'thenti,kāt, ȯ-\ *vb* **-cated; -cat•ing** : prove genuine **—au•then•ti•ca•tion** \-,thenti'kāshən\ *n*

au•thor \'ȯthər\ *n* **1** : writer **2** : creator **—au•thor•ship** *n*

au•thor•i•tar•i•an \ə,thärə'terēən, ə-, -,thȯr-\ *adj* : marked by blind obedience to authority

au•thor•i•ta•tive \ə'thärə,tātiv, ȯ-, -'thȯr-\ *adj* : being an authority **—au•thor•i•ta•tive•ly** *adv* **au•thor•i•ta•tive•ness** *n*

au•thor•i•ty \ə'thärətē, ȯ-, -'thȯr-\ *n, pl* **-ties** **1** : expert **2** : right, responsibility, or power to influence **3** *pl* : persons in official positions

au•tho•rize \'ȯthə,rīz\ *vb* **-rized; -rizing** : permit or give official approval for **—au•tho•ri•za•tion** \,ȯthərə'zāshən\ *n*

au•to \'ȯtō\ *n, pl* **autos** : automobile

au•to•bi•og•ra•phy \,ȯtəbī'ägrəfē, -bē-\ *n* : writer's own life story **—au•to•bi•og•ra•pher** \-fər\ *n* **—au•to•bio•graph•i•cal** \-,bīə'grafikəl\ *adj*

au•toc•ra•cy \ȯ'täkrəsē\ *n, pl* **-cies** : government by one person having unlimited power **—au•to•crat** \'ȯtə,krat\ *n* **—au•to•crat•ic** \,ȯtə'kratik\ *adj* **—au•to•crat•i•cal•ly** \-iklē\ *adv*

au•to•graph \'ȯtə,graf\ *n* : signature ~ *vb* : write one's name on

au•to•mate \'ȯtə,māt\ *vb* **-mat•ed; -mating** : make automatic **—au•to•ma•tion** \,ȯtə'māshən\ *n*

au•to•mat•ic \,ȯtə'matik\ *adj* **1** : involuntary **2** : designed to function without human intervention ~ *n* : automatic device (as a firearm) **—au•to•mat•i•cal•ly** \-iklē\ *adv*

au•tom•a•ton \ȯ'tämətən, -,tän\ *n, pl* **-a•tons** *or* **-a•ta** \-tə, -,tä\ : robot

au•to•mo•bile \,ȯtəmō'bēl, -'mō,bēl\ *n* : 4-wheeled passenger vehicle with its own power source

au•to•mo•tive \,ȯtə'mōtiv\ *adj* : relating to automobiles

au•ton•o•mous \ȯ'tänəməs\ *adj* : self-governing **—au•ton•o•mous•ly** *adv* **—au•ton•o•my** \-mē\ *n*

au•top•sy \'ȯ,täpsē, 'ȯtəp-\ *n, pl* **-sies** : medical examination of a corpse

au•tumn \'ȯtəm\ *n* : season between summer and winter **—au•tum•nal** \ȯ'təmnəl\ *adj*

aux•il•ia•ry \ȯg'zilyərē, -lərē\ *adj* **1** : being a supplement or reserve **2** : accompanying a main verb form to express person, number, mood, or tense **—auxiliary** *n*

avail \ə'vāl\ *vb* : be of use or make use ~ *n* : use

avail•able \ə'vāləbəl\ *adj* **1** : usable **2** : accessible **—avail•abil•i•ty** \-,vālə'bilətē\ *n*

av•a•lanche \'avə,lanch\ *n* : mass of sliding or falling snow or rock

av•a•rice \'avərəs\ *n* : greed **—av•a•ri•cious** \,avə'rishəs\ *adj*

avenge \ə'venj\ *vb* **avenged; aveng•ing** : take vengeance for **—aveng•er** *n*

av•e•nue \'avə,nü, -,nyü\ *n* **1** : way of approach **2** : broad street

av•er•age \'avrij\ *adj* **1** : being about midway between extremes **2** : ordinary ~ *vb* **1** : be usually **2** : find the mean of ~ *n* : mean

averse \ə'vərs\ *adj* : feeling dislike or reluctance **—aver•sion** \-'vərzhən\ *n*

avert \ə'vərt\ *vb* : turn away

avi•ary \'āvē,erē\ *n, pl* **-ar•ies** : place where birds are kept

avi•a•tion \,āvē'āshən, ,av-\ *n* : operation or manufacture of airplanes **—avi•a•tor** \'āvē,ātər, 'av-\ *n*

av•id \'avəd\ *adj* **1** : greedy **2** : enthusiastic **—avid•i•ty** \ə'vidətē, a-\ *n* **—av•id•ly** *adv*

av•o•ca•do \,avə'kädō, ,äv-\ *n, pl* **-dos** : tropical fruit with green pulp

av•o•ca•tion \,avə'kāshən\ *n* : hobby

avoid \ə'vȯid\ *vb* **1** : keep away from **2** : prevent the occurrence of **3** : refrain from **—avoid•able** *adj* **—avoidance** \-ᵊns\ *n*

av•oir•du•pois \,avərdə'pȯiz\ *n* : system of weight based on the pound of 16 ounces

avow \ə'vau̇\ *vb* : declare openly **—avow•al** \-'vau̇əl\ *n*

await \ə'wāt\ *vb* : wait for

awake \ə'wāk\ *vb* **awoke** \-'wōk\; **awok•en** \-'wōkən\ *or* **awaked; awak•ing** : wake up **—awake** *adj*

awak•en \ə'wākən\ *vb* **-ened; -en•ing** : wake up

award \ə'wȯrd\ *vb* : give (something won or deserved) ~ *n* **1** : judgment **2** : prize

aware \ə'war\ *adj* : having realization or consciousness **—aware•ness** *n*

awash \ə'wȯsh, -'wäsh\ *adv or adj* : flooded

away \ə'wā\ *adv* **1** : from this or that place or time **2** : out of the way **3** : in another direction **4** : from one's possession ~ *adj* **1** : absent **2** : distant

awe \'ȯ\ *n* : respectful fear or wonder ~ *vb* **awed; aw•ing** : fill with awe **—awe•some** \-səm\ *adj* **—awe•struck** *adj*

aw•ful \'ȯfəl\ *adj* **1** : inspiring awe **2** : extremely disagreeable **3** : very great **—aw•ful•ly** *adv*

awhile \ə'hwīl\ *adv* : for a while

awk•ward \'ȯkwərd\ *adj* **1** : clumsy **2** : embarrassing **—awk•ward•ly** *adv* **—awk•ward•ness** *n*

awl \'ȯl\ *n* : hole-making tool

aw•ning \'ȯniŋ\ *n* : window cover

awry \ə'rī\ *adv or adj* : wrong

ax, axe \'aks\ *n* : chopping tool

ax•i•om \'aksēəm\ *n* : generally accepted truth **—ax•i•om•at•ic** \,aksēə'matik\ *adj*

ax•is \'aksəs\ *n, pl* **ax•es** \-,sēz\ : center of rotation **—ax•i•al** \-sēəl\ *adj* **—ax•i•al•ly** *adv*

ax•le \'aksəl\ *n* : shaft on which a wheel revolves

aye \'ī\ *adv* : yes ~ *n* : a vote of yes

aza•lea \ə'zālyə\ *n* : rhododendron with funnel-shaped blossoms

az•i•muth \'azəməth\ *n* : horizontal direction expressed as an angle

azure \'azhər\ *n* : blue of the sky **—azure** *adj*

B

b \'bē\ *n, pl* **b's** *or* **bs** \'bēz\ : 2d letter of the alphabet

bab•ble \'babəl\ *vb* **-bled; -bling** **1** : utter meaningless sounds **2** : talk foolishly or too much **—babble** *n* **—bab•bler** *n*

babe \'bāb\ *n* : baby

ba•bel \'babəl, 'bab-\ *n* : noisy confusion

ba•boon \ba'bün\ *n* : large Asian or African ape with a doglike muzzle

ba•by \'bābē\ *n, pl* **-bies** : very young child ~ *vb* **-bied; -by•ing** : pamper **—baby** *adj* **—ba•by•hood** *n* **—ba•by•ish** *adj*

ba•by–sit *vb* **-sat; -sit•ting** : care for children while parents are away **—baby–sit•ter** *n*

bac•ca•lau•re•ate \,bakə'lȯrēət\ *n* : bachelor's degree

bac•cha•na•lia \,bakə'nālyə\ *n, pl* **-lia** : drunken orgy **—bac•cha•na•lian** \-yən\ *adj or n*

bach•e•lor \'bachələr\ *n* **1** : holder of lowest 4-year college degree **2** : unmarried man **—bach•e•lor•hood** *n*

ba•cil•lus \bə'siləs\ *n, pl* **-li** \-,ī\ : rod-shaped bacterium **—bac•il•lary** \'basə,lerē\ *adj*

back \'bak\ *n* **1** : part of a human or animal body nearest the spine **2** : part opposite the front **3** : player farthest from the opponent's goal ~ *adv* **1** : to or at the back **2** : ago **3** : to or in a former place or state **4** : in reply ~ *adj* **1** : located at the back **2** : not paid on time **3** : moving or working backward **4** : not current ~ *vb* **1** : support **2** : go or cause to go back **3** : form the back of **—back•ache** *n* **—backer** *n* **—back•ing** *n* **—back•less** *adj* **—back•rest** *n*

back•bite *vb* **-bit; -bit•ten; -bit•ing** : say spiteful things about someone absent **—back•bit•er** *n*

back•bone *n* **1** : bony column in the back that encloses the spinal cord **2** : firm character

back•drop *n* : painted cloth hung across the rear of a stage

back•fire *n* : loud noise from the wrongly timed explosion of fuel in an engine ~ *vb* **1** : make or undergo a backfire **2** : have a result opposite of that intended

back•gam•mon \'bak,gamən\ *n* : board game

back•ground *n* **1** : scenery behind something **2** : sum of a person's experience or training

back•hand *n* : stroke (as in tennis) made with the back of the hand turned forward **—backhand** *adj or vb* **—back•hand•ed** *adj*

back•lash *n* : adverse reaction

back•log *n* : accumulation of things to be done **—backlog** *vb*

back•pack *n* : camping pack carried on the back ~ *vb* : hike with a backpack **—back•pack•er** *n*

back•slide *vb* **-slid; -slid** *or* **-slid•den** \-,slidᵊn\; **-slid•ing** : lapse in morals or religious practice **—back•slid•er** *n*

back•stage *adv or adj* : in or to an area behind a stage

back•up *n* : substitute

back•ward \'bakwərd\, **back•wards** *adv* **1** : toward the back **2** : with the back foremost **3** : in a reverse direction **4** : toward an earlier or worse state ~ *adj* **1** : directed, turned, or done backward **2** : retarded in development **—back•ward•ness** *n*

back•woods *n pl* : remote or isolated place

ba•con \'bākən\ *n* : salted and smoked meat from a pig

bac•te•ri•um \bak'tirēəm\ *n, pl* **-ria** \-ēə\ : microscopic plant **—bac•te•ri•al** \-ēəl\ *adj* **—bac•te•ri•o•log•ic** \-,tirēə'läjik\, **bac•te•ri•o•log•i•cal** \-əl\ *adj* **—bac•te•ri•ol•o•gist** \-ē'äləjist\ *n* **—bac•te•ri•ol•o•gy** \-jē\ *n*

bad \'bad\ *adj* **worse** \'wərs\; **worst** \'wərst\ **1** : not good **2** : naughty **3** : faulty **4**

: spoiled —**bad** *n or adv* —**bad•ly** *adv* —**bad•ness** *n*

bade *past of* BID

badge \'baj\ *n* : symbol of status

bad•ger \'bajər\ *n* : burrowing mammal ~ *vb* : harass

bad•min•ton \'bad,mintᵊn\ *n* : tennis-like game played with a shuttlecock

baf•fle \'bafəl\ *vb* **-fled; -fling** : perplex ~ *n* : device to alter flow (as of liquid or sound) —**baf•fle•ment** *n*

bag \'bag\ *n* : flexible usu. closable container ~ *vb* **-gg- 1** : bulge out **2** : put in a bag **3** : catch in hunting

bag•a•telle \,bagə'tel\ *n* : trifle

ba•gel \'bāgəl\ *n* : hard doughnut-shaped roll

bag•gage \'bagij\ *n* : traveler's bags and belongings

bag•gy \'bagē\ *adj* **-gi•er; -est** : puffed out like a bag —**bag•gi•ly** *adv* —**bag•gi•ness** *n*

bag•pipe *n* : musical instrument with a bag, a tube with valves, and sounding pipes —often pl.

¹**bail** \'bāl\ *n* : container for scooping water out of a boat —**bail** *vb* —**bail•er** *n*

²**bail** *n* **1** : security given to guarantee a prisoner's appearance in court **2** : release secured by bail ~ *vb* : bring about the release of by giving bail

bai•liff \'bāləf\ *n* **1** : British sheriff's aide **2** : minor officer of a U.S. court

bai•li•wick \'bāli,wik\ *n* : one's special field or domain

bail•out \'bā,laut\ *n* : rescue from financial distress

bait \'bāt\ *vb* **1** : harass with dogs usu. for sport **2** : furnish (a hook or trap) with bait ~ *n* : lure esp. for catching animals

bake \'bāk\ *vb* **baked; bak•ing** : cook in dry heat esp. in an oven ~ *n* : party featuring baked food —**baker** *n* —**bak•ery** \'bākərē\ *n* —**bake•shop** *n*

bal•ance \'baləns\ *n* **1** : weighing device **2** : counteracting weight, force, or influence **3** : equilibrium **4** : that which remains ~ *vb* **-anced; -anc•ing 1** : compute the balance **2** : equalize **3** : bring into harmony or proportion —**bal•anced** *adj*

bal•co•ny \'balkənē\ *n, pl* **-nies** : platform projecting from a wall

bald \'bold\ *adj* **1** : lacking a natural or usual covering (as of hair) **2** : plain —**bald•ing** *adj* —**bald•ly** *adv* —**bald•ness** *n*

bal•der•dash \'boldər,dash\ *n* : nonsense

bale \'bāl\ *n* : large bundle ~ *vb* **baled; bal•ing** : pack in a bale —**bal•er** *n*

bale•ful \'bālfəl\ *adj* **1** : deadly **2** : ominous

balk \'bok\ *n* : hindrance ~ *vb* **1** : thwart **2** : stop short and refuse to go on —**balky** *adj*

¹**ball** \'bol\ *n* **1** : rounded mass **2** : game played with a ball ~ *vb* : form into a ball

²**ball** *n* : large formal dance —**ballroom** *n*

bal•lad \'baləd\ *n* **1** : narrative poem **2** : slow romantic song —**bal•lad•eer** \,balə'diər\ *n*

bal•last \'baləst\ *n* : heavy material to steady a ship or balloon ~ *vb* : provide with ballast

bal•le•ri•na \,balə'rēnə\ *n* : female ballet dancer

bal•let \'ba,lā, ba'lā\ *n* : theatrical dancing

bal•lis•tics \bə'listiks\ *n sing or pl* : science of projectile motion —**ballistic** *adj*

bal•loon \bə'lün\ *n* : inflated bag ~ *vb* **1** : travel in a balloon **2** : swell out —**bal•loon•ist** *n*

bal•lot \'balət\ *n* **1** : paper used to cast a vote **2** : system of voting ~ *vb* : vote

bal•ly•hoo \'balē,hü\ *n* : publicity —**bally•hoo** *vb*

balm \'bäm, 'bälm\ *n* **1** : fragrant healing or soothing preparation **2** : spicy fragrant herb

balmy \'bämē, 'bälmē\ *adj* **balm•i•er; -est** : gently soothing —**balm•i•ness** *n*

ba•lo•ney \bə'lōnē\ *n* : nonsense

bal•sa \'bölsə\ *n* : very light wood of a tropical tree

bal•sam \'bölsəm\ *n* **1** : aromatic resinous plant substance **2** : balsam-yielding plant —**bal•sam•ic** \böl'samik\ *adj*

bal•us•ter \'baləstər\ *n* : upright support for a rail

bal•us•trade \-,strād\ *n* : row of balusters topped by a rail

bam•boo \bam'bü\ *n* : tall tropical grass with strong hollow stems

bam•boo•zle \bam'büzəl\ *vb* **-zled; -zling** : deceive

ban \'ban\ *vb* **-nn-** : prohibit ~ *n* : legal prohibition

ba•nal \bə'näl, -'nal; 'bānᵊl\ *adj* : ordinary and uninteresting —**ba•nal•i•ty** \bə'nal-tē\ *n*

ba•nana \bə'nanə\ *n* : elongated fruit of a treelike tropical plant

¹**band** \'band\ *n* **1** : something that ties or binds **2** : strip or stripe different (as in color) from nearby matter **3** : range of radio wavelengths ~ *vb* **1** : enclose with a band **2** : unite for a common end —**band•ed** *adj* —**band•er** *n*

²**band** *n* **1** : group **2** : musicians playing together

ban•dage \'bandij\ *n* : material used esp. in dressing wounds ~ *vb* : dress or cover with a bandage

ban•dan•na, ban•dana \ban'danə\ *n* : large colored figured handkerchief

ban•dit \'bandət\ *n* : outlaw or robber —**ban•dit•ry** \-,dətrē\ *n*

band•stand *n* : stage for band concerts

band•wag•on *n* : candidate, side, or movement gaining support

¹**ban•dy** \'bandē\ *vb* **-died; -dy•ing** : exchange in rapid succession

²**bandy** *adj* : curved outward

bane \'bān\ *n* **1** : poison **2** : cause of woe —**bane•ful** *adj*

¹**bang** \'baŋ\ *vb* : strike, thrust, or move usu. with a loud noise ~ *n* **1** : blow **2** : sudden loud noise ~ *adv* : directly

²**bang** *n* : fringe of short hair over the forehead —usu. pl. ~ *vb* **1** : cut in bangs

ban•gle \'baŋgəl\ *n* : bracelet

ban•ish \'banish\ *vb* **1** : force by authority to leave a country **2** : expel —**ban•ish•ment** *n*

ban•is•ter \-əstər\ *n* **1** : baluster **2** : handrail

ban•jo \'ban,jō\ *n, pl* **-jos** : stringed instrument with a drumlike body —**banjo•ist** *n*

¹**bank** \'baŋk\ *n* **1** : piled-up mass **2** : rising ground along a body of water **3** : sideways slope along a curve ~ *vb* **1** : form a bank **2** : cover (as a fire) to keep inactive **3** : incline (an airplane) laterally

²**bank** *n* : tier of objects

³**bank** *n* **1** : money institution **2** : reserve supply ~ *vb* : conduct business in a bank —**bank•book** *n* —**bank•er** *n* —**bank•ing** *n*

bank•rupt \'baŋ,krəpt\ *n* : one required by law to forfeit assets to pay off debts ~ *adj* **1** : legally a bankrupt **2** : lacking something essential —**bankrupt** *vb* —**bank•rupt•cy** \-,krəpsē\ *n*

ban•ner \'banər\ *n* : flag ~ *adj* : excellent

banns \'banz\ *n pl* : announcement in church of a proposed marriage

ban•quet \'baŋkwət\ *n* : ceremonial dinner —**banquet** *vb*

ban•shee \'banshē\ *n* : wailing female spirit that foretells death

ban•tam \'bantəm\ *n* : miniature domestic fowl

ban•ter \'bantər\ *n* : good-natured joking —**banter** *vb*

ban•yan \'banyən\ *n* : large tree that grows new trunks from the limbs

bap•tism \'bap,tizəm\ *n* : Christian rite signifying spiritual cleansing —**baptis•mal** \bap'tizməl\ *adj*

bap•tize \'bap'tīz, 'bap,tīz\ *vb* **-tized; -tiz•ing** : administer baptism to

bar \'bär\ *n* **1** : long narrow object used esp. as a lever, fastening, or support **2** : barrier **3** : body of practicing lawyers **4** : wide stripe **5** : food counter **6** : place where liquor is served **7** : vertical line across the musical staff ~ *vb* **-rr- 1** : obstruct with a bar **2** : shut out **3** : prohibit ~ *prep* : excluding —**barred** *adj* —**barroom** *n* —**bar•tend•er** *n*

barb \'bärb\ *n* : sharp projection pointing backward —**barbed** *adj*

bar•bar•ian \bär'barēən\ *adj* **1** : relating to people considered backward **2** : not refined —**barbarian** *n*

bar•bar•ic \-'barik\ *adj* : barbarian

bar•ba•rous \'bärbərəs\ *adj* **1** : lacking refinement **2** : mercilessly cruel —**bar•bar•ism** \-bə,rizəm\ *n* —**bar•bar•i•ty** \bär'barətē\ *n* —**bar•ba•rous•ly** *adv*

bar•be•cue \'bärbi,kyü\ *n* : gathering at which barbecued food is served ~ *vb* **-cued; -cu•ing** : cook over hot coals or on a spit often with a highly seasoned sauce

bar•ber \'bärbər\ *n* : one who cuts hair

bar•bi•tu•rate \bär'bichərət\ *n* : sedative or hypnotic drug

bard \'bärd\ *n* : poet

bare \'bar\ *adj* **bar•er; bar•est 1** : naked **2** : not concealed **3** : empty **4** : leaving nothing to spare **5** : plain ~ *vb* **bared; bar•ing** : make or lay bare —**bare•foot, bare•foot•ed** *adv or adj* —**bare•hand•ed** *adv or adj* —**bare•head•ed** *adv or adj* —**bare•ly** *adv* —**bare•ness** *n*

bare•back, bare•backed *adv or adj* : without a saddle

bare•faced *adj* : open and esp. brazen

bar•gain \'bärgən\ *n* **1** : agreement **2** : something bought for less than its value ~ *vb* **1** : negotiate **2** : barter

barge \'bärj\ *n* : broad flat-bottomed boat ~ *vb* **barged; barg•ing** : move rudely or clumsily —**barge•man** *n*

bari•tone \'barə,tōn\ *n* : male voice between bass and tenor

bar•i•um \'barēəm\ *n* : silver-white metallic chemical element

¹**bark** \'bärk\ *vb* **1** : make the sound of a dog **2** : speak in a loud curt tone ~ *n* : sound of a barking dog

²**bark** *n* **1** : tough corky outer covering of a woody stem or root ~ *vb* : remove bark or skin from

³**bark** *n* : sailing ship with a fore-and-aft rear sail

bark•er \'bärkər\ *n* : one who calls out to attract people to a show

bar•ley \'bärlē\ *n* : cereal grass or its seeds

barn \'bärn\ *n* : building for keeping hay or livestock —**barn•yard** *n*

bar•na•cle \'bärnikəl\ *n* : marine crustacean

barn•storm *vb* : tour through rural districts giving performances

ba•rom•e•ter \bə'rämətər\ *n* : instrument for measuring atmospheric pressure —**baro•met•ric** \,barə'metrik\ *adj*

bar•on \'barən\ *n* : British peer —**bar•on•age** \-ij\ *n* —**ba•ro•ni•al** \bə'rōnēəl\ *adj* —**bar•ony** \'barənē\ *n*

bar•on•ess \-ənəs\ *n* **1** : baron's wife **2** : woman holding a baronial title

bar•on•et \-ənət\ *n* : man holding a rank between a baron and a knight —**bar•on•et•cy** \-sē\ *n*

ba•roque \bə'rōk, -'räk\ *adj* : elaborately ornamented

bar•racks \'barəks\ *n sing or pl* : soldiers' housing

bar•ra•cu•da \,barə'küdə\ *n, pl* **-da** *or* **-das** : large predatory sea fish

bar•rage \bə'räzh, -'räj\ *n* : heavy artillery fire

bar•rel \'barəl\ *n* **1** : closed cylindrical container **2** : amount held by a barrel **3** : cylindrical part ~ *vb* **-reled** *or* **-relled; -rel•ing** *or* **-rel•ling 1** : pack in a barrel **2** : move at high speed —**bar•reled** *adj*

bar•ren \'barən\ *adj* **1** : unproductive of life **2** : uninteresting —**bar•ren•ness** *n*

bar•rette \bä'ret, bə-\ *n* : clasp for a woman's hair

bar•ri•cade \'barə,kād, ,barə'-\ *n* : barrier —**barricade** *vb*

bar•ri•er \'barēər\ *n* : something that separates or obstructs

bar•ring \'bäriŋ\ *prep* : omitting

bar•ris•ter \'barəstər\ *n* : British trial lawyer

bar•row \'barō\ *n* : wheelbarrow

bar•ter \'bärtər\ *vb* : trade by exchange of goods —**barter** *n*

ba•salt \bə'sólt, 'bā,-\ *n* : dark fine-grained igneous rock —**ba•sal•tic** \bə'sóltik\ *adj*

¹**base** \'bās\ *n, pl* **bas•es 1** : bottom **2** : fundamental part **3** : beginning point **4** : supply source of a force **5** : compound that reacts with an acid to form a salt ~ *vb* **based; bas•ing** : establish —**base•less** *adj*

²**base** *adj* **bas•er; bas•est 1** : inferior **2** : contemptible —**base•ly** *adv* —**baseness** *n*

base•ball *n* : game played with a bat and ball by 2 teams

base•ment \-mənt\ *n* : part of a building below ground level

bash \'bash\ *vb* : strike violently ~ *n* : heavy blow

bash•ful \-fəl\ *adj* : self-conscious —**bash•ful•ness** *n*

ba•sic \'bāsik\ *adj* **1** : relating to or forming the base or essence **2** : relating to a chemical base —**ba•si•cal•ly** *adv* —**ba•sic•i•ty** \bā'sisətē\ *n*

ba•sil \'bazəl, 'bās-, 'bāz-\ *n* : aromatic mint

ba•sil•i•ca \bə'silikə\ *n* : important church or cathedral

ba•sin \'bāsᵊn\ *n* **1** : large bowl or pan **2** : region drained by a river

ba•sis \'bāsəs\ *n, pl* **ba•ses** \-,sēz\ **1** : something that supports **2** : fundamental principle

bask \'bask\ *vb* : enjoy pleasant warmth

bas•ket \'baskət\ *n* : woven container —**bas•ket•ful** *n*

bas•ket•ball *n* : game played with a ball on a court by 2 teams

bas-re•lief \,bäri'lēf\ *n* : flat sculpture with slightly raised design

¹**bass** \'bas\ *n, pl* **bass** *or* **bass•es** : spiny-finned sport and food fish

²**bass** \'bās\ *n* **1** : deep tone **2** : lowest choral voice

bas•set hound \'basət-\ *n* : short-legged dog with long ears

bas•si•net \,basə'net\ *n* : baby's bed

bas•soon \bə'sün, ba-\ *n* : low-pitched wind instrument

bas•tard \'bastərd\ *n* **1** : illegitimate child **2** : offensive person ~ *adj* **1** : illegitimate **2** : inferior —**bas•tardize** *vb* —**bas•tardy** *n*

¹**baste** \'bāst\ *vb* **bast•ed; bast•ing** : sew temporarily with long stitches

²**baste** *vb* **bast•ed; bast•ing** : moisten at intervals while cooking

bas•tion \'baschən\ *n* : fortified position

¹**bat** \'bat\ *n* **1** : stick or club **2** : sharp blow ~ *vb* **-tt-** : hit with a bat

²**bat** *n* : small flying mammal

³**bat** *vb* **-tt-** : wink or blink

batch \'bach\ *n* : quantity used or produced at one time

bate \'bāt\ *vb* **bat•ed; bat•ing** : moderate or reduce

bath \'bath, 'bäth\ *n, pl* **baths** \'bathz, 'baths, 'bäthz, 'bäths\ **1** : a washing of the body **2** : water for washing the body **3** : liquid in which something is immersed **4** : bathroom **5** : large financial loss —**bath•tub** *n*

bathe \'bāth\ *vb* **bathed; bath•ing 1** : wash in liquid **2** : flow against so as to wet **3** : shine light over **4** : take a bath or a swim —**bath•er** *n*

bath•robe *n* : robe worn around the house

bath•room *n* : room with a bathtub and shower and usu. a sink and toilet

ba•tiste \bə'tēst\ *n* : fine sheer fabric

ba•ton \bə'tän\ *n* : musical conductor's stick

bat•tal•ion \bə'talyən\ *n* : military unit composed of a headquarters and two or more companies

bat•ten \'batᵊn\ *n* : strip of wood used to seal or reinforce ~ *vb* : furnish or fasten with battens

¹**bat•ter** \'batər\ *vb* : beat or damage with repeated blows

²**batter** *n* : mixture of flour and liquid

³**batter** *n* : player who bats

bat•tery \'batərē\ *n, pl* **-ter•ies 1** : illegal beating of a person **2** : group of artillery guns **3** : group of electric cells

bat•ting \'batiŋ\ *n* : layers of cotton or wool for stuffing

bat•tle \'batᵊl\ *n* : military fighting ~ *vb* **-tled; -tling** : engage in battle —**battle•field** *n*

bat•tle•ax *n* : long-handled ax formerly used as a weapon

bat•tle•ment \-mənt\ *n* : parapet on top of a wall

bat•tle•ship *n* : heavily armed warship

bat•ty \'batē\ *adj* **-ti•er; -est** : crazy

bau•ble \'bóbəl\ *n* : trinket

bawdy \'bódē\ *adj* **bawd•i•er; -est** : obscene or lewd —**bawd•i•ly** *adv* —**bawd•i•ness** *n*

bawl \'ból\ *vb* : cry loudly ~ *n* : long loud cry

¹**bay** \'bā\ *adj* : reddish brown ~ *n* : bay-colored animal

²**bay** *n* : European laurel

³**bay** *n* **1** : compartment **2** : area projecting out from a building and containing a window (**bay window**)

⁴**bay** *vb* : bark with deep long tones ~ *n* **1** : position of one unable to escape danger **2** : baying of dogs

⁵**bay** *n* : body of water smaller than a gulf and nearly surrounded by land

bay•ber•ry \-,berē\ *n* : shrub bearing small waxy berries

bay•o•net \'bāənət, ,bāə'net\ *n* : dagger that fits on the end of a rifle ~ *vb* **-net•ed; -net•ing** : stab with a bayonet

bay•ou \'bīü, -ō\ *n* : creek flowing through marshy land

ba•zaar \bə'zär\ *n* **1** : market **2** : fair for charity

ba•zoo•ka \-'zükə\ *n* : weapon that shoots armor-piercing rockets

BB *n* : small shot pellet

be \'bē\ *vb* **was** \'wəz, 'wäz\, **were** \'wər\; **been** \'bin\; **be•ing** \'bēiŋ\; **am** \'am, əm, 'am\, **is** \'iz, əz\, **are** \ər, 'är\ **1** : equal **2** : exist **3** : occupy a certain place **4** : occur ~ *verbal auxiliary* —used to show continuous action or to form the passive voice

beach \'bēch\ *n* : sandy shore of a sea, lake, or river ~ *vb* : drive ashore

beach•comb•er \-,kōmər\ *n* : one who searches the shore for useful objects

beach•head *n* : shore area held by an attacking force in an invasion

bea•con \'bēkən\ *n* : guiding or warning light or signal

bead \'bēd\ *n* : small round body esp. strung on a thread ~ *vb* : form into a bead —**bead•ing** *n* —**beady** *adj*

bea•gle \'bēgəl\ *n* : small short-legged hound

beak \'bēk\ *n* : bill of a bird —**beaked** *adj*

bea•ker \'bēkər\ *n* **1** : large drinking cup **2** : laboratory vessel

beam \'bēm\ *n* **1** : large long piece of timber or metal **2** : ray of light **3** : directed radio signals for the guidance of pilots ~ *vb* **1** : send out light **2** : smile **3** : aim a radio broadcast

bean \'bēn\ *n* : edible plant seed borne in pods

¹**bear** \'bar\ *n, pl* **bears** *or pl* **bear** : large heavy mammal with shaggy hair **2** : gruff or sullen person —**bearish** *adj*

²**bear** *vb* **bore** \'bōr\; **borne** \'bōrn\; **bear•ing 1** : carry **2** : give birth to or produce **3** : endure **4** : press **5** : go in an indicated direction —**bear•able** *adj* —**bear•er** *n*

beard \'bird\ *n* **1** : facial hair on a man **2** : tuft like a beard ~ *vb* : confront boldly —**beard•ed** *adj* —**beard•less** *adj*

bear•ing *n* **1** : way of carrying oneself **2** : supporting object or purpose **3** : significance **4** : machine part in which an-

other part turns **5** : direction with respect esp. to compass points
beast \'bēst\ *n* **1** : animal **2** : brutal person —**beast·li·ness** *n* —**beast·ly** *adj*
beat \'bēt\ *vb* **beat; beat·en** \'bētᵊn\ *or* **beat; beat·ing 1** : strike repeatedly **2** : defeat **3** : act or arrive before **4** : throb ~ *n* **1** : single stroke or pulsation **2** : rhythmic stress in poetry or music ~ *adj* : exhausted —**beat·er** *n*
be·atif·ic \ˌbēə'tifik\ *adj* : blissful
be·at·i·fy \bē'atəˌfī\ *vb* **-fied; -fy·ing** : make happy or blessed —**be·at·i·fi·ca·tion** \-ˌatəfə'kāshən\ *n*
be·at·i·tude \-'atəˌtüd, -ˌtyüd\ *n* : saying in the Sermon on the Mount (Matthew 5:3-12) beginning "Blessed are"
beau \'bō\ *n, pl* **beaux** \'bōz\ *or* **beaus** : suitor
beau·ty \'byütē\ *n, pl* **-ties** : qualities that please the senses or mind —**beau·te·ous** \-ēəs\ *adj* —**beau·te·ous·ly** *adv* —**beau·ti·fi·ca·tion** \ˌbyütəfə'kāshən\ *n* —**beau·ti·fi·er** \'byütəˌfīər\ *n* —**beau·ti·ful** \-ifəl\ *adj* —**beau·ti·ful·ly** *adv* —**beau·ti·fy** \-əˌfī\ *vb*
bea·ver \'bēvər\ *n* : large fur-bearing rodent
be·cause \bi'kȯz, -'kəz\ *conj* : for the reason that
because of *prep* : by reason of
beck \'bek\ *n* : summons
beck·on \'bekən\ *vb* : summon esp. by a nod or gesture
be·come \bi'kəm\ *vb* **-came** \-'kām\; **-come; -com·ing 1** : come to be **2** : be suitable —**be·com·ing** *adj* —**be·com·ing·ly** *adv*
bed \'bed\ *n* **1** : piece of furniture to sleep on **2** : flat or level surface ~ *vb* **-dd-** : put or go to bed —**bed·spread** *n*
bed·bug *n* : wingless bloodsucking insect
bed·clothes *n pl* : bedding
bed·ding *n* **1** : sheets and blankets for a bed **2** : soft material (as hay) for an animal's bed
be·deck \bi'dek\ *vb* : adorn
be·dev·il \-'devəl\ *vb* : harass
bed·lam \'bedləm\ *n* : uproar and confusion
be·drag·gled \bi'dragəld\ *adj* : dirty and disordered
bed·rid·den \'bedˌridᵊn\ *adj* : kept in bed by illness
bed·rock *n* : solid subsurface rock —**bedrock** *adj*
[1]**bee** \'bē\ *n* : 4-winged honey-producing insect —**bee·hive** *n* —**bee·keep·er** *n* —**bees·wax** *n*
[2]**bee** *n* : neighborly work session
beech \'bēch\ *n, pl* **beech·es** *or* **beech** : tree with smooth gray bark and edible nuts (**beech·nuts**) —**beech·en** \-ən\ *adj*
beef \'bēf\ *n, pl* **beefs** \'bēfs\ *or* **beeves** \'bēvz\ : flesh of a steer, cow, or bull ~ *vb* : strengthen —used with *up* —**beef·steak** *n*
bee·line *n* : straight course
been *past part of* BE
beep \'bēp\ *n* : short usu. high-pitched warning sound —**beep** *vb* —**beep·er** *n*
beer \'bir\ *n* : alcoholic drink brewed from malt and hops —**beery** *adj*
beet \'bēt\ *n* : garden root vegetable
bee·tle \'bētəl\ *n* : 4-winged insect
be·fall \bi'fȯl\ *vb* **-fell; -fall·en** : happen to
be·fit \bi'fit\ *vb* : be suitable to
be·fore \bi'fōr\ *adv* **1** : in front **2** : earlier ~ *prep* **1** : in front of **2** : earlier than ~ *conj* : earlier than
be·fore·hand *adv or adj* : in advance
be·friend \bi'frend\ *vb* : act as friend to
be·fud·dle \-'fədᵊl\ *vb* : confuse
beg \'beg\ *vb* **-gg-** : ask earnestly
be·get \bi'get\ *vb* **-got; -got·ten** *or* **-got; -get·ting** : become the father of
beg·gar \'begər\ *n* : one that begs ~ *vb* : make poor —**beg·gar·ly** *adj* —**beg·gary** *n*
be·gin \bi'gin\ *vb* **-gan** \-'gan\; **-gun** \-'gən\; **-gin·ning 1** : start **2** : come into being —**be·gin·ner** *n*
be·gone \bi'gȯn\ *vb* : go away
be·go·nia \-'gōnyə\ *n* : tropical herb with waxy flowers
be·grudge \-'grəj\ *vb* **1** : concede reluctantly **2** : look upon disapprovingly
be·guile \-'gīl\ *vb* **-guiled; -guil·ing 1** : deceive **2** : amuse
be·half \-'haf, -'häf\ *n* : benefit
be·have \-'hāv\ *vb* **-haved; -hav·ing** : act in a certain way
be·hav·ior \-'hāvyər\ *n* : way of behaving —**be·hav·ior·al** \-əl\ *adj*
be·head \-'hed\ *vb* : cut off the head of
be·hest \-'hest\ *n* : command
be·hind \bi'hīnd\ *adv* : at the back ~ *prep* **1** : in back of **2** : less than **3** : supporting
be·hold \-'hōld\ *vb* **-held; -hold·ing** : see —**be·hold·er** *n*
be·hold·en \-'hōldən\ *adj* : indebted
be·hoove \-'hüv\ *vb* **-hooved; -hoov·ing** : be necessary for
beige \'bāzh\ *n* : yellowish brown —**beige** *adj*
be·ing \'bēiŋ\ *n* **1** : existence **2** : living thing
be·la·bor \bi'lābər\ *vb* : carry on to absurd lengths
be·lat·ed \-'lātəd\ *adj* : delayed
belch \'belch\ *vb* **1** : expel stomach gas orally **2** : emit forcefully —**belch** *n*
be·lea·guer \bi'lēgər\ *vb* **1** : besiege **2** : harass
bel·fry \'belfrē\ *n, pl* **-fries** : bell tower
be·lie \bi'lī\ *vb* **-lied; -ly·ing 1** : misrepresent **2** : prove false
be·lief \bə'lēf\ *n* **1** : trust **2** : something believed
be·lieve \-'lēv\ *vb* **-lieved; -liev·ing 1** : trust in **2** : accept as true **3** : hold as an opinion —**be·liev·able** *adj* —**be·liev·ably** *adv* —**be·liev·er** *n*
be·lit·tle \bi'litᵊl\ *vb* **-lit·tled; -lit·tling 1** : disparage **2** : make seem less
bell \'bel\ *n* : hollow metallic device that rings when struck ~ *vb* : provide with a bell
bel·la·don·na \ˌbelə'dänə\ *n* : poisonous herb yielding a drug
belle \'bel\ *n* : beautiful woman
bel·li·cose \'beliˌkōs\ *adj* : pugnacious —**bel·li·cos·i·ty** \ˌbeli'käsətē\ *n*
bel·lig·er·ent \bə'lijərənt\ *adj* **1** : waging war **2** : truculent —**bel·lig·er·ence** \-rəns\ *n* —**bel·lig·er·en·cy** \-rənsē\ *n* —**belligerent** *n*
bel·low \'belō\ *vb* : make a loud deep roar or shout —**bellow** *n*
bel·lows \-ōz, -əz\ *n sing or pl* : device with sides that can be compressed to expel air
bell·weth·er \'bel'weth̲ər, -ˌweth̲-\ *n* : leader
bel·ly \'belē\ *n, pl* **-lies** : abdomen ~ *vb* **-lied; -ly·ing** : bulge
be·long \bi'lȯŋ\ *vb* **1** : be suitable **2** : be owned **3** : be a part of
be·long·ings \-iŋz\ *n pl* : possessions
be·loved \bi'ləvəd, -'ləvd\ *adj* : dearly loved —**beloved** *n*
be·low \-'lō\ *adv* : in or to a lower place ~ *prep* : lower than
belt \'belt\ *n* **1** : strip (as of leather) worn about the waist **2** : endless band to impart motion **3** : distinct region ~ *vb* **1** : put a belt around **2** : thrash
be·moan \bi'mōn\ *vb* : lament
be·muse \-'myüz\ *vb* : confuse
bench \'bench\ *n* **1** : long seat **2** : judge's seat **3** : court
bend \'bend\ *vb* **bent** \'bent\; **bending 1** : curve or cause a change of shape in **2** : turn in a certain direction ~ *n* **1** : act of bending **2** : curve
be·neath \bi'nēth\ *adv or prep* : below
bene·dic·tion \ˌbenə'dikshən\ *n* : closing blessing
bene·fac·tor \'benəˌfaktər\ *n* : one who gives esp. charitable aid
be·nef·i·cence \bə'nefəsəns\ *n* : quality of doing good —**be·nef·i·cent** \-sənt\ *adj*
ben·e·fi·cial \ˌbenə'fishəl\ *adj* : being of benefit —**ben·e·fi·cial·ly** *adv*
ben·e·fi·cia·ry \-'fishēˌerē, -'fishərē\ *n, pl* **-ries** : one who receives benefits
ben·e·fit \'benəˌfit\ *n* **1** : something that does good **2** : help **3** : fund-raising event —**benefit** *vb*
be·nev·o·lence \bə'nevələns\ *n* **1** : charitable nature **2** : act of kindness —**be·nev·o·lent** \-lənt\ *adj* —**be·nev·o·lent·ly** *adv*
be·night·ed \bi'nītəd\ *adj* : ignorant
be·nign \bi'nīn\ *adj* **1** : gentle or kindly **2** : not malignant —**be·nig·ni·ty** \-'nignətē\ *n*
be·nig·nant \-'nignənt\ *adj* : benign
bent \'bent\ *n* : aptitude or interest
be·numb \bi'nəm\ *vb* : make numb esp. by cold
ben·zene \'benˌzēn\ *n* : colorless flammable liquid
be·queath \bi'kwēth, -'kwēth̲\ *vb* **1** : give by will **2** : hand down
be·quest \bi'kwest\ *n* : something bequeathed
be·rate \-'rāt\ *vb* : scold harshly
be·reaved \-'rēvd\ *adj* : suffering the death of a loved one ~ *n, pl* **bereaved** : one who is bereaved —**be·reave·ment** *n*
be·reft \-'reft\ *adj* : deprived of or lacking something
be·ret \bə'rā\ *n* : round soft visorless cap
beri·beri \ˌberē'berē\ *n* : thiamine-deficiency disease
berm \'bərm\ *n* : bank of earth
ber·ry \'berē\ *n, pl* **-ries** : small pulpy fruit
ber·serk \bər'sərk, -'zərk\ *adj* : crazed —**berserk** *adv*
berth \'bərth\ *n* **1** : place where a ship is anchored **2** : place to sit or sleep esp. on a ship **3** : job ~ *vb* : to bring or come into a berth
ber·yl \'berəl\ *n* : light-colored silicate mineral
be·seech \bi'sēch\ *vb* **-sought** \-'sȯt\ *or* **-seeched; -seech·ing** : entreat
be·set \-'set\ *vb* **1** : harass **2** : hem in
be·side \-'sīd\ *prep* **1** : by the side of **2** : besides
be·sides \-'sīdz\ *adv* **1** : in addition **2** : moreover ~ *prep* **1** : other than **2** : in addition to
be·siege \-'sēj\ *vb* : lay siege to —**be·sieg·er** *n*
be·smirch \-'smərch\ *vb* : soil
be·sot \-'sät\ *vb* **-tt-** : become drunk
be·speak \bi'spēk\ *vb* **-spoke; -spo·ken; -speak·ing 1** : address **2** : indicate
best \'best\ *adj, superlative of* GOOD **1** : excelling all others **2** : most productive **3** : largest ~ *adv, superlative of* WELL **1** : in the best way **2** : most ~ *n* : one that is best ~ *vb* : outdo
bes·tial \'beschəl, 'bēs-\ *adj* **1** : relating to beasts **2** : brutish —**bes·ti·al·i·ty** \ˌbeschē'alətē, ˌbēs-\ *n*
be·stir \bi'stər\ *vb* : rouse to action
best man *n* : chief male attendant at a wedding
be·stow \bi'stō\ *vb* : give —**be·stow·al** \-əl\ *n*
bet \'bet\ *n* **1** : something risked or pledged on the outcome of a contest **2** : the making of a bet ~ *vb* **bet; betting 1** : risk (as money) on an outcome **2** : make a bet with
be·tide \bi'tīd\ *vb* : happen to
be·to·ken \bi'tōkən\ *vb* : give an indication of
be·tray \bi'trā\ *vb* **1** : seduce **2** : report or reveal to an enemy by treachery **3** : abandon **4** : prove unfaithful to **5** : reveal unintentionally —**be·tray·al** *n* —**be·tray·er** *n*
be·troth \-'träth, -'trȯth, -'trōth, *or with* th̲\ *vb* : promise to marry —**be·troth·al** *n* —**be·trothed** *n*
bet·ter \'betər\ *adj, comparative of* GOOD **1** : more than half **2** : improved in health **3** : of higher quality ~ *adv, comparative of* WELL **1** : in a superior manner **2** : more ~ *n* **1** : one that is better **2** : advantage ~ *vb* **1** : improve **2** : surpass —**bet·ter·ment** \-mənt\ *n*
bet·tor, bet·ter \'betər\ *n* : one who bets
be·tween \bi'twēn\ *prep* **1** —used to show two things considered together **2** : in the space separating **3** —used to indicate a comparison or choice ~ *adv* : in an intervening space or interval
bev·el \'bevəl\ *n* : slant on an edge ~ *vb* **-eled** *or* **-elled; -el·ing** *or* **-el·ling 1** : cut or shape to a bevel **2** : incline
bev·er·age \'bevrij\ *n* : drink
bevy \'bevē\ *n, pl* **bev·ies** : large group
be·wail \bi'wāl\ *vb* : lament
be·ware \-'war\ *vb* : be cautious
be·wil·der \-'wildər\ *vb* : confuse —**be·wil·der·ment** *n*
be·witch \-'wich\ *vb* **1** : affect by witchcraft **2** : charm —**be·witch·ment** *n*
be·yond \bē'yänd\ *adv* **1** : farther **2** : besides ~ *prep* **1** : on or to the farther side of **2** : out of the reach of **3** : besides
bi- \'bī, ˌbī\ *prefix* **1** : two **2** : coming or occurring every two **3** : twice, doubly, or on both sides

bicolored	**bifunctional**
biconcave	**bimetal**
biconcavity	**bimetallic**
biconvex	**binational**
biconvexity	**biparental**
bicultural	**bipolar**
bidirectional	**biracial**

bi·an·nu·al \bī'anyəwəl\ *adj* : occurring twice a year —**bi·an·nu·al·ly** *adv*
bi·as \'bīəs\ *n* **1** : line diagonal to the grain of a fabric **2** : prejudice ~ *vb* **-ased** *or* **-assed; -as·ing** *or* **-as·sing** : prejudice
bib \'bib\ *n* : shield tied under the chin to protect the clothes while eating
Bi·ble \'bībəl\ *n* **1** : sacred scriptures of Christians **2** : sacred scriptures of Judaism or of some other religion —**bib·li·cal** \'biblikəl\ *adj*
bib·li·og·ra·phy \ˌbiblē'ägrəfē\ *n, pl* **-phies** : list of writings on a subject or of an author —**bib·li·og·ra·pher** \-fər\ *n* —**bib·li·o·graph·ic** \-lēə'grafik\ *adj*
bi·cam·er·al \'bī'kamərəl\ *adj* : having 2 legislative chambers
bi·car·bon·ate \-'kärbəˌnāt, -nət\ *n* : acid carbonate
bi·cen·ten·ni·al \ˌbīsen'tenēəl\ *n* : 200th anniversary —**bicentennial** *adj*
bi·ceps \'bīˌseps\ *n* : large muscle of the upper arm
bick·er \'bikər\ *vb or n* : squabble
bi·cus·pid \bī'kəspəd\ *n* : double-pointed tooth
bi·cy·cle \'bīˌsikəl\ *n* : 2-wheeled vehicle moved by pedaling ~ *vb* **-cled; -cling** : ride a bicycle —**bi·cy·cler** \-klər\ *n* —**bi·cy·clist** \-list\ *n*
bid \'bid\ *vb* **bade** \'bad, 'bād\ *or* **bid; bid·den** \'bidᵊn\ *or* **bid; bid·ding 1** : order **2** : invite **3** : express **4** : make a bid ~ *n* **1** : act of bidding **2** : buyer's proposed price —**bid·da·ble** \-əbəl\ *adj* —**bid·der** *n*
bide \'bīd\ *vb* **bode** \'bōd\ *or* **bid·ed; bided; bid·ing 1** : wait **2** : dwell
bi·en·ni·al \bī'enēəl\ *adj* **1** : occurring once in 2 years **2** : lasting 2 years —**biennial** *n* —**bi·en·ni·al·ly** *adv*
bier \'bir\ *n* : stand for a coffin
bifocals \'bīˌfōkəlz\ *n pl* : eyeglasses that correct for near and distant vision
big \'big\ *adj* **-gg-** : large in size, amount, or scope —**big·ness** *n*
big·a·my \'bigəmē\ *n* : marrying one person while still married to another —**big·a·mist** \-mist\ *n* —**big·a·mous** \-məs\ *adj*
big·horn *n, pl* **-horn** *or* **-horns** : wild mountain sheep
bight \'bīt\ *n* **1** : loop of a rope **2** : bay
big·ot \'bigət\ *n* : one who is intolerant of others —**big·ot·ed** \-ətəd\ *adj* —**big·ot·ry** \-ətrē\ *n*
big shot *n* : important person
big·wig *n* : big shot
bike \'bīk\ *n* : bicycle or motorcycle
bi·ki·ni \bə'kēnē\ *n* : woman's brief 2-piece bathing suit
bi·lat·er·al \bī'latərəl\ *adj* : involving 2 sides —**bi·lat·er·al·ly** *adv*
bile \'bīl\ *n* **1** : greenish liver secretion that aids digestion **2** : bad temper
bi·lin·gual \bī'liŋgwəl\ *adj* : using 2 languages
bil·ious \'bilyəs\ *adj* : irritable —**bilious·ness** *n*
bilk \'bilk\ *vb* : cheat
[1]**bill** \'bil\ *n* : jaws of a bird together with their horny covering ~ *vb* : caress fondly —**billed** *adj*
[2]**bill** *n* **1** : draft of a law **2** : list of things to be paid for **3** : printed advertisement **4** : piece of paper money ~ *vb* : submit a bill or account to
bill·board *n* : surface for displaying advertising bills
bil·let \'bilət\ *n* : soldiers' quarters ~ *vb* : lodge in a billet
bill·fold *n* : wallet
bil·liards \'bilyərdz\ *n* : game of driving balls into one another or into pockets on a table
bil·lion \'bilyən\ *n, pl* **billions** *or* **billion** : 1000 millions —**billion** *adj* —**billionth** \-yənth\ *adj or n*
bil·low \'bilō\ *n* **1** : great wave **2** : rolling mass ~ *vb* : swell out —**bil·lowy** \'biləwē\ *adj*
billy goat *n* : male goat
bin \'bin\ *n* : storage box
bi·na·ry \'bīnərē\ *adj* : consisting of 2 things —**binary** *n*
bind \'bīnd\ *vb* **bound** \'bau̇nd\; **binding 1** : tie **2** : obligate **3** : unite into a mass **4** : bandage —**bind·er** *n* —**binding** *n*
binge \'binj\ *n* : spree
bin·go \'biŋgō\ *n, pl* **-gos** : game of covering numbers on a card
bin·oc·u·lar \bī'näkyələr, bə-\ *adj* : of or relating to both eyes ~ *n* : binocular optical instrument —usu. pl.
bio·chem·is·try \ˌbīō'keməstrē\ *n* : chemistry dealing with organisms —**bio·chemi·cal** *adj or n* —**bio·chem·ist** *n*
bio·de·grad·able \ˌbīōdi'grādəbəl\ *adj* : able to be reduced to harmless products by organisms —**bio·de·grad·abil·i·ty** *n* —**bio·deg·ra·da·tion** *n* —**bio·de·grade** *vb*
bi·og·ra·phy \bī'ägrəfē, bē-\ *n, pl* **-phies** : written history of a person's life —**bi·og·ra·pher** \-fər\ *n* —**bi·o·graph·i·cal** \ˌbīə'grafikəl\ *adj*
bi·ol·o·gy \bī'äləjē\ *n* : science of living beings and life processes —**bi·o·log·ic** \ˌbīə'läjik\, **bi·o·log·i·cal** \-əl\ *adj* —**bi·ol·o·gist** \bī'äləjist\ *n*
bio·phys·ics \ˌbīō'fiziks\ *n* : application of physics to biological problems —**bio·phys·i·cal** *adj* —**bio·phys·i·cist** *n*
bi·op·sy \'bīˌäpsē\ *n, pl* **-sies** : removal of live bodily tissue for examination
bio·tech·nol·o·gy \ˌbīōtek'näləjē\ *n* : manufacture of products using techniques involving the manipulation of DNA
bi·par·ti·san \bī'pärtəzən, -sən\ *adj* : involving members of 2 parties
bi·ped \'bīˌped\ *n* : 2-footed animal
birch \'bərch\ *n* : deciduous tree with close-grained wood —**birch, birch·en** \-ən\ *adj*
bird \'bərd\ *n* : warm-blooded egg-laying vertebrate with wings and feathers —**bird·bath** *n* —**bird·house** *n* —**bird·seed** *n*
bird's–eye \'bərdzˌī\ *adj* **1** : seen from above **2** : cursory
birth \'bərth\ *n* **1** : act or fact of being born or of producing young **2** : origin —**birth·day** *n* —**birth·place** *n* —**birth·rate** *n*
birth·mark *n* : unusual blemish on the skin at birth
birth·right *n* : something one is entitled to by birth
bis·cuit \'biskət\ *n* : small bread made with leavening other than yeast
bi·sect \'bīˌsekt\ *vb* : divide into 2 parts —**bi·sec·tion** \'bīˌsekshən\ *n* —**bi·sec·tor** \-tər\ *n*
bish·op \'bishəp\ *n* : clergy member higher than a priest

bish•op•ric \-shə,prik\ *n* **1** : diocese **2** : office of bishop

bis•muth \'bizməth\ *n* : heavy brittle metallic chemical element

bi•son \'bīsᵊn, 'bīz-\ *n, pl* **-son** : large shaggy wild ox of central U.S.

bis•tro \'bēstrō, 'bis-\ *n, pl* **-tros** : small restaurant or bar

1bit \'bit\ *n* **1** : part of a bridle that goes in a horse's mouth **2** : drilling tool

2bit *n* **1** : small piece or quantity **2** : small degree

bitch \'bich\ *n* : female dog ~ *vb* : complain

bite \'bīt\ *vb* **bit** \'bit\; **bit•ten** \'bitᵊn\; **bit•ing** \'bītiŋ\ **1** : to grip or cut with teeth or jaws **2** : dig in or grab and hold **3** : sting **4** : take bait ~ *n* **1** : act of biting **2** : bit of food **3** : wound made by biting **—bit•ing** *adj*

bit•ter \'bitər\ *adj* **1** : having an acrid lingering taste **2** : intense or severe **3** : extremely harsh or resentful **—bit•ter•ly** *adv* **—bit•ter•ness** *n*

bit•tern \'bitərn\ *n* : small heron

bi•tu•mi•nous coal \bə'tümənəs-, -'tyü-\ *n* : coal that yields volatile waste matter when heated

bi•valve \'bī,valv\ *n* : animal (as a clam) with a shell of 2 parts **—bivalve** *adj*

biv•ouac \'bivə,wak\ *n* : temporary camp ~ *vb* **-ouacked; -ouack•ing** : camp

bi•zarre \bə'zär\ *adj* : very strange **—bi•zarre•ly** *adv*

blab \'blab\ *vb* **-bb-** : talk too much

black \'blak\ *adj* **1** : of the color black **2** : Negro **3** : soiled **4** : lacking light **5** : wicked or evil **6** : gloomy ~ *n* **1** : black pigment or dye **2** : something black **3** : color of least lightness **4** : person of a dark-skinned race ~ *vb* : blacken **—black•ing** *n* **—black•ish** *adj* **—black•ly** *adv* **—black•ness** *n*

black–and–blue *adj* : darkly discolored from bruising

black•ball \'blak,bȯl\ *vb* **1** : ostracize **2** : boycott **—blackball** *n*

black•ber•ry \'blak,berē\ *n* : black or purple fruit of a bramble

black•bird *n* : bird of which the male is largely or wholly black

black•board *n* : dark surface for writing on with chalk

black•en \'blakən\ *vb* **1** : make or become black **2** : defame

black•guard \'blagərd, -,ärd\ *n* : scoundrel

black•head *n* : small dark oily mass plugging the outlet of a skin gland

black hole *n* : invisible extremely massive celestial object

black•jack *n* **1** : flexible leather-covered club **2** : card game ~ *vb* : hit with a blackjack

black•list *n* : list of persons to be punished or boycotted **—blacklist** *vb*

black•mail *n* **1** : extortion by threat of exposure **2** : something extorted by blackmail **—blackmail** *vb* **—blackmail•er** *n*

black•out *n* **1** : darkness due to electrical failure **2** : brief fainting spell **—black out** *vb*

black•smith *n* : one who forges iron

black•top *n* : dark tarry material for surfacing roads **—blacktop** *vb*

blad•der \'bladər\ *n* : sac into which urine passes from the kidneys

blade \'blād\ *n* **1** : leaf esp. of grass **2** : something resembling the flat part of a leaf **3** : cutting part of an instrument or tool **—blad•ed** \'blādəd\ *adj*

blame \'blām\ *vb* **blamed; blam•ing** **1** : find fault with **2** : hold responsible or responsible for **—blam•able** *adj* **—blame** *n* **—blame•less** *adj* **—blameless•ly** *adv* **—blame•wor•thi•ness** *n* **—blame•worthy** *adj*

blanch \'blanch\ *vb* : make or become white or pale

bland \'bland\ *adj* **1** : smooth in manner **2** : soothing **3** : tasteless **—bland•ly** *adv* **—bland•ness** *n*

blan•dish•ment \'blandishmənt\ *n* : flattering or coaxing speech or act

blank \'blaŋk\ *adj* **1** : showing or causing a dazed look **2** : lacking expression **3** : empty **4** : free from writing **5** : downright ~ *n* **1** : an empty space **2** : form with spaces to write in **3** : unfinished form (as of a key) **4** : cartridge with no bullet ~ *vb* : cover or close up **—blank•ly** *adv* **—blank•ness** *n*

blan•ket \'blaŋkət\ *n* **1** : heavy covering for a bed **2** : covering layer ~ *vb* : cover ~ *adj* : applying to a group

blare \'blar\ *vb* **blared; blar•ing** : make a loud harsh sound **—blare** *n*

blar•ney \'blärnē\ *n* : skillful flattery

bla•sé \blä'zā\ *adj* : indifferent to pleasure or excitement

blas•pheme \blas'fēm\ *vb* **-phemed; -phem•ing** : speak blasphemy **—blas•phem•er** *n*

blas•phe•my \'blasfəmē\ *n, pl* **-mies** : irreverence toward God or anything sacred **—blas•phe•mous** *adj*

blast \'blast\ *n* **1** : violent gust of wind **2** : explosion ~ *vb* : shatter by or as if by explosive **—blast off** *vb* : take off esp. in a rocket

bla•tant \'blātᵊnt\ *adj* : offensively showy **—bla•tan•cy** \-ᵊnsē\ *n* **—blatant•ly** *adv*

1blaze \'blāz\ *n* **1** : fire **2** : intense direct light **3** : strong display ~ *vb* **blazed; blaz•ing** : burn or shine brightly

2blaze *n* **1** : white stripe on an animal's face **2** : trail marker esp. on a tree ~ *vb* **blazed; blaz•ing** : mark with blazes

blaz•er \-ər\ *n* : sports jacket

bleach \'blēch\ *vb* : whiten **—bleach** *n*

bleach•ers \-ərz\ *n sing or pl* : uncovered stand for spectators

bleak \'blēk\ *adj* **1** : desolately barren **2** : lacking cheering qualities **—bleak•ish** *adj* **—bleak•ly** *adv* **—bleak•ness** *n*

blear \'blir\ *adj* : dim with water or tears

bleary \'blirē\ *adj* : dull or dimmed esp. from fatigue

bleat \'blēt\ *n* : cry of a sheep or goat or a sound like it **—bleat** *vb*

bleed \'blēd\ *vb* **bled** \'bled\; **bleed•ing** **1** : lose or shed blood **2** : feel distress **3** : flow from a wound **4** : draw fluid from **5** : extort money from **—bleed•er** *n*

blem•ish \'blemish\ *vb* : spoil by a flaw ~ *n* : noticeable flaw

1blench \'blench\ *vb* : flinch

2blench *vb* : grow or make pale

blend \'blend\ *vb* **1** : mix thoroughly **2** : combine into an integrated whole **—blend** *n* **—blend•er** *n*

bless \'bles\ *vb* **blessed** \'blest\; **bless•ing** **1** : consecrate by religious rite **2** : invoke divine care for **3** : make happy **—bless•ed** \'blesəd\, **blest** \'blest\ *adj* **—bless•ed•ly** \'blesədlē\ *adv* **—bless•ed•ness** \'blesədnəs\ *n* **—bless•ing** *n*

blew *past of* BLOW

blight \'blīt\ *n* **1** : plant disorder marked by withering or an organism causing it **2** : harmful influence **3** : deteriorated condition ~ *vb* : affect with or suffer from blight

blimp \'blimp\ *n* : airship holding form by pressure of contained gas

blind \'blīnd\ *adj* **1** : lacking or quite deficient in ability to see **2** : not intelligently controlled **3** : having no way out ~ *vb* **1** : to make blind **2** : dazzle ~ *n* **1** : something to conceal or darken **2** : place of concealment **—blind•ly** *adv* **—blind•ness** *n*

blind•fold *vb* : cover the eyes of **—blind•fold** *n*

blink \'bliŋk\ *vb* **1** : wink **2** : shine intermittently ~ *n* : wink

blink•er *n* : a blinking light

bliss \'blis\ *n* **1** : complete happiness **2** : heaven or paradise **—bliss•ful** *adj* **—bliss•ful•ly** *adv*

blis•ter \'blistər\ *n* **1** : raised area of skin containing watery fluid **2** : raised or swollen spot ~ *vb* : develop or cause blisters

blithe \'blīth, 'blīth\ *adj* **blith•er; blithest** : cheerful **—blithe•ly** *adv* **—blithe•some** \-səm\ *adj*

blitz \'blits\ *n* **1** : series of air raids **2** : fast intensive campaign **—blitz** *vb*

bliz•zard \'blizərd\ *n* : severe snowstorm

bloat \'blōt\ *vb* : swell

blob \'bläb\ *n* : small lump or drop

bloc \'bläk\ *n* : group working together

block \'bläk\ *n* **1** : solid piece **2** : frame enclosing a pulley **3** : quantity considered together **4** : large building divided into separate units **5** : a city square or the distance along one of its sides **6** : obstruction **7** : interruption of a bodily or mental function ~ *vb* : obstruct or hinder

block•ade \blä'kād\ *n* : isolation of a place usu. by troops or ships **—blockade** *vb* **—block•ad•er** *n*

block•head *n* : stupid person

blond, blonde \'bländ\ *adj* **1** : fair in complexion **2** : of a light color **—blond, blonde** *n*

blood \'bləd\ *n* **1** : red liquid that circulates in the heart, arteries, and veins of animals **2** : lifeblood **3** : lineage **—blood•ed** *adj* **—blood•less** *adj* **—blood•stain** *n* **—blood•stained** *adj* **—blood•suck•er** *n* **—blood•suck•ing** *n* **—bloody** *adj*

blood•cur•dling *adj* : terrifying

blood•hound *n* : large hound with a keen sense of smell

blood•mo•bile \-mō,bēl\ *n* : truck for collecting blood from donors

blood•shed *n* : slaughter

blood•shot *adj* : inflamed to redness

blood•stream *n* : blood in a circulatory system

blood•thirsty *adj* : eager to shed blood **—blood•thirst•i•ly** *adv* **—blood•thirst•i•ness** *n*

bloom \'blüm\ *n* **1** : flower **2** : period of flowering **3** : fresh or healthy look ~ *vb* **1** : yield flowers **2** : mature **—bloomy** *adj*

bloo•mers \'blümərz\ *n pl* : woman's underwear of short loose trousers

bloop•er \'blüpər\ *n* : public blunder

blos•som \'bläsəm\ *n or vb* : flower

blot \'blät\ *n* **1** : stain **2** : blemish ~ *vb* **-tt-** **1** : spot **2** : dry with absorbent paper **—blot•ter** *n*

blotch \'bläch\ *n* : large spot **—blotch** *vb* **—blotchy** *adj*

blouse \'blaůs, 'blaůz\ *n* : loose garment reaching from the neck to the waist

1blow \'blō\ *vb* **blew** \'blü\; **blown** \'blōn\; **blow•ing** **1** : move forcibly **2** : send forth a current of air **3** : sound **4** : shape by blowing **5** : explode **6** : bungle ~ *n* **1** : gale **2** : act of blowing **—blow•er** *n* **—blowy** *adj*

2blow *n* **1** : forcible stroke **2** *pl* : fighting **3** : calamity

blow•out *n* : bursting of a tire

blow•torch *n* : small torch that uses a blast of air

1blub•ber \'bləbər\ *n* : fat of whales

2blubber *vb* : cry noisily

blud•geon \'bləjən\ *n* : short club ~ *vb* : hit with a bludgeon

blue \'blü\ *adj* **blu•er; blu•est** **1** : of the color blue **2** : melancholy ~ *n* : color of the clear sky **—blu•ish** \-ish\ *adj*

blue•bell *n* : plant with blue bell-shaped flowers

blue•ber•ry \-,berē\ *n* : edible blue or blackish berry

blue•bird *n* : small bluish songbird

blue•fish *n* : bluish marine food fish

blue jay *n* : American crested jay

blue•print *n* **1** : photographic print in white on blue of a mechanical drawing **2** : plan of action **—blueprint** *vb*

blues \'blüz\ *n pl* **1** : depression **2** : music in a melancholy style

1bluff \'bləf\ *adj* **1** : rising steeply with a broad flat front **2** : frank ~ *n* : cliff

2bluff *vb* : deceive by pretense ~ *n* : act of bluffing **—bluff•er** \-ər\ *n*

blu•ing, blue•ing \'blüiŋ\ *n* : laundry preparation to keep fabrics white

blun•der \'bləndər\ *vb* **1** : move clumsily **2** : make a stupid mistake ~ *n* : bad mistake

blun•der•buss \-,bəs\ *n* : obsolete short-barreled firearm

blunt \'blənt\ *adj* **1** : not sharp **2** : tactless ~ *vb* : make dull **—blunt•ly** *adv* **—blunt•ness** *n*

blur \'blər\ *n* **1** : smear **2** : something perceived indistinctly ~ *vb* **-rr-** : cloud or obscure **—blur•ry** \-ē\ *adj*

blurb \'blərb\ *n* : short publicity notice

blurt \'blərt\ *vb* : utter suddenly

blush \'bləsh\ *n* : reddening of the face **—blush** *vb* **—blush•ful** *adj*

blus•ter \'bləstər\ *vb* **1** : blow violently **2** : talk or act with boasts or threats **—blus•ter** *n* **—blus•tery** *adj*

boa \'bōə\ *n* **1** : a large snake (as the **boa con•stric•tor** \-kən'striktər\) that crushes its prey **2** : fluffy scarf

boar \'bōr\ *n* : male swine

board \'bōrd\ *n* **1** : long thin piece of sawed lumber **2** : flat thin sheet esp. for games **3** : daily meals furnished for pay **4** : official body ~ *vb* **1** : go aboard **2** : cover with boards **3** : supply meals to **—board•er** *n*

board•walk *n* : wooden walk along a beach

boast \'bōst\ *vb* : praise oneself or one's possessions **—boast** *n* **—boast•er** *n* **—boast•ful** *adj* **—boast•ful•ly** *adv*

boat \'bōt\ *n* : small vessel for traveling on water **—boat** *vb* **—boat•man** \-mən\ *n*

boat•swain \'bōsᵊn\ *n* : ship's officer in charge of the hull

1bob \'bäb\ *vb* **-bb-** **1** : move up and down **2** : appear suddenly

2bob *n* **1** : float **2** : woman's short haircut ~ *vb* : cut hair in a bob

bob•bin \'bäbən\ *n* : spindle for holding thread

bob•ble \'bäbəl\ *vb* **-bled; -bling** : fumble **—bobble** *n*

bob•cat *n* : small American lynx

bob•o•link \'bäbə,liŋk\ *n* : American songbird

bob•sled \'bäb,sled\ *n* : racing sled **—bob•sled** *vb*

bob•white \'bäb'hwīt\ *n* : quail

bock \'bäk\ *n* : dark beer

1bode \'bōd\ *vb* **bod•ed; bod•ing** : indicate by signs

2bode *past of* BIDE

bod•ice \'bädəs\ *n* : close-fitting top of dress

bodi•ly \'bädᵊlē\ *adj* : relating to the body ~ *adv* **1** : in the flesh **2** : as a whole

body \'bädē\ *n, pl* **bod•ies** **1** : the physical whole of an organism **2** : human being **3** : main part **4** : mass of matter **5** : group **—bod•ied** *adj* **—bodi•less** \-iləs, -ᵊləs\ *adj* **—body•guard** *n*

bog \'bäg, 'bȯg\ *n* : swamp ~ *vb* **-gg-** : sink in or as if in a bog **—bog•gy** *adj*

bo•gey \'bůgē, 'bō-\ *n, pl* **-geys** : someone or something frightening

bog•gle \'bägəl\ *vb* **-gled; -gling** : overwhelm with amazement

bo•gus \'bōgəs\ *adj* : fake

bo•he•mi•an \bō'hēmēən\ *n* : one living unconventionally **—bohemian** *adj*

1boil \'bȯil\ *n* : inflamed swelling

2boil *vb* **1** : heat to a temperature (**boiling point**) at which vapor forms **2** : cook in boiling liquid **3** : be agitated **—boil** *n*

boil•er \'bȯilər\ *n* : tank holding hot water or steam

bois•ter•ous \'bȯistərəs\ *adj* : noisily turbulent **—bois•ter•ous•ly** *adv*

bold \'bōld\ *adj* **1** : courageous **2** : insolent **3** : daring **—bold•ly** *adv* **—bold•ness** *n*

bo•le•ro \bə'lerō\ *n, pl* **-ros** **1** : Spanish dance **2** : short open jacket

boll \'bōl\ *n* : seed pod

boll weevil *n* : small grayish weevil that infests the cotton plant

bo•lo•gna \bə'lōnē\ *n* : large smoked sausage

bol•ster \'bōlstər\ *n* : long pillow ~ *vb* **-stered; -ster•ing** : support

bolt \'bōlt\ *n* **1** : flash of lightning **2** : sliding bar used to fasten a door **3** : roll of cloth **4** : threaded pin used with a nut ~ *vb* **1** : move suddenly **2** : fasten with a bolt **3** : swallow hastily

bomb \'bäm\ *n* : explosive device ~ *vb* : attack with bombs **—bomb•proof** *adj*

bom•bard \bäm'bärd, bəm-\ *vb* : attack with or as if with artillery **—bom•bard•ment** *n*

bom•bar•dier \,bämbə'dir\ *n* : one who releases the bombs from a bomber

bom•bast \'bäm,bast\ *n* : pretentious language **—bom•bas•tic** \bäm'bastik\ *adj*

bomb•er *n* **1** : one that bombs **2** : airplane for dropping bombs

bomb•shell *n* **1** : bomb **2** : great surprise

bona fide \'bōnə,fīd, 'bän-; ,bōnə'fīdē\ *adj* **1** : made in good faith **2** : genuine

bo•nan•za \bə'nanzə\ *n* : something yielding a rich return

bon•bon \'bän,bän\ *n* : piece of candy

bond \'bänd\ *n* **1** *pl* : fetters **2** : uniting force **3** : obligation made binding by money **4** : interest-bearing certificate ~ *vb* **1** : insure **2** : cause to adhere **—bond•hold•er** *n*

bond•age \'bändij\ *n* : slavery **—bond•man** \-mən\ *n* **—bond•wom•an** *n*

1bonds•man \'bändzmən\ *n* : slave

2bondsman *n* : surety

bone \'bōn\ *n* : skeletal material ~ *vb* **boned; bon•ing** : to free from bones **—bone•less** *adj* **—bony** \'bōnē\ *adj*

bon•er \'bōnər\ *n* : blunder

bon•fire \'bän,fīr\ *n* : outdoor fire

bo•ni•to \bə'nētō\ *n, pl* **-tos** *or* **-to** : medium-sized tuna

bon•net \'bänət\ *n* : hat for a woman or infant

bo•nus \'bōnəs\ *n* : extra payment

boo \'bü\ *n, pl* **boos** : shout of disapproval **—boo** *vb*

boo•by \'bübē\ *n, pl* **-bies** : dunce

book \'bůk\ *n* **1** : paper sheets bound into a volume **2** : long literary work or a subdivision of one ~ *vb* : reserve **—book•case** *n* **—book•let** \-lət\ *n* **—book•mark** *n* **—book•sell•er** *n* **—book•shelf** *n*

book•end *n* : support to hold up a row of books

book•ie \-ē\ *n* : bookmaker

book•ish \-ish\ *adj* : fond of books and reading

book•keep•er *n* : one who keeps business accounts **—book•keep•ing** *n*

book•mak•er *n* : one who takes bets **—book•mak•ing** *n*

book•worm *n* : one devoted to reading

1boom \'büm\ *n* **1** : long spar to extend the bottom of a sail **2** : beam projecting from the pole of a derrick

2boom *vb* **1** : make a deep hollow sound **2** : grow rapidly esp. in value ~ *n* **1** : booming sound **2** : rapid growth

boo•mer•ang \'bümə,raŋ\ *n* : angular club that returns to the thrower

1boon \'bün\ *n* : benefit

2boon *adj* : congenial

boon•docks \'bün,däks\ *n pl* : rural area

boor \'bůr\ *n* : rude person **—boor•ish** *adj*

boost \'büst\ *vb* **1** : raise **2** : promote **—boost** *n* **—boost•er** *n*

boot \'büt\ *n* **1** : covering for the foot and leg **2** : kick ~ *vb* : kick

boo•tee, boo•tie \'bütē\ *n* : infant's knitted sock

booth \'büth\ *n, pl* **booths** \'büthz, 'büths\ : small enclosed stall or seating area

boot•leg \'büt,leg\ *vb* : make or sell liquor illegally **—bootleg** *adj or n* **—boot•leg•ger** *n*

boo•ty \'bütē\ *n, pl* **-ties** : plunder

booze \'büz\ *vb* **boozed; booz•ing** : drink liquor to excess ~ *n* : liquor **—booz•er** *n* **—boozy** *adj*

bo•rax \'bōr,aks\ *n* : crystalline compound of boron

bor•der \'bȯrdər\ *n* **1** : edge **2** : boundary ~ *vb* **1** : put a border on **2** : be close

1bore \'bōr\ *vb* **bored; bor•ing** **1** : pierce **2** : make by piercing ~ *n* : cylindrical hole or its diameter **—bor•er** *n*

2bore *past of* BEAR

3bore *n* : one that is dull ~ *vb* **bored; bor-**

ing : tire with dullness —**bore•dom** \'bōrdəm\ *n*

born \'bōrn\ *adj* **1** : brought into life **2** : being such by birth

borne *past part of* BEAR

bo•ron \'bōr,än\ *n* : dark-colored chemical element

bor•ough \'bərō\ *n* : incorporated town or village

bor•row \'bärō\ *vb* **1** : take as a loan **2** : take into use

bo•som \'bu̇zəm, 'bü-\ *n* : breast ~ *adj* : intimate —**bo•somed** *adj*

boss \'bȯs\ *n* : employer or supervisor ~ *vb* : supervise —**bossy** *adj*

bot•a•ny \'bätᵊnē\ *n* : plant biology —**bo•tan•i•cal** \bə'tanikəl\ *adj* —**bot•a•nist** \'bätᵊnist\ *n* —**bot•a•nize** \-ᵊn,īz\ *vb*

botch \'bäch\ *vb* : do clumsily —**botch** *n*

both \'bōth\ *adj or pron* : the one and the other ~ *conj* —used to show each of two is included

both•er \'bäth̲ər\ *vb* **1** : annoy or worry **2** : take the trouble —**bother** *n* —**both•er•some** \-səm\ *adj*

bot•tle \'bätᵊl\ *n* : container with a narrow neck and no handles ~ *vb* **bottled; bot•tling** : put into a bottle

bot•tle•neck *n* : place or cause of congestion

bot•tom \'bätəm\ *n* **1** : supporting surface **2** : lowest part or place —**bottom** *adj* —**bot•tomed** *adj* —**bot•tom•less** *adj*

bot•u•lism \'bächə,lizəm\ *n* : acute food poisoning

bou•doir \'bü,dwär, 'bu̇-, ,bü'-, ,bu̇'-\ *n* : woman's private room

bough \'bau̇\ *n* : large tree branch

bought *past of* BUY

bouil•lon \'bü,yän; 'bu̇l,yän, -yən\ *n* : clear soup

boul•der \'bōldər\ *n* : large rounded rock —**boul•dered** *adj*

bou•le•vard \'bu̇lə,värd, 'bü-\ *n* : broad thoroughfare

bounce \'bau̇ns\ *vb* **bounced; bounc•ing** **1** : spring back **2** : make bounce —**bounce** *n* —**bouncy** \'bau̇nsē\ *adj*

1bound \'bau̇nd\ *adj* : intending to go

2bound *n* : limit or boundary ~ *vb* : be a boundary of —**bound•less** *adj* —**bound•less•ness** *n*

3bound *adj* **1** : obliged **2** : having a binding **3** : determined **4** : incapable of failing

4bound *n* : leap ~ *vb* : move by springing

bound•ary \'bau̇ndrē\ *n, pl* **-aries** : line marking extent or separation

boun•ty \'bau̇ntē\ *n, pl* **-ties** **1** : generosity **2** : reward —**boun•te•ous** \-ēəs\ *adj* —**boun•te•ous•ly** *adv* —**boun•ti•ful** \-ifəl\ *adj* —**boun•ti•ful•ly** *adv*

bou•quet \bō'kā, bü-\ *n* **1** : bunch of flowers **2** : fragrance

bour•bon \'bərbən\ *n* : corn whiskey

bour•geoi•sie \,bu̇rzh,wä'zē\ *n* : middle class of society —**bour•geois** \'bu̇rzh,wä, bu̇rzh'wä\ *n or adj*

bout \'bau̇t\ *n* **1** : contest **2** : outbreak

bou•tique \bü'tēk\ *n* : specialty shop

bo•vine \'bō,vīn, -,vēn\ *adj* : relating to cattle —**bovine** *n*

1bow \'bau̇\ *vb* **1** : submit **2** : bend the head or body ~ *n* : act of bowing

2bow \'bō\ *n* **1** : bend or arch **2** : weapon for shooting arrows **3** : knot with loops **4** : rod with stretched horsehairs for playing a stringed instrument ~ *vb* : curve or bend —**bow•man** \-mən\ *n* —**bow•string** *n*

3bow \'bau̇\ *n* : forward part of a ship —**bow** *adj*

bow•els \'bau̇əls\ *n pl* **1** : intestines **2** : inmost parts

bow•er \'bau̇ər\ *n* : arbor

1bowl \'bōl\ *n* : concave vessel or part —**bowl•ful** \-,fu̇l\ *n*

2bowl *n* : round ball for bowling ~ *vb* : roll a ball in bowling —**bowl•er** *n*

bowl•ing *n* : game in which balls are rolled to knock down pins

1box \'bäks\ *n, pl* **box** *or* **box•es** : evergreen shrub —**box•wood** \-,wu̇d\ *n*

2box *n* **1** : container usu. with 4 sides and a cover **2** : small compartment ~ *vb* : put in a box

3box *n* : slap ~ *vb* **1** : slap **2** : fight with the fists —**box•er** *n* —**box•ing** *n*

box•car *n* : roofed freight car

box office *n* : theater ticket office

boy \'bȯi\ *n* : male child —**boy•hood** *n* —**boy•ish** *adj* —**boy•ish•ly** *adv* —**boy•ish•ness** *n*

boy•cott \-,kät\ *vb* : refrain from dealing with —**boycott** *n*

boy•friend \'bȯi,frend\ *n* **1** : male friend **2** : woman's regular male companion

brace \'brās\ *n* **1** : crank for turning a bit **2** : something that resists weight or supports **3** : punctuation mark {or} ~ *vb* **braced; brac•ing** **1** : make taut or steady **2** : invigorate **3** : strengthen

brace•let \'brāslət\ *n* : ornamental band for the wrist or arm

brack•et \'brakət\ *n* **1** : projecting support **2** : punctuation mark [or] **3** : class ~ *vb* **1** : furnish or fasten with brackets **2** : place within brackets **3** : group

brack•ish \-ish\ *adj* : salty

brad \'brad\ *n* : nail with a small head

brag \'brag\ *vb* **-gg-** : boast —**brag** *n*

brag•gart \'bragərt\ *n* : boaster

braid \'brād\ *vb* : interweave ~ *n* : something braided

braille \'brāl\ *n* : system of writing for the blind using raised dots

brain \'brān\ *n* **1** : organ of thought and nervous coordination enclosed in the skull **2** : intelligence ~ *vb* : smash the skull of —**brained** *adj* —**brain•less** *adj* —**brainy** *adj*

braise \'brāz\ *vb* **braised; brais•ing** : cook (meat) slowly in a covered dish

brake \'brāk\ *n* : device for slowing or stopping ~ *vb* **braked; brak•ing** : slow or stop by a brake

bram•ble \'brambəl\ *n* : prickly shrub

bran \'bran\ *n* : edible cracked grain husks

branch \'branch\ *n* **1** : division of a plant stem **2** : part ~ *vb* **1** : develop branches **2** : diverge —**branched** *adj*

brand \'brand\ *n* **1** : identifying mark made by burning **2** : stigma **3** : distinctive kind (as of goods from one firm) ~ *vb* : mark with a brand

bran•dish \'brandish\ *vb* : wave

brand–new *adj* : unused

bran•dy \'brandē\ *n, pl* **-dies** : liquor distilled from wine

brash \'brash\ *adj* **1** : impulsive **2** : aggressively self-assertive

brass \'bras\ *n* **1** : alloy of copper and zinc **2** : brazen self-assurance **3** : high-ranking military officers —**brassy** *adj*

bras•siere \brə'zir\ *n* : woman's undergarment to support the breasts

brat \'brat\ *n* : ill-behaved child —**brat•ti•ness** *n* —**brat•ty** *adj*

bra•va•do \brə'vädō\ *n, pl* **-does** *or* **-dos** : false bravery

1brave \'brāv\ *adj* **brav•er; brav•est** : showing courage ~ *vb* **braved; brav•ing** : face with courage —**brave•ly** *adv* —**brav•ery** \-ərē\ *n*

2brave *n* : American Indian warrior

bra•vo \'brävō\ *n, pl* **-vos** : shout of approval

brawl \'brȯl\ *n* : noisy quarrel or violent fight —**brawl** *vb* —**brawl•er** *n*

brawn \'brȯn\ *n* : muscular strength —**brawny** \-ē\ *adj* —**brawn•i•ness** *n*

bray \'brā\ *n* : harsh cry of a donkey —**bray** *vb*

bra•zen \'brāzᵊn\ *adj* **1** : made of brass **2** : bold —**bra•zen•ly** *adv* —**bra•zenness** *n*

bra•zier \'brāzhər\ *n* : charcoal grill

breach \'brēch\ *n* **1** : breaking of a law, obligation, or standard **2** : gap ~ *vb* : make a breach in

bread \'bred\ *n* : baked food made of flour ~ *vb* : cover with bread crumbs

breadth \'bredth\ *n* : width

bread•win•ner *n* : wage earner

break \'brāk\ *vb* **broke** \'brōk\; **bro•ken** \'brōkən\; **break•ing** **1** : knock into pieces **2** : transgress **3** : force a way into or out of **4** : exceed **5** : interrupt **6** : fail ~ *n* **1** : act or result of breaking **2** : stroke of good luck —**break•able** *adj or n* —**break•age** \'brākij\ *n* —**break•er** *n* —**break in** *vb* **1** : enter by force **2** : interrupt **3** : train —**break out** *vb* **1** : erupt with force **2** : develop a rash

break•down *n* : physical or mental failure —**break down** *vb*

break•fast \'brekfəst\ *n* : first meal of the day —**breakfast** *vb*

breast \'brest\ *n* **1** : milk-producing gland esp. of a woman **2** : front part of the chest

breast•bone *n* : sternum

breath \'breth\ *n* **1** : slight breeze **2** : air breathed in or out —**breath•less** *adj* —**breath•less•ly** *adv* —**breath•less•ness** *n* —**breathy** \'brethē\ *adj*

breathe \'brēth̲\ *vb* **breathed; breathing** **1** : draw air into the lungs and expel it **2** : live **3** : utter

breath•tak•ing *adj* : exciting

breech•es \'brichəz\ *n pl* : trousers ending near the knee

breed \'brēd\ *vb* **bred** \'bred\; **breed•ing** **1** : give birth to **2** : propagate **3** : raise ~ *n* **1** : kind of plant or animal usu. developed by humans **2** : class —**breed•er** *n*

breeze \'brēz\ *n* : light wind ~ *vb* **breezed; breez•ing** : move fast —**breezy** *adj*

breth•ren \'breth̲rən, -ərn\ *pl of* BROTHER

bre•via•ry \'brēvərē, 'bre-, -vyərē, -vē,erē\ *n, pl* **-ries** : prayer book used by Roman Catholic priests

brev•i•ty \'brevətē\ *n, pl* **-ties** : shortness or conciseness

brew \'brü\ *vb* : make by fermenting or steeping —**brew** *n* —**brew•er** *n* —**brew•ery** \'brüərē, 'bru̇rē\ *n*

bri•ar *var of* BRIER

bribe \'brīb\ *vb* **bribed; brib•ing** : corrupt or influence by gifts ~ *n* : something offered or given in bribing —**brib•able** *adj* —**brib•ery** \-ərē\ *n*

bric–a–brac \'brikə,brak\ *n pl* : small ornamental articles

brick \'brik\ *n* : building block of baked clay —**brick** *vb* —**brick•lay•er** *n* —**brick•lay•ing** *n*

bride \'brīd\ *n* : woman just married or about to be married —**brid•al** \-ᵊl\ *adj*

bride•groom *n* : man just married or about to be married

brides•maid *n* : woman who attends a bride at her wedding

1bridge \'brij\ *n* **1** : structure built for passage over a depression or obstacle **2** : upper part of the nose **3** : compartment from which a ship is navigated **4** : artificial replacement for missing teeth ~ *vb* : build a bridge over —**bridge•able** *adj*

2bridge *n* : card game for 4 players

bri•dle \'brīdᵊl\ *n* : headgear to control a horse ~ *vb* **-dled; -dling** **1** : put a bridle on **2** : restrain **3** : show hostility or scorn

brief \'brēf\ *adj* : short or concise ~ *n* : concise summary (as of a legal case) ~ *vb* : give final instructions or essential information to —**brief•ly** *adv* —**brief•ness** *n*

brief•case *n* : case for papers

1bri•er \'brīər\ *n* : thorny plant

2brier *n* : heath of southern Europe

1brig \'brig\ *n* : 2-masted ship

2brig *n* : jail on a naval ship

bri•gade \brig'ād\ *n* **1** : large military unit **2** : group organized for a special activity

brig•a•dier general \,brigə'dir-\ *n* : officer ranking next below a major general

brig•and \'brigənd\ *n* : bandit —**brig•and•age** \-ij\ *n*

bright \'brīt\ *adj* **1** : radiating or reflecting light **2** : cheerful **3** : intelligent —**bright•en** \-ᵊn\ *vb* —**bright•en•er** \'brītᵊnər\ *n* —**bright•ly** *adv* —**bright•ness** *n*

bril•liant \'brilyənt\ *adj* **1** : very bright **2** : splendid **3** : very intelligent —**bril•li•ance** \-yəns\ *n* —**bril•lian•cy** \-yənsē\ *n* —**bril•liant•ly** *adv*

brim \'brim\ *n* : edge or rim ~ *vb* : be or become full —**brim•less** *adj* —**brimmed** *adj*

brim•ful \-'fu̇l\ *adj* : full to the brim

brim•stone *n* : sulfur

brin•dled \'brindᵊld\ *adj* : gray or tawny with dark streaks or flecks

brine \'brīn\ *n* **1** : salt water **2** : ocean —**brin•i•ness** *n* —**briny** *adj*

bring \'briŋ\ *vb* **brought** \'brȯt\; **bring•ing** **1** : cause to come with one **2** : persuade **3** : produce **4** : sell for —**bring•er** *n* —**bring about** *vb* : make happen —**bring up** *vb* **1** : care for and educate **2** : cause to be noticed

brink \'briŋk\ *n* : edge

bri•quette, bri•quet \bri'ket\ *n* : pressed mass (as of charcoal)

brisk \'brisk\ *adj* **1** : lively **2** : invigorating —**brisk•ly** *adv* —**brisk•ness** *n*

bris•ket \'briskət\ *n* : breast or lower chest of a quadruped

bris•tle \'brisəl\ *n* : short stiff hair ~ *vb* **-tled; -tling** **1** : stand erect **2** : show angry defiance **3** : appear as if covered with bristles —**bris•tly** *adj*

brit•tle \'britᵊl\ *adj* **-tler; -tlest** : easily broken —**brit•tle•ness** *n*

broach \'brōch\ *n* : pointed tool (as for opening casks) ~ *vb* **1** : pierce (as a cask) to open **2** : introduce for discussion

broad \'brȯd\ *adj* **1** : wide **2** : spacious **3** : clear or open **4** : obvious **5** : tolerant in outlook **6** : widely applicable **7** : dealing with essential points —**broad•en** \-ᵊn\ *vb* —**broad•ly** *adv* —**broad•ness** *n*

broad•cast *n* **1** : transmission by radio waves **2** : radio or television program ~ *vb* **-cast; -cast•ing** **1** : scatter or sow in all directions **2** : make widely known **3** : send out on a broadcast —**broad•cast•er** *n*

broad•cloth *n* : fine cloth

broad•loom *adj* : woven on a wide loom esp. in solid color

broad–mind•ed *adj* : tolerant of varied opinions —**broad–mind•ed•ly** *adv* —**broad–mind•ed•ness** *n*

broad•side *n* **1** : simultaneous firing of all guns on one side of a ship **2** : verbal attack

bro•cade \brō'kād\ *n* : usu. silk fabric with a raised design

broc•co•li \'bräkəlē\ *n* : green vegetable akin to cauliflower

bro•chure \brō'shu̇r\ *n* : pamphlet

brogue \'brōg\ *n* : Irish accent

broil \'brȯil\ *vb* : cook by radiant heat —**broil** *n*

broil•er *n* **1** : utensil for broiling **2** : chicken fit for broiling

1broke \'brōk\ *past of* BREAK

2broke *adj* : out of money

bro•ken \'brōkən\ *adj* : imperfectly spoken —**bro•ken•ly** *adv*

bro•ken•heart•ed \-'härtəd\ *adj* : overcome by grief or despair

bro•ker \'brōkər\ *n* : agent who buys and sells for a fee —**broker** *vb* —**bro•ker•age** \-kərij\ *n*

bro•mine \'brō,mēn\ *n* : deep red liquid corrosive chemical element

bron•chi•tis \brän'kītəs, bräŋ-\ *n* : inflammation of the bronchi

bron•chus \'bräŋkəs\ *n, pl* **-chi** \-,kī, -,kē\ : division of the windpipe leading to a lung —**bron•chi•al** \-kēəl\ *adj*

bronze \'bränz\ *vb* **bronzed; bronz•ing** : make bronze in color ~ *n* **1** : alloy of copper and tin **2** : yellowish brown —**bronzy** \-ē\ *adj*

brooch \'brōch, 'brüch\ *n* : ornamental clasp or pin

brood \'brüd\ *n* : family of young ~ *vb* **1** : sit on eggs to hatch them **2** : ponder ~ *adj* : kept for breeding —**brood•er** *n* —**brood•ing•ly** *adv*

1brook \'bru̇k\ *vb* : tolerate

2brook *n* : small stream

broom \'brüm, 'bru̇m\ *n* **1** : flowering shrub **2** : implement for sweeping —**broom•stick** *n*

broth \'brȯth\ *n, pl* **broths** \'brȯths, 'brȯth̲z\ : liquid in which meat has been cooked

broth•el \'bräthəl, 'brȯth-\ *n* : house of prostitutes

broth•er \'brəth̲ər\ *n, pl* **brothers** *also* **breth•ren** \'breth̲rən, -ərn\ **1** : male sharing one or both parents with another person **2** : kinsman —**broth•er•hood** *n* —**broth•er•li•ness** *n* —**broth•er•ly** *adj*

broth•er–in–law *n, pl* **brothers–in–law** : brother of one's spouse or husband of one's sister or of one's spouse's sister

brought *past of* BRING

brow \'brau̇\ *n* **1** : eyebrow **2** : forehead **3** : edge of a steep place

brow•beat *vb* **-beat; -beat•en** *or* **-beat; -beat•ing** : intimidate

brown \'brau̇n\ *adj* **1** : of the color brown **2** : of dark or tanned complexion ~ *n* : a color like that of coffee ~ *vb* : make or become brown —**brown•ish** *adj*

browse \'brau̇z\ *vb* **browsed; brows•ing** **1** : graze **2** : look over casually —**brows•er** *n*

bru•in \'brüən\ *n* : bear

bruise \'brüz\ *vb* **bruised; bruis•ing** **1** : make a bruise on **2** : become bruised ~ *n* : surface injury to flesh

brunch \'brənch\ *n* : late breakfast, early lunch, or combination of both

bru•net, bru•nette \brü'net\ *adj* : having dark hair and usu. dark skin —**brunet, brunette** *n*

brunt \'brənt\ *n* : main impact

1brush \'brəsh\ *n* **1** : small cut branches **2** : coarse shrubby vegetation

2brush *n* **1** : bristles set in a handle used esp. for cleaning or painting **2** : light touch ~ *vb* **1** : apply a brush to **2** : remove with or as if with a brush **3** : dismiss in an offhand way **4** : touch lightly —**brush up** *vb* : renew one's skill

3brush *n* : skirmish

brush–off *n* : curt dismissal

brusque \'brəsk\ *adj* : curt or blunt in manner —**brusque•ly** *adv*

bru•tal \'brütᵊl\ *adj* : like a brute and esp. cruel —**bru•tal•i•ty** \brü'talətē\ *n* —**bru•tal•ize** \'brütᵊl,īz\ *vb* —**bru•tal•ly** \-ᵊlē\ *adv*

brute \'brüt\ *adj* **1** : relating to beasts **2** : unreasoning **3** : purely physical ~ *n* **1** : beast **2** : brutal person —**brut•ish** \-ish\ *adj*

bub•ble \'bəbəl\ *vb* **-bled; -bling** : form, rise in, or give off bubbles ~ *n* : globule of gas in or covered with a liquid —**bub•bly** \-əlē\ *adj*

bu•bo \'bübō, 'byü-\ *n, pl* **buboes** : inflammatory swelling of a lymph gland —**bu•bon•ic** \bü'bänik, 'byü-\ *adj*

buc•ca•neer \,bəkə'nir\ *n* : pirate

buck \'bək\ *n, pl* **buck** *or* **bucks** **1** : male animal (as a deer) **2** : dollar ~ *vb* **1** : jerk forward **2** : oppose

buck•et \'bəkət\ *n* : pail —**buck•et•ful** *n*

buck•le \'bəkəl\ *n* **1** : clasp (as on a belt) for two loose ends **2** : bend or fold ~ *vb* **-led; -ling** **1** : fasten with a buckle **2** : apply oneself **3** : bend or crumple

buck•ler \'bəklər\ *n* : shield

buck•shot *n* : coarse lead shot

buck•skin *n* : soft leather (as from the skin of a buck) —**buckskin** *adj*

buck•tooth *n* : large projecting front tooth —**buck–toothed** *adj*

buck•wheat *n* : herb whose seeds are used as a cereal grain or the seeds themselves

bu•col•ic \byü'kälik\ *adj* : pastoral

bud \'bəd\ *n* **1** : undeveloped plant shoot **2** : partly opened flower ~ *vb* **-dd-** **1** : form or put forth buds **2** : be or develop like a bud

Bud•dhism \'bü,dizəm, 'bu̇-\ *n* : religion of eastern and central Asia —**Bud•dhist** \'büdist, 'bu̇d-\ *n or adj*

bud•dy \'bədē\ *n, pl* **-dies** : friend

budge \'bəj\ *vb* **budged; budg•ing** : move from a place

bud•get \'bəjət\ *n* **1 :** estimate of income and expenses **2 :** plan for coordinating income and expenses **3 :** money available for a particular use **—budget** *vb or adj* **—bud•get•ary** \-ə,terē\ *adj*

buff \'bəf\ *n* **1 :** yellow to orange yellow color **2 :** enthusiast ~ *adj* **:** of the color buff ~ *vb* **:** polish

buf•fa•lo \'bəfə,lō\ *n, pl* **-lo** *or* **-loes :** wild ox (as a bison)

[1]**buff•er** \'bəfər\ *n* **:** shield or protector

[2]**buffer** *n* **:** one that buffs

[1]**buf•fet** \'bəfət\ *n* **:** blow or slap ~ *vb* **:** hit esp. repeatedly

[2]**buf•fet** \,bə'fā, bü-\ *n* **1 :** sideboard **2 :** meal at which people serve themselves

buf•foon \,bə'fün\ *n* **:** clown **—buf•foon•ery** \-ərē\ *n*

bug \'bəg\ *n* **1 :** small usu. obnoxious crawling creature **2 :** 4-winged sucking insect **3 :** unexpected imperfection **4 :** disease-producing germ **5 :** hidden microphone ~ *vb* **-gg- 1 :** pester **2 :** conceal a microphone in

bug•a•boo \'bəgə,bü\ *n, pl* **-boos :** bogey

bug•bear *n* **:** source of dread

bug•gy \'bəgē\ *n, pl* **-gies :** light carriage

bu•gle \'byügəl\ *n* **:** trumpetlike brass instrument **—bu•gler** \-glər\ *n*

build \'bild\ *vb* **built** \'bilt\; **build•ing 1 :** put together **2 :** establish **3 :** increase ~ *n* **:** physique **—build•er** *n*

build•ing \'bildiŋ\ *n* **1 :** roofed and walled structure **2 :** art or business of constructing buildings

bulb \'bəlb\ *n* **1 :** large underground plant bud **2 :** rounded or pear-shaped object **—bul•bous** \-əs\ *adj*

bulge \'bəlj\ *n* **:** swelling projecting part ~ *vb* **bulged; bulg•ing :** swell out

bulk \'bəlk\ *n* **1 :** magnitude **2 :** indigestible food material **3 :** large mass **4 :** major portion ~ *vb* **:** cause to swell or bulge **—bulky** \-ē\ *adj*

bulk•head *n* **:** ship's partition

[1]**bull** \'bu̇l\ *n* **:** large adult male animal (as of cattle) ~ *adj* **:** male

[2]**bull** *n* **1 :** papal letter **2 :** decree

bull•dog *n* **:** compact short-haired dog

bull•doze \-,dōz\ *vb* **1 :** move or level with a tractor (**bull•doz•er**) having a broad blade **2 :** force

bul•let \'bu̇lət\ *n* **:** missile to be shot from a gun **—bul•let•proof** *adj*

bul•le•tin \'bu̇lətən\ *n* **1 :** brief public report **2 :** periodical

bull•fight *n* **:** sport of taunting and killing bulls **—bull•fight•er** *n*

bull•frog *n* **:** large deep-voiced frog

bull•head•ed *adj* **:** stupidly stubborn

bul•lion \'bu̇lyən\ *n* **:** gold or silver esp. in bars

bull•ock \'bu̇lək\ *n* **1 :** young bull **2 :** steer

bull's–eye *n, pl* **bull's–eyes :** center of a target

bul•ly \'bu̇lē\ *n, pl* **-lies :** one who hurts or intimidates others ~ *vb* **-lied; -ly•ing :** act like a bully toward

bul•rush \'bu̇l,rəsh\ *n* **:** tall coarse rush or sedge

bul•wark \'bu̇l,wərk, -,wȯrk; 'bəl,wərk\ *n* **1 :** wall-like defense **2 :** strong support or protection

bum \'bəm\ *vb* **-mm- 1 :** wander as a tramp **2 :** get by begging ~ *n* **:** idle worthless person ~ *adj* **:** bad

bum•ble•bee \'bəmbəl,bē\ *n* **:** large hairy bee

bump \'bəmp\ *vb* **:** strike or knock forcibly ~ *n* **1 :** sudden blow **2 :** small bulge or swelling **—bumpy** *adj*

[1]**bum•per** \'bəmpər\ *adj* **:** unusually large

[2]**bump•er** \'bəmpər\ *n* **:** shock-absorbing bar at either end of a car

bump•kin \'bəmpkən\ *n* **:** awkward country person

bun \'bən\ *n* **:** sweet biscuit or roll

bunch \'bənch\ *n* **:** group ~ *vb* **:** form into a group **—bunchy** *adj*

bun•dle \'bəndᵊl\ *n* **1 :** several items bunched together **2 :** something wrapped for carrying **3 :** large amount ~ *vb* **-dled; -dling :** gather into a bundle

bun•ga•low \'bəŋgə,lō\ *n* **:** one-story house

bun•gle \'bəŋgəl\ *vb* **-gled; -gling :** do badly **—bungle** *n* **—bun•gler** *n*

bun•ion \'bənyən\ *n* **:** inflamed swelling of the first joint of the big toe

[1]**bunk** \'bəŋk\ *n* **:** built-in bed that is often one of a tier ~ *vb* **:** sleep

[2]**bunk** *n* **:** nonsense

bun•ker \-ər\ *n* **1 :** storage compartment **2 :** protective embankment

bun•kum, bun•combe \'bəŋkəm\ *n* **:** nonsense

bun•ny \'bənē\ *n, pl* **-nies :** rabbit

[1]**bun•ting** \'bəntiŋ\ *n* **:** small finch

[2]**bunting** *n* **:** flag material

buoy \'büē, 'bȯi\ *n* **:** floating marker anchored in water ~ *vb* **1 :** keep afloat **2 :** raise the spirits of **—buoy•an•cy** \'bȯiənsē, 'büyən-\ *n* **—buoy•ant** \-yənt\ *adj*

bur, burr \'bər\ *n* **:** rough or prickly covering of a fruit **—bur•ry** *adj*

bur•den \'bərdᵊn\ *n* **1 :** something carried **2 :** something oppressive **3 :** cargo ~ *vb* **:** load or oppress **—burden•some** \-səm\ *adj*

bur•dock \'bər,däk\ *n* **:** tall coarse herb with prickly flower heads

bu•reau \'byu̇rō\ *n* **1 :** chest of drawers **2 :** administrative unit **3 :** business office

bu•reau•cra•cy \byu̇'räkrəsē\ *n, pl* **-cies 1 :** body of government officials **2 :** unwieldy administrative system **—bu•reau•crat** \'byu̇rə,krat\ *n* **—bu•reau•crat•ic** \,byu̇rə'kratik\ *adj*

bur•geon \'bərjən\ *vb* **:** grow

bur•glary \'bərglərē\ *n, pl* **-glar•ies :** forcible entry into a building to steal **—bur•glar** \-glər\ *n* **—bur•glar•ize** \'bərglə,rīz\ *vb*

bur•gle \'bərgəl\ *vb* **-gled; -gling :** commit burglary on or in

Bur•gun•dy \'bərgəndē\ *n, pl* **-dies :** kind of table wine

buri•al \'berēəl\ *n* **:** act of burying

bur•lap \'bər,lap\ *n* **:** coarse fabric usu. of jute or hemp

bur•lesque \bər'lesk\ *n* **1 :** witty or derisive imitation **2 :** broadly humorous variety show ~ *vb* **-lesqued; -lesqu•ing :** mock

bur•ly \'bərlē\ *adj* **-li•er; -est :** strongly and heavily built

burn \'bərn\ *vb* **burned** \'bərnd, 'bərnt\ *or* **burnt** \'bərnt\; **burn•ing 1 :** be on fire **2 :** feel or look as if on fire **3 :** alter or become altered by or as if by fire or heat **4 :** cause or make by fire ~ *n* **:** injury or effect produced by burning **—burn•er** *n*

bur•nish \'bərnish\ *vb* **:** polish

burp \'bərp\ *n or vb* **:** belch

bur•ro \'bərō, 'bu̇r-\ *n, pl* **-os :** small donkey

bur•row \'bərō\ *n* **:** hole in the ground made by an animal ~ *vb* **:** make a burrow **—bur•row•er** *n*

bur•sar \'bərsər\ *n* **:** treasurer esp. of a college

bur•si•tis \bər'sītəs\ *n* **:** inflammation of a sac (**bur•sa** \'bərsə\) in a joint

burst \'bərst\ *vb* **burst** *or* **burst•ed; burst•ing 1 :** fly apart or into pieces **2 :** enter or emerge suddenly ~ *n* **:** sudden outbreak or effort

bury \'berē\ *vb* **bur•ied; bury•ing 1 :** deposit in the earth **2 :** hide

bus \'bəs\ *n, pl* **bus•es** *or* **bus•ses :** large motor-driven passenger vehicle ~ *vb* **bused** *or* **bussed; bus•ing** *or* **bus•sing :** travel or transport by bus

bus•boy *n* **:** waiter's helper

bush \'bu̇sh\ *n* **1 :** shrub **2 :** rough uncleared country **3 :** a thick tuft or mat **—bushy** *adj*

bush•el \'bu̇shəl\ *n* **:** 4 pecks

bush•ing \'bu̇shiŋ\ *n* **:** metal lining used as a guide or bearing

busi•ness \'biznəs, -nəz\ *n* **1 :** vocation **2 :** commercial or industrial enterprise **3 :** personal concerns **—busi•ness•man** \-,man\ *n* **—busi•ness•wom•an** \-,wu̇mən\ *n*

[1]**bust** \'bəst\ *n* **1 :** sculpture of the head and upper torso **2 :** breasts of a woman

[2]**bust** *vb* **1 :** burst or break **2 :** tame ~ *n* **1 :** punch **2 :** failure

[1]**bus•tle** \'bəsəl\ *vb* **-tled; -tling :** move or work briskly ~ *n* **:** energetic activity

[2]**bustle** *n* **:** pad or frame formerly worn under a woman's skirt

busy \'bizē\ *adj* **busi•er; -est 1 :** engaged in action **2 :** being in use **3 :** full of activity ~ *vb* **bus•ied; busy•ing :** make or keep busy **—busi•ly** *adv*

busy•body *n* **:** meddler

but \'bət\ *conj* **1 :** if not for the fact **2 :** that **3 :** without the certainty that **4 :** rather **5 :** yet ~ *prep* **:** other than

butch•er \'bu̇chər\ *n* **1 :** one who slaughters animals or dresses their flesh **2 :** brutal killer **3 :** bungler **—butcher** *vb* **—butch•ery** \-ərē\ *n*

but•ler \'bətlər\ *n* **:** chief male household servant

[1]**butt** \'bət\ *vb* **:** strike with a butt ~ *n* **:** blow with the head or horns

[2]**butt** *n* **1 :** target **2 :** victim

[3]**butt** *vb* **:** join edge to edge

[4]**butt** *n* **:** large end or bottom

[5]**butt** *n* **:** large cask

butte \'byüt\ *n* **:** isolated steep hill

but•ter \'bətər\ *n* **:** solid edible fat churned from cream ~ *vb* **:** spread with butter **—but•tery** *adj*

but•ter•cup *n* **:** yellow-flowered herb

but•ter•fat *n* **:** natural fat of milk and of butter

but•ter•fly *n* **:** insect with 4 broad wings

but•ter•milk *n* **:** liquid remaining after butter is churned

but•ter•nut *n* **:** edible nut of a tree related to the walnut or this tree

but•ter•scotch \-,skäch\ *n* **:** candy made from sugar, corn syrup, and water

but•tocks \'bətəks\ *n pl* **:** rear part of the hips

but•ton \'bətᵊn\ *n* **1 :** small knob for fastening clothing **2 :** buttonlike object ~ *vb* **:** fasten with buttons

but•ton•hole *n* **:** hole or slit for a button ~ *vb* **:** hold in talk

but•tress \'bətrəs\ *n* **1 :** projecting structure to support a wall **2 :** support **—buttress** *vb*

bux•om \'bəksəm\ *adj* **:** full-bosomed

buy \'bī\ *vb* **bought** \'bȯt\; **buy•ing :** purchase ~ *n* **:** bargain **—buy•er** *n*

buzz \'bəz\ *vb* **:** make a low humming sound ~ *n* **:** act or sound of buzzing

buz•zard \'bəzərd\ *n* **:** large bird of prey

buzz•er *n* **:** signaling device that buzzes

buzz•word \'bəz,wərd\ *n* **:** word or phrase in vogue

by \'bī\ *prep* **1 :** near **2 :** through **3 :** beyond **4 :** throughout **5 :** no later than ~ *adv* **1 :** near **2 :** farther

by•gone \'bī,gȯn\ *adj* **:** past **—bygone** *n*

by•law, bye•law *n* **:** organization's rule

by–line *n* **:** writer's name on an article

by•pass *n* **:** alternate route ~ *vb* **:** go around

by–prod•uct *n* **:** product in addition to the main product

by•stand•er *n* **:** spectator

by•way \'bī,wā\ *n* **:** side road

by•word *n* **:** proverb

C

c \'sē\ *n, pl* **c's** *or* **cs** \'sēz\ **:** 3d letter of the alphabet

cab \'kab\ *n* **1 :** light closed horse-drawn carriage **2 :** taxicab **3 :** compartment for a driver **—cab•bie, cabby** *n* **—cab•stand** *n*

ca•bal \kə'bal\ *n* **:** group of conspirators

ca•bana \kə'banə, -nyə\ *n* **:** shelter at a beach or pool

cab•a•ret \,kabə'rā\ *n* **:** nightclub

cab•bage \'kabij\ *n* **:** vegetable with a dense head of leaves

cab•in \-ən\ *n* **1 :** private room on a ship **2 :** small house **3 :** airplane compartment

cab•i•net \'kabnət\ *n* **1 :** display case or cupboard **2 :** advisory council of a head of state **—cab•i•net•mak•er** *n* **—cab•i•net•mak•ing** *n* **—cab•i•net•work** *n*

ca•ble \'kābəl\ *n* **1 :** strong rope, wire, or chain **2 :** cablegram **3 :** bundle of electrical wires ~ *vb* **-bled; -bling :** send a cablegram to

ca•ble•gram \-,gram\ *n* **:** message sent by a submarine telegraph cable

ca•boose \kə'büs\ *n* **:** crew car on a train

ca•cao \kə'kau̇, -'kāō\ *n, pl* **cacaos :** So. American tree whose seeds (**cacao beans**) yield cocoa and chocolate

cache \'kash\ *n* **1 :** hiding place **2 :** something hidden **—cache** *vb*

ca•chet \ka'shā\ *n* **:** prestige or a feature conferring this

cack•le \'kakəl\ *vb* **-led; -ling :** make a cry or laugh like the sound of a hen **—cackle** *n* **—cack•ler** *n*

ca•coph•o•ny \ka'käfənē\ *n, pl* **-nies :** harsh noise **—ca•coph•o•nous** \-nəs\ *adj*

cac•tus \'kaktəs\ *n, pl* **cac•ti** \-,tī\ *or* **-tus•es :** drought-resistant flowering plant with scales or prickles

cad \'kad\ *n* **:** ungentlemanly person **—cad•dish** \-ish\ *adj* **—cad•dish•ly** *adv* **—cad•dish•ness** *n*

ca•dav•er \kə'davər\ *n* **:** dead body **—ca•dav•er•ous** \-ərəs\ *adj*

cad•die, cad•dy \'kadē\ *n, pl* **-dies :** golfer's helper **—caddie, caddy** *vb*

cad•dy \'kadē\ *n, pl* **-dies :** small tea chest

ca•dence \'kādᵊns\ *n* **:** measure of a rhythmical flow **—ca•denced** \-ᵊnst\ *adj*

ca•det \kə'det\ *n* **:** student in a military academy

cadge \'kaj\ *vb* **cadged; cadg•ing :** beg **—cadg•er** *n*

cad•mi•um \'kadmēəm\ *n* **:** grayish metallic chemical element

ca•dre \-rē\ *n* **:** nucleus of highly trained people

ca•fé \ka'fā, kə-\ *n* **:** restaurant

caf•e•te•ria \,kafə'tirēə\ *n* **:** self-service restaurant

caf•feine \ka'fēn, 'ka,fēn\ *n* **:** stimulating alkaloid in coffee and tea

cage \'kāj\ *n* **:** box of wire or bars for confining an animal ~ *vb* **caged; caging :** put or keep in a cage

ca•gey \-ē\ *adj* **-gi•er; -est :** shrewd **—ca•gi•ly** *adv* **—ca•gi•ness** *n*

cais•son \'kā,sän, -sən\ *n* **1:** ammunition carriage **2 :** watertight chamber for underwater construction

ca•jole \kə'jōl\ *vb* **-joled; -jol•ing :** persuade or coax **—ca•jol•ery** \-ərē\ *n*

cake \'kāk\ *n* **1 :** food of baked or fried usu. sweet batter **2 :** compacted mass ~ *vb* **caked; cak•ing 1 :** form into a cake **2 :** encrust

cal•a•bash \'kalə,bash\ *n* **:** gourd

cal•a•mine \'kalə,mīn\ *n* **:** lotion of oxides of zinc and iron

ca•lam•i•ty \kə'lamətē\ *n, pl* **-ties :** disaster **—ca•lam•i•tous** \-ətəs\ *adj* **—ca•lam•i•tous•ly** *adv* **—ca•lam•i•tous•ness** *n*

cal•ci•fy \'kalsə,fī\ *vb* **-fied; -fy•ing :** harden **—cal•ci•fi•ca•tion** \,kalsəfə'kāshən\ *n*

cal•ci•um \'kalsēəm\ *n* **:** silver-white soft metallic chemical element

cal•cu•late \'kalkyə,lāt\ *vb* **-lat•ed; -lating 1 :** determine by mathematical processes **2 :** judge **—cal•cu•la•ble** \-ləbəl\ *adj* **—cal•cu•la•tion** \,kalkyə'lāshən\ *n* **—cal•cu•la•tor** \'kalkyə,lātər\ *n*

cal•cu•lat•ing *adj* **:** shrewd

cal•cu•lus \'kalkyələs\ *n, pl* **-li** \-,lī\ **:** higher mathematics dealing with rates of change

cal•dron *var of* CAULDRON

cal•en•dar \'kaləndər\ *n* **:** list of days, weeks, and months

[1]**calf** \'kaf, 'kåf\ *n, pl* **calves** \'kavz, 'kåvz\ **:** young cow or related mammal **—calf•skin** *n*

[2]**calf** *n, pl* **calves :** back part of the leg below the knee

cal•i•ber, cal•i•bre \'kaləbər\ *n* **1 :** diameter of a bullet or shell or of a gun bore **2 :** degree of mental or moral excellence

cal•i•brate \'kalə,brāt\ *vb* **-brat•ed; -brat•ing :** adjust precisely **—cal•i•bra•tion** \,kalə'brāshən\ *n*

cal•i•co \'kali,kō\ *n, pl* **-coes** *or* **-cos 1 :** printed cotton fabric **2 :** animal with fur having patches of different colors

cal•i•pers \'kaləpərz\ *n* **:** measuring instrument with two adjustable legs

ca•liph \'kāləf, 'kal-\ *n* **:** title of head of Islam **—ca•liph•ate** \-,āt, -ət\ *n*

cal•is•then•ics \,kaləs'theniks\ *n sing or pl* **:** stretching and jumping exercises **—cal•is•then•ic** *adj*

calk \'kȯk\ *var of* CAULK

call \'kȯl\ *vb* **1 :** shout **2 :** summon **3 :** demand **4 :** telephone **5 :** make a visit **6 :** name **—call** *n* **—call•er** *n* **—call down** *vb* **:** reprimand **—call off** *vb* **:** cancel

call•ing *n* **:** vocation

cal•li•ope \kə'līə,pē, 'kalē,ōp\ *n* **:** musical instrument of steam whistles

cal•lous \'kaləs\ *adj* **1 :** thickened and hardened **2 :** unfeeling ~ *vb* **:** make callous **—cal•los•i•ty** \ka'läsətē\ *n* **—cal•lous•ly** *adv* **—cal•lous•ness** *n*

cal•low \'kalō\ *adj* **:** inexperienced or innocent **—cal•low•ness** *n*

cal•lus \'kaləs\ *n* **:** callous area on skin or bark ~ *vb* **:** form a callus

calm \'käm, 'kälm\ *n* **1 :** period or condition of peacefulness or stillness ~ *adj* **:** still or tranquil ~ *vb* **:** make calm **—calm•ly** *adv* **—calm•ness** *n*

ca•lor•ic \kə'lȯrik\ *adj* **:** relating to heat or calories

cal•o•rie \'kalərē\ *n* **:** unit for measuring heat and energy value of food

ca•lum•ni•ate \kə'ləmnē,āt\ *vb* **-at•ed; -at•ing :** slander **—ca•lum•ni•a•tion** \-,ləmnē'āshən\ *n*

cal•um•ny \'kaləmnē\ *n, pl* **-nies :** false and malicious charge **—ca•lum•ni•ous** \kə'ləmnēəs\ *adj*

calve \'kav, 'kåv\ *vb* **calved; calv•ing :** give birth to a calf

calves *pl of* CALF

ca•lyp•so \kə'lipsō\ *n, pl* **-sos :** West Indian style of music

ca•lyx \'kāliks, 'kal-\ *n, pl* **-lyx•es** *or* **-ly•ces** \-lə,sēz\ **:** sepals of a flower

cam \'kam\ *n* **:** machine part that slides or rotates irregularly to transmit linear motion

ca•ma•ra•de•rie \,käm'rädərē, ,kam-, -mə'-, -'rad-\ *n* **:** fellowship

cam•bric \'kāmbrik\ *n* **:** fine thin linen or cotton fabric

came *past of* COME

cam•el \'kaməl\ *n* **:** large hoofed mammal of desert areas

ca•mel•lia \kə'mēlyə\ *n* **:** shrub or tree grown for its showy roselike flowers or the flower itself

cam•eo \'kamē,ō\ *n, pl* **-eos :** gem carved in relief

cam•era \'kamrə\ *n* **:** box with a lens for taking pictures **—cam•era•man** \-,man, -mən\ *n*

cam•ou•flage \'kamə,fläzh, -,fläj\ *vb* **:** hide by disguising **—camouflage** *n*

camp \'kamp\ *n* **1 :** place to stay temporarily esp. in a tent **2 :** group living in a camp ~ *vb* **:** make or live in a camp **—camp•er** *n* **—camp•ground** *n* **—camp•site** *n*

cam•paign \kam'pān\ *n* : series of military operations or of activities meant to gain a result —**campaign** *vb*

cam•pa•ni•le \ˌkampə'nēlē, -'nēl\ *n, pl* **-ni•les** *or* **-ni•li** \-'nēlē\ : bell tower

cam•phor \'kamfər\ *n* : gummy volatile aromatic compound from an evergreen tree (**cam•phor tree**)

cam•pus \'kampəs\ *n* : grounds and buildings of a college or school

1**can** \kən, 'kan\ *vb, past* **could** \kəd, 'ku̇d\; *pres sing & pl* **can 1** : be able to **2** : be permitted to by conscience or feeling **3** : have permission or liberty to

2**can** \'kan\ *n* : metal container ~ *vb* **-nn-** : preserve by sealing in airtight cans or jars —**can•ner** *n* —**can•nery** \-ərē\ *n*

ca•nal \kə'nal\ *n* **1** : tubular passage in the body **2** : channel filled with water

ca•na•pé \'kanəpē, -ˌpā\ *n* : appetizer

ca•nard \kə'närd\ *n* : false report

ca•nary \-'nerē\ *n, pl* **-nar•ies** : yellow or greenish finch often kept as a pet

can•cel \'kansəl\ *vb* **-celed** *or* **-celled; -cel•ing** *or* **-cel•ling 1** : cross out **2** : destroy, neutralize, or match the force or effect of —**cancel** *n* —**cancel•la•tion** \ˌkansə'lāshən\ *n* —**cancel•er, can•cel•ler** *n*

can•cer \'kansər\ *n* **1** : malignant tumor that tends to spread **2** : slowly destructive evil —**can•cer•ous** \-ərəs\ *adj* —**can•cer•ous•ly** *adv*

can•de•la•bra \ˌkandə'läbrə, -'lab-\ *n* : candelabrum

can•de•la•brum \-rəm\ *n, pl* **-bra** \-rə\ : ornamental branched candlestick

can•did \'kandəd\ *adj* **1** : frank **2** : unposed —**can•did•ly** *adv* —**can•did•ness** *n*

can•di•date \'kandəˌdāt, -dət\ *n* : one who seeks an office or membership —**can•di•da•cy** \-dəsē\ *n*

can•dle \'kandəl\ *n* : tallow or wax molded around a wick and burned to give light —**can•dle•light** *n* —**candle•stick** *n*

can•dor \'kandər\ *n* : frankness

can•dy \-dē\ *n, pl* **-dies** : food made from sugar ~ *vb* **-died; -dy•ing** : encrust in sugar

cane \'kān\ *n* **1** : slender plant stem **2** : a tall woody grass or reed **3** : stick for walking or beating ~ *vb* **caned; can•ing 1** : beat with a cane **2** : weave or make with cane —**can•er** *n*

ca•nine \'kāˌnīn\ *adj* : relating to dogs ~ *n* **1** : pointed tooth next to the incisors **2** : dog

can•is•ter \'kanəstər\ *n* : cylindrical container

can•ker \'kaŋkər\ *n* : mouth ulcer —**can•ker•ous** \-kərəs\ *adj*

can•na•bis \'kanəbəs\ *n* : preparation derived from hemp

can•ni•bal \'kanəbəl\ *n* : human or animal that eats its own kind —**can•ni•bal•ism** \-bəˌlizəm\ *n* —**can•ni•bal•is•tic** \ˌkanəbə'listik\ *adj*

can•ni•bal•ize \'kanəbəˌlīz\ *vb* **-ized; -iz•ing 1** : take usable parts from **2** : practice cannibalism

can•non \'kanən\ *n, pl* **-nons** *or* **-non** : large heavy gun —**can•non•ball** *n* —**can•non•eer** \ˌkanə'nir\ *n*

can•non•ade \ˌkanə'nād\ *n* : heavy artillery fire ~ *vb* **-ad•ed; -ad•ing** : bombard

can•not \'kanˌät; kə'nät\ : can not —**cannot but** : be bound to

can•ny \'kanē\ *adj* **-ni•er; -est** : shrewd —**can•ni•ly** *adv* —**can•ni•ness** *n*

ca•noe \kə'nü\ *n* : narrow sharp-ended boat propelled by paddles —**canoe** *vb* —**ca•noe•ist** *n*

1**can•on** \'kanən\ *n* **1** : regulation governing a church **2** : authoritative list **3** : an accepted principle

2**canon** *n* : clergy member in a cathedral

ca•non•i•cal \kə'nänikəl\ *adj* **1** : relating to or conforming to a canon **2** : orthodox —**ca•non•i•cal•ly** *adv*

can•on•ize \'kanəˌnīz\ *vb* **-ized** \-ˌnīzd\; **-iz•ing** : recognize as a saint —**can•on•iza•tion** \ˌkanənə'zāshən\ *n*

can•o•py \'kanəpē\ *n, pl* **-pies** : overhanging cover —**canopy** *vb*

1**cant** \'kant\ *n* **1** : slanting surface **2** : slant ~ *vb* **1** : tip up **2** : lean to one side

2**cant** *vb* : talk hypocritically ~ *n* **1** : jargon **2** : insincere talk

can't \'kant, 'kánt\ : can not

can•ta•loupe \'kantəlˌōp\ *n* : muskmelon with orange flesh

can•tan•ker•ous \kan'taŋkərəs\ *adj* : hard to deal with —**can•tan•ker•ous•ly** *adv* —**can•tan•ker•ous•ness** *n*

can•ta•ta \kən'tätə\ *n* : choral work

can•teen \kan'tēn\ *n* **1** : place of recreation for service personnel **2** : water container

can•ter \'kantər\ *n* : slow gallop —**canter** *vb*

can•ti•cle \'kantikəl\ *n* : liturgical song

can•ti•le•ver \'kantəlˌēvər, -ˌev-\ *n* : beam or structure supported at only one end

can•to \'kanˌtō\ *n, pl* **-tos** : major division of a long poem

can•tor \'kantər\ *n* : synagogue official who sings liturgical music

can•vas \'kanvəs\ *n* **1** : strong cloth orig. used for making tents and sails **2** : set of sails **3** : oil painting

can•vass \-vəs\ *vb* : solicit votes, orders, or opinions from ~ *n* : act of canvassing —**can•vass•er** *n*

can•yon \'kanyən\ *n* : deep valley with steep sides

cap \'kap\ *n* **1** : covering for the head **2** : top or cover like a cap **3** : upper limit ~ *vb* **-pp- 1** : provide or protect with a cap **2** : climax —**cap•ful** \-ˌfu̇l\ *n*

ca•pa•ble \'kāpəbəl\ *adj* : able to do something —**ca•pa•bil•i•ty** \ˌkāpə'bilətē\ *n* —**ca•pa•bly** \'kāpəblē\ *adv*

ca•pa•cious \kə'pāshəs\ *adj* : able to contain much

ca•pac•i•tance \kə'pasətəns\ *n* : ability to store electrical energy

ca•pac•i•tor \-sətər\ *n* : device for storing electrical energy

ca•pac•i•ty \-sətē\ *n, pl* **-ties 1** : ability to contain **2** : volume **3** : ability **4** : role or job ~ *adj* : equaling maximum capacity

1**cape** \'kāp\ *n* : point of land jutting out into water

2**cape** *n* : garment that drapes over the shoulders

1**ca•per** \'kāpər\ *n* : flower bud of a shrub pickled for use as a relish

2**caper** *vb* : leap or prance about ~ *n* **1** : frolicsome leap **2** : escapade

cap•il•lary \'kapəˌlerē\ *adj* **1** : resembling a hair **2** : having a very small bore ~ *n, pl* **-lar•ies** : tiny thin-walled blood vessel

1**cap•i•tal** \'kapətəl\ *adj* **1** : punishable by death **2** : being in the series A, B, C rather than a, b, c **3** : relating to capital **4** : excellent ~ *n* **1** : capital letter **2** : seat of government **3** : wealth **4** : total face value of a company's stock **5** : investors as a group

2**capital** *n* : top part of a column

cap•i•tal•ism \-ˌizəm\ *n* : economic system of private ownership of capital

cap•i•tal•ist \-ist\ *n* **1** : person with capital invested in business **2** : believer in capitalism ~ *adj* **1** : owning capital **2** : practicing, advocating, or marked by capitalism —**cap•i•tal•is•tic** \ˌkapətəl'istik\ *adj* —**cap•i•tal•is•ti•cal•ly** \-klē\ *adv*

cap•i•tal•ize \-ˌīz\ *vb* **-ized; -iz•ing 1** : write or print with a capital letter **2** : use as capital **3** : supply capital for **4** : turn something to advantage —**cap•i•tal•iza•tion** \ˌkapətələ'zāshən\ *n*

cap•i•tol \'kapətəl\ *n* : building in which a legislature sits

ca•pit•u•late \kə'pichəˌlāt\ *vb* **-lat•ed; -lat•ing** : surrender —**ca•pit•u•la•tion** \-ˌpichə'lāshən\ *n*

ca•pon \'kāˌpän, -pən\ *n* : castrated male chicken

ca•price \kə'prēs\ *n* : whim —**ca•pri•cious** \-'prishəs\ *adj* —**ca•pri•cious•ly** *adv* —**ca•pri•cious•ness** *n*

cap•size \'kapˌsīz, kap'sīz\ *vb* **-sized; -siz•ing** : overturn

cap•stan \'kapstən, -ˌstan\ *n* : upright winch

cap•sule \'kapsəl, -sül\ *n* **1** : enveloping cover (as for medicine) **2** : small pressurized compartment for astronauts ~ *adj* : very brief or compact —**cap•su•lar** \-sələr\ *adj* —**cap•su•lat•ed** \-səˌlātəd\ *adj*

cap•tain \'kaptən\ *n* **1** : commander of a body of troops **2** : officer in charge of a ship **3** : commissioned officer in the navy ranking next below a rear admiral or a commodore **4** : commissioned officer (as in the army) ranking next below a major **5** : leader ~ *vb* : be captain of —**captain•cy** *n*

cap•tion \'kapshən\ *n* **1** : title **2** : explanation with an illustration —**caption** *vb*

cap•tious \'kapshəs\ *adj* : tending to find fault —**cap•tious•ly** *adv*

cap•ti•vate \'kaptəˌvāt\ *vb* **-vat•ed; -vat•ing** : attract and charm —**cap•ti•va•tion** \ˌkaptə'vāshən\ *n* —**cap•ti•va•tor** \'kaptəˌvātər\ *n*

cap•tive \-tiv\ *adj* **1** : made prisoner **2** : confined or under control —**captive** *n* —**cap•tiv•i•ty** \kap'tivətē\ *n*

cap•tor \'kaptər\ *n* : one that captures

cap•ture \-chər\ *n* : seizure by force or trickery ~ *vb* **-tured; -tur•ing** : take captive

car \'kär\ *n* **1** : vehicle moved on wheels **2** : cage of an elevator

ca•rafe \kə'raf, -'räf\ *n* : decanter

car•a•mel \'karəməl, 'kärməl\ *n* **1** : burnt sugar used for flavoring and coloring **2** : firm chewy candy

1**carat** *var of* KARAT

2**car•at** \'karət\ *n* : unit of weight for precious stones

car•a•van \'karəˌvan\ *n* : travelers journeying together (as in a line)

car•a•way \'karəˌwā\ *n* : aromatic herb with seeds used in seasoning

car•bine \'kärˌbēn, -ˌbīn\ *n* : short-barreled rifle

car•bo•hy•drate \ˌkärbō'hīˌdrāt, -drət\ *n* : compound of carbon, hydrogen, and oxygen

car•bon \'kärbən\ *n* **1** : chemical element occurring in nature esp. as diamond and graphite **2** : piece of carbon paper or a copy made with it

1**car•bon•ate** \'kärbəˌnāt, -nət\ *n* : salt or ester of a carbon-containing acid

2**car•bon•ate** \-ˌnāt\ *vb* **-at•ed; -at•ing** : impregnate with carbon dioxide —**car•bon•ation** \ˌkärbə'nāshən\ *n*

carbon paper *n* : thin paper coated with a pigment for making copies

car•bun•cle \'kärˌbəŋkəl\ *n* : painful inflammation of the skin and underlying tissue

car•bu•re•tor \'kärbəˌrātər, -byə-\ *n* : device for mixing fuel and air

car•cass \'kärkəs\ *n* : dead body

car•cin•o•gen \kär'sinəjən\ *n* : agent causing cancer —**car•ci•no•gen•ic** \ˌkärsənō'jenik\ *adj*

car•ci•no•ma \ˌkärsən'ōmə\ *n, pl* **-mas** *or* **-ma•ta** \-mətə\ : malignant tumor —**car•ci•no•ma•tous** \-mətəs\ *adj*

1**card** \'kärd\ *vb* : comb (fibers) before spinning ~ *n* : device for carding fibers —**card•er** *n*

2**card** *n* **1** : playing card **2** *pl* : game played with playing cards **3** : small flat piece of paper

card•board *n* : stiff material like paper

car•di•ac \'kärdēˌak\ *adj* : relating to the heart

car•di•gan \'kärdigən\ *n* : sweater with an opening in the front

1**car•di•nal** \'kärdənəl\ *n* **1** : official of the Roman Catholic Church **2** : bright red songbird

2**cardinal** *adj* : of basic importance

cardinal number *n* : number (as 1, 82, 357) used in counting

car•di•ol•o•gy \ˌkärdē'äləjē\ *n* : study of the heart —**car•di•ol•o•gist** \-jist\ *n*

car•dio•vas•cu•lar \-ō'vaskyələr\ *adj* : relating to the heart and blood vessels

care \'ker\ *n* **1** : anxiety **2** : watchful attention **3** : supervision ~ *vb* **cared; car•ing 1** : feel anxiety or concern **2** : like **3** : provide care —**care•free** *adj* —**care•ful** \-fəl\ *adj* —**care•ful•ly** *adv* —**care•ful•ness** *n* —**care•giv•er** \-ˌgivər\ *n* —**care•less** *adj* —**care•less•ly** *adv* —**care•less•ness** *n*

ca•reen \kə'rēn\ *vb* **1** : sway from side to side **2** : career

ca•reer \kə'rir\ *n* : vocation ~ *vb* : go at top speed

ca•ress \kə'res\ *n* : tender touch ~ *vb* : touch lovingly or tenderly

car•et \'karət\ *n* : mark ‸ showing where something is to be inserted

care•tak•er *n* : one in charge for another or temporarily

car•go \'kärgō\ *n, pl* **-goes** *or* **-gos** : transported goods

car•i•bou \'karəˌbü\ *n, pl* **-bou** *or* **-bous** : large No. American deer

car•i•ca•ture \'karikəˌchu̇r\ *n* : distorted representation for humor or ridicule —**caricature** *vb* —**car•i•ca•tur•ist** \-ist\ *n*

car•ies \'karēz\ *n, pl* **caries** : tooth decay

car•il•lon \'karəˌlän\ *n* : set of tuned bells

car•mine \'kärmən, -ˌmīn\ *n* : vivid red

car•nage \'kärnij\ *n* : slaughter

car•nal \'kärnəl\ *adj* : sensual —**car•nal•i•ty** \kär'nalətē\ *n* —**car•nal•ly** *adv*

car•na•tion \kär'nāshən\ *n* : showy flower

car•ni•val \'kärnəvəl\ *n* **1** : festival **2** : traveling enterprise offering amusements

car•ni•vore \-ˌvōr\ *n* : flesh-eating animal —**car•niv•o•rous** \kär'nivərəs\ *adj* —**car•niv•o•rous•ly** *adv* —**car•niv•o•rous•ness** *n*

car•ol \'karəl\ *n* : song of joy —**carol** *vb* —**car•ol•er, car•ol•ler** \-ələr\ *n*

car•om \-əm\ *n or vb* : rebound

ca•rouse \kə'rau̇z\ *vb* **-roused; -rous•ing** : drink and be boisterous —**ca•rouse** *n* —**ca•rous•er** *n*

car•ou•sel, car•rou•sel \ˌkarə'sel, 'karəˌ-\ *n* : merry-go-round

1**carp** \'kärp\ *vb* : find fault

2**carp** *n, pl* **carp** *or* **carps** : freshwater fish

car•pel \'kärpəl\ *n* : modified leaf forming part of the ovary of a flower

car•pen•ter \'kärpəntər\ *n* : one who builds with wood —**carpenter** *vb* —**car•pen•try** \-trē\ *n*

car•pet \'kärpət\ *n* : fabric floor covering ~ *vb* : cover with a carpet —**car•pet•ing** \-iŋ\ *n*

car•port *n* : open-sided automobile shelter

car•riage \'karij\ *n* **1** : conveyance **2** : manner of holding oneself **3** : wheeled vehicle

car•ri•on \'karēən\ *n* : dead and decaying flesh

car•rot \'karət\ *n* : orange root vegetable

car•ry \'karē\ *vb* **-ried; -ry•ing 1** : move while supporting **2** : hold (oneself) in a specified way **3** : support **4** : keep in stock **5** : reach to a distance **6** : win —**car•ri•er** \-ēər\ *n* —**carry on** *vb* **1** : conduct **2** : behave excitedly —**carry out** *vb* : put into effect

cart \'kärt\ *n* : wheeled vehicle ~ *vb* : carry in a cart —**cart•age** \-ij\ *n* —**cart•er** *n*

car•tel \kär'tel\ *n* : business combination designed to limit competition

car•ti•lage \'kärtəlij\ *n* : elastic skeletal tissue —**car•ti•lag•i•nous** \ˌkärtəl'ajənəs\ *adj*

car•tog•ra•phy \kär'tägrəfē\ *n* : making of maps —**car•tog•ra•pher** \-fər\ *n*

car•ton \'kärtən\ *n* : cardboard box

car•toon \kär'tün\ *n* **1** : humorous drawing **2** : comic strip —**cartoon** *vb* —**car•toon•ist** *n*

car•tridge \'kärtrij\ *n* **1** : tube containing powder and a bullet or shot for a firearm **2** : container of material for insertion into an apparatus

carve \'kärv\ *vb* **carved; carv•ing 1** : cut with care **2** : cut into pieces or slices —**carv•er** *n*

cas•cade \kas'kād\ *n* : small steep waterfall ~ *vb* **-cad•ed; -cad•ing** : fall in a cascade

1**case** \'kās\ *n* **1** : particular instance **2** : convincing argument **3** : inflectional form esp. of a noun or pronoun **4** : fact **5** : lawsuit **6** : instance of disease —**in case** : as a precaution —**in case of** : in the event of

2**case** *n* **1** : box **2** : outer covering ~ *vb* **cased; cas•ing 1** : enclose **2** : inspect

case•ment \-mənt\ *n* : window that opens like a door

cash \'kash\ *n* **1** : ready money **2** : money paid at the time of purchase ~ *vb* : give or get cash for

ca•shew \'kashü, kə'shü\ *n* : tropical American tree or its nut

1**ca•shier** \ka'shir\ *vb* : dismiss in disgrace

2**cash•ier** *n* : person who receives and records payments

cash•mere \'kazhˌmir, 'kash-\ *n* : fine goat's wool or a fabric of this

ca•si•no \kə'sēnō\ *n, pl* **-nos** : place for gambling

cask \'kask\ *n* : barrel-shaped container for liquids

cas•ket \'kaskət\ *n* : coffin

cas•se•role \'kasəˌrōl\ *n* : baking dish or the food cooked in this

cas•sette \kə'set, ka-\ *n* : case containing magnetic tape

cas•sock \'kasək\ *n* : long clerical garment

cast \'kast\ *vb* **cast; cast•ing 1** : throw **2** : deposit (a ballot) **3** : assign parts in a play **4** : mold ~ *n* **1** : throw **2** : appearance **3** : rigid surgical dressing **4** : actors in a play

cas•ta•nets \ˌkastə'nets\ *n pl* : shells clicked together in the hand

cast•away \'kastəˌwā\ *n* : survivor of a shipwreck —**castaway** *adj*

caste \'kast\ *n* : social class or rank

cast•er \'kastər\ *n* : small wheel on furniture

cas•ti•gate \'kastəˌgāt\ *vb* **-gat•ed; -gating** : chastise severely —**cas•ti•ga•tion** \ˌkastə'gāshən\ *n* —**cas•ti•ga•tor** \'kastəˌgātər\ *n*

cast iron *n* : hard brittle alloy of iron

cas•tle \'kasəl\ *n* : fortified building

cast–off *adj* : thrown away —**cast•off** *n*

cas•trate \'kasˌtrāt\ *vb* **-trat•ed; -trat•ing** : remove the testes of —**cas•tra•tion** \ka'strāshən\ *n*

ca•su•al \'kazhəwəl\ *adj* **1** : happening by chance **2** : showing little concern **3** : informal —**ca•su•al•ly** \-ē\ *adv* —**ca•su•al•ness** *n*

ca•su•al•ty \-tē\ *n, pl* **-ties 1** : serious or fatal accident **2** : one injured, lost, or destroyed

ca•su•ist•ry \'kazhəwəstrē\ *n, pl* **-ries** : rationalization —**ca•su•ist** \-wist\ *n*

cat \'kat\ *n* **1** : small domestic mammal **2** : related animal (as a lion) —**cat•like** *adj*

cat•a•clysm \'katəˌklizəm\ *n* : violent change —**cat•a•clys•mal** \ˌkatə'klizməl\, **cat•a•clys•mic** \-'klizmik\ *adj*

cat•a•comb \'katəˌkōm\ *n* : underground burial place

cat•a•log, cat•a•logue \'katəlˌȯg\ *n* **1** : list **2** : book containing a description of items ~ *vb* **-loged** *or* **-logued; -log•ing** *or* **-logu•ing 1** : make a catalog of **2** : enter in a catalog —**cat•a•log•er, cat•a•logu•er** *n*

ca•tal•pa \kə'talpə\ *n* : tree with broad leaves and long pods

ca•tal•y•sis \kə'taləsəs\ *n, pl* **-y•ses** \-ˌsēz\ : increase in the rate of chemical reaction caused by a substance (**cat•a•lyst** \'katəlist\) that is itself unchanged —**cat•a•lyt•ic** \ˌkatəl'itik\ *adj*

cat•a•ma•ran \ˌkatəmə'ran\ *n* : boat with twin hulls

cat•a•mount \'katəˌmau̇nt\ *n* : cougar

cat•a•pult \'katəˌpəlt, -ˌpu̇lt\ *n* : device for hurling or launching —**catapult** *vb*

cat•a•ract \'katəˌrakt\ *n* **1** : large waterfall **2** : cloudiness of the lens of the eye

ca•tarrh \kə'tär\ *n* : inflammation of the nose and throat

ca•tas•tro•phe \kəˈtastrəˌfē\ *n* **1 :** great disaster or misfortune **2 :** utter failure —**cat•a•stroph•ic** \ˌkatəˈsträfik\ *adj* —**cat•a•stroph•i•cal•ly** \-iklē\ *adv*

cat•bird *n* **:** American songbird

cat•call *n* **:** noise of disapproval

catch \ˈkach, ˈkech\ *vb* **caught** \ˈkȯt\; **catch•ing 1 :** capture esp. after pursuit **2 :** trap **3 :** detect esp. by surprise **4 :** grasp **5 :** get entangled **6 :** become affected with or by **7 :** seize and hold firmly ~ *n* **1 :** act of catching **2 :** something caught **3 :** something that fastens **4 :** hidden difficulty —**catch•er** *n*

catch•ing \-iŋ\ *adj* **:** infectious

catch•up \ˈkechəp, ˈkach-; ˈkatsəp\ *var of* KETCHUP

catch•word *n* **:** slogan

catchy \-ē\ *adj* **catch•i•er; -est :** likely to catch interest

cat•e•chism \ˈkatəˌkizəm\ *n* **:** set of questions and answers esp. to teach religious doctrine

cat•e•gor•i•cal \ˌkatəˈgȯrikəl\ *adj* **:** absolute —**cat•e•gor•i•cal•ly** \-klē\ *adv*

cat•e•go•ry \ˈkatəˌgōrē\ *n, pl* **-ries :** group or class —**cat•e•go•ri•za•tion** \ˌkatigərəˈzāshən\ *n* —**cat•e•go•rize** \ˈkatigəˌrīz\ *vb*

ca•ter \ˈkātər\ *vb* **1 :** provide food for **2 :** supply what is wanted —**ca•ter•er** *n*

cat•er•cor•ner \ˌkatēˈkȯrnər, ˌkatə-, ˌkitē-\, **cat•er–cor•nered** *adv or adj* **:** in a diagonal position

cat•er•pil•lar \ˈkatərˌpilər\ *n* **:** butterfly or moth larva

cat•er•waul \ˈkatərˌwȯl\ *vb* **:** make the harsh cry of a cat —**caterwaul** *n*

cat•fish *n* **:** big-headed fish with feelers about the mouth

cat•gut *n* **:** tough cord made usu. from sheep intestines

ca•thar•sis \kəˈthärsəs\ *n, pl* **ca•thar•ses** \-ˌsēz\ **:** a purging —**ca•thar•tic** \kəˈthärtik\ *adj or n*

ca•the•dral \-ˈthēdrəl\ *n* **:** principal church of a diocese

cath•e•ter \ˈkathətər\ *n* **:** tube for insertion into a body cavity

cath•ode \ˈkathˌōd\ *n* **1 :** negative electrode **2 :** positive battery terminal —**ca•thod•ic** \kaˈthädik\ *adj*

cath•o•lic \ˈkathəlik\ *adj* **1 :** universal **2** *cap* **:** relating to Roman Catholics

Cath•o•lic *n* **:** member of the Roman Catholic Church —**Ca•thol•i•cism** \kəˈthäləˌsizəm\ *n*

cat•kin \ˈkatkən\ *n* **:** long dense flower cluster

cat•nap *n* **:** short light nap —**catnap** *vb*

cat•nip \-ˌnip\ *n* **:** aromatic mint relished by cats

cat's–paw *n, pl* **cat's–paws :** person used as if a tool

cat•sup \ˈkechəp, ˈkach-; ˈkatsəp\ *var of* KETCHUP

cat•tail *n* **:** marsh herb with furry brown spikes

cat•tle \ˈkatᵊl\ *n pl* **:** domestic bovines —**cat•tle•man** \-mən, -ˌman\ *n*

cat•ty \ˈkatē\ *adj* **-ti•er; -est :** mean or spiteful —**cat•ti•ly** *adv* —**cat•ti•ness** *n*

cat•walk *n* **:** high narrow walk

Cau•ca•sian \kȯˈkāzhən\ *adj* **:** relating to the white race —**Caucasian** *n*

cau•cus \ˈkȯkəs\ *n* **:** political meeting —**caucus** *vb*

caught *past of* CATCH

cauldron \ˈkȯldrən\ *n* **:** large kettle

cau•li•flow•er \ˈkȯliˌflaùər, ˈkäl-\ *n* **:** vegetable having a compact head of usu. white undeveloped flowers

caulk \ˈkȯk\ *vb* **:** make seams watertight —**caulk** *n* —**caulk•er** *n*

caus•al \ˈkȯzəl\ *adj* **:** relating to or being a cause —**cau•sal•i•ty** \kȯˈzalətē\ *n* —**caus•al•ly** \ˈkȯzəlē\ *adv*

cause \ˈkȯz\ *n* **1 :** something that brings about a result **2 :** reason **3 :** lawsuit **4 :** principle or movement to support ~ *vb* **caused; caus•ing :** be the cause of —**cau•sa•tion** \kȯˈzāshən\ *n* —**caus•ative** \ˈkȯzətiv\ *adj* —**cause•less** *adj* —**caus•er** *n*

cause•way *n* **:** raised road esp. over water

caus•tic \ˈkȯstik\ *adj* **1 :** corrosive **2 :** sharp or biting —**caustic** *n*

cau•ter•ize \ˈkȯtəˌrīz\ *vb* **-ized; -iz•ing :** burn to prevent infection or bleeding —**cau•ter•i•za•tion** \ˌkȯtərəˈzāshən\ *n*

cau•tion \ˈkȯshən\ *n* **1 :** warning **2 :** care or prudence ~ *vb* **:** warn —**cau•tion•ary** \-shəˌnerē\ *adj*

cau•tious \ˈkȯshəs\ *adj* **:** taking caution —**cau•tious•ly** *adv* —**cau•tious•ness** *n*

cav•al•cade \ˌkavəlˈkād, ˈkavəlˌ-\ *n* **1 :** procession on horseback **2 :** series

cav•a•lier \ˌkavəˈlir\ *n* **:** mounted soldier ~ *adj* **:** disdainful or arrogant —**cav•a•lier•ly** *adv*

cav•al•ry \ˈkavəlrē\ *n, pl* **-ries :** troops on horseback or in vehicles —**cav•al•ry•man** \-mən, -ˌman\ *n*

cave \ˈkāv\ *n* **:** natural underground chamber —**cave in** *vb* **:** collapse

cav•ern \ˈkavərn\ *n* **:** large cave —**cavern•ous** *adj* —**cav•ern•ous•ly** *adv*

cav•i•ar, cav•i•are \ˈkavēˌär, ˈkäv-\ *n* **:** salted fish roe

cav•il \ˈkavəl\ *vb* **-iled** *or* **-illed; -il•ing** *or* **-il•ling :** raise trivial objections —**cavil** *n* —**cav•il•er, cav•il•ler** *n*

cav•i•ty \ˈkavətē\ *n, pl* **-ties 1 :** unfilled place within a mass **2 :** decay in a tooth

ca•vort \kəˈvȯrt\ *vb* **:** prance or caper

caw \ˈkȯ\ *vb* **:** utter the harsh call of the crow —**caw** *n*

cay•enne pepper \ˌkīˈen-, ˌkā-\ *n* **:** ground dried fruits of a hot pepper

CD \ˌsēˈdē\ *n* **:** compact disc

cease \ˈsēs\ *vb* **ceased; ceas•ing :** stop

cease•less \-ləs\ *adj* **:** continuous

ce•dar \ˈsēdər\ *n* **:** cone-bearing tree with fragrant durable wood

cede \ˈsēd\ *vb* **ced•ed; ced•ing :** surrender —**ced•er** *n*

ceil•ing \ˈsēliŋ\ *n* **1 :** overhead surface of a room **2 :** upper limit

cel•e•brate \ˈseləˌbrāt\ *vb* **-brat•ed; -brat•ing 1 :** perform with appropriate rites **2 :** honor with ceremonies **3 :** extol —**cel•e•brant** \-brənt\ *n* —**cel•e•bra•tion** \ˌseləˈbrāshən\ *n* —**cel•e•bra•tor** \ˈseləˌbrātər\ *n*

cel•e•brat•ed \-əd\ *adj* **:** renowned

ce•leb•ri•ty \səˈlebrətē\ *n, pl* **-ties 1 :** renown **2 :** well-known person

ce•ler•i•ty \səˈlerətē\ *n* **:** speed

cel•ery \ˈselərē\ *n, pl* **-er•ies :** herb grown for crisp edible stalks

ce•les•ta \səˈlestə\, **ce•leste** \səˈlest\ *n* **:** keyboard musical instrument

ce•les•tial \səˈleschəl\ *adj* **1 :** relating to the sky **2 :** heavenly

cel•i•ba•cy \ˈseləbəsē\ *n* **1 :** state of being unmarried **2 :** abstention from sexual intercourse —**cel•i•bate** \ˈseləbət\ *n or adj*

cell \ˈsel\ *n* **1 :** small room **2 :** tiny mass of protoplasm that forms the fundamental unit of living matter **3 :** container holding an electrolyte for generating electricity —**celled** *adj*

cel•lar \ˈselər\ *n* **:** room or area below ground

cel•lo \ˈchelō\ *n, pl* **-los :** bass member of the violin family —**cel•list** \-ist\ *n*

cel•lo•phane \ˈseləˌfān\ *n* **:** thin transparent cellulose wrapping

cel•lu•lar \ˈselyələr\ *adj* **:** relating to or consisting of cells

cel•lu•lose \ˈselyəˌlōs\ *n* **:** complex plant carbohydrate

Cel•sius \ˈselsēəs\ *adj* **:** relating to a thermometer scale on which the freezing point of water is 0° and the boiling point is 100°

ce•ment \siˈment\ *n* **1 :** powdery mixture of clay and limestone that hardens when wetted **2 :** binding agent ~ *vb* **:** unite or cover with cement —**ce•ment•er** *n*

cem•e•tery \ˈseməˌterē\ *n, pl* **-ter•ies :** burial ground

cen•ser \ˈsensər\ *n* **:** vessel for burning incense

cen•sor \ˈsensər\ *n* **:** one with power to suppress anything objectionable (as in printed matter) ~ *vb* **:** be a censor of —**cen•so•ri•al** \senˈsōrēəl\ *adj* —**cen•sor•ship** \-ˌship\ *n*

cen•so•ri•ous \senˈsōrēəs\ *adj* **:** critical —**cen•so•ri•ous•ly** *adv* —**cen•so•ri•ous•ness** *n*

cen•sure \ˈsenchər\ *n* **:** official reprimand ~ *vb* **-sured; -sur•ing :** find blameworthy —**cen•sur•able** *adj*

cen•sus \ˈsensəs\ *n* **:** periodic population count —**census** *vb*

cent \ˈsent\ *n* **:** monetary unit equal to 1/100 of a basic unit of value

cen•taur \ˈsenˌtȯr\ *n* **:** mythological creature that is half man and half horse

cen•ten•ni•al \senˈtenēəl\ *n* **:** 100th anniversary —**centennial** *adj*

cen•ter \ˈsentər\ *n* **1 :** middle point **2 :** point of origin or greatest concentration **3 :** region of concentrated population **4 :** player near the middle of the team ~ *vb* **1 :** place, fix, or concentrate at or around a center **2 :** have a center —**cen•ter•piece** *n*

cen•ti•grade \ˈsentəˌgrād, ˈsänt-\ *adj* **:** Celsius

cen•ti•me•ter \ˈsentəˌmētər, ˈsänt-\ *n* **:** 1/100 meter

cen•ti•pede \ˈsentəˌpēd\ *n* **:** long flat many-legged arthropod

cen•tral \ˈsentrəl\ *adj* **1 :** constituting or being near a center **2 :** essential or principal —**cen•tral•ly** *adv*

cen•tral•ize \-trəˌlīz\ *vb* **-ized; -iz•ing :** bring to a central point or under central control —**cen•tral•i•za•tion** \ˌsentrələˈzāshən\ *n* —**cen•tral•iz•er** *n*

cen•tre *chiefly Brit var of* CENTER

cen•trif•u•gal \senˈtrifyəgəl, -ˈtrifigəl\ *adj* **:** acting in a direction away from a center or axis

cen•tri•fuge \ˈsentrəˌfyüj\ *n* **:** machine that separates substances by spinning

cen•trip•e•tal \senˈtripətᵊl\ *adj* **:** acting in a direction toward a center or axis

cen•tu•ri•on \senˈchùrēən, -ˈtùr-\ *n* **:** Roman military officer

cen•tu•ry \ˈsenchərē\ *n, pl* **-ries :** 100 years

ce•ram•ic \səˈramik\ *n* **1** *pl* **:** art or process of shaping and hardening articles from clay **2 :** product of ceramics —**ceramic** *adj*

ce•re•al \ˈsirēəl\ *adj* **:** made of or relating to grain or to the plants that produce it ~ *n* **1 :** grass yielding edible grain **2 :** food prepared from a cereal grain

cer•e•bel•lum \ˌserəˈbeləm\ *n, pl* **-bellums** *or* **-bel•la** \-ˈbelə\ **:** part of the brain controlling muscular coordination —**cer•e•bel•lar** \-ər\ *adj*

ce•re•bral \səˈrēbrəl, ˈserə-\ *adj* **1 :** relating to the brain, intellect, or cerebrum **2 :** appealing to the intellect

cerebral palsy *n* **:** disorder caused by brain damage and marked esp. by defective muscle control

cer•e•brate \ˈserəˌbrāt\ *vb* **-brat•ed; -brat•ing :** think —**cer•e•bra•tion** \ˌserəˈbrāshən\ *n*

ce•re•brum \səˈrēbrəm, ˈserə-\ *n, pl* **-brums** *or* **-bra** \-brə\ **:** part of the brain that contains the higher nervous centers

cer•e•mo•ny \ˈserəˌmōnē\ *n, pl* **-nies 1 :** formal act prescribed by law, ritual, or convention **2 :** prescribed procedures —**cer•e•mo•ni•al** \ˌserəˈmōnēəl\ *adj or n* —**cer•e•mo•ni•ous** \-nēəs\ *adj*

ce•rise \səˈrēs\ *n* **:** moderate red

cer•tain \ˈsərtᵊn\ *adj* **1 :** settled **2 :** true **3 :** specific but not named **4 :** bound **5 :** assured ~ *pron* **:** certain ones —**cer•tain•ly** *adv* —**cer•tain•ty** \-tē\ *n*

cer•tif•i•cate \sərˈtifikət\ *n* **:** document establishing truth or fulfillment

cer•ti•fy \ˈsərtəˌfī\ *vb* **-fied; -fy•ing 1 :** verify **2 :** endorse —**cer•ti•fi•able** \-ˌfīəbəl\ *adj* —**cer•ti•fi•ably** \-blē\ *adv* —**cer•ti•fi•ca•tion** \ˌsərtəfəˈkāshən\ *n* —**cer•ti•fi•er** *n*

cer•ti•tude \ˈsərtəˌtüd, -ˌtyüd\ *n* **:** state of being certain

cer•vix \ˈsərviks\ *n, pl* **-vi•ces** \-vəˌsēz\ *or* **-vix•es 1 :** neck **2 :** narrow end of the uterus —**cer•vi•cal** \-vikəl\ *adj*

ce•sar•e•an \siˈzarēən\ *n* **:** surgical operation to deliver a baby —**cesarean** *adj*

ce•si•um \ˈsēzēəm\ *n* **:** silver-white soft ductile chemical element

ces•sa•tion \seˈsāshən\ *n* **:** a halting

ces•sion \ˈseshən\ *n* **:** a yielding

cess•pool \ˈsesˌpül\ *n* **:** underground sewage pit

Cha•blis \ˈshabˌlē; shaˈblē\ *n, pl* **Chablis** \-ˌlēz, -ˈblēz\ **:** dry white wine

chafe \ˈchāf\ *vb* **chafed; chaf•ing 1 :** fret **2 :** make sore by rubbing

chaff \ˈchaf\ *n* **1 :** debris separated from grain **2 :** something worthless

chaf•ing dish \ˈchāfiŋ-\ *n* **:** utensil for cooking at the table

cha•grin \shəˈgrin\ *n* **:** embarrassment or humiliation ~ *vb* **:** cause to feel chagrin

chain \ˈchān\ *n* **1 :** flexible series of connected links **2** *pl* **:** fetters **3 :** linked series ~ *vb* **:** bind or connect with a chain

chair \ˈcher\ *n* **1 :** seat with a back **2 :** position of authority or dignity **3 :** chairman ~ *vb* **:** act as chairman of

chair•man \-mən\ *n* **:** presiding officer —**chair•man•ship** *n*

chair•wom•an \-ˌwùmən\ *n* **:** woman who acts as a presiding officer

chaise longue \ˈshāzˈlȯŋ\ *n, pl* **chaise longues** \-lȯŋ, -ˈlȯŋz\ **:** long chair for reclining

cha•let \shaˈlā\ *n* **:** Swiss mountain cottage with overhanging roof

chal•ice \ˈchaləs\ *n* **:** eucharistic cup

chalk \ˈchȯk\ *n* **1 :** soft limestone **2 :** chalky material used as a crayon ~ *vb* **:** mark with chalk —**chalky** *adj* —**chalk up** *vb* **1 :** credit **2 :** achieve

chalk•board *n* **:** blackboard

chal•lenge \ˈchalənj\ *vb* **-lenged; -leng•ing 1 :** dispute **2 :** invite or dare to act or compete —**challenge** *n* —**challeng•er** *n*

cham•ber \ˈchāmbər\ *n* **1 :** room **2 :** enclosed space **3 :** legislative meeting place or body **4** *pl* **:** judge's consultation room —**cham•bered** *adj*

cham•ber•maid *n* **:** bedroom maid

chamber music *n* **:** music by a small group for a small audience

cha•me•leon \kəˈmēlyən\ *n* **:** small lizard whose skin changes color

cham•ois \ˈshamē\ *n, pl* **cham•ois** \-ē, -ēz\ **1 :** goatlike antelope **2 :** soft leather

1**champ** \ˈchamp, ˈchämp\ *vb* **:** chew noisily

2**champ** \ˈchamp\ *n* **:** champion

cham•pagne \shamˈpān\ *n* **:** sparkling white wine

cham•pi•on \ˈchampēən\ *n* **1 :** advocate or defender **2 :** winning contestant ~ *vb* **:** protect or fight for

cham•pi•on•ship \-ˌship\ *n* **1 :** title of a champion **2 :** contest to pick a champion

chance \ˈchans\ *n* **1 :** unpredictable element of existence **2 :** opportunity **3 :** probability **4 :** risk **5 :** raffle ticket ~ *vb* **chanced; chanc•ing 1 :** happen **2 :** encounter unexpectedly **3 :** risk —**chance** *adj*

chan•cel \ˈchansəl\ *n* **:** part of a church around the altar

chan•cel•lery, chan•cel•lory \ˈchansələrē\ *n, pl* **-ler•ies** *or* **-lor•ies 1 :** position of a chancellor **2 :** chancellor's office

chan•cel•lor \-sələr\ *n* **1 :** chief or high state official **2 :** head of a university —**chan•cel•lor•ship** *n*

chan•cre \ˈshaŋkər\ *n* **:** skin ulcer esp. from syphilis

chancy \ˈchansē\ *adj* **chanc•i•er; -est :** risky

chan•de•lier \ˌshandəˈlir\ *n* **:** hanging lighting fixture

chan•dler \ˈchandlər\ *n* **:** provisions dealer —**chan•dlery** *n*

change \ˈchānj\ *vb* **changed; chang•ing 1 :** make or become different **2 :** exchange **3 :** give or receive change for ~ *n* **1 :** a changing **2 :** excess from a payment **3 :** money in smaller denominations **4 :** coins —**change•able** *adj* —**change•less** *adj* —**chang•er** *n*

chan•nel \ˈchanᵊl\ *n* **1 :** deeper part of a waterway **2 :** means of passage or communication **3 :** strait **4 :** broadcast frequency ~ *vb* **-neled** *or* **-nelled; -nel•ing** *or* **-nel•ling :** make or direct through a channel

chant \ˈchant\ *vb* **:** sing or speak in one tone —**chant** *n* —**chant•er** *n*

chan•tey, chan•ty \ˈshantē, ˈchant-\ *n, pl* **-teys** *or* **-ties :** sailors' work song

Cha•nu•kah \ˈkänəkə, ˈhän-\ *var of* HANUKKAH

cha•os \ˈkāˌäs\ *n* **:** complete disorder —**cha•ot•ic** \kāˈätik\ *adj* —**cha•ot•i•cal•ly** \-iklē\ *adv*

1**chap** \ˈchap\ *n* **:** fellow

2**chap** *vb* **-pp- :** dry and crack open usu. from wind and cold

cha•pel \ˈchapəl\ *n* **:** private or small place of worship

chap•er•on, chap•er•one \ˈshapəˌrōn\ *n* **:** older person who accompanies young people at a social gathering ~ *vb* **-oned; -on•ing :** act as chaperon at or for —**chap•er•on•age** \-ij\ *n*

chap•lain \ˈchaplən\ *n* **:** clergy member in a military unit or a prison —**chap•lain•cy** \-sē\ *n*

chap•ter \ˈchaptər\ *n* **1 :** main book division **2 :** branch of a society

char \ˈchär\ *vb* **-rr- 1 :** burn to charcoal **2 :** scorch

char•ac•ter \ˈkariktər\ *n* **1 :** letter or graphic mark **2 :** trait or distinctive combination of traits **3 :** peculiar person **4 :** fictional person —**char•ac•ter•i•za•tion** \ˌkariktərəˈzāshən\ *n* —**char•ac•ter•ize** \ˈkariktəˌrīz\ *vb*

char•ac•ter•is•tic \ˌkariktəˈristik\ *adj* **:** typical ~ *n* **:** distinguishing quality —**char•ac•ter•is•ti•cal•ly** \-tiklē\ *adv*

cha•rades \shəˈrādz\ *n sing or pl* **:** pantomime guessing game

char•coal \ˈchärˌkōl\ *n* **:** porous carbon prepared by partial combustion

chard \ˈchärd\ *n* **:** leafy vegetable

charge \ˈchärj\ *vb* **charged; charg•ing 1 :** give an electric charge to **2 :** impose a task or responsibility on **3 :** command **4 :** accuse **5 :** rush forward in assault **6 :** assume a debt for **7 :** fix as a price ~ *n* **1 :** excess or deficiency of electrons in a body **2 :** tax **3 :** responsibility **4 :** accusation **5 :** cost **6 :** attack —**charge•able** *adj*

charg•er \-ər\ *n* **:** horse ridden in battle

char•i•ot \ˈcharēət\ *n* **:** ancient 2-wheeled vehicle —**char•i•o•teer** \ˌcharēəˈtir\ *n*

cha•ris•ma \kəˈrizmə\ *n* **:** special ability to lead —**char•is•mat•ic** \ˌkarəzˈmatik\ *adj*

char•i•ty \ˈcharətē\ *n, pl* **-ties 1 :** love for mankind **2 :** generosity or leniency **3 :** alms **4 :** institution for relief of the needy —**char•i•ta•ble** \-əbəl\ *adj* —**char•i•ta•ble•ness** *n* —**char•i•ta•bly** \-blē\ *adv*

char•la•tan \ˈshärlətən\ *n* **:** impostor

charm \ˈchärm\ *n* **1 :** something with magic power **2 :** appealing trait **3 :** small ornament ~ *vb* **:** fascinate —**charm•er** *n* —**charm•ing** *adj* —**charm•ing•ly** *adv*

char•nel house \ˈchärnᵊl-\ *n* **:** place for dead bodies

chart \ˈchärt\ *n* **1 :** map **2 :** diagram ~ *vb* **1 :** make a chart of **2 :** plan

char•ter \-ər\ *n* **1 :** document granting rights **2 :** constitution ~ *vb* **1 :** establish by charter **2 :** rent —**char•ter•er** *n*

char•treuse \shärˈtrüz, -ˈtrüs\ *n* **:** brilliant yellow green

char•wom•an \ˈchärˌwùmən\ *n* **:** cleaning woman

chary \ˈcharē\ *adj* **chari•er; -est :** cautious —**char•i•ly** \ˈcharəlē\ *adv*

1**chase** \ˈchās\ *vb* **chased; chas•ing 1 :** follow trying to catch **2 :** drive away —**chase** *n* —**chas•er** *n*

2chase *vb* **chased; chas•ing** : decorate (metal) by embossing or engraving
chasm \'kazəm\ *n* : gorge
chas•sis \'chasē, 'shasē\ *n, pl* **chas•sis** \-ēz\ : supporting structural frame
chaste \'chāst\ *adj* **chast•er; chast•est** 1 : abstaining from all or unlawful sexual relations 2 : modest or decent 3 : severely simple —**chaste•ly** *adv* —**chaste•ness** *n* —**chas•ti•ty** \'chastətē\ *n*
chas•ten \'chāsᵊn\ *vb* : discipline
chas•tise \chas'tīz\ *vb* **-tised; -tis•ing** 1 : punish 2 : censure — **chas•tise•ment** \-mənt, 'chastəz-\ *n*
chat \'chat\ *n* : informal talk —**chat** *vb* —**chat•ty** \-ē\ *adj*
châ•teau \sha'tō\ *n, pl* **-teaus** \-'tōz\ *or* **-teaux** \-'tō, -'tōz\ 1 : large country house 2 : French vineyard estate
chat•tel \'chatᵊl\ *n* : item of tangible property other than real estate
chat•ter \'chatər\ *vb* 1 : utter rapidly succeeding sounds 2 : talk fast or too much —**chatter** *n* —**chat•ter•er** *n*
chat•ter•box *n* : incessant talker
chauf•feur \'shōfər, shō'fər\ *n* : hired car driver ~ *vb* : work as a chauffeur
chau•vin•ism \'shōvəˌnizəm\ *n* : excessive patriotism —**chau•vin•ist** \-vənist\ *n* —**chau•vin•is•tic** \ˌshōvə'nistik\ *adj*
cheap \'chēp\ *adj* 1 : inexpensive 2 : shoddy —**cheap** *adv* —**cheap•en** \'chēpən\ *vb* —**cheap•ly** *adv* —**cheap•ness** *n*
cheap•skate *n* : stingy person
cheat \'chēt\ *n* 1 : act of deceiving 2 : one that cheats ~ *vb* 1 : deprive through fraud or deceit 2 : violate rules dishonestly —**cheat•er** *n*
check \'chek\ *n* 1 : sudden stoppage 2 : restraint 3 : test or standard for testing 4 : written order to a bank to pay money 5 : ticket showing ownership 6 : slip showing an amount due 7 : pattern in squares or fabric in such a pattern 8 : mark placed beside an item noted ~ *vb* 1 : slow down or stop 2 : restrain 3 : compare or correspond with a source or original 4 : inspect or test for condition 5 : mark with a check 6 : leave or accept for safekeeping or shipment 7 : checker —**check in** *vb* : report one's arrival —**check out** *vb* : settle one's account and leave
1check•er \-ər\ *n* : piece in checkers ~ *vb* : mark with different colors or into squares
2checker *n* : one that checks
check•er•board \-ˌbōrd\ *n* : board of 64 squares of alternate colors
check•ers \'chekərz\ *n* : game for 2 played on a checkerboard
check•mate *vb* : thwart completely —**checkmate** *n*
check•point *n* : place where traffic is checked
check•up *n* : physical examination
ched•dar \'chedər\ *n* : hard smooth cheese
cheek \'chēk\ *n* 1 : fleshy side part of the face 2 : impudence —**cheeked** \'chēkt\ *adj* —**cheeky** *adj*
cheep \'chēp\ *vb* : utter faint shrill sounds —**cheep** *n*
cheer \'chir\ *n* 1 : good spirits 2 : food and drink for a feast 3 : shout of applause or encouragement ~ *vb* 1 : give hope or courage to 2 : make or become glad 3 : urge on or applaud with shouts —**cheer•er** *n* —**cheer•ful** \-fəl\ *adj* —**cheer•ful•ly** *adv* —**cheer•ful•ness** *n* —**cheer•lead•er** *n* —**cheer•less** *adj* —**cheer•less•ly** *adv* —**cheer•less•ness** *n*
cheery \'chirē\ *adj* **cheer•i•er; -est** : cheerful —**cheer•i•ly** *adv* —**cheer•i•ness** *n*
cheese \'chēz\ *n* : curd of milk usu. pressed and cured —**cheesy** *adj*
cheese•cloth *n* : lightweight coarse cotton gauze
chee•tah \'chētə\ *n* : spotted swift-moving African cat
chef \'shef\ *n* : chief cook
chem•i•cal \'kemikəl\ *adj* 1 : relating to chemistry 2 : working or produced by chemicals ~ *n* : substance obtained by chemistry —**chem•i•cal•ly** \-klē\ *adv*
che•mise \shə'mēz\ *n* 1 : woman's one-piece undergarment 2 : loose dress
chem•ist \'kemist\ *n* 1 : one trained in chemistry 2 *Brit* : pharmacist
chem•is•try \-istrē\ *n, pl* **-tries** : science that deals with the composition and properties of substances
che•mo•ther•a•py \ˌkēmō'therəpē, ˌkemō-\ *n* : use of chemicals in the treatment of disease —**che•mo•ther•a•peu•tic** *adj*
che•nille \shə'nēl\ *n* : yarn with protruding pile or fabric of such yarn
cheque \'chek\ *chiefly Brit var of* CHECK 4
cher•ish \'cherish\ *vb* : hold dear
cher•ry \'cherē\ *n, pl* **-ries** : small fleshy fruit of a tree related to the roses or the tree or its wood
cher•ub \'cherəb\ *n* 1 *pl* **-u•bim** \-əˌbim, -yə-\ : angel 2 *pl* **-ubs** : chubby child —**che•ru•bic** \chə'rübik\ *adj*
chess \'ches\ *n* : game for 2 played on a checkerboard —**chess•board** *n* —**chess•man** *n*
chest \'chest\ *n* 1 : boxlike container 2 : part of the body enclosed by the ribs and breastbone —**chest•ed** *adj*
chest•nut \'chesˌnət\ *n* : nut of a tree related to the beech or the tree
chev•i•ot \'shevēət\ *n* 1 : heavy rough wool fabric 2 : soft-finished cotton fabric
chev•ron \'shevrən\ *n* : V-shaped insignia
chew \'chü\ *vb* : crush or grind with the teeth ~ *n* : something to chew —**chew•able** *adj* —**chew•er** *n* —**chewy** *adj*
chic \'shēk\ *n* : smart elegance of dress or manner ~ *adj* 1 : stylish 2 : currently fashionable
chi•ca•nery \shik'ānərē\ *n, pl* **-ner•ies** : trickery
chick \'chik\ *n* : young chicken or bird
chick•a•dee \-əˌdē\ *n* : small grayish American bird
chick•en \'chikən\ *n* 1 : common domestic fowl or its flesh used as food 2 : coward
chicken pox *n* : acute contagious virus disease esp. of children
chi•cle \'chikəl\ *n* : gum from a tropical evergreen tree
chic•o•ry \'chikərē\ *n, pl* **-ries** : herb used in salad or its dried ground root used to adulterate coffee
chide \'chīd\ *vb* **chid** \'chid\ *or* **chid•ed** \'chīdəd\; **chid** *or* **chid•den** \'chidᵊn\ *or* **chided; chid•ing** \'chīdiŋ\ : scold
chief \'chēf\ *n* : leader ~ *adj* 1 : highest in rank 2 : most important —**chiefdom** *n* —**chief•ly** *adv*
chief•tain \'chēftən\ *n* : chief
chif•fon \shif'än, 'shifˌ-\ *n* : sheer fabric
chig•ger \'chigər\ *n* : bloodsucking mite
chi•gnon \'shēnˌyän\ *n* : knot of hair
chil•blain \'chilˌblān\ *n* : sore or inflamed swelling caused by cold
child \'chīld\ *n, pl* **chil•dren** \'childrən\ 1 : unborn or recently born person 2 : son or daughter —**child•bear•ing** *n or adj* —**child•birth** *n* —**child•hood** *n* —**child•ish** *adj* —**child•ish•ly** *adv* —**child•ish•ness** *n* —**child•less** *adj* —**child•less•ness** *n* —**child•like** *adj* —**child•proof** \-ˌprüf\ *adj*
chili, chile, chil•li \'chilē\ *n, pl* **chil•ies** *or* **chil•es** *or* **chil•lies** 1 : hot pepper 2 : spicy stew of ground beef, chilies, and beans
chill \'chil\ *vb* : make or become cold or chilly ~ *adj* : moderately cold ~ *n* 1 : feeling of coldness with shivering 2 : moderate coldness
chilly \-ē\ *adj* **chill•i•er; -est** : noticeably cold —**chill•i•ness** *n*
chime \'chīm\ *n* : set of tuned bells or their sound ~ *vb* : make bell-like sounds —**chime in** *vb* : break into or join in a conversation
chi•me•ra, chi•mae•ra \kī'mirə, kə-\ *n* 1 : imaginary monster 2 : illusion —**chi•me•ri•cal** \-'merikəl\ *adj*
chim•ney \'chimnē\ *n, pl* **-neys** 1 : passage for smoke 2 : glass tube around a lamp flame
chimp \'chimp, 'shimp\ *n* : chimpanzee
chim•pan•zee \ˌchimˌpan'zē, ˌshim-; chim'panzē, shim-\ *n* : small ape
chin \'chin\ *n* : part of the face below the mouth —**chin•less** *adj*
chi•na \'chīnə\ *n* 1 : porcelain ware 2 : domestic pottery
chin•chil•la \chin'chilə\ *n* : small So. American rodent with soft pearl-gray fur or this fur
chink \'chiŋk\ *n* : small crack ~ *vb* : fill chinks of
chintz \'chints\ *n* : printed cotton cloth
chip \'chip\ *n* 1 : small thin flat piece cut or broken off 2 : thin crisp morsel of food 3 : counter used in games 4 : flaw where a chip came off 5 : small slice of semiconductor containing electronic circuits ~ *vb* **-pp-** : cut or break chips from —**chip in** *vb* : contribute
chip•munk \-ˌməŋk\ *n* : small striped ground-dwelling rodent
chip•per \-ər\ *adj* : lively and cheerful
chi•rop•o•dy \kə'räpədē, shə-\ *n* : podiatry —**chi•rop•o•dist** \-ədist\ *n*
chi•ro•prac•tic \'kīrəˌpraktik\ *n* : system of healing based esp. on manipulation of body structures —**chi•ro•prac•tor** \-tər\ *n*
chirp \'chərp\ *n* : short sharp sound like that of a bird or cricket —**chirp** *vb*
chis•el \'chizəl\ *n* : sharp-edged metal tool ~ *vb* **-eled** *or* **-elled; -el•ing** *or* **-el•ling** 1 : work with a chisel 2 : cheat —**chis•el•er** \-ələr\ *n*
chit \'chit\ *n* : signed voucher for a small debt
chit•chat \-ˌchat\ *n* : casual conversation —**chitchat** *vb*
chiv•al•rous \'shivəlrəs\ *adj* 1 : relating to chivalry 2 : honest, courteous, or generous —**chiv•al•rous•ly** *adv* —**chiv•al•rous•ness** *n*
chiv•al•ry \-rē\ *n, pl* **-ries** 1 : system or practices of knighthood 2 : spirit or character of the ideal knight —**chi•val•ric** \shə'valrik\ *adj*
chive \'chīv\ *n* : herb related to the onion
chlo•ride \'klōrˌīd\ *n* : compound of chlorine
chlo•ri•nate \-əˌnāt\ *vb* **-nat•ed; -nat•ing** : treat or combine with chlorine —**chlo•ri•na•tion** \ˌklōrə'nāshən\ *n*
chlo•rine \'klōrˌēn\ *n* : chemical element that is a heavy strong-smelling greenish yellow irritating gas
chlo•ro•form \'klōrəˌfórm\ *n* : etherlike colorless heavy fluid ~ *vb* : anesthetize or kill with chloroform
chlo•ro•phyll \'klōrəˌfil\ *n* : green coloring matter of plants
chock \'chäk\ *n* : wedge for blocking the movement of a wheel —**chock** *vb*
chock–full \'chək'fu̇l, 'chäk-\ *adj* : full to the limit
choc•o•late \'chäkələt, 'chók-\ *n* 1 : ground roasted cacao beans or a beverage made from them 2 : candy made of or with chocolate 3 : dark brown
choice \'chóis\ *n* 1 : act or power of choosing 2 : one selected 3 : variety offered for selection ~ *adj* **choic•er; choic•est** 1 : worthy of being chosen 2 : selected with care 3 : of high quality
choir \'kwīr\ *n* : group of singers esp. in church —**choir•boy** *n* —**choir•mas•ter** *n*
choke \'chōk\ *vb* **choked; chok•ing** 1 : hinder breathing 2 : clog or obstruct ~ *n* 1 : a choking or sound of choking 2 : valve for controlling air intake in a gasoline engine
chok•er \-ər\ *n* : tight necklace
cho•ler \'kälər, 'kō-\ *n* : bad temper —**cho•ler•ic** \'kälərik, kə'ler-\ *adj*
chol•era \'kälərə\ *n* : disease marked by severe vomiting and dysentery
cho•les•ter•ol \kə'lestəˌról, -ˌrōl\ *n* : waxy substance in animal tissues
choose \'chüz\ *vb* **chose** \'chōz\; **cho•sen** \'chōzᵊn\; **choos•ing** 1 : select after consideration 2 : decide 3 : prefer —**choos•er** *n*
choosy, choos•ey \'chüzē\ *adj* **choos•i•er; -est** : fussy in making choices
chop \'chäp\ *vb* **-pp-** 1 : cut by repeated blows 2 : cut into small pieces ~ *n* 1 : sharp downward blow 2 : small cut of meat often with part of a rib
chop•per \-ər\ *n* 1 : one that chops 2 : helicopter
chop•py \-ē\ *adj* **-pi•er; -est** 1 : rough with small waves 2 : jerky or disconnected —**chop•pi•ly** *adv* —**chop•piness** *n*
chops \'chäps\ *n pl* : fleshy covering of the jaws
chop•sticks *n pl* : pair of sticks used in eating in oriental countries
cho•ral \'kōrəl\ *adj* : relating to or sung by a choir or chorus or in chorus —**cho•ral•ly** *adv*
cho•rale \kə'ral, -'räl\ *n* 1 : hymn tune or harmonization of a traditional melody 2 : chorus or choir
1chord \'kórd\ *n* : harmonious tones sounded together
2chord *n* 1 : cordlike anatomical structure 2 : straight line joining 2 points on a curve
chore \'chōr\ *n* 1 *pl* : daily household or farm work 2 : routine or disagreeable task
cho•re•og•ra•phy \ˌkōrē'ägrəfē\ *n, pl* **-phies** : art of composing and arranging dances —**cho•reo•graph** \'kōrēəˌgraf\ *vb* —**cho•re•og•ra•pher** \ˌkōrē'ägrəfər\ *n* —**cho•reo•graph•ic** \-ēə'grafik\ *adj*
cho•ris•ter \'kōrəstər\ *n* : choir singer
chor•tle \'chórtᵊl\ *vb* **-tled; -tling** : laugh or chuckle —**chortle** *n*
cho•rus \'kōrəs\ *n* 1 : group of singers or dancers 2 : part of a song repeated at intervals 3 : composition for a chorus ~ *vb* : sing or utter together
chose *past of* CHOOSE
cho•sen \'chōzᵊn\ *adj* : favored
1chow \'chau̇\ *n* : food
2chow *n* : thick-coated muscular dog
chow•der \'chau̇dər\ *n* : thick soup usu. of seafood and milk
chow mein \'chau̇'mān\ *n* : thick stew of shredded vegetables and meat
chris•ten \'krisᵊn\ *vb* 1 : baptize 2 : name —**chris•ten•ing** *n*
Chris•ten•dom \-dəm\ *n* : areas where Christianity prevails
Chris•tian \'krischən\ *n* : adherent of Christianity ~ *adj* : relating to or professing a belief in Christianity or Jesus Christ —**Chris•tian•ize** \'krischəˌnīz\ *vb*
Chris•ti•an•i•ty \ˌkrischē'anətē\ *n* : religion derived from the teachings of Jesus Christ
Christian name *n* : first name
Christ•mas \'krisməs\ *n* : December 25 celebrated as the birthday of Christ
chro•mat•ic \krō'matik\ *adj* 1 : relating to color 2 : proceeding by half steps of the musical scale
chrome \'krōm\ *n* : chromium or something plated with it
chro•mi•um \-ēəm\ *n* : a bluish white metallic element used esp. in alloys
chro•mo•some \'krōməˌsōm, -ˌzōm\ *n* : part of a cell nucleus that contains the genes —**chro•mo•som•al** \ˌkrōmə'sōməl, -'zō-\ *adj*
chron•ic \'kränik\ *adj* : frequent or persistent —**chron•i•cal•ly** \-iklē\ *adv*
chron•i•cle \'kränikəl\ *n* : history ~ *vb* **-cled; -cling** : record —**chron•i•cler** \-iklər\ *n*
chro•nol•o•gy \krə'näləjē\ *n, pl* **-gies** : list of events in order of their occurrence —**chron•o•log•i•cal** \ˌkränᵊl'äjikəl\ *adj* —**chron•o•log•i•cal•ly** \-iklē\ *adv*
chro•nom•e•ter \krə'nämətər\ *n* : very accurate timepiece
chrys•a•lis \'krisələs\ *n, pl* **chry•sal•i•des** \kris'aləˌdēz\ *or* **chrys•a•lis•es** : insect pupa enclosed in a shell
chry•san•the•mum \kris'anthəməm\ *n* : plant with showy flowers
chub•by \'chəbē\ *adj* **-bi•er; -est** : fat —**chub•bi•ness** *n*
1chuck \'chək\ *vb* 1 : tap 2 : toss ~ *n* 1 : light pat under the chin 2 : toss
2chuck *n* 1 : cut of beef 2 : machine part that holds work or another part
chuck•le \'chəkəl\ *vb* **-led; -ling** : laugh quietly —**chuckle** *n*
chug \'chəg\ *n* : sound of a laboring engine ~ *vb* **-gg-** : work or move with chugs
chum \'chəm\ *n* : close friend ~ *vb* **-mm-** : be chums —**chum•my** \-ē\ *adj*
chump \'chəmp\ *n* : fool
chunk \'chəŋk\ *n* 1 : short thick piece 2 : sizable amount
chunky \-ē\ *adj* **chunk•i•er; -est** 1 : stocky 2 : containing chunks
church \'chərch\ *n* 1 : building esp. for Christian public worship 2 : whole body of Christians 3 : denomination 4 : congregation —**church•go•er** *n* —**church•go•ing** *adj or n*
church•yard *n* : cemetery beside a church
churl \'chərl\ *n* : rude ill-bred person —**churl•ish** *adj*
churn \'chərn\ *n* : container in which butter is made ~ *vb* 1 : agitate in a churn 2 : shake violently
chute \'shüt\ *n* : trough or passage
chut•ney \'chətnē\ *n, pl* **-neys** : sweet and sour relish
chutz•pah \'hu̇tspə, 'ku̇t-, -ˌspä\ *n* : nerve or insolence
ci•ca•da \sə'kādə\ *n* : stout-bodied insect with transparent wings
ci•der \'sīdər\ *n* : apple juice
ci•gar \sig'är\ *n* : roll of leaf tobacco for smoking
cig•a•rette \ˌsigə'ret, 'sigəˌret\ *n* : cut tobacco rolled in paper for smoking
cinch \'sinch\ *n* 1 : strap holding a saddle or pack in place 2 : sure thing —**cinch** *vb*
cin•cho•na \siŋ'kōnə\ *n* : So. American tree that yields quinine
cinc•ture \'siŋkchər\ *n* : belt or sash
cin•der \'sindər\ *n* 1 *pl* : ashes 2 : piece of partly burned wood or coal
cin•e•ma \'sinəmə\ *n* : movies or a movie theater —**cin•e•mat•ic** \ˌsinə'matik\ *adj*
cin•na•mon \'sinəmən\ *n* : spice from an aromatic tree bark
ci•pher \'sīfər\ *n* 1 : zero 2 : code
cir•ca \'sərkə\ *prep* : about
cir•cle \'sərkəl\ *n* 1 : closed symmetrical curve 2 : cycle 3 : group with a common tie ~ *vb* **-cled; -cling** 1 : enclose in a circle 2 : move or revolve around
cir•cuit \'sərkət\ *n* 1 : boundary 2 : regular tour of a territory 3 : complete path of an electric current 4 : group of electronic components
cir•cu•itous \ˌsər'kyüətəs\ *adj* : circular or winding
cir•cuit•ry \'sərkətrē\ *n, pl* **-ries** : arrangement of an electric circuit
cir•cu•lar \'sərkyələr\ *adj* 1 : round 2 : moving in a circle ~ *n* : advertising leaflet —**cir•cu•lar•i•ty** \ˌsərkyə'larətē\ *n*
cir•cu•late \'sərkyəˌlāt\ *vb* **-lat•ed; -lating** : move or cause to move in a circle or from place to place or person to person —**cir•cu•la•tion** \ˌsərkyə'lāshən\ *n* —**cir•cu•la•to•ry** \'sərkyələˌtōrē\ *adj*
cir•cum•cise \'sərkəmˌsīz\ *vb* **-cised; -cis•ing** : cut off the foreskin of —**cir•cum•ci•sion** \ˌsərkəm'sizhən\ *n*
cir•cum•fer•ence \sər'kəmfrəns\ *n* : perimeter of a circle
cir•cum•flex \'sərkəmˌfleks\ *n* : phonetic mark (as ^)
cir•cum•lo•cu•tion \ˌsərkəmlō'kyüshən\ *n* : excessive use of words
cir•cum•nav•i•gate \ˌsərkəm'navəˌgāt\ *vb* : sail completely around —**cir•cum•nav•i•ga•tion** *n*
cir•cum•scribe \'sərkəmˌskrīb\ *vb* 1 : draw a line around 2 : limit
cir•cum•spect \'sərkəmˌspekt\ *adj* : careful —**cir•cum•spec•tion** \ˌsərkəm'spekshən\ *n*
cir•cum•stance \'sərkəmˌstans\ *n* 1 : fact or event 2 *pl* : surrounding conditions 3 *pl* : financial situation —**cir•cum•stan•tial** \ˌsərkəm'stanchəl\ *adj*

cir•cum•vent \ˌsərkəm'vent\ *vb* : get around esp. by trickery —**cir•cum•ven•tion** \-'venchən\ *n*
cir•cus \'sərkəs\ *n* : show with feats of skill, animal acts, and clowns
cir•rho•sis \sə'rōsəs\ *n, pl* **-rho•ses** \-ˌsēz\ : fibrosis of the liver —**cir•rhot•ic** \-'rätik\ *adj or n*
cir•rus \'sirəs\ *n, pl* **-ri** \-ˌī\ : wispy white cloud
cis•tern \'sistərn\ *n* : underground water tank
cit•a•del \'sitədᵊl, -əˌdel\ *n* : fortress
cite \'sīt\ *vb* **cit•ed; cit•ing** **1** : summon before a court **2** : quote **3** : refer to esp. in commendation —**ci•ta•tion** \sī'tāshən\ *n*
cit•i•zen \'sitəzən\ *n* : member of a country —**cit•i•zen•ry** \-rē\ *n* —**cit•i•zen•ship** *n*
cit•ron \'sitrən\ *n* : lemonlike fruit
cit•rus \'sitrəs\ *n, pl* **-rus** *or* **-rus•es** : evergreen tree or shrub grown for its fruit (as the orange or lemon)
city \'sitē\ *n, pl* **cit•ies** : place larger or more important than a town
civ•ic \'sivik\ *adj* : relating to citizenship or civil affairs
civ•ics \-iks\ *n* : study of citizenship
civ•il \'sivəl\ *adj* **1** : relating to citizens **2** : polite **3** : relating to or being a lawsuit —**civ•il•ly** *adv*
ci•vil•ian \sə'vilyən\ *n* : person not in a military, police, or fire-fighting force
ci•vil•i•ty \sə'vilətē\ *n, pl* **-ties** : courtesy
civ•i•li•za•tion \ˌsivələ'zāshən\ *n* **1** : high level of cultural development **2** : culture of a time or place
civ•i•lize \'sivəˌlīz\ *vb* **-lized; -liz•ing** : raise from a primitive stage of cultural development —**civ•i•lized** *adj*
civil liberty *n* : freedom from arbitrary governmental interference —usu. pl.
civil rights *n pl* : nonpolitical rights of a citizen
civil service *n* : government service
civil war *n* : war among citizens of one country
clack \'klak\ *vb* : make or cause a clatter — **clack** *n*
clad \'klad\ *adj* : covered
claim \'klām\ *vb* **1** : demand or take as the rightful owner **2** : maintain ~ *n* **1** : demand of right or ownership **2** : declaration **3** : something claimed — **claim•ant** \-ənt\ *n*
clair•voy•ant \klar'vòiənt\ *adj* : able to perceive things beyond the senses —**clair•voy•ance** \-əns\ *n* —**clairvoyant** *n*
clam \'klam\ *n* : bivalve mollusk
clam•ber \'klambər\ *vb* : climb awkwardly
clam•my \'klamē\ *adj* **-mi•er; -est** : being damp, soft, and usu. cool —**clam•mi•ness** *n*
clam•or \-ər\ *n* **1** : uproar **2** : protest — **clamor** *vb* —**clam•or•ous** *adj*
clamp \'klamp\ *n* : device for holding things together —**clamp** *vb*
clan \'klan\ *n* : group of related families — **clan•nish** *adj* —**clan•nish•ness** *n*
clan•des•tine \klan'destən\ *adj* : secret
clang \'klaŋ\ *n* : loud metallic ringing — **clang** *vb*
clan•gor \-ər, -gər\ *n* : jumble of clangs
clank \'klaŋk\ *n* : brief sound of struck metal —**clank** *vb*
clap \'klap\ *vb* **-pp- 1** : strike noisily **2** : applaud ~ *n* **1** : loud crash **2** : noise made by clapping the hands
clap•board \'klabərd, 'klap-, -ˌbōrd\ *n* : narrow tapered board used for siding
clap•per \'klapər\ *n* : tongue of a bell
claque \'klak\ *n* **1** : group hired to applaud at a performance **2** : group of sycophants
clar•et \'klarət\ *n* : dry red wine
clar•i•fy \'klarəˌfī\ *vb* **-fied; -fy•ing** : make or become clear —**clar•i•fi•ca•tion** \ˌklarəfə'kāshən\ *n*
clar•i•net \ˌklarə'net\ *n* : woodwind instrument shaped like a tube —**clar•i•net•ist, clar•i•net•tist** \-ist\ *n*
clar•i•on \'klarēən\ *adj* : loud and clear
clar•i•ty \'klarətē\ *n* : clearness
clash \'klash\ *vb* **1** : make or cause a clash **2** : be in opposition or disharmony ~ *n* **1** : crashing sound **2** : hostile encounter
clasp \'klasp\ *n* **1** : device for holding things together **2** : embrace or grasp ~ *vb* **1** : fasten **2** : embrace or grasp
class \'klas\ *n* **1** : group of the same status or nature **2** : social rank **3** : course of instruction **4** : group of students ~ *vb* : classify —**class•less** *adj* —**class•mate** *n* —**class•room** *n*
clas•sic \'klasik\ *adj* **1** : serving as a standard of excellence **2** : classical ~ *n* : work of enduring excellence and esp. of ancient Greece or Rome —**clas•si•cal** \-ikəl\ *adj* —**clas•si•cal•ly** \-klē\ *adv* —**clas•si•cism** \'klasəˌsizəm\ *n* —**clas•si•cist** \-sist\ *n*
clas•si•fied \'klasəˌfīd\ *adj* : restricted for security reasons
clas•si•fy \-ˌfī\ *vb* **-fied; -fy•ing** : arrange in or assign to classes —**clas•si•fi•ca•tion** \ˌklasəfə'kāshən\ *n* —**clas•si•fi•er** \'klasəˌfīər\ *n*
clat•ter \'klatər\ *n* : rattling sound —**clatter** *vb*
clause \'klòz\ *n* **1** : separate part of a document **2** : part of a sentence with a subject and predicate
claus•tro•pho•bia \ˌklòstrə'fōbēə\ *n* : fear of closed or narrow spaces —**claus•tro•pho•bic** \-bik\ *adj*
clav•i•chord \'klavəˌkòrd\ *n* : early keyboard instrument
clav•i•cle \'klavikəl\ *n* : collarbone
claw \'klò\ *n* : sharp curved nail or process (as on the toe of an animal) ~ *vb* : scratch or dig —**clawed** *adj*
clay \'klā\ *n* : plastic earthy material —**clay•ey** \-ē\ *adj*
clean \'klēn\ *adj* **1** : free from dirt or disease **2** : pure or honorable **3** : thorough ~ *vb* : make or become clean —**clean** *adv* — **clean•er** *n* —**clean•ly** \-lē\ *adv* —**clean•ness** *n*
clean•ly \'klenlē\ *adj* **-li•er; -est** : clean — **clean•li•ness** *n*
cleanse \'klenz\ *vb* **cleansed; cleans•ing** : make clean —**cleans•er** *n*
clear \'klir\ *adj* **1** : bright **2** : free from clouds **3** : transparent **4** : easily heard, seen or understood **5** : free from doubt **6** : free from restriction or obstruction ~ *vb* **1** : make or become clear **2** : go away **3** : free from accusation or blame **4** : explain or settle **5** : net **6** : jump or pass without touching ~ *n* : clear space or part —**clear** *adv* —**clear•ance** \'klirəns\ *n*
clear•ing \'kliriŋ\ *n* : land cleared of wood
clear•ly *adv* **1** : in a clear manner **2** : it is obvious that
cleat \'klēt\ *n* : projection that strengthens or prevents slipping
cleav•age \'klēvij\ *n* **1** : a splitting apart **2** : depression between a woman's breasts
[1]**cleave** \'klēv\ *vb* **cleaved** \'klēvd\ *or* **clove** \'klōv\; **cleav•ing** : adhere
[2]**cleave** *vb* **cleaved** \'klēvd\; **cleav•ing** : split apart
cleav•er \'klēvər\ *n* : heavy chopping knife
clef \'klef\ *n* : sign on the staff in music to show pitch
cleft \'kleft\ *n* : crack
clem•ent \'klemənt\ *adj* **1** : merciful **2** : temperate or mild —**clem•en•cy** \-ənsē\ *n*
clench \'klench\ *vb* **1** : hold fast **2** : close tightly
cler•gy \'klərjē\ *n* : body of religious officials —**cler•gy•man** \-jimən\ *n*
cler•ic \'klerik\ *n* : member of the clergy
cler•i•cal \-ikəl\ *adj* **1** : relating to the clergy **2** : relating to a clerk or office worker
clerk \'klərk, *Brit* 'klärk\ *n* **1** : official responsible for record-keeping **2** : person doing general office work **3** : salesperson in a store —**clerk** *vb* —**clerk•ship** *n*
clev•er \'klevər\ *adj* **1** : resourceful **2** : marked by wit or ingenuity —**clev•er•ly** *adv* —**clev•er•ness** *n*
clew *var of* CLUE
cli•ché \kli'shā\ *n* : trite phrase —**cli•chéd** \-'shād\ *adj*
click \'klik\ *n* : slight sharp noise ~ *vb* : make or cause to make a click
cli•ent \'klīənt\ *n* **1** : person who engages professional services **2** : customer
cli•en•tele \ˌklīən'tel, ˌklē-\ *n* : body of customers
cliff \'klif\ *n* : high steep face of rock
cli•mate \'klīmət\ *n* : average weather conditions over a period of years —**cli•mat•ic** \klī'matik\ *adj*
cli•max \'klīˌmaks\ *n* : the highest point ~ *vb* : come to a climax —**cli•mac•tic** \klī'maktik\ *adj*
climb \'klīm\ *vb* **1** : go up or down by use of hands and feet **2** : rise ~ *n* : a climbing —**climb•er** *n*
clinch \'klinch\ *vb* **1** : fasten securely **2** : settle **3** : hold fast or firmly —**clinch** *n* —**clinch•er** *n*
cling \'kliŋ\ *vb* **clung** \'kləŋ\; **cling•ing** **1** : adhere firmly **2** : hold on tightly
clin•ic \'klinik\ *n* : facility for diagnosis and treatment of outpatients —**clin•i•cal** \-əl\ *adj* —**clin•i•cal•ly** \-klē\ *adv*
clink \'kliŋk\ *vb* : make a slight metallic sound —**clink** *n*
clin•ker \'kliŋkər\ *n* : fused stony matter esp. in a furnace
[1]**clip** \'klip\ *vb* **-pp-** : fasten with a clip ~ *n* : device to hold things together
[2]**clip** *vb* **-pp- 1** : cut or cut off **2** : hit ~ *n* **1** : clippers **2** : sharp blow **3** : rapid pace
clip•per \'klipər\ *n* **1** *pl* : implement for clipping **2** : fast sailing ship
clique \'klēk, 'klik\ *n* : small exclusive group of people
cli•to•ris \'klitərəs, kli'tòrəs\ *n, pl* **cli•to•ri•des** \-'tòrəˌdēz\ : small organ at the front of the vulva
cloak \'klōk\ *n* **1** : loose outer garment **2** : something that conceals ~ *vb* : cover or hide with a cloak
clob•ber \'kläbər\ *vb* : hit hard
clock \'kläk\ *n* : timepiece not carried on the person ~ *vb* : record the time of
clock•wise \-ˌwīz\ *adv or adj* : in the same direction as a clock's hands move
clod \'kläd\ *n* **1** : lump esp. of earth **2** : dull insensitive person
clog \'kläg\ *n* **1** : restraining weight **2** : thick-soled shoe ~ *vb* **-gg- 1** : impede with a clog **2** : obstruct passage through **3** : become plugged up
clois•ter \'klòistər\ *n* **1** : monastic establishment **2** : covered passage ~ *vb* : shut away from the world
clone \'klōn\ *n* **1** : offspring produced from a single organism **2** : copy
[1]**close** \'klōz\ *vb* **closed; clos•ing** **1** : shut **2** : cease operation **3** : terminate **4** : bring or come together ~ *n* : conclusion or end
[2]**close** \'klōs\ *adj* **clos•er; clos•est** **1** : confining **2** : secretive **3** : strict **4** : stuffy **5** : having little space between items **6** : fitting tightly **7** : near **8** : intimate **9** : accurate **10** : nearly even —**close** *adv* —**close•ly** *adv* —**close•ness** *n*
clos•et \'kläzət, 'klòz-\ *n* : small compartment for household utensils or clothing ~ *vb* : take into a private room for a talk
clo•sure \'klōzhər\ *n* **1** : act of closing **2** : something that closes
clot \'klät\ *n* : dried mass of a liquid —**clot** *vb*
cloth \'klòth\ *n, pl* **cloths** \'klòthz, 'klòths\ **1** : fabric **2** : tablecloth
clothe \'klōth\ *vb* **clothed** *or* **clad** \'klad\; **cloth•ing** : dress
clothes \'klōthz, 'klōz\ *n pl* **1** : clothing **2** : bedclothes
cloth•ier \'klōthyər, -thēər\ *n* : maker or seller of clothing
cloth•ing \'klōthiŋ\ *n* : covering for the human body
cloud \'klaud\ *n* **1** : visible mass of particles in the air **2** : something that darkens, hides, or threatens ~ *vb* : darken or hide —**cloud•i•ness** *n* —**cloud•less** *adj* — **cloudy** *adj*
cloud•burst *n* : sudden heavy rain
clout \'klaut\ *n* **1** : blow **2** : influence ~ *vb* : hit forcefully
[1]**clove** \'klōv\ *n* : section of a bulb
[2]**clove** *past of* CLEAVE
[3]**clove** *n* : dried flower bud of an East Indian tree used as a spice
clo•ver \'klōvər\ *n* : leguminous herb with usu. 3-part leaves
clo•ver•leaf *n, pl* **-leafs** *or* **-leaves** : highway interchange
clown \'klaun\ *n* : funny costumed entertainer esp. in a circus ~ *vb* : act like a clown —**clown•ish** *adj* —**clown•ish•ly** *adv* —**clown•ish•ness** *n*
cloy \'klòi\ *vb* : disgust with excess **cloy•ing•ly** \-iŋlē\ *adv*
club \'kləb\ *n* **1** : heavy wooden stick **2** : playing card of a suit marked with a black figure like a clover leaf **3** : group associated for a common purpose ~ *vb* **-bb-** : hit with a club
club•foot *n* : misshapen foot twisted out of position from birth —**club•foot•ed** \-ˌfutəd\ *adj*
cluck \'klək\ *n* : sound made by a hen — **cluck** *vb*
clue \'klü\ *n* : piece of evidence that helps solve a problem ~ *vb* **clued; clue•ing** *or* **clu•ing** : provide with a clue
clump \'kləmp\ *n* **1** : cluster **2** : heavy tramping sound ~ *vb* : tread heavily
clum•sy \'kləmzē\ *adj* **-si•er; -est 1** : lacking dexterity, nimbleness, or grace **2** : tactless —**clum•si•ly** *adv* —**clum•si•ness** *n*
clung *past of* CLING
clunk•er \'kləŋkər\ *n* : old automobile
clus•ter \'kləstər\ *n* : group ~ *vb* : grow or gather in a cluster
clutch \'kləch\ *vb* : grasp ~ *n* **1** : grasping hand or claws **2** : control or power **3** : coupling for connecting two working parts in machinery
clut•ter \'klətər\ *vb* : fill with things that get in the way —**clutter** *n*
co- *prefix* : with, together, joint, or jointly

coact	coexistence
coactor	coexistent
coauthor	cofeature
coauthorship	cofinance
cocaptain	cofound
cochairman	cofounder
cochampion	coheir
cocomposer	coheiress
coconspirator	cohost
cocreator	cohostess
codefendant	coinvent
codesign	coinventor
codevelop	coinvestigator
codeveloper	coleader
codirect	comanagement
codirector	comanager
codiscoverer	co-organizer
codrive	co-own
codriver	co-owner
coedit	copartner
coeditor	copartnership
coexecutor	copresident
coexist	coprincipal
coprisoner	coresident
coproduce	cosignatory
coproducer	cosigner
coproduction	cosponsor
copromoter	costar
coproprietor	cowinner
copublish	coworker
copublisher	cowrite
corecipient	

coach \'kōch\ *n* **1** : closed 2-door 4-wheeled carriage **2** : railroad passenger car **3** : bus **4** : 2d-class air travel **5** : one who instructs or trains performers ~ *vb* : instruct or direct as a coach
co•ag•u•late \kō'agyəˌlāt\ *vb* **-lat•ed; -lat•ing** : clot —**co•ag•u•lant** \-lənt\ *n* —**co•ag•u•la•tion** \-ˌagyə'lāshən\ *n*
coal \'kōl\ *n* **1** : ember **2** : black solid mineral used as fuel —**coal•field** *n*
co•alesce \ˌkōə'les\ *vb* **-alesced; -alesc•ing** : grow together —**co•ales•cence** \-'lesᵊns\ *n*
co•ali•tion \-'lishən\ *n* : temporary alliance
coarse \'kōrs\ *adj* **coars•er; coars•est 1** : composed of large particles **2** : rough or crude —**coarse•ly** *adv* —**coars•en** \-ᵊn\ *vb* —**coarse•ness** *n*
coast \'kōst\ *n* : seashore ~ *vb* : move without effort —**coast•al** \-ᵊl\ *adj*
coast•er \-ər\ *n* **1** : one that coasts **2** : plate or mat to protect a surface
coast guard *n* : military force that guards or patrols a coast —**coast•guards•man** \'kōstˌgärdzmən\ *n*
coast•line *n* : shape of a coast
coat \'kōt\ *n* **1** : outer garment for the upper body **2** : external growth of fur or feathers **3** : covering layer ~ *vb* : cover with a coat —**coat•ed** *adj* —**coat•ing** *n*
coax \'kōks\ *vb* : move to action or achieve by gentle urging or flattery
cob \'käb\ *n* : corncob
co•balt \'kōˌbòlt\ *n* : shiny silver-white magnetic metallic chemical element
cob•ble \'käbəl\ *vb* **cob•bled; cob•bling** : make or put together hastily
cob•bler \'käblər\ *n* **1** : shoemaker **2** : deep-dish fruit pie
cob•ble•stone *n* : small round paving stone
co•bra \'kōbrə\ *n* : venomous snake
cob•web \'käbˌweb\ *n* : network spun by a spider or a similar filament
co•caine \kō'kān, 'kōˌkān\ *n* : drug obtained from the leaves of a So. American shrub (**co•ca** \'kōkə\)
co•chlea \'kōklēə, 'käk-\ *n, pl* **-chle•as** *or* **-chle•ae** \-lēˌē, -ˌī\ : the usu. spiral part of the inner ear —**coch•le•ar** \-lēər\ *adj*
cock \'käk\ *n* **1** : male fowl **2** : valve or faucet ~ *vb* **1** : draw back the hammer of a firearm **2** : tilt to one side —**cock•fight** *n*
cock•ade \kä'kād\ *n* : badge on a hat
cock•a•too \'käkəˌtü\ *n, pl* **-toos** : large Australian crested parrot
cock•eyed \'käk'īd\ *adj* **1** : tilted to one side **2** : slightly crazy
cock•le \'käkəl\ *n* : edible shellfish
cock•pit \'käkˌpit\ *n* : place for a pilot, driver, or helmsman
cock•roach *n* : nocturnal insect often infesting houses
cock•tail \'käkˌtāl\ *n* **1** : iced drink of liquor and flavorings **2** : appetizer
cocky \'käkē\ *adj* **cock•i•er; -est** : overconfident —**cock•i•ly** \-əlē\ *adv* —**cock•i•ness** *n*
co•coa \'kōkō\ *n* **1** : cacao **2** : powdered chocolate or a drink made from this
co•co•nut \'kōkəˌnət\ *n* : large nutlike fruit of a tropical palm (**coconut palm**)
co•coon \kə'kün\ *n* : case protecting an insect pupa
cod \'käd\ *n, pl* **cod** : food fish of the No. Atlantic
cod•dle \'kädᵊl\ *vb* **-dled; -dling** : pamper
code \'kōd\ *n* **1** : system of laws or rules **2** : system of signals
co•deine \'kōˌdēn\ *n* : narcotic drug used in cough remedies
cod•ger \'käjər\ *n* : odd fellow
cod•i•cil \'kädəsəl, -ˌsil\ *n* : postscript to a will
cod•i•fy \'kädəˌfī, 'kōd-\ *vb* **-fied; -fy•ing** : arrange systematically —**cod•i•fi•ca•tion** \ˌkädəfə'kāshən, ˌkōd-\ *n*
co•ed \'kōˌed\ *n* : female student in a coeducational institution —**coed** *adj*
co•ed•u•ca•tion \ˌkō-\ *n* : education of the sexes together —**co•ed•u•ca•tion•al** *adj*
co•ef•fi•cient \ˌkōə'fishənt\ *n* **1** : number that is a multiplier of another **2** : number that serves as a measure of some property
co•erce \kō'ərs\ *vb* **-erced; -erc•ing** : force —**co•er•cion** \-'ərzhən, -shən\ *n* —**co•er•cive** \-'ərsiv\ *adj*
cof•fee \'kòfē\ *n* : drink made from the roasted and ground seeds (**coffee beans**) of a tropical shrub —**cof•fee•house** *n* — **cof•fee•pot** *n*
cof•fer \'kòfər\ *n* : box for valuables
cof•fin \-fən\ *n* : box for burial

cog \\käg\ *n* : tooth on the rim of a gear — **cogged** \\kägd\ *adj* —**cog•wheel** *n*

co•gent \\kōjənt\ *adj* : compelling or convincing —**co•gen•cy** \-jənsē\ *n*

cog•i•tate \\käjə‚tāt\ *vb* **-tat•ed; -tat•ing** : think over —**cog•i•ta•tion** \-käjə'tāshən\ *n* —**cog•i•ta•tive** \\käjə‚tātiv\ *adj*

co•gnac \\kōn‚yak\ *n* : French brandy

cog•nate \\käg‚nāt\ *adj* : related —**cognate** *n*

cog•ni•tion \käg'nishən\ *n* : act or process of knowing —**cog•ni•tive** \\kägnətiv\ *adj*

cog•ni•zance \\kägnəzəns\ *n* : notice or awareness —**cog•ni•zant** \\kägnəzənt\ *adj*

co•hab•it \kō'habət\ *vb* : live together as husband and wife —**co•hab•i•ta•tion** \-‚habə'tāshən\ *n*

co•here \kō'hir\ *vb* **-hered; -her•ing** : stick together

co•her•ent \-'hirənt\ *adj* **1** : able to stick together **2** : logically consistent —**co•her•ence** \-əns\ *n* —**co•her•ent•ly** *adv*

co•he•sion \-'hēzhən\ *n* : a sticking together —**co•he•sive** \-siv\ *adj* —**co•he•sive•ly** *adv* —**co•he•sive•ness** *n*

co•hort \\kō‚hört\ *n* **1** : group of soldiers **2** : companion

coif•fure \kwä'fyùr\ *n* : hair style

coil \\kóil\ *vb* : wind in a spiral ~ *n* : series of loops (as of rope)

coin \\kóin\ *n* : piece of metal used as money ~ *vb* **1** : make (a coin) by stamping **2** : create —**coin•age** \-ij\ *n* —**coin•er** *n*

co•in•cide \\kōən'sīd, 'kōən‚sīd\ *vb* **-cid•ed; -cid•ing 1** : be in the same place **2** : happen at the same time **3** : be alike —**co•in•ci•dence** \kō'insədəns\ *n* —**co•in•ci•dent** \-ənt\ *adj* —**co•in•ci•den•tal** \-‚insə'dentəl\ *adj*

co•itus \\kōətəs\ *n* : sexual intercourse —**co•ital** \-ətəl\ *adj*

coke \\kōk\ *n* : fuel made by heating soft coal

co•la \\kōlə\ *n* : carbonated soft drink

col•an•der \\kələndər, 'käl-\ *n* : perforated utensil for draining food

cold \\kōld\ *adj* **1** : having a low or below normal temperature **2** : lacking warmth of feeling **3** : suffering from lack of warmth ~ *n* **1** : low temperature **2** : minor respiratory illness —**cold•ly** *adv* —**cold•ness** *n* **in cold blood** : with premeditation

cold–blood•ed *adj* **1** : cruel or merciless **2** : having a body temperature that varies with the temperature of the environment

cole•slaw \\kōl‚sló\ *n* : cabbage salad

col•ic \\kälik\ *n* : sharp abdominal pain —**col•icky** *adj*

col•i•se•um \\kälə'sēəm\ *n* : arena

col•lab•o•rate \kə'labə‚rāt\ *vb* **-rat•ed; -rat•ing 1** : work jointly with others **2** : help the enemy —**col•lab•o•ra•tion** \-‚labə'rāshən\ *n* —**col•lab•o•ra•tor** \-'labə‚rātər\ *n*

col•lapse \kə'laps\ *vb* **-lapsed; -laps•ing 1** : fall in **2** : break down physically or mentally **3** : fold down ~ *n* : breakdown —**col•laps•ible** *adj*

col•lar \\kälər\ *n* : part of a garment around the neck ~ *vb* **1** : seize by the collar **2** : grab —**col•lar•less** *adj*

col•lar•bone *n* : bone joining the breastbone and the shoulder blade

col•lards \\kälərdz\ *n pl* : kale

col•late \kə'lāt; 'käl‚āt, 'kōl-\ *vb* **-lat•ed; -lat•ing 1** : compare carefully **2** : assemble in order

col•lat•er•al \kə'latərəl\ *adj* **1** : secondary **2** : descended from the same ancestors but not in the same line **3** : similar ~ *n* : property used as security for a loan

col•league \\käl‚ēg\ *n* : associate

col•lect \kə'lekt\ *vb* **1** : bring, come, or gather together **2** : receive payment of ~ *adv or adj* **1** : to be paid for by the receiver —**col•lect•ible, col•lect•able** *adj* —**col•lec•tion** \-'lekshən\ *n* —**col•lec•tor** \-'lektər\ *n*

col•lec•tive \-tiv\ *adj* : denoting or shared by a group ~ *n* : a cooperative unit —**col•lec•tive•ly** *adv*

col•lege \\kälij\ *n* : institution of higher learning granting a bachelor's degree —**col•le•gian** \kə'lējən\ *n* —**col•le•giate** \kə'lējət\ *adj*

col•lide \kə'līd\ *vb* **-lid•ed; -lid•ing** : strike together —**col•li•sion** \-'lizhən\ *n*

col•lie \\kälē\ *n* : large long-haired dog

col•loid \\käl‚óid\ *n* : tiny particles in suspension in a fluid —**col•loi•dal** \kə'lóidəl\ *adj*

col•lo•qui•al \kə'lōkwēəl\ *adj* : used in informal conversation —**col•lo•qui•al•ism** \-ə‚lizəm\ *n*

col•lo•quy \\käləkwē\ *n, pl* **-quies** : formal conversation or conference

col•lu•sion \kə'lüzhən\ *n* : secret cooperation for deceit —**col•lu•sive** \-'lüsiv\ *adj*

co•logne \kə'lōn\ *n* : perfumed liquid

1co•lon \\kōlən\ *n, pl* **colons** *or* **co•la** \-lə\ : lower part of the large intestine —**co•lon•ic** \kō'länik\ *adj*

2colon *n, pl* **colons** : punctuation mark : used esp. to direct attention to following matter

col•o•nel \\kərnəl\ *n* : commissioned officer (as in the army) ranking next below a brigadier general

col•o•nize \\kälə‚nīz\ *vb* **-nized; -niz•ing 1** : establish a colony in **2** : settle —**col•o•ni•za•tion** \‚kälənə'zāshən\ *n* —**col•o•niz•er** *n*

col•on•nade \\kälə'nād\ *n* : row of supporting columns

col•o•ny \\kälənē\ *n, pl* **-nies 1** : people who inhabit a new territory or the territory itself **2** : animals of one kind (as bees) living together —**co•lo•nial** \kə'lōnēəl\ *adj or n* —**co•lo•nist** \\kälənist\ *n*

col•or \\kälər\ *n* **1** : quality of visible things distinct from shape that results from light reflection **2** *pl* : flag **3** : liveliness ~ *vb* **1** : give color to **2** : blush —**col•or•fast** *adj* —**col•or•ful** *adj* —**col•or•less** *adj*

col•or–blind *adj* : unable to distinguish colors —**color blindness** *n*

col•ored \\kälərd\ *adj* **1** : having color **2** : of a race other than the white ~ *n, pl* **colored** *or* **coloreds** : colored person

co•los•sal \kə'läsəl\ *adj* : very large or great

co•los•sus \-əs\ *n, pl* **-si** \-‚sī, -‚läs,ī\ : something of great size or scope

colt \\kōlt\ *n* : young male horse —**colt•ish** *adj*

col•umn \\käləm\ *n* **1** : vertical section of a printed page **2** : regular feature article (as in a newspaper) **3** : pillar **4** : row (as of soldiers) —**col•um•nar** \kə'ləmnər\ *adj* —**col•um•nist** \\käləmnist\ *n*

co•ma \\kōmə\ *n* : deep prolonged unconsciousness —**co•ma•tose** \-‚tōs, 'kämə-\ *adj*

comb \\kōm\ *n* **1** : toothed instrument for arranging the hair **2** : crest on a fowl's head —**comb** *vb* —**combed** \\kōmd\ *adj*

com•bat \kəm'bat, 'käm,bat\ *vb* **-bat•ed** *or* **-bat•ted; -bat•ing** *or* **-bat•ting** : fight —**com•bat** \\käm‚bat\ *n* —**com•bat•ant** \kəm'batᵊnt\ *n* —**com•bat•ive** \kəm'bativ\ *adj*

com•bi•na•tion \\kämbə'nāshən\ *n* **1** : process or result of combining **2** : code for opening a lock

com•bine \kəm'bīn\ *vb* **-bined; -bin•ing** : join together ~ \'käm‚bīn\ *n* **1** : association for business or political advantage **2** : harvesting machine

com•bus•ti•ble \kəm'bəstəbəl\ *adj* : apt to catch fire —**com•bus•ti•bil•i•ty** \-‚bəstə'bilətē\ *n* —**combustible** *n*

com•bus•tion \-'bəschən\ *n* : process of burning

come \\kəm\ *vb* **came** \\kām\; **come; com•ing 1** : move toward or arrive at something **2** : reach a state **3** : originate or exist **4** : amount —**come clean** *vb* : confess —**come into** *vb* : acquire, achieve —**come off** *vb* : succeed —**come to** *vb* : regain consciousness —**come to pass** : happen —**come to terms** : reach an agreement

come•back *n* **1** : retort **2** : return to a former position —**come back** *vb*

co•me•di•an \kə'mēdēən\ *n* **1** : comic actor **2** : funny person **3** : entertainer specializing in comedy

co•me•di•enne \-‚mēdē'en\ *n* : a woman who is a comedian

com•e•dy \\kämədē\ *n, pl* **-dies 1** : an amusing play **2** : humorous entertainment

come•ly \\kəmlē\ *adj* **-li•er; -est** : attractive —**come•li•ness** *n*

com•et \\kämət\ *n* : small bright celestial body having a tail

com•fort \\kəmfərt\ *n* **1** : consolation **2** : well-being or something that gives it ~ *vb* **1** : give hope to **2** : console —**com•fort•able** \\kəmftəbəl, 'kəmfərt-\ *adj* —**com•fort•ably** \-blē\ *adv* —**com•fort•less** *adj*

com•fort•er \\kəmfərtər\ *n* **1** : one that comforts **2** : quilt

com•ic \\kämik\ *adj* **1** : relating to comedy **2** : funny ~ *n* **1** : comedian **2** : sequence of cartoons —**com•i•cal** *adj*

com•ing \\kəmiŋ\ *adj* : next

com•ma \\kämə\ *n* : punctuation mark , used esp. to separate sentence parts

com•mand \kə'mand\ *vb* **1** : order **2** : control ~ *n* **1** : act of commanding **2** : an order given **3** : mastery **4** : troops under a commander —**com•man•dant** \\kämən‚dant, -‚dänt\ *n*

com•man•deer \\kämən'dir\ *vb* : seize by force

com•mand•er \kə'mandər\ *n* **1** : officer commanding an army or subdivision of an army **2** : commissioned officer in the navy ranking next below a captain

com•mand•ment \-'mandmənt\ *n* : order

command sergeant major *n* : noncommissioned officer in the army ranking above a first sergeant

com•mem•o•rate \kə'memə‚rāt\ *vb* **-rat•ed; -rat•ing** : celebrate or honor —**com•mem•o•ra•tion** \-‚memə'rāshən\ *n* —**com•mem•o•ra•tive** \-'memrətiv, -'memə‚rāt-\ *adj*

com•mence \kə'mens\ *vb* **-menced; -menc•ing** : start

com•mence•ment \-mənt\ *n* **1** : beginning **2** : graduation ceremony

com•mend \kə'mend\ *vb* **1** : entrust **2** : recommend **3** : praise —**commendable** \-əbəl\ *adj* —**com•men•da•tion** \‚kämən'dāshən, -‚en-\ *n*

com•men•su•rate \kə'mensərət, -'mench-\ *adj* : equal in measure or extent

com•ment \\käm‚ent\ *n* : statement of opinion or remark —**comment** *vb*

com•men•tary \-ən‚terē\ *n, pl* **-tar•ies** : series of comments

com•men•ta•tor \-ən‚tātər\ *n* : one who discusses news

com•merce \\kämərs\ *n* : business

com•mer•cial \kə'mərshəl\ *adj* : designed for profit or for mass appeal ~ *n* : broadcast advertisement —**com•mer•cial•ize** \-‚īz\ *vb* —**com•mer•cial•ly** \-ē\ *adv*

com•min•gle \kə'miŋgəl\ *vb* : mix

com•mis•er•ate \kə'mizə‚rāt\ *vb* **-at•ed; at•ing** : sympathize —**com•mis•er•a•tion** \-‚mizə'rāshən\ *n*

com•mis•sary \\kämə‚serē\ *n, pl* **-sar•ies** : store esp. for military personnel

com•mis•sion \kə'mishən\ *n* **1** : order granting power or rank **2** : panel to judge, approve, or act **3** : the doing of an act **4** : agent's fee ~ *vb* **1** : confer rank or authority to or for **2** : request something be done

com•mis•sion•er \-shənər\ *n* **1** : member of a commission **2** : head of a government department

com•mit \kə'mit\ *vb* **-tt- 1** : turn over to someone for safekeeping or confinement **2** : perform or do **3** : pledge —**com•mit•ment** *n*

com•mit•tee \kə'mitē\ *n* : panel that examines or acts on something

com•mo•di•ous \kə'mōdēəs\ *adj* : spacious

com•mod•i•ty \kə'mädətē\ *n, pl* **-ties** : article for sale

com•mo•dore \\kämə‚dōr\ *n* **1** : former commissioned officer in the navy ranking next below a rear admiral **2** : officer commanding a group of merchant ships

com•mon \\kämən\ *adj* **1** : public **2** : shared by several **3** : widely known, found, or observed **4** : ordinary ~ *n* : community land —**com•mon•ly** *adv* **in common** : shared together

com•mon•place \\kämən‚plās\ *n* : cliché ~ *adj* : ordinary

common sense *n* : good judgment

com•mon•weal \-‚wēl\ *n* : general welfare

com•mon•wealth \-‚welth\ *n* : state

com•mo•tion \kə'mōshən\ *n* : disturbance

1com•mune \kə'myün\ *vb* **-muned; -mun•ing** : communicate intimately

2com•mune \\käm‚yün, kə'myün\ *n* : community that shares all ownership and duties —**com•mu•nal** \-əl\ *adj*

com•mu•ni•cate \kə'myünə‚kāt\ *vb* **-cat•ed; -cat•ing 1** : make known **2** : transmit **3** : exchange information or opinions —**com•mu•ni•ca•ble** \-'myünikəbəl\ *adj* —**com•mu•ni•ca•tion** \-‚myünə'kāshən\ *n* —**com•mu•ni•ca•tive** \-'myüni‚kātiv, -kət-\ *adj*

Com•mu•nion \kə'myünyən\ *n* **1** : Christian sacrament of partaking of bread and wine

com•mu•ni•qué \kə'myünə‚kā, -‚myünə'kā\ *n* : official bulletin

com•mu•nism \\kämyə‚nizəm\ *n* **1** : social organization in which goods are held in common **2** *cap* : political doctrine based on revolutionary Marxist socialism —**com•mu•nist** \-nist\ *n or adj, often cap* —**com•mu•nis•tic** \‚kämyə'nistik\ *adj, often cap*

com•mu•ni•ty \kə'myünətē\ *n, pl* **-ties** : body of people living in the same place under the same laws

com•mute \kə'myüt\ *vb* **-mut•ed; -mut•ing 1** : reduce (a punishment) **2** : travel back and forth regularly ~ *n* : trip made in commuting —**com•mu•ta•tion** \‚kämyə'tāshən\ *n* —**com•mut•er** *n*

1com•pact \kəm'pakt, 'käm‚pakt\ *adj* **1** : hard **2** : small or brief ~ *vb* : pack together ~ \'käm‚pakt\ *n* **1** : cosmetics case **2** : small car —**com•pact•ly** *adv* —**com•pact•ness** *n*

2com•pact \\käm‚pakt\ *n* : agreement

compact disc *n* : plastic-coated disc with laser-readable recorded music

com•pan•ion \kəm'panyən\ *n* **1** : close friend **2** : one of a pair —**com•pan•ion•able** *adj* —**com•pan•ion•ship** *n*

com•pa•ny \\kəmpənē\ *n, pl* **-nies 1** : business organization **2** : group of performers **3** : guests **4** : infantry unit

com•par•a•tive \kəm'parətiv\ *adj* **1** : relating to or being an adjective or adverb form that denotes increase **2** : relative —**comparative** *n* —**com•par•a•tive•ly** *adv*

com•pare \kəm'par\ *vb* **-pared; -par•ing 1** : represent as similar **2** : check for likenesses or differences ~ *n* : comparison —**com•pa•ra•ble** \\kämprəbəl\ *adj*

com•par•i•son \kəm'parəsən\ *n* **1** : act of comparing **2** : change in the form and meaning of an adjective or adverb to show different levels of quality, quantity, or relation

com•part•ment \kəm'pärtmənt\ *n* : section or room

com•pass \\kəmpəs, 'käm-\ *n* **1** : scope **2** : device for drawing circles **3** : device for determining direction

com•pas•sion \kəm'pashən\ *n* : pity —**com•pas•sion•ate** \-ənət\ *adj*

com•pat•i•ble \-'patəbəl\ *adj* : harmonious —**com•pat•i•bil•i•ty** \-‚patə'bilətē\ *n*

com•pa•tri•ot \kəm'pātrēət, -trē‚ät\ *n* : fellow countryman

com•pel \kəm'pel\ *vb* **-ll-** : cause through necessity

com•pen•di•ous \kəm'pendēəs\ *adj* **1** : concise and comprehensive **2** : comprehensive

com•pen•di•um \-'pendēəm\ *n, pl* **-di•ums** *or* **-dia** \-dēə\ : summary

com•pen•sate \\kämpən‚sāt\ *vb* **-sat•ed; -sat•ing 1** : offset or balance **2** : repay —**com•pen•sa•tion** \‚kämpən'sāshən\ *n* —**com•pen•sa•to•ry** \kəm'pensə‚tōrē\ *adj*

com•pete \kəm'pēt\ *vb* **-pet•ed; -pet•ing** : strive to win —**com•pe•ti•tion** \‚kämpə'tishən\ *n* —**com•pet•i•tive** \kəm'petətiv\ *adj* —**com•pet•i•tive•ness** *n* —**com•pet•i•tor** \kəm'petətər\ *n*

com•pe•tent \\kämpətənt\ *adj* : capable —**com•pe•tence** \-əns\ *n* —**com•pe•ten•cy** \-ənsē\ *n*

com•pile \kəm'pīl\ *vb* **-piled; -pil•ing** : collect or compose from several sources —**com•pi•la•tion** \‚kämpə'lāshən\ *n* —**com•pil•er** \kəm'pīlər\ *n*

com•pla•cen•cy \kəm'plāsᵊnsē\ *n* : self-satisfaction —**com•pla•cent** \-ᵊnt\ *adj*

com•plain \kəm'plān\ *vb* **1** : express grief, pain, or discontent **2** : make an accusation —**com•plain•ant** *n* —**com•plain•er** *n*

com•plaint \-'plānt\ *n* **1** : expression of grief or discontent **2** : ailment **3** : formal accusation

com•ple•ment \\kämpləmənt\ *n* **1** : something that completes **2** : full number or amount ~ \-‚ment\ *vb* : complete —**com•ple•men•ta•ry** \‚kämplə'mentərē\ *adj*

com•plete \kəm'plēt\ *adj* **-plet•er; -est 1** : having all parts **2** : finished **3** : total ~ *vb* **-plet•ed; -plet•ing 1** : make whole **2** : finish —**com•plete•ly** *adv* —**com•plete•ness** *n* —**com•ple•tion** \-'plēshən\ *n*

com•plex \käm'pleks, kəm-; 'käm‚pleks\ *adj* **1** : having many parts **2** : intricate ~ \'käm‚pleks\ *n* **1** : psychological problem —**com•plex•i•ty** \käm'pleksətē, kəm-\ *n*

com•plex•ion \kəm'plekshən\ *n* : hue or appearance of the skin esp. of the face —**com•plex•ioned** *adj*

com•pli•cate \\kämplə‚kāt\ *vb* **-cat•ed; -cat•ing** : make complex or hard to understand —**com•pli•cat•ed** \-əd\ *adj* —**com•pli•ca•tion** \‚kämplə'kāshən\ *n*

com•plic•i•ty \kəm'plisətē\ *n, pl* **-ties** : participation in guilt

com•pli•ment \\kämpləmənt\ *n* **1** : flattering remark **2** *pl* : greeting ~ \-‚ment\ *vb* : pay a compliment to

com•pli•men•ta•ry \‚kämplə'mentərē\ *adj* **1** : praising **2** : free

com•ply \kəm'plī\ *vb* **-plied; -ply•ing** : conform or yield —**com•pli•ance** \-əns\ *n* —**com•pli•ant** \-ənt\ *n*

com•po•nent \kəm'pōnənt, 'käm‚pō-\ *n* : part of something larger ~ *adj* : serving as a component

com•port \kəm'pōrt\ *vb* **1** : agree **2** : behave —**com•port•ment** \-mənt\ *n*

com•pose \kəm'pōz\ *vb* **-posed; -pos•ing 1** : create (as by writing) or put together **2** : calm **3** : set type —**com•pos•er** *n* —**com•po•si•tion** \‚kämpə'zishən\ *n*

com•pos•ite \käm'päzət, kəm-\ *adj* : made up of diverse parts —**composite** *n*

com•post \\käm‚pōst\ *n* : decayed organic fertilizing material

com•po•sure \kəm'pōzhər\ *n* : calmness

com•pote \\käm‚pōt\ *n* : fruits cooked in syrup

1com•pound \\käm‚paund, kəm'paund\ *vb* **1** : combine or add **2** : pay (interest) on principal and accrued interest ~ \'käm‚paund\ *adj* : made up of 2 or more parts ~ \'käm‚paund\ *n* : something that is compound

2com•pound \\käm‚paund\ *n* : enclosure

com•pre•hend \‚kämpri'hend\ *vb* **1** : understand **2** : include —**com•pre•hen•si•ble** \-'hensəbəl\ *adj* —**com•pre•hen•sion** \-'henchən\ *n* —**com•pre•hen•sive** \-siv\ *adj*

com•press \kəm'pres\ *vb* : squeeze together ~ \'käm‚pres\ *n* : pad for pressing on a wound —**com•pres•sion** \-'preshən\ *n* —**com•pres•sor** \-'presər\ *n*

compressed air *n* : air under pressure greater than that of the atmosphere

com•prise \kəm'prīz\ vb -prised; -prising 1 : contain or cover 2 : be made up of

com•pro•mise \'kämprə,mīz\ vb -mised; -mis•ing : settle differences by mutual concessions —compromise n

comp•trol•ler \kən'trōlər, 'kämp,trō-\ n : financial officer

com•pul•sion \kəm'pəlshən\ n 1 : coercion 2 : irresistible impulse —com•pul•sive \-siv\ adj —com•pul•so•ry \-'pəlsərē\ adj

com•punc•tion \-'pəŋkshən\ n : remorse

com•pute \-'pyüt\ vb -put•ed; -put•ing : calculate —com•pu•ta•tion \,kämpyü'tāshən\ n

com•put•er \kəm'pyütər\ n : electronic data processing machine —com•put•er•i•za•tion \-,pyütərə'zāshən\ n —com•put•er•ize \-'pyütə,rīz\ vb

com•rade \'käm,rad, -rəd\ n : companion —com•rade•ship n

1con \'kän\ adv : against ~ n : opposing side or person

2con vb -nn- : swindle

con•cave \kän'kāv, 'kän,kāv\ adj : curved like the inside of a sphere —con•cav•i•ty \kän'kavətē\ n

con•ceal \kən'sēl\ vb : hide —con•ceal•ment n

con•cede \-'sēd\ vb -ced•ed; -ced•ing : grant

con•ceit \-'sēt\ n : excessively high opinion of oneself —con•ceit•ed \-əd\ adj

con•ceive \-'sēv\ vb -ceived; -ceiv•ing 1 : become pregnant 2 : think of —con•ceiv•able \-'sēvəbəl\ adj —con•ceiv•ably \-blē\ adv

con•cen•trate \'känsən,trāt\ vb -trat•ed; -trat•ing 1 : gather together 2 : make stronger 3 : fix one's attention ~ n : something concentrated —con•cen•tra•tion \,känsən'trāshən\ n

con•cen•tric \kən'sentrik\ adj : having a common center

con•cept \'kän,sept\ n : thought or idea

con•cep•tion \kən'sepshən\ n 1 : act of conceiving 2 : idea

con•cern \kən'sərn\ vb 1 : relate to 2 : involve ~ n 1 : affair 2 : worry 3 : business —con•cerned \-'sərnd\ adj —con•cern•ing \-'sərniŋ\ prep

con•cert \'kän,sərt\ n 1 : agreement or joint action 2 : public performance of music —con•cert•ed \kən'sərtəd\ adj

con•cer•ti•na \,känsər'tēnə\ n : accordion-like instrument

con•cer•to \kən'chertō\ n, pl -ti \-tē\ or -tos : orchestral work with solo instruments

con•ces•sion \-'seshən\ n 1 : act of conceding 2 : something conceded 3 : right to do business on a property

conch \'käŋk, 'känch\ n, pl conchs \'käŋks\ or conch•es \'känchəz\ : large spiral-shelled marine mollusk

con•cil•ia•to•ry \kən'silēə,tōrē\ adj : mollifying

con•cise \kən'sīs\ adj : said in few words —con•cise•ly adv —con•cise•ness n —con•ci•sion \kən'sizhən\ n

con•clave \'kän,klāv\ n : private meeting

con•clude \kən'klüd\ vb -clud•ed; -clud•ing 1 : end 2 : decide —con•clu•sion \-'klüzhən\ n —con•clu•sive \-siv\ adj —con•clu•sive•ly adv

con•coct \kən'käkt, kän-\ vb : prepare or devise —con•coc•tion \-'käkshən\ n

con•com•i•tant \-'kämətənt\ adj : accompanying —concomitant n

con•cord \'kän,kȯrd, 'käŋ-\ n : agreement

con•cor•dance \kən'kȯrdᵊns\ n 1 : agreement 2 : index of words —con•cor•dant \-ᵊnt\ adj

con•course \'kän,kōrs\ n : open space where crowds gather

con•crete \kän'krēt, 'kän,krēt\ adj 1 : naming something real 2 : actual or substantial 3 : made of concrete ~ \'kän,krēt, kän'krēt\ n : hard building material made of cement, sand, gravel, and water

con•cre•tion \kän'krēshən\ n : hard mass

con•cu•bine \'käŋkyù,bīn\ n : mistress

con•cur \kən'kər\ vb -rr- : agree —con•cur•rence \-'kərəns\ n

con•cur•rent \-ənt\ adj : happening at the same time

con•cus•sion \kən'kəshən\ n 1 : shock 2 : brain injury from a blow

con•demn \-'dem\ vb 1 : declare to be wrong, guilty, or unfit for use 2 : sentence —con•dem•na•tion \,kän,dem'nāshən\ n

con•dense \kən'dens\ vb -densed; -dens•ing 1 : make or become more compact 2 : change from vapor to liquid —con•den•sa•tion \,kän,den'sāshən, -dən-\ n —con•dens•er n

con•de•scend \,kändi'send\ vb 1 : lower oneself 2 : act haughtily —con•de•scen•sion \-'senchən\ n

con•di•ment \'kändəmənt\ n : pungent seasoning

con•di•tion \kən'dishən\ n 1 : necessary situation or stipulation 2 pl : state of affairs 3 : state of being ~ vb : put into proper condition —con•di•tion•al \kən'dishənəl\ adj —con•di•tion•al•ly \-ē\ adv

con•do•lence \kən'dōləns\ n : expression of sympathy—usu. pl.

con•do•min•i•um \,kändə'minēəm\ n, pl -ums : individually owned apartment

con•done \kən'dōn\ vb -doned; -don•ing : overlook or forgive

con•dor \'kändər, -,dȯr\ n : large western American vulture

con•du•cive \kən'düsiv, -'dyü-\ adj : tending to help or promote

con•duct \'kän,dəkt\ n 1 : management 2 : behavior ~ \kən'dəkt\ vb 1 : guide 2 : manage or direct 3 : be a channel for 4 : behave —con•duc•tion \-'dəkshən\ n —con•duc•tive \-'dəktiv\ adj —con•duc•tiv•i•ty \,kän,dək'tivətē\ n —con•duc•tor \-'dəktər\ n

con•duit \'kän,düət, -,dyü-\ n : channel (as for conveying fluid)

cone \'kōn\ n 1 : scaly fruit of pine and related trees 2 : solid figure having a circular base and tapering sides

con•fec•tion \kən'fekshən\ n : sweet dish or candy —con•fec•tion•er \-shənər\ n

con•fed•er•a•cy \kən'fedərəsē\ n, pl -cies 1 : league 2 cap : 11 southern states that seceded from the U.S. in 1860 and 1861

con•fed•er•ate \-rət\ adj 1 : united in a league 2 cap : relating to the Confederacy ~ n 1 : ally 2 cap : adherent of the Confederacy ~ \-'fedə,rāt\ vb -at•ed; -at•ing : unite —con•fed•er•a•tion \-,fedə'rāshən\ n

con•fer \kən'fər\ vb -rr- 1 : give 2 : meet to exchange views —con•fer•ee \,känfə'rē\ n —con•fer•ence \'känfərəns\ n

con•fess \kən'fes\ vb 1 : acknowledge or disclose one's misdeed, fault, or sin 2 : declare faith in —con•fes•sion \-'feshən\ n —con•fes•sion•al \-'feshənəl\ n or adj

con•fes•sor \kən'fesər, 2 also 'kän,fes-\ n 1 : one who confesses 2 : priest who hears confessions

con•fet•ti \kən'fetē\ n : bits of paper or ribbon thrown in celebration

con•fi•dant \'känfə,dant, -,dänt\ n : one to whom secrets are confided

con•fide \kən'fīd\ vb -fid•ed; -fid•ing 1 : share private thoughts 2 : reveal in confidence

con•fi•dence \'känfədəns\ n 1 : trust 2 : self-assurance 3 : something confided —con•fi•dent \-ənt\ adj —con•fi•den•tial \,känfə'denchəl\ adj —con•fi•den•tial•ly \-ē\ adv —con•fi•dent•ly adv

con•fig•u•ra•tion \kən,figyə'rāshən\ n : arrangement

con•fine \kən'fīn\ vb -fined; -fin•ing 1 : restrain or restrict to a limited area 2 : imprison —con•fine•ment n —con•fin•er n

con•fines \'kän,fīnz\ n pl : bounds

con•firm \kən'fərm\ vb 1 : ratify 2 : verify 3 : admit as a full member of a church or synagogue —con•fir•ma•tion \,känfər'māshən\ n

con•fis•cate \'känfə,skāt\ vb -cat•ed; -cat•ing : take by authority —con•fis•ca•tion \,känfə'skāshən\ n —con•fis•ca•to•ry \kən'fiskə,tōrē\ adj

con•fla•gra•tion \,känflə'grāshən\ n : great fire

con•flict \'kän,flikt\ n 1 : war 2 : clash of ideas ~ \kən'flikt\ vb : clash

con•form \kən'fȯrm\ vb 1 : make or be like 2 : obey —con•for•mi•ty \kən'fȯrmətē\ n

con•found \kən'faund, kän-\ vb : confuse

con•front \kən'frənt\ vb : oppose or face —con•fron•ta•tion \,känfrən'tāshən\ n

con•fuse \kən'fyüz\ vb -fused; -fus•ing 1 : make mentally uncertain 2 : jumble —con•fu•sion \-'fyüzhən\ n

con•fute \-'fyüt\ vb -fut•ed; -fut•ing : overwhelm by argument

con•geal \kən'jēl\ vb 1 : freeze 2 : become thick and solid

con•ge•nial \kən'jēnēəl\ adj : kindred or agreeable —con•ge•ni•al•i•ty n

con•gen•i•tal \kən'jenətᵊl\ adj : existing from birth

con•gest \kən'jest\ vb : overcrowd or overfill —con•ges•tion \-'jeschən\ n —con•ges•tive \-'jestiv\ adj

con•glom•er•ate \kən'glämərət\ adj : made up of diverse parts ~ \-ə,rāt\ vb -at•ed; -at•ing : form into a mass ~ \-ərət\ n : diversified corporation —con•glom•er•a•tion \-,glämə'rāshən\ n

con•grat•u•late \kən'grachə,lāt, -'graj-\ vb -lat•ed; -lat•ing : express pleasure to for good fortune —con•grat•u•la•tion \-,grachə'lāshən, -,graj-\ n —con•grat•u•la•to•ry \-'grachələ,tōrē- 'graj-\ adj

con•gre•gate \'käŋgri,gāt\ vb -gat•ed; -gat•ing : assemble

con•gre•ga•tion \,käŋgri'gāshən\ n 1 : assembly of people at worship 2 : religious group —con•gre•ga•tion•al \-shənəl\ adj

con•gress \'käŋgrəs\ n : assembly of delegates or of senators and representatives —con•gres•sio•nal \kən'greshənəl, kän-\ adj —con•gress•man \'käŋgrəsmən\ n —con•gress•wom•an n

con•gru•ence \kən'grüəns, 'käŋgrəwəns\ n : likeness —con•gru•ent \-ənt\ adj

con•gru•ity \kən'grüətē, kän-\ n : correspondence between things —con•gru•ous \'käŋgrəwəs\ adj

con•ic \'känik\ adj : relating to or like a cone —con•i•cal \-ikəl\ adj

co•ni•fer \'känəfər, 'kōn-\ n : cone-bearing tree —co•nif•er•ous \kō'nifərəs\ adj

con•jec•ture \kən'jekchər\ n or vb : guess —con•jec•tur•al \-əl\ adj

con•join \kən'jȯin\ vb : join together —con•joint \-'jȯint\ adj

con•ju•gal \'känjigəl, kən'jü-\ adj : relating to marriage

con•ju•gate \'känjə,gāt\ vb -gat•ed; -gat•ing : give the inflected forms of (a verb) —con•ju•ga•tion \,känjə'gāshən\ n

con•junc•tion \kən'jəŋkshən\ n 1 : combination 2 : occurrence at the same time 3 : a word that joins other words together —con•junc•tive \-tiv\ adj

con•jure \'känjər, 'kən-\ vb -jured; -jur•ing 1 : summon by sorcery 2 : practice sleight of hand 3 : entreat —con•jur•er, con•ju•ror \'känjərər, 'kən-\ n

con•nect \kə'nekt\ vb : join or associate —con•nect•able adj —con•nec•tion \-'nekshən\ n —con•nec•tive \-tiv\ n or adj —con•nec•tor n

con•nive \kə'nīv\ vb -nived; -niv•ing 1 : pretend ignorance of wrongdoing 2 : cooperate secretly —con•niv•ance n

con•nois•seur \,känə'sər, -'sůr\ n : expert judge esp. of art

con•note \kə'nōt\ vb -not•ed; -not•ing : suggest additional meaning —con•no•ta•tion \,känə'tāshən\ n

con•nu•bi•al \kə'nübēəl, -'nyü-\ adj : relating to marriage

con•quer \'käŋkər\ vb : defeat or overcome —con•quer•or \-kərər\ n

con•quest \'kän,kwest, 'käŋ-\ n 1 : act of conquering 2 : something conquered

con•science \'känchəns\ n : awareness of right and wrong

con•sci•en•tious \,känchē'enchəs\ adj : honest and hard-working —con•sci•en•tious•ly adv

con•scious \'känchəs\ adj 1 : aware 2 : mentally awake or alert 3 : intentional —con•scious•ly adv —con•scious•ness n

con•script \kən'skript\ vb : draft for military service —con•script \'kän,skript\ n —con•scrip•tion \kən'skripshən\ n

con•se•crate \'känsə,krāt\ vb -crat•ed; -crat•ing 1 : declare sacred 2 : devote to a solemn purpose —con•se•cra•tion \,känsə'krāshən\ n

con•sec•u•tive \kən'sekyətiv\ adj : following in order —con•sec•u•tive•ly adv

con•sen•sus \-'sensəs\ n 1 : agreement in opinion 2 : collective opinion

con•sent \-'sent\ vb : give permission or approval —consent n

con•se•quence \'känsə,kwens\ n 1 : result or effect 2 : importance —con•se•quent \-kwənt, -,kwent\ adj —con•se•quent•ly adv

con•se•quen•tial \,känsə'kwenchəl\ adj : important

con•ser•va•tion \,känsər'vāshən\ n : planned management of natural resources —con•ser•va•tion•ist \-shənist\ n

con•ser•va•tive \kən'sərvətiv\ adj 1 : disposed to maintain the status quo 2 : cautious —con•ser•va•tism \-və,tizəm\ n —conservative n —con•ser•va•tive•ly adv

con•ser•va•to•ry \kən'sərvə,tōrē\ n, pl -ries : school for art or music

con•serve \-'sərv\ vb -served; -serv•ing : keep from wasting ~ \'kän,sərv\ n : candied fruit or fruit preserves

con•sid•er \kən'sidər\ vb 1 : think about 2 : give thoughtful attention to 3 : think that —con•sid•er•ate \-'sidərət\ adj —con•sid•er•ation \-,sidə'rāshən\ n

con•sid•er•able \-'sidərəbəl\ adj 1 : significant 2 : noticeably large —con•sid•er•a•bly \-blē\ adv

con•sid•er•ing prep : taking notice of

con•sign \kən'sīn\ vb 1 : transfer 2 : send to an agent for sale —con•sign•ee \,känsə'nē, -,sī-; kən,sī-\ n —con•sign•ment \kən'sīnmənt\ n —con•sign•or \,känsə'nȯr, -,sī-; kən,sī-\ n

con•sist \kən'sist\ vb 1 : be inherent —used with in 2 : be made up —used with of

con•sis•ten•cy \-'sistənsē\ n, pl -cies 1 : degree of thickness or firmness 2 : quality of being consistent

con•sis•tent \-tənt\ adj : being steady and regular —con•sis•tent•ly adv

1con•sole \kən'sōl\ vb -soled; -sol•ing : soothe the grief of —con•so•la•tion \,känsə'lāshən\ n

2con•sole \'kän,sōl\ n : cabinet or part with controls

con•sol•i•date \kən'sälə,dāt\ vb -dat•ed; -dat•ing : unite or compact —con•sol•i•da•tion \-,sälə'dāshən\ n

con•som•mé \,känsə'mā\ n : clear soup

con•so•nance \'känsənəns\ n : agreement or harmony —con•so•nant \-nənt\ adj —con•so•nant•ly adv

con•so•nant \-nənt\ n 1 : speech sound marked by constriction or closure in the breath channel 2 : letter other than a, e, i, o, and u —con•so•nan•tal \,känsə'nantᵊl\ adj

con•sort \'kän,sȯrt\ n : spouse ~ \kən'sȯrt\ vb : keep company

con•spic•u•ous \kən'spikyəwəs\ adj : very noticeable —con•spic•u•ous•ly adv

con•spire \kən'spīr\ vb -spired; -spir•ing : secretly plan an unlawful act —con•spir•a•cy \-'spirəsē\ n —con•spir•a•tor \-'spirətər\ n —con•spir•a•to•ri•al \-,spirə'tōrēəl\ adj

con•sta•ble \'känstəbəl, 'kən-\ n : police officer

con•stab•u•lary \kən'stabyə,lerē\ n, pl -lar•ies : police force

con•stant \'känstənt\ adj 1 : steadfast or faithful 2 : not varying 3 : continually recurring ~ n : something unchanging —con•stan•cy \-stənsē\ n —con•stant•ly adv

con•stel•la•tion \,känstə'lāshən\ n : group of stars

con•ster•na•tion \-stər'nāshən\ n : amazed dismay

con•sti•pa•tion \-stə'pāshən\ n : difficulty of defecation —con•sti•pate \'känstə,pāt\ vb

con•stit•u•ent \kən'stichəwənt\ adj 1 : component 2 : having power to elect ~ n 1 : component part 2 : one who may vote for a representative —con•stit•u•en•cy \-wənsē\ n

con•sti•tute \'känstə,tüt, -,tyüt\ vb -tut•ed; -tut•ing 1 : establish 2 : be all or a basic part of

con•sti•tu•tion \,känstə'tüshən, -'tyü-\ n 1 : physical composition or structure 2 : the basic law of an organized body or the document containing it —con•sti•tu•tion•al \-əl\ adj —con•sti•tu•tion•al•i•ty \-,tüshə'nalətē, -,tyü-\ n

con•strain \kən'strān\ vb 1 : compel 2 : confine 3 : restrain —con•straint \-'strānt\ n

con•strict \-'strikt\ vb : draw or squeeze together —con•stric•tion \-'strikshən\ n —con•stric•tive \-'striktiv\ adj

con•struct \kən'strəkt\ vb : build or make —con•struc•tion \-'strəkshən\ n —con•struc•tive \-tiv\ adj

con•strue \kən'strü\ vb -strued; -stru•ing : explain or interpret

con•sul \'känsəl\ n 1 : Roman magistrate 2 : government commercial official in a foreign country —con•sul•ar \-sələr\ adj —con•sul•ate \-lət\ n

con•sult \kən'səlt\ vb 1 : ask the advice or opinion of 2 : confer —con•sul•tant \-ənt\ n —con•sul•ta•tion \,känsəl'tāshən\ n

con•sume \kən'süm\ vb -sumed; -suming : eat or use up —con•sum•able adj —con•sum•er n

con•sum•mate \kən'səmət\ adj : complete or perfect ~ \'känsə,māt\ vb -mat•ed; -mat•ing : make complete —con•sum•ma•tion \,känsə'māshən\ n

con•sump•tion \kən'səmpshən\ n 1 : act of consuming 2 : use of goods 3 : tuberculosis —con•sump•tive \-tiv\ adj or n

con•tact \'kän,takt\ n 1 : a touching 2 : association or relationship 3 : connection or communication ~ vb 1 : come or bring into contact 2 : communicate with

con•ta•gion \kən'tājən\ n 1 : spread of disease by contact 2 : disease spread by contact —con•ta•gious \-jəs\ adj

con•tain \-'tān\ vb 1 : enclose or include 2 : have or hold within 3 : restrain —con•tain•er n —con•tain•ment n

con•tam•i•nate \kən'tamə,nāt\ vb -nated; -nat•ing : soil or infect by contact or association —con•tam•i•na•tion \-,tamə'nāshən\ n

con•tem•plate \'käntəm,plāt\ vb -pla•ted; -plat•ing : view or consider thoughtfully —con•tem•pla•tion \,käntəm'plāshən\ n —con•tem•plative \kən'templətiv, 'käntəm,plāt-\ adj

con•tem•po•ra•ne•ous \kən,tempə'rānēəs\ adj : contemporary

con•tem•po•rary \-'tempə,rerē\ adj 1 : occurring or existing at the same time 2 : of the same age —contemporary n

con•tempt \kən'tempt\ n 1 : feeling of scorn 2 : state of being despised 3 : disobedience to a court or legislature —con•tempt•ible \-'temptəbəl\ adj

con•temp•tu•ous \-'tempchəwəs\ adj : feeling or expressing contempt —con•temp•tu•ous•ly adv

con•tend \-'tend\ vb 1 : strive against rivals or difficulties 2 : argue 3 : maintain or claim —con•tend•er n

1con•tent \kən'tent\ adj : satisfied ~ vb : satisfy ~ n : ease of mind —content-

ed *adj* —**con•tent•ed•ly** *adv* —**con•tent•ed•ness** *n* —**con•tent•ment** *n*

2**con•tent** \'kän,tent\ *n* **1** *pl* : something contained **2** *pl* : subject matter (as of a book) **3** : essential meaning **4** : proportion contained

con•ten•tion \kən'tenchən\ *n* : state of contending —**con•ten•tious** \-chəs\ *adj* —**con•ten•tious•ly** *adv*

con•test \kən'test\ *vb* : dispute or challenge ~ \'kän,test\ *n* **1** : struggle **2** : game —**con•test•able** \kən'testəbəl\ *adj* —**con•tes•tant** \-'testənt\ *n*

con•text \'kän,tekst\ *n* : words surrounding a word or phrase

con•tig•u•ous \kən'tigyəwəs\ *adj* : connected to or adjoining —**con•ti•gu•i•ty** \,käntə'gyüətē\ *n*

con•ti•nence \'käntᵊnəns\ *n* : self-restraint —**con•ti•nent** \-ənt\ *adj*

con•ti•nent \'käntᵊnənt\ *n* : great division of land on the globe —**con•ti•nen•tal** \,käntᵊn'entᵊl\ *adj*

con•tin•gen•cy \kən'tinjənsē\ *n, pl* **-cies** : possible event

con•tin•gent \-jənt\ *adj* : dependent on something else ~ *n* : a quota from an area or group

con•tin•u•al \kən'tinyəwəl\ *adj* **1** : continuous **2** : steadily recurring —**con•tin•u•al•ly** \-ē\ *adv*

con•tin•ue \kən'tinyü\ *vb* **-tin•ued; -tin•u•ing 1** : remain in a place or condition **2** : endure **3** : resume after an intermission **4** : extend —**con•tin•u•ance** \-yəwəns\ *n* —**con•tin•u•a•tion** \-,tinyə'wāshən\ *n*

con•tin•u•ous \-'tinyəwəs\ *adj* : continuing without interruption —**con•ti•nu•ity** \,käntᵊn'üətē, -'yü-\ *n* —**con•tin•u•ous•ly** *adv*

con•tort \kən'tȯrt\ *vb* : twist out of shape —**con•tor•tion** \-'tȯrshən\ *n*

con•tour \'kän,tu̇r\ *n* **1** : outline **2** *pl* : shape

con•tra•band \'käntrə,band\ *n* : illegal goods

con•tra•cep•tion \,käntrə'sepshən\ *n* : prevention of conception —**con•tra•cep•tive** \-'septiv\ *adj or n*

con•tract \'kän,trakt\ *n* : binding agreement ~ \kən'trakt, *1 usu* 'kän,trakt\ *vb* **1** : establish or undertake by contract **2** : become ill with **3** : make shorter —**con•trac•tion** \kən'trakshən\ *n* —**con•trac•tor** \'kän,traktər, kən'trak-\ *n* —**con•trac•tu•al** \kən'trakchəwəl\ *adj* —**con•trac•tu•al•ly** *adv*

con•tra•dict \,käntrə'dikt\ *vb* : state the contrary of —**con•tra•dic•tion** \-'dikshən\ *n* —**con•tra•dic•to•ry** \-'diktərē\ *adj*

con•tral•to \kən'traltō\ *n, pl* **-tos** : lowest female singing voice

con•trap•tion \kən'trapshən\ *n* : device or contrivance

con•trary \'kän,trerē; *4 often* kən'trerē\ *adj* **1** : opposite in character, nature, or position **2** : mutually opposed **3** : unfavorable **4** : uncooperative or stubborn —**con•trari•ly** \-,trerəlē, -'trer-\ *adv* —**con•trari•wise** \-,wīz\ *adv* —**contrary** \'kän,trerē\ *n*

con•trast \'kän,trast\ *n* **1** : unlikeness shown by comparing **2** : unlike color or tone of adjacent parts ~ \kən'trast\ *vb* **1** : show differences **2** : compare so as to show differences

con•tra•vene \,käntrə'vēn\ *vb* **-vened; -ven•ing** : go or act contrary to

con•trib•ute \kən'tribyət\ *vb* **-ut•ed; -ut•ing** : give or help along with others —**con•tri•bu•tion** \,käntrə'byüshən\ *n* —**con•trib•u•tor** \kən'tribyətər\ *n* —**con•trib•u•to•ry** \-yə,tōrē\ *adj*

con•trite \'kän,trīt, kən'trīt\ *adj* : repentant —**con•tri•tion** \kən'trishən\ *n*

con•trive \kən'trīv\ *vb* **-trived; -triv•ing 1** : devise or make with ingenuity **2** : bring about —**con•triv•ance** \-'trīvəns\ *n* —**con•triv•er** *n*

con•trol \-'trōl\ *vb* **-ll- 1** : exercise power over **2** : dominate or rule ~ *n* **1** : power to direct or regulate **2** : restraint **3** : regulating device —**con•trol•la•ble** *adj* —**con•trol•ler** \-'trōlər, 'kän,-\ *n*

con•tro•ver•sy \'käntrə,vərsē\ *n, pl* **-sies** : clash of opposing views —**con•tro•ver•sial** \,käntrə'vərshəl, -sēəl\ *adj*

con•tro•vert \'käntrə,vərt, ,käntrə'-\ *vb* : contradict —**con•tro•vert•ible** *adj*

con•tu•ma•cious \,käntə'māshəs, -tyə-\ *adj* : rebellious

con•tu•me•ly \kən'tüməlē, 'käntü,mēlē, -tyü-\ *n* : rudeness

con•tu•sion \kən'tüzhən, -tyü-\ *n* : bruise —**con•tuse** \-'tüz, -'tyüz\ *vb*

co•nun•drum \kə'nəndrəm\ *n* : riddle

con•va•lesce \,känvə'les\ *vb* **-lesced; -lesc•ing** : gradually recover health —**con•va•les•cence** \-ᵊns\ *n* —**con•va•les•cent** \-ᵊnt\ *adj or n*

con•vec•tion \kən'vekshən\ *n* : circulation in fluids due to warmer portions rising and colder ones sinking —**con•vec•tion•al** \-'vekshənəl\ *adj* —**con•vec•tive** \-'vektiv\ *adj*

con•vene \kən'vēn\ *vb* **-vened; -ven•ing** : assemble or meet

con•ve•nience \-'vēnyəns\ *n* **1** : personal comfort or ease **2** : device that saves work

con•ve•nient \-nyənt\ *adj* **1** : suited to one's convenience **2** : near at hand —**con•ve•nient•ly** *adv*

con•vent \'känvənt, -,vent\ *n* : community of nuns

con•ven•tion \kən'venchən\ *n* **1** : agreement esp. between nations **2** : large meeting **3** : body of delegates **4** : accepted usage or way of behaving —**con•ven•tion•al** \-'venchənəl\ *adj* —**con•ven•tion•al•ly** *adv*

con•verge \kən'vərj\ *vb* **-verged; -verg•ing** : approach a single point —**con•ver•gence** \-'vərjəns\ *n* —**con•ver•gent** \-jənt\ *adj*

con•ver•sant \-'vərsᵊnt\ *adj* : having knowledge and experience

con•ver•sa•tion \,känvər'sāshən\ *n* : an informal talking together —**con•ver•sa•tion•al** \-shənəl\ *adj*

1**con•verse** \kən'vərs\ *vb* **-versed; -vers•ing** : engage in conversation —**con•verse** \'kän,vərs\ *n*

2**con•verse** \kən'vərs, 'kän,vers\ *adj* : opposite —**con•verse** \'kän,vərs\ *n* —**con•verse•ly** *adv*

con•ver•sion \kən'vərzhən\ *n* **1** : change **2** : adoption of religion

con•vert \kən'vərt\ *vb* **1** : turn from one belief or party to another **2** : change ~ \'kän,vərt\ *n* : one who has undergone religious conversion —**con•vert•er, con•ver•tor** \kən'vərtər\ *n* —**con•vert•ible** *adj*

con•vert•ible \kən'vərtəbəl\ *n* : automobile with a removable top

con•vex \kän'veks, 'kän,-, kən'-\ *adj* : curved or rounded like the outside of a sphere —**con•vex•i•ty** \kən'veksətē, kän-\ *n*

con•vey \kən'vā\ *vb* **-veyed; -vey•ing** : transport or transmit —**con•vey•ance** \-'vāəns\ *n* —**con•vey•or** \-ər\ *n*

con•vict \kən'vikt\ *vb* : find guilty ~ \'kän,vikt\ *n* : person in prison

con•vic•tion \kən'vikshən\ *n* **1** : act of convicting **2** : strong belief

con•vince \-'vins\ *vb* **-vinced; -vinc•ing** : cause to believe —**con•vinc•ing•ly** *adv*

con•viv•ial \-'vivyəl, -'vivēəl\ *adj* : cheerful or festive —**con•viv•i•al•i•ty** \-,vivē'alətē\ *n*

con•voke \kən'vōk\ *vb* **-voked; -vok•ing** : call together to a meeting —**con•vo•ca•tion** \,känvə'kāshən\ *n*

con•vo•lut•ed \'känvə,lütəd\ *adj* **1** : intricately folded **2** : intricate

con•vo•lu•tion \,känvə'lüshən\ *n* : convoluted structure

con•voy \'kän,vȯi, kən'vȯi\ *vb* : accompany for protection ~ \'kän,vȯi\ *n* : group of vehicles or ships moving together

con•vul•sion \kən'vəlshən\ *n* : violent involuntary muscle contraction —**con•vulse** \-'vəls\ *vb* —**con•vul•sive** \-'vəlsiv\ *adj*

coo \'kü\ *n* : sound of a pigeon —**coo** *vb*

cook \'ku̇k\ *n* : one who prepares food ~ *vb* : prepare food —**cook•book** *n* —**cook•er** *n* —**cook•ery** \-ərē\ *n* —**cook•ware** *n*

cook•ie, cooky \'ku̇kē\ *n, pl* **-ies** : small sweet flat cake

cool \'kül\ *adj* **1** : moderately cold **2** : not excited **3** : unfriendly ~ *vb* : make or become cool ~ *n* **1** : cool time or place **2** : composure —**cool•ant** \-ənt\ *n* —**cool•er** *n* —**cool•ly** *adv* —**cool•ness** *n*

coo•lie \'külē\ *n* : unskilled Oriental laborer

coop \'küp, 'ku̇p\ *n* : enclosure usu. for poultry ~ *vb* : confine in or as if in a coop

co–op \'kō,äp\ *n* : cooperative

coo•per \'küpər, 'ku̇p-\ *n* : barrel maker —**cooper** *vb*

co•op•er•ate \kō'äpə,rāt\ *vb* : act jointly —**co•op•er•a•tion** \-,äpə'rāshən\ *n*

co•op•er•a•tive \kō'äpərətiv, -'äpə,rāt-\ *adj* : willing to work with others ~ *n* : enterprise owned and run by those using its services

co–opt \kō'äpt\ *vb* **1** : elect as a colleague **2** : take over

co•or•di•nate \-'ȯrdᵊnət\ *adj* : equal esp. in rank ~ *n* : any of a set of numbers used in specifying the location of a point on a surface or in space ~ \-ᵊn,āt\ *vb* **-nat•ed; -nat•ing 1** : make or become coordinate **2** : work or act together harmoniously —**co•or•di•nate•ly** *adv* —**co•or•di•na•tion** \-,ȯrdᵊn'āshən\ *n* —**co•or•di•na•tor** \-ᵊn,ātər\ *n*

coot \'küt\ *n* **1** : dark-colored ducklike bird **2** : harmless simple person

cop \'käp\ *n* : police officer

1**cope** \'kōp\ *n* : cloaklike ecclesiastical vestment

2**cope** *vb* **coped; cop•ing** : deal with difficulties

co•pi•lot \'kō,pīlət\ *n* : assistant airplane pilot

cop•ing \'kōpiŋ\ *n* : top layer of a wall

co•pi•ous \'kōpēəs\ *adj* : very abundant —**co•pi•ous•ly** *adv* —**co•pi•ous•ness** *n*

cop•per \'käpər\ *n* **1** : malleable reddish metallic chemical element **2** : penny —**cop•pery** *adj*

cop•per•head *n* : largely coppery brown venomous snake

co•pra \'kōprə\ *n* : dried coconut meat

copse \'käps\ *n* : thicket

cop•u•la \'käpyələ\ *n* : verb linking subject and predicate —**cop•u•la•tive** \-,lātiv\ *adj*

cop•u•late \'käpyə,lāt\ *vb* **-lat•ed; -lat•ing** : engage in sexual intercourse —**cop•u•la•tion** \,käpyə'lāshən\ *n*

copy \'käpē\ *n, pl* **cop•ies 1** : imitation or reproduction of an original **2** : writing to be set for printing ~ *vb* **cop•ied; copy•ing 1** : make a copy of **2** : imitate —**copi•er** \-ər\ *n* —**copy•ist** *n*

copy•right *n* : sole right to a literary or artistic work ~ *vb* : get a copyright on

co•quette \kō'ket\ *n* : flirt

cor•al \'kȯrəl\ *n* **1** : skeletal material of colonies of tiny sea polyps **2** : deep pink —**coral** *adj*

cord \'kȯrd\ *n* **1** : usu. heavy string **2** : long slender anatomical structure **3** : measure of firewood equal to 128 cu. ft. **4** : small electrical cable ~ *vb* **1** : tie or furnish with a cord **2** : pile (wood) in cords

cor•dial \'kȯrjəl\ *adj* : warmly welcoming ~ *n* : liqueur —**cor•di•al•i•ty** \,kȯrjē'alətē, kȯrd'yal-\ *n* —**cor•dial•ly** \'kȯrjəlē\ *adv*

cor•don \'kȯrdᵊn\ *n* : encircling line of troops or police —**cordon** *vb*

cor•do•van \'kȯrdəvən\ *n* : soft fine-grained leather

cor•du•roy \'kȯrdə,rȯi\ *n* **1** : heavy ribbed fabric **2** *pl* : trousers of corduroy

core \'kōr\ *n* **1** : central part of some fruits **2** : inmost part ~ *vb* **cored; cor•ing** : take out the core of —**cor•er** *n*

cork \'kȯrk\ *n* **1** : tough elastic bark of a European oak (**cork oak**) **2** : stopper of cork ~ *vb* : stop up with a cork —**corky** *adj*

cork•screw *n* : device for drawing corks from bottles

cor•mo•rant \'kȯrmərənt, -,rant\ *n* : dark seabird

1**corn** \'kȯrn\ *n* : cereal grass or its seeds ~ *vb* : cure or preserve in brine —**corn•meal** *n* —**corn•stalk** *n* —**corn•starch** *n*

2**corn** *n* : local hardening and thickening of skin

corn•cob *n* : axis on which the kernels of Indian corn are arranged

cor•nea \'kȯrnēə\ *n* : transparent part of the coat of the eyeball —**cor•ne•al** *adj*

cor•ner \'kȯrnər\ *n* **1** : point or angle formed by the meeting of lines or sides **2** : place where two streets meet **3** : inescapable position **4** : control of the supply of something ~ *vb* **1** : drive into a corner **2** : get a corner on **3** : turn a corner

cor•ner•stone *n* **1** : stone at a corner of a wall **2** : something basic

cor•net \kȯr'net\ *n* : trumpetlike instrument

cor•nice \'kȯrnəs\ *n* : horizontal wall projection

cor•nu•co•pia \,kȯrnə'kōpēə, -nyə-\ *n* : goat's horn filled with fruits and grain emblematic of abundance

co•rol•la \kə'rälə\ *n* : petals of a flower

cor•ol•lary \'kȯrə,lerē\ *n, pl* **-lar•ies 1** : logical deduction **2** : consequence or result

co•ro•na \kə'rōnə\ *n* : shining ring around the sun seen during eclipses

cor•o•nary \'kȯrə,nerē\ *adj* : relating to the heart or its blood vessels ~ *n* **1** : thrombosis of an artery supplying the heart **2** : heart attack

cor•o•na•tion \,kȯrə'nāshən\ *n* : crowning of a monarch

cor•o•ner \'kȯrənər\ *n* : public official who investigates causes of suspicious deaths

1**cor•po•ral** \'kȯrpərəl\ *adj* : bodily

2**corporal** *n* : noncommissioned officer ranking next below a sergeant

cor•po•ra•tion \,kȯrpə'rāshən\ *n* : legal creation with the rights and liabilities of a person —**cor•po•rate** \'kȯrpərət\ *adj*

cor•po•re•al \kȯr'pōrēəl\ *adj* : physical or material —**cor•po•re•al•ly** *adv*

corps \'kōr\ *n, pl* **corps** \'kōrz\ **1** : subdivision of a military force **2** : working group

corpse \'kȯrps\ *n* : dead body

cor•pu•lence \'kȯrpyələns\ *n* : obesity —**cor•pu•lent** \-lənt\ *adj*

cor•pus \'kȯrpəs\ *n, pl* **-po•ra** \-pərə\ **1** : corpse **2** : body of writings

cor•pus•cle \'kȯr,pəsəl\ *n* : blood cell

cor•ral \kə'ral\ *n* : enclosure for animals —**corral** *vb*

cor•rect \kə'rekt\ *vb* **1** : make right **2** : chastise ~ *adj* **1** : true or factual **2** : conforming to a standard —**cor•rec•tion** \-'rekshən\ *n* —**cor•rec•tive** \-'rektiv\ *adj* —**cor•rect•ly** *adv* —**cor•rect•ness** *n*

cor•re•late \'kȯrə,lāt\ *vb* **-lat•ed; -lat•ing** : show a connection between —**cor•re•late** \-lət, -,lāt\ *n* —**cor•re•la•tion** \,kȯrə'lāshən\ *n*

cor•rel•a•tive \kə'relətiv\ *adj* : regularly used together —**correlative** *n*

cor•re•spond \,kȯrə'spänd\ *vb* **1** : match **2** : communicate by letter —**cor•re•spon•dence** \-'spändəns\ *n* —**cor•re•spond•ing•ly** \-'spändiŋlē\ *adv*

cor•re•spon•dent \-'spändənt\ *n* **1** : person one writes to **2** : reporter

cor•ri•dor \'kȯrədər, -,dȯr\ *n* : passageway connecting rooms

cor•rob•o•rate \kə'räbə,rāt\ *vb* **-rat•ed; -rat•ing** : support with evidence —**cor•rob•o•ra•tion** \-,räbə'rāshən\ *n*

cor•rode \kə'rōd\ *vb* **-rod•ed; -rod•ing** : wear away by chemical action —**cor•ro•sion** \-'rōzhən\ *n* —**cor•ro•sive** \-'rōsiv\ *adj or n*

cor•ru•gate \'kȯrə,gāt\ *vb* **-gat•ed; -gat•ing** : form into ridges and grooves —**cor•ru•gat•ed** *adj* —**cor•ru•ga•tion** \,kȯrə'gāshən\ *n*

cor•rupt \kə'rəpt\ *vb* **1** : change from good to bad **2** : bribe ~ *adj* : morally debased —**cor•rupt•ible** *adj* —**cor•rup•tion** \-'rəpshən\ *n*

cor•sage \kȯr'säzh, -'säj\ *n* : bouquet worn by a woman

cor•set \'kȯrsət\ *n* : woman's stiffened undergarment

cor•tege \kȯr'tezh, 'kȯr,-\ *n* : funeral procession

cor•tex \'kȯr,teks\ *n, pl* **-ti•ces** \'kȯrtə,sēz\ *or* **-tex•es** : outer or covering layer of an organism or part (as the brain) —**cor•ti•cal** \'kȯrtikəl\ *adj*

cor•ti•sone \'kȯrtə,sōn, -zōn\ *n* : adrenal hormone

cos•met•ic \käz'metik\ *n* : beautifying preparation ~ *adj* : relating to beautifying

cos•mic \'käzmik\ *adj* **1** : relating to the universe **2** : vast or grand

cos•mo•naut \'käzmə,nȯt\ *n* : Soviet or Russian astronaut

cos•mo•pol•i•tan \,käzmə'pälətᵊn\ *adj* : belonging to all the world —**cosmopolitan** *n*

cos•mos \'käzməs, -,mōs, -,mäs\ *n* : universe

cos•sack \'käs,ak, -ək\ *n* : Russian czarist cavalryman

cost \'kȯst\ *n* **1** : amount paid for something **2** : loss or penalty ~ *vb* **cost; cost•ing 1** : require so much in payment **2** : cause to pay, suffer, or lose —**cost•li•ness** \-lēnəs\ *n* —**cost•ly** \-lē\ *adj*

cos•tume \'käs,tüm, -,tyüm\ *n* : clothing

co•sy \'kōzē\ *var of* COZY

cot \'kät\ *n* : small bed

cote \'kōt, 'kät\ *n* : small shed or coop

co•te•rie \'kōtə,rē, ,kōtə'-\ *n* : exclusive group of persons

co•til•lion \kō'tilyən\ *n* : formal ball

cot•tage \'kätij\ *n* : small house

cot•ton \'kätᵊn\ *n* : soft fibrous plant substance or thread or cloth made of it —**cot•ton•seed** *n* —**cot•tony** *adj*

cot•ton•mouth *n* : poisonous snake

couch \'kau̇ch\ *vb* **1** : lie or place on a couch **2** : phrase ~ *n* : bed or sofa

cou•gar \'kügər, -,gär\ *n* : large tawny wild American cat

cough \'kȯf\ *vb* : force air from the lungs with short sharp noises —**cough** *n*

could \'ku̇d\ *past of* CAN

coun•cil \'kau̇nsəl\ *n* **1** : assembly or meeting **2** : body of lawmakers —**coun•cil•lor, coun•cil•or** \-sələr\ *n* —**coun•cil•man** \-mən\ *n* —**coun•cil•wom•an** *n*

coun•sel \'kau̇nsəl\ *n* **1** : advice **2** : deliberation together **3** *pl* **-sel** : lawyer ~ *vb* **-seled** *or* **-selled; -sel•ing** *or* **-sel•ling 1** : advise **2** : consult together —**coun•sel•or, coun•sel•lor** \-sələr\ *n*

1**count** \'kau̇nt\ *vb* **1** : name or indicate one by one to find the total number **2** : recite numbers in order **3** : rely **4** : be of value or account ~ *n* **1** : act of counting or the total obtained by counting **2** : charge in an indictment —**count•able** *adj*

2**count** *n* : European nobleman

coun•te•nance \'kau̇ntᵊnəns\ *n* : face or facial expression ~ *vb* **-nanced; -nanc•ing** : allow or encourage

1**count•er** \'kau̇ntər\ *n* **1** : piece for reckoning or games **2** : surface over which business is transacted

2**count•er** *n* : one that counts

3**coun•ter** *vb* : oppose ~ *adv* : in an opposite direction ~ *n* : offsetting force or move ~ *adj* : contrary

counter- *prefix* **1** : contrary or opposite **2** : opposing **3** : retaliatory

counteraccusation
counteraggression
counterargue
counterassault
counterattack
counterbid
counterblockade
counterblow
countercampaign
countercharge
counterclaim
countercomplaint
countercoup
countercriticism

counterdemand
counterdemonstration
counterdemonstrator
countereffort
counterevidence
counterguerrilla
counterinflationary
counterinfluence
countermeasure
countermove
countermovement
counteroffer
counterpetition
counterploy
counterpower
counterpressure
counterpropaganda
counterproposal
counterprotest
counterquestion
counterraid
counterrally
counterreform
counterresponse
counterretaliation
counterrevolution
counterrevolutionary
counterstrategy
counterstyle
countersue
countersuggestion
countersuit
countertendency
counterterror
counterterrorism
counterterrorist
counterthreat
counterthrust
countertrend

coun•ter•act *vb* : lessen the force of —**coun•ter•ac•tive** *adj*
coun•ter•bal•ance *n* : balancing influence or weight ~ *vb* : oppose or balance
coun•ter•clock•wise *adv or adj* : opposite to the way a clock's hands move
coun•ter•feit \'kau̇ntər,fit\ *vb* **1** : copy in order to deceive **2** : pretend ~ *adj* : spurious ~ *n* : fraudulent copy —**coun•ter•feit•er** *n*
coun•ter•mand \-,mand\ *vb* : supersede with a contrary order
coun•ter•pane \-,pān\ *n* : bedspread
coun•ter•part *n* : one that is similar or corresponds
coun•ter•point *n* : music with interwoven melodies
coun•ter•sign *n* : secret signal ~ *vb* : add a confirming signature to
count•ess \'kau̇ntəs\ *n* : wife or widow of a count or an earl or a woman holding that rank in her own right
count•less \-ləs\ *adj* : too many to be numbered
coun•try \'kəntrē\ *n, pl* **-tries 1** : nation **2** : rural area ~ *adj* : rural —**coun•try•man** \-mən\ *n*
coun•try•side *n* : rural area or its people
coun•ty \'kau̇ntē\ *n, pl* **-ties** : local government division esp. of a state
coup \'kü\ *n, pl* **coups** \'küz\ **1** : brilliant sudden action or plan **2** : sudden overthrow of a government
coupe \'küp\ *n* : 2-door automobile with an enclosed body
cou•ple \'kəpəl\ *vb* **-pled; -pling** : link together ~ *n* **1** : pair **2** : two persons closely associated or married
cou•pling \'kəpliŋ\ *n* : connecting device
cou•pon \'kü,pän, 'kyü-\ *n* : certificate redeemable for goods or a cash discount
cour•age \'kərij\ *n* : ability to conquer fear or despair —**cou•ra•geous** \kə'rājəs\ *adj*
cou•ri•er \'ku̇rēər, 'kərē-\ *n* : messenger
course \'kōrs\ *n* **1** : progress **2** : ground over which something moves **3** : part of a meal served at one time **4** : method of procedure **5** : subject taught in a series of classes ~ *vb* **coursed; cours•ing 1** : hunt with dogs **2** : run speedily —**of course** : as might be expected
court \'kōrt\ *n* **1** : residence of a sovereign **2** : sovereign and his or her officials and advisers **3** : area enclosed by a building **4** : space marked for playing a game **5** : place where justice is administered ~ *vb* : woo —**court•house** *n* —**court•room** *n* —**court•ship** \-,ship\ *n*
cour•te•ous \'kərtēəs\ *adj* : showing politeness and respect for others —**cour•te•ous•ly** *adv*
cour•te•san \'kōrtəzən, 'kərt-\ *n* : prostitute
cour•te•sy \'kərtəsē\ *n, pl* **-sies** : courteous behavior
court•ier \'kōrtēər, 'kōrtyər\ *n* : person in attendance at a royal court
court•ly \'kōrtlē\ *adj* **-li•er; -est** : polite or elegant —**court•li•ness** *n*
court–mar•tial *n, pl* **courts–martial** : military trial court —**court–martial** *vb*
court•yard *n* : enclosure open to the sky that is attached to a house
cous•in \'kəzᵊn\ *n* : child of one's uncle or aunt
cove \'kōv\ *n* : sheltered inlet or bay
co•ven \'kəvən\ *n* : group of witches
cov•e•nant \'kəvənənt\ *n* : binding agreement —**cov•e•nant** \-nənt, -,nant\ *vb*
cov•er \'kəvər\ *vb* **1** : place something over or upon **2** : protect or hide **3** : include or deal with ~ *n* : something that covers —**cov•er•age** \-ərij\ *n*
cov•er•let \-lət\ *n* : bedspread
co•vert \'kō,vərt, 'kəvərt\ *adj* : secret ~ \'kəvərt, 'kō-\ *n* : thicket that shelters animals
cov•et \'kəvət\ *vb* : desire enviously —**cov•et•ous** *adj*
cov•ey \'kəvē\ *n, pl* **-eys 1** : bird with her young **2** : small flock (as of quail)

1**cow** \'kau̇\ *n* : large adult female animal (as of cattle) —**cow•hide** *n*
2**cow** *vb* : intimidate
cow•ard \'kau̇ərd\ *n* : one who lacks courage —**cow•ard•ice** \-əs\ *n* —**cow•ard•ly** *adv or adj*
cow•boy *n* : a mounted ranch hand who tends cattle
cow•er \'kau̇ər\ *vb* : shrink from fear or cold
cow•girl *n* : woman ranch hand who tends cattle
cowl \'kau̇l\ *n* : monk's hood
cow•lick \'kau̇,lik\ *n* : turned-up tuft of hair that resists control
cow•slip \-,slip\ *n* : yellow flower
cox•swain \'käksən, -,swān\ *n* : person who steers a boat
coy \'kȯi\ *adj* : shy or pretending shyness
coy•ote \'kī,ōt, kī'ōtē\ *n, pl* **coy•otes** *or* **coy•ote** : small No. American wolf
coz•en \'kəzᵊn\ *vb* : cheat
co•zy \'kōzē\ *adj* **-zi•er; -est** : snug
crab \'krab\ *n* : short broad shellfish with pincers
crab•by \'krabē\ *adj* **-bi•er; -est** : cross
1**crack** \'krak\ *vb* **1** : break with a sharp sound **2** : fail in tone **3** : break without completely separating ~ *n* **1** : sudden sharp noise **2** : witty remark **3** : narrow break **4** : sharp blow **5** : try
2**crack** *adj* : extremely proficient
crack•down *n* : disciplinary action —**crack down** *vb*
crack•er \-ər\ *n* : thin crisp bakery product
crack•le \'krakəl\ *vb* **-led; -ling 1** : make snapping noises **2** : develop fine cracks in a surface —**crackle** *n*
crack•pot \'krak,pät\ *n* : eccentric
crack–up *n* : crash
cra•dle \'krādᵊl\ *n* : baby's bed ~ *vb* **-dled; -dling 1** : place in a cradle **2** : hold securely
craft \'kraft\ *n* **1** : occupation requiring special skill **2** : craftiness **3** *pl usu* **craft** : structure designed to provide transportation **4** *pl usu* **craft** : small boat —**crafts•man** \'kraftsmən\ *n* —**crafts•man•ship** \-,ship\ *n*
crafty \'kraftē\ *adj* **craft•i•er; -est** : sly —**craft•i•ness** *n*
crag \'krag\ *n* : steep cliff —**crag•gy** \-ē\ *adj*
cram \'kram\ *vb* **-mm- 1** : eat greedily **2** : pack in tight **3** : study intensely for a test
cramp \'kramp\ *n* **1** : sudden painful contraction of muscle **2** *pl* : sharp abdominal pains ~ *vb* **1** : affect with cramp **2** : restrain
cran•ber•ry \'kran,berē\ *n* : red acid berry of a trailing plant
crane \'krān\ *n* **1** : tall wading bird **2** : machine for lifting heavy objects ~ *vb* **craned; cran•ing** : stretch one's neck to see
cra•ni•um \'krānēəm\ *n, pl* **-ni•ums** *or* **-nia** \-nēə\ : skull —**cra•ni•al** \-əl\ *adj*
crank \'kraŋk\ *n* **1** : bent lever turned to operate a machine **2** : eccentric ~ *vb* : start or operate by turning a crank
cranky \'kraŋkē\ *adj* **crank•i•er; -est** : irritable
cran•ny \'kranē\ *n, pl* **-nies** : crevice
craps \'kraps\ *n* : dice game
crash \'krash\ *vb* **1** : break noisily **2** : fall and hit something with noise and damage ~ *n* **1** : loud sound **2** : action of crashing **3** : failure
crass \'kras\ *adj* : crude or unfeeling
crate \'krāt\ *n* : wooden shipping container —**crate** *vb*
cra•ter \'krātər\ *n* : volcanic depression
cra•vat \krə'vat\ *n* : necktie
crave \'krāv\ *vb* **craved; crav•ing** : long for —**crav•ing** *n*
cra•ven \'krāvən\ *adj* : cowardly —**craven** *n*
craw•fish \'krȯ,fish\ *n* : crayfish
crawl \'krȯl\ *vb* **1** : move slowly (as by drawing the body along the ground) **2** : swarm with creeping things ~ *n* : very slow pace
cray•fish \'krā,fish\ *n* : lobsterlike freshwater crustacean
cray•on \'krā,än, -ən\ *n* : stick of chalk or wax used for drawing or coloring —**crayon** *vb*
craze \'krāz\ *vb* **crazed; craz•ing** : make or become insane ~ *n* : fad
cra•zy \'krāzē\ *adj* **cra•zi•er; -est 1** : mentally disordered **2** : wildly impractical —**cra•zi•ly** *adv* —**cra•zi•ness** *n*
creak \'krēk\ *vb or n* : squeak —**creaky** *adj*
cream \'krēm\ *n* **1** : yellowish fat-rich part of milk **2** : thick smooth sauce, confection, or cosmetic **3** : choicest part ~ *vb* : beat into creamy consistency —**creamy** *adj*
cream•ery \-ərē\ *n, pl* **-er•ies** : place where butter and cheese are made
crease \'krēs\ *n* : line made by folding —**crease** *vb*
cre•ate \krē'āt\ *vb* **-at•ed; -at•ing** : bring into being —**cre•a•tion** \krē'āshən\ *n* —**cre•a•tive** \-'ātiv\ *adj* —**cre•a•tiv•i•ty** \,krēā'tivətē\ *n* —**cre•a•tor** \krē'ātər\ *n*
crea•ture \'krēchər\ *n* : lower animal or human being
cre•dence \'krēdᵊns\ *n* : belief
cre•den•tials \kri'denchəlz\ *n* : evidence of qualifications or authority
cred•i•ble \'kredəbəl\ *adj* : believable —**cred•i•bil•i•ty** \,kredə'bilətē\ *n*
cred•it \'kredət\ *n* **1** : balance in a person's favor **2** : time given to pay for goods **3** : belief **4** : esteem **5** : source of honor ~ *vb* **1** : believe **2** : give credit to
cred•it•able \-əbəl\ *adj* : worthy of esteem or praise —**cred•it•ably** \-əblē\ *adv*
cred•i•tor \-ər\ *n* : person to whom money is owed
cred•u•lous \'krejələs\ *adj* : easily convinced —**cre•du•li•ty** \kri'dülətē, -'dyü-\ *n*
creed \'krēd\ *n* : statement of essential beliefs
creek \'krēk, 'krik\ *n* : small stream
creel \'krēl\ *n* : basket for carrying fish
creep \'krēp\ *vb* **crept** \'krept\; **creep•ing 1** : crawl **2** : grow over a surface like ivy —**creep** *n* —**creep•er** *n*
cre•mate \'krē,māt\ *vb* **-mat•ed; -mat•ing** : burn up (a corpse) —**cre•ma•tion** \kri'māshən\ *n* —**cre•ma•to•ry** \'krēmə,tōrē, 'krem-\ *n*
cre•o•sote \'krēə,sōt\ *n* : oily wood preservative
crepe, crêpe \'krāp\ *n* : light crinkled fabric
cre•scen•do \krə'shendō\ *adv or adj* : growing louder —**crescendo** *n*
cres•cent \'kresᵊnt\ *n* : shape of the moon between new moon and first quarter
crest \'krest\ *n* **1** : tuft on a bird's head **2** : top of a hill or wave **3** : part of a coat of arms ~ *vb* : rise to a crest —**crest•ed** \-əd\ *adj*
crest•fall•en *adj* : sad
cre•tin \'krētᵊn\ *n* : stupid person
cre•vasse \kri'vas\ *n* : deep fissure esp. in a glacier
crev•ice \'krevəs\ *n* : narrow fissure
crew \'krü\ *n* : body of workers (as on a ship) —**crew•man** \-mən\ *n*
crib \'krib\ *n* **1** : manger **2** : grain storage bin **3** : baby's bed ~ *vb* **-bb-** : put in a crib
crib•bage \'kribij\ *n* : card game scored by moving pegs on a board (**cribbage board**)
crick \'krik\ *n* : muscle spasm
1**crick•et** \'krikət\ *n* : insect noted for the chirping of the male
2**cricket** *n* : bat and ball game played on a field with wickets
cri•er \'krīər\ *n* : one who calls out announcements
crime \'krīm\ *n* : serious violation of law
crim•i•nal \'krimənᵊl\ *adj* : relating to or being a crime or its punishment ~ *n* : one who commits a crime
crimp \'krimp\ *vb* : cause to become crinkled, wavy, or bent —**crimp** *n*
crim•son \'krimzən\ *n* : deep red —**crimson** *adj*
cringe \'krinj\ *vb* **cringed; cring•ing** : shrink in fear
crin•kle \'kriŋkəl\ *vb* **-kled; -kling** : wrinkle —**crinkle** *n* —**crin•kly** \-klē\ *adj*
crin•o•line \'krinᵊlən\ *n* **1** : stiff cloth **2** : full stiff skirt or petticoat
crip•ple \'kripəl\ *n* : disabled person ~ *vb* **-pled; -pling** : disable
cri•sis \'krīsəs\ *n, pl* **cri•ses** \-,sēz\ : decisive or critical moment
crisp \'krisp\ *adj* **1** : easily crumbled **2** : firm and fresh **3** : lively **4** : invigorating —**crisp** *vb* —**crisp•ly** *adv* —**crisp•ness** *n* —**crispy** *adj*
criss•cross \'kris,krȯs\ *n* : pattern of crossed lines ~ *vb* : mark with or follow a crisscross
cri•te•ri•on \krī'tirēən\ *n, pl* **-ria** \-ēə\ : standard
crit•ic \'kritik\ *n* : judge of literary or artistic works
crit•i•cal \-ikəl\ *adj* **1** : inclined to criticize **2** : being a crisis **3** : relating to criticism or critics —**crit•i•cal•ly** \-iklē\ *adv*
crit•i•cize \'kritə,sīz\ *vb* **-cized; -ciz•ing 1** : judge as a critic **2** : find fault —**crit•i•cism** \-ə,sizəm\ *n*
cri•tique \krə'tēk\ *n* : critical estimate
croak \'krōk\ *n* : hoarse harsh cry (as of a frog) —**croak** *vb*
cro•chet \krō'shā\ *n* : needlework done with a hooked needle —**crochet** *vb*
crock \'kräk\ *n* : thick earthenware pot or jar —**crock•ery** \-ərē\ *n*
croc•o•dile \'kräkə,dīl\ *n* : large reptile of tropical waters
cro•cus \'krōkəs\ *n, pl* **-cus•es** : herb with spring flowers
crone \'krōn\ *n* : ugly old woman
cro•ny \'krōnē\ *n, pl* **-nies** : chum
crook \'kru̇k\ *n* **1** : bent or curved tool or part **2** : thief ~ *vb* : curve sharply
crook•ed \'kru̇kəd\ *adj* **1** : bent **2** : dishonest —**crook•ed•ness** *n*

croon \'krün\ *vb* : sing softly —**croon•er** *n*
crop \'kräp\ *n* **1** : pouch in the throat of a bird or insect **2** : short riding whip **3** : something that can be harvested ~ *vb* **-pp- 1** : trim **2** : appear unexpectedly :—used with *up*
cro•quet \krō'kā\ *n* : lawn game of driving balls through wickets
cro•quette \-'ket\ *n* : mass of minced food deep-fried
cro•sier \'krōzhər\ *n* : bishop's staff
cross \'krȯs\ *n* **1** : figure or structure consisting of an upright and a cross piece **2** : interbreeding of unlike strains ~ *vb* **1** : intersect **2** : cancel **3** : go or extend across **4** : interbreed ~ *adj* **1** : going across **2** : contrary **3** : marked by bad temper —**cross•ing** *n* —**cross•ly** *adv*
cross•bow \-,bō\ *n* : short bow mounted on a rifle stock
cross•breed *vb* **-bred; -breed•ing** : hybridize
cross–ex•am•ine *vb* : question about earlier testimony —**cross–ex•am•i•na•tion** *n*
cross–eyed *adj* : having the eye turned toward the nose
cross–re•fer *vb* : refer to another place (as in a book) —**cross–ref•er•ence** *n*
cross•roads *n* : place where 2 roads cross
cross section *n* : representative portion
cross•walk *n* : path for pedestrians crossing a street
cross•ways *adv* : crosswise
cross•wise \-,wīz\ *adv* : so as to cross something —**crosswise** *adj*
crotch \'kräch\ *n* : angle formed by the parting of 2 legs or branches
crotch•ety \'krächətē\ *adj* : cranky, ill-natured
crouch \'krau̇ch\ *vb* : stoop over —**crouch** *n*
croup \'krüp\ *n* : laryngitis of infants
crou•ton \'krü,tän\ *n* : bit of toast
1**crow** \'krō\ *n* : large glossy black bird
2**crow** *vb* **1** : make the loud sound of the cock **2** : gloat ~ *n* : cry of the cock
crow•bar *n* : metal bar used as a pry or lever
crowd \'krau̇d\ *vb* : collect or cram together ~ *n* : large number of people
crown \'krau̇n\ *n* **1** : wreath of honor or victory **2** : royal headdress **3** : top or highest part ~ *vb* **1** : place a crown on **2** : honor —**crowned** \'krau̇nd\ *adj*
cru•cial \'krüshəl\ *adj* : vitally important
cru•ci•ble \'krüsəbəl\ *n* : heat-resisting container
cru•ci•fix \'krüsə,fiks\ *n* : representation of Christ on the cross
cru•ci•fix•ion \,krüsə'fikshən\ *n* : act of crucifying
cru•ci•fy \'krüsə,fī\ *vb* **-fied; -fy•ing 1** : put to death on a cross **2** : persecute
crude \'krüd\ *adj* **crud•er; -est 1** : not refined **2** : lacking grace or elegance ~ *n* : unrefined petroleum —**crude•ly** *adv* —**cru•di•ty** \-ətē\ *n*
cru•el \'krüəl\ *adj* **-el•er** *or* **-el•ler; -el•est** *or* **-el•lest** : causing suffering to others —**cru•el•ly** \-ē\ *adv* —**cru•el•ty** \tē\ *n*
cru•et \'krüət\ *n* : bottle for salad dressings
cruise \'krüz\ *vb* **cruised; cruis•ing 1** : sail to several ports **2** : travel at the most efficient speed —**cruise** *n*
cruis•er \'krüzər\ *n* **1** : warship **2** : police car
crumb \'krəm\ *n* : small fragment
crum•ble \'krəmbəl\ *vb* **-bled; -bling** : break into small pieces —**crum•bly** \-blē\ *adj*
crum•ple \'krəmpəl\ *vb* **-pled; -pling 1** : crush together **2** : collapse
crunch \'krənch\ *vb* : chew or press with a crushing noise ~ *n* : crunching sound —**crunchy** *adj*
cru•sade \krü'sād\ *n* **1** *cap* : medieval Christian expedition to the Holy Land **2** : reform movement —**crusade** *vb* —**cru•sad•er** *n*
crush \'krəsh\ *vb* **1** : squeeze out of shape **2** : grind or pound to bits **3** : suppress ~ *n* **1** : severe crowding **2** : infatuation
crust \'krəst\ *n* **1** : hard outer part of bread or a pie **2** : hard surface layer —**crust•al** *adj* —**crusty** *adj*
crus•ta•cean \,krəs'tāshən\ *n* : aquatic arthropod having a firm shell
crutch \'krəch\ *n* : support for use by the disabled in walking
crux \'krəks, 'kru̇ks\ *n, pl* **crux•es 1** : hard problem **2** : crucial point
cry \'krī\ *vb* **cried; cry•ing 1** : call out **2** : weep ~ *n, pl* **cries 1** : shout **2** : fit of weeping **3** : characteristic sound of an animal
crypt \'kript\ *n* : underground chamber
cryp•tic \'kriptik\ *adj* : enigmatic
cryp•tog•ra•phy \krip'tägrəfē\ *n* : coding and decoding of messages —**cryp•tog•ra•pher** \-fər\ *n*
crys•tal \'kristᵊl\ *n* **1** : transparent quartz **2** : something (as glass) like crystal **3** : body formed by solidification that has a regular repeating atomic arrangement —**crys•tal•line** \-tələn\ *adj*

crys·tal·lize \-tə,līz\ *vb* **-lized; -liz·ing** : form crystals or a definite shape —**crys·tal·li·za·tion** \,kristələ'zāshən\ *n*
cub \'kəb\ *n* : young animal
cub·by·hole \'kəbē,hōl\ *n* : small confined space
cube \'kyüb\ *n* **1** : solid having 6 equal square sides **2** : product obtained by taking a number 3 times as a factor ~ *vb* **cubed; cub·ing 1** : raise to the 3d power **2** : form into a cube **3** : cut into cubes —**cu·bic** \'kyübik\ *adj*
cu·bi·cle \-bikəl\ *n* : small room
cu·bit \'kyübət\ *n* : ancient unit of length equal to about 18 inches
cuck·old \'kəkəld, 'kuk-\ *n* : man whose wife is unfaithful —**cuckold** *vb*
cuck·oo \'kükü, 'kuk-\ *n, pl* **-oos** : brown European bird ~ *adj* : silly
cu·cum·ber \'kyü,kəmbər\ *n* : fleshy fruit related to the gourds
cud \'kəd\ *n* : food chewed again by ruminating animals
cud·dle \'kədəl\ *vb* **-dled; -dling** : lie close
cud·gel \'kəjəl\ *n or vb* : club
¹cue \'kyü\ *n* : signal —**cue** *vb*
²cue *n* : stick used in pool
¹cuff \'kəf\ *n* **1** : part of a sleeve encircling the wrist **2** : folded trouser hem
²cuff *vb or n* : slap
cui·sine \kwi'zēn\ *n* : manner of cooking
cu·li·nary \'kələ,nerē, 'kyülə-\ *adj* : of or relating to cookery
cull \'kəl\ *vb* : select
cul·mi·nate \'kəlmə,nāt\ *vb* **-nat·ed; -nat·ing** : rise to the highest point —**cul·mi·na·tion** \,kəlmə'nāshən\ *n*
cul·pa·ble \'kəlpəbəl\ *adj* : deserving blame
cul·prit \'kəlprət\ *n* : guilty person
cult \'kəlt\ *n* **1** : religious system **2** : faddish devotion —**cult·ist** *n*
cul·ti·vate \'kəltə,vāt\ *vb* **-vat·ed; -vat·ing 1** : prepare for crops **2** : foster the growth of 3 : refine —**cul·ti·va·tion** \kəltə'vā-shən\ *n*
cul·ture \'kəlchər\ *n* **1** : cultivation **2** : refinement of intellectual and artistic taste **3** : particular form or stage of civilization —**cul·tur·al** \'kəlchərəl\ *adj*—**cul·tured** \'kəlchərd\ *adj*
cul·vert \'kəlvərt\ *n* : drain crossing under a road or railroad
cum·ber·some \'kəmbərsəm\ *adj* : awkward to handle due to bulk
cu·mu·la·tive \'kyümyələtiv, -,lāt-\ *adj* : increasing by additions
cu·mu·lus \'kyümyələs\ *n, pl* **-li** \-,lī, -,lē\ : massive rounded cloud
cun·ning \'kəniŋ\ *adj* **1** : crafty **2** : clever **3** : appealing ~ *n* **1** : skill **2** : craftiness
cup \'kəp\ *n* **1** : small drinking vessel **2** : contents of a cup **3** : a half pint ~ *vb* **-pp-** : shape like a cup —**cup·ful** *n*
cup·board \'kəbərd\ *n* : small storage closet
cup·cake *n* : small cake
cu·pid·i·ty \kyu'pidətē\ *n, pl* **-ties** : excessive desire for money
cu·po·la \'kyüpələ, -,lō\ *n* : small rooftop structure
cur \'kər\ *n* : mongrel dog
cu·rate \'kyurət\ *n* : member of the clergy —**cu·ra·cy** \-əsē\ *n*
cu·ra·tor \kyu'rātər\ *n* : one in charge of a museum or zoo
curb \'kərb\ *n* **1** : restraint **2** : raised edging along a street ~ *vb* : hold back
curd \'kərd\ *n* : coagulated milk
cur·dle \'kərdəl\ *vb* **-dled; -dling 1** : form curds **2** : sour
cure \'kyur\ *n* **1** : recovery from disease **2** : remedy ~ *vb* **cured; cur·ing 1** : restore to health **2** : process for storage or use —**cur·able** *adj*
cur·few \'kər,fyü\ *n* : requirement to be off the streets at a set hour
cu·rio \'kyurē,ō\ *n, pl* **-ri·os** : rare or unusual article
cu·ri·ous \'kyurēəs\ *adj* **1** : eager to learn **2** : strange —**cu·ri·os·i·ty** \,kyurē'äsətē\ *n* —**cu·ri·ous·ness** *n*
curl \'kərl\ *vb* **1** : form into ringlets **2** : curve ~ *n* **1** : ringlet of hair **2** : something with a spiral form —**curl·er** *n* —**curly** *adj*
cur·lew \'kərlü, -lyü\ *n, pl* **-lews** *or* **-lew** : long-legged brownish bird
curl·i·cue \'kərli,kyü\ *n* : fanciful curve
cur·rant \'kərənt\ *n* **1** : small seedless raisin **2** : berry of a shrub
cur·ren·cy \'kərənsē\ *n, pl* **-cies 1** : general use or acceptance **2** : money
cur·rent \'kərənt\ *adj* : occurring in or belonging to the present ~ *n* **1** : swiftest part of a stream **2** : flow of electricity
cur·ric·u·lum \kə'rikyələm\ *n, pl* **-la** \-lə\ : course of study
¹cur·ry \'kərē\ *vb* **-ried; -ry·ing** : brush (a horse) with a wire brush (**cur·ry·comb** \-,kōm\) —**curry favor** : seek favor by flattery
²curry *n, pl* **-ries** : blend of pungent spices or a food seasoned with this
curse \'kərs\ *n* **1** : a calling down of evil or harm upon one **2** : affliction ~ *vb* **cursed;**

curs·ing 1 : call down injury upon **2** : swear at **3** : afflict
cur·sor \'kərsər\ *n* : indicator on a computer screen
cur·so·ry \'kərsərē\ *adj* : hastily done
curt \'kərt\ *adj* : rudely abrupt —**curt·ly** *adv* —**curt·ness** *n*
cur·tail \kər'tāl\ *vb* : shorten —**cur·tail·ment** *n*
cur·tain \'kərtən\ *n* : hanging screen that can be drawn back or raised —**curtain** *vb*
curt·sy, curt·sey \'kərtsē\ *n, pl* **-sies** *or* **-seys** : courteous bow made by bending the knees —**curtsy, curtsey** *vb*
cur·va·ture \'kərvə,chur\ *n* : amount or state of curving
curve \'kərv\ *vb* **curved; curv·ing** : bend from a straight line or course ~ *n* **1** : a bending without angles **2** : something curved
cush·ion \'kushən\ *n* **1** : soft pillow **2** : something that eases or protects ~ *vb* **1** : provide with a cushion **2** : soften the force of
cusp \'kəsp\ *n* : pointed end
cus·pid \'kəspəd\ *n* : a canine tooth
cus·pi·dor \'kəspə,dor\ *n* : spittoon
cus·tard \'kəstərd\ *n* : sweetened cooked mixture of milk and eggs
cus·to·dy \'kəstədē\ *n, pl* **-dies** : immediate care or charge —**cus·to·di·al** \,kəs'tō-dēəl\ *adj* —**cus·to·di·an** \-ēən\ *n*
cus·tom \'kəstəm\ *n* **1** : habitual course of action **2** *pl* : import taxes ~ *adj* : made to personal order —**cus·tom·ar·i·ly** \,kəstə'merəlē\ *adv* —**cus·tom·ary** \'kəstə,merē\ *adj* —**cus·tom-built** *adj* —**cus·tom-made** *adj*
cus·tom·er \'kəstəmər\ *n* : buyer
cut \'kət\ *vb* **cut; cut·ting 1** : penetrate or divide with a sharp edge **2** : experience the growth of (a tooth) through the gum **3** : shorten **4** : remove by severing **5** : intersect ~ *n* **1** : something separated by cutting **2** : reduction —**cut in** *vb* : thrust oneself between others
cu·ta·ne·ous \kyu'tānēəs\ *adj* : relating to the skin
cute \'kyüt\ *adj* **cut·er; -est** : pretty
cu·ti·cle \'kyütikəl\ *n* : outer layer (as of skin)
cut·lass \'kətləs\ *n* : short heavy curved sword
cut·lery \-lərē\ *n* : cutting utensils
cut·let \-lət\ *n* : slice of meat
cut·ter \'kətər\ *n* **1** : tool or machine for cutting **2** : small armed motorboat **3** : light sleigh
cut·throat *n* : murderer ~ *adj* : ruthless
-cy \sē\ *n suffix* **1** : action or practice **2** : rank or office **3** : body **4** : state or quality
cy·a·nide \'sīə,nīd, -nəd\ *n* : poisonous chemical salt
cy·cle \'sīkəl, 4 *also* 'sikəl\ *n* **1** : period of time for a series of repeated events **2** : recurring round of events **3** : long period of time **4** : bicycle or motorcycle ~ *vb* **-cled; -cling** : ride a cycle —**cy·clic** \'sīklik, 'sik-\, **cy·cli·cal** \-əl\ *adj* —**cy·clist** \'sīklist, 'sik-\ *n*
cy·clone \'sī,klōn\ *n* : tornado —**cy·clon·ic** \sī'klänik\ *adj*
cy·clo·pe·dia, cy·clo·pae·dia \,sīklə'pēdēə\ *n* : encyclopedia
cyl·in·der \'siləndər\ *n* **1** : long round body or figure **2** : rotating chamber in a revolver **3** : piston chamber in an engine —**cy·lin·dri·cal** \sə'lindrikəl\ *adj*
cym·bal \'simbəl\ *n* : one of 2 concave brass plates clashed together
cyn·ic \'sinik\ *n* : one who attributes all actions to selfish motives —**cyn·i·cal** \-ikəl\ *adj* —**cyn·i·cism** \-ə,sizəm\ *n*
cy·no·sure \'sīnə,shur, 'sin-\ *n* : center of attraction
cy·press \'sīprəs\ *n* : evergreen tree related to the pines
cyst \'sist\ *n* : abnormal bodily sac —**cys·tic** \'sistik\ *adj*
czar \'zär\ *n* : ruler of Russia until 1917 —**czar·ist** *n or adj*

D

d \'dē\ *n, pl* **d's** *or* **ds** \'dēz\ : 4th letter of the alphabet
¹dab \'dab\ *n* : gentle touch or stroke ~ *vb* **-bb-** : touch or apply lightly

²dab *n* : small amount
dab·ble \'dabəl\ *vb* **-bled; -bling 1** : splash **2** : work without serious effort —**dab·bler** \-blər\ *n*
dachs·hund \'däks,hunt\ *n* : small dog with a long body and short legs
dad \'dad\ *n* : father
dad·dy \'dadē\ *n, pl* **-dies** : father
daf·fo·dil \'dafə,dil\ *n* : narcissus with trumpetlike flowers
daft \'daft\ *adj* : foolish —**daft·ness** *n*
dag·ger \'dagər\ *n* : knife for stabbing
dahl·ia \'dalyə, 'däl-\ *n* : tuberous herb with showy flowers
dai·ly \'dālē\ *adj* **1** : occurring, done, or used every day or every weekday **2** : computed in terms of one day ~ *n, pl* **-lies** : daily newspaper —**daily** *adv*
dain·ty \'dāntē\ *n, pl* **-ties** : something delicious ~ *adj* **-ti·er; -est** : delicately pretty —**dain·ti·ly** *adv* —**dain·ti·ness** *n*
dairy \'darē\ *n, pl* **-ies** : farm that produces or company that processes milk —**dairy-maid** *n* —**dairy·man** \-mən, -,man\ *n*
da·is \'dāəs\ *n* : raised platform (as for a speaker)
dai·sy \'dāzē\ *n, pl* **-sies** : tall leafy-stemmed plant bearing showy flowers
dale \'dāl\ *n* : valley
dal·ly \'dalē\ *vb* **-lied; -ly·ing 1** : flirt **2** : dawdle —**dal·li·ance** \-əns\ *n*
dal·ma·tian \dal'māshən\ *n* : large dog having a spotted white coat
¹dam \'dam\ *n* : female parent of a domestic animal
²dam *n* : barrier to hold back water —**dam** *vb*
dam·age \'damij\ *n* **1** : loss or harm due to injury **2** *pl* : compensation for loss or injury ~ *vb* **-aged; -ag·ing** : do damage to
dam·ask \'daməsk\ *n* : firm lustrous figured fabric
dame \'dām\ *n* : woman of rank or authority
damn \'dam\ *vb* **1** : condemn to hell **2** : curse —**damn·able** \-nəbəl\ *adj* —**dam·na·tion** \dam'nāshən\ *n* —**damned** *adj*
damp \'damp\ *n* : moisture ~ *vb* **1** : reduce the draft in **2** : restrain **3** : moisten ~ *adj* : moist —**damp·ness** *n*
damp·en \'dampən\ *vb* **1** : diminish in activity or vigor **2** : make or become damp
damp·er \'dampər\ *n* : movable plate to regulate a flue draft
dam·sel \'damzəl\ *n* : young woman
dance \'dans\ *vb* **danced; danc·ing** : move rhythmically to music ~ *n* : act of dancing or a gathering for dancing —**danc·er** *n*
dan·de·li·on \'dandə,līən\ *n* : common yellow-flowered herb
dan·der \'dandər\ *n* : temper
dan·druff \'dandrəf\ *n* : whitish thin dry scales of skin on the scalp
dan·dy \'dandē\ *n, pl* **-dies 1** : man too concerned with clothes **2** : something excellent ~ *adj* **-di·er; -est** : very good
dan·ger \'dānjər\ *n* **1** : exposure to injury or evil **2** : something that may cause injury —**dan·ger·ous** \'dānjərəs\ *adj*
dan·gle \'daŋgəl\ *vb* **-gled; -gling 1** : hang and swing freely **2** : be left without support or connection **3** : allow or cause to hang **4** : offer as an inducement
dank \'daŋk\ *adj* : unpleasantly damp
dap·per \'dapər\ *adj* : neat and stylishly dressed
dap·ple \'dapəl\ *vb* **-pled; -pling** : mark with colored spots
dare \'dar\ *vb* **dared; dar·ing 1** : have sufficient courage **2** : urge or provoke to contend —**dare** *n* —**dar·ing** \'dariŋ\ *n or adj*
dare·dev·il *n* : recklessly bold person
dark \'därk\ *adj* **1** : having little or no light **2** : not light in color **3** : gloomy ~ *n* : absence of light —**dark·en** \-ən\ *vb* —**dark·ly** *adv* —**dark·ness** *n*
dar·ling \'därliŋ\ *n* **1** : beloved **2** : favorite ~ *adj* **1** : dearly loved **2** : very pleasing
darn \'därn\ *vb* : mend with interlacing stitches —**darn·er** *n*
dart \'därt\ *n* **1** : small pointed missile **2** *pl* : game of throwing darts at a target **3** : tapering fold in a garment **4** : quick movement ~ *vb* : move suddenly or rapidly
dash \'dash\ *vb* **1** : smash **2** : knock or hurl violently **3** : ruin **4** : perform or finish hastily **5** : move quickly ~ *n* **1** : sudden burst, splash, or stroke **2** : punctuation mark — **3** : tiny amount **4** : showiness or liveliness **5** : sudden rush **6** : short race **7** : dashboard
dash·board *n* : instrument panel
dash·ing \'dashiŋ\ *adj* : dapper and charming
das·tard \'dastərd\ *n* : one who sneakingly commits malicious acts
das·tard·ly \-lē\ *adj* : base or malicious
da·ta \'dātə, 'dat-, 'dät-\ *n sing or pl* : factual information
da·ta·base \-,bās\ *n* : data organized for computer search
¹date \'dāt\ *n* : edible fruit of a palm

²date *n* **1** : day, month, or year when something is done or made **2** : historical time period **3** : social engagement or the person one goes out with ~ *vb* **dat·ed; dat·ing 1** : determine or record the date of **2** : have a date with **3** : originate —**to date** : up to now
dat·ed \-əd\ *adj* : old-fashioned
da·tum \'dātəm, 'dat-, 'dät-\ *n, pl* **-ta** \-ə\ *or* **-tums** : piece of data
daub \'dob\ *vb* : smear ~ *n* : something daubed on —**daub·er** *n*
daugh·ter \'dotər\ *n* : human female offspring
daugh·ter-in-law *n, pl* **daughters-in- law** : wife of one's son
daunt \'dont\ *vb* : lessen the courage of
daunt·less \-ləs\ *adj* : fearless
dav·en·port \'davən,pōrt\ *n* : sofa
daw·dle \'dodəl\ *vb* **-dled; -dling 1** : waste time **2** : loiter
dawn \'don\ *vb* **1** : grow light as the sun rises **2** : begin to appear, develop, or be understood ~ *n* : first appearance (as of daylight)
day \'dā\ *n* **1** : period of light between one night and the next **2** : 24 hours **3** : specified date **4** : particular time or age **5** : period of work for a day —**day·light** *n* —**day·time** *n*
day·break *n* : dawn
day·dream *n* : fantasy of wish fulfillment —**daydream** *vb*
daylight saving time *n* : time one hour ahead of standard time
daze \'dāz\ *vb* **dazed; daz·ing 1** : stun by a blow **2** : dazzle —**daze** *n*
daz·zle \'dazəl\ *vb* **-zled; -zling 1** : overpower with light **2** : impress greatly —**dazzle** *n*
DDT \,dē,dē'tē\ *n* : long-lasting insecticide
dea·con \'dēkən\ *n* : subordinate church officer
dea·con·ess \'dēkənəs\ *n* : woman who assists in church ministry
dead \'ded\ *adj* **1** : lifeless **2** : unresponsive or inactive **3** : exhausted **4** : obsolete **5** : precise ~ *n, pl* **dead 1** : one that is dead —usu. with the **2** : most lifeless time ~ *adv* **1** : completely **2** : directly —**dead·en** \'dedən\ *vb*
dead·beat *n* : one who will not pay debts
dead end *n* : end of a street with no exit —**dead-end** *adj*
dead heat *n* : tie in a contest
dead·line *n* : time by which something must be finished
dead·lock *n* : struggle that neither side can win —**deadlock** *vb*
dead·ly \'dedlē\ *adj* **-li·er; -est 1** : capable of causing death **2** : very accurate **3** : fatal to spiritual progress **4** : suggestive of death **5** : very great ~ *adv* : extremely —**dead·li·ness** *n*
dead·pan *adj* : expressionless —**deadpan** *n or adv or adj*
dead·wood *n* : something useless
deaf \'def\ *adj* : unable or unwilling to hear —**deaf·en** \-ən\ *vb* —**deaf·ness** *n*
deaf-mute *n* : deaf person unable to speak
deal \'dēl\ *n* **1** : indefinite quantity **2** : distribution of playing cards **3** : negotiation or agreement **4** : treatment received **5** : bargain ~ *vb* **dealt** \'delt\; **deal·ing** \'dēliŋ\ **1** : distribute playing cards **2** : be concerned with **3** : administer or deliver **4** : take action **5** : sell **6** : reach a state of acceptance —**deal·er** *n* —**deal·ing** *n*
dean \'dēn\ *n* **1** : head of a group of clergy members **2** : university or school administrator **3** : senior member
dear \'dir\ *adj* **1** : highly valued or loved **2** : expensive ~ *n* : loved one —**dear·ly** *adv* —**dear·ness** *n*
dearth \'dərth\ *n* : scarcity
death \'deth\ *n* **1** : end of life **2** : cause of loss of life **3** : state of being dead **4** : destruction or extinction —**death·less** *adj* —**death·ly** *adj or adv*
de·ba·cle \di'bäkəl, -'bakəl\ *n* : disaster or fiasco
de·bar \di'bär\ *vb* : bar from something
de·bark \-'bärk\ *vb* : disembark —**de·bar·ka·tion** \,dē,bär'käshən\ *n*
de·base \di'bās\ *vb* : disparage —**de·base·ment** *n*
de·bate \-'bāt\ *vb* **-bat·ed; -bat·ing** : discuss a question by argument —**de·bat·able** *adj* —**debate** *n* —**de·bat·er** *n*
de·bauch \-'boch\ *vb* : seduce or corrupt —**de·bauch·ery** \-ərē\ *n*
de·bil·i·tate \-'bilə,tāt\ *vb* **-tat·ed; -tat·ing** : make ill or weak
de·bil·i·ty \-'bilətē\ *n, pl* **-ties** : physical weakness
deb·it \'debət\ *n* : account entry of a payment or debt ~ *vb* : record as a debit
deb·o·nair \,debə'nar\ *adj* : suave
de·bris \də'brē, dā-; 'dā,brē\ *n, pl* **-bris** \-'brēz, -,brēz\ : remains of something destroyed
debt \'det\ *n* **1** : sin **2** : something owed **3** : state of owing —**debt·or** \-ər\ *n*

de•bunk \dē'bəŋk\ *vb* : expose as false
de•but \'dā,byü, dā'byü\ *n* **1** : first public appearance **2** : formal entrance into society **—debut** *vb* **—deb•u•tante** \'debyù,tänt\ *n*
de•cade \'dek,ād, -əd; de'kād\ *n* : 10 years
dec•a•dence \'dekədəns, di'kādəns\ *n* : deterioration **—dec•a•dent** \-ənt, -ənt\ *adj or n*
de•cal \'dē,kal, di'kal, 'dekəl\ *n* : picture or design for transfer from prepared paper
de•camp \di'kamp\ *vb* : depart suddenly
de•cant \di'kant\ *vb* : pour gently
de•cant•er \-ər\ *n* : ornamental bottle
de•cap•i•tate \di'kapə,tāt\ *vb* **-tat•ed; -tat•ing** : behead **—de•cap•i•ta•tion** \-,kapə'tāshən\ *n*
de•cay \di'kā\ *vb* **1** : decline in condition **2** : decompose **—decay** *n*
de•cease \-'sēs\ *n* : death **—decease** *vb*
de•ceit \-'sēt\ *n* **1** : deception **2** : dishonesty **—de•ceit•ful** \-fəl\ *adj* **—de•ceit•ful•ly** *adv* **—de•ceit•ful•ness** *n*
de•ceive \-'sēv\ *vb* **-ceived; -ceiv•ing** : trick or mislead **—de•ceiv•er** *n*
de•cel•er•ate \dē'selə,rāt\ *vb* **-at•ed; -at•ing** : slow down
De•cem•ber \di'sembər\ *n* : 12th month of the year having 31 days
de•cent \'dēsənt\ *adj* **1** : good, right, or just **2** : clothed **3** : not obscene **4** : fairly good **—de•cen•cy** \-ənsē\ *n* **—de•cent•ly** *adv*
de•cep•tion \di'sepshən\ *n* **1** : act or fact of deceiving **2** : fraud **—de•cep•tive** \-'septiv\ *adj* **—de•cep•tive•ly** *adv* **—de•cep•tive•ness** *n*
de•cide \di'sīd\ *vb* **-cid•ed; -cid•ing** **1** : make a choice or judgment **2** : bring to a conclusion **3** : cause to decide
de•cid•ed *adj* **1** : unquestionable **2** : resolute **—de•cid•ed•ly** *adv*
de•cid•u•ous \di'sijəwəs\ *adj* : having leaves that fall annually
dec•i•mal \'desəməl\ *n* : fraction in which the denominator is a power of 10 expressed by a point **(decimal point)** placed at the left of the numerator **—decimal** *adj*
de•ci•pher \di'sīfər\ *vb* : make out the meaning of **—de•ci•pher•able** *adj*
de•ci•sion \-'sizhən\ *n* **1** : act or result of deciding **2** : determination
de•ci•sive \-'sīsiv\ *adj* **1** : having the power to decide **2** : conclusive **3** : showing determination **—de•ci•sive•ly** *adv* **—de•ci•sive•ness** *n*
deck \'dek\ *n* **1** : floor of a ship **2** : pack of playing cards ~ *vb* **1** : array or dress up **2** : knock down
de•claim \di'klām\ *vb* : speak loudly or impressively **—dec•la•ma•tion** \,dekləmāshən\ *n*
de•clare \di'klar\ *vb* **-clared; -clar•ing** **1** : make known formally **2** : state emphatically **—dec•la•ra•tion** \,deklə'rāshən\ *n* **—de•clar•a•tive** \di'klarətiv\ *adj* **—de•clar•a•to•ry** \di'klarə,tōrē\ *adj* **—de•clar•er** *n*
de•clen•sion \di'klenchən\ *n* : inflectional forms of a noun, pronoun, or adjective
de•cline \di'klīn\ *vb* **-clined; -clin•ing** **1** : turn or slope downward **2** : wane **3** : refuse to accept **4** : inflect ~ *n* **1** : gradual wasting away **2** : change to a lower state or level **3** : a descending slope **—dec•li•na•tion** \,deklə'nāshən\ *n*
de•code \dē'kōd\ *vb* : decipher (a coded message) **—de•cod•er** *n*
de•com•mis•sion \,dēkə'mishən\ *vb* : remove from service
de•com•pose \,dēkəm'pōz\ *vb* **1** : separate into parts **2** : decay **—de•com•po•si•tion** \dē,kämpə'zishən\ *n*
de•con•ges•tant \,dēkən'jestənt\ *n* : agent that relieves congestion
de•cor, dé•cor \dā'kòr, 'dā,kòr\ *n* : room design or decoration
dec•o•rate \'dekə,rāt\ *vb* **-rat•ed; -rat•ing** **1** : add something attractive to **2** : honor with a medal **—dec•o•ra•tion** \,dekə'rāshən\ *n* **—dec•o•ra•tive** \'dekərətiv\ *adj* **—dec•o•ra•tor** \'dekə,rātər\ *n*
de•co•rum \di'kōrəm\ *n* : proper behavior **—dec•o•rous** \'dekərəs, di'kōrəs\ *adj*
de•coy \'dē,kòi, di'-\ *n* : something that tempts or draws attention from another ~ *vb* : tempt
de•crease \di'krēs\ *vb* **-creased; -creas•ing** : grow or cause to grow less **—decrease** \'dē,krēs\ *n*
de•cree \di'krē\ *n* : official order **—decree** *vb*
de•crep•it \di'krepət\ *adj* : impaired by age
de•cre•scen•do \,dākrə'shendō\ *adv or adj* : with a decrease in volume
de•cry \di'krī\ *vb* : express strong disapproval of
ded•i•cate \'dedi,kāt\ *vb* **-cat•ed; -cat•ing** **1** : set apart for a purpose (as honor or worship) **2** : address to someone as a compliment **—ded•i•ca•tion** \,dedi'kāshən\ *n* **—ded•i•ca•to•ry** \'dedikə,tōrē\ *adj*
de•duce \di'düs, -'dyüs\ *vb* **-duced; -duc•ing** : derive by reasoning **—de•duc•ible** *adj*
de•duct \-'dəkt\ *vb* : subtract **—de•duct•ible** *adj*
de•duc•tion \-'dəkshən\ *n* **1** : subtraction **2** : reasoned conclusion **—de•duc•tive** \-'dəktiv\ *adj*
deed \'dēd\ *n* **1** : exploit **2** : document showing ownership ~ *vb* : convey by deed
deem \'dēm\ *vb* : think
deep \'dēp\ *adj* **1** : extending far or a specified distance down, back, within, or outward **2** : occupied **3** : dark and rich in color **4** : low in tone ~ *adv* **1** : deeply **2** : far along in time ~ *n* : deep place **—deep•en** \'dēpən\ *vb* **—deep•ly** *adv*
deep–seat•ed \-'sētəd\ *adj* : firmly established
deer \'dir\ *n, pl* **deer** : ruminant mammal with antlers in the male **—deer•skin** *n*
de•face \di'fās\ *vb* : mar the surface of **—de•face•ment** *n* **—de•fac•er** *n*
de•fame \di'fām\ *vb* **-famed; -fam•ing** : injure the reputation of **—def•a•ma•tion** \,defə'māshən\ *n* **—de•fam•a•to•ry** \di'famə,tōrē\ *adj*
de•fault \di'fòlt\ *n* : failure in a duty **—default** *vb* **—de•fault•er** *n*
de•feat \di'fēt\ *vb* **1** : frustrate **2** : win victory over ~ *n* : loss of a battle or contest
def•e•cate \'defi,kāt\ *vb* **-cat•ed; -cat•ing** : discharge feces from the bowels **—def•e•ca•tion** \,defi'kāshən\ *n*
de•fect \'dē,fekt, di'fekt\ *n* : imperfection ~ \di'-\ *vb* : desert **—de•fec•tion** \-'fekshən\ *n* **—de•fec•tor** \-'fektər\ *n*
de•fec•tive \di'fektiv\ *adj* : faulty or deficient **—defective** *n*
de•fend \-'fend\ *vb* **1** : protect from danger or harm **2** : take the side of **—de•fend•er** *n*
de•fen•dant \-'fendənt\ *n* : person charged or sued in a court
de•fense \-'fens\ *n* **1** : act of defending **2** : something that defends **3** : party, group, or team that opposes another **—de•fense•less** *adj* **—de•fen•si•ble** *adj* **—de•fen•sive** *adj or n*
1**de•fer** \di'fər\ *vb* **-rr-** : postpone **—de•fer•ment** \di'fərmənt\ *n* **—de•fer•ra•ble** \-əbəl\ *adj*
2**defer** *vb* **-rr-** : yield to the opinion or wishes of another **—def•er•ence** \'defrəns\ *n* **—def•er•en•tial** \,defə'renchəl\ *adj*
de•fi•ance \di'fīəns\ *n* : disposition to resist **—de•fi•ant** \-ənt\ *adj*
de•fi•cient \di'fishənt\ *adj* **1** : lacking something necessary **2** : not up to standard **—de•fi•cien•cy** \-'fishənsē\ *n*
def•i•cit \'defəsət\ *n* : shortage esp. in money
de•file \di'fīl\ *vb* **-filed; -fil•ing** **1** : make filthy or corrupt **2** : profane or dishonor **—de•file•ment** *n*
de•fine \di'fīn\ *vb* **-fined; -fin•ing** **1** : fix or mark the limits of **2** : clarify in outline **3** : set forth the meaning of **—de•fin•able** *adj* **—de•fin•ably** *adv* **—de•fin•er** *n* **—def•i•ni•tion** \,defə'nishən\ *n*
def•i•nite \'defənət\ *adj* **1** : having distinct limits **2** : clear in meaning, intent, or identity **3** : typically designating an identified or immediately identifiable person or thing **—def•i•nite•ly** *adv*
de•fin•i•tive \di'finətiv\ *adj* **1** : conclusive **2** : authoritative
de•flate \di'flāt\ *vb* **-flat•ed; -flat•ing** **1** : release air or gas from **2** : reduce **—de•fla•tion** \-'flāshən\ *n*
de•flect \-'flekt\ *vb* : turn aside **—de•flec•tion** \-'flekshən\ *n*
de•fog \-'fòg, -'fäg\ *vb* : remove condensed moisture from **—de•fog•ger** *n*
de•fo•li•ate \dē'fōlē,āt\ *vb* **-at•ed; -at•ing** : deprive of leaves esp. prematurely **—de•fo•li•ant** \-lēənt\ *n* **—de•fo•li•a•tion** \-,fōlē'āshən\ *n*
de•form \di'fòrm\ *vb* **1** : distort **2** : disfigure **—de•for•ma•tion** \,dē,fòr'māshən, ,defər-\ *n* **—de•for•mi•ty** \di'fòrmətē\ *n*
de•fraud \di'fròd\ *vb* : cheat
de•fray \-'frā\ *vb* : pay
de•frost \-'fròst\ *vb* **1** : thaw out **2** : free from ice **—de•frost•er** *n*
deft \'deft\ *adj* : quick and skillful **—deft•ly** *adv* **—deft•ness** *n*
de•funct \di'fəŋkt\ *adj* : dead
de•fy \-'fī\ *vb* **-fied; -fy•ing** **1** : challenge **2** : boldly refuse to obey
de•gen•er•ate \di'jenərət\ *adj* : degraded or corrupt ~ *n* : degenerate person ~ \-ə,rāt\ *vb* : become degenerate **—de•gen•er•a•cy** \-ərəsē\ *n* **—de•gen•er•a•tion** \-,jenə'rāshən\ *n* **—de•gen•er•a•tive** \-'jenə,rātiv\ *adj*
de•grade \di'grād\ *vb* **1** : reduce from a higher to a lower rank or degree **2** : debase **3** : decompose **—de•grad•able** \-əbəl\ *adj* **—deg•ra•da•tion** \,degrə'dāshən\ *n*
de•gree \di'grē\ *n* **1** : step in a series **2** : extent, intensity, or scope **3** : title given to a college graduate **4** : a 360th part of the circumference of a circle **5** : unit for measuring temperature
de•hy•drate \dē'hī,drāt\ *vb* **1** : remove water from **2** : lose liquid **—de•hy•dra•tion** \,dēhī'drāshən\ *n*
de•i•fy \'dēə,fī, 'dā-\ *vb* **-fied; -fy•ing** : make a god of **—de•i•fi•ca•tion** \,dēəfə'kāshən, ,dā-\ *n*
deign \'dān\ *vb* : condescend
de•i•ty \'dēətē, 'dā-\ *n, pl* **-ties** **1** *cap* : God **2** : a god or goddess
de•ject•ed \di'jektəd\ *adj* : sad **—de•jec•tion** \-shən\ *n*
de•lay \di'lā\ *n* : a putting off of something ~ *vb* **1** : postpone **2** : stop or hinder for a time
de•lec•ta•ble \di'lektəbəl\ *adj* : delicious
del•e•gate \'deligət, -,gāt\ *n* : representative ~ \-,gāt\ *vb* **-gat•ed; -gat•ing** **1** : entrust to another **2** : appoint as one's delegate **—del•e•ga•tion** \,deli'gāshən\ *n*
de•lete \di'lēt\ *vb* **-let•ed; -let•ing** : eliminate something written **—de•le•tion** \-'lēshən\ *n*
del•e•te•ri•ous \,delə'tirēəs\ *adj* : harmful
de•lib•er•ate \di'libərət\ *adj* **1** : determined after careful thought **2** : intentional **3** : not hurried ~ \-ə,rāt\ *vb* **-at•ed; -at•ing** : consider carefully **—de•lib•er•ate•ly** *adv* **—de•lib•er•ate•ness** *n* **—de•lib•er•a•tion** \-,libə'rāshən\ *n* **—de•lib•er•a•tive** \-'libə,rātiv, -rət-\ *adj*
del•i•ca•cy \'delikəsē\ *n, pl* **-cies** **1** : something special and pleasing to eat **2** : fineness **3** : frailty
del•i•cate \'delikət\ *adj* **1** : subtly pleasing to the senses **2** : dainty and charming **3** : sensitive or fragile **4** : requiring fine skill or tact **—del•i•cate•ly** *adv*
del•i•ca•tes•sen \,delikə'tesən\ *n* : store that sells ready-to-eat food
de•li•cious \di'lishəs\ *adj* : very pleasing esp. in taste or aroma **—de•li•cious•ly** *adv* **—de•li•cious•ness** *n*
de•light \di'līt\ *n* **1** : great pleasure **2** : source of great pleasure ~ *vb* **1** : take great pleasure **2** : satisfy greatly **—de•light•ful** \-fəl\ *adj* **—de•light•ful•ly** *adv*
de•lin•eate \di'linē,āt\ *vb* **-eat•ed; -eat•ing** : sketch or portray **—de•lin•ea•tion** \-,linē'āshən\ *n*
de•lin•quent \-'liŋkwənt\ *n* : delinquent person ~ *adj* **1** : violating duty or law **2** : overdue in payment **—de•lin•quen•cy** \-kwənsē\ *n*
de•lir•i•um \di'lirēəm\ *n* : mental disturbance **—de•lir•i•ous** \-ēəs\ *adj*
de•liv•er \di'livər\ *vb* **1** : set free **2** : hand over **3** : assist in birth **4** : say or speak **5** : send to an intended destination **—de•liv•er•ance** \-ərəns\ *n* **—de•liv•er•er** *n* **—de•liv•ery** \-ərē\ *n*
dell \'del\ *n* : small secluded valley
del•ta \'deltə\ *n* : triangle of land at the mouth of a river
de•lude \di'lüd\ *vb* **-lud•ed; -lud•ing** : mislead or deceive
del•uge \'delyüj\ *n* **1** : flood **2** : drenching rain ~ *vb* **-uged; -ug•ing** **1** : flood **2** : overwhelm
de•lu•sion \di'lüzhən\ *n* : false belief
de•luxe \di'lùks, -'ləks, -'lüks\ *adj* : very luxurious or elegant
delve \'delv\ *vb* **delved; delv•ing** **1** : dig **2** : seek information in records
dem•a•gogue, dem•a•gog \'demə,gäg\ *n* : politician who appeals to emotion and prejudice **—dem•a•gogu•ery** \-,gägərē\ *n* **—dem•a•gogy** \-,gägē, -,gäjē\ *n*
de•mand \di'mand\ *n* **1** : act of demanding **2** : something claimed as due **3** : ability and desire to buy **4** : urgent need ~ *vb* **1** : ask for with authority **2** : require
de•mar•cate \di'mär,kāt, 'dē,mär-\ *vb* **-cat•ed; -cat•ing** : mark the limits of **—de•mar•ca•tion** \,dē,mär'kāshən\ *n*
de•mean \di'mēn\ *vb* : degrade
de•mean•or \-'mēnər\ *n* : behavior
de•ment•ed \-'mentəd\ *adj* : crazy
de•mer•it \-'merət\ *n* : mark given an offender
demi•god \'demi,gäd\ *n* : mythological being less powerful than a god
de•mise \di'mīz\ *n* **1** : death **2** : loss of status
demi•tasse \'demi,tas\ *n* : small cup of coffee
de•mo•bi•lize \di'mōbə,līz, dē-\ *vb* : disband from military service **—de•mo•bi•li•za•tion** \-,mōbələ'zāshən\ *n*
de•moc•ra•cy \di'mäkrəsē\ *n, pl* **-cies** **1** : government in which the supreme power is held by the people **2** : political unit with democratic government
dem•o•crat \'demə,krat\ *n* : adherent of democracy
dem•o•crat•ic \,demə'kratik\ *adj* : relating to or favoring democracy **—dem•o•crat•i•cal•ly** \-tiklē\ *adv* **—de•moc•ra•tize** \di'mäkrə,tīz\ *vb*
de•mol•ish \di'mälish\ *vb* **1** : tear down or smash **2** : put an end to **—de•mo•li•tion** \,demə'lishən, ,dē-\ *n*
de•mon \'dēmən\ *n* : evil spirit **—de•mon•ic** \di'mänik\ *adj*
dem•on•strate \'demən,strāt\ *vb* **-strat•ed; -strat•ing** **1** : show clearly or publicly **2** : prove **3** : explain **—de•mon•stra•ble** \di'mänstrəbəl\ *adj* **—de•mon•stra•bly** \-blē\ *adv* **—dem•on•stra•tion** \,demən'strāshən\ *n* **—de•mon•stra•tive** \di'mänstrətiv\ *adj or n* **—dem•on•stra•tor** \'demən,strātər\ *n*
de•mor•al•ize \di'mòrə,līz\ *vb* : destroy the enthusiasm of
de•mote \di'mōt\ *vb* **-mot•ed; -mot•ing** : reduce to a lower rank **—de•mo•tion** \-'mōshən\ *n*
de•mur \di'mər\ *vb* **-rr-** : object **—demur** *n*
de•mure \di'myùr\ *adj* : modest **—de•mure•ly** *adv*
den \'den\ *n* **1** : animal's shelter **2** : hiding place **3** : cozy private little room
de•na•ture \dē'nāchər\ *vb* **-tured; -tur•ing** : make (alcohol) unfit for drinking
de•ni•al \di'nīəl\ *n* : rejection of a request or of the validity of a statement
den•i•grate \'deni,grāt\ *vb* **-grat•ed; -grat•ing** : speak ill of
den•im \'denəm\ *n* **1** : durable twilled cotton fabric **2** *pl* : pants of denim
den•i•zen \'denəzən\ *n* : inhabitant
de•nom•i•na•tion \di,nämə'nāshən\ *n* **1** : religious body **2** : value or size in a series **—de•nom•i•na•tion•al** \-shənəl\ *adj*
de•nom•i•na•tor \-'nämə,nātər\ *n* : part of a fraction below the line
de•note \di'nōt\ *vb* **1** : mark out plainly **2** : mean **—de•no•ta•tion** \,dēnō'tāshən\ *n* **—de•no•ta•tive** \'dēnō,tātiv, di'nōtətiv\ *adj*
de•noue•ment \,dā,nü'män\ *n* : final outcome (as of a drama)
de•nounce \di'naùns\ *vb* **-nounced; -nounc•ing** **1** : pronounce blameworthy or evil **2** : inform against
dense \'dens\ *adj* **dens•er; -est** **1** : thick, compact, or crowded **2** : stupid **—dense•ly** *adv* **—dense•ness** *n* **—den•si•ty** \'densətē\ *n*
dent \'dent\ *n* : small depression **—dent** *vb*
den•tal \'dentəl\ *adj* : relating to teeth or dentistry
den•ti•frice \'dentəfrəs\ *n* : preparation for cleaning teeth
den•tin \'dentən\, **den•tine** \'den,tēn, ,den'-\ *n* : bonelike component of teeth
den•tist \'dentist\ *n* : one who cares for and replaces teeth **—den•tist•ry** *n*
den•ture \'denchər\ *n* : artificial teeth
de•nude \di'nüd, -'nyüd\ *vb* **-nud•ed; -nud•ing** : strip of covering
de•nun•ci•a•tion \di,nənsē'āshən\ *n* : act of denouncing
de•ny \-'nī\ *vb* **-nied; -ny•ing** **1** : declare untrue **2** : disavow **3** : refuse to grant
de•odor•ant \dē'ōdərənt\ *n* : preparation to prevent unpleasant odors **—de•odor•ize** \-,rīz\ *vb*
de•part \di'pärt\ *vb* **1** : go away or away from **2** : die **—de•par•ture** \-'pärchər\ *n*
de•part•ment \di'pärtmənt\ *n* **1** : area of responsibility or interest **2** : functional division **—de•part•men•tal** \di,pärt'mentəl, ,dē-\ *adj*
de•pend \di'pend\ *vb* **1** : rely for support **2** : be determined by or based on something else **—de•pend•abil•i•ty** \-,pendə'bilətē\ *n* **—de•pend•able** *adj* **—de•pen•dence** \di'pendəns\ *n* **—de•pen•den•cy** \-dənsē\ *n* **—de•pen•dent** \-ənt\ *adj or n*
de•pict \di'pikt\ *vb* : show by or as if by a picture **—de•pic•tion** \-'pikshən\ *n*
de•plete \di'plēt\ *vb* **-plet•ed; -plet•ing** : use up resources of **—de•ple•tion** \-'plēshən\ *n*
de•plore \-'plōr\ *vb* **-plored; -plor•ing** : regret strongly **—de•plor•able** \-əbəl\ *adj*
de•ploy \-'plòi\ *vb* : spread out for battle **—de•ploy•ment** \-mənt\ *n*
de•port \di'pōrt\ *vb* **1** : behave **2** : send out of the country **—de•por•ta•tion** \,dē,pōr'tāshən\ *n* **—de•port•ment** \di'pōrtmənt\ *n*
de•pose \-'pōz\ *vb* **-posed; -pos•ing** **1** : remove (a ruler) from office **2** : testify **—de•po•si•tion** \,depə'zishən, ,dē-\ *n*
de•pos•it \di'päzət\ *vb* **-it•ed; -it•ing** : place esp. for safekeeping ~ *n* **1** : state of being deposited **2** : something deposited **3** : act of depositing **4** : natural accumulation **—de•pos•i•tor** \-'päzətər\ *n*
de•pos•i•to•ry \di'päzə,tōrē\ *n, pl* **-ries** : place for deposit
de•pot \1 *usu* 'depō, 2 *usu* 'dēp-\ *n* **1** : place for storage **2** : bus or railroad station
de•prave \di'prāv\ *vb* **-praved; -prav•ing** : corrupt morally **—de•praved** *adj* **—de•prav•i•ty** \-'pravətē\ *n*
dep•re•cate \'depri,kāt\ *vb* **-cat•ed; -cat•ing** **1** : express disapproval of **2** : belittle **—dep•re•ca•tion** \,depri'kāshən\ *n* **—dep•re•ca•to•ry** \'deprikə,tōrē\ *adj*
de•pre•ci•ate \di'prēshē,āt\ *vb* **-at•ed; -at•ing** **1** : lessen in value **2** : belittle **—de•pre•ci•a•tion** \-,prēshē'āshən\ *n*
dep•re•da•tion \,deprə'dāshən\ *n* : a laying waste or plundering **—dep•re•date** \'deprə,dāt\ *vb*

de•press \di'pres\ *vb* **1 :** press down **2 :** lessen the activity or force of **3 :** discourage **4 :** decrease the market value of **—de•pres•sant** \-ənt\ *n or adj* **—de•pressed** *adj* **—de•pres•sive** \-iv\ *adj or n* **—de•pres•sor** \-ər\ *n*

de•pres•sion \di'preshən\ *n* **1 :** act of depressing or state of being depressed **2 :** depressed place **3 :** period of low economic activity

de•prive \-'prīv\ *vb* **-prived; -priv•ing :** take or keep something away from **—de•pri•va•tion** \ˌdeprə'vāshən\ *n*

depth \'depth\ *n, pl* **depths 1 :** something that is deep **2 :** distance down from a surface **3 :** distance from front to back **4 :** quality of being deep

dep•u•ta•tion \ˌdepyə'tāshən\ *n* **:** delegation

dep•u•ty \'depyətē\ *n, pl* **-ties :** person appointed to act for another **—dep•u•tize** \-yəˌtīz\ *vb*

de•rail \di'rāl\ *vb* **:** leave the rails **—de•rail•ment** *n*

de•range \-'rānj\ *vb* **-ranged; -rang•ing 1 :** disarrange or upset **2 :** make insane **—de•range•ment** *n*

der•by \'dərbē, *Brit* 'där-\ *n, pl* **-bies 1 :** horse race **2 :** stiff felt hat with dome-shaped crown

de•reg•u•late \dē'regyuˌlāt\ *vb* **:** remove restrictions on **—de•reg•u•la•tion** \-ˌregyu'lāshən\ *n*

der•e•lict \'derəˌlikt\ *adj* **1 :** abandoned **2 :** negligent ~ *n* **1 :** something abandoned **2 :** bum **—der•e•lic•tion** \ˌderə'likshən\ *n*

de•ride \di'rīd\ *vb* **-rid•ed; -rid•ing :** make fun of **—de•ri•sion** \-'rizhən\ *n* **—de•ri•sive** \-'rīsiv\ *adj* **—de•ri•sive•ly** *adv* **—de•ri•sive•ness** *n*

de•rive \di'rīv\ *vb* **-rived; -riv•ing 1 :** obtain from a source or parent **2 :** come from a certain source **3 :** infer or deduce **—der•i•va•tion** \ˌderə'vāshən\ *n* **—de•riv•a•tive** \di'rivətiv\ *adj or n*

der•ma•tol•o•gy \ˌdərmə'täləjē\ *n* **:** study of the skin and its disorders **—der•ma•tol•o•gist** \-jist\ *n*

de•ro•ga•tive \di'rägətiv\ *adj* **:** derogatory

de•rog•a•to•ry \di'rägəˌtōrē\ *adj* **:** intended to lower the reputation

der•rick \'derik\ *n* **1 :** hoisting apparatus **2 :** framework over an oil well

de•scend \di'send\ *vb* **1 :** move or climb down **2 :** derive **3 :** extend downward **4 :** appear suddenly (as in an attack) **—de•scen•dant, de•scen•dent** \-ənt\ *adj or n* **—de•scent** \di'sent\ *n*

de•scribe \-'skrīb\ *vb* **-scribed; -scrib•ing :** represent in words **—de•scrib•able** *adj* **—de•scrip•tion** \-'skripshən\ *n* **—de•scrip•tive** \-'skriptiv\ *adj*

de•scry \di'skrī\ *vb* **-scried; -scry•ing :** catch sight of

des•e•crate \'desiˌkrāt\ *vb* **-crat•ed; -crat•ing :** treat (something sacred) with disrespect **—des•e•cra•tion** \ˌdesi'krāshən\ *n*

de•seg•re•gate \dē'segrəˌgāt\ *vb* **:** eliminate esp. racial segregation in **—de•seg•re•ga•tion** *n*

1des•ert \'dezərt\ *n* **:** dry barren region **—desert** *adj*

2de•sert \di'zərt\ *n* **:** what one deserves

3de•sert \di'zərt\ *vb* **:** abandon **—de•sert•er** *n* **—de•ser•tion** \-'zərshən\ *n*

de•serve \-'zərv\ *vb* **-served; -serv•ing :** be worthy of

des•ic•cate \'desiˌkāt\ *vb* **-cat•ed; -cat•ing :** dehydrate **—des•ic•ca•tion** \ˌdesi'kāshən\ *n*

de•sign \di'zīn\ *vb* **1 :** create and work out the details of **2 :** make a pattern or sketch of ~ *n* **1 :** mental project or plan **2 :** purpose **3 :** preliminary sketch **4 :** underlying arrangement of elements **5 :** decorative pattern **—de•sign•er** *n*

des•ig•nate \'dezigˌnāt\ *vb* **-nat•ed; -nat•ing 1 :** indicate, specify, or name **2 :** appoint **—des•ig•na•tion** \ˌdezig'nāshən\ *n*

de•sire \di'zīr\ *vb* **-sired; -sir•ing 1 :** feel desire for **2 :** request ~ *n* **1 :** strong conscious impulse to have, be, or do something **2 :** something desired **—de•sir•abil•i•ty** \-ˌzīrə'bilətē\ *n* **—de•sir•able** \-'zīrəbəl\ *adj* **—de•sir•able•ness** *n* **—de•sir•ous** \-'zīrəs\ *adj*

de•sist \di'zist, -'sist\ *vb* **:** stop

desk \'desk\ *n* **:** table esp. for writing and reading

des•o•late \'desələt, 'dez-\ *adj* **1 :** lifeless **2 :** disconsolate ~ \-ˌlāt\ *vb* **-lat•ed; -lat•ing :** lay waste **—des•o•la•tion** \ˌdesə'lāshən, ˌdez-\ *n*

de•spair \di'spar\ *vb* **:** lose all hope ~ *n* **:** loss of hope

des•per•a•do \ˌdespə'rädō, -'rād-\ *n, pl* **-does** *or* **-dos :** desperate criminal

des•per•ate \'desprət\ *adj* **1 :** hopeless **2 :** rash **3 :** extremely intense **—des•per•ate•ly** *adv* **—des•per•a•tion** \ˌdespə'rāshən\ *n*

de•spi•ca•ble \di'spikəbel, 'despik-\ *adj* **:** deserving scorn

de•spise \di'spīz\ *vb* **-spised; -spis•ing :** feel contempt for

de•spite \-'spīt\ *prep* **:** in spite of

de•spoil \-'spȯil\ *vb* **:** strip of possessions or value

de•spon•den•cy \-'spändənsē\ *n* **:** dejection **—de•spon•dent** \-dənt\ *adj*

des•pot \'despət, -ˌpät\ *n* **:** tyrant **—des•pot•ic** \des'pätik\ *adj* **—des•po•tism** \'despəˌtizəm\ *n*

des•sert \di'zərt\ *n* **:** sweet food, fruit, or cheese ending a meal

des•ti•na•tion \ˌdestə'nāshən\ *n* **:** place where something or someone is going

des•tine \'destən\ *vb* **-tined; -tin•ing 1 :** designate, assign, or determine in advance **2 :** direct

des•ti•ny \'destənē\ *n, pl* **-nies :** that which is to happen in the future

des•ti•tute \'destəˌtüt, -ˌtyüt\ *adj* **1 :** lacking something **2 :** very poor **—des•ti•tu•tion** \ˌdestə'tüshən, -'tyü-\ *n*

de•stroy \di'strȯi\ *vb* **:** kill or put an end to

de•stroy•er \-'strȯiər\ *n* **1 :** one that destroys **2 :** small speedy warship

de•struc•tion \-'strəkshən\ *n* **1 :** action of destroying **2 :** ruin **—de•struc•ti•bil•i•ty** \-ˌstrəktə'bilətē\ *n* **—de•struc•ti•ble** \-'strəktəbəl\ *adj* **—de•struc•tive** \-'strəktiv\ *adj*

des•ul•to•ry \'desəlˌtōrē\ *adj* **:** aimless

de•tach \di'tach\ *vb* **:** separate

de•tached \-'tacht\ *adj* **1 :** separate **2 :** aloof or impartial

de•tach•ment \-'tachmənt\ *n* **1 :** separation **2 :** troops or ships on special service **3 :** aloofness **4 :** impartiality

de•tail \di'tāl, 'dēˌtāl\ *n* **:** small item or part ~ *vb* **:** give details of

de•tain \di'tān\ *vb* **1 :** hold in custody **2 :** delay

de•tect \di'tekt\ *vb* **:** discover **—de•tect•able** *adj* **—de•tec•tion** \-'tekshən\ *n* **—de•tec•tor** \-tər\ *n*

de•tec•tive \-'tektiv\ *n* **:** one who investigates crime

dé•tente \dā'tänt\ *n* **:** relaxation of tensions between nations

de•ten•tion \di'tenchən\ *n* **:** confinement

de•ter \-'tər\ *vb* **-rr- :** discourage or prevent **—de•ter•rence** \-əns\ *n* **—de•ter•rent** \-ənt\ *adj or n*

de•ter•gent \di'tərjənt\ *n* **:** cleansing agent

de•te•ri•o•rate \-'tirēəˌrāt\ *vb* **-rat•ed; -rat•ing :** make or become worse **—de•te•ri•o•ra•tion** \-ˌtirēə'rāshən\ *n*

de•ter•mi•na•tion \diˌtərmə'nāshən\ *n* **1 :** act of deciding or fixing **2 :** firm purpose

de•ter•mine \-'tərmən\ *vb* **-mined; -min•ing 1 :** decide on, establish, or settle **2 :** find out **3 :** bring about as a result

de•test \-'test\ *vb* **:** hate **—de•test•able** *adj* **—de•tes•ta•tion** \ˌdēˌtes'tāshən\ *n*

det•o•nate \'detənˌāt\ *vb* **-nat•ed; -nat•ing :** explode **—det•o•na•tion** \ˌdetən'āshən\ *n* **—det•o•na•tor** \'detənˌātər\ *n*

de•tour \'dēˌtu̇r\ *n* **:** temporary indirect route **—detour** *vb*

de•tract \di'trakt\ *vb* **:** take away **—de•trac•tion** \-'trakshən\ *n* **—de•trac•tor** \-'traktər\ *n*

det•ri•ment \'detrəmənt\ *n* **:** damage **—det•ri•men•tal** \ˌdetrə'mentəl\ *adj* **—det•ri•men•tal•ly** *adv*

deuce \'düs, 'dyüs\ *n* **1 :** 2 in cards or dice **2 :** tie in tennis **3 :** devil —used as an oath

deut•sche mark \'dȯichə-\ *n* **:** monetary unit of Germany

de•val•ue \dē'valˌyü\ *vb* **:** reduce the value of **—de•val•u•a•tion** *n*

dev•as•tate \'devəˌstāt\ *vb* **-tat•ed; -tat•ing :** ruin **—dev•as•ta•tion** \ˌdevə'stāshən\ *n*

de•vel•op \di'veləp\ *vb* **1 :** grow, increase, or evolve gradually **2 :** cause to grow, increase, or reach full potential **—de•vel•op•er** *n* **—de•vel•op•ment** *n* **—de•vel•op•men•tal** \-ˌveləp'mentəl\ *adj*

de•vi•ate \'dēvēˌāt\ *vb* **-at•ed; -at•ing :** change esp. from a course or standard **—de•vi•ant** \-vēənt\ *adj or n* **—de•vi•ate** \-vēət, -vēˌāt\ *n* **—de•vi•a•tion** \ˌdēvē'āshən\ *n*

de•vice \di'vīs\ *n* **1 :** specialized piece of equipment or tool **2 :** design

dev•il \'devəl\ *n* **1 :** personified supreme spirit of evil **2 :** demon **3 :** wicked person ~ *vb* **-iled** *or* **-illed; -il•ing** *or* **-il•ling 1 :** season highly **2 :** pester **—dev•il•ish** \'devəlish\ *adj* **—dev•il•ry** \'devəlrē\, **dev•il•try** \-trē\ *n*

de•vi•ous \'dēvēəs\ *adj* **:** tricky

de•vise \di'vīz\ *vb* **-vised; -vis•ing 1 :** invent **2 :** plot **3 :** give by will

de•void \-'vȯid\ *adj* **:** entirely lacking

de•vote \di'vōt\ *vb* **-vot•ed; -vot•ing :** set apart for a special purpose

de•vot•ed *adj* **:** faithful

dev•o•tee \ˌdevə'tē, -'tā\ *n* **:** ardent follower

de•vo•tion \di'vōshən\ *n* **1 :** prayer —usu. pl. **2 :** loyalty and dedication **—de•vo•tion•al** \-shənəl\ *adj*

de•vour \di'vau̇ər\ *vb* **:** consume ravenously **—de•vour•er** *n*

de•vout \-'vau̇t\ *adj* **1 :** devoted to religion **2 :** serious **—de•vout•ly** *adv* **—de•vout•ness** *n*

dew \'dü, 'dyü\ *n* **:** moisture condensed at night **—dew•drop** *n* **—dewy** *adj*

dex•ter•ous \'dekstrəs\ *adj* **:** skillful with the hands **—dex•ter•i•ty** \dek'sterətē\ *n* **—dex•ter•ous•ly** *adv*

dex•trose \'dekˌstrōs\ *n* **:** plant or blood sugar

di•a•be•tes \ˌdīə'bētēz, -'bētəs\ *n* **:** disorder in which the body has too little insulin and too much sugar **—di•a•bet•ic** \-'betik\ *adj or n*

di•a•bol•ic \-'bälik\, **di•a•bol•i•cal** \-ikəl\ *adj* **:** fiendish

di•a•crit•ic \-'kritik\ *n* **:** mark accompanying a letter and indicating a specific sound value **—di•a•crit•i•cal** \-'kritikəl\ *adj*

di•a•dem \'dīəˌdem\ *n* **:** crown

di•ag•no•sis \ˌdīig'nōsəs, -əg-\ *n, pl* **-no•ses** \-ˌsēz\ **:** identifying of a disease from its symptoms **—di•ag•nose** \'dīigˌnōs, -əg-\ *vb* **—di•ag•nos•tic** \ˌdīig'nästik, -əg-\ *adj*

di•ag•o•nal \dī'agənəl\ *adj* **:** extending from one corner to the opposite corner ~ *n* **:** diagonal line, direction, or arrangement **—di•ag•o•nal•ly** *adv*

di•a•gram \'dīəˌgram\ *n* **:** explanatory drawing or plan ~ *vb* **-gramed** *or* **-grammed; -gram•ing** *or* **gram•ming :** represent by a diagram **—di•a•gram•mat•ic** \ˌdīəgrə'matik\ *adj*

di•al \'dīəl\ *n* **1 :** face of a clock, meter, or gauge **2 :** control knob or wheel ~ *vb* **-aled** *or* **-alled; -al•ing** *or* **-al•ling :** turn a dial to call, operate, or select

di•a•lect \'dīəˌlekt\ *n* **:** variety of language confined to a region or group

di•a•logue \-ˌlȯg\ *n* **:** conversation

di•am•e•ter \dī'amətər\ *n* **1 :** straight line through the center of a circle **2 :** thickness

di•a•met•ric \ˌdīə'metrik\, **di•a•met•ri•cal** \-trikəl\ *adj* **:** completely opposite **—di•a•met•ri•cal•ly** \-iklē\ *adv*

di•a•mond \'dīmənd, 'dīə-\ *n* **1 :** hard brilliant mineral that consists of crystalline carbon **2 :** flat figure having 4 equal sides, 2 acute angles, and 2 obtuse angles **3 :** playing card of a suit marked with a red diamond **4 :** baseball field

di•a•per \'dīpər\ *n* **:** baby's garment for receiving bodily wastes ~ *vb* **:** put a diaper on

di•a•phragm \'dīəˌfram\ *n* **1 :** sheet of muscle between the chest and abdominal cavity **2 :** contraceptive device

di•ar•rhea \ˌdīə'rēə\ *n* **:** abnormally watery discharge from bowels

di•a•ry \'dīərē\ *n, pl* **-ries :** daily record of personal experiences **—di•a•rist** \'dīərist\ *n*

di•a•tribe \'dīəˌtrīb\ *n* **:** biting or abusive denunciation

dice \'dīs\ *n, pl* **dice :** die or a game played with dice ~ *vb* **diced; dic•ing :** cut into small cubes

dick•er \'dikər\ *vb* **:** bargain

dic•tate \'dikˌtāt\ *vb* **-tat•ed; -tat•ing 1 :** speak for a person or a machine to record **2 :** command ~ *n* **:** order **—dic•ta•tion** \dik'tāshən\ *n*

dic•ta•tor \'dikˌtātər\ *n* **:** person ruling absolutely and often brutally **—dic•ta•to•ri•al** \ˌdiktə'tōrēəl\ *adj* **—dic•ta•tor•ship** \dik'tātərˌship, 'dikˌ-\ *n*

dic•tion \'dikshən\ *n* **1 :** choice of the best word **2 :** precise pronunciation

dic•tio•nary \-shəˌnerē\ *n, pl* **-nar•ies :** reference book of words with information about their meanings

dic•tum \'diktəm\ *n, pl* **-ta** \-tə\ **:** authoritative or formal statement

did *past of* DO

di•dac•tic \dī'daktik\ *adj* **:** intended to teach a moral lesson

1die \'dī\ *vb* **died; dy•ing** \'dīiŋ\ **1 :** stop living **2 :** pass out of existence **3 :** stop or subside **4 :** long

2die \'dī\ *n* **1** *pl* **dice** \'dīs\ **:** small marked cube used in gambling **2** *pl* **dies** \'dīz\ **:** form for stamping or cutting

die•sel \'dēzəl, -səl\ *n* **:** engine in which high compression causes ignition of the fuel

di•et \'dīət\ *n* **:** food and drink regularly consumed (as by a person) ~ *vb* **:** eat less or according to certain rules **—di•e•tary** \'dīəˌterē\ *adj or n* **—di•et•er** *n*

di•e•tet•ics \ˌdīə'tetiks\ *n sing or pl* **:** science of nutrition **—di•e•tet•ic** *adj* **—di•e•ti•tian, di•e•ti•cian** \-'tishən\ *n*

dif•fer \'difər\ *vb* **1 :** be unlike **2 :** vary **3 :** disagree **—dif•fer•ence** \'difrəns\ *n*

dif•fer•ent \-rənt\ *adj* **:** not the same **—dif•fer•ent•ly** *adv*

dif•fer•en•ti•ate \ˌdifə'renchēˌāt\ *vb* **-at•ed; -at•ing 1 :** make or become different **2 :** distinguish **—dif•fer•en•ti•a•tion** \-ˌrenchē'āshən\ *n*

dif•fi•cult \'difikəlt\ *adj* **:** hard to do, understand, or deal with

dif•fi•cul•ty \-kəltē\ *n, pl* **-ties 1 :** difficult nature **2 :** great effort **3 :** something hard to do, understand, or deal with

dif•fi•dent \'difədənt\ *adj* **:** reserved **—dif•fi•dence** \-əns\ *n*

dif•fuse \dif'yüs\ *adj* **1 :** wordy **2 :** not concentrated ~ \-'yüz\ *vb* **-fused; -fus•ing :** pour out or spread widely **—dif•fu•sion** \-'yüzhən\ *n*

dig \'dig\ *vb* **dug** \'dəg\ **dig•ging 1 :** turn up soil **2 :** hollow out or form by removing earth **3 :** uncover by turning up earth ~ *n* **1 :** thrust **2 :** cutting remark **—dig in** *vb* **1 :** establish a defensive position **2 :** begin working or eating **—dig up** *vb* **:** discover

1di•gest \'dīˌjest\ *n* **:** body of information in shortened form

2di•gest \dī'jest, də-\ *vb* **1 :** think over **2 :** convert (food) into a form that can be absorbed **3 :** summarize **—di•gest•ible** *adj* **—di•ges•tion** \-'jeschən\ *n* **—di•ges•tive** \-'jestiv\ *adj*

dig•it \'dijət\ *n* **1 :** any of the figures 1 to 9 inclusive and usu. the symbol 0 **2 :** finger or toe

dig•i•tal \-əl\ *adj* **:** providing information in numerical digits **—dig•i•tal•ly** *adv*

dig•ni•fy \'dignəˌfī\ *vb* **-fied; -fy•ing :** give dignity or attention to

dig•ni•tary \-ˌterē\ *n, pl* **-taries :** person of high position

dig•ni•ty \'dignətē\ *n, pl* **-ties 1 :** quality or state of being worthy or honored **2 :** formal reserve (as of manner)

di•gress \dī'gres, də-\ *vb* **:** wander from the main subject **—di•gres•sion** \-'greshən\ *n*

dike \'dīk\ *n* **:** earth bank or dam

di•lap•i•dat•ed \də'lapəˌdātəd\ *adj* **:** fallen into partial ruin **—di•lap•i•da•tion** \-ˌlapə'dāshən\ *n*

di•late \dī'lāt, 'dīˌlāt\ *vb* **-lat•ed; -lat•ing :** swell or expand **—dil•a•ta•tion** \ˌdilə'tāshən\ *n* **—di•la•tion** \dī'lāshən\ *n*

dil•a•to•ry \'diləˌtōrē\ *adj* **1 :** delaying **2 :** tardy or slow

di•lem•ma \də'lemə\ *n* **1 :** undesirable choice **2 :** predicament

dil•et•tante \'diləˌtänt, -ˌtant; ˌdilə'tänt, -'tant\ *n, pl* **-tantes** *or* **-tan•ti** \-'täntē, -'tantē\ **:** one who dabbles in a field of interest

dil•i•gent \'diləjənt\ *adj* **:** attentive and busy **—dil•i•gence** \-jəns\ *n* **—dil•i•gent•ly** *adv*

dill \'dil\ *n* **:** herb with aromatic leaves and seeds

dil•ly•dal•ly \'dilēˌdalē\ *vb* **:** waste time by delay

di•lute \dī'lüt, də-\ *vb* **-lut•ed; -lut•ing :** lessen the consistency or strength of by mixing with something else ~ *adj* **:** weak **—di•lu•tion** \-'lüshən\ *n*

dim \'dim\ *adj* **-mm- 1 :** not bright or distinct **2 :** having no luster **3 :** not seeing or understanding clearly **—dim** *vb* **—dim•ly** *adv* **—dim•mer** *n* **—dim•ness** *n*

dime \'dīm\ *n* **:** U.S. coin worth 1/10 dollar

di•men•sion \də'menchən, dī-\ *n* **1 :** measurement of extension (as in length, height, or breadth) **2 :** extent **—di•men•sion•al** \-'menchənəl\ *adj*

di•min•ish \də'minish\ *vb* **1 :** make less or cause to appear less **2 :** dwindle

di•min•u•tive \də'minyətiv\ *adj* **:** extremely small

dim•ple \'dimpəl\ *n* **:** small depression esp. in the cheek or chin

din \'din\ *n* **:** loud noise

dine \'dīn\ *vb* **dined; din•ing :** eat dinner

din•er \'dīnər\ *n* **1 :** person eating dinner **2 :** railroad dining car or restaurant resembling one

din•ghy \'diŋē, -gē, -kē\ *n, pl* **-ghies :** small boat

din•gy \'dinjē\ *adj* **-gi•er; -est 1 :** dirty **2 :** shabby **—din•gi•ness** *n*

din•ner \'dinər\ *n* **:** main daily meal

di•no•saur \'dīnəˌsȯr\ *n* **:** extinct often huge reptile

dint \'dint\ *n* **:** force—in the phrase *by dint of*

di•o•cese \'dīəsəs, -ˌsēz, -ˌsēs\ *n, pl* **-ces•es** \-əz; 'dīəˌsēz\ **:** territorial jurisdiction of a bishop **—di•oc•e•san** \dī'äsəsən, ˌdīə'sēzən\ *adj or n*

dip \'dip\ *vb* **-pp- 1 :** plunge into a liquid **2 :** take out with a ladle **3 :** lower and quickly raise again **4 :** sink or slope downward suddenly ~ *n* **1 :** plunge into water for sport **2 :** sudden downward movement or incline **—dip•per** *n*

diph•the•ria \dif'thirēə\ *n* **:** acute contagious disease

diph•thong \'difˌthȯŋ\ *n* **:** two vowel sounds joined to form one speech sound (as *ou* in *out*)

di•plo•ma \də'plōmə\ *n, pl* **-mas :** record of graduation from a school

di•plo•ma•cy \-məsē\ *n* **1 :** business of conducting negotiations between nations **2 :** tact **—dip•lo•mat** \'dipləˌmat\ *n* **—dip•lo•mat•ic** \ˌdiplə'matik\ *adj*

dire \'dīr\ *adj* **dir•er; -est 1 :** very horrible **2 :** extreme

di•rect \də'rekt, dī-\ *vb* **1 :** address **2 :** cause to move or to follow a certain course **3 :** show (someone) the way **4 :** regulate the activities or course of **5 :** request with authority ~ *adj* **1 :** leading to or coming from a point without deviation or inter-

ruption 2 : frank —**direct** adv —**di•rect•ly** adv —**di•rect•ness** n —**di•rec•tor** \-tər\ n

direct current n : electric current flowing in one direction only

di•rec•tion \də'rekshən, dī-\ n 1 : supervision 2 : order 3 : course along which something moves —**di•rec•tion•al** \-shənəl\ adj

di•rec•tive \-tiv\ n : order

di•rec•to•ry \-tərē\ n, pl -ries : alphabetical list of names and addresses

dirge \'dərj\ n : funeral hymn

di•ri•gi•ble \dirəjəbəl, də'rijə-\ n : airship

dirt \'dərt\ n 1 : mud, dust, or grime that makes something unclean 2 : soil

dirty \-ē\ adj **dirt•i•er; -est** 1 : not clean 2 : unfair 3 : indecent ~ vb **dirt•ied; dirty•ing** : make or become dirty —**dirt•i•ness** n

dis•able \dis'ābəl\ vb **-abled; -abling** : make unable to function —**dis•abil•i•ty** \disə'bilətē\ n

dis•abuse \disə'byüz\ vb : free from error or misconception

dis•ad•van•tage \disəd'vantij\ n : something that hinders success —**dis•ad•van•ta•geous** adj

dis•af•fect \disə'fekt\ vb : cause discontent in —**dis•af•fec•tion** n

dis•agree \disə'grē\ vb 1 : fail to agree 2 : differ in opinion —**dis•agree•ment** n

dis•agree•able \-əbəl\ adj : unpleasant

dis•al•low \disə'lau̇\ vb : refuse to admit or recognize

dis•ap•pear \disə'pir\ vb 1 : pass out of sight 2 : cease to be —**dis•ap•pear•ance** n

dis•ap•point \disə'point\ vb : fail to fulfill the expectation or hope of —**dis•ap•point•ment** n

dis•ap•prove \-ə'prüv\ vb 1 : condemn or reject 2 : feel or express dislike or rejection —**dis•ap•prov•al** n —**dis•ap•prov•ing•ly** adv

dis•arm \dis'ärm\ vb 1 : take weapons from 2 : reduce armed forces 3 : make harmless or friendly —**dis•ar•ma•ment** \-'ärməmənt\ n

dis•ar•range \disə'rānj\ vb : throw into disorder —**dis•ar•range•ment** n

dis•ar•ray \disə'rā\ n : disorder

dis•as•ter \diz'astər, dis-\ n : sudden great misfortune —**di•sas•trous** \-'astrəs\ adj

dis•avow \disə'vau̇\ vb : deny responsibility for —**dis•avow•al** \-'vau̇əl\ n

dis•band \dis'band\ vb : break up the organization of

dis•bar \dis'bär\ vb : expel from the legal profession —**dis•bar•ment** n

dis•be•lieve \disbi'lēv\ vb : hold not worthy of belief —**dis•be•lief** n

dis•burse \dis'bərs\ vb **-bursed; -burs•ing** : pay out —**dis•burse•ment** n

disc var of DISK

dis•card \dis'kärd, 'dis,kärd\ vb : get rid of as unwanted —**dis•card** \'dis,kärd\ n

dis•cern \dis'ərn, diz-\ vb : discover with the eyes or the mind —**dis•cern•ible** adj —**dis•cern•ment** n

dis•charge \dis'chärj, 'dis,chärj\ vb 1 : unload 2 : shoot 3 : set free 4 : dismiss from service 5 : let go or let off 6 : give forth fluid ~ \'dis,-, dis'-\ n 1 : act of discharging 2 : a flowing out (as of blood) 3 : dismissal

dis•ci•ple \di'sīpəl\ n : one who helps spread another's teachings

dis•ci•pli•nar•i•an \disəplə'nerēən\ n : one who enforces order

dis•ci•pline \'disəplən\ n 1 : field of study 2 : training that corrects, molds, or perfects 3 : punishment 4 : control gained by obedience or training ~ vb **-plined; -plin•ing** 1 : punish 2 : train in self-control —**dis•ci•plin•ary** \'disəplə,nerē\ adj

dis•claim \dis'klām\ vb : disavow

dis•close \-'klōz\ vb : reveal —**dis•clo•sure** \-'klōzhər\ n

dis•col•or \dis'kələr\ vb : change the color of esp. for the worse —**dis•col•or•ation** \dis,kələ'rāshən\ n

dis•com•fit \dis'kəmfət\ vb : upset —**dis•com•fi•ture** \dis'kəmfə,chu̇r\ n

dis•com•fort \dis'kəmfərt\ n : uneasiness

dis•con•cert \diskən'sərt\ vb : upset

dis•con•nect \diskə'nekt\ vb : undo the connection of

dis•con•so•late \dis'känsələt\ adj : hopelessly sad

dis•con•tent \diskən'tent\ n : uneasiness of mind —**dis•con•tent•ed** adj

dis•con•tin•ue \diskən'tinyü\ vb : end —**dis•con•tin•u•ance** n —**dis•con•ti•nu•ity** \dis,käntə'nüətē, -'nyü-\ n —**dis•con•tin•u•ous** \diskən'tinyəwəs\ adj

dis•cord \'dis,kȯrd\ n : lack of harmony —**dis•cor•dant** \dis'kȯrdᵊnt\ adj —**dis•cor•dant•ly** adv

dis•count \'dis,kau̇nt\ n : reduction from a regular price ~ \'dis,-, dis'-\ vb 1 : reduce the amount of 2 : disregard —**discount** adj —**dis•count•er** n

dis•cour•age \dis'kərij\ vb **-aged; -ag•ing** 1

: deprive of courage, confidence, or enthusiasm 2 : dissuade —**dis•cour•age•ment** n

dis•course \'dis,kȯrs\ n 1 : conversation 2 : formal treatment of a subject ~ \dis'-\ vb **-coursed; -cours•ing** : talk at length

dis•cour•te•ous \dis'kərtēəs\ adj : lacking courtesy —**dis•cour•te•ous•ly** adv —**dis•cour•te•sy** n

dis•cov•er \dis'kəvər\ vb 1 : make known 2 : obtain the first sight or knowledge of 3 : find out —**dis•cov•er•er** n —**dis•cov•ery** \-ərē\ n

dis•cred•it \dis'kredət\ vb 1 : disbelieve 2 : destroy confidence in ~ n 1 : loss of reputation 2 : disbelief —**dis•cred•it•able** adj

dis•creet \dis'krēt\ adj : capable of keeping a secret —**dis•creet•ly** adv

dis•crep•an•cy \dis'krepənsē\ n, pl -cies : difference or disagreement

dis•crete \dis'krēt, 'dis,-\ adj : individually distinct

dis•cre•tion \dis'kreshən\ n 1 : discreet quality 2 : power of decision or choice —**dis•cre•tion•ary** adj

dis•crim•i•nate \dis'krimə,nāt\ vb **-nat•ed; -nat•ing** 1 : distinguish 2 : show favor or disfavor unjustly —**dis•crim•i•na•tion** \-,krimə'nāshən\ n —**dis•crim•i•na•to•ry** \-'krimənə,tȯrē\ adj

dis•cur•sive \dis'kərsiv\ adj : passing from one topic to another —**dis•cur•sive•ly** adv —**dis•cur•sive•ness** n

dis•cus \'diskəs\ n, pl -cus•es : disk hurled for distance in a contest

dis•cuss \dis'kəs\ vb : talk about or present —**dis•cus•sion** \-'kəshən\ n

dis•dain \dis'dān\ n : feeling of contempt ~ vb : look upon or reject with disdain —**dis•dain•ful** \-fəl\ adj —**dis•dain•ful•ly** adv

dis•ease \di'zēz\ n : condition of a body that impairs its functioning —**dis•eased** \-'zēzd\ adj

dis•em•bark \disəm'bärk\ vb : get off a ship —**dis•em•bar•ka•tion** \dis,em,bär'kāshən\ n

dis•em•bodied \disəm'bädēd\ adj : having no substance or reality

dis•en•chant \disᵊn'chant\ vb : to free from illusion —**dis•en•chant•ment** n

dis•en•chant•ed \-'chantəd\ adj : disappointed

dis•en•gage \-ᵊn'gāj\ vb : release —**dis•en•gage•ment** n

dis•en•tan•gle \-ᵊn'taŋgəl\ vb : free from entanglement

dis•fa•vor \dis'fāvər\ n : disapproval

dis•fig•ure \dis'figyər\ vb : spoil the appearance of —**dis•fig•ure•ment** n

dis•fran•chise \dis'fran,chīz\ vb : deprive of the right to vote —**dis•fran•chise•ment** n

dis•gorge \dis'gȯrj\ vb : spew forth

dis•grace \dis'grās\ vb : bring disgrace to ~ n 1 : shame 2 : cause of shame —**dis•grace•ful** \-fəl\ adj —**dis•grace•ful•ly** adv

dis•grun•tle \dis'grəntᵊl\ vb **-tled; -tling** : put in bad humor

dis•guise \dis'gīz\ vb **-guised; -guis•ing** : hide the true identity or nature of ~ n : something that conceals

dis•gust \dis'gəst\ n : strong aversion ~ vb : provoke disgust in —**dis•gust•ed•ly** adv —**dis•gust•ing•ly** adv

dish \'dish\ n 1 : vessel for serving food or the food it holds 2 : food prepared in a particular way ~ vb : put in a dish —**dish•cloth** n —**dish•rag** n —**dish•wash•er** n —**dish•wa•ter** n

dis•har•mo•ny \dis'härmənē\ n : lack of harmony —**dis•har•mo•ni•ous** \dishär'mōnēəs\ adj

dis•heart•en \dis'härtᵊn\ vb : discourage

di•shev•el \di'shevəl\ vb **-eled or -elled; -el•ing or -el•ling** : throw into disorder —**di•shev•eled, di•shev•elled** adj

dis•hon•est \dis'änəst\ adj : not honest —**dis•hon•est•ly** adv —**dis•hon•es•ty** n

dis•hon•or \dis'änər\ n or vb : disgrace —**dis•hon•or•able** adj —**dis•hon•or•ably** adv

dis•il•lu•sion \disə'lüzhən\ vb : to free from illusion —**dis•il•lu•sion•ment** n

dis•in•cli•na•tion \dis,inklə'nāshən\ n : slight aversion —**dis•in•cline** \disᵊn'klīn\ vb

dis•in•fect \disᵊn'fekt\ vb : destroy disease germs in or on —**dis•in•fec•tant** \-'fektənt\ adj or n —**dis•in•fec•tion** \-'fekshən\ n

dis•in•gen•u•ous \disᵊn'jenyəwəs\ adj : lacking in candor

dis•in•her•it \disᵊn'herət\ vb : prevent from inheriting property

dis•in•te•grate \dis'intə,grāt\ vb : break into parts or small bits —**dis•in•te•gra•tion** \dis,intə'grāshən\ n

dis•in•ter•est•ed \dis'intərəstəd, -,res-\ adj 1 : not interested 2 : not prejudiced —**dis•in•ter•est•ed•ness** n

dis•joint•ed \dis'jȯintəd\ adj 1 : separated at the joint 2 : incoherent

disk \'disk\ n : something round and flat

dis•like \dis'līk\ vb : regard with dislike ~ n : feeling that something is unpleasant and to be avoided

dis•lo•cate \'dislō,kāt, dis'-\ vb : move out of the usual or proper place —**dis•lo•ca•tion** \dislō'kāshən\ n

dis•lodge \dis'läj\ vb : force out of a place

dis•loy•al \dis'lȯiəl\ adj : not loyal —**dis•loy•al•ty** n

dis•mal \'dizməl\ adj : showing or causing gloom —**dis•mal•ly** adv

dis•man•tle \dis'mantᵊl\ vb **-tled; -tling** : take apart

dis•may \dis'mā\ vb **-mayed; -may•ing** : discourage —**dismay** n

dis•mem•ber \dis'membər\ vb : cut into pieces —**dis•mem•ber•ment** n

dis•miss \dis'mis\ vb 1 : send away 2 : remove from service 3 : put aside or out of mind —**dis•miss•al** n

dis•mount \dis'mau̇nt\ vb 1 : get down from something 2 : take apart

dis•obey \disə'bā\ vb : refuse to obey —**dis•obe•di•ence** \-'bēdēəns\ n —**dis•obe•di•ent** \-ənt\ adj

dis•or•der \dis'ȯrdər\ n 1 : lack of order 2 : breach of public order 3 : abnormal state of body or mind —**disorder** vb —**dis•or•der•li•ness** n —**dis•or•der•ly** adj

dis•or•ga•nize \dis'ȯrgə,nīz\ vb : throw into disorder —**dis•or•ga•ni•za•tion** n

dis•own \dis'ōn\ vb : repudiate

dis•par•age \dis'parij\ vb **-aged; -ag•ing** : say bad things about —**dis•par•age•ment** n

dis•pa•rate \dis'parət, 'dispərət\ adj : different in quality or character —**dis•par•i•ty** \dis'parətē\ n

dis•pas•sion•ate \dis'pashənət\ adj : not influenced by strong feeling —**dis•pas•sion•ate•ly** adv

dis•patch \dis'pach\ vb 1 : send 2 : kill 3 : attend to rapidly 4 : defeat ~ n 1 : message 2 : news item from a correspondent 3 : promptness and efficiency —**dis•patch•er** n

dis•pel \dis'pel\ vb **-ll-** : clear away

dis•pen•sa•ry \dis'pensərē\ n, pl -ries : place where medical or dental aid is provided

dis•pen•sa•tion \dispən'sāshən\ n 1 : system of principles or rules 2 : exemption from a rule 3 : act of dispensing

dis•pense \dis'pens\ vb **-pensed; -pens•ing** 1 : portion out 2 : make up and give out (remedies) —**dis•pens•er** n —**dispense with** : do without

dis•perse \dis'pərs\ vb **-persed; -pers•ing** : scatter —**dis•per•sal** \-'pərsəl\ n —**dis•per•sion** \-'pərzhən\ n

dis•place \dis'plās\ vb 1 : expel or force to flee from home or native land 2 : take the place of —**dis•place•ment** \-mənt\ n

dis•play \-'plā\ vb : present to view —**display** n

dis•please \-'plēz\ vb : arouse the dislike of —**dis•plea•sure** \-'plezhər\ n

dis•port \dis'pȯrt\ vb 1 : amuse 2 : frolic

dis•pose \dis'pōz\ vb **-posed; -pos•ing** 1 : give a tendency to 2 : settle —**dis•pos•able** \-'pōzəbəl\ adj —**dis•pos•al** \-'pōzəl\ n —**dispose of** : dispose of 1 : determine the fate, condition, or use of 2 : get rid of

dis•po•si•tion \dispə'zishən\ n 1 : act or power of disposing of 2 : arrangement 3 : natural attitude

dis•pos•sess \dispə'zes\ vb : deprive of possession or occupancy —**dis•pos•ses•sion** \-'zeshən\ n

dis•pro•por•tion \disprə'pȯrshən\ n : lack of proportion —**dis•pro•por•tion•ate** \-shənət\ adj

dis•prove \dis'prüv\ vb : prove false —**dis•proof** n

dis•pute \dis'pyüt\ vb **-put•ed; -put•ing** 1 : argue 2 : deny the truth or rightness of 3 : struggle against or over ~ n : debate or quarrel —**dis•put•able** \-əbəl, dis'pyət-\ adj —**dis•pu•ta•tion** \dispyə'tāshən\ n

dis•qual•i•fy \dis'kwälə,fī\ vb : make ineligible —**dis•qual•i•fi•ca•tion** n

dis•qui•et \dis'kwīət\ vb : make uneasy or restless ~ n : anxiety

dis•re•gard \disri'gärd\ vb : pay no attention to ~ n : neglect

dis•re•pair \disri'par\ n : need of repair

dis•rep•u•ta•ble \dis'repyətəbəl\ adj : having a bad reputation

dis•re•pute \disri'pyüt\ n : low regard

dis•re•spect \disri'spekt\ n : lack of respect —**dis•re•spect•ful** adj

dis•robe \dis'rōb\ vb : undress

dis•rupt \dis'rəpt\ vb : throw into disorder —**dis•rup•tion** \-'rəpshən\ n —**dis•rup•tive** \-'rəptiv\ adj

dis•sat•is•fac•tion \dis,satəs'fakshən\ n : lack of satisfaction

dis•sat•is•fy \dis'satəs,fī\ vb : fail to satisfy

dis•sect \di'sekt\ vb : cut into parts esp. to examine —**dis•sec•tion** \-'sekshən\ n

dis•sem•ble \di'sembəl\ vb **-bled; -bling** : disguise feelings or intention —**dis•sem•bler** n

dis•sem•i•nate \di'semə,nāt\ vb **-nat•ed; -nat•ing** : spread around —**dis•sem•i•na•tion** \-,semə'nāshən\ n

dis•sen•sion \di'senchən\ n : discord

dis•sent \di'sent\ vb : object or disagree ~ n : difference of opinion —**dis•sent•er** n —**dis•sen•tient** \-'senchənt\ adj or n

dis•ser•ta•tion \disər'tāshən\ n : long written study of a subject

dis•ser•vice \dis'sərvəs\ n : injury

dis•si•dent \'disədənt\ n : one who differs openly with an establishment —**dis•si•dence** \-əns\ n —**dissident** adj

dis•sim•i•lar \di'simələr\ adj : different —**dis•sim•i•lar•i•ty** \di,simə'larətē\ n

dis•si•pate \disə,pāt\ vb **-pat•ed; -pat•ing** 1 : break up and drive off 2 : squander —**dis•si•pa•tion** \disə'pāshən\ n

dis•so•ci•ate \dis'ōsē,āt, -shē-\ vb **-at•ed; -at•ing** : separate from association —**dis•so•ci•a•tion** \dis,ōsē'āshən, -shē-\ n

dis•so•lute \disə,lüt\ adj : loose in morals or conduct

dis•so•lu•tion \disə'lüshən\ n : act or process of dissolving

dis•solve \di'zälv\ vb 1 : break up or bring to an end 2 : pass or cause to pass into solution

dis•so•nance \'disənəns\ n : discord —**dis•so•nant** \-nənt\ adj

dis•suade \di'swād\ vb **-suad•ed; -suad•ing** : persuade not to do something —**dis•sua•sion** \-'swāzhən\ n

dis•tance \'distəns\ n 1 : measure of separation in space or time 2 : reserve

dis•tant \-tənt\ adj 1 : separate in space 2 : remote in time, space, or relationship 3 : reserved —**dis•tant•ly** adv

dis•taste \dis'tāst\ n : dislike —**dis•taste•ful** adj

dis•tem•per \dis'tempər\ n : serious virus disease of dogs

dis•tend \dis'tend\ vb : swell out —**disten•sion, dis•ten•tion** \-'tenchən\ n

dis•till \di'stil\ vb : obtain by distillation —**dis•til•late** \distə,lāt, -lət\ n —**dis•till•er** n —**dis•till•ery** \di'stilərē\ n

dis•til•la•tion \distə'lāshən\ n : purification of liquid by evaporating then condensing

dis•tinct \dis'tiŋkt\ adj 1 : distinguishable from others 2 : readily discerned —**dis•tinc•tive** \-tiv\ adj —**dis•tinc•tive•ly** adv —**dis•tinc•tive•ness** n —**dis•tinct•ly** adv —**dis•tinct•ness** n

dis•tinc•tion \-'tiŋkshən\ n 1 : act of distinguishing 2 : difference 3 : special recognition

dis•tin•guish \-'tiŋgwish\ vb 1 : perceive as different 2 : set apart 3 : discern 4 : make outstanding —**dis•tin•guish•able** adj —**dis•tin•guished** \-gwisht\ adj

dis•tort \dis'tȯrt\ vb : twist out of shape, condition, or true meaning —**dis•tor•tion** \-'tȯrshən\ n

dis•tract \di'strakt\ vb : divert the mind or attention of —**dis•trac•tion** \-'strakshən\ n

dis•traught \dis'trȯt\ adj : agitated with mental conflict

dis•tress \-'tres\ n 1 : suffering 2 : misfortune 3 : state of danger or great need ~ vb : subject to strain or distress —**dis•tress•ful** adj

dis•trib•ute \-'tribyət\ vb **-ut•ed; -ut•ing** 1 : divide among many 2 : spread or hand out —**dis•tri•bu•tion** \distrə'byüshən\ n —**dis•trib•u•tive** \dis'tribyətiv\ adj —**dis•trib•u•tor** \-ər\ n

dis•trict \'dis,trikt\ n : territorial division

dis•trust \dis'trəst\ vb or n : mistrust —**dis•trust•ful** \-fəl\ adj

dis•turb \dis'tərb\ vb 1 : interfere with 2 : destroy the peace, composure, or order of —**dis•tur•bance** \-'tərbəns\ n —**dis•turb•er** n

dis•use \dis'yüs\ n : lack of use

ditch \'dich\ n : trench ~ vb 1 : dig a ditch in 2 : get rid of

dith•er \'dithər\ n : highly nervous or excited state

dit•to \'ditō\ n, pl -tos : more of the same

dit•ty \'ditē\ n, pl -ties : short simple song

di•uret•ic \dīyu̇'retik\ adj : tending to increase urine flow —**diuretic** n

di•ur•nal \dī'ərnᵊl\ adj 1 : daily 2 : of or occurring in the daytime

di•van \'dī,van, dī'-\ n : couch

dive \'dīv\ vb **dived or dove** \'dōv\; **dived; div•ing** 1 : plunge into water head-first 2 : submerge 3 : descend quickly ~ n 1 : act of diving 2 : sharp decline —**div•er** n

di•verge \də'vərj, dī-\ vb **-verged; -verg•ing** 1 : move in different directions 2 : differ —**di•ver•gence** \-'vərjəns\ n —**di•ver•gent** \-jənt\ adj

di•vers \'dīvərz\ adj : various

di•verse \dī'vərs, də-, 'dī,vərs\ adj : involving different forms —**di•ver•si•fi•ca•tion** \də,vərsəfə'kāshən, dī-\ n —**di•ver•si•fy** \-'vərsə,fī\ vb —**di•ver•si•ty** \-sətē\ n

di•vert \də'vərt, dī-\ vb 1 : turn from a

course or purpose 2 : distract 3 : amuse —**di•ver•sion** \-ˈvərzhən\ *n*

di•vest \dīˈvest, də-\ *vb* : strip of clothing, possessions, or rights

di•vide \dəˈvīd\ *vb* **-vid•ed; -vid•ing** 1 : separate 2 : distribute 3 : share 4 : subject to mathematical division ~ *n* : watershed —**di•vid•er** *n*

div•i•dend \ˈdivəˌdend\ *n* 1 : individual share 2 : bonus 3 : number to be divided

div•i•na•tion \ˌdivəˈnāshən\ *n* : practice of trying to foretell future events

di•vine \dəˈvīn\ *adj* **-vin•er; -est** 1 : relating to or being God or a god 2 : supremely good ~ *n* : clergy member ~ *vb* **-vined; -vin•ing** 1 : infer 2 : prophesy —**di•vine•ly** *adv* —**di•vin•er** *n* —**di•vin•i•ty** \dəˈvinətē\ *n*

di•vis•i•ble \-ˈvizəbəl\ *adj* : capable of being divided —**di•vis•i•bil•i•ty** \-ˌvizəˈbilətē\ *n*

di•vi•sion \-ˈvizhən\ *n* 1 : distribution 2 : part of a whole 3 : disagreement 4 : process of finding out how many times one number is contained in another

di•vi•sive \dəˈvīsiv, -ˈvi-, -ziv\ *adj* : creating dissension

di•vi•sor \-ˈvīzər\ *n* : number by which a dividend is divided

di•vorce \dəˈvōrs\ *n* : legal breaking up of a marriage —**divorce** *vb*

di•vor•cée \-ˌvōrˈsā, -ˈsē\ *n* : divorced woman

di•vulge \dəˈvəlj, dī-\ *vb* **-vulged; -vulg•ing** : reveal

diz•zy \ˈdizē\ *adj* **-zi•er; -est** 1 : having a sensation of whirling 2 : causing or caused by giddiness —**diz•zi•ly** *adv* —**diz•zi•ness** *n*

DNA \ˌdēˌenˈā\ *n* : compound in cell nuclei that is the basis of heredity

do \ˈdü\ *vb* **did** \ˈdid\; **done** \ˈdən\; **do•ing** \ˈdüiŋ\; **does** \ˈdəz\ 1 : work to accomplish (an action or task) 2 : behave 3 : prepare or fix up 4 : fare 5 : finish 6 : serve the needs or purpose of 7 —used as an auxiliary verb —**do away with** 1 : get rid of 2 : destroy —**do by** : deal with —**do•er** \ˈdüər\ *n* —**do in** *vb* 1 : ruin 2 : kill

doc•ile \ˈdäsəl\ *adj* : easily managed —**do•cil•i•ty** \däˈsilətē\ *n*

[1]**dock** \ˈdäk\ *vb* 1 : shorten 2 : reduce

[2]**dock** *n* 1 : berth between 2 piers to receive ships 2 : loading wharf or platform ~ *vb* : bring or come into dock —**dock•work•er** *n*

[3]**dock** *n* : place in a court for a prisoner

dock•et \ˈdäkət\ *n* 1 : record of the proceedings in a legal action 2 : list of legal causes to be tried —**docket** *vb*

doc•tor \ˈdäktər\ *n* 1 : person holding one of the highest academic degrees 2 : one (as a surgeon) skilled in healing arts ~ *vb* 1 : give medical treatment to 2 : repair or alter —**doc•tor•al** \-tərəl\ *adj*

doc•trine \ˈdäktrən\ *n* : something taught —**doc•tri•nal** \-trənᵊl\ *adj*

doc•u•ment \ˈdäkyəmənt\ *n* : paper that furnishes information or legal proof —**doc•u•ment** \-ˌment\ *vb* —**doc•u•men•ta•tion** \ˌdäkyəmənˈtāshən\ *n* —**doc•u•ment•er** *n*

doc•u•men•ta•ry \ˌdäkyəˈmentərē\ *adj* 1 : of or relating to documents 2 : giving a factual presentation —**documentary** *n*

dod•der \ˈdädər\ *vb* : become feeble usu. from age

dodge \ˈdäj\ *vb* **dodged; dodg•ing** 1 : move quickly aside or out of the way of 2 : evade —**dodge** *n*

do•do \ˈdōdō\ *n, pl* **-does** *or* **-dos** 1 : heavy flightless extinct bird 2 : stupid person

doe \ˈdō\ *n, pl* **does** *or* **doe** : adult female deer —**doe•skin** \-ˌskin\ *n*

does *pres 3d sing of* DO

doff \ˈdäf\ *vb* : remove

dog \ˈdȯg\ *n* : flesh-eating domestic mammal ~ *vb* 1 : hunt down or track like a hound 2 : harass —**dog•catch•er** *n* —**dog•gy** \-ē\ *n or adj* —**dog•house** *n*

dog–ear \ˈdȯgˌir\ *n* : turned-down corner of a page —**dog–ear** *vb* —**dog–eared** \-ˌird\ *adj*

dog•ged \ˈdȯgəd\ *adj* : stubbornly determined

dog•ma \ˈdȯgmə\ *n* : tenet or code of tenets

dog•ma•tism \-ˌtizəm\ *n* : unwarranted stubbornness of opinion —**dog•ma•tic** \dȯgˈmatik\ *adj*

dog•wood *n* : flowering tree

doi•ly \ˈdȯilē\ *n, pl* **-lies** : small decorative mat

do•ings \ˈdüiŋz\ *n pl* : events

dol•drums \ˈdōldrəmz, ˈdäl-\ *n pl* : spell of listlessness, despondency, or stagnation

dole \ˈdōl\ *n* : distribution esp. of money to the needy or unemployed —**dole out** *vb* : give out esp. in small portions

dole•ful \ˈdōlfəl\ *adj* : sad —**dole•ful•ly** *adv*

doll \ˈdäl, ˈdȯl\ *n* : small figure of a person used esp. as a child's toy

dol•lar \ˈdälər\ *n* : any of various basic monetary units (as in the U.S. and Canada)

dol•ly \ˈdälē\ *n, pl* **-lies** : small cart or wheeled platform

dol•phin \ˈdälfən\ *n* 1 : sea mammal related to the whales 2 : saltwater food fish

dolt \ˈdōlt\ *n* : stupid person —**dolt•ish** *adj*

-dom \dəm\ *n suffix* 1 : office or realm 2 : state or fact of being 3 : those belonging to a group

do•main \dōˈmān, də-\ *n* 1 : territory over which someone reigns 2 : sphere of activity or knowledge

dome \ˈdōm\ *n* 1 : large hemispherical roof 2 : roofed stadium

do•mes•tic \dəˈmestik\ *adj* 1 : relating to the household or family 2 : relating and limited to one's own country 3 : tame ~ *n* : household servant —**do•mes•ti•cal•ly** \-tiklē\ *adv*

do•mes•ti•cate \-tiˌkāt\ *vb* **-cat•ed; -cat•ing** : tame —**do•mes•ti•ca•tion** \-ˌmestiˈkāshən\ *n*

do•mi•cile \ˈdäməˌsīl, ˈdō-; ˈdäməsəl\ *n* : home —**domicile** *vb*

dom•i•nance \ˈdämənəns\ *n* : control —**dom•i•nant** \-nənt\ *adj*

dom•i•nate \-ˌnāt\ *vb* **-nat•ed; -nat•ing** 1 : have control over 2 : rise high above —**dom•i•na•tion** \ˌdäməˈnāshən\ *n*

dom•i•neer \ˌdäməˈnir\ *vb* : exercise arbitrary control

do•min•ion \dəˈminyən\ *n* 1 : supreme authority 2 : governed territory

dom•i•no \ˈdäməˌnō\ *n, pl* **-noes** *or* **-nos** : flat rectangular block used as a piece in a game (**dominoes**)

don \ˈdän\ *vb* **-nn-** : put on (clothes)

do•nate \ˈdōˌnāt\ *vb* **-nat•ed; -nat•ing** : make a gift of —**do•na•tion** \dōˈnāshən\ *n*

[1]**done** \ˈdən\ *past part of* DO

[2]**done** *adj* 1 : finished or ended 2 : cooked sufficiently

don•key \ˈdäŋkē, ˈdəŋ-\ *n, pl* **-keys** : sturdy domestic ass

do•nor \ˈdōnər\ *n* : one that gives

doo•dle \ˈdüdᵊl\ *vb* **-dled; -dling** : draw or scribble aimlessly —**doodle** *n*

doom \ˈdüm\ *n* 1 : judgment 2 : fate 3 : ruin —**doom** *vb*

door \ˈdōr\ *n* : passage for entrance or a movable barrier that can open or close such a passage —**door•jamb** *n* —**door•knob** *n* —**door•mat** *n* —**door•step** *n* —**door•way** *n*

dope \ˈdōp\ 1 : narcotic preparation 2 : stupid person 3 : information ~ *vb* **doped; dop•ing** : drug

dor•mant \ˈdȯrmənt\ *adj* : not actively growing or functioning —**dor•man•cy** \-mənsē\ *n*

dor•mer \ˈdȯrmər\ *n* : window built upright in a sloping roof

dor•mi•to•ry \ˈdȯrməˌtōrē\ *n, pl* **-ries** : residence hall (as at a college)

dor•mouse \ˈdȯrˌmau̇s\ *n* : squirrellike rodent

dor•sal \ˈdȯrsəl\ *adj* : relating to or on the back —**dor•sal•ly** *adv*

do•ry \ˈdōrē\ *n, pl* **-ries** : flat-bottomed boat

dose \ˈdōs\ *n* : quantity (as of medicine) taken at one time ~ *vb* **dosed; dosing** : give medicine to —**dos•age** \ˈdōsij\ *n*

dot \ˈdät\ *n* 1 : small spot 2 : small round mark made with or as if with a pen ~ *vb* **-tt-** : mark with dots

dot•age \ˈdōtij\ *n* : senility

dote \ˈdōt\ *vb* **dot•ed; dot•ing** 1 : act feebleminded 2 : be foolishly fond

dou•ble \ˈdəbəl\ *adj* 1 : consisting of 2 members or parts 2 : being twice as great or as many 3 : folded in two ~ *n* 1 : something twice another 2 : one that resembles another ~ *adv* : doubly ~ *vb* **-bled; -bling** 1 : make or become twice as great 2 : fold or bend 3 : clench

dou•ble–cross *vb* : deceive by trickery —**dou•ble–cross•er** *n*

dou•bly \ˈdəblē\ *adv* : to twice the degree

doubt \ˈdau̇t\ *vb* 1 : be uncertain about 2 : mistrust 3 : consider unlikely ~ *n* 1 : uncertainty 2 : mistrust 3 : inclination not to believe —**doubt•ful** \-fəl\ *adj* —**doubt•ful•ly** *adv* —**doubt•less** \-ləs\ *adv*

douche \ˈdüsh\ *n* : jet of fluid for cleaning a body part

dough \ˈdō\ *n* : stiff mixture of flour and liquid —**doughy** \ˈdōē\ *adj*

dough•nut \-ˌnət\ *n* : small fried ring-shaped cake

dough•ty \ˈdau̇tē\ *adj* **-ti•er; -est** : able, strong, or valiant

dour \ˈdau̇ər, ˈdu̇r\ *adj* 1 : severe 2 : gloomy or sullen —**dour•ly** *adv*

douse \ˈdau̇s, ˈdau̇z\ *vb* **doused; dous•ing** 1 : plunge into or drench with water 2 : extinguish

[1]**dove** \ˈdəv\ *n* : small wild pigeon

[2]**dove** \ˈdōv\ *past of* DIVE

dove•tail \ˈdəvˌtāl\ *vb* : fit together neatly

dow•a•ger \ˈdau̇ijər\ *n* 1 : widow with wealth or a title 2 : dignified elderly woman

dowdy \ˈdau̇dē\ *adj* **dowd•i•er; -est** : lacking neatness and charm

dow•el \ˈdau̇əl\ *n* 1 : peg used for fastening two pieces 2 : wooden rod

dow•er \ˈdau̇ər\ *n* : property given a widow for life ~ *vb* : supply with a dower

[1]**down** \ˈdau̇n\ *adv* 1 : toward or in a lower position or state 2 : to a lying or sitting position 3 : as a cash deposit 4 : on paper ~ *adj* 1 : lying on the ground 2 : directed or going downward 3 : being at a low level ~ *prep* : toward the bottom of ~ *vb* 1 : cause to go down 2 : defeat

[2]**down** *n* : fluffy feathers

down•cast *adj* 1 : sad 2 : directed down

down•fall *n* : ruin or cause of ruin

down•grade *n* : downward slope ~ *vb* : lower in grade or position

down•heart•ed *adj* : sad

down•pour *n* : heavy rain

down•right *adv* : thoroughly ~ *adj* : absolute or thorough

downs \ˈdau̇nz\ *n pl* : rolling treeless uplands

down•size \ˈdau̇nˌsīz\ *vb* : reduce in size

down•stairs *adv* : on or to a lower floor and esp. the main floor —**downstairs** *adj or n*

down–to–earth *adj* : practical

down•town *adv* : to, toward, or in the business center of a town —**downtown** *n or adj*

down•trod•den \ˈdau̇nˌträdᵊn\ *adj* : suffering oppression

down•ward \ˈdau̇nwərd\, **down•wards** \-wərdz\ *adv* : to a lower place or condition —**downward** *adj*

down•wind *adv or adj* : in the direction the wind is blowing

downy \ˈdau̇nē\ *adj* **-i•er; -est** : resembling or covered with down

dow•ry \ˈdau̇rē\ *n, pl* **-ries** : property a woman gives her husband in marriage

dox•ol•o•gy \däkˈsäləjē\ *n, pl* **-gies** : hymn of praise to God

doze \ˈdōz\ *vb* **dozed; doz•ing** : sleep lightly —**doze** *n*

doz•en \ˈdəzᵊn\ *n, pl* **-ens** *or* **-en** : group of 12 —**doz•enth** \-ᵊnth\ *adj*

drab \ˈdrab\ *adj* **-bb-** : dull —**drab•ly** *adv* —**drab•ness** *n*

dra•co•ni•an \drāˈkōnēən, dra-\ *adj, often cap* : harsh, cruel

draft \ˈdraft, ˈdräft\ *n* 1 : act of drawing or hauling 2 : act of drinking 3 : amount drunk at once 4 : preliminary outline or rough sketch 5 : selection from a pool or the selection process 6 : order for the payment of money 7 : air current ~ *vb* 1 : select usu. on a compulsory basis 2 : make a preliminary sketch, version, or plan of ~ *adj* : drawn from a container —**draft•ee** \drafˈtē, dräf-\ *n* —**drafty** \ˈdraftē\ *adj*

drafts•man \ˈdraftsmən, ˈdräft-\ *n* : person who draws plans

drag \ˈdrag\ *n* 1 : something dragged over a surface or through water 2 : something that hinders progress or is boring 3 : act or an instance of dragging ~ *vb* **-gg-** 1 : haul 2 : move or work with difficulty 3 : pass slowly 4 : search or fish with a drag —**drag•ger** *n*

drag•net \-ˌnet\ *n* 1 : trawl 2 : planned actions for finding a criminal

drag•on \ˈdragən\ *n* : fabled winged serpent

drag•on•fly *n* : large 4-winged insect

drain \ˈdrān\ *vb* 1 : draw off or flow off gradually or completely 2 : exhaust ~ *n* : means or act of draining —**drain•age** \-ij\ *n* —**drain•er** *n* —**drain•pipe** *n*

drake \ˈdrāk\ *n* : male duck

dra•ma \ˈdrämə, ˈdram-\ *n* 1 : composition for theatrical presentation esp. on a serious subject 2 : series of events involving conflicting forces —**dra•mat•ic** \drəˈmatik\ *adj* —**dra•mat•i•cal•ly** \-iklē\ *adv* —**dram•a•tist** \ˈdramətist, ˈdräm-\ *n* —**dram•a•ti•za•tion** \ˌdramətəˈzāshən, ˌdräm-\ *n* —**dra•ma•tize** \ˈdraməˌtīz, ˈdräm-\ *vb*

drank *past of* DRINK

drape \ˈdrāp\ *vb* **draped; drap•ing** 1 : cover or adorn with folds of cloth 2 : cause to hang in flowing lines or folds ~ *n* : curtain

drap•ery \ˈdrāpərē\ *n, pl* **-er•ies** : decorative fabric hung esp. as a heavy curtain

dras•tic \ˈdrastik\ *adj* : extreme or harsh —**dras•ti•cal•ly** \-tiklē\ *adj*

draught \ˈdraft\, **draughty** \ˈdraftē\ *chiefly Brit var of* DRAFT, DRAFTY

draw \ˈdrȯ\ *vb* **drew** \ˈdrü\; **drawn** \ˈdrȯn\; **draw•ing** 1 : move or cause to move (as by pulling) 2 : attract or provoke 3 : extract 4 : take or receive (as money) 5 : bend a bow in preparation for shooting 6 : leave a contest undecided 7 : sketch 8 : write out 9 : deduce ~ *n* 1 : act, process, or result of drawing 2 : tie —**draw out** : cause to speak candidly —**draw up** 1 : write out 2 : pull oneself erect 3 : bring or come to a stop

draw•back *n* : disadvantage

draw•bridge *n* : bridge that can be raised

draw•er \ˈdrȯr, ˈdrȯər\ *n* 1 : one that draws 2 : sliding boxlike compartment 3 *pl* : underpants

draw•ing \ˈdrȯiŋ\ *n* 1 : occasion of choosing by lot 2 : act or art of making a figure, plan, or sketch with lines 3 : something drawn

drawl \ˈdrȯl\ *vb* : speak slowly —**drawl** *n*

dread \ˈdred\ *vb* : feel extreme fear or reluctance ~ *n* : great fear ~ *adj* : causing dread —**dread•ful** \-fəl\ *adj* —**dread•ful•ly** *adv*

dream \ˈdrēm\ *n* 1 : series of thoughts or visions during sleep 2 : dreamlike vision 3 : something notable 4 : ideal ~ *vb* **dreamed** \ˈdremt, ˈdrēmd\ *or* **dreamt** \ˈdremt\ **dream•ing** 1 : have a dream 2 : imagine —**dream•er** *n* —**dream•like** *adj* —**dreamy** *adj*

drea•ry \ˈdrirē\ *adj* **-ri•er; -est** : dismal —**drea•ri•ly** \ˈdrirəlē\ *adv*

[1]**dredge** \ˈdrej\ *n* : machine for removing earth esp. from under water ~ *vb* **dredged; dredg•ing** : dig up or search with a dredge —**dredg•er** *n*

[2]**dredge** *vb* **dredged; dredg•ing** : coat (food) with flour

dregs \ˈdregz\ *n pl* 1 : sediment 2 : most worthless part

drench \ˈdrench\ *vb* : wet thoroughly

dress \ˈdres\ *vb* 1 : put clothes on 2 : decorate 3 : prepare (as a carcass) for use 4 : apply dressings, remedies, or fertilizer to ~ *n* 1 : apparel 2 : single garment of bodice and skirt ~ *adj* : suitable for a formal event —**dress•mak•er** *n* —**dress•mak•ing** *n*

dress•er \ˈdresər\ *n* : bureau with a mirror

dress•ing *n* 1 : act or process of dressing 2 : sauce or a seasoned mixture 3 : material to cover an injury

dressy \ˈdresē\ *adj* **dress•i•er; -est** 1 : showy in dress 2 : stylish

drew *past of* DRAW

drib•ble \ˈdribəl\ *vb* **-bled; -bling** 1 : fall or flow in drops 2 : drool —**dribble** *n*

drier *comparative of* DRY

driest *superlative of* DRY

drift \ˈdrift\ *n* 1 : motion or course of something drifting 2 : mass piled up by wind 3 : general intention or meaning ~ *vb* 1 : float or be driven along (as by a current) 2 : wander without purpose 3 : pile up under force —**drift•er** *n* —**drift•wood** *n*

[1]**drill** \ˈdril\ *vb* 1 : bore with a drill 2 : instruct by repetition ~ *n* 1 : tool for boring holes 2 : regularly practiced exercise —**drill•er** *n*

[2]**drill** *n* : seed-planting implement

[3]**drill** *n* : twill-weave cotton fabric

drily *var of* DRYLY

drink \ˈdriŋk\ *vb* **drank** \ˈdraŋk\; **drunk** \ˈdrəŋk\ *or* **drank; drink•ing** 1 : swallow liquid 2 : absorb 3 : drink alcoholic beverages esp. to excess ~ *n* 1 : beverage 2 : alcoholic liquor —**drink•able** *adj* —**drink•er** *n*

drip \ˈdrip\ *vb* **-pp-** : fall or let fall in drops ~ *n* 1 : a dripping 2 : sound of falling drops

drive \ˈdrīv\ *vb* **drove** \ˈdrōv\; **driv•en** \ˈdrivən\; **driv•ing** 1 : urge or force onward 2 : direct the movement or course of 3 : compel 4 : cause to become 5 : propel forcefully ~ *n* 1 : trip in a vehicle 2 : intensive campaign 3 : aggressive or dynamic quality 4 : basic need —**driv•er** *n*

drive–in *adj* : accommodating patrons in cars —**drive–in** *n*

driv•el \ˈdrivəl\ *vb* **-eled** *or* **-elled; -el•ing** *or* **el•ling** 1 : drool 2 : talk stupidly ~ *n* : nonsense

drive•way *n* : usu. short private road from the street to a house

driz•zle \ˈdrizəl\ *n* : fine misty rain —**driz•zle** *vb*

droll \ˈdrōl\ *adj* : humorous or whimsical —**droll•ery** *n* —**drol•ly** *adv*

drom•e•dary \ˈdräməˌderē\ *n, pl* **-dar•ies** : speedy one-humped camel

drone \ˈdrōn\ *n* 1 : male honeybee 2 : deep hum or buzz ~ *vb* **droned; dron•ing** : make a dull monotonous sound

drool \ˈdrül\ *vb* : let liquid run from the mouth

droop \ˈdrüp\ *vb* 1 : hang or incline downward 2 : lose strength or spirit —**droop** *n* —**droopy** \-ē\ *adj*

drop \ˈdräp\ *n* 1 : quantity of fluid in one spherical mass 2 *pl* : medicine used by drops 3 : decline or fall 4 : distance something drops ~ *vb* **-pp-** 1 : fall in drops 2 : let fall 3 : convey 4 : go lower or become less strong or less active —**drop•let** \-lət\ *n* —**drop back** *vb* : move toward the rear —**drop behind** : fail to keep up —**drop in** *vb* : pay an unexpected visit

drop•per *n* : device that dispenses liquid by drops

drop•sy \ˈdräpsē\ *n* : edema

dross \ˈdräs\ *n* : waste matter

drought \ˈdrau̇t\ *n* : long dry spell

1drove \'drōv\ n : crowd of moving people or animals

2drove past of DRIVE

drown \'draůn\ vb **1** : suffocate in water **2** : overpower or become overpowered

drowse \'draůz\ vb **drowsed; drows•ing** : doze —**drowse** n

drowsy \'draůzē\ adj **drows•i•er; -est** : sleepy —**drows•i•ly** adv —**drows•i•ness** n

drub \'drəb\ vb **-bb-** : beat severely

drudge \'drəj\ vb **drudged; drudg•ing** : do hard or boring work —**drudge** n —**drudg•ery** \-ərē\ n

drug \'drəg\ n **1** : substance used as or in medicine **2** : narcotic ~ vb **-gg-** : affect with drugs —**drug•gist** \-ist\ n —**drug•store** n

dru•id \'drüəd\ n : ancient Celtic priest

drum \'drəm\ n **1** : musical instrument that is a skin-covered cylinder beaten usu. with sticks **2** : drum-shaped object (as a container) ~ vb **-mm- 1** : beat a drum **2** : drive, force, or bring about by steady effort —**drum•beat** n —**drum•mer** n

drum•stick n **1** : stick for beating a drum **2** : lower part of a fowl's leg

drunk \'drəŋk\ adj : having the faculties impaired by alcohol ~ n : one who is drunk —**drunk•ard** \'drəŋkərd\ n —**drunk•en** \-kən\ adj —**drunk•en•ly** adv —**drunk•en•ness** n

dry \'drī\ adj **dri•er** \'drīər\; **dri•est** \'drīəst\ **1** : lacking water or moisture **2** : thirsty **3** : marked by the absence of alcoholic beverages **4** : uninteresting **5** : not sweet ~ vb **dried; dry•ing** : make or become dry —**dry•ly** adv —**dry•ness** n

dry–clean vb : clean (fabrics) chiefly with solvents other than water —**dry cleaning** n

dry•er \'drīər\ n : device for drying

dry goods n pl : textiles, clothing, and notions

dry ice n : solid carbon dioxide

du•al \'düəl, 'dyü-\ adj : twofold —**du•al•ism** \-ə,lizəm\ n —**du•al•i•ty** \dü'alətē, dyü-\ n

dub \'dəb\ vb **-bb-** : name

du•bi•ous \'dübēəs, 'dyü-\ adj **1** : uncertain **2** : questionable —**du•bi•ous•ly** adv —**du•bi•ous•ness** n

du•cal \'dükəl, 'dyü-\ adj : relating to a duke or dukedom

duch•ess \'dəchəs\ n **1** : wife of a duke **2** : woman holding a ducal title

duchy \-ē\ n, pl **-ies** : territory of a duke or duchess

1duck \'dək\ n, pl : swimming bird related to the goose and swan ~ vb **1** : thrust or plunge under water **2** : lower the head or body suddenly **3** : evade —**duck•ling** \-liŋ\ n

2duck n : cotton fabric

duct \'dəkt\ n : canal for conveying a fluid —**duct•less** \-ləs\ adj

duc•tile \'dəktᵊl\ adj : able to be drawn out or shaped —**duc•til•i•ty** \,dək'tilətē\ n

dude \'düd, 'dyüd\ n **1** : dandy **2** : guy

dud•geon \'dəjən\ n : ill humor

due \'dü, 'dyü\ adj **1** : owed **2** : appropriate **3** : attributable **4** : scheduled ~ n **1** : something due **2** pl : fee ~ adv : directly

du•el \'düəl, 'dyü-\ n : combat between 2 persons —**duel** vb —**du•el•ist** n

du•et \dü'et, dyü-\ n : musical composition for 2 performers

due to prep : because of

dug past of DIG

dug•out \'dəg,aůt\ n **1** : boat made by hollowing out a log **2** : shelter made by digging

duke \'dük, 'dyük\ n : nobleman of the highest rank —**duke•dom** n

dull \'dəl\ adj **1** : mentally slow **2** : blunt **3** : not brilliant or interesting —**dull** vb —**dul•lard** \'dələrd\ n —**dull•ness** n —**dul•ly** adv

du•ly \'dülē, 'dyü-\ adv : in a due manner or time

dumb \'dəm\ adj **1** : mute **2** : stupid —**dumb•ly** adv

dumb•bell \'dəm,bel\ n **1** : short bar with weights on the ends used for exercise **2** : stupid person

dumb•found, dum•found \,dəm'faůnd\ vb : amaze

dum•my \'dəmē\ n, pl **-mies 1** : stupid person **2** : imitative substitute

dump \'dəmp\ vb : let fall in a pile ~ n : place for dumping something (as refuse) —**in the dumps** : sad

dump•ling \'dəmpliŋ\ n : small mass of boiled or steamed dough

dumpy \'dəmpē\ adj **dump•i•er; -est** : short and thick in build

1dun \'dən\ adj : brownish gray

2dun vb **-nn-** : hound for payment of a debt

dunce \'dəns\ n : stupid person

dune \'dün, 'dyün\ n : hill of sand

dung \'dəŋ\ n : manure

dun•ga•ree \,dəŋgə'rē\ n **1** : blue denim **2** pl : work clothes made of dungaree

dun•geon \'dənjən\ n : underground prison

dunk \'dəŋk\ vb : dip or submerge temporarily in liquid

duo \'düō, 'dyüō\ n, pl **du•os** : pair

du•o•de•num \,düə'dēnəm, ,dyü-; dů'ädᵊnəm, dyů-\ n, pl **-na** \-'dēnə, -ᵊnə\ or **-nums** : part of the small intestine nearest the stomach —**du•o•de•nal** \-'dēnᵊl, -ᵊnəl\ adj

dupe \'düp, dyüp\ n : one easily deceived or cheated —**dupe** vb

du•plex \'dü,pleks, 'dyü-\ adj : double ~ n : 2-family house

du•pli•cate \'düplikət, 'dyü-\ adj **1** : consisting of 2 identical items **2** : being just like another ~ n : exact copy ~ \-,kāt\ vb **-cat•ed; -cat•ing 1** : make an exact copy of **2** : repeat or equal —**du•pli•ca•tion** \,düpli'kāshən, ,dyü-\ n —**du•pli•ca•tor** \'düpli,kātər, dyü-\ n

du•plic•i•ty \dů'plisətē, ,dyü-\ n, pl **-ties** : deception

du•ra•ble \'důrəbəl, 'dyůr-\ adj : lasting a long time —**du•ra•bil•i•ty** \,důrə'bilətē, ,dyůr-\ n

du•ra•tion \dů'rāshən, dyů-\ n : length of time something lasts

du•ress \dů'res, dyů-\ n : coercion

dur•ing \'důriŋ, 'dyůr-\ prep **1** : throughout **2** : at some point in

dusk \'dəsk\ n : twilight —**dusky** adj

dust \'dəst\ n : powdered matter ~ vb **1** : remove dust from **2** : sprinkle with fine particles —**dust•er** n —**dust•pan** n —**dusty** adj

du•ty \'dütē, 'dyü-\ n, pl **-ties 1** : action required by one's occupation or position **2** : moral or legal obligation **3** : tax —**du•te•ous** \-əs\ adj —**du•ti•able** \-ēəbəl\ adj —**du•ti•ful** \'dütifəl, 'dyü-\ adj

dwarf \'dwȯrf\ n, pl **dwarfs** \'dwȯrfs\ or **dwarves** \'dwȯrvz\ : one that is much below normal size ~ vb **1** : stunt **2** : cause to seem smaller —**dwarf•ish** adj

dwell \'dwel\ vb **dwelt** \'dwelt\ or **dwelled** \'dweld, 'dwelt\; **dwell•ing 1** : reside **2** : keep the attention directed —**dwell•er** n —**dwell•ing** n

dwin•dle \'dwindᵊl\ vb **-dled; -dling** : become steadily less

dye \'dī\ n : coloring material ~ vb **dyed; dye•ing** : give a new color to

dying pres part of DIE

dyke var of DIKE

dy•nam•ic \dī'namik\ adj **1** : relating to physical force producing motion **2** : energetic or forceful

dy•na•mite \'dīnə,mīt\ n : explosive made of nitroglycerin —**dynamite** vb

dy•na•mo \-,mō\ n, pl **-mos** : electrical generator

dy•nas•ty \'dīnəstē, -,nas-\ n, pl **-ties** : succession of rulers of the same family —**dy•nas•tic** \dī'nastik\ adj

dys•en•tery \'disᵊn,terē\ n, pl **-ter•ies** : disease marked by diarrhea

dys•lex•ia \dis'leksēə\ n : disturbance of the ability to read —**dys•lex•ic** \-sik\ adj

dys•pep•sia \-'pepshə, -sēə\ n : indigestion —**dys•pep•tic** \-'peptik\ adj or n

dys•tro•phy \'distrəfē\ n, pl **-phies** : disorder involving nervous and muscular tissue

E

e \'ē\ n, pl **e's** or **es** \'ēz\ : 5th letter of the alphabet

each \'ēch\ adj : being one of the class named ~ pron : every individual one ~ adv : apiece

ea•ger \'ēgər\ adj : enthusiastic or anxious —**ea•ger•ly** adv —**ea•ger•ness** n

ea•gle \'ēgəl\ n : large bird of prey

-ean —see -AN

1ear \'ir\ n : organ of hearing or the outer part of this —**ear•ache** n —**eared** adj —**ear•lobe** \-,lōb\ n

2ear n : fruiting head of a cereal

ear•drum n : thin membrane that receives and transmits sound waves in the ear

earl \'ərl\ n : British nobleman —**earl•dom** \-dəm\ n

ear•ly \'ərlē\ adj **-li•er; -li•est 1** : relating to or occurring near the beginning or before the usual time **2** : ancient —**early** adv

ear•mark vb : designate for a specific purpose

earn \'ərn\ vb **1** : receive as a return for service **2** : deserve

ear•nest \'ərnəst\ n : serious state of mind —**earnest** adj —**ear•nest•ly** adv —**ear•nest•ness** n

earn•ings \'ərniŋz\ n pl : something earned

ear•phone n : device that reproduces sound and is worn over or in the ear

ear•ring n : earlobe ornament

ear•shot n : range of hearing

earth \'ərth\ n **1** : soil or land **2** : planet inhabited by man —**earth•li•ness** n —**earth•ly** adj —**earth•ward** \-wərd\ adv

earth•en \'ərthən\ adj : made of earth or baked clay —**earth•en•ware** \-,war\ n

earth•quake n : shaking or trembling of the earth

earth•worm n : long segmented worm

earthy \'ərthē\ adj **earth•i•er; -est 1** : relating to or consisting of earth **2** : practical **3** : coarse —**earth•i•ness** n

ease \'ēz\ n **1** : comfort **2** : naturalness of manner **3** : freedom from difficulty ~ vb **eased; eas•ing 1** : relieve from distress **2** : lessen the tension of **3** : make easier

ea•sel \'ēzəl\ n : frame to hold a painter's canvas

east \'ēst\ adv : to or toward the east ~ adj : situated toward or at or coming from the east ~ n **1** : direction of sunrise **2** cap : regions to the east —**east•er•ly** \'ēstərlē\ adv or adj —**east•ward** adv or adj —**east•wards** adv

Eas•ter \'ēstər\ n : church feast celebrating Christ's resurrection

east•ern \'ēstərn\ adj **1** cap : relating to a region designated East **2** : lying toward or coming from the east —**East•ern•er** n

easy \'ēzē\ adj **eas•i•er; -est 1** : marked by ease **2** : lenient —**eas•i•ly** \'ēzəlē\ adv —**eas•i•ness** \-ēnəs\ n

easy•go•ing adj : relaxed and casual

eat \'ēt\ vb **ate** \'āt\; **eat•en** \'ētᵊn\; **eat•ing 1** : take in as food **2** : use up or corrode —**eat•able** adj or n —**eat•er** n

eaves \'ēvz\ n pl : overhanging edge of a roof

eaves•drop vb : listen secretly —**eaves•drop•per** n

ebb \'eb\ n **1** : outward flow of the tide **2** : decline ~ vb **1** : recede from the flood state **2** : wane

eb•o•ny \'ebənē\ n, pl **-nies** : hard heavy wood of tropical trees ~ adj **1** : made of ebony **2** : black

ebul•lient \i'bůlyənt, -'bəl-\ adj : exuberant —**ebul•lience** \-yəns\ n

ec•cen•tric \ik'sentrik\ adj **1** : odd in behavior **2** : being off center —**eccentric** n —**ec•cen•tri•cal•ly** \-triklē\ adv —**ec•cen•tric•i•ty** \,ek,sen'trisətē\ n

ec•cle•si•as•tic \ik,lēzē'astik\ n : clergyman

ec•cle•si•as•ti•cal \-tikəl\, **ecclesiastic** adj : relating to a church —**ec•cle•si•as•ti•cal•ly** \-tiklē\ adv

ech•e•lon \'eshə,län\ n **1** : steplike arrangement **2** : level of authority

echo \'ekō\ n, pl **ech•oes** : repetition of a sound caused by a reflection of the sound waves —**echo** vb

éclair \ā'klar\ n : custard-filled pastry

eclec•tic \e'klektik, i-\ adj : drawing or drawn from varied sources

eclipse \i'klips\ n : total or partial obscuring of one celestial body by another —**eclipse** vb

ecol•o•gy \i'käləjē, e-\ n, pl **-gies** : science concerned with the interaction of organisms and their environment —**eco•log•i•cal** \,ēkə'läjikəl, ,ek-\ adj —**eco•log•i•cal•ly** adv —**ecol•o•gist** \i'käləjist, e-\ n

eco•nom•ic \,ekə'nämik, ,ēkə-\ adj : relating to the producing and the buying and selling of goods and services

eco•nom•ics \-'nämiks\ n : branch of knowledge dealing with goods and services —**econ•o•mist** \i'känəmist\ n

econ•o•mize \i'känə,mīz\ vb **-mized; -miz•ing** : be thrifty —**econ•o•miz•er** n

econ•o•my \-əmē\ n, pl **-mies 1** : thrifty use of resources **2** : economic system —**eco•nom•i•cal** \,ekə'nämikəl, ,ēkə-\ adj —**eco•nom•i•cal•ly** adv —**economy** adj

ecru \'ekrü, 'ākrü\ n : beige

ec•sta•sy \'ekstəsē\ n, pl **-sies** : extreme emotional excitement —**ec•stat•ic** \ek'statik, ik-\ adj —**ec•stat•i•cal•ly** \-iklē\ adv

ec•u•men•i•cal \,ekyə'menikəl\ adj : promoting worldwide Christian unity

ec•ze•ma \ig'zēmə, 'egzəmə, 'eksə-\ n : itching skin inflammation

1-ed \d after a vowel or b, g, j, l, m, n, ŋ, r, th, v, z, zh; əd, id after d, t; t after other sounds\ vb suffix or adj suffix **1** —used to form the past participle of regular verbs **2** : having or having the characteristics of

2-ed vb suffix —used to form the past tense of regular verbs

ed•dy \'edē\ n, pl **-dies** : whirlpool —**eddy** vb

ede•ma \i'dēmə\ n : abnormal accumulation of fluid in the body tissues —**edem•a•tous** \-'demətəs\ adj

Eden \'ēdᵊn\ n : paradise

edge \'ej\ n **1** : cutting side of a blade **2** : line where something begins or ends ~ vb **edged; edg•ing 1** : give or form an edge **2** : move gradually **3** : narrowly defeat —**edg•er** n

edge•wise \-,wīz\ adv : sideways

edgy \'ejē\ adj **edg•i•er; -est** : nervous —**edg•i•ness** n

ed•i•ble \'edəbəl\ adj : fit or safe to be eaten —**ed•i•bil•i•ty** \,edə'bilətē\ n —**edible** n

edict \'ē,dikt\ n : order or decree

ed•i•fi•ca•tion \,edəfə'kāshən\ n : instruction or information —**ed•i•fy** \'edə,fī\ vb

ed•i•fice \'edəfəs\ n : large building

ed•it \'edət\ vb **1** : revise and prepare for publication **2** : delete —**ed•i•tor** \-ər\ n —**ed•i•tor•ship** n

edi•tion \i'dishən\ n **1** : form in which a text is published **2** : total number published at one time

ed•i•to•ri•al \,edə'tōrēəl\ adj **1** : relating to an editor or editing **2** : expressing opinion ~ n : article (as in a newspaper) expressing the views of an editor —**ed•i•to•ri•al•ize** \-ēə,līz\ vb —**ed•i•to•ri•al•ly** adv

ed•u•cate \'ejə,kāt\ vb **-cat•ed; -cat•ing 1** : give instruction to **2** : develop mentally and morally **3** : provide with information —**ed•u•ca•ble** \'ejəkəbəl\ adj —**ed•u•ca•tion** \,ejə'kāshən\ n —**ed•u•ca•tion•al** \-shənᵊl\ adj —**ed•u•ca•tor** \-ər\ n

eel \'ēl\ n : snakelike fish

ee•rie \'irē\ adj **-ri•er; -est** : weird —**ee•ri•ly** \'irəlē\ adv

ef•face \i'fās, e-\ vb **-faced; -fac•ing** : obliterate by rubbing out —**ef•face•ment** n

ef•fect \i'fekt\ n **1** : result **2** : meaning **3** : influence **4** pl : goods or possessions ~ vb : cause to happen —**in effect** : in substance

ef•fec•tive \i'fektiv\ adj **1** : producing a strong or desired effect **2** : being in operation —**ef•fec•tive•ly** adv —**ef•fec•tive•ness** n

ef•fec•tu•al \i'fekchəwəl\ adj : producing an intended effect —**ef•fec•tu•al•ly** adv —**ef•fec•tu•al•ness** n

ef•fem•i•nate \ə'femənət\ adj : unsuitably womanish —**ef•fem•i•na•cy** \-nəsē\ n

ef•fer•vesce \,efər'ves\ vb **-vesced; -vesc•ing 1** : bubble and hiss as gas escapes **2** : show exhilaration —**ef•fer•ves•cence** \-'vesᵊns\ n —**ef•fer•ves•cent** \-ᵊnt\ adj —**ef•fer•ves•cent•ly** adv

ef•fete \e'fēt\ adj **1** : worn out **2** : weak or decadent **3** : effeminate

ef•fi•ca•cious \,efə'kāshəs\ adj : effective —**ef•fi•ca•cy** \'efikəsē\ n

ef•fi•cient \i'fishənt\ adj : working well with little waste —**ef•fi•cien•cy** \-ənsē\ n —**ef•fi•cient•ly** adv

ef•fi•gy \'efəjē\ n, pl **-gies** : usu. crude image of a person

ef•flu•ent \'e,flüənt, e'flü-\ n : something that flows out —**effluent** adj

ef•fort \'efərt\ n **1** : a putting forth of strength **2** : use of resources toward a goal **3** : product of effort —**ef•fort•less** adj —**ef•fort•less•ly** adv

ef•fron•tery \i'frəntərē\ n, pl **-ter•ies** : insolence

ef•fu•sion \i'fyüzhən, e-\ n : a gushing forth —**ef•fu•sive** \-'fyüsiv\ adj —**ef•fu•sive•ly** adv

1egg \'eg, 'āg\ vb : urge to action

2egg n **1** : rounded usu. hard-shelled reproductive body esp. of birds and reptiles from which the young hatches **2** : ovum —**egg•shell** n

egg•nog \-,näg\ n : rich drink of eggs and cream

egg•plant n : edible purplish fruit of a plant related to the potato

ego \'ēgō\ n, pl **egos** : self-esteem

ego•cen•tric \,ēgō'sentrik\ adj : self-centered

ego•tism \'ēgə,tizəm\ n : exaggerated sense of self-importance —**ego•tist** \-tist\ n —**ego•tis•tic** \,ēgə'tistik\ **ego•tis•ti•cal** \-tikəl\ adj —**ego•tis•ti•cal•ly** adv

egre•gious \i'grējəs\ adj : notably bad —**egre•gious•ly** adv

egress \'ē,gres\ n : a way out

egret \'ēgrət, i'gret, 'egrət\ n : long-plumed heron

ei•der•down \'īdər,daůn\ n : soft down obtained from a northern sea duck (**eider**)

eight \'āt\ n **1** : one more than 7 **2** : 8th in a set or series **3** : something having 8 units —**eight** adj or pron —**eighth** \'ātth\ adj or adv or n

eigh•teen \āt'tēn\ n : one more than 17 —**eigh•teen** adj or pron —**eigh•teenth** \-'tēnth\ adj or n

eighty \'ātē\ n, pl **eight•ies** : 8 times 10 —**eight•i•eth** \'ātēəth\ adj or n —**eighty** adj or pron

ei•ther \'ēthər, 'ī-\ adj **1** : both **2** : being the one or the other of two ~ pron : one of two or more ~ conj : one or the other

ejac•u•late \i'jakyə,lāt\ *vb* **-lat•ed; -lat•ing** **1** : say suddenly **2** : eject a fluid (as semen) **—ejac•u•la•tion** \-,jakyə'lāshən\ *n*

eject \i'jekt\ *vb* : drive or throw out **—ejec•tion** \-'jekshən\ *n*

eke \'ēk\ *vb* **eked; ek•ing** : barely gain with effort —usu. with *out*

elab•o•rate \i'labərət\ *adj* **1** : planned in detail **2** : complex and ornate ~ \-ə,rāt\ *vb* **-rat•ed; -rat•ing** : work out in detail **—elab•o•rate•ly** *adv* **—elab•o•rate•ness** *n* **—elab•o•ra•tion** \-,labə'rāshən\ *n*

elapse \i'laps\ *vb* **elapsed; elaps•ing** : slip by

elas•tic \i'lastik\ *adj* **1** : springy **2** : flexible ~ *n* **1** : elastic material **2** : rubber band **—elas•tic•i•ty** \-,las'tisətē, ,ē,las-\ *n*

elate \i'lāt\ *vb* **elat•ed; elat•ing** : fill with joy **—ela•tion** \-'lāshən\ *n*

el•bow \'el,bō\ *n* **1** : joint of the arm **2** : elbow-shaped bend or joint ~ *vb* : push aside with the elbow

el•der \'eldər\ *adj* : older ~ *n* **1** : one who is older **2** : church officer

el•der•ber•ry \'eldər,berē\ *n* : edible black or red fruit or a tree or shrub bearing these

el•der•ly \'eldərlē\ *adj* : past middle age

el•dest \'eldəst\ *adj* : oldest

elect \i'lekt\ *adj* : elected but not yet in office ~ *n* **elect** *pl* : exclusive group ~ *vb* : choose esp. by vote **—elec•tion** \i'lekshən\ *n* **—elec•tive** \i'lektiv\ *n or adj* **—elec•tor** \i'lektər\ *n* **—elec•tor•al** \-tərəl\ *adj*

elec•tor•ate \i'lektərət\ *n* : body of persons entitled to vote

elec•tric \i'lektrik\ *adj* **1** : *or* **elec•tri•cal** \-trikəl\ : relating to or run by electricity **2** : thrilling **—elec•tri•cal•ly** *adv*

elec•tri•cian \i,lek'trishən\ *n* : person who installs or repairs electrical equipment

elec•tric•i•ty \-'trisətē\ *n, pl* **-ties** **1** : fundamental form of energy occurring naturally (as in lightning) or produced artificially **2** : electric current

elec•tri•fy \i'lektrə,fī\ *vb* **-fied; -fy•ing** **1** : charge with electricity **2** : equip for use of electric power **3** : thrill **—elec•tri•fi•ca•tion** \-,lektrəfə'kāshən\ *n*

elec•tro•car•dio•gram \i,lektrō'kärdēə,gram\ *n* : tracing made by an electrocardiograph

elec•tro•car•dio•graph \-,graf\ *n* : instrument for monitoring heart function

elec•tro•cute \i'lektrə,kyüt\ *vb* **-cut•ed; -cut•ing** : kill by an electric shock **—elec•tro•cu•tion** \-,lektrə'kyüshən\ *n*

elec•trode \i'lek,trōd\ *n* : conductor at a nonmetallic part of a circuit

elec•trol•y•sis \i,lek'träləsəs\ *n* **1** : production of chemical changes by passage of an electric current through a substance **2** : destruction of hair roots with an electric current **—elec•tro•lyt•ic** \-trə'litik\ *adj*

elec•tro•lyte \i'lektrə,līt\ *n* : nonmetallic electric conductor

elec•tro•mag•net \i,lektrō'magnət\ *n* : magnet made using electric current

elec•tro•mag•ne•tism \-nə,tizəm\ *n* : natural force responsible for interactions between charged particles **—elec•tro•mag•net•ic** \-mag'netik\ *adj* **—elec•tro•mag•net•i•cal•ly** \-iklē\ *adv*

elec•tron \i'lek,trän\ *n* : negatively charged particle within the atom

elec•tron•ic \i,lek'tränik\ *adj* : relating to electrons or electronics **—elec•tron•i•cal•ly** \-iklē\ *adv*

elec•tron•ics \-iks\ *n* : physics of electrons and their use esp. in devices

elec•tro•plate \i'lektrə,plāt\ *vb* : coat (as with metal) by electrolysis

el•e•gance \'eligəns\ *n* : refined gracefulness **—el•e•gant** \-gənt\ *adj* **—el•e•gant•ly** *adv*

el•e•gy \'eləjē\ *n, pl* **-gies** : poem expressing grief for one who is dead **—ele•gi•ac** \,elə'jīək, -,ak\ *adj*

el•e•ment \'eləmənt\ *n* **1** *pl* : weather conditions **2** : natural environment **3** : constituent part **4** *pl* : simplest principles **5** : substance that has atoms of only one kind **—el•e•men•tal** \,elə'mentᵊl\ *adj*

el•e•men•ta•ry \,elə'mentrē\ *adj* **1** : simple **2** : relating to the basic subjects of education

el•e•phant \'eləfənt\ *n* : huge mammal with a trunk and 2 ivory tusks

el•e•vate \'elə,vāt\ *vb* **-vat•ed; -vat•ing** **1** : lift up **2** : exalt

el•e•va•tion \,elə'vāshən\ *n* : height or a high place

el•e•va•tor \'elə,vātər\ *n* **1** : cage or platform for raising or lowering something **2** : grain storehouse

elev•en \i'levən\ *n* **1** : one more than 10 **2** : 11th in a set or series **3** : something having 11 units **—eleven** *adj or pron* **—elev•enth** \-ənth\ *adj or n*

elf \'elf\ *n, pl* **elves** \'elvz\ : mischievous fairy **—elf•in** \'elfən\ *adj* **—elf•ish** \'elfish\ *adj*

elic•it \i'lisət\ *vb* : draw forth

el•i•gi•ble \'eləjəbəl\ *adj* : qualified to participate or to be chosen **—el•i•gibil•i•ty** \,eləjə'bilətē\ *n* **—eligible** *n*

elim•i•nate \i'limə,nāt\ *vb* **-nat•ed; -nat•ing** : get rid of **—elim•i•na•tion** \i,limə'nāshən\ *n*

elite \ā'lēt\ *n* : choice or select group

elix•ir \i'liksər\ *n* : medicinal solution

elk \'elk\ *n* : large deer

el•lipse \i'lips, e-\ *n* : oval

el•lip•sis \-'lipsəs\ *n, pl* **-lip•ses** \-,sēz\ **1** : omission of a word **2** : marks (as . . .) to show omission

el•lip•ti•cal \-tikəl\, **el•lip•tic** \-tik\ *adj* **1** : relating to or shaped like an ellipse **2** : relating to or marked by ellipsis

elm \'elm\ *n* : tall shade tree

el•o•cu•tion \,elə'kyüshən\ *n* : art of public speaking

elon•gate \i'lȯŋ,gāt\ *vb* **-gat•ed; -gat•ing** : make or grow longer **—elon•ga•tion** \,ē,lȯŋ'gāshən\ *n*

elope \i'lōp\ *vb* **eloped; elop•ing** : run away esp. to be married **—elope•ment** *n* **—elop•er** *n*

el•o•quent \'eləkwənt\ *adj* : forceful and persuasive in speech **—el•o•quence** \-kwəns\ *n* **—el•o•quent•ly** *adv*

else \'els\ *adv* **1** : in a different way, time, or place **2** : otherwise ~ *adj* **1** : other **2** : more

else•where *adv* : in or to another place

elu•ci•date \i'lüsə,dāt\ *vb* **-dat•ed; -dat•ing** : explain **—elu•ci•da•tion** \i,lüsə'dāshən\ *n*

elude \ē'lüd\ *vb* **elud•ed; elud•ing** : evade **—elu•sive** \ē'lüsiv\ *adj* **—elu•sive•ly** *adv* **—elu•sive•ness** *n*

elves *pl of* ELF

ema•ci•ate \i'māshē,āt\ *vb* **-at•ed; -at•ing** : become or make very thin **—ema•ci•a•tion** \i,māsē'āshən, -shē-\ *n*

em•a•nate \'emə,nāt\ *vb* **-nat•ed; -nat•ing** : come forth **—em•a•na•tion** \,emə'nāshən\ *n*

eman•ci•pate \i'mansə,pāt\ *vb* **-pat•ed; -pat•ing** : set free **—eman•ci•pa•tion** \i,mansə'pāshən\ *n* **—eman•ci•pa•tor** \i'mansə,pātər\ *n*

emas•cu•late \i'maskyə,lāt\ *vb* **-lat•ed; -lat•ing** **1** : castrate **2** : weaken **—emas•cu•la•tion** \i,maskyə'lāshən\ *n*

em•balm \im'bäm, -'bälm\ *vb* : preserve (a corpse) **—em•balm•er** *n*

em•bank•ment \im'baŋkmənt\ *n* : protective barrier of earth

em•bar•go \im'bärgō\ *n, pl* **-goes** : ban on trade **—embargo** *vb*

em•bark \-'bärk\ *vb* **1** : go on board a ship or airplane **2** : make a start **—em•bar•ka•tion** \,em,bär'kāshən\ *n*

em•bar•rass \im'barəs\ *vb* : cause distress and self-consciousness **—em•bar•rass•ment** *n*

em•bas•sy \'embəsē\ *n, pl* **-sies** : residence and offices of an ambassador

em•bed \im'bed\ *vb* **-dd-** : fix firmly

em•bel•lish \-'belish\ *vb* : decorate **—em•bel•lish•ment** *n*

em•ber \'embər\ *n* : smoldering fragment from a fire

em•bez•zle \im'bezəl\ *vb* **-zled; -zling** : steal (money) by falsifying records **—em•bez•zle•ment** *n* **—em•bez•zler** \-ələr\ *n*

em•bit•ter \im'bitər\ *vb* : make bitter

em•bla•zon \-'blāzᵊn\ *vb* : display conspicuously

em•blem \'embləm\ *n* : symbol **—em•blem•at•ic** \,emblə'matik\ *adj*

em•body \im'bädē\ *vb* **-bod•ied; -body•ing** : give definite form or expression to **—em•bodi•ment** \-'bädimənt\ *n*

em•boss \-'bäs, -'bȯs\ *vb* : ornament with raised work

em•brace \-'brās\ *vb* **-braced; -brac•ing** **1** : clasp in the arms **2** : welcome **3** : include **—embrace** *n*

em•broi•der \-'brȯidər\ *vb* : ornament with or do needlework **—em•broi•dery** \-ərē\ *n*

em•broil \im'brȯil\ *vb* : involve in conflict or difficulties

em•bryo \'embrē,ō\ *n* : living being in its earliest stages of development **—em•bry•on•ic** \,embrē'änik\ *adj*

emend \ē'mend\ *vb* : correct **—emen•da•tion** \,ē,men'dāshən\ *n*

em•er•ald \'emrəld, 'emə-\ *n* : green gem ~ *adj* : bright green

emerge \i'mərj\ *vb* **emerged; emerg•ing** : rise, come forth, or appear **—emer•gence** \-'mərjəns\ *n* **—emer•gent** \-jənt\ *adj*

emer•gen•cy \i'mərjənsē\ *n, pl* **-cies** : condition requiring prompt action

em•ery \'emərē\ *n, pl* **-er•ies** : dark granular mineral used for grinding

emet•ic \i'metik\ *n* : agent that induces vomiting **—emetic** *adj*

em•i•grate \'emə,grāt\ *vb* **-grat•ed; -grat•ing** : leave a country to settle elsewhere **—em•i•grant** \-igrənt\ *n* **—em•i•gra•tion** \,emə'grāshən\ *n*

em•i•nence \'emənəns\ *n* **1** : prominence or superiority **2** : person of high rank

em•i•nent \-nənt\ *adj* : prominent **—em•i•nent•ly** *adv*

em•is•sary \'emə,serē\ *n, pl* **-sar•ies** : agent

emis•sion \ē'mishən\ *n* : substance discharged into the air

emit \ē'mit\ *vb* **-tt-** : give off or out

emol•u•ment \i'mälyəmənt\ *n* : salary or fee

emote \i'mōt\ *vb* **emot•ed; emot•ing** : express emotion

emo•tion \i'mōshən\ *n* : intense feeling **—emo•tion•al** \-shənəl\ *adj* **—emo•tion•al•ly** *adv*

em•per•or \'empərər\ *n* : ruler of an empire

em•pha•sis \'emfəsəs\ *n, pl* **-pha•ses** \-,sēz\ : stress

em•pha•size \-,sīz\ *vb* **-sized; -siz•ing** : stress

em•phat•ic \im'fatik, em-\ *adj* : uttered with emphasis **—em•phat•i•cal•ly** \-iklē\ *adv*

em•pire \'em,pīr\ *n* : large state or a group of states

em•pir•i•cal \im'pirikəl\ *adj* : based on observation **—em•pir•i•cal•ly** \-iklē\ *adv*

em•ploy \im'plȯi\ *vb* **1** : use **2** : occupy ~ *n* : paid occupation **—em•ploy•ee, em•ploye** \im,plȯi'ē, -'plȯi,ē\ *n* **—em•ploy•er** *n* **—em•ploy•ment** \-mənt\ *n*

em•pow•er \im'paủər\ *vb* : give power to **—em•pow•er•ment** *n*

em•press \'emprəs\ *n* **1** : wife of an emperor **2** : woman emperor

emp•ty \'emptē\ *adj* **1** : containing nothing **2** : not occupied **3** : lacking value, sense, or purpose ~ *vb* **-tied; -ty•ing** : make or become empty **—emp•ti•ness** \-tēnəs\ *n*

emu \'ēmyü\ *n* : Australian bird related to the ostrich

em•u•late \'emyə,lāt\ *vb* **-lat•ed; -lat•ing** : try to equal or excel **—em•u•la•tion** \,emyə'lāshən\ *n*

emul•si•fy \i'məlsə,fī\ *vb* **-fied; -fy•ing** : convert into an emulsion **—emul•si•fi•ca•tion** \i,məlsəfə'kāshən\ *n* **—emul•si•fi•er** \-'məlsə,fīər\ *n*

emul•sion \i'məlshən\ *n* **1** : mixture of mutually insoluble liquids **2** : light-sensitive coating on photographic film

-en \ən, ᵊn\ *vb suffix* **1** : become or cause to be **2** : cause or come to have

en•able \in'ābəl\ *vb* **-abled; -abling** : give power, capacity, or ability to

en•act \in'akt\ *vb* **1** : make into law **2** : act out **—en•act•ment** *n*

enam•el \in'aməl\ *n* **1** : glasslike substance used to coat metal or pottery **2** : hard outer layer of a tooth **3** : glossy paint **—enamel** *vb*

en•am•or \in'amər\ *vb* : excite with love

en•camp \in'kamp\ *vb* : make camp **—en•camp•ment** *n*

en•case \in'kās\ *vb* : enclose in or as if in a case

-ence \əns, ᵊns\ *n suffix* **1** : action or process **2** : quality or state

en•ceph•a•li•tis \in,sefə'lītəs\ *n, pl* **-lit•i•des** \-'litə,dēz\ : inflammation of the brain

en•chant \in'chant\ *vb* **1** : bewitch **2** : fascinate **—en•chant•er** *n* **—en•chant•ment** *n* **—en•chant•ress** \-'chantrəs\ *n*

en•cir•cle \in'sərkəl\ *vb* : surround

en•close \in'klōz\ *vb* **1** : shut up or surround **2** : include **—en•clo•sure** \in'klōzhər\ *n*

en•co•mi•um \en'kōmēəm\ *n, pl* **-mi•ums** *or* **-mia** \-mēə\ : high praise

en•com•pass \in'kəmpəs, -'käm-\ *vb* : surround or include

en•core \'än,kōr\ *n* : further performance

en•coun•ter \in'kaủntər\ *vb* **1** : fight **2** : meet unexpectedly **—encounter** *n*

en•cour•age \in'kərij\ *vb* **-aged; -ag•ing** **1** : inspire with courage and hope **2** : foster **—en•cour•age•ment** *n*

en•croach \in'krōch\ *vb* : enter upon another's property or rights **—en•croach•ment** *n*

en•crust \in'krəst\ *vb* : form a crust on

en•cum•ber \in'kəmbər\ *vb* : burden **—en•cum•brance** \-brəns\ *n*

-en•cy \ənsē, ᵊn-\ *n suffix* : -ence

en•cyc•li•cal \in'siklikəl, en-\ *n* : papal letter to bishops

en•cy•clo•pe•dia \in,sīklə'pēdēə\ *n* : reference work on many subjects **—en•cy•clo•pe•dic** \-'pēdik\ *adj*

end \'end\ *n* **1** : point at which something stops or no longer exists **2** : cessation **3** : purpose ~ *vb* **1** : stop or finish **2** : be at the end of **—end•ed** *adj* **—end•less** *adj* **—end•less•ly** *adv*

en•dan•ger \in'dānjər\ *vb* : bring into danger

en•dear \in'dir\ *vb* : make dear **—en•dear•ment** \-mənt\ *n*

en•deav•or \in'devər\ *vb or n* : attempt

end•ing \'endiŋ\ *n* : end

en•dive \'en,dīv\ *n* : salad plant

en•do•crine \'endəkrən, -,krīn, -,krēn\ *adj* : producing secretions distributed by the bloodstream

en•dorse \in'dȯrs\ *vb* **-dorsed; -dors•ing** **1** : sign one's name to **2** : approve **—en•dorse•ment** *n*

en•dow \in'daủ\ *vb* **1** : furnish with funds **2** : furnish naturally **—en•dow•ment** *n*

en•dure \in'dủr, -'dyủr\ *vb* **-dured; -dur•ing** **1** : last **2** : suffer patiently **3** : tolerate **—en•dur•able** *adj* **—en•dur•ance** \-əns\ *n*

en•e•ma \'enəmə\ *n* : injection of liquid into the rectum

en•e•my \-mē\ *n, pl* **-mies** : one that attacks or tries to harm another

en•er•get•ic \,enər'jetik\ *adj* : full of energy or activity **—en•er•get•i•cal•ly** \-iklē\ *adv*

en•er•gize \'enər,jīz\ *vb* **-gized; -giz•ing** : give energy to

en•er•gy \'enərjē\ *n, pl* **-gies** **1** : capacity for action **2** : vigorous action **3** : capacity for doing work

en•er•vate \'enər,vāt\ *vb* **-vat•ed; -va•ting** : make weak or listless **—en•er•va•tion** \,enər'vāshən\ *n*

en•fold \in'fōld\ *vb* : surround or embrace

en•force \-'fōrs\ *vb* **1** : compel **2** : carry out **—en•force•able** \-əbəl\ *adj* **—en•force•ment** *n*

en•fran•chise \-'fran,chīz\ *vb* **-chised; -chis•ing** : grant voting rights to **—en•fran•chise•ment** \-,chīzmənt, -chəz-\ *n*

en•gage \in'gāj\ *vb* **-gaged; -gag•ing** **1** : participate or cause to participate **2** : bring or come into working contact **3** : bind by a pledge to marry **4** : hire **5** : bring or enter into conflict **—en•gage•ment** \-mənt\ *n*

en•gag•ing *adj* : attractive

en•gen•der \in'jendər\ *vb* **-dered; -der•ing** : create

en•gine \'enjən\ *n* **1** : machine that converts energy into mechanical motion **2** : locomotive

en•gi•neer \,enjə'nir\ *n* **1** : one trained in engineering **2** : engine operator ~ *vb* : lay out or manage as an engineer

en•gi•neer•ing \-iŋ\ *n* : practical application of science and mathematics

en•grave \in'grāv\ *vb* **-graved; -grav•ing** : cut into a surface **—en•grav•er** *n* **—en•grav•ing** *n*

en•gross \-'grōs\ *vb* : occupy fully

en•gulf \-'gəlf\ *vb* : swallow up

en•hance \-'hans\ *vb* **-hanced; -hanc•ing** : improve in value **—en•hance•ment** *n*

enig•ma \i'nigmə\ *n* : puzzle or mystery **—enig•mat•ic** \,enig'matik, ,ē-\ *adj* **—enig•mat•i•cal•ly** *adv*

en•join \in'jȯin\ *vb* **1** : command **2** : forbid

en•joy \-'jȯi\ *vb* : take pleasure in **—en•joy•able** *adj* **—en•joy•ment** *n*

en•large \-'lärj\ *vb* **-larged; -larg•ing** : make or grow larger **—en•large•ment** *n* **—en•larg•er** *n*

en•light•en \-'lītᵊn\ *vb* : give knowledge or spiritual insight to **—en•light•en•ment** *n*

en•list \-'list\ *vb* **1** : join the armed forces **2** : get the aid of **—en•list•ee** \-,lis'tē\ *n* **—en•list•ment** \-'listmənt\ *n*

en•liv•en \in'līvən\ *vb* : give life or spirit to

en•mi•ty \'enmətē\ *n, pl* **-ties** : mutual hatred

en•no•ble \in'ōbəl\ *vb* **-bled; -bling** : make noble

en•nui \,än'wē\ *n* : boredom

enor•mi•ty \i'nȯrmətē\ *n, pl* **-ties** **1** : great wickedness **2** : huge size

enor•mous \i'nȯrməs\ *adj* : great in size, number, or degree **—enor•mous•ly** *adv* **—enor•mous•ness** *n*

enough \i'nəf\ *adj* : adequate ~ *adv* **1** : in an adequate manner **2** : in a tolerable degree ~ *pron* : adequate number, quantity, or amount

en•quire \in'kwīr\, **en•qui•ry** \'in,kwīrē, in'-; 'inkwərē, 'iŋ-\ *var of* INQUIRE, INQUIRY

en•rage \in'rāj\ *vb* : fill with rage

en•rich \-'rich\ *vb* : make rich **—en•rich•ment** *n*

en•roll, en•rol \-'rōl\ *vb* **-rolled; -roll•ing** **1** : enter on a list **2** : become enrolled **—en•roll•ment** *n*

en route \äⁿ'rüt, en-, in-\ *adv or adj* : on or along the way

en•sconce \in'skäns\ *vb* **-sconced; -sconc•ing** : settle snugly

en•sem•ble \än'sämbəl\ *n* **1** : small group **2** : complete costume

en•shrine \in'shrīn\ *vb* **1** : put in a shrine **2** : cherish

en•sign \'ensən, *1 also* 'en,sīn\ *n* **1** : flag **2** : lowest ranking commissioned officer in the navy

en•slave \in'slāv\ *vb* : make a slave of **—en•slave•ment** *n*

en•snare \-'snar\ *vb* : trap

en•sue \-'sü\ *vb* **-sued; -su•ing** : follow as a consequence

en•sure \-'shủr\ *vb* **-sured; -sur•ing** : guarantee

en•tail \-'tāl\ *vb* : involve as a necessary result

en•tan•gle \-'taŋgəl\ *vb* : tangle **—entan•gle•ment** *n*

en•ter \'entər\ *vb* **1** : go or come in or into **2** : start **3** : set down (as in a list)

en•ter•prise \'entər,prīz\ *n* **1** : an undertaking **2** : business organization **3** : initiative

en•ter•pris•ing \-ˌprīziŋ\ *adj* : showing initiative

en•ter•tain \ˌentər'tān\ *vb* **1** : treat or receive as a guest **2** : hold in mind **3** : amuse —**en•ter•tain•er** *n* —**en•ter•tain•ment** *n*

en•thrall, en•thral \in'thrȯl\ *vb* **-thralled; -thrall•ing** : hold spellbound

en•thu•si•asm \-'thüzēˌazəm, -'thyü-\ *n* : strong excitement of feeling or its cause —**en•thu•si•ast** \-ˌast, -əst\ *n* —**en•thu•si•as•tic** \-ˌthüzē'astik, -ˌthyü-\ *adj* —**en•thu•si•as•ti•cal•ly** \-tiklē\ *adv*

en•tice \-'tīs\ *vb* **-ticed; -tic•ing** : tempt —**en•tice•ment** *n*

en•tire \in'tīr\ *adj* : complete or whole —**en•tire•ly** *adv* —**en•tire•ty** \-'tīrətē, -'tīrtē\ *n*

en•ti•tle \-'tītᵊl\ *vb* **-tled; -tling 1** : name **2** : give a right to

en•ti•ty \'entətē\ *n, pl* **-ties** : something with separate existence

en•to•mol•o•gy \ˌentə'mäləjē\ *n* : study of insects —**en•to•mo•log•i•cal** \-mə'läjikəl\ *adj* —**en•to•mol•o•gist** \-'mäləjist\ *n*

en•tou•rage \ˌäntü'räzh\ *n* : retinue

en•trails \'entrəlz, -ˌtrālz\ *n pl* : intestines

1en•trance \'entrəns\ *n* **1** : act of entering **2** : means or place of entering —**en•trant** \'entrənt\ *n*

2en•trance \in'trans\ *vb* **-tranced; -tranc•ing** : fascinate or delight

en•trap \in'trap\ *vb* : trap —**en•trap•ment** *n*

en•treat \-'trēt\ *vb* : ask urgently —**en•treaty** \-'trētē\ *n*

en•trée, en•tree \'änˌtrā\ *n* : principal dish of the meal

en•trench \in'trench\ *vb* : establish in a strong position —**en•trench•ment** *n*

en•tre•pre•neur \ˌäntrəprə'nər\ *n* : organizer or promoter of an enterprise

en•trust \in'trəst\ *vb* : commit to another with confidence

en•try \'entrē\ *n, pl* **-tries 1** : entrance **2** : an entering in a record or an item so entered

en•twine \in'twīn\ *vb* : twine together or around

enu•mer•ate \i'nüməˌrāt, -'nyü-\ *vb* **-at•ed; -at•ing 1** : count **2** : list —**enu•mer•a•tion** \iˌnümə'rāshən, -ˌnyü-\ *n*

enun•ci•ate \ē'nənsēˌāt\ *vb* **-at•ed; -ating 1** : announce **2** : pronounce —**enun•ci•a•tion** \-ˌnənsē'āshən\ *n*

en•vel•op \in'veləp\ *vb* : surround —**en•vel•op•ment** *n*

en•ve•lope \'envəˌlōp, 'än-\ *n* : paper container for a letter

en•vi•ron•ment \in'vīrənmənt\ *n* : surroundings —**en•vi•ron•men•tal** \-ˌvīrən'mentᵊl\ *adj*

en•vi•ron•men•tal•ist \-ᵊlist\ *n* : person concerned about the environment

en•vi•rons \in'vīrənz\ *n pl* : vicinity

en•vis•age \in'vizij\ *vb* **-aged; -ag•ing** : have a mental picture of

en•vi•sion \-'vizhən\ *vb* : picture to oneself

en•voy \'enˌvȯi, 'än-\ *n* : diplomat

en•vy \'envē\ *n* **1** : resentful awareness of another's advantage **2** : object of envy ~ *vb* **-vied; -vy•ing** : feel envy toward or on account of —**en•vi•able** \-vēəbəl\ *adj* —**en•vi•ous** \-vēəs\ *adj* —**en•vi•ous•ly** *adv*

en•zyme \'enˌzīm\ *n* : biological catalyst

eon \'ēən, ēˌän\ *var of* AEON

ep•au•let \ˌepə'let\ *n* : shoulder ornament on a uniform

ephem•er•al \i'femərəl\ *adj* : short-lived

ep•ic \'epik\ *n* : long poem about a hero —**epic** *adj*

ep•i•cure \'epiˌkyu̇r\ *n* : person with fastidious taste esp. in food and wine —**ep•i•cu•re•an** \ˌepikyu̇'rēən, -'kyu̇rē-\ *n or adj*

ep•i•dem•ic \ˌepə'demik\ *adj* : affecting many persons at one time —**epidemic** *n*

epi•der•mis \ˌepə'dərməs\ *n* : outer layer of skin

ep•i•gram \'epəˌgram\ *n* : short witty poem or saying —**ep•i•gram•mat•ic** \ˌepəgrə'matik\ *adj*

ep•i•lep•sy \'epəˌlepsē\ *n, pl* **-sies** : nervous disorder marked by convulsive attacks —**ep•i•lep•tic** \ˌepə'leptik\ *adj or n*

epis•co•pal \i'piskəpəl\ *adj* : governed by bishops

ep•i•sode \'epəˌsōd, -ˌzōd\ *n* : occurrence —**ep•i•sod•ic** \ˌepə'sädik, -'zäd-\ *adj*

epis•tle \i'pisəl\ *n* : letter

ep•i•taph \'epəˌtaf\ *n* : inscription in memory of a dead person

ep•i•thet \'epəˌthet, -thət\ *n* : characterizing often abusive word or phrase

epit•o•me \i'pitəmē\ *n* **1** : summary **2** : ideal example —**epit•o•mize** \-ˌmīz\ *vb*

ep•och \'epək, 'epˌäk\ *n* : extended period —**ep•och•al** \'epəkəl, 'epˌäkəl\ *adj*

ep•oxy \'epˌäksē, ep'äksē\ *n* : synthetic resin used esp. in adhesives ~ *vb* **-ox•ied** *or* **-oxyed; -oxy•ing** : glue with epoxy

equa•ble \'ekwəbəl, 'ēkwə-\ *adj* : free from unpleasant extremes —**eq•ua•bil•i•ty** \ˌekwə'bilətē, ˌē-\ *n* —**eq•ua•bly** \-blē\ *adv*

equal \'ēkwəl\ *adj* : of the same quantity, value, quality, number, or status as another ~ *n* : one that is equal ~ *vb* **equaled** *or* **equalled; equal•ing** *or* **equal•ling** : be or become equal to —**equal•i•ty** \i'kwälətē\ *n* —**equal•ize** \'ēkwəˌlīz\ *vb* —**equal•ly** \'ēkwəlē\ *adv*

equa•nim•i•ty \ˌēkwə'nimətē, ek-\ *n, pl* **-ties** : calmness

equate \i'kwāt\ *vb* **equat•ed; equat•ing** : treat or regard as equal

equa•tion \i'kwāzhən, -shən\ *n* : mathematical statement that two things are equal

equa•tor \i'kwātər\ *n* : imaginary circle that separates the northern and southern hemispheres —**equa•to•ri•al** \ˌēkwə'tōrēəl, ˌek-\ *adj*

eques•tri•an \i'kwestrēən\ *adj* : relating to horseback riding ~ *n* : horseback rider

equi•lat•er•al \ˌēkwə'latərəl\ *adj* : having equal sides

equi•lib•ri•um \-'librēəm\ *n, pl* **-ri•ums** *or* **-ria** \-rēə\ : state of balance

equine \'ēˌkwīn, 'ekˌwīn\ *adj* : relating to the horse —**equine** *n*

equi•nox \'ēkwəˌnäks, 'ek-\ *n* : time when day and night are everywhere of equal length

equip \i'kwip\ *vb* **-pp-** : furnish with needed resources —**equip•ment** \-mənt\ *n*

eq•ui•ta•ble \'ekwətəbəl\ *adj* : fair

eq•ui•ty \'ekwətē\ *n, pl* **-ties 1** : justice **2** : value of a property less debt

equiv•a•lent \i'kwivələnt\ *adj* : equal —**equiv•a•lence** \-ləns\ *n* —**equivalent** *n*

equiv•o•cal \i'kwivəkəl\ *adj* : ambiguous or uncertain

equiv•o•cate \i'kwivəˌkāt\ *vb* **-cat•ed; -cat•ing 1** : use misleading language **2** : avoid answering definitely —**equiv•o•ca•tion** \-ˌkwivə'kāshən\ *n*

1-er \ər\ *adj suffix or adv suffix* —used to form the comparative degree of adjectives and adverbs and esp. those of one or two syllables

2-er \ər\, **-ier** \ēər, yər\, **-yer** \yər\ *n suffix* **1** : one that is associated with **2** : one that performs or is the object of an action **3** : one that is

era \'irə, 'erə, 'ērə\ *n* : period of time associated with something

erad•i•cate \i'radəˌkāt\ *vb* **-cat•ed; -cat•ing** : do away with

erase \i'rās\ *vb* **erased; eras•ing** : rub or scratch out —**eras•er** *n* —**era•sure** \i'rāshər\ *n*

ere \'er\ *prep or conj* : before

erect \i'rekt\ *adj* : not leaning or lying down ~ *vb* **1** : build **2** : bring to an upright position —**erec•tion** \i'rekshən\ *n*

er•mine \'ərmən\ *n* : weasel with white winter fur or its fur

erode \i'rōd\ *vb* **erod•ed; erod•ing** : wear away gradually

ero•sion \i'rōzhən\ *n* : process of eroding

erot•ic \i'rätik\ *adj* : sexually arousing —**erot•i•cal•ly** \-iklē\ *adv* —**erot•i•cism** \i'rätəˌsizəm\ *n*

err \'er, 'ər\ *vb* : be or do wrong

er•rand \'erənd\ *n* : short trip taken to do something often for another

er•rant \-ənt\ *adj* **1** : traveling about **2** : going astray

er•rat•ic \ir'atik\ *adj* **1** : eccentric **2** : inconsistent —**er•rat•i•cal•ly** \-iklē\ *adv*

er•ro•ne•ous \ir'ōnēəs, e'rō-\ *adj* : wrong —**er•ro•ne•ous•ly** *adv*

er•ror \'erər\ *n* **1** : something that is not accurate **2** : state of being wrong

er•satz \'erˌsäts\ *adj* : phony

erst•while \'ərstˌhwīl\ *adv* : in the past ~ *adj* : former

er•u•di•tion \ˌerə'dishən, ˌeryə-\ *n* : great learning —**er•u•dite** \'erəˌdīt, 'eryə-\ *adj*

erupt \i'rəpt\ *vb* : burst forth esp. suddenly and violently —**erup•tion** \i'rəpshən\ *n* —**erup•tive** \-tiv\ *adj*

-ery \ərē\ *n suffix* **1** : character or condition **2** : practice **3** : place of doing

1-es \əz, iz *after* s, z, sh, ch; z *after* v *or a vowel*\ *n pl suffix* —used to form the plural of some nouns

2-es *vb suffix* —used to form the 3d person singular present of some verbs

es•ca•late \'eskəˌlāt\ *vb* **-lat•ed; -lat•ing** : become quickly larger or greater —**es•ca•la•tion** \ˌeskə'lāshən\ *n*

es•ca•la•tor \'eskəˌlātər\ *n* : moving stairs

es•ca•pade \'eskəˌpād\ *n* : mischievous adventure

es•cape \is'kāp\ *vb* **-caped; -cap•ing** : get away or get away from ~ *n* **1** : flight from or avoidance of something unpleasant **2** : leakage **3** : means of escape ~ *adj* : providing means of escape —**es•cap•ee** \isˌkā'pē, ˌes-\ *n*

es•ca•role \'eskəˌrōl\ *n* : salad green

es•carp•ment \is'kärpmənt\ *n* : cliff

es•chew \is'chü\ *vb* : shun

es•cort \'esˌkȯrt\ *n* : one accompanying another —**es•cort** \is'kȯrt, es-\ *vb*

es•crow \'esˌkrō\ *n* : deposit to be delivered upon fulfillment of a condition

esoph•a•gus \i'säfəgəs\ *n, pl* **-gi** \-ˌgī, -ˌjī\ : muscular tube connecting the mouth and stomach

es•o•ter•ic \ˌesə'terik\ *adj* : mysterious or secret

es•pe•cial•ly \is'peshəlē\ *adv* : particularly or notably

es•pi•o•nage \'espēəˌnäzh, -nij\ *n* : practice of spying

es•pous•al \is'pau̇zəl\ *n* **1** : betrothal **2** : wedding **3** : a taking up as a supporter —**es•pouse** \-'pau̇z\ *vb*

espres•so \e'spresō\ *n, pl* **-sos** : strong steam-brewed coffee

es•py \is'pī\ *vb* **-pied; -py•ing** : catch sight of

es•quire \'esˌkwīr\ *n* —used as a title of courtesy

-ess \əs, ˌes\ *n suffix* : female

es•say \'esˌā\ *n* : literary composition ~ *vb* \e'sā, 'esˌā\ : attempt —**es•say•ist** \'esˌāist\ *n*

es•sence \'esᵊns\ *n* **1** : fundamental nature or quality **2** : extract **3** : perfume

es•sen•tial \i'senchəl\ *adj* : basic or necessary —**essential** *n* —**es•sen•tial•ly** *adv*

-est \əst, ist\ *adj suffix or adv suffix* —used to form the superlative degree of adjectives and adverbs and esp. those of 1 or 2 syllables

es•tab•lish \is'tablish\ *vb* **1** : bring into existence **2** : put on a firm basis **3** : cause to be recognized

es•tab•lish•ment \-mənt\ *n* **1** : business or a place of business **2** : an establishing or being established **3** : controlling group

es•tate \is'tāt\ *n* **1** : one's possessions **2** : large piece of land with a house

es•teem \is'tēm\ *n or vb* : regard

es•ter \'estər\ *n* : organic chemical compound

esthetic *var of* AESTHETIC

es•ti•ma•ble \'estəməbəl\ *adj* : worthy of esteem

es•ti•mate \'estəˌmāt\ *vb* **-mat•ed; -mat•ing** : judge the approximate value, size, or cost ~ \-mət\ *n* **1** : rough or approximate calculation **2** : statement of the cost of a job —**es•ti•ma•tion** \ˌestə'māshən\ *n* —**es•ti•ma•tor** \'estəˌmātər\ *n*

es•trange \is'trānj\ *vb* **-tranged; -trang•ing** : make hostile —**es•trange•ment** *n*

es•tro•gen \'estrəjən\ *n* : hormone that produces female characteristics

es•tu•ary \'eschəˌwerē\ *n, pl* **-ar•ies** : arm of the sea at a river's mouth

et cet•era \et'setərə, -'setrə\ : and others esp. of the same kind

etch \'ech\ *vb* : produce by corroding parts of a surface with acid —**etch•er** *n* —**etch•ing** *n*

eter•nal \i'tərnᵊl\ *adj* : lasting forever —**eter•nal•ly** *adv*

eter•ni•ty \-nətē\ *n, pl* **-ties** : infinite duration

eth•ane \'ethˌān\ *n* : gaseous hydrocarbon

eth•a•nol \'ethəˌnȯl, -ˌnōl\ *n* : alcohol

ether \'ēthər\ *n* : light flammable liquid used as an anesthetic

ethe•re•al \i'thirēəl\ *adj* **1** : celestial **2** : exceptionally delicate

eth•i•cal \'ethikəl\ *adj* **1** : relating to ethics **2** : honorable —**eth•i•cal•ly** *adv*

eth•ics \-iks\ *n sing or pl* **1** : study of good and evil and moral duty **2** : moral principles or practice

eth•nic \'ethnik\ *adj* : relating to races or groups of people with common customs ~ *n* : member of a minority ethnic group

eth•nol•o•gy \eth'näləjē\ *n* : study of the races of human beings —**eth•no•log•i•cal** \ˌethnə'läjikəl\ *adj* —**eth•nol•o•gist** \eth'näləjist\ *n*

et•i•quette \'etikət, -ˌket\ *n* : good manners

et•y•mol•o•gy \ˌetə'mäləjē\ *n, pl* **-gies 1** : history of a word **2** : study of etymologies —**et•y•mo•log•i•cal** \-mə'läjikəl\ *adj* —**et•y•mol•o•gist** \-'mäləjist\ *n*

eu•ca•lyp•tus \ˌyükə'liptəs\ *n, pl* **-ti** \-ˌtī\ *or* **-tus•es** : Australian evergreen tree

Eu•cha•rist \'yükərəst\ *n* : Communion —**eu•cha•ris•tic** \ˌyükə'ristik\ *adj*

eu•lo•gy \'yüləjē\ *n, pl* **-gies** : speech in praise —**eu•lo•gis•tic** \ˌyülə'jistik\ *adj* —**eu•lo•gize** \'yüləˌjīz\ *vb*

eu•nuch \'yünək\ *n* : castrated man

eu•phe•mism \'yüfəˌmizəm\ *n* : substitution of a pleasant expression for an unpleasant or offensive one —**euphe•mis•tic** \ˌyüfə'mistik\ *adj*

eu•pho•ni•ous \yu̇'fōnēəs\ *adj* : pleasing to the ear —**eu•pho•ny** \'yüfənē\ *n*

eu•pho•ria \yu̇'fōrēə\ *n* : elation —**euphor•ic** \-'fȯrik\ *adj*

eu•tha•na•sia \ˌyüthə'nāzhə, -zhēə\ *n* : mercy killing

evac•u•ate \i'vakyəˌwāt\ *vb* **-at•ed; -at•ing 1** : discharge wastes from the body **2** : remove or withdraw from —**evac•u•a•tion** \iˌvakyə'wāshən\ *n*

evade \i'vād\ *vb* **evad•ed; evad•ing** : manage to avoid

eval•u•ate \i'valyəˌwāt\ *vb* **-at•ed; -at•ing** : appraise —**eval•u•a•tion** \iˌvalyə'wāshən\ *n*

evan•gel•i•cal \ˌēˌvan'jelikəl, ˌevən-\ *adj* : relating to the Christian gospel

evan•ge•lism \i'vanjəˌlizəm\ *n* : the winning or revival of personal commitments to Christ —**evan•ge•list** \i'vanjəlist\ *n* —**evan•ge•lis•tic** \iˌvanjə'listik\ *adj*

evap•o•rate \i'vapəˌrāt\ *vb* **-rat•ed; -rat•ing 1** : pass off in or convert into vapor **2** : disappear quickly —**evap•o•ra•tion** \iˌvapə'rāshən\ *n* —**evap•o•ra•tor** \i'vapəˌrātər\ *n*

eva•sion \i'vāzhən\ *n* : act or instance of evading —**eva•sive** \i'vāsiv\ *adj* —**eva•sive•ness** *n*

eve \'ēv\ *n* : evening

even \'ēvən\ *adj* **1** : smooth **2** : equal or fair **3** : fully revenged **4** : divisible by 2 ~ *adv* **1** : already **2** —used for emphasis ~ *vb* : make or become even —**even•ly** *adv* —**even•ness** *n*

eve•ning \'ēvniŋ\ *n* : early part of the night

event \i'vent\ *n* **1** : occurrence **2** : noteworthy happening **3** : eventuality —**event•ful** *adj*

even•tu•al \i'venchəwəl\ *adj* : later —**even•tu•al•ly** *adv*

even•tu•al•i•ty \iˌvenchə'walətē\ *n, pl* **-ties** : possible occurrence or outcome

ev•er \'evər\ *adv* **1** : always **2** : at any time **3** : in any case

ev•er•green *adj* : having foliage that remains green —**evergreen** *n*

ev•er•last•ing \ˌevər'lastiŋ\ *adj* : lasting forever

ev•ery \'evrē\ *adj* **1** : being each one of a group **2** : all possible

ev•ery•body \'evriˌbädē, -bəd-\ *pron* : every person

ev•ery•day *adj* : ordinary

ev•ery•one \-ˌwən\ *pron* : every person

ev•ery•thing *pron* : all that exists

ev•ery•where *adv* : in every place or part

evict \i'vikt\ *vb* : force (a person) to move from a property —**evic•tion** \i'vikshən\ *n*

ev•i•dence \'evədəns\ *n* **1** : outward sign **2** : proof or testimony

ev•i•dent \-ənt\ *adj* : clear or obvious —**ev•i•dent•ly** \-ədəntlē, -əˌdent-\ *adv*

evil \'ēvəl\ *adj* **evil•er** *or* **evil•ler; evil•est** *or* **evil•lest** : wicked ~ *n* **1** : sin **2** : source of sorrow or distress —**evil•do•er** \ˌēvəl'düər\ *n* —**evil•ly** *adv*

evince \i'vins\ *vb* **evinced; evinc•ing** : show

evis•cer•ate \i'visəˌrāt\ *vb* **-at•ed; -at•ing** : remove the viscera of —**evis•cer•a•tion** \iˌvisə'rāshən\ *n*

evoke \i'vōk\ *vb* **evoked; evok•ing** : call forth or up —**evo•ca•tion** \ˌēvō'kāshən, ˌevə-\ *n* —**evoc•a•tive** \i'väkətiv\ *adj*

evo•lu•tion \ˌevə'lüshən\ *n* : process of change by degrees —**evo•lu•tion•ary** \-shəˌnerē\ *adj*

evolve \i'välv\ *vb* **evolved; evolv•ing** : develop or change by degrees

ewe \'yü\ *n* : female sheep

ew•er \'yüər\ *n* : water pitcher

ex•act \ig'zakt\ *vb* : compel to furnish ~ *adj* : precisely correct —**ex•act•ing** *adj* —**ex•ac•tion** \-'zakshən\ *n* —**ex•ac•ti•tude** \-'zaktəˌtüd, -ˌtyüd\ *n* —**ex•act•ly** *adv* —**ex•act•ness** *n*

ex•ag•ger•ate \ig'zajəˌrāt\ *vb* **-at•ed; -at•ing** : say more than is true —**ex•ag•ger•at•ed•ly** *adv* —**ex•ag•ger•a•tion** \-ˌzajə'rāshən\ *n* —**ex•ag•ger•a•tor** \-'zajəˌrātər\ *n*

ex•alt \ig'zȯlt\ *vb* : glorify —**ex•al•ta•tion** \ˌegˌzȯl'tāshən, ˌekˌsȯl-\ *n*

ex•am \ig'zam\ *n* : examination

ex•am•ine \-ən\ *vb* **-ined; -in•ing 1** : inspect closely **2** : test by questioning —**ex•am•i•na•tion** \-ˌzamə'nāshən\ *n*

ex•am•ple \ig'zampəl\ *n* **1** : representative sample **2** : model **3** : problem to be solved for teaching purposes

ex•as•per•ate \ig'zaspəˌrāt\ *vb* **-at•ed; -at•ing** : thoroughly annoy —**ex•as•per•a•tion** \-ˌzaspə'rāshən\ *n*

ex•ca•vate \'ekskəˌvāt\ *vb* **-vat•ed; -vat•ing** : dig or hollow out —**ex•ca•va•tion** \ˌekskə'vāshən\ *n* —**ex•ca•va•tor** \'ekskəˌvātər\ *n*

ex•ceed \ik'sēd\ *vb* **1** : go or be beyond the limit of **2** : do better than

ex•ceed•ing•ly *adv* : extremely

ex•cel \ik'sel\ *vb* **-ll-** : do extremely well or far better than

ex•cel•lence \'eksələns\ *n* : quality of being excellent

ex•cel•len•cy \-lənsē\ *n, pl* **-cies** —used as a title of honor

ex•cel•lent \'eksələnt\ *adj* : very good —**ex•cel•lent•ly** *adv*

ex•cept \ik'sept\ *vb* : omit ~ *prep* : excluding ~ *conj* : but —**ex•cep•tion** \-'sepshən\ *n*

ex•cep•tion•al \-'sepshənəl\ *adj* : superior —**ex•cep•tion•al•ly** *adv*

ex•cerpt \'ekˌsərpt, 'egˌzərpt\ *n* : brief passage ~ \ek'-, eg'-, 'ekˌ-, 'egˌ-\ *vb* : select an excerpt

ex•cess \ik'ses, 'ek,ses\ *n* **:** amount left over **—excess** *adj* **—ex•ces•sive** \ik'sesiv\ *adj* **—ex•ces•sive•ly** *adv*

ex•change \iks'chānj, 'eks,chānj\ *n* **1 :** the giving or taking of one thing in return for another **2 :** marketplace esp. for securities ~ *vb* **-changed; -chang•ing :** transfer in return for some equivalent **—ex•change•able** \iks'chānjəbəl\ *adj*

¹ex•cise \'ek,sīz, -,sīs\ *n* **:** tax

²ex•cise \ik'sīz\ *vb* **-cised; -cis•ing :** cut out **—ex•ci•sion** \-'sizhən\ *n*

ex•cite \ik'sīt\ *vb* **-cit•ed; -cit•ing 1 :** stir up **2 :** kindle the emotions of **—ex•cit•abil•i•ty** \-,sītə'bilətē\ *n* **—ex•cit•able** \-'sītəbəl\ *adj* **—ex•ci•ta•tion** \,ek,sī'tāshən, -sə-\ *n* **—ex•cit•ed•ly** *adv* **—ex•cite•ment** \ik'sītmənt\ *n*

ex•claim \iks'klām\ *vb* **:** cry out esp. in delight **—ex•cla•ma•tion** \,eksklə'māshən\ *n* **—ex•clam•a•to•ry** \iks'klamə,tōrē\ *adj*

exclamation point *n* **:** punctuation mark ! used esp. after an interjection or exclamation

ex•clude \iks'klüd\ *vb* **-clud•ed; -clud•ing :** leave out **—ex•clu•sion** \-'klüzhən\ *n*

ex•clu•sive \-'klüsiv\ *adj* **1 :** reserved for particular persons **2 :** stylish **3 :** sole **—exclusive** *n* **—ex•clu•sive•ly** *adv* **—ex•clu•sive•ness** *n*

ex•com•mu•ni•cate \,ekskə'myünə,kāt\ *vb* **:** expel from a church **—excom•mu•ni•ca•tion** \-,myünə'kāshən\ *n*

ex•cre•ment \'ekskrəmənt\ *n* **:** bodily waste **—ex•cre•men•tal** \,ekskrə-'mentᵊl\ *adj*

ex•crete \ik'skrēt\ *vb* **-cret•ed; -cret•ing :** eliminate wastes from the body **—ex•cre•tion** \-'skrēshən\ *n* **—ex•cre•to•ry** \'ekskrə,tōrē\ *adj*

ex•cru•ci•at•ing \ik'skrüshē,ātiŋ\ *adj* **:** intensely painful **—ex•cru•ci•at•ing•ly** *adv*

ex•cul•pate \'ekskəl,pāt\ *vb* **-pat•ed; -pat•ing :** clear from alleged fault

ex•cur•sion \ik'skərzhən\ *n* **:** pleasure trip

ex•cuse \ik'skyüz\ *vb* **-cused; -cus•ing 1 :** pardon **2 :** release from an obligation **3 :** justify ~ \-'skyüs\ *n* **1 :** justification **2 :** apology

ex•e•cute \'eksi,kyüt\ *vb* **-cut•ed; -cut•ing 1 :** carry out fully **2 :** enforce **3 :** put to death **—ex•e•cu•tion** \,eksi'kyüshən\ *n* **—ex•e•cu•tion•er** \-shənər\ *n*

ex•ec•u•tive \ig'zekyətiv\ *adj* **:** relating to the carrying out of decisions, plans, or laws ~ *n* **1 :** branch of government with executive duties **2 :** administrator

ex•ec•u•tor \-yətər\ *n* **:** person named in a will to execute it

ex•ec•u•trix \ig'zekyə,triks\ *n, pl* **ex•ec•u•tri•ces** \-,zekyə'trī,sēz\ *or* **ex•ec•u•trix•es :** woman executor

ex•em•pla•ry \ig'zemplərē\ *adj* **:** so commendable as to serve as a model

ex•em•pli•fy \-plə,fī\ *vb* **-fied; -fy•ing :** serve as an example of **—ex•em•pli•fi•ca•tion** \-,zempləfə'kāshən\ *n*

ex•empt \ig'zempt\ *adj* **:** being free from some liability ~ *vb* **:** make exempt **—ex•emp•tion** \-'zempshən\ *n*

ex•er•cise \'eksər,sīz\ *n* **1 :** a putting into action **2 :** exertion to develop endurance or a skill **3** *pl* **:** public ceremony ~ *vb* **-cised; -cis•ing 1 :** exert **2 :** engage in exercise **—ex•er•cis•er** *n*

ex•ert \ig'zərt\ *vb* **:** put into action **—ex•er•tion** \-'zərshən\ *n*

ex•hale \eks'hāl\ *vb* **-haled; -hal•ing :** breathe out **—ex•ha•la•tion** \ekshə'lāshən\ *n*

ex•haust \ig'zȯst\ *vb* **1 :** draw out or develop completely **2 :** use up **3 :** tire or wear out ~ *n* **:** waste steam or gas from an engine or a system for removing it **—ex•haus•tion** \-'zȯschən\ *n* **—ex•haus•tive** \-'zȯstiv\ *adj*

ex•hib•it \ig'zibət\ *vb* **:** display esp. publicly ~ *n* **1 :** act of exhibiting **2 :** something exhibited **—ex•hi•bi•tion** \,eksə'bishən\ *n* **—ex•hib•i•tor** \ig'zibətər\ *n*

ex•hil•a•rate \ig'zilə,rāt\ *vb* **-rat•ed; -rat•ing :** thrill **—ex•hil•a•ra•tion** \-,zilə'rāshən\ *n*

ex•hort \-'zȯrt\ *vb* **:** urge earnestly **—ex•hor•ta•tion** \,eks,ȯr'tāshən, ,egz-, -ər-\ *n*

ex•hume \igz'üm, -'yüm; iks'yüm, -'hyüm\ *vb* **-humed; -hum•ing :** dig up (a buried corpse) **—ex•hu•ma•tion** \,eksyü'māshən, -hyü-; ,egzü-, -zyü-\ *n*

ex•i•gen•cies \'eksəjənsēz, ig'zijən-\ *n pl* **:** requirements (as of a situation)

ex•ile \'eg,zīl, 'ek,sīl\ *n* **1 :** banishment **2 :** person banished from his or her country **—exile** *vb*

ex•ist \ig'zist\ *vb* **1 :** have real or actual being **2 :** live **—ex•is•tence** \-əns\ *n* **—ex•is•tent** \-ənt\ *adj*

ex•it \'egzət, 'eksət\ *n* **1 :** departure **2 :** way out of an enclosed space **3 :** way off an expressway **—exit** *vb*

ex•o•dus \'eksədəs\ *n* **:** mass departure

ex•on•er•ate \ig'zänə,rāt\ *vb* **-at•ed; -at•ing :** free from blame **—ex•on•er•a•tion** \-,zänə'rāshən\ *n*

ex•or•bi•tant \ig'zȯrbətənt\ *adj* **:** exceeding what is usual or proper

ex•or•cise \'ek,sȯr,sīz, -sər-\ *vb* **-cised; -cis•ing :** drive out (as an evil spirit) **—ex•or•cism** \-,sizəm\ *n* **—ex•or•cist** \-,sist\ *n*

ex•ot•ic \ig'zätik\ *adj* **:** foreign or strange **—exotic** *n* **—ex•ot•i•cal•ly** \-iklē\ *adv*

ex•pand \ik'spand\ *vb* **:** enlarge

ex•panse \-'spans\ *n* **:** very large area

ex•pan•sion \-'spanchən\ *n* **1 :** act or process of expanding **2 :** expanded part

ex•pan•sive \-'spansiv\ *adj* **1 :** tending to expand **2 :** warmly benevolent **3 :** of large extent **—ex•pan•sive•ly** *adv* **—ex•pan•sive•ness** *n*

ex•pa•tri•ate \ek'spātrē,āt, -ət\ *n* **:** exile **—expatriate** \-,āt\ *adj or vb*

ex•pect \ik'spekt\ *vb* **1 :** look forward to **2 :** consider probable or one's due **—ex•pec•tan•cy** \-ənsē\ *n* **—ex•pec•tant** \-ənt\ *adj* **—ex•pec•tant•ly** *adv* **—ex•pec•ta•tion** \,ek,spek'tāshən\ *n*

ex•pe•di•ent \ik'spēdēənt\ *adj* **:** convenient or advantageous rather than right or just ~ *n* **:** convenient often makeshift means to an end

ex•pe•dite \'ekspə,dīt\ *vb* **-dit•ed; -dit•ing :** carry out or handle promptly **—ex•pe•dit•er** *n*

ex•pe•di•tion \,ekspə'dishən\ *n* **:** long journey for work or research or the people making this

ex•pe•di•tious \-əs\ *adj* **:** prompt and efficient

ex•pel \ik'spel\ *vb* **-ll- :** force out

ex•pend \-'spend\ *vb* **1 :** pay out **2 :** use up **—ex•pend•able** *adj*

ex•pen•di•ture \-'spendichər, -də,chu̇r\ *n* **:** act of using or spending

ex•pense \ik'spens\ *n* **:** cost **—ex•pen•sive** \-'spensiv\ *adj* **—ex•pen•sive•ly** *adv*

ex•pe•ri•ence \ik'spirēəns\ *n* **1 :** a participating in or living through an event **2 :** an event that affects one **3 :** knowledge from doing ~ *vb* **-enced; -enc•ing :** undergo

ex•per•i•ment \ik'sperəmənt\ *n* **:** test to discover something ~ *vb* **:** make experiments **—ex•per•i•men•tal** \-,sperə'mentᵊl\ *adj* **—ex•per•i•men•ta•tion** \-mən'tāshən\ *n* **—ex•per•i•men•ter** \-'sperə,mentər\ *n*

ex•pert \'ek,spərt\ *adj* **:** thoroughly skilled ~ *n* **:** person with special skill **—ex•pert•ly** *adv* **—ex•pert•ness** *n*

ex•per•tise \,ekspər'tēz\ *n* **:** skill

ex•pi•ate \'ekspē,āt\ *vb* **:** make amends for **—ex•pi•a•tion** \,ekspē'āshən\ *n*

ex•pire \ik'spīr, ek-\ *vb* **-pired; -pir•ing 1 :** breathe out **2 :** die **3 :** end **—ex•pi•ra•tion** \,ekspə'rāshən\ *n*

ex•plain \ik'splān\ *vb* **1 :** make clear **2 :** give the reason for **—ex•plain•able** \-əbəl\ *adj* **—ex•pla•na•tion** \,eksplə'nāshən\ *n* **—ex•plan•a•to•ry** \ik'splanə,tōrē\ *adj*

ex•ple•tive \'eksplətiv\ *n* **:** usu. profane exclamation

ex•pli•ca•ble \ek'splikəbəl, 'eksplik-\ *adj* **:** capable of being explained

ex•plic•it \ik'splisət\ *adj* **:** absolutely clear or precise **—ex•plic•it•ly** *adv* **—ex•plic•it•ness** *n*

ex•plode \ik'splōd\ *vb* **-plod•ed; -plod•ing 1 :** discredit **2 :** burst or cause to burst violently **3 :** increase rapidly

ex•ploit \'ek,splȯit\ *n* **:** heroic act ~ \ik'splȯit\ *vb* **1 :** utilize **2 :** use unfairly **—ex•ploi•ta•tion** \,ek,splȯi'tāshən\ *n*

ex•plore \ik'splōr\ *vb* **-plored; -plor•ing :** examine or range over thoroughly **—ex•plo•ra•tion** \,eksplə'rāshən\ *n* **—ex•plor•ato•ry** \ik'splōrə,tōrē\ *adj* **—ex•plor•er** *n*

ex•plo•sion \ik'splōzhən\ *n* **:** process or instance of exploding

ex•plo•sive \-siv\ *adj* **1 :** able to cause explosion **2 :** likely to explode **—explosive** *n* **—ex•plo•sive•ly** *adv*

ex•po•nent \ik'spōnənt, 'ek,spō-\ *n* **1 :** mathematical symbol showing how many times a number is to be repeated as a factor **2 :** advocate **—ex•po•nen•tial** \,ekspə'nenchəl\ *adj* **—ex•po•nen•tial•ly** *adv*

ex•port \ek'spōrt, 'ek,spōrt\ *vb* **:** send to foreign countries **—export** \'ek,-\ *n* **—ex•por•ta•tion** \,ek,spōr'tāshən\ *n* **—ex•port•er** \ek'spōrtər, 'ek,spōrt-\ *n*

ex•pose \ik'spōz\ *vb* **-posed; -pos•ing 1 :** deprive of shelter or protection **2 :** subject (film) to light **3 :** make known **—ex•po•sure** \-'spōzhər\ *n*

ex•po•sé, ex•po•se \,ekspō'zā\ *n* **:** exposure of something discreditable

ex•po•si•tion \,ekspə'zishən\ *n* **:** public exhibition

ex•pound \ik'spau̇nd\ *vb* **:** set forth or explain in detail

¹ex•press \-'spres\ *adj* **1 :** clear **2 :** specific **3 :** traveling at high speed with few stops **—express** *adv or n* **—ex•press•ly** *adv*

²express *vb* **1 :** make known in words or appearance **2 :** press out (as juice)

ex•pres•sion \-'spreshən\ *n* **1 :** utterance **2 :** mathematical symbol **3 :** significant word or phrase **4 :** look on one's face **—ex•pres•sion•less** *adj* **—ex•pres•sive** \-'spresiv\ *adj* **—ex•pres•sive•ness** *n*

ex•press•way \ik'spres,wā\ *n* **:** high-speed divided highway with limited access

ex•pul•sion \ik'spəlshən\ *n* **:** an expelling or being expelled

ex•pur•gate \'ekspər,gāt\ *vb* **-gat•ed; -gat•ing :** censor **—ex•pur•ga•tion** \,ekspər'gāshən\ *n*

ex•qui•site \ek'skwizət, 'ekskwiz-\ *adj* **1 :** flawlessly beautiful and delicate **2 :** keenly discriminating

ex•tant \'ekstənt, ek'stant\ *adj* **:** existing

ex•tem•po•ra•ne•ous \ek,stempə'rānēəs\ *adj* **:** impromptu **—ex•tem•po•ra•ne•ous•ly** *adv*

ex•tend \ik'stend\ *vb* **1 :** stretch forth or out **2 :** prolong **3 :** enlarge **—ex•tend•able, ex•tend•ible** \-'stendəbəl\ *adj*

ex•ten•sion \-'stenchən\ *n* **1 :** an extending or being extended **2 :** additional part **3 :** extra telephone line

ex•ten•sive \-'stensiv\ *adj* **:** of considerable extent **—ex•ten•sive•ly** *adv*

ex•tent \-'stent\ *n* **:** range, space, or degree to which something extends

ex•ten•u•ate \ik'stenyə,wāt\ *vb* **-at•ed; -at•ing :** lessen the seriousness of **—ex•ten•u•a•tion** \-,stenyə'wāshən\ *n*

ex•te•ri•or \ek'stirēər\ *adj* **:** external ~ *n* **:** external part or surface

ex•ter•mi•nate \ik'stərmə,nāt\ *vb* **-nat•ed; -nat•ing :** destroy utterly **—ex•ter•mi•na•tion** \-,stərmə'nāshən\ *n* **—ex•ter•mi•na•tor** \-'stərmə,nātər\ *n*

ex•ter•nal \ek'stərnᵊl\ *adj* **:** relating to or on the outside **—ex•ter•nal•ly** *adv*

ex•tinct \ik'stiŋkt\ *adj* **:** no longer existing **—ex•tinc•tion** \-'stiŋkshən\ *n*

ex•tin•guish \-'stiŋgwish\ *vb* **:** cause to stop burning **—ex•tin•guish•able** *adj* **—ex•tin•guish•er** *n*

ex•tir•pate \'ekstər,pāt\ *vb* **-pat•ed; -pat•ing :** destroy

ex•tol \ik'stōl\ *vb* **-ll- :** praise highly

ex•tort \-'stȯrt\ *vb* **:** obtain by force or improper pressure **—ex•tor•tion** \-'stȯrshən\ *n* **—ex•tor•tion•er** *n* **—ex•tor•tion•ist** *n*

ex•tra \'ekstrə\ *adj* **1 :** additional **2 :** superior **—extra** *n or adv*

extra- *prefix* **:** outside or beyond

ex•tract \ik'strakt\ *vb* **1 :** pull out forcibly **2 :** withdraw (as a juice) ~ \'ek,-\ *n* **1 :** excerpt **2 :** product (as a juice) obtained by extracting **—ex•tract•able** *adj* **—ex•trac•tion** \ik'strakshən\ *n* **—ex•trac•tor** \-tər\ *n*

ex•tra•cur•ric•u•lar \,ekstrəkə'rikyələr\ *adj* **:** lying outside the regular curriculum

ex•tra•dite \'ekstrə,dīt\ *vb* **-dit•ed; -dit•ing :** bring or deliver a suspect to a different jurisdiction for trial **—ex•tra•di•tion** \,ekstrə'dishən\ *n*

ex•tra•mar•i•tal \,ekstrə'marətᵊl\ *adj* **:** relating to sexual relations of a married person outside of the marriage

ex•tra•ne•ous \ek'strānēəs\ *adj* **:** not essential or relevant **—ex•tra•ne•ous•ly** *adv*

ex•traor•di•nary \ik'strȯrdᵊn,erē, ,ekstrə'ȯrd-\ *adj* **:** notably unusual or exceptional **—ex•traor•di•nari•ly** \ik,strȯrdᵊn'erəlē, ,ekstrə,ȯrd-\ *adv*

ex•tra•sen•so•ry \,ekstrə'sensərē\ *adj* **:** outside the ordinary senses

ex•tra•ter•res•tri•al \,ekstrətə'restrēəl\ *n* **:** one existing or coming from outside the earth ~ *adj* **:** relating to an extraterrestrial

ex•trav•a•gant \ik'stravigənt\ *adj* **:** wildly excessive, lavish, or costly **—ex•trav•a•gance** \-gəns\ *n* **—ex•trav•a•gant•ly** *adv*

ex•trav•a•gan•za \-,stravə'ganzə\ *n* **:** spectacular event

ex•tra•ve•hic•u•lar \,ekstrəvē'hikyələr\ *adj* **:** occurring outside a spacecraft

ex•treme \ik'strēm\ *adj* **1 :** very great or intense **2 :** very severe **3 :** not moderate **4 :** most remote ~ *n* **1 :** extreme state **2 :** something located at one end or the other of a range **—ex•treme•ly** *adv*

ex•trem•i•ty \-'stremətē\ *n, pl* **-ties 1 :** most remote part **2 :** human hand or foot **3 :** extreme degree or state (as of need)

ex•tri•cate \'ekstrə,kāt\ *vb* **-cat•ed; -cat•ing :** set or get free from an entanglement or difficulty **—ex•tri•ca•ble** \ik'strikəbəl, ek-; 'ekstrik-\ *adj* **ex•tri•ca•tion** \,ekstrə'kāshən\ *n*

ex•tro•vert \'ekstrə,vərt\ *n* **:** gregarious person **—ex•tro•ver•sion** \,ekstrə'vərzhən\ *n* **—ex•tro•vert•ed** \'ekstrə,vərtəd\ *adj*

ex•trude \ik'strüd\ *vb* **-trud•ed; -trud•ing :** to force or push out

ex•u•ber•ant \ig'zübərənt\ *adj* **:** joyously unrestrained **—ex•u•ber•ance** \-rəns\ *n* **—ex•u•ber•ant•ly** *adv*

ex•ude \ig'züd\ *vb* **-ud•ed; -ud•ing 1 :** discharge slowly through pores **2 :** display conspicuously

ex•ult \ig'zəlt\ *vb* **:** rejoice **—ex•ul•tant** \-'zəltᵊnt\ *adj* **—ex•ul•tant•ly** *adv* **—ex•ul•ta•tion** \,eksəl'tāshən, ,egzəl-\ *n*

-ey —see -Y

eye \'ī\ *n* **1 :** organ of sight consisting of a globular structure (**eye•ball**) in a socket of the skull with thin movable covers (**eye•lids**) bordered with hairs (**eye•lash•es**) **2 :** vision **3 :** judgment **4 :** something suggesting an eye ~ *vb* **eyed; eye•ing** *or* **ey•ing :** look at **—eye•brow** \-,brau̇\ *n* **—eyed** \'īd\ *adj* **—eye•strain** *n*

eye•drop•per *n* **:** dropper

eye•glass•es *n pl* **:** glasses

eye•let \'īlət\ *n* **:** hole (as in cloth) for a lacing or rope

eye–open•er *n* **:** something startling **—eye–open•ing** *adj*

eye•piece *n* **:** lens at the eye end of an optical instrument

eye•sight *n* **:** sight

eye•sore *n* **:** unpleasant sight

eye•tooth *n* **:** upper canine tooth

eye•wit•ness *n* **:** person who actually sees something happen

ey•rie \'īrē, *or like* AERIE\ *var of* AERIE

F

f \'ef\ *n, pl* **f's** *or* **fs** \'efs\ **:** 6th letter of the alphabet

fa•ble \'fābəl\ *n* **1 :** legendary story **2 :** story that teaches a lesson **—fa•bled** \-bəld\ *adj*

fab•ric \'fabrik\ *n* **1 :** structure **2 :** material made usu. by weaving or knitting fibers

fab•ri•cate \'fabri,kāt\ *vb* **-cat•ed; -cat•ing 1 :** construct **2 :** invent **—fab•ri•ca•tion** \,fabri'kāshən\ *n*

fab•u•lous \'fabyələs\ *adj* **1 :** like, told in, or based on fable **2 :** incredible or marvelous **—fab•u•lous•ly** *adv*

fa•cade \fə'säd\ *n* **1 :** principal face of a building **2 :** false or superficial appearance

face \'fās\ *n* **1 :** front or principal surface (as of the head) **2 :** presence **3 :** facial expression **4 :** grimace **5 :** outward appearance ~ *vb* **faced; fac•ing 1 :** challenge or resist firmly or brazenly **2 :** cover with different material **3 :** sit or stand with the face toward **4 :** have the front oriented toward **—faced** \'fāst\ *adj* **—face•less** *adj* *n* **—fa•cial** \'fāshəl\ *adj or n*

face•down *adv* **:** with the face downward

face–lift \'fās,lift\ *n* **1 :** cosmetic surgery on the face **2 :** modernization

fac•et \'fasət\ *n* **1 :** surface of a cut gem **2 :** phase **—fac•et•ed** *adj*

fa•ce•tious \fə'sēshəs\ *adj* **:** jocular **—fa•ce•tious•ly** *adv* **—fa•ce•tious•ness** *n*

fac•ile \'fasəl\ *adj* **1 :** easy **2 :** fluent

fa•cil•i•tate \fə'silə,tāt\ *vb* **-tat•ed; -tat•ing :** make easier

fa•cil•i•ty \fə'silətē\ *n, pl* **-ties 1 :** ease in doing or using **2 :** something built or installed to serve a purpose or facilitate an activity

fac•ing \'fāsiŋ\ *n* **:** lining or covering or material for this

fac•sim•i•le \fak'siməlē\ *n* **:** exact copy

fact \'fakt\ *n* **1 :** act or action **2 :** something that exists or is real **3 :** piece of information **—fac•tu•al** \'fakchəwəl\ *adj* **—fac•tu•al•ly** *adv*

fac•tion \'fakshən\ *n* **:** part of a larger group **—fac•tion•al•ism** \-shənə,lizəm\ *n*

fac•tious \'fakshəs\ *adj* **:** causing discord

fac•ti•tious \fak'tishəs\ *adj* **:** artificial

fac•tor \'faktər\ *n* **1 :** something that has an effect **2 :** gene **3 :** number used in multiplying

fac•to•ry \'faktərē\ *n, pl* **-ries :** place for manufacturing

fac•to•tum \fak'tōtəm\ *n* **:** person (as a servant) with varied duties

fac•ul•ty \'fakəltē\ *n, pl* **-ties 1 :** ability to act **2 :** power of the mind or body **3 :** body of teachers or department of instruction

fad \'fad\ *n* **:** briefly popular practice or interest **—fad•dish** *adj* **—fad•dist** *n*

fade \'fād\ *vb* **fad•ed; fad•ing 1 :** wither **2 :** lose or cause to lose freshness or brilliance **3 :** grow dim **4 :** vanish

fag \'fag\ *vb* **-gg- 1 :** drudge **2 :** tire or exhaust

fag•ot, fag•got \'fagət\ *n* **:** bundle of twigs

Fahr•en•heit \'farən,hīt\ *adj* **:** relating to a thermometer scale with the boiling point at 212 degrees and the freezing point at 32 degrees

fail \'fāl\ *vb* **1 :** decline in health **2 :** die away

3 : stop functioning 4 : be unsuccessful 5 : become bankrupt 6 : disappoint 7 : neglect ~ *n* : act of failing
fail·ing \'fāl·ing\ *n* : slight defect in character or conduct ~ *prep* : in the absence or lack of
faille \'fīl\ *n* : closely woven ribbed fabric
fail·ure \'fālyər\ *n* 1 : absence of expected action or performance 2 : bankruptcy 3 : deficiency 4 : one that has failed
faint \'fānt\ *adj* 1 : cowardly or spiritless 2 : weak and dizzy 3 : lacking vigor 4 : indistinct ~ *vb* : lose consciousness ~ *n* : act or condition of fainting —**faint·heart·ed** *adj* —**faint·ly** *adv* —**faint·ness** *n*
¹**fair** \'far\ *adj* 1 : pleasing in appearance 2 : not stormy or cloudy 3 : just or honest 4 : conforming with the rules 5 : open to legitimate pursuit or attack 6 : light in color 7 : adequate —**fair·ness** *n*
²**fair** *adv, chiefly Brit* : FAIRLY
³**fair** *n* : exhibition for judging or selling —**fair·ground** *n*
fair·ly \'farlē\ *adv* 1 : in a manner of speaking 2 : without bias 3 : somewhat
fairy \'farē\ *n, pl* **fair·ies** : usu. small imaginary being —**fairy tale** *n*
fairy·land \-,land\ *n* 1 : land of fairies 2 : beautiful or charming place
faith \'fāth\ *n, pl* **faiths** \'fāths, 'fāthz\ 1 : allegiance 2 : belief and trust in God 3 : confidence 4 : system of religious beliefs —**faith·ful** \-fəl\ *adj* —**faith·ful·ly** *adv* —**faith·ful·ness** *n* —**faith·less** *adj* —**faith·less·ly** *adv* —**faith·less·ness** *n*
fake \'fāk\ *vb* **faked; fak·ing** 1 : falsify 2 : counterfeit ~ *n* : copy, fraud, or impostor ~ *adj* : not genuine —**fak·er** *n*
fa·kir \fə'kir\ *n* : wandering beggar of India
fal·con \'falkən, 'fol-\ *n* : small long-winged hawk used esp. for hunting —**fal·con·ry** \-rē\ *n*
fall \'fol\ *vb* **fell** \'fel\; **fall·en** \'folən\; **fall·ing** 1 : go down by gravity 2 : hang freely 3 : go lower 4 : be defeated or ruined 5 : commit a sin 6 : happen at a certain time 7 : become gradually ~ *n* 1 : act of falling 2 : autumn 3 : downfall 4 *pl* : waterfall 5 : distance something falls
fal·la·cy \'faləsē\ *n, pl* **-cies** 1 : false idea 2 : false reasoning —**fal·la·cious** \fə'lāshəs\ *adj*
fal·li·ble \'faləbəl\ *adj* : capable of making a mistake —**fal·li·bly** \-blē\ *adv*
fall·out *n* 1 : radioactive particles from a nuclear explosion 2 : secondary effects
fal·low \'falō\ *adj* 1 : plowed but not planted 2 : dormant —**fallow** *n or vb*
false \'fols\ *adj* **fals·er; fals·est** 1 : not genuine, true, faithful, or permanent 2 : misleading —**false·ly** *adv* —**false·ness** *n* —**fal·si·fi·ca·tion** \,folsəfə'kāshən\ *n* —**fal·si·fy** \'folsə,fī\ *vb* —**fal·si·ty** \'folsətē\ *n*
false·hood \'fols,hud\ *n* : lie
fal·set·to \fol'setō\ *n, pl* **-tos** : artificially high singing voice
fal·ter \'foltər\ *vb* **-tered; -ter·ing** 1 : move unsteadily 2 : hesitate —**fal·ter·ing·ly** *adv*
fame \'fām\ *n* : public reputation —**famed** \'fāmd\ *adj*
fa·mil·ial \fə'milyəl\ *adj* : relating to a family
¹**fa·mil·iar** \fə'milyər\ *n* 1 : companion 2 : guardian spirit
²**familiar** *adj* 1 : closely acquainted 2 : forward 3 : frequently seen or experienced —**fa·mil·iar·i·ty** \fə,milē'arətē, -,milē'yar-\ *n* —**fa·mil·iar·ize** \fə'milyə,rīz\ *vb* —**fa·mil·iar·ly** *adv*
fam·i·ly \'famlē\ *n, pl* **-lies** : persons of common ancestry 2 : group living together 3 : parents and children 4 : group of related individuals
fam·ine \'famən\ *n* : extreme scarcity of food
fam·ish \'famish\ *vb* : starve
fa·mous \'fāməs\ *adj* : widely known or celebrated
fa·mous·ly *adv* : very well
¹**fan** \'fan\ *n* : device for producing a current of air ~ *vb* **-nn-** 1 : move air with a fan 2 : direct a current of air upon 3 : stir to activity
²**fan** *n* : enthusiastic follower or admirer
fa·nat·ic \fə'natik\, **fa·nat·i·cal** \-ikəl\ *adj* : excessively enthusiastic or devoted —**fanatic** *n* —**fa·nat·i·cism** \-'natə,sizəm\ *n*
fan·ci·er \'fansēər\ *n* : one devoted to raising a particular plant or animal
fan·cy \'fansē\ *n, pl* **-cies** 1 : liking 2 : whim 3 : imagination ~ *vb* **-cied; -cy·ing** 1 : like 2 : imagine ~ *adj* **-cier; -est** 1 : not plain 2 : of superior quality —**fan·ci·ful** \-sifəl\ *adj* —**fan·ci·ful·ly** \-fəlē\ *adv* —**fan·ci·ly** *adv*
fan·dan·go \fan'daŋgō\ *n, pl* **-gos** : lively Spanish dance
fan·fare \'fan,far\ *n* 1 : a sounding of trumpets 2 : showy display
fang \'faŋ\ *n* : long sharp tooth
fan·light *n* : semicircular window

: music written to fancy rather than to form
fan·tas·tic \fan'tastik\ *adj* 1 : imaginary or unrealistic 2 : exceedingly or unbelievably great —**fan·tas·ti·cal·ly** \-tiklē\ *adv*
fan·ta·sy \'fantəsē\ *n* 1 : imagination 2 : product (as a daydream) of the imagination 3 : fantasia —**fan·ta·size** \'fantə,sīz\ *vb*
far \'fär\ *adv* **far·ther** \-thər\ *or* **fur·ther** \'fər-\; **far·thest** *or* **fur·thest** \-thəst\ 1 : at or to a distance 2 : much 3 : to a degree 4 : to an advanced point or extent ~ *adj* **farther** *or* **further; farthest** *or* **furthest** 1 : remote 2 : long 3 : being more distant
far·away *adj* : distant
farce \'färs\ *n* 1 : satirical comedy with an improbable plot 2 : ridiculous display —**far·ci·cal** \-sikəl\ *adj*
¹**fare** \'far\ *vb* **fared; far·ing** : get along
²**fare** *n* 1 : price of transportation 2 : range of food
fare·well \far'wel\ *n* 1 : wish of welfare at parting 2 : departure —**farewell** *adj*
far–fetched \'fär'fecht\ *adj* : improbable
fa·ri·na \fə'rēnə\ *n* : fine meal made from cereal grains
farm \'färm\ *n* : place where something is raised for food ~ *vb* 1 : use (land) as a farm 2 : raise plants or animals for food —**farm·er** *n* —**farm·hand** \-,hand\ *n* —**farm·house** *n* —**farm·ing** *n* —**farm·land** \-,land\ *n* —**farm·yard** *n*
far–off *adj* : remote in time or space
far·ri·er \'farēər\ *n* : blacksmith who shoes horses
far·row \'farō\ *vb* : give birth to a litter of pigs —**farrow** *n*
far·sight·ed *adj* 1 : better able to see distant things than near 2 : judicious or shrewd —**far·sight·ed·ness** *n*
far·ther \'färthər\ *adv* 1 : at or to a greater distance or more advanced point 2 : to a greater degree or extent ~ *adj* : more distant
far·ther·most *adj* : most distant
far·thest \'färthəst\ *adj* : most distant ~ *adv* 1 : to or at the greatest distance 2 : to the most advanced point 3 : by the greatest extent
fas·ci·cle \'fasikəl\ *n* 1 : small bundle 2 : division of a book published in parts —**fas·ci·cled** \-kəld\ *adj*
fas·ci·nate \'fasᵊn,āt\ *vb* **-nat·ed; -nat·ing** : transfix and hold spellbound —**fas·ci·na·tion** \,fasᵊn'āshən\ *n*
fas·cism \'fash,izəm\ *n* : dictatorship that exalts nation and race —**fas·cist** \-ist\ *n or adj* —**fas·cis·tic** \fa'shistik\ *adj*
fash·ion \'fashən\ *n* 1 : manner 2 : prevailing custom or style ~ *vb* : form or construct —**fash·ion·able** \-ənəbəl\ *adj* —**fash·ion·ably** \-blē\ *adv*
¹**fast** \'fast\ *adj* 1 : firmly fixed, bound, or shut 2 : faithful 3 : moving or acting quickly 4 : indicating ahead of the correct time 5 : deep and undisturbed 6 : permanently dyed 7 : wild or promiscuous ~ *adv* 1 : so as to be secure or bound 2 : soundly or deeply 3 : swiftly
²**fast** *vb* : abstain from food or eat sparingly ~ *n* : act or time of fasting
fas·ten \'fasᵊn\ *vb* : attach esp. by pinning or tying —**fas·ten·er** *n* —**fas·ten·ing** *n*
fas·tid·i·ous \fas'tidēəs\ *adj* : hard to please —**fas·tid·i·ous·ly** *adv* —**fas·tid·i·ous·ness** *n*
¹**fat** \'fat\ *adj* **-tt-** 1 : having much or fat 2 : thick ~ *n* : animal tissue rich in greasy or oily matter —**fat·ness** *n* —**fat·ten** \'fatᵊn\ *vb* —**fat·ty** *adj or n*
fa·tal \'fātᵊl\ *adj* : causing death or ruin —**fa·tal·i·ty** \fā'talətē, fə-\ *n* —**fa·tal·ly** *adv*
fa·tal·ism \'fātᵊl,izəm\ *n* : belief that fate determines events —**fa·tal·ist** \-ist\ *n* —**fa·tal·is·tic** \,fātᵊl'istik\ *adj* —**fa·tal·is·ti·cal·ly** \-tiklē\ *adv*
fate \'fāt\ *n* 1 : principle, cause, or will held to determine events 2 : end or outcome —**fat·ed** *adj* —**fate·ful** \-fəl\ *adj* —**fate·ful·ly** *adv*
fa·ther \'fäthər, 'fåth-\ *n* 1 : male parent 2 *cap* : God 3 : originator —**father** *vb* —**fa·ther·hood** \-,hud\ *n* —**fa·ther·land** \-,land\ *n* —**fa·ther·less** *adj* —**fa·ther·ly** *adj*
father–in–law *n, pl* **fathers–in–law** : father of one's spouse
fath·om \'fathəm\ *n* : nautical unit of length equal to 6 feet ~ *vb* : understand —**fath·om·able** *adj* —**fath·om·less** *adj*
fa·tigue \fə'tēg\ *n* 1 : weariness from labor or use 2 : tendency to break under repeated stress ~ *vb* **-tigued; -tigu·ing** : tire
fat·u·ous \'fachəwəs\ *adj* : foolish or stupid —**fat·u·ous·ly** *adv* —**fat·u·ous·ness** *n*
fau·cet \'fosət, 'fäs-\ *n* : fixture for drawing off a liquid
fault \'folt\ *n* 1 : weakness in character 2 : something wrong or imperfect 3 : responsibility for something wrong 4 : fracture in the earth's crust ~ *vb* : find fault in or with —**fault·find·er** *n* —**fault·**

find·ing *n* —**fault·i·ly** \'foltəlē\ *adv* —**fault·less** *adj* —**fault·less·ly** *adv* —**faulty** *adj*
fau·na \'fonə\ *n* : animals or animal life esp. of a region —**fau·nal** \-ᵊl\ *adj*
faux pas \'fō'pä\ *n, pl* **faux pas** *same or* -'päz\ : social blunder
fa·vor \'fāvər\ *n* 1 : approval 2 : partiality 3 : act of kindness ~ *vb* : regard or treat with favor —**fa·vor·able** \'fāvərəbəl\ *adj* —**fa·vor·ably** \-blē\ *adv*
fa·vor·ite \'fāvrət\ *n* : one favored —**fa·vorite** *adj* —**fa·vor·it·ism** \-,izəm\ *n*
¹**fawn** \'fon\ *vb* : seek favor by groveling
²**fawn** *n* : young deer
faze \'fāz\ *vb* **fazed; faz·ing** : disturb the composure of
fear \'fir\ *n* : unpleasant emotion caused by expectation or awareness of danger ~ *vb* : be afraid of —**fear·ful** \-fəl\ *adj* —**fear·ful·ly** *adv* —**fear·less** *adj* —**fear·less·ly** *adv* —**fear·less·ness** *n* —**fear·some** \-səm\ *adj*
fea·si·ble \'fēzəbəl\ *adj* : capable of being done —**fea·si·bil·i·ty** \,fēzə'bilətē\ *n* —**fea·si·bly** \'fēzəblē\ *adv*
feast \'fēst\ *n* 1 : large or fancy meal 2 : religious festival ~ *vb* : eat plentifully
feat \'fēt\ *n* : notable deed
feath·er \'fethər\ *n* : one of the light horny outgrowths that form the external covering of a bird's body —**feather** *vb* —**feath·ered** \-ərd\ *adj* —**feath·er·less** *adj* —**feath·ery** *adj*
fea·ture \'fēchər\ *n* 1 : shape or appearance of the face 2 : part of the face 3 : prominent characteristic 4 : special attraction ~ *vb* : give prominence to —**fea·ture·less** *adj*
Feb·ru·ary \'febyə,werē, 'febə-, 'febrə-\ *n* : 2d month of the year having 28 and in leap years 29 days
fe·ces \'fē,sēz\ *n pl* : intestinal body waste —**fe·cal** \-kəl\ *adj*
feck·less \'fekləs\ *adj* : irresponsible
fe·cund \'fekənd, 'fē-\ *adj* : prolific —**fe·cun·di·ty** \fi'kəndətē, fe-\ *n*
fed·er·al \'fedrəl, -dərəl\ *adj* : of or constituting a government with power distributed between a central authority and constituent units —**fed·er·al·ism** \-rə,lizəm\ *n* —**fed·er·al·ist** \-list\ *n or adj* —**fed·er·al·ly** *adv*
fed·er·ate \'fedə,rāt\ *vb* **-at·ed; -at·ing** : join in a federation
fed·er·a·tion \,fedə'rāshən\ *n* : union of organizations
fe·do·ra \fi'dōrə\ *n* : soft felt hat
fed up *adj* : out of patience
fee \'fē\ *n* : fixed charge
fee·ble \'fēbəl\ *adj* **-bler; -blest** : weak or ineffective —**fee·ble·mind·ed** \,fēbəl'mīndəd\ *adj* —**fee·ble·mind·ed·ness** *n* —**fee·ble·ness** *n* —**fee·bly** \-blē\ *adv*
feed \'fēd\ *vb* **fed** \'fed\; **feed·ing** 1 : give food to 2 : eat 3 : furnish ~ *n* : food for livestock —**feed·er** *n*
feel \'fēl\ *vb* **felt** \'felt\; **feel·ing** 1 : perceive or examine through physical contact 2 : think or believe 3 : be conscious of 4 : seem 5 : have sympathy ~ *n* 1 : sense of touch 2 : quality of a thing imparted through touch —**feel·er** *n*
feel·ing \'fēliŋ\ *n* 1 : sense of touch 2 : state of mind 3 *pl* : sensibilities 4 : opinion
feet *pl of* FOOT
feign \'fān\ *vb* : pretend
feint \'fānt\ *n* : mock attack intended to distract attention —**feint** *vb*
fe·lic·i·tate \fi'lisə,tāt\ *vb* **-tat·ed; -tat·ing** : congratulate —**fe·lic·i·ta·tion** \-,lisə'tāshən\ *n*
fe·lic·i·tous \fi'lisətəs\ *adj* : aptly expressed —**fe·lic·i·tous·ly** *adv*
fe·lic·i·ty \-'lisətē\ *n, pl* **-ties** 1 : great happiness 2 : pleasing faculty esp. in art or language
fe·line \'fē,līn\ *adj* : relating to cats —**feline** *n*
¹**fell** \'fel\ *vb* : cut or knock down
²**fell** *past of* FALL
fel·low \'felō\ *n* 1 : companion or associate 2 : man or boy —**fel·low·ship** \-,ship\ *n*
fel·low·man \,felō'man\ *n* : kindred human being
fel·on \'felən\ *n* : one who has committed a felony
fel·o·ny \'felənē\ *n, pl* **-nies** : serious crime —**fe·lo·ni·ous** \fə'lōnēəs\ *adj*
¹**felt** \'felt\ *n* : cloth made of pressed wool and fur
²**felt** *past of* FEEL
fe·male \'fē,māl\ *adj* : relating to or being the sex that bears young —**female** *n*
fem·i·nine \'femənən\ *adj* : relating to the female sex —**fem·i·nin·i·ty** \,femə'ninətē\ *n*
fem·i·nism \'femə,nizəm\ *n* : organized activity on behalf of women's rights —**fem·i·nist** \-nist\ *n or adj*
fe·mur \'fēmər\ *n, pl* **fe·murs** *or* **fem·o·ra** \'femərə\ : long bone of the thigh —**fem·o·ral** \'femərəl\ *adj*
fence \'fens\ *n* : enclosing barrier esp. of

wood or wire ~ *vb* **fenced; fenc·ing** 1 : enclose with a fence 2 : practice fencing —**fenc·er** *n*
fenc·ing \'fensiŋ\ *n* 1 : combat with swords for sport 2 : material for building fences
fend \'fend\ *vb* : ward off
fend·er \'fendər\ *n* : guard over an automobile wheel
fen·nel \'fenᵊl\ *n* : herb related to the carrot
fer·ment \fər'ment\ *vb* : cause or undergo fermentation ~ \'fər,ment\ *n* : agitation
fer·men·ta·tion \,fərmən'tāshən, -,men-\ *n* : chemical decomposition of an organic substance in the absence of oxygen
fern \'fərn\ *n* : flowerless seedless green plant
fe·ro·cious \fə'rōshəs\ *adj* : fierce or savage —**fe·ro·cious·ly** *adv* —**fe·ro·cious·ness** *n* —**fe·roc·i·ty** \-'räsətē\ *n*
fer·ret \'ferət\ *n* : white European polecat ~ *vb* : find out by searching
fer·ric \'ferik\, **fer·rous** \'ferəs\ *adj* : relating to or containing iron
fer·rule \'ferəl\ *n* : metal band or ring
fer·ry \'ferē\ *vb* **-ried; -ry·ing** : carry by boat over water ~ *n, pl* **-ries** : boat used in ferrying —**fer·ry·boat** *n*
fer·tile \'fərtᵊl\ *adj* 1 : producing plentifully 2 : capable of developing or reproducing —**fer·til·i·ty** \fər'tilətē\ *n*
fer·til·ize \'fərtᵊl,īz\ *vb* **-ized; -iz·ing** : make fertile —**fer·til·iza·tion** \,fərtᵊlə'zāshən\ *n* —**fer·til·iz·er** *n*
fer·vid \'fərvəd\ *adj* : ardent or zealous —**fer·vid·ly** *adv*
fer·vor \'fərvər\ *n* : passion —**fer·ven·cy** \-vənsē\ *n* —**fer·vent** \-vənt\ *adj* —**fer·vent·ly** *adv*
fes·ter \'festər\ *vb* 1 : form pus 2 : become more bitter or malignant
fes·ti·val \'festəvəl\ *n* : time of celebration
fes·tive \-tiv\ *adj* : joyous or happy —**fes·tive·ly** *adv* —**fes·tiv·i·ty** \fes'tivətē\ *n*
fes·toon \fes'tün\ *n* : decorative chain or strip hanging in a curve —**festoon** *vb*
fe·tal \'fētᵊl\ *adj* : of, relating to, or being a fetus
fetch \'fech\ *vb* 1 : go or come after and bring or take back 2 : sell for
fetch·ing \'fechiŋ\ *adj* : attractive —**fetch·ing·ly** *adv*
fête \'fāt, 'fet\ *n* : lavish party ~ *vb* **fêt·ed; fêt·ing** : honor or commemorate with a fête
fet·id \'fetəd\ *adj* : having an offensive smell
fe·tish \'fetish\ *n* 1 : object believed to have magical powers 2 : object of unreasoning devotion or concern
fet·lock \'fet,läk\ *n* : projection on the back of a horse's leg above the hoof
fet·ter \'fetər\ *n* : chain or shackle for the feet —**fetter** *vb*
fet·tle \'fetᵊl\ *n* : state of fitness
fe·tus \'fētəs\ *n* : vertebrate not yet born or hatched
feud \'fyüd\ *n* : prolonged quarrel —**feud** *vb*
feu·dal \'fyüdᵊl\ *adj* : of or relating to feudalism
feu·dal·ism \-,izəm\ *n* : medieval political order in which land is granted in return for service —**feu·dal·is·tic** \,fyüdᵊl'istik\ *adj*
fe·ver \'fēvər\ *n* 1 : abnormal rise in body temperature 2 : state of heightened emotion —**fe·ver·ish** *adj* —**fe·ver·ish·ly** *adv*
few \'fyü\ *pron* : not many ~ *adj* : some but not many —often with *a* ~ *n* : small number —often with *a*
few·er \-ər\ *pron* : smaller number of things
fez \'fez\ *n, pl* **fez·zes** : round flat-crowned hat
fi·an·cé \,fē,än'sā\ *n* : man one is engaged to
fi·an·cée \,fē,än'sā\ *n* : woman one is engaged to
fi·as·co \fē'askō\ *n, pl* **-coes** : ridiculous failure
fi·at \'fēat, -,at, -,ät; 'fīət, -,at\ *n* : decree
fib \'fib\ *n* : trivial lie —**fib** *vb* —**fib·ber** *n*
fi·ber, fi·bre \'fībər\ *n* 1 : threadlike substance or structure (as a muscle cell or fine root) 2 : indigestible material in food 3 : element that gives texture or substance —**fi·brous** \-brəs\ *adj*
fi·ber·board *n* : construction material made of compressed fibers
fi·ber·glass *n* : glass in fibrous form in various products (as insulation)
fi·bril·la·tion \,fibrə'lāshən, ,fīb-\ *n* : rapid irregular contractions of heart muscle —**fi·bril·late** \'fibrə,lāt, 'fīb-\ *vb*
fib·u·la \'fibyələ\ *n, pl* **-lae** \-,lē, -,lī\ *or* **-las** : outer of the two leg bones below the knee —**fib·u·lar** \-lər\ *adj*
fick·le \'fikəl\ *adj* : unpredictably changeable —**fick·le·ness** *n*
fic·tion \'fikshən\ *n* : a made-up story or literature consisting of these —**fic·tion·al** \-shənəl\ *adj*
fic·ti·tious \fik'tishəs\ *adj* : made up or pretended
fid·dle \'fidᵊl\ *n* : violin ~ *vb* **-dled; -dling**

1 : play on the fiddle 2 : move the hands restlessly —**fid•dler** \'fidlər, -ələr\ *n*

fid•dle•sticks *n* : nonsense —used as an interjection

fi•del•i•ty \fə'delətē, fī-\ *n, pl* **-ties** 1 : quality or state of being faithful 2 : quality of reproduction

fid•get \'fijət\ *n* 1 *pl* : restlessness 2 : one that fidgets ~ *vb* : move restlessly —**fid•gety** *adj*

fi•du•cia•ry \fə'düshē,erē, -'dyü-, -shərē\ *adj* : held or holding in trust —**fiduciary** *n*

field \'fēld\ *n* 1 : open country 2 : cleared land 3 : land yielding some special product 4 : sphere of activity 5 : area for sports 6 : region or space in which a given effect (as magnetism) exists ~ *vb* : put into the field —**field** *adj* —**field•er** *n*

fiend \'fēnd\ *n* 1 : devil 2 : extremely wicked person —**fiend•ish** *adj* —**fiend•ish•ly** *adv*

fierce \'firs\ *adj* **fierc•er; -est** 1 : violently hostile or aggressive 2 : intense 3 : menacing looking —**fierce•ly** *adv* —**fierce•ness** *n*

fi•ery \'fīərē\ *adj* **fi•er•i•er; -est** 1 : burning 2 : hot or passionate —**fi•eri•ness** \'fīərēnəs\ *n*

fi•es•ta \fē'estə\ *n* : festival

fife \'fīf\ *n* : small flute

fif•teen \fif'tēn\ *n* : one more than 14 —**fifteen** *adj or pron* —**fif•teenth** \-'tēnth\ *adj or n*

fifth \'fifth\ *n* 1 : one that is number 5 in a countable series 2 : one of 5 equal parts of something —**fifth** *adj or adv*

fif•ty \'fiftē\ *n, pl* **-ties** : 5 times 10 —**fif•ti•eth** \-tēəth\ *adj or n* —**fifty** *adj or pron*

fif•ty–fif•ty *adv or adj* : shared equally

fig \'fig\ *n* : pear-shaped edible fruit

fight \'fīt\ *vb* **fought** \'fȯt\; **fight•ing** 1 : contend against another in battle 2 : box 3 : struggle ~ *n* 1 : hostile encounter 2 : boxing match 3 : verbal disagreement —**fight•er** *n*

fig•ment \'figmənt\ *n* : something imagined or made up

fig•u•ra•tive \'figyərətiv, -gə-\ *adj* : metaphorical —**fig•u•ra•tive•ly** *adv*

fig•ure \'figyər, -gər\ *n* 1 : symbol representing a number 2 *pl* : arithmetical calculations 3 : price 4 : shape or outline 5 : illustration 6 : pattern or design 7 : prominent person ~ *vb* **-ured; -ur•ing** 1 : be important 2 : calculate —**fig•ured** *adj*

fig•u•rine \,figyə'rēn\ *n* : small statue

fil•a•ment \'filəmənt\ *n* : fine thread or threadlike part —**fil•a•men•tous** \,filə'mentəs\ *adj*

fil•bert \'filbərt\ *n* : edible nut of a European hazel

filch \'filch\ *vb* : steal furtively

1file \'fīl\ *n* : tool for smoothing or sharpening ~ *vb* **filed; fil•ing** : rub or smooth with a file

2file *vb* **filed; fil•ing** 1 : arrange in order 2 : enter or record officially ~ *n* : device for keeping papers in order

3file *n* : row of persons or things one behind the other ~ *vb* **filed; fil•ing** : march in file

fil•ial \'filēəl, 'filyəl\ *adj* : relating to a son or daughter

fil•i•bus•ter \'filə,bəstər\ *n* : long speeches to delay a legislative vote —**filibuster** *vb* —**fil•i•bus•ter•er** *n*

fil•i•gree \'filə,grē\ *n* : ornamental designs of fine wire —**fil•i•greed** \-,grēd\ *adj*

fill \'fil\ *vb* 1 : make or become full 2 : stop up 3 : feed 4 : satisfy 5 : occupy fully 6 : spread through ~ *n* 1 : full supply 2 : material for filling —**fill•er** *n* —**fill in** *vb* 1 : provide information to or for 2 : substitute

fil•let \'filət, fi'lā, 'fil,ā\ *n* : piece of boneless meat or fish ~ *vb* : cut into fillets

fill•ing *n* : material used to fill something

fil•ly \'filē\ *n, pl* **-lies** : young female horse

film \'film\ *n* 1 : thin skin or membrane 2 : thin coating or layer 3 : strip of material used in taking pictures 4 : movie ~ *vb* : make a movie of —**filmy** *adj*

film•strip *n*: strip of film with photographs for still projection

fil•ter \'filtər\ *n* 1 : device for separating matter from a fluid 2 : device (as on a camera lens) that absorbs light ~ *vb* 1 : pass through a filter 2 : remove by means of a filter —**fil•ter•able** *adj* —**fil•tra•tion** \fil'trāshən\ *n*

filth \'filth\ *n* : repulsive dirt or refuse —**filth•i•ness** *n* —**filthy** \'filthē\ *adj*

fin \'fin\ *n* 1 : thin external process controlling movement in an aquatic animal 2 : fin-shaped part (as on an airplane) 3 : flipper —**finned** \'find\ *adj*

fi•na•gle \fə'nāgəl\ *vb* **-gled; -gling** : get by clever or tricky means —**fi•na•gler** *n*

fi•nal \'fīnᵊl\ *adj* 1 : not to be changed 2 : ultimate 3 : coming at the end —**final** *n* —**fi•nal•ist** \'fīnᵊlist\ *n* —**fi•nal•i•ty** \fī'nalətē, fə-\ *n* —**fi•nal•ize** \-,īz\ *vb* —**fi•nal•ly** *adv*

fi•na•le \fə'nalē, fi'näl-\ *n* : last or climactic part

fi•nance \fə'nans, 'fī,nans\ *n* 1 *pl* : money resources 2 : management of money affairs ~ *vb* **-nanced; -nanc•ing** 1 : raise funds for 2 : give necessary funds to 3 : sell on credit

fi•nan•cial \fə'nanchəl, fī-\ *adj* : relating to finance —**fi•nan•cial•ly** *adv*

fi•nan•cier \,finən'sir, ,fī,nan-\ *n* : person who invests large sums of money

finch \'finch\ *n* : songbird (as a sparrow or linnet) with a strong bill

find \'fīnd\ *vb* **found** \'faund\; **find•ing** 1 : discover or encounter 2 : obtain by effort 3 : experience or feel 4 : gain or regain the use of 5 : decide on (a verdict) ~ *n* 1 : act or instance of finding 2 : something found —**find•er** *n* —**find•ing** *n* —**find out** *vb* : learn, discover, or verify something

fine \'fīn\ *n* : money paid as a penalty ~ *vb* **fined; fin•ing** : impose a fine on ~ *adj* **fin•er; -est** 1 : free from impurity 2 : small or thin 3 : not coarse 4 : superior in quality or appearance ~ *adv* : finely —**fine•ly** *adv* —**fine•ness** *n*

fin•ery \'fīnərē\ *n, pl* **-er•ies** : showy clothing and jewels

fi•nesse \fə'nes\ *n* 1 : delicate skill 2 : craftiness —**finesse** *vb*

fin•ger \'fiŋgər\ *n* 1 : one of the 5 divisions at the end of the hand and esp. one other than the thumb 2 : something like a finger 3 : part of a glove for a finger ~ *vb* 1 : touch with the fingers 2 : identify as if by pointing —**fin•gered** *adj* —**fin•ger•nail** *n* —**fin•ger•tip** *n*

fin•ger•ling \-gərliŋ\ *n* : small fish

fin•ger•print *n* : impression of the pattern of marks on the tip of a finger —**fingerprint** *vb*

fin•icky \'finikē\ *adj* : excessively particular in taste or standards

fin•ish \'finish\ *vb* 1 : come or bring to an end 2 : use or dispose of entirely 3 : put a final coat or surface on ~ *n* 1 : end 2 : final treatment given a surface —**fin•ish•er** *n*

fi•nite \'fī,nīt\ *adj* : having definite limits

fink \'fiŋk\ *n* : contemptible person

fiord *var of* FJORD

fir \'fər\ *n* : erect evergreen tree or its wood

fire \'fīr\ *n* 1 : light or heat and esp. the flame of something burning 2 : destructive burning (as of a house) 3 : enthusiasm 4 : the shooting of weapons ~ *vb* **fired; fir•ing** 1 : kindle 2 : stir up or enliven 3 : dismiss from employment 4 : shoot 5 : bake —**fire•bomb** *n or vb* —**fire•fight•er** *n* —**fire•less** *adj* —**fire•proof** *adj or vb* —**fire•wood** *n*

fire•arm *n* : weapon (as a rifle) that works by an explosion of gunpowder

fire•ball *n* 1 : ball of fire 2 : brilliant meteor

fire•boat *n* : boat equipped for fighting fire

fire•box *n* 1 : chamber (as of a furnace) that contains a fire 2 : fire-alarm box

fire•break *n* : cleared land for checking a forest fire

fire•bug *n* : person who deliberately sets destructive fires

fire•crack•er *n* : small firework that makes noise

fire•fly *n* : night-flying beetle that produces a soft light

fire•man \'fīrmən\ *n* 1 : person trained to put out fires 2 : stoker

fire•place *n* : opening made in a chimney to hold an open fire

fire•plug *n* : hydrant

fire•side *n* 1 : place near the fire or hearth 2 : home ~ *adj* : having an informal quality

fire•trap *n* : place apt to catch on fire

fire•work *n* : device that explodes to produce noise or a display of light

1firm \'fərm\ *adj* 1 : securely fixed in place 2 : strong or vigorous 3 : not subject to change 4 : resolute ~ *vb* : make or become firm —**firm•ly** *adv* —**firm•ness** *n*

2firm *n* : business enterprise

fir•ma•ment \'fərməmənt\ *n* : sky

first \'fərst\ *adj* 1 : being number one 2 : foremost ~ *adv* 1 : before any other 2 : for the first time ~ *n* 1 : number one 2 : one that is first —**first class** *n* —**first–class** *adj or adv* —**first•ly** *adv* —**first–rate** *adj or adv*

first aid *n* : emergency care

first lieutenant *n* : commissioned officer ranking next below a captain

first sergeant *n* 1 : noncommissioned officer serving as the chief assistant to the commander of a military unit 2 : rank in the army below a command sergeant major and in the marine corps below a sergeant major

firth \'fərth\ *n* : estuary

fis•cal \'fiskəl\ *adj* : relating to money —**fis•cal•ly** *adv*

fish \'fish\ *n, pl* **fish** *or* **fish•es** : water animal with fins, gills, and usu. scales ~ *vb* 1 : try to catch fish 2 : grope —**fish•er** *n* —**fish•hook** *n* —**fish•ing** *n*

fish•er•man \-mən\ *n* : one who fishes

fish•ery \'fishərē\ *n, pl* **-er•ies** : fishing business or a place for this

fishy \'fishē\ *adj* **fish•i•er; -est** 1 : relating to or like fish 2 : questionable

fis•sion \'fishən, 'fizh-\ *n* : splitting of an atomic nucleus —**fis•sion•able** \-ənəbəl\ *adj*

fis•sure \'fishər\ *n* : crack

fist \'fist\ *n* : hand doubled up —**fist•ed** \'fistəd\ *adj* —**fist•ful** \-,fu̇l\ *n*

fist•i•cuffs \'fisti,kəfs\ *n pl* : fist fight

1fit \'fit\ *n* : sudden attack of illness or emotion

2fit *adj* **-tt-** 1 : suitable 2 : qualified 3 : sound in body ~ *vb* **-tt-** 1 : be suitable to 2 : insert or adjust correctly 3 : make room for 4 : supply or equip 5 : belong ~ *n* : state of fitting or being fitted —**fit•ly** *adv* —**fit•ness** *n* —**fit•ter** *n*

fit•ful \'fitfəl\ *adj* : restless —**fit•ful•ly** *adv*

fit•ting *adj* : suitable ~ *n* : a small part

five \'fīv\ *n* 1 : one more than 4 2 : 5th in a set or series 3 : something having 5 units —**five** *adj or pron*

fix \'fiks\ *vb* 1 : attach 2 : establish 3 : make right 4 : prepare 5 : improperly influence ~ *n* 1 : predicament 2 : determination of location —**fix•er** *n*

fix•a•tion \fik'sāshən\ *n* : obsessive attachment —**fix•ate** \'fik,sāt\ *vb*

fixed \'fikst\ *adj* 1 : stationary 2 : settled —**fixed•ly** \'fiksədlē\ *adv* —**fixed•ness** \-nəs\ *n*

fix•ture \'fikschər\ *n* : permanent part of something

fizz \'fiz\ *vb* : make a hissing sound ~ *n* : effervescence

fiz•zle \'fizəl\ *vb* **-zled; -zling** 1 : fizz 2 : fail ~ *n* : failure

fjord \fē'ȯrd\ *n* : inlet of the sea between cliffs

flab \'flab\ *n* : flabby flesh

flab•ber•gast \'flabər,gast\ *vb* : astound

flab•by \'flabē\ *adj* **-bi•er; -est** : not firm —**flab•bi•ness** *n*

flac•cid \'flaksəd, 'flasəd\ *adj* : not firm

1flag \'flag\ *n* : flat stone

2flag *n* 1 : fabric that is a symbol (as of a country) 2 : something used to signal ~ *vb* **-gg-** : signal with a flag —**flag•pole** *n* —**flag•staff** *n*

3flag *vb* **-gg-** : lose strength or spirit

flag•el•late \'flajə,lāt\ *vb* **-lat•ed; -lat•ing** : whip —**flag•el•la•tion** \,flajə'lāshən\ *n*

flag•on \'flagən\ *n* : container for liquids

fla•grant \'flāgrənt\ *adj* : conspicuously bad —**fla•grant•ly** *adv*

flag•ship *n* : ship carrying a commander

flag•stone *n* : flag

flail \'flāl\ *n* : tool for threshing grain ~ *vb* : beat with or as if with a flail

flair \'flar\ *n* : natural aptitude

flak \'flak\ *n, pl* **flak** 1 : antiaircraft fire 2 : criticism

flake \'flāk\ *n* : small flat piece ~ *vb* **flaked; flak•ing** : separate or form into flakes

flam•boy•ant \flam'bȯiənt\ *adj* : showy —**flam•boy•ance** \-əns\ *n* —**flam•boy•ant•ly** *adv*

flame \'flām\ *n* 1 : glowing part of a fire 2 : state of combustion 3 : burning passion —**flame** *vb* —**flam•ing** *adj*

fla•min•go \flə'miŋgō\ *n, pl* **-gos** : long-legged long-necked tropical water bird

flam•ma•ble \'flaməbəl\ *adj* : easily ignited

flange \'flanj\ *n* : rim

flank \'flaŋk\ *n* : side of something ~ *vb* 1 : attack or go around the side of 2 : be at the side of

flan•nel \'flanᵊl\ *n* : soft napped fabric

flap \'flap\ *n* 1 : slap 2 : something flat that hangs loose ~ *vb* **-pp-** 1 : move (wings) up and down 2 : swing back and forth noisily

flap•jack \-,jak\ *n* : pancake

flare \'flar\ *vb* **flared; flar•ing** : become suddenly bright or excited ~ *n* : blaze of light

flash \'flash\ *vb* 1 : give off a sudden flame or burst of light 2 : appear or pass suddenly ~ *n* 1 : sudden burst of light or inspiration 2 : instant ~ *adj* : coming suddenly

flash•light *n* : small battery-operated light

flashy \'flashē\ *adj* **flash•i•er; -est** : showy —**flash•i•ly** *adv* —**flash•i•ness** *n*

flask \'flask\ *n* : flattened bottle

flat \'flat\ *adj* **-tt-** 1 : smooth 2 : broad and thin 3 : definite 4 : uninteresting 5 : deflated 6 : below the true pitch ~ *n* 1 : level surface of land 2 : flat note in music 3 : apartment 4 : deflated tire ~ *adv* **-tt-** 1 : exactly 2 : below the true pitch ~ *vb* **-tt-** : make flat —**flat•ly** *adv* —**flat•ness** *n* —**flat•ten** \-ᵊn\ *vb*

flat•car *n* : railroad car without sides

flat•fish *n* : flattened fish with both eyes on the upper side

flat•foot *n, pl* **flat•feet** : foot condition in which the arch is flattened —**flat–foot•ed** *adj*

flat–out *adj* 1 : being maximum effort or speed 2 : downright

flat•ter \'flatər\ *vb* 1 : praise insincerely 2 : judge or represent too favorably —**flat•ter•er** *n* —**flat•tery** \'flatərē\ *n*

flat•u•lent \'flachələnt\ *adj* : full of gas —**flat•u•lence** \-ləns\ *n*

flat•ware *n* : eating utensils

flaunt \'flȯnt\ *vb* : display ostentatiously —**flaunt** *n*

fla•vor \'flāvər\ *n* 1 : quality that affects the sense of taste 2 : something that adds flavor ~ *vb* : give flavor to —**fla•vor•ful** *adj* —**fla•vor•ing** *n* —**fla•vor•less** *adj*

flaw \'flȯ\ *n* : fault —**flaw•less** *adj* —**flaw•less•ly** *adv* —**flaw•less•ness** *n*

flax \'flaks\ *n* : plant from which linen is made

flax•en \'flaksən\ *adj* : made of or like flax

flay \'flā\ *vb* 1 : strip off the skin of 2 : criticize harshly

flea \'flē\ *n* : leaping bloodsucking insect

fleck \'flek\ *vb or n* : streak or spot

fledg•ling \'flejliŋ\ *n* : young bird

flee \'flē\ *vb* **fled** \'fled\; **flee•ing** : run away

fleece \'flēs\ *n* : sheep's wool ~ *vb* **fleeced; fleec•ing** 1 : shear 2 : get money from dishonestly —**fleecy** *adj*

1fleet \'flēt\ *vb* : pass rapidly ~ *adj* : swift —**fleet•ing** *adj* —**fleet•ness** *n*

2fleet *n* : group of ships

fleet admiral *n* : commissioned officer of the highest rank in the navy

flesh \'flesh\ *n* 1 : soft parts of an animal's body 2 : soft plant tissue (as fruit pulp) —**fleshed** \'flesht\ *adj* —**flesh out** *vb* : make fuller —**fleshy** *adj*

flesh•ly \'fleshlē\ *adj* : sensual

flew *past of* FLY

flex \'fleks\ *vb* : bend

flex•i•ble \'fleksəbəl\ *adj* 1 : capable of being flexed 2 : adaptable —**flex•i•bil•i•ty** \,fleksə'bilətē\ *n* —**flex•i•bly** \-əblē\ *adv*

flick \'flik\ *n* : light jerky stroke ~ *vb* 1 : strike lightly 2 : flutter

flick•er \'flikər\ *vb* 1 : waver 2 : burn unsteadily ~ *n* 1 : sudden movement 2 : wavering light

fli•er \'flīər\ *n* 1 : aviator 2 : advertising circular

1flight \'flīt\ *n* 1 : act or instance of flying 2 : ability to fly 3 : a passing through air or space 4 : series of stairs —**flight•less** *adj*

2flight *n* : act or instance of running away

flighty \-ē\ *adj* **flight•i•er; -est** : capricious or silly —**flight•i•ness** *n*

flim•flam \'flim,flam\ *n* : trickery

flim•sy \-zē\ *adj* **-si•er; -est** 1 : not strong or well made 2 : not believable —**flim•si•ly** *adv* —**flim•si•ness** *n*

flinch \'flinch\ *vb* : shrink from pain

fling \'fliŋ\ *vb* **flung** \'fləŋ\; **fling•ing** 1 : move brusquely 2 : throw ~ *n* 1 : act or instance of flinging 2 : attempt 3 : period of self-indulgence

flint \'flint\ *n* : hard quartz that gives off sparks when struck with steel —**flinty** *adj*

flip \'flip\ *vb* **-pp-** 1 : cause to turn over quickly or many times 2 : move with a quick push ~ *adj* : insolent —**flip** *n*

flip•pant \'flipənt\ *adj* : not serious enough —**flip•pan•cy** \-ənsē\ *n*

flip•per \'flipər\ *n* : paddlelike limb (as of a seal) for swimming

flirt \'flərt\ *vb* 1 : be playfully romantic 2 : show casual interest ~ *n* : one who flirts —**flir•ta•tion** \,flər'tāshən\ *n* —**flir•ta•tious** \-shəs\ *adj*

flit \'flit\ *vb* **-tt-** : dart

float \'flōt\ *n* 1 : something that floats 2 : vehicle carrying an exhibit ~ *vb* 1 : rest on or in a fluid without sinking 2 : wander 3 : finance by issuing stock or bonds —**float•er** *n*

flock \'fläk\ *n* : group of animals (as birds) or people ~ *vb* : gather or move as a group

floe \'flō\ *n* : mass of floating ice

flog \'fläg\ *vb* **-gg-** : beat with a rod or whip —**flog•ger** *n*

flood \'fləd\ *n* 1 : great flow of water over the land 2 : overwhelming volume ~ *vb* : cover or fill esp. with water —**flood•wa•ter** *n*

floor \'flōr\ *n* 1 : bottom of a room on which one stands 2 : story of a building 3 : lower limit ~ *vb* 1 : furnish with a floor 2 : knock down 3 : amaze —**floor•board** *n* —**floor•ing** \-iŋ\ *n*

floo•zy, floo•zie \'flüzē\ *n, pl* **-zies** : promiscuous young woman

flop \'fläp\ *vb* **-pp-** 1 : flap 2 : slump heavily 3 : fail —**flop** *n*

flop•py \'fläpē\ *adj* **-pi•er; -est** : soft and flexible

flo•ra \'flōrə\ *n* : plants or plant life of a region

flo•ral \'flōrəl\ *adj* : relating to flowers

flor•id \'flȯrəd\ *adj* 1 : very flowery in style 2 : reddish

flo•rist \'flōrist\ *n* : flower dealer

floss \ˈfläs\ n 1 : soft thread for embroidery 2 : thread used to clean between teeth —floss vb

flo·ta·tion \flōˈtāshən\ n : process or instance of floating

flo·til·la \flōˈtilə\ n : small fleet

flot·sam \ˈflätsəm\ n : floating wreckage

1flounce \ˈflau̇ns\ vb flounced; flounc·ing : move with exaggerated jerky motions —flounce n

2flounce n : fabric border or wide ruffle

1floun·der \ˈflau̇ndər\ n, pl flounder or flounders : flatfish

2flounder vb 1 : struggle for footing 2 : proceed clumsily

flour \ˈflau̇ər\ n : finely ground meal ~ vb : coat with flour —floury adj

flour·ish \ˈflərish\ vb 1 : thrive 2 : wave threateningly ~ n 1 : embellishment 2 : fanfare 3 : wave 4 : showiness of action

flout \ˈflau̇t\ vb : treat with disdain

flow \ˈflō\ vb 1 : move in a stream 2 : proceed smoothly and readily ~ n : uninterrupted stream

flow·er \ˈflau̇ər\ n 1 : showy plant shoot that bears seeds 2 : state of flourishing ~ vb 1 : produce flowers 2 : flourish —flow·ered adj —flow·er·i·ness n —flow·er·less adj —flow·er·pot n —flow·ery \-ē\ adj

flown past part of FLY

flu \ˈflü\ n 1 : influenza 2 : minor virus ailment

flub \ˈfləb\ vb -bb- : bungle —flub n

fluc·tu·ate \ˈfləkchəˌwāt\ vb -at·ed; -at·ing : change rapidly esp. up and down —fluc·tu·a·tion \ˌfləkchəˈwāshən\ n

flue \ˈflü\ n : smoke duct

flu·ent \ˈflüənt\ adj : speaking with ease —flu·en·cy \-ənsē\ n —flu·ent·ly adv

fluff \ˈfləf\ n 1 : something soft and light 2 : blunder ~ vb 1 : make fluffy 2 : make a mistake —fluffy \-ē\ adj

flu·id \ˈflüəd\ adj : flowing ~ n : substance that can flow —flu·id·i·ty \flüˈidətē\ n —flu·id·ly adv

fluid ounce n : unit of liquid measure equal to 1/16 pint

fluke \ˈflük\ n : stroke of luck

flume \ˈflüm\ n : channel for water

flung past of FLING

flunk \ˈfləŋk\ vb : fail in school work

flun·ky, flun·key \ˈfləŋkē\ n, pl -kies or -keys : lackey

flu·o·res·cence \ˌflu̇rˈesᵊns, ˌflȯr-\ n : emission of light after initial absorption —flu·o·resce \-ˈes\ vb —flu·o·res·cent \-ˈesᵊnt\ adj

flu·o·ri·date \ˈflȯrəˌdāt, ˈflu̇r-\ vb -dat·ed; -dat·ing : add fluoride to —flu·o·ri·da·tion \ˌflȯrəˈdāshən, ˌflu̇r-\ n

flu·o·ride \ˈflȯrˌīd, ˈflu̇r-\ n : compound of fluorine

flu·o·rine \ˈflu̇rˌēn, -ən\ n : toxic gaseous chemical element

flu·o·ro·car·bon \ˌflȯrōˈkärbən, ˌflu̇r-\ n : compound containing fluorine and carbon

flu·o·ro·scope \ˈflu̇rəˌskōp\ n : instrument for internal examination —flu·o·ro·scop·ic \ˌflu̇rəˈskäpik\ adj —flu·o·ros·co·py \ˌflu̇rˈäskəpē\ n

flur·ry \ˈflərē\ n, pl -ries 1 : light snowfall 2 : bustle 3 : brief burst of activity —flurry vb

1flush \ˈfləsh\ vb : cause (a bird) to fly from cover

2flush n 1 : sudden flow (as of water) 2 : surge of emotion 3 : blush ~ vb 1 : blush 2 : wash out with a rush of liquid ~ adj 1 : filled to overflowing 2 : of a reddish healthy color 3 : smooth or level 4 : abutting —flush adv

3flush n : cards of the same suit

flus·ter \ˈfləstər\ vb : upset —fluster n

flute \ˈflüt\ n 1 : pipelike musical instrument 2 : groove —flut·ed adj —flut·ing n —flut·ist \-ist\ n

flut·ter \ˈflətər\ vb 1 : flap the wings rapidly 2 : move with quick wavering or flapping motions 3 : behave in an agitated manner ~ n 1 : a fluttering 2 : state of confusion —flut·tery \-ərē\ adj

flux \ˈfləks\ n : state of continuous change

1fly \ˈflī\ vb flew \ˈflü\; flown \ˈflōn\; fly·ing 1 : move through the air with wings 2 : float or soar 3 : flee 4 : move or pass swiftly 5 : operate an airplane

2fly n, pl flies : garment closure

3fly n, pl flies : winged insect

fly·er var of FLIER

fly·pa·per n : sticky paper for catching flies

fly·speck n 1 : speck of fly dung 2 : something tiny

fly·wheel n : rotating wheel that regulates the speed of machinery

foal \ˈfōl\ n : young horse —foal vb

foam \ˈfōm\ n 1 : mass of bubbles on top of a liquid 2 : material of cellular form ~ vb : form foam —foamy adj

fob \ˈfäb\ n : short chain for a pocket watch

fo'·c'sle var of FORECASTLE

fo·cus \ˈfōkəs\ n, pl -ci \-ˌsī\ 1 : point at which reflected or refracted rays meet 2 : adjustment (as of eyeglasses) for clear vision 3 : central point ~ vb : bring to a focus —fo·cal \-kəl\ adj —fo·cal·ly adv

fod·der \ˈfädər\ n : food for livestock

foe \ˈfō\ n : enemy

fog \ˈfȯg, ˈfäg\ n 1 : fine particles of water suspended near the ground 2 : mental confusion ~ vb -gg- : obscure or be obscured with fog —fog·gy adj

fog·horn n : warning horn sounded in a fog

fo·gy \ˈfōgē\ n, pl -gies : person with old-fashioned ideas

foi·ble \ˈfȯibəl\ n : minor character fault

1foil \ˈfȯil\ vb : defeat ~ n : light fencing sword

2foil n 1 : thin sheet of metal 2 : one that sets off another by contrast

foist \ˈfȯist\ vb : force another to accept

1fold \ˈfōld\ n 1 : enclosure for sheep 2 : group with a common interest

2fold vb 1 : lay one part over another 2 : embrace ~ n : part folded

fold·er \ˈfōldər\ n 1 : one that folds 2 : circular 3 : folded cover or envelope for papers

fol·de·rol \ˈfäldəˌräl\ n : nonsense

fo·liage \ˈfōlēij, -lij\ n : plant leaves

fo·lio \ˈfōlēˌō\ n, pl -li·os : sheet of paper folded once

folk \ˈfōk\ n, pl folk or folks 1 : people in general 2 folks pl : one's family ~ adj : relating to the common people

folk·lore n : customs and traditions of a people —folk·lor·ist n

folksy \ˈfōksē\ adj folks·i·er; -est : friendly and informal

fol·li·cle \ˈfälikəl\ n : small anatomical cavity or gland

fol·low \ˈfälō\ vb 1 : go or come after 2 : pursue 3 : obey 4 : proceed along 5 : keep one's attention fixed on 6 : result from —fol·low·er n

fol·low·ing \ˈfäləwiŋ\ adj : next ~ n : group of followers ~ prep : after

fol·ly \ˈfälē\ n, pl -lies : foolishness

fo·ment \fōˈment\ vb : incite

fond \ˈfänd\ adj 1 : strongly attracted 2 : affectionate 3 : dear —fond·ly adv —fond·ness n

fon·dle \ˈfändᵊl\ vb -dled; -dling : touch lovingly

fon·due \fänˈdü, -ˈdyü\ n : preparation of melted cheese

font \ˈfänt\ n 1 : baptismal basin 2 : fountain

food \ˈfüd\ n : material eaten to sustain life

fool \ˈfül\ n 1 : stupid person 2 : jester ~ vb 1 : waste time 2 : meddle 3 : deceive —fool·ery \ˈfülərē\ n —fool·ish \ˈfülish\ adj —fool·ish·ly adv —fool·ish·ness n —fool·proof adj

fool·har·dy \ˈfülˌhärdē\ adj : rash —fool·har·di·ness n

foot \ˈfu̇t\ n, pl feet \ˈfēt\ 1 : end part of a leg 2 : unit of length equal to 1/3 yard 3 : unit of verse meter 4 : bottom —foot·age \-ij\ n —foot·ed adj —foot·path n —foot·print n —foot·race n —foot·rest n —foot·wear n

foot·ball n : ball game played by 2 teams on a rectangular field

foot·bridge n : bridge for pedestrians

foot·hill n : hill at the foot of higher hills

foot·hold n : support for the feet

foot·ing n 1 : foothold 2 : basis

foot·lights n pl : stage lights along the floor

foot·lock·er n : small trunk

foot·loose adj : having no ties

foot·man \ˈfu̇tmən\ n : male servant

foot·note n : note at the bottom of a page

foot·step n 1 : step 2 : distance covered by a step 3 : footprint

foot·stool n : stool to support the feet

foot·work n : skillful movement of the feet (as in boxing)

fop \ˈfäp\ n : dandy —fop·pery \-ərē\ n —fop·pish adj

for \ˈfȯr\ prep 1 —used to show preparation or purpose 2 : because of 3 —used to show a recipient 4 : in support of 5 : so as to support or help cure 6 : so as to be equal to 7 : concerning 8 : through the period of ~ conj : because

for·age \ˈfȯrij\ n : food for animals ~ vb -aged; -ag·ing 1 : hunt food 2 : search for provisions

for·ay \ˈfȯrˌā\ n or vb : raid

1for·bear \fȯrˈbar\ vb -bore \-ˈbōr\; -borne \-ˈbōrn\; -bear·ing 1 : refrain from 2 : be patient —for·bear·ance \-ˈbarəns\ n

2forbear var of FOREBEAR

for·bid \fərˈbid\ vb -bade \-ˈbad, -ˈbād\ or -bad \-ˈbad\; -bid·den \-ˈbidᵊn\; -bid·ding 1 : prohibit 2 : order not to do something

for·bid·ding adj : tending to discourage

force \ˈfōrs\ n 1 : exceptional strength or energy 2 : military strength 3 : body (as of persons) available for a purpose 4 : violence 5 : influence (as a push or pull) that causes motion ~ vb forced; forc·ing 1 : compel 2 : gain against resistance 3 : break open —force·ful \-fəl\ adj —force·ful·ly adv —in force 1 : in great numbers 2 : valid

for·ceps \ˈfȯrsəps\ n, pl forceps : surgical instrument for grasping objects

forc·ible \ˈfōrsəbəl\ adj 1 : done by force 2 : showing force —forc·i·bly \-blē\ adv

ford \ˈfōrd\ n : place to wade across a stream ~ vb : wade across

fore \ˈfōr\ adv : in or toward the front ~ adj : being or coming before in time, place, or order ~ n : front

fore–and–aft adj : lengthwise

fore·arm \ˈfōrˌärm\ n : part of the arm between the elbow and the wrist

fore·bear \ˈfōrˌbar\ n : ancestor

fore·bod·ing \fōrˈbōdiŋ\ n : premonition of disaster —fore·bod·ing adj

fore·cast \ˈfōrˌkast\ vb -cast; -cast·ing : predict —forecast n —fore·cast·er n

fore·cas·tle \ˈfōksəl\ n : forward part of a ship

fore·close \fōrˈklōz\ vb : take legal measures to terminate a mortgage —fore·clo·sure \-ˈklōzhər\ n

fore·fa·ther \ˈfōrˌfäthər\ n : ancestor

fore·fin·ger \ˈfōrˌfiŋgər\ n : finger next to the thumb

fore·foot \ˈfōrˌfu̇t\ n : front foot of a quadruped

fore·front \ˈfōrˌfrənt\ n : foremost position or place

1fore·go \fōrˈgō\ vb -went; -gone; -go·ing : precede

2forego var of FORGO

fore·go·ing adj : preceding

fore·gone adj : determined in advance

fore·ground \ˈfōrˌgrau̇nd\ n : part of a scene nearest the viewer

fore·hand \ˈfōrˌhand\ n : stroke (as in tennis) made with the palm of the hand turned forward —forehand adj

fore·head \ˈfȯrəd, ˈfōrˌhed\ n : part of the face above the eyes

for·eign \ˈfȯrən\ adj 1 : situated outside a place or country and esp. one's own country 2 : belonging to a different place or country 3 : not pertinent 4 : related to or dealing with other nations —for·eign·er \-ər\ n

fore·know \fōrˈnō\ vb -knew; -known; -know·ing : know beforehand —fore·knowl·edge n

fore·leg \ˈfōrˌleg\ n : front leg

fore·lock \ˈfōrˌläk\ n : front lock of hair

fore·man \ˈfōrmən\ n 1 : spokesman of a jury 2 : workman in charge

fore·most \ˈfōrˌmōst\ adj : first in time, place, or order —foremost adv

fore·noon \ˈfōrˌnün\ n : morning

fo·ren·sic \fəˈrensik\ adj : relating to courts or public speaking or debate

fo·ren·sics \-siks\ n pl : art or study of speaking or debating

fore·or·dain \ˌfōrȯrˈdān\ vb : decree beforehand

fore·quar·ter \ˈfōrˌkwȯrtər\ n : front half on one side of the body of a quadruped

fore·run·ner \ˈfōrˌrənər\ n : one that goes before

fore·see \fōrˈsē\ vb -saw; -seen; -see·ing : see or realize beforehand —fore·see·able adj

fore·shad·ow \fōrˌshadō\ vb : hint or suggest beforehand

fore·sight \ˈfōrˌsīt\ n : care or provision for the future —fore·sight·ed adj —fore·sight·ed·ness n

for·est \ˈfȯrəst\ n : large thick growth of trees and underbrush —for·est·ed \ˈfȯrəstəd\ adj —for·est·er \-əstər\ n —for·est·land \-ˌland\ n —for·est·ry \-əstrē\ n

fore·stall \fōrˈstȯl, fȯr-\ vb : prevent by acting in advance

foreswear var of FORSWEAR

fore·taste \ˈfōrˌtāst\ n : advance indication or notion ~ vb : anticipate

fore·tell \fōrˈtel\ vb -told; -tell·ing : predict

fore·thought \ˈfōrˌthȯt\ n : foresight

for·ev·er \fȯrˈevər\ adv 1 : for a limitless time 2 : always

for·ev·er·more \-ˌevərˈmōr\ adv : forever

fore·warn \fōrˈwȯrn\ vb : warn beforehand

fore·word \ˈfōrwərd\ n : preface

for·feit \ˈfȯrfət\ n : something forfeited ~ vb : lose or lose the right to by an error or crime —for·fei·ture \-fəˌchu̇r\ n

1forge \ˈfōrj\ n : smithy ~ vb forged; forg·ing 1 : form (metal) by heating and hammering 2 : imitate falsely esp. to defraud —forg·er n —forg·ery \-ərē\ n

2forge vb forged; forg·ing : move ahead steadily

for·get \fərˈget\ vb -got \-ˈgät\; -got·ten \-ˈgätᵊn\ or -got; -get·ting 1 : be unable to think of or recall 2 : fail to think of at the proper time —for·get·ta·ble adj —for·get·ful \-fəl\ adj —for·get·ful·ly adv

forget–me–not n : small herb with blue or white flowers

for·give \fərˈgiv\ vb -gave \-ˈgāv\; -giv·en \-ˈgivən\; -giv·ing : pardon —for·giv·able adj —for·give·ness n

for·giv·ing adj 1 : able to forgive 2 : allowing room for error or weakness

for·go, fore·go \fōrˈgō\ vb -went; -gone; -go·ing : do without

fork \ˈfȯrk\ n 1 : implement with prongs for lifting, holding, or digging 2 : forked part 3 : a dividing into branches or a place where something branches ~ vb 1 : divide into branches 2 : move with a fork —forked \ˈfȯrkt, ˈfȯrkəd\ adj

fork·lift n : machine for lifting with steel fingers

for·lorn \fərˈlȯrn\ adj 1 : deserted 2 : wretched —for·lorn·ly adv

form \ˈfȯrm\ n 1 : shape 2 : set way of doing or saying something 3 : document with blanks to be filled in 4 : manner of performing with respect to what is expected 5 : mold 6 : kind or variety 7 : one of the ways in which a word is changed to show difference in use ~ vb 1 : give form or shape to 2 : train 3 : develop 4 : constitute —for·ma·tive \ˈfȯrmətiv\ adj —form·less \-ləs\ adj

for·mal \ˈfȯrməl\ adj : following established custom ~ n : formal social event —for·mal·i·ty \fȯrˈmalətē\ n —for·mal·ize \ˈfȯrməˌlīz\ vb —for·mal·ly adv

form·al·de·hyde \fȯrˈmaldəˌhīd\ n : colorless pungent gas used as a preservative and disinfectant

for·mat \ˈfȯrˌmat\ n : general style or arrangement of something —format vb

for·ma·tion \fȯrˈmāshən\ n 1 : a giving form to something 2 : something formed 3 : arrangement

for·mer \ˈfȯrmər\ adj : coming before in time —for·mer·ly adv

for·mi·da·ble \ˈfȯrmədəbəl, fȯrˈmid-\ adj 1 : causing fear or dread 2 : very difficult —for·mi·da·bly \-blē\ adv

for·mu·la \ˈfȯrmyələ\ n, pl -las or -lae \-ˌlē, -ˌlī\ 1 : set form of words for ceremonial use 2 : recipe 3 : milk mixture for a baby 4 : group of symbols or figures briefly expressing information 5 : set form or method

for·mu·late \-ˌlāt\ vb -lat·ed; -lat·ing : design, devise —for·mu·la·tion \ˌfȯrmyəˈlāshən\ n

for·ni·ca·tion \ˌfȯrnəˈkāshən\ n : illicit sexual intercourse —for·ni·cate \ˈfȯrnəˌkāt\ vb —for·ni·ca·tor \-ˌkātər\ n

for·sake \fərˈsāk\ vb -sook \-ˈsu̇k\; -sak·en \-ˈsākən\; -sak·ing : renounce completely

for·swear \fȯrˈswar\ vb -swore; -sworn; -swear·ing 1 : renounce under oath 2 : perjure

for·syth·ia \fərˈsithēə\ n : shrub grown for its yellow flowers

fort \ˈfōrt\ n 1 : fortified place 2 : permanent army post

forte \ˈfōrt, ˈfȯrˌtā\ n : something at which a person excels

forth \ˈfōrth\ adv : forward

forth·com·ing adj 1 : coming or available soon 2 : open and direct

forth·right adj : direct —forth·right·ly adv —forth·right·ness n

forth·with adv : immediately

for·ti·fy \ˈfȯrtəˌfī\ vb -fied; -fy·ing : make strong —for·ti·fi·ca·tion \ˌfȯrtəfəˈkāshən\ n

for·ti·tude \ˈfȯrtəˌtüd, -ˌtyüd\ n : ability to endure

fort·night \ˈfȯrtˌnīt\ n : 2 weeks —fort·night·ly adj or adv

for·tress \ˈfȯrtrəs\ n : strong fort

for·tu·itous \fȯrˈtüətəs, -ˈtyü-\ adj : accidental

for·tu·nate \ˈfȯrchənət\ adj 1 : coming by good luck 2 : lucky —for·tu·nate·ly adv

for·tune \ˈfȯrchən\ n 1 : prosperity attained partly through luck 2 : good or bad luck 3 : destiny 4 : wealth

for·tune–tell·er \-ˌtelər\ n : one who foretells a person's future —for·tune–tell·ing \-iŋ\ n or adj

for·ty \ˈfȯrtē\ n, pl forties : 4 times 10 —for·ti·eth \-ēəth\ adj or n —forty adj or pron

fo·rum \ˈfōrəm\ n, pl -rums 1 : Roman marketplace 2 : medium for open discussion

for·ward \ˈfȯrwərd\ adj 1 : being near or at or belonging to the front 2 : brash ~ adv : toward what is in front ~ n : player near the front of his team ~ vb 1 : help onward 2 : send on —for·ward·er \-wərdər\ n —for·ward·ness n

for·wards \ˈfȯrwərdz\ adv : forward

fos·sil \ˈfäsəl\ n : preserved trace of an ancient plant or animal ~ adj : being or originating from a fossil —fos·sil·ize vb

fos·ter \ˈfȯstər\ adj : being, having, or relating to substitute parents ~ vb : help to grow or develop

fought past of FIGHT

foul \ˈfau̇l\ adj 1 : offensive 2 : clogged with dirt 3 : abusive 4 : wet and stormy 5 : unfair ~ n : a breaking of the rules in a game ~ adv : foully ~ vb 1 : make or become foul or filthy 2 : tangle —foul·ly adv —foul·mouthed \-ˈmau̇thd, -ˈmau̇tht\ adj —foul·ness n

fou·lard \fu̇ˈlärd\ n : lightweight silk

foul–up n : error or state of confusion —foul up vb : bungle

1found \ˈfau̇nd\ past of FIND

2found *vb* : establish **—found•er** *n*
foun•da•tion \fau̇n'dāshən\ *n* **1** : act of founding **2** : basis for something **3** : endowed institution **4** : supporting structure **—foun•da•tion•al** \-shənəl\ *adj*
foun•der \'fau̇ndər\ *vb* : sink
found•ling \'fau̇ndliŋ\ *n* : abandoned infant that is found
found•ry \'fau̇ndrē\ *n, pl* **-dries** : place where metal is cast
fount \'fau̇nt\ *n* : fountain
foun•tain \'fau̇ntən\ *n* **1** : spring of water **2** : source **3** : artificial jet of water
four \'fōr\ *n* **1** : one more than 3 **2** : 4th in a set or series **3** : something having 4 units **—four** *adj or pron*
four•fold *adj* : quadruple **—four•fold** *adv*
four•score *adj* : 80
four•some \'fōrsəm\ *n* : group of 4
four•teen \fōr'tēn\ *n* : one more than 13 **—fourteen** *adj or pron* **—four•teenth** \-'tēnth\ *adj or n*
fourth \'fōrth\ *n* **1** : one that is 4th **2** : one of 4 equal parts of something **—fourth** *adj or adv*
fowl \'fau̇l\ *n, pl* **fowl** *or* **fowls 1** : bird **2** : chicken
fox \'fäks\ *n, pl* **fox•es 1** : small mammal related to wolves **2** : clever person ~ *vb* : trick **—foxy** \'fäksē\ *adj*
fox•glove *n* : flowering plant that provides digitalis
fox•hole \'fäks,hōl\ *n* : pit for protection against enemy fire
foy•er \'fȯiər, 'fȯi,yā\ *n* : entrance hallway
fra•cas \'frākəs, 'frak-\ *n, pl* **-cas•es** \-əsəz\ : brawl
frac•tion \'frakshən\ *n* **1** : number indicating one or more equal parts of a whole **2** : portion **—frac•tion•al** \-shənəl\ *adj* **—frac•tion•al•ly** *adv*
frac•tious \'frakshəs\ *adj* : hard to control
frac•ture \'frakchər\ *n* : a breaking of something **—fracture** *vb*
frag•ile \'frajəl, -ˌīl\ *adj* : easily broken **—fra•gil•i•ty** \frə'jilətē\ *n*
frag•ment \'fragmənt\ *n* : part broken off ~ \-ˌment\ *vb* : break into parts **—frag•men•tary** \'fragmən,terē\ *adj* **—frag•men•ta•tion** \ˌfragmən'tāshən, -ˌmen-\ *n*
fra•grant \'frāgrənt\ *adj* : sweet-smelling **—fra•grance** \-grəns\ *n* **—fra•grant•ly** *adv*
frail \'frāl\ *adj* : weak or delicate **—frail•ty** \-tē\ *n*
frame \'frām\ *vb* **framed; fram•ing 1** : plan **2** : formulate **3** : construct or arrange **4** : enclose in a frame **5** : make appear guilty ~ *n* **1** : makeup of the body **2** : supporting or enclosing structure **3** : state or disposition (as of mind) **—frame•work** *n*
franc \'fraŋk\ *n* : monetary unit (as of France)
fran•chise \'fran,chīz\ *n* **1** : special privilege **2** : the right to vote **—fran•chi•see** \ˌfran,chī'zē, -chə-\ *n*
fran•gi•ble \'franjəbəl\ *adj* : breakable **—fran•gi•bil•i•ty** \ˌfranjə'bilətē\ *n*
1frank \'fraŋk\ *adj* : direct and sincere **—frank•ly** *adv* **—frank•ness** *n*
2frank *vb* : mark (mail) with a sign showing it can be mailed free ~ *n* : sign on franked mail
frank•furt•er \'fraŋkfərtər, -ˌfərt-\, **frank•furt** \-fərt\ *n* : cooked sausage
frank•in•cense \'fraŋkən,sens\ *n* : incense resin
fran•tic \'frantik\ *adj* : wildly excited **—fran•ti•cal•ly** \-iklē\ *adv*
fra•ter•nal \frə'tərnəl\ *adj* **1** : brotherly **2** : of a fraternity **—fra•ter•nal•ly** *adv*
fra•ter•ni•ty \frə'tərnətē\ *n, pl* **-ties** : men's student social group
frat•er•nize \'fratər,nīz\ *vb* **-nized; -niz•ing 1** : mingle as friends **2** : associate with members of a hostile group **—frat•er•ni•za•tion** \ˌfratərnə'zāshən\ *n*
frat•ri•cide \'fratrə,sīd\ *n* : killing of a sibling **—frat•ri•cid•al** \ˌfratrə'sīdəl\ *adj*
fraud \'frȯd\ *n* : trickery **—fraud•u•lent** \'frȯjələnt\ *adj* **—fraud•u•lent•ly** *adv*
fraught \'frȯt\ *adj* : full of or accompanied by something specified
1fray \'frā\ *n* : fight
2fray *vb* **1** : wear by rubbing **2** : separate the threads of **3** : irritate
fraz•zle \'frazəl\ *vb* **-zled; -zling** : wear out ~ *n* : exhaustion
freak \'frēk\ *n* **1** : something abnormal or unusual **2** : enthusiast **—freak•ish** *adj* **—freak out** *vb* **1** : experience nightmarish hallucinations from drugs **2** : distress or become distressed
freck•le \'frekəl\ *n* : brown spot on the skin **—freckle** *vb*
free \'frē\ *adj* **fre•er; fre•est 1** : having liberty or independence **2** : not taxed **3** : given without charge **4** : voluntary **5** : not in use **6** : not fastened ~ *adv* : without charge ~ *vb* **freed; free•ing** : set free **—free** *adv* **—free•born** *adj* **—free•dom** \'frēdəm\ *n* **—free•ly** *adv*
free•boot•er \-ˌbütər\ *n* : pirate
free–for–all *n* : fight with no rules
free•load *vb* : live off another's generosity **—free•load•er** *n*
free•stand•ing *adj* : standing without support
free•way \'frē,wā\ *n* : expressway
free will *n* : independent power to choose **—free•will** *adj*
freeze \'frēz\ *vb* **froze** \'frōz\; **fro•zen** \'frōzən\; **freez•ing 1** : harden into ice **2** : become chilled **3** : damage by frost **4** : stick fast **5** : become motionless **6** : fix at one stage or level ~ *n* **1** : very cold weather **2** : state of being frozen **—freez•er** *n*
freeze–dry *vb* : preserve by freezing then drying **—freeze–dried** *adj*
freight \'frāt\ *n* **1** : carrying of goods or payment for this **2** : shipped goods ~ *vb* : load or ship goods **—freight•er** *n*
french fry *vb* : fry in deep fat **—french fry** *n*
fre•net•ic \fri'netik\ *adj* : frantic **—fre•net•i•cal•ly** \-iklē\ *adv*
fren•zy \'frenzē\ *n, pl* **-zies** : violent agitation **—fren•zied** \-zēd\ *adj*
fre•quen•cy \'frēkwənsē\ *n, pl* **-cies 1** : frequent or regular occurrence **2** : number of cycles or sound waves per second
fre•quent \'frēkwənt\ *adj* : happening often ~ \frē'kwent, 'frēkwənt\ *vb* : go to habitually **—fre•quent•er** *n* **—fre•quent•ly** *adv*
fres•co \'freskō\ *n, pl* **-coes** : painting on fresh plaster
fresh \'fresh\ *adj* **1** : not salt **2** : pure **3** : not preserved **4** : not stale **5** : like new **6** : insolent **—fres•hen** \-ən\ *vb* **—fresh•ly** *adv* **—fresh•ness** *n*
fresh•et \-ət\ *n* : overflowing stream
fresh•man \-mən\ *n* : first-year student
fresh•wa•ter *n* : water that is not salty
fret \'fret\ *vb* **-tt- 1** : worry or become irritated **2** : fray **3** : agitate ~ *n* **1** : worn spot **2** : irritation **—fret•ful** \-fəl\ *adj* **—fret•ful•ly** *adv* **—fret•ful•ness** *n*
fri•a•ble \'frīəbəl\ *adj* : easily pulverized
fri•ar \'frīər\ *n* : member of a religious order
fri•ary \-ē\ *n, pl* **-ar•ies** : monastery of friars
fric•as•see \'frikə,sē, ˌfrikə'-\ *n* : meat stewed in a gravy ~ *vb* **-seed; -see•ing** : stew in gravy
fric•tion \'frikshən\ *n* **1** : a rubbing between 2 surfaces **2** : clash of opinions **—fric•tion•al** *adj*
Fri•day \'frīdā\ *n* : 6th day of the week
friend \'frend\ *n* : person one likes **—friend•less** \-ləs\ *adj* **—friend•li•ness** \-lēnəs\ *n* **—friend•ly** *adj* **—friend•ship** \-ˌship\ *n*
frieze \'frēz\ *n* : ornamental band around a room
frig•ate \'frigət\ *n* : warship smaller than a destroyer
fright \'frīt\ *n* : sudden fear **—frigh•ten** \-ən\ *vb* **—fright•ful** \-fəl\ *adj* **—fright•ful•ly** *adv* **—fright•ful•ness** *n*
frig•id \'frijəd\ *adj* : intensely cold **—fri•gid•i•ty** \frij'idətē\ *n*
frill \'fril\ *n* **1** : ruffle **2** : pleasing but nonessential addition **—frilly** *adj*
fringe \'frinj\ *n* **1** : ornamental border of short hanging threads or strips **2** : edge **—fringe** *vb*
frisk \'frisk\ *vb* **1** : leap about **2** : search (a person) esp. for weapons
frisky \'friskē\ *adj* **frisk•i•er; -est** : playful **—frisk•i•ly** *adv* **—frisk•i•ness** *n*
1frit•ter \'fritər\ *n* : fried batter containing fruit or meat
2fritter *vb* : waste little by little
friv•o•lous \'frivələs\ *adj* : not important or serious **—fri•vol•i•ty** \friv'älətē\ *n* **—friv•o•lous•ly** *adv*
frizz \'friz\ *vb* : curl tightly **—frizz** *n* **—frizzy** *adj*
fro \'frō\ *adv* : away
frock \'fräk\ *n* **1** : loose outer garment **2** : dress
frog \'frȯg, 'fräg\ *n* **1** : leaping amphibian **2** : hoarseness **3** : ornamental braid fastener **4** : small holder for flowers
frog•man \-ˌman, -mən\ *n* : underwater swimmer
frol•ic \'frälik\ *vb* **-icked; -ick•ing** : romp ~ *n* : fun **—frol•ic•some** \-səm\ *adj*
from \'frəm, 'främ\ *prep* —used to show a starting point
frond \'fränd\ *n* : fern or palm leaf
front \'frənt\ *n* **1** : face **2** : behavior **3** : main side of a building **4** : forward part **5** : boundary between air masses ~ *vb* **1** : have the main side adjacent to something **2** : serve as a front **—fron•tal** \-əl\ *adj*
front•age \'frəntij\ *n* : length of boundary line on a street
fron•tier \ˌfrən'tir\ *n* : outer edge of settled territory **—fron•tiers•man** \-'tirzmən\ *n*
fron•tis•piece \'frəntə,spēs\ *n* : illustration facing a title page
frost \'frȯst\ *n* **1** : freezing temperature **2** : ice crystals on a surface ~ *vb* **1** : cover with frost **2** : put icing on (a cake) **—frosty** *adj*
frost•bite \-ˌbīt\ *n* : partial freezing of part of the body **—frost•bit•ten** \-ˌbitən\ *adj*
frost•ing *n* : icing
froth \'frȯth\ *n, pl* **froths** \'frȯths, 'frȯthz\ : bubbles on a liquid **—frothy** *adj*
fro•ward \'frōwərd\ *adj* : willful
frown \'frau̇n\ *vb or n* : scowl
frow•sy, frow•zy \'frau̇zē\ *adj* **-si•er** *or* **-zi•er; -est** : untidy
froze *past of* FREEZE
frozen *past part of* FREEZE
fru•gal \'frügəl\ *adj* : thrifty **—fru•gal•i•ty** \frü'galətē\ *n* **—fru•gal•ly** *adv*
fruit \'früt\ *n* **1** : usu. edible and sweet part of a seed plant **2** : result ~ *vb* : bear fruit **—fruit•cake** *n* **—fruit•ed** \-əd\ *adj* **—fruit•ful** *adj* **—fruit•ful•ness** *n* **—fruit•less** *adj* **—fruit•less•ly** *adv* **—fruity** *adj*
fru•ition \frü'ishən\ *n* : completion
frumpy \'frəmpē\ *adj* **frump•i•er; -est** : dowdy
frus•trate \'frəs,trāt\ *vb* **-trat•ed; -trat•ing 1** : block **2** : cause to fail **—frus•trat•ing•ly** *adv* **—frus•tra•tion** \ˌfrəs'trāshən\ *n*
1fry \'frī\ *vb* **fried; fry•ing 1** : cook esp. with fat or oil **2** : be cooked by frying ~ *n, pl* **fries 1** : something fried **2** : social gathering with fried food
2fry *n, pl* **fry** : recently hatched fish
fud•dle \'fədəl\ *vb* **-dled; -dling** : muddle
fud•dy–dud•dy \'fədē,dədē\ *n, pl* **-dies** : one who is old-fashioned or unimaginative
fudge \'fəj\ *vb* **fudged; fudg•ing** : cheat or exaggerate ~ *n* : creamy candy
fu•el \'fyüəl\ *n* : material burned to produce heat or power ~ *vb* **-eled** *or* **-elled; -el•ing** *or* **-el•ling** : provide with or take in fuel
fu•gi•tive \'fyüjətiv\ *adj* **1** : running away or trying to escape **2** : not lasting **—fugitive** *n*
-ful \'fəl\ *adj suffix* **1** : full of **2** : having the qualities of **3** : -able ~ *n suffix* : quantity that fills
ful•crum \'fu̇lkrəm, 'fəl-\ *n, pl* **-crums** *or* **-cra** \-krə\ : support on which a lever turns
ful•fill, ful•fil \fu̇l'fil\ *vb* **-filled; -fill•ing 1** : perform **2** : satisfy **—ful•fill•ment** *n*
1full \'fu̇l\ *adj* **1** : filled **2** : complete **3** : rounded **4** : having an abundance of something ~ *adv* : entirely ~ *n* : utmost degree **—full•ness** *n* **—ful•ly** *adv*
2full *vb* : shrink and thicken woolen cloth **—full•er** *n*
full–fledged \'fu̇l'flejd\ *adj* : fully developed
ful•some \'fu̇lsəm\ *adj* : copious verging on excessive
fum•ble \'fəmbəl\ *vb* **-bled; -bling** : fail to hold something properly **—fumble** *n*
fume \'fyüm\ *n* : irritating gas ~ *vb* **fumed; fum•ing 1** : give off fumes **2** : show annoyance
fu•mi•gate \'fyümə,gāt\ *vb* **-gat•ed; -gat•ing** : treat with pest-killing fumes **—fu•mi•gant** \'fyümigənt\ *n* **—fu•mi•ga•tion** \ˌfyümə'gāshən\ *n*
fun \'fən\ *n* **1** : something providing amusement or enjoyment **2** : enjoyment ~ *adj* : full of fun
func•tion \'fəŋkshən\ *n* **1** : special purpose **2** : formal ceremony or social affair ~ *vb* : have or carry on a function **—func•tion•al** \-shənəl\ *adj* **—func•tion•al•ly** *adv*
func•tion•ary \-shə,nerē\ *n, pl* **-ar•ies** : official
fund \'fənd\ *n* **1** : store **2** : sum of money intended for a special purpose **3** *pl* : available money ~ *vb* : provide funds for
fun•da•men•tal \ˌfəndə'mentəl\ *adj* **1** : basic **2** : of central importance or necessity **—fundamental** *n* **—fun•da•men•tal•ly** *adv*
fu•ner•al \'fyünərəl\ *n* : ceremony for a dead person **—funeral** *adj* **—fu•ne•re•al** \fyü'nirēəl\ *adj*
fun•gi•cide \'fənjə,sīd, 'fəŋgə-\ *n* : agent that kills fungi **—fun•gi•cid•al** \ˌfənjə'sīdəl, ˌfəŋgə-\ *adj*
fun•gus \'fəŋgəs\ *n, pl* **fun•gi** \'fən,jī, 'fəŋ,gī\ : lower plant that lacks chlorophyll **—fun•gal** \'fəŋgəl\ *adj* **—fun•gous** \-gəs\ *adj*
funk \'fəŋk\ *n* : state of depression
funky \'fəŋkē\ *adj* **funk•i•er; -est** : unconventional and unsophisticated
fun•nel \'fənəl\ *n* **1** : cone-shaped utensil with a tube for directing the flow of a liquid **2** : ship's smokestack ~ *vb* **-neled; -nel•ing** : move to a central point or into a central channel
fun•nies \'fənēz\ *n pl* : section of comic strips
fun•ny \'fənē\ *adj* **-ni•er; -est 1** : amusing **2** : strange
fur \'fər\ *n* **1** : hairy coat of a mammal **2** : article of clothing made with fur **—fur** *adj* **—furred** \'fərd\ *adj* **—fur•ry** \-ē\ *adj*
fur•bish \'fərbish\ *vb* : make lustrous or new looking
fu•ri•ous \'fyu̇rēəs\ *adj* : fierce or angry **—fu•ri•ous•ly** *adv*
fur•long \'fər,lȯŋ\ *n* : a unit of distance equal to 220 yards
fur•lough \'fərlō\ *n* : authorized absence from duty **—furlough** *vb*
fur•nace \'fərnəs\ *n* : enclosed structure in which heat is produced
fur•nish \'fərnish\ *vb* **1** : provide with what is needed **2** : make available for use
fur•nish•ings \-iŋs\ *n pl* **1** : articles or accessories of dress **2** : furniture
fur•ni•ture \'fərnichər\ *n* : movable articles for a room
fu•ror \'fyu̇r,ȯr\ *n* **1** : anger **2** : sensational craze
fur•ri•er \'fərēər\ *n* : dealer in furs
fur•row \'fərō\ *n* **1** : trench made by a plow **2** : wrinkle or groove **—furrow** *vb*
fur•ther \'fərthər\ *adv* **1** : at or to a more advanced point **2** : more ~ *adj* : additional ~ *vb* : promote **—fur•ther•ance** \-ərəns\ *n*
fur•ther•more \'fərthər,mōr\ *adv* : in addition
fur•ther•most \-ˌmōst\ *adj* : most distant
fur•thest \'fərthəst\ *adv or adj* : farthest
fur•tive \'fərtiv\ *adj* : slyly or secretly done **—fur•tive•ly** *adv* **—fur•tive•ness** *n*
fu•ry \'fyu̇rē\ *n, pl* **-ries 1** : intense rage **2** : violence
1fuse \'fyüz\ *n* **1** : cord lighted to transmit fire to an explosive **2** *usu* **fuze** : device for exploding a charge ~, **fuze** *vb* **fused** *or* **fuzed; fus•ing** *or* **fuz•ing** : equip with a fuse
2fuse *vb* **fused; fus•ing 1** : melt and run together **2** : unite ~ *n* : electrical safety device **—fus•ible** *adj*
fu•se•lage \'fyüsə,läzh, -zə-\ *n* : main body of an aircraft
fu•sil•lade \'fyüsə,läd, -ˌlād, ˌfyüsə'-, -zə-\ *n* : volley of fire
fu•sion \'fyüzhən\ *n* **1** : process of merging by melting **2** : union of atomic nuclei
fuss \'fəs\ *n* **1** : needless bustle or excitement **2** : show of attention **3** : objection or protest ~ *vb* : make a fuss
fuss•bud•get \-ˌbəjət\ *n* : one who fusses or is fussy about trifles
fussy \'fəsē\ *adj* **fuss•i•er; -est 1** : irritable **2** : paying very close attention to details **—fuss•i•ly** *adv* **—fuss•i•ness** *n*
fu•tile \'fyütəl, 'fyü,tīl\ *adj* : useless or vain **—fu•til•i•ty** \fyü'tilətē\ *n*
fu•ture \'fyüchər\ *adj* : coming after the present ~ *n* **1** : time yet to come **2** : what will happen **—fu•tur•is•tic** \ˌfyüchə'ristik\ *adj*
fuze *var of* FUSE
fuzz \'fəz\ *n* : fine particles or fluff
fuzzy \-ē\ *adj* **fuzz•i•er; -est 1** : covered with or like fuzz **2** : indistinct **—fuzz•i•ness** *n*
-fy \ˌfī\ *vb suffix* : make **—-fi•er** \ˌfīər\ *n suffix*

G

g \'jē\ *n, pl* **g's** *or* **gs** \'jēz\ **1** : 7th letter of the alphabet **2** : unit of gravitational force
gab \'gab\ *vb* **-bb-** : chatter **—gab** *n* **—gab•by** \'gabē\ *adj*
gab•ar•dine \'gabər,dēn\ *n* : durable twilled fabric
ga•ble \'gābəl\ *n* : triangular part of the end of a building **—ga•bled** \-bəld\ *adj*
gad \'gad\ *vb* **-dd-** : roam about **—gad•der** *n*
gad•fly *n* : persistently critical person
gad•get \'gajət\ *n* : device **—gad•get•ry** \'gajətrē\ *n*
gaff \'gaf\ *n* : metal hook for lifting fish **—gaff** *vb*
gaffe \'gaf\ *n* : social blunder
gag \'gag\ *vb* **-gg- 1** : prevent from speaking or crying out by stopping up the mouth **2** : retch or cause to retch ~ *n* **1** : something that stops up the mouth **2** : laugh-provoking remark or act
gage *var of* GAUGE
gag•gle \'gagəl\ *n* : flock of geese
gai•ety \'gāətē\ *n, pl* **-eties** : high spirits
gai•ly \'gālē\ *adv* : in a gay manner
gain \'gān\ *n* **1** : profit **2** : obtaining of profit or possessions **3** : increase ~ *vb* **1** : get possession of **2** : win **3** : arrive at **4**

: increase or increase in **5** : profit **—gain·er** *n* **—gain·ful** *adj* **—gain·ful·ly** *adv*

gain·say \gān'sā\ *vb* **-said** \-'sād, -'sed\; **-say·ing; -says** \-'sāz, -'sez\ : deny or dispute **—gain·say·er** *n*

gait \'gāt\ *n* : manner of walking or running **—gait·ed** *adj*

gal \'gal\ *n* : girl

ga·la \'gālə, 'galə, 'gälə\ *n* : festive celebration **—gala** *adj*

gal·axy \'galəksē\ *n, pl* **-ax·ies** : very large group of stars **—ga·lac·tic** \gə'laktik\ *adj*

gale \'gāl\ *n* **1** : strong wind **2** : outburst

1gall \'gȯl\ *n* **1** : bile **2** : insolence

2gall *n* **1** : skin sore caused by chafing **2** : swelling of plant tissue caused by parasites ~ *vb* **1** : chafe **2** : irritate or vex

gal·lant \gə'lant, -'länt; 'galənt\ *n* : man very attentive to women ~ \'galənt; gə'lant, -'länt\ *adj* **1** : splendid **2** : brave **3** : polite and attentive to women **—gal·lant·ly** *adv* **—gal·lant·ry** \'galəntrē\ *n*

gall·blad·der *n* : pouch attached to the liver in which bile is stored

gal·le·on \'galyən\ *n* : large sailing ship formerly used esp. by the Spanish

gal·lery \'galərē\ *n, pl* **-ler·ies 1** : outdoor balcony **2** : long narrow passage or hall **3** : room or building for exhibiting art **4** : spectators **—gal·ler·ied** \-rēd\ *adj*

gal·ley \'galē\ *n, pl* **-leys 1** : old ship propelled esp. by oars **2** : kitchen of a ship or airplane

gal·li·um \'galēəm\ *n* : bluish white metallic chemical element

gal·li·vant \'galə,vant\ *vb* : travel or roam about for pleasure

gal·lon \'galən\ *n* : unit of liquid measure equal to 4 quarts

gal·lop \'galəp\ *n* : fast 3-beat gait of a horse **—gallop** *vb* **—gal·lop·er** *n*

gal·lows \'galōz\ *n, pl* **-lows** *or* **-lows·es** : upright frame for hanging criminals

gall·stone *n* : abnormal concretion in the gallbladder or bile passages

ga·lore \gə'lōr\ *adj* : in abundance

ga·losh \gə'läsh\ *n* : overshoe —usu. pl.

gal·va·nize \'galvə,nīz\ *vb* **-nized; -niz·ing 1** : shock into action **2** : coat (iron or steel) with zinc **—gal·va·ni·za·tion** \,galvənə'zāshən\ *n* **—gal·va·niz·er** *n*

gam·bit \'gambit\ *n* **1** : opening tactic in chess **2** : stratagem

gam·ble \'gambəl\ *vb* **-bled; -bling 1** : play a game for stakes **2** : bet **3** : take a chance ~ *n* : risky undertaking **—gam·bler** \-blər\ *n*

gam·bol \'gambəl\ *vb* **-boled** *or* **-bolled; -bol·ing** *or* **-bol·ling** : skip about in play **—gambol** *n*

game \'gām\ *n* **1** : playing activity **2** : competition according to rules **3** : animals hunted for sport or food ~ *vb* **gamed; gam·ing** : gamble ~ *adj* **1** : plucky **2** : lame **—game·ly** *adv* **—game·ness** *n*

game·cock *n* : fighting cock

game·keep·er *n* : person in charge of game animals or birds

gam·ete \gə'mēt, 'gam,ēt\ *n* : mature germ cell **—ga·met·ic** \gə'metik\ *adj*

ga·mine \ga'mēn\ *n* : charming tomboy

gam·ut \'gamət\ *n* : entire range or series

gamy *or* **gam·ey** \'gāmē\ *adj* **gam·i·er; -est** : having the flavor of game esp. when slightly tainted **—gam·i·ness** *n*

1gan·der \'gandər\ *n* : male goose

2gander *n* : glance

gang \'gaŋ\ *n* **1** : group of persons working together **2** : group of criminals ~ *vb* : attack in a gang —with *up*

gan·gling \'gaŋgliŋ\ *adj* : lanky

gan·gli·on \'gaŋglēən\ *n, pl* **-glia** \-glēə\ : mass of nerve cells

gang·plank *n* : platform used in boarding or leaving a ship

gan·grene \'gaŋ,grēn, gaŋ'-; 'gan-, gan-\ *n* : local death of body tissue **—gangrene** *vb* **—gan·gre·nous** \'gaŋgrənəs\ *adj*

gang·ster \'gaŋstər\ *n* : member of criminal gang

gang·way \-,wā\ *n* : passage in or out

gan·net \'ganət\ *n* : large fish-eating marine bird

gan·try \'gantrē\ *n, pl* **-tries** : frame structure supported over or around something

gap \'gap\ *n* **1** : break in a barrier **2** : mountain pass **3** : empty space

gape \'gāp\ *vb* **gaped; gap·ing 1** : open widely **2** : stare with mouth open **—gape** *n*

ga·rage \gə'räzh, -'räj\ *n* : shelter or repair shop for automobiles ~ *vb* **-raged; -rag·ing** : put or keep in a garage

garb \'gärb\ *n* : clothing ~ *vb* : dress

gar·bage \'gärbij\ *n* **1** : food waste **2** : trash **—gar·bage·man** *n*

gar·ble \'gärbəl\ *vb* **-bled; -bling** : distort the meaning of

gar·den \'gärdᵊn\ *n* **1** : plot for growing fruits, flowers, or vegetables **2** : public recreation area ~ *vb* : work in a garden **—gar·den·er** \'gärdᵊnər\ *n*

gar·de·nia \gär'dēnyə\ *n* : tree or shrub with fragrant white or yellow flowers or the flower

gar·gan·tuan \gär'ganchəwən\ *adj* : having tremendous size or volume

gar·gle \'gärgəl\ *vb* **-gled; -gling** : rinse the throat with liquid **—gargle** *n*

gar·goyle \'gär,gȯil\ *n* : waterspout in the form of a grotesque human or animal

gar·ish \'garish\ *adj* : offensively bright or gaudy

gar·land \'gärlənd\ *n* : wreath ~ *vb* : form into or deck with a garland

gar·lic \'gärlik\ *n* : herb with pungent bulbs used in cooking **—gar·licky** \-likē\ *adj*

gar·ment \'gärmənt\ *n* : article of clothing

gar·ner \'gärnər\ *vb* : acquire by effort

gar·net \'gärnət\ *n* : deep red mineral

gar·nish \'gärnish\ *vb* : add decoration to (as food) **—garnish** *n*

gar·nish·ee \,gärnə'shē\ *vb* **-eed; -ee·ing** : take (as a debtor's wages) by legal authority

gar·nish·ment \'gärnishmənt\ *n* : attachment of property to satisfy a creditor

gar·ret \'garət\ *n* : attic

gar·ri·son \'garəsən\ *n* : military post or the troops stationed there **—garrison** *vb*

gar·ru·lous \'garələs\ *adj* : talkative **—gar·ru·li·ty** \gə'rülətē\ *n* **—gar·ru·lous·ly** *adv* **—gar·ru·lous·ness** *n*

gar·ter \'gärtər\ *n* : band to hold up a stocking or sock

gas \'gas\ *n, pl* **gas·es 1** : fluid (as hydrogen or air) that tends to expand indefinitely **2** : gasoline ~ *vb* **gassed; gas·sing 1** : treat with gas **2** : fill with gasoline **—gas·eous** \'gasēəs, 'gashəs\ *adj*

gash \'gash\ *n* : deep long cut **—gash** *vb*

gas·ket \'gaskət\ *n* : material or a part used to seal a joint

gas·light *n* : light of burning illuminating gas

gas·o·line \'gasə,lēn, ,gasə'-\ *n* : flammable liquid from petroleum

gasp \'gasp\ *vb* **1** : catch the breath audibly **2** : breathe laboriously **—gasp** *n*

gas·tric \'gastrik\ *adj* : relating to or located near the stomach

gas·tron·o·my \gas'tränəmē\ *n* : art of good eating **—gas·tro·nom·ic** \,gastrə'nämik\ *adj*

gate \'gāt\ *n* : an opening for passage in a wall or fence **—gate·keep·er** *n* **—gate·post** *n*

gate·way *n* : way in or out

gath·er \'gathər\ *vb* **1** : bring or come together **2** : harvest **3** : pick up little by little **4** : deduce **—gath·er·er** *n* **—gath·er·ing** *n*

gauche \'gōsh\ *adj* : crude or tactless

gaudy \'gȯdē\ *adj* **gaud·i·er; -est** : tastelessly showy **—gaud·i·ly** \'gȯdᵊlē\ *adv* **—gaud·i·ness** *n*

gauge \'gāj\ *n* : instrument for measuring ~ *vb* **gauged; gaug·ing** : measure

gaunt \'gȯnt\ *adj* : thin or emaciated **—gaunt·ness** *n*

1gaunt·let \-lət\ *n* **1** : protective glove **2** : challenge to combat

2gauntlet *n* : ordeal

gauze \'gȯz\ *n* : thin often transparent fabric **—gauzy** *adj*

gave *past of* GIVE

gav·el \'gavəl\ *n* : mallet of a presiding officer, auctioneer, or judge

gawk \'gȯk\ *vb* : stare stupidly

gawky \-ē\ *adj* **gawk·i·er; -est** : clumsy

gay \'gā\ *adj* **1** : merry **2** : bright and lively **3** : homosexual **—gay** *n*

gaze \'gāz\ *vb* **gazed; gaz·ing** : fix the eyes in a steady intent look **—gaze** *n* **—gaz·er** *n*

ga·zelle \gə'zel\ *n* : small swift antelope

ga·zette \-'zet\ *n* : newspaper

gaz·et·teer \,gazə'tir\ *n* : geographical dictionary

gear \'gir\ *n* **1** : clothing **2** : equipment **3** : toothed wheel **—gear** *vb*

gear·shift *n* : mechanism by which automobile gears are shifted

geek \'gēk\ *n* : socially inept person

geese *pl of* GOOSE

gei·sha \'gāshə, 'gē-\ *n, pl* **-sha** *or* **-shas** : Japanese girl or woman trained to entertain men

gel·a·tin \'jelətᵊn\ *n* : sticky substance obtained from animal tissues by boiling **—ge·lat·i·nous** \jə'latᵊnəs\ *adj*

geld \'geld\ *vb* : castrate

geld·ing \-iŋ\ *n* : castrated horse

gem \'jem\ *n* : cut and polished valuable stone **—gem·stone** *n*

gen·der \'jendər\ *n* **1** : sex **2** : division of a class of words (as nouns) that determines agreement of other words

gene \'jēn\ *n* : segment of DNA that controls inheritance of a trait

ge·ne·al·o·gy \,jēnē'äləjē, ,jen-, -'al-\ *n, pl* **-gies** : study of family pedigrees **—ge·ne·a·log·i·cal** \-ēə'läjikəl\ *adj* **—ge·ne·a·log·i·cal·ly** *adv* **—ge·ne·al·o·gist** \-ē'äləjist, -'al-\ *n*

genera *pl of* GENUS

gen·er·al \'jenrəl, 'jenə-\ *adj* **1** : relating to the whole **2** : applicable to all of a group **3** : common or widespread ~ *n* **1** : something that involves or is applicable to the whole **2** : commissioned officer in the army, air force, or marine corps ranking above a lieutenant general **—gen·er·al·ly** *adv* **—in general** : for the most part

gen·er·al·i·ty \,jenə'ralətē\ *n, pl* **-ties** : general statement

gen·er·al·ize \'jenrə,līz, 'jenə-\ *vb* **-ized; -iz·ing** : reach a general conclusion esp. on the basis of particular instances **—gen·er·al·iza·tion** \,jenrələ'zāshən, ,jenə-\ *n*

general of the air force : commissioned officer of the highest rank in the air force

general of the army : commissioned officer of the highest rank in the army

gen·er·ate \'jenə,rāt\ *vb* **-at·ed; -at·ing** : create or produce

gen·er·a·tion \,jenə'rāshən\ *n* **1** : living beings constituting a single step in a line of descent **2** : production **—gen·er·a·tive** \'jenə,rātiv, -rət-\ *adj*

gen·er·a·tor \'jenə,rātər\ *n* **1** : one that generates **2** : machine that turns mechanical into electrical energy

ge·ner·ic \jə'nerik\ *adj* **1** : general **2** : not protected by a trademark **3** : relating to a genus **—generic** *n*

gen·er·ous \'jenərəs\ *adj* : freely giving or sharing **—gen·er·os·i·ty** \,jenə'räsətē\ *n* **—gen·er·ous·ly** *adv* **—gen·er·ous·ness** *n*

ge·net·ics \jə'netiks\ *n* : biology dealing with heredity and variation **—ge·net·ic** \-ik\ *adj* **—ge·net·i·cal·ly** *adv* **—ge·net·i·cist** \-'netəsist\ *n*

ge·nial \'jēnēəl\ *adj* : cheerful **—ge·nial·i·ty** \,jēnē'alətē\ *n* **—ge·nial·ly** *adv*

ge·nie \'jēnē\ *n* : supernatural spirit that often takes human form

gen·i·tal \'jenətᵊl\ *adj* : concerned with reproduction **—gen·i·tal·ly** \-tᵊlē\ *adv*

gen·i·ta·lia \,jenə'tālyə\ *n pl* : external genital organs

gen·i·tals \'jenətᵊlz\ *n pl* : genitalia

ge·nius \'jēnyəs\ *n* **1** : single strongly marked capacity **2** : extraordinary intellectual power or a person having such power

geno·cide \'jenə,sīd\ *n* : systematic destruction of a racial or cultural group

genre \'zhänrə, 'zhäⁿrə\ *n* : category esp. of literary composition

gen·teel \jen'tēl\ *adj* : polite or refined

gen·tile \'jen,tīl\ *n* : person who is not Jewish **—gentile** *adj*

gen·til·i·ty \jen'tilətē\ *n, pl* **-ties 1** : good birth and family **2** : good manners

gen·tle \'jentᵊl\ *adj* **-tler; -tlest 1** : of a family of high social station **2** : not harsh, stern, or violent **3** : soft or delicate ~ *vb* **-tled; -tling** : make gentle **—gen·tle·ness** *n* **—gen·tly** *adv*

gen·tle·man \-mən\ *n* : man of good family or manners **—gen·tle·man·ly** *adv*

gen·tle·wom·an \-,wu̇mən\ *n* : woman of good family or breeding

gen·try \'jentrē\ *n, pl* **-tries** : people of good birth or breeding

gen·u·flect \'jenyə,flekt\ *vb* : bend the knee in worship **—gen·u·flec·tion** \,jenyə'flekshən\ *n*

gen·u·ine \'jenyəwən\ *adj* : being the same in fact as in appearance **—gen·u·ine·ly** *adv* **—gen·u·ine·ness** *n*

ge·nus \'jēnəs\ *n, pl* **gen·era** \'jenərə\ : category of biological classification

ge·ode \'jē,ōd\ *n* : stone having a mineral-lined cavity

geo·de·sic \,jēə'desik, -'dēs-\ *adj* : made of a framework of linked polygons

ge·og·ra·phy \jē'ägrəfē\ *n* **1** : study of the earth and its climate, products, and inhabitants **2** : natural features of a region **—ge·og·ra·pher** \-fər\ *n* **—geo·graph·ic** \,jēə'grafik\, **geo·graph·i·cal** \-ikəl\ *adj* **—geo·graph·i·cal·ly** *adv*

ge·ol·o·gy \jē'äləjē\ *n* : study of the history of the earth and its life esp. as recorded in rocks **—geo·log·ic** \,jēə'läjik\, **geo·log·i·cal** \-ikəl\ *adj* **—geo·log·i·cal·ly** *adv* **—ge·ol·o·gist** \jē'äləjist\ *n*

ge·om·e·try \jē'ämətrē\ *n, pl* **-tries** : mathematics of the relations, properties, and measurements of solids, surfaces, lines, and angles **—geo·met·ric** \,jēə'metrik\, **geo·met·ri·cal** \-rikəl\ *adj*

geo·ther·mal \,jēō'thərməl\ *adj* : relating to or derived from the heat of the earth's interior

ge·ra·ni·um \jə'rānēəm\ *n* : garden plant with clusters of white, pink, or scarlet flowers

ger·bil \'jərbəl\ *n* : burrowing desert rodent

ge·ri·at·ric \,jerē'atrik\ *adj* **1** : relating to aging or the aged **2** : old

ge·ri·at·rics \-triks\ *n* : medicine dealing with the aged and aging

germ \'jərm\ *n* **1** : microorganism **2** : source or rudiment

ger·mane \jər'mān\ *adj* : relevant

ger·ma·ni·um \-'mānēəm\ *n* : grayish white hard chemical element

ger·mi·cide \'jərmə,sīd\ *n* : agent that destroys germs **—ger·mi·cid·al** \,jərmə'sīdᵊl\ *adj*

ger·mi·nate \'jərmə,nāt\ *vb* **-nat·ed; -nat·ing** : begin to develop **—ger·mi·na·tion** \,jərmə'nāshən\ *n*

ger·ry·man·der \,jerē'mandər, 'jerē,-, ,gerē'-, 'gerē,-\ *vb* : divide into election districts so as to give one political party an advantage **—gerrymander** *n*

ger·und \'jerənd\ *n* : word having the characteristics of both verb and noun

ge·sta·po \gə'stäpō\ *n, pl* **-pos** : secret police

ges·ta·tion \je'stāshən\ *n* : pregnancy or incubation **—ges·tate** \'jes,tāt\ *vb*

ges·ture \'jeschər\ *n* **1** : movement of the body or limbs that expresses something **2** : something said or done for its effect on the attitudes of others **—ges·tur·al** \-chərəl\ *adj* **—gesture** *vb*

ge·sund·heit \gə'zu̇nt,hīt\ *interj* —used to wish good health to one who has just sneezed

get \'get\ *vb* **got** \'gät\; **got** *or* **got·ten** \'gätᵊn\; **get·ting 1** : gain or be in possession of **2** : succeed in coming or going **3** : cause to come or go or to be in a certain condition or position **4** : become **5** : be subjected to **6** : understand **7** : be obliged **—get along** *vb* **1** : get by **2** : be on friendly terms **—get by** *vb* : meet one's needs

get·away \'getə,wā\ *n* **1** : escape **2** : a starting or getting under way

gey·ser \'gīzər\ *n* : spring that intermittently shoots up hot water and steam

ghast·ly \'gastlē\ *adj* **-li·er; -est** : horrible or shocking

gher·kin \'gərkən\ *n* : small pickle

ghet·to \'getō\ *n, pl* **-tos** *or* **-toes** : part of a city in which members of a minority group live

ghost \'gōst\ *n* : disembodied soul **—ghost·ly** *adv*

ghost·write *vb* **-wrote; -writ·ten** : write for and in the name of another **—ghost·writ·er** *n*

ghoul \'gül\ *n* : legendary evil being that feeds on corpses **—ghoul·ish** *adj*

GI \,jē'ī\ *n, pl* **GI's** *or* **GIs** : member of the U.S. armed forces

gi·ant \'jīənt\ *n* **1** : huge legendary being **2** : something very large or very powerful **—giant** *adj*

gib·ber \'jibər\ *vb* **-bered; -ber·ing** : speak rapidly and foolishly

gib·ber·ish \'jibərish\ *n* : unintelligible speech or language

gib·bon \'gibən\ *n* : manlike ape

gibe \'jīb\ *vb* **gibed; gib·ing** : jeer at **—gibe** *n*

gib·lets \'jibləts\ *n pl* : edible fowl viscera

gid·dy \'gidē\ *adj* **-di·er; -est 1** : silly **2** : dizzy **—gid·di·ness** *n*

gift \'gift\ *n* **1** : something given **2** : talent **—gift·ed** *adj*

gi·gan·tic \jī'gantik\ *adj* : very big

gig·gle \'gigəl\ *vb* **-gled; -gling** : laugh in a silly manner **—giggle** *n* **—gig·gly** \-əlē\ *adj*

gig·o·lo \'jigə,lō\ *n, pl* **-los** : man living on the earnings of a woman

Gi·la monster \'hēlə-\ *n* : large venomous lizard

gild \'gild\ *vb* **gild·ed** \'gildəd\ *or* **gilt** \'gilt\; **gild·ing** : cover with or as if with gold

gill \'gil\ *n* : organ of a fish for obtaining oxygen from water

gilt \'gilt\ *adj* : gold-colored ~ *n* : gold or goldlike substance on the surface of an object

gim·bal \'gimbəl, 'jim-\ *n* : device that allows something to incline freely

gim·let \'gimlət\ *n* : small tool for boring holes

gim·mick \'gimik\ *n* : new and ingenious scheme, feature, or device **—gim·mick·ry** *n* **—gim·micky** \-ikē\ *adj*

gimpy \'gimpē\ *adj* : lame

1gin \'jin\ *n* : machine to separate seeds from cotton **—gin** *vb*

2gin *n* : clear liquor flavored with juniper berries

gin·ger \'jinjər\ *n* : pungent aromatic spice from a tropical plant **—gin·ger·bread** *n*

gin·ger·ly *adj* : very cautious or careful **—gingerly** *adv*

ging·ham \'giŋəm\ *n* : cotton clothing fabric

gin·gi·vi·tis \,jinjə'vītəs\ *n* : inflammation of the gums

gink·go \'giŋkō\ *n, pl* **-goes** *or* **-gos** : tree of eastern China

gin·seng \'jin,siŋ, -,seŋ, -saŋ\ *n* : aromatic root of a Chinese herb

gi·raffe \jə'raf\ *n* : African mammal with a very long neck

gird \'gərd\ *vb* **gird·ed** \'gərdəd\ *or* **girt** \'gərt\; **gird·ing 1** : encircle or fasten with or as if with a belt **2** : prepare

gird·er \'gərdər\ *n* : horizontal supporting beam

gir·dle \'gərdᵊl\ *n* : woman's supporting undergarment ~ *vb* : surround

girl \'gərl\ *n* **1** : female child **2** : young

woman 3 : sweetheart —girl•hood \-ˌhu̇d\ n —girl•ish adj

girlfriend n : frequent or regular female companion of a boy or man

girth \ˈgərth\ n : measure around something

gist \ˈjist\ n : main point or part

give \ˈgiv\ vb gave \ˈgāv\; giv•en \ˈgivən\; giv•ing 1 : put into the possession or keeping of another 2 : pay 3 : perform 4 : contribute or donate 5 : produce 6 : utter 7 : yield to force, strain, or pressure ~ n : capacity or tendency to yield to force or strain —give in vb : surrender —give out vb : become used up or exhausted —give up vb 1 : let out of one's control 2 : cease from trying, doing, or hoping

give•away n 1 : unintentional betrayal 2 : something given free

giv•en \ˈgivən\ adj 1 : prone or disposed 2 : having been specified

giz•zard \ˈgizərd\ n : muscular usu. horny-lined enlargement following the crop of a bird

gla•cial \ˈglāshəl\ adj 1 : relating to glaciers 2 : very slow —gla•cial•ly adv

gla•cier \ˈglāshər\ n : large body of ice moving slowly

glad \ˈglad\ adj -dd- 1 : experiencing or causing pleasure, joy, or delight 2 : very willing —glad•den \-ᵊn\ vb —glad•ly adv —glad•ness n

glade \ˈglād\ n : grassy open space in a forest

glad•i•a•tor \ˈgladēˌātər\ n : one who fought to the death for the entertainment of ancient Romans —glad•i•a•to•ri•al \ˌgladēəˈtōrēəl\ adj

glad•i•o•lus \ˌgladēˈōləs\ n, pl -li \-lē, -ˌlī\ : plant related to the irises

glam•our, glam•or \ˈglamər\ n : romantic or exciting attractiveness —glam•or•ize \-əˌrīz\ vb —glam•or•ous \-ərəs\ adj

glance \ˈglans\ vb glanced; glanc•ing 1 : strike and fly off to one side 2 : give a quick look ~ n : quick look

gland \ˈgland\ n : group of cells that secretes a substance —glan•du•lar \ˈglanjələr\ adj

glans \ˈglanz\ n, pl glan•des \ˈglanˌdēz\ : conical vascular body forming the end of the penis or clitoris

glare \ˈglar\ vb glared; glar•ing 1 : shine with a harsh dazzling light 2 : stare angrily ~ n 1 : harsh dazzling light 2 : angry stare

glar•ing \ˈglariŋ\ adj : painfully obvious —glar•ing•ly adv

glass \ˈglas\ n 1 : hard usu. transparent material made by melting sand and other materials 2 : something made of glass 3 pl : lenses used to correct defects of vision —glass adj —glass•ful \-ˌfu̇l\ n —glass•ware \-ˌwar\ n —glassy adj

glass•blow•ing n : art of shaping a mass of molten glass by blowing air into it —glass•blow•er n

glau•co•ma \glau̇ˈkōmə, glȯ-\ n : state of increased pressure within the eyeball

glaze \ˈglāz\ vb glazed; glaz•ing 1 : furnish with glass 2 : apply glaze to ~ n : glassy surface or coating

gla•zier \ˈglāzhər\ n : one who sets glass in window frames

gleam \ˈglēm\ n 1 : transient or partly obscured light 2 : faint trace ~ vb : send out gleams

glean \ˈglēn\ vb : collect little by little —glean•able adj —glean•er n

glee \ˈglē\ n : joy —glee•ful adj

glen \ˈglen\ n : narrow hidden valley

glib \ˈglib\ adj -bb- : speaking or spoken with ease —glib•ly adv

glide \ˈglīd\ vb glid•ed; glid•ing : move or descend smoothly and effortlessly —glide n

glid•er \ˈglīdər\ n 1 : winged aircraft having no engine 2 : swinging porch seat

glim•mer \ˈglimər\ vb : shine faintly or unsteadily ~ n 1 : faint light 2 : small amount

glimpse \ˈglimps\ vb glimpsed; glimps•ing : take a brief look at —glimpse n

glint \ˈglint\ vb : gleam or sparkle —glint n

glis•ten \ˈglisᵊn\ vb : shine or sparkle by reflection —glisten n

glit•ter \ˈglitər\ vb : shine with brilliant or metallic luster ~ n : small glittering ornaments —glit•tery adj

gloat \ˈglōt\ vb : think of something with triumphant delight

glob \ˈgläb\ n : large rounded lump

glob•al \ˈglōbəl\ adj : worldwide —glob•al•ly adv

globe \ˈglōb\ n 1 : sphere 2 : the earth or a model of it

glob•u•lar \ˈgläbyələr\ adj 1 : round 2 : made up of globules

glob•ule \ˈgläbyül\ n : tiny ball

glock•en•spiel \ˈgläkənˌshpēl\ n : portable musical instrument consisting of tuned metal bars

gloom \ˈglüm\ n 1 : darkness 2 : sadness —gloom•i•ly adv —gloom•i•ness n —gloomy adj

glop \ˈgläp\ n : messy mass or mixture

glo•ri•fy \ˈglōrəˌfī\ vb -fied; -fy•ing 1 : make to seem glorious 2 : worship —glo•ri•fi•ca•tion \ˌglōrəfəˈkāshən\ n

glo•ry \ˈglōrē\ n, pl -ries 1 : praise or honor offered in worship 2 : cause for praise or renown 3 : magnificence 4 : heavenly bliss ~ vb -ried; -ry•ing : rejoice proudly —glo•ri•ous \ˈglōrēəs\ adj —glo•ri•ous•ly adv

[1]**gloss** \ˈgläs, ˈglȯs\ n : luster —gloss•i•ly \-əlē\ adv —gloss•i•ness \-ēnəs\ n —gloss over vb 1 : mask the true nature of 2 : deal with only superficially —glossy \-ē\ adj

[2]**gloss** n : brief explanation or translation ~ vb : translate or explain

glos•sa•ry \ˈgläsərē, ˈglȯs-\ n, pl -ries : dictionary —glos•sar•i•al \gläˈsarēəl, glȯ-\ adj

glove \ˈgləv\ n : hand covering with sections for each finger

glow \ˈglō\ vb 1 : shine with or as if with intense heat 2 : show exuberance ~ n : brightness or warmth of color or feeling

glow•er \ˈglau̇ər\ vb : stare angrily —glower n

glow•worm n : insect or insect larva that emits light

glu•cose \ˈglüˌkōs\ n : sugar found esp. in blood, plant sap, and fruits

glue \ˈglü\ n : substance used for sticking things together —glue vb —glu•ey \ˈglüē\ adj

glum \ˈgləm\ adj -mm- 1 : sullen 2 : dismal

glut \ˈglət\ vb -tt- : fill to excess —glut n

glu•ten \ˈglütᵊn\ n : gluey protein substance in flour

glu•ti•nous \ˈglütᵊnəs\ adj : sticky

glut•ton \ˈglətᵊn\ n : one who eats to excess —glut•ton•ous \ˈglətᵊnəs\ adj —glut•tony \ˈglətᵊnē\ n

gnarled \ˈnärld\ adj 1 : knotty 2 : gloomy or sullen

gnash \ˈnash\ vb : grind (as teeth) together

gnat \ˈnat\ n : small biting fly

gnaw \ˈnȯ\ vb : bite or chew on —gnaw•er n

gnome \ˈnōm\ n : dwarf of folklore —gnom•ish adj

gnu \ˈnü, ˈnyü\ n, pl gnu or gnus : large African antelope

go \ˈgō\ vb went \ˈwent\; gone \ˈgȯn, ˈgän\; go•ing \ˈgōiŋ\; goes \ˈgōz\ 1 : move, proceed, run, or pass 2 : leave 3 : extend or lead 4 : sell or amount —with for 5 : happen 6 —used in present participle to show intent or imminent action 7 : become 8 : fit or harmonize 9 : belong ~ n, pl goes 1 : act or manner of going 2 : vigor 3 : attempt —go back on : betray —go by the board : be discarded —go for : favor —go off : explode —go one better : outdo —go over 1 : examine 2 : study —go to town : be very successful —on the go : constantly active

goad \ˈgōd\ n : something that urges —goad vb

goal \ˈgōl\ n 1 : mark to reach in a race 2 : purpose 3 : object in a game through which a ball is propelled

goal•ie \ˈgōlē\ n : player who defends the goal

goal•keep•er n : goalie

goat \ˈgōt\ n : horned ruminant mammal related to the sheep —goat•skin n

goa•tee \gōˈtē\ n : small pointed beard

gob \ˈgäb\ n : lump

[1]**gob•ble** \ˈgäbəl\ vb -bled; -bling : eat greedily

[2]**gobble** vb -bled; -bling : make the noise of a turkey (gob•bler)

gob•ble•dy•gook \ˈgäbəldēˌgu̇k, -ˈgük\ n : nonsense

gob•let \ˈgäblət\ n : large stemmed drinking glass

gob•lin \ˈgäblən\ n : ugly mischievous sprite

god \ˈgäd, ˈgȯd\ n 1 cap : supreme being 2 : being with supernatural powers —god•like adj —god•ly adj

god•child n : person one sponsors at baptism —god•daugh•ter n —god•son n

god•dess \ˈgädəs, ˈgȯd-\ n : female god

god•less \-ləs\ adj : not believing in God —god•less•ness n

god•par•ent n : sponsor at baptism —god•fa•ther n —god•moth•er n

god•send \-ˌsend\ n : something needed that comes unexpectedly

goes pres 3d sing of GO

go–get•ter \ˈgōˌgetər\ n : enterprising person —go–get•ting \-iŋ\ adj or n

gog•gle \ˈgägəl\ vb -gled; -gling : stare wide-eyed

gog•gles \-əlz\ n pl : protective glasses

go•ings–on \ˌgōiŋzˈȯn, -ˈän\ n pl : events

goi•ter \ˈgȯitər\ n : abnormally enlarged thyroid gland

gold \ˈgōld\ n : malleable yellow metallic chemical element —gold•smith \-ˌsmith\ n

gold•brick \-ˌbrik\ n : person who shirks duty —goldbrick vb

gold•en \ˈgōldən\ adj 1 : made of, containing, or relating to gold 2 : having the color of gold 3 : precious or favorable

gold•en•rod \ˈgōldənˌräd\ n : herb having tall stalks with tiny yellow flowers

gold•finch \ˈgōldˌfinch\ n : yellow American finch

gold•fish \-ˌfish\ n : small usu. orange or golden carp

golf \ˈgälf, ˈgȯlf\ n : game played by hitting a small ball (golf ball) with clubs (golf clubs) into holes placed in a field (golf course) —golf vb —golf•er n

go•nad \ˈgōˌnad\ n : sex gland

gon•do•la \ˈgändələ (usual for 1), gänˈdō-\ n 1 : long narrow boat used on the canals of Venice 2 : car suspended from a cable

gon•do•lier \ˌgändəˈlir\ n : person who propels a gondola

gone \ˈgȯn\ adj 1 : past 2 : involved

gon•er \ˈgȯnər\ n : hopeless case

gong \ˈgäŋ, ˈgȯŋ\ n : metallic disk that makes a deep sound when struck

gon•or•rhea \ˌgänəˈrēə\ n : bacterial inflammatory venereal disease of the genital tract —gon•or•rhe•al \-ˈrēəl\ adj

goo \ˈgü\ n : thick or sticky substance —goo•ey \-ē\ adj

good \ˈgu̇d\ adj bet•ter \ˈbetər\; best \ˈbest\ 1 : satisfactory 2 : salutary 3 : considerable 4 : desirable 5 : well-behaved, kind, or virtuous ~ n 1 : something good 2 : benefit 3 pl : personal property 4 pl : wares ~ adv : well —good–heart•ed \-ˈhärtəd\ adj —good–look•ing adj —good–na•tured adj —good•ness n —good–tem•pered \-ˈtempərd\ adj —for good : forever

good–bye, good–by \gu̇dˈbī\ n : parting remark

good–for–noth•ing n : idle worthless person

Good Friday n : Friday before Easter observed as the anniversary of the crucifixion of Christ

good•ly adj -li•er; -est : considerable

good•will n 1 : good intention 2 : kindly feeling

goody \ˈgu̇dē\ n, pl good•ies : something that is good esp. to eat

goody–goody adj : affectedly or annoyingly sweet or self-righteous —goody–goody n

goof \ˈgüf\ vb 1 : blunder 2 : waste time —usu. with off or around —goof n —goof–off n

goofy \ˈgüfē\ adj goof•i•er; -est : crazy —goof•i•ness n

goose \ˈgüs\ n, pl geese \ˈgēs\ : large bird with webbed feet

goose•ber•ry \ˈgüsˌberē, ˈgüz-\ n : berry of a shrub related to the currant

goose bumps n pl : roughening of the skin caused by fear, excitement, or cold

goose•flesh n : goose bumps

goose pimples n pl : goose bumps

go•pher \ˈgōfər\ n : burrowing rodent

[1]**gore** \ˈgōr\ n : blood

[2]**gore** vb gored; gor•ing : pierce or wound with a horn or tusk

[1]**gorge** \ˈgȯrj\ n : narrow ravine

[2]**gorge** vb gorged; gorg•ing : eat greedily

gor•geous \ˈgȯrjəs\ adj : supremely beautiful

go•ril•la \gəˈrilə\ n : African manlike ape

gory \ˈgōrē\ adj gor•i•er; -est : bloody

gos•hawk \ˈgäsˌhȯk\ n : long-tailed hawk with short rounded wings

gos•ling \ˈgäzliŋ, ˈgȯz-\ n : young goose

gos•pel \ˈgäspəl\ n 1 : teachings of Christ and the apostles 2 : something accepted as infallible truth —gospel adj

gos•sa•mer \ˈgäsəmər, ˈgäz-\ n 1 : film of cobweb 2 : light filmy substance

gos•sip \ˈgäsəp\ n 1 : person who reveals personal information 2 : rumor or report of an intimate nature ~ vb : spread gossip —gos•sipy \-ē\ adj

got past of GET

Goth•ic \ˈgäthik\ adj : relating to a medieval style of architecture

gotten past part of GET

gouge \ˈgau̇j\ n 1 : rounded chisel 2 : cavity or groove scooped out ~ vb gouged; goug•ing 1 : cut or scratch a groove in 2 : overcharge

gou•lash \ˈgüˌläsh, -ˌlash\ n : beef stew with vegetables and paprika

gourd \ˈgōrd, ˈgu̇rd\ n 1 : any of a group of vines including the cucumber, squash, and melon 2 : inedible hard-shelled fruit of a gourd

gour•mand \ˈgu̇rˌmänd\ n : person who loves good food and drink

gour•met \ˈgu̇rˌmā, gu̇rˈmā\ n : connoisseur of food and drink

gout \ˈgau̇t\ n : disease marked by painful inflammation and swelling of the joints —gouty adj

gov•ern \ˈgəvərn\ vb 1 : control and direct policy in 2 : guide or influence strongly 3 : restrain —gov•ern•ment \-ərmənt\ n —gov•ern•men•tal \ˌgəvərˈmentᵊl\ adj

gov•ern•ess \ˈgəvərnəs\ n : female teacher in a private home

gov•er•nor \ˈgəvənər, ˈgəvər-\ n 1 : head of a political unit 2 : automatic speed-control device —gov•er•nor•ship n

gown \ˈgau̇n\ n 1 : loose flowing outer garment 2 : woman's formal evening dress —gown vb

grab \ˈgrab\ vb -bb- : take by sudden grasp —grab n

grace \ˈgrās\ n 1 : unmerited divine assistance 2 : short prayer before or after a meal 3 : respite 4 : ease of movement or bearing ~ vb graced; grac•ing 1 : honor 2 : adorn —grace•ful \-fəl\ adj —grace•ful•ly adv —grace•ful•ness n —grace•less adj

gra•cious \ˈgrāshəs\ adj : marked by kindness and courtesy or charm and taste —gra•cious•ly adv —gra•cious•ness n

grack•le \ˈgrakəl\ n : American blackbird

gra•da•tion \grāˈdāshən, grə-\ n : step, degree, or stage in a series

grade \ˈgrād\ n 1 : stage in a series, order, or ranking 2 : division of school representing one year's work 3 : mark of accomplishment in school 4 : degree of slope ~ vb grad•ed; grad•ing 1 : arrange in grades 2 : make level or evenly sloping 3 : give a grade to —grad•er n

grade school n : school including the first 4 or 8 grades

gra•di•ent \ˈgrādēənt\ n : slope

grad•u•al \ˈgrajəwəl\ adj : going by steps or degrees —grad•u•al•ly adv

grad•u•ate \ˈgrajəwət\ n : holder of a diploma ~ adj : of or relating to studies beyond the bachelor's degree ~ \-əˌwāt\ vb -at•ed; -at•ing 1 : grant or receive a diploma 2 : mark with degrees of measurement —grad•u•a•tion \ˌgrajəˈwāshən\ n

graf•fi•to \graˈfētō, grə-\ n, pl -ti \-ē\ : inscription on a wall

graft \ˈgraft\ vb : join one thing to another so that they grow together ~ n 1 : grafted plant 2 : the getting of money dishonestly or the money so gained —graft•er n

grain \ˈgrān\ n 1 : seeds or fruits of cereal grasses 2 : small hard particle 3 : arrangement of fibers in wood —grained \ˈgrānd\ adj —grainy adj

gram \ˈgram\ n : metric unit of weight equal to 1/1000 kilogram

gram•mar \ˈgramər\ n : study of words and their functions and relations in the sentence —gram•mar•i•an \grəˈmarēən\ n —gram•mat•i•cal \-ˈmatikəl\ adj —gram•mat•i•cal•ly adv

grammar school n : grade school

gra•na•ry \ˈgrānərē, ˈgran-\ n, pl -ries : storehouse for grain

grand \ˈgrand\ adj 1 : large or striking in size or scope 2 : fine and imposing 3 : very good —grand•ly adv —grand•ness n

grand•child \-ˌchīld\ n : child of one's son or daughter —grand•daugh•ter n —grand•son n

gran•deur \ˈgranjər\ n : quality or state of being grand

gran•dil•o•quence \granˈdiləkwəns\ n : pompous speaking —gran•dil•o•quent \-kwənt\ adj

gran•di•ose \ˈgrandēˌōs, ˌgrandēˈ-\ adj 1 : impressive 2 : affectedly splendid —gran•di•ose•ly adv

grand•par•ent \ˈgrandˌparənt\ n : parent of one's father or mother —grand•fa•ther \-ˌfäthər, -ˌfȧth-\ n —grand•moth•er \-ˌməthər\ n

grand•stand \-ˌstand\ n : usu. roofed stand for spectators

grange \ˈgrānj\ n : farmers association

gran•ite \ˈgranət\ n : hard igneous rock

grant \ˈgrant\ vb 1 : consent to 2 : give 3 : admit as true ~ n 1 : act of granting 2 : something granted —grant•ee \grantˈē\ n —grant•er \ˈgrantər\ n —grant•or \-ər, -ˌȯr\ n

gran•u•late \ˈgranyəˌlāt\ vb -lat•ed; -lat•ing : form into grains or crystals —gran•u•la•tion \ˌgranyəˈlāshən\ n

gran•ule \ˈgranyül\ n : small particle —gran•u•lar \-yələr\ adj —gran•u•lar•i•ty \ˌgranyəˈlarətē\ n

grape \ˈgrāp\ n : smooth juicy edible berry of a woody vine (grape•vine)

grape•fruit n : large edible yellow-skinned citrus fruit

graph \ˈgraf\ n : diagram that shows relationships between things —graph vb

graph•ic \ˈgrafik\ adj 1 : vividly described 2 : relating to the arts (graphic arts) of representation and printing on flat surfaces ~ n 1 : picture used for illustration 2 pl : computer screen display —graph•i•cal•ly \-iklē\ adv

graph•ite \ˈgrafˌīt\ n : soft carbon used for lead pencils and lubricants

grap•nel \ˈgrapnəl\ n : small anchor with several claws

grap•ple \ˈgrapəl\ vb -pled; -pling 1 : seize or hold with or as if with a hooked implement 2 : wrestle

grasp \ˈgrasp\ *vb* **1 :** take or seize firmly **2 :** understand ~ *n* **1 :** one's hold or control **2 :** one's reach **3 :** comprehension
grass \ˈgras\ *n* **:** plant with jointed stem and narrow leaves **—grassy** *adj*
grass•hop•per \-ˌhäpər\ *n* **:** leaping plant-eating insect
grass•land *n* **:** land covered with grasses
1grate \ˈgrāt\ *n* **1 :** grating **2 :** frame of iron bars to hold burning fuel
2grate *vb* **grat•ed; -ing 1 :** pulverize by rubbing against something rough **2 :** irritate **—grat•er** *n* **—grat•ing•ly** *adv*
grate•ful \ˈgrātfəl\ *adj* **:** thankful or appreciative **—grate•ful•ly** *adv* **—grate•ful•ness** *n*
grat•i•fy \ˈgratəˌfī\ *vb* **-fied; -fy•ing :** give pleasure to **—grat•i•fi•ca•tion** \ˌgratəfəˈkāshən\ *n*
grat•ing \ˈgrātiŋ\ *n* **:** framework with bars across it
gra•tis \ˈgratəs, ˈgrāt-\ *adv or adj* **:** free
grat•i•tude \ˈgratəˌtüd, -ˌtyüd\ *n* **:** state of being grateful
gra•tu•itous \grəˈtüətəs, -ˈtyü-\ *adj* **1 :** free **2 :** uncalled-for
gra•tu•ity \-ətē\ *n, pl* **-ities :** tip
1grave \ˈgrāv\ *n* **:** place of burial **—grave•stone** *n* **—grave•yard** *n*
2grave *adj* **grav•er; grav•est 1 :** threatening great harm or danger **2 :** solemn **—grave•ly** *adv* **—grave•ness** *n*
grav•el \ˈgravəl\ *n* **:** loose rounded fragments of rock **—grav•el•ly** *adj*
grav•i•tate \ˈgravəˌtāt\ *vb* **-tat•ed; -tat•ing :** move toward something
grav•i•ta•tion \ˌgravəˈtāshən\ *n* **:** natural force of attraction that tends to draw bodies together **—grav•i•ta•tion•al** \-shənəl\ *adj* **—grav•i•ta•tion•al•ly** *adv*
grav•i•ty \ˈgravətē\ *n, pl* **-ties 1 :** serious importance **2 :** gravitation
gra•vy \ˈgrāvē\ *n, pl* **-vies :** sauce made from thickened juices of cooked meat
gray \ˈgrā\ *adj* **1 :** of the color gray **2 :** having gray hair ~ *n* **:** neutral color between black and white ~ *vb* **:** make or become gray **—gray•ish** \-ish\ *adj* **—gray•ness** *n*
1graze \ˈgrāz\ *vb* **grazed; graz•ing :** feed on herbage or pasture **—graz•er** *n*
2graze *vb* **grazed; graz•ing :** touch lightly in passing
grease \ˈgrēs\ *n* **:** thick oily material or fat ~ \ˈgrēs, ˈgrēz\ *vb* **greased; greas•ing :** smear or lubricate with grease **—greasy** \ˈgrēsē, -zē\ *adj*
great \ˈgrāt\ *adj* **1 :** large in size or number **2 :** larger than usual **—great•ly** *adv* **—great•ness** *n*
grebe \ˈgrēb\ *n* **:** diving bird related to the loon
greed \ˈgrēd\ *n* **:** selfish desire beyond reason **—greed•i•ly** \-əlē\ *adv* **—greed•i•ness** \-ēnəs\ *n* **—greedy** \ˈgrēdē\ *adj*
green \ˈgrēn\ *adj* **1 :** of the color green **2 :** unripe **3 :** inexperienced ~ *vb* **:** become green ~ *n* **1 :** color between blue and yellow **2** *pl* **:** leafy parts of plants **—green•ish** *adj* **—green•ness** *n*
green•ery \ˈgrēnərē\ *n, pl* **-er•ies :** green foliage or plants
green•horn *n* **:** inexperienced person
green•house *n* **:** glass structure for the growing of plants
greet \ˈgrēt\ *vb* **1 :** address with expressions of kind wishes **2 :** react to **—greet•er** *n*
greet•ing *n* **1 :** friendly address on meeting **2** *pl* **:** best wishes
gre•gar•i•ous \griˈgarēəs\ *adj* **:** social or companionable **—gre•gar•i•ous•ly** *adv* **—gre•gar•i•ous•ness** *n*
grem•lin \ˈgremlən\ *n* **:** small mischievous gnome
gre•nade \grəˈnād\ *n* **:** small missile filled with explosive or chemicals
grew *past of* GROW
grey *var of* GRAY
grey•hound \ˈgrāˌhaůnd\ *n* **:** tall slender dog noted for speed
grid \ˈgrid\ *n* **1 :** grating **2 :** evenly spaced horizontal and vertical lines (as on a map)
grid•dle \ˈgridᵊl\ *n* **:** flat metal surface for cooking
grid•iron \ˈgridˌīərn\ *n* **1 :** grate for broiling **2 :** football field
grief \ˈgrēf\ *n* **1 :** emotional suffering caused by or as if by bereavement **2 :** disaster
griev•ance \ˈgrēvəns\ *n* **:** complaint
grieve \ˈgrēv\ *vb* **grieved; griev•ing :** feel or cause to feel grief or sorrow
griev•ous \ˈgrēvəs\ *adj* **1 :** oppressive **2 :** causing grief or sorrow **—griev•ous•ly** *adv*
grill \ˈgril\ *vb* **1 :** cook on a grill **2 :** question intensely ~ *n* **1 :** griddle **2 :** informal restaurant
grille, grill \ˈgril\ *n* **:** grating forming a barrier or screen **—grill•work** *n*
grim \ˈgrim\ *adj* **-mm- 1 :** harsh and forbidding in appearance **2 :** relentless **—grim•ly** *adv* **—grim•ness** *n*
gri•mace \ˈgriməs, grimˈās\ *n* **:** facial expression of disgust **—grimace** *vb*
grime \ˈgrīm\ *n* **:** embedded or accumulated dirt **—grimy** *adj*
grin \ˈgrin\ *vb* **-nn- :** smile so as to show the teeth **—grin** *n*
grind \ˈgrīnd\ *vb* **ground** \ˈgraůnd**; grind•ing 1 :** reduce to powder **2 :** wear down or sharpen by friction **3 :** operate or produce by turning a crank ~ *n* **:** monotonous labor or routine **—grind•er** *n* **—grind•stone** \ˈgrīnˌstōn\ *n*
grip \ˈgrip\ *vb* **-pp- :** seize or hold firmly ~ *n* **1 :** grasp **2 :** control **3 :** device for holding
gripe \ˈgrīp\ *vb* **griped; grip•ing 1 :** cause pains in the bowels **2 :** complain **—gripe** *n*
grippe \ˈgrip\ *n* **:** influenza
gris•ly \ˈgrizlē\ *adj* **-li•er; -est :** horrible or gruesome
grist \ˈgrist\ *n* **:** grain to be ground or already ground **—grist•mill** *n*
gris•tle \ˈgrisəl\ *n* **:** cartilage **—gris•tly** \-lē\ *adj*
grit \ˈgrit\ *n* **1 :** hard sharp granule **2 :** material composed of granules **3 :** unyielding courage ~ *vb* **-tt- :** press with a grating noise **—grit•ty** *adj*
grits \ˈgrits\ *n pl* **:** coarsely ground hulled grain
griz•zled \ˈgrizəld\ *adj* **:** streaked with gray
groan \ˈgrōn\ *vb* **1 :** moan **2 :** creak under a strain **—groan** *n*
gro•cer \ˈgrōsər\ *n* **:** food dealer **—grocery** \ˈgrōsrē, ˈgrōsh-, -ərē\ *n*
grog \ˈgräg\ *n* **:** rum diluted with water
grog•gy \-ē\ *adj* **-gi•er; -est :** dazed and unsteady on the feet **—grog•gi•ly** *adv* **—grog•gi•ness** *n*
groin \ˈgrȯin\ *n* **:** juncture of the lower abdomen and inner thigh
grom•met \ˈgrämət, ˈgrəm-\ *n* **:** eyelet
groom \ˈgrüm, ˈgrům\ *n* **1 :** one who cares for horses **2 :** bridegroom ~ *vb* **1 :** clean and care for (as a horse) **2 :** make neat or attractive **3 :** prepare
groove \ˈgrüv\ *n* **1 :** long narrow channel **2 :** fixed routine **—groove** *vb*
grope \ˈgrōp\ *vb* **groped; grop•ing :** search for by feeling
gros•beak \ˈgrōsˌbēk\ *n* **:** finch with large conical bill
1gross \ˈgrōs\ *adj* **1 :** glaringly noticeable **2 :** bulky **3 :** consisting of an overall total exclusive of deductions **4 :** vulgar ~ *n* **:** the whole before any deductions ~ *vb* **:** earn as a total **—gross•ly** *adv* **—gross•ness** *n*
2gross *n, pl* **gross :** 12 dozen
gro•tesque \grōˈtesk\ *adj* **1 :** absurdly distorted or repulsive **2 :** ridiculous **—gro•tesque•ly** *adv*
grot•to \ˈgrätō\ *n, pl* **-toes :** cave
grouch \ˈgraůch\ *n* **:** complaining person **—grouch** *vb* **—grouchy** *adj*
1ground \ˈgraůnd\ *n* **1 :** bottom of a body of water **2** *pl* **:** sediment **3 :** basis for something **4 :** surface of the earth **5 :** conductor that makes electrical connection with the earth or a framework ~ *vb* **1 :** force or bring down to the ground **2 :** give basic knowledge to **3 :** connect with an electrical ground **—ground•less** *adj*
2ground *past of* GRIND
ground•hog *n* **:** woodchuck
ground•wa•ter *n* **:** underground water
ground•work *n* **:** foundation
group \ˈgrüp\ *n* **:** number of associated individuals ~ *vb* **:** gather or collect into groups
grou•per \ˈgrüpər\ *n* **:** large fish of warm seas
grouse \ˈgraůs\ *n, pl* **grouse** *or* **grouses :** ground-dwelling game bird
grout \ˈgraůt\ *n* **:** mortar for filling cracks **—grout** *vb*
grove \ˈgrōv\ *n* **:** small group of trees
grov•el \ˈgrävəl, ˈgrəv-\ *vb* **-eled** *or* **-elled; -el•ing** *or* **-el•ling :** abase oneself
grow \ˈgrō\ *vb* **grew** \ˈgrü\ **grown** \ˈgrōn**; grow•ing 1 :** come into existence and develop to maturity **2 :** be able to grow **3 :** advance or increase **4 :** become **5 :** cultivate **—grow•er** *n*
growl \ˈgraůl\ *vb* **:** utter a deep threatening sound **—growl** *n*
grown–up \ˈgrōnˌəp\ *n* **:** adult **—grown–up** *adj*
growth \ˈgrōth\ *n* **1 :** stage in growing **2 :** process of growing **3 :** result of something growing
grub \ˈgrəb\ *vb* **-bb- 1 :** root out by digging **2 :** search about ~ *n* **1 :** thick wormlike larva **2 :** food
grub•by \ˈgrəbē\ *adj* **-bi•er; -est :** dirty **—grub•bi•ness** *n*
grub•stake *n* **:** supplies for a prospector
grudge \ˈgrəj\ *vb* **grudged; grudg•ing :** be reluctant to give ~ *n* **:** feeling of ill will
gru•el \ˈgrüəl\ *n* **:** thin porridge
gru•el•ing, gru•el•ling \-əliŋ\ *adj* **:** requiring extreme effort
grue•some \ˈgrüsəm\ *adj* **:** horribly repulsive
gruff \ˈgrəf\ *adj* **:** rough in speech or manner **—gruff•ly** *adv*
grum•ble \ˈgrəmbəl\ *vb* **-bled; -bling :** mutter in discontent **—grum•bler** \-blər\ *n*
grumpy \-pē\ *adj* **grump•i•er; -est :** cross **—grump•i•ly** *adv* **—grump•i•ness** *n*
grun•ion \ˈgrənyən\ *n* **:** fish of the California coast
grunt \ˈgrənt\ *n* **:** deep guttural sound **—grunt** *vb*
gua•no \ˈgwänō\ *n* **:** excrement of seabirds used as fertilizer
guar•an•tee \ˌgarənˈtē\ *n* **1 :** assurance of the fulfillment of a condition **2 :** something given or held as a security ~ *vb* **-teed; -tee•ing 1 :** promise to be responsible for **2 :** state with certainty **—guar•an•tor** \ˌgarənˈtȯr\ *n*
guar•an•ty \ˈgarəntē\ *n, pl* **-ties 1 :** promise to answer for another's failure to pay a debt **2 :** guarantee **3 :** pledge ~ *vb* **-tied; -ty•ing :** guarantee
guard \ˈgärd\ *n* **1 :** defensive position **2 :** act of protecting **3 :** an individual or group that guards against danger **4 :** protective or safety device ~ *vb* **1 :** protect or watch over **2 :** take precautions **—guard•house** *n* **—guard•room** *n*
guard•ian \ˈgärdēən\ *n* **:** one who has responsibility for the care of the person or property of another **—guard•ian•ship** *n*
gua•va \ˈgwävə\ *n* **:** shrubby tropical tree or its mildly acid fruit
gu•ber•na•to•ri•al \ˌgübənəˈtōrēəl, ˌgyü-\ *adj* **:** relating to a governor
guer•ril•la, gue•ril•la \gəˈrilə\ *n* **:** soldier engaged in small-scale harassing tactics
guess \ˈges\ *vb* **1 :** form an opinion from little evidence **2 :** state correctly solely by chance **3 :** think or believe **—guess** *n*
guest \ˈgest\ *n* **1 :** person to whom hospitality (as of a house) is extended **2 :** patron of a commercial establishment (as a hotel) **3 :** person not a regular cast member who appears on a program
guf•faw \gəˈfȯ, ˈgəfˌȯ\ *n* **:** loud burst of laughter **—guf•faw** \gəˈfȯ\ *vb*
guide \ˈgīd\ *n* **1 :** one that leads or gives direction to another **2 :** device on a machine to direct motion ~ *vb* **guid•ed; guid•ing 1 :** show the way to **2 :** direct **—guid•able** *adj* **—guid•ance** \ˈgīdᵊns\ *n* **—guide•book** *n*
guide•line \-ˌlīn\ *n* **:** summary of procedures regarding policy or conduct
guild \ˈgild\ *n* **:** association
guile \ˈgīl\ *n* **:** craftiness **—guile•ful** *adj* **—guile•less** *adj* **—guile•less•ness** *n*
guil•lo•tine \ˈgiləˌtēn; ˌgēyəˈtēn, ˈgēyəˌ-\ *n* **:** machine for beheading persons **—guillotine** *vb*
guilt \ˈgilt\ *n* **1 :** fact of having committed an offense **2 :** feeling of responsibility for offenses **—guilt•i•ly** *adv* **—guilt•i•ness** *n* **—guilty** \ˈgiltē\ *adj*
guin•ea \ˈginē\ *n* **1 :** old gold coin of United Kingdom **2 :** 21 shillings
guinea pig *n* **:** small So. American rodent
guise \ˈgīz\ *n* **:** external appearance
gui•tar \gəˈtär, gi-\ *n* **:** 6-stringed musical instrument played by plucking
gulch \ˈgəlch\ *n* **:** ravine
gulf \ˈgəlf\ *n* **1 :** extension of an ocean or a sea into the land **2 :** wide gap
1gull \ˈgəl\ *n* **:** seabird with webbed feet
2gull *vb* **:** make a dupe of ~ *n* **:** dupe **—gull•ible** *adj*
gul•let \ˈgələt\ *n* **:** throat
gul•ly \ˈgəlē\ *n, pl* **-lies :** trench worn by running water
gulp \ˈgəlp\ *vb* **:** swallow hurriedly or greedily **—gulp** *n*
1gum \ˈgəm\ *n* **:** tissue along the jaw at the base of the teeth
2gum *n* **1 :** sticky plant substance **2 :** gum usu. of sweetened chicle prepared for chewing **—gum•my** *adj*
gum•bo \ˈgəmbō\ *n* **:** thick soup
gum•drop *n* **:** gumlike candy
gump•tion \ˈgəmpshən\ *n* **:** initiative
gun \ˈgən\ *n* **1 :** cannon **2 :** portable firearm **3 :** discharge of a gun **4 :** something like a gun ~ *vb* **-nn- :** hunt with a gun **—gun•fight** *n* **—gun•fight•er** *n* **—gun•fire** *n* **—gun•man** \-mən\ *n* **—gun•pow•der** *n* **—gun•shot** *n* **—gun•smith** *n*
gun•boat *n* **:** small armed ship
gun•ner \ˈgənər\ *n* **:** person who uses a gun
gun•nery sergeant \ˈgənərē-\ *n* **:** noncommissioned officer in the marine corps ranking next below a first sergeant
gun•ny•sack \ˈgənēˌsak\ *n* **:** burlap sack
gun•sling•er \ˈgənˌsliŋər\ *n* **:** skilled gunman in the old West
gun•wale \ˈgənᵊl\ *n* **:** upper edge of a boat's side
gup•py \ˈgəpē\ *n, pl* **-pies :** tiny tropical fish
gur•gle \ˈgərgəl\ *vb* **-gled; -gling :** make a sound like that of a flowing and gently splashing liquid **—gurgle** *n*
gu•ru \ˈgüˌrü\ *n, pl* **-rus 1 :** personal religious teacher in Hinduism **2 :** expert
gush \ˈgəsh\ *vb* **:** pour forth violently or enthusiastically **—gush•er** \ˈgəshər\ *n*
gushy \-ē\ *adj* **gush•i•er; -est :** effusively sentimental
gust \ˈgəst\ *n* **1 :** sudden brief rush of wind **2 :** sudden outburst **—gust** *vb* **—gusty** *adj*
gus•ta•to•ry \ˈgəstəˌtōrē\ *adj* **:** relating to the sense of taste
gus•to \ˈgəstō\ *n* **:** zest
gut \ˈgət\ *n* **1** *pl* **:** intestines **2 :** digestive canal **3** *pl* **:** courage ~ *vb* **-tt- :** eviscerate
gut•ter \ˈgətər\ *n* **:** channel for carrying off rainwater
gut•tur•al \ˈgətərəl\ *adj* **:** sounded in the throat **—guttural** *n*
1guy \ˈgī\ *n* **:** rope, chain, or rod attached to something to steady it **—guy** *vb*
2guy *n* **:** person
guz•zle \ˈgəzəl\ *vb* **-zled; -zling :** drink greedily
gym \ˈjim\ *n* **:** gymnasium
gym•na•si•um \jimˈnāzēəm, -zhəm\ *n, pl* **-si•ums** *or* **-sia** \-zēə, -zhə\ **:** place for indoor sports
gym•nas•tics \jimˈnastiks\ *n* **:** physical exercises performed in a gymnasium **—gym•nast** \ˈjimˌnast\ *n* **—gym•nas•tic** *adj*
gy•ne•col•o•gy \ˌgīnəˈkäləjē, ˌjin-\ *n* **:** branch of medicine dealing with the diseases of women **—gy•ne•co•log•ic** \-ikəˈläjik\, **gy•ne•co•log•i•cal** \-ikəl\ *adj* **—gy•ne•col•o•gist** \-əˈkäləjist\ *n*
gyp \ˈjip\ *n* **1 :** cheat **2 :** trickery **—gyp** *vb*
gyp•sum \ˈjipsəm\ *n* **:** calcium-containing mineral
gy•rate \ˈjīˌrāt\ *vb* **-rat•ed; -rat•ing :** revolve around a center **—gy•ra•tion** \jīˈrāshən\ *n*
gy•ro•scope \ˈjīrəˌskōp\ *n* **:** wheel mounted to spin rapidly about an axis that is free to turn in various directions

H

h \ˈāch\ *n, pl* **h's** *or* **hs** \ˈāchəz\ **:** 8th letter of the alphabet
hab•er•dash•er \ˈhabərˌdashər\ *n* **:** men's clothier **—hab•er•dash•ery** \-ərē\ *n*
hab•it \ˈhabət\ *n* **1 :** monk's or nun's clothing **2 :** usual behavior **3 :** addiction **—hab•it–form•ing** *adj*
hab•it•able \-əbəl\ *adj* **:** capable of being lived in
hab•i•tat \ˈhabəˌtat\ *n* **:** place where a plant or animal naturally occurs
hab•i•ta•tion \ˌhabəˈtāshən\ *n* **1 :** occupancy **2 :** dwelling place
ha•bit•u•al \həˈbichəwəl\ *adj* **1 :** commonly practiced or observed **2 :** doing, practicing, or acting by habit **—ha•bit•u•al•ly** *adv* **—ha•bit•u•al•ness** *n*
ha•bit•u•ate \həˈbichəˌwāt\ *vb* **-at•ed; -at•ing :** accustom
ha•ci•en•da \ˌhäsēˈendə\ *n* **:** ranch house
1hack \ˈhak\ *vb* **1 :** cut with repeated irregular blows **2 :** cough in a short dry manner **3 :** manage successfully **—hack** *n* **—hack•er** *n*
2hack *n* **1 :** horse or vehicle for hire **2 :** saddle horse **3 :** writer for hire **—hack** *adj* **—hack•man** \-mən\ *n*
hack•le \ˈhakəl\ *n* **1 :** long feather on the neck or back of a bird **2** *pl* **:** hairs that can be erected **3** *pl* **:** temper
hack•ney \-nē\ *n, pl* **-neys 1 :** horse for riding or driving **2 :** carriage for hire
hack•neyed \-nēd\ *adj* **:** trite
hack•saw *n* **:** saw for metal
had *past of* HAVE
had•dock \ˈhadək\ *n, pl* **haddock :** Atlantic food fish
Ha•des \ˈhādēz\ *n* **1 :** mythological abode of the dead **2 :** *often not cap* **:** hell
haft \ˈhaft\ *n* **:** handle of a weapon or tool
hag \ˈhag\ *n* **1 :** witch **2 :** ugly old woman
hag•gard \ˈhagərd\ *adj* **:** worn or emaciated **—hag•gard•ly** *adv*
hag•gle \ˈhagəl\ *vb* **-gled; -gling :** argue in bargaining **—hag•gler** *n*
1hail \ˈhāl\ *n* **1 :** precipitation in small lumps of ice **2 :** something like a rain of hail ~ *vb* **:** rain hail **—hail•stone** *n* **—hail•storm** *n*
2hail *vb* **1 :** greet or salute **2 :** summon ~ *n* **:** expression of greeting or praise **—often used as an interjection**
hair \ˈhar\ *n* **:** threadlike growth from the

skin —**hair•brush** *n* —**hair•cut** *n* —**hair•dress•er** *n* —**haired** *adj* —**hair•i•ness** *n* —**hair•less** *adj* —**hairpin** *n* —**hair•style** *n* —**hair•styl•ing** *n* —**hair•styl•ist** *n* —**hairy** *adj*

hair•breadth \-ˌbredth\, **hairs•breadth** \'harz-\ *n* : tiny distance or margin

hair•do \-ˌdü\ *n, pl* **-dos** : style of wearing hair

hair•line *n* **1** : thin line **2** : outline of the hair on the head

hair•piece *n* : toupee

hair–rais•ing *adj* : causing terror or astonishment

hake \'hāk\ *n* : marine food fish

hal•cy•on \'halsēən\ *adj* : prosperous or most pleasant

1**hale** \'hāl\ *adj* : healthy or robust

2**hale** *vb* **haled; hal•ing 1** : haul **2** : compel to go

half \'haf, 'háf\ *n, pl* **halves** \'havz, 'hávz\ : either of 2 equal parts ~ *adj* **1** : being a half or nearly a half **2** : partial —**half** *adv*

half brother *n* : brother related through one parent only

half•heart•ed \-'härtəd\ *adj* : without enthusiasm —**half•heart•ed•ly** *adv* —**half•heart•ed•ness** *n*

half–life *n* : time for half of something to undergo a process

half sister *n* : sister related through one parent only

half•way *adj* : midway between 2 points —**half•way** *adv*

half–wit \-ˌwit\ *n* : foolish person —**half–wit•ted** \-ˌwitəd\ *adj*

hal•i•but \'haləbət\ *n, pl* **halibut** : large edible marine flatfish

hal•i•to•sis \ˌhalə'tōsəs\ *n* : bad breath

hall \'hól\ *n* **1** : large public or college or university building **2** : lobby **3** : auditorium

hal•le•lu•jah \ˌhalə'lüyə\ *interj* —used to express praise, joy, or thanks

hall•mark \'hólˌmärk\ *n* : distinguishing characteristic

hal•low \'halō\ *vb* : consecrate —**hallowed** \-ōd, -əwəd\ *adj*

Hal•low•een \ˌhalə'wēn, ˌhäl-\ *n* : evening of October 31 observed esp. by children in merrymaking and masquerading

hal•lu•ci•na•tion \həˌlüsən'āshən\ *n* : perception of objects that are not real —**hal•lu•ci•nate** \hə'lüsənˌāt\ *vb* —**hal•lu•ci•na•to•ry** \-'lüsənəˌtōrē\ *adj*

hal•lu•ci•no•gen \hə'lüsənəjən\ *n* : substance that induces hallucinations —**hal•lu•ci•no•gen•ic** \-ˌlüsənə'jenik\ *adj*

hall•way *n* : entrance hall

ha•lo \'hālō\ *n, pl* **-los** *or* **-loes** : circle of light appearing to surround a shining body

1**halt** \'hólt\ *adj* : lame

2**halt** *vb* : stop or cause to stop —**halt** *n*

hal•ter \'hóltər\ *n* **1** : rope or strap for leading or tying an animal **2** : brief blouse held up by straps ~ *vb* : catch (an animal) with a halter

halt•ing \'hóltiŋ\ *adj* : uncertain —**halt•ing•ly** *adv*

halve \'hav, 'háv\ *vb* **halved; halv•ing 1** : divide into halves **2** : reduce to half

halves *pl of* HALF

ham \'ham\ *n* **1** : thigh—usu. pl. **2** : cut esp. of pork from the thigh **3** : showy actor **4** : amateur radio operator ~ *vb* **-mm-** : overplay a part —**ham** *adj*

ham•burg•er \'hamˌbərgər\, **ham•burg** \-ˌbərg\ *n* : ground beef or a sandwich made with this

ham•let \'hamlət\ *n* : small village

ham•mer \'hamər\ *n* **1** : hand tool for pounding **2** : gun part whose striking explodes the charge ~ *vb* : beat, drive, or shape with a hammer —**hammer out** *vb* : produce with effort

ham•mer•head *n* **1** : striking part of a hammer **2** : shark with a hammerlike head

ham•mock \'hamək\ *n* : swinging bed hung by cords at each end

1**ham•per** \'hampər\ *vb* : impede

2**hamper** *n* : large covered basket

ham•ster \'hamstər\ *n* : stocky shorttailed rodent

ham•string \'hamˌstriŋ\ *vb* **-strung** \-ˌstrəŋ\; **-string•ing** \-ˌstriŋiŋ\ **1** : cripple by cutting the leg tendons **2** : make ineffective or powerless

hand \'hand\ *n* **1** : end of a front limb adapted for grasping **2** : side **3** : promise of marriage **4** : handwriting **5** : assistance or participation **6** : applause **7** : cards held by a player **8** : worker ~ *vb* : lead, assist, give, or pass with the hand —**hand•clasp** *n* —**hand•craft** *vb* —**hand•ful** *n* —**hand•gun** *n* —**hand•less** *adj* —**hand•made** *adj* —**hand•rail** *n* —**hand•saw** *n* —**hand•wo•ven** *adj* —**hand•writ•ing** *n* —**hand•writ•ten** *adj*

hand•bag *n* : woman's purse

hand•ball *n* : game played by striking a ball with the hand

hand•bill *n* : printed advertisement or notice distributed by hand

hand•book *n* : concise reference book

hand•cuffs *n pl* : locking bracelets that bind the wrists together —**handcuff** *vb*

hand•i•cap \'handēˌkap\ *n* **1** : advantage given or disadvantage imposed to equalize a competition **2** : disadvantage —**handicap** *vb* —**hand•i•capped** *adj* —**hand•i•cap•per** *n*

hand•i•craft \'handēˌkraft\ *n* **1** : manual skill **2** : article made by hand —**hand•i•craft•er** *n* —**hand•i•crafts•man** \-ˌkraftsmən\ *n*

hand•i•work \-ˌwərk\ *n* : work done personally or by the hands

hand•ker•chief \'haŋkərchəf, -ˌchēf\ *n, pl* **-chiefs** \-chəfs, -ˌchēfs\ : small piece of cloth carried for personal use

han•dle \'handəl\ *n* : part to be grasped ~ *vb* **-dled; -dling 1** : touch, hold, or manage with the hands **2** : deal with **3** : deal or trade in —**han•dle•bar** *n* —**han•dled** \-dəld\ *adj* —**han•dler** \'handlər\ *n*

hand•maid•en *n* : female attendant

hand•out *n* : something given out

hand•pick *vb* : select personally

hand•shake *n* : clasping of hands (as in greeting)

hand•some \'hansəm\ *adj* **-som•er; -est 1** : sizable **2** : generous **3** : nice-looking —**hand•some•ly** *adv* —**hand•some•ness** *n*

hand•spring *n* : somersault on the hands

hand•stand *n* : a balancing upside down on the hands

handy \'handē\ *adj* **hand•i•er; -est 1** : conveniently near **2** : easily used **3** : dexterous —**hand•i•ly** *adv* —**hand•i•ness** *n*

handy•man \-ˌman\ *n* : one who does odd jobs

hang \'haŋ\ *vb* **hung** \'həŋ\ **hang•ing 1** : fasten or remain fastened to an elevated point without support from below **2** : suspend by the neck until dead—past tense often *hanged* **3** : droop ~ *n* **1** : way a thing hangs **2** : an understanding of something —**hang•er** *n* —**hang•ing** *n*

han•gar \'haŋər\ *n* : airplane shelter

hang•dog \'haŋˌdóg\ *adj* : ashamed or guilty

hang•man \-mən\ *n* : public executioner

hang•nail *n* : loose skin near a fingernail

hang•out *n* : place where one likes to spend time

hang•over *n* : sick feeling following heavy drinking

hank \'haŋk\ *n* : coil or loop

han•ker \'haŋkər\ *vb* : desire strongly —**han•ker•ing** *n*

han•ky–pan•ky \ˌhaŋkē'paŋkē\ *n* : questionable or underhanded activity

han•som \'hansəm\ *n* : 2-wheeled covered carriage

Ha•nuk•kah \'känəkə, 'hän-\ *n* : 8-day Jewish holiday commemorating the rededication of the Temple of Jerusalem after its defilement by Antiochus of Syria

hap•haz•ard \hap'hazərd\ *adj* : having no plan or order —**hap•haz•ard•ly** *adv*

hap•less \'hapləs\ *adj* : unfortunate —**hap•less•ly** *adv* —**hap•less•ness** *n*

hap•pen \'hapən\ *vb* **1** : take place **2** : be fortunate to encounter something unexpectedly —often used with infinitive

hap•pen•ing \-əniŋ\ *n* : occurrence

hap•py \'hapē\ *adj* **-pi•er; -est 1** : fortunate **2** : content, pleased, or joyous —**hap•pi•ly** \'hapəlē\ *adv* —**hap•pi•ness** *n*

ha•rangue \hə'raŋ\ *n* : ranting or scolding speech —**harangue** *vb* —**ha•rangu•er** \-'raŋər\ *n*

ha•rass \hə'ras, 'harəs\ *vb* **1** : disturb and impede by repeated raids **2** : annoy continually —**ha•rass•ment** *n*

har•bin•ger \'härbənjər\ *n* : one that announces or foreshadows what is coming

har•bor \-bər\ *n* : protected body of water suitable for anchorage ~ *vb* **1** : give refuge to **2** : hold as a thought or feeling

hard \'härd\ *adj* **1** : not easily penetrated **2** : firm or definite **3** : close or searching **4** : severe or unfeeling **5** : strenuous or difficult **6** : physically strong or intense —**hard** *adv* —**hard•ness** *n*

hard•en \'härdən\ *vb* : make or become hard or harder —**hard•en•er** *n*

hard•head•ed \ˌhärd'hedəd\ *adj* **1** : stubborn **2** : realistic —**hard•head•ed•ly** *adv* —**hard•head•ed•ness** *n*

hard–heart•ed \-'härtəd\ *adj* : lacking sympathy —**hard–heart•ed•ly** *adv* —**hard–heart•ed•ness** *n*

hard•ly \'härdlē\ *adv* **1** : only just **2** : certainly not

hard–nosed \-ˌnōzd\ *adj* : tough or uncompromising

hard•ship \-ˌship\ *n* : suffering or privation

hard•tack \-ˌtak\ *n* : hard biscuit

hard•ware *n* **1** : cutlery or tools made of metal **2** : physical components of a vehicle or apparatus

hard•wood *n* : wood of a broad-leaved usu. deciduous tree —**hardwood** *adj*

har•dy \'härdē\ *adj* **-di•er; -est** : able to withstand adverse conditions —**har•di•ly** *adv* —**har•di•ness** *n*

hare \'har\ *n, pl* **hare** *or* **hares** : long-eared mammal related to the rabbit

hare•brained \-ˌbrānd\ *adj* : foolish

hare•lip *n* : deformity in which the upper lip is vertically split —**harelipped** \-ˌlipt\ *adj*

ha•rem \'harəm\ *n* : house or part of a house allotted to women in a Muslim household or the women and servants occupying it

hark \'härk\ *vb* : listen

har•le•quin \'härlikən, -kwən\ *n* : clown

har•lot \'härlət\ *n* : prostitute

harm \'härm\ *n* **1** : physical or mental damage **2** : mischief ~ *vb* : cause harm —**harm•ful** \-fəl\ *adj* —**harmful•ly** *adv* —**harm•ful•ness** *n* —**harm•less** *adj* —**harm•less•ly** *adv* —**harm•less•ness** *n*

har•mon•ic \här'mänik\ *adj* **1** : of or relating to musical harmony **2** : pleasing to hear —**har•mon•i•cal•ly** \-iklē\ *adv*

har•mon•i•ca \här'mänikə\ *n* : small wind instrument with metallic reeds

har•mo•ny \'härmənē\ *n, pl* **-nies 1** : musical combination of sounds **2** : pleasing arrangement of parts **3** : lack of conflict **4** : internal calm —**har•mo•ni•ous** \här'mōnēəs\ *adj* —**har•mo•ni•ous•ly** *adv* —**har•mo•ni•ous•ness** *n* —**har•mo•ni•za•tion** \ˌhärmənə'zāshən\ *n* —**har•mo•nize** \'härməˌnīz\ *vb*

har•ness \'härnəs\ *n* : gear of a draft animal ~ *vb* **1** : put a harness on **2** : put to use

harp \'härp\ *n* : musical instrument with many strings plucked by the fingers ~ *vb* **1** : play on a harp **2** : dwell on a subject tiresomely —**harp•er** *n* —**harp•ist** *n*

har•poon \här'pün\ *n* : barbed spear used in hunting whales —**harpoon** *vb* —**har•poon•er** *n*

harp•si•chord \'härpsiˌkórd\ *n* : keyboard instrument with strings that are plucked

har•py \'härpē\ *n, pl* **-pies** : shrewish woman

har•row \'harō\ *n* : implement used to break up soil ~ *vb* **1** : cultivate with a harrow **2** : distress

har•ry \'harē\ *vb* **-ried; -ry•ing** : torment by or as if by constant attack

harsh \'härsh\ *adj* **1** : disagreeably rough **2** : severe —**harsh•ly** *adv* —**harsh•ness** *n*

har•um–scar•um \ˌharəm'skarəm\ *adv* : recklessly

har•vest \'härvəst\ *n* **1** : act or time of gathering in a crop **2** : mature crop —**harvest** *vb* —**har•vest•er** *n*

has *pres 3d sing of* HAVE

hash \'hash\ *vb* : chop into small pieces ~ *n* : chopped meat mixed with potatoes and browned

hasp \'hasp\ *n* : hinged strap fastener esp. for a door

has•sle \'hasəl\ *n* **1** : quarrel **2** : struggle **3** : cause of annoyance —**hassle** *vb*

has•sock \'hasək\ *n* : cushion used as a seat or leg rest

haste \'hāst\ *n* **1** : rapidity of motion **2** : rash action **3** : excessive eagerness —**hast•i•ly** \'hāstəlē\ *adv* —**hast•i•ness** \-stēnəs\ *n* —**hasty** \-stē\ *adj*

has•ten \'hāsən\ *vb* : hurry

hat \'hat\ *n* : covering for the head

1**hatch** \'hach\ *n* : small door or opening —**hatch•way** *n*

2**hatch** *vb* : emerge from an egg —**hatch•ery** \-ərē\ *n*

hatch•et \'hachət\ *n* : short-handled ax

hate \'hāt\ *n* : intense hostility and aversion ~ *vb* **hat•ed; hat•ing 1** : express or feel hate **2** : dislike —**hate•ful** \-fəl\ *adj* —**hate•ful•ly** *adv* —**hate•ful•ness** *n* —**hat•er** *n*

ha•tred \'hātrəd\ *n* : hate

hat•ter \'hatər\ *n* : one that makes or sells hats

haugh•ty \'hótē\ *adj* **-ti•er; -est** : disdainfully proud —**haugh•ti•ly** *adv* —**haugh•ti•ness** *n*

haul \'hól\ *vb* **1** : draw or pull **2** :transport or carry ~ *n* **1** : amount collected **2** : load or the distance it is transported —**haul•er** *n*

haunch \'hónch\ *n* : hip or hindquarter —usu. pl.

haunt \'hónt\ *vb* **1** : visit often **2** : visit or inhabit as a ghost ~ *n* : place frequented —**haunt•er** *n* —**haunt•ing•ly** *adv*

have \'hav, *in sense 2 before "to" usu* 'haf\ *vb* **had** \'had\; **hav•ing** \'haviŋ\; **has** \'haz, *in sense 2 before "to" usu* 'has\ **1** : hold in possession, service, or affection **2** : be compelled or forced to **3** —used as an auxiliary with the past participle to form the present perfect, past perfect, or future perfect **4** : obtain or receive **5** : undergo **6** : cause to **7** : bear —**have to do with** : have in the way of connection or relation with or effect on

ha•ven \'hāvən\ *n* : place of safety

hav•oc \'havək\ *n* **1** : wide destruction **2** : great confusion

1**hawk** \'hók\ *n* : bird of prey with a strong hooked bill and sharp talons

2**hawk** *vb* : offer for sale by calling out in the street —**hawk•er** *n*

haw•ser \'hózər\ *n* : large rope

haw•thorn \'hóˌthórn\ *n* : spiny shrub or tree with pink or white fragrant flowers

hay \'hā\ *n* : herbs (as grass) cut and dried for use as fodder —**hay** *vb* —**hay•loft** *n* —**hay•mow** \-ˌmaü\ *n* —**hay•stack** *n*

hay•cock \'hāˌkäk\ *n* : small pile of hay

hay•rick \-ˌrik\ *n* : large outdoor stack of hay

hay•seed \'hāˌsēd\ *n* : bumpkin

hay•wire *adj* : being out of order

haz•ard \'hazərd\ *n* **1** : source of danger **2** : chance ~ *vb*: venture or risk —**haz•ard•ous** *adj*

1**haze** \'hāz\ *n* : fine dust, smoke, or light vapor in the air that reduces visibility

2**haze** *vb* **hazed; haz•ing** : harass by abusive and humiliating tricks

ha•zel \'hāzəl\ *n* **1** : shrub or small tree bearing edible nuts (**ha•zel•nuts**) **2** : light brown color

hazy \'hāzē\ *adj* **haz•i•er; -est 1** : obscured by haze **2** : vague or indefinite —**haz•i•ly** *adv* —**haz•i•ness** *n*

he \'hē\ *pron* **1** : that male one **2** : a or the person

head \'hed\ *n* **1** : front or upper part of the body **2** : mind **3** : upper or higher end **4** : director or leader **5** : place of leadership or honor ~ *adj* : principal or chief ~ *vb* **1** : provide with or form a head **2** : put, stand, or be at the head **3** : point or proceed in a certain direction —**head•ache** *n* —**head•band** *n* —**head•dress** *n* —**head•ed** *adj* —**head•first** *adv or adj* —**head•gear** *n* —**head•less** *adj* —**head•rest** *n* —**head•ship** *n* —**head•wait•er** *n*

head•ing \-iŋ\ *n* **1** : direction in which a plane or ship heads **2** : something (as a title) standing at the top or beginning

head•land \'hedlənd, -ˌland\ *n* : promontory

head•light *n* : light on the front of a vehicle

head•line *n* : introductory line of a newspaper story printed in large type

head•long \-'lóŋ\ *adv* **1** : head foremost **2** : in a rash or reckless manner —**head•long** \-ˌlóŋ\ *adj*

head•mas•ter *n* : man who is head of a private school

head•mis•tress *n* : woman who is head of a private school

head–on *adj* : having the front facing in the direction of initial contact —**head–on** *adv*

head•phone *n* : an earphone held on by a band over the head—usu. pl.

head•quar•ters *n sing or pl* : command or administrative center

head•stone *n* : stone at the head of a grave

head•strong *adj* : stubborn or willful

head•wa•ters *n pl* : source of a stream

head•way *n* : forward motion

heady \'hedē\ *adj* **head•i•er; -est 1** : intoxicating **2** : shrewd

heal \'hēl\ *vb* : make or become sound or whole —**heal•er** *n*

health \'helth\ *n* : sound physical or mental condition

health•ful \-fəl\ *adj* : beneficial to health —**health•ful•ly** *adv* —**health•ful•ness** *n*

healthy \'helthē\ *adj* **health•i•er; -est** : enjoying or typical of good health —**health•i•ly** *adv* —**health•i•ness** *n*

heap \'hēp\ *n* : pile ~ *vb* : throw or lay in a heap

hear \'hir\ *vb* **heard** \'hərd\; **hear•ing** \'hiriŋ\ **1** : perceive by the ear **2** : heed **3** : learn

hear•ing *n* **1** : process or power of perceiving sound **2** : earshot **3** : session in which witnesses are heard

hear•ken \'härkən\ *vb* : give attention

hear•say *n* : rumor

hearse \'hərs\ *n* : vehicle for carrying the dead to the grave

heart \'härt\ *n* **1** : hollow muscular organ that keeps up the circulation of the blood **2** : playing card of a suit marked with a red heart **3** : whole personality or the emotional or moral part of it **4** : courage **5** : essential part —**heart•beat** *n* —**heart•ed** *adj*

heart•ache *n* : anguish of mind

heart•break *n* : crushing grief —**heart•break•er** *n* —**heart•break•ing** *adj* —**heart•bro•ken** *adj*

heart•burn *n* : burning distress in the heart area after eating

heart•en \'härtən\ *vb* : encourage

hearth \'härth\ *n* **1** : area in front of a fireplace **2** : home —**hearth•stone** *n*

heart•less \'härtləs\ *adj* : cruel

heart•rend•ing \-ˌrendiŋ\ *adj* : causing intense grief or anguish

heart•sick *adj* : very despondent —**heart•sick•ness** *n*

heart•strings *n pl* : deepest emotions

heart•throb *n* : sweetheart

heart•warm•ing *adj* : inspiring sympathetic feeling

heart•wood *n* : central portion of wood

hearty \ˈhärtē\ *adj* **heart•i•er; -est 1** : vigorously healthy **2** : nourishing —**heart•i•ly** *adv* —**heart•i•ness** *n*

heat \ˈhēt\ *vb* : make or become warm or hot ~ *n* **1** : condition of being hot **2** : form of energy that causes a body to rise in temperature **3** : intensity of feeling —**heat•ed•ly** *adv* —**heat•er** *n*

heath \ˈhēth\ *n* **1** : often evergreen shrubby plant of wet acid soils **2** : tract of wasteland —**heathy** *adj*

hea•then \ˈhēthən\ *n, pl* **-thens** *or* **-then** : uncivilized or godless person —**heathen** *adj*

heath•er \ˈhethər\ *n* : evergreen heath with lavender flowers —**heath•ery** *adj*

heat•stroke *n* : disorder that follows prolonged exposure to excessive heat

heave \ˈhēv\ *vb* **heaved** *or* **hove** \ˈhōv\; **heav•ing 1** : rise or lift upward **2** : throw **3** : rise and fall ~ *n* **1** : an effort to lift or raise **2** : throw

heav•en \ˈhevən\ *n* **1** *pl* : sky **2** : abode of the Deity and of the blessed dead **3** : place of supreme happiness —**heav•en•ly** *adj* —**heav•en•ward** *adv or adj*

heavy \ˈhevē\ *adj* **heavi•er; -est 1** : having great weight **2** : hard to bear **3** : greater than the average —**heav•i•ly** *adv* —**heavi•ness** *n* —**heavy•weight** *n*

heavy–du•ty *adj* : able to withstand unusual strain

heavy•set *adj* : stocky and compact in build

heck•le \ˈhekəl\ *vb* **-led; -ling** : harass with gibes —**heck•ler** \-ˈheklər\ *n*

hec•tic \ˈhektik\ *adj* : filled with excitement, activity, or confusion —**hec•ti•cal•ly** \-tiklē\ *adv*

hedge \ˈhej\ *n* **1** : fence or boundary of shrubs or small trees **2** : means of protection ~ *vb* **hedged; hedg•ing 1** : protect oneself against loss **2** : evade the risk of commitment —**hedg•er** *n*

hedge•hog *n* : spiny mammal (as a porcupine)

he•do•nism \ˈhēdᵊnˌizəm\ *n* : way of life devoted to pleasure —**he•do•nist** \-ᵊnist\ *n* —**he•do•nis•tic** \ˌhēdᵊnˈistik\ *adj*

heed \ˈhēd\ *vb* : pay attention ~ *n* : attention —**heed•ful** \-fəl\ *adj* —**heed•ful•ly** *adv* —**heed•ful•ness** *n* —**heed•less** *adj* —**heed•less•ly** *adv* —**heed•less•ness** *n*

[1]**heel** \ˈhēl\ *n* **1** : back of the foot **2** : crusty end of a loaf of bread **3** : solid piece forming the back of the sole of a shoe —**heelless** \ˈhēlləs\ *adj*

[2]**heel** *vb* : tilt to one side

heft \ˈheft\ *n* : weight ~ *vb* : judge the weight of by lifting

hefty \ˈheftē\ *adj* **heft•i•er; -est** : big and bulky

he•gem•o•ny \hiˈjemənē\ *n* : preponderant influence over others

heif•er \ˈhefər\ *n* : young cow

height \ˈhīt, ˈhītth\ *n* **1** : highest part or point **2** : distance from bottom to top **3** : altitude

height•en \ˈhītᵊn\ *vb* : increase in amount or degree

hei•nous \ˈhānəs\ *adj* : shockingly evil —**hei•nous•ly** *adv* —**hei•nous•ness** *n*

heir \ˈar\ *n* : one who inherits or is entitled to inherit property

heir•ess \ˈarəs\ *n* : female heir esp. to great wealth

heir•loom \ˈarˌlüm\ *n* : something handed on from one generation to another

held *past of* HOLD

he•li•cal \ˈhelikəl, ˈhē-\ *adj* : spiral

he•li•cop•ter \ˈheləˌkäptər, ˈhē-\ *n* : aircraft supported in the air by rotors

he•lio•trope \ˈhēlyəˌtrōp\ *n* : garden herb with small fragrant white or purple flowers

he•li•um \ˈhēlēəm\ *n* : very light nonflammable gaseous chemical element

he•lix \ˈhēliks\ *n, pl* **-li•ces** \ˈheləˌsēz, ˈhē-\ : something spiral

hell \ˈhel\ *n* **1** : nether world in which the dead continue to exist **2** : realm of the devil **3** : place or state of torment or destruction —**hell•ish** *adj*

hell•gram•mite \ˈhelgrəˌmīt\ *n* : aquatic insect larva

hel•lion \ˈhelyən\ *n* : troublesome person

hel•lo \həˈlō, he-\ *n, pl* **-los** : expression of greeting

helm \ˈhelm\ *n* : lever or wheel for steering a ship —**helms•man** \ˈhelmzmən\ *n*

hel•met \ˈhelmət\ *n* : protective covering for the head

help \ˈhelp\ *vb* **1** : supply what is needed **2** : be of use **3** : refrain from or prevent ~ *n* **1** : something that helps or a source of help **2** : one who helps another —**help•er** *n* —**help•ful** \-fəl\ *adj* —**help•ful•ly** *adv* —**help•ful•ness** *n* —**help•less** *adj* —**help•less•ly** *adv* —**help•less•ness** *n*

help•ing \ˈhelpiŋ\ *n* : portion of food

help•mate *n* **1** : helper **2** : wife

help•meet \-ˌmēt\ *n* : helpmate

hel•ter–skel•ter \ˌheltərˈskeltər\ *adv* : in total disorder

hem \ˈhem\ *n* : border of an article of cloth doubled back and stitched down ~ *vb* **-mm- 1** : sew a hem **2** : surround restrictively —**hem•line** *n*

he•ma•tol•o•gy \ˌhēməˈtäləjē\ *n* : study of the blood and blood-forming organs —**hema•to•log•ic** \-mətᵊlˈäjik\ *adj* —**hema•tol•o•gist** \-ˈtäləjist\ *n*

hemi•sphere \ˈheməˌsfir\ *n* : one of the halves of the earth divided by the equator into northern and southern parts (**northern hemisphere, southern hemisphere**) or by a meridian into eastern and western parts (**eastern hemisphere, western hemisphere**) —**hemi•spher•ic** \ˌheməˈsfirik, -ˈsfer-\, **hemi•spher•i•cal** \-ˈsfirikəl, -ˈsfer-\ *adj*

hem•lock \ˈhemˌläk\ *n* **1** : poisonous herb related to the carrot **2** : evergreen tree related to the pines

he•mo•glo•bin \ˈhēməˌglōbən\ *n* : iron-containing compound found in red blood cells

he•mo•phil•ia \ˌhēməˈfilēə\ *n* : hereditary tendency to severe prolonged bleeding —**he•mo•phil•i•ac** \-ēˌak\ *adj or n*

hem•or•rhage \ˈhemərij\ *n* : large discharge of blood —**hemorrhage** *vb* —**hem•or•rhag•ic** \ˌheməˈrajik\ *adj*

hem•or•rhoids \ˈheməˌròidz\ *n pl* : swollen mass of dilated veins at or just within the anus

hemp \ˈhemp\ *n* : tall Asian herb grown for its tough fiber —**hemp•en** \ˈhempən\ *adj*

hen \ˈhen\ *n* : female domestic fowl

hence \ˈhens\ *adv* **1** : away **2** : therefore **3** : from this source or origin

hence•forth *adv* : from this point on

hence•for•ward *adv* : henceforth

hench•man \ˈhenchmən\ *n* : trusted follower

hen•na \ˈhenə\ *n* : reddish brown dye from a tropical shrub used esp. on hair

hen•peck \ˈhenˌpek\ *vb* : subject (one's husband) to persistent nagging

he•pat•ic \hiˈpatik\ *adj* : relating to or resembling the liver

hep•a•ti•tis \ˌhepəˈtītəs\ *n, pl* **-tit•i•des** \-ˈtitəˌdēz\ : disease in which the liver becomes inflamed

her \ˈhər\ *adj* : of or relating to her or herself ~ \ər, (ˈ)hər\ *pron, objective case of* SHE

her•ald \ˈherəld\ *n* **1** : official crier or messenger **2** : harbinger ~ *vb* : give notice

her•ald•ry \ˈherəldrē\ *n, pl* **-ries** : practice of devising and granting stylized emblems (as for a family) —**he•ral•dic** \heˈraldik, hə-\ *adj*

herb \ˈərb, ˈhərb\ *n* **1** : seed plant that lacks woody tissue **2** : plant or plant part valued for medicinal or savory qualities —**herba•ceous** \ˌərˈbāshəs, ˌhər-\ *adj* —**herb•age** \ˈərbij, ˈhər-\ *n* —**herb•al** \-bəl\ *n or adj* —**herb•al•ist** \-bəlist\ *n*

her•bi•cide \ˈərbəˌsīd, ˈhər-\ *n* : agent that destroys plants —**her•bi•cid•al** \ˌərbəˈsīdᵊl, ˌhər-\ *adj*

her•biv•o•rous \ˌərˈbivərəs, ˌhər-\ *adj* : feeding on plants —**her•bi•vore** \ˈərbəˌvōr, ˈhər-\ *n*

her•cu•le•an \ˌhərkyəˈlēən, ˌhərˈkyülēən\ *adj* : of extraordinary power, size, or difficulty

herd \ˈhərd\ *n* : group of animals of one kind ~ *vb* : assemble or move in a herd —**herd•er** *n* —**herds•man** \ˈhərdzmən\ *n*

here \ˈhir\ *adv* **1** : in, at, or to this place **2** : now **3** : at or in this point or particular **4** : in the present life or state ~ *n* : this place —**here•abouts** \ˈhirəˌbaùts\, **here•about** \-ˌbaùt\ *adv*

here•af•ter *adv* : in some future time or state ~ *n* : existence beyond earthly life

here•by *adv* : by means of this

he•red•i•tary \həˈredəˌterē\ *adj* **1** : genetically passed or passable from parent to offspring **2** : passing by inheritance

he•red•i•ty \-ətē\ *n* : the passing of characteristics from parent to offspring

here•in *adv* : in this

here•of *adv* : of this

here•on *adv* : on this

her•e•sy \ˈherəsē\ *n, pl* **-sies** : opinion or doctrine contrary to church dogma —**her•e•tic** \-ˌtik\ *n* —**he•re•ti•cal** \həˈretikəl\ *adj*

here•to *adv* : to this document

here•to•fore \ˈhirtüˌfōr\ *adv* : up to this time

here•un•der *adv* : under this

here•un•to *adv* : to this

here•upon *adv* : on this

here•with *adv* **1** : with this **2** : hereby

her•i•tage \ˈherətij\ *n* **1** : inheritance **2** : birthright

her•maph•ro•dite \hərˈmafrəˌdīt\ *n* : animal or plant having both male and female reproductive organs —**hermaphrodite** *adj* —**her•maph•ro•dit•ic** \-ˌmafrəˈditik\ *adj*

her•met•ic \hərˈmetik\ *adj* : sealed airtight —**her•met•i•cal•ly** \-iklē\ *adv*

her•mit \ˈhərmət\ *n* : one who lives in solitude

her•nia \ˈhərnēə\ *n, pl* **-ni•as** *or* **-ni•ae** \-nēˌē, -nēˌī\ : protrusion of a bodily part through the weakened wall of its enclosure —**her•ni•ate** \-nēˌāt\ *vb*

he•ro \ˈhērō, ˈhirō\ *n, pl* **-roes** : one that is much admired or shows great courage —**he•ro•ic** \hiˈrōik\ *adj* —**he•ro•i•cal•ly** \-iklē\ *adv* —**he•ro•ics** \-iks\ *n pl* —**her•o•ism** \ˈherəˌwizəm\ *n*

her•o•in \ˈherəwən\ *n* : strongly addictive narcotic

her•o•ine \ˈherəwən\ *n* : woman of heroic achievements or qualities

her•on \ˈherən\ *n* : long-legged long-billed wading bird

her•pes \ˈhərpēz\ *n* : virus disease characterized by the formation of blisters

her•pe•tol•o•gy \ˌhərpəˈtäləjē\ *n* : study of reptiles and amphibians —**her•pe•tol•o•gist** \-pəˈtäləjist\ *n*

her•ring \ˈheriŋ\ *n, pl* **-ring** *or* **-rings** : narrow-bodied Atlantic food fish

hers \ˈhərz\ *pron* : one or the ones belonging to her

her•self \hərˈself\ *pron* : she, her —used reflexively or for emphasis

hertz \ˈherts, ˈhərts\ *n, pl* **hertz** : unit of frequency equal to one cycle per second

hes•i•tant \ˈhezətənt\ *adj* : tending to hesitate —**hes•i•tance** \-təns\ *n* —**hes•i•tan•cy** \-tənsē\ *n* —**hes•i•tant•ly** *adv*

hes•i•tate \ˈhezəˌtāt\ *vb* **-tat•ed; -tat•ing 1** : hold back esp. in doubt **2** : pause —**hes•i•ta•tion** \ˌhezəˈtāshən\ *n*

het•er•o•ge•neous \ˌhetərəˈjēnēəs, -nyəs\ *adj* : consisting of dissimilar ingredients or constituents —**het•er•o•ge•ne•ity** \-jəˈnēətē\ *n* —**het•ero•ge•neous•ly** *adv*

het•ero•sex•u•al \ˌhetərōˈsekshəwəl\ *adj* : oriented toward the opposite sex —**heterosexual** *n* —**het•ero•sex•u•al•i•ty** \-ˌsekshəˈwalətē\ *n*

hew \ˈhyü\ *vb* **hewed; hewed** *or* **hewn** \ˈhyün\; **hew•ing 1** : cut or shape with or as if with an ax **2** : conform strictly —**hew•er** *n*

hex \ˈheks\ *vb* : put an evil spell on —**hex** *n*

hexa•gon \ˈheksəˌgän\ *n* : 6-sided polygon —**hex•ag•o•nal** \hekˈsagənᵊl\ *adj*

hey•day \ˈhāˌdā\ *n* : time of flourishing

hi•a•tus \hīˈātəs\ *n* : lapse in continuity

hi•ba•chi \hiˈbächē\ *n* : brazier

hi•ber•nate \ˈhībərˌnāt\ *vb* **-nat•ed; -nat•ing** : pass the winter in a torpid or resting state —**hi•ber•na•tion** \ˌhībərˈnāshən\ *n* —**hi•ber•na•tor** \ˈhībərˌnātər\ *n*

hic•cup \ˈhikəp\ *vb* **-cuped; -cup•ing** : to inhale spasmodically and make a peculiar sound ~ *n pl* : attack of hiccuping

hick \ˈhik\ *n* : awkward provincial person —**hick** *adj*

hick•o•ry \ˈhikərē\ *n, pl* **-ries** : No. American hardwood tree —**hickory** *adj*

[1]**hide** \ˈhīd\ *vb* **hid** \ˈhid\; **hid•den** \ˈhidᵊn\ *or* **hid; hid•ing** : put or remain out of sight —**hid•er** *n*

[2]**hide** *n* : animal skin

hide•bound \ˈhīdˌbaùnd\ *adj* : inflexible or conservative

hid•eous \ˈhidēəs\ *adj* : very ugly —**hid•eous•ly** *adv* —**hid•eous•ness** *n*

hie \ˈhī\ *vb* **hied; hy•ing** *or* **hie•ing** : hurry

hi•er•ar•chy \ˈhīəˌrärkē\ *n, pl* **-chies** : persons or things arranged in a graded series —**hi•er•ar•chi•cal** \ˌhīəˈrärkikəl\ *adj*

hi•er•o•glyph•ic \ˌhīərəˈglifik\ *n* : character in the picture writing of the ancient Egyptians

high \ˈhī\ *adj* **1** : having large extension upward **2** : elevated in pitch **3** : exalted in character **4** : of greater degree or amount than average **5** : expensive **6** : excited or stupefied by alcohol or a drug ~ *adv* : at or to a high place or degree ~ *n* **1** : elevated point or level **2** : automobile gear giving the highest speed —**high•ly** *adv*

high•boy *n* : high chest of drawers on legs

high•brow \-ˌbraù\ *n* : person of superior learning or culture —**highbrow** *adj*

high–flown *adj* : pretentious

high–hand•ed *adj* : willful and arrogant —**high–hand•ed•ly** *adv* —**high–hand•ed•ness** *n*

high•land \ˈhīlənd\ *n* : hilly country —**high•land•er** \-ləndər\ *n*

high•light *n* : event or detail of major importance ~ *vb* **1** : emphasize **2** : be a highlight of

high•ness \-nəs\ *n* **1** : quality or degree of being high **2** —used as a title (as for kings)

high–rise *adj* : having several stories

high school *n* : school usu. including grades 9 to 12 or 10 to 12

high–spir•it•ed *adj* : lively

high–strung \ˌhīˈstrəŋ\ *adj* : very nervous or sensitive

high•way *n* : public road

high•way•man \-mən\ *n* : one who robs travelers on a road

hi•jack \ˈhīˌjak\ *vb* : steal esp. by commandeering a vehicle —**hijack** *n* —**hi•jack•er** *n*

hike \ˈhīk\ *vb* **hiked; hik•ing 1** : raise quickly **2** : take a long walk ~ *n* **1** : long walk **2** : increase —**hik•er** *n*

hi•lar•i•ous \hiˈlarēəs, hīˈ-\ *adj* : extremely funny —**hi•lar•i•ous•ly** *adv* —**hi•lar•i•ty** \-ətē\ *n*

hill \ˈhil\ *n* : place where the land rises —**hill•side** *n* —**hill•top** *n* —**hilly** *adj*

hill•bil•ly \ˈhilˌbilē\ *n, pl* **-lies** : person from a backwoods area

hill•ock \ˈhilək\ *n* : small hill

hilt \ˈhilt\ *n* : handle of a sword

him \ˈhim\ *pron, objective case of* HE

him•self \himˈself\ *pron* : he, him —used reflexively or for emphasis

[1]**hind** \ˈhīnd\ *n* : female deer

[2]**hind** *adj* : back

hin•der \ˈhindər\ *vb* : obstruct or hold back

hind•most *adj* : farthest to the rear

hind•quar•ter *n* : back half of a complete side of a carcass

hin•drance \ˈhindrəns\ *n* : something that hinders

hind•sight *n* : understanding of an event after it has happened

Hin•du•ism \ˈhindüˌizəm\ *n* : body of religious beliefs and practices native to India —**Hin•du** *n or adj*

hinge \ˈhinj\ *n* : jointed piece on which a swinging part (as a door) turns ~ *vb* **hinged; hing•ing 1** : attach by or furnish with hinges **2** : depend

hint \ˈhint\ *n* **1** : indirect suggestion **2** : clue **3** : very small amount —**hint** *vb*

hin•ter•land \ˈhintərˌland\ *n* : remote region

hip \ˈhip\ *n* : part of the body on either side just below the waist —**hip•bone** *n*

hip•po•pot•a•mus \ˌhipəˈpätəməs\ *n, pl* **-mus•es** *or* **-mi** \-ˌmī\ : large thick-skinned African river animal

hire \ˈhīr\ *n* **1** : payment for labor **2** : employment **3** : one who is hired ~ *vb* **hired; hir•ing** : employ for pay

hire•ling \-liŋ\ *n* : one who serves another only for gain

hir•sute \ˈhərˌsüt, ˈhir-\ *adj* : hairy

his \ˈhiz\ *adj* : of or belonging to him ~ *pron* : ones belonging to him

hiss \ˈhis\ *vb* **1** : make a sibilant sound **2** : show dislike by hissing —**hiss** *n*

his•to•ri•an \hisˈtōrēən\ *n* : writer of history

his•to•ry \ˈhistərē\ *n, pl* **-ries 1** : chronological record of significant events **2** : study of past events **3** : an established record —**his•tor•ic** \hisˈtòrik\, **his•tor•i•cal** \-ikəl\ *adj* —**his•tor•i•cal•ly** \-klē\ *adv*

his•tri•on•ics \ˌhistrēˈäniks\ *n pl* : exaggerated display of emotion

hit \ˈhit\ *vb* **hit; hit•ting 1** : reach with a blow **2** : come or cause to come in contact **3** : affect detrimentally ~ *n* **1** : blow **2** : great success —**hit•ter** *n*

hitch \ˈhich\ *vb* **1** : move by jerks **2** : catch by a hook **3** : hitchhike ~ *n* **1** : jerk **2** : sudden halt

hitch•hike \ˈhichˌhīk\ *vb* : travel by securing free rides from passing vehicles —**hitch•hik•er** *n*

hith•er \ˈhithər\ *adv* : to this place

hith•er•to \-ˌtü\ *adv* : up to this time

hive \ˈhīv\ *n* **1** : container housing honeybees **2** : colony of bees —**hive** *vb*

hives \ˈhīvz\ *n sing or pl* : allergic disorder with itchy skin patches

HMO \ˌāchˌemˈō\ *n* : comprehensive health-care organization financed by clients

hoard \ˈhōrd\ *n* : hidden accumulation —**hoard** *vb* —**hoard•er** *n*

hoar•frost \ˈhōrˌfròst\ *n* : frost

hoarse \ˈhōrs\ *adj* **hoars•er; -est 1** : harsh in sound **2** : speaking in a harsh strained voice —**hoarse•ly** *adv* —**hoarse•ness** *n*

hoary \ˈhōrē\ *adj* **hoar•i•er; -est** : gray or white with age —**hoar•i•ness** *n*

hoax \ˈhōks\ *n* : act intended to trick or dupe —**hoax** *vb* —**hoax•er** *n*

hob•ble \ˈhäbəl\ *vb* **-bled; -bling** : limp along ~ *n* : hobbling movement

hob•by \ˈhäbē\ *n, pl* **-bies** : interest engaged in for relaxation —**hob•by•ist** \-ēist\ *n*

hob•gob•lin \ˈhäbˌgäblən\ *n* **1** : mischievous goblin **2** : bogey

hob•nail \-ˌnāl\ *n* : short nail for studding shoe soles —**hob•nailed** \-ˌnāld\ *adj*

hob•nob \-ˌnäb\ *vb* **-bb-** : associate socially

ho•bo \ˈhōbō\ *n, pl* **-boes** : tramp

[1]**hock** \ˈhäk\ *n* : joint or region in the hind limb of a quadruped corresponding to the human ankle

[2]**hock** *n or vb* : pawn

hock•ey \ˈhäkē\ *n* : game played on ice or a field by 2 teams

hod \ˈhäd\ *n* : carrier for bricks or mortar

hodge•podge \ˈhäjˌpäj\ *n* : heterogeneous mixture

hoe \ˈhō\ *n* : long-handled tool for cultivating or weeding —**hoe** *vb*

hog \ˈhòg, ˈhäg\ *n* **1** : domestic adult swine **2** : glutton ~ *vb* : take selfishly —**hog•gish** *adj*

hogs•head \ˈhògzˌhed, ˈhägz-\ *n* : large cask or barrel

hog•wash *n* : nonsense

hoist \'hȯist\ *vb* **:** lift ~ *n* **1 :** lift **2 :** apparatus for hoisting
hok•ey \'hōkē\ *adj* **hok•i•er; -est 1 :** tiresomely simple or sentimental **2 :** phony
[1]hold \'hōld\ *vb* **held** \'held\; **hold•ing 1 :** possess **2 :** restrain **3 :** have a grasp on **4 :** remain or keep in a particular situation or position **5 :** contain **6 :** regard **7 :** cause to occur **8 :** occupy esp. by appointment or election ~ *n* **1 :** act or manner of holding **2 :** restraining or controlling influence **—hold•er** *n* **—hold forth :** speak at length **—hold to :** adhere to **—hold with :** agree with
[2]hold *n* **:** cargo area of a ship
hold•ing \'hōldiŋ\ *n* **:** property owned —usu. pl.
hold•up *n* **1 :** robbery at the point of a gun **2 :** delay
hole \'hōl\ *n* **1 :** opening into or through something **2 :** hollow place (as a pit) **3 :** den **—hole** *vb*
hol•i•day \'hälə,dā\ *n* **1 :** day of freedom from work **2 :** vacation **—holiday** *vb*
ho•li•ness \'hōlēnəs\ *n* **:** quality or state of being holy—used as a title for a high religious official
ho•lis•tic \hō'listik\ *adj* **:** relating to a whole (as the body)
hol•ler \'hälər\ *vb* **:** cry out **—holler** *n*
hol•low \'hälō\ *adj* **-low•er** \-əwər\; **-est 1 :** sunken **2 :** having a cavity within **3 :** sounding like a noise made in an empty place **4 :** empty of value or meaning ~ *vb* **:** make or become hollow ~ *n* **1 :** surface depression **2 :** cavity **—hol•low•ness** *n*
hol•ly \'hälē\ *n, pl* **-lies :** evergreen tree or shrub with glossy leaves
hol•ly•hock \-,häk, -,hȯk\ *n* **:** tall perennial herb with showy flowers
ho•lo•caust \'hälə,kȯst, 'hō-, 'hȯ-\ *n* **:** thorough destruction esp. by fire
hol•stein \'hōl,stēn, -,stīn\ *n* **:** large black-and-white dairy cow
hol•ster \'hōlstər\ *n* **:** case for a pistol
ho•ly \'hōlē\ *adj* **-li•er; -est 1 :** sacred **2 :** spiritually pure
hom•age \'ämij, 'hä-\ *n* **:** reverent regard
home \'hōm\ *n* **1 :** residence **2 :** congenial environment **3 :** place of origin or refuge ~ *vb* **homed; hom•ing :** go or return home **—home•bred** *adj* **—home•com•ing** *n* **—home•grown** *adj* **—home•land** \-,land\ *n* **—home•less** *adj* **—home•made** \-'mād\ *adj*
home•ly \-lē\ *adj* **-li•er; -est :** plain or unattractive **—home•li•ness** *n*
home•mak•er *n* **:** one who manages a household **—home•mak•ing** *n*
home•sick *adj* **:** longing for home **—home•sick•ness** *n*
home•spun \-,spən\ *adj* **:** simple
home•stead \-,sted\ *n* **:** home and land occupied and worked by a family **—home•stead•er** \-ər\ *n*
home•stretch *n* **1 :** last part of a racetrack **2 :** final stage
home•ward \-wərd\, **home•wards** \-wərdz\ *adv* **:** toward home **—homeward** *adj*
home•work *n* **:** school lessons to be done outside the classroom
hom•ey \'hōmē\ *adj* **hom•i•er; -est :** characteristic of home
ho•mi•cide \'hämə,sīd, 'hō-\ *n* **:** the killing of one human being by another **—hom•i•cid•al** \,hämə'sīdᵊl, ,hō-\ *adj*
hom•i•ly \'häməlē\ *n, pl* **-lies :** sermon
hom•i•ny \'hämənē\ *n* **:** type of processed hulled corn
ho•mo•ge•neous \,hōmə'jēnēəs, -nyəs\ *adj* **:** of the same or a similar kind **—ho•mo•ge•ne•i•ty** \-jə'nēətē\ *n* **—ho•mo•ge•neous•ly** *adv*
ho•mog•e•nize \hō'mäjə,nīz, hə-\ *vb* **-nized; -niz•ing :** make the particles in (as milk) of uniform size and even distribution **—ho•mog•e•ni•za•tion** \-,mäjənə'zāshən\ *n* **—ho•mog•e•niz•er** *n*
ho•mo•graph \'hämə,graf, 'hō-\ *n* **:** one of 2 or more words (as the noun *conduct* and the verb *conduct*) spelled alike but different in origin or meaning or pronunciation
hom•onym \'hämə,nim, 'hō-\ *n* **1 :** homophone **2 :** homograph **3 :** one of 2 or more words (as *pool* of water and *pool* the game) spelled and pronounced alike but different in meaning
ho•mo•phone \'hämə,fōn, 'hō-\ *n* **:** one of 2 or more words (as *to, too,* and *two*) pronounced alike but different in origin or meaning or spelling
Ho•mo sa•pi•ens \,hōmō'sapēənz, -'sā-\ *n* **:** humankind
ho•mo•sex•u•al \,hōmə'sekshəwəl\ *adj* **:** oriented toward one's own sex **—ho•mosexual** *n* **—ho•mo•sex•u•al•i•ty** \-,sekshə'walətē\ *n*
hone \'hōn\ *vb* **:** sharpen with or as if with an abrasive stone
hon•est \'änəst\ *adj* **1 :** free from deception **2 :** trustworthy **3 :** frank **—hon•est•ly** *adv* **—hon•esty** \-əstē\ *n*
hon•ey \'hənē\ *n, pl* **-eys :** sweet sticky substance made by bees (**hon•ey•bees**) from the nectar of flowers
hon•ey•comb *n* **:** mass of 6-sided wax cells built by honeybees or something like it ~ *vb* **:** make or become full of holes like a honeycomb
hon•ey•moon *n* **:** holiday taken by a newly married couple **—honeymoon** *vb*
hon•ey•suck•le \-,səkəl\ *n* **:** shrub or vine with flowers rich in nectar
honk \'häŋk, 'hȯŋk\ *n* **:** cry of a goose or a similar sound **—honk** *vb* **—honk•er** *n*
hon•or \'änər\ *n* **1 :** good name **2 :** outward respect or symbol of this **3 :** privilege **4 :** person of superior rank or position —used esp. as a title **5 :** something or someone worthy of respect **6 :** integrity ~ *vb* **1 :** regard with honor **2 :** confer honor on **3 :** fulfill the terms of **—hon•or•able** \'änərəbəl\ *adj* **—hon•or•ably** \-blē\ *adv* **—hon•or•ari•ly** \,änə'rerəlē\ *adv* **—hon•or•ary** \'änə,rerē\ *adj* **—hon•or•ee** \,änə'rē\ *n*
hood \'hu̇d\ *n* **1 :** part of a garment that covers the head **2 :** covering over an automobile engine compartment **—hood•ed** *adj*
-hood \,hu̇d\ *n suffix* **1 :** state, condition, or quality **2 :** individuals sharing a state or character
hood•lum \'hu̇dləm, 'hüd-\ *n* **:** thug
hood•wink \'hu̇d,wiŋk\ *vb* **:** deceive
hoof \'hu̇f, 'hüf\ *n, pl* **hooves** \'hu̇vz, 'hüvz\ *or* **hoofs :** horny covering of the toes of some mammals (as horses or cattle) **—hoofed** \'hu̇ft, 'hüft\ *adj*
hook \'hu̇k\ *n* **:** curved or bent device for catching, holding, or pulling ~ *vb* **:** seize or make fast with a hook **—hook•er** *n*
hook•worm *n* **:** parasitic intestinal worm
hoo•li•gan \'hüligən\ *n* **:** thug
hoop \'hüp\ *n* **:** circular strip, figure, or object
hoot \'hüt\ *vb* **1 :** shout in contempt **2 :** make the cry of an owl **—hoot** *n* **—hoot•er** *n*
[1]hop \'häp\ *vb* **-pp- :** move by quick springy leaps **—hop** *n*
[2]hop *n* **:** vine whose ripe dried flowers are used to flavor malt liquors
hope \'hōp\ *vb* **hoped; hop•ing :** desire with expectation of fulfillment ~ *n* **1 :** act of hoping **2 :** something hoped for **—hope•ful** \-fəl\ *adj* **—hope•ful•ly** *adv* **—hope•ful•ness** *n* **—hope•less** *adj* **—hope•less•ly** *adv* **—hope•less•ness** *n*
hop•per \'häpər\ *n* **:** container that releases its contents through the bottom
horde \'hōrd\ *n* **:** throng or swarm
ho•ri•zon \hə'rīzᵊn\ *n* **:** apparent junction of earth and sky
hor•i•zon•tal \,hȯrə'zäntᵊl\ *adj* **:** parallel to the horizon **—hor•i•zon•tal•ly** *adv*
hor•mone \'hȯr,mōn\ *n* **:** cell product in body fluids that has a specific effect on other cells **—hor•mon•al** \hȯr'mōnᵊl\ *adj*
horn \'hȯrn\ *n* **1 :** hard bony projection on the head of a hoofed animal **2 :** brass wind instrument **—horned** *adj* **—horn•less** *adj*
hor•net \'hȯrnət\ *n* **:** large social wasp
horny \'hȯrnē\ *adj* **horn•i•er; -est 1 :** made of horn **2 :** hard or callous **3 :** sexually aroused
horo•scope \'hȯrə,skōp\ *n* **:** astrological forecast
hor•ren•dous \hȯ'rendəs\ *adj* **:** horrible
hor•ri•ble \'hȯrəbəl\ *adj* **1 :** having or causing horror **2 :** highly disagreeable **—hor•ri•ble•ness** *n* **—hor•ri•bly** \-blē\ *adv*
hor•rid \'hȯrəd\ *adj* **:** horrible **—hor•rid•ly** *adv*
hor•ri•fy \'hȯrə,fī\ *vb* **-fied; -fy•ing :** cause to feel horror
hor•ror \'hȯrər\ *n* **1 :** intense fear, dread, or dismay **2 :** intense repugnance **3 :** something horrible
hors d'oeuvre \ȯr'dərv\ *n, pl* **hors d'oeuvres** \-'dərvz\ **:** appetizer
horse \'hȯrs\ *n* **:** large solid-hoofed domesticated mammal **—horse•back** *n or adv* **—horse•hair** *n* **—horse•hide** *n* **—horse•less** *adj* **—horse•man** \-mən\ *n* **—horse•man•ship** *n* **—horse•wom•an** *n* **—hors•ey, horsy** *adj*
horse•fly *n* **:** large fly with bloodsucking female
horse•play *n* **:** rough boisterous play
horse•pow•er *n* **:** unit of mechanical power
horse•rad•ish *n* **:** herb with a pungent root used as a condiment
horse•shoe *n* **:** U-shaped protective metal plate fitted to the rim of a horse's hoof
hor•ti•cul•ture \'hȯrtə,kəlchər\ *n* **:** science of growing fruits, vegetables, and flowers **—hor•ti•cul•tur•al** \,hȯrtə'kəlchərəl\ *adj* **—hor•ti•cul•tur•ist** \-rist\ *n*
ho•san•na \hō'zanə, -'zän-\ *interj* —used as a cry of acclamation and adoration **—hosanna** *n*
hose \'hōz\ *n* **1** *pl* **hose :** stocking or sock **2** *pl* **hos•es :** flexible tube for conveying fluids ~ *vb* **hosed; hos•ing :** spray, water, or wash with a hose
ho•siery \'hōzhərē, 'hōzə-\ *n* **:** stockings or socks
hos•pice \'häspəs\ *n* **1 :** lodging (as for travelers) maintained by a religious order **2 :** facility or program for caring for dying persons
hos•pi•ta•ble \hä'spitəbəl, 'häs,pit-\ *adj* **:** given to generous and cordial reception of guests **—hos•pi•ta•bly** \-blē\ *adv*
hos•pi•tal \'häs,pitᵊl\ *n* **:** institution where the sick or injured receive medical care **—hos•pi•tal•i•za•tion** \,häs,pitᵊlə'zāshən\ *n* **—hos•pi•tal•ize** \'häs,pitᵊl,īz\ *vb*
hos•pi•tal•i•ty \,häspə'talətē\ *n, pl* **-ties :** hospitable treatment, reception, or disposition
[1]host \'hōst\ *n* **1 :** army **2 :** multitude
[2]host *n* **:** one who receives or entertains guests **—host** *vb*
[3]host *n* **:** eucharistic bread
hos•tage \'hästij\ *n* **:** person held to guarantee that promises be kept or demands met
hos•tel \'hästᵊl\ *n* **:** lodging for youth **—hos•tel•er** *n*
hos•tel•ry \-rē\ *n, pl* **-ries :** hotel
host•ess \'hōstəs\ *n* **:** woman who is host
hos•tile \'hästᵊl, -,tīl\ *adj* **:** openly or actively unfriendly or opposed to someone or something **—hostile** *n* **—hos•tile•ly** *adv* **—hos•til•i•ty** \häs'tilətē\ *n*
hot \'hät\ *adj* **-tt- 1 :** having a high temperature **2 :** giving a sensation of heat or burning **3 :** ardent **4 :** pungent **—hot** *adv* **—hot•ly** *adv* **—hot•ness** *n*
hot•bed *n* **:** environment that favors rapid growth
hot dog *n* **:** frankfurter
ho•tel \hō'tel\ *n* **:** building where lodging and personal services are provided
hot•head•ed *adj* **:** impetuous **—hot•head** *n* **—hot•head•ed•ly** *adv* **—hot•head•ed•ness** *n*
hot•house *n* **:** greenhouse
hound \'hau̇nd\ *n* **:** long-eared hunting dog ~ *vb* **:** pursue relentlessly
hour \'au̇r\ *n* **1 :** 24th part of a day **2 :** time of day **—hour•ly** *adv or adj*
hour•glass *n* **:** glass vessel for measuring time
house \'hau̇s\ *n, pl* **hous•es** \'hau̇zəz\ **1 :** building to live in **2 :** household **3 :** legislative body **4 :** business firm ~ \'hau̇z\ *vb* **housed; hous•ing :** provide with or take shelter **—house•boat** \'hau̇s,bōt\ *n* **—house•clean** \'hau̇s,klēn\ *vb* **—house•cleaning** *n* **—house•ful** \-,fu̇l\ *n* **—house•maid** *n* **—house•wares** *n pl* **—house•work** *n*
house•bro•ken \-,brōkən\ *adj* **:** trained in excretory habits acceptable in indoor living
house•fly *n* **:** two-winged fly common about human habitations
house•hold \-,hōld\ *n* **:** those who dwell as a family under the same roof ~ *adj* **1 :** domestic **2 :** common or familiar **—house•hold•er** *n*
house•keep•ing \-,kēpiŋ\ *n* **:** care and management of a house or institution **—house•keep•er** *n*
house•warm•ing *n* **:** party to celebrate moving into a house
house•wife \'hau̇s,wīf\ *n* **:** married woman in charge of a household **—house•wife•ly** *adj* **—house•wif•ery** \-,wīfərē\ *n*
hous•ing \'hau̇ziŋ\ *n* **1 :** dwellings for people **2 :** protective covering
hove *past of* HEAVE
hov•el \'həvəl, 'häv-\ *n* **:** small wretched house
hov•er \'həvər, 'häv-\ *vb* **1 :** remain suspended in the air **2 :** move about in the vicinity
how \'hau̇\ *adv* **1 :** in what way or condition **2 :** for what reason **3 :** to what extent ~ *conj* **:** the way or manner in which
how•ev•er \hau̇'evər\ *conj* **:** in whatever manner ~ *adv* **1 :** to whatever degree or in whatever manner **2 :** in spite of that
how•it•zer \'hau̇ətsər\ *n* **:** short cannon
howl \'hau̇l\ *vb* **:** emit a loud long doleful sound like a dog **—howl** *n* **—howl•er** *n*
hoy•den \'hȯidᵊn\ *n* **:** girl or woman of saucy or carefree behavior
hub \'həb\ *n* **:** central part of a circular object (as of a wheel) **—hub•cap** *n*
hub•bub \'həb,əb\ *n* **:** uproar
hu•bris \'hyübrəs\ *n* **:** excessive pride
huck•le•ber•ry \'həkəl,berē\ *n* **1 :** shrub related to the blueberry or its berry **2 :** blueberry
huck•ster \'həkstər\ *n* **:** peddler
hud•dle \'hədᵊl\ *vb* **-dled; -dling 1 :** crowd together **2 :** confer **—huddle** *n*
hue \'hyü\ *n* **:** color or gradation of color **—hued** \'hyüd\ *adj*
huff \'həf\ *n* **:** fit of pique **—huffy** *adj*
hug \'həg\ *vb* **-gg- 1 :** press tightly in the arms **2 :** stay close to **—hug** *n*
huge \'hyüj\ *adj* **hug•er; hug•est :** very large or extensive **—huge•ly** *adv* **—huge•ness** *n*
hu•la \'hülə\ *n* **:** Polynesian dance
hulk \'həlk\ *n* **1 :** bulky or unwieldy person or thing **2 :** old ship unfit for service **—hulk•ing** *adj*
hull \'həl\ *n* **1 :** outer covering of a fruit or seed **2 :** frame or body of a ship or boat ~ *vb* **:** remove the hulls of **—hull•er** *n*
hul•la•ba•loo \'hələbə,lü\ *n, pl* **-loos :** uproar
hum \'həm\ *vb* **-mm- 1 :** make a prolonged sound like that of the speech sound \m\ **2 :** be busily active **3 :** run smoothly **4 :** sing with closed lips **—hum** *n* **—hum•mer** *n*
hu•man \'hyümən, 'yü-\ *adj* **1 :** of or relating to the species people belong to **2 :** by, for, or like people **—human** *n* **—hu•man•kind** *n* **—hu•man•ly** *adv* **—hu•man•ness** *n*
hu•mane \hyü'mān, ,yü-\ *adj* **:** showing compassion or consideration for others **—hu•mane•ly** *adv* **—hu•mane•ness** *n*
hu•man•ism \'hyümə,nizəm, 'yü-\ *n* **:** doctrine or way of life centered on human interests or values **—hu•man•ist** \-nist\ *n or adj* **—hu•man•is•tic** \,hyümə'nistik, ,yü-\ *adj*
hu•man•i•tar•i•an \hyü,manə'terēən, yü-\ *n* **:** person promoting human welfare **—humanitarian** *adj* **—hu•man•i•tari•an•ism** *n*
hu•man•i•ty \hyü'manətē, yü-\ *n, pl* **-ties 1 :** human or humane quality or state **2 :** the human race
hu•man•ize \'hyümə,nīz, 'yü-\ *vb* **-ized; -iz•ing :** make human or humane **—hu•man•iza•tion** \,hyümənə'zāshən, ,yü-\ *n* **—hu•man•iz•er** *n*
hu•man•oid \'hyümə,nȯid, 'yü-\ *adj* **:** having human form **—humanoid** *n*
hum•ble \'həmbəl\ *adj* **-bler; -blest 1 :** not proud or haughty **2 :** not pretentious ~ *vb* **-bled; -bling :** make humble **—hum•ble•ness** *n* **—hum•bler** *n* **—hum•bly** \-blē\ *adv*
hum•bug \'həm,bəg\ *n* **:** nonsense
hum•drum \-,drəm\ *adj* **:** monotonous
hu•mid \'hyüməd, 'yü-\ *adj* **:** containing or characterized by moisture **—hu•mid•i•fi•ca•tion** \hyü,midəfə'kāshən\ *n* **—hu•mid•i•fi•er** \-'midə,fīər\ *n* **—hu•mid•i•fy** \-,fī\ *vb* **—hu•mid•ly** *adv*
hu•mid•i•ty \hyü'midətē, yü-\ *n, pl* **-ties :** atmospheric moisture
hu•mi•dor \'hyümə,dȯr, 'yü-\ *n* **:** humidified storage case (as for cigars)
hu•mil•i•ate \hyü'milē,āt, yü-\ *vb* **-at•ed; -at•ing :** injure the self-respect of **—hu•mil•i•at•ing•ly** *adv* **—hu•mil•i•ation** \-,milē'āshən\ *n*
hu•mil•i•ty \hyü'milətē, yü-\ *n* **:** humble quality or state
hum•ming•bird \'həmiŋ,bərd\ *n* **:** tiny American bird that can hover
hum•mock \'həmək\ *n* **:** mound or knoll **—hum•mocky** \-məkē\ *adj*
hu•mor \'hyümər, 'yü-\ *n* **1 :** mood **2 :** quality of being laughably ludicrous or incongruous **3 :** appreciation of what is ludicrous or incongruous **4 :** something intended to be funny ~ *vb* **:** comply with the wishes or mood of **—hu•mor•ist** \-ərist\ *n* **—hu•mor•less** *adj* **—hu•mor•less•ly** *adv* **—hu•mor•less•ness** *n* **—hu•mor•ous** \'hyümərəs, 'yü-\ *adj* **—hu•mor•ous•ly** *adv* **—hu•mor•ous•ness** *n*
hump \'həmp\ *n* **:** rounded protuberance **—humped** *adj*
hump•back *n* **:** hunchback **—humpbacked** *adj*
hu•mus \'hyüməs, 'yü-\ *n* **:** dark organic part of soil
hunch \'hənch\ *vb* **:** assume or cause to assume a bent or crooked posture ~ *n* **:** strong intuitive feeling
hunch•back *n* **1 :** back with a hump **2 :** person with a crooked back **—hunch•backed** *adj*
hun•dred \'həndrəd\ *n, pl* **-dreds** *or* **-dred :** 10 times 10 **—hundred** *adj* **—hun•dredth** \-drədth\ *adj or n*
[1]hung *past of* HANG
[2]hung *adj* **:** unable to reach a verdict
hun•ger \'həŋgər\ *n* **1 :** craving or urgent need for food **2 :** strong desire **—hunger** *vb* **—hun•gri•ly** \-grəlē\ *adv* **—hun•gry** *adj*
hunk \'həŋk\ *n* **:** large piece
hun•ker \'həŋkər\ *vb* **:** settle in for a sustained period—used with *down*
hunt \'hənt\ *vb* **1 :** pursue for food or sport **2 :** try to find ~ *n* **:** act or instance of hunting **—hunt•er** *n*
hur•dle \'hərdᵊl\ *n* **1 :** barrier to leap over in a race **2 :** obstacle **—hurdle** *vb* **—hur•dler** *n*
hurl \'hərl\ *vb* **:** throw with violence **—hurl** *n* **—hurl•er** *n*
hur•rah \hu̇'rä, -'rȯ\ *interj* —used to express joy or approval
hur•ri•cane \'hərə,kān\ *n* **:** tropical storm with winds of 74 miles per hour or greater
hur•ry \'hərē\ *vb* **-ried; -ry•ing :** go or cause to go with haste ~ *n* **:** extreme haste **—hur•ried•ly** *adv* **—hur•ried•ness** *n*

hurt \'hərt\ *vb* **hurt; hurt•ing 1 :** feel or cause pain **2 :** do harm to ~ *n* **1 :** bodily injury **2 :** harm **—hurt•ful** \-fəl\ *adj* **—hurt•ful•ness** *n*

hur•tle \'hərtəl\ *vb* **-tled; -tling :** move rapidly or forcefully

hus•band \'həzbənd\ *n* **:** married man ~ *vb* **:** manage prudently

hus•band•ry \-bəndrē\ *n* **1 :** careful use **2 :** agriculture

hush \'həsh\ *vb* **:** make or become quiet ~ *n* **:** silence

husk \'həsk\ *n* **:** outer covering of a seed or fruit ~ *vb* **:** strip the husk from **—husk•er** *n*

1**hus•ky** \'həskē\ *adj* **-ki•er; -est :** hoarse **—hus•ki•ly** *adv* **—hus•ki•ness** *n*

2**husky** *adj* **-ki•er; -est :** burly **—husk•i•ness** *n*

3**husky** *n, pl* **-kies :** working dog of the arctic

hus•sy \'həsē, -zē\ *n, pl* **-sies 1 :** brazen woman **2 :** mischievous girl

hus•tle \'həsəl\ *vb* **-tled; -tling 1 :** hurry **2 :** work energetically **—hustle** *n* **—hus•tler** \'həslər\ *n*

hut \'hət\ *n* **:** small often temporary dwelling

hutch \'həch\ *n* **1 :** cupboard with open shelves **2 :** pen for an animal

hy•a•cinth \'hīə‚sinth\ *n* **:** bulbous herb grown for bell-shaped flowers

hy•brid \'hībrəd\ *n* **:** offspring of genetically differing parents **—hybrid** *adj* **—hy•brid•iza•tion** \‚hībrədə'zāshən\ *n* **—hy•brid•ize** \'hībrəd‚īz\ *vb* **—hy•brid•iz•er** *n*

hy•drant \'hīdrənt\ *n* **:** pipe from which water may be drawn to fight fires

hy•drau•lic \hī'drȯlik\ *adj* **:** operated by liquid forced through a small hole **—hy•drau•lics** \-liks\ *n*

hy•dro•car•bon \‚hīdrə'kärbən\ *n* **:** organic compound of carbon and hydrogen

hy•dro•elec•tric \‚hīdrōi'lektrik\ *adj* **:** producing electricity by waterpower **—hy•dro•elec•tric•i•ty** \-‚lek'trisətē\ *n*

hy•dro•gen \'hīdrəjən\ *n* **:** very light gaseous colorless odorless flammable chemical element

hydrogen bomb *n* **:** powerful bomb that derives its energy from the union of atomic nuclei

hy•dro•pho•bia \‚hīdrə'fōbēə\ *n* **:** rabies

hy•dro•plane \'hīdrə‚plān\ *n* **:** speedboat that skims the water

hy•drous \'hīdrəs\ *adj* **:** containing water

hy•e•na \hī'ēnə\ *n* **:** nocturnal carnivorous mammal of Asia and Africa

hy•giene \'hī‚jēn\ *n* **:** conditions or practices conducive to health **—hy•gien•ic** \hī'jenik, -'jēn-; ‚hījē'enik\ *adj* **—hy•gien•i•cal•ly** \-iklē\ *adv* **—hy•gien•ist** \hī'jēnist, -'jen-; 'hī‚jen-\ *n*

hy•grom•e•ter \hī'grämətər\ *n* **:** instrument for measuring atmospheric humidity

hying *pres part of* HIE

hymn \'him\ *n* **:** song of praise esp. to God **—hymn** *vb*

hym•nal \'himnəl\ *n* **:** book of hymns

hype \'hīp\ *vb* **hyped; hyp•ing :** publicize extravagantly**—hype** *n*

hyper- *prefix* **1 :** above or beyond **2 :** excessively or excessive

hyperacid
hyperacidity
hyperactive
hyperacute
hyperaggressive
hypercautious
hypercorrect
hypercritical
hyperemotional
hyperenergetic
hyperexcitable
hyperfastidious
hyperintense
hypermasculine
hypernationalistic
hyperreactive
hyperrealistic
hyperromantic
hypersensitive
hypersensitiveness
hypersensitivity
hypersexual
hypersusceptible
hypertense
hypervigilant

hy•per•bo•le \hī'pərbəlē\ *n* **:** extravagant exaggeration

hy•per•ten•sion \'hīpər‚tenchən\ *n* **:** high blood pressure **—hy•per•ten•sive** \‚hīpər'tensiv\ *adj or n*

hy•phen \'hīfən\ *n* **:** punctuation mark - used to divide or compound words **—hyphen** *vb*

hy•phen•ate \'hīfə‚nāt\ *vb* **-at•ed; -at•ing :** connect or divide with a hyphen **—hy•phen•ation** \‚hīfə'nāshən\ *n*

hyp•no•sis \hip'nōsəs\ *n, pl* **-no•ses** \-‚sēz\ **:** induced state like sleep in which the subject is responsive to suggestions of the inducer (**hyp•no•tist** \'hipnətist\) **—hyp•no•tism** \'hipnə‚tizəm\ *n* **—hyp•no•tiz•able** \‚hipnə'tīzəbəl\ *adj* **—hyp•no•tize** \'hipnə‚tīz\ *vb*

hyp•not•ic \hip'nätik\ *adj* **:** relating to hypnosis **—hypnotic** *n* **—hyp•not•i•cal•ly** \-iklē\ *adv*

hy•po•chon•dria \‚hīpə'kändrēə\ *n* **:** morbid concern for one's health **—hy•po•chon•dri•ac** \-drē‚ak\ *adj or n*

hy•poc•ri•sy \hip'äkrəsē\ *n, pl* **-sies :** a feigning to be what one is not **—hyp•o•crite** \'hipə‚krit\ *n* **—hyp•o•crit•i•cal** \‚hipə'kritikəl\ *adj* **—hyp•o•crit•i•cal•ly** *adv*

hy•po•der•mic \‚hīpə'dərmik\ *adj* **:** administered or used in making an injection beneath the skin ~ *n* **:** hypodermic syringe

hy•pot•e•nuse \hī'pätə‚nüs, -‚nüz, -‚nyüs, -‚nyüz\ *n* **:** side of a right-angled triangle opposite the right angle

hy•poth•e•sis \hī'päthəsəs\ *n, pl* **-e•ses** \-‚sēz\ **:** assumption made in order to test its consequences **—hy•poth•e•size** \-‚sīz\ *vb* **—hy•po•thet•i•cal** \‚hīpə'thetikəl\ *adj* **—hy•po•thet•i•cal•ly** *adv*

hys•ter•ec•to•my \‚histə'rektəmē\ *n, pl* **-mies :** surgical removal of the uterus

hys•te•ria \his'terēə, -tir-\ *n* **:** uncontrollable fear or outburst of emotion **—hys•ter•i•cal** \-'terikəl\ *adj* **—hys•ter•i•cal•ly** *adv*

hys•ter•ics \-'teriks\ *n pl* **:** uncontrollable laughter or crying

I

i \'ī\ *n, pl* **i's** *or* **is** \'īz\ **:** 9th letter of the alphabet

I \'ī\ *pron* **:** the speaker

-ial *adj suffix* **:** of, relating to, or characterized by

-ian —see -AN

ibis \'ībəs\ *n, pl* **ibis** *or* **ibis•es :** wading bird with a down-curved bill

-ible —see -ABLE

ibu•pro•fen \‚ībyu'prōfən\ *n* **:** drug used to relieve inflammation, pain, and fever

-ic \ik\ *adj suffix* **1 :** of, relating to, or being **2 :** containing **3 :** characteristic of **4 :** marked by **5 :** caused by

-i•cal \ikəl\ *adj suffix* **:** -ic **— -i•cal•ly** \iklē, -kəlē\ *adv suffix*

ice \'īs\ *n* **1 :** frozen water **2 :** flavored frozen dessert ~ *vb* **iced; ic•ing 1 :** freeze **2 :** chill **3 :** cover with icing

ice•berg \'īs‚bərg\ *n* **:** large floating mass of ice

ice•box *n* **:** refrigerator

ice•break•er *n* **:** ship equipped to cut through ice

ice cream *n* **:** sweet frozen food

ice–skate *vb* **:** skate on ice **—ice skat•er** *n*

ich•thy•ol•o•gy \‚ikthē'äləjē\ *n* **:** study of fishes **—ich•thy•ol•o•gist** \-jist\ *n*

ici•cle \'ī‚sikəl\ *n* **:** hanging mass of ice

ic•ing \'īsiŋ\ *n* **:** sweet usu. creamy coating for baked goods

icon \'ī‚kän\ *n* **1 :** religious image **2 :** small picture on a computer screen identified with an available function

icon•o•clast \ī'känə‚klast\ *n* **:** attacker of cherished beliefs or institutions **—icon•o•clasm** \-‚klazəm\ *n*

icy \'īsē\ *adj* **ic•i•er; -est 1 :** covered with or consisting of ice **2 :** very cold **—ic•i•ly** *adv* **—ic•i•ness** *n*

id \'id\ *n* **:** unconscious instinctual part of the mind

idea \ī'dēə\ *n* **1 :** something imagined in the mind **2 :** purpose or plan

ide•al \ī'dēəl\ *adj* **1 :** imaginary **2 :** perfect ~ *n* **1 :** standard of excellence **2 :** model **3 :** aim **—ide•al•ly** *adv*

ide•al•ism \ī'dēə‚lizəm\ *n* **:** adherence to ideals **—ide•al•ist** \-list\ *n* **—ide•al•is•tic** \ī‚dēə'listik\ *adj* **—ide•al•is•ti•cal•ly** \-tiklē\ *adv*

ide•al•ize \ī'dēə‚līz\ *vb* **-ized; -iz•ing :** think of or represent as ideal **—ide•al•i•za•tion** \-‚dēələ'zāshən\ *n*

iden•ti•cal \ī'dentikəl\ *adj* **1 :** being the same **2 :** exactly or essentially alike

iden•ti•fi•ca•tion \ī‚dentəfə'kāshən\ *n* **1 :** act of identifying **2 :** evidence of identity

iden•ti•fy \ī'dentə‚fī\ *vb* **-fied; -fy•ing 1 :** associate **2 :** establish the identity of **—iden•ti•fi•able** \ī‚dentə'fīəbəl\ *adj* **—iden•ti•fi•er** \ī'dentə‚fīər\ *n*

iden•ti•ty \ī'dentətē\ *n, pl* **-ties 1 :** sameness of essential character **2 :** individuality **3 :** fact of being what is supposed

ide•ol•o•gy \‚īdē'äləjē, ‚id-\ *n, pl* **-gies :** body of beliefs **—ide•o•log•i•cal** \‚īdēə'läjikəl, ‚id-\ *adj*

id•i•om \'idēəm\ *n* **1 :** language peculiar to a person or group **2 :** expression with a special meaning **—id•i•om•at•ic** \‚idēə'matik\ *adj* **—id•i•om•at•i•cal•ly** \-iklē\ *adv*

id•io•syn•cra•sy \‚idēō'siŋkrəsē\ *n, pl* **-sies :** personal peculiarity **—id•io•syn•crat•ic** \-sin'kratik\ *adj* **—id•io•syn•crat•i•cal•ly** \-'kratiklē\ *adv*

id•i•ot \'idēət\ *n* **:** mentally retarded or foolish person **—id•i•o•cy** \-əsē\ *n* **—id•i•ot•ic** \‚idē'ätik\ *adj* **—id•i•ot•i•cal•ly** \-iklē\ *adv*

idle \'īdəl\ *adj* **idler; idlest 1 :** worthless **2 :** inactive **3 :** lazy ~ *vb* **idled; idling :** spend time doing nothing **—idle•ness** *n* **—idler** *n* **—idly** \'īdlē\ *adv*

idol \'īdəl\ *n* **1 :** image of a god **2 :** object of devotion **—idol•iza•tion** \‚īdələ'zāshən\ *n* **—idol•ize** \'īdəl‚īz\ *vb*

idol•a•ter, idol•a•tor \ī'dälətər\ *n* **:** worshiper of idols **—idol•a•trous** \-trəs\ *adj* **—idol•a•try** \-trē\ *n*

idyll \'īdəl\ *n* **:** period of peace and contentment **—idyl•lic** \ī'dilik\ *adj*

-ier —see -ER

if \'if\ *conj* **1 :** in the event that **2 :** whether **3 :** even though

-i•fy \ə‚fī\ *vb suffix* **:** -fy

ig•loo \'iglü\ *n, pl* **-loos :** hut made of snow blocks

ig•nite \ig'nīt\ *vb* **-nit•ed; -nit•ing :** set afire or catch fire **—ig•nit•able** \-'nītəbəl\ *adj*

ig•ni•tion \ig'nishən\ *n* **1 :** a setting on fire **2 :** process or means of igniting fuel

ig•no•ble \ig'nōbəl\ *adj* **:** not honorable **—ig•no•bly** \-blē\ *adv*

ig•no•min•i•ous \‚ignə'minēəs\ *adj* **1 :** dishonorable **2 :** humiliating **—ig•no•min•i•ous•ly** *adv* **—ig•no•mi•ny** \'ignə‚minē, ig'nämənē\ *n*

ig•no•ra•mus \‚ignə'rāməs\ *n* **:** ignorant person

ig•no•rant \'ignərənt\ *adj* **1 :** lacking knowledge **2 :** showing a lack of knowledge or intelligence **3 :** unaware **—ig•no•rance** \-rəns\ *n* **—ig•no•rant•ly** *adv*

ig•nore \ig'nōr\ *vb* **-nored; -nor•ing :** refuse to notice

igua•na \i'gwänə\ *n* **:** large tropical American lizard

ilk \'ilk\ *n* **:** kind

ill \'il\ *adj* **worse** \'wərs\; **worst** \'wərst\ **1 :** sick **2 :** bad **3 :** rude or unacceptable **4 :** hostile ~ *adv* **worse; worst 1 :** with displeasure **2 :** harshly **3 :** scarcely **4 :** badly ~ *n* **1 :** evil **2 :** misfortune **3 :** sickness

il•le•gal \il'lēgəl\ *adj* **:** not lawful **—il•le•gal•i•ty** \ili'galətē\ *n* **—il•le•gal•ly** \il'lēgəlē\ *adv*

il•leg•i•ble \il'lejəbəl\ *adj* **:** not legible **—il•leg•i•bil•i•ty** \il‚lejə'bilətē\ *n* **—il•leg•i•bly** \il'lejəblē\ *adv*

il•le•git•i•mate \‚ili'jitəmət\ *adj* **1 :** born of unmarried parents **2 :** illegal **—il•le•git•i•ma•cy** \-əməsē\ *n* **—il•le•git•i•mate•ly** *adv*

il•lic•it \il'lisət\ *adj* **:** not lawful **—il•lic•it•ly** *adv*

il•lim•it•able \il'limətəbəl\ *adj* **:** boundless **—il•lim•it•ably** \-blē\ *adv*

il•lit•er•ate \il'litərət\ *adj* **:** unable to read or write **—il•lit•er•a•cy** \-ərəsē\ *n* **—illiterate** *n*

ill–na•tured \-'nāchərd\ *adj* **:** cross **—ill–na•tured•ly** *adv*

ill•ness \'ilnəs\ *n* **:** sickness

il•log•i•cal \il'läjikəl\ *adj* **:** contrary to sound reasoning **—il•log•i•cal•ly** *adv*

ill–starred \'il'stärd\ *adj* **:** unlucky

il•lu•mi•nate \il'ümə‚nāt\ *vb* **-nat•ed; -nat•ing 1 :** light up **2 :** make clear **—il•lu•mi•nat•ing•ly** \-‚nātiŋlē\ *adv* **—il•lu•mi•na•tion** \-‚ümə'nāshən\ *n*

ill–use \-'yüz\ *vb* **:** abuse **—ill–use** \-'yüs\ *n*

il•lu•sion \il'üzhən\ *n* **1 :** mistaken idea **2 :** misleading visual image

il•lu•so•ry \il'üsərē, -'üz-\ *adj* **:** based on or producing illusion

il•lus•trate \'iləs‚trāt\ *vb* **-trat•ed; -trat•ing 1 :** explain by example **2 :** provide with pictures or figures **—il•lus•tra•tor** \-ər\ *n*

il•lus•tra•tion \‚iləs'trāshən\ *n* **1 :** example that explains **2 :** pictorial explanation

il•lus•tra•tive \il'əstrətiv\ *adj* **:** designed to illustrate **—il•lus•tra•tive•ly** *adv*

il•lus•tri•ous \-trēəs\ *adj* **:** notably or brilliantly outstanding **—il•lus•tri•ous•ness** *n*

ill will *n* **:** unfriendly feeling

im•age \'imij\ *n* **1 :** likeness **2 :** visual counterpart of an object formed by a lens or mirror **3 :** mental picture ~ *vb* **-aged; -ag•ing :** create a representation of

im•ag•ery \'imijrē\ *n* **1 :** images **2 :** figurative language

imag•i•nary \im'ajə‚nerē\ *adj* **:** existing only in the imagination

imag•i•na•tion \im‚ajə'nāshən\ *n* **1 :** act or power of forming a mental image **2 :** creative ability **—imag•i•na•tive** \im'ajənətiv, -ə‚nātiv\ *adj* **—imag•i•na•tive•ly** *adv*

imag•ine \im'ajən\ *vb* **-ined; -in•ing :** form a mental picture of something not present **—imag•in•able** \-'ajənəbəl\ *adj* **—imag•in•ably** \-blē\ *adv*

im•bal•ance \im'baləns\ *n* **:** lack of balance

im•be•cile \'imbəsəl, -‚sil\ *n* **:** idiot **—imbecile, im•be•cil•ic** \‚imbə'silik\ *adj* **—im•be•cil•i•ty** \-'silətē\ *n*

im•bibe \im'bīb\ *vb* **-bibed; -bib•ing :** drink **—im•bib•er** *n*

im•bro•glio \im'brōlyō\ *n, pl* **-glios :** complicated situation

im•bue \-'byü\ *vb* **-bued; -bu•ing :** fill (as with color or a feeling)

im•i•tate \'imə‚tāt\ *vb* **-tat•ed; -tat•ing 1 :** follow as a model **2 :** mimic **—im•i•ta•tive** \-‚tātiv\ *adj* **—im•i•ta•tor** \-ər\ *n*

im•i•ta•tion \‚imə'tāshən\ *n* **1 :** act of imitating **2 :** copy **—imitation** *adj*

im•mac•u•late \im'akyələt\ *adj* **:** without stain or blemish **—im•mac•u•late•ly** *adv*

im•ma•te•ri•al \‚imə'tirēəl\ *adj* **1 :** spiritual **2 :** not relevant **—im•ma•te•ri•al•i•ty** \-‚tirē'alətē\ *n*

im•ma•ture \‚imə'tür, -'tyür\ *adj* **:** not yet mature **—im•ma•tu•ri•ty** \-ətē\ *n*

im•mea•sur•able \im'ezhərəbəl\ *adj* **:** indefinitely extensive **—im•mea•sur•ably** \-blē\ *adv*

im•me•di•a•cy \im'ēdēəsē\ *n, pl* **-cies :** quality or state of being urgent

im•me•di•ate \-ēət\ *adj* **1 :** direct **2 :** being next in line **3 :** made or done at once **4 :** not distant **—im•me•di•ate•ly** *adv*

im•me•mo•ri•al \‚imə'mōrēəl\ *adj* **:** old beyond memory

im•mense \im'ens\ *adj* **:** vast **—im•mense•ly** *adv* **—im•men•si•ty** \-'ensətē\ *n*

im•merse \im'ərs\ *vb* **-mersed; -mers•ing 1 :** plunge or dip esp. into liquid **2 :** engross **—im•mer•sion** \-'ərzhən\ *n*

im•mi•grant \'imigrənt\ *n* **:** one that immigrates

im•mi•grate \'imə‚grāt\ *vb* **-grat•ed; -grat•ing :** come into a place and take up residence **—im•mi•gra•tion** \‚imə'grāshən\ *n*

im•mi•nent \'imənənt\ *adj* **:** ready to take place **—im•mi•nence** \-nəns\ *n* **—im•mi•nent•ly** *adv*

im•mo•bile \im'ōbəl\ *adj* **:** incapable of being moved **—im•mo•bil•i•ty** \‚imō'bilətē\ *n* **—im•mo•bi•lize** \im'ōbə‚līz\ *vb*

im•mod•er•ate \im'ädərət\ *adj* **:** not moderate **—im•mod•er•a•cy** \-ərəsē\ *n* **—im•mod•er•ate•ly** *adv*

im•mod•est \im'ädəst\ *adj* **:** not modest **—im•mod•est•ly** *adv* **—im•mod•es•ty** \-əstē\ *n*

im•mo•late \'imə‚lāt\ *vb* **-lat•ed; -lat•ing :** offer in sacrifice **—im•mo•la•tion** \‚imə'lāshən\ *n*

im•mor•al \im'ȯrəl\ *adj* **:** not moral **—im•mo•ral•i•ty** \‚imȯ'ralətē, ‚imə-\ *n* **—im•mor•al•ly** *adv*

im•mor•tal \im'ȯrtəl\ *adj* **1 :** not mortal **2 :** having lasting fame ~ *n* **:** one exempt from death or oblivion **—im•mor•tal•i•ty** \‚im‚ȯr'talətē\ *n* **—im•mor•tal•ize** \im'ȯrtəl‚īz\ *vb*

im•mov•able \im'üvəbəl\ *adj* **1 :** stationary **2 :** unyielding **—im•mov•abil•ity** \‚im‚üvə'bilətē\ *n* **—im•mov•ably** *adv*

im•mune \im'yün\ *adj* **:** not liable esp. to disease **—im•mu•ni•ty** \im'yünətē\ *n* **—im•mu•ni•za•tion** \‚imyənə'zāshən\ *n* **—im•mu•nize** \'imyə‚nīz\ *vb*

im•mu•nol•o•gy \‚imyə'näləjē\ *n* **:** science of immunity to disease **—im•mu•no•log•ic** \-yənəl'äjik\, **im•mu•no•log•i•cal** \-ikəl\ *adj* **—im•mu•nol•o•gist** \‚imyə'näləjist\ *n*

im•mu•ta•ble \im'yütəbəl\ *adj* **:** unchangeable **—im•mu•ta•bil•i•ty** \im‚yütə'bilətē\ *n* **—im•mu•ta•bly** *adv*

imp \'imp\ *n* **1 :** demon **2 :** mischievous child

im•pact \im'pakt\ *vb* **1 :** press close **2 :** have an effect on ~ \'im‚pakt\ *n* **1 :** forceful contact **2 :** influence

im•pact•ed \im'paktəd\ *adj* **:** wedged between the jawbone and another tooth

im•pair \im'par\ *vb* **:** diminish in quantity, value, or ability **—im•pair•ment** *n*

im•pa•la \im'palə\ *n, pl* **impalas** *or* **impala :** large African antelope

im•pale \im'pāl\ *vb* **-paled; -pal•ing :** pierce with something pointed

im•pal•pa•ble \im'palpəbəl\ *adj* **:** incapable of being felt **—im•pal•pa•bly** *adv*

im•pan•el \im'panəl\ *vb* **:** enter in or on a panel

im•part \-'pärt\ *vb* **:** give from or as if from a store

im•par•tial \im'pärshəl\ *adj* **:** not partial **—im•par•tial•i•ty** \im‚pärshē'alətē\ *n* **—im•par•tial•ly** *adv*

im•pass•able \im'pasəbəl\ *adj* **:** not passable **—im•pass•ably** \-'pasəblē\ *adv*

im•passe \'im‚pas\ *n* **:** inescapable predicament

im•pas•sioned \im'pashənd\ *adj* **:** filled with passion

im•pas•sive \im'pasiv\ *adj* **:** showing no feeling or interest **—im•pas•sive•ly** *adv* **—im•pas•siv•i•ty** \‚im‚pas'ivətē\ *n*

im•pa•tiens \im'pāshənz, -shəns\ *n* **:** annual herb with showy flowers

im•pa•tient \im'pāshənt\ *adj* **:** not patient **—im•pa•tience** \-shəns\ *n* **—im•pa•tient•ly** *adv*

im•peach \im'pēch\ *vb* **1** : charge (an official) with misconduct **2** : cast doubt on **3** : remove from office for misconduct —**im•peach•ment** *n*

im•pec•ca•ble \im'pekəbəl\ *adj* : faultless —**im•pec•ca•bly** *adv*

im•pe•cu•nious \ˌimpi'kyünēəs\ *adj* : broke —**im•pe•cu•nious•ness** *n*

im•pede \im'pēd\ *vb* **-ped•ed; -ped•ing** : interfere with

im•ped•i•ment \-'pedəmənt\ *n* **1** : hindrance **2** : speech defect

im•pel \-'pel\ *vb* **-pelled; -pel•ling** : urge forward

im•pend \-'pend\ *vb* : be about to occur

im•pen•e•tra•ble \im'penətrəbəl\ *adj* : incapable of being penetrated or understood —**im•pen•e•tra•bil•i•ty** \imˌpenətrə'bilətē\ *n* —**im•pen•e•tra•bly** *adv*

im•pen•i•tent \im'penətənt\ *adj* : not penitent —**im•pen•i•tence** \-təns\ *n*

im•per•a•tive \im'perətiv\ *adj* **1** : expressing a command **2** : urgent ~ *n* **1** : imperative mood or verb form **2** : unavoidable fact, need, or obligation —**im•per•a•tive•ly** *adv*

im•per•cep•ti•ble \ˌimpər'septəbəl\ *adj* : not perceptible —**im•per•cep•ti•bly** *adv*

im•per•fect \im'pərfikt\ *adj* : not perfect —**im•per•fec•tion** *n* —**im•per•fect•ly** *adv*

im•pe•ri•al \im'pirēəl\ *adj* **1** : relating to an empire or an emperor **2** : royal

im•pe•ri•al•ism \im'pirēəˌlizəm\ *n* : policy of controlling other nations —**im•pe•ri•al•ist** \-list\ *n or adj* —**im•pe•ri•al•is•tic** \-ˌpirēə'listik\ *adj* —**im•pe•ri•al•is•ti•cal•ly** \-tiklē\ *adv*

im•per•il \im'perəl\ *vb* **-iled** *or* **-illed; -il•ing** *or* **-il•ling** : endanger

im•pe•ri•ous \im'pirēəs\ *adj* : arrogant or domineering —**im•pe•ri•ous•ly** *adv*

im•per•ish•able \im'perishəbəl\ *adj* : not perishable

im•per•ma•nent \-'pərmənənt\ *adj* : not permanent —**im•per•ma•nent•ly** *adv*

im•per•me•able \-'pərmēəbəl\ *adj* : not permeable

im•per•mis•si•ble \ˌimpər'misəbəl\ *adj* : not permissible

im•per•son•al \im'pərsᵊnəl\ *adj* : not involving human personality or emotion —**im•per•son•al•i•ty** \imˌpərsᵊn'alətē\ *n* —**im•per•son•al•ly** *adv*

im•per•son•ate \im'pərsᵊnˌāt\ *vb* **-at•ed; -at•ing** : assume the character of —**im•per•son•ation** \-ˌpərsᵊn'āshən\ *n* —**im•per•son•ator** \-'pərsᵊnˌātər\ *n*

im•per•ti•nent \im'pərtᵊnənt\ *adj* **1** : irrelevant **2** : insolent —**im•per•ti•nence** \-ᵊnəns\ *n* —**im•per•ti•nent•ly** *adv*

im•per•turb•able \ˌimpər'tərbəbəl\ *adj* : calm and steady

im•per•vi•ous \im'pərvēəs\ *adj* : incapable of being penetrated or affected

im•pet•u•ous \im'pechəwəs\ *adj* : impulsive —**im•pet•u•os•i•ty** \imˌpechə'wäsətē\ *n* —**im•pet•u•ous•ly** *adv*

im•pe•tus \'impətəs\ *n* : driving force

im•pi•ety \im'pīətē\ *n* : quality or state of being impious

im•pinge \im'pinj\ *vb* **-pinged; -ping•ing** : encroach —**im•pinge•ment** \-mənt\ *n*

im•pi•ous \'impēəs, im'pī-\ *adj* : not pious

imp•ish \'impish\ *adj* : mischievous —**imp•ish•ly** *adv* —**imp•ish•ness** *n*

im•pla•ca•ble \im'plakəbəl, -'plā-\ *adj* : not capable of being appeased or changed —**im•pla•ca•bil•i•ty** \imˌplakə'bilətē, -ˌplā-\ *n* —**im•pla•ca•bly** \im'plakəblē\ *adv*

im•plant \im'plant\ *vb* **1** : set firmly or deeply **2** : fix in the mind or spirit ~ \'imˌplant\ *n* : something implanted in tissue —**im•plan•ta•tion** \ˌimˌplan'tāshən\ *n*

im•plau•si•ble \im'plȯzəbəl\ *adj* : not plausible —**im•plau•si•bil•i•ty** \imˌplȯzə'bilətē\ *n*

im•ple•ment \'impləmənt\ *n* : tool, utensil ~ \-ˌment\ *vb* : put into practice —**im•ple•men•ta•tion** \ˌimpləmən'tāshən\ *n*

im•pli•cate \'impləˌkāt\ *vb* **-cat•ed; -cat•ing** : involve

im•pli•ca•tion \ˌimplə'kāshən\ *n* **1** : an implying **2** : something implied

im•plic•it \im'plisət\ *adj* **1** : understood though only implied **2** : complete and unquestioning —**im•plic•it•ly** *adv*

im•plode \im'plōd\ *vb* **-plod•ed; -plod•ing** : burst inward —**im•plo•sion** \-'plōzhən\ *n* —**im•plo•sive** \-'plōsiv\ *adj*

im•plore \im'plōr\ *vb* **-plored; -plor•ing** : entreat

im•ply \-'plī\ *vb* **-plied; -ply•ing** : express indirectly

im•po•lite \ˌimpə'līt\ *adj* : not polite

im•pol•i•tic \im'päləˌtik\ *adj* : not politic

im•pon•der•a•ble \im'pändərəbəl\ *adj* : incapable of being precisely evaluated —**imponderable** *n*

im•port \im'pōrt\ *vb* **1** : mean **2** : bring in from an external source ~ \'imˌpōrt\ *n* **1** : meaning **2** : importance **3** : something imported —**im•por•ta•tion** \ˌimˌpōr'tāshən\ *n* —**im•port•er** *n*

im•por•tant \im'pȯrtᵊnt\ *adj* : having great worth, significance, or influence —**im•por•tance** \-ᵊns\ *n* —**im•por•tant•ly** *adv*

im•por•tu•nate \im'pȯrchənət\ *adj* : troublesomely persistent or urgent

im•por•tune \ˌimpər'tün, -'tyün; im'pȯrchən\ *vb* **-tuned; -tun•ing** : urge or beg persistently —**im•por•tu•ni•ty** \ˌimpər'tünətē, -'tyü-\ *n*

im•pose \im'pōz\ *vb* **-posed; -pos•ing 1** : establish as compulsory **2** : take unwarranted advantage of —**im•po•si•tion** \ˌimpə'zishən\ *n*

im•pos•ing \im'pōziŋ\ *adj* : impressive —**im•pos•ing•ly** *adv*

im•pos•si•ble \im'päsəbəl\ *adj* **1** : incapable of occurring **2** : enormously difficult —**im•pos•si•bil•i•ty** \imˌpäsə'bilətē\ *n* —**im•pos•si•bly** \im'päsəblē\ *adv*

im•post \'imˌpōst\ *n* : tax

im•pos•tor, im•pos•ter \im'pästər\ *n* : one who assumes an identity or title to deceive —**im•pos•ture** \-'päschər\ *n*

im•po•tent \'impətənt\ *adj* **1** : lacking power **2** : sterile —**im•po•tence** \-pətəns\ *n* —**im•po•ten•cy** \-ənsē\ *n* —**im•po•tent•ly** *adv*

im•pound \im'paůnd\ *vb* : seize and hold in legal custody —**im•pound•ment** *n*

im•pov•er•ish \im'pävərish\ *vb* : make poor —**im•pov•er•ish•ment** *n*

im•prac•ti•ca•ble \im'praktikəbəl\ *adj* : not practicable

im•prac•ti•cal \-'praktikəl\ *adj* : not practical

im•pre•cise \ˌimpri'sīs\ *adj* : not precise —**im•pre•cise•ly** *adv* —**im•pre•cise•ness** *n* —**im•pre•ci•sion** \-'sizhən\ *n*

im•preg•na•ble \im'pregnəbəl\ *adj* : able to resist attack —**im•preg•na•bil•i•ty** \imˌpregnə'bilətē\ *n*

im•preg•nate \im'pregˌnāt\ *vb* **-nat•ed; -nat•ing 1** : make pregnant **2** : cause to be filled, permeated, or saturated —**im•preg•na•tion** \ˌimˌpreg'nāshən\ *n*

im•pre•sa•rio \ˌimprə'särēˌō\ *n, pl* **-ri•os** : one who sponsors an entertainment

¹im•press \im'pres\ *vb* **1** : apply with or produce by pressure **2** : press, stamp, or print in or upon **3** : produce a vivid impression of **4** : affect (as the mind) forcibly

²im•press \im'pres\ *vb* : force into naval service —**im•press•ment** *n*

im•pres•sion \im'preshən\ *n* **1** : mark made by impressing **2** : marked influence or effect **3** : printed copy **4** : vague notion or recollection —**im•pres•sion•able** \-'preshənəbəl\ *adj*

im•pres•sive \im'presiv\ *adj* : making a marked impression —**im•pres•sive•ly** *adv* —**im•pres•sive•ness** *n*

im•pri•ma•tur \ˌimprə'mäˌtůr\ *n* : official approval (as of a publication by a censor)

im•print \im'print, 'imˌ-\ *vb* : stamp or mark by or as if by pressure ~ \'imˌ-\ *n* : something imprinted or printed

im•pris•on \im'prizᵊn\ *vb* : put in prison —**im•pris•on•ment** \-mənt\ *n*

im•prob•a•ble \im'präbəbəl\ *adj* : unlikely to be true or to occur —**im•prob•a•bil•i•ty** \imˌpräbə'bilətē\ *n* —**im•prob•a•bly** *adv*

im•promp•tu \im'prämptü, -tyü\ *adj* : not planned beforehand —**impromptu** *adv or n*

im•prop•er \im'präpər\ *adj* : not proper —**im•prop•er•ly** *adv*

im•pro•pri•ety \ˌimprə'prīətē\ *n, pl* **-eties** : state or instance of being improper

im•prove \im'prüv\ *vb* **-proved; -prov•ing** : grow or make better —**im•prov•able** \-'prüvəbəl\ *adj* —**im•prove•ment** *n*

im•prov•i•dent \im'prävədənt\ *adj* : not providing for the future —**im•prov•i•dence** \-əns\ *n*

im•pro•vise \'imprəˌvīz\ *vb* **-vised; -vis•ing** : make, invent, or arrange offhand —**im•pro•vi•sa•tion** \imˌprävə'zāshən, ˌimprəvə-\ *n* —**im•pro•vis•er, im•pro•vi•sor** \'imprəˌvīzər\ *n*

im•pru•dent \im'prüdᵊnt\ *adj* : not prudent —**im•pru•dence** \-ᵊns\ *n*

im•pu•dent \'impyədənt\ *adj* : insolent —**im•pu•dence** \-əns\ *n* —**im•pu•dent•ly** *adv*

im•pugn \im'pyün\ *vb* : attack as false

im•pulse \'imˌpəls\ *n* **1** : moving force **2** : sudden inclination

im•pul•sive \im'pəlsiv\ *adj* : acting on impulse —**im•pul•sive•ly** *adv* —**impul•sive•ness** *n*

im•pu•ni•ty \im'pyünətē\ *n* : exemption from punishment or harm

im•pure \im'pyůr\ *adj* : not pure —**im•pu•ri•ty** \-'pyůrətē\ *n*

im•pute \im'pyüt\ *vb* **-put•ed; -put•ing** : credit to or blame on a person or cause —**im•pu•ta•tion** \ˌimpyə'tāshən\ *n*

in \'in\ *prep* **1** —used to indicate location, inclusion, situation, or manner **2** : into **3** : during ~ *adv* : to or toward the inside ~ *adj* : located inside

in- \in\ *prefix* **1** : not **2** : lack of

inability
inaccessibility
inaccessible
inaccuracy
inaccurate
inaction
inactive
inactivity
inadequacy
inadequate
inadequately
inadmissibility
inadmissible
inadvisability
inadvisable
inapparent
inapplicable
inapposite
inappositely
inappositeness
inappreciative
inapproachable
inappropriate
inappropriately
inappropriateness
inapt
inarguable
inartistic
inartistically
inattentive
inattentively
inattentiveness
inaudible
inaudibly
inauspicious
inauthentic
incapability
incapable
incautious
incoherence
incoherent
incoherently
incombustible
incommensurate
incommodious
incommunicable
incompatibility
incompatible
incomplete
incompletely
incompleteness
incomprehensible
inconclusive
incongruent
inconsecutive
inconsiderate
inconsiderately
inconsiderateness
inconsistency
inconsistent
inconsistently
inconspicuous
inconspicuously
inconstancy
inconstant
inconstantly
inconsumable
incontestable
incontestably
incorporeal
incorporeally
incorrect
incorrectly
incorrectness
incorruptible
inculpable
incurable
incurious
indecency
indecent
indecently
indecipherable
indecisive
indecisively
indecisiveness
indecorous
indecorously
indecorousness
indefensible
indefinable
indefinably
indescribable
indescribably
indestructibility
indestructible
indigestible
indiscernible
indiscreet
indiscreetly
indiscretion
indisputable
indisputably
indistinct
indistinctly
indistinctness
indivisibility
indivisible
ineducable
ineffective
ineffectively
ineffectiveness
ineffectual
ineffectually
ineffectualness
inefficiency
inefficient
inefficiently
inelastic
inelasticity
inelegance
inelegant
ineligibility
ineligible
ineradicable
inessential
inexact
inexactly
inexpedient
inexpensive
inexperience
inexperienced
inexpert
inexpertly
inexpertness
inexplicable
inexplicably
inexplicit
inexpressible
inexpressibly
inextinguishable
inextricable
infeasibility
infeasible
infelicitous
infelicity
infertile
infertility
inflexibility
inflexible
inflexibly
infrequent
infrequently
inglorious
ingloriously
ingratitude
inhumane
inhumanely
injudicious
injudiciously
injudiciousness
inoffensive
inoperable
inoperative
insalubrious
insensitive
insensitivity
inseparable
insignificant
insincere
insincerely
insincerity
insolubility
insoluble
instability
insubstantial
insufficiency
insufficient
insufficiently
insupportable
intangibility
intangible
intangibly
intolerable
intolerably
intolerance
intolerant
intractable
invariable
invariably
inviable
invisibility
invisible
invisibly
involuntarily
involuntary
invulnerability
invulnerable
invulnerably

in•ad•ver•tent \ˌinəd'vərtᵊnt\ *adj* : unintentional —**in•ad•ver•tence** \-ᵊns\ *n* —**in•ad•ver•ten•cy** \-ᵊnsē\ *n* —**in•ad•ver•tent•ly** *adv*

in•alien•able \in'ālyənəbəl, -'ālēənə-\ *adj* : incapable of being transferred or given up —**in•alien•abil•i•ty** \inˌālyənə'bilətē, -ˌālēənə-\ *n* —**in•alien•ably** *adv*

inane \in'ān\ *adj* **inan•er; -est** : silly or stupid —**inan•i•ty** \in'anətē\ *n*

in•an•i•mate \in'anəmət\ *adj* : not animate or animated —**in•an•i•mate•ly** *adv* —**in•an•i•mate•ness** *n*

in•ap•pre•cia•ble \ˌinə'prēshəbəl\ *adj* : too small to be perceived —**in•ap•pre•cia•bly** *adv*

in•ar•tic•u•late \ˌinär'tikyələt\ *adj* : without the power of speech or effective expression —**in•ar•tic•u•lately** *adv*

in•as•much as \ˌinaz'məchaz\ *conj* : because

in•at•ten•tion \ˌinə'tenchən\ *n* : failure to pay attention

in•au•gu•ral \in'ȯgyərəl, -gərəl\ *adj* : relating to an inauguration ~ *n* **1** : inaugural speech **2** : inauguration

in•au•gu•rate \in'ȯgyəˌrāt, -gə-\ *vb* **-rat•ed; -rat•ing 1** : install in office **2** : start —**in•au•gu•ra•tion** \-ˌȯgyə'rāshən, -gə-\ *n*

in•board \ˌinˌbōrd\ *adv* : inside a vehicle or craft —**inboard** *adj*

in•born \'inˌbȯrn\ *adj* : present from birth

in•bred \'inˌbred\ *adj* : deeply ingrained in one's nature

in•breed•ing \'inˌbrēdiŋ\ *n* : interbreeding of closely related individuals —**in•breed** \-ˌbrēd\ *vb*

in•cal•cu•la•ble \in'kalkyələbəl\ *adj* : too large to be calculated —**in•cal•cu•la•bly** *adv*

in•can•des•cent \ˌinkən'desᵊnt\ *adj* **1** : glowing with heat **2** : brilliant —**in•can•des•cence** \-ᵊns\ *n*

in•can•ta•tion \ˌinˌkan'tāshən\ *n* : use of spoken or sung charms or spells as a magic ritual

in•ca•pac•i•tate \ˌinkə'pasəˌtāt\ *vb* **-tat•ed; -tat•ing** : disable

in•ca•pac•i•ty \ˌinkə'pasətē\ *n, pl* **-ties** : quality or state of being incapable

in•car•cer•ate \in'kärsəˌrāt\ *vb* **-at•ed; -at•ing** : imprison —**in•car•cer•a•tion** \inˌkärsə'rāshən\ *n*

in•car•nate \in'kärnət, -ˌnāt\ *adj* : having bodily form and substance —**in•car•nate** \-ˌnāt\ *vb* —**in•car•na•tion** \-ˌkär'nāshən\ *n*

in•cen•di•ary \in'sendēˌerē\ *adj* **1** : pertaining to or used to ignite fire **2** : tending to excite —**incendiary** *n*

in•cense \'inˌsens\ *n* : material burned to produce a fragrant odor or its smoke ~ \in'sens\ *vb* **-censed; -cens•ing** : make very angry

in•cen•tive \in'sentiv\ *n* : inducement to do something

in•cep•tion \in'sepshən\ *n* : beginning

in•ces•sant \in'sesᵊnt\ *adj* : continuing without interruption —**in•ces•sant•ly** *adv*

in•cest \'inˌsest\ *n* : sexual intercourse between close relatives —**in•ces•tu•ous** \in'seschəwəs\ *adj*

inch \'inch\ *n* : unit of length equal to 1/12 foot ~ *vb* : move by small degrees

in•cho•ate \in'kōət, 'inkəˌwāt\ *adj* : new and not fully formed or ordered

in•ci•dent \'insədənt\ *n* : occurrence —**in•ci•dence** \-əns\ *n* —**incident** *adj*

in•ci•den•tal \ˌinsə'dentᵊl\ *adj* **1** : subordinate, nonessential, or attendant **2** : met by chance ~ *n* **1** : something incidental **2** *pl* : minor expenses that are not itemized —**in•ci•den•tal•ly** *adv*

in•cin•er•ate \in'sinəˌrāt\ *vb* **-at•ed; -at•ing** : burn to ashes —**in•cin•er•a•tor** \-ˌrātər\ *n*

in•cip•i•ent \in'sipēənt\ *adj* : beginning to be or appear

in•cise \in'sīz\ *vb* **-cised; -cis•ing** : carve into

in•ci•sion \in'sizhən\ *n* : surgical cut

in•ci•sive \in'sīsiv\ *adj* : keen and discerning —**in•ci•sive•ly** *adv*

in•ci•sor \in'sīzər\ *n* : tooth for cutting

in•cite \in'sīt\ *vb* **-cit•ed; -cit•ing** : arouse to action —**in•cite•ment** *n*

in•ci•vil•i•ty \ˌinsə'vilətē\ *n* : rudeness

in•clem•ent \in'klemənt\ *adj* : stormy —**in•clem•en•cy** \-ənsē\ *n*

in•cline \in'klīn\ *vb* **-clined; -clin•ing 1** : bow **2** : tend toward an opinion **3** : slope ~ *n* : slope —**in•cli•na•tion** \ˌinklə'nāshən\ *n* —**in•clin•er** *n*

inclose, inclosure *var of* ENCLOSE, ENCLOSURE

in•clude \in'klüd\ *vb* **-clud•ed; -clud•ing** : take in or comprise —**in•clu•sion** \in'klüzhən\ *n* —**in•clu•sive** \-'klüsiv\ *adj*

in•cog•ni•to \ˌinˌkäg'nētō, in'kägnəˌtō\ *adv or adj* : with one's identity concealed

in•come \'inˌkəm\ *n* : money gained (as from work or investment)

in•com•ing \'inˌkəmiŋ\ *adj* : coming in

in•com•mu•ni•ca•do \ˌinkəˌmyünə'kädō\ *adv or adj* : without means of communication

in•com•pa•ra•ble \in'kämpərəbəl\ *adj* : eminent beyond comparison

in•com•pe•tent \in'kämpətənt\ *adj* : lacking sufficient knowledge or skill —**in•com•pe•tence** \-pətəns\ *n* —**in•com•pe•ten•cy** \-ənsē\ *n* —**incompetent** *n*

in•con•ceiv•able \ˌinkən'sēvəbəl\ *adj* **1** : impossible to comprehend **2** : unbelievable —**in•con•ceiv•ably** \-blē\ *adv*

in•con•gru•ous \in'käŋgrəwəs\ *adj* : inappropriate or out of place —**in•con•gru•i•ty** \ˌinkən'grüətē, -ˌkän-\ *n* —**in•con•gru•ous•ly** *adv*

in·con·se·quen·tial \in,känsə'kwenchəl\ adj : unimportant —**in·con·se·quence** \in'känsə,kwens\ n —**in·con·se·quen·tial·ly** adv

in·con·sid·er·able \inkən'sidərəbəl\ adj : trivial

in·con·sol·able \inkən'sōləbəl\ adj : incapable of being consoled —**in·con·sol·ably** adv

in·con·ve·nience \inkən'vēnyəns\ n 1 : discomfort 2 : something that causes trouble or annoyance ~ vb : cause inconvenience to —**in·con·ve·nient** \inkən'vēnyənt\ adj —**in·con·ve·nient·ly** adv

in·cor·po·rate \in'kórpə,rāt\ vb -rat·ed; -rat·ing 1 : blend 2 : form into a legal body —**in·cor·po·rat·ed** adj —**in·cor·po·ra·tion** \-,kórpə'rāshən\ n

in·cor·ri·gi·ble \in'kórəjəbəl\ adj : incapable of being corrected or reformed —**in·cor·ri·gi·bil·i·ty** \in,kórəjə'bilətē\ n

in·crease \in'krēs, 'in,krēs\ vb -creased; -creas·ing : make or become greater ~ \'in,-, in'-\ n 1 : enlargement in size 2 : something added —**in·creas·ing·ly** \-'krēsiŋlē\ adv

in·cred·i·ble \in'kredəbəl\ adj : too extraordinary to be believed —**in·cred·i·bil·i·ty** \in,kredə'bilətē\ n —**in·cred·i·bly** \-'kredəblē\ adv

in·cred·u·lous \in'krejələs\ adj : skeptical —**in·cre·du·li·ty** \inkri'dülətē, -'dyü-\ n —**in·cred·u·lous·ly** adv

in·cre·ment \'iŋkrəmənt, 'in-\ n : increase or amount of increase —**in·cre·men·tal** \,iŋkrə'mentəl, in-\ adj

in·crim·i·nate \in'krimə,nāt\ vb -nat·ed; -nat·ing : show to be guilty of a crime —**in·crim·i·na·tion** \-,krimə'nāshən\ n —**in·crim·i·na·to·ry** \-'krimənə,tōrē\ adj

in·cu·bate \'iŋkyə,bāt, 'in-\ vb -bat·ed; -bat·ing : keep (as eggs) under conditions favorable for development —**in·cu·ba·tion** \iŋkyə'bāshən, in-\ n —**in·cu·ba·tor** \'iŋkyə,bātər, 'in-\ n

in·cul·cate \in'kəl,kāt, 'in,kəl-\ vb -cat·ed; -cat·ing : instill by repeated teaching —**in·cul·ca·tion** \in,kəl'kāshən\ n

in·cum·bent \in'kəmbənt\ n : holder of an office ~ adj : obligatory —**in·cum·ben·cy** \-bənsē\ n

in·cur \in'kər\ vb -rr- : become liable or subject to

in·cur·sion \in'kərzhən\ n : invasion

in·debt·ed \in'detəd\ adj : owing something —**in·debt·ed·ness** n

in·de·ci·sion \indi'sizhən\ n : inability to decide

in·deed \in'dēd\ adv : without question

in·de·fat·i·ga·ble \indi'fatigəbəl\ adj : not tiring —**in·de·fat·i·ga·bly** \-blē\ adv

in·def·i·nite \in'defənət\ adj 1 : not defining or identifying 2 : not precise 3 : having no fixed limit —**in·def·i·nite·ly** adv

in·del·i·ble \in'deləbəl\ adj : not capable of being removed or erased —**in·del·i·bly** adv

in·del·i·cate \in'delikət\ adj : improper —**in·del·i·ca·cy** \in'deləkəsē\ n

in·dem·ni·fy \in'demnə,fī\ vb -fied; -fy·ing : repay for a loss —**in·dem·ni·fi·ca·tion** \-,demnəfə'kāshən\ n

in·dem·ni·ty \in'demnətē\ n, pl -ties : security against loss or damage

1in·dent \in'dent\ vb : leave a space at the beginning of a paragraph

2indent vb : force inward so as to form a depression or dent

in·den·ta·tion \in,den'tashən\ n 1 : notch, recess, or dent 2 : action of indenting 3 : space at the beginning of a paragraph

in·den·ture \in'denchər\ n : contract binding one person to work for another for a given period —usu. in pl. ~ vb -tured; -tur·ing : bind by indentures

Independence Day n : July 4 observed as a legal holiday in commemoration of the adoption of the Declaration of Independence in 1776

in·de·pen·dent \ində'pendənt\ adj 1 : not governed by another 2 : not requiring or relying on something or somebody else 3 : not easily influenced —**in·de·pen·dence** \-dəns\ n —**independent** n —**in·de·pen·dent·ly** adv

in·de·ter·mi·nate \indi'tərmənət\ adj : not definitely determined —**in·de·ter·mi·nate·ly** adv

in·dex \'in,deks\ n, pl -dex·es or -di·ces \-də,sēz\ 1 : alphabetical list of items (as topics in a book) 2 : a number that serves as a measure or indicator of something ~ vb 1 : provide with an index 2 : serve as an index of

index finger : forefinger

in·di·cate \'ində,kāt\ vb -cat·ed; -cat·ing 1 : point out or to 2 : show indirectly 3 : state briefly —**in·di·ca·tion** \ində'kā-shən\ n —**in·di·ca·tor** \'ində,kātər\ n

in·dic·a·tive \in'dikətiv\ adj : serving to indicate

in·dict \in'dīt\ vb : charge with a crime —**in·dict·able** adj —**in·dict·ment** n

in·dif·fer·ent \in'difrənt\ adj 1 : having no preference 2 : showing neither interest nor dislike 3 : mediocre —**in·dif·fer·ence** \-'difrəns\ n —**in·dif·fer·ent·ly** adv

in·dig·e·nous \in'dijənəs\ adj : native to a particular region

in·di·gent \'indijənt\ adj : needy —**in·di·gence** \-jəns\ n

in·di·ges·tion \,indī'jeschən, -də-\ n : discomfort from inability to digest food

in·dig·na·tion \indig'nāshən\ n : anger aroused by something unjust or unworthy —**in·dig·nant** \in'dignənt\ adj —**in·dig·nant·ly** adv

in·dig·ni·ty \in'dignətē\ n, pl -ties 1 : offense against self-respect 2 : humiliating treatment

in·di·go \'indi,gō\ n, pl -gos or -goes 1 : blue dye 2 : deep reddish blue color

in·di·rect \ində'rekt, -dī-\ adj : not straight or straightforward —**in·di·rec·tion** \-'rekshən\ n —**in·di·rect·ly** adv —**in·di·rect·ness** n

in·dis·crim·i·nate \indis'krimənət\ adj 1 : not careful or discriminating 2 : haphazard —**in·dis·crim·i·nate·ly** adv

in·dis·pens·able \indis'pensəbəl\ adj : absolutely essential —**in·dis·pens·abil·i·ty** \-,pensə'bilətē\ n —**indispensable** n —**in·dis·pens·ably** \-'pensəblē\ adv

in·dis·posed \-'pōzd\ adj : slightly ill —**dis·po·si·tion** \in,dispə'zishən\ n

in·dis·sol·u·ble \indis'älyəbəl\ adj : not capable of being dissolved or broken

in·di·vid·u·al \ində'vijəwəl\ n 1 : single member of a category 2 : person —**individual** adj —**in·di·vid·u·al·ly** adv

in·di·vid·u·al·ist \-əwəlist\ n : person who is markedly independent in thought or action

in·di·vid·u·al·i·ty \-,vijə'walətē\ n : special quality that distinguishes an individual

in·di·vid·u·al·ize \-'vijəwə,līz\ vb -ized; -iz·ing 1 : make individual 2 : treat individually

in·doc·tri·nate \in'däktrə,nāt\ vb -nat·ed; -nat·ing : instruct in fundamentals (as of a doctrine) —**in·doc·tri·na·tion** \in-,däktrə'nāshən\ n

in·do·lent \'indələnt\ adj : lazy —**in·do·lence** \-ləns\ n

in·dom·i·ta·ble \in'dämətəbəl\ adj : invincible —**in·dom·i·ta·bly** \-blē\ adv

in·door \'in,dōr\ adj : relating to the inside of a building

in·doors \in'dōrz\ adv : in or into a building

in·du·bi·ta·ble \in'dübətəbəl, -'dyü-\ adj : being beyond question —**in·du·bi·ta·bly** \-blē\ adv

in·duce \in'düs, -'dyüs\ vb -duced; -duc·ing 1 : persuade 2 : bring about —**in·duce·ment** n —**in·duc·er** n

in·duct \in'dəkt\ vb 1 : put in office 2 : admit as a member 3 : enroll (as for military service) —**in·duct·ee** \in,dək'tē\ n

in·duc·tion \in'dəkshən\ n 1 : act or instance of inducting 2 : reasoning from particular instances to a general conclusion

in·duc·tive \in'dəktiv\ adj : reasoning by induction

in·dulge \in'dəlj\ vb -dulged; -dulg·ing : yield to the desire of or for —**in·dul·gence** \-'dəljəns\ n —**in·dul·gent** \-jənt\ adj —**in·dul·gent·ly** adv

in·dus·tri·al \in'dəstrēəl\ adj 1 : relating to industry 2 : heavy-duty —**in·dus·tri·al·ist** \-əlist\ n —**in·dus·tri·al·iza·tion** \-,dəstrēələ'zāshən\ n —**in·dus·tri·al·ize** \-'dəstrēə,līz\ vb —**in·dus·tri·al·ly** adv

in·dus·tri·ous \in'dəstrēəs\ adj : diligent or busy —**in·dus·tri·ous·ly** adv —**in·dus·tri·ous·ness** n

in·dus·try \'indəstrē\ n, pl -tries 1 : diligence 2 : manufacturing enterprises or activity

in·ebri·at·ed \in'ēbrē,ātəd\ adj : drunk —**in·ebri·a·tion** \-,ēbrē'āshən\ n

in·ef·fa·ble \in'efəbəl\ adj : incapable of being expressed in words —**in·ef·fa·bly** \-blē\ adv

in·ept \in'ept\ adj 1 : inappropriate or foolish 2 : generally incompetent —**in·ep·ti·tude** \in'eptə,tüd, -,tyüd\ n —**in·ept·ly** adv —**in·ept·ness** n

in·equal·i·ty \ini'kwälətē\ n : quality of being unequal or uneven

in·ert \in'ərt\ adj 1 : powerless to move or act 2 : sluggish —**in·ert·ly** adv —**in·ert·ness** n

in·er·tia \in'ərshə\ n : tendency of matter to remain at rest or in motion —**in·er·tial** \-shəl\ adj

in·es·cap·able \inə'skāpəbəl\ adj : inevitable —**in·es·cap·ably** \-blē\ adv

in·es·ti·ma·ble \in'estəməbəl\ adj : incapable of being estimated —**in·es·ti·ma·bly** \-blē\ adv

in·ev·i·ta·ble \in'evətəbəl\ adj : incapable of being avoided or escaped —**in·ev·i·ta·bil·i·ty** \in,evətə'bilətē\ n —**in·ev·i·ta·bly** \in'evətəblē\ adv

in·ex·cus·able \inik'skyüzəbəl\ adj : being without excuse or justification —**in·ex·cus·ably** \-blē\ adv

in·ex·haust·ible \inig'zóstəbəl\ adj : incapable of being used up or tired out —**in·ex·haust·ibly** \-blē\ adv

in·ex·o·ra·ble \in'eksərəbəl\ adj : unyielding or relentless —**in·ex·o·ra·bly** adv

in·fal·li·ble \in'faləbəl\ adj : incapable of error —**in·fal·li·bil·i·ty** \in,falə'bilətē\ n —**in·fal·li·bly** adv

in·fa·mous \'infəməs\ adj : having the worst kind of reputation —**in·fa·mous·ly** adv

in·fa·my \-mē\ n, pl -mies : evil reputation

in·fan·cy \'infənsē\ n, pl -cies 1 : early childhood 2 : early period of existence

in·fant \'infənt\ n : baby

in·fan·tile \'infən,tīl, -təl, -,tēl\ adj 1 : relating to infants 2 : childish

in·fan·try \'infəntrē\ n, pl -tries : soldiers that fight on foot

in·fat·u·ate \in'facha,wāt\ vb -at·ed; -at·ing : inspire with foolish love or admiration —**in·fat·u·a·tion** \-,facha'wāshən\ n

in·fect \in'fekt\ vb : contaminate with disease-producing matter —**in·fec·tion** \-'fekshən\ n —**in·fec·tious** \-shəs\ adj —**in·fec·tive** \-'fektiv\ adj

in·fer \in'fər\ vb -rr- : deduce —**in·fer·ence** \'infərəns\ n —**in·fer·en·tial** \infə'ren-chəl\ adj

in·fe·ri·or \in'firēər\ adj 1 : being lower in position, degree, rank, or merit 2 : of lesser quality —**inferior** n —**in·fe·ri·or·i·ty** \in,firē'órətē\ n

in·fer·nal \in'fərnəl\ adj : of or like hell—often used as a general expression of disapproval —**in·fer·nal·ly** adv

in·fer·no \in'fərnō\ n, pl -nos : place or condition suggesting hell

in·fest \in'fest\ vb : swarm or grow in or over —**in·fes·ta·tion** \in,fes'tāshən\ n

in·fi·del \'infəd²l, -fə,del\ n : one who does not believe in a particular religion

in·fi·del·i·ty \infə'delətē, -fī-\ n, pl -ties : lack of faithfulness

in·field \'in,fēld\ n : baseball field inside the base lines —**in·field·er** n

in·fil·trate \in'fil,trāt, 'infil-\ vb -trat·ed; -trat·ing : enter or become established in without being noticed —**in·fil·tra·tion** \infil'trāshən\ n

in·fi·nite \'infənət\ adj 1 : having no limit or extending indefinitely 2 : vast —**infinite** n —**in·fi·nite·ly** adv —**in·fi·ni·tude** \in'finə,tüd, -,tyüd\ n

in·fin·i·tes·i·mal \in,finə'tesəməl\ adj : immeasurably small —**in·fin·i·tes·i·mal·ly** adv

in·fin·i·tive \in'finətiv\ n : verb form in English usu. used with to

in·fin·i·ty \in'finətē\ n, pl -ties 1 : quality or state of being infinite 2 : indefinitely great number or amount

in·firm \in'fərm\ adj : feeble from age —**in·fir·mi·ty** \-'fərmətē\ n

in·fir·ma·ry \in'fərmərē\ n, pl -ries : place for the care of the sick

in·flame \in'flām\ vb -flamed; -flam·ing 1 : excite to intense action or feeling 2 : affect or become affected with inflammation —**in·flam·ma·to·ry** \-'flamə,tōrē\ adj

in·flam·ma·ble \in'flaməbəl\ adj : flammable

in·flam·ma·tion \,inflə'māshən\ n : response to injury in which an affected area becomes red and painful and congested with blood

in·flate \in'flāt\ vb -flat·ed; -flat·ing 1 : swell or puff up (as with gas) 2 : expand or increase abnormally —**in·flat·able** adj

in·fla·tion \in'flāshən\ n 1 : act of inflating 2 : continual rise in prices —**in·fla·tion·ary** \-shə,nerē\ adj

in·flec·tion \in'flekshən\ n 1 : change in pitch or loudness of the voice 2 : change in form of a word —**in·flect** \-'flekt\ vb —**in·flec·tion·al** \-'flekshənəl\ adj

in·flict \in'flikt\ vb : give by or as if by hitting —**in·flic·tion** \-'flikshən\ n

in·flu·ence \'in,flüəns\ n 1 : power or capacity of causing an effect in indirect or intangible ways 2 : one that exerts influence ~ vb -enced; -enc·ing : affect or alter by influence —**in·flu·en·tial** \influ-'enchəl\ adj

in·flu·en·za \,influ'enzə\ n : acute very contagious virus disease

in·flux \'in,fləks\ n : a flowing in

in·form \in'fórm\ vb : give information or knowledge to —**in·for·mant** \-ənt\ n —**in·form·er** n

in·for·mal \in'fórmal\ adj 1 : without formality or ceremony 2 : for ordinary or familiar use —**in·for·mal·i·ty** \infór-'malətē, -fər-\ n —**in·for·mal·ly** adv

in·for·ma·tion \infər'māshən\ n : knowledge obtained from investigation, study, or instruction —**in·for·ma·tion·al** \-shə-nəl\ adj

in·for·ma·tive \in'fórmətiv\ adj : giving knowledge

in·frac·tion \in'frakshən\ n : violation

in·fra·red \infrə'red\ adj : being, relating to, or using radiation of wavelengths longer than those of red light —**infrared** n

in·fra·struc·ture \'infrə,strəkchər\ n : foundation of a system or organization

in·fringe \in'frinj\ vb -fringed; -fring·ing : violate another's right or privilege —**in·fringe·ment** n

in·fu·ri·ate \in'fyúrē,āt\ vb -at·ed; -at·ing : make furious —**in·fu·ri·at·ing·ly** \-,ātiŋlē\ adv

in·fuse \in'fyüz\ vb -fused; -fus·ing 1 : instill a principle or quality in 2 : steep in liquid without boiling —**in·fu·sion** \-'fyüzhən\ n

1-ing \iŋ\ vb suffix or adj suffix —used to form the present participle and sometimes an adjective resembling a present participle

2-ing n suffix 1 : action or process 2 : something connected with or resulting from an action or process

in·ge·nious \in'jēnyəs\ adj : very clever —**in·ge·nious·ly** adv —**in·ge·nious·ness** n

in·ge·nue, in·gé·nue \'anjə,nü, 'än-; 'anzhə-, 'än-\ n : naive young woman

in·ge·nu·i·ty \injə'nüətē, -'nyü-\ n, pl -ties : skill or cleverness in planning or inventing

in·gen·u·ous \in'jenyəwəs\ adj : innocent and candid —**in·gen·u·ous·ly** adv —**in·gen·u·ous·ness** n

in·gest \in'jest\ vb : eat —**in·ges·tion** \-'jeschən\ n

in·gle·nook \'iŋgəl,núk\ n : corner by the fireplace

in·got \'iŋgət\ n : block of metal

in·grained \in'grānd\ adj : deep-seated

in·grate \'in,grāt\ n : ungrateful person

in·gra·ti·ate \in'grāshē,āt\ vb -at·ed; -at·ing : gain favor for (oneself) —**in·gra·ti·at·ing** adj

in·gre·di·ent \in'grēdēənt\ n : one of the substances that make up a mixture

in·grown \'in,grōn\ adj : grown in and esp. into the flesh

in·hab·it \in'habət\ vb : live or dwell in —**in·hab·it·able** adj —**in·hab·it·ant** \-ə-tənt\ n

in·hale \in'hāl\ vb -haled; -hal·ing : breathe in —**in·hal·ant** \-ənt\ n —**in·ha·la·tion** \inhə'lāshən, inə-\ n —**in·hal·er** n

in·here \in'hir\ vb -hered; -her·ing : be inherent

in·her·ent \in'hirənt, -'her-\ adj : being an essential part of something —**in·her·ent·ly** adv

in·her·it \in'herət\ vb : receive from one's ancestors —**in·her·it·able** \-əbəl\ adj —**in·her·i·tance** \-ətəns\ n —**in·her·i·tor** \-ətər\ n

in·hib·it \in'hibət\ vb : hold in check —**in·hi·bi·tion** \inhə'bishən, inə-\ n

in·hu·man \in'hyümən, -'yü-\ adj : cruel or impersonal —**in·hu·man·i·ty** \-hyü'manətē, -yü-\ n —**in·hu·man·ly** adv —**in·hu·man·ness** n

in·im·i·cal \in'imikəl\ adj : hostile or harmful —**in·im·i·cal·ly** adv

in·im·i·ta·ble \in'imətəbəl\ adj : not capable of being imitated

in·iq·ui·ty \in'ikwətē\ n, pl -ties : wickedness —**in·iq·ui·tous** \-wətəs\ adj

ini·tial \in'ishəl\ adj 1 : of or relating to the beginning 2 : first ~ n : 1st letter of a word or name ~ vb -tialed or -tialled; -tial·ing or -tial·ling : put initials on —**ini·tial·ly** adv

ini·ti·ate \in'ishē,āt\ vb -at·ed; -at·ing 1 : start 2 : induct into membership 3 : instruct in the rudiments of something —**initiate** \-'ishēət\ n —**ini·ti·a·tion** \-,ishē'āshən\ n —**ini·ti·a·to·ry** \-'ishēə,tōrē\ adj

ini·tia·tive \in'ishətiv\ n 1 : first step 2 : readiness to undertake something on one's own

in·ject \in'jekt\ vb : force or introduce into something —**in·jec·tion** \-'jekshən\ n

in·junc·tion \in'jəŋkshən\ n : court writ requiring one to do or to refrain from doing a specified act

in·jure \'injər\ vb -jured; -jur·ing : do damage, hurt, or a wrong to

in·ju·ry \'injərē\ n, pl -ries 1 : act that injures 2 : hurt, damage, or loss sustained —**in·ju·ri·ous** \in'júrēəs\ adj

in·jus·tice \in'jəstəs\ n : unjust act

ink \'iŋk\ n : usu. liquid and colored material for writing and printing ~ vb : put ink on —**ink·well** \-,wel\ n —**inky** adj

in·kling \'iŋkliŋ\ n : hint or idea

in·land \'in,land, -lənd\ n : interior of a country —**inland** adj or adv

in-law \'in,ló\ n : relative by marriage

in·lay \in'lā, 'in,lā\ vb -laid \-'lād\ -lay·ing : set into a surface for decoration ~ \'in,-\ n 1 : inlaid work 2 : shaped filling cemented into a tooth

in·let \'in,let, -lət\ n : small bay

in·mate \'in,māt\ n : person confined to an asylum or prison

in me•mo•ri•am \ˌinmə'mōrēəm\ *prep* : in memory of
in•most \'inˌmōst\ *adj* : deepest within
inn \'in\ *n* : hotel
in•nards \'inərdz\ *n pl* : internal parts
in•nate \in'āt\ *adj* **1** : inborn **2** : inherent —**in•nate•ly** *adv*
in•ner \'inər\ *adj* : being on the inside
in•ner•most \'inərˌmōst\ *adj* : farthest inward
in•ner•sole \ˌinər'sōl\ *n* : insole
in•ning \'iniŋ\ *n* : baseball team's turn at bat
inn•keep•er \'inˌkēpər\ *n* : owner of an inn
in•no•cent \'inəsənt\ *adj* **1** : free from guilt **2** : harmless **3** : not sophisticated —**in•no•cence** \-səns\ *n* —**innocent** *n* —**in•no•cent•ly** *adv*
in•noc•u•ous \in'äkyəwəs\ *adj* **1** : harmless **2** : inoffensive
in•no•va•tion \ˌinə'vāshən\ *n* : new idea or method —**in•no•vate** \'inəˌvāt\ *vb* —**in•no•va•tive** \'inəˌvātiv\ *adj* —**in•no•va•tor** \-ˌvātər\ *n*
in•nu•en•do \ˌinyə'wendō\ *n, pl* **-dos** *or* **-does** : insinuation
in•nu•mer•a•ble \in'ümərəbəl, -'yüm-\ *adj* : countless
in•oc•u•late \in'äkyəˌlāt\ *vb* **-lat•ed; -lat•ing** : treat with something esp. to establish immunity —**in•oc•u•la•tion** \-ˌäkyə'lāshən\ *n*
in•op•por•tune \inˌäpər'tün, -'tyün\ *adj* : inconvenient —**in•op•por•tune•ly** *adv*
in•or•di•nate \in'ȯrd^{ə}nət\ *adj* : unusual or excessive —**in•or•di•nate•ly** *adv*
in•or•gan•ic \ˌinˌȯr'ganik\ *adj* : made of mineral matter
in•pa•tient \'inˌpāshənt\ *n* : patient who stays in a hospital
in•put \'inˌpu̇t\ *n* : something put in —**input** *vb*
in•quest \'inˌkwest\ *n*: inquiry esp. before a jury
in•quire \in'kwīr\ *vb* **-quired; -quir•ing 1** : ask **2** : investigate —**in•quir•er** *n* —**in•quir•ing•ly** *adv* —**in•qui•ry** \'inˌkwīrē, in'kwīrē; 'inkwərē, 'iŋ-\ *n*
in•qui•si•tion \ˌinkwə'zishən, ˌiŋ-\ *n* **1** : official inquiry **2** : severe questioning —**in•quis•i•tor** \in'kwizətər\ *n* —**in•quis•i•to•ri•al** \-ˌkwizə'tōrēəl\ *adj*
in•quis•i•tive \in'kwizətiv\ *adj* : curious —**in•quis•i•tive•ly** *adv* —**in•quis•i•tive•ness** *n*
in•road \'inˌrōd\ *n* : encroachment
in•rush \'inˌrəsh\ *n* : influx
in•sane \in'sān\ *adj* **1** : not sane **2** : absurd —**in•sane•ly** *adv* —**in•san•i•ty** \in'sanətē\ *n*
in•sa•tia•ble \in'sāshəbəl\ *adj* : incapable of being satisfied —**in•sa•tia•bil•i•ty** \inˌsāshə'bilətē\ *n* —**in•sa•tia•bly** *adv*
in•scribe \in'skrīb\ *vb* **1** : write **2** : engrave **3** : dedicate (a book) to someone —**in•scrip•tion** \-'skripshən\ *n*
in•scru•ta•ble \in'skrütəbəl\ *adj* : mysterious —**in•scru•ta•bly** *adv*
in•seam \'inˌsēm\ *n* : inner seam (of a garment)
in•sect \'inˌsekt\ *n* : small usu. winged animal with 6 legs
in•sec•ti•cide \in'sektəˌsīd\ *n* : insect poison —**in•sec•ti•cid•al** \inˌsektə'sīd^{ə}l\ *adj*
in•se•cure \ˌinsi'kyu̇r\ *adj* **1** : uncertain **2** : unsafe **3** : fearful —**in•se•cure•ly** *adv* —**in•se•cu•ri•ty** \-'kyu̇rətē\ *n*
in•sem•i•nate \in'seməˌnāt\ *vb* **-nat•ed; -nat•ing** : introduce semen into —**in•sem•i•na•tion** \-ˌsemə'nāshən\ *n*
in•sen•si•ble \in'sensəbəl\ *adj* **1** : unconscious **2** : unable to feel **3** : unaware —**in•sen•si•bil•i•ty** \inˌsensə'bilətē\ *n* —**in•sen•si•bly** *adv*
in•sen•tient \in'senchənt\ *adj* : lacking feeling —**in•sen•tience** \-chəns\ *n*
in•sert \in'sərt\ *vb* : put in —**insert** \'inˌsərt\ *n* —**in•ser•tion** \in'sərshən\ *n*
in•set \'inˌset\ *vb* **inset** *or* **in•set•ted; in•set•ting** : set in —**inset** *n*
in•shore \'in'shōr\ *adj* **1** : situated near shore **2** : moving toward shore ~ *adv* : toward shore
in•side \in'sīd, 'inˌsīd\ *n* **1** : inner side **2** *pl* : innards ~ *prep* **1** : in or into the inside of **2** : within ~ *adv* **1** : on the inner side **2** : into the interior —**inside** *adj* —**in•sid•er** \in'sīdər\ *n*
inside of *prep* : inside
in•sid•i•ous \in'sidēəs\ *adj* **1** : treacherous **2** : seductive —**in•sid•i•ous•ly** *adv* —**in•sid•i•ous•ness** *n*
in•sight \'inˌsīt\ *n* : understanding —**in•sight•ful** \'inˌsītfəl, in'sīt-\ *adj*
in•sig•nia \in'signēə\, **in•sig•ne** \-ˌnē\ *n, pl* **-nia** *or* **-ni•as** : badge of authority or office
in•sin•u•ate \in'sinyəˌwāt\ *vb* **-at•ed; -at•ing 1** : imply **2** : bring in artfully —**in•sin•u•a•tion** \inˌsinyə'wāshən\ *n*
in•sip•id \in'sipəd\ *adj* **1** : tasteless **2** : not stimulating —**in•si•pid•i•ty** \ˌinsə'pidətē\ *n*
in•sist \in'sist\ *vb* : be firmly demanding —**in•sis•tence** \in'sistəns\ *n* —**in•sis•tent** \-tənt\ *adj* —**in•sis•tent•ly** *adv*
in•so•far as \ˌinsō'färaz\ *conj* : to the extent that
in•sole \'inˌsōl\ *n* : inside sole of a shoe
in•so•lent \'insələnt\ *adj* : contemptuously rude —**in•so•lence** \-ləns\ *n*
in•sol•vent \in'sälvənt\ *adj* : unable or insufficient to pay debts —**in•sol•ven•cy** \-vənsē\ *n*
in•som•nia \in'sämnēə\ *n* : inability to sleep
in•so•much as \ˌinsō'məchaz\ *conj* : inasmuch as
insomuch that *conj* : to such a degree that
in•sou•ci•ance \in'süsēəns, a^{n}sü'syä^{n}s\ *n* : lighthearted indifference —**in•sou•ci•ant** \in'süsēənt, a^{n}sü'syä^{n}\ *adj*
in•spect \in'spekt\ *vb* : view closely and critically —**in•spec•tion** \-'spekshən\ *n* —**in•spec•tor** \-tər\ *n*
in•spire \in'spīr\ *vb* **-spired; -spir•ing 1** : inhale **2** : influence by example **3** : bring about **4** : stir to action —**in•spi•ra•tion** \ˌinspə'rāshən\ *n* —**in•spi•ra•tion•al** \-'rāshənəl\ *adj* —**in•spir•er** *n*
in•stall, in•stal \in'stȯl\ *vb* **-stalled; -stall•ing 1** : induct into office **2** : set up for use —**in•stal•la•tion** \ˌinstə'lāshən\ *n*
in•stall•ment \in'stȯlmənt\ *n* : partial payment
in•stance \'instəns\ *n* **1** : request or instigation **2** : example
in•stant \'instənt\ *n* : moment ~ *adj* **1** : immediate **2** : ready to mix —**in•stan•ta•neous** \ˌinstən'tānēəs\ *adj* —**in•stan•ta•neous•ly** *adv* —**in•stant•ly** *adv*
in•stead \in'sted\ *adv* : as a substitute or alternative
instead of *prep* : as a substitute for or alternative to
in•step \'inˌstep\ *n* : part of the foot in front of the ankle
in•sti•gate \'instəˌgāt\ *vb* **-gat•ed; -gat•ing** : incite —**in•sti•ga•tion** \ˌinstə'gāshən\ *n* —**in•sti•ga•tor** \'instəˌgātər\ *n*
in•still \in'stil\ *vb* **-stilled; -still•ing** : impart gradually
in•stinct \'inˌstiŋkt\ *n* **1** : natural talent **2** : natural inherited or subconsciously motivated behavior —**in•stinc•tive** \in'stiŋktiv\ *adj* —**in•stinc•tive•ly** *adv* —**in•stinc•tu•al** \in'stiŋkchəwəl\ *adj*
in•sti•tute \'instəˌtüt, -ˌtyüt\ *vb* **-tut•ed; -tut•ing** : establish, start, or organize ~ *n* **1** : organization promoting a cause **2** : school
in•sti•tu•tion \ˌinstə'tüshən, -'tyü-\ *n* **1** : act of instituting **2** : custom **3** : corporation or society of a public character —**in•sti•tu•tion•al** \-shənəl\ *adj* —**in•sti•tu•tion•al•ize** \-ˌīz\ *vb* —**in•sti•tu•tion•al•ly** *adv*
in•struct \in'strəkt\ *vb* **1** : teach **2** : give an order to —**in•struc•tion** \in'strəkshən\ *n* —**in•struc•tion•al** \-shənəl\ *adj* —**in•struc•tive** \in'strəktiv\ *adj* —**in•struc•tor** \in'strəktər\ *n* —**in•struc•tor•ship** *n*
in•stru•ment \'instrəmənt\ *n* **1** : something that produces music **2** : means **3** : device for doing work and esp. precision work **4** : legal document —**in•stru•men•tal** \ˌinstrə'ment^{ə}l\ *adj* —**in•stru•men•tal•ist** \-ist\ *n* —**in•stru•men•tal•i•ty** \ˌinstrəmən'talətē, -ˌmen-\ *n* —**in•stru•men•ta•tion** \ˌinstrəmən'tāshən, -ˌmen-\ *n*
in•sub•or•di•nate \ˌinsə'bȯrd^{ə}nət\ *adj* : not obeying —**in•sub•or•di•na•tion** \-ˌbȯrd^{ə}n'āshən\ *n*
in•suf•fer•able \in'səfərəbəl\ *adj* : unbearable —**in•suf•fer•ably** \-blē\ *adv*
in•su•lar \'insülər, -syu̇-\ *adj* **1** : relating to or residing on an island **2** : narrow-minded —**in•su•lar•i•ty** \ˌinsü'larətē, -syu̇-\ *n*
in•su•late \'insəˌlāt\ *vb* **-lat•ed; -lat•ing** : protect from heat loss or electricity —**in•su•la•tion** \ˌinsə'lāshən\ *n* —**in•su•la•tor** \'insəˌlātər\ *n*
in•su•lin \'insələn\ *n* : hormone used by diabetics
in•sult \in'səlt\ *vb* : treat with contempt ~ \'inˌsəlt\ *n* : insulting act or remark —**in•sult•ing•ly** \-iŋlē\ *adv*
in•su•per•a•ble \in'süpərəbəl\ *adj* : too difficult —**in•su•per•a•bly** \-blē\ *adv*
in•sure \in'shu̇r\ *vb* **-sured; -sur•ing 1** : guarantee against loss **2** : make certain —**in•sur•able** \-əbəl\ *adj* —**in•sur•ance** \-əns\ *n* —**in•sured** \in'shu̇rd\ *n* —**in•sur•er** *n*
in•sur•gent \in'sərjənt\ *n* : rebel —**in•sur•gence** \-jəns\ *n* —**in•sur•gen•cy** \-jənsē\ *n* —**in•sur•gent** *adj*
in•sur•mount•able \ˌinsər'mau̇ntəbəl\ *adj* : too great to be overcome —**in•sur•mount•ably** \-blē\ *adv*
in•sur•rec•tion \ˌinsə'rekshən\ *n* : revolution —**in•sur•rec•tion•ist** *n*
in•tact \in'takt\ *adj* : undamaged
in•take \'inˌtāk\ *n* **1** : opening through which something enters **2** : act of taking in **3** : amount taken in
in•te•ger \'intijər\ *n* : number that is not a fraction and does not include a fraction
in•te•gral \'intigrəl\ *adj* : essential
in•te•grate \'intəˌgrāt\ *vb* **-grat•ed; -grat•ing 1** : unite **2** : end segregation of or at —**in•te•gra•tion** \ˌintə'grāshən\ *n*
in•teg•ri•ty \in'tegrətē\ *n* **1** : soundness **2** : adherence to a code of values **3** : completeness
in•tel•lect \'int^{ə}lˌekt\ *n* : power of knowing or thinking —**in•tel•lec•tu•al** \ˌint^{ə}l'ekchəwəl\ *adj or n* —**in•tel•lec•tu•al•ism** \-chəwəˌlizəm\ *n* —**in•tel•lec•tu•al•ly** *adv*
in•tel•li•gence \in'teləjəns\ *n* **1** : ability to learn and understand **2** : mental acuteness **3** : information
in•tel•li•gent \in'teləjənt\ *adj* : having or showing intelligence —**in•tel•li•gent•ly** *adv*
in•tel•li•gi•ble \in'teləjəbəl\ *adj* : understandable —**in•tel•li•gi•bil•i•ty** \-ˌteləjə'bilətē\ *n* —**in•tel•li•gi•bly** *adv*
in•tem•per•ance \in'tempərəns\ *n* : lack of moderation —**in•tem•per•ate** \-pərət\ *adj* —**in•tem•per•ate•ness** *n*
in•tend \in'tend\ *vb* : have as a purpose
in•tend•ed \-'tendəd\ *n* : engaged person —**intended** *adj*
in•tense \in'tens\ *adj* **1** : extreme **2** : deeply felt —**in•tense•ly** *adv* —**inten•si•fi•ca•tion** \-ˌtensəfə'kāshən\ *n* —**in•ten•si•fy** \-'tensəˌfī\ *vb* —**in•ten•si•ty** \in'tensətē\ *n* —**in•ten•sive** \in'tensiv\ *adj* —**in•ten•sive•ly** *adv*
[1]**in•tent** \in'tent\ *n* : purpose —**in•ten•tion** \-'tenchən\ *n* —**in•ten•tion•al** \-'tenchənəl\ *adj* —**in•ten•tion•al•ly** *adv*
[2]**intent** *adj* : concentrated —**in•tent•ly** *adv* —**in•tent•ness** *n*
in•ter \in'tər\ *vb* **-rr-** : bury
inter- *prefix* : between or among

interagency
interatomic
interbank
interborough
intercampus
interchurch
intercity
interclass
intercoastal
intercollegiate
intercolonial
intercommunal
intercommunity
intercompany
intercontinental
intercounty
intercultural
interdenominational
interdepartmental
interdivisional
interelectronic
interethnic
interfaculty
interfamily
interfiber
interfraternity
intergalactic
intergang
intergovernmental
intergroup
interhemispheric
interindustry
interinstitutional
interisland
interlibrary
intermolecular
intermountain
interoceanic
interoffice
interparticle
interparty
interpersonal
interplanetary
interpopulation
interprovincial
interracial
interregional
interreligious
interscholastic
intersectional
interstate
interstellar
intersystem
interterm
interterminal
intertribal
intertroop
intertropical
interuniversity
interurban
intervalley
intervillage
interwar
interzonal
interzone

in•ter•ac•tion \ˌintər'akshən\ *n* : mutual influence —**in•ter•act** \-'akt\ *vb* —**in•ter•ac•tive** *adj*
in•ter•breed \ˌintər'brēd\ *vb* **-bred** \-'bred\; **-breed•ing** : breed together
in•ter•ca•late \in'tərkəˌlāt\ *vb* **-lat•ed; -lat•ing** : insert —**in•ter•ca•la•tion** \-ˌtərkə'lāshən\ *n*
in•ter•cede \ˌintər'sēd\ *vb* **-ced•ed; -ced•ing** : act to reconcile —**in•ter•ces•sion** \-'seshən\ *n* —**in•ter•ces•sor** \-'sesər\ *n*
in•ter•cept \ˌintər'sept\ *vb* : interrupt the progress of —**intercept** \'intərˌsept\ *n* —**in•ter•cep•tion** \ˌintər'sepshən\ *n* —**in•ter•cep•tor** \-'septər\ *n*
in•ter•change \ˌintər'chānj\ *vb* **1** : exchange **2** : change places ~ \'intərˌchānj\ *n* **1** : exchange **2** : junction of highways —**in•ter•change•able** \ˌintər'chānjəbəl\ *adj*
in•ter•course \'intərˌkōrs\ *n* **1** : relations between persons or nations **2** : copulation
in•ter•de•pen•dent \ˌintərdi'pendənt\ *adj* : mutually dependent —**in•ter•de•pen•dence** \-dəns\ *n*
in•ter•dict \ˌintər'dikt\ *vb* **1** : prohibit **2** : destroy or cut (an enemy supply line) —**in•ter•dic•tion** \-'dikshən\ *n*
in•ter•est \'intrəst, -təˌrest\ *n* **1** : right **2** : benefit **3** : charge for borrowed money **4** : readiness to pay special attention **5** : quality that causes interest ~ *vb* **1** : concern **2** : get the attention of —**in•ter•est•ing** *adj* —**in•ter•est•ing•ly** *adv*
in•ter•face \'intərˌfās\ *n* : common boundary —**in•ter•fa•cial** \ˌintər'fāshəl\ *adj*
in•ter•fere \ˌintər'fir\ *vb* **-fered; -fer•ing 1** : collide or be in opposition **2** : try to run the affairs of others —**inter•fer•ence** \-'firəns\ *n*
in•ter•im \'intərəm\ *n* : time between —**interim** *adj*
in•te•ri•or \in'tirēər\ *adj* : being on the inside ~ *n* **1** : inside **2** : inland area
in•ter•ject \ˌintər'jekt\ *vb* : stick in between
in•ter•jec•tion \-'jekshən\ *n* : an exclamatory word —**in•ter•jec•tion•al•ly** \-shənəlē\ *adv*
in•ter•lace \ˌintər'lās\ *vb* : cross or cause to cross one over another
in•ter•lin•ear \ˌintər'linēər\ *adj* : between written or printed lines
in•ter•lock \ˌintər'läk\ *vb* **1** : interlace **2** : connect for mutual effect —**inter•lock** \'intərˌläk\ *n*
in•ter•lop•er \ˌintər'lōpər\ *n* : intruder or meddler
in•ter•lude \'intərˌlüd\ *n* : intervening period
in•ter•mar•ry \ˌintər'marē\ *vb* **1** : marry each other **2** : marry within a group —**in•ter•mar•riage** \-'marij\ *n*
in•ter•me•di•ary \ˌintər'mēdēˌerē\ *n, pl* **-ar•ies** : agent between individuals or groups —**intermediary** *adj*
in•ter•me•di•ate \ˌintər'mēdēət\ *adj* : between extremes —**intermediate** *n*
in•ter•ment \in'tərmənt\ *n* : burial
in•ter•mi•na•ble \in'tərmənəbəl\ *adj* : endless —**in•ter•mi•na•bly** *adv*
in•ter•min•gle \ˌintər'miŋgəl\ *vb* : mingle
in•ter•mis•sion \ˌintər'mishən\ *n* : break in a performance
in•ter•mit•tent \-'mit^{ə}nt\ *adj* : coming at intervals —**in•ter•mit•tent•ly** *adv*
in•ter•mix \ˌintər'miks\ *vb* : mix together —**in•ter•mix•ture** \-'mikschər\ *n*
[1]**in•tern** \'inˌtərn, in'tərn\ *vb* : confine esp. during a war —**in•tern•ee** \ˌinˌtər'nē\ *n* —**in•tern•ment** *n*
[2]**in•tern** \'inˌtərn\ *n* : advanced student (as in medicine) gaining supervised experience ~ *vb* : act as an intern —**in•tern•ship** *n*
in•ter•nal \in'tərn^{ə}l\ *adj* **1** : inward **2** : inside of the body **3** : relating to or existing in the mind —**in•ter•nal•ly** *adv*
in•ter•na•tion•al \ˌintər'nashənəl\ *adj* : affecting 2 or more nations ~ *n* : something having international scope —**in•ter•na•tion•al•ism** \-ˌizəm\ *n* —**in•ter•na•tion•al•ize** \-ˌīz\ *vb* —**in•ter•na•tion•ally** *adv*
in•ter•nist \'inˌtərnist\ *n* : specialist in nonsurgical medicine
in•ter•play \'intərˌplā\ *n* : interaction
in•ter•po•late \in'tərpəˌlāt\ *vb* **-lat•ed; -lat•ing** : insert —**in•ter•po•la•tion** \-ˌtərpə'lāshən\ *n*
in•ter•pose \ˌintər'pōz\ *vb* **-posed; -pos•ing 1** : place between **2** : intrude —**in•ter•po•si•tion** \-pə'zishən\ *n*
in•ter•pret \in'tərprət\ *vb* : explain the meaning of —**in•ter•pre•ta•tion** \inˌtərprə'tāshən\ *n* —**in•ter•pre•ta•tive** \-'tərprəˌtātiv\ *adj* —**in•ter•pret•er** *n* —**in•ter•pre•tive** \-'tərprətiv\ *adj*
in•ter•re•late \ˌintəri'lāt\ *vb* : have a mutual relationship —**in•ter•re•lat•ed•ness** \-'lātədnəs\ *n* —**in•ter•re•la•tion** \-'lāshən\ *n* —**in•ter•re•la•tion•ship** *n*
in•ter•ro•gate \in'terəˌgāt\ *vb* **-gat•ed; -gat•ing** : question —**in•ter•ro•ga•tion** \-ˌterə'gāshən\ *n* —**in•ter•rog•a•tive** \ˌintə'rägətiv\ *adj or n* —**in•ter•ro•ga•tor** \-'terəˌgātər\ *n* —**in•ter•rog•a•to•ry** \ˌintə'rägəˌtȯrē\ *adj*
in•ter•rupt \ˌintə'rəpt\ *vb* : intrude so as to hinder or end continuity —**in•ter•rupt•er** *n* —**in•ter•rup•tion** \-'rəpshən\ *n* —**in•ter•rup•tive** \-'rəptiv\ *adv*
in•ter•sect \ˌintər'sekt\ *vb* **1** : cut across or divide **2** : cross —**in•ter•sec•tion** \-'sekshən\ *n*
in•ter•sperse \ˌintər'spərs\ *vb* **-spersed; -spers•ing** : insert at intervals —**in•ter•sper•sion** \-'spərzhən\ *n*
in•ter•stice \in'tərstəs\ *n, pl* **-stic•es** \-stəˌsēz, -stəsəz\ : space between —**in•ter•sti•tial** \ˌintər'stishəl\ *adj*
in•ter•twine \ˌintər'twīn\ *vb* : twist together —**in•ter•twine•ment** *n*
in•ter•val \'intərvəl\ *n* **1** : time between **2** : space between
in•ter•vene \ˌintər'vēn\ *vb* **-vened; -ven•ing 1** : happen between events **2** : intercede —**in•ter•ven•tion** \-'venchən\ *n*
in•ter•view \'intərˌvyü\ *n* : a meeting to get information —**interview** *vb* —**in•ter•view•er** *n*
in•ter•weave \ˌintər'wēv\ *vb* **-wove** \-'wōv\; **-wo•ven** \-'wōvən\; **-weav•ing** : weave together —**in•ter•wo•ven** \-'wōvən\ *adj*
in•tes•tate \in'tesˌtāt, -tət\ *adj* : not leaving a will
in•tes•tine \in'testən\ *n* : tubular part of the digestive system after the stomach including a long narrow upper part (**small intestine**) followed by a broader shorter lower part (**large intestine**) —**in•tes•ti•nal** \-tən^{ə}l\ *adj*

in•ti•mate \'intə,māt\ *vb* **-mat•ed; -mat•ing** : hint ~ \'intəmət\ *adj* **1** : very friendly **2** : suggesting privacy **3** : very personal ~ *n* : close friend —**in•ti•ma•cy** \'intəməsē\ *n* —**in•ti•mate•ly** *adv* —**in•ti•ma•tion** \,intə'māshən\ *n*

in•tim•i•date \in'timə,dāt\ *vb* **-dat•ed; -dat•ing** : make fearful —**in•tim•i•da•tion** \-,timə'dāshən\ *n*

in•to \'intü\ *prep* **1** : to the inside of **2** : to the condition of **3** : against

in•to•na•tion \,intō'nāshən\ *n* : way of singing or speaking

in•tone \in'tōn\ *vb* **-toned; -ton•ing** : chant

in•tox•i•cate \in'täksə,kāt\ *vb* **-cat•ed; -cat•ing** : make drunk —**in•tox•i•cant** \-sikənt\ *n or adj* —**in•tox•i•ca•tion** \-,täksə'kāshən\ *n*

in•tra•mu•ral \,intrə'myu̇rəl\ *adj* : within a school

in•tran•si•gent \in'transəjənt\ *adj* : uncompromising —**in•tran•si•gence** \-jəns\ *n* —**intransigent** *n*

in•tra•ve•nous \,intrə'vēnəs\ *adj* : by way of the veins —**in•tra•ve•nous•ly** *adv*

in•trep•id \in'trepəd\ *adj* : fearless —**in•tre•pid•i•ty** \,intrə'pidətē\ *n*

in•tri•cate \'intrikət\ *adj* : very complex and delicate —**in•tri•ca•cy** \-trikəsē\ *n* —**in•tri•cate•ly** *adv*

in•trigue \in'trēg\ *vb* **-trigued; -trigu•ing 1** : scheme **2** : arouse curiosity of ~ *n* : secret scheme —**in•trigu•ing•ly** \-iŋlē\ *adv*

in•trin•sic \in'trinzik, -sik\ *adj* : essential —**in•trin•si•cal•ly** \-ziklē, -si-\ *adv*

in•tro•duce \,intrə'düs, -'dyüs\ *vb* **-duced; -duc•ing 1** : bring in esp. for the 1st time **2** : cause to be acquainted **3** : bring to notice **4** : put in —**in•tro•duc•tion** \'dəkshən\ *n* —**in•tro•duc•to•ry** \-'dəktərē\ *adj*

in•tro•spec•tion \,intrə'spekshən\ *n* : examination of one's own thoughts or feelings —**in•tro•spec•tive** \-'spektiv\ *adj* —**in•tro•spec•tive•ly** *adv*

in•tro•vert \'intrə,vərt\ *n* : shy or reserved person —**in•tro•ver•sion** \,intrə'vərzhən\ *n* —**introvert** *adj* —**in•tro•vert•ed** \'intrə,vərtəd\ *adj*

in•trude \in'trüd\ *vb* **-trud•ed; -trud•ing 1** : thrust in **2** : encroach —**in•trud•er** *n* —**in•tru•sion** \-'trüzhən\ *n* —**in•tru•sive** \-'trüsiv\ *adj* —**in•tru•sive•ness** *n*

in•tu•ition \,intu̇'ishən, -tyü-\ *n* : quick and ready insight —**in•tu•it** \in'tüət, -'tyü-\ *vb* —**in•tu•i•tive** \-ətiv\ *adj* —**in•tu•i•tive•ly** *adv*

in•un•date \'inən,dāt\ *vb* **-dat•ed; -dat•ing** : flood —**in•un•da•tion** \,inən'dāshən\ *n*

in•ure \in'u̇r, -'yu̇r\ *vb* **-ured; -ur•ing** : accustom to accept something undesirable

in•vade \in'vād\ *vb* **-vad•ed; -vad•ing** : enter for conquest —**in•vad•er** *n* —**in•va•sion** \-'vāzhən\ *n*

[1]**in•val•id** \in'valəd\ *adj* : not true or legal —**in•va•lid•i•ty** \,invə'lidətē\ *n* —**in•val•id•ly** *adv*

[2]**in•va•lid** \'invələd\ *adj* : sickly ~ *n* : one chronically ill

in•val•i•date \in'valə,dāt\ *vb* : make invalid —**in•val•i•da•tion** \in,valə'dāshən\

in•valu•able \in'valyəwəbəl\ *adj* : extremely valuable

in•va•sive \in'vāsiv\ *adj* : involving entry into the body

in•vec•tive \in'vektiv\ *n* : abusive language —**invective** *adj*

in•veigh \in'vā\ *vb* : protest or complain forcefully

in•vei•gle \in'vāgəl, -'vē-\ *vb* **-gled; -gling** : win over or get by flattery

in•vent \in'vent\ *vb* **1** : think up **2** : create for the 1st time —**in•ven•tion** \-'venchən\ *n* —**in•ven•tive** \-'ventiv\ *adj* —**in•ven•tive•ness** *n* —**in•ven•tor** \-'ventər\ *n*

in•ven•to•ry \'invən,tōrē\ *n, pl* **-ries 1** : list of goods **2** : stock —**inventory** *vb*

in•verse \in'vərs, 'in,vərs\ *adj or n* : opposite —**in•verse•ly** *adv*

in•vert \in'vərt\ *vb* **1** : turn upside down or inside out **2** : reverse —**in•ver•sion** \-'verzhən\ *n*

in•ver•te•brate \in'vərtəbrət, -,brāt\ *adj* : lacking a backbone ~ *n* : invertebrate animal

in•vest \in'vest\ *vb* **1** : give power or authority to **2** : endow with a quality **3** : commit money to someone else's use in hope of profit —**in•vest•ment** \-mənt\ *n* —**in•ves•tor** \-'vestər\ *n*

in•ves•ti•gate \in'vestə,gāt\ *vb* **-gat•ed; -gat•ing** : study closely and systematically —**in•ves•ti•ga•tion** \-,vestə'gāshən\ *n* —**in•ves•ti•ga•tive** \-'vestə,gātiv\ *adj* —**in•ves•ti•ga•tor** \-'vestə,gātər\ *n*

in•ves•ti•ture \in'vestə,chu̇r, -chər\ *n* : act of establishing in office

in•vet•er•ate \in'vetərət\ *adj* : acting out of habit

in•vid•i•ous \in'vidēəs\ *adj* : harmful or obnoxious —**in•vid•i•ous•ly** *adv*

in•vig•o•rate \in'vigə,rāt\ *vb* **-rat•ed; -rat•ing** : give life and energy to —**in•vig•o•ra•tion** \-,vigə'rāshən\ *n*

in•vin•ci•ble \in'vinsəbəl\ *adj* : incapable of being conquered —**in•vin•ci•bil•i•ty** \in,vinsə'bilətē\ *n* —**in•vin•ci•bly** \in'vinsəblē\ *adv*

in•vi•o•la•ble \in'vīələbəl\ *adj* : safe from violation or desecration —**in•vi•o•la•bil•i•ty** \in,vīələ'bilətē\ *n*

in•vi•o•late \in'vīələt\ *adj* : not violated or profaned

in•vite \in'vīt\ *vb* **-vit•ed; -vit•ing 1** : entice **2** : increase the likelihood of **3** : request the presence or participation of **4** : encourage —**in•vi•ta•tion** \,invə'tāshən\ *n* —**in•vit•ing** \in'vītiŋ\ *adj*

in•vo•ca•tion \,invə'kāshən\ *n* **1** : prayer **2** : incantation

in•voice \'in,vȯis\ *n* : itemized bill for goods shipped ~ *vb* **-voiced; -voic•ing** : bill

in•voke \in'vōk\ *vb* **-voked; -vok•ing 1** : call on for help **2** : cite as authority **3** : conjure **4** : carry out

in•volve \in'välv\ *vb* **-volved; -volv•ing 1** : draw in as a participant **2** : relate closely **3** : require as a necessary part **4** : occupy fully —**in•volve•ment** *n*

in•volved \-'välvd\ *adj* : intricate

[1]**in•ward** \'inwərd\ *adj* : inside

[2]**inward, in•wards** \-wərdz\ *adv* : toward the inside, center, or inner being

in•ward•ly *adv* **1** : mentally or spiritually **2** : internally **3** : to oneself

io•dide \'īə,dīd\ *n* : compound of iodine

io•dine \'īə,dīn, -əd[ə]n\ *n* **1** : nonmetallic chemical element **2** : solution of iodine used as an antiseptic

io•dize \'īə,dīz\ *vb* **-dized; -diz•ing** : treat with iodine or an iodide

ion \'īən, 'ī,än\ *n* : electrically charged particle —**ion•ic** \ī'änik\ *adj* —**ion•iz•able** \'īə,nīzəbəl\ *adj* —**ion•iza•tion** \,īənə'zāshən\ *n* —**ion•ize** \'īə,nīz\ *vb* —**ion•iz•er** \'īə,nīzər\ *n*

-ion *n suffix* **1** : act or process **2** : state or condition

ion•o•sphere \ī'änə,sfir\ *n* : layer of the upper atmosphere containing ionized gases —**ion•o•spher•ic** \ī,änə'sfirik, -'sfer-\ *adj*

io•ta \ī'ōtə\ *n* : small quantity

IOU \,ī,ō'yü\ *n* : acknowledgment of a debt

iras•ci•ble \ir'asəbəl, ī'ras-\ *adj* : marked by hot temper —**iras•ci•bil•i•ty** \-,asə'bilətē, -,ras-\ *n*

irate \ī'rāt\ *adj* : roused to intense anger —**irate•ly** *adv*

ire \'īr\ *n* : anger

ir•i•des•cence \,irə'des[ə]ns\ *n* : rainbowlike play of colors —**ir•i•des•cent** \-[ə]nt\ *adj*

iris \'īrəs\ *n, pl* **iris•es** *or* **iri•des** \'īrə,dēz, 'ir-\ **1** : colored part around the pupil of the eye **2** : plant with long leaves and large showy flowers

irk \'ərk\ *vb* : annoy —**irk•some** \-səm\ *adj* —**irk•some•ly** *adv*

iron \'īərn\ *n* **1** : heavy metallic chemical element **2** : something made of iron **3** : heated device for pressing clothes **4** : hardness, determination ~ *vb* : press or smooth out with an iron —**iron•ware** *n* —**iron•work** *n* —**iron•work•er** *n* —**iron•works** *n pl*

iron•clad \-'klad\ *adj* **1** : sheathed in iron armor **2** : strict or exacting

iron•ing \'īərniŋ\ *n* : clothes to be ironed

iron•wood \-,wu̇d\ *n* : tree or shrub with very hard wood or this wood

iro•ny \'īrənē\ *n, pl* **-nies 1** : use of words to express the opposite of the literal meaning **2** : incongruity between the actual and expected result of events —**iron•ic** \ī'ränik\ **iron•i•cal** \-ikəl\ *adj* —**iron•i•cal•ly** \-iklē\ *adv*

ir•ra•di•ate \ir'ādē,āt\ *vb* **-at•ed; -at•ing** : treat with radiation —**ir•ra•di•a•tion** \-,ādē'āshən\ *n*

ir•ra•tio•nal \ir'ashənəl\ *adj* **1** : incapable of reasoning **2** : not based on reason —**ir•ra•tio•nal•i•ty** \ir,ashə'nalətē\ *n* —**ir•ra•tio•nal•ly** *adv*

ir•rec•on•cil•able \ir,ekən'sīləbəl\ *adj* : impossible to reconcile —**irrec•on•cil•abil•i•ty** \-,sīlə'bilətē\ *n*

ir•re•cov•er•able \,iri'kəvərəbəl\ *adj* : not capable of being recovered —**ir•re•cov•er•ably** \-blē\ *adv*

ir•re•deem•able \,iri'dēməbəl\ *adj* : not redeemable

ir•re•duc•ible \,iri'düsəbəl, -'dyü-\ *adj* : not reducible —**ir•re•duc•ibly** \-blē\ *adv*

ir•re•fut•able \,iri'fyütəbəl, ir'refyət-\ *adj* : impossible to refute

ir•reg•u•lar \ir'egyələr\ *adj* : not regular or normal —**irregular** *n* —**ir•reg•u•lar•i•ty** \ir,egyə'larətē\ *n* —**ir•reg•u•lar•ly** *adv*

ir•rel•e•vant \ir'eləvənt\ *adj* : not relevant —**ir•rel•e•vance** \-vəns\ *n*

ir•re•li•gious \,iri'lijəs\ *adj* : not following religious practices

ir•rep•a•ra•ble \ir'epərəbəl\ *adj* : impossible to make good, undo, or remedy

ir•re•place•able \,iri'plāsəbəl\ *adj* : not replaceable

ir•re•press•ible \-'presəbəl\ *adj* : impossible to repress or control

ir•re•proach•able \-'prōchəbəl\ *adj* : blameless

ir•re•sist•ible \-'zistəbəl\ *adj* : impossible to successfully resist —**ir•re•sist•ibly** \-blē\ *adv*

ir•res•o•lute \ir'ezəlüt\ *adj* : uncertain —**ir•res•o•lute•ly** *adv* —**ir•res•o•lu•tion** \-,ezə'lüshən\ *n*

ir•re•spec•tive of \,iri'spektiv-\ *prep* : without regard to

ir•re•spon•si•ble \,iri'spänsəbəl\ *adj* : not responsible —**ir•re•spon•si•bil•i•ty** \-,spänsə'bilətē\ *n* —**ir•re•spon•si•bly** *adv*

ir•re•triev•able \,iri'trēvəbəl\ *adj* : not retrievable

ir•rev•er•ence \ir'evərəns\ *n* **1** : lack of reverence **2** : irreverent act or utterance —**ir•rev•er•ent** \-rənt\ *adj*

ir•re•vers•ible \,iri'vərsəbəl\ *adj* : incapable of being reversed

ir•rev•o•ca•ble \ir'evəkəbəl\ *adj* : incapable of being revoked —**ir•rev•o•ca•bly** \-blē\ *adv*

ir•ri•gate \'irə,gāt\ *vb* **-gat•ed; -gat•ing** : supply with water by artificial means —**ir•ri•ga•tion** \,irə'gāshən\ *n*

ir•ri•tate \'irə,tāt\ *vb* **-tat•ed; -tat•ing 1** : excite to anger **2** : make sore or inflamed —**ir•ri•ta•bil•i•ty** \,irətə'bilətē\ *n* —**ir•ri•ta•ble** \'irətəbəl\ *adj* —**ir•ri•ta•bly** \'irətəblē\ *adv* —**ir•ri•tant** \'irətənt\ *adj or n* —**ir•ri•tat•ing•ly** *adv* —**ir•ri•ta•tion** \,irə'tāshən\ *n*

is *pres 3d sing of* BE

-ish \ish\ *adj suffix* **1** : characteristic of **2** : somewhat

Is•lam \is'läm, iz-, -'lam\ *n* : religious faith of Muslims —**Is•lam•ic** \-ik\ *adj*

is•land \'īlənd\ *n* : body of land surrounded by water —**is•land•er** \'īləndər\ *n*

isle \'īl\ *n* : small island

is•let \'īlət\ *n* : small island

-ism \,izəm\ *n suffix* **1** : act or practice **2** : characteristic manner **3** : condition **4** : doctrine

iso•late \'īsə,lāt\ *vb* **-lat•ed; -lat•ing** : place or keep by itself —**iso•la•tion** \,īsə'lāshən\ *n*

iso•met•rics \,īsə'metriks\ *n sing or pl* : exercise against unmoving resistance —**isometric** *adj*

isos•ce•les \ī'säsə,lēz\ *adj* : having 2 equal sides

iso•tope \'īsə,tōp\ *n* : species of atom of a chemical element —**iso•to•pic** \,īsə'täpik, -'tō-\ *adj*

is•sue \'ishü\ *vb* **-sued; -su•ing 1** : go, come, or flow out **2** : descend from a specified ancestor **3** : emanate or result **4** : put forth or distribute officially ~ *n* **1** : action of issuing **2** : offspring **3** : result **4** : point of controversy **5** : act of giving out or printing **6** : quantity given out or printed —**is•su•ance** \'ishəwəns\ *n* —**is•su•er** *n*

-ist \ist\ *n suffix* **1** : one that does **2** : one that plays **3** : one that specializes in **4** : follower of a doctrine

isth•mus \'isməs\ *n* : narrow strip of land connecting 2 larger portions

it \'it\ *pron* **1** : that one —used of a lifeless thing or an abstract entity **2** —used as an anticipatory subject or object ~ *n* : player who tries to catch others (as in a game of tag)

ital•ic \ə'talik, i-, ī-\ *n* : style of type with slanting letters —**italic** *adj* —**ital•i•ci•za•tion** \ə,taləsə'zāshən, i-, ī-\ *n* —**ital•i•cize** \ə'talə,sīz, i-, ī-\ *vb*

itch \'ich\ *n* **1** : uneasy irritating skin sensation **2** : skin disorder **3** : persistent desire —**itch** *vb* —**itchy** *adj*

item \'ītəm\ *n* **1** : particular in a list, account, or series **2** : piece of news —**item•iza•tion** \,ītəmə'zāshən\ *n* —**item•ize** \'ītə,mīz\ *vb*

itin•er•ant \ī'tinərənt, ə-\ *adj* : traveling from place to place

itin•er•ary \ī'tinə,rerē, ə-\ *n, pl* **-ar•ies** : route or outline of a journey

its \'its\ *adj* : relating to it

it•self \it'self\ *pron* : it—used reflexively or for emphasis

-ity \ətē\ *n suffix* : quality, state, or degree

-ive \iv\ *adj suffix* : that performs or tends toward an action

ivo•ry \'īvrē\ *n, pl* **-ries 1** : hard creamy-white material of elephants' tusks **2** : pale yellow color

ivy \'īvē\ *n, pl* **ivies** : trailing woody vine with evergreen leaves

-ize \,īz\ *vb suffix* **1** : cause to be, become, or resemble **2** : subject to an action **3** : treat or combine with **4** : engage in an activity

J

j \'jā\ *n, pl* **j's** *or* **js** \'jāz\ : 10th letter of the alphabet

jab \'jab\ *vb* **-bb-** : thrust quickly or abruptly ~ *n* : short straight punch

jab•ber \'jabər\ *vb* : talk rapidly or unintelligibly —**jabber** *n*

jack \'jak\ *n* **1** : mechanical device to raise a heavy body **2** : small flag **3** : small 6-pointed metal object used in a game **(jacks) 4** : electrical socket ~ *vb* **1** : raise with a jack **2** : increase

jack•al \'jakəl, -,ȯl\ *n* : wild dog

jack•ass *n* **1** : male ass **2** : stupid person

jack•et \'jakət\ *n* : garment for the upper body

jack•ham•mer \'jak,hamər\ *n* : pneumatic tool for drilling

jack•knife \'jak,nīf\ *n* : pocketknife ~ *vb* : fold like a jackknife

jack–o'–lan•tern \'jakə,lantərn\ *n* : lantern made of a carved pumpkin

jack•pot \'jak,pät\ *n* : sum of money won

jack•rab•bit \-,rabət\ *n* : large hare of western No. America

jade \'jād\ *n* : usu. green gemstone

jad•ed \'jādəd\ *adj* : dulled or bored by having too much

jag•ged \'jagəd\ *adj* : sharply notched

jag•uar \'jag,wär, 'jagyə-\ *n* : black-spotted tropical American cat

jai alai \'hī,lī\ *n* : game with a ball propelled by a basket on the hand

jail \'jāl\ *n* : prison —**jail** *vb* —**jail•break** *n* —**jail•er, jail•or** *n*

ja•la•pe•ño \,hälə'pān,yō, -,pēnō\ *n* : Mexican hot pepper

ja•lopy \jə'läpē\ *n, pl* **-lop•ies** : dilapidated vehicle

jal•ou•sie \'jaləsē\ *n* : door or window with louvers

jam \'jam\ *vb* **-mm- 1** : press into a tight position **2** : cause to become wedged and unworkable ~ *n* **1** : crowded mass that blocks or impedes **2** : difficult situation **3** : thick sweet food made of cooked fruit

jamb \'jam\ *n* : upright framing piece of a door

jam•bo•ree \,jambə'rē\ *n* : large festive gathering

jan•gle \'jaŋgəl\ *vb* **-gled; -gling** : make a harsh ringing sound —**jangle** *n*

jan•i•tor \'janətər\ *n* : person who has the care of a building —**jan•i•to•ri•al** \,janə'tōrēəl\ *adj*

Jan•u•ary \'janyə,werē\ *n* : 1st month of the year having 31 days

[1]**jar** \'jär\ *vb* **-rr- 1** : have a harsh or disagreeable effect **2** : vibrate or shake ~ *n* **1** : jolt **2** : painful effect

[2]**jar** *n* : wide-mouthed container

jar•gon \'järgən, -,gän\ *n* : special vocabulary of a group

jas•mine \'jazmən\ *n* : climbing shrub with fragrant flowers

jas•per \'jaspər\ *n* : red, yellow, or brown opaque quartz

jaun•dice \'jȯndəs\ *n* : yellowish discoloration of skin, tissues, and body fluids

jaun•diced \-dəst\ *adj* : exhibiting envy or hostility

jaunt \'jȯnt\ *n* : short pleasure trip

jaun•ty \'jȯntē\ *adj* **-ti•er; -est** : lively in manner or appearance —**jaun•ti•ly** \'jȯnt[ə]lē\ *adv* —**jaun•ti•ness** *n*

jav•e•lin \'javələn\ *n* : light spear

jaw \'jȯ\ *n* **1** : either of the bony or cartilaginous structures that support the mouth **2** : one of 2 movable parts for holding or crushing ~ *vb* : talk indignantly or at length —**jaw•bone** \-,bōn\ *n* —**jawed** \'jȯd\ *adj*

jay \'jā\ *n* : noisy brightly colored bird

jay•bird *n* : jay

jay•walk *vb* : cross a street carelessly —**jay•walk•er** *n*

jazz \'jaz\ *vb* : enliven ~ *n* **1** : kind of American music involving improvisation **2** : empty talk —**jazzy** *adj*

jeal•ous \'jeləs\ *adj* : suspicious of a rival or of one believed to enjoy an advantage —**jeal•ous•ly** *adv* —**jeal•ous•y** \-əsē\ *n*

jeans \'jēnz\ *n pl* : pants made of durable twilled cotton cloth

jeep \'jēp\ *n* : 4-wheel army vehicle

jeer \'jir\ *vb* **1** : speak or cry out in derision **2** : ridicule ~ *n* : taunt

Je•ho•vah \ji'hōvə\ *n* : God

je•june \ji'jün\ *adj* : dull or childish

jell \'jel\ *vb* **1** : come to the consistency of jelly **2** : take shape

jel•ly \'jelē\ *n, pl* **-lies** : a substance (as food) with a soft somewhat elastic consistency —**jelly** *vb*

jel•ly•fish *n* : sea animal with a saucer-shaped jellylike body

jen•ny \ˈjenē\ *n, pl* **-nies** : female bird or donkey

jeop•ar•dy \ˈjepərdē\ *n* : exposure to death, loss, or injury —**jeop•ar•dize** \-ər͵dīz\ *vb*

jerk \ˈjərk\ *vb* **1** : give a sharp quick push, pull, or twist **2** : move in short abrupt motions ~ *n* **1** : short quick pull or twist **2** : stupid or foolish person —**jerk•i•ly** *adv* —**jerky** *adj*

jer•kin \ˈjərkən\ *n* : close-fitting sleeveless jacket

jer•ry–built \ˈjerē͵bilt\ *adj* : built cheaply and flimsily

jer•sey \ˈjərzē\ *n, pl* **-seys 1** : plain knit fabric **2** : knitted shirt

jest \ˈjest\ *n* : witty remark —**jest** *vb*

jest•er \ˈjestər\ *n* : one employed to entertain a court

1jet \ˈjet\ *n* : velvet-black coal used for jewelry

2jet *vb* **-tt- 1** : spout or emit in a stream **2** : travel by jet ~ *n* **1** : forceful rush of fluid through a narrow opening **2** : jet-propelled airplane

jet–propelled *adj* : driven by an engine (**jet engine**) that produces propulsion (**jet propulsion**) by the rearward discharge of a jet of fluid

jet•sam \ˈjetsəm\ *n* : jettisoned goods

jet•ti•son \ˈjetəsən\ *vb* **1** : throw (goods) overboard **2** : discard —**jettison** *n*

jet•ty \ˈjetē\ *n, pl* **-ties** : pier or wharf

Jew \ˈjü\ *n* : one whose religion is Judaism —**Jew•ish** *adj*

jew•el \ˈjüəl\ *n* **1** : ornament of precious metal **2** : gem ~ *vb* **-eled** *or* **-elled; -el•ing** *or* **-el•ling** : adorn with jewels —**jew•el•er, jew•el•ler** \-ər\ *n* —**jew•el•ry** \-rē\ *n*

jib \ˈjib\ *n* : triangular sail

jibe \ˈjīb\ *vb* **jibed; jib•ing** : be in agreement

jif•fy \ˈjifē\ *n, pl* **-fies** : short time

jig \ˈjig\ *n* : lively dance ~ *vb* **-gg-** : dance a jig

jig•ger \ˈjigər\ *n* : measure used in mixing drinks

jig•gle \ˈjigəl\ *vb* **-gled; -gling** : move with quick little jerks —**jiggle** *n*

jig•saw *n* : machine saw with a narrow blade that moves up and down

jilt \ˈjilt\ *vb* : drop (a lover) unfeelingly

jim•my \ˈjimē\ *n, pl* **-mies** : small crowbar ~ *vb* **-mied; -my•ing** : pry open

jim•son•weed \ˈjimsən͵wēd\ *n* : coarse poisonous weed

jin•gle \ˈjiŋgəl\ *vb* **-gled; -gling** : make a light tinkling sound ~ *n* **1** : light tinkling sound **2** : short verse or song

jin•go•ism \ˈjiŋgō͵izəm\ *n* : extreme chauvinism or nationalism —**jin•go•ist** \-ist\ *n* —**jin•go•is•tic** \͵jiŋgōˈistik\ *adj*

jinx \ˈjiŋks\ *n* : one that brings bad luck —**jinx** *vb*

jit•ney \ˈjitnē\ *n, pl* **-neys** : small bus

jit•ters \ˈjitərz\ *n pl* : extreme nervousness —**jit•tery** \-ərē\ *adj*

job \ˈjäb\ *n* **1** : something that has to be done **2** : regular employment —**job•hold•er** *n* —**job•less** *adj*

job•ber \ˈjäbər\ *n* : middleman

jock•ey \ˈjäkē\ *n, pl* **-eys** : one who rides a horse in a race ~ *vb* **-eyed; -ey•ing** : manipulate or maneuver adroitly

jo•cose \jōˈkōs\ *adj* : jocular

joc•u•lar \ˈjäkyələr\ *adj* : marked by jesting —**joc•u•lar•i•ty** \͵jäkyəˈlarətē\ *n* —**joc•u•lar•ly** *adv*

jo•cund \ˈjäkənd\ *adj* : full of mirth or gaiety

jodh•purs \ˈjädpərz\ *n pl* : riding breeches

1jog \ˈjäg\ *vb* **-gg- 1** : give a slight shake or push to **2** : run or ride at a slow pace ~ *n* **1** : slight shake **2** : slow pace —**jog•ger** *n*

2jog *n* : brief abrupt change in direction or line

join \ˈjȯin\ *vb* **1** : come or bring together **2** : become a member of —**join•er** *n*

joint \ˈjȯint\ *n* **1** : point of contact between bones **2** : place where 2 parts connect **3** : often disreputable place ~ *adj* : common to 2 or more —**joint•ed** *adj* —**joint•ly** *adv*

joist \ˈjȯist\ *n* : beam supporting a floor or ceiling

joke \ˈjōk\ *n* : something said or done to provoke laughter ~ *vb* **joked; jok•ing** : make jokes —**jok•er** *n* —**jok•ing•ly** \ˈjōkiŋlē\ *adv*

jol•li•ty \ˈjälətē\ *n, pl* **-ties** : gaiety or merriment

jol•ly \ˈjälē\ *adj* **-li•er; -est** : full of high spirits

jolt \ˈjōlt\ *vb* **1** : move with a sudden jerky motion **2** : give a jolt to ~ *n* **1** : abrupt jerky blow or movement **2** : sudden shock —**jolt•er** *n*

jon•quil \ˈjänkwəl\ *n* : narcissus with white or yellow flowers

josh \ˈjäsh\ *vb* : tease or joke

jos•tle \ˈjäsəl\ *vb* **-tled; -tling** : push or shove

jot \ˈjät\ *n* : least bit ~ *vb* **-tt-** : write briefly and hurriedly

jounce \ˈjau̇ns\ *vb* **jounced; jounc•ing** : jolt —**jounce** *n*

jour•nal \ˈjərnəl\ *n* **1** : brief account of daily events **2** : periodical (as a newspaper)

jour•nal•ism \ˈjərnəl͵izəm\ *n* : business of reporting or printing news —**jour•nal•ist** \-ist\ *n* —**jour•nal•is•tic** \͵jərnəlˈistik\ *adj*

jour•ney \ˈjərnē\ *n, pl* **-neys** : a going from one place to another ~ *vb* **-neyed; -ney•ing** : make a journey

jour•ney•man \-mən\ *n* : worker who has learned a trade and works for another person

joust \ˈjau̇st\ *n* : combat on horseback between 2 knights with lances —**joust** *vb*

jo•vial \ˈjōvēəl\ *adj* : marked by good humor —**jo•vi•al•i•ty** \͵jōvēˈalətē\ *n* —**jo•vi•al•ly** \ˈjōvēəlē\ *adv*

1jowl \ˈjau̇l\ *n* : loose flesh about the lower jaw or throat

2jowl *n* **1** : lower jaw **2** : cheek

joy \ˈjȯi\ *n* **1** : feeling of happiness **2** : source of happiness —**joy** *vb* —**joy•ful** *adj* —**joy•ful•ly** *adv* —**joy•less** *adj* —**joy•ous** \ˈjȯiəs\ *adj* —**joy•ous•ly** *adv* —**joy•ous•ness** *n*

joy•ride *n* : reckless ride for pleasure —**joy•rid•er** *n* —**joy•rid•ing** *n*

ju•bi•lant \ˈjübələnt\ *adj* : expressing great joy —**ju•bi•lant•ly** *adv* —**ju•bi•la•tion** \͵jübəˈlāshən\ *n*

ju•bi•lee \ˈjübə͵lē\ *n* **1** : 50th anniversary **2** : season or occasion of celebration

Ju•da•ism \ˈjüdə͵izəm\ *n* : religion developed among the ancient Hebrews —**Ju•da•ic** \ju̇ˈdāik\ *adj*

judge \ˈjəj\ *vb* **judged; judg•ing 1** : form an opinion **2** : decide as a judge ~ *n* **1** : public official authorized to decide questions brought before a court **2** : one who gives an authoritative opinion —**judge•ship** *n*

judg•ment, judge•ment \ˈjəjmənt\ *n* **1** : decision or opinion given after judging **2** : capacity for judging —**judg•men•tal** \͵jəjˈmentəl\ *adj* —**judg•men•tal•ly** *adv*

ju•di•ca•ture \ˈjüdikə͵chu̇r\ *n* : administration of justice

ju•di•cial \ju̇ˈdishəl\ *adj* : relating to judicature or the judiciary —**ju•di•cial•ly** *adv*

ju•di•cia•ry \ju̇ˈdishē͵erē, -ˈdishərē\ *n* : system of courts of law or the judges of them —**judiciary** *adj*

ju•di•cious \ju̇ˈdishəs\ *adj* : having or characterized by sound judgment —**ju•di•cious•ly** *adv*

ju•do \ˈjüdō\ *n* : form of wrestling —**judo•ist** *n*

jug \ˈjəg\ *n* : large deep container with a narrow mouth and a handle

jug•ger•naut \ˈjəgər͵nȯt\ *n* : massive inexorable force or object

jug•gle \ˈjəgəl\ *vb* **-gled; -gling 1** : keep several objects in motion in the air at the same time **2** : manipulate for an often tricky purpose —**jug•gler** \ˈjəglər\ *n*

jug•u•lar \ˈjəgyələr\ *adj* : in or on the throat or neck

juice \ˈjüs\ *n* **1** : extractable fluid contents of cells or tissues **2** : electricity —**juic•er** *n* —**juic•i•ly** \ˈjüsəlē\ *adv* —**juic•i•ness** \-sēnəs\ *n* —**juicy** \ˈjüsē\ *adj*

ju•jube \ˈjü͵jüb, ˈjüju̇͵bē\ *n* : gummy candy

juke•box \ˈjük͵bäks\ *n* : coin-operated machine for playing music recordings

ju•lep \ˈjüləp\ *n* : mint-flavored bourbon drink

Ju•ly \ju̇ˈlī\ *n* : 7th month of the year having 31 days

jum•ble \ˈjəmbəl\ *vb* **-bled; -bling** : mix in a confused mass —**jumble** *n*

jum•bo \ˈjəmbō\ *n, pl* **-bos** : very large version —**jumbo** *adj*

jump \ˈjəmp\ *vb* **1**: rise into or through the air esp. by muscular effort **2** : pass over **3** : give a start **4** : rise or increase sharply ~ *n* **1** : a jumping **2** : sharp sudden increase **3** : initial advantage

1jump•er \ˈjəmpər\ *n* : one that jumps

2jumper *n* : sleeveless one-piece dress

jumpy \ˈjəmpē\ *adj* **jump•i•er; -est** : nervous or jittery

junc•tion \ˈjəŋkshən\ *n* **1** : a joining **2** : place or point of meeting

junc•ture \ˈjəŋkchər\ *n* **1** : joint or connection **2** : critical time or state of affairs

June \ˈjün\ *n* : 6th month of the year having 30 days

jun•gle \ˈjəŋgəl\ *n* : thick tangled mass of tropical vegetation

ju•nior \ˈjünyər\ *n* **1** : person who is younger or of lower rank than another **2** : student in the next-to-last year ~ *adj* : younger or lower in rank

ju•ni•per \ˈjünəpər\ *n* : evergreen shrub or tree

1junk \ˈjəŋk\ *n* **1** : discarded articles **2** : shoddy product ~ *vb* : discard or scrap —**junky** *adj*

2junk *n* : flat-bottomed ship of Chinese waters

jun•ket \ˈjəŋkət\ *n* : trip made by an official at public expense

jun•ta \ˈhu̇ntə, ˈjəntə, ˈhəntə\ *n* : group of persons controlling a government

ju•ris•dic•tion \͵ju̇rəsˈdikshən\ *n* **1** : right or authority to interpret and apply the law **2** : limits within which authority may be exercised —**ju•ris•dic•tion•al** \-shənəl\ *adj*

ju•ris•pru•dence \-ˈprüdəns\ *n* **1** : system of laws **2** : science or philosophy of law

ju•rist \ˈju̇rist\ *n* : judge

ju•ror \ˈju̇rər\ *n* : member of a jury

ju•ry \ˈju̇rē\ *n, pl* **-ries** : body of persons sworn to give a verdict on a matter

just \ˈjəst\ *adj* **1** : reasonable **2** : correct or proper **3** : morally or legally right **4** : deserved ~ *adv* **1** : exactly **2** : very recently **3** : barely **4** : only **5** : quite **6** : possibly —**just•ly** *adv* —**just•ness** *n*

jus•tice \ˈjəstəs\ *n* **1** : administration of what is just **2** : judge **3** : administration of law **4** : fairness

jus•ti•fy \ˈjəstə͵fī\ *vb* **-fied; -fy•ing** : prove to be just, right, or reasonable —**jus•ti•fi•able** *adj* —**jus•ti•fi•ca•tion** \͵jəstəfəˈkāshən\ *n*

jut \ˈjət\ *vb* **-tt-** : stick out

jute \ˈjüt\ *n* : strong glossy fiber from a tropical plant

ju•ve•nile \ˈjüvə͵nīl, -vənəl\ *adj* : relating to children or young people ~ *n* : young person

jux•ta•pose \ˈjəkstə͵pōz\ *vb* **-posed; -pos•ing** : place side by side —**jux•ta•po•si•tion** \͵jəkstəpəˈzishən\ *n*

K

k \ˈkā\ *n, pl* **k's** *or* **ks** \ˈkāz\ : 11th letter of the alphabet

kai•ser \ˈkīzər\ *n* : German ruler

kale \ˈkāl\ *n* : curly cabbage

ka•lei•do•scope \kəˈlīdə͵skōp\ *n* : device containing loose bits of colored material reflecting in many patterns —**ka•lei•do•scop•ic** \-͵līdəˈskäpik\ *adj* —**ka•lei•do•scop•i•cal•ly** \-iklē\ *adv*

kan•ga•roo \͵kaŋgəˈrü\ *n, pl* **-roos** : large leaping Australian mammal

ka•o•lin \ˈkāələn\ *n* : fine white clay

kar•at \ˈkarət\ *n* : unit of gold content

ka•ra•te \kəˈrätē\ *n* : art of self-defense by crippling kicks and punches

ka•ty•did \ˈkātē͵did\ *n* : large American grasshopper

kay•ak \ˈkī͵ak\ *n* : Eskimo canoe

ka•zoo \kəˈzü\ *n, pl* **-zoos** : toy musical instrument

keel \ˈkēl\ *n* : central lengthwise strip on the bottom of a ship —**keeled** \ˈkēld\ *adj*

keen \ˈkēn\ *adj* **1** : sharp **2** : severe **3** : enthusiastic **4** : mentally alert —**keen•ly** *adv* —**keen•ness** *n*

keep \ˈkēp\ *vb* **kept** \ˈkept\; **keep•ing 1** : perform **2** : guard **3** : maintain **4** : retain in one's possession **5** : detain **6** : continue in good condition **7** : refrain ~ *n* **1** : fortress **2** : means by which one is kept —**keep•er** *n*

keep•ing \ˈkēpiŋ\ *n* : conformity

keep•sake \ˈkēp͵sāk\ *n* : souvenir

keg \ˈkeg\ *n* : small cask or barrel

kelp \ˈkelp\ *n* : coarse brown seaweed

ken \ˈken\ *n* : range of sight or understanding

ken•nel \ˈkenəl\ *n* : dog shelter —**kennel** *vb*

ker•chief \ˈkərchəf, -͵chēf\ *n* : square of cloth worn as a head covering

ker•nel \ˈkərnəl\ *n* **1** : inner softer part of a seed or nut **2** : whole seed of a cereal **3** : central part

ker•o•sene, ker•o•sine \ˈkerə͵sēn, ͵kerəˈ-\ *n* : thin flammable oil from petroleum

ketch•up \ˈkechəp, ˈka-\ *n* : spicy tomato sauce

ket•tle \ˈketəl\ *n* : vessel for boiling liquids

ket•tle•drum \-͵drum\ *n* : brass or copper kettle-shaped drum

1key \ˈkē\ *n* **1** : usu. metal piece to open a lock **2** : explanation **3** : lever pressed by a finger in playing an instrument or operating a machine **4** : leading individual or principle **5** : system of musical tones or pitch ~ *vb* : attune ~ *adj* : basic —**key•hole** *n* —**key up** *vb* : make nervous

2key *n* : low island or reef

key•board *n* : arrangement of keys

key•note \-͵nōt\ *n* **1** : 1st note of a scale **2** : central fact, idea, or mood ~ *vb* **1** : set the keynote of **2** : deliver the major speech

key•stone *n* : wedge-shaped piece at the crown of an arch

kha•ki \ˈkakē, ˈkäk-\ *n* : light yellowish brown color

khan \ˈkän, ˈkan\ *n* : Mongol leader

kib•butz \kibˈu̇ts, -ˈüts\ *n, pl* **-but•zim** \-͵u̇tˈsēm, -͵üt-\ : Israeli communal farm or settlement

ki•bitz•er \ˈkibətsər, kəˈbit-\ *n* : one who offers unwanted advice —**kib•itz** \ˈkibəts\ *vb*

kick \ˈkik\ *vb* **1** : strike out or hit with the foot **2** : object strongly **3** : recoil ~ *n* **1** : thrust with the foot **2** : recoil of a gun **3** : stimulating effect —**kick•er** *n*

kid \ˈkid\ *n* **1** : young goat **2** : child ~ *vb* **-dd- 1** : deceive as a joke **2** : tease —**kid•der** *n* —**kid•ding•ly** *adv*

kid•nap \ˈkid͵nap\ *vb* **-napped** *or* **-naped** \-͵napt\; **-nap•ping** *or* **-nap•ing** : carry a person away by illegal force —**kid•nap•per, kid•nap•er** *n*

kid•ney \ˈkidnē\ *n, pl* **-neys** : either of a pair of organs that excrete urine

kill \ˈkil\ *vb* **1** : deprive of life **2** : finish **3** : use up (time) ~ *n* : act of killing —**kill•er** *n*

kiln \ˈkil, ˈkiln\ *n* : heated enclosure for burning, firing, or drying —**kiln** *vb*

ki•lo \ˈkēlō\ *n, pl* **-los** : kilogram

kilo•cy•cle \ˈkilə͵sīkəl\ *n* : kilohertz

ki•lo•gram \ˈkēlə͵gram, ˈkilə-\ *n* : basic metric mass unit nearly equal to the mass of 1000 cubic centimeters of water at its maximum density

ki•lo•hertz \ˈkilə͵hərts, ˈkēlə-, -͵herts\ *n* : 1000 hertz

ki•lo•me•ter \kilˈämətər, ˈkilə͵mēt-\ *n* : 1000 meters

ki•lo•volt \ˈkilə͵vōlt\ *n* : 1000 volts

ki•lo•watt \ˈkilə͵wät\ *n* : 1000 watts

kilt \ˈkilt\ *n* : knee-length pleated skirt

kil•ter \ˈkiltər\ *n* : proper condition

ki•mo•no \kəˈmōnō\ *n, pl* **-nos** : loose robe

kin \ˈkin\ *n* **1** : one's relatives **2** : kinsman

kind \ˈkīnd\ *n* **1** : essential quality **2** : group with common traits **3** : variety ~ *adj* **1** : of a sympathetic nature **2** : arising from sympathy —**kind•heart•ed** *adj* —**kind•ness** *n*

kin•der•gar•ten \ˈkindər͵gärtən\ *n* : class for young children —**kin•der•gart•ner** \-͵gärtnər\ *n*

kin•dle \ˈkindəl\ *vb* **-dled; -dling 1** : set on fire or start burning **2** : stir up

kin•dling \ˈkindliŋ, ˈkinlən\ *n* : material for starting a fire

kind•ly \ˈkīndlē\ *adj* **-li•er; -est** : of a sympathetic nature ~ *adv* **1** : sympathetically **2** : courteously —**kind•li•ness** *n*

kin•dred \ˈkindrəd\ *n* **1** : related individuals **2** : kin ~ *adj* : of a like nature

kin•folk \ˈkin͵fōk\, **kinfolks** *n pl* : kin

king \ˈkiŋ\ *n* : male sovereign —**king•dom** \-dəm\ *n* —**king•less** *adj* —**king•ly** *adj* —**king•ship** *n*

king•fish•er \-͵fishər\ *n* : bright-colored crested bird

kink \ˈkiŋk\ *n* **1** : short tight twist or curl **2** : cramp —**kinky** *adj*

kin•ship *n* : relationship

kins•man \ˈkinzmən\ *n* : male relative

kins•wom•an \-͵wu̇mən\ *n* : female relative

kip•per \ˈkipər\ *n* : dried or smoked fish —**kipper** *vb*

kiss \ˈkis\ *vb* : touch with the lips as a mark of affection —**kiss** *n*

kit \ˈkit\ *n* : set of articles (as tools or parts)

kitch•en \ˈkichən\ *n* : room with cooking facilities

kite \ˈkīt\ *n* **1** : small hawk **2** : covered framework flown at the end of a string

kith \ˈkith\ *n* : familiar friends

kit•ten \ˈkitən\ *n* : young cat —**kit•ten•ish** *adj*

1kit•ty \ˈkitē\ *n, pl* **-ties** : kitten

2kitty *n, pl* **-ties** : fund or pool (as in a card game)

kit•ty–cor•ner, kit•ty–cor•nered *var of* CATERCORNER

ki•wi \ˈkē͵wē\ *n* : small flightless New Zealand bird

klep•to•ma•nia \͵kleptəˈmānēə\ *n* : neurotic impulse to steal —**klep•to•ma•ni•ac** \-nē͵ak\ *n*

knack \ˈnak\ *n* **1** : clever way of doing something **2** : natural aptitude

knap•sack \ˈnap͵sak\ *n* : bag for carrying supplies on one's back

knave \ˈnāv\ *n* : rogue —**knav•ery** \ˈnāvərē\ *n* —**knav•ish** \ˈnāvish\ *adj*

knead \ˈnēd\ *vb* **1** : work and press with the hands **2** : massage —**knead•er** *n*

knee \ˈnē\ *n* : joint in the middle part of the leg —**kneed** \ˈnēd\ *adj*

knee•cap \ˈnē͵kap\ *n* : bone forming the front of the knee

kneel \ˈnēl\ *vb* **knelt** \ˈnelt\ *or* **kneeled; kneel•ing** : rest on one's knees

knell \ˈnel\ *n* : stroke of a bell

knew *past of* KNOW

knick•ers \ˈnikərz\ *n pl* **:** pants gathered at the knee
knick•knack \ˈnikˌnak\ *n* **:** small decorative object
knife \ˈnīf\ *n, pl* **knives** \ˈnīvz\ **:** sharp blade with a handle ~ *vb* **knifed; knif•ing :** stab or cut with a knife
knight \ˈnīt\ *n* **1 :** mounted warrior of feudal times **2 :** man honored by a sovereign ~ *vb* **:** make a knight of **—knight•hood** *n* **—knight•ly** *adv*
knit \ˈnit\ *vb* **knit** *or* **knit•ted; knit•ting 1 :** link firmly or closely **2 :** form a fabric by interlacing yarn or thread ~ *n* **:** knitted garment **—knit•ter** *n*
knob \ˈnäb\ *n* **:** rounded protuberance or handle **—knobbed** \ˈnäbd\ *adj* **—knob•by** \ˈnäbē\ *adj*
knock \ˈnäk\ *vb* **1 :** strike with a sharp blow **2 :** collide **3 :** find fault with ~ *n* **:** sharp blow **—knock out** *vb* **:** make unconscious
knock•er *n* **:** device hinged to a door to knock with
knoll \ˈnōl\ *n* **:** small round hill
knot \ˈnät\ *n* **1 :** interlacing (as of string) that forms a lump **2 :** base of a woody branch in the stem **3 :** group **4 :** one nautical mile per hour ~ *vb* **-tt- :** tie in or with a knot **—knot•ty** *adj*
know \ˈnō\ *vb* **knew** \ˈnü, ˈnyü\; **known** \ˈnōn\; **know•ing 1 :** perceive directly or understand **2 :** be familiar with **—know•able** *adj* **—know•er** *n*
know•ing \ˈnōiŋ\ *adj* **:** shrewdly and keenly alert **—know•ing•ly** *adv*
knowl•edge \ˈnälij\ *n* **1 :** understanding gained by experience **2 :** range of information **—knowl•edge•able** *adj*
knuck•le \ˈnəkəl\ *n* **:** rounded knob at a finger joint
ko•ala \kōˈälə\ *n* **:** gray furry Australian animal
kohl•ra•bi \kōlˈrabē, -ˈräb-\ *n, pl* **-bies :** cabbage that forms no head
Ko•ran \kəˈran, -ˈrän\ *n* **:** book of Islam containing revelations made to Muhammad by Allah
ko•sher \ˈkōshər\ *adj* **:** ritually fit for use according to Jewish law
kow•tow \kaúˈtaú, ˈkaúˌtaú\ *vb* **:** show excessive deference
kryp•ton \ˈkripˌtän\ *n* **:** gaseous chemical element used in lamps
ku•dos \ˈkyüˌdäs, ˈkü-, -ˌdōz\ *n* **:** fame and renown
kum•quat \ˈkəmˌkwät\ *n* **:** small citrus fruit

L

l \ˈel\ *n, pl* **l's** *or* **ls** \ˈelz\ **:** 12th letter of the alphabet
lab \ˈlab\ *n* **:** laboratory
la•bel \ˈlābəl\ *n* **1 :** identification slip **2 :** identifying word or phrase ~ *vb* **-beled** *or* **-belled; -bel•ing** *or* **-bel•ling :** put a label on
la•bi•al \ˈlābēəl\ *adj* **:** of or relating to the lips
la•bor \ˈlābər\ *n* **1 :** physical or mental effort **2 :** physical efforts of childbirth **3 :** task **4 :** people who work manually ~ *vb* **:** work esp. with great effort **—la•bor•er** *n*
lab•o•ra•to•ry \ˈlabrəˌtōrē\ *n, pl* **-ries :** place for experimental testing
Labor Day *n* **:** 1st Monday in September observed as a legal holiday in recognition of working people
la•bo•ri•ous \ləˈbōrēəs\ *adj* **:** requiring great effort **—la•bo•ri•ous•ly** *adv*
lab•y•rinth \ˈlabəˌrinth\ *n* **:** maze **—lab•y•rin•thine** \ˌlabəˈrinthən\ *adj*
lace \ˈlās\ *n* **1 :** cord or string for tying **2 :** fine net usu. figured fabric ~ *vb* **laced; lac•ing 1 :** tie **2 :** adorn with lace **—lacy** \ˈlāsē\ *adj*
lac•er•ate \ˈlasəˌrāt\ *vb* **-at•ed; -at•ing :** tear roughly **—lac•er•a•tion** \ˌlasəˈrāshən\ *n*
lach•ry•mose \ˈlakrəˌmōs\ *adj* **:** tearful
lack \ˈlak\ *vb* **:** be missing or deficient in ~ *n* **:** deficiency
lack•a•dai•si•cal \ˌlakəˈdāzikəl\ *adj* **:** lacking spirit **—lack•a•dai•si•cal•ly** \-klē\ *adv*
lack•ey \ˈlakē\ *n, pl* **-eys 1 :** footman or servant **2 :** toady
lack•lus•ter \ˈlakˌləstər\ *adj* **:** dull
la•con•ic \ləˈkänik\ *adj* **:** sparing of words **—la•con•i•cal•ly** \-iklē\ *adv*
lac•quer \ˈlakər\ *n* **:** glossy surface coating **—lacquer** *vb*
la•crosse \ləˈkrös\ *n* **:** ball game played with long-handled rackets
lac•tate \ˈlakˌtāt\ *vb* **-tat•ed; -tat•ing :** secrete milk **—lac•ta•tion** \lakˈtāshən\ *n*
lac•tic \ˈlaktik\ *adj* **:** relating to milk
la•cu•na \ləˈkünə, -ˈkyü-\ *n, pl* **-nae** \-ˌnē\ *or* **-nas :** blank space or missing part
lad \ˈlad\ *n* **:** boy
lad•der \ˈladər\ *n* **:** device with steps or rungs for climbing
lad•en \ˈlādᵊn\ *adj* **:** loaded
la•dle \ˈlādᵊl\ *n* **:** spoon with a deep bowl **—ladle** *vb*
la•dy \ˈlādē\ *n, pl* **-dies 1 :** woman of rank or authority **2 :** woman
la•dy•bird \ˈlādēˌbərd\ *n* **:** ladybug
la•dy•bug \-ˌbəg\ *n* **:** brightly colored beetle
lag \ˈlag\ *vb* **-gg- :** fail to keep up ~ *n* **1 :** a falling behind **2 :** interval
la•ger \ˈlägər\ *n* **:** beer
lag•gard \ˈlagərd\ *adj* **:** slow ~ *n* **:** one that lags **—lag•gard•ly** *adv or adj* **—lag•gard•ness** *n*
la•gniappe \ˈlanˌyap\ *n* **:** bonus
la•goon \ləˈgün\ *n* **:** shallow sound, channel, or pond near or connecting with a larger body of water
laid *past of* LAY
lain *past part of* LIE
lair \ˈlar\ *n* **:** den
lais•sez–faire \ˌlesˌāˈfar\ *n* **:** doctrine opposing government interference in business
la•ity \ˈlāətē\ *n* **:** people of a religious faith who are not clergy members
lake \ˈlāk\ *n* **:** inland body of water
la•ma \ˈlämə\ *n* **:** Buddhist monk
lamb \ˈlam\ *n* **:** young sheep or its flesh used as food
lam•baste, lam•bast \lamˈbāst, -ˈbast\ *vb* **1 :** beat **2 :** censure
lam•bent \ˈlambənt\ *adj* **:** light or bright **—lam•ben•cy** \-bənsē\ *n* **—lam•bent•ly** *adv*
lame \ˈlām\ *adj* **lam•er; lam•est 1 :** having a limb disabled **2 :** weak ~ *vb* **lamed; lam•ing :** make lame **—lame•ly** *adv* **—lame•ness** *n*
la•mé \läˈmā, la-\ *n* **:** cloth with tinsel threads
lame•brain \ˈlāmˌbrān\ *n* **:** fool
la•ment \ləˈment\ *vb* **1 :** mourn **2 :** express sorrow for ~ *n* **1 :** mourning **2 :** complaint **—lam•en•ta•ble** \ˈlaməntəbəl, ləˈmentə-\ *adj* **—lam•en•ta•bly** \-blē\ *adv* **—lam•en•ta•tion** \ˌlamənˈtāshən\ *n*
lam•i•nat•ed \ˈlaməˌnātəd\ *adj* **:** made of thin layers of material **—lam•i•nate** \-ˌnāt\ *vb* **—lam•i•nate** \-nət\ *n or adj* **—lam•i•na•tion** \ˌlaməˈnāshən\ *n*
lamp \ˈlamp\ *n* **:** device for producing light or heat
lam•poon \lamˈpün\ *n* **:** satire **—lampoon** *vb*
lam•prey \ˈlamprē\ *n, pl* **-preys :** sucking eellike fish
lance \ˈlans\ *n* **:** spear ~ *vb* **lanced; lanc•ing :** pierce or open with a lancet
lance corporal *n* **:** enlisted man in the marine corps ranking above a private first class and below a corporal
lan•cet \ˈlansət\ *n* **:** pointed surgical instrument
land \ˈland\ *n* **1 :** solid part of the surface of the earth **2 :** country ~ *vb* **1 :** go ashore **2 :** catch or gain **3 :** touch the ground or a surface **—land•less** *adj* **—land•own•er** *n*
land•fill *n* **:** dump
land•ing \ˈlandiŋ\ *n* **1 :** action of one that lands **2 :** place for loading passengers and cargo **3 :** level part of a staircase
land•la•dy \ˈlandˌlādē\ *n* **:** woman landlord
land•locked *adj* **:** enclosed by land
land•lord *n* **:** owner of property
land•lub•ber \-ˌləbər\ *n* **:** one with little sea experience
land•mark \-ˌmärk\ *n* **1 :** object that marks a boundary or serves as a guide **2 :** event that marks a turning point
land•scape \-ˌskāp\ *n* **:** view of natural scenery ~ *vb* **-scaped; -scap•ing :** beautify a piece of land (as by decorative planting)
land•slide *n* **1 :** slipping down of a mass of earth **2 :** overwhelming victory
land•ward \ˈlandwərd\ *adj* **:** toward the land **—landward** *adv*
lane \ˈlān\ *n* **:** narrow way
lan•guage \ˈlaŋgwij\ *n* **:** words and the methods of combining them for communication
lan•guid \ˈlaŋgwəd\ *adj* **1 :** weak **2 :** sluggish **—lan•guid•ly** *adv* **—languid•ness** *n*
lan•guish \ˈlaŋgwish\ *vb* **:** become languid or discouraged
lan•guor \ˈlaŋgər\ *n* **:** listless indolence **—lan•guor•ous** *adj* **—lan•guor•ous•ly** *adv*
lank \ˈlaŋk\ *adj* **1 :** thin **2 :** limp
lanky *adj* **lank•i•er; -est :** tall and thin
lan•o•lin \ˈlanᵊlən\ *n* **:** fatty wax from sheep's wool used in ointments
lan•tern \ˈlantərn\ *n* **:** enclosed portable light
[1]**lap** \ˈlap\ *n* **1 :** front part of the lower trunk and thighs of a seated person **2 :** overlapping part **3 :** one complete circuit completing a course (as around a track or pool) ~ *vb* **-pp- :** fold over
[2]**lap** *vb* **-pp- 1 :** scoop up with the tongue **2 :** splash gently
lap•dog *n* **:** small dog
la•pel \ləˈpel\ *n* **:** fold of the front of a coat
lap•i•dary \ˈlapəˌderē\ *n* **:** one who cuts and polishes gems ~ *adj* **:** relating to gems
lapse \ˈlaps\ *n* **1 :** slight error **2 :** termination of a right or privilege **3 :** interval ~ *vb* **lapsed; laps•ing 1 :** slip **2 :** subside **3 :** cease
lap•top \ˈlapˌtäp\ *adj* **:** of a size that may be used on one's lap
lar•board \ˈlärbərd\ *n* **:** port side
lar•ce•ny \ˈlärsᵊnē\ *n, pl* **-nies :** theft **—lar•ce•nous** \ˈlärsᵊnəs\ *adj*
larch \ˈlärch\ *n* **:** tree like a pine that loses its needles
lard \ˈlärd\ *n* **:** pork fat
lar•der \ˈlärdər\ *n* **:** pantry
large \ˈlärj\ *adj* **larg•er; larg•est :** greater than average **—large•ly** *adv* **—large•ness** *n*
lar•gesse, lar•gess \lärˈzhes, -ˈjes; ˈlärˌ-\ *n* **:** liberal giving
lar•i•at \ˈlarēət\ *n* **:** lasso
[1]**lark** \ˈlärk\ *n* **:** small songbird
[2]**lark** *vb or n* **:** romp
lar•va \ˈlärvə\ *n, pl* **-vae** \-ˌvē\ **:** wormlike form of an insect **—lar•val** \-vəl\ *adj*
lar•yn•gi•tis \ˌlarənˈjītəs\ *n* **:** inflammation of the larynx
lar•ynx \ˈlariŋks\ *n, pl* **-ryn•ges** \ləˈrinˌjēz\ *or* **-ynx•es :** upper part of the trachea **—la•ryn•ge•al** \ˌlarənˈjēəl, ləˈrinjēəl\ *adj*
la•sa•gna \ləˈzänyə\ *n* **:** flat noodles baked usu. with tomato sauce, meat, and cheese
las•civ•i•ous \ləˈsivēəs\ *adj* **:** lewd **—las•civ•i•ous•ness** *n*
la•ser \ˈlāzər\ *n* **:** device that produces an intense light beam
[1]**lash** \ˈlash\ *vb* **:** whip ~ *n* **1 :** stroke esp. of a whip **2 :** eyelash
[2]**lash** *vb* **:** bind with a rope or cord
lass \ˈlas\ *n* **:** girl
lass•ie \ˈlasē\ *n* **:** girl
las•si•tude \ˈlasəˌtüd, -ˌtyüd\ *n* **1 :** fatigue **2 :** listlessness
las•so \ˈlasō, laˈsü\ *n, pl* **-sos** *or* **-soes :** rope with a noose for catching livestock **—lasso** *vb*
[1]**last** \ˈlast\ *vb* **:** continue in existence or operation
[2]**last** *adj* **1 :** final **2 :** previous **3 :** least likely ~ *adv* **1 :** at the end **2 :** most recently **3 :** in conclusion ~ *n* **:** something that is last **—last•ly** *adv* **—at last :** finally
[3]**last** *n* **:** form on which a shoe is shaped
latch \ˈlach\ *vb* **:** catch or get hold ~ *n* **:** catch that holds a door closed
late \ˈlāt\ *adj* **lat•er; lat•est 1 :** coming or staying after the proper time **2 :** advanced toward the end **3 :** recently deceased **4 :** recent **—late** *adv* **—late•com•er** \-ˌkəmər\ *n* **—late•ly** *adv* **—late•ness** *n*
la•tent \ˈlātᵊnt\ *adj* **:** present but not visible or expressed **—la•ten•cy** \-ᵊnsē\ *n*
lat•er•al \ˈlatərəl\ *adj* **:** on or toward the side **—lat•er•al•ly** *adv*
la•tex \ˈlāˌteks\ *n, pl* **-ti•ces** \ˈlātəˌsēz, ˈlat-\ *or* **-tex•es :** emulsion of synthetic rubber or plastic
lath \ˈlath, ˈla<u>th</u>\ *n, pl* **laths** *or* **lath :** building material (as a thin strip of wood) used as a base for plaster **—lath** *vb* **—lath•ing** \-iŋ\ *n*
lathe \ˈlā<u>th</u>\ *n* **:** machine that rotates material for shaping
lath•er \ˈla<u>th</u>ər\ *n* **:** foam ~ *vb* **:** form or spread lather
lat•i•tude \ˈlatəˌtüd, -ˌtyüd\ *n* **1 :** distance north or south from the earth's equator **2 :** freedom of action
la•trine \ləˈtrēn\ *n* **:** toilet
lat•ter \ˈlatər\ *adj* **1 :** more recent **2 :** being the second of 2 **—lat•ter•ly** *adv*
lat•tice \ˈlatəs\ *n* **:** framework of crossed strips
laud *vb or n* **:** praise **—laud•able** *adj* **—laud•ably** *adv*
laugh \ˈlaf, ˈláf\ *vb* **:** show mirth, joy, or scorn with a smile and explosive sound **—laugh** *n* **—laugh•able** *adj* **—laugh•ing•ly** \-iŋlē\ *adv*
laugh•ing•stock \ˈlafiŋˌstäk, ˈláf-\ *n* **:** object of ridicule
laugh•ter \ˈlaftər, ˈláf-\ *n* **:** action or sound of laughing
[1]**launch** \ˈlónch\ *vb* **1 :** hurl or send off **2 :** set afloat **3 :** start **—launch** *n* **—launch•er** *n*
[2]**launch** *n* **:** small open boat
laun•der \ˈlóndər\ *vb* **:** wash or iron fabrics **—laun•der•er** *n* **—laun•dress** \-drəs\ *n* **—laun•dry** \-drē\ *n*
lau•re•ate \ˈlórēət\ *n* **:** recipient of honors **—laureate** *adj*
lau•rel \ˈlórəl\ *n* **1 :** small evergreen tree **2 :** honor
la•va \ˈlävə, ˈlav-\ *n* **:** volcanic molten rock
lav•a•to•ry \ˈlavəˌtōrē\ *n, pl* **-ries :** bathroom
lav•en•der \ˈlavəndər\ *n* **1 :** aromatic plant used for perfume **2 :** pale purple color
lav•ish \ˈlavish\ *adj* **:** expended profusely ~ *vb* **:** expend or give freely **—lav•ish•ly** *adv* **—lav•ish•ness** *n*
law \ˈló\ *n* **1 :** established rule of conduct **2 :** body of such rules **3 :** principle of construction or procedure **4 :** rule stating uniform behavior under uniform conditions **5 :** lawyer's profession **—law•break•er** *n* **—law•giv•er** *n* **—law•less** *adj* **—law•less•ly** *adv* **—law•less•ness** *n* **—law•mak•er** *n* **—law•man** \-mən\ *n* **—law•suit** *n*
law•ful \ˈlófəl\ *adj* **:** permitted by law **—law•ful•ly** *adv*
lawn \ˈlón\ *n* **:** grass-covered yard
law•yer \ˈlóyər\ *n* **:** legal practitioner
lax \ˈlaks\ *adj* **:** not strict or tense **—lax•i•ty** \ˈlaksətē\ *n* **—lax•ly** *adv*
lax•a•tive \ˈlaksətiv\ *n* **:** drug relieving constipation
[1]**lay** \ˈlā\ *vb* **laid** \ˈlād\; **lay•ing 1 :** put or set down **2 :** produce eggs **3 :** bet **4 :** impose as a duty or burden **5 :** put forward ~ *n* **:** way something lies or is laid
[2]**lay** *past of* LIE
[3]**lay** *n* **:** song
[4]**lay** *adj* **:** of the laity **—lay•man** \-mən\ *n* **—lay•wom•an** \-ˌwúmən\ *n*
lay•er \ˈlāər\ *n* **1 :** one that lays **2 :** one thickness over or under another
lay•off \ˈlāˌóf\ *n* **:** temporary dismissal of a worker
lay•out \ˈlāˌaút\ *n* **:** arrangement
la•zy \ˈlāzē\ *adj* **-zi•er; -est :** disliking activity or exertion **—la•zi•ly** \ˈlāzəlē\ *adv* **—la•zi•ness** *n*
lea \ˈlē, ˈlā\ *n* **:** meadow
leach \ˈlēch\ *vb* **:** remove (a soluble part) with a solvent
[1]**lead** \ˈlēd\ *vb* **led** \ˈled\; **lead•ing 1 :** guide on a way **2 :** direct the activity of **3 :** go at the head of **4 :** tend to a definite result ~ *n* **:** position in front **—lead•er** *n* **—lead•er•less** *adj* **—lead•er•ship** *n*
[2]**lead** \ˈled\ *n* **1 :** heavy bluish white chemical element **2 :** marking substance in a pencil **—lead•en** \ˈledᵊn\ *adj*
leaf \ˈlēf\ *n, pl* **leaves** \ˈlēvz\ **1 :** green outgrowth of a plant stem **2 :** leaflike thing ~ *vb* **1 :** produce leaves **2 :** turn book pages **—leaf•age** \ˈlēfij\ *n* **—leafed** \ˈlēft\ *adj* **—leaf•less** *adj* **—leafy** *adj* **—leaved** \ˈlēfd\ *adj*
leaf•let \ˈlēflət\ *n* **:** pamphlet
[1]**league** \ˈlēg\ *n* **:** unit of distance equal to about 3 miles
[2]**league** *n* **:** association for a common purpose **—league** *vb* **—leagu•er** *n*
leak \ˈlēk\ *vb* **1 :** enter or escape through a leak **2 :** become or make known ~ *n* **:** opening that accidentally admits or lets out a substance **—leak•age** \ˈlēkij\ *n* **—leaky** *adj*
[1]**lean** \ˈlēn\ *vb* **1 :** bend from a vertical position **2 :** rely on for support **3 :** incline in opinion **—lean** *n*
[2]**lean** *adj* **1 :** lacking in flesh **2 :** lacking richness **—lean•ness** \ˈlēnnəs\ *n*
leap \ˈlēp\ *vb* **leapt** *or* **leaped** \ˈlēpt, ˈlept\; **leap•ing :** jump **—leap** *n*
leap year *n* **:** 366-day year
learn \ˈlərn\ *vb* **1 :** gain understanding or skill by study or experience **2 :** memorize **3 :** find out **—learn•er** *n*
learn•ed \-əd\ *adj* **:** having great learning **—learn•ed•ness** *n*
learn•ing \-iŋ\ *n* **:** knowledge
lease \ˈlēs\ *n* **:** contract transferring real estate for a term and usu. for rent ~ *vb* **leased; leas•ing :** grant by or hold under a lease
leash \ˈlēsh\ *n* **:** line to hold an animal **—leash** *vb*
least \ˈlēst\ *adj* **1 :** lowest in importance or position **2 :** smallest **3 :** scantiest ~ *n* **:** one that is least ~ *adv* **:** in the smallest or lowest degree
leath•er \ˈle<u>th</u>ər\ *n* **:** dressed animal skin **—leath•ern** \-ərn\ *adj* **—leath•ery** *adj*
[1]**leave** \ˈlēv\ *vb* **left** \ˈleft\; **leav•ing 1 :** bequeath **2 :** allow or cause to remain **3 :** have as a remainder **4 :** go away ~ *n* **1 :** permission **2 :** authorized absence **3 :** departure
[2]**leave** *vb* **leaved; leav•ing :** leaf
leav•en \ˈlevən\ *n* **:** substance for producing fermentation ~ *vb* **:** raise dough with a leaven
leaves *pl of* LEAF
lech•ery \ˈlechərē\ *n* **:** inordinate indulgence in sex **—lech•er** \ˈlechər\ *n* **—lech•er•ous** \-chərəs\ *adj* **—lech•er•ous•ly** *adv* **—lech•er•ous•ness** *n*
lec•ture \ˈlekchər\ *n* **1 :** instructive talk **2 :** reprimand **—lecture** *vb* **—lec•tur•er** *n* **—lec•ture•ship** *n*
led *past of* LEAD
ledge \ˈlej\ *n* **:** shelflike projection

led•ger \'lejər\ *n* : account book

lee \'lē\ *n* : side sheltered from the wind —**lee** *adj*

leech \'lēch\ *n* : segmented freshwater worm that feeds on blood

leek \'lēk\ *n* : onionlike herb

leer \'lir\ *n* : suggestive or malicious look —**leer** *vb*

leery \'lirē\ *adj* : suspicious or wary

lees \'lēz\ *n pl* : dregs

lee•ward \'lēwərd, 'lüərd\ *adj* : situated away from the wind ~ *n* : the lee side

lee•way \'lē,wā\ *n* : allowable margin

1left \'left\ *adj* : on the same side of the body as the heart ~ *n* : left hand —**left** *adv*

2left *past of* LEAVE

leg \'leg\ *n* **1** : limb of an animal that supports the body **2** : something like a leg **3** : clothing to cover the leg ~ *vb* **-gg-** : walk or run —**legged** \'legəd\ *adj* —**leg•less** *adj*

leg•a•cy \'legəsē\ *n, pl* **-cies** : inheritance

le•gal \'lēgəl\ *adj* **1** : relating to law or lawyers **2** : lawful —**le•gal•is•tic** \,lēgə'listik\ *adj* —**le•gal•i•ty** \li'galətē\ *n* —**le•gal•ize** \'lēgə,līz\ *vb* —**le•gal•ly** \-gəlē\ *adv*

leg•ate \'legət\ *n* : official representative

le•ga•tion \li'gāshən\ *n* **1** : diplomatic mission **2** : official residence and office of a diplomat

leg•end \'lejənd\ *n* **1** : story handed down from the past **2** : inscription **3** : explanation of map symbols —**leg•end•ary** \-ən,derē\ *adj*

leg•er•de•main \,lejərdə'mān\ *n* : sleight of hand

leg•ging, leg•gin \'legən, -iŋ\ *n* : leg covering

leg•i•ble \'lejəbəl\ *adj* : capable of being read —**leg•i•bil•i•ty** \,lejə'bilətē\ *n* —**leg•i•bly** \'lejəblē\ *adv*

le•gion \'lējən\ *n* **1** : large army unit **2** : multitude **3** : association of former servicemen —**le•gion•ary** \-,erē\ *n* —**le•gion•naire** \,lējən'ar\ *n*

leg•is•late \'lejə,slāt\ *vb* **-lat•ed; -lat•ing** : enact or bring about with laws —**leg•is•la•tion** \,lejə'slāshən\ *n* —**leg•is•la•tive** \'lejə,slātiv\ *adj* —**leg•is•la•tor** \-ər\ *n*

leg•is•la•ture \'lejə,slāchər\ *n* : organization with authority to make laws

le•git•i•mate \li'jitəmət\ *adj* **1** : lawfully begotten **2** : genuine **3** : conforming with law or accepted standards —**le•git•i•ma•cy** \-məsē\ *n* —**le•git•i•mate•ly** *adv* —**le•git•i•mize** \-mīz\ *vb*

le•gume \'leg,yüm, li'gyüm\ *n* : plant bearing pods —**le•gu•mi•nous** \li'gyümənəs\ *adj*

lei \'lā\ *n* : necklace of flowers

lei•sure \'lēzhər, 'lezh-, 'lāzh-\ *n* **1** : free time **2** : ease **3** : convenience —**lei•sure•ly** *adj or adv*

lem•ming \'lemiŋ\ *n* : short-tailed rodent

lem•on \'lemən\ *n* : yellow citrus fruit —**lem•ony** *adj*

lem•on•ade \,lemə'nād\ *n* : sweetened lemon beverage

lend \'lend\ *vb* **lent** \'lent\; **lend•ing 1** : give for temporary use **2** : furnish —**lend•er** *n*

length \'leŋth\ *n* **1** : longest dimension **2** : duration in time **3** : piece to be joined to others —**length•en** \'leŋthən\ *vb* —**length•wise** *adv or adj* —**lengthy** *adj*

le•nient \'lēnēənt, -nyənt\ *adj* : of mild and tolerant disposition or effect —**le•ni•en•cy** \'lēnēənsē -nyənsē\ *n* —**le•ni•ent•ly** *adv*

len•i•ty \'lenətē\ *n* : leniency

lens \'lenz\ *n* **1** : curved piece for forming an image in an optical instrument **2** : transparent body in the eye that focuses light rays

Lent \'lent\ *n* : 40-day period of penitence and fasting from Ash Wednesday to Easter —**Lent•en** \-ən\ *adj*

len•til \'lentəl\ *n* : legume with flat edible seeds

le•o•nine \'lēə,nīn\ *adj* : like a lion

leop•ard \'lepərd\ *n* : large tawny black-spotted cat

le•o•tard \'lēə,tärd\ *n* : close-fitting garment

lep•er \'lepər\ *n* : person with leprosy

lep•re•chaun \'leprə,kän\ *n* : mischievous Irish elf

lep•ro•sy \'leprəsē\ *n* : chronic bacterial disease —**lep•rous** \-rəs\ *adj*

les•bi•an \'lezbēən\ *n* : female homosexual —**lesbian** *adj* —**les•bi•an•ism** \-,izəm\ *n*

le•sion \'lēzhən\ *n* : abnormal area in the body due to injury or disease

less \'les\ *adj* **1** : fewer **2** : of lower rank, degree, or importance **3** : smaller ~ *adv* : to a lesser degree ~ *n, pl* **less** : smaller portion ~ *prep* : minus —**less•en** \-ən\ *vb*

-less \ləs\ *adj suffix* **1** : not having **2** : unable to act or be acted on

les•see \le'sē\ *n* : tenant under a lease

less•er \'lesər\ *adj* : of less size, quality, or significance

les•son \'lesən\ *n* **1** : reading or exercise to be studied by a pupil **2** : something learned

les•sor \'les,ȯr, le'sȯr\ *n* : one who transfers property by a lease

lest \,lest\ *conj* : for fear that

1let \'let\ *n* : hindrance or obstacle

2let *vb* **let; let•ting 1** : cause to **2** : rent **3** : permit

-let \lət\ *n suffix* : small one

le•thal \'lēthəl\ *adj* : deadly —**le•thal•ly** *adv*

leth•ar•gy \'lethərjē\ *n* **1** : drowsiness **2** : state of being lazy or indifferent —**le•thar•gic** \li'thärjik\ *adj*

let•ter \'letər\ *n* **1** : unit of an alphabet **2** : written or printed communication **3** *pl* : literature or learning **4** : literal meaning ~ *vb* : mark with letters —**let•ter•er** *n*

let•tuce \'letəs\ *n* : garden plant with crisp leaves

leu•ke•mia \lü'kēmēə\ *n* : cancerous blood disease —**leu•ke•mic** \-mik\ *adj or n*

lev•ee \'levē\ *n* : embankment to prevent flooding

lev•el \'levəl\ *n* **1** : device for establishing a flat surface **2** : horizontal surface **3** : position in a scale ~ *vb* **-eled** *or* **-elled; -el•ing** *or* **-el•ling 1** : make flat or level **2** : aim **3** : raze ~ *adj* **1** : having an even surface **2** : of the same height or rank —**lev•el•er** *n* —**lev•el•ly** *adv* —**lev•el•ness** *n*

le•ver \'levər, 'lē-\ *n* : bar for prying or dislodging something —**le•ver•age** \'levərij, 'lēv-\ *n*

le•vi•a•than \li'vīəthən\ *n* **1** : large sea animal **2** : enormous thing

lev•i•ty \'levətē\ *n* : unseemly frivolity

levy \'levē\ *n, pl* **lev•ies** : imposition or collection of a tax ~ *vb* **lev•ied; levy•ing 1** : impose or collect legally **2** : enlist for military service **3** : wage

lewd \'lüd\ *adj* **1** : sexually unchaste **2** : vulgar —**lewd•ly** *adv* —**lewd•ness** *n*

lex•i•cog•ra•phy \,leksə'kägrəfē\ *n* : dictionary making —**lex•i•cog•ra•pher** \-fər\ *n* —**lex•i•co•graph•i•cal** \-kō'grafikəl\ *or* **lex•i•co•graph•ic** \-ik\ *adj*

lex•i•con \'leksə,kän\ *n, pl* **-i•ca** \-sikə\ *or* **-icons** : dictionary

li•a•ble \'līəbəl\ *adj* **1** : legally obligated **2** : probable **3** : susceptible —**li•a•bil•i•ty** \,līə'bilətē\ *n*

li•ai•son \'lēə,zän, lē'ā-\ *n* **1** : close bond **2** : communication between groups

li•ar \'līər\ *n* : one who lies

li•bel \'lībəl\ *n* : action, crime, or an instance of injuring a person's reputation esp. by something written ~ *vb* **-beled** *or* **-belled; -bel•ing** *or* **-bel•ling** : make or publish a libel —**li•bel•er** *n* —**li•bel•ist** *n* —**li•bel•ous, li•bel•lous** \-bələs\ *adj*

lib•er•al \'librəl, 'libə-\ *adj* : not stingy, narrow, or conservative —**liberal** *n* —**lib•er•al•ism** \-,izəm\ *n* —**lib•er•al•i•ty** \,libə'ralətē\ *n* —**lib•er•al•ize** \'librə,līz, 'libə-\ *vb* —**lib•er•al•ly** \-rəlē\ *adv*

lib•er•ate \'libə,rāt\ *vb* **-at•ed; -at•ing** : set free —**lib•er•a•tion** \,libə'rāshən\ *n* —**lib•er•a•tor** \'libə,rātər\ *n*

lib•er•tine \'libər,tēn\ *n* : one who leads a dissolute life

lib•er•ty \'libərtē\ *n, pl* **-ties 1** : quality or state of being free **2** : action going beyond normal limits

li•bi•do \lə'bēdō, -'bīd-\ *n, pl* **-dos** : sexual drive —**li•bid•i•nal** \lə'bidənəl\ *adj* —**li•bid•i•nous** \-əs\ *adj*

li•brary \'lī,brerē\ *n, pl* **-brar•ies 1** : place where books are kept for use **2** : collection of books —**li•brar•i•an** \lī'brerēən\ *n*

li•bret•to \lə'bretō\ *n, pl* **-tos** *or* **-ti** \-ē\ : text of an opera —**li•bret•tist** \-ist\ *n*

lice *pl of* LOUSE

li•cense, li•cence \'līsəns\ *n* **1** : legal permission to engage in some activity **2** : document or tag providing proof of a license **3** : irresponsible use of freedom —**license** *vb* —**li•cens•ee** \,līsən'sē\ *n*

li•cen•tious \lī'senchəs\ *adj* : disregarding sexual restraints —**li•cen•tious•ly** *adv* —**li•cen•tious•ness** *n*

li•chen \'līkən\ *n* : complex lower plant made up of an alga and a fungus

lic•it \'lisət\ *adj* : lawful

lick \'lik\ *vb* **1** : draw the tongue over **2** : beat ~ *n* **1** : stroke of the tongue **2** : small amount

lic•o•rice \'likərish, -rəs\ *n* : dried root of a European legume or candy flavored by it

lid \'lid\ *n* **1** : movable cover **2** : eyelid

1lie \'lī\ *vb* **lay** \'lā\; **lain** \'lān\; **ly•ing** \'līiŋ\ **1** : be in, rest in, or assume a horizontal position **2** : occupy a certain relative position ~ *n* : position in which something lies

2lie *vb* **lied; ly•ing** \'līiŋ\ : tell a lie ~ *n* : untrue statement

liege \'lēj\ *n* : feudal superior or vassal

lien \'lēn, 'lēən\ *n* : legal claim on the property of another

lieu•ten•ant \lü'tenənt\ *n* **1** : representative **2** : first lieutenant or second lieutenant **3** : commissioned officer in the navy ranking next below a lieutenant commander —**lieu•ten•an•cy** \-ənsē\ *n*

lieutenant colonel *n* : commissioned officer (as in the army) ranking next below a colonel

lieutenant commander *n* : commissioned officer in the navy ranking next below a commander

lieutenant general *n* : commissioned officer (as in the army) ranking next below a general

lieutenant junior grade *n, pl* **lieutenants junior grade** : commissioned officer in the navy ranking next below a lieutenant

life \'līf\ *n, pl* **lives** \'līvz\ **1** : quality that distinguishes a vital and functional being from a dead body or inanimate matter **2** : physical and mental experiences of an individual **3** : biography **4** : period of existence **5** : way of living **6** : liveliness —**life•less** *adj* —**life•like** *adj*

life•blood *n* : basic source of strength and vitality

life•boat *n* : boat for saving lives at sea

life•guard *n* : one employed to safeguard bathers

life•long *adj* : continuing through life

life•sav•ing *n* : art or practice of saving lives —**life•sav•er** \-,sāvər\ *n*

life•style \'līf,stīl\ *n* : a way of life

life•time *n* : duration of an individual's existence

lift \'lift\ *vb* **1** : move upward or cause to move upward **2** : put an end to —**lift** *n* —**lift•er** *n*

lift•off \'lift,ȯf\ *n* : vertical takeoff by a rocket

lig•a•ment \'ligəmənt\ *n* : band of tough tissue that holds bones together

lig•a•ture \'ligə,chu̇r, -chər\ *n* : something that binds or ties

1light \'līt\ *n* **1** : radiation that makes vision possible **2** : daylight **3** : source of light **4** : public knowledge **5** : aspect **6** : celebrity **7** : flame for lighting ~ *adj* **1** : bright **2** : weak in color ~ *vb* **lit** \'lit\ *or* **light•ed; light•ing 1** : make or become light **2** : cause to burn —**light•er** *n* —**light•ness** *n* —**light•proof** *adj*

2light *adj* : not heavy, serious, or abundant —**light** *adv* —**light•ly** *adv* —**light•ness** *n* —**light•weight** *adj*

3light *vb* **light•ed** *or* **lit** \'lit\; **light•ing** : settle or dismount

1light•en \'lītən\ *vb* **1** : make light or bright **2** : give out flashes of lightning

2lighten *vb* **1** : relieve of a burden **2** : become lighter

light•heart•ed \-'härtəd\ *adj* : free from worry —**light•heart•ed•ly** *adv* —**light•heart•ed•ness** *n*

light•house *n* : structure with a powerful light for guiding sailors

light•ning \'lītniŋ\ *n* : flashing discharge of atmospheric electricity

light–year \'līt,yir\ *n* : distance traveled by light in one year equal to about 5.88 trillion miles

lig•nite \'lig,nīt\ *n* : brownish black soft coal

1like \'līk\ *vb* **liked; lik•ing 1** : enjoy **2** : desire ~ *n* : preference —**lik•able, like•able** \'līkəbəl\ *adj*

2like *adj* : similar ~ *prep* **1** : similar or similarly to **2** : typical of **3** : such as ~ *n* : counterpart ~ *conj* : as or as if —**like•ness** *n* —**like•wise** *adv*

-like \,līk\ *adj comb form* : resembling or characteristic of

like•li•hood \'līklē,hu̇d\ *n* : probability

like•ly \'līklē\ *adj* **-li•er; -est 1** : probable **2** : believable ~ *adv* : in all probability

lik•en \'līkən\ *vb* : compare

lik•ing \'līkiŋ\ *n* : favorable regard

li•lac \'līlək, -,lak, -,läk\ *n* : shrub with clusters of fragrant pink, purple, or white flowers

lilt \'lilt\ *n* : rhythmical swing or flow

lily \'lilē\ *n, pl* **lil•ies** : tall bulbous herb with funnel-shaped flowers

lima bean \'līmə-\ *n* : flat edible seed of a plant or the plant itself

limb \'lim\ *n* **1** : projecting appendage used in moving or grasping **2** : tree branch —**limb•less** *adj*

lim•ber \'limbər\ *adj* : supple or agile ~ *vb* : make or become limber

lim•bo \'limbō\ *n, pl* **-bos** : place or state of confinement or oblivion

1lime \'līm\ *n* : caustic white oxide of calcium

2lime *n* : small green lemonlike citrus fruit —**lime•ade** \-,ād\ *n*

lime•light *n* : center of public attention

lim•er•ick \'limərik\ *n* : light poem of 5 lines

lime•stone *n* : rock that yields lime when burned

lim•it \'limət\ *n* **1** : boundary **2** : something that restrains or confines ~ *vb* : set limits on —**lim•i•ta•tion** \,limə'tāshən\ *n* —**lim•it•less** *adj*

lim•ou•sine \'limə,zēn, ,limə'-\ *n* : large luxurious sedan

limp \'limp\ *vb* : walk lamely ~ *n* : limping movement or gait ~ *adj* : lacking firmness and body —**limp•ly** *adv* —**limp•ness** *n*

lim•pid \'limpəd\ *adj* : clear or transparent

lin•den \'lindən\ *n* : tree with large heart-shaped leaves

1line \'līn\ *vb* **lined; lin•ing** : cover the inner surface of —**lin•ing** *n*

2line *n* **1** : cord, rope, or wire **2** : row or something like a row **3** : note **4** : course of action or thought **5** : state of agreement **6** : occupation **7** : limit **8** : transportation system **9** : long narrow mark ~ *vb* **lined; lin•ing 1** : mark with a line **2** : place in a line **3** : form a line

lin•eage \'linēij\ *n* : descent from a common ancestor

lin•eal \'linēəl\ *adj* **1** : linear **2** : in a direct line of ancestry

lin•ea•ments \'linēəmənts\ *n pl* : features or contours esp. of a face

lin•ear \'linēər\ *adj* **1** : straight **2** : long and narrow

lin•en \'linən\ *n* **1** : cloth or thread made of flax **2** : household articles made of linen cloth

lin•er \'līnər\ *n* **1** : one that lines **2** : ship or airplane belonging to a line

line•up \'līn,əp\ *n* **1** : line of persons for inspection or identification **2** : list of players in a game

-ling \liŋ\ *n suffix* **1** : one linked with **2** : young, small, or minor one

lin•ger \'liŋgər\ *vb* : be slow to leave or act —**lin•ger•er** *n*

lin•ge•rie \,länjə'rā, ,lanzhə-, -'rē\ *n* : women's underwear

lin•go \'liŋgō\ *n, pl* **-goes** : usu. strange language

lin•guist \'liŋgwist\ *n* **1** : person skilled in speech or languages **2** : student of language —**lin•guis•tic** \liŋ'gwistik\ *adj* —**lin•guis•tics** *n pl*

lin•i•ment \'linəmənt\ *n* : liquid medication rubbed on the skin

link \'liŋk\ *n* **1** : connecting structure (as a ring of a chain) **2** : bond —**link** *vb* —**link•age** \-ij\ *n* —**link•er** *n*

li•no•leum \lə'nōlēəm\ *n* : floor covering with hard surface

lin•seed \'lin,sēd\ *n* : seeds of flax yielding an oil (**linseed oil**)

lint \'lint\ *n* : fine fluff or loose short fibers from fabric

lin•tel \'lintəl\ *n* : horizontal piece over a door or window

li•on \'līən\ *n* : large cat of Africa and Asia —**li•on•ess** \'līənəs\ *n*

li•on•ize \'līə,nīz\ *vb* **-ized; -iz•ing** : treat as very important —**li•on•iza•tion** \,līənə'zāshən\ *n*

lip \'lip\ *n* **1** : either of the 2 fleshy folds surrounding the mouth **2** : edge of something hollow —**lipped** \'lipt\ *adj* —**lip•read•ing** *n*

li•po•suc•tion \'lipə,səkshən, 'lī-\ *n* : surgical removal of fat deposits (as from the thighs)

lip•stick \'lip,stik\ *n* : stick of cosmetic to color lips

liq•ue•fy \'likwə,fī\ *vb* **-fied; -fy•ing** : make or become liquid —**liq•ue•fi•er** \'likwə,fīər\ *n*

li•queur \li'kər\ *n* : sweet or aromatic alcoholic liquor

liq•uid \'likwəd\ *adj* **1** : flowing freely like water **2** : neither solid nor gaseous **3** : of or convertible to cash —**liquid** *n* —**li•quid•i•ty** \lik'widətē\ *n*

liq•ui•date \'likwə,dāt\ *vb* **-dat•ed; -dat•ing 1** : pay off **2** : dispose of —**liq•ui•da•tion** \,likwə'dāshən\ *n*

li•quor \'likər\ *n* : liquid substance and esp. a distilled alcoholic beverage

lisp \'lisp\ *vb* : pronounce *s* and *z* imperfectly —**lisp** *n*

lis•some \'lisəm\ *adj* : supple or agile

1list \'list\ *n* **1** : series of names or items ~ *vb* **1** : make a list of **2** : put on a list

2list *vb* : tilt or lean over ~ *n* : slant

lis•ten \'lisən\ *vb* **1** : pay attention in order to hear **2** : heed —**lis•ten•er** \'lisənər\ *n*

list•less \'listləs\ *adj* : having no desire to act —**list•less•ly** *adv* —**list•less•ness** *n*

lit \'lit\ *past of* LIGHT

lit•a•ny \'litənē\ *n, pl* **-nies 1** : prayer said as a series of responses to a leader **2** : long recitation

li•ter \'lētər\ *n* : unit of liquid measure equal to about 1.06 quarts

lit•er•al \'litərəl\ *adj* : being exactly as stated —**lit•er•al•ly** *adv*

lit•er•ary \'litə,rerē\ *adj* : relating to literature

lit•er•ate \'litərət\ *adj* : able to read and write —**lit•er•a•cy** \'litərəsē\ *n*

lit•er•a•ture \'litərə,chu̇r, -chər\ *n* : writings of enduring interest

lithe \'līth, 'līth\ *adj* **1** : supple **2** : graceful —**lithe•some** \-səm\ *adj*

lith•o•graph \'lithə,graf\ *n* : print from a drawing on metal or stone —**li•thog•ra•pher** \lith'ägrəfər, 'lithə,grafər\ *n* —**lith•o•graph•ic** \,lithə'grafik\ *adj* —**li•thog•ra•phy** \lith'ägrəfē\ *n*

lit•i•gate \'litə,gāt\ *vb* **-gat•ed; -gat•ing** : carry on a lawsuit **—lit•i•gant** \'litigənt\ *n* **—lit•i•ga•tion** \,litə'gāshən\ *n* **—li•ti•gious** \lə'tijəs, li-\ *adj* **—li•ti•gious•ness** *n*

lit•mus \'litməs\ *n* : coloring matter that turns red in acid solutions and blue in alkaline

lit•ter \'litər\ *n* **1** : animal offspring of one birth **2** : stretcher **3** : rubbish **4** : material to absorb animal waste ~ *vb* **1** : give birth to young **2** : strew with litter

lit•tle \'litəl\ *adj* **lit•tler** *or* **less** \'les\ *or* **less•er** \'lesər\; **lit•tlest** *or* **least** \'lēst\ **1** : not big **2** : not much **3** : not important ~ *adv* **less** \'les\; **least** \'lēst\ **1** : slightly **2** : not often ~ *n* : small amount **—lit•tle•ness** *n*

lit•ur•gy \'litərjē\ *n, pl* **-gies** : rite of worship **—li•tur•gi•cal** \lə'tərjikəl\ *adj* **—li•tur•gi•cal•ly** \-klē\ *adv* **—lit•ur•gist** \'litərjist\ *n*

liv•able \'livəbəl\ *adj* : suitable for living in or with **—liv•a•bil•i•ty** \,livə'bilətē\ *n*

1live \'liv\ *vb* **lived; liv•ing 1** : be alive **2** : conduct one's life **3** : subsist **4** : reside

2live \'līv\ *adj* **1** : having life **2** : burning **3** : connected to electric power **4** : not exploded **5** : of continuing interest **6** : involving the actual presence of real people

live•li•hood \'līvlē,hu̇d\ *n* : means of subsistence

live•long \'liv'lȯŋ\ *adj* : whole

live•ly \'līvlē\ *adj* **-li•er; -est** : full of life and vigor **—live•li•ness** *n*

liv•en \'līvən\ *vb* : enliven

liv•er \'livər\ *n* : organ that secretes bile

liv•ery \'livərē\ *n, pl* **-er•ies 1** : servant's uniform **2** : care of horses for pay **—liv•er•ied** \-rēd\ *adj* **—liv•ery•man** \-mən\ *n*

lives *pl of* LIFE

live•stock \'līv,stäk\ *n* : farm animals

liv•id \'livəd\ *adj* **1** : discolored by bruising **2** : pale **3** : enraged

liv•ing \'liviŋ\ *adj* : having life ~ *n* : livelihood

liz•ard \'lizərd\ *n* : reptile with 4 legs and a long tapering tail

lla•ma \'lämə\ *n* : So. American mammal related to the camel

load \'lōd\ *n* **1** : cargo **2** : supported weight **3** : burden **4** : a large quantity—usu. pl. ~ *vb* **1** : put a load on **2** : burden **3** : put ammunition in

1loaf \'lōf\ *n, pl* **loaves** \'lōvz\ : mass of bread

2loaf *vb* : waste time **—loaf•er** *n*

loam \'lōm, 'lüm\ *n* : soil **—loamy** *adj*

loan \'lōn\ *n* **1** : money borrowed at interest **2** : something lent temporarily **3** : grant of use ~ *vb* : lend

loath \'lōth, 'lōth\ *adj* : very reluctant

loathe \'lōth\ *vb* **loathed; loath•ing** : hate

loath•ing \'lōthiŋ\ *n* : extreme disgust

loath•some \'lōthsəm, 'lōth-\ *adj* : repulsive

lob \'läb\ *vb* **-bb-** : throw or hit in a high arc **—lob** *n*

lob•by \'läbē\ *n, pl* **-bies 1** : public waiting room at the entrance of a building **2** : persons lobbying ~ *vb* **-bied; -by•ing** : try to influence legislators **—lob•by•ist** *n*

lobe \'lōb\ *n* : rounded part **—lo•bar** \'lōbər\ *adj* **—lobed** \'lōbd\ *adj*

lo•bot•o•my \lō'bätəmē\ *n, pl* **-mies** : surgical severance of nerve fibers in the brain

lob•ster \'läbstər\ *n* : marine crustacean with 2 large pincerlike claws

lo•cal \'lōkəl\ *adj* : confined to or serving a limited area **—local** *n* **—lo•cal•ly** *adv*

lo•cale \lō'kal\ *n* : setting for an event

lo•cal•i•ty \lō'kalətē\ *n, pl* **-ties** : particular place

lo•cal•ize \'lōkə,līz\ *vb* **-ized; -iz•ing** : confine to a definite place **—lo•cal•i•za•tion** \,lōkələ'zāshən\ *n*

lo•cate \'lō,kāt, lō'kāt\ *vb* **-cat•ed; -cat•ing 1** : settle **2** : find a site for **3** : discover the place of **—lo•ca•tion** \lō'kāshən\ *n*

1lock \'läk\ *n* : tuft or strand of hair

2lock *n* **1** : fastener using a bolt **2** : enclosure in a canal to raise or lower boats ~ *vb* **1** : make fast with a lock **2** : confine **3** : interlock

lock•er \'läkər\ *n* : storage compartment

lock•et \'läkət\ *n* : small case worn on a necklace

lock•jaw *n* : tetanus

lock•out *n* : closing of a plant by an employer during a labor dispute

lock•smith \-,smith\ *n* : one who makes or repairs locks

lo•co•mo•tion \,lōkə'mōshən\ *n* : power of moving **—lo•co•mo•tive** \-'mōtiv\ *adj*

lo•co•mo•tive \-'mōtiv\ *n* : vehicle that moves railroad cars

lo•co•weed \'lōkō,wēd\ *n* : western plant poisonous to livestock

lo•cust \'lōkəst\ *n* **1** : migratory grasshopper **2** : cicada **3** : tree with hard wood or this wood

lo•cu•tion \lō'kyüshən\ *n* : way of saying something

lode \'lōd\ *n* : ore deposit

lode•stone *n* : magnetic rock

lodge \'läj\ *vb* **lodged; lodg•ing 1** : provide quarters for **2** : come to rest **3** : file ~ *n* **1** : special house (as for hunters) **2** : animal's den **3** : branch of a fraternal organization **—lodg•er** \'läjər\ *n* **—lodg•ing** *n* **—lodg•ment, lodge•ment** \-mənt\ *n*

loft \'lȯft\ *n* **1** : attic **2** : upper floor (as of a warehouse)

lofty \'lȯftē\ *adj* **loft•i•er; -est 1** : noble **2** : proud **3** : tall or high **—loft•i•ly** *adv* **—loft•i•ness** *n*

log \'lȯg, 'läg\ *n* **1** : unshaped timber **2** : daily record of a ship's or plane's progress ~ *vb* **-gg- 1** : cut (trees) for lumber **2** : enter in a log **—log•ger** \-ər\ *n*

log•a•rithm \'lȯgə,rithəm, 'läg-\ *n* : exponent to which a base number is raised to produce a given number

loge \'lōzh\ *n* : box in a theater

log•ger•head \'lȯgər,hed, 'läg-\ *n* : large Atlantic sea turtle **—at loggerheads** : in disagreement

log•ic \'läjik\ *n* **1** : science of reasoning **2** : sound reasoning **—log•i•cal** \-ikəl\ *adj* **—log•i•cal•ly** *adv* **—lo•gi•cian** \lō'jishən\ *n*

lo•gis•tics \lō'jistiks\ *n sing or pl* : procurement and movement of people and supplies **—lo•gis•tic** *adj*

logo \'lōgō, 'lȯg-, 'läg-\ *n, pl* **log•os** \-ōz\ : advertising symbol

loin \'lȯin\ *n* **1** : part of the body on each side of the spine between the hip and lower ribs **2** *pl* : pubic regions

loi•ter \'lȯitər\ *vb* : remain around a place idly **—loi•ter•er** *n*

loll \'läl\ *vb* : lounge

lol•li•pop, lol•ly•pop \'läli,päp\ *n* : hard candy on a stick

lone \'lōn\ *adj* **1** : alone or isolated **2** : only **—lone•li•ness** *n* **—lone•ly** *adj* **—lon•er** \'lōnər\ *n*

lone•some \-səm\ *adj* : sad from lack of company **—lone•some•ly** *adv* **—lone•some•ness** *n*

long \'lȯŋ\ *adj* **lon•ger** \'lȯŋgər\; **long•est** \'lȯŋgəst\ **1** : extending far or for a considerable time **2** : having a specified length **3** : tedious **4** : well supplied—used with *on* ~ *adv* : for a long time ~ *n* : long period ~ *vb* : feel a strong desire **—long•ing** \'lȯŋiŋ\ *n* **—long•ing•ly** *adv*

lon•gev•i•ty \län'jevətē\ *n* : long life

long•hand *n* : handwriting

long•horn *n* : cattle with long horns

lon•gi•tude \'länjə,tüd, -,tyüd\ *n* : angular distance east or west from a meridian

lon•gi•tu•di•nal \,länjə'tüdənəl, -'tyüd-\ *adj* : lengthwise **—lon•gi•tu•di•nal•ly** *adv*

long•shore•man \'lȯŋ'shōrmən\ *n* : one who loads and unloads ships

look \'lu̇k\ *vb* **1** : see **2** : seem **3** : direct one's attention **4** : face ~ *n* **1** : action of looking **2** : appearance of the face **3** : aspect **—look after** : take care of **—look for 1** : expect **2** : search for

look•out *n* **1** : one who watches **2** : careful watch

1loom \'lüm\ *n* : frame or machine for weaving

2loom *vb* : appear large and indistinct or impressive

loon \'lün\ *n* : black-and-white diving bird

loo•ny, loo•ney \'lünē\ *adj* **-ni•er; -est** : crazy

loop \'lüp\ *n* **1** : doubling of a line that leaves an opening **2** : something like a loop **—loop** *vb*

loop•hole \'lüp,hōl\ *n* : means of evading

loose \'lüs\ *adj* **loos•er; -est 1** : not fixed tight **2** : not restrained **3** : not dense **4** : slack **5** : not exact ~ *vb* **loosed; loos•ing 1** : release **2** : untie or relax **—loose** *adv* **—loose•ly** *adv* **—loos•en** \'lüsən\ *vb* **—loose•ness** *n*

loot \'lüt\ *n or vb* : plunder **—loot•er** *n*

lop \'läp\ *vb* **-pp-** : cut off

lope \'lōp\ *n* : bounding gait **—lope** *vb*

lop•sid•ed \'läp'sīdəd\ *adj* **1** : leaning to one side **2** : not symmetrical **—lop•sid•ed•ly** *adv* **—lop•sid•ed•ness** *n*

lo•qua•cious \lō'kwāshəs\ *adj* : very talkative **—lo•quac•i•ty** \-'kwasətē\ *n*

lord \'lȯrd\ *n* **1** : one with authority over others **2** : British nobleman

lord•ly \-lē\ *adj* **-li•er; -est** : haughty

lord•ship \-,ship\ *n* : rank of a lord

Lord's Supper *n* : Communion

lore \'lōr\ *n* : traditional knowledge

lose \'lüz\ *vb* **lost** \'lȯst\; **los•ing** \'lüziŋ\ **1** : have pass from one's possession **2** : be deprived of **3** : waste **4** : be defeated in **5** : fail to keep to or hold **6** : get rid of **—los•er** *n*

loss \'lȯs\ *n* **1** : something lost **2** *pl* : killed, wounded, or captured soldiers **3** : failure to win

lost \'lȯst\ *adj* **1** : not used, won, or claimed **2** : unable to find the way

lot \'lät\ *n* **1** : object used in deciding something by chance **2** : share **3** : fate **4** : plot of land **5** : much

loth \'lōth, 'lōth\ *var of* LOATH

lo•tion \'lōshən\ *n* : liquid to rub on the skin

lot•tery \'lätərē\ *n, pl* **-ter•ies** : drawing of lots with prizes going to winners

lo•tus \'lōtəs\ *n* **1** : legendary fruit that causes forgetfulness **2** : water lily

loud \'lau̇d\ *adj* **1** : high in volume of sound **2** : noisy **3** : obtrusive in color or pattern **—loud** *adv* **—loud•ly** *adv* **—loud•ness** *n*

loud•speak•er *n* : device that amplifies sound

lounge \'lau̇nj\ *vb* **lounged; loung•ing** : act or move lazily ~ *n* : room with comfortable furniture

lour \'lau̇ər\ *var of* LOWER

louse \'lau̇s\ *n, pl* **lice** \'līs\ : parasitic wingless usu. flat insect

lousy \'lau̇zē\ *adj* **lous•i•er; -est 1** : infested with lice **2** : not good **—lous•i•ly** *adv* **—lous•i•ness** *n*

lout \'lau̇t\ *n* : stupid awkward person **—lout•ish** *adj* **—lout•ish•ly** *adv*

lou•ver, lou•vre \'lüvər\ *n* : opening having parallel slanted slats for ventilation or such a slat

love \'ləv\ *n* **1** : strong affection **2** : warm attachment **3** : beloved person ~ *vb* **loved; lov•ing 1** : feel affection for **2** : enjoy greatly **—lov•able** \-əbəl\ *adj* **—love•less** *adj* **—lov•er** *n* **—lov•ing•ly** *adv*

love•lorn \-,lȯrn\ *adj* : deprived of love or of a lover

love•ly \'ləvlē\ *adj* **-li•er; -est** : beautiful **—love•li•ness** *n* **—lovely** *adv*

1low \'lō\ *vb or n* : moo

2low *adj* **low•er; low•est 1** : not high or tall **2** : below normal level **3** : not loud **4** : humble **5** : sad **6** : less than usual **7** : falling short of a standard **8** : unfavorable ~ *n* **1** : something low **2** : automobile gear giving the slowest speed **—low** *adv* **—low•ness** *n*

low•brow \'lō,brau̇\ *n* : person with little taste or intellectual interest

1low•er \'lau̇ər\ *vb* **1** : scowl **2** : become dark and threatening

2low•er \'lōər\ *adj* : relatively low (as in rank)

3low•er \'lōər\ *vb* **1** : drop **2** : let descend **3** : reduce in amount

low•land \'lōlənd, -,land\ *n* : low flat country

low•ly \'lōlē\ *adj* **-li•er; -est 1** : humble **2** : low in rank **—low•li•ness** *n*

loy•al \'lȯiəl\ *adj* : faithful to a country, cause, or friend **—loy•al•ist** *n* **—loy•al•ly** *adv* **—loy•al•ty** \'lȯiəltē\ *n*

loz•enge \'läzənj\ *n* : small medicated candy

lu•bri•cant \'lübrikənt\ *n* : material (as grease) to reduce friction

lu•bri•cate \-,kāt\ *vb* **-cat•ed; -cat•ing** : apply a lubricant to **—lu•bri•ca•tion** \,lübrə'kāshən\ *n* **—lu•bri•ca•tor** \'lübrə,kātər\ *n*

lu•cid \'lüsəd\ *adj* **1** : mentally sound **2** : easily understood **—lu•cid•i•ty** \lü'sidətē\ *n* **—lu•cid•ly** *adv* **—lu•cid•ness** *n*

luck \'lək\ *n* **1** : chance **2** : good fortune **—luck•i•ly** *adv* **—luck•i•ness** *n* **—luck•less** *adj* **—lucky** *adj*

lu•cra•tive \'lükrətiv\ *adj* : profitable **—lu•cra•tive•ly** *adv* **—lu•cra•tive•ness** *n*

lu•di•crous \'lüdəkrəs\ *adj* : comically ridiculous **—lu•di•crous•ly** *adv* **—lu•di•crous•ness** *n*

lug \'ləg\ *vb* **-gg-** : drag or carry laboriously

lug•gage \'ləgij\ *n* : baggage

lu•gu•bri•ous \lu̇'gübrēəs\ *adj* : mournful often to an exaggerated degree **—lu•gu•bri•ous•ly** *adv* **—lu•gu•bri•ous•ness** *n*

luke•warm \'lük'wȯrm\ *adj* **1** : moderately warm **2** : not enthusiastic

lull \'ləl\ *vb* : make or become quiet or relaxed ~ *n* : temporary calm

lul•la•by \'lələ,bī\ *n, pl* **-bies** : song to lull children to sleep

lum•ba•go \,ləm'bāgō\ *n* : rheumatic back pain

lum•ber \'ləmbər\ *n* : timber dressed for use ~ *vb* : cut logs **—lum•ber•man** *n* **—lum•ber•yard** *n*

lum•ber•jack \-,jak\ *n* : logger

lu•mi•nary \'lümə,nerē\ *n, pl* **-nar•ies** : very famous person

lu•mi•nes•cence \,lümə'nesəns\ *n* : low-temperature emission of light **—lu•mi•nes•cent** \-ənt\ *adj*

lu•mi•nous \'lümənəs\ *adj* : emitting light **—lu•mi•nance** \-nəns\ *n* **—lu•mi•nos•i•ty** \,lümə'näsətē\ *n* **—lu•mi•nous•ly** *adv*

lump \'ləmp\ *n* **1** : mass of irregular shape **2** : abnormal swelling ~ *vb* : heap together **—lump•ish** *adj* **—lumpy** *adj*

lu•na•cy \'lünəsē\ *n, pl* **-cies** : state of insanity

lu•nar \'lünər\ *adj* : of the moon

lu•na•tic \'lünə,tik\ *adj* : insane **—lunatic** *n*

lunch \'lənch\ *n* : noon meal ~ *vb* : eat lunch

lun•cheon \'lənchən\ *n* : usu. formal lunch

lung \'ləŋ\ *n* : breathing organ in the chest **—lunged** \'ləŋd\ *adj*

lunge \'lənj\ *n* **1** : sudden thrust **2** : sudden move forward **—lunge** *vb*

lurch \'lərch\ *n* : sudden swaying **—lurch** *vb*

lure \'lu̇r\ *n* **1** : something that attracts **2** : artificial fish bait ~ *vb* **lured; lur•ing** : attract

lu•rid \'lu̇rəd\ *adj* **1** : gruesome **2** : sensational **—lu•rid•ly** *adv*

lurk \'lərk\ *vb* : lie in wait

lus•cious \'ləshəs\ *adj* **1** : pleasingly sweet in taste or smell **2** : sensually appealing **—lus•cious•ly** *adv* **—lus•cious•ness** *n*

lush \'ləsh\ *adj* : covered with abundant growth

lust \'ləst\ *n* **1** : intense sexual desire **2** : intense longing **—lust** *vb* **—lust•ful** *adj*

lus•ter, lus•tre \'ləstər\ *n* **1** : brightness from reflected light **2** : magnificence **—lus•ter•less** *adj* **—lus•trous** \-trəs\ *adj*

lusty \'ləstē\ *adj* **lust•i•er; -est** : full of vitality **—lust•i•ly** *adv* **—lust•i•ness** *n*

lute \'lüt\ *n* : pear-shaped stringed instrument **—lute•nist, lu•ta•nist** \'lütənist\ *n*

lux•u•ri•ant \,ləg'zhu̇rēənt, ,lək'shu̇r-\ *adj* **1** : growing plentifully **2** : rich and varied **—lux•u•ri•ance** \-ēəns\ *n* **—lux•u•ri•ant•ly** *adv*

lux•u•ri•ate \-ē,āt\ *vb* **-at•ed; -at•ing** : revel

lux•u•ry \'ləkshərē, 'ləgzh-\ *n, pl* **-ries 1** : great comfort **2** : something adding to pleasure or comfort **—lux•u•ri•ous** \,ləg'zhu̇rēəs, ,lək'shu̇r-\ *adj* **—lux•u•ri•ous•ly** *adv*

-ly \lē\ *adv suffix* **1** : in a specified way **2** : from a specified point of view

ly•ce•um \lī'sēəm, 'līsē-\ *n* : hall for public lectures

lye \'lī\ *n* : caustic alkaline substance

lying *pres part of* LIE

lymph \'limf\ *n* : bodily liquid consisting chiefly of blood plasma and white blood cells **—lym•phat•ic** \lim'fatik\ *adj*

lynch \'linch\ *vb* : put to death by mob action **—lynch•er** *n*

lynx \'liŋks\ *n, pl* **lynx** *or* **lynx•es** : wildcat

lyre \'līr\ *n* : ancient Greek stringed instrument

lyr•ic \'lirik\ *adj* **1** : suitable for singing **2** : expressing direct personal emotion ~ *n* **1** : lyric poem **2** *pl* : words of a song **—lyr•i•cal** \-ikəl\ *adj*

M

m \'em\ *n, pl* **m's** *or* **ms** \'emz\ : 13th letter of the alphabet

ma'am \'mam\ *n* : madam

ma•ca•bre \mə'käb, -'käbər, -'käbrə\ *adj* : gruesome

mac•ad•am \mə'kadəm\ *n* : pavement of cemented broken stone **—mac•ad•am•ize** \-,īz\ *vb*

mac•a•ro•ni \,makə'rōnē\ *n* : tube-shaped pasta

mac•a•roon \,makə'rün\ *n* : cookie of ground almonds or coconut

ma•caw \mə'kȯ\ *n* : large long-tailed parrot

1mace \'mās\ *n* **1** : heavy spiked club **2** : ornamental staff as a symbol of authority

2mace *n* : spice from the fibrous coating of the nutmeg

ma•chete \mə'shetē\ *n* : large heavy knife

mach•i•na•tion \,makə'nāshən, ,mashə-\ *n* : plot or scheme **—mach•i•nate** \'makə,nāt, 'mash-\ *vb*

ma•chine \mə'shēn\ *n* : combination of mechanical or electrical parts ~ *vb* **-chined; -chin•ing** : modify by machine-operated tools **—ma•chin•able** *adj* **—ma•chin•ery** \-ərē\ *n* **—ma•chin•ist** *n*

mack•er•el \'makərəl\ *n, pl* **-el** *or* **-els** : No. Atlantic food fish

mack•i•naw \'makə,nȯ\ *n* : short heavy plaid coat

mac•ra•mé \,makrə'mā\ *n* : coarse lace or fringe made by knotting

mac•ro \'makrō\ *adj* : very large

mac•ro•cosm \'makrə,käzəm\ *n* : universe

mad \'mad\ *adj* **-dd- 1** : insane or rabid **2** : rash and foolish **3** : angry **4** : carried away by enthusiasm **—mad•den** \'madən\ *vb* **—mad•den•ing•ly** \'madəniŋlē\ *adv* **—mad•ly** *adv* **—mad•ness** *n*

mad•am \'madəm\ *n, pl* **mes•dames** \mā'däm\ —used in polite address to a woman

ma•dame \mə'dam, *before a surname also* 'madəm\ *n, pl* **mes•dames** \mā'däm\ —

used as a title for a woman not of English-speaking nationality

mad•cap \ˈmad,kap\ *adj* **:** wild or zany —**madcap** *n*

made *past of* MAKE

Ma•dei•ra \məˈdirə\ *n* **:** amber-colored dessert wine

ma•de•moi•selle \,madmwəˈzel, -məˈzel\ *n, pl* **ma•de•moi•selles** \-ˈzelz\ *or* **mes•de•moi•selles** \,mādmwəˈzel\ **:** an unmarried girl or woman —used as a title for a woman esp. of French nationality

mad•house *n* **1 :** insane asylum **2 :** place of great uproar or confusion

mad•man \-,man, -mən\ *n* **:** lunatic

mad•ri•gal \ˈmadrigəl\ *n* **:** elaborate song for several voice parts

mad•wom•an \ˈmad,wu̇mən\ *n* **:** woman who is insane

mael•strom \ˈmālstrəm\ *n* **1 :** whirlpool **2 :** tumult

mae•stro \ˈmīstrō\ *n, pl* **-stros** *or* **-stri** \-,strē\ **:** eminent composer or conductor

Ma•fia \ˈmäfēə\ *n* **:** secret criminal organization

ma•fi•o•so \,mäfēˈōsō\ *n, pl* **-si** \-sē\ **:** member of the Mafia

mag•a•zine \ˈmagə,zēn\ *n* **1 :** storehouse **2 :** publication issued at regular intervals **3 :** cartridge container in a gun

ma•gen•ta \məˈjentə\ *n* **:** deep purplish red color

mag•got \ˈmagət\ *n* **:** wormlike fly larva —**mag•goty** *adj*

mag•ic \ˈmajik\ *n* **1 :** art of using supernatural powers **2 :** extraordinary power or influence **3 :** sleight of hand —**magic, mag•i•cal** \-ikəl\ *adj* —**mag•i•cal•ly** *adv* —**ma•gi•cian** \məˈjishən\ *n*

mag•is•te•ri•al \,majəˈstirēəl\ *adj* **1 :** authoritative **2 :** relating to a magistrate

mag•is•trate \ˈmajə,strāt\ *n* **:** judge —**mag•is•tra•cy** \-strəsē\ *n*

mag•ma \ˈmagmə\ *n* **:** molten rock

mag•nan•i•mous \magˈnanəməs\ *adj* **:** noble or generous —**mag•na•nim•i•ty** \,magnəˈnimətē\ *n* —**mag•nan•i•mous•ly** *adv* —**mag•nan•i•mous•ness** *n*

mag•ne•sia \magˈnēzhə, -shə\ *n* **:** oxide of magnesium used as a laxative

mag•ne•sium \magˈnēzēəm, -zhəm\ *n* **:** silver-white metallic chemical element

mag•net \ˈmagnət\ *n* **1 :** body that attracts iron **2 :** something that attracts —**mag•net•ic** \magˈnetik\ *adj* —**mag•net•i•cal•ly** \-iklē\ *adv* —**mag•ne•tism** \ˈmagnə,tizəm\ *n*

mag•ne•tite \ˈmagnə,tīt\ *n* **:** black iron ore

mag•ne•tize \ˈmagnə,tīz\ *vb* **-tized; -tiz•ing 1 :** attract like a magnet **2 :** give magnetic properties to —**mag•ne•tiz•able** *adj* —**mag•ne•ti•za•tion** \,magnətəˈzāshən\ *n* —**mag•ne•tiz•er** *n*

mag•nif•i•cent \magˈnifəsənt\ *adj* **:** splendid —**mag•nif•i•cence** \-səns\ *n* —**mag•nif•i•cent•ly** *adv*

mag•ni•fy \ˈmagnə,fī\ *vb* **-fied; -fy•ing 1 :** intensify **2 :** enlarge —**mag•ni•fi•ca•tion** \,magnəfəˈkāshən\ *n* —**mag•ni•fi•er** \ˈmagnə,fīər\ *n*

mag•ni•tude \ˈmagnə,tüd, -,tyüd\ *n* **1 :** greatness of size or extent **2 :** quantity

mag•no•lia \magˈnōlyə\ *n* **:** shrub with large fragrant flowers

mag•pie \ˈmag,pī\ *n* **:** long-tailed black-and-white bird

ma•hog•a•ny \məˈhägənē\ *n, pl* **-nies :** tropical evergreen tree or its reddish brown wood

maid \ˈmād\ *n* **1 :** unmarried young woman **2 :** female servant

maid•en \ˈmādən\ *n* **:** unmarried young woman ~ *adj* **1 :** unmarried **2 :** first —**maid•en•hood** \-,hu̇d\ *n* —**maid•en•ly** *adj*

maid•en•hair \-,har\ *n* **:** fern with delicate feathery fronds

1mail \ˈmāl\ *n* **1 :** something sent or carried in the postal system **2 :** postal system ~ *vb* **:** send by mail —**mail•box** *n* —**mail•man** \-,man, -mən\ *n*

2mail *n* **:** armor of metal links or plates

maim \ˈmām\ *vb* **:** seriously wound or disfigure

main \ˈmān\ *n* **1 :** force **2 :** ocean **3 :** principal pipe, duct, or circuit of a utility system ~ *adj* **:** chief —**main•ly** *adv*

main•frame \ˈmān,frām\ *n* **:** large fast computer

main•land \ˈmān,land, -lənd\ *n* **:** part of a country on a continent

main•stay *n* **:** chief support

main•stream *n* **:** prevailing current or direction of activity or influence —**mainstream** *adj*

main•tain \mānˈtān\ *vb* **1 :** keep in an existing state (as of repair) **2 :** sustain **3 :** declare —**main•tain•abil•i•ty** \-,tānəˈbilətē\ *n* —**main•tain•able** \-ˈtānəbəl\ *adj* —**main•te•nance** \ˈmāntənəns\ *n*

mai•tre d'hô•tel \,mātrədōˈtel, ,me-\ *n* **:** head of a dining room staff

maize \ˈmāz\ *n* **:** corn

maj•es•ty \ˈmajəstē\ *n, pl* **-ties 1 :** sovereign power or dignity —used as a title **2 :** grandeur or splendor —**ma•jes•tic** \məˈjestik\ *adj* —**ma•jes•ti•cal•ly** \-tiklē\ *adv*

ma•jor \ˈmājər\ *adj* **1 :** larger or greater **2 :** noteworthy or conspicuous ~ *n* **1 :** commissioned officer (as in the army) ranking next below a lieutenant colonel **2 :** main field of study ~ *vb* **-jored; -jor•ing :** pursue an academic major

ma•jor•do•mo \,mājərˈdōmō\ *n, pl* **-mos :** head steward

major general *n* **:** commissioned officer (as in the army) ranking next below a lieutenant general

ma•jor•i•ty \məˈjȯrətē\ *n, pl* **-ties 1 :** age of full civil rights **2 :** quantity more than half

make \ˈmāk\ *vb* **made** \ˈmād\; **mak•ing 1 :** cause to exist, occur, or appear **2 :** fashion or manufacture **3 :** formulate in the mind **4 :** constitute **5 :** prepare **6 :** cause to be or become **7 :** carry out or perform **8 :** compel **9 :** gain **10 :** have an effect —used with *for* ~ *n* **:** brand —**mak•er** *n* —**make do** *vb* **:** get along with what is available —**make good** *vb* **1 :** repay **2 :** succeed —**make out** *vb* **1 :** draw up or write **2 :** discern or understand **3 :** fare —**make up** *vb* **1 :** invent **2 :** become reconciled **3 :** compensate for

make–be•lieve *n* **:** a pretending to believe ~ *adj* **:** imagined or pretended

make•shift *n* **:** temporary substitute —**makeshift** *adj*

make•up \-,əp\ *n* **1 :** way in which something is constituted **2 :** cosmetics

mal•ad•just•ed \,maləˈjəstəd\ *adj* **:** poorly adjusted (as to one's environment) —**mal•ad•just•ment** \-ˈjəstmənt\ *n*

mal•adroit \,maləˈdrȯit\ *adj* **:** clumsy or inept

mal•a•dy \ˈmalədē\ *n, pl* **-dies :** disease or disorder

mal•aise \məˈlāz, ma-\ *n* **:** sense of being unwell

mal•a•mute \ˈmalə,myüt\ *n* **:** powerful heavy-coated dog

mal•a•prop•ism \ˈmalə,präp,izəm\ *n* **:** humorous misuse of a word

ma•lar•ia \məˈlerēə\ *n* **:** disease transmitted by a mosquito —**ma•lar•i•al** \-əl\ *adj*

ma•lar•key \məˈlärkē\ *n* **:** foolishness

mal•con•tent \,malkənˈtent\ *n* **:** discontented person —**malcontent** *adj*

male \ˈmāl\ *adj* **1 :** relating to the sex that performs a fertilizing function **2 :** masculine ~ *n* **:** male individual —**male•ness** *n*

male•dic•tion \,maləˈdikshən\ *n* **:** curse

male•fac•tor \ˈmalə,faktər\ *n* **:** one who commits an offense esp. against the law

ma•lef•i•cent \məˈlefəsənt\ *adj* **:** harmful

ma•lev•o•lent \məˈlevələnt\ *adj* **:** malicious or spiteful —**ma•lev•o•lence** \-ləns\ *n*

mal•fea•sance \malˈfēzəns\ *n* **:** misconduct by a public official

mal•for•ma•tion \,malfȯrˈmāshən\ *n* **:** distortion or faulty formation —**mal•formed** \malˈfȯrmd\ *adj*

mal•func•tion \malˈfəŋkshən\ *vb* **:** fail to operate properly —**malfunction** *n*

mal•ice \ˈmaləs\ *n* **:** desire to cause pain or injury to another —**ma•li•cious** \məˈlishəs\ *adj* —**ma•li•cious•ly** *adv*

ma•lign \məˈlīn\ *adj* **1 :** wicked **2 :** malignant ~ *vb* **:** speak evil of

ma•lig•nant \məˈlignənt\ *adj* **1 :** harmful **2 :** likely to cause death —**ma•lig•nan•cy** \-nənsē\ *n* —**ma•lig•nant•ly** *adv* —**ma•lig•ni•ty** \-nətē\ *n*

ma•lin•ger \məˈliŋgər\ *vb* **:** pretend illness to avoid duty —**ma•lin•ger•er** *n*

mall \ˈmȯl\ *n* **1 :** shaded promenade **2 :** concourse providing access to rows of shops

mal•lard \ˈmalərd\ *n, pl* **-lard** *or* **-lards :** common wild duck

mal•lea•ble \ˈmalēəbəl\ *adj* **1 :** easily shaped **2 :** adaptable —**mal•le•a•bil•i•ty** \,malēəˈbilətē\ *n*

mal•let \ˈmalət\ *n* **:** hammerlike tool

mal•nour•ished \malˈnərisht\ *adj* **:** poorly nourished

mal•nu•tri•tion \,malnu̇ˈtrishən, -nyu̇-\ *n* **:** inadequate nutrition

mal•odor•ous \malˈōdərəs\ *adj* **:** foul-smelling —**mal•odor•ous•ly** *adv* —**mal•odor•ous•ness** *n*

mal•prac•tice \-ˈpraktəs\ *n* **:** failure of professional duty

malt \ˈmȯlt\ *n* **:** sprouted grain used in brewing

mal•treat \malˈtrēt\ *vb* **:** treat badly —**mal•treat•ment** *n*

ma•ma, mam•ma \ˈmämə\ *n* **:** mother

mam•mal \ˈmaməl\ *n* **:** warm-blooded vertebrate animal that nourishes its young with milk —**mam•ma•li•an** \məˈmālēən, ma-\ *adj or n*

mam•ma•ry \ˈmamərē\ *adj* **:** relating to the milk-secreting glands **(mammary glands)** of mammals

mam•mo•gram \ˈmamə,gram\ *n* **:** X-ray photograph of the breasts

mam•moth \ˈmaməth\ *n* **:** large hairy extinct elephant ~ *adj* **:** enormous

man \ˈman\ *n, pl* **men** \ˈmen\ **1 :** human being **2 :** adult male **3 :** mankind ~ *vb* **-nn- :** supply with people for working —**man•hood** *n* —**man•hunt** *n* —**man•like** *adj* —**man•li•ness** *n* —**man•ly** *adj or adv* —**man–made** *adj* —**man•nish** *adj* —**man•nish•ly** *adv* —**man•nish•ness** *n* —**man-size, man–sized** *adj*

man•a•cle \ˈmanikəl\ *n* **:** shackle for the hands or wrists —**manacle** *vb*

man•age \ˈmanij\ *vb* **-aged; -ag•ing 1 :** control **2 :** direct or carry on business or affairs **3 :** cope —**man•age•abil•i•ty** \,manijəˈbilətē\ *n* —**man•age•able** \ˈmanijəbəl\ *adj* —**man•age•able•ness** *n* —**man•age•ably** \-blē\ *adv* —**man•age•ment** \ˈmanijmənt\ *n* —**man•ag•er** \ˈmanijər\ *n* —**man•a•ge•ri•al** \,manəˈjirēəl\ *adj*

man•da•rin \ˈmandərən\ *n* **:** Chinese imperial official

man•date \ˈman,dāt\ *n* **:** authoritative command

man•da•to•ry \ˈmandə,tōrē\ *adj* **:** obligatory

man•di•ble \ˈmandəbəl\ *n* **:** lower jaw —**man•dib•u•lar** \manˈdibyələr\ *adj*

man•do•lin \,mandəˈlin, ˈmandələn\ *n* **:** stringed musical instrument

man•drake \ˈman,drāk\ *n* **:** herb with a large forked root

mane \ˈmān\ *n* **:** animal's neck hair —**maned** \ˈmānd\ *adj*

ma•neu•ver \məˈnüvər, -ˈnyü-\ *n* **1 :** planned movement of troops or ships **2 :** military training exercise **3 :** clever or skillful move or action —**maneuver** *vb* —**ma•neu•ver•abil•i•ty** \-,nüvərəˈbilətē, -,nyü-\ *n*

man•ful \ˈmanfəl\ *adj* **:** courageous —**man•ful•ly** *adv*

man•ga•nese \ˈmaŋgə,nēz, -,nēs\ *n* **:** gray metallic chemical element

mange \ˈmānj\ *n* **:** skin disease of domestic animals —**mangy** \ˈmānjē\ *adj*

man•ger \ˈmānjər\ *n* **:** feeding trough for livestock

man•gle \ˈmaŋgəl\ *vb* **-gled; -gling 1 :** mutilate **2 :** bungle —**man•gler** *n*

man•go \ˈmaŋgō\ *n, pl* **-goes :** juicy yellowish red tropical fruit

man•grove \ˈman,grōv, ˈmaŋ-\ *n* **:** tropical tree growing in salt water

man•han•dle *vb* **:** handle roughly

man•hole *n* **:** entry to a sewer

ma•nia \ˈmānēə, -nyə\ *n* **1 :** insanity marked by uncontrollable emotion or excitement **2 :** excessive enthusiasm —**ma•ni•ac** \-nē,ak\ *n* —**ma•ni•a•cal** \məˈnīəkəl\ *adj* —**man•ic** \ˈmanik\ *adj or n*

man•i•cure \ˈmanə,kyu̇r\ *n* **:** treatment for the fingernails ~ *vb* **-cured; -cur•ing 1 :** do manicure work on **2 :** trim precisely —**man•i•cur•ist** \-,kyu̇rist\ *n*

1man•i•fest \ˈmanə,fest\ *adj* **:** clear to the senses or to the mind ~ *vb* **:** make evident —**man•i•fes•ta•tion** \,manəfəˈstāshən\ *n* —**man•i•fest•ly** *adv*

2manifest *n* **:** invoice of cargo or list of passengers

man•i•fes•to \,manəˈfestō\ *n, pl* **-tos** *or* **-toes :** public declaration of policy or views

man•i•fold \ˈmanə,fōld\ *adj* **:** marked by diversity or variety ~ *n* **:** pipe fitting with several outlets for connections

ma•nila paper \məˈnilə-\ *n* **:** durable brownish paper

ma•nip•u•late \məˈnipyə,lāt\ *vb* **-lat•ed; -lat•ing 1 :** treat or operate manually or mechanically **2 :** influence esp. by cunning —**ma•nip•u•la•tion** \mə,nipyəˈlāshən\ *n* —**ma•nip•u•la•tive** \-ˈnipyə,lātiv, -lətiv\ *adj* —**ma•nip•u•la•tor** \-,lātər\ *n*

man•kind \ˈmanˈkīnd\ *n* **:** human race

man•na \ˈmanə\ *n* **:** something valuable that comes unexpectedly

manned \ˈmand\ *adj* **:** carrying or performed by a man

man•ne•quin \ˈmanikən\ *n* **:** dummy used to display clothes

man•ner \ˈmanər\ *n* **1 :** kind **2 :** usual way of acting **3 :** artistic method **4** *pl* **:** social conduct

man•nered \-ərd\ *adj* **1 :** having manners of a specified kind **2 :** artificial

man•ner•ism \ˈmanə,rizəm\ *n* **:** individual peculiarity of action

man•ner•ly \-lē\ *adj* **:** polite —**man•ner•li•ness** *n* —**mannerly** *adv*

man–of–war \,manəˈwȯr, -əvˈwȯr\ *n, pl* **men–of–war** \,men-\ **:** warship

man•or \ˈmanər\ *n* **:** country estate —**ma•no•ri•al** \məˈnōrēəl\ *adj*

man•pow•er *n* **:** supply of people available for service

man•sard \ˈman,särd\ *n* **:** roof with two slopes on all sides and the lower slope the steeper

manse \ˈmans\ *n* **:** parsonage

man•ser•vant *n, pl* **men•ser•vants :** a male servant

man•sion \ˈmanchən\ *n* **:** very big house

man•slaugh•ter *n* **:** unintentional killing of a person

man•tel \ˈmantəl\ *n* **:** shelf above a fireplace

man•tis \ˈmantəs\ *n, pl* **-tis•es** *or* **-tes** \ˈman,tēz\ **:** large green insect-eating insect with stout forelegs

man•tle \ˈmantəl\ *n* **1 :** sleeveless cloak **2 :** something that covers, enfolds, or envelops —**mantle** *vb*

man•tra \ˈmantrə\ *n* **:** mystical chant

man•u•al \ˈmanyəwəl\ *adj* **:** involving the hands or physical force ~ *n* **:** handbook —**man•u•al•ly** *adv*

man•u•fac•ture \,manyəˈfakchər, ,manə-\ *n* **:** process of making wares by hand or by machinery ~ *vb* **-tured; -tur•ing :** make from raw materials —**man•u•fac•tur•er** *n*

ma•nure \məˈnu̇r, -ˈnyu̇r\ *n* **:** animal excrement used as fertilizer

manu•script \ˈmanyə,skript\ *n* **1 :** something written or typed **2 :** document submitted for publication

many \ˈmenē\ *adj* **more** \ˈmōr\; **most** \ˈmōst\ **:** consisting of a large number —**many** *n or pron*

map \ˈmap\ *n* **:** representation of a geographical area ~ *vb* **-pp- 1 :** make a map of **2 :** plan in detail —**map•pa•ble** \-əbəl\ *adj* —**map•per** *n*

ma•ple \ˈmāpəl\ *n* **:** tree with hard light-colored wood

mar \ˈmär\ *vb* **-rr- :** damage

mar•a•schi•no \,marəˈskēnō, -ˈshē-\ *n, pl* **-nos :** preserved cherry

mar•a•thon \ˈmarə,thän\ *n* **1 :** long-distance race **2 :** test of endurance —**mar•a•thon•er** \-,thänər\ *n*

ma•raud \məˈrȯd\ *vb* **:** roam about in search of plunder —**ma•raud•er** *n*

mar•ble \ˈmärbəl\ *n* **1 :** crystallized limestone **2 :** small glass ball used in a children's game **(marbles)**

mar•bling \-bəliŋ\ *n* **:** intermixture of fat and lean in meat

march \ˈmärch\ *vb* **:** move with regular steps or in a purposeful manner ~ *n* **1 :** distance covered in a march **2 :** measured stride **3 :** forward movement **4 :** music for marching —**march•er** *n*

March *n* **:** 3d month of the year having 31 days

mar•chio•ness \ˈmärshənəs\ *n* **:** woman holding the rank of a marquess

Mar•di Gras \ˈmärdē,grä\ *n* **:** Tuesday before the beginning of Lent often observed with parades and merrymaking

mare \ˈmar\ *n* **:** female horse

mar•ga•rine \ˈmärjərən\ *n* **:** butter substitute made usu. from vegetable oils

mar•gin \ˈmärjən\ *n* **1 :** edge **2 :** spare amount, measure, or degree

mar•gin•al \-jənəl\ *adj* **1 :** relating to or situated at a border or margin **2 :** close to the lower limit of acceptability —**mar•gin•al•ly** *adv*

mari•gold \ˈmarə,gōld\ *n* **:** garden plant with showy flower heads

mar•i•jua•na \,marəˈwänə, -ˈhwä-\ *n* **:** intoxicating drug obtained from the hemp plant

ma•ri•na \məˈrēnə\ *n* **:** place for mooring pleasure boats

mar•i•nate \ˈmarə,nāt\ *vb* **-nat•ed; -nat•ing :** soak in a savory sauce

ma•rine \məˈrēn\ *adj* **1 :** relating to the sea **2 :** relating to marines ~ *n* **:** infantry soldier associated with a navy

mar•i•ner \ˈmarənər\ *n* **:** sailor

mar•i•o•nette \,marēəˈnet\ *n* **:** puppet

mar•i•tal \ˈmarətəl\ *adj* **:** relating to marriage

mar•i•time \ˈmarə,tīm\ *adj* **:** relating to the sea or commerce on the sea

mar•jo•ram \ˈmärjərəm\ *n* **:** aromatic mint used as a seasoning

mark \ˈmärk\ *n* **1 :** something aimed at **2 :** something (as a line) designed to record position **3 :** visible sign **4 :** written symbol **5 :** grade **6 :** lasting impression **7 :** blemish ~ *vb* **1 :** designate or set apart by a mark or make a mark on **2 :** characterize **3 :** remark —**mark•er** *n*

marked \ˈmärkt\ *adj* **:** noticeable —**mark•ed•ly** \ˈmärkədlē\ *adv*

mar•ket \ˈmärkət\ *n* **1 :** buying and selling of goods or the place this happens **2 :** demand for commodities **3 :** store ~ *vb* **:** sell —**mar•ket•able** *adj*

mar•ket•place *n* **1 :** market **2 :** world of trade or economic activity

marks•man \ˈmärksmən\ *n* **:** good shooter —**marks•man•ship** *n*

mar•lin \ˈmärlən\ *n* **:** large oceanic fish

mar•ma•lade \ˈmärmə,lād\ *n* **:** jam with pieces of fruit and rind

mar•mo•set \ˈmärmə,set\ *n* **:** small bushy-tailed monkey

mar•mot \ˈmärmət\ *n* **:** burrowing rodent

1ma•roon \məˈrün\ *vb* **:** isolate without hope of escape

2maroon *n* **:** dark red color

mar•quee \märˈkē\ *n* **:** canopy over an entrance

mar•quess \ˈmärkwəs\, **mar•quis** \ˈmärk-

wəs, mär'kē\ *n, pl* **-quess•es** *or* **-quis•es** *or* **-quis** : British noble ranking next below a duke
mar•quise \mär'kēz\ *n, pl* **mar•quises** \-'kēz, -'kēzəz\ : marchioness
mar•riage \'marij\ *n* **1** : state of being married **2** : wedding ceremony —**mar•riage•able** *adj*
mar•row \'marō\ *n* : soft tissue in the cavity of bone
mar•ry \'marē\ *vb* **-ried; -ry•ing 1** : join as husband and wife **2** : take or give in marriage —**mar•ried** *adj or n*
marsh \'märsh\ *n* : soft wet land —**marshy** *adj*
mar•shal \'märshəl\ *n* **1** : leader of ceremony **2** : usu. high military or administrative officer ~ *vb* **-shaled** *or* **-shalled; -shal•ing** *or* **-shal•ling 1** : arrange in order, rank, or position **2** : lead with ceremony
marsh•mal•low \'märsh,melō, -,malō\ *n* : spongy candy
mar•su•pi•al \mär'süpēəl\ *n* : mammal that nourishes young in an abdominal pouch —**marsupial** *adj*
mart \'märt\ *n* : market
mar•ten \'märtᵊn\ *n, pl* **-ten** *or* **-tens** : weasellike mammal with soft fur
mar•tial \'märshəl\ *adj* **1** : relating to war or an army **2** : warlike
mar•tin \'märtᵊn\ *n* : small swallow
mar•ti•net \,märtᵊn'et\ *n* : strict disciplinarian
mar•tyr \'märtər\ *n* : one who dies or makes a great sacrifice for a cause ~ *vb* : make a martyr of —**mar•tyr•dom** \-dəm\ *n*
mar•vel \'märvəl\ *vb* **-veled** *or* **-velled; -vel•ing** *or* **-vel•ling** : feel surprise or wonder ~ *n* : something amazing —**mar•vel•ous, mar•vel•lous** \'märvələs\ *adj* —**mar•vel•ous•ly** *adv* —**mar•vel•ous•ness** *n*
Marx•ism \'märk,sizəm\ *n* : political and social principles of Karl Marx —**Marx•ist** \-sist\ *n or adj*
mas•cara \mas'karə\ *n* : eye cosmetic
mas•cot \'mas,kät, -kət\ *n* : one believed to bring good luck
mas•cu•line \'maskyələn\ *adj* : relating to the male sex —**mas•cu•lin•i•ty** \,maskyə'linətē\ *n*
mash \'mash\ *n* **1** : crushed steeped grain for fermenting **2** : soft pulpy mass ~ *vb* **1** : reduce to a pulpy mass **2** : smash —**mash•er** *n*
mask \'mask\ *n* : disguise for the face ~ *vb* **1** : disguise **2** : cover to protect —**mask•er** *n*
mas•och•ism \'masə,kizəm, 'maz-\ *n* : pleasure in being abused —**mas•och•ist** \-kist\ *n* —**mas•och•is•tic** \,masə'kistik, ,maz-\ *adj*
ma•son \'māsᵊn\ *n* : workman who builds with stone or brick —**ma•son•ry** \-rē\ *n*
mas•quer•ade \,maskə'rād\ *n* **1** : costume party **2** : disguise ~ *vb* **-ad•ed; -ad•ing 1** : disguise oneself **2** : take part in a costume party —**mas•quer•ad•er** *n*
mass \'mas\ *n* **1** : large amount of matter or number of things **2** : expanse or magnitude **3** : great body of people —usu. pl. ~ *vb* : form into a mass —**mass•less** \-ləs\ *adj* —**massy** *adj*
Mass *n* : worship service of the Roman Catholic Church
mas•sa•cre \'masikər\ *n* : wholesale slaughter —**massacre** *vb*
mas•sage \mə'säzh, -'säj\ *n* : a rubbing of the body —**massage** *vb*
mas•seur \ma'sər\ *n* : man who massages
mas•seuse \-'sœz, -'süz\ *n* : woman who massages
mas•sive \'masiv\ *adj* **1** : being a large mass **2** : large in scope —**mas•sive•ly** *adv* —**mas•sive•ness** *n*
mast \'mast\ *n* : tall pole esp. for supporting sails —**mast•ed** *adj*
mas•ter \'mastər\ *n* **1** : male teacher **2** : holder of an academic degree between a bachelor's and a doctor's **3** : one highly skilled **4** : one in authority ~ *vb* **1** : subdue **2** : become proficient in —**mas•ter•ful** \-fəl\ *adj* —**mas•ter•ful•ly** *adv* —**mas•ter•ly** *adj* —**mas•tery** \'mastərē\ *n*
master chief petty officer *n* : petty officer of the highest rank in the navy
master gunnery sergeant *n* : noncommissioned officer in the marine corps ranking above a master sergeant
mas•ter•piece \'mastər,pēs\ *n* : great piece of work
master sergeant *n* **1** : noncommissioned officer in the army ranking next below a sergeant major **2** : noncommissioned officer in the air force ranking next below a senior master sergeant **3** : noncommissioned officer in the marine corps ranking next below a master gunnery sergeant
mas•ter•work *n* : masterpiece
mas•tic \'mastik\ *n* : pasty glue
mas•ti•cate \'mastə,kāt\ *vb* **-cat•ed; -cat•ing** : chew —**mas•ti•ca•tion** \,mastə'kāshən\ *n*
mas•tiff \'mastəf\ *n* : large dog
mast•odon \'mastə,dän\ *n* : extinct elephantlike animal
mas•toid \'mas,tȯid\ *n* : bone behind the ear —**mastoid** *adj*
mas•tur•ba•tion \,mastər'bāshən\ *n* : stimulation of sex organs by hand —**mas•tur•bate** \'mastər,bāt\ *vb*
1mat \'mat\ *n* **1** : coarse woven or plaited fabric **2** : mass of tangled strands **3** : thick pad ~ *vb* **-tt-** : form into a mat
2mat *vb* **-tt- 1** : make matte **2** : provide (a picture) with a mat ~ *or* **matt** *or* **matte** *n* : border around a picture
3mat *var of* MATTE
mat•a•dor \'matə,dȯr\ *n* : bullfighter
1match \'mach\ *n* **1** : one equal to another **2** : one able to cope with another **3** : suitable pairing **4** : game **5** : marriage ~ *vb* **1** : set in competition **2** : marry **3** : be or provide the equal of **4** : fit or go together —**match•less** *adj* —**match•mak•er** *n*
2match *n* : piece of wood or paper material with a combustible tip
mate \'māt\ *n* **1** : companion **2** : subordinate officer on a ship **3** : one of a pair ~ *vb* **mat•ed; mat•ing 1** : fit together **2** : come together as a pair **3** : copulate
ma•te•ri•al \mə'tirēəl\ *adj* **1** : natural **2** : relating to matter **3** : important **4** : of a physical or worldly nature ~ *n* : stuff something is made of —**ma•te•ri•al•ly** *adv*
ma•te•ri•al•ism \mə'tirēə,lizəm\ *n* **1** : theory that matter is the only reality **2** : preoccupation with material and not spiritual things —**ma•te•ri•al•ist** \-list\ *n or adj* —**ma•te•ri•al•is•tic** \-,tirēə'listik\ *adj*
ma•te•ri•al•ize \mə'tirēə,līz\ *vb* **-ized; -iz•ing** : take or cause to take bodily form —**ma•te•ri•al•i•za•tion** \mə,tirēələ'zāshən\ *n*
ma•té•ri•el, ma•te•ri•el \mə,tirē'el\ *n* : military supplies
ma•ter•nal \mə'tərnᵊl\ *adj* : motherly —**ma•ter•nal•ly** *adv*
ma•ter•ni•ty \mə'tərnətē\ *n, pl* **-ties 1** : state of being a mother **2** : hospital's childbirth facility ~ *adj* **1** : worn during pregnancy **2** : relating to the period close to childbirth
math \'math\ *n* : mathematics
math•e•mat•ics \,mathə'matiks\ *n pl* : science of numbers and of shapes in space —**math•e•mat•i•cal** \-ikəl\ *adj* —**math•e•mat•i•cal•ly** *adv* —**math•e•ma•ti•cian** \,mathəmə'tishən\ *n*
mat•i•nee, mat•i•née \,matᵊn'ā\ *n* : afternoon performance
mat•ins \'matᵊnz\ *n* : morning prayers
ma•tri•arch \'mātrē,ärk\ *n* : woman who rules a family —**ma•tri•ar•chal** \,mātrē'ärkəl\ *adj* —**ma•tri•ar•chy** \'mātrē,ärkē\ *n*
ma•tri•cide \'matrə,sīd, 'mā-\ *n* : murder of one's mother —**ma•tri•cid•al** \,matrə'sīdᵊl, ,mā-\ *adj*
ma•tric•u•late \mə'trikyə,lāt\ *vb* **-lat•ed; -lat•ing** : enroll in school —**ma•tric•u•la•tion** \-,trikyə'lāshən\ *n*
mat•ri•mo•ny \'matrə,mōnē\ *n* : marriage —**mat•ri•mo•ni•al** \,matrə'mōnēəl\ *adj* —**mat•ri•mo•ni•al•ly** *adv*
ma•trix \'mātriks\ *n, pl* **-tri•ces** \'mātrə,sēz, 'ma-\ *or* **-trix•es** \'mātriksəz\ : something (as a mold) that gives form, foundation, or origin to something else enclosed in it
ma•tron \'mātrən\ *n* **1** : dignified mature woman **2** : woman supervisor —**ma•tron•ly** *adj*
matte \'mat\ *adj* : not shiny
mat•ter \'matər\ *n* **1** : subject of interest **2** *pl* : circumstances **3** : trouble **4** : physical substance ~ *vb* : be important
mat•tock \'matək\ *n* : a digging tool
mat•tress \'matrəs\ *n* : pad to sleep on
ma•ture \mə'tür, -'tyür, -'chür\ *adj* **-tur•er; -est 1** : carefully considered **2** : fully grown or developed **3** : due for payment ~ *vb* **-tured; -tur•ing** : become mature —**mat•u•ra•tion** \,machə'rāshən\ *n* —**ma•ture•ly** *adv* —**ma•tu•ri•ty** \-ətē\ *n*
maud•lin \'mȯdlən\ *adj* : excessively sentimental
maul \'mȯl\ *n* : heavy hammer ~ *vb* **1** : beat **2** : handle roughly
mau•so•le•um \,mȯsə'lēəm, ,mȯzə-\ *n, pl* **-leums** *or* **-lea** \-'lēə\ : large aboveground tomb
mauve \'mōv, 'mȯv\ *n* : lilac color
ma•ven, ma•vin \'māvən\ *n* : expert
mav•er•ick \'mavrik\ *n* **1** : unbranded range animal **2** : nonconformist
maw \'mȯ\ *n* **1** : stomach **2** : throat, esophagus, or jaws
mawk•ish \'mȯkish\ *adj* : sickly sentimental —**mawk•ish•ly** *adv* —**mawk•ish•ness** *n*
max•im \'maksəm\ *n* : proverb
max•i•mum \'maksəməm\ *n, pl* **-ma** \-səmə\ *or* **-mums 1** : greatest quantity **2** : upper limit **3** : largest number —**maximum** *adj* —**max•i•mize** \-sə-,mīz\ *vb*
may \'mā\ *verbal auxiliary, past* **might** \'mīt\; *pres sing & pl* **may 1** : have permission **2** : be likely to **3** —used to express desire, purpose, or contingency
May \'mā\ *n* : 5th month of the year having 31 days
may•ap•ple *n* : woodland herb having edible fruit
may•be \'mābē\ *adv* : perhaps
may•flow•er *n* : spring-blooming herb
may•fly *n* : fly with an aquatic larva
may•hem \'mā,hem, 'māəm\ *n* **1** : crippling or mutilation of a person **2** : needless damage
may•on•naise \'māə,nāz\ *n* : creamy white sandwich spread
may•or \'māər, 'mer\ *n* : chief city official —**may•or•al** \-əl\ *adj* —**may•or•al•ty** \-əltē\ *n*
maze \'māz\ *n* : confusing network of passages —**mazy** *adj*
ma•zur•ka \mə'zərkə\ *n* : Polish dance
me \'mē\ *pron, objective case of* I
mead \'mēd\ *n* : alcoholic beverage brewed from honey
mead•ow \'medō\ *n* : low-lying usu. level grassland —**mead•ow•land** \-,land\ *n*
mead•ow•lark *n* : songbird with a yellow breast
mea•ger, mea•gre \'mēgər\ *adj* **1** : thin **2** : lacking richness or strength —**mea•ger•ly** *adv* —**mea•ger•ness** *n*
1meal \'mēl\ *n* **1** : food to be eaten at one time **2** : act of eating —**meal•time** *n*
2meal *n* : ground grain —**mealy** *adj*
1mean \'mēn\ *adj* **1** : humble **2** : worthy of or showing little regard **3** : stingy **4** : malicious —**mean•ly** *adv* —**mean•ness** *n*
2mean \'mēn\ *vb* **meant** \'ment\; **mean•ing** \'mēniŋ\ **1** : intend **2** : serve to convey, show, or indicate **3** : be important
3mean *n* **1** : middle point **2** *pl* : something that helps gain an end **3** *pl* : material resources **4** : sum of several quantities divided by the number of quantities ~ *adj* : being a mean
me•an•der \mē'andər\ *vb* **-dered; -der•ing 1** : follow a winding course **2** : wander aimlessly —**meander** *n*
mean•ing \'mēniŋ\ *n* **1** : idea conveyed or intended to be conveyed **2** : aim —**mean•ing•ful** \-fəl\ *adj* —**mean•ing•ful•ly** *adv* —**mean•ing•less** *adj*
mean•time \'mēn,tīm\ *n* : intervening time —**meantime** *adv*
mean•while \-,hwīl\ *n* : meantime ~ *adv* **1** : meantime **2** : at the same time
mea•sles \'mēzəlz\ *n pl* : disease that is marked by red spots on the skin
mea•sly \'mēzlē\ *adj* **-sli•er; -est** : contemptibly small in amount
mea•sure \'mezhər, 'māzh-\ *n* **1** : moderate amount **2** : dimensions or amount **3** : something to show amount **4** : unit or system of measurement **5** : act of measuring **6** : means to an end ~ *vb* **-sured; -sur•ing 1** : find out or mark off size or amount of **2** : have a specified measurement —**mea•sur•able** \'mezhərəbəl, 'māzh-\ *adj* —**mea•sur•ably** \-blē\ *adv* —**mea•sure•less** *adj* —**mea•sure•ment** *n* —**mea•sur•er** *n*
meat \'mēt\ *n* **1** : food **2** : animal flesh used as food —**meat•ball** *n* —**meaty** *adj*
me•chan•ic \mi'kanik\ *n* : worker who repairs cars
me•chan•i•cal \mi'kanikəl\ *adj* **1** : relating to machines or mechanics **2** : involuntary —**me•chan•i•cal•ly** *adv*
me•chan•ics \-iks\ *n sing or pl* **1** : branch of physics dealing with energy and forces in relation to bodies **2** : mechanical details
mech•a•nism \'mekə,nizəm\ *n* **1** : piece of machinery **2** : technique for gaining a result **3** : basic processes producing a phenomenon —**mech•a•nis•tic** \,mekə'nistik\ *adj* —**mech•a•ni•za•tion** \,mekənə'zāshən\ *n* —**mech•a•nize** \'mekə,nīz\ *vb* —**mech•a•niz•er** *n*
med•al \'medᵊl\ *n* **1** : religious pin or pendant **2** : coinlike commemorative metal piece
med•al•ist, med•al•list \'medᵊlist\ *n* : person awarded a medal
me•dal•lion \mə'dalyən\ *n* : large medal
med•dle \'medᵊl\ *vb* **-dled; -dling** : interfere —**med•dler** \'medᵊlər\ *n* —**med•dle•some** \'medᵊlsəm\ *adj*
me•dia \'mēdēə\ *n pl* : communications organizations
me•di•an \'mēdēən\ *n* : middle value in a range —**median** *adj*
me•di•ate \'mēdē,āt\ *vb* **-at•ed; -at•ing** : help settle a dispute —**me•di•a•tion** \,mēdē'āshən\ *n* —**me•di•a•tor** \'mēdē,ātər\ *n*
med•ic \'medik\ *n* : medical worker esp. in the military
med•i•ca•ble \'medikəbəl\ *adj* : curable
med•ic•aid \'medi,kād\ *n* : government program of medical aid for the poor
med•i•cal \'medikəl\ *adj* : relating to medicine —**med•i•cal•ly** \-klē\ *adv*
medi•care \'medi,ker\ *n* : government program of medical care for the aged
med•i•cate \'medə,kāt\ *vb* **-cat•ed; -cat•ing** : treat with medicine
med•i•ca•tion \,medə'kāshən\ *n* **1** : act of medicating **2** : medicine
med•i•cine \'medəsən\ *n* **1** : preparation used to treat disease **2** : science dealing with the cure of disease —**me•dic•i•nal** \mə'disᵊnəl\ *adj* —**me•dic•i•nal•ly** *adv*
me•di•e•val, me•di•ae•val \,mēdē'ēval, ,med-, ,mid-; ,mē'dē-, ,me-, ,mi-\ *adj* : of or relating to the Middle Ages —**me•di•eval•ist** \-ist\ *n*
me•di•o•cre \,mēdē'ōkər\ *adj* : not very good —**me•di•oc•ri•ty** \-'äkrətē\ *n*
med•i•tate \'medə,tāt\ *vb* **-tat•ed; -tat•ing** : contemplate —**med•i•ta•tion** \,medə'tāshən\ *n* —**med•i•ta•tive** \'medə,tātiv\ *adj* —**med•i•ta•tive•ly** *adv*
me•di•um \'mēdēəm\ *n, pl* **-diums** *or* **-dia** \-ēə\ **1** : middle position or degree **2** : means of effecting or conveying something **3** : surrounding substance **4** : means of communication **5** : mode of artistic expression —**medium** *adj*
med•ley \'medlē\ *n, pl* **-leys** : series of songs performed as one
meek \'mēk\ *adj* **1** : mild-mannered **2** : lacking spirit —**meek•ly** *adv* —**meek•ness** *n*
meer•schaum \'mirshəm, -,shȯm\ *n* : claylike tobacco pipe
1meet \'mēt\ *vb* **met** \'met\; **meet•ing 1** : run into **2** : join **3** : oppose **4** : assemble **5** : satisfy **6** : be introduced to ~ *n* : sports team competition
2meet *adj* : proper
meet•ing \'mētiŋ\ *n* : a getting together —**meet•ing•house** *n*
mega•byte \'megə,bīt\ *n* : unit of computer storage capacity
mega•hertz \-,hərts, -,herts\ *n* : one million hertz
mega•phone \'megə,fōn\ *n* : cone-shaped device to intensify or direct the voice
mel•an•choly \'melən,kälē\ *n* : depression —**mel•an•chol•ic** \,melən'kälik\ *adj* —**melancholy** *adj*
mel•a•no•ma \,melə'nōmə\ *n, pl* **-mas** : usu. malignant skin tumor
me•lee \'mā,lā, mā'lā\ *n* : brawl
me•lio•rate \'mēlyə,rāt, 'mēlēə-\ *vb* **-rat•ed; -rat•ing** : improve —**me•lio•ra•tion** \,mēlyə'rāshən, ,mēlēə-\ *n* —**me•lio•ra•tive** \'mēlyə,rātiv, 'mē-lēə-\ *adj*
mel•lif•lu•ous \me'lifləwəs, mə-\ *adj* : sweetly flowing —**mel•lif•lu•ous•ly** *adv* —**mel•lif•lu•ous•ness** *n*
mel•low \'melō\ *adj* **1** : grown gentle or mild **2** : rich and full —**mellow** *vb* —**mel•low•ness** *n*
melo•dra•ma \'melə,drämə, -,dram-\ *n* : overly theatrical play —**melo•dra•mat•ic** \,melədrə'matik\ *adj* —**melo•dra•mat•i•cal•ly** \-tiklē\ *adv*
mel•o•dy \'melədē\ *n, pl* **-dies 1** : agreeable sound **2** : succession of musical notes —**me•lod•ic** \mə'lädik\ *adj* —**me•lod•i•cal•ly** \-iklē\ *adv* —**me•lo•di•ous** \mə'lōdēəs\ *adj* —**me•lo•di•ous•ly** *adv* —**me•lo•di•ous•ness** *n*
mel•on \'melən\ *n* : gourdlike fruit
melt \'melt\ *vb* **1** : change from solid to liquid usu. by heat **2** : dissolve or disappear gradually **3** : move or be moved emotionally
mem•ber \'membər\ *n* **1** : part of a person, animal, or plant **2** : one of a group **3** : part of a whole —**mem•ber•ship** \-,ship\ *n*
mem•brane \'mem,brān\ *n* : thin layer esp. in an organism —**mem•bra•nous** \-brənəs\ *adj*
me•men•to \mi'mentō\ *n, pl* **-tos** *or* **-toes** : souvenir
memo \'memō\ *n, pl* **mem•os** : memorandum
mem•oirs \'mem,wärz\ *n pl* : autobiography
mem•o•ra•bil•ia \,memərə'bilēə, -'bil-yə\ *n pl* **1** : memorable things **2** : mementos
mem•o•ra•ble \'memərəbəl\ *adj* : worth remembering —**mem•o•ra•bil•i•ty** \,memərə'bilətē\ *n* —**mem•o•ra•ble•ness** *n* —**mem•o•ra•bly** \-blē\ *adv*
mem•o•ran•dum \,memə'randəm\ *n, pl* **-dums** *or* **-da** \-də\ : informal note
me•mo•ri•al \mə'mōrēəl\ *n* : something (as a monument) meant to keep remembrance alive —**memorial** *adj* —**me•mo•ri•al•ize** *vb*
Memorial Day *n* : last Monday in May or formerly May 30 observed as a legal holiday in commemoration of dead servicemen
mem•o•ry \'memrē, 'memə-\ *n, pl* **-ries 1** : power of remembering **2** : something remembered **3** : commemoration **4** : time within which past events are remembered —**mem•o•ri•za•tion** \,memərə'zāshən\ *n* —**mem•o•rize** \'memə,rīz\ *vb* —**mem•o•riz•er** *n*
men *pl of* MAN
men•ace \'menəs\ *n* : threat of danger ~ *vb*

-aced; -ac•ing 1 : threaten **2 :** endanger **—men•ac•ing•ly** *adv*
me•nag•er•ie \məˈnajərē\ *n* **:** collection of wild animals
mend \ˈmend\ *vb* **1 :** improve **2 :** repair **3 :** heal **—mend** *n* **—mend•er** *n*
men•da•cious \menˈdāshəs\ *adj* **:** dishonest **—men•da•cious•ly** *adv* **—men•dac•i•ty** \-ˈdasətē\ *n*
men•di•cant \ˈmendikənt\ *n* **:** beggar **—men•di•can•cy** \-kənsē\ *n* **—mendicant** *adj*
men•ha•den \menˈhādᵊn, mən-\ *n, pl* **-den :** fish related to the herring
me•nial \ˈmēnēəl, -nyəl\ *adj* **1 :** relating to servants **2 :** humble ~ *n* **:** domestic servant **—me•ni•al•ly** *adv*
men•in•gi•tis \ˌmenənˈjītəs\ *n, pl* **-git•i•des** \-ˈjitəˌdēz\ **:** disease of the brain and spinal cord
meno•pause \ˈmenəˌpȯz\ *n* **:** time when menstruation ends **—meno•paus•al** \ˌmenəˈpȯzəl\ *adj*
me•no•rah \məˈnōrə\ *n* **:** candelabrum used in Jewish worship
men•stru•a•tion \ˌmenstrəˈwāshən, menˈstrā-\ *n* **:** monthly discharge of blood from the uterus **—men•stru•al** \ˈmenstrəwəl\ *adj* **—men•stru•ate** \ˈmenstrəˌwāt, -ˌstrāt\ *vb*
-ment \mənt\ *n suffix* **1 :** result or means of an action **2 :** action or process **3 :** place of an action **4 :** state or condition
men•tal \ˈmentᵊl\ *adj* **:** relating to the mind or its disorders **—men•tal•i•ty** \menˈtalətē\ *n* **—men•tal•ly** *adv*
men•thol \ˈmenˌthȯl, -ˌthōl\ *n* **:** soothing substance from oil of peppermint **—men•tho•lat•ed** \-thəˌlātəd\ *adj*
men•tion \ˈmenchən\ *vb* **:** refer to **—mention** *n*
men•tor \ˈmenˌtȯr, ˈmentər\ *n* **:** instructor
menu \ˈmenyü\ *n* **1 :** restaurant's list of food **2 :** list of offerings
me•ow \mēˈau̇\ *n* **:** characteristic cry of a cat **—meow** *vb*
mer•can•tile \ˈmərkənˌtēl, -ˌtīl\ *adj* **:** relating to merchants or trade
mer•ce•nary \ˈmərsᵊnˌerē\ *n, pl* **-nar•ies :** hired soldier ~ *adj* **:** serving only for money
mer•chan•dise \ˈmərchənˌdīz, -ˌdīs\ *n* **:** goods bought and sold ~ *vb* **-dised; -dis•ing :** buy and sell **— mer•chan•dis•er** *n*
mer•chant \ˈmərchənt\ *n* **:** one who buys and sells
merchant marine *n* **:** commercial ships
mer•cu•ri•al \ˌmərˈkyu̇rēəl\ *adj* **:** unpredictable **—mer•cu•ri•al•ly** *adv* **—mer•cu•ri•al•ness** *n*
mer•cu•ry \ˈmərkyərē\ *n* **:** heavy liquid metallic chemical element
mer•cy \ˈmərsē\ *n, pl* **-cies 1 :** show of pity or leniency **2 :** divine blessing **—mer•ci•ful** \-sifəl\ *adj* **—mer•ci•ful•ly** *adv* **—mer•ci•less** \-siləs\ *adj* **—mer•ci•less•ly** *adv* **—mercy** *adj*
mere \ˈmir\ *adj, superlative* **mer•est :** nothing more than **—mere•ly** *adv*
merge \ˈmərj\ *vb* **merged; merg•ing 1 :** unite **2 :** blend **—merg•er** \ˈmərjər\ *n*
me•rid•i•an \məˈridēən\ *n* **:** imaginary circle on the earth's surface passing through the poles **—meridian** *adj*
me•ringue \məˈraŋ\ *n* **:** baked dessert topping of beaten egg whites
me•ri•no \məˈrēnō\ *n, pl* **-nos 1 :** kind of sheep **2 :** fine soft woolen yarn
mer•it \ˈmerət\ *n* **1 :** praiseworthy quality **2** *pl* **:** rights and wrongs of a legal case ~ *vb* **:** deserve **—mer•i•to•ri•ous** \ˌmerəˈtōrēəs\ *adj* **—mer•i•to•ri•ous•ly** *adv* **—mer•i•to•ri•ous•ness** *n*
mer•maid \ˈmərˌmād\ *n* **:** legendary female sea creature
mer•ry \ˈmerē\ *adj* **-ri•er; -est :** full of high spirits **—mer•ri•ly** *adv* **—mer•ri•ment** \ˈmerimənt\ *n* **—mer•ry•mak•er** \ˈmerēˌmākər\ *n* **—mer•ry•mak•ing** \ˈmerēˌmākiŋ\ *n*
merry–go–round *n* **:** revolving amusement ride
me•sa \ˈmāsə\ *n* **:** steep flat-topped hill
mesdames *pl of* MADAM *or of* MADAME *or of* MRS.
mesdemoiselles *pl of* MADEMOISELLE
mesh \ˈmesh\ *n* **1 :** one of the openings in a net **2 :** net fabric **3 :** working contact ~ *vb* **:** fit together properly **—meshed** \ˈmesht\ *adj*
mes•mer•ize \ˈmezməˌrīz\ *vb* **-ized; -iz•ing :** hypnotize
mess \ˈmes\ *n* **1 :** meal eaten by a group **2 :** confused, dirty, or offensive state ~ *vb* **1 :** make dirty or untidy **2 :** putter **3 :** interfere **—messy** *adj*
mes•sage \ˈmesij\ *n* **:** news, information, or a command sent by one person to another
mes•sen•ger \ˈmesᵊnjər\ *n* **:** one who carries a message or does an errand
Mes•si•ah \məˈsīə\ *n* **1 :** expected deliverer of the Jews **2 :** Jesus Christ **3** *not cap* **:** great leader
messieurs *pl of* MONSIEUR
Messrs. *pl of* MR.
mes•ti•zo \meˈstēzō\ *n, pl* **-zos :** person of mixed blood
met *past of* MEET
me•tab•o•lism \məˈtabəˌlizəm\ *n* **:** biochemical processes necessary to life **—met•a•bol•ic** \ˌmetəˈbälik\ *adj* **—me•tab•o•lize** \məˈtabəˌlīz\ *vb*
met•al \ˈmetᵊl\ *n* **:** shiny substance that can be melted and shaped and conducts heat and electricity **—me•tal•lic** \məˈtalik\ *adj* **—met•al•ware** *n* **—met•al•work** *n* **—met•al•work•er** *n* **—met•al•work•ing** *n*
met•al•lur•gy \ˈmetᵊlˌərjē\ *n* **:** science of metals **—met•al•lur•gi•cal** \ˌmetᵊlˈərjikəl\ *adj* **—met•al•lur•gist** \ˈmetᵊlˌərjist\ *n*
meta•mor•pho•sis \ˌmetəˈmȯrfəsəs\ *n, pl* **-pho•ses** \-ˌsēz\ **:** sudden and drastic change (as of form) **—metamorphose** \-ˌfōz, -ˌfōs\ *vb*
met•a•phor \ˈmetəˌfȯr, -fər\ *n* **:** use of a word denoting one kind of object or idea in place of another to suggest a likeness between them **—met•a•phor•i•cal** \ˌmetəˈfȯrikəl\ *adj*
meta•phys•ics \ˌmetəˈfiziks\ *n* **:** study of the causes and nature of things **—meta•phys•i•cal** \-ˈfizəkəl\ *adj*
mete \ˈmēt\ *vb* **met•ed; met•ing :** allot
me•te•or \ˈmētēər, -ēˌȯr\ *n* **:** small body that produces a streak of light as it burns up in the atmosphere
me•te•or•ic \ˌmētēˈȯrik\ *adj* **1 :** relating to a meteor **2 :** sudden and spectacular **—me•te•or•i•cal•ly** \-iklē\ *adv*
me•te•or•ite \ˈmētēəˌrīt\ *n* **:** meteor that reaches the earth
me•te•o•rol•o•gy \ˌmētēəˈräləjē\ *n* **:** science of weather **—me•te•o•ro•log•ic** \ˌmētēˌȯrəˈläjik\, **me•te•o•ro•log•i•cal** \-ˈläjikəl\ *adj* **—me•te•o•rol•o•gist** \-ēəˈräləjist\ *n*
1me•ter \ˈmētər\ *n* **:** rhythm in verse or music
2meter *n* **:** unit of length equal to 39.37 inches
3meter *n* **:** measuring instrument
meth•a•done \ˈmethəˌdōn\ *n* **:** synthetic addictive narcotic
meth•ane \ˈmethˌān\ *n* **:** colorless odorless flammable gas
meth•a•nol \ˈmethəˌnȯl, -ˌnōl\ *n* **:** volatile flammable poisonous liquid
meth•od \ˈmethəd\ *n* **1 :** procedure for achieving an end **2 :** orderly arrangement or plan **—me•thod•i•cal** \məˈthädikəl\ *adj* **—me•thod•i•cal•ly** \-klē\ *adv* **—me•thod•i•cal•ness** *n*
me•tic•u•lous \məˈtikyələs\ *adj* **:** extremely careful in attending to details **—me•tic•u•lous•ly** *adv* **—me•tic•u•lous•ness** *n*
met•ric \ˈmetrik\, **met•ri•cal** \-trikəl\ *adj* **:** relating to meter or the metric system **—met•ri•cal•ly** *adv*
metric system *n* **:** system of weights and measures using the meter and kilogram
met•ro•nome \ˈmetrəˌnōm\ *n* **:** instrument that ticks regularly to mark a beat in music
me•trop•o•lis \məˈträpələs\ *n* **:** major city **—met•ro•pol•i•tan** \ˌmetrəˈpälətᵊn\ *adj*
met•tle \ˈmetᵊl\ *n* **:** spirit or courage **—met•tle•some** \-səm\ *adj*
mez•za•nine \ˈmezᵊnˌēn, ˌmezᵊnˈēn\ *n* **1 :** intermediate level between 2 main floors **2 :** lowest balcony
mez•zo–so•pra•no \ˌmetsōsəˈpranō, ˌmedz-\ *n* **:** voice between soprano and contralto
mi•as•ma \mīˈazmə\ *n* **1 :** noxious vapor **2 :** harmful influence **—mi•as•mic** \-mik\ *adj*
mi•ca \ˈmīkə\ *n* **:** mineral separable into thin transparent sheets
mice *pl of* MOUSE
mi•cro \ˈmīkrō\ *adj* **:** very small
mi•crobe \ˈmīˌkrōb\ *n* **:** disease-causing microorganism **—mi•cro•bi•al** \mīˈkrōbēəl\ *adj*
mi•cro•bi•ol•o•gy \ˌmīkrōbīˈäləjē\ *n* **:** biology dealing with microscopic life **—mi•cro•bi•o•log•i•cal** \ˈmīkrōˌbīəˈläjikəl\ *adj* **—mi•cro•bi•ol•o•gist** \ˌmīkrōbīˈäləjist\ *n*
mi•cro•com•put•er \ˈmīkrōkəmˌpyütər\ *n* **:** small computer that uses a microprocessor
mi•cro•cosm \ˈmīkrəˌkäzəm\ *n* **:** one thought of as a miniature universe
mi•cro•film \-ˌfilm\ *n* **:** small film recording printed matter **—microfilm** *vb*
mi•crom•e•ter \mīˈkrämətər\ *n* **:** instrument for measuring minute distances
mi•cro•min•i•a•tur•ized \ˌmīkrōˈminēəchəˌrīzd, -ˈminichə-\ *adj* **:** reduced to a very small size **—mi•cro•min•i•a•tur•iza•tion** \-ˌminēəˌchu̇rəˈzāshən, -ˌminiˌchu̇r-, -chər-\ *n*
mi•cron \ˈmīˌkrän\ *n* **:** one millionth of a meter
mi•cro•or•gan•ism \ˌmīkrōˈȯrgəˌnizəm\ *n* **:** very tiny living thing
mi•cro•phone \ˈmīkrəˌfōn\ *n* **:** instrument for changing sound waves into variations of an electric current
mi•cro•pro•ces•sor \ˈmīkrōˌpräsesər\ *n* **:** miniaturized computer processing unit on a single chip
mi•cro•scope \-ˌskōp\ *n* **:** optical device for magnifying tiny objects **—mi•cro•scop•ic** \ˌmīkrəˈskäpik\ *adj* **—mi•cro•scop•i•cal•ly** *adv* **—mi•cros•copy** \mīˈkräskəpē\ *n*
mi•cro•wave \ˈmīkrəˌwāv\ *n* **1 :** short radio wave **2 :** oven that cooks food using microwaves ~ *vb* **:** heat or cook in a microwave oven **—mi•cro•wav•able, mi•cro•wave•able** \ˌmīkrəˈwāvəbəl\ *adj*
mid \ˈmid\ *adj* **:** middle **—mid•point** *n* **—mid•stream** *n* **—mid•sum•mer** *n* **—mid•town** *n or adj* **—mid•week** *n* **—mid•win•ter** *n* **—mid•year** *n*
mid•air *n* **:** a point in the air well above the ground
mid•day *n* **:** noon
mid•dle \ˈmidᵊl\ *adj* **1 :** equally distant from the extremes **2 :** being at neither extreme ~ *n* **:** middle part or point
Middle Ages *n pl* **:** period from about A.D. 500 to about 1500
mid•dle•man \-ˌman\ *n* **:** dealer or agent between the producer and consumer
mid•dling \ˈmidliŋ, -lən\ *adj* **1 :** of middle or medium size, degree, or quality **2 :** mediocre
midge \ˈmij\ *n* **:** very tiny fly
midg•et \ˈmijət\ *n* **:** very small person or thing
mid•land \ˈmidlənd, -ˌland\ *n* **:** interior of a country
mid•most *adj* **:** being nearest the middle **—midmost** *adv*
mid•night *n* **:** 12 o'clock at night
mid•riff \ˈmidˌrif\ *n* **:** mid-region of the torso
mid•ship•man \ˈmidˌshipmən, ˌmidˈship-\ *n* **:** student naval officer
midst \ˈmidst\ *n* **:** position close to or surrounded by others **—midst** *prep*
mid•way \ˈmidˌwā\ *n* **:** concessions and amusements at a carnival ~ *adv* **:** in the middle
mid•wife \ˈmidˌwīf\ *n* **:** person who aids at childbirth **—mid•wife•ry** \midˈwifərē, -ˈwīf-\ *n*
mien \ˈmēn\ *n* **:** appearance
miff \ˈmif\ *vb* **:** upset or peeve
1might \ˈmīt\ *past of* MAY —used to express permission or possibility or as a polite alternative to *may*
2might *n* **:** power or resources
mighty \ˈmītē\ *adj* **might•i•er; -est 1 :** very strong **2 :** great **—might•i•ly** *adv* **—might•i•ness** *n* **—mighty** *adv*
mi•graine \ˈmīˌgrān\ *n* **:** severe headache often with nausea
mi•grant \ˈmīgrənt\ *n* **:** one who moves frequently to find work
mi•grate \ˈmīˌgrāt\ *vb* **-grat•ed; -grat•ing 1 :** move from one place to another **2 :** pass periodically from one region or climate to another **—mi•gra•tion** \mīˈgrāshən\ *n* **—mi•gra•to•ry** \ˈmīgrəˌtōrē\ *adj*
mild \ˈmīld\ *adj* **1 :** gentle in nature or behavior **2 :** moderate in action or effect **—mild•ly** *adv* **—mild•ness** *n*
mil•dew \ˈmilˌdü, -ˌdyü\ *n* **:** whitish fungal growth **—mildew** *vb*
mile \ˈmīl\ *n* **:** unit of length equal to 5280 feet
mile•age \ˈmīlij\ *n* **1 :** allowance per mile for traveling expenses **2 :** amount or rate of use expressed in miles
mile•stone *n* **:** significant point in development
mi•lieu \mēlˈyü, -ˈyœ\ *n, pl* **-lieus** *or* **-lieux** \-ˈyüz, -ˈyœ\ **:** surroundings or setting
mil•i•tant \ˈmilətənt\ *adj* **:** aggressively active or hostile **—mil•i•tan•cy** \-tənsē\ *n* **—militant** *n* **—mil•i•tant•ly** *adv*
mil•i•ta•rism \ˈmilətəˌrizəm\ *n* **:** dominance of military ideals or of a policy of aggressive readiness for war **—mil•i•ta•rist** \-rist\ *n* **—mil•i•ta•ris•tic** \ˌmilətəˈristik\ *adj*
mil•i•tary \ˈmiləˌterē\ *adj* **1 :** relating to soldiers, arms, or war **2 :** relating to or performed by armed forces ~ *n* **:** armed forces or the people in them **—mil•i•tar•i•ly** \ˌmiləˈterəlē\ *adv*
mil•i•tate \-ˌtāt\ *vb* **-tat•ed; -tat•ing :** have an effect
mi•li•tia \məˈlishə\ *n* **:** civilian soldiers **—mi•li•tia•man** \-mən\ *n*
milk \ˈmilk\ *n* **:** white nutritive fluid secreted by female mammals for feeding their young ~ *vb* **1 :** draw off the milk of **2 :** draw something from as if by milking **—milk•er** *n* **—milk•i•ness** \-ēnəs\ *n* **—milky** *adj*
milk•man \-ˌman, -mən\ *n* **:** man who sells or delivers milk
milk•weed *n* **:** herb with milky juice
1mill \ˈmil\ *n* **1 :** building in which grain is ground into flour **2 :** manufacturing plant **3 :** machine used esp. for forming or processing ~ *vb* **1 :** subject to a process in a mill **2 :** move in a circle **—mill•er** *n*
2mill *n* **:** 1/10 cent
mil•len•ni•um \məˈlenēəm\ *n, pl* **-nia** \-ēə\ *or* **-niums :** a period of 1000 years
mil•let \ˈmilət\ *n* **:** cereal and forage grass with small seeds
mil•li•gram \ˈmiləˌgram\ *n* **:** 1/1000 gram
mil•li•li•ter \-ˌlētər\ *n* **:** 1/1000 liter
mil•li•me•ter \-ˌmētər\ **:** 1/1000 meter
mil•li•ner \ˈmilənər\ *n* **:** person who makes or sells women's hats **—mil•li•nery** \ˈmiləˌnerē\ *n*
mil•lion \ˈmilyən\ *n, pl* **millions** *or* **million :** 1000 thousands **—million** *adj* **—mil•lionth** \-yənth\ *adj or n*
mil•lion•aire \ˌmilyəˈnar, ˈmilyəˌnar\ *n* **:** person worth a million or more (as of dollars)
mil•li•pede \ˈmiləˌpēd\ *n* **:** longbodied arthropod with 2 pairs of legs on most segments
mill•stone *n* **:** either of 2 round flat stones used for grinding grain
mime \ˈmīm\ *n* **1 :** mimic **2 :** pantomime **—mime** *vb*
mim•eo•graph \ˈmimēəˌgraf\ *n* **:** machine for making many stencil copies **—mimeograph** *vb*
mim•ic \ˈmimik\ *n* **:** one that mimics ~ *vb* **-icked; -ick•ing 1 :** imitate closely **2 :** ridicule by imitation **—mim•ic•ry** \ˈmimikrē\ *n*
min•a•ret \ˌminəˈret\ *n* **:** tower attached to a mosque
mince \ˈmins\ *vb* **minced; minc•ing 1 :** cut into small pieces **2 :** choose (one's words) carefully **3 :** walk in a prim affected manner
mind \ˈmīnd\ *n* **1 :** memory **2 :** the part of an individual that feels, perceives, and esp. reasons **3 :** intention **4 :** normal mental condition **5 :** opinion **6 :** intellectual ability ~ *vb* **1 :** attend to **2 :** obey **3 :** be concerned about **4 :** be careful **—mind•ed** *adj* **—mind•less** \ˈmīndləs\ *adj* **—mind•less•ly** *adv* **—mind•less•ness** *n*
mind•ful \-fəl\ *adj* **:** aware or attentive **—mind•ful•ly** *adv* **—mind•ful•ness** *n*
1mine \ˈmīn\ *pron* **:** that which belongs to me
2mine \ˈmīn\ *n* **1 :** excavation from which minerals are taken **2 :** explosive device placed in the ground or water for destroying enemy vehicles or vessels that later pass ~ *vb* **mined; min•ing 1 :** get ore from **2 :** place military mines in **—mine•field** *n* **—min•er** *n*
min•er•al \ˈminərəl\ *n* **1 :** crystalline substance not of organic origin **2 :** useful natural substance (as coal) obtained from the ground **—mineral** *adj*
min•er•al•o•gy \ˌminəˈräləjē, -ˈral-\ *n* **:** science dealing with minerals **—min•er•al•og•i•cal** \ˌminərəˈläjikəl\ *adj* **—min•er•al•o•gist** \ˌminəˈräləjist, -ˈral-\ *n*
min•gle \ˈmiŋgəl\ *vb* **-gled; -gling :** bring together or mix
mini- *comb form* **:** miniature or of small dimensions
min•ia•ture \ˈminēəˌchu̇r, ˈminiˌchu̇r, -chər\ *n* **:** tiny copy or very small version **—miniature** *adj* **—min•ia•tur•ist** \-ˌchu̇rist, -chər-\ *n* **—min•ia•tur•ize** \-ēəchəˌrīz, -ichə-\ *vb*
mini•bike \ˈminēˌbīk\ *n* **:** small motorcycle
mini•bus \-ˌbəs\ *n* **:** small bus
mini•com•put•er \-kəmˌpyütər\ *n* **:** computer intermediate between a mainframe and a microcomputer in size and speed
mini•course \-ˌkōrs\ *n* **:** short course of study
min•i•mal \ˈminəməl\ *adj* **:** relating to or being a minimum **—min•i•mal•ly** *adv*
min•i•mize \ˈminəˌmīz\ *vb* **-mized; -miz•ing 1 :** reduce to a minimum **2 :** underestimate intentionally
min•i•mum \ˈminəməm\ *n, pl* **-ma** \-mə\ *or* **-mums :** lowest quantity or amount **—minimum** *adj*
min•ion \ˈminyən\ *n* **1 :** servile dependent **2 :** subordinate official
mini•se•ries \ˈminēˌsirēz\ *n* **:** television story in several parts
mini•skirt \-ˌskərt\ *n* **:** very short skirt
min•is•ter \ˈminəstər\ *n* **1 :** Protestant member of the clergy **2 :** high officer of state **3 :** diplomatic representative ~ *vb* **:** give aid or service **—min•is•te•ri•al** \ˌminəˈstirēəl\ *adj* **—min•is•tra•tion** *n*
min•is•try \ˈminəstrē\ *n, pl* **-tries 1 :** office or duties of a minister **2 :** body of ministers **3 :** government department headed by a minister
mini•van \ˈminēˌvan\ *n* **:** small van
mink \ˈmiŋk\ *n, pl* **mink** *or* **minks :** weasellike mammal or its soft brown fur
min•now \ˈminō\ *n, pl* **-nows :** small freshwater fish
mi•nor \ˈmīnər\ *adj* **1 :** less in size, importance, or value **2 :** not serious ~ *n* **1 :** person not yet of legal age **2 :** secondary field of academic specialization
mi•nor•i•ty \məˈnȯrətē, mī-\ *n, pl* **-ties 1 :** time or state of being a minor **2 :** smaller number (as of votes) **3 :** part of a popu-

lation differing from others (as in race or religion)

min•strel \'minstrəl\ *n* **1 :** medieval singer of verses **2 :** performer in a program usu. of black American songs and jokes —**min•strel•sy** \-sē\ *n*

1**mint** \'mint\ *n* **1 :** fragrant herb that yields a flavoring oil **2 :** mint-flavored piece of candy —**minty** *adj*

2**mint** *n* **1 :** place where coins are made **2 :** vast sum ~ *adj* **:** unused —**mint** *vb* —**mint•er** *n*

min•u•et \ˌminyə'wet\ *n* **:** slow graceful dance

mi•nus \'mīnəs\ *prep* **1 :** diminished by **2 :** lacking ~ *n* **:** negative quantity or quality

mi•nus•cule \'minəsˌkyül, min'əs-\, **min•is•cule** \'minəs-\ *adj* **:** very small

1**min•ute** \'minət\ *n* **1 :** 60th part of an hour or of a degree **2 :** short time **3** *pl* **:** official record of a meeting

2**mi•nute** \mī'nüt, mə-, -'nyüt\ *adj* **-nut•er; -est 1 :** very small **2 :** marked by close attention to details —**mi•nute•ly** *adv* —**mi•nute•ness** *n*

mir•a•cle \'mirikəl\ *n* **1 :** extraordinary event taken as a sign of divine intervention in human affairs **2 :** marvel —**mi•rac•u•lous** \mə'rakyələs\ *adj* —**mi•rac•u•lous•ly** *adv*

mi•rage \mə'räzh\ *n* **:** distant illusion caused by atmospheric conditions (as in the desert)

mire \'mīr\ *n* **:** heavy deep mud ~ *vb* **mired; mir•ing :** stick or sink in mire —**miry** *adj*

mir•ror \'mirər\ *n* **:** smooth surface (as of glass) that reflects images ~ *vb* **:** reflect in or as if in a mirror

mirth \'mərth\ *n* **:** gladness and laughter —**mirth•ful** \-fəl\ *adj* —**mirth•ful•ly** *adv* —**mirth•ful•ness** *n* —**mirth•less** *adj*

mis•an•thrope \'misənˌthrōp\ *n* **:** one who hates mankind —**mis•an•throp•ic** \ˌmisən'thräpik\ *adj* —**mis•an•thro•py** \mis'anthrəpē\ *n*

mis•ap•pre•hend \ˌmisˌaprə'hend\ *vb* **:** misunderstand —**mis•ap•pre•hen•sion** *n*

mis•ap•pro•pri•ate \ˌmisə'prōprēˌāt\ *vb* **:** take dishonestly for one's own use —**mis•ap•pro•pri•a•tion** *n*

mis•be•got•ten \-bi'gätən\ *adj* **1 :** illegitimate **2 :** ill-conceived

mis•be•have \ˌmisbi'hāv\ *vb* **:** behave improperly —**mis•be•hav•er** *n* —**mis•be•hav•ior** *n*

mis•cal•cu•late \mis'kalkyəˌlāt\ *vb* **:** calculate wrongly —**mis•cal•cu•la•tion**

mis•car•ry \ˌmis'karē, 'misˌkarē\ *vb* **1 :** give birth prematurely before the fetus can survive **2 :** go wrong or be unsuccessful —**mis•car•riage** \-rij\ *n*

mis•ce•ge•na•tion \misˌejə'nāshən, ˌmisijə'nā-\ *n* **:** marriage between persons of different races

mis•cel•la•neous \ˌmisə'lānēəs\ *adj* **:** consisting of many things of different kinds —**mis•cel•la•neous•ly** *adv* —**mis•cel•la•neous•ness** *n*

mis•cel•la•ny \'misəˌlānē\ *n, pl* **-nies :** collection of various things

mis•chance \mis'chans\ *n* **:** bad luck

mis•chief \'mischəf\ *n* **:** conduct esp. of a child that annoys or causes minor damage

mis•chie•vous \'mischəvəs\ *adj* **1 :** causing annoyance or minor injury **2 :** irresponsibly playful —**mis•chie•vous•ly** *adv* —**mis•chie•vous•ness** *n*

mis•con•ceive \ˌmiskən'sēv\ *vb* **:** interpret incorrectly —**mis•con•cep•tion** *n*

mis•con•duct \mis'kändəkt\ *n* **1 :** mismanagement **2 :** bad behavior

mis•con•strue \ˌmiskən'strü\ *vb* **:** misinterpret —**mis•con•struc•tion** *n*

mis•cre•ant \'miskrēənt\ *n* **:** one who behaves criminally or viciously —**miscreant** *adj*

mis•deed \mis'dēd\ *n* **:** wrong deed

mis•de•mean•or \ˌmisdi'mēnər\ *n* **:** crime less serious than a felony

mi•ser \'mīzər\ *n* **:** person who hoards and is stingy with money —**mi•ser•li•ness** \-lēnəs\ *n* —**mi•ser•ly** *adj*

mis•er•a•ble \'mizərəbəl\ *adj* **1 :** wretchedly deficient **2 :** causing extreme discomfort **3 :** shameful —**mis•er•a•ble•ness** *n* —**mis•er•a•bly** \-blē\ *adv*

mis•ery \'mizərē\ *n, pl* **-er•ies :** suffering and want caused by distress or poverty

mis•fire \mis'fīr\ *vb* **1 :** fail to fire **2 :** miss an intended effect —**mis•fire** \'misˌfīr\ *n*

mis•fit \'misˌfit, mis'fit\ *n* **:** person poorly adjusted to his environment

mis•for•tune \mis'fórchən\ *n* **1 :** bad luck **2 :** unfortunate condition or event

mis•giv•ing \mis'giviŋ\ *n* **:** doubt or concern

mis•guid•ed \mis'gīdəd\ *adj* **:** mistaken, uninformed, or deceived

mis•hap \'misˌhap\ *n* **:** accident

mis•in•form \ˌmisən'fórm\ *vb* **:** give wrong information to —**mis•in•for•ma•tion** \ˌmisˌinfər'māshən\ *n*

mis•in•ter•pret \ˌmisən'tərprət\ *vb* **:** understand or explain wrongly —**mis•in•ter•pre•ta•tion** \-ˌtərprə'tāshən\ *n*

mis•judge \mis'jəj\ *vb* **:** judge incorrectly or unjustly —**mis•judg•ment** *n*

mis•lay \mis'lā\ *vb* **-laid; -lay•ing :** misplace

mis•lead \mis'lēd\ *vb* **-led; -lead•ing :** lead in a wrong direction or into error —**mis•lead•ing•ly** *adv*

mis•man•age \mis'manij\ *vb* **:** manage badly —**mis•man•age•ment** *n*

mis•no•mer \mis'nōmər\ *n* **:** wrong name

mi•sog•y•nist \mə'säjənist\ *n* **:** one who hates or distrusts women —**mi•sog•y•nis•tic** \məˌsäjə'nistik\ *adj* —**mi•sog•y•ny** \-nē\ *n*

mis•place \mis'plās\ *vb* **:** put in a wrong or unremembered place

mis•print \'misˌprint, mis'-\ *n* **:** error in printed matter

mis•pro•nounce \ˌmisprə'naùns\ *vb* **:** pronounce incorrectly —**mis•pro•nun•ci•a•tion** *n*

mis•quote \mis'kwōt\ *vb* **:** quote incorrectly —**mis•quo•ta•tion** \ˌmiskwō'tāshən\ *n*

mis•read \mis'rēd\ *vb* **-read; -read•ing :** read or interpret incorrectly

mis•rep•re•sent \ˌmisˌrepri'zent\ *vb* **:** represent falsely or unfairly —**mis•rep•re•sen•ta•tion** *n*

mis•rule \mis'rül\ *vb* **:** govern badly ~ *n* **1 :** bad or corrupt government **2 :** disorder

1**miss** \'mis\ *vb* **1 :** fail to hit, reach, or contact **2 :** notice the absence of **3 :** fail to obtain **4 :** avoid **5 :** omit —**miss** *n*

2**miss** *n* **:** young unmarried woman or girl —often used as a title

mis•sal \'misəl\ *n* **:** book containing what is said at mass during the year

mis•shap•en \mis'shāpən\ *adj* **:** distorted

mis•sile \'misəl\ *n* **:** object (as a stone or rocket) thrown or shot

miss•ing \'misiŋ\ *adj* **:** absent or lost

mis•sion \'mishən\ *n* **1 :** ministry sent by a church to spread its teaching **2 :** group of diplomats sent to a foreign country **3 :** task

mis•sion•ary \'mishəˌnerē\ *adj* **:** relating to religious missions ~ *n, pl* **-ar•ies :** person sent to spread religious faith

mis•sive \'misiv\ *n* **:** letter

mis•spell \mis'spel\ *vb* **:** spell incorrectly —**mis•spell•ing** *n*

mis•state \mis'stāt\ *vb* **:** state incorrectly —**mis•state•ment** *n*

mis•step \'misˌstep\ *n* **1 :** wrong step **2 :** mistake

mist \'mist\ *n* **:** particles of water falling as fine rain

mis•take \mə'stāk\ *n* **1 :** misunderstanding or wrong belief **2 :** wrong action or statement —**mistake** *vb*

mis•tak•en \-'stākən\ *adj* **:** having a wrong opinion or incorrect information —**mis•tak•en•ly** *adv*

mis•ter \'mistər\ *n* **:** sir —used without a name in addressing a man

mis•tle•toe \'misəlˌtō\ *n* **:** parasitic green shrub with waxy white berries

mis•treat \mis'trēt\ *vb* **:** treat badly —**mis•treat•ment** *n*

mis•tress \'mistrəs\ *n* **1 :** woman in control **2 :** a woman not his wife with whom a married man has recurrent sexual relations

mis•tri•al \mis'trīəl\ *n* **:** trial that has no legal effect

mis•trust \-'trəst\ *n* **:** lack of confidence ~ *vb* **:** have no confidence in —**mis•trust•ful** \-fəl\ *adj* —**mis•trust•ful•ly** *adv* —**mis•trust•ful•ness** *n*

misty \'mistē\ *adj* **mist•i•er; -est 1 :** obscured by mist **2 :** tearful—**mist•i•ly** *adv* —**mist•i•ness** *n*

mis•un•der•stand \ˌmisˌəndər'stand\ *vb* **1 :** fail to understand **2 :** interpret incorrectly

mis•un•der•stand•ing \-'standiŋ\ *n* **1 :** wrong interpretation **2 :** disagreement

mis•use \mis'yüz\ *vb* **1 :** use incorrectly **2 :** mistreat —**mis•use** \-'yüs\ *n*

mite \'mīt\ *n* **1 :** tiny spiderlike animal **2 :** small amount

mi•ter, mi•tre \'mītər\ *n* **1 :** bishop's headdress **2 :** angular joint in wood ~ *vb* **-tered** *or* **-tred; -ter•ing** *or* **-tring** \'mītəriŋ\ **:** bevel the ends of for a miter joint

mit•i•gate \'mitəˌgāt\ *vb* **-gat•ed; -gat•ing :** make less severe —**mit•i•ga•tion** \ˌmitə'gāshən\ *n* —**mit•i•ga•tive** \'mitəˌgātiv\ *adj*

mi•to•sis \mī'tōsəs\ *n, pl* **-to•ses** \-ˌsēz\ **:** process of forming 2 cell nuclei from one —**mi•tot•ic** \-'tätik\ *adj*

mitt \'mit\ *n* **:** mittenlike baseball glove

mit•ten \'mitən\ *n* **:** hand covering without finger sections

mix \'miks\ *vb* **:** combine or join into one mass or group ~ *n* **:** commercially prepared food mixture —**mix•able** *adj* —**mix•er** *n* —**mix up** *vb* **:** confuse

mix•ture \'mikschər\ *n* **:** act or product of mixing

mix–up *n* **:** instance of confusion

mne•mon•ic \ni'mänik\ *adj* **:** relating to or assisting memory

moan \'mōn\ *n* **:** low prolonged sound of pain or grief —**moan** *vb*

moat \'mōt\ *n* **:** deep wide trench around a castle

mob \'mäb\ *n* **1 :** large disorderly crowd **2 :** criminal gang ~ *vb* **-bb- :** crowd around and attack or annoy

mo•bile \'mōbəl, -ˌbēl, -ˌbīl\ *adj* **:** capable of moving or being moved ~ \'mōˌbēl\ *n* **:** suspended art construction with freely moving parts —**mo•bil•i•ty** \mō'bilətē\ *n*

mo•bi•lize \'mōbəˌlīz\ *vb* **-lized; -liz•ing :** assemble and make ready for war duty —**mo•bi•li•za•tion** \ˌmōbələ'zāshən\ *n*

moc•ca•sin \'mäkəsən\ *n* **1 :** heelless shoe **2 :** venomous U.S. snake

mo•cha \'mōkə\ *n* **1 :** mixture of coffee and chocolate **2 :** dark brown color

mock \'mäk, 'mók\ *vb* **1 :** ridicule **2 :** mimic in derision ~ *adj* **1 :** simulated **2 :** phony —**mock•er** *n* —**mock•ery** \-ərē\ *n* —**mock•ing•ly** *adv*

mock•ing•bird \'mäkiŋˌbərd, 'mók-\ *n* **:** songbird that mimics other birds

mode \'mōd\ *n* **1 :** particular form or variety **2 :** style —**mod•al** \-əl\ *adj* —**mod•ish** \'mōdish\ *adj*

mod•el \'mädəl\ *n* **1 :** structural design **2 :** miniature representation **3 :** something worthy of copying **4 :** one who poses for an artist or displays clothes **5 :** type or design ~ *vb* **-eled** *or* **-elled; -el•ing** *or* **-el•ling 1 :** shape **2 :** work as a model ~ *adj* **1 :** serving as a pattern **2 :** being a miniature representation of

mo•dem \'mōdəm, -ˌdem\ *n* **:** device by which a computer communicates with another computer over telephone lines

mod•er•ate \'mädərət\ *adj* **:** avoiding extremes ~ \'mädəˌrāt\ *vb* **-at•ed; -at•ing 1 :** lessen the intensity of **2 :** act as a moderator —**moderate** *n* —**mod•er•ate•ly** *adv* —**mod•er•ate•ness** *n* —**mod•er•a•tion** \ˌmädə'rāshən\ *n*

mod•er•a•tor \'mädəˌrātər\ *n* **:** one who presides

mod•ern \'mädərn\ *adj* **:** relating to or characteristic of the present —**modern** *n* —**mo•der•ni•ty** \mə'dərnətē\ *n* —**mod•ern•iza•tion** \ˌmädərnə'zāshən\ *n* —**mod•ern•ize** \'mädərˌnīz\ *vb* —**mod•ern•iz•er** \'mädərˌnīzər\ *n* —**mod•ern•ly** *adv* —**mod•ern•ness** *n*

mod•est \'mädəst\ *adj* **1 :** having a moderate estimate of oneself **2 :** reserved or decent in thoughts or actions **3 :** limited in size, amount, or aim —**mod•est•ly** *adv* —**mod•es•ty** \-əstē\ *n*

mod•i•cum \'mädikəm\ *n* **:** small amount

mod•i•fy \'mädəˌfī\ *vb* **-fied; -fy•ing 1 :** limit the meaning of **2 :** change —**mod•i•fi•ca•tion** \ˌmädəfə'kāshən\ *n* —**mod•i•fi•er** \'mädəˌfīər\ *n*

mod•u•lar \'mäjələr\ *adj* **:** built with standardized units —**mod•u•lar•ized** \-ləˌrīzd\ *adj*

mod•u•late \'mäjəˌlāt\ *vb* **-lat•ed; -lat•ing 1 :** keep in proper measure or proportion **2 :** vary a radio wave —**mod•u•la•tion** \ˌmäjə'lāshən\ *n* —**mod•u•la•tor** \'mäjəˌlātər\ *n* —**mod•u•la•to•ry** \-ləˌtōrē\ *adj*

mod•ule \'mäjül\ *n* **:** standardized unit

mo•gul \'mōgəl\ *n* **:** important person

mo•hair \'mōˌhar\ *n* **:** fabric made from the hair of the Angora goat

moist \'móist\ *adj* **:** slightly or moderately wet —**moist•en** \'móisən\ *vb* —**moist•en•er** \'móisənər\ *n* —**moist•ly** *adv* —**moist•ness** *n*

mois•ture \'móischər\ *n* **:** small amount of liquid that causes dampness —**mois•tur•ize** \-chəˌrīz\ *vb* —**mois•tur•iz•er** *n*

mo•lar \'mōlər\ *n* **:** grinding tooth —**molar** *adj*

mo•las•ses \mə'lasəz\ *n* **:** thick brown syrup from raw sugar

1**mold** \'mōld\ *n* **:** crumbly organic soil

2**mold** *n* **:** frame or cavity for forming ~ *vb* **:** shape in or as if in a mold —**mold•er** *n*

3**mold** *n* **:** surface growth of fungus ~ *vb* **:** become moldy —**mold•i•ness** \'mōldēnəs\ *n* —**moldy** *adj*

mold•er \'mōldər\ *vb* **:** crumble

mold•ing \'mōldiŋ\ *n* **:** decorative surface, plane, or strip

1**mole** \'mōl\ *n* **:** spot on the skin

2**mole** *n* **:** small burrowing mammal —**mole•hill** *n*

mol•e•cule \'mäliˌkyül\ *n* **:** small particle of matter —**mo•lec•u•lar** \mə'lekyələr\ *adj*

mole•skin \-ˌskin\ *n* **:** heavy cotton fabric

mo•lest \mə'lest\ *vb* **1 :** annoy or disturb **2 :** force physical and usu. sexual contact on —**mo•les•ta•tion** \ˌmōlˌes'tāshən, ˌmäl-\ *n* —**mo•lest•er** *n*

mol•li•fy \'mäləˌfī\ *vb* **-fied; -fy•ing :** soothe in temper —**mol•li•fi•ca•tion** \ˌmäləfə'kāshən\ *n*

mol•lusk, mol•lusc \'mäləsk\ *n* **:** shelled aquatic invertebrate —**mol•lus•can** \mə'ləskən\ *adj*

mol•ly•cod•dle \'mälēˌkädəl\ *vb* **-dled; -dling :** pamper

molt \'mōlt\ *vb* **:** shed hair, feathers, outer skin, or horns periodically —**molt** *n* —**molt•er** *n*

mol•ten \'mōltən\ *adj* **:** fused or liquefied by heat

mom \'mäm, 'məm\ *n* **:** mother

mo•ment \'mōmənt\ *n* **1 :** tiny portion of time **2 :** time of excellence **3 :** importance

mo•men•tari•ly \ˌmōmən'terəlē\ *adv* **1 :** for a moment **2 :** at any moment

mo•men•tary \'mōmənˌterē\ *adj* **:** continuing only a moment —**mo•men•tar•i•ness** *n*

mo•men•tous \mō'mentəs\ *adj* **:** very important —**mo•men•tous•ly** *adv* —**mo•men•tous•ness** *n*

mo•men•tum \-əm\ *n, pl* **-ta** \-ə\ *or* **-tums :** force of a moving body

mon•arch \'mänərk, -ˌärk\ *n* **:** ruler of a kingdom or empire —**mo•nar•chi•cal** \mə'närkikəl\ *adj*

mon•ar•chist \'mänərkist\ *n* **:** believer in monarchical government —**mon•ar•chism** \-ˌkizəm\ *n*

mon•ar•chy \'mänərkē\ *n, pl* **-chies :** realm of a monarch

mon•as•tery \'mänəˌsterē\ *n, pl* **-ter•ies :** house for monks

mo•nas•tic \mə'nastik\ *adj* **:** relating to monasteries, monks, or nuns —**monastic** *n* —**mo•nas•ti•cal•ly** \-tiklē\ *adv* —**mo•nas•ti•cism** \-təˌsizəm\ *n*

Mon•day \'məndā, -dē\ *n* **:** 2d day of the week

mon•e•tary \'mänəˌterē, 'mən-\ *adj* **:** relating to money

mon•ey \'mənē\ *n, pl* **-eys** *or* **-ies** \'mənēz\ **1 :** something (as coins or paper currency) used in buying **2 :** wealth —**mon•eyed** \-ēd\ *adj* —**mon•ey•lend•er** *n*

mon•ger \'məŋgər, 'mäŋ-\ *n* **:** dealer

mon•gol•ism \'mäŋgəˌlizəm\ *n* **:** congenital mental retardation —**Mon•gol•oid** \-gəˌlòid\ *adj or n*

mon•goose \'mänˌgüs, 'mäŋ-\ *n, pl* **-goos•es :** small agile mammal esp. of India

mon•grel \'mäŋgrəl, 'məŋ-\ *n* **:** offspring of mixed breed

mon•i•tor \'mänətər\ *n* **1 :** student assistant **2 :** television screen ~ *vb* **:** watch or observe esp. for quality

monk \'məŋk\ *n* **:** member of a religious order living in a monastery —**monk•ish** *adj*

mon•key \'məŋkē\ *n, pl* **-keys :** small long-tailed arboreal primate ~ *vb* **1 :** fool **2 :** tamper

mon•key•shines \-ˌshīnz\ *n pl* **:** pranks

monks•hood \'məŋksˌhùd\ *n* **:** poisonous herb with showy flowers

mon•o•cle \'mänikəl\ *n* **:** eyeglass for one eye

mo•nog•a•my \mə'nägəmē\ *n* **1 :** marriage with one person at a time **2 :** practice of having a single mate for a period of time —**mo•nog•a•mist** \mə'nägəmist\ *n* —**mo•nog•a•mous** \-məs\ *adj*

mono•gram \'mänəˌgram\ *n* **:** sign of identity made of initials —**monogram** *vb*

mono•graph \-ˌgraf\ *n* **:** learned treatise

mono•lin•gual \ˌmänə'liŋgwəl\ *adj* **:** using only one language

mono•lith \'mänəlˌith\ *n* **1 :** single great stone **2 :** single uniform massive whole —**mono•lith•ic** \ˌmänəl'ithik\ *adj*

mono•logue \'mänəlˌòg\ *n* **:** long speech —**mono•logu•ist** \-ˌògist\, **mo•no•lo•gist** \mə'näləjist, 'mänəlˌògist\ *n*

mono•nu•cle•o•sis \ˌmänōˌnüklē'ōsəs, -ˌnyü-\ *n* **:** acute infectious disease

mo•nop•o•ly \mə'näpəlē\ *n, pl* **-lies 1 :** exclusive ownership or control of a commodity **2 :** one controlling a monopoly —**mo•nop•o•list** \-list\ *n* —**mo•nop•o•lis•tic** \məˌnäpə'listik\ *adj* —**mo•nop•o•li•za•tion** \-lə'zāshən\ *n* —**mo•nop•o•lize** \mə'näpəˌlīz\ *vb*

mono•rail \'mänəˌrāl\ *n* **:** single rail for a vehicle or a vehicle or system using it

mono•syl•lab•ic \ˌmänəsə'labik\ *adj* **:** consisting of or using words of only one syllable —**mono•syl•la•ble** \'mänəˌsiləbəl\ *n*

mono•the•ism \'mänōthēˌizəm\ *n* **:** doctrine or belief that there is only one deity —**mono•the•ist** \-ˌthēist\ *n* —**mono•the•is•tic** \ˌmänōthē'istik\ *adj*

mono•tone \'mänəˌtōn\ *n* **:** succession of words in one unvarying tone

mo•not•o•nous \mə'nätənəs\ *adj* **1 :** sounded in one unvarying tone **2 :** tediously uniform —**mo•not•o•nous•ly** *adv* —**mo•not•o•nous•ness** *n* —**mo•not•o•ny** \-ənē\ *n*

mon•ox•ide \mə'näkˌsīd\ *n* **:** oxide containing one atom of oxygen in a molecule

mon•sieur \məs'yər, məsh-\ *n, pl* **mes•sieurs** \-yərz, māˈsyərz\ **:** man of high rank or station —used as a title for a man esp. of French nationality

mon•si•gnor \män'sēnyər\ *n, pl* **monsignors** *or* **mon•si•gno•ri** \ˌmänˌsēn'yōrē\ **:** Roman Catholic prelate —used as a title

mon•soon \män'sün\ *n* : periodic rainy season
mon•ster \'mänstər\ *n* 1 : abnormal or terrifying animal 2 : ugly, wicked, or cruel person —**mon•stros•i•ty** \män'sträsətē\ *n* —**mon•strous** \'mänstrəs\ *adj* —**mon•strous•ly** *adv*
mon•tage \män'täzh\ *n* : artistic composition of several different elements
month \'mənth\ *n* : 12th part of a year —**month•ly** *adv or adj or n*
mon•u•ment \'mänyəmənt\ *n* : structure erected in remembrance
mon•u•men•tal \ˌmänyə'mentᵊl\ *adj* 1 : serving as a monument 2 : outstanding 3 : very great —**mon•u•men•tal•ly** *adv*
moo \'mü\ *vb* : make the noise of a cow —**moo** *n*
mood \'müd\ *n* : state of mind or emotion
moody \'müdē\ *adj* **mood•i•er; -est** 1 : sad 2 : subject to changing moods and esp. to bad moods — **mood•i•ly** \'müdᵊlē\ *adv* —**mood•i•ness** \-ēnəs\ *n*
moon \'mün\ *n* : natural satellite (as of earth) —**moon•beam** *n* —**moon•light** *n* —**moon•lit** *adj*
moon•light \-ˌlīt\ *vb* **-ed; -ing** : hold a 2d job —**moon•light•er** *n*
moon•shine *n* 1 : moonlight 2 : meaningless talk 3 : illegally distilled liquor
1**moor** \'mu̇r\ *n* : open usu. swampy wasteland —**moor•land** \-lənd, -ˌland\ *n*
2**moor** *vb* : fasten with line or anchor
moor•ing \-iŋ\ *n* : place where boat can be moored
moose \'müs\ *n, pl* **moose** : large heavy-antlered deer
moot \'müt\ *adj* : open to question
mop \'mäp\ *n* : floor-cleaning implement ~ *vb* **-pp-** : use a mop on
mope \'mōp\ *vb* **moped; mop•ing** : be sad or listless
mo•ped \'mōˌped\ *n* : low-powered motorbike
mo•raine \mə'rān\ *n* : glacial deposit of earth and stones
mor•al \'mȯrəl\ *adj* 1 : relating to principles of right and wrong 2 : conforming to a standard of right behavior 3 : relating to or acting on the mind, character, or will ~ *n* 1 : point of a story 2 *pl* : moral practices or teachings —**mor•al•ist** \'mȯrəlist\ *n* —**mor•al•is•tic** \ˌmȯrə'listik\ *adj* —**mor•al•i•ty** \mə'ralətē\ *n* —**mor•al•ize** \'mȯrəˌlīz\ *vb* —**mor•al•ly** *adv*
mo•rale \mə'ral\ *n* : emotional attitude
mo•rass \mə'ras\ *n* : swamp
mor•a•to•ri•um \ˌmȯrə'tōrēəm\ *n, pl* **-riums** *or* **-ria** \-ēə\ : suspension of activity
mo•ray \'mȯrˌā, mə'rā\ *n* : savage eel
mor•bid \'mȯrbəd\ *adj* 1 : relating to disease 2 : gruesome —**mor•bid•i•ty** \mȯr'bidətē\ *n* —**mor•bid•ly** *adv* —**mor•bid•ness** *n*
mor•dant \'mȯrdᵊnt\ *adj* : sarcastic —**mor•dant•ly** *adv*
more \'mōr\ *adj* 1 : greater 2 : additional ~ *adv* 1 : in addition 2 : to a greater degree ~ *n* 1 : greater quantity 2 : additional amount ~ *pron* : additional ones
mo•rel \mə'rel\ *n* : pitted edible mushroom
more•over \mōr'ōvər\ *adv* : in addition
mo•res \'mȯrˌāz, -ēz\ *n, pl* : customs
morgue \'mȯrg\ *n* : temporary holding place for dead bodies
mor•i•bund \'mȯrəˌbənd\ *adj* : dying
morn \'mȯrn\ *n* : morning
morn•ing \'mȯrniŋ\ *n* : time from sunrise to noon
mo•ron \'mōrˌän\ *n* 1 : mentally retarded person 2 : very stupid person —**mo•ron•ic** \mə'ränik\ *adj* —**mo•ron•i•cal•ly** *adv*
mo•rose \mə'rōs\ *adj* : sullen —**mo•rose•ly** *adv* —**mo•rose•ness** *n*
mor•phine \'mȯrˌfēn\ *n* : addictive painkilling drug
mor•row \'märō\ *n* : next day
Morse code \'mȯrs-\ *n* : code of dots and dashes or long and short sounds used for transmitting messages
mor•sel \'mȯrsəl\ *n* : small piece or quantity
mor•tal \'mȯrtᵊl\ *adj* 1 : causing or subject to death 2 : extreme —**mortal** *n* —**mor•tal•i•ty** \mȯr'talətē\ *n* —**mor•tal•ly** \'mȯrtᵊlē\ *adv*
mor•tar \'mȯrtər\ *n* 1 : strong bowl 2 : short-barreled cannon 3 : masonry material used to cement bricks or stones in place —**mortar** *vb*
mort•gage \'mȯrgij\ *n* : transfer of property rights as security for a loan —**mortgage** *vb* —**mort•gag•ee** \ˌmȯrgi'jē\ *n* —**mort•ga•gor** \ˌmȯrgi'jȯr\ *n*
mor•ti•fy \'mȯrtəˌfī\ *vb* **-fied; -fy•ing** 1 : subdue by abstinence or self-inflicted pain 2 : humiliate —**mor•ti•fi•ca•tion** \ˌmȯrtəfə'kāshən\ *n*
mor•tu•ary \'mȯrchəˌwerē\ *n, pl* **-ar•ies** : place where dead bodies are kept until burial
mo•sa•ic \mō'zāik\ *n* : inlaid stone decoration —**mosaic** *adj*
Mos•lem \'mäzləm\ *var of* MUSLIM
mosque \'mäsk\ *n* : building where Muslims worship
mos•qui•to \mə'skētō\ *n, pl* **-toes** : biting bloodsucking insect
moss \'mȯs\ *n* : green seedless plant —**mossy** *adj*
most \'mōst\ *adj* 1 : majority of 2 : greatest ~ *adv* : to the greatest or a very great degree ~ *n* : greatest amount ~ *pron* : greatest number or part
-most \ˌmōst\ *adj suffix* : most : most toward
most•ly \'mōstlē\ *adv* : mainly
mote \'mōt\ *n* : small particle
mo•tel \mō'tel\ *n* : hotel with rooms accessible from the parking lot
moth \'mȯth\ *n* : small pale insect related to the butterflies
moth•er \'mət͟hər\ *n* 1 : female parent 2 : source ~ *vb* 1 : give birth to 2 : cherish or protect —**moth•er•hood** \-ˌhu̇d\ *n* —**moth•er•land** \-ˌland\ *n* —**moth•er•less** *adj* —**moth•er•ly** *adj*
moth•er–in–law *n, pl* **mothers–in–law** : spouse's mother
mo•tif \mō'tēf\ *n* : dominant theme
mo•tion \'mōshən\ *n* 1 : act or instance of moving 2 : proposal for action ~ *vb* : direct by a movement —**mo•tion•less** *adj* —**mo•tion•less•ly** *adv* —**mo•tion•less•ness** *n*
motion picture *n* : movie
mo•ti•vate \'mōtəˌvāt\ *vb* **-vat•ed; -vat•ing** : provide with a motive —**mo•ti•va•tion** \ˌmōtə'vāshən\ *n* —**mo•ti•va•tor** \'mōtəˌvātər\ *n*
mo•tive \'mōtiv\ *n* : cause of a person's action ~ *adj* 1 : moving to action 2 : relating to motion —**mo•tive•less** *adj*
mot•ley \'mätlē\ *adj* : of diverse colors or elements
mo•tor \'mōtər\ *n* : unit that supplies power or motion ~ *vb* : travel by automobile —**mo•tor•ist** \-ist\ *n* —**mo•tor•ize** \'mōtəˌrīz\ *vb*
mo•tor•bike *n* : lightweight motorcycle
mo•tor•boat *n* : engine-driven boat
mo•tor•car *n* : automobile
mo•tor•cy•cle *n* : 2-wheeled automotive vehicle —**mo•tor•cy•clist** *n*
mo•tor•truck *n* : automotive truck
mot•tle \'mätᵊl\ *vb* **-tled; -tling** : mark with spots of different color
mot•to \'mätō\ *n, pl* **-toes** : brief guiding rule
mould \'mōld\ *var of* MOLD
mound \'mau̇nd\ *n* : pile (as of earth)
1**mount** \'mau̇nt\ *n* : mountain
2**mount** *vb* 1 : increase in amount 2 : get up on 3 : put in position ~ *n* 1 : frame or support 2 : horse to ride —**mount•able** *adj* —**mount•er** *n*
moun•tain \'mau̇ntᵊn\ *n* : elevated land higher than a hill —**moun•tain•ous** \'mau̇ntᵊnəs\ *adj* —**moun•tain•top** *n*
moun•tain•eer \ˌmau̇ntᵊn'ir\ *n* : mountain resident or climber
moun•te•bank \'mau̇ntiˌbaŋk\ *n* : impostor
mourn \'mōrn\ *vb* : feel or express grief —**mourn•er** *n* —**mourn•ful** \-fəl\ *adj* —**mourn•ful•ly** *adv* —**mourn•ful•ness** *n* —**mourn•ing** *n*
mouse \'mau̇s\ *n, pl* **mice** \'mīs\ 1 : small rodent 2 : device for controlling cursor movement on a computer display —**mouse•trap** *n or vb* —**mousy, mous•ey** \'mau̇sē, -zē\ *adj*
mousse \'müs\ *n* 1 : light chilled dessert 2 : foamy hair-styling preparation
mous•tache \'məsˌtash, məs'tash\ *var of* MUSTACHE
mouth \'mau̇th\ *n* : opening through which an animal takes in food ~ \'mau̇t͟h\ *vb* 1 : speak 2 : repeat without comprehension or sincerity 3 : form soundlessly with the lips —**mouthed** \'mau̇t͟hd, 'mau̇tht\ *adj* —**mouth•ful** \-ˌfu̇l\ *n*
mouth•piece *n* 1 : part (as of a musical instrument) held in or to the mouth 2 : spokesman
mou•ton \'müˌtän\ *n* : processed sheepskin
move \'müv\ *vb* **moved; mov•ing** 1 : go or cause to go to another point 2 : change residence 3 : change or cause to change position 4 : take or cause to take action 5 : make a formal request 6 : stir the emotions ~ *n* 1 : act or instance of moving 2 : step taken to achieve a goal—**mov•able, move•able** \-əbəl\ *adj* —**move•ment** *n* —**mov•er** *n*
mov•ie \'müvē\ *n* : projected picture in which persons and objects seem to move
1**mow** \'mau̇\ *n* : part of a barn where hay or straw is stored
2**mow** \'mō\ *vb* **mowed; mowed** *or* **mown** \'mōn\; **mow•ing** : cut with a machine —**mow•er** *n*
Mr. \'mistər\ *n, pl* **Messrs.** \'mesərz\—conventional title for a man
Mrs. \'misəz, -əs, *esp South* 'mizəz, -əs\ *n, pl* **Mes•dames** \mā'däm, -'dam\ —conventional title for a married woman
Ms. \'miz\ *n* —conventional title for a woman
much \'məch\ *adj* **more** \'mōr\; **most** \'mōst\ : great in quantity, extent, or degree ~ *adv* **more; most** : to a great degree or extent ~ *n* : great quantity, extent, or degree
mu•ci•lage \'myüsəlij\ *n* : weak glue
muck \'mək\ *n* : manure, dirt, or mud —**mucky** *adj*
mu•cus \'myükəs\ *n* : slippery protective secretion of membranes (**mucous membranes**) lining body cavities —**mu•cous** \-kəs\ *adj*
mud \'məd\ *n* : soft wet earth —**mud•di•ly** \'mədᵊlē\ *adv* —**mud•di•ness** \-ēnəs\ *n* —**mud•dy** *adj or vb*
mud•dle \'mədᵊl\ *vb* **-dled; -dling** 1 : make, be, or act confused 2 : make a mess of —**muddle** *n* —**mud•dle•head•ed** \ˌmədᵊl'hedəd\ *adj*
mu•ez•zin \mü'ezᵊn, myü-\ *n* : Muslim who calls the hour of daily prayer
1**muff** \'məf\ *n* : tubular hand covering
2**muff** *vb* : bungle —**muff** *n*
muf•fin \'məfən\ *n* : soft cake baked in a cup-shaped container
muf•fle \'məfəl\ *vb* **-fled; -fling** 1 : wrap up 2 : dull the sound of —**muf•fler** \'məflər\ *n*
muf•ti \'məftē\ *n* : civilian clothes
1**mug** \'məg\ *n* : drinking cup ~ *vb* **-gg-** : make faces
2**mug** *vb* **-gg-** : assault with intent to rob —**mug•ger** *n*
mug•gy \'məgē\ *adj* **-gi•er; -est** : hot and humid —**mug•gi•ness** *n*
Mu•ham•mad•an \mō'hamədən, -'häm-; mü-\ *n* : Muslim —**Mu•ham•mad•an•ism** \-ˌizəm\ *n*
mu•lat•to \mu̇'lätō, -'lat-\ *n, pl* **-toes** *or* **-tos** : person of mixed black and white ancestry
mul•ber•ry \'məlˌberē\ *n* : tree with small edible fruit
mulch \'məlch\ *n* : protective ground covering —**mulch** *vb*
mulct \'məlkt\ *n or vb* : fine
1**mule** \'myül\ *n* 1 : offspring of a male ass and a female horse 2 : stubborn person —**mul•ish** \'myülish\ *adj* —**mul•ish•ly** *adv* —**mu•lish•ness** *n*
2**mule** *n* : backless shoe
mull \'məl\ *vb* : ponder
mul•let \'mələt\ *n, pl* **-let** *or* **-lets** : marine food fish
multi- *comb form* 1 : many or multiple 2 : many times over

multiarmed	**multimillion**
multibarreled	**multimillionaire**
multibillion	**multipart**
multibranched	**multipartite**
multibuilding	**multiparty**
multicenter	**multiplant**
multichambered	**multipolar**
multichannel	**multiproblem**
multicolored	**multiproduct**
multicounty	**multipurpose**
multicultural	**multiracial**
multidimensional	**multiroom**
multidirectional	**multisense**
multidisciplinary	**multiservice**
multidiscipline	**multisided**
multidivisional	**multispeed**
multifaceted	**multistage**
multifamily	**multistep**
multifilament	**multistory**
multifunction	**multisyllabic**
multifunctional	**multitalented**
multigrade	**multitrack**
multiheaded	**multiunion**
multihospital	**multiunit**
multihued	**multiuse**
multilane	**multivitamin**
multilevel	**multiwarhead**
multimedia	**multiyear**
multimember	

mul•ti•far•i•ous \ˌməltə'farēəs\ *adj* : diverse
mul•ti•lat•er•al \ˌməlti'latərəl, -ˌtī-\ *adj* : having many sides or participants
mul•ti•lin•gual \-'liŋgwəl\ *adj* : knowing or using several languages —**mul•ti•lin•gual•ism** \-gwəˌlizəm\ *n*
mul•ti•na•tion•al \-'nashənəl\ *adj* 1 : relating to several nations or nationalities 2 : having divisions in several countries —**multinational** *n*
mul•ti•ple \'məltəpəl\ *adj* 1 : several or many 2 : various ~ *n* : product of one number by another
multiple sclerosis \-sklə'rōsəs\ *n* : brain or spinal disease affecting muscle control
mul•ti•pli•ca•tion \ˌməltəplə'kāshən\ *n* 1 : increase 2 : short method of repeated addition
mul•ti•plic•i•ty \ˌməltə'plisətē\ *n, pl* **-ties** : great number or variety
mul•ti•ply \'məltəˌplī\ *vb* **-plied; -ply•ing** 1 : increase in number 2 : perform multiplication —**mul•ti•pli•er** \-ˌplīər\ *n*
mul•ti•tude \'məltəˌtüd, -ˌtyüd\ *n* : great number —**mul•ti•tu•di•nous** \ˌməltə'tüdᵊnəs, -'tyü-\ *adj*
1**mum** \'məm\ *adj* : silent
2**mum** *n* : chrysanthemum
mum•ble \'məmbəl\ *vb* **-bled; -bling** : speak indistinctly —**mumble** *n* —**mum•bler** *n*
mum•mer \'məmər\ *n* 1 : actor esp. in a pantomime 2 : disguised merrymaker —**mum•mery** *n*
mum•my \'məmē\ *n, pl* **-mies** : embalmed body —**mum•mi•fi•ca•tion** \ˌməmifə'kāshən\ *n* —**mum•mi•fy** \'məmiˌfī\ *vb*
mumps \'məmps\ *n sing or pl* : virus disease with swelling esp. of the salivary glands
munch \'mənch\ *vb* : chew
mun•dane \ˌmən'dān, 'mənˌ-\ *adj* 1 : relating to the world 2 : lacking concern for the ideal or spiritual —**mun•dane•ly** *adv*
mu•nic•i•pal \myu̇'nisəpəl\ *adj* : of or relating to a town or city —**mu•nic•i•pal•i•ty** \myu̇ˌnisə'palətē\ *n*
mu•nif•i•cent \myu̇'nifəsənt\ *adj* : generous —**mu•nif•i•cence** \-səns\ *n*
mu•ni•tion \myu̇'nishən\ *n* : armaments
mu•ral \'myu̇rəl\ *adj* : relating to a wall ~ *n* : wall painting —**mu•ral•ist** *n*
mur•der \'mərdər\ *n* : unlawful killing of a person ~ *vb* : commit a murder —**mur•der•er** *n* —**mur•der•ess** \-əs\ *n* —**mur•der•ous** \-əs\ *adj* —**mur•der•ous•ly** *adv*
murk \'mərk\ *n* : darkness —**murk•i•ly** \'mərkəlē\ *adv* —**murk•i•ness** \-kēnəs\ *n* —**murky** *adj*
mur•mur \'mərmər\ *n* 1 : muttered complaint 2 : low indistinct sound —**murmur** *vb* —**mur•mur•er** *n* —**mur•mur•ous** *adj*
mus•ca•tel \ˌməskə'tel\ *n* : sweet wine
mus•cle \'məsəl\ *n* 1 : body tissue capable of contracting to produce motion 2 : strength ~ *vb* **-cled; -cling** : force one's way —**mus•cled** *adj* —**mus•cu•lar** \'məskyələr\ *adj*—**mus•cu•lar•i•ty** \ˌməskyə'larətē\ *n*
muscular dystrophy *n* : disease marked by progressive wasting of muscles
mus•cu•la•ture \'məskyələˌchu̇r\ *n* : bodily muscles
1**muse** \'myüz\ *vb* **mused; mus•ing** : ponder —**mus•ing•ly** *adv*
2**muse** *n* : source of inspiration
mu•se•um \myu̇'zēəm\ *n* : institution displaying objects of interest
mush \'məsh\ *n* 1 : corn meal boiled in water or something of similar consistency 2 : sentimental nonsense —**mushy** *adj*
mush•room \'məshˌrüm, -ˌru̇m\ *n* : caplike organ of a fungus ~ *vb* : grow rapidly
mu•sic \'myüzik\ *n* : vocal or instrumental sounds —**mu•si•cal** \-zikəl\ *adj or n* —**mu•si•cal•ly** *adv*
mu•si•cian \myu̇'zishən\ *n* : composer or performer of music —**mu•si•cian•ly** *adj* —**mu•si•cian•ship** *n*
musk \'məsk\ *n* : strong-smelling substance from an Asiatic deer used in perfume —**musk•i•ness** \'məskēnəs\ *n* —**musky** *adj*
mus•kel•lunge \'məskəˌlənj\ *n, pl* **-lunge** : large No. American pike
mus•ket \'məskət\ *n* : former shoulder firearm —**mus•ke•teer** \ˌməskə'tir\ *n*
musk•mel•on \'məskˌmelən\ *n* : small edible melon
musk–ox \'məskˌäks\ *n* : shaggy-coated wild ox of the arctic
musk•rat \-ˌrat\ *n, pl* **-rat** *or* **-rats** : No. American aquatic rodent
Mus•lim \'məzləm, 'mu̇s-, 'mu̇z-\ *n* : adherent of Islam —**Muslim** *adj*
mus•lin \'məzlən\ *n* : cotton fabric
muss \'məs\ *n* : untidy state ~ *vb* : disarrange —**muss•i•ly** \'məsəlē\ *adv* —**muss•i•ness** \-ēnəs\ *n* —**mussy** *adj*
mus•sel \'məsəl\ *n* : edible mollusk
must \'məst\ *vb* —used as an auxiliary esp. to express a command, obligation, or necessity ~ \'məst\ *n* : something necessary
mus•tache \'məsˌtash, məs'-\ *n* : hair of the human upper lip
mus•tang \'məsˌtaŋ\ *n* : wild horse of Western America
mus•tard \'məstərd\ *n* : pungent yellow seasoning
mus•ter \'məstər\ *vb* 1 : assemble 2 : rouse ~ *n* : assembled group
musty \'məstē\ *adj* **mus•ti•er; -est** : stale —**must•i•ly** *adv* —**must•i•ness** *n*
mu•ta•ble \'myütəbəl\ *adj* : changeable —**mu•ta•bil•i•ty** \ˌmyütə'bilətē\ *n*
mu•tant \'myütᵊnt\ *adj* : relating to or produced by mutation —**mutant** *n*
mu•tate \'myüˌtāt\ *vb* **-tat•ed; -tat•ing** : undergo mutation —**mu•ta•tive** \'myüˌtātiv, 'myütət-\ *adj*
mu•ta•tion \myü'tāshən\ *n* : change in a hereditary character —**mu•ta•tion•al** *adj*
mute \'myüt\ *adj* **mut•er; mut•est** 1 : unable to speak 2 : silent ~ *n* 1 : one who is mute 2 : muffling device ~ *vb* **mut•ed; mut•ing** : muffle —**mute•ly** *adv* —**mute•ness** *n*
mu•ti•late \'myütᵊlˌāt\ *vb* **-lat•ed; -lat•ing** : damage seriously (as by cutting off or altering an essential part) —**mu•ti•la•tion** \ˌmyütᵊl'āshən\ *n* —**mu•ti•la•tor** \'myütᵊlˌātər\ *n*

mu•ti•ny \'myütənē\ n, pl -nies : rebellion —mu•ti•neer \ˌmyütən'ir\ n —mu•ti•nous \'myütənəs\ adj —mu•ti•nous•ly adv —mutiny vb
mutt \'mət\ n : mongrel
mut•ter \'mətər\ vb 1 : speak indistinctly or softly 2 : grumble —mutter n
mut•ton \'mətən\ n : flesh of a mature sheep —mut•tony adj
mu•tu•al \'myüchəwəl\ adj 1 : given or felt by one another in equal amount 2 : common —mu•tu•al•ly adv
muz•zle \'məzəl\ n 1 : nose and jaws of an animal 2 : muzzle covering to immobilize an animal's jaws 3 : discharge end of a gun ~ vb -zled; -zling : restrain with or as if with a muzzle
my \'mī\ adj 1 : relating to me or myself 2 —used interjectionally esp. to express surprise
my•nah, my•na \'mīnə\ n : dark crested Asian bird
my•o•pia \mī'ōpēə\ n : nearsightedness —my•o•pic \-'ōpik, -'äpik\ adj —my•o•pi•cal•ly adv
myr•i•ad \'mirēəd\ n : indefinitely large number —myriad adj
myrrh \'mər\ n : aromatic plant gum
myr•tle \'mərtəl\ n : shiny evergreen
my•self \mī'self\ pron : I, me —used reflexively or for emphasis
mys•tery \'mistərē\ n, pl -ter•ies 1 : religious truth 2 : something not understood 3 : puzzling or secret quality or state —mys•te•ri•ous \mis'tirēəs\ adj —mys•te•ri•ous•ly adv —mys•te•ri•ous•ness n
mys•tic \'mistik\ adj : mystical or mysterious ~ n : one who has mystical experiences —mys•ti•cism \-təˌsizəm\ n
mys•ti•cal \'mistikəl\ adj 1 : spiritual 2 : relating to direct communion with God —mys•ti•cal•ly adj
mys•ti•fy \'mistəˌfī\ vb -fied; -fy•ing : perplex —mys•ti•fi•ca•tion \ˌmistəfə'kāshən\ n
mys•tique \mis'tēk\ n : aura of mystery surrounding something
myth \'mith\ n 1 : legendary narrative explaining a belief or phenomenon 2 : imaginary person or thing —myth•i•cal \-ikəl\ adj
my•thol•o•gy \mith'äləjē\ n, pl -gies : body of myths —myth•o•log•i•cal \ˌmithə'läjikəl\ adj —my•thol•o•gist \mith'äləjist\ n

N

n \'en\ n, pl n's or ns \'enz\ : 14th letter of the alphabet
nab \'nab\ vb -bb- : seize or arrest
na•dir \'nāˌdir, 'nādər\ n : lowest point
1nag \'nag\ n : old or decrepit horse
2nag vb -gg- 1 : complain 2 : scold or urge continually 3 : be persistently annoying ~ n : one who nags habitually
na•iad \'nāəd, 'nī-, -ˌad\ n, pl -iads or -ia•des \-əˌdēz\ : mythological water nymph
nail \'nāl\ n 1 : horny sheath at the end of each finger and toe 2 : pointed metal fastener ~ vb : fasten with a nail —nail•er n
na•ive, na•ïve \nä'ēv\ adj -iv•er; -est 1 : innocent and unsophisticated 2 : easily deceived —na•ive•ly adv — na•ive•ness n
na•ïve•té \ˌnäˌēvə'tā, nä'ēvəˌ-\ n : quality or state of being naive
na•ked \'nākəd, 'nekəd\ adj 1 : having no clothes on 2 : uncovered 3 : plain or obvious 4 : unaided —na•ked•ly adv —na•ked•ness n
nam•by–pam•by \ˌnambē'pambē\ adj : weak or indecisive
name \'nām\ n 1 : word by which a person or thing is known 2 : disparaging word for someone 3 : distinguished reputation ~ vb named; nam•ing 1 : give a name to 2 : mention or identify by name 3 : nominate or appoint ~ adj 1 : relating to a name 2 : prominent —name•able adj —name•less adj —name•less•ly adv
name•ly \'nāmlē\ adv : that is to say
name•sake \-ˌsāk\ n : one named after another
1nap \'nap\ vb -pp- 1 : sleep briefly 2 : be off guard ~ n : short sleep
2nap n : soft downy surface —nap•less adj —napped \'napt\ adj
na•palm \'nāˌpälm, -ˌpäm\ n : gasoline in the form of a jelly
nape \'nāp, 'nap\ n : back of the neck
naph•tha \'nafthə\ n : flammable solvent
nap•kin \'napkən\ n : small cloth for use at the table
nar•cis•sism \'närsəˌsizəm\ n : self-love —nar•cis•sist \-sist\ n or adj —nar•cis•sis•tic \ˌnärsə'sistik\ adj
nar•cis•sus \när'sisəs\ n, pl -cis•sus or -cis•sus•es or -cis•si \-'sisˌī, -ˌē\ : plant with flowers usu. borne separately
nar•cot•ic \när'kätik\ n : painkilling addictive drug —narcotic adj
nar•rate \'narˌāt\ vb nar•rat•ed; nar•rat•ing : tell (a story) —nar•ra•tion \na'rāshən\ n —nar•ra•tive \'narətiv\ n or adj —nar•ra•tor \'narˌātər\ n
nar•row \'narō\ adj 1 : of less than standard width 2 : limited 3 : not liberal 4 : barely successful ~ vb : make narrow—nar•row•ly adv —nar•row•ness n
nar•row–mind•ed \ˌnarō'mīndəd\ adj : shallow, provincial, or bigoted
nar•rows \'narōz\ n pl : narrow passage
nar•whal \'närˌhwäl, 'närwəl\ n : sea mammal with a tusk
nasal \'nāzəl\ adj : relating to or uttered through the nose —na•sal•ly adv
nas•tur•tium \nə'stərshəm, na-\ n : herb with showy flowers
nas•ty \'nastē\ adj nas•ti•er; -est 1 : filthy 2 : indecent 3 : malicious or spiteful 4 : difficult or disagreeable 5 : unfair —nas•ti•ly \'nastəlē\ adv —nas•ti•ness \-tēnəs\ n
na•tal \'nātəl\ adj : relating to birth
na•tion \'nāshən\ n 1 : people of similar characteristics 2 : community with its own territory and government —na•tion•al \'nashənəl\ adj or n —na•tion•al•ly adv —na•tion•hood n —na•tion•wide adj
na•tion•al•ism \'nashənəlˌizəm\ n : devotion to national interests, unity, and independence —na•tion•al•ist \-ist\ n or adj —na•tion•al•is•tic \ˌnashənəl'istik\ adj
na•tion•al•i•ty \ˌnashə'nalətē\ n, pl -ties 1 : national character 2 : membership in a nation 3 : political independence 4 : ethnic group
na•tion•al•ize \'nashənəlˌīz\ vb -ized; -iz•ing 1 : make national 2 : place under government control —na•tion•al•i•za•tion \ˌnashənələ'zāshən\ n
na•tive \'nātiv\ adj 1 : belonging to a person at or by way of birth 2 : born or produced in a particular place ~ n : one who belongs to a country by birth
Na•tiv•i•ty \nə'tivətē, nā-\ n, pl -ties 1 : birth of Christ 2 not cap : birth
nat•ty \'natē\ adj -ti•er; -est : smartly dressed —nat•ti•ly \'natəlē\ adv —nat•ti•ness \-ēnəs\ n
nat•u•ral \'nachərəl\ adj 1 : relating to or determined by nature 2 : not artificial 3 : simple and sincere 4 : lifelike ~ n : one having an innate talent —nat•u•ral•ness n
nat•u•ral•ism \'nachərəˌlizəm\ n : realism in art and literature —nat•u•ral•is•tic \ˌnachərə'listik\ adj
nat•u•ral•ist \-list\ n 1 : one who practices naturalism 2 : student of animals or plants
nat•u•ral•ize \-ˌlīz\ vb -ized; -iz•ing 1 : become or cause to become established 2 : confer citizenship on —nat•u•ral•i•za•tion \ˌnachərələ'zāshən\ n
nat•u•ral•ly \'nachərəlē\ adv 1 : in a natural way 2 : as might be expected
na•ture \'nāchər\ n 1 : basic quality of something 2 : kind 3 : disposition 4 : physical universe 5 : natural environment
naught \'nȯt, 'nät\ n 1 : nothing 2 : zero
naugh•ty \'nȯtē, 'nät-\ adj -ti•er; -est 1 : disobedient or misbehaving 2 : improper —naught•i•ly \'nȯtəlē, 'nät-\ adv —naught•i•ness \-ēnəs\ n
nau•sea \'nȯzēə, -shə\ n 1 : sickness of the stomach with a desire to vomit 2 : extreme disgust —nau•seous \-shəs, -zēəs\ adj
nau•se•ate \'nȯzēˌāt, -zhē-, -sē-, -shē-\ vb -ated; -at•ing : affect or become affected with nausea —nau•se•at•ing•ly \-ˌātiŋlē\ adv
nau•ti•cal \'nȯtikəl\ adj : relating to ships and sailing —nau•ti•cal•ly adv
nau•ti•lus \'nȯtələs\ n, pl -lus•es or -li \-əlˌī, -ˌē\ : sea mollusk with a spiral shell
na•val \'nāvəl\ adj : relating to a navy
nave \'nāv\ n : central part of a church
na•vel \'nāvəl\ n : depression in the abdomen
nav•i•ga•ble \'navigəbəl\ adj : capable of being navigated —nav•i•ga•bil•i•ty \ˌnavigə'bilətē\ n
nav•i•gate \'navəˌgāt\ vb -gat•ed; -gat•ing 1 : sail on or through 2 : direct the course of —nav•i•ga•tion \ˌnavə'gāshən\ n —nav•i•ga•tor \'navəˌgātər\ n
na•vy \'nāvē\ n, pl -vies 1 : fleet 2 : nation's organization for sea warfare
nay \'nā\ adv : no—used in oral voting ~ n : negative vote
Na•zi \'nätsē, 'nat-\ n : member of a German fascist party from 1933 to 1945 —Nazi adj —Na•zism \'nätˌsizəm, 'nat-\, Na•zi•ism \-sēˌizəm\ n
near \'nir\ adv : at or close to ~ prep : close to ~ adj 1 : not far away 2 : very much like ~ vb : approach —near•ly adv —near•ness n
near•by \nir'bī, 'nirˌbī\ adv or adj : near
near•sight•ed \'nir'sītəd\ adj : seeing well at short distances only —nearsight•ed•ly adv —near•sight•ed•ness n
neat \'nēt\ adj 1 : not diluted 2 : tastefully simple 3 : orderly and clean —neat adv —neat•ly adv —neat•ness n
neb•u•la \'nebyələ\ n, pl -lae \-ˌlē, -ˌlī\ : large cloud of interstellar gas —neb•u•lar \-lər\ adj
neb•u•lous \-ləs\ adj : indistinct
nec•es•sary \'nesəˌserē\ n, pl -saries : indispensable item ~ adj 1 : inevitable 2 : compulsory 3 : positively needed —nec•es•sar•i•ly \ˌnesə'serəlē\ adv
ne•ces•si•tate \ni'sesəˌtāt\ vb -tat•ed; -tat•ing : make necessary
ne•ces•si•ty \ni'sesətē\ n, pl -ties 1 : very great need 2 : something that is necessary 3 : poverty 4 : circumstances that cannot be changed
neck \'nek\ n 1 : body part connecting the head and trunk 2 : part of a garment at the neck 3 : narrow part ~ vb : kiss and caress —necked \'nekt\ adj
neck•er•chief \'nekərchəf, -ˌchēf\ n, pl -chiefs \-chəfs, -ˌchēfs\ : cloth worn tied about the neck
neck•lace \'nekləs\ n : ornament worn around the neck
neck•tie n : ornamental cloth tied under a collar
nec•ro•man•cy \'nekrəˌmansē\ n : art of conjuring up the spirits of the dead —nec•ro•man•cer \-sər\ n
ne•cro•sis \nə'krōsəs, ne-\ n, pl -cro•ses \-ˌsēz\ : death of body tissue
nec•tar \'nektər\ n : sweet plant secretion
nec•tar•ine \ˌnektə'rēn\ n : smooth-skinned peach
née, nee \'nā\ adj—used to identify a married woman by maiden name
need \'nēd\ n 1 : obligation 2 : lack of something or what is lacking 3 : poverty ~ vb 1 : be in want 2 : have cause for 3 : be under obligation —need•ful \-fəl\ adj —need•less adj —need•less•ly adv —needy adj
nee•dle \'nēdəl\ n 1 : pointed sewing implement or something like it 2 : movable bar in a compass 3 : hollow instrument for injecting or withdrawing material ~ vb -dled; -dling : incite to action by repeated gibes —nee•dle•work \-ˌwərk\ n
nee•dle•point \'nēdəlˌpȯint\ n 1 : lace fabric 2 : embroidery on canvas —needlepoint adj
ne•far•i•ous \ni'farēəs\ adj : very wicked —ne•far•i•ous•ly adv
ne•gate \ni'gāt\ vb -gat•ed; -gat•ing 1 : deny 2 : nullify —ne•ga•tion \-'gāshən\ n
neg•a•tive \'negətiv\ adj 1 : marked by denial or refusal 2 : showing a lack of something suspected or desirable 3 : less than zero 4 : having more electrons than protons 5 : having light and shadow images reversed ~ n 1 : negative word or vote 2 : a negative number 3 : negative photographic image —neg•ative•ly adv —neg•a•tive•ness n —neg•a•tiv•i•ity \ˌnegə'tivətē\ n
ne•glect \ni'glekt\ vb 1 : disregard 2 : leave unattended to ~ n 1 : act of neglecting 2 : condition of being neglected —ne•glect•ful adj
neg•li•gee \ˌneglə'zhā\ n : woman's loose robe
neg•li•gent \'neglijənt\ adj : marked by neglect —neg•li•gence \-jəns\ n —neg•li•gent•ly adv
neg•li•gi•ble \'neglijəbəl\ adj : insignificant
ne•go•ti•ate \ni'gōshēˌāt\ vb -at•ed; -at•ing 1 : confer with another to settle a matter 2 : obtain cash for 3 : get through successfully —ne•go•tia•ble \-shəbəl, -shēə-\ adj —ne•go•ti•a•tion \-ˌgōshē'āshən, -shē'ā-\ n —ne•go•ti•a•tor \-'gōshēˌātər\ n
Ne•gro \'nēgrō\ n, pl -groes : member of the black race —Negro adj —Negroid \'nēˌgrȯid\ n or adj, often not cap
neigh \'nā\ n : cry of a horse —neigh vb
neigh•bor \'nābər\ n 1 : one living nearby 2 : fellowman ~ vb : be near or next to —neigh•bor•hood \-ˌhu̇d\ n —neigh•bor•li•ness n —neigh•bor•ly adv
nei•ther \'nēthər, 'nī-\ pron or adj : not the one or the other ~ conj 1 : not either 2 : nor
nem•e•sis \'neməsəs\ n, pl -e•ses \-əˌsēz\ 1 : old and usu. frustrating rival 2 : retaliation
ne•ol•o•gism \nē'äləˌjizəm\ n : new word
ne•on \'nēˌän\ n : gaseous colorless chemical element that emits a reddish glow in electric lamps —neon adj
neo•phyte \'nēəˌfīt\ n : beginner
neph•ew \'nefyü, chiefly Brit 'nev-\ n : a son of one's brother, sister, brother-in-law, or sister-in-law
nep•o•tism \'nepəˌtizəm\ n : favoritism shown in hiring a relative
nerd \'nərd\ n : one who is not stylish or socially at ease —nerdy adj
nerve \'nərv\ n 1 : strand of body tissue that connects the brain with other parts of the body 2 : self-control 3 : daring 4 pl : nervousness —nerved \'nərvd\ adj —nerve•less adj
ner•vous \'nərvəs\ adj 1 : relating to or made up of nerves 2 : easily excited 3 : timid or fearful —ner•vous•ly adv —ner•vous•ness n
nervy \'nərvē\ adj nerv•i•er; -est : insolent or presumptuous
-ness \nəs\ n suffix : condition or quality
nest \'nest\ n 1 : shelter prepared by a bird for its eggs 2 : place where eggs (as of insects or fish) are laid and hatched 3 : snug retreat 4 : set of objects fitting one inside or under another ~ vb : build or occupy a nest
nes•tle \'nesəl\ vb -tled; -tling : settle snugly (as in a nest)
1net \'net\ n : fabric with spaces between strands or something made of this ~ vb -tt- : cover with or catch in a net
2net adj : remaining after deductions ~ vb -tt- : have as profit
neth•er \'nethər\ adj : situated below
net•tle \'netəl\ n : coarse herb with stinging hairs ~ vb -tled; -tling : provoke or vex —net•tle•some adj
net•work n : system of crossing or connected elements
neu•ral \'nu̇rəl, 'nyu̇r-\ adj : relating to a nerve
neu•ral•gia \nu̇'raljə, nyu̇-\ n : pain along a nerve —neu•ral•gic \-jik\ adj
neu•ri•tis \nu̇'rītəs, nyu̇-\ n, pl -rit•i•des \-'ritəˌdēz\ or -ri•tis•es : inflammation of a nerve
neu•rol•o•gy \nu̇'räləjē, nyu̇-\ n : study of the nervous system —neu•ro•log•i•cal \ˌnu̇rə'läjikəl, ˌnyu̇r-\, neu•ro•log•ic \-ik\ adj —neu•rol•o•gist \nu̇'räləjist, nyu̇-\ n
neu•ro•sis \nu̇'rōsəs, nyu̇-\ n, pl -ro•ses \-ˌsēz\ : nervous disorder
neu•rot•ic \nu̇'rätik, nyu̇-\ adj : relating to neurosis ~ n : unstable person —neu•rot•i•cal•ly adv
neu•ter \'nütər, 'nyü-\ adj : neither masculine nor feminine ~ vb : castrate or spay
neu•tral \-trəl\ adj 1 : not favoring either side 2 : being neither one thing nor the other 3 : not decided in color 4 : not electrically charged ~ n 1 : one that is neutral 2 : position of gears that are not engaged —neu•tral•i•za•tion \ˌnütrələ'zāshən, ˌnyü-\ n —neu•tral•ize \'nütrəˌlīz, 'nyü-\ vb
neu•tral•i•ty \nü'tralətē, nyü-\ n : state of being neutral
neu•tron \'nüˌträn, 'nyü-\ n : uncharged atomic particle
nev•er \'nevər\ adv 1 : not ever 2 : not in any degree, way, or condition
nev•er•more adv : never again
nev•er•the•less adv : in spite of that
new \'nü, 'nyü\ adj 1 : not old or familiar 2 : different from the former 3 : recently discovered or learned 4 : not accustomed 5 : refreshed or regenerated 6 : being such for the first time ~ adv : newly —new•ish adj —new•ness n
new•born adj 1 : recently born 2 : born anew ~ n, pl -born or -borns : newborn individual
new•ly \-lē\ adv : recently
news \'nüz, 'nyüz\ n : report of recent events —news•let•ter n —news•mag•a•zine n —news•man \-mən, -ˌman\ n —news•pa•per n —news•pa•per•man \-ˌman\ n —news•stand n —news•wom•an \-ˌwu̇mən\ n —news•wor•thy adj
news•cast \-ˌkast\ n : broadcast of news —news•cast•er \-ˌkastər\ n
news•print n : paper made from wood pulp
newsy \'nüzē, 'nyü-\ adj news•i•er; -est : filled with news
newt \'nüt, 'nyüt\ n : small salamander
New Year n : New Year's Day
New Year's Day n : January 1 observed as a legal holiday
next \'nekst\ adj : immediately preceding or following ~ adv 1 : in the time or place nearest 2 : at the first time yet to come ~ prep : nearest to
nex•us \'neksəs\ n, pl -us•es \-səsəz\ or -us \-səs, -ˌsüs\ : connection
nib \'nib\ n : pen point
nib•ble \'nibəl\ vb -bled; -bling : bite gently or bit by bit ~ n : small bite
nice \'nīs\ adj nic•er; nic•est 1 : fastidious 2 : very precise or delicate 3 : pleasing 4 : respectable —nice•ly adv —nice•ness n

nice•ty \ˈnīsətē\ *n, pl* **-ties** **1 :** dainty or elegant thing **2 :** fine detail **3 :** exactness
niche \ˈnich\ *n* **1 :** recess in a wall **2 :** fitting place, work, or use
nick \ˈnik\ *n* **1 :** small broken area or chip **2 :** critical moment ~ *vb* **:** make a nick in
nick•el \ˈnikəl\ *n* **1 :** hard silver-white metallic chemical element used in alloys **2 :** U.S. 5-cent piece
nick•name \ˈnikˌnām\ *n* **:** informal substitute name **—nickname** *vb*
nic•o•tine \ˈnikəˌtēn\ *n* **:** poisonous and addictive substance in tobacco
niece \ˈnēs\ *n* **:** a daughter of one's brother, sister, brother-in-law, or sister-in-law
nig•gard•ly \ˈnigərdlē\ *adj* **:** stingy **—nig•gard** *n* **—nig•gard•li•ness** *n*
nig•gling \ˈnigəliŋ\ *adj* **:** petty and annoying
nigh \ˈnī\ *adv or adj or prep* **:** near
night \ˈnīt\ *n* **1 :** period between dusk and dawn **2 :** the coming of night **—night** *adj* **—night•ly** *adj or adv* **—night•time** *n*
night•clothes *n pl* **:** garments worn in bed
night•club \-ˌkləb\ *n* **:** place for drinking and entertainment open at night
night crawler *n* **:** earthworm
night•fall *n* **:** the coming of night
night•gown *n* **:** gown worn for sleeping
night•in•gale \ˈnītᵊnˌgāl, -iŋ-\ *n* **:** Old World thrush that sings at night
night•mare \ˈnītˌmar\ *n* **:** frightening dream **—nightmare** *adj* **—night•mar•ish** \-ˌmarish\ *adj*
night•shade \ˈnītˌshād\ *n* **:** group of plants that include poisonous forms and food plants (as the potato and eggplant)
nil \ˈnil\ *n* **:** nothing
nim•ble \ˈnimbəl\ *adj* **-bler; -blest 1 :** agile **2 :** clever **—nim•ble•ness** *n* **—nim•bly** \-blē\ *adv*
nine \ˈnīn\ *n* **1 :** one more than 8 **2 :** 9th in a set or series **—nine** *adj or pron* **—ninth** \ˈnīnth\ *adj or adv or n*
nine•pins *n* **:** bowling game using 9 pins
nine•teen \nīnˈtēn\ *n* **:** one more than 18 **—nineteen** *adj or pron* **—nine•teenth** \-ˈtēnth\ *adj or n*
nine•ty \ˈnīntē\ *n, pl* **-ties :** 9 times 10 **—nine•ti•eth** \-ēəth\ *adj or n* **—ninety** *adj or pron*
nin•ny \ˈninē\ *n, pl* **nin•nies :** fool
¹nip \ˈnip\ *vb* **-pp- 1 :** catch hold of and squeeze tightly **2 :** pinch or bite off **3 :** destroy the growth or fulfillment of ~ *n* **1 :** biting cold **2 :** tang **3 :** pinch or bite
²nip *n* **:** small quantity of liquor ~ *vb* **-pp- :** take liquor in nips
nip•per \ˈnipər\ *n* **1 :** one that nips **2** *pl* **:** pincers **3 :** small boy
nip•ple \ˈnipəl\ *n* **:** tip of the breast or something resembling it
nip•py \ˈnipē\ *adj* **-pi•er; -est 1 :** pungent **2 :** chilly
nir•va•na \nirˈvänə\ *n* **:** state of blissful oblivion
nit \ˈnit\ *n* **:** egg of a parasitic insect
ni•ter \ˈnītər\ *n* **:** potassium nitrate used in gunpowder or fertilizer or in curing meat
ni•trate \ˈnīˌtrāt, -trət\ *n* **:** chemical salt used esp. in curing meat
ni•tric acid \ˈnītrik-\ *n* **:** liquid acid used in making dyes, explosives, and fertilizers
ni•trite \-ˌtrīt\ *n* **:** chemical salt used in curing meat
ni•tro•gen \ˈnītrəjən\ *n* **:** tasteless odorless gaseous chemical element
ni•tro•glyc•er•in, ni•tro•glyc•er•ine \ˌnītrōˈglisərən\ *n* **:** heavy oily liquid used as an explosive and as a blood-vessel relaxer
nit•wit \ˈnitˌwit\ *n* **:** stupid person
no \ˈnō\ *adv* **1**—used to express the negative **2 :** in no respect or degree **3 :** not so **4**—used as an interjection of surprise or doubt ~ *adj* **1 :** not any **2 :** not a ~ *n, pl* **noes** *or* **nos** \ˈnōz\ **1 :** refusal **2 :** negative vote
no•bil•i•ty \nōˈbilətē\ *n* **1 :** quality or state of being noble **2 :** class of people of noble rank
no•ble \ˈnōbəl\ *adj* **-bler; -blest 1 :** illustrious **2 :** aristocratic **3 :** stately **4 :** of outstanding character ~ *n* **:** nobleman **—no•ble•ness** *n* **—no•bly** *adv*
no•ble•man \-mən\ *n* **:** member of the nobility
no•ble•wom•an \-ˌwu̇mən\ *n* **:** a woman of noble rank
no•body \ˈnōbədē, -ˌbädē\ *pron* **:** no person ~ *n, pl* **-bod•ies :** person of no influence or importance
noc•tur•nal \näkˈtərnᵊl\ *adj* **:** relating to, occurring at, or active at night
noc•turne \ˈnäkˌtərn\ *n* **:** dreamy musical composition
nod \ˈnäd\ *vb* **-dd- 1 :** bend the head downward or forward (as in bowing or going to sleep or as a sign of assent) **2 :** move up and down **3 :** show by a nod of the head **—nod** *n*
node \ˈnōd\ *n* **:** stem part from which a leaf arises **—nod•al** \-ᵊl\ *adj*
nod•ule \ˈnäjül\ *n* **:** small lump or swelling **—nod•u•lar** \ˈnäjələr\ *adj*
no•el \nōˈel\ *n* **1 :** Christmas carol **2** *cap* **:** Christmas season
noes *pl of* NO
nog•gin \ˈnägən\ *n* **1 :** small mug **2 :** person's head
no•how \ˈnōˌhau̇\ *adv* **:** in no manner
noise \ˈnȯiz\ *n* **:** loud or unpleasant sound ~ *vb* **noised; nois•ing :** spread by rumor **—noise•less** *adj* **—noise•less•ly** *adv* **—noise•mak•er** *n* **—nois•i•ly** \ˈnȯizəlē\ *adv* **—nois•i•ness** \-zēnəs\ *n* **—noisy** \ˈnȯizē\ *adj*
noi•some \ˈnȯisəm\ *adj* **:** harmful or offensive
no•mad \ˈnōˌmad\ *n* **:** one who has no permanent home **—nomad** *adj* **—no•mad•ic** \nōˈmadik\ *adj*
no•men•cla•ture \ˈnōmənˌklāchər\ *n* **:** system of names
nom•i•nal \ˈnämənᵊl\ *adj* **1 :** being something in name only **2 :** small or negligible **—nom•i•nal•ly** *adv*
nom•i•nate \ˈnäməˌnāt\ *vb* **-nat•ed; -nat•ing :** propose or choose as a candidate **—nom•i•na•tion** \ˌnäməˈnāshən\ *n*
nom•i•na•tive \ˈnämənətiv\ *adj* **:** relating to or being a grammatical case marking typically the subject of a verb **—nominative** *n*
nom•i•nee \ˌnäməˈnē\ *n* **:** person nominated
non- \ˈnän, ˌnän\ *prefix* **1 :** not, reverse of, or absence of **2 :** not important

nonabrasive
nonabsorbent
nonacademic
nonaccredited
nonacid
nonaddictive
nonadhesive
nonadjacent
nonadjustable
nonaffiliated
nonaggression
nonalcoholic
nonaligned
nonappearance
nonautomatic
nonbeliever
nonbinding
nonbreakable
noncancerous
noncandidate
non-Catholic
non-Christian
nonchurchgoer
noncitizen
nonclassical
nonclassified
noncombat
noncombatant
noncombustible
noncommercial
noncommunist
noncompliance
nonconflicting
nonconforming
nonconsecutive
nonconstructive
noncontagious
noncontrollable
noncontroversial
noncorrosive
noncriminal
noncritical
noncumulative
noncurrent
nondeductible
nondeferrable
nondegradable
nondelivery
nondemocratic
nondenominational
nondestructive
nondiscrimination
nondiscriminatory
noneducational
nonelastic
nonelected
nonelective
nonelectric
nonelectronic
nonemotional
nonenforcement
nonessential
nonexclusive
nonexistence
nonexistent
nonexplosive
nonfat
nonfatal
nonfattening
nonfictional
nonflammable
nonflowering
nonfunctional
nongovernmental
nongraded
nonhazardous
nonhereditary
nonindustrial
nonindustrialized
noninfectious
noninflationary
nonintegrated
nonintellectual
noninterference
nonintoxicating
noninvasive
non-Jewish
nonlegal
nonlethal
nonliterary
nonliving
nonmagnetic
nonmalignant
nonmedical
nonmember
nonmetal
nonmetallic
nonmilitary
nonmusical
nonnative
nonnegotiable
nonobjective
nonobservance
nonorthodox
nonparallel
nonparticipant
nonparticipating
nonpaying
nonpayment
nonperformance
nonperishable
nonphysical
nonpoisonous
nonpolitical
nonpolluting
nonporous
nonpregnant
nonproductive
nonprofessional
nonprofit
nonracial
nonradioactive
nonrated
nonrealistic
nonrecurring
nonrefillable
nonrefundable
nonreligious
nonrenewable
nonrepresentative
nonresident
nonresponsive
nonrestricted
nonreversible
nonsalable
nonscientific
nonscientist
nonsegregated
non-self-governing
nonsexist
nonsexual
nonsignificant
nonskier
nonsmoker
nonsmoking
nonspeaking
nonspecialist
nonspecific
nonstandard
nonstick
nonstop
nonstrategic
nonstudent
nonsugar
nonsurgical
nonswimmer
nontaxable
nonteaching
nontechnical
nontoxic
nontraditional
nontransferable
nontropical
nontypical
nonunion
nonuser
nonvenomous
nonverbal
nonvoter
nonwhite
nonworker

non•age \ˈnänij, ˈnōnij\ *n* **:** period of youth and esp. legal minority
nonce \ˈnäns\ *n* **:** present occasion ~ *adj* **:** occurring, used, or made only once
non•cha•lant \ˌnänshəˈlänt\ *adj* **:** showing indifference **—non•cha•lance** \-ˈläns\ *n* **—non•cha•lant•ly** *adv*
non•com•mis•sioned officer \ˌnänkəˈmishənd-\ *n* **:** subordinate officer in the armed forces appointed from enlisted personnel
non•com•mit•tal \ˌnänkəˈmitᵊl\ *adj* **:** indicating neither consent nor dissent
non•con•duc•tor *n* **:** substance that is a very poor conductor
non•con•form•ist *n* **:** one who does not conform to an established belief or mode of behavior **—non•con•for•mi•ty** *n*
non•de•script \ˌnändiˈskript\ *adj* **:** lacking distinctive qualities
none \ˈnən\ *pron* **:** not any ~ *adv* **:** not at all
non•en•ti•ty *n* **:** one of no consequence
none•the•less \ˌnən<u>th</u>əˈles\ *adv* **:** nevertheless
non•pa•reil \ˌnänpəˈrel\ *adj* **:** having no equal ~ *n* **1 :** one who has no equal **2 :** chocolate candy disk
non•par•ti•san *adj* **:** not influenced by political party bias
non•per•son *n* **:** person without social or legal status
non•plus \ˌnänˈpləs\ *vb* **-ss- :** perplex
non•pre•scrip•tion *adj* **:** available without a doctor's prescription
non•pro•lif•er•a•tion *adj* **:** aimed at ending increased use of nuclear arms
non•sched•uled *adj* **:** licensed to carry by air without a regular schedule
non•sense \ˈnänˌsens, -səns\ *n* **:** foolish or meaningless words or actions **—non•sen•si•cal** \nänˈsensikəl\ *adj* **—non•sen•si•cal•ly** *adv*
non•sup•port *n* **:** failure in a legal obligation to provide for someone's needs
non•vi•o•lence *n* **:** avoidance of violence esp. in political demonstrations **—non•vi•o•lent** *adj*
noo•dle \ˈnüdᵊl\ *n* **:** ribbon-shaped food paste
nook \ˈnu̇k\ *n* **1 :** inside corner **2 :** private place
noon \ˈnün\ *n* **:** middle of the day **—noon** *adj*
noon•day \-ˌdā\ *n* **:** noon
no one *pron* **:** no person
noon•time *n* **:** noon
noose \ˈnüs\ *n* **:** rope loop that slips down tight
nor \nȯr\ *conj* **:** and not—used esp. after *neither* to introduce and negate the 2d member of a series
norm \ˈnȯrm\ *n* **1 :** standard usu. derived from an average **2 :** typical widespread practice or custom
nor•mal \ˈnȯrməl\ *adj* **:** average, regular, or standard **—nor•mal•cy** \-sē\ *n* **—nor•mal•i•ty** \nȯrˈmalətē\ *n* **—nor•mal•i•za•tion** \ˌnȯrmələˈzāshən\ *n* **—nor•mal•ize** \ˈnȯrməˌlīz\ *vb* **—nor•mal•ly** *adv*
north \ˈnȯrth\ *adv* **:** to or toward the north ~ *adj* **:** situated toward, at, or coming from the north ~ *n* **1 :** direction to the left of one facing east **2** *cap* **:** regions to the north **—north•er•ly** \ˈnȯr<u>th</u>ərlē\ *adv or adj* **—north•ern** \-ərn\ *adj* **—North•ern•er** *n* **—north•ern•most** \-ˌmōst\ *adj* **—north•ward** \-wərd\ *adv or adj* **—north•wards** \-wərdz\ *adv*
north•east \nȯrthˈēst\ *n* **1 :** direction between north and east **2** *cap* **:** regions to the northeast **—northeast** *adj or adv* **—north•east•er•ly** \-ərlē\ *adv or adj* **—north•east•ern** \-ərn\ *adj*
northern lights *n pl* **:** aurora borealis
north pole *n* **:** northernmost point of the earth
north•west \-ˈwest\ *n* **1 :** direction between north and west **2** *cap* **:** regions to the northwest **—northwest** *adj or adv* **—north•west•er•ly** \-ərlē\ *adv or adj* **—north•west•ern** \-ərn\ *adj*
nose \ˈnōz\ *n* **1 :** part of the face containing the nostrils **2 :** sense of smell **3 :** front part ~ *vb* **nosed; nos•ing 1 :** detect by smell **2 :** push aside with the nose **3 :** pry **4 :** inch ahead **—nose•bleed** *n* **—nosed** \ˈnōzd\ *adj* **—nose out** *vb* **:** narrowly defeat
nose•gay \-ˌgā\ *n* **:** small bunch of flowers
nos•tal•gia \näˈstaljə, nə-\ *n* **:** wistful yearning for something past **—nos•tal•gic** \-jik\ *adj*
nos•tril \ˈnästrəl\ *n* **:** opening of the nose
nos•trum \-trəm\ *n* **:** questionable remedy
nosy, nos•ey \ˈnōzē\ *adj* **nos•i•er; -est :** tending to pry
not \ˈnät\ *adv*—used to make a statement negative
no•ta•ble \ˈnōtəbəl\ *adj* **1 :** noteworthy **2 :** distinguished ~ *n* **:** notable person **—no•ta•bil•i•ty** \ˌnōtəˈbilətē\ *n* **—no•ta•bly** \ˈnōtəblē\ *adv*
no•ta•rize \ˈnōtəˌrīz\ *vb* **-rized; -riz•ing :** attest as a notary public
no•ta•ry public \ˈnōtərē-\ *n, pl* **-ries public** *or* **-ry publics :** public official who attests writings to make them legally authentic
no•ta•tion \nōˈtāshən\ *n* **1 :** note **2 :** act, process, or method of marking things down
notch \ˈnäch\ *n* **:** V-shaped hollow **—notch** *vb*
note \ˈnōt\ *vb* **not•ed; not•ing 1 :** notice **2 :** write down ~ *n* **1 :** musical tone **2 :** written comment or record **3 :** short informal letter **4 :** notice or heed **—note•book** *n*
not•ed \ˈnōtəd\ *adj* **:** famous
note•wor•thy \-ˌwər<u>th</u>ē\ *adj* **:** worthy of special mention
noth•ing \ˈnəthiŋ\ *pron* **1 :** no thing **2 :** no part **3 :** one of no value or importance ~ *adv* **:** not at all ~ *n* **1 :** something that does not exist **2 :** zero **3 :** one of little or no importance **—noth•ing•ness** *n*
no•tice \ˈnōtəs\ *n* **1 :** warning or announcement **2 :** attention ~ *vb* **-ticed; -tic•ing :** take notice of **—no•tice•able** *adj* **—no•tice•ably** *adv*
no•ti•fy \ˈnōtəˌfī\ *vb* **-fied; -fy•ing :** give notice of or to **—no•ti•fi•ca•tion** \ˌnōtəfəˈkāshən\ *n*
no•tion \ˈnōshən\ *n* **1 :** idea or opinion **2 :** whim
no•to•ri•ous \nōˈtōrēəs\ *adj* **:** widely and unfavorably known **—no•to•ri•ety** \ˌnōtəˈrīətē\ *n* **—no•to•ri•ous•ly** *adv*
not•with•stand•ing \ˌnätwithˈstandiŋ, -wi<u>th</u>-\ *prep* **:** in spite of ~ *adv* **:** nevertheless ~ *conj* **:** although
nou•gat \ˈnügət\ *n* **:** nuts or fruit pieces in a sugar paste
nought \ˈnȯt, ˈnät\ *var of* NAUGHT
noun \ˈnau̇n\ *n* **:** word that is the name of a person, place, or thing
nour•ish \ˈnərish\ *vb* **:** promote the growth of **—nour•ish•ing** *adj* **—nour•ish•ment** *n*
no•va \ˈnōvə\ *n, pl* **-vas** *or* **-vae** \-ˌvē, -ˌvī\ **:** star that suddenly brightens and then fades gradually
nov•el \ˈnävəl\ *adj* **:** new or strange ~ *n* **:** long invented prose story **—nov•el•ist** \-əlist\ *n*
nov•el•ty \ˈnävəltē\ *n, pl* **-ties 1 :** something new or unusual **2 :** newness **3 :** small manufactured article—usu. pl.
No•vem•ber \nōˈvembər\ *n* **:** 11th month of the year having 30 days
nov•ice \ˈnävəs\ *n* **1 :** one preparing to take vows in a religious order **2 :** one who is inexperienced or untrained
no•vi•tiate \nōˈvishət, nə-\ *n* **:** period or state of being a novice
now \ˈnau̇\ *adv* **1 :** at the present time or moment **2 :** forthwith **3 :** under these circumstances ~ *conj* **:** in view of the fact ~ *n* **:** present time
now•a•days \ˈnau̇əˌdāz\ *adv* **:** now
no•where \-ˌhwer\ *adv* **:** not anywhere **—no•where** *n*
nox•ious \ˈnäkshəs\ *adj* **:** harmful
noz•zle \ˈnäzəl\ *n* **:** device to direct or control a flow of fluid
nu•ance \ˈnüˌäns, ˈnyü-\ *n* **:** subtle distinction or variation
nub \ˈnəb\ *n* **1 :** knob or lump **2 :** gist
nu•bile \ˈnüˌbīl, ˈnyü-, -bəl\ *adj* **1 :** of marriageable condition or age **2 :** sexually attractive
nu•cle•ar \ˈnüklēər, ˈnyü-\ *adj* **1 :** relating to the atomic nucleus or atomic energy **2 :** relating to a weapon whose power is from a nuclear reaction
nu•cle•us \ˈnüklēəs, ˈnyü-\ *n, pl* **-clei** \-klēˌī\ **:** central mass or part (as of a cell or an atom)
nude \ˈnüd, ˈnyüd\ *adj* **nud•er; nud•est :** naked ~ *n* **:** nude human figure **—nu•di•ty** \ˈnüdətē, ˈnyü-\ *n*
nudge \ˈnəj\ *vb* **nudged; nudg•ing :** touch or push gently **—nudge** *n*
nud•ism \ˈnüdˌizəm, ˈnyü-\ *n* **:** practice of going nude **—nud•ist** \ˈnüdist, ˈnyü-\ *n*
nug•get \ˈnəgət\ *n* **:** lump of gold
nui•sance \ˈnüsᵊns, ˈnyü-\ *n* **:** something annoying
null \ˈnəl\ *adj* **:** having no legal or binding force **—nul•li•ty** \ˈnələtē\ *n*
nul•li•fy \ˈnələˌfī\ *vb* **-fied; -fy•ing :** make null or valueless **—nul•li•fi•ca•tion** \ˌnələfəˈkāshən\ *n*
numb \ˈnəm\ *adj* **:** lacking feeling **—numb** *vb* **—numb•ly** *adv* **—numb•ness** *n*
num•ber \ˈnəmbər\ *n* **1 :** total of individuals taken together **2 :** indefinite total **3 :** unit of a mathematical system **4 :** numeral **5 :** one in a sequence ~ *vb* **1 :** count **2 :** assign a number to **3 :** comprise in number **—num•ber•less** *adj*
nu•mer•al \ˈnümərəl, ˈnyü-\ *n* **:** conventional symbol representing a number

nu•mer•a•tor \ˈnüməˌrātər, ˈnyü-\ *n* : part of a fraction above the line

nu•mer•i•cal \nu̇ˈmerikəl, nyu̇-\, **nu•meric** \-ˈmerik\ *adj* **1** : relating to numbers **2** : expressed in or involving numbers —**nu•mer•i•cal•ly** *adv*

nu•mer•ol•o•gy \ˌnüməˈräləjē, ˌnyü-\ *n* : occult study of numbers —**nu•mer•ol•o•gist** \-jist\ *n*

nu•mer•ous \ˈnümərəs, ˈnyü-\ *adj* : consisting of a great number

nu•mis•mat•ics \ˌnüməzˈmatiks, ˌnyü-\ *n* : study or collection of monetary objects —**nu•mis•mat•ic** \-ik\ *adj* —**nu•mis•ma•tist** \nüˈmizmətist, nyü-\ *n*

num•skull \ˈnəmˌskəl\ *n* : stupid person

nun \ˈnən\ *n* : woman belonging to a religious order —**nun•nery** \-ərē\ *n*

nup•tial \ˈnəpshəl\ *adj* : relating to marriage or a wedding ~ *n* : marriage or wedding—usu. pl.

nurse \ˈnərs\ *n* **1** : one hired to care for children **2** : person trained to care for sick people ~ *vb* **nursed; nurs•ing 1** : suckle **2** : care for

nurs•ery \ˈnərsərē\ *n, pl* **-er•ies 1** : place where children are cared for **2** : place where young plants are grown

nursing home *n* : private establishment providing care for persons who are unable to care for themselves

nur•ture \ˈnərchər\ *n* **1** : training or upbringing **2** : food or nourishment ~ *vb* **-tured; -tur•ing 1** : care for or feed **2** : educate

nut \ˈnət\ *n* **1** : dry hard-shelled fruit or seed with a firm inner kernel **2** : metal block with a screw hole through it **3** : foolish, eccentric, or crazy person **4** : enthusiast —**nut•crack•er** *n* —**nut•shell** *n* —**nut•ty** *adj*

nut•hatch \ˈnətˌhach\ *n* : small bird

nut•meg \ˈnətˌmeg, -ˌmāg\ *n* : nutlike aromatic seed of a tropical tree

nu•tri•ent \ˈnütrēənt, ˈnyü-\ *n* : something giving nourishment —**nutrient** *adj*

nu•tri•ment \-trəmənt\ *n* : nutrient

nu•tri•tion \nu̇ˈtrishən, nyu̇-\ *n* : act or process of nourishing esp. with food —**nu•tri•tion•al** \-ˈtrishənəl\ *adj* —**nu•tri•tious** \-ˈtrishəs\ *adj* —**nu•tri•tive** \ˈnütrətiv, ˈnyü-\ *adj*

nuts \ˈnəts\ *adj* **1** : enthusiastic **2** : crazy

nuz•zle \ˈnəzəl\ *vb* **-zled; -zling 1** : touch with or as if with the nose **2** : snuggle

ny•lon \ˈnīˌlän\ *n* **1** : tough synthetic material used esp. in textiles **2** *pl* : stockings made of nylon

nymph \ˈnimf\ *n* **1** : lesser goddess in ancient mythology **2** : girl **3** : immature insect

O

o \ˈō\ *n, pl* **o's** *or* **os** \ˈōz\ **1** : 15th letter of the alphabet **2** : zero

O *var of* OH

oaf \ˈōf\ *n* : stupid or awkward person —**oaf•ish** \ˈōfish\ *adj*

oak \ˈōk\ *n, pl* **oaks** *or* **oak** : tree bearing a thin-shelled nut or its wood —**oak•en** \ˈōkən\ *adj*

oar \ˈōr\ *n* : pole with a blade at the end used to propel a boat

oar•lock \-ˌläk\ *n* : u-shaped device for holding an oar

oa•sis \ōˈāsəs\ *n, pl* **oa•ses** \-ˌsēz\ : fertile area in a desert

oat \ˈōt\ *n* : cereal grass or its edible seed —**oat•cake** *n* —**oat•en** \-ən\ *adj* —**oat•meal** *n*

oath \ˈōth\ *n, pl* **oaths** \ˈōt͟hz, ˈōths\ **1** : solemn appeal to God as a pledge of sincerity **2** : profane utterance

ob•du•rate \ˈäbdu̇rət, -dyu̇-\ *adj* : stubbornly resistant —**ob•du•ra•cy** \-rəsē\ *n*

obe•di•ent \ōˈbēdēənt\ *adj* : willing to obey —**obe•di•ence** \-əns\ *n* —**obe•di•ent•ly** *adv*

obei•sance \ōˈbēsəns, -ˈbās-\ *n* : bow of respect or submission

obe•lisk \ˈäbəˌlisk\ *n* : 4-sided tapering pillar

obese \ōbēs\ *adj* : extremely fat —**obe•si•ty** \-ˈbēsətē\ *n*

obey \ōˈbā\ *vb* **obeyed; obey•ing 1** : follow the commands or guidance of **2** : behave in accordance with

ob•fus•cate \ˈäbfəˌskāt\ *vb* **-cat•ed; -cat•ing** : confuse —**ob•fus•ca•tion** \ˌäbfəsˈkāshən\ *n*

obit•u•ary \əˈbichəˌwerē\ *n, pl* **-ar•ies** : death notice

[1]ob•ject \ˈäbjikt\ *n* **1** : something that may be seen or felt **2** : purpose **3** : noun or equivalent toward which the action of a verb is directed or which follows a preposition

[2]ob•ject \əbˈjekt\ *vb* : offer opposition or disapproval —**ob•jec•tion** \-ˈjekshən\ *n* —**ob•jec•tion•able** \-shənəbəl\ *adj* —**ob•jec•tion•ably** \-blē\ *adv* —**ob•jec•tor** \-ˈjektər\ *n*

ob•jec•tive \əbˈjektiv\ *adj* **1** : relating to an object or end **2** : existing outside an individual's thoughts or feelings **3** : treating facts without distortion **4** : relating to or being a grammatical case marking objects ~ *n* : aim or end of action —**ob•jec•tive•ly** *adv* —**ob•jec•tive•ness** *n* —**ob•jec•tiv•i•ty** \ˌäbˌjekˈtivətē\ *n*

ob•li•gate \ˈäbləˌgāt\ *vb* **-gat•ed; -gat•ing** : bind legally or morally —**ob•liga•tion** \ˌäbləˈgāshən\ *n* —**ob•lig•a•to•ry** \əˈbligəˌtōrē, ˈäbligə-\ *adj*

oblige \əˈblīj\ *vb* **obliged; oblig•ing 1** : compel **2** : do a favor for —**oblig•ing** *adj* —**oblig•ing•ly** *adv*

oblique \ōˈblēk, -ˈblīk\ *adj* **1** : lying at a slanting angle **2** : indirect —**oblique•ly** *adv* —**oblique•ness** *n* — **obliq•ui•ty** \-ˈblikwətē\ *n*

oblit•er•ate \əˈblitəˌrāt\ *vb* **-at•ed; -at•ing** : completely remove or destroy —**oblit•er•a•tion** \-ˌblitəˈrāshən\ *n*

obliv•i•on \əˈblivēən\ *n* **1** : state of having lost conscious awareness **2** : state of being forgotten

obliv•i•ous \-ēəs\ *adj* : not aware or mindful—with *to* or *of* —**obliv•i•ous•ly** *adv* —**obliv•i•ous•ness** *n*

ob•long \ˈäbˌlȯŋ\ *adj* : longer in one direction than in the other with opposite sides parallel —**oblong** *n*

ob•lo•quy \ˈäbləkwē\ *n, pl* **-quies 1** : strongly condemning utterance **2** : bad repute

ob•nox•ious \äbˈnäkshəs, əb-\ *adj* : repugnant —**ob•nox•ious•ly** *adv* —**ob•nox•ious•ness** *n*

oboe \ˈōbō\ *n* : slender woodwind instrument with a reed mouthpiece —**obo•ist** \ˈōˌbōist\ *n*

ob•scene \äbˈsēn, əb-\ *adj* : repugnantly indecent —**ob•scene•ly** *adv* —**ob•scen•i•ty** \-ˈsenətē\ *n*

ob•scure \äbˈskyu̇r, əb-\ *adj* **1** : dim or hazy **2** : not well known **3** : vague ~ *vb* : make indistinct or unclear —**obscure•ly** *adv* —**ob•scu•ri•ty** \-ˈskyu̇rətē\ *n*

ob•se•quies \ˈäbsəkwēz\ *n pl* : funeral or burial rite

ob•se•qui•ous \əbˈsēkwēəs\ *adj* : excessively attentive or flattering —**ob•se•qui•ous•ly** *adv* —**ob•se•qui•ous•ness** *n*

ob•ser•va•to•ry \əbˈzərvəˌtōrē\ *n, pl* **-ries** : place for observing astronomical phenomena

ob•serve \əbˈzərv\ *vb* **-served; -serv•ing 1** : conform to **2** : celebrate **3** : see, watch, or notice **4** : remark —**ob•serv•able** *adj* —**ob•ser•vance** \-ˈzərvəns\ *n* —**ob•ser•vant** \-vənt\ *adj* —**ob•ser•va•tion** \ˌäbsərˈvāshən, -zər-\ *n*

ob•sess \əbˈses\ *vb* : preoccupy intensely or abnormally —**ob•ses•sion** \äbˈseshən, əb-\ *n* —**ob•ses•sive** \-ˈsesiv\ *adj* —**ob•ses•sive•ly** *adv*

ob•so•les•cent \ˌäbsəˈlesənt\ *adj* : going out of use —**ob•so•les•cence** \-əns\ *n*

ob•so•lete \ˌäbsəˈlēt, ˈäbsəˌ-\ *adj* : no longer in use

ob•sta•cle \ˈäbstikəl\ *n* : something that stands in the way or opposes

ob•stet•rics \əbˈstetriks\ *n sing or pl* : branch of medicine that deals with childbirth —**ob•stet•ric** \-rik\, **ob•stet•ri•cal** \-rikəl\ *adj* —**ob•ste•tri•cian** \ˌäbstəˈtrishən\ *n*

ob•sti•nate \ˈäbstənət\ *adj* : stubborn —**ob•sti•na•cy** \-nəsē\ *n* —**ob•sti•nate•ly** *adv*

ob•strep•er•ous \əbˈstrepərəs\ *adj* : uncontrollably noisy or defiant —**ob•strep•er•ous•ness** *n*

ob•struct \əbˈstrəkt\ *vb* : block or impede —**ob•struc•tion** \-ˈstrəkshən\ *n* —**ob•struc•tive** \-ˈstrəktiv\ *adj* —**ob•struc•tor** \-tər\ *n*

ob•tain \əbˈtān\ *vb* **1** : gain by effort **2** : be generally recognized —**ob•tain•able** *adj*

ob•trude \əbˈtrüd\ *vb* **-trud•ed; -trud•ing 1** : thrust out **2** : intrude —**ob•tru•sion** \-ˈtrüzhən\ *n* —**ob•tru•sive** \-ˈtrüsiv\ *adj* —**ob•tru•sive•ly** *adv* —**ob•tru•sive•ness** *n*

ob•tuse \äbˈtüs, əb-, -ˈtyüs\ *adj* **1** : slow-witted **2** : exceeding 90 but less than 180 degrees —**ob•tuse•ly** *adv* —**ob•tuse•ness** *n*

ob•verse \ˈäbˌvərs, äbˈ-\ *n* : principal side (as of a coin)

ob•vi•ate \ˈäbvēˌāt\ *vb* **-at•ed; -at•ing** : make unnecessary —**ob•vi•a•tion** \ˌäbvēˈāshən\ *n*

ob•vi•ous \ˈäbvēəs\ *adj* : plain or unmistakable —**ob•vi•ous•ly** *adv* —**obvi•ous•ness** *n*

oc•ca•sion \əˈkāzhən\ *n* **1** : favorable opportunity **2** : cause **3** : time of an event **4** : special event ~ *vb* : cause —**oc•ca•sion•al** \-ˈkāzhənəl\ *adj* —**oc•ca•sion•al•ly** *adv*

oc•ci•den•tal \ˌäksəˈdentəl\ *adj* : western —**Occidental** *n*

oc•cult \əˈkəlt, ˈäkˌəlt\ *adj* **1** : secret or mysterious **2** : relating to supernatural agencies —**oc•cult•ism** \-ˈkəlˌtizəm\ *n* —**oc•cult•ist** \-tist\ *n*

oc•cu•pan•cy \ˈäkyəpənsē\ *n, pl* **-cies** : an occupying

oc•cu•pant \-pənt\ *n* : one who occupies

oc•cu•pa•tion \ˌäkyəˈpāshən\ *n* **1** : vocation **2** : action or state of occupying —**oc•cu•pa•tion•al** \-shənəl\ *adj* —**oc•cu•pa•tion•al•ly** *adv*

oc•cu•py \ˈäkyəˌpī\ *vb* **-pied; -py•ing 1** : engage the attention of **2** : fill up **3** : take or hold possession of **4** : reside in —**oc•cu•pi•er** \-ˌpīər\ *n*

oc•cur \əˈkər\ *vb* **-rr- 1** : be found or met with **2** : take place **3** : come to mind

oc•cur•rence \əˈkərəns\ *n* : something that takes place

ocean \ˈōshən\ *n* **1** : whole body of salt water **2** : very large body of water —**ocean•front** *n* —**ocean•go•ing** *adj* —**oce•an•ic** \ˌōshēˈanik\ *adj*

ocean•og•ra•phy \ˌōshəˈnägrəfē\ *n* : science dealing with the ocean —**ocean•og•ra•pher** \-fər\ *n* —**ocean•o•graph•ic** \-nəˈgrafik\ *adj*

oce•lot \ˈäsəˌlät, ˈōsə-\ *n* : medium-sized American wildcat

ocher, ochre \ˈōkər\ *n* : red or yellow pigment

o'•clock \əˈkläk\ *adv* : according to the clock

oc•ta•gon \ˈäktəˌgän\ *n* : 8-sided polygon —**oc•tag•o•nal** \äkˈtagənəl\ *adj*

oc•tave \ˈäktiv\ *n* : musical interval of 8 steps or the notes within this interval

Oc•to•ber \äkˈtōbər\ *n* : 10th month of the year having 31 days

oc•to•pus \ˈäktəpəs\ *n, pl* **-pus•es** *or* **-pi** \-ˌpī\ : sea mollusk with 8 arms

oc•u•lar \ˈäkyələr\ *adj* : relating to the eye

oc•u•list \ˈäkyəlist\ *n* **1** : ophthalmologist **2** : optometrist

odd \ˈäd\ *adj* **1** : being only one of a pair or set **2** : not divisible by two without a remainder **3** : additional to what is usual or to the number mentioned **4** : queer —**odd•ly** *adv* —**odd•ness** *n*

odd•i•ty \ˈädətē\ *n, pl* **-ties** : something odd

odds \ˈädz\ *n pl* **1** : difference by which one thing is favored **2** : disagreement **3** : ratio between winnings and the amount of the bet

ode \ˈōd\ *n* : solemn lyric poem

odi•ous \ˈōdēəs\ *adj* : hated —**odi•ous•ly** *adv* —**odi•ous•ness** *n*

odi•um \ˈōdēəm\ *n* **1** : merited loathing **2** : disgrace

odor \ˈōdər\ *n* : quality that affects the sense of smell —**odor•less** *adj* —**odor•ous** *adj*

od•ys•sey \ˈädəsē\ *n, pl* **-seys** : long wandering

o'er \ˈōr\ *adv or prep* : OVER

of \əv, ˈäv\ *prep* **1** : from **2** : distinguished by **3** : because of **4** : made or written by **5** : made with, being, or containing **6** : belonging to or connected with **7** : about **8** : that is **9** : concerning **10** : before

off \ˈȯf\ *adv* **1** : from a place **2** : unattached or removed **3** : to a state of being no longer in use **4** : away from work **5** : at a distance in time or space ~ *prep* **1** : away from **2** : at the expense of **3** : not engaged in or abstaining from **4** : below the usual level of ~ *adj* **1** : not operating, up to standard, or correct **2** : remote **3** : provided for

of•fal \ˈōfəl\ *n* **1** : waste **2** : viscera and trimmings of a butchered animal

of•fend \əˈfend\ *vb* **1** : sin or act in violation **2** : hurt, annoy, or insult —**of•fend•er** *n*

of•fense, of•fence \əˈfens, ˈäfˌens\ *n* : attack, misdeed, or insult

of•fen•sive \əˈfensiv, ˈäfˌen-\ *adj* : causing offense ~ *n* : attack —**offen•sive•ly** *adv* —**of•fen•sive•ness** *n*

of•fer \ˈȯfər\ *vb* **1** : present for acceptance **2** : propose **3** : put up (an effort) ~ *n* **1** : proposal **2** : bid —**of•fer•ing** *n*

of•fer•to•ry \ˈȯfərˌtōrē\ *n, pl* **-ries** : presentation of offerings or its musical accompaniment

off•hand *adv or adj* : without previous thought or preparation

of•fice \ˈȯfəs\ *n* **1** : position of authority (as in government) **2** : rite **3** : place where a business is transacted —**of•fice•hold•er** *n*

of•fi•cer \ˈȯfəsər\ *n* **1** : one charged with law enforcement **2** : one who holds an office of trust or authority **3** : one who holds a commission in the armed forces

of•fi•cial \əˈfishəl\ *n* : one in office ~ *adj* : authorized or authoritative —**of•fi•cial•dom** \-dəm\ *n* —**of•fi•cial•ly** *adv*

of•fi•ci•ant \əˈfishēənt\ *n* : clergy member who officiates at a religious rite

of•fi•ci•ate \əˈfishēˌāt\ *vb* **-at•ed; -at•ing** : perform a ceremony or function

of•fi•cious \əˈfishəs\ *adj* : volunteering one's services unnecessarily —**of•fi•cious•ly** *adv* —**of•fi•cious•ness** *n*

off•ing \ˈȯfiŋ\ *n* : future

off•set \ˈȯfˌset\ *vb* **-set; -set•ting** : provide an opposite or equaling effect to

off•shoot \ˈȯfˌshüt\ *n* : outgrowth

off•shore *adv* : at a distance from the shore ~ *adj* : moving away from or situated off the shore

off•spring \ˈȯfˌspriŋ\ *n, pl* **offspring** : one coming into being through animal or plant reproduction

of•ten \ˈȯfən, ˈȯft-\ *adv* : many times —**of•ten•times, oft•times** *adv*

ogle \ˈōgəl\ *vb* **ogled; ogling** : stare at lustily —**ogle** *n* —**ogler** \-ələr\ *n*

ogre \ˈōgər\ *n* **1** : monster **2** : dreaded person

oh \ˈō\ *interj* **1**—used to express an emotion **2**—used in direct address

ohm \ˈōm\ *n* : unit of electrical resistance —**ohm•ic** \ˈōmik\ *adj* —**ohm•me•ter** \ˈōmˌmētər\ *n*

oil \ˈȯil\ *n* **1** : greasy liquid substance **2** : petroleum ~ *vb* : put oil in or on —**oil•er** *n* —**oil•i•ness** \ˈȯilēnəs\ *n* —**oily** \ˈȯilē\ *adj*

oil•cloth *n* : cloth treated with oil or paint and used for coverings

oil•skin *n* : oiled waterproof cloth

oink \ˈȯiŋk\ *n* : natural noise of a hog —**oink** *vb*

oint•ment \ˈȯintmənt\ *n* : oily medicinal preparation

OK *or* **okay** \ōˈkā\ *adv or adj* : all right ~ *vb* **OK'd** *or* **okayed; OK'•ing** *or* **okay•ing** : approve ~ *n* : approval

okra \ˈōkrə, *South also* -krē\ *n* : leafy vegetable with edible green pods

old \ˈōld\ *adj* **1** : of long standing **2** : of a specified age **3** : relating to a past era **4** : having existed a long time —**old•ish** \ˈōldish\ *adj*

old•en \ˈōldən\ *adj* : of or relating to a bygone era

old–fash•ioned \-ˈfashənd\ *adj* **1** : out-of-date **2** : conservative

old maid *n* : spinster

old–tim•er \ōldˈtīmər\ *n* **1** : veteran **2** : one who is old

ole•an•der \ˈōlēˌandər\ *n* : poisonous evergreen shrub

oleo•mar•ga•rine \ˌōlēōˈmärjərən\ *n* : margarine

ol•fac•to•ry \älˈfaktərē, ōl-\ *adj* : relating to the sense of smell

oli•gar•chy \ˈäləˌgärkē, ˈōlə-\ *n, pl* **-chies 1** : government by a few people **2** : those holding power in an oligarchy —**oli•garch** \-ˌgärk\ *n* —**oli•gar•chic** \äləˈgärkik, ˌōlə-\, **oli•gar•chi•cal** \-kikəl\ *adj*

ol•ive \ˈäliv, -əv\ *n* **1** : evergreen tree bearing small edible fruit or the fruit **2** : dull yellowish green color

om•buds•man \ˈämˌbu̇dzmən, ämˈbu̇dz-\ *n, pl* **-men** \-mən\ : complaint investigator

om•e•let, om•e•lette \ˈämələt\ *n* : beaten eggs lightly fried and folded

omen \ˈōmən\ *n* : sign or warning of the future

om•i•nous \ˈämənəs\ *adj* : presaging evil —**om•i•nous•ly** *adv* —**om•i•nous•ness** *n*

omit \ōˈmit\ *vb* **-tt- 1** : leave out **2** : fail to perform —**omis•si•ble** \ōˈmisəbəl\ *adj* —**omis•sion** \-ˈmishən\ *n*

om•nip•o•tent \ämˈnipətənt\ *adj* : almighty —**om•nip•o•tence** \-əns\ *n* —**om•nip•o•tent•ly** *adv*

om•ni•pres•ent \ˌämniˈprezənt\ *adj* : ever-present —**om•ni•pres•ence** \-əns\ *n*

om•ni•scient \ämˈnishənt\ *adj* : all-knowing —**om•ni•science** \-əns\ *n* —**om•ni•scient•ly** *adv*

om•niv•o•rous \ämˈnivərəs\ *adj* **1** : eating both meat and vegetables **2** : avid —**om•niv•o•rous•ly** *adv*

on \ˈȯn, ˈän\ *prep* **1** : in or to a position over and in contact with **2** : at or to **3** : about **4** : from **5** : with regard to **6** : in a state or process **7** : during the time of ~ *adv* **1** : in or into contact with **2** : forward **3** : into operation

once \ˈwəns\ *adv* **1** : one time only **2** : at any one time **3** : formerly ~ *n* : one time ~ *conj* : as soon as ~ *adj* : former —**at once 1** : simultaneously **2** : immediately

once–over *n* : swift examination

on•com•ing *adj* : approaching

one \ˈwən\ *adj* **1** : being a single thing **2** : being one in particular **3** : being the same in kind ~ *pron* **1** : certain indefinitely indicated person or thing **2** : a person in general ~ *n* **1** : 1st in a series **2** : single person or thing —**one•ness** *n*

oner•ous \ˈänərəs, ˈōnə-\ *adj* : imposing a burden

one•self \ˌwənˈself\ *pron* : one's own self—usu. used reflexively or for emphasis

one–sid•ed \-'sīdəd\ *adj* **1 :** occurring on one side only **2 :** partial
one•time *adj* **:** former
one–way *adj* **:** made or for use in only one direction
on•go•ing *adj* **:** continuing
on•ion \'ənyən\ *n* **:** plant grown for its pungent edible bulb or this bulb
on•ly \'ōnlē\ *adj* **:** alone in its class ~ *adv* **1 :** merely or exactly **2 :** solely **3 :** at the very least **4 :** as a result ~ *conj* **:** but
on•set *n* **:** start
on•shore *adj* **1 :** moving toward shore **2 :** lying on or near the shore **—onshore** *adv*
on•slaught \'än,slȯt, 'ȯn-\ *n* **:** attack
on•to \'ȯntü, 'än-\ *prep* **:** to a position or point on
onus \'ōnəs\ *n* **:** burden (as of obligation or blame)
on•ward \'ȯnwərd, 'än-\ *adv or adj* **:** forward
on•yx \'äniks\ *n* **:** quartz used as a gem
[1]**ooze** \'üz\ *n* **:** soft mud ~ *vb* **oozed; ooz•ing :** flow or leak out slowly **—oozy** \'üzē\ *adj*
opac•i•ty \ō'pasətē\ *n* **:** quality or state of being opaque or an opaque spot
opal \'ōpəl\ *n* **:** gem with delicate colors
opaque \ō'pāk\ *adj* **1 :** blocking light **2 :** not easily understood **3 :** dull-witted **—opaque•ly** *adv*
open \'ōpən\ *adj* **1 :** not shut or shut up **2 :** not secret or hidden **3 :** frank or generous **4 :** extended **5 :** free from controls **6 :** not decided ~ *vb* **1 :** make or become open **2 :** make or become functional **3 :** start ~ *n* **:** outdoors **—open•er** \-ər\ *n* **—open•ly** *adv* **—open•ness** *n*
open•hand•ed \-'handəd\ *adj* **:** generous **—open•hand•ed•ly** *adv*
open•ing \'ōpəniŋ\ *n* **1 :** act or instance of making open **2 :** something that is open **3 :** opportunity
op•era \'äpərə, 'äprə\ *n* **:** drama set to music **—op•er•at•ic** \,äpə'ratik\ *adj*
op•er•a•ble \'äpərəbəl\ *adj* **1 :** usable or in working condition **2 :** suitable for surgical treatment
op•er•ate \'äpə,rāt\ *vb* **-at•ed; -at•ing 1 :** perform work **2 :** perform an operation **3 :** manage **—op•er•a•tor** \-,rātər\ *n*
op•er•a•tion \,äpə'rāshən\ *n* **1 :** act or process of operating **2 :** surgical work on a living body **3 :** military action or mission **—op•er•a•tion•al** \-shənəl\ *adj*
op•er•a•tive \'äpərətiv, -,rāt-\ *adj* **:** working or having an effect
op•er•et•ta \,äpə'retə\ *n* **:** light opera
oph•thal•mol•o•gy \,äf,thal'mäləjē\ *n* **:** branch of medicine dealing with the eye **—oph•thal•mol•o•gist** \-jist\ *n*
opi•ate \'ōpēət, -pē,āt\ *n* **:** preparation or derivative of opium
opine \ō'pīn\ *vb* **opined; opin•ing :** express an opinion
opin•ion \ə'pinyən\ *n* **1 :** belief **2 :** judgment **3 :** formal statement by an expert
opin•ion•at•ed \-yə,nātəd\ *adj* **:** stubborn in one's opinions
opi•um \'ōpēəm\ *n* **:** addictive narcotic drug that is the dried juice of a poppy
opos•sum \ə'päsəm\ *n* **:** common tree-dwelling nocturnal mammal
op•po•nent \ə'pōnənt\ *n* **:** one that opposes
op•por•tune \,äpər'tün, -'tyün\ *adj* **:** suitable or timely **—op•por•tune•ly** *adv*
op•por•tun•ism \-'tü,nizəm, -'tyü-\ *n* **:** a taking advantage of opportunities **—op•por•tun•ist** \-nist\ *n* **—op•por•tu•nis•tic** \-tü'nistik, -tyü-\ *adj*
op•por•tu•ni•ty \-'tünətē, -'tyü-\ *n, pl* **-ties :** favorable time
op•pose \ə'pōz\ *vb* **-posed; -pos•ing 1 :** place opposite or against something **2 :** resist **—op•po•si•tion** \,äpə'zishən\ *n*
op•po•site \'äpəzət\ *n* **:** one that is opposed ~ *adj* **1 :** set facing something that is at the other side or end **2 :** opposed or contrary ~ *adv* **:** on opposite sides ~ *prep* **:** across from **—op•po•site•ly** *adv*
op•press \ə'pres\ *vb* **1 :** persecute **2 :** weigh down **—op•pres•sion** \ə'preshən\ *n* **—op•pres•sive** \-'presiv\ *adj* **—op•pres•sive•ly** *adv* **—op•pres•sor** \-'presər\ *n*
op•pro•bri•ous \ə'prōbrēəs\ *adj* **:** expressing or deserving opprobrium **—op•pro•bri•ous•ly** *adv*
op•pro•bri•um \-brēəm\ *n* **1 :** something that brings disgrace **2 :** infamy
opt \'äpt\ *vb* **:** choose
op•tic \'äptik\ *adj* **:** relating to vision or the eye
op•ti•cal \'äptikəl\ *adj* **:** relating to optics, vision, or the eye
op•ti•cian \äp'tishən\ *n* **:** maker of or dealer in eyeglasses
op•tics \'äptiks\ *n pl* **:** science of light and vision
op•ti•mal \'äptəməl\ *adj* **:** most favorable **—op•ti•mal•ly** *adv*
op•ti•mism \'äptə,mizəm\ *n* **:** tendency to hope for the best **—op•ti•mist** \-mist\ *n* **—op•ti•mis•tic** \,äptə'mistik\ *adj* **—op•ti•mis•ti•cal•ly** *adv*
op•ti•mum \'äptəməm\ *n, pl* **-ma** \-mə\ **:** amount or degree of something most favorable to an end **—optimum** *adj*
op•tion \'äpshən\ *n* **1 :** ability to choose **2 :** right to buy or sell a stock **3 :** alternative **—op•tion•al** \-shənəl\ *adj*
op•tom•e•try \äp'tämətrē\ *n* **:** profession of examining the eyes **—op•tom•e•trist** \-trist\ *n*
op•u•lent \'äpyələnt\ *adj* **:** lavish **—op•u•lence** \-ləns\ *n* **—op•u•lent•ly** *adv*
opus \'ōpəs\ *n, pl* **opera** \'ōpərə, 'äpə-\ **:** work esp. of music
or \'ȯr\ *conj*—used to indicate an alternative
-or \ər\ *n suffix* **:** one that performs an action
or•a•cle \'ȯrəkəl\ *n* **1 :** one held to give divinely inspired answers or revelations **2 :** wise person or an utterance of such a person **—orac•u•lar** \ȯ'rakyələr\ *adj*
oral \'ōrəl\ *adj* **1 :** spoken **2 :** relating to the mouth **—oral•ly** *adv*
or•ange \'ȯrinj\ *n* **1 :** reddish yellow citrus fruit **2 :** color between red and yellow **—or•ange•ade** \,ȯrinj'ād\ *n*
orang•u•tan \ə'raŋə,taŋ, -,tan\ *n* **:** large reddish brown ape
ora•tion \ə'rāshən\ *n* **:** elaborate formal speech
or•a•tor \'ȯrətər\ *n* **:** one noted as a public speaker
or•a•to•rio \,ȯrə'tōrē,ō\ *n, pl* **-ri•os :** major choral work
or•a•to•ry \'ȯrə,tōrē\ *n* **:** art of public speaking **—or•a•tor•i•cal** \,ȯrə'tȯrikəl\ *adj*
orb \'ȯrb\ *n* **:** spherical body
or•bit \'ȯrbət\ *n* **:** path made by one body revolving around another ~ *vb* **:** revolve around **—or•bit•al** \-ᵊl\ *adj* **—or•bit•er** *n*
or•chard \'ȯrchərd\ *n* **:** place where fruit or nut trees are grown **—or•chard•ist** \-ist\ *n*
or•ches•tra \'ȯrkəstrə\ *n* **1 :** group of musicians **2 :** front seats of a theater's main floor **—or•ches•tral** \ȯr'kestrəl\ *adj* **—or•ches•tral•ly** *adv*
or•ches•trate \'ȯrkə,strāt\ *vb* **-trat•ed; -trat•ing 1 :** compose or arrange for an orchestra **2 :** arrange or combine for best effect **—or•ches•tra•tion** \,ȯrkə'strāshən\ *n*
or•chid \'ȯrkəd\ *n* **:** plant with showy 3-petal flowers or its flower
or•dain \ȯr'dān\ *vb* **1 :** admit to the clergy **2 :** decree
or•deal \ȯr'dēl, 'ȯr,dēl\ *n* **:** severely trying experience
or•der \'ȯrdər\ *n* **1 :** rank, class, or special group **2 :** arrangement **3 :** rule of law **4 :** authoritative regulation or instruction **5 :** working condition **6 :** special request for a purchase or what is purchased ~ *vb* **1 :** arrange **2 :** give an order to **3 :** place an order for
or•der•ly \-lē\ *adj* **1 :** being in order or tidy **2 :** well behaved ~ *n, pl* **-lies 1 :** officer's attendant **2 :** hospital attendant **—or•der•li•ness** *n*
or•di•nal \'ȯrdᵊnəl\ *n* **:** number indicating order in a series
or•di•nance \-ᵊnəns\ *n* **:** municipal law
or•di•nary \'ȯrdᵊn,erē\ *adj* **:** of common occurrence, quality, or ability **—or•di•nar•i•ly** \,ȯrdᵊn'erəlē\ *adv*
or•di•na•tion \,ȯrdᵊn'āshən\ *n* **:** act of ordaining
ord•nance \'ȯrdnəns\ *n* **:** military supplies
ore \'ōr\ *n* **:** mineral containing a valuable constituent
oreg•a•no \ə'regə,nō\ *n* **:** mint used as a seasoning and source of oil
or•gan \'ȯrgən\ *n* **1 :** air-powered or electronic keyboard instrument **2 :** animal or plant structure with special function **3 :** periodical
or•gan•ic \ȯr'ganik\ *adj* **1 :** relating to a bodily organ **2 :** relating to living things **3 :** relating to or containing carbon or its compounds **4 :** relating to foods produced without the use of laboratory-made products **—or•gan•i•cal•ly** *adv*
or•gan•ism \'ȯrgə,nizəm\ *n* **:** a living thing
or•gan•ist \'ȯrgənist\ *n* **:** organ player
or•ga•nize \'ȯrgə,nīz\ *vb* **-nized; -niz•ing :** form parts into a functioning whole **—or•ga•ni•za•tion** \,ȯrgənə'zāshən\ *n* **—or•ga•ni•za•tion•al** \-shənəl\ *adj* **—or•ga•niz•er** *n*
or•gasm \'ȯr,gazəm\ *n* **:** climax of sexual excitement **—or•gas•mic** \ȯr'gazmik\ *adj*
or•gy \'ȯrjē\ *n, pl* **-gies :** unrestrained indulgence (as in sexual activity)
ori•ent \'ōrē,ent\ *vb* **1 :** set in a definite position **2 :** acquaint with a situation **—ori•en•ta•tion** \,ōrēən'tāshən\ *n*
ori•en•tal \,ōrē'entᵊl\ *adj* **:** Eastern **—Oriental** *n*
or•i•fice \'ȯrəfəs\ *n* **:** opening
or•i•gin \'ȯrəjən\ *n* **1 :** ancestry **2 :** rise, beginning, or derivation from a source **—orig•i•nate** \ə'rijə,nāt\ *vb* **—orig•i•na•tor** \-ər\ *n*
orig•i•nal \ə'rijənəl\ *n* **:** something from which a copy is made ~ *adj* **1 :** first **2 :** not copied from something else **3 :** inventive **—orig•i•nal•i•ty** *n* **—orig•i•nal•ly** *adv*
ori•ole \'ōrē,ōl, -ēəl\ *n* **:** American songbird
or•na•ment \'ȯrnəmənt\ *n* **:** something that adorns ~ *vb* **:** provide with ornament **—or•na•men•tal** \,ȯrnə'mentᵊl\ *adj* **—or•na•men•ta•tion** \-mən'tāshən\ *n*
or•nate \ȯr'nāt\ *adj* **:** elaborately decorated **—or•nate•ly** *adv* **—or•nate•ness** *n*
or•nery \'ȯrnərē, 'än-\ *adj* **:** irritable
or•ni•thol•o•gy \,ȯrnə'thäləjē\ *n, pl* **-gies :** study of birds **—or•ni•tho•log•i•cal** \-thə'läjikəl\ *adj* **—or•ni•thol•o•gist** \-'thäləjist\ *n*
or•phan \'ȯrfən\ *n* **:** child whose parents are dead **—orphan** *vb* **—or•phan•age** \-ənij\ *n*
or•tho•don•tics \,ȯrthə'däntiks\ *n* **:** dentistry dealing with straightening teeth **—or•tho•don•tist** \-'däntist\ *n*
or•tho•dox \'ȯrthə,däks\ *adj* **1 :** conforming to established doctrine **2** *cap* **:** of or relating to a Christian church originating in the Eastern Roman Empire **—or•tho•doxy** \-,däksē\ *n*
or•thog•ra•phy \ȯr'thägrəfē\ *n* **:** spelling **—or•tho•graph•ic** \,ȯrthə'grafik\ *adj*
or•tho•pe•dics \,ȯrthə'pēdiks\ *n sing or pl* **:** correction or prevention of skeletal deformities **—or•tho•pe•dic** \-ik\ *adj* **—or•tho•pe•dist** \-'pēdist\ *n*
-o•ry \,ōrē, ,ȯrē, ərē\ *adj suffix* **1 :** of, relating to, or characterized by **2 :** serving for, producing, or maintaining
os•cil•late \'äsə,lāt\ *vb* **-lat•ed; -lat•ing :** swing back and forth **—os•cil•la•tion** \,äsə'lāshən\ *n*
os•mo•sis \äz'mōsəs, äs-\ *n* **:** diffusion esp. of water through a membrane **—os•mot•ic** \-'mätik\ *adj*
os•prey \'äsprē, -,prā\ *n, pl* **-preys :** large fish-eating hawk
os•si•fy \'äsə,fī\ *vb* **-fied; -fy•ing :** make or become hardened or set in one's ways
os•ten•si•ble \ä'stensəbəl\ *adj* **:** seeming **—os•ten•si•bly** \-blē\ *adv*
os•ten•ta•tion \,ästən'tāshən\ *n* **:** pretentious display **—os•ten•ta•tious** \-shəs\ *adj* **—os•ten•ta•tious•ly** *adv*
os•te•op•a•thy \,ästē'äpəthē\ *n* **:** system of healing that emphasizes manipulation (as of joints) **—os•te•o•path** \'ästēə,path\ *n* **—os•te•o•path•ic** \,ästēə'pathik\ *adj*
os•te•o•po•ro•sis \,ästēōpə'rōsəs\ *n, pl* **-ro•ses** \-,sēz\ **:** condition characterized by fragile and porous bones
os•tra•cize \'ästrə,sīz\ *vb* **-cized; -ciz•ing :** exclude by common consent **—ostra•cism** \-,sizəm\ *n*
os•trich \'ästrich, 'ȯs-\ *n* **:** very large flightless bird
oth•er \'əthər\ *adj* **1 :** being the one left **2 :** alternate **3 :** additional ~ *pron* **1 :** remaining one **2 :** different one
oth•er•wise *adv* **1 :** in a different way **2 :** in different circumstances **3 :** in other respects **—otherwise** *adj*
ot•ter \'ätər\ *n* **:** fish-eating mammal with webbed feet
ot•to•man \'ätəmən\ *n* **:** upholstered footstool
ought \'ȯt\ *verbal auxiliary*—used to express obligation, advisability, or expectation
ounce \'au̇ns\ *n* **1 :** unit of weight equal to about 28.3 grams **2 :** unit of capacity equal to about 29.6 milliliters
our \'är, 'au̇r\ *adj* **:** of or relating to us
ours \'au̇rz, 'ärz\ *pron* **:** that which belongs to us
our•selves \är'selvz, au̇r-\ *pron* **:** we, us—used reflexively or for emphasis
-ous \əs\ *adj suffix* **:** having or having the qualities of
oust \'au̇st\ *vb* **:** expel or eject
oust•er \'au̇stər\ *n* **:** expulsion
out \'au̇t\ *adv* **1 :** away from the inside or center **2 :** beyond control **3 :** to extinction, exhaustion, or completion **4 :** in or into the open ~ *vb* **:** become known ~ *adj* **1 :** situated outside **2 :** absent ~ *prep* **1 :** out through **2 :** outward on or along **—out•bound** *adj* **—out•build•ing** *n*
out•age \'au̇tij\ *n* **:** period of no electricity
out•board \'au̇t,bōrd\ *adv* **:** outside a boat or ship **—outboard** *adj*
out•break \'au̇t,brāk\ *n* **:** sudden occurrence
out•burst \-,bərst\ *n* **:** violent expression of feeling
out•cast \-,kast\ *n* **:** person cast out by society
out•come \-,kəm\ *n* **:** result
out•crop \'au̇t,kräp\ *n* **:** part of a rock stratum that appears above the ground **—outcrop** *vb*
out•cry \-,krī\ *n* **:** loud cry
out•dat•ed \au̇t'dātəd\ *adj* **:** out-of-date
out•dis•tance *vb* **:** go far ahead of
out•do \au̇t'dü\ *vb* **-did** \-'did\; **-done** \-'dən\; **-do•ing** \-'düiŋ\; **-does** \-'dəz\ **:** do better than
out•doors \au̇t'dōrz\ *adv* **:** in or into the open air ~ *n* **:** open air **—out•door** *adj*
out•er \'au̇tər\ *adj* **1 :** external **2 :** farther out **—out•er•most** *adj*
out•field \'au̇t,fēld\ *n* **:** baseball field beyond the infield **—out•field•er** \-,fēldər\ *n*
out•fit \'au̇t,fit\ *n* **1 :** equipment for a special purpose **2 :** group ~ *vb* **-tt- :** equip **—out•fit•ter** *n*
out•go \'au̇t,gō\ *n, pl* **outgoes :** expenditure
out•go•ing \'au̇t,gōiŋ\ *adj* **1 :** retiring from a position **2 :** friendly
out•grow \au̇t'grō\ *vb* **-grew** \-'grü\; **-grown** \-'grōn\; **-grow•ing 1 :** grow faster than **2 :** grow too large for
out•growth \'au̇t,grōth\ *n* **1 :** product of growing out **2 :** consequence
out•ing \'au̇tiŋ\ *n* **:** excursion
out•land•ish \au̇t'landish\ *adj* **:** very strange **—out•land•ish•ly** *adv*
outlast *vb* **:** last longer than
out•law \'au̇t,lȯ\ *n* **:** lawless person ~ *vb* **:** make illegal
out•lay \'au̇t,lā\ *n* **:** expenditure
out•let \'au̇t,let, -lət\ *n* **1 :** exit **2 :** means of release **3 :** market for goods **4 :** electrical device that gives access to wiring
out•line \'au̇t,līn\ *n* **1 :** line marking the outer limits **2 :** summary ~ *vb* **1 :** draw the outline of **2 :** indicate the chief parts of
out•live \au̇t'liv\ *vb* **:** live longer than
out•look \'au̇t,lu̇k\ *n* **1 :** viewpoint **2 :** prospect for the future
out•ly•ing \'au̇t,līiŋ\ *adj* **:** far from a central point
out•ma•neu•ver \,au̇tmə'nüvər, -'nyü-\ *vb* **:** defeat by more skillful maneuvering
out•mod•ed \au̇t'mōdəd\ *adj* **:** out-of-date
out•num•ber \-'nəmbər\ *vb* **:** exceed in number
out of *prep* **1 :** out from within **2 :** beyond the limits of **3 :** among **4** —used to indicate absence or loss **5 :** because of **6 :** from or with
out–of–date *adj* **:** no longer in fashion or in use
out•pa•tient *n* **:** person treated at a hospital who does not stay overnight
out•post *n* **:** remote military post
out•put *n* **:** amount produced ~ *vb* **-put•ted** *or* **-put; -put•ting :** produce
out•rage \'au̇t,rāj\ *n* **1 :** violent or shameful act **2 :** injury or insult **3 :** extreme anger ~ *vb* **-raged; -rag•ing 1 :** subject to violent injury **2 :** make very angry
out•ra•geous \au̇t'rājəs\ *adj* **:** extremely offensive or shameful **—out•ra•geous•ly** *adv* **—out•ra•geous•ness** *n*
out•right *adv* **1 :** completely **2 :** instantly ~ *adj* **1 :** complete **2 :** given without reservation
out•set *n* **:** beginning
out•side \au̇t'sīd, 'au̇t,-\ *n* **1 :** place beyond a boundary **2 :** exterior **3 :** utmost limit ~ *adj* **1 :** outer **2 :** coming from without **3 :** remote ~ *adv* **:** on or to the outside ~ *prep* **1 :** on or to the outside of **2 :** beyond the limits of
outside of *prep* **1 :** outside **2 :** besides
out•sid•er \-'sīdər\ *n* **:** one who does not belong to a group
out•skirts *n pl* **:** outlying parts (as of a city)
out•smart \au̇t'smärt\ *vb* **:** outwit
out•spo•ken *adj* **:** direct and open in speech **—out•spo•ken•ness** *n*
out•stand•ing *adj* **1 :** unpaid **2 :** very good **—out•stand•ing•ly** *adv*
out•strip \au̇t'strip\ *vb* **1 :** go faster than **2 :** surpass
[1]**out•ward** \'au̇twərd\ *adj* **1 :** being toward the outside **2 :** showing outwardly
[2]**outward, out•wards** \-wərdz\ *adv* **:** toward the outside **—out•ward•ly** *adv*
out•wit \au̇t'wit\ *vb* **:** get the better of by superior cleverness
ova *pl of* OVUM
oval \'ōvəl\ *adj* **:** egg-shaped **—oval** *n*
ova•ry \'ōvərē\ *n, pl* **-ries 1 :** egg-producing organ **2 :** seed-producing part of a flower **—ovar•i•an** \ō'varēən\ *adj*
ova•tion \ō'vāshən\ *n* **:** enthusiastic applause
ov•en \'əvən\ *n* **:** chamber (as in a stove) for baking
over \'ōvər\ *adv* **1 :** across **2 :** upside down **3 :** in excess or addition **4 :** above **5 :** at an end **6 :** again ~ *prep* **1 :** above in position or authority **2 :** more than **3 :** along, through, or across **4 :** because of ~ *adj* **1 :** upper **2 :** remaining **3 :** ended
over- *prefix* **1 :** so as to exceed or surpass **2 :** excessive or excessively

overabundance
overabundant
overachiever
overactive
overaggressive
overambitious
overanalyze
overanxiety
overanxious
overarousal
overassertive
overbake
overbid
overbill
overbold
overborrow
overbright
overbroad
overbuild
overburden

overbusy
overbuy
overcapacity
overcapitalize
overcareful
overcautious
overcharge
overcivilized
overclean
overcommit
overcompensate
overcomplicate
overconcern
overconfidence
overconfident
overconscientious
overconsume
overconsumption
overcontrol
overcook
overcorrect
overcritical
overcrowd
overdecorate
overdependence
overdependent
overdevelop
overdose
overdramatic
overdramatize
overdress
overdrink
overdue
overeager
overeat
overeducated
overelaborate
overemotional
overemphasis
overemphasize
overenergetic
overenthusiastic
overestimate
overexaggerate
overexaggeration
overexcite
overexcited
overexercise
overexert
overexertion
overexpand
overexpansion
overexplain
overexploit
overexpose
overextend
overextension
overexuberant
overfamiliar
overfatigued
overfeed
overfertilize
overfill
overfond
overgeneralization
overgeneralize
overgenerous
overglamorize
overgraze
overharvest
overhasty
overheat
overidealize
overimaginative
overimpress
overindebtedness
overindulge
overindulgence
overindulgent
overinflate
overinsistent
overintense
overintensity
overinvestment
overladen
overlarge
overlend
overload
overlong
overloud
overmedicate
overmodest
overmuch
overobvious
overoptimistic
overorganize
overparticular
overpay
overpayment
overplay
overpopulated
overpraise
overprescribe
overpressure
overprice
overprivileged
overproduce
overproduction
overpromise
overprotect
overprotective
overqualified
overrate
overreact
overreaction
overrefined
overregulate
overregulation
overreliance
overrepresented
overrespond
overripe
oversaturate
oversell
oversensitive
overserious
oversexed
oversimple
oversimplify
oversolicitous
overspecialize
overspend
overstaff
overstimulation
overstock
overstrain
overstress
overstretch
oversubtle
oversupply
oversuspicious
oversweeten
overtax
overtighten
overtip
overtired
overtrain
overtreat
overuse
overutilize
overvalue
overweight
overwork
overzealous

[1]**over•age** \ˌōvər'āj\ *adj* : too old

[2]**over•age** \'ōvərij\ *n* : surplus

over•all \ˌōvər'ȯl\ *adj* : including everything

over•alls \'ōvərˌȯlz\ *n pl* : pants with an extra piece covering the chest

over•awe *vb* : subdue by awe

over•bear•ing \-'bariŋ\ *adj* : arrogant

over•blown \-'blōn\ *adj* : pretentious

over•board *adv* : over the side into the water

over•cast *adj* : clouded over ~ *n* : cloud covering

over•coat *n* : outer coat

over•come *vb* **-came** \-'kām\; **-come; -com•ing 1** : defeat **2** : make helpless or exhausted

over•do *vb* **-did; -done; -do•ing; -does** : do too much

over•draft *n* : overdrawn sum

over•draw *vb* **-drew; -drawn; -draw•ing** : write checks for more than one's bank balance

over•flow \ˌōvər'flō\ *vb* **1** : flood **2** : flow over **—over•flow** \'ōvərˌflō\ *n*

over•grow *vb* **-grew; -grown; -grow•ing** : grow over

over•hand *adj* : made with the hand brought down from above **—overhand** *adv* **—over•hand•ed** \-ˌhandəd\ *adv or adj*

over•hang *vb* **-hung; -hang•ing** : jut out over ~ *n* : something that overhangs

over•haul *vb* **1** : repair **2** : overtake

over•head \ˌōvər'hed\ *adv* : aloft ~ \'ōvərˌ-\ *adj* : situated above ~ \'ōvərˌ-\ *n* : general business expenses

over•hear *vb* **-heard; -hear•ing** : hear without the speaker's knowledge

over•joyed *adj* : filled with joy

over•kill \'ōvərˌkil\ *n* : large excess

over•land \-ˌland, -lənd\ *adv or adj* : by, on, or across land

over•lap *vb* : lap over **—over•lap** \'ōvərˌlap\ *n*

over•lay \ˌōvər'lā\ *vb* **-laid; -lay•ing** : lay over or across **—over•lay** \'ōvərˌlā\ *n*

over•look \ˌōvər'lu̇k\ *vb* **1** : look down on **2** : fail to see **3** : ignore **4** : pardon **5** : supervise ~ \'ōvərˌ-\ *n* : observation point

over•ly \'ōvərlē\ *adv* : excessively

over•night *adv* **1** : through the night **2** : suddenly **—overnight** *adj*

over•pass *n* : bridge over a road

over•pow•er *vb* : conquer

over•reach \ˌōvər'rēch\ *vb* : try or seek too much

over•ride *vb* **-rode; -rid•den; -rid•ing** : neutralize action of

over•rule *vb* : rule against or set aside

over•run *vb* **-ran; -run•ning 1** : swarm or flow over **2** : go beyond ~ *n* : an exceeding of estimated costs

over•seas *adv or adj* : beyond or across the sea

over•see \ˌōvər'sē\ *vb* **-saw; -seen; -see•ing** : supervise **—over•seer** \'ōvərˌsiər\ *n*

over•shad•ow *vb* : exceed in importance

over•shoe *n* : protective outer shoe

over•shoot *vb* **-shot; -shoot•ing** : shoot or pass beyond

over•sight *n* : inadvertent omission or error

over•sleep *vb* **-slept; -sleep•ing** : sleep longer than intended

over•spread *vb* **-spread; -spread•ing** : spread over or above

over•state *vb* : exaggerate **—over•state•ment** *n*

over•stay *vb* : stay too long

over•step *vb* : exceed

overt \ō'vərt, 'ōˌvərt\ *adj* : not secret **—overt•ly** *adv*

over•take *vb* **-took; -tak•en; -tak•ing** : catch up with

over•throw \ˌōvər'thrō\ *vb* **-threw; -thrown; -throw•ing 1** : upset **2** : defeat **—over•throw** \'ōvərˌ-\ *n*

over•time *n* : extra working time **—over•time** *adv*

over•tone *n* **1** : higher tone in a complex musical tone **2** : suggestion

over•ture \'ōvərˌchu̇r, -chər\ *n* **1** : opening offer **2** : musical introduction

over•turn *vb* **1** : turn over **2** : nullify

over•view *n* : brief survey

over•ween•ing \ˌōvər'wēniŋ\ *adj* **1** : arrogant **2** : excessive

over•whelm \ˌōvər'hwelm\ *vb* : overcome completely **—over•whelm•ing•ly** \-'hwelmiŋlē\ *adv*

over•wrought \ˌōvər'rȯt\ *adj* : extremely excited

ovoid \'ōˌvȯid\, **ovoi•dal** \ō'vȯidᵊl\ *adj* : egg-shaped

ovu•late \'ävyəˌlāt, 'ōv-\ *vb* **-lat•ed; -lat•ing** : produce eggs from an ovary **—ovu•la•tion** \ˌävyə'lāshən, ˌōv-\ *n*

ovum \'ōvəm\ *n, pl* **ova** \-və\ : female germ cell

owe \'ō\ *vb* **owed; ow•ing 1** : have an obligation to pay **2** : be indebted to or for

owing to *prep* : because of

owl \'au̇l\ *n* : nocturnal bird of prey **—owl•ish** *adj* **—owl•ish•ly** *adv*

own \'ōn\ *adj* : belonging to oneself ~ *vb* **1** : have as property **2** : acknowledge ~ *pron* : one or ones belonging to oneself **—own•er** *n* **—own•er•ship** *n*

ox \'äks\ *n, pl* **ox•en** \'äksən\ : bovine mammal and esp. a castrated bull

ox•ide \'äkˌsīd\ *n* : compound of oxygen

ox•i•dize \'äksəˌdīz\ *vb* **-dized; -diz•ing** : combine with oxygen **—ox•i•da•tion** \ˌäksə'dāshən\ *n* **—ox•i•diz•er** *n*

ox•y•gen \'äksijən\ *n* : gaseous chemical element essential for life

oys•ter \'ȯistər\ *n* : bivalve mollusk **—oys•ter•ing** \-riŋ\ *n*

ozone \'ōˌzōn\ *n* : very reactive bluish form of oxygen

P

p \'pē\ *n, pl* **p's** *or* **ps** \'pēz\ : 16th letter of the alphabet

pace \'pās\ *n* **1** : walking step **2** : rate of progress ~ *vb* **paced; pac•ing 1** : go at a pace **2** : cover with slow steps **3** : set the pace of

pace•mak•er *n* : electrical device to regulate heartbeat

pachy•derm \'pakiˌdərm\ *n* : elephant

pa•cif•ic \pə'sifik\ *adj* : calm or peaceful

pac•i•fism \'pasəˌfizəm\ *n* : opposition to war or violence **—pac•i•fist** \-fist\ *n or adj* **—pac•i•fis•tic** \ˌpasə'fistik\ *adj*

pac•i•fy \'pasəˌfī\ *vb* **-fied; -fy•ing** : make calm **—pac•i•fi•ca•tion** \ˌpasəfə'kāshən\ *n* **—pac•i•fi•er** \'pasəˌfīər\ *n*

pack \'pak\ *n* **1** : compact bundle **2** : group of animals ~ *vb* **1** : put into a container **2** : fill tightly or completely **3** : send without ceremony **—pack•er** *n*

pack•age \'pakij\ *n* : items bundled together ~ *vb* **-aged; -ag•ing** : enclose in a package

pack•et \'pakət\ *n* : small package

pact \'pakt\ *n* : agreement

pad \'pad\ *n* **1** : cushioning part or thing **2** : floating leaf of a water plant **3** : tablet of paper ~ *vb* **-dd- 1** : furnish with a pad **2** : expand with needless matter **—pad•ding** *n*

pad•dle \'padᵊl\ *n* : implement with a flat blade ~ *vb* **-dled; -dling** : move, beat, or stir with a paddle

pad•dock \'padək\ *n* : enclosed area for racehorses

pad•dy \'padē\ *n, pl* **-dies** : wet land where rice is grown

pad•lock *n* : lock with a U-shaped catch **—padlock** *vb*

pae•an \'pēən\ *n* : song of praise

pa•gan \'pāgən\ *n or adj* : heathen **—pa•gan•ism** \-ˌizəm\ *n*

[1]**page** \'pāj\ *n* : messenger ~ *vb* **paged; pag•ing** : summon by repeated calls **—pag•er** *n*

[2]**page** *n* : single leaf (as of a book) or one side of the leaf

pag•eant \'pajənt\ *n* : elaborate spectacle or procession **—pag•eant•ry** \-əntrē\ *n*

pa•go•da \pə'gōdə\ *n* : tower with roofs curving upward

paid *past of* PAY

pail \'pāl\ *n* : cylindrical container with a handle **—pail•ful** \-ˌfu̇l\ *n*

pain \'pān\ *n* **1** : punishment or penalty **2** : suffering of body or mind **3** *pl* : great care ~ *vb* : cause or experience pain **—pain•ful** \-fəl\ *adj* **—pain•ful•ly** *adv* **—pain•kill•er** *n* **—pain•kill•ing** *adj* **—pain•less** *adj* **—pain•less•ly** *adv*

pains•tak•ing \'pānˌstākiŋ\ *adj* : taking pains **—painstaking** *n* **—pains•tak•ing•ly** *adv*

paint \'pānt\ *vb* **1** : apply color or paint to **2** : portray esp. in color ~ *n* : mixture of pigment and liquid **—paint•brush** *n* **—paint•er** *n* **—paint•ing** *n*

pair \'par\ *n* : a set of two ~ *vb* : put or go together as a pair

pa•ja•mas \pə'jäməz, -'jam-\ *n pl* : loose suit for sleeping

pal \'pal\ *n* : close friend

pal•ace \'paləs\ *n* **1** : residence of a chief of state **2** : mansion **—pa•la•tial** \pə'lāshəl\ *adj*

pal•at•able \'palətəbəl\ *adj* : agreeable to the taste

pal•ate \'palət\ *n* **1** : roof of the mouth **2** : taste **—pal•a•tal** \-ətᵊl\ *adj*

pa•la•ver \pə'lavər, -'läv-\ *n* : talk **—palaver** *vb*

[1]**pale** \'pāl\ *adj* **pal•er; pal•est 1** : lacking in color or brightness **2** : light in color or shade ~ *vb* **paled; pal•ing** : make or become pale **—pale•ness** *n*

[2]**pale** *n* **1** : fence stake **2** : enclosed place

pa•le•on•tol•o•gy \ˌpālēˌän'täləjē\ *n* : branch of biology dealing with ancient forms of life known from fossils **—pa•le•on•tol•o•gist** \-ˌän'täləjist, -ən-\ *n*

pal•ette \'palət\ *n* : board on which paints are laid and mixed

pal•i•sade \ˌpalə'sād\ *n* **1** : high fence **2** : line of cliffs

[1]**pall** \'pȯl\ *n* **1** : cloth draped over a coffin **2** : something that produces gloom

[2]**pall** *vb* : lose in interest or attraction

pall•bear•er *n* : one who attends the coffin at a funeral

[1]**pal•let** \'palət\ *n* : makeshift bed

[2]**pallet** *n* : portable storage platform

pal•li•ate \'palēˌāt\ *vb* **-at•ed; -at•ing 1** : ease without curing **2** : cover or conceal by excusing **—pal•li•a•tion** \ˌpalē'āshən\ *n* **—pal•li•a•tive** \'palēˌātiv\ *adj or n*

pal•lid \'paləd\ *adj* : pale

pal•lor \'palər\ *n* : paleness

[1]**palm** \'päm, 'pälm\ *n* **1** : tall tropical tree crowned with large leaves **2** : symbol of victory

[2]**palm** *n* : underside of the hand ~ *vb* **1** : conceal in the hand **2** : impose by fraud

palm•ist•ry \'päməstrē, 'pälmə-\ *n* : reading a person's character or future in his palms **—palm•ist** \'pämist, 'pälm-\ *n*

palmy \'pämē, 'pälmē\ *adj* **palm•i•er; -est** : flourishing

pal•o•mi•no \ˌpalə'mēnō\ *n, pl* **-nos** : light-colored horse

pal•pa•ble \'palpəbəl\ *adj* **1** : capable of being touched **2** : obvious **—pal•pa•bly** \-blē\ *adv*

pal•pi•tate \'palpəˌtāt\ *vb* **-tat•ed; -tat•ing** : beat rapidly **—pal•pi•ta•tion** \ˌpalpə'tāshən\ *n*

pal•sy \'pȯlzē\ *n, pl* **-sies 1** : paralysis **2** : condition marked by tremor **—pal•sied** \-zēd\ *adj*

pal•try \'pȯltrē\ *adj* **-tri•er; -est** : trivial

pam•per \'pampər\ *vb* : spoil or indulge

pam•phlet \'pamflət\ *n* : unbound publication **—pam•phle•teer** \ˌpamflə'tir\ *n*

pan \'pan\ *n* : broad, shallow, and open container ~ *vb* **1** : wash gravel in a pan to search for gold **2** : criticize severely

pan•a•cea \ˌpanə'sēə\ *n* : remedy for all ills or difficulties

pan•cake *n* : fried flat cake

pan•cre•as \'paŋkrēəs, 'pan-\ *n* : gland that produces insulin **—pan•cre•at•ic** \ˌpaŋkrē'atik, ˌpan-\ *adj*

pan•da \'pandə\ *n* : black-and-white bear-like animal

pan•de•mo•ni•um \ˌpandə'mōnēəm\ *n* : wild uproar

pan•der \'pandər\ *n* **1** : pimp **2** : one who caters to others' desires or weaknesses ~ *vb* : act as a pander

pane \'pān\ *n* : sheet of glass

pan•e•gy•ric \ˌpanə'jirik\ *n* : eulogistic oration **—pan•e•gyr•ist** \-'jirist\ *n*

pan•el \'panᵊl\ *n* **1** : list of persons (as jurors) **2** : discussion group **3** : flat piece of construction material **4** : board with instruments or controls ~ *vb* **-eled** *or* **-elled; -el•ing** *or* **-el•ling** : decorate with panels **—pan•el•ing** *n* **—pan•el•ist** \-ist\ *n*

pang \'paŋ\ *n* : sudden sharp pain

pan•han•dle \'panˌhandᵊl\ *vb* **-dled; -dling** : ask for money on the street **—pan•han•dler** \-ər\ *n*

pan•ic \'panik\ *n* : sudden overpowering fright ~ *vb* **-icked; -ick•ing** : affect or be affected with panic **—pan•icky** \-ikē\ *adj*

pan•o•ply \'panəplē\ *n, pl* **-plies 1** : full suit of armor **2** : impressive array

pan•o•ra•ma \ˌpanə'ramə, -'räm-\ *n* : view in every direction **—pan•o•ram•ic** \-'ramik\ *adj*

pan•sy \'panzē\ *n, pl* **-sies** : low-growing garden herb with showy flowers

pant \'pant\ *vb* **1** : breathe with great effort **2** : yearn ~ *n* : panting sound

pan•ta•loons \ˌpantᵊl'ünz\ *n pl* : pants

pan•the•on \'panthēˌän, -ən\ *n* **1** : the gods of a people **2** : group of famous people

pan•ther \'panthər\ *n* : large wild cat

pant•ies \'pantēz\ *n pl* : woman's or child's short underpants

pan•to•mime \'pantəˌmīm\ *n* **1** : play without words **2** : expression by bodily or facial movements ~ *vb* : represent by pantomime

pan•try \'pantrē\ *n, pl* **-tries** : storage room for food and dishes

pants \'pants\ *n pl* **1** : 2-legged outer garment **2** : panties

pap \'pap\ *n* : soft food

pa•pa•cy \'pāpəsē\ *n, pl* **-cies 1** : office of pope **2** : reign of a pope

pa•pal \'pāpəl\ *adj* : relating to the pope

pa•pa•ya \pə'pīə\ *n* : tropical tree with large yellow edible fruit

pa•per \'pāpər\ *n* **1** : pliable substance used to write or print on, to wrap things in, or to cover walls **2** : printed or written document **3** : newspaper **—paper** *adj or vb* **— pa•per•hang•er** *n* **—pa•per•weight** *n* **—pa•pery** \'pāpərē\ *adj*

pa•per•board *n* : cardboard

pa•pier–mâ•ché \ˌpāpərmə'shā, ˌpapˌyāmə-, -ma-\ *n* : molding material of waste paper

pa•poose \pa'püs, pə-\ *n* : young child of American Indian parents

pa•pri•ka \pə'prēkə, pa-\ *n* : mild red spice from sweet peppers

pa•py•rus \pə'pīrəs\ *n, pl* **-rus•es** *or* **-ri** \-ˌrē, -ˌrī\ **1** : tall grasslike plant **2** : paper from papyrus

par \'pär\ *n* **1** : stated value **2** : common level **3** : accepted standard or normal condition **—par** *adj*

par•a•ble \'parəbəl\ *n* : simple story illustrating a moral truth

para•chute \'parəˌshüt\ *n* : large umbrella-shaped device for making a descent through air **—parachute** *vb* **—para•chut•ist** \-ˌshütist\ *n*

pa•rade \pə'rād\ *n* **1** : pompous display **2** : ceremonial formation and march ~ *vb* **-rad•ed; -rad•ing 1** : march in a parade **2** : show off

par•a•digm \'parəˌdīm, -ˌdim\ *n* : model

par•a•dise \'parəˌdīs, -ˌdīz\ *n* : place of bliss

par•a•dox \'parəˌdäks\ *n* : statement that seems contrary to common sense yet is perhaps true **—par•a•dox•i•cal** \ˌparə'däksikəl\ *adj* **—par•a•dox•i•cal•ly** *adv*

par•af•fin \'parəfən\ *n* : white waxy substance used esp. for making candles and sealing foods

par·a·gon \ˈparəˌgän, -gən\ *n* : model of perfection

para·graph \ˈparəˌgraf\ *n* : unified division of a piece of writing ~ *vb* : divide into paragraphs

par·a·keet \ˈparəˌkēt\ *n* : small slender parrot

par·al·lel \ˈparəˌlel\ *adj* **1** : lying or moving in the same direction but always the same distance apart **2** : similar ~ *n* **1** : parallel line, curve, or surface **2** : line of latitude **3** : similarity ~ *vb* **1** : compare **2** : correspond to **—par·al·lel·ism** \-ˌizəm\ *n*

par·al·lel·o·gram \ˌparəˈleləˌgram\ *n* : 4-sided polygon with opposite sides equal and parallel

pa·ral·y·sis \pəˈraləsəs\ *n, pl* **-y·ses** \-ˌsēz\ : loss of function and esp. of voluntary motion **—par·a·lyt·ic** \ˌparəˈlitik\ *adj or n*

par·a·lyze \ˈparəˌlīz\ *vb* **-lyzed; -lyz·ing** : affect with paralysis **—par·a·lyz·ing·ly** *adv*

para·med·ic \ˌparəˈmedik\ *n* : person trained to provide initial emergency medical treatment

pa·ram·e·ter \pəˈramətər\ *n* : characteristic element **—para·met·ric** \ˌparəˈmetrik\ *adj*

par·a·mount \ˈparəˌmau̇nt\ *adj* : superior to all others

par·amour \ˈparəˌmu̇r\ *n* : illicit lover

para·noia \ˌparəˈnȯiə\ *n* : mental disorder marked by irrational suspicion **—para·noid** \ˈparəˌnȯid\ *adj or n*

par·a·pet \ˈparəpət, -ˌpet\ *n* : protecting rampart in a fort

par·a·pher·na·lia \ˌparəfəˈnālyə, -fər-\ *n sing or pl* : equipment

para·phrase \ˈparəˌfrāz\ *n* : restatement of a text giving the meaning in different words **—paraphrase** *vb*

para·ple·gia \ˌparəˈplējə, -jēə\ *n* : paralysis of the lower trunk and legs **—para·ple·gic** \-jik\ *adj or n*

par·a·site \ˈparəˌsīt\ *n* : organism living on another **—par·a·sit·ic** \ˌparəˈsitik\ *adj* **—par·a·sit·ism** \ˈparəsəˌtizəm, -ˌsīt,iz-\ *n*

para·sol \ˈparəˌsȯl\ *n* : umbrella used to keep off the sun

para·troops \-ˌtrüps\ *n pl* : troops trained to parachute from an airplane **—para·troop·er** \-ˌtrüpər\ *n*

par·boil \ˈpärˌbȯil\ *vb* : boil briefly

par·cel \ˈpärsəl\ *n* **1** : lot **2** : package ~ *vb* **-celed** *or* **-celled; -cel·ing** *or* **-cel·ling** : divide into portions

parch \ˈpärch\ *vb* : toast or shrivel with dry heat

parch·ment \ˈpärchmənt\ *n* : animal skin prepared to write on

par·don \ˈpärdᵊn\ *n* : excusing of an offense ~ *vb* : free from penalty **—par·don·able** \ˈpärdᵊnəbəl\ *adj* **—par·don·er** \-ᵊnər\ *n*

pare \ˈpar\ *vb* **pared; par·ing** **1** : trim off an outside part **2** : reduce as if by paring **—par·er** *n*

par·e·gor·ic \ˌparəˈgȯrik\ *n* : tincture of opium and camphor

par·ent \ˈparənt\ *n* : one that begets or brings up offspring **—par·ent·age** \-ij\ *n* **—pa·ren·tal** \pəˈrentᵊl\ *adj* **—par·ent·hood** *n*

pa·ren·the·sis \pəˈrenthəsəs\ *n, pl* **-the·ses** \-ˌsēz\ **1** : word or phrase inserted in a passage **2** : one of a pair of punctuation marks ( ) **—par·en·thet·ic** \ˌparənˈthetik\, **par·en·thet·i·cal** \-ikəl\ *adj* **—par·en·thet·i·cal·ly** *adv*

par·fait \pärˈfā\ *n* : layered cold dessert

pa·ri·ah \pəˈrīə\ *n* : outcast

par·ish \ˈparish\ *n* : local church community

pa·rish·io·ner \pəˈrishənər\ *n* : member of a parish

par·i·ty \ˈparətē\ *n, pl* **-ties** : equality

park \ˈpärk\ *n* : land set aside for recreation or for its beauty ~ *vb* : leave a vehicle standing

par·ka \ˈpärkə\ *n* : usu. hooded heavy jacket

park·way \ˈpärkˌwā\ *n* : broad landscaped thoroughfare

par·lance \ˈpärləns\ *n* : manner of speaking

par·lay \ˈpärˌlā\ *n* : the risking of a stake plus its winnings **—parlay** *vb*

par·ley \ˈpärlē\ *n, pl* **-leys** : conference about a dispute **—parley** *vb*

par·lia·ment \ˈpärləmənt\ *n* : legislative assembly **—par·lia·men·tar·i·an** *n* **—par·lia·men·ta·ry** \ˌpärləˈmentərē\ *adj*

par·lor \ˈpärlər\ *n* **1** : reception room **2** : place of business

pa·ro·chi·al \pəˈrōkēəl\ *adj* **1** : relating to a church parish **2** : provincial **—pa·ro·chi·al·ism** \-əˌlizəm\ *n*

par·o·dy \ˈparədē\ *n, pl* **-dies** : humorous or satirical imitation **—parody** *vb*

pa·role \pəˈrōl\ *n* : conditional release of a prisoner **—parole** *vb* **—pa·rol·ee** \-ˌrōˈlē, -ˈrōˌlē\ *n*

par·ox·ysm \ˈparəkˌsizəm, pəˈräk-\ *n* : convulsion

par·quet \ˈpärˌkā, pärˈkā\ *n* : flooring of patterned wood inlay

par·ra·keet *var of* PARAKEET

par·rot \ˈparət\ *n* : bright-colored tropical bird

par·ry \ˈparē\ *vb* **-ried; -ry·ing** **1** : ward off a blow **2** : evade adroitly **—parry** *n*

parse \ˈpärs\ *vb* **parsed; pars·ing** : analyze grammatically

par·si·mo·ny \ˈpärsəˌmōnē\ *n* : extreme frugality **—par·si·mo·ni·ous** \ˌpärsəˈmōnēəs\ *adj* **—par·si·mo·ni·ous·ly** *adv*

pars·ley \ˈpärslē\ *n* : garden plant used as a seasoning or garnish

pars·nip \ˈpärsnəp\ *n* : carrotlike vegetable with a white edible root

par·son \ˈpärsᵊn\ *n* : minister

par·son·age \ˈpärsᵊnij\ *n* : parson's house

part \ˈpärt\ *n* **1** : one of the units into which a larger whole is divided **2** : function or role ~ *vb* **1** : take leave **2** : separate **3** : go away **4** : give up

par·take \pärˈtāk, pər-\ *vb* **-took; -tak·en; -tak·ing** : have or take a share **—par·tak·er** *n*

par·tial \ˈpärshəl\ *adj* **1** : favoring one over another **2** : affecting a part only **—par·tial·i·ty** \ˌpärshēˈalətē\ *n* **—par·tial·ly** \ˈpärshəlē\ *adv*

par·tic·i·pate \pərˈtisəˌpāt, pär-\ *vb* **-pat·ed; -pat·ing** : take part in something **—par·tic·i·pant** \-pənt\ *adj or n* **—par·tic·i·pa·tion** \-ˌtisəˈpāshən\ *n* **—par·tic·i·pa·to·ry** \-ˈtisəpəˌtōrē\ *adj*

par·ti·ci·ple \ˈpärtəˌsipəl\ *n* : verb form with functions of both verb and adjective **—par·ti·cip·i·al** \ˌpärtəˈsipēəl\ *adj*

par·ti·cle \ˈpärtikəl\ *n* : small bit

par·tic·u·lar \pärˈtikyələr\ *adj* **1** : relating to a specific person or thing **2** : individual **3** : hard to please ~ *n* : detail **—par·tic·u·lar·ly** *adv*

par·ti·san \ˈpärtəzən, -sən\ *n* **1** : adherent **2** : guerrilla **—partisan** *adj* **—par·ti·san·ship** *n*

par·tite \ˈpärˌtīt\ *adj* : divided into parts

par·ti·tion \pərˈtishən, pär-\ *n* **1** : distribution **2** : something that divides **—partition** *vb*

part·ly \ˈpärtlē\ *adv* : in some degree

part·ner \ˈpärtnər\ *n* **1** : associate **2** : companion **3** : business associate **—part·ner·ship** *n*

part of speech : class of words distinguished esp. according to function

par·tridge \ˈpärtrij\ *n, pl* **-tridge** *or* **-tridg·es** : stout-bodied game bird

par·ty \ˈpärtē\ *n, pl* **-ties** **1** : political organization **2** : participant **3** : company of persons esp. with a purpose **4** : social gathering

par·ve·nu \ˈpärvəˌnü, -ˌnyü\ *n* : social upstart

pass \ˈpas\ *vb* **1** : move past, over, or through **2** : go away or die **3** : allow to elapse **4** : go unchallenged **5** : transfer or undergo transfer **6** : render a judgment **7** : occur **8** : enact **9** : undergo testing successfully **10** : be regarded **11** : decline ~ *n* **1** : low place in a mountain range **2** : act of passing **3** : accomplishment **4** : permission to leave, enter, or move about **—pass·able** *adj* **—pass·ably** *adv* **—pass·er** *n* **—pass·er·by** *n*

pas·sage \ˈpasij\ *n* **1** : process of passing **2** : means of passing **3** : voyage **4** : right to pass **5** : literary selection **—pas·sage·way** *n*

pass·book *n* : bankbook

pas·sé \paˈsā\ *adj* : out-of-date

pas·sen·ger \ˈpasᵊnjər\ *n* : traveler in a conveyance

pass·ing \ˈpasiŋ\ *n* : death

pas·sion \ˈpashən\ *n* **1** : strong feeling esp. of anger, love, or desire **2** : object of affection or enthusiasm **—pas·sion·ate** \ˈpashənət\ *adj* **—pas·sion·ate·ly** *adv* **—pas·sion·less** *adj*

pas·sive \ˈpasiv\ *adj* **1** : not active but acted upon **2** : submissive **—passive** *n* **—pas·sive·ly** *adv* **—pas·siv·i·ty** \paˈsivətē\ *n*

Pass·over \ˈpasˌōvər\ *n* : Jewish holiday celebrated in March or April in commemoration of the Hebrews' liberation from slavery in Egypt

pass·port \ˈpasˌpōrt\ *n* : government document needed for travel abroad

pass·word *n* **1** : word or phrase spoken to pass a guard **2** : sequence of characters needed to get into a computer system

past \ˈpast\ *adj* **1** : ago **2** : just gone by **3** : having existed before the present **4** : expressing past time ~ *prep or adv* : beyond ~ *n* **1** : time gone by **2** : verb tense expressing time gone by **3** : past life

pas·ta \ˈpästə\ *n* : fresh or dried shaped dough

paste \ˈpāst\ *n* **1** : smooth ground food **2** : moist adhesive ~ *vb* **past·ed; past·ing** : attach with paste **—pasty** *adj*

paste·board *n* : cardboard

pas·tel \pasˈtel\ *n* : light color **—pastel** *adj*

pas·teur·ize \ˈpaschəˌrīz, ˈpastə-\ *vb* **-ized; -iz·ing** : heat (as milk) so as to kill germs **—pas·teur·i·za·tion** \ˌpaschərəˈzāshən, ˌpastə-\ *n*

pas·time \ˈpasˌtīm\ *n* : amusement

pas·tor \ˈpastər\ *n* : priest or minister serving a church or parish **—pas·tor·ate** \-tərət\ *n*

pas·to·ral \ˈpastərəl\ *adj* **1** : relating to rural life **2** : of or relating to spiritual guidance or a pastor ~ *n* : literary work dealing with rural life

past·ry \ˈpāstrē\ *n, pl* **-ries** : sweet baked goods

pas·ture \ˈpaschər\ *n* : land used for grazing ~ *vb* **-tured; -tur·ing** : graze

pat \ˈpat\ *n* **1** : light tap **2** : small mass ~ *vb* **-tt-** : tap gently ~ *adj or adv* **1** : apt or glib **2** : unyielding

patch \ˈpach\ *n* **1** : piece used for mending **2** : small area distinct from surrounding area ~ *vb* **1** : mend with a patch **2** : make of fragments **3** : repair hastily **—patchy** \-ē\ *adj*

patch·work *n* : something made of pieces of different materials, shapes, or colors

pate \ˈpāt\ *n* : crown of the head

pa·tel·la \pəˈtelə\ *n, pl* **-lae** \-ˈtelˌē, -ˌī\ *or* **-las** : kneecap

pa·tent *adj* **1** \ˈpatᵊnt, ˈpāt-\ : obvious **2** \ˈpat-\ : protected by a patent ~ \ˈpat-\ *n* : document conferring or securing a right ~ \ˈpat-\ *vb* : secure by patent **—pat·ent·ly** *adv*

pa·ter·nal \pəˈtərnᵊl\ *adj* **1** : fatherly **2** : related through or inherited from a father **—pa·ter·nal·ly** *adv*

pa·ter·ni·ty \pəˈtərnətē\ *n* : fatherhood

path \ˈpath, ˈpa̐th\ *n* **1** : trodden way **2** : route or course **—path·find·er** *n* **—path·way** *n* **—path·less** *adj*

pa·thet·ic \pəˈthetik\ *adj* : pitiful **—pa·thet·i·cal·ly** *adv*

pa·thol·o·gy \pəˈthäləjē\ *n, pl* **-gies** **1** : study of disease **2** : physical abnormality **—path·o·log·i·cal** \ˌpathəˈläjikəl\ *adj* **—pa·thol·o·gist** \pəˈthäləjist\ *n*

pa·thos \ˈpāˌthäs\ *n* : element evoking pity

pa·tience \ˈpāshəns\ *n* : habit or fact of being patient

pa·tient \ˈpāshənt\ *adj* : bearing pain or trials without complaint ~ *n* : one under medical care **—pa·tient·ly** *adv*

pa·ti·na \pəˈtēnə, ˈpatənə\ *n, pl* **-nas** \-nəz\ *or* **-nae** \-ˌnē, -ˌnī\ : green film formed on copper and bronze

pa·tio \ˈpatēˌō, ˈpät-\ *n, pl* **-ti·os** **1** : courtyard **2** : paved recreation area near a house

pa·tri·arch \ˈpātrēˌärk\ *n* **1** : man revered as father or founder **2** : venerable old man **—pa·tri·ar·chal** \ˌpātrēˈärkəl\ *adj* **—pa·tri·ar·chy** \-ˌärkē\ *n*

pa·tri·cian \pəˈtrishən\ *n* : person of high birth **—patrician** *adj*

pat·ri·mo·ny \ˈpatrəˌmōnē\ *n* : something inherited **—pat·ri·mo·ni·al** \ˌpatrəˈmōnēəl\ *adj*

pa·tri·ot \ˈpātrēət, -ˌät\ *n* : one who loves his or her country **—pa·tri·ot·ic** \ˌpātrēˈätik\ *adj* **—pa·tri·ot·i·cal·ly** *adv* **—pa·tri·o·tism** \ˈpātrēəˌtizəm\ *n*

pa·trol \pəˈtrōl\ *n* **1** : a going around for observation or security **2** : group on patrol ~ *vb* **-ll-** : carry out a patrol

pa·trol·man \-mən\ *n* : police officer

pa·tron \ˈpātrən\ *n* **1** : special protector **2** : wealthy supporter **3** : customer

pa·tron·age \ˈpatrənij, ˈpā-\ *n* **1** : support or influence of a patron **2** : trade of customers **3** : control of government appointments

pa·tron·ess \ˈpātrənəs\ *n* : woman who is a patron

pa·tron·ize \ˈpātrəˌnīz, ˈpa-\ *vb* **-ized; -iz·ing** **1** : be a customer of **2** : treat with condescension

[1]pat·ter \ˈpatər\ *vb* : talk glibly or mechanically ~ *n* : rapid talk

[2]patter *vb* : pat or tap rapidly ~ *n* : quick succession of pats or taps

pat·tern \ˈpatərn\ *n* **1** : model for imitation or for making things **2** : artistic design **3** : noticeable formation or set of characteristics ~ *vb* : form according to a pattern

pat·ty \ˈpatē\ *n, pl* **-ties** : small flat cake

pau·ci·ty \ˈpȯsətē\ *n* : shortage

paunch \ˈpȯnch\ *n* : large belly **—paunchy** *adj*

pau·per \ˈpȯpər\ *n* : poor person **—pau·per·ism** \-pəˌrizəm\ *n* **—pau·per·ize** \-pəˌrīz\ *vb*

pause \ˈpȯz\ *n* : temporary stop ~ *vb* **paused; paus·ing** : stop briefly

pave \ˈpāv\ *vb* **paved; pav·ing** : cover to smooth or firm the surface **—pave·ment** \-mənt\ *n* **—pav·ing** *n*

pa·vil·ion \pəˈvilyən\ *n* **1** : large tent **2** : light structure used for entertainment or shelter

paw \ˈpȯ\ *n* : foot of a 4-legged clawed animal ~ *vb* **1** : handle clumsily or rudely **2** : touch or strike with a paw

pawn \ˈpȯn\ *n* **1** : goods deposited as security for a loan **2** : state of being pledged ~ *vb* : deposit as a pledge **—pawn·bro·ker** *n* **—pawn·shop** *n*

pay \ˈpā\ *vb* **paid** \ˈpād\; **pay·ing** **1** : make due return for goods or services **2** : discharge indebtedness for **3** : requite **4** : give freely or as fitting **5** : be profitable ~ *n* **1** : status of being paid **2** : something paid **—pay·able** *adj* **—pay·check** *n* **—pay·ee** \pāˈē\ *n* **—pay·er** *n* **—pay·ment** *n*

PC \ˌpēˈsē\ *n, pl* **PCs** *or* **PC's** : microcomputer

pea \ˈpē\ *n* : round edible seed of a leguminous vine

peace \ˈpēs\ *n* **1** : state of calm and quiet **2** : absence of war or strife **—peace·able** \-əbəl\ *adj* **—peace·ably** \-blē\ *adv* **—peace·ful** \-fəl\ *adj* **—peace·ful·ly** *adv* **—peace·keep·er** *n* **—peace·keep·ing** *n* **—peace·mak·er** *n* **—peace·time** *n*

peach \ˈpēch\ *n* : sweet juicy fruit of a flowering tree or this tree

pea·cock \ˈpēˌkäk\ *n* : brilliantly colored male pheasant

peak \ˈpēk\ *n* **1** : pointed or projecting part **2** : top of a hill **3** : highest level ~ *vb* : reach a maximum **—peak** *adj*

peak·ed \ˈpēkəd\ *adj* : sickly

peal \ˈpēl\ *n* : loud sound (as of ringing bells) ~ *vb* : give out peals

pea·nut \ˈpēˌnət\ *n* : annual herb that bears underground pods or the pod or the edible seed inside

pear \ˈpar\ *n* : fleshy fruit of a tree related to the apple

pearl \ˈpərl\ *n* : gem formed within an oyster **—pearly** \ˈpərlē\ *adj*

peas·ant \ˈpezᵊnt\ *n* : tiller of the soil **—peas·ant·ry** \-ᵊntrē\ *n*

peat \ˈpēt\ *n* : decayed organic deposit often dried for fuel **—peaty** *adj*

peb·ble \ˈpebəl\ *n* : small stone **—pebbly** *adj*

pe·can \piˈkän, -ˈkan\ *n* : hickory tree bearing a smooth-shelled nut or the nut

pec·ca·dil·lo \ˌpekəˈdilō\ *n, pl* **-loes** *or* **-los** : slight offense

[1]peck \ˈpek\ *n* : unit of dry measure equal to 8 quarts

[2]peck *vb* : strike or pick up with the bill ~ *n* : quick sharp stroke

pec·tin \ˈpektən\ *n* : water-soluble plant substance that causes fruit jellies to set **—pec·tic** \-tik\ *adj*

pec·to·ral \ˈpektərəl\ *adj* : relating to the breast or chest

pe·cu·liar \piˈkyülyər\ *adj* **1** : characteristic of only one **2** : strange **—pe·cu·liar·i·ty** \-ˌkyülˈyarətē, -ēˈar-\ *n* **—pe·cu·liar·ly** *adv*

pe·cu·ni·ary \piˈkyünēˌerē\ *adj* : relating to money

ped·a·go·gy \ˈpedəˌgōjē, -ˌgäj-\ *n* : art or profession of teaching **—ped·a·gog·ic** \ˌpedəˈgäjik, -ˈgōj-\, **ped·a·gog·i·cal** \-ikəl\ *adj* **—ped·a·gogue** \ˈpedəˌgäg\ *n*

ped·al \ˈpedᵊl\ *n* : lever worked by the foot ~ *adj* : relating to the foot ~ *vb* : use a pedal

ped·ant \ˈpedᵊnt\ *n* : learned bore **—pe·dan·tic** \piˈdantik\ *adj* **—ped·ant·ry** \ˈpedᵊntrē\ *n*

ped·dle \ˈpedᵊl\ *vb* **-dled; -dling** : offer for sale **—ped·dler** \ˈpedlər\ *n*

ped·es·tal \ˈpedəstᵊl\ *n* : support or foot of something upright

pe·des·tri·an \pəˈdestrēən\ *adj* **1** : ordinary **2** : walking ~ *n* : person who walks

pe·di·at·rics \ˌpēdēˈatriks\ *n* : branch of medicine dealing with children **—pe·di·at·ric** \-trik\ *adj* **—pe·di·a·tri·cian** \ˌpēdēəˈtrishən\ *n*

ped·i·gree \ˈpedəˌgrē\ *n* : line of ancestors or a record of it

ped·i·ment \ˈpedəmənt\ *n* : triangular gablelike decoration on a building

peek \ˈpēk\ *vb* **1** : look furtively **2** : glance **—peek** *n*

peel \ˈpēl\ *vb* **1** : strip the skin or rind from **2** : lose the outer layer ~ *n* : skin or rind **—peel·ing** *n*

[1]peep \ˈpēp\ *vb or n* : cheep

[2]peep *vb* **1** : look slyly **2** : begin to emerge ~ *n* : brief look **—peep·er** *n* **—peep·hole** *n*

[1]peer \ˈpir\ *n* **1** : one's equal **2** : nobleman **—peer·age** \-ij\ *n*

[2]peer *vb* : look intently or curiously

peer·less \-ləs\ *adj* : having no equal

peeve \ˈpēv\ *vb* **peeved; peev·ing** : make resentful ~ *n* : complaint **—peev·ish** \-ish\ *adj* **—peev·ish·ly** *adv* **—peev·ish·ness** *n*

peg \ˈpeg\ *n* : small pinlike piece ~ *vb* **-gg-** **1** : put a peg into **2** : fix or mark with or as if with pegs

pei·gnoir \pānˈwär, pen-\ *n* : negligee

pe·jo·ra·tive \piˈjȯrətiv\ *adj* : having a negative or degrading effect ~ *n* : a degrading word or phrase **—pe·jo·ra·tive·ly** *adv*

pel·i·can \ˈpelikən\ *n* : large-billed seabird

pel·la·gra \pəˈlagrə, -ˈlāg-\ *n* : protein-deficiency disease

pel·let \ˈpelət\ *n* : little ball **—pel·let·al** \-ᵊl\ *adj* **—pel·let·ize** \-ˌīz\ *vb*

pell–mell \ˈpelˈmel\ *adv* : in confusion or haste

pel•lu•cid \pə'lüsəd\ *adj* : very clear

1**pelt** \'pelt\ *n* : skin of a fur-bearing animal

2**pelt** *vb* : strike with blows or missiles

pel•vis \'pelvəs\ *n, pl* **-vis•es** \-vəsəz\ *or* **-ves** \-ˌvēz\ : cavity formed by the hip bones —**pel•vic** \-vik\ *adj*

1**pen** \'pen\ *n* : enclosure for animals ~ *vb* **-nn-** : shut in a pen

2**pen** *n* : tool for writing with ink ~ *vb* **-nn-** : write

pe•nal \'pēnᵊl\ *adj* : relating to punishment

pe•nal•ize \'pēnᵊlˌīz, 'pen-\ *vb* **-ized; -iz•ing** : put a penalty on

pen•al•ty \'penᵊltē\ *n, pl* **-ties 1** : punishment for crime **2** : disadvantage, loss, or hardship due to an action

pen•ance \'penəns\ *n* : act performed to show repentance

pence \'pens\ *pl of* PENNY

pen•chant \'penchənt\ *n* : strong inclination

pen•cil \'pensəl\ *n* : writing or drawing tool with a solid marking substance (as graphite) as its core ~ *vb* **-ciled** *or* **-cilled; -cil•ing** *or* **-cil•ling** : draw or write with a pencil

pen•dant \'pendənt\ *n* : hanging ornament

pen•dent, pen•dant \'pendənt\ *adj* : hanging

pend•ing \'pendiŋ\ *prep* : while awaiting ~ *adj* : not yet decided

pen•du•lous \'penjələs, -dyùləs\ *adj* : hanging loosely

pen•du•lum \-ləm\ *n* : a hanging weight that is free to swing

pen•e•trate \'penəˌtrāt\ *vb* **-trat•ed; -trat•ing 1** : enter into **2** : permeate **3** : see into —**pen•e•tra•ble** \-trəbəl\ *adj* —**pen•e•tra•tion** \ˌpenə'trāshən\ *n* —**pen•e•tra•tive** \'penəˌtrātiv\ *adj*

pen•guin \'pengwən, 'peŋ-\ *n* : short-legged flightless seabird

pen•i•cil•lin \ˌpenə'silən\ *n* : antibiotic usu. produced by a mold

pen•in•su•la \pə'ninsələ, -'ninchə-\ *n* : land extending out into the water —**pen•in•su•lar** \-lər\ *adj*

pe•nis \'pēnəs\ *n, pl* **-nes** \-ˌnēz\ *or* **-nis•es** : male organ of copulation

pen•i•tent \'penətənt\ *adj* : feeling sorrow for sins or offenses ~ *n* : penitent person —**pen•i•tence** \-təns\ *n* —**pen•i•ten•tial** \ˌpenə'tenchəl\ *adj*

pen•i•ten•tia•ry \ˌpenə'tenchərē\ *n, pl* **-ries** : state or federal prison

pen•man•ship \'penmənˌship\ *n* : art or practice of writing

pen•nant \'penənt\ *n* : nautical or championship flag

pen•ny \'penē\ *n, pl* **-nies** \-ēz\ *or* **pence** \'pens\ **1** : monetary unit equal to 1/100 pound **2** *pl* **-nies** : cent —**pen•ni•less** \'peniləs\ *adj*

pen•sion \'penchən\ *n* : retirement income ~ *vb* : pay a pension to —**pen•sion•er** *n*

pen•sive \'pensiv\ *adj* : thoughtful —**pen•sive•ly** *adv*

pent \'pent\ *adj* : confined

pent•a•gon \'pentəˌgän\ *n* : 5-sided polygon —**pen•tag•o•nal** \pen'tagənᵊl\ *adj*

pen•tam•e•ter \pen'tamətər\ *n* : line of verse containing 5 metrical feet

pent•house \'pentˌhaùs\ *n* : rooftop apartment

pen•u•ry \'penyərē\ *n* **1** : poverty **2** : thrifty or stingy manner —**pe•nu•ri•ous** \pə'nùrēəs, -'nyùr-\ *adj*

pe•on \'pēˌän, -ən\ *n, pl* **-ons** *or* **-o•nes** \pā'ōnēz\ : landless laborer in Spanish America —**pe•on•age** \-ənij\ *n*

pe•o•ny \'pēənē\ *n, pl* **-nies** : garden plant having large flowers

peo•ple \'pēpəl\ *n, pl* **people 1** *pl* : human beings in general **2** *pl* : human beings in a certain group (as a family) or community **3** *pl* **peoples** : tribe, nation, or race ~ *vb* **-pled; -pling** : constitute the population of

pep \'pep\ *n* : brisk energy ~ *vb* **pepped; pep•ping** : put pep into —**pep•py** *adj*

pep•per \'pepər\ *n* **1** : pungent seasoning from the berry (**pep•per•corn**) of a shrub **2** : vegetable grown for its hot or sweet fruit ~ *vb* : season with pepper —**pep•pery** \-ərē\ *adj*

pep•per•mint \-ˌmint, -mənt\ *n* : pungent aromatic mint

pep•per•o•ni \ˌpepə'rōnē\ *n* : spicy beef and pork sausage

pep•tic \'peptik\ *adj* : relating to digestion or the effect of digestive juices

per \'pər\ *prep* **1** : by means of **2** : for each **3** : according to

per•am•bu•late \pə'rambyəˌlāt\ *vb* **-lat•ed; -lat•ing** : walk —**per•am•bu•la•tion** \-ˌrambyə'lāshən\ *n*

per•cale \ˌpər'kāl, 'pərˌ-; ˌpər'kal\ *n* : fine woven cotton cloth

per•ceive \pər'sēv\ *vb* **-ceived; -ceiv•ing 1** : realize **2** : become aware of through the senses —**per•ceiv•able** *adj*

per•cent \pər'sent\ *adv* : in each hundred ~ *n, pl* **-cent** *or* **-cents 1** : one part in a hundred **2** : percentage

per•cent•age \pər'sentij\ *n* : part expressed in hundredths

per•cen•tile \pər'senˌtīl\ *n* : a standing on a scale of 0–100

per•cep•ti•ble \pər'septəbəl\ *adj* : capable of being perceived —**per•cep•ti•bly** \-blē\ *adv*

per•cep•tion \pər'sepshən\ *n* **1** : act or result of perceiving **2** : ability to understand

per•cep•tive \pər'septiv\ *adj* : showing keen perception —**per•cep•tive•ly** *adv*

1**perch** \'pərch\ *n* : roost for birds ~ *vb* : roost

2**perch** *n, pl* **perch** *or* **perch•es** : freshwater spiny-finned food fish

per•co•late \'pərkəˌlāt\ *vb* **-lat•ed; -lat•ing** : trickle or filter down through a substance —**per•co•la•tor** \-ˌlātər\ *n*

per•cus•sion \pər'kəshən\ *n* **1** : sharp blow **2** : musical instrument sounded by striking

pe•remp•to•ry \pə'remptərē\ *adj* **1** : imperative **2** : domineering —**pe•remp•to•ri•ly** \-tərəlē\ *adv*

pe•ren•ni•al \pə'renēəl\ *adj* **1** : present at all seasons **2** : continuing from year to year **3** : recurring regularly ~ *n* : perennial plant —**pe•ren•ni•al•ly** *adv*

per•fect \'pərfikt\ *adj* **1** : being without fault or defect **2** : exact **3** : complete ~ \pər'fekt\ *vb* : make perfect —**per•fect•ibil•i•ty** \pərˌfektə'bilətē\ *n* —**per•fect•ible** \pər'fektəbəl\ *adj* —**per•fect•ly** *adv* —**per•fect•ness** *n*

per•fec•tion \pər'fekshən\ *n* **1** : quality or state of being perfect **2** : highest degree of excellence —**per•fec•tion•ist** \-shənist\ *n*

per•fid•i•ous \pər'fidēəs\ *adj* : treacherous —**per•fid•i•ous•ly** *adv*

per•fo•rate \'pərfəˌrāt\ *vb* **-rat•ed; -rat•ing** : make a hole in —**per•fo•ra•tion** \ˌpərfə'rāshən\ *n*

per•force \pər'fōrs\ *adv* : of necessity

per•form \pər'fòrm\ *vb* **1** : carry out **2** : do in a set manner **3** : give a performance —**per•form•er** *n*

per•for•mance \pər'fòrməns\ *n* **1** : act or process of performing **2** : public presentation

per•fume \'pərˌfyüm, pər'-\ *n* **1** : pleasant odor **2** : something that gives a scent ~ \pər'-, 'pərˌ-\ *vb* **-fumed; -fum•ing** : add scent to

per•func•to•ry \pər'fəŋktərē\ *adj* : done merely as a duty —**per•func•to•ri•ly** \-tərəlē\ *adv*

per•haps \pər'haps\ *adv* : possibly but not certainly

per•il \'perəl\ *n* : danger —**per•il•ous** *adj* —**per•il•ous•ly** *adv*

pe•rim•e•ter \pə'rimətər\ *n* : outer boundary of a body or figure

pe•ri•od \'pirēəd\ *n* **1** : punctuation mark . used esp. to mark the end of a declarative sentence or an abbreviation **2** : division of time **3** : stage in a process or development

pe•ri•od•ic \ˌpirē'ädik\ *adj* : occurring at regular intervals —**pe•ri•od•i•cal•ly** *adv*

pe•ri•od•i•cal \ˌpirē'ädikəl\ *n* : newspaper or magazine

pe•riph•ery \pə'rifərē\ *n, pl* **-er•ies** : outer boundary —**pe•riph•er•al** \-ərəl\ *adj*

peri•scope \'perəˌskōp\ *n* : optical instrument for viewing from a submarine

per•ish \'perish\ *vb* : die or spoil —**per•ish•able** \-əbəl\ *adj or n*

per•ju•ry \'pərjərē\ *n* : lying under oath —**per•jure** \'pərjər\ *vb* —**per•jur•er** *n*

1**perk** \'pərk\ *vb* **1** : thrust (as the head) up jauntily **2** : freshen **3** : gain vigor or spirit —**perky** *adj*

2**perk** *vb* : percolate

3**perk** *n* : privilege or benefit in addition to regular pay

per•ma•nent \'pərmənənt\ *adj* : lasting ~ *n* : hair wave —**per•ma•nence** \-nəns\ *n* —**per•ma•nent•ly** *adv*

per•me•able \'pərmēəbəl\ *adj* : permitting fluids to seep through —**per•me•a•bil•i•ty** \ˌpərmēə'bilətē\ *n*

per•me•ate \'pərmēˌāt\ *vb* **-at•ed; -at•ing 1** : seep through **2** : pervade —**per•me•ation** \ˌpərmē'āshən\ *n*

per•mis•si•ble \pər'misəbəl\ *adj* : that may be permitted

per•mis•sion \pər'mishən\ *n* : formal consent

per•mis•sive \pər'misiv\ *adj* : granting freedom esp. to excess —**per•miss•ive•ly** *adv* —**per•mis•sive•ness** *n*

per•mit \pər'mit\ *vb* **-tt- 1** : approve **2** : make possible ~ \'pərˌ-, pər'-\ *n* : license

per•ni•cious \pər'nishəs\ *adj* : very harmful —**per•ni•cious•ly** *adv*

per•ox•ide \pə'räkˌsīd\ *n* : compound (as hydrogen peroxide) in which oxygen is joined to oxygen

per•pen•dic•u•lar \ˌpərpən'dikyələr\ *adj* **1** : vertical **2** : meeting at a right angle — **perpendicular** *n* —**per•pen•dic•u•lar•i•ty** \-ˌdikyə'larətē\ *n* —**per•pen•dic•u•lar•ly** *adv*

per•pe•trate \'pərpəˌtrāt\ *vb* **-trat•ed; -trat•ing** : be guilty of doing —**per•pe•tra•tion** \ˌpərpə'trāshən\ *n* —**per•pe•tra•tor** \'pərpəˌtrātər\ *n*

per•pet•u•al \pər'pechəwəl\ *adj* **1** : continuing forever **2** : occurring continually —**per•pet•u•al•ly** *adv* —**per•pe•tu•ity** \ˌpərpə'tüətē, -'tyü-\ *n*

per•pet•u•ate \pər'pechəˌwāt\ *vb* **-at•ed; -at•ing** : make perpetual —**per•pet•u•a•tion** \-ˌpechə'wāshən\ *n*

per•plex \pər'pleks\ *vb* : confuse —**per•plex•i•ty** \-ətē\ *n*

per•se•cute \'pərsiˌkyüt\ *vb* **-cut•ed; -cut•ing** : harass, afflict —**per•se•cu•tion** \ˌpərsi'kyüshən\ *n* —**per•se•cu•tor** \'pərsiˌkyütər\ *n*

per•se•vere \ˌpərsə'vir\ *vb* **-vered; -ver•ing** : persist —**per•se•ver•ance** \-'virəns\ *n*

per•sist \pər'sist, -'zist\ *vb* **1** : go on resolutely in spite of difficulties **2** : continue to exist —**per•sis•tence** \-'sistəns, -'zis-\ *n* —**per•sis•ten•cy** \-tənsē\ *n* —**per•sis•tent** \-tənt\ *adj* —**per•sis•tent•ly** *adv*

per•son \'pərsᵊn\ *n* **1** : human being **2** : human being's body or individuality **3** : reference to the speaker, one spoken to, or one spoken of

per•son•able \'pərsᵊnəbəl\ *adj* : having a pleasing personality

per•son•age \'pərsᵊnij\ *n* : person of rank or distinction

per•son•al \'pərsᵊnəl\ *adj* **1** : relating to a particular person **2** : done in person **3** : affecting one's body **4** : offensive to a certain individual —**per•son•al•ly** *adv*

per•son•al•i•ty \ˌpərsᵊn'alətē\ *n, pl* **-ties 1** : manner and disposition of an individual **2** : distinctive or well-known person

per•son•al•ize \'pərsᵊnəˌlīz\ *vb* **-ized; -iz•ing** : mark as belonging to a particular person

per•son•i•fy \pər'sänəˌfī\ *vb* **-fied; -fy•ing 1** : represent as a human being **2** : be the embodiment of —**per•son•i•fi•ca•tion** \-ˌsänəfə'kāshən\ *n*

per•son•nel \ˌpərsᵊn'el\ *n* : body of persons employed

per•spec•tive \pər'spektiv\ *n* **1** : apparent depth and distance in painting **2** : view of things in their true relationship or importance

per•spi•ca•cious \ˌpərspə'kāshəs\ *adj* : showing keen understanding or discernment —**per•spi•cac•i•ty** \-'kasətē\ *n*

per•spire \pər'spīr\ *vb* **-spired; -spir•ing** : sweat —**per•spi•ra•tion** \ˌpərspə'rāshən\ *n*

per•suade \pər'swād\ *vb* **-suad•ed; -suad•ing** : win over to a belief or course of action by argument or entreaty —**per•sua•sion** \pər'swāzhən\ *n* —**per•sua•sive** \-'swāsiv, -ziv\ *adj* —**per•sua•sive•ly** *adv* —**per•sua•sive•ness** *n*

pert \'pərt\ *adj* : flippant or irreverent

per•tain \pər'tān\ *vb* **1** : belong **2** : relate

per•ti•nent \'pərtᵊnənt\ *adj* : relevant —**per•ti•nence** \-əns\ *n*

per•turb \pər'tərb\ *vb* : make uneasy —**per•tur•ba•tion** \ˌpərtər'bāshən\ *n*

pe•ruse \pə'rüz\ *vb* **-rused; -rus•ing** : read attentively —**pe•rus•al** \-'rüzəl\ *n*

per•vade \pər'vād\ *vb* **-vad•ed; -vad•ing** : spread through every part of —**per•va•sive** \-'vāsiv, -ziv\ *adj*

per•verse \pər'vərs\ *adj* **1** : corrupt **2** : unreasonably contrary —**per•verse•ly** *adv* —**per•verse•ness** *n* — **per•ver•sion** \pər'vərzhən\ *n* — **per•ver•si•ty** \-'vərsətē\ *n*

per•vert \pər'vərt\ *vb* : corrupt or distort ~ \'pərˌ-\ *n* : one that is perverted

pe•so \'pāsō\ *n, pl* **-sos** : monetary unit (as of Mexico)

pes•si•mism \'pesəˌmizəm\ *n* : inclination to expect the worst —**pes•simist** \-mist\ *n* —**pes•si•mis•tic** \ˌpesə'mistik\ *adj*

pest \'pest\ *n* **1** : nuisance **2** : plant or animal detrimental to humans or their crops —**pes•ti•cide** \'pestəˌsīd\ *n*

pes•ter \'pestər\ *vb* **-tered; -ter•ing** : harass with petty matters

pes•ti•lence \'pestələns\ *n* : plague —**pes•ti•lent** \-lənt\ *adj*

pes•tle \'pesəl, 'pestᵊl\ *n* : implement for grinding substances in a mortar

pet \'pet\ *n* **1** : domesticated animal kept for pleasure **2** : favorite ~ *vb* **-tt-** : stroke gently or lovingly

pet•al \'petᵊl\ *n* : modified leaf of a flower head

pe•tite \pə'tēt\ *adj* : having a small trim figure

pe•ti•tion \pə'tishən\ *n* : formal written request ~ *vb* : make a request —**pe•ti•tion•er** *n*

pet•ri•fy \'petrəˌfī\ *vb* **-fied; -fy•ing 1** : change into stony material **2** : make rigid or inactive (as from fear) —**pet•ri•fac•tion** \ˌpetrə'fakshən\ *n*

pe•tro•leum \pə'trōlēəm\ *n* : raw oil obtained from the ground

pet•ti•coat \'petēˌkōt\ *n* : skirt worn under a dress

pet•ty \'petē\ *adj* **-ti•er; -est 1** : minor **2** : of no importance **3** : narrow-minded or mean —**pet•ti•ly** \'petᵊlē\ *adv* —**pet•ti•ness** *n*

petty officer *n* : subordinate officer in the navy or coast guard

pet•u•lant \'pechələnt\ *adj* : irritable —**pet•u•lance** \-ləns\ *n* —**pet•u•lant•ly** *adv*

pe•tu•nia \pi'tünyə, -'tyü-\ *n* : tropical herb with bright flowers

pew \'pyü\ *n* : bench with a back used in a church

pew•ter \'pyütər\ *n* : alloy of tin used for household utensils

pH \ˌpē'āch\ *n* : number expressing relative acidity and alkalinity

pha•lanx \'fāˌlaŋks\ *n, pl* **-lanx•es** *or* **-lan•ges** \fə'lanˌjēz\ **1** : body (as of troops) in compact formation **2** *pl* *phalanges* : digital bone of the hand or foot

phal•lus \'faləs\ *n, pl* **-li** \'falˌī\ *or* **-lus•es** : penis —**phal•lic** *adj*

phantasy *var of* FANTASY

phan•tom \'fantəm\ *n* : something that only appears to be real —**phantom** *adj*

pha•raoh \'ferō, 'fārō\ *n* : ruler of ancient Egypt

phar•ma•ceu•ti•cal \ˌfärmə'sütikəl\ *adj* : relating to pharmacy or the making and selling of medicinal drugs —**pharmaceutical** *n*

phar•ma•col•o•gy \ˌfärmə'käləjē\ *n* : science of drugs esp. as related to medicinal uses —**phar•ma•co•log•i•cal** \-ikəl\ *adj* —**phar•ma•col•o•gist** \-'käləjist\ *n*

phar•ma•cy \'färməsē\ *n, pl* **-cies 1** : art or practice of preparing and dispensing medical drugs **2** : drugstore —**phar•ma•cist** \-sist\ *n*

phar•ynx \'fariŋks\ *n, pl* **pha•ryn•ges** \fə'rinˌjēz\ : space behind the mouth into which the nostrils, esophagus, and windpipe open —**pha•ryn•ge•al** \fə'rinjəl, ˌfarən'jēəl\ *adj*

phase \'fāz\ *n* **1** : particular appearance or stage in a recurring series of changes **2** : stage in a process —**phase in** *vb* : introduce in stages —**phase out** *vb* : discontinue gradually

pheas•ant \'fezᵊnt\ *n, pl* **-ant** *or* **-ants** : long-tailed brilliantly colored game bird

phe•nom•e•non \fi'näməˌnän, -nən\ *n, pl* **-na** \-nə\ *or* **-nons 1** : observable fact or event **2** *pl* **-nons** : prodigy —**phe•nom•e•nal** \-'nämənᵊl\ *adj*

phi•lan•der•er \fə'landərər\ *n* : one who makes love without serious intent

phi•lan•thro•py \fə'lanthrəpē\ *n, pl* **-pies** : charitable act or gift or an organization that distributes such gifts —**phil•an•throp•ic** \ˌfilən'thräpik\ *adj* —**phi•lan•thro•pist** \fə'lanthrəpist\ *n*

phi•lat•e•ly \fə'latᵊlē\ *n* : collection and study of postage stamps —**phi•lat•e•list** \-ᵊlist\ *n*

phi•lis•tine \'filəˌstēn, fə'listən\ *n* : one who is smugly indifferent to intellectual or artistic values —**philistine** *adj*

philo•den•dron \ˌfilə'dendrən\ *n, pl* **-drons** *or* **-dra** \-drə\ : plant grown for its showy leaves

phi•los•o•pher \fə'läsəfər\ *n* **1** : reflective thinker **2** : student of philosophy

phi•los•o•phy \fə'läsəfē\ *n, pl* **-phies 1** : critical study of fundamental beliefs **2** : sciences and liberal arts exclusive of medicine, law, and theology **3** : system of ideas **4** : sum of personal convictions —**phil•o•soph•ic** \ˌfilə'säfik\, **phil•o•soph•i•cal** \-ikəl\ *adj* —**phil•o•soph•i•cal•ly** \-klē\ *adv* —**phi•los•o•phize** \fə'läsəˌfīz\ *vb*

phle•bi•tis \fli'bītəs\ *n* : inflammation of a vein

phlegm \'flem\ *n* : thick mucus in the nose and throat

phlox \'fläks\ *n, pl* **phlox** *or* **phlox•es** : herb grown for its flower clusters

pho•bia \'fōbēə\ *n* : irrational persistent fear

phoe•nix \'fēniks\ *n* : legendary bird held to burn itself to death and rise fresh and young from its ashes

phone \'fōn\ *n* : telephone ~ *vb* **phoned; phon•ing** : call on a telephone

pho•neme \'fōˌnēm\ *n* : basic distinguishable unit of speech —**pho•ne•mic** \fō'nēmik\ *adj*

pho•net•ics \fə'netiks\ *n* : study of speech sounds —**pho•net•ic** \-ik\ *adj* —**pho•ne•ti•cian** \ˌfōnə'tishən\ *n*

pho•nics \'fäniks\ *n* : method of teaching reading by stressing sound values of syllables and words

pho•no•graph \'fōnəˌgraf\ *n* : instrument that reproduces sounds from a grooved disc

pho•ny, pho•ney \'fōnē\ *adj* **-ni•er; -est** : not sincere or genuine —**phony** *n*

phos•phate \'fäsˌfāt\ *n* : chemical salt used in fertilizers —**phos•phat•ic** \fäs'fatik\ *adj*

phos•phor \'fäsfər\ *n* : phosphorescent substance

phos•pho•res•cence \,fäsfə'resəns\ *n* : luminescence from absorbed radiation —**phos•pho•res•cent** \-ənt\ *adj* —**phos•pho•res•cent•ly** *adv*

phos•pho•rus \'fäsfərəs\ *n* : poisonous waxy chemical element —**phos•phor•ic** \fäs'fȯrik, -'fär-\ *adj* —**phos•pho•rous** \'fäsfərəs, fäs'fōrəs\ *adj*

pho•to \'fōtō\ *n, pl* **-tos** : photograph — **photo** *vb or adj*

pho•to•copy \'fōtə,käpē\ *n* : photographic copy (as of a printed page) —**photocopy** *vb*

pho•to•elec•tric \,fōtōi'lektrik\ *adj* : relating to an electrical effect due to the interaction of light with matter

pho•to•ge•nic \,fōtə'jenik\ *adj* : suitable for being photographed

pho•to•graph \'fōtə,graf\ *n* : picture taken by photography —**photograph** *vb* — **pho•tog•ra•pher** \fə'tägrəfər\ *n*

pho•tog•ra•phy \fə'tägrəfē\ *n* : process of using light to produce images on a sensitized surface —**pho•to•graph•ic** \,fōtə'grafik\ *adj* —**pho•to•graph•i•cal•ly** *adv*

pho•to•syn•the•sis \,fōtō'sinthəsəs\ *n* : formation of carbohydrates by chlorophyll-containing plants exposed to sunlight — **pho•to•syn•the•size** \-,sīz\ *vb* —**pho•to•syn•thet•ic** \-sin'thetik\ *adj*

phrase \'frāz\ *n* **1** : brief expression **2** : group of related words that express a thought ~ *vb* **phrased; phras•ing** : express in a particular manner

phrase•ol•o•gy \,frāzē'äləjē\ *n, pl* **-gies** : manner of phrasing

phy•lum \'fīləm\ *n, pl* **-la** \-lə\ : major division of the plant or animal kingdom

phys•i•cal \'fizikəl\ *adj* **1** : relating to nature **2** : material as opposed to mental or spiritual **3** : relating to the body ~ *n* : medical examination —**phys•i•cal•ly** \-klē\ *adv*

phy•si•cian \fə'zishən\ *n* : doctor of medicine

physician's assistant *n* : person certified to provide basic medical care under a physician's supervision

phys•i•cist \'fizəsist\ *n* : specialist in physics

phys•ics \'fiziks\ *n* : science that deals with matter and motion

phys•i•og•no•my \,fizē'ägnəmē\ *n, pl* **-mies** : facial appearance esp. as a reflection of inner character

phys•i•ol•o•gy \,fizē'äləjē\ *n* : functional processes in an organism —**phys•i•o•log•i•cal** \-ēə'läjikəl\, **phys•i•o•log•ic** \-ik\ *adj* —**phys•i•ol•o•gist** \-ē'äləjist\ *n*

phy•sique \fə'zēk\ *n* : build of a person's body

pi \'pī\ *n, pl* **pis** \'pīz\ : symbol π denoting the ratio of the circumference of a circle to its diameter or the ratio itself

pi•a•nist \pē'anist, 'pēənist\ *n* : one who plays the piano

pi•ano \pē'anō\ *n, pl* **-anos** : musical instrument with strings sounded by hammers operated from a keyboard

pi•az•za \pē'azə, -'äz-, -tsə\ *n, pl* **-zas** *or* **-ze** \-tsā\ : public square in a town

pic•a•yune \,pikē'yün\ *adj* : trivial or petty

pic•co•lo \'pikə,lō\ *n, pl* **-los** : small shrill flute

1**pick** \'pik\ *vb* **1** : break up with a pointed instrument **2** : remove bit by bit **3** : gather by plucking **4** : select **5** : rob **6** : provoke **7** : unlock with a wire **8** : eat sparingly ~ *n* **1** : act of choosing **2** : choicest one — **pick•er** *n* —**pick up** *vb* **1** : improve **2** : put in order

2**pick** *n* : pointed digging tool

pick•ax *n* : pick

pick•er•el \'pikərəl\ *n, pl* **-el** *or* **-els** : small pike

pick•et \'pikət\ *n* **1** : pointed stake (as for a fence) **2** : worker demonstrating on strike ~ *vb* : demonstrate as a picket

pick•le \'pikəl\ *n* **1** : brine or vinegar solution for preserving foods or a food preserved in a pickle **2** : bad state —**pickle** *vb*

pick•pock•et *n* : one who steals from pockets

pick•up \'pik,əp\ *n* **1** : revival or acceleration **2** : light truck with an open body

pic•nic \'pik,nik\ *n* : outing with food usu. eaten in the open ~ *vb* **-nicked; -nick•ing** : go on a picnic

pic•to•ri•al \pik'tōrēəl\ *adj* : relating to pictures

pic•ture \'pikchər\ *n* **1** : representation by painting, drawing, or photography **2** : vivid description **3** : copy **4** : movie ~ *vb* **-tured; -tur•ing** : form a mental image of

pic•tur•esque \,pikchə'resk\ *adj* : attractive or charming enough for a picture —**pic•tur•esque•ness** *n*

pie \'pī\ *n* : pastry crust and a filling

pie•bald \'pī,bȯld\ *adj* : blotched with white and black

piece \'pēs\ *n* **1** : part of a whole **2** : one of a group or set **3** : single item **4** : product of creative work ~ *vb* **pieced; piec•ing** : join into a whole

piece•meal \'pēs,mēl\ *adv or adj* : gradually

pied \'pīd\ *adj* : colored in blotches

pier \'pir\ *n* **1** : support for a bridge span **2** : deck or wharf built out over water **3** : pillar

pierce \'pirs\ *vb* **pierced; pierc•ing 1** : enter or thrust into or through **2** : penetrate **3** : see through

pi•ety \'pīətē\ *n, pl* **-eties** : devotion to religion

pig \'pig\ *n* **1** : young swine **2** : dirty or greedy individual **3** : iron casting —**pig•gish** \-ish\ *adj* —**pig•let** \-lət\ *n* —**pig•pen** *n* —**pig•sty** *n*

pi•geon \'pijən\ *n* : stout-bodied short-legged bird

pi•geon•hole *n* : small open compartment for letters or documents ~ *vb* **1** : place in a pigeonhole **2** : classify

pig•gy•back \'pigē,bak\ *adv or adj* : up on the back and shoulders

pig•head•ed \-'hedəd\ *adj* : stubborn

pig•ment \'pigmənt\ *n* : coloring matter — **pig•men•ta•tion** *n*

pigmy *var of* PYGMY

pig•tail *n* : tight braid of hair

1**pike** \'pīk\ *n, pl* **pike** *or* **pikes** : large freshwater fish

2**pike** *n* : former weapon consisting of a long wooden staff with a steel point

3**pike** *n* : turnpike

pi•laf, pi•laff \pi'läf, 'pē,läf\, **pi•lau** \pi'lō, -'lō; 'pēlō, -lō\ *n* : dish of seasoned rice

1**pile** \'pīl\ *n* : supporting pillar driven into the ground

2**pile** *n* : quantity of things thrown on one another ~ *vb* **piled; pil•ing** : heap up, accumulate

3**pile** *n* : surface of fine hairs or threads — **piled** *adj*

piles \'pīlz\ *n pl* : hemorrhoids

pil•fer \'pilfər\ *vb* : steal in small quantities

pil•grim \'pilgrəm\ *n* **1** : one who travels to a shrine or holy place in devotion **2** *cap* : one of the English settlers in America in 1620

pil•grim•age \-grəmij\ *n* : pilgrim's journey

pill \'pil\ *n* : small rounded mass of medicine —**pill•box** *n*

pil•lage \'pilij\ *vb* **-laged; -lag•ing** : loot and plunder —**pillage** *n*

pil•lar \'pilər\ *n* : upright usu. supporting column —**pil•lared** *adj*

pil•lo•ry \'pilərē\ *n, pl* **-ries** : wooden frame for public punishment with holes for the head and hands ~ *vb* **-ried; -ry•ing 1** : set in a pillory **2** : expose to public scorn

pil•low \'pilō\ *n* : soft cushion for the head —**pil•low•case** *n*

pi•lot \'pīlət\ *n* **1** : helmsman **2** : person licensed to take ships into and out of a port **3** : guide **4** : one that flies an aircraft or spacecraft ~ *vb* : act as pilot of —**pi•lot•less** *adj*

pi•men•to \pə'mentō\ *n, pl* **-tos** *or* **-to 1** : allspice **2** : pimiento

pi•mien•to \pə'mentō, -'myen-\ *n, pl* **-tos** : mild red sweet pepper

pimp \'pimp\ *n* : man who solicits clients for a prostitute —**pimp** *vb*

pim•ple \'pimpəl\ *n* : small inflamed swelling on the skin —**pim•ply** \-pəlē\ *adj*

pin \'pin\ *n* **1** : fastener made of a small pointed piece of wire **2** : ornament or emblem fastened to clothing with a pin **3** : wooden object used as a target in bowling ~ *vb* **-nn- 1** : fasten with a pin **2** : hold fast or immobile —**pin•hole** *n*

pin•a•fore \'pinə,fōr\ *n* : sleeveless dress or apron fastened at the back

pin•cer \'pinsər\ *n* **1** *pl* : gripping tool with 2 jaws **2** : pincerlike claw

pinch \'pinch\ *vb* **1** : squeeze between the finger and thumb or between the jaws of a tool **2** : compress painfully **3** : restrict **4** : steal ~ *n* **1** : emergency **2** : painful effect **3** : act of pinching **4** : very small quantity

pin•cush•ion *n* : cushion for storing pins

1**pine** \'pīn\ *n* : evergreen cone-bearing tree or its wood

2**pine** *vb* **pined; pin•ing 1** : lose health through distress **2** : yearn for intensely

pine•ap•ple *n* : tropical plant bearing an edible juicy fruit

pin•feath•er *n* : new feather just coming through the skin

1**pinion** \'pinyən\ *vb* : restrain by binding the arms

2**pinion** *n* : small gear

1**pink** \'piŋk\ *n* **1** : plant with narrow leaves and showy flowers **2** : highest degree

2**pink** *n* : light red color —**pink** *adj* —**pink•ish** *adj*

pink•eye *n* : contagious eye inflammation

pin•na•cle \'pinikəl\ *n* : highest point

pi•noch•le \'pē,nəkəl\ *n* : card game played with a 48-card deck

pin•point *vb* : locate, hit, or aim with great precision

pint \'pīnt\ *n* : 1/2 quart

pin•to \'pin,tō\ *n, pl* **pintos** : spotted horse or pony

pin•worm *n* : small parasitic intestinal worm

pi•o•neer \,pīə'nir\ *n* **1** : one that originates or helps open up a new line of thought or activity **2** : early settler ~ *vb* : act as a pioneer

pi•ous \'pīəs\ *adj* **1** : conscientious in religious practices **2** : affectedly religious — **pi•ous•ly** *adv*

pipe \'pīp\ *n* **1** : tube that produces music when air is forced through **2** : bagpipe **3** : long tube for conducting a fluid **4** : smoking tool ~ *vb* **piped; pip•ing 1** : play on a pipe **2** : speak in a high voice **3** : convey by pipes —**pip•er** *n*

pipe•line *n* **1** : line of pipe **2** : channel for information

pip•ing \'pīpiŋ\ *n* **1** : music of pipes **2** : narrow fold of material used to decorate edges or seams

pi•quant \'pēkənt\ *adj* **1** : tangy **2** : provocative or charming —**pi•quan•cy** \-kənsē\ *n*

pique \'pēk\ *n* : resentment ~ *vb* **piqued; piqu•ing 1** : offend **2** : arouse by provocation

pi•qué, pi•que \pi'kā\ *n* : durable ribbed clothing fabric

pi•ra•cy \'pīrəsē\ *n, pl* **-cies 1** : robbery on the seas **2** : unauthorized use of another's production or invention

pi•ra•nha \pə'ranyə, -'ränə\ *n* : small So. American fish with sharp teeth

pi•rate \'pīrət\ *n* : one who commits piracy —**pirate** *vb* —**pi•rat•i•cal** \pə'ratikəl, pī-\ *adj*

pir•ou•ette \,pirə'wet\ *n* : ballet turn on the toe or ball of one foot —**pirouette** *vb*

pis *pl of* PI

pis•ta•chio \pə'stashē,ō, -'stäsh-\ *n, pl* **-chios** : small tree bearing a greenish edible seed or its seed

pis•til \'pistəl\ *n* : female reproductive organ in a flower —**pis•til•late** \'pistə,lāt\ *adj*

pis•tol \'pistəl\ *n* : firearm held with one hand

pis•ton \'pistən\ *n* : sliding piece that receives and transmits motion usu. inside a cylinder

1**pit** \'pit\ *n* **1** : hole or shaft in the ground **2** : sunken or enclosed place for a special purpose **3** : hell **4** : hollow or indentation ~ *vb* **-tt- 1** : form pits in **2** : become marred with pits

2**pit** *n* : stony seed of some fruits ~ *vb* **-tt-** : remove the pit from

pit bull *n* : powerful compact dog bred for fighting

1**pitch** \'pich\ *n* : resin from conifers — **pitchy** *adj*

2**pitch** *vb* **1** : erect and fix firmly in place **2** : throw **3** : set at a particular tone level **4** : fall headlong ~ *n* **1** : action or manner of pitching **2** : degree of slope **3** : relative highness of a tone **4** : sales talk —**pitched** *adj*

1**pitch•er** \'pichər\ *n* : container for liquids

2**pitcher** *n* : one that pitches (as in baseball)

pitch•fork *n* : long-handled fork for pitching hay

pit•e•ous \'pitēəs\ *adj* : arousing pity —**pit•e•ous•ly** *adv*

pit•fall \'pit,fȯl\ *n* : hidden danger

pith \'pith\ *n* **1** : spongy plant tissue **2** : essential or meaningful part —**pithy** *adj*

piti•able \'pitēəbəl\ *adj* : pitiful

piti•ful \'pitifəl\ *adj* **1** : arousing or deserving pity **2** : contemptible —**piti•ful•ly** *adv*

pit•tance \'pitəns\ *n* : small portion or amount

pi•tu•itary \pə'tüə,terē, -'tyü-\ *adj* : relating to or being a small gland attached to the brain

pity \'pitē\ *n, pl* **pit•ies 1** : sympathetic sorrow **2** : something to be regretted ~ *vb* **pit•ied; pity•ing** : feel pity for —**piti•less** *adj* —**piti•less•ly** *adv*

piv•ot \'pivət\ *n* : fixed pin on which something turns ~ *vb* : turn on or as if on a pivot —**piv•ot•al** *adj*

pix•ie, pixy \'piksē\ *n, pl* **pix•ies** : mischievous sprite

piz•za \'pētsə\ *n* : thin pie of bread dough spread with a spiced mixture (as of tomatoes, cheese, and meat)

piz•zazz, pi•zazz \pə'zaz\ *n* : glamour

piz•ze•ria \,pētsə'rēə\ *n* : pizza restaurant

plac•ard \'plakərd, -,ärd\ *n* : poster ~ *vb* : display placards in or on

pla•cate \'plā,kāt, 'plak,āt\ *vb* **-cat•ed; -cat•ing** : appease —**pla•ca•ble** \'plakəbəl, 'plākə-\ *adj*

place \'plās\ *n* **1** : space or room **2** : indefinite area **3** : a particular building, locality, area, or part **4** : relative position in a scale or sequence **5** : seat **6** : job ~ *vb* **placed; plac•ing 1** : put in a place **2** : identify —**place•ment** *n*

pla•ce•bo \plə'sēbō\ *n, pl* **—bos** : something inactive prescribed as a remedy for its psychological effect

pla•cen•ta \plə'sentə\ *n, pl* **-tas** *or* **-tae** \-,ē\ : structure in a uterus by which a fetus is nourished —**pla•cen•tal** \-'sentəl\ *adj*

plac•id \'plasəd\ *adj* : undisturbed or peaceful —**pla•cid•i•ty** \pla'sidətē\ *n* —**plac•id•ly** *adv*

pla•gia•rize \'plājə,rīz\ *vb* **-rized; -riz•ing** : use (words or ideas) of another as if your own —**pla•gia•rism** \-,rizəm\ *n* —**pla•gia•rist** \-rist\ *n*

plague \'plāg\ *n* **1** : disastrous evil **2** : destructive contagious bacterial disease ~ *vb* **plagued; plagu•ing 1** : afflict with disease or disaster **2** : harass

plaid \'plad\ *n* : woolen fabric with a pattern of crossing stripes or the pattern itself — **plaid** *adj*

plain \'plān\ *n* : expanse of relatively level treeless country ~ *adj* **1** : lacking ornament **2** : not concealed or disguised **3** : easily understood **4** : frank **5** : not fancy or pretty —**plain•ly** *adv* —**plain•ness** \'plānnəs\ *n*

plain•tiff \'plāntəf\ *n* : complaining party in a lawsuit

plain•tive \'plāntiv\ *adj* : expressive of suffering or woe —**plain•tive•ly** *adv*

plait \'plāt, 'plat\ *n* **1** : pleat **2** : braid of hair or straw —**plait** *vb*

plan \'plan\ *n* **1** : drawing or diagram **2** : method for accomplishing something ~ *vb* **-nn- 1** : form a plan of **2** : intend — **plan•less** *adj* —**plan•ner** *n*

1**plane** \'plān\ *vb* **planed; plan•ing** : smooth or level off with a plane ~ *n* : smoothing or shaping tool —**plan•er** *n*

2**plane** *n* **1** : level surface **2** : level of existence, consciousness, or development **3** : airplane ~ *adj* **1** : flat **2** : dealing with flat surfaces or figures

plan•et \'planət\ *n* : celestial body that revolves around the sun —**plan•e•tary** \-ə,terē\ *adj*

plan•e•tar•i•um \,planə'terēəm\ *n, pl* **-iums** *or* **-ia** \-ēə\ : building or room housing a device to project images of celestial bodies

plank \'plaŋk\ *n* **1** : heavy thick board **2** : article in the platform of a political party —**plank•ing** *n*

plank•ton \'plaŋktən\ *n* : tiny aquatic animal and plant life —**plank•ton•ic** \plaŋk'tänik\ *adj*

plant \'plant\ *vb* **1** : set in the ground to grow **2** : place firmly or forcibly ~ *n* **1** : living thing without sense organs that cannot move about **2** : land, buildings, and machinery used esp. in manufacture

1**plan•tain** \'plantən\ *n* : short-stemmed herb with tiny greenish flowers

2**plantain** *n* : banana plant with starchy greenish fruit

plan•ta•tion \plan'tāshən\ *n* : agricultural estate usu. worked by resident laborers

plant•er \'plantər\ *n* **1** : plantation owner **2** : plant container

plaque \'plak\ *n* **1** : commemorative tablet **2** : film layer on a tooth

plas•ma \'plazmə\ *n* : watery part of blood —**plas•mat•ic** \plaz'matik\ *adj*

plas•ter \'plastər\ *n* **1** : medicated dressing **2** : hardening paste for coating walls and ceilings ~ *vb* : cover with plaster —**plas•ter•er** *n*

plas•tic \'plastik\ *adj* : capable of being molded ~ *n* : material that can be formed into rigid objects, films, or filaments — **plas•tic•i•ty** \plas'tisətē\ *n*

plate \'plāt\ *n* **1** : flat thin piece **2** : plated metalware **3** : shallow usu. circular dish **4** : denture or the part of it that fits to the mouth **5** : something printed from an engraving ~ *vb* **plat•ed; plat•ing** : overlay with metal —**plat•ing** *n*

pla•teau \pla'tō\ *n, pl* **-teaus** *or* **-teaux** \-'tōz\ : large level area of high land

plat•form \'plat,fȯrm\ *n* **1** : raised flooring or stage **2** : declaration of principles for a political party

plat•i•num \'platənəm\ *n* : heavy grayish-white metallic chemical element

plat•i•tude \'platə,tüd, -,tyüd\ *n* : trite remark —**plat•i•tu•di•nous** \,platə'tüdənəs, -'tyüd-\ *adj*

pla•toon \plə'tün\ *n* : small military unit

platoon sergeant *n* : noncommissioned officer in the army ranking below a first sergeant

plat•ter \'platər\ *n* : large serving plate

platy•pus \'platipəs\ *n* : small aquatic egg-laying mammal

plau•dit \'plȯdət\ *n* : act of applause

plau•si•ble \'plȯzəbəl\ *adj* : reasonable or believeable —**plau•si•bil•i•ty** \,plȯzə'bilətē\ *n* —**plau•si•bly** \-blē\ *adv*

play \'plā\ *n* **1** : action in a game **2** : recreational activity **3** : light or fitful movement **4** : free movement **5** : stage representation of a drama ~ *vb* **1** : engage in recreation **2** : move or toy with aimlessly **3** : perform music **4** : act in a drama —**play•act•ing** *n* —**play•er** *n* —**play•ful** \-fəl\ *adj* —**play•ful•ly** *adv* —**play•ful-**

ness *n* —**play•pen** *n* —**play•suit** *n* —**play•thing** *n*

play•ground *n* : place for children to play

play•house *n* **1** : theater **2** : small house for children to play in

playing card *n* : one of a set of 24 to 78 cards marked to show its rank and suit and used to play a game of cards

play•mate *n* : companion in play

play–off *n* : contest or series of contests to determine a champion

play•wright \-ˌrīt\ *n* : writer of plays

pla•za \'plazə, 'pläz-\ *n* **1** : public square **2** : shopping mall

plea \'plē\ *n* **1** : defendant's answer to charges **2** : urgent request

plead \'plēd\ *vb* **plead•ed** \'plēdəd\ *or* **pled** \'pled\; **plead•ing 1** : argue for or against in court **2** : answer to a charge or indictment **3** : appeal earnestly —**plead•er** *n*

pleas•ant \'plezᵊnt\ *adj* **1** : giving pleasure **2** : marked by pleasing behavior or appearance —**pleas•ant•ly** *adv* —**pleas•ant•ness** *n*

pleas•ant•ries \-ᵊntrēz\ *n pl* : pleasant and casual conversation

please \'plēz\ *vb* **pleased; pleas•ing 1** : give pleasure or satisfaction to **2** : desire or intend

pleas•ing \'plēziŋ\ *adj* : giving pleasure —**pleas•ing•ly** *adv*

plea•sur•able \'plezhərəbəl\ *adj* : pleasant —**plea•sur•ably** \-blē\ *adv*

plea•sure \'plezhər\ *n* **1** : desire or inclination **2** : enjoyment **3** : source of delight

pleat \'plēt\ *vb* : arrange in pleats ~ *n* : fold in cloth

ple•be•ian \pli'bēən\ *n* : one of the common people ~ *adj* : ordinary

pledge \'plej\ *n* **1** : something given as security **2** : promise or vow ~ *vb* **pledged; pledg•ing 1** : offer as or bind by a pledge **2** : promise

ple•na•ry \'plēnərē, 'plen-\ *adj* : full

pleni•po•ten•tia•ry \ˌplenəpə'tenchərē, -'tenchēˌerē\ *n* : diplomatic agent having full authority —**plenipotentiary** *adj*

plen•i•tude \'plenəˌtüd, -ˌtyüd\ *n* **1** : completeness **2** : abundance

plen•te•ous \'plentēəs\ *adj* : existing in plenty

plen•ty \'plentē\ *n* : more than adequate number or amount —**plen•ti•ful** \'plentifəl\ *adj* —**plen•ti•ful•ly** *adv*

pleth•o•ra \'plethərə\ *n* : excess

pleu•ri•sy \'plu̇rəsē\ *n* : inflammation of the chest membrane

pli•able \'plīəbəl\ *adj* : flexible

pli•ant \'plīənt\ *adj* : flexible —**pli•an•cy** \-ənsē\ *n*

pli•ers \'plīərz\ *n pl* : pinching or gripping tool

[1]**plight** \'plīt\ *vb* : pledge

[2]**plight** *n* : bad state

plod \'pläd\ *vb* **-dd- 1** : walk heavily or slowly **2** : work laboriously and monotonously —**plod•der** *n* —**plod•ding•ly** \-iŋlē\ *adv*

plot \'plät\ *n* **1** : small area of ground **2** : ground plan **3** : main story development (as of a book or movie) **4** : secret plan for doing something ~ *vb* **-tt- 1** : make a plot or plan of **2** : plan or contrive —**plot•ter** *n*

plo•ver \'pləvər, 'plōvər\ *n, pl* **-ver** *or* **-vers** : shorebird related to the sandpiper

plow, plough \'plau̇\ *n* **1** : tool used to turn soil **2** : device for pushing material aside ~ *vb* **1** : break up with a plow **2** : cleave or move through like a plow —**plow•man** \-mən, -ˌman\ *n*

plow•share \-ˌsher\ *n* : plow part that cuts the earth

ploy \'plȯi\ *n* : clever maneuver

pluck \'plək\ *vb* **1** : pull off or out **2** : tug or twitch ~ *n* **1** : act or instance of plucking **2** : spirit or courage

plucky \'pləkē\ *adj* **pluck•i•er; -est** : courageous or spirited

plug \'pləg\ *n* **1** : something for sealing an opening **2** : electrical connector at the end of a cord **3** : piece of favorable publicity ~ *vb* **-gg- 1** : stop or make tight or secure by inserting a plug **2** : publicize

plum \'pləm\ *n* **1** : smooth-skinned juicy fruit **2** : fine reward

plum•age \'plümij\ *n* : feathers of a bird —**plum•aged** \-mijd\ *adj*

plumb \'pləm\ *n* : weight on the end of a line (**plumb line**) to show vertical direction ~ *adv* **1** : vertically **2** : completely ~ *vb* : sound or test with a plumb ~ *adj* : vertical

plumb•er \'pləmər\ *n* : one who repairs usu. water pipes and fixtures

plumb•ing \'pləmiŋ\ *n* : system of water pipes in a building

plume \'plüm\ *n* : large, conspicuous, or showy feather ~ *vb* **plumed; plum•ing 1** : provide or deck with feathers **2** : indulge in pride —**plumed** \'plümd\ *adj*

plum•met \'pləmət\ *vb* : drop straight down

[1]**plump** \'pləmp\ *vb* : drop suddenly or heavily ~ *adv* **1** : straight down **2** : in a direct manner

[2]**plump** *adj* : having a full rounded form —**plump•ness** *n*

plun•der \'pləndər\ *vb* : rob or take goods by force (as in war) ~ *n* : something taken in plundering —**plun•der•er** *n*

plunge \'plənj\ *vb* **plunged; plung•ing 1** : thrust or drive with force **2** : leap or dive into water **3** : begin an action suddenly **4** : dip or move suddenly forward or down ~ *n* : act or instance of plunging —**plung•er** *n*

plu•ral \'plu̇rəl\ *adj* : relating to a word form denoting more than one —**plural** *n*

plu•ral•i•ty \plu̇'ralətē\ *n, pl* **-ties** : greatest number of votes cast when not a majority

plu•ral•ize \'plu̇rəˌlīz\ *vb* **-ized; -iz•ing** : make plural —**plu•ral•i•za•tion** \ˌplu̇rələ'zāshən\ *n*

plus \'pləs\ *prep* : with the addition of ~ *n* **1** : sign + (**plus sign**) in mathematics to indicate addition **2** : added or positive quantity **3** : advantage ~ *adj* : being more or in addition ~ *conj* : and

plush \'pləsh\ *n* : fabric with a long pile ~ *adj* : luxurious —**plush•ly** *adv* —**plushy** *adj* —**plush•ness** *n*

plu•toc•ra•cy \plü'täkrəsē\ *n, pl* **-cies 1** : government by the wealthy **2** : a controlling class of the wealthy —**plu•to•crat** \'plütəˌkrat\ *n* —**plu•to•crat•ic** \ˌplütə'kratik\ *adj*

plu•to•ni•um \plü'tōnēəm\ *n* : radioactive chemical element

[1]**ply** \'plī\ *n, pl* **plies** : fold, thickness, or strand of which something is made

[2]**ply** *vb* **plied; ply•ing 1** : use or work at **2** : keep supplying something to **3** : travel regularly usu. by sea

ply•wood *n* : sheets of wood glued and pressed together

pneu•mat•ic \nu̇'matik, nyu̇-\ *adj* **1** : moved by air pressure **2** : filled with compressed air —**pneu•mat•i•cal•ly** *adv*

pneu•mo•nia \nu̇'mōnyə, nyu̇-\ *n* : inflammatory lung disease

[1]**poach** \'pōch\ *vb* : cook in simmering liquid

[2]**poach** *vb* : hunt or fish illegally —**poach•er** *n*

pock \'päk\ *n* : small swelling on the skin or its scar —**pock•mark** *n* —**pock•marked** *adj*

pock•et \'päkət\ *n* **1** : small open bag sewn into a garment **2** : container or receptacle **3** : isolated area or group ~ *vb* : put in a pocket —**pock•et•ful** \-ˌfu̇l\ *n*

pock•et•book *n* **1** : purse **2** : financial resources

pock•et•knife *n* : knife with a folding blade carried in the pocket

pod \'päd\ *n* **1** : dry fruit that splits open when ripe **2** : compartment on a ship or craft

po•di•a•try \pə'dīətrē, pō-\ *n* : branch of medicine dealing with the foot —**po•di•a•trist** \pə'dīətrist, pō-\ *n*

po•di•um \'pōdēəm\ *n, pl* **-di•ums** *or* **-dia** \-ēə\ : dais

po•em \'pōəm\ *n* : composition in verse

po•et \'pōət\ *n* : writer of poetry

po•et•ry \'pōətrē\ *n* **1** : metrical writing **2** : poems —**po•et•ic** \pō'etik\, **po•et•i•cal** \-ikəl\ *adj*

po•grom \'pōgrəm, pə'gräm, 'pägrəm\ *n* : organized massacre

poi•gnant \'pȯinyənt\ *adj* **1** : emotionally painful **2** : deeply moving —**poi•gnan•cy** \-nyənsē\ *n*

poin•set•tia \pȯin'setēə, -'setə\ *n* : showy tropical American plant

point \'pȯint\ *n* **1** : individual often essential detail **2** : purpose **3** : particular place, time, or stage **4** : sharp end **5** : projecting piece of land **6** : dot or period **7** : division of the compass **8** : unit of counting ~ *vb* **1** : sharpen **2** : indicate direction by extending a finger **3** : direct attention to **4** : aim —**point•ed•ly** \-ədlē\ *adv* —**point•less** *adj*

point–blank *adj* **1** : so close to a target that a missile fired goes straight to it **2** : direct —**point–blank** *adv*

point•er \'pȯintər\ *n* **1** : one that points out **2** : large short-haired hunting dog **3** : hint or tip

poise \'pȯiz\ *vb* **poised; pois•ing** : balance ~ *n* : self-possessed calmness

poi•son \'pȯizᵊn\ *n* : chemical that can injure or kill ~ *vb* **1** : injure or kill with poison **2** : apply poison to **3** : affect destructively —**poi•son•er** *n* —**poi•son•ous** \'pȯizᵊnəs\ *adj*

poke \'pōk\ *vb* **poked; pok•ing 1** : prod **2** : dawdle ~ *n* : quick thrust

[1]**pok•er** \'pōkər\ *n* : rod for stirring a fire

[2]**po•ker** *n* : card game for gambling

po•lar \'pōlər\ *adj* : relating to a geographical or magnetic pole

po•lar•ize \'pōləˌrīz\ *vb* **-ized; -iz•ing 1** : cause to have magnetic poles **2** : break up into opposing groups — **po•lar•i•za•tion** \ˌpōlərə'zāshən\ *n*

[1]**pole** \'pōl\ *n* : long slender piece of wood or metal

[2]**pole** *n* **1** : either end of the earth's axis **2** : battery terminal **3** : either end of a magnet

pole•cat \'pōlˌkat\ *n, pl* **polecats** *or* **polecat 1** : European carnivorous mammal **2** : skunk

po•lem•ics \pə'lemiks\ *n sing or pl* : practice of disputation —**po•lem•i•cal** \-ikəl\ *adj* —**po•lem•i•cist** \-əsist\ *n*

po•lice \pə'lēs\ *n, pl* **police 1** : department of government that keeps public order and enforces the laws **2** : members of the police ~ *vb* **-liced; -lic•ing** : regulate and keep in order —**po•lice•man** \-mən\ *n* —**po•lice•wom•an** *n*

police officer *n* : member of the police

[1]**pol•i•cy** \'päləsē\ *n, pl* **-cies** : course of action selected to guide decisions

[2]**policy** *n, pl* **-cies** : insurance contract —**pol•i•cy•hold•er** *n*

po•lio \'pōlēˌō\ *n* : poliomyelitis —**polio** *adj*

po•lio•my•eli•tis \-ˌmīə'lītəs\ *n* : acute virus disease of the spinal cord

pol•ish \'pälish\ *vb* **1** : make smooth and glossy **2** : develop or refine ~ *n* **1** : shiny surface **2** : refinement

po•lite \pə'līt\ *adj* **-lit•er; -est** : marked by courteous social conduct —**po•lite•ly** *adv* —**po•lite•ness** *n*

pol•i•tic \'päləˌtik\ *adj* : shrewdly tactful

politically correct *adj* : seeking to avoid offending members of a different group

pol•i•tics \'päləˌtiks\ *n sing or pl* : practice of government and managing of public affairs —**po•lit•i•cal** \pə'litikəl\ *adj* —**po•lit•i•cal•ly** *adv* —**pol•i•ti•cian** \ˌpälə'tishən\ *n*

pol•ka \'pōlkə\ *n* : lively couple dance —**polka** *vb*

pol•ka dot \'pōkəˌdät\ *n* : one of a series of regular dots in a pattern

poll \'pōl\ *n* **1** : head **2** : place where votes are cast —usu. pl. **3** : a sampling of opinion ~ *vb* **1** : cut off **2** : receive or record votes **3** : question in a poll —**poll•ster** \-stər\ *n*

pol•len \'pälən\ *n* : spores of a seed plant

pol•li•na•tion \ˌpälə'nāshən\ *n* : the carrying of pollen to fertilize the seed —**pol•li•nate** \'päləˌnāt\ *vb* —**pol•li•na•tor** \-ər\ *n*

pol•lute \pə'lüt\ *vb* **-lut•ed; -lut•ing** : contaminating with waste products —**pol•lut•ant** \-'lütᵊnt\ *n* —**pol•lut•er** *n* —**pol•lu•tion** \-'lüshən\ *n*

pol•ly•wog, pol•li•wog \'pälēˌwäg\ *n* : tadpole

po•lo \'pōlō\ *n* : game played by 2 teams on horseback using long-handled mallets to drive a wooden ball

pol•ter•geist \'pōltərˌgīst\ *n* : mischievous ghost

pol•troon \päl'trün\ *n* : coward

poly•es•ter \'pälēˌestər\ *n* : synthetic fiber

po•lyg•a•my \pə'ligəmē\ *n* : marriage to several spouses at the same time —**po•lyg•a•mist** \-mist\ *n* —**po•lyg•a•mous** \-məs\ *adj*

poly•gon \'päliˌgän\ *n* : closed plane figure with straight sides

poly•mer \'päləmər\ *n* : chemical compound of molecules joined in long strings —**po•lym•er•i•za•tion** \pəˌlimərə'zāshən\ *n* —**po•lym•er•ize** \pə'liməˌrīz\ *vb*

poly•tech•nic \ˌpäli'teknik\ *adj* : relating to many technical arts or applied sciences

poly•the•ism \'pälithēˌizəm\ *n* : worship of many gods —**poly•the•ist** \-ˌthēist\ *adj or n*

poly•un•sat•u•rat•ed \ˌpäleˌən'sachəˌrātəd\ *adj* : having many double or triple bonds in a molecule

pome•gran•ate \'pämˌgranət, 'pämə-\ *n* : tropical reddish fruit with many seeds

pom•mel \'pəməl, 'päm-\ *n* **1** : knob on the hilt of a sword **2** : knob at the front of a saddle ~ \'pəməl\ *vb* **-meled** *or* **-melled; -mel•ing** *or* **-mel•ling** : pummel

pomp \'pämp\ *n* **1** : brilliant display **2** : ostentation

pomp•ous \'pämpəs\ *adj* : pretentiously dignified —**pom•pos•i•ty** \päm'päsətē\ *n* —**pomp•ous•ly** *adv*

pon•cho \'pänchō\ *n, pl* **-chos** : blanketlike cloak

pond \'pänd\ *n* : small body of water

pon•der \'pändər\ *vb* : consider

pon•der•ous \'pändərəs\ *adj* **1** : very heavy **2** : clumsy **3** : oppressively dull

pon•tiff \'päntəf\ *n* : pope —**pon•tif•i•cal** \pän'tifikəl\ *adj*

pon•tif•i•cate \pän'tifəˌkāt\ *vb* **-cat•ed; -cat•ing** : talk pompously

pon•toon \pän'tün\ *n* : flat-bottomed boat or float

po•ny \'pōnē\ *n, pl* **-nies** : small horse

po•ny•tail \-ˌtāl\ *n* : hair arrangement like the tail of a pony

poo•dle \'püdᵊl\ *n* : dog with a curly coat

[1]**pool** \'pül\ *n* **1** : small body of water **2** : puddle

[2]**pool** *n* **1** : amount contributed by participants in a joint venture **2** : game of pocket billiards ~ *vb* : combine in a common fund

poor \'pu̇r, 'pōr\ *adj* **1** : lacking material possessions **2** : less than adequate **3** : arousing pity **4** : unfavorable —**poor•ly** *adv*

[1]**pop** \'päp\ *vb* **-pp- 1** : move suddenly **2** : burst with or make a sharp sound **3** : protrude ~ *n* **1** : sharp explosive sound **2** : flavored soft drink

[2]**pop** *adj* : popular

pop•corn \'päpˌkȯrn\ *n* : corn whose kernels burst open into a light mass when heated

pope \'pōp\ *n, often cap* : head of the Roman Catholic Church

pop•lar \'päplər\ *n* : slender quick-growing tree

pop•lin \'päplən\ *n* : strong plain-woven fabric with crosswise ribs

pop•over \'päpˌōvər\ *n* : hollow muffin made from egg-rich batter

pop•py \'päpē\ *n, pl* **-pies** : herb with showy flowers

pop•u•lace \'päpyələs\ *n* **1** : common people **2** : population

pop•u•lar \'päpyələr\ *adj* **1** : relating to the general public **2** : widely accepted **3** : commonly liked —**pop•u•lar•i•ty** \ˌpäpyə'larətē\ *n* —**pop•u•lar•ize** \'päpyələˌrīz\ *vb* —**pop•u•lar•ly** \-lərlē\ *adv*

pop•u•late \'päpyəˌlāt\ *vb* **-lat•ed; -lat•ing** : inhabit or occupy

pop•u•la•tion \ˌpäpyə'lāshən\ *n* : people or number of people in an area

pop•u•list \'päpyəlist\ *n* : advocate of the rights of the common people —**pop•u•lism** \-ˌlizəm\ *n*

pop•u•lous \'päpyələs\ *adj* : densely populated —**pop•u•lous•ness** *n*

por•ce•lain \'pōrsələn\ *n* : fine-grained ceramic ware

porch \'pōrch\ *n* : covered entrance

por•cu•pine \'pȯrkyəˌpīn\ *n* : mammal with sharp quills

[1]**pore** \'pōr\ *vb* **pored; por•ing** : read attentively

[2]**pore** *n* : tiny hole (as in the skin) —**pored** *adj*

pork \'pōrk\ *n* : pig meat

pork barrel *n* : government projects benefiting political patrons

por•nog•ra•phy \pȯr'nägrəfē\ *n* : depiction of erotic behavior intended to cause sexual excitement —**por•no•graph•ic** \ˌpȯrnə'grafik\ *adj*

po•rous \'pōrəs\ *adj* : permeable to fluids —**po•ros•i•ty** \pə'räsətē\ *n*

por•poise \'pȯrpəs\ *n* **1** : small whale with a blunt snout **2** : dolphin

por•ridge \'pȯrij\ *n* : soft boiled cereal

por•rin•ger \'pȯrənjər\ *n* : low one-handled metal bowl or cup

[1]**port** \'pōrt\ *n* **1** : harbor **2** : city with a harbor

[2]**port** *n* **1** : inlet or outlet (as in an engine) for a fluid **2** : porthole

[3]**port** *n* : left side of a ship or airplane looking forward —**port** *adj*

[4]**port** *n* : sweet wine

por•ta•ble \'pōrtəbəl\ *adj* : capable of being carried —**portable** *n*

por•tage \'pōrtij, pȯr'täzh\ *n* : carrying of boats overland between navigable bodies of water or the route where this is done —**portage** *vb*

por•tal \'pōrtᵊl\ *n* : entrance

por•tend \pȯr'tend\ *vb* : give a warning of beforehand

por•tent \'pōrˌtent\ *n* : something that foreshadows a coming event —**por•ten•tous** \pȯr'tentəs\ *adj*

por•ter \'pōrtər\ *n* : baggage carrier

por•ter•house \-ˌhau̇s\ *n* : choice cut of steak

port•fo•lio \pōrt'fōlēˌō\ *n, pl* **-lios 1** : portable case for papers **2** : office or function of a diplomat **3** : investor's securities

port•hole \'pōrtˌhōl\ *n* : window in the side of a ship or aircraft

por•ti•co \'pōrtiˌkō\ *n, pl* **-coes** *or* **-cos** : colonnade forming a porch

por•tion \'pōrshən\ *n* : part or share of a whole ~ *vb* : divide into or allot portions

port•ly \'pōrtlē\ *adj* **-li•er; -est** : somewhat stout

por•trait \'pōrtrət, -ˌtrāt\ *n* : picture of a person —**por•trait•ist** \-ist\ *n* —**por•trai•ture** \'pōrtrəˌchu̇r\ *n*

por•tray \pōr'trā\ *vb* **1** : make a picture of **2** : describe in words **3** : play the role of —**por•tray•al** *n*

por•tu•laca \ˌpōrchə'lakə\ *n* : tropical herb with showy flowers

pose \'pōz\ *vb* **posed; pos•ing 1** : assume a posture or attitude **2** : propose **3** : pretend to be what one is not ~ *n* **1** : sustained posture **2** : pretense —**pos•er** *n*

posh \'päsh\ *adj* : elegant

po•si•tion \pə'zishən\ *n* **1** : stand taken on a question **2** : place or location **3** : status **4** : job —**position** *vb*

pos•i•tive \'päzətiv\ *adj* **1 :** definite **2 :** confident **3 :** relating to or being an adjective or adverb form that denotes no increase **4 :** greater than zero **5 :** having a deficiency of electrons **6 :** affirmative **—pos•i•tive•ly** *adv* **—pos•i•tive•ness** *n*
pos•se \'päsē\ *n* **:** emergency assistants of a sheriff
pos•sess \pə'zes\ *vb* **1 :** have as property or as a quality **2 :** control **—pos•ses•sion** \-'zeshən\ *n* **—pos•ses•sor** \-'zesər\ *n*
pos•ses•sive \pə'zesiv\ *adj* **1 :** relating to a grammatical case denoting ownership **2 :** jealous **—possessive** *n* **—pos•ses•sive•ness** *n*
pos•si•ble \'päsəbəl\ *adj* **1 :** that can be done **2 :** potential **—pos•si•bil•i•ty** \,päsə'bilətē\ *n* **—pos•si•bly** *adv*
pos•sum \'päsəm\ *n* **:** opossum
[1]**post** \'pōst\ *n* **:** upright stake serving to support or mark ~ *vb* **:** put up or announce by a notice
[2]**post** *vb* **1 :** mail **2 :** inform
[3]**post** *n* **1 :** sentry's station **2 :** assigned task **3 :** army camp ~ *vb* **:** station
post- *prefix* **:** after or subsequent to

postadolescent	**postinoculation**
postattack	**postmarital**
postbaccalaureate	**postmenopausal**
postbiblical	**postnatal**
postcollege	**postnuptial**
postcolonial	**postproduction**
postelection	**postpuberty**
postexercise	**postrecession**
postflight	**postretirement**
postgame	**postrevolutionary**
postgraduate	**postseason**
postgraduation	**postsecondary**
postharvest	**postsurgical**
posthospital	**posttreatment**
postimperial	**posttrial**
postinaugural	**postvaccination**
postindustrial	**postwar**

post•age \'pōstij\ *n* **:** fee for mail
post•al \'pōstᵊl\ *adj* **:** relating to the mail
post•card *n* **:** card for mailing a message
post•date \,pōst'dāt\ *vb* **:** assign a date to that is later than the actual date of execution
post•er \'pōstər\ *n* **:** large usu. printed notice
pos•te•ri•or \pō'stirēər, pä-\ *adj* **1 :** later **2 :** situated behind ~ *n* **:** buttocks
pos•ter•i•ty \pä'sterətē\ *n* **:** all future generations
post•haste \'pōst'hāst\ *adv* **:** speedily
post•hu•mous \'päschəməs\ *adj* **:** occurring after one's death **—post•hu•mous•ly** *adv*
post•man \'pōstmən, -,man\ *n* **:** mail carrier
post•mark *n* **:** official mark on mail **—postmark** *vb*
post•mas•ter *n* **:** chief of a post office
post me•ri•di•em \'pōstmə'ridēəm, -ē,em\ *adj* **:** being after noon
post•mor•tem \,pōst'mórtəm\ *adj* **:** occurring or done after death ~ *n* **1 :** medical examination of a corpse **2 :** analysis after an event
post office *n* **:** agency or building for mail service
post•op•er•a•tive \,pōst'äpərətiv, -'äpə,rāt-\ *adj* **:** following surgery
post•paid *adv* **:** with postage paid by the sender
post•par•tum \-'pärtəm\ *adj* **:** following childbirth **—postpartum** *adv*
post•pone \-'pōn\ *vb* **-poned; -pon•ing :** put off to a later time **—post•pone•ment** *n*
post•script \'pōst,skript\ *n* **:** added note
pos•tu•lant \'päschələnt\ *n* **:** candidate for a religious order
pos•tu•late \'päschə,lāt\ *vb* **-lat•ed; -lat•ing :** assume as true ~ *n* **:** assumption
pos•ture \'päschər\ *n* **:** bearing of the body ~ *vb* **-tured; -tur•ing :** strike a pose
po•sy \'pōzē\ *n, pl* **-sies :** flower or bunch of flowers
pot \'pät\ *n* **:** rounded container ~ *vb* **-tt- :** place in a pot **—pot•ful** *n*
po•ta•ble \'pōtəbəl\ *adj* **:** drinkable
pot•ash \'pät,ash\ *n* **:** white chemical salt of potassium used esp. in agriculture
po•tas•si•um \pə'tasēəm\ *n* **:** silver-white metallic chemical element
po•ta•to \pə'tātō\ *n, pl* **-toes :** edible plant tuber
pot•bel•ly *n* **:** paunch **—pot•bel•lied** *adj*
po•tent \'pōtᵊnt\ *adj* **:** powerful or effective **—po•ten•cy** \-ᵊnsē\ *n*
po•ten•tate \'pōtᵊn,tāt\ *n* **:** powerful ruler
po•ten•tial \pə'tenchəl\ *adj* **:** capable of becoming actual ~ *n* **1 :** something that can become actual **2 :** degree of electrification with reference to a standard **—po•ten•ti•al•i•ty** \pə,tenchē'alətē\ *n* **—po•ten•tial•ly** *adv*
poth•er \'päthər\ *n* **:** fuss
pot•hole \'pät,hōl\ *n* **:** large hole in a road surface
po•tion \'pōshən\ *n* **:** liquid medicine or poison
pot•luck *n* **:** whatever food is available
pot•pour•ri \,pōpù'rē\ *n* **1 :** mix of flowers, herbs, and spices used for scent **2 :** miscellaneous collection
pot•shot *n* **1 :** casual or easy shot **2 :** random critical remark
pot•ter \'pätər\ *n* **:** pottery maker
pot•tery \'pätərē\ *n, pl* **-ter•ies :** objects (as dishes) made from clay
pouch \'paùch\ *n* **1 :** small bag **2 :** bodily sac
poul•tice \'pōltəs\ *n* **:** warm medicated dressing **—poultice** *vb*
poul•try \'pōltrē\ *n* **:** domesticated fowl
pounce \'paùns\ *vb* **pounced; pounc•ing :** spring or swoop upon and seize
[1]**pound** \'paùnd\ *n* **1 :** unit of weight equal to 16 ounces **2 :** monetary unit (as of the United Kingdom) **—pound•age** \-ij\ *n*
[2]**pound** *n* **:** shelter for stray animals
[3]**pound** *vb* **1 :** crush by beating **2 :** strike heavily **3 :** drill **4 :** move along heavily
pour \'pōr\ *vb* **1 :** flow or supply esp. copiously **2 :** rain hard
pout \'paùt\ *vb* **:** look sullen **—pout** *n*
pov•er•ty \'pävərtē\ *n* **1 :** lack of money or possessions **2 :** poor quality
pow•der \'paùdər\ *n* **:** dry material of fine particles ~ *vb* **:** sprinkle or cover with powder **—pow•dery** *adj*
pow•er \'paùər\ *n* **1 :** position of authority **2 :** ability to act **3 :** one that has power **4 :** physical might **5 :** force or energy used to do work ~ *vb* **:** supply with power **—pow•er•ful** \-fəl\ *adj* **—pow•er•ful•ly** *adv* **—pow•er•less** *adj*
pow•er•house *n* **:** dynamic or energetic person
pow•wow \'paù,waù\ *n* **:** conference
pox \'päks\ *n, pl* **pox** *or* **pox•es :** disease marked by skin rash
prac•ti•ca•ble \'praktikəbəl\ *adj* **:** feasible **—prac•ti•ca•bil•i•ty** \,praktikə'bilətē\ *n*
prac•ti•cal \'praktikəl\ *adj* **1 :** relating to practice **2 :** virtual **3 :** capable of being put to use **4 :** inclined to action as opposed to speculation **—prac•ti•cal•i•ty** \,prakti'kalətē\ *n* **—prac•ti•cal•ly** \'praktiklē\ *adv*
prac•tice, prac•tise \'praktəs\ *vb* **-ticed** *or* **-tised; -tic•ing** *or* **-tis•ing 1 :** perform repeatedly to become proficient **2 :** do or perform customarily **3 :** be professionally engaged in ~ *n* **1 :** actual performance **2 :** habit **3 :** exercise for proficiency **4 :** exercise of a profession
prac•ti•tio•ner \prak'tishənər\ *n* **:** one who practices a profession
prag•ma•tism \'pragmə,tizəm\ *n* **:** practical approach to problems **—prag•mat•ic** \prag'matik\ *adj* **—prag•mat•i•cal•ly** *adv*
prai•rie \'prerē\ *n* **:** broad grassy rolling tract of land
praise \'prāz\ *vb* **praised; prais•ing 1 :** express approval of **2 :** glorify **—praise** *n* **—praise•wor•thy** *adj*
prance \'prans\ *vb* **pranced; pranc•ing 1 :** spring from the hind legs **2 :** swagger **—prance** *n* **—pranc•er** *n*
prank \'praŋk\ *n* **:** playful or mischievous act **—prank•ster** \-stər\ *n*
prate \'prāt\ *vb* **prat•ed; prat•ing :** talk long and foolishly
prat•fall \'prat,fòl\ *n* **:** fall on the buttocks
prat•tle \'pratᵊl\ *vb* **-tled; -tling :** babble **—prattle** *n*
prawn \'pròn\ *n* **:** shrimplike crustacean
pray \'prā\ *vb* **1 :** entreat **2 :** ask earnestly for something **3 :** address God or a god
prayer \'prer\ *n* **1 :** earnest request **2 :** an addressing of God or a god **3 :** words used in praying **—prayer•ful** *adj* **—prayer•ful•ly** *adv*
praying mantis *n* **:** mantis
pre- *prefix* **:** before, prior to, or in advance

preadmission	**precut**
preadolescence	**predawn**
preadolescent	**predefine**
preadult	**predeparture**
preanesthetic	**predesignate**
prearrange	**predetermine**
prearrangement	**predischarge**
preassembled	**predrill**
preassign	**preelection**
prebattle	**preelectric**
prebiblical	**preemployment**
prebreakfast	**preestablish**
precalculus	**preexist**
precancel	**preexistence**
precancellation	**preexistent**
preclear	**prefight**
preclearance	**preform**
precollege	**pregame**
precolonial	**preheat**
precombustion	**preinaugural**
precompute	**preindustrial**
preconceive	**preinterview**
preconception	**prejudge**
preconcert	**prekindergarten**
precondition	**prelaunch**
preconstructed	**prelife**
preconvention	**premarital**
precook	**premenopausal**
precool	**premenstrual**
premix	**prerelease**
premodern	**preretirement**
premodify	**prerevolutionary**
premoisten	**prerinse**
premold	**presale**
prenatal	**preschool**
prenotification	**preseason**
prenotify	**preselect**
prenuptial	**preset**
preopening	**preshrink**
preoperational	**preshrunk**
preoperative	**presoak**
preordain	**presort**
prepackage	**prestamp**
prepay	**presterilize**
preplan	**prestrike**
preprocess	**presurgery**
preproduction	**presweeten**
preprofessional	**pretape**
preprogram	**pretelevision**
prepubertal	**pretournament**
prepublication	**pretreat**
prepunch	**pretreatment**
prepurchase	**pretrial**
prerecorded	**prewar**
preregister	**prewash**
preregistration	**prewrap**
prerehearsal	

preach \'prēch\ *vb* **1 :** deliver a sermon **2 :** advocate earnestly **—preach•er** *n* **—preach•ment** *n*
pre•am•ble \'prē,ambəl\ *n* **:** introduction
pre•can•cer•ous \,prē'kansərəs\ *adj* **:** likely to become cancerous
pre•car•i•ous \pri'karēəs\ *adj* **:** dangerously insecure **—pre•car•i•ous•ly** *adv* **—pre•car•i•ous•ness** *n*
pre•cau•tion \pri'kòshən\ *n* **:** care taken beforehand **—pre•cau•tion•ary** \-shə,nerē\ *adj*
pre•cede \pri'sēd\ *vb* **-ced•ed; -ced•ing :** be, go, or come ahead of **—pre•ce•dence** \'presədəns, pri'sēdᵊns\ *n*
prec•e•dent \'presədənt\ *n* **:** something said or done earlier that serves as an example
pre•cept \'prē,sept\ *n* **:** rule of action or conduct
pre•cinct \'prē,siŋkt\ *n* **1 :** district of a city **2** *pl* **:** vicinity
pre•cious \'preshəs\ *adj* **1 :** of great value **2 :** greatly cherished **3 :** affected
prec•i•pice \'presəpəs\ *n* **:** steep cliff
pre•cip•i•tate \pri'sipə,tāt\ *vb* **-tat•ed; -tat•ing 1 :** cause to happen quickly or abruptly **2 :** cause to separate out of a liquid **3 :** fall as rain, snow, or hail ~ *n* **:** solid matter precipitated from a liquid ~ \-'sipətət, -ə,tāt\ *adj* **:** unduly hasty **—pre•cip•i•tate•ly** *adv* **—pre•cip•i•tate•ness** *n* **—pre•cip•i•tous** \pri'sipətəs\ *adj* **—pre•cip•i•tous•ly** *adv*
pre•cip•i•ta•tion \pri,sipə'tāshən\ *n* **1 :** rash haste **2 :** rain, snow, or hail
pré•cis \prā'sē\ *n, pl* **pré•cis** \-'sēz\ **:** concise summary of essentials
pre•cise \pri'sīs\ *adj* **1 :** definite **2 :** highly accurate **—pre•cise•ly** *adv* **—pre•cise•ness** *n*
pre•ci•sion \pri'sizhən\ *n* **:** quality or state of being precise
pre•clude \pri'klüd\ *vb* **-clud•ed; -clud•ing :** make impossible
pre•co•cious \pri'kōshəs\ *adj* **:** exceptionally advanced **—pre•co•cious•ly** *adv* **—pre•coc•i•ty** \pri'käsətē\ *n*
pre•cur•sor \pri'kərsər\ *n* **:** harbinger
pred•a•to•ry \'predə,tōrē\ *adj* **:** preying upon others **—pred•a•tor** \'predətər\ *n*
pre•de•ces•sor \'predə,sesər, 'prēd-\ *n* **:** a previous holder of a position
pre•des•tine \prē'destən\ *vb* **:** settle beforehand **—pre•des•ti•na•tion** \-,destə'nāshən\ *n*
pre•dic•a•ment \pri'dikəmənt\ *n* **:** difficult situation
pred•i•cate \'predikət\ *n* **:** part of a sentence that states something about the subject ~ \'predə,kāt\ *vb* **-cat•ed; -cat•ing 1 :** affirm **2 :** establish **—pred•i•ca•tion** \,predə'kāshən\ *n*
pre•dict \pri'dikt\ *vb* **:** declare in advance **—pre•dict•abil•i•ty** \-,diktə'bilətē\ *n* **—pre•dict•able** \-'diktəbəl\ *adj* **—pre•dict•ably** \-blē\ *adv* **—pre•dic•tion** \-'dikshən\ *n*
pre•di•lec•tion \,predᵊl'ekshən, ,prēd-\ *n* **:** established preference
pre•dis•pose \,prēdis'pōz\ *vb* **:** cause to be favorable or susceptible to something beforehand **—pre•dis•po•si•tion** \,prē,dispə'zishən\ *n*
pre•dom•i•nate \pri'dämə,nāt\ *vb* **:** be superior **—pre•dom•i•nance** \-nəns\ *n* **—pre•dom•i•nant** \-nənt\ *adj* **—pre•dom•i•nant•ly** *adv*
pre•em•i•nent \prē'emənənt\ *adj* **:** having highest rank **—pre•em•i•nence** \-nəns\ *n* **—pre•em•i•nent•ly** *adv*
pre•empt \prē'empt\ *vb* **1 :** seize for oneself **2 :** take the place of **—pre•emp•tion** \-'empshən\ *n* **—pre•emp•tive** \-'emptiv\ *adj*
preen \'prēn\ *vb* **:** dress or smooth up (as feathers)
pre•fab•ri•cat•ed \'prē'fabrə,kātəd\ *adj* **:** manufactured for rapid assembly elsewhere **—pre•fab•ri•ca•tion** \,prē,fabri'kāshən\ *n*
pref•ace \'prefəs\ *n* **:** introductory comments ~ *vb* **-aced; -ac•ing :** introduce with a preface **—pref•a•to•ry** \'prefə,tōrē\ *adj*
pre•fect \'prē,fekt\ *n* **:** chief officer or judge **—pre•fec•ture** \-,fekchər\ *n*
pre•fer \pri'fər\ *vb* **-rr- 1 :** like better **2 :** bring (as a charge) against a person **—pref•er•a•ble** \'prefərəbəl\ *adj* **—pref•er•a•bly** *adv* **—pref•er•ence** \-ərəns\ *n* **—pref•er•en•tial** \,prefə'renchəl\ *adj*
pre•fer•ment \pri'fərmənt\ *n* **:** promotion
pre•fig•ure \prē'figyər\ *vb* **:** foreshadow
[1]**pre•fix** \'prē,fiks, prē'fiks\ *vb* **:** place before
[2]**pre•fix** \'prē,fiks\ *n* **:** affix at the beginning of a word
preg•nant \'pregnənt\ *adj* **1 :** containing unborn young **2 :** meaningful **—preg•nan•cy** \-nənsē\ *n*
pre•hen•sile \prē'hensəl, -,sīl\ *adj* **:** adapted for grasping
pre•his•tor•ic \,prēhis'tòrik\, **pre•his•tor•i•cal** \-ikəl\ *adj* **:** relating to the period before written history
prej•u•dice \'prejədəs\ *n* **1 :** damage esp. to one's rights **2 :** unreasonable attitude for or against something ~ *vb* **-diced; -dic•ing 1 :** damage **2 :** cause to have prejudice **—prej•u•di•cial** \,prejə'dishəl\ *adj*
prel•ate \'prelət\ *n* **:** clergy member of high rank **—prel•a•cy** \-əsē\ *n*
pre•lim•i•nary \pri'limə,nerē\ *n, pl* **-nar•ies :** something that precedes or introduces **—preliminary** *adj*
pre•lude \'prel,üd, -,yüd; 'prā,lüd\ *n* **:** introductory performance, event, or musical piece
pre•ma•ture \,prēmə'tüər, -'tyùr, -'chùr\ *adj* **:** coming before the usual or proper time **—pre•ma•ture•ly** *adv*
pre•med•i•tate \pri'medə,tāt\ *vb* **:** plan beforehand **—pre•med•i•ta•tion** \-,medə'tāshən\ *n*
pre•mier \pri'mir, -'myir; 'prēmēər\ *adj* **:** first in rank or importance ~ *n* **:** prime minister **—pre•mier•ship** *n*
pre•miere \pri'myer, -'mir\ *n* **:** 1st performance ~ *vb* **-miered; -mier•ing :** give a 1st performance of
prem•ise \'preməs\ *n* **1 :** statement made or implied as a basis of argument **2** *pl* **:** piece of land with the structures on it
pre•mi•um \'prēmēəm\ *n* **1 :** bonus **2 :** sum over the stated value **3 :** sum paid for insurance **4 :** high value
pre•mo•ni•tion \,prēmə'nishən, ,premə-\ *n* **:** feeling that something is about to happen **—pre•mon•i•to•ry** \pri'mänə,tōrē\ *adj*
pre•oc•cu•pied \prē'äkyə,pīd\ *adj* **:** lost in thought
pre•oc•cu•py \-,pī\ *vb* **:** occupy the attention of **—pre•oc•cu•pa•tion** \prē,äkyə'pāshən\ *n*
pre•pare \pri'par\ *vb* **-pared; -par•ing 1 :** make or get ready often beforehand **2 :** put together or compound **—prep•a•ra•tion** \,prepə'rāshən\ *n* **—pre•pa•ra•to•ry** \pri'parə,tōrē\ *adj* **—pre•pared•ness** \-'parədnəs\ *n*
pre•pon•der•ant \pri'pändərənt\ *adj* **:** having great weight, power, importance, or numbers **—pre•pon•der•ance** \-rəns\ *n* **—pre•pon•der•ant•ly** *adv*
prep•o•si•tion \,prepə'zishən\ *n* **:** word that combines with a noun or pronoun to form a phrase **—prep•o•si•tion•al** \-'zishənəl\ *adj*
pre•pos•sess•ing \,prēpə'zesiŋ\ *adj* **:** tending to create a favorable impression
pre•pos•ter•ous \pri'pästərəs\ *adj* **:** absurd
pre•req•ui•site \prē'rekwəzət\ *n* **:** something required beforehand **—prerequisite** *adj*
pre•rog•a•tive \pri'rägətiv\ *n* **:** special right or power
pre•sage \'presij, pri'sāj\ *vb* **-saged; -sag•ing 1 :** give a warning of **2 :** predict **—pres•age** \'presij\ *n*
pres•by•ter \'prezbətər\ *n* **:** priest or minister
pre•science \'prēshəns, 'presh-\ *n* **:** foreknowledge of events **—pre•scient** \-ənt\ *adj*
pre•scribe \pri'skrīb\ *vb* **-scribed; -scrib•ing 1 :** lay down as a guide **2 :** direct the use of as a remedy
pre•scrip•tion \pri'skripshən\ *n* **:** written direction for the preparation and use of a medicine or the medicine prescribed
pres•ence \'prezᵊns\ *n* **1 :** fact or condition of being present **2 :** appearance or bearing
[1]**pres•ent** \'prezᵊnt\ *n* **:** gift
[2]**pre•sent** \pri'zent\ *vb* **1 :** introduce **2 :** bring before the public **3 :** make a gift to or of **4 :** bring before a court for inquiry **—pre•sent•able** *adj* **—pre•sen•ta•tion** \,prē,zen'tāshən, ,prezᵊn-\ *n* **—pre•sent•ment** \pri'zentmənt\ *n*

³pres·ent \'prez°nt\ adj : now existing, in progress, or attending ~ n : present time

pre·sen·ti·ment \pri'zentəmənt\ n : premonition

pres·ent·ly \'prez°ntlē\ adv 1 : soon 2 : now

present participle n : participle that typically expresses present action

pre·serve \pri'zərv\ vb -served; -serv·ing 1 : keep safe from danger or spoilage 2 : maintain ~ n 1 : preserved fruit —often in pl. 2 : area for protection of natural resources —pres·er·va·tion \prezər'vāshən\ n —pre·ser·va·tive \pri'zərvətiv\ adj or n —pre·serv·er \-'zərvər\ n

pre·side \pri'zīd\ vb -sid·ed; -sid·ing 1 : act as chairman 2 : exercise control

pres·i·dent \'prezədənt\ n 1 : one chosen to preside 2 : chief official (as of a company or nation) —pres·i·den·cy \-ənsē\ n —pres·i·den·tial \prezə'denchəl\ adj

press \'pres\ n 1 : crowded condition 2 : machine or device for exerting pressure and esp. for printing 3 : pressure 4 : printing or publishing establishment 5 : news media and esp. newspapers ~ vb 1 : lie against and exert pressure on 2 : smooth with an iron or squeeze with something heavy 3 : urge 4 : crowd 5 : force one's way —press·er n

press·ing adj : urgent

pres·sure \'preshər\ n 1 : burden of distress or urgent business 2 : direct application of force —pressure vb —pres·sur·i·za·tion \preshərə'zāshən\ n —pres·sur·ize \-,īz\ vb

pres·ti·dig·i·ta·tion \prestə,dijə'tāshən\ n : sleight of hand

pres·tige \pres'tēzh, -'tēj\ n : estimation in the eyes of people —pres·ti·gious \-'tijəs\ adj

pres·to \'prestō\ adv or adj : quickly

pre·sume \pri'züm\ vb -sumed; -sum·ing 1 : assume authority without right to do so 2 : take for granted —pre·sum·ably \-'züməbəl\ adj —pre·sum·ably \-blē\ adv

pre·sump·tion \pri'zəmpshən\ n 1 : presumptuous attitude or conduct 2 : belief supported by probability —pre·sump·tive \-tiv\ adj

pre·sump·tu·ous \pri'zəmpchəwəs\ adj : too bold or forward —pre·sump·tu·ous·ly adv

pre·sup·pose \,prēsə'pōz\ vb : take for granted —pre·sup·po·si·tion \,prē,səpə'zishən\ n

pre·tend \pri'tend\ vb 1 : act as if something is real or true when it is not 2 : act in a way that is false 3 : lay claim —pre·tend·er n

pre·tense, pre·tence \'prē,tens, pri'tens\ n 1 : insincere effort 2 : deception —pre·ten·sion \pri'tenchən\ n

pre·ten·tious \pri'tenchəs\ adj : overly showy or self-important —pre·ten·tious·ly adv —pre·ten·tious·ness n

pre·ter·nat·u·ral \prētər'nachərəl\ adj 1 : exceeding what is natural 2 : inexplicable by ordinary means —pre·ter·nat·u·ral·ly adv

pre·text \'prē,tekst\ n : falsely stated purpose

pret·ty \'pritē, 'purt-\ adj -ti·er; -est : pleasing by delicacy or attractiveness ~ adv : in some degree ~ vb -tied; -ty·ing : make pretty —pret·ti·ly \'pritl'ē\ adv —pret·ti·ness n

pret·zel \'pretsəl\ n : twisted thin bread that is glazed and salted

pre·vail \pri'vāl\ vb 1 : triumph 2 : urge successfully 3 : be frequent, widespread, or dominant

prev·a·lent \'prevələnt\ adj : widespread —prev·a·lence \-ləns\ n

pre·var·i·cate \pri'varə,kāt\ vb -cat·ed; -cat·ing : deviate from the truth —pre·var·i·ca·tion \-,varə'kāshən\ n —pre·var·i·ca·tor \-'varə,kātər\ n

pre·vent \pri'vent\ vb : keep from happening or acting —pre·vent·able adj —pre·ven·tion \-'venchən\ n —pre·ven·tive \-'ventiv\ adj or n —pre·ven·ta·tive \-'ventətiv\ adj or n

pre·view \'prē,vyü\ vb : view or show beforehand —preview n

pre·vi·ous \'prēvēəs\ adj : having gone, happened, or existed before —pre·vi·ous·ly adv

prey \'prā\ n, pl preys 1 : animal taken for food by another 2 : victim ~ vb 1 : seize and devour animals as prey 2 : have a harmful effect on

price \'prīs\ n : cost ~ vb priced; pric·ing : set a price on

price·less \-ləs\ adj : too precious to have a price

pric·ey \'prīsē\ adj pric·i·er; -est : expensive

prick \'prik\ n 1 : tear or small wound made by a point 2 : something sharp or pointed ~ vb : pierce slightly with a sharp point —prick·er n

prick·le \'prikəl\ n 1 : small sharp spine or

thorn 2 : slight stinging pain ~ vb -led; -ling : tingle —prick·ly \'priklē\ adj

pride \'prīd\ n : quality or state of being proud ~ vb prid·ed; prid·ing : indulge in pride —pride·ful adj

priest \'prēst\ n : person having authority to perform the sacred rites of a religion —priest·hood n —priest·li·ness \-lēnəs\ n —priest·ly adj

priest·ess \'prēstəs\ n : woman who is a priest

prig \'prig\ n : one who irritates by rigid or pointed observance of proprieties —prig·gish \-ish\ adj —prig·gish·ly adv

prim \'prim\ adj -mm- : stiffly formal and proper —prim·ly adv —prim·ness n

pri·mal \'prīməl\ adj 1 : original or primitive 2 : most important

pri·ma·ry \'prī,merē, 'prīmərē\ adj : first in order of time, rank, or importance ~ n, pl -ries : preliminary election —pri·mar·i·ly \prī'merəlē\ adv

primary school n : elementary school

pri·mate n 1 \'prī,māt, -mət\ : highest-ranking bishop 2 \-,māt\ : mammal of the group that includes humans and monkeys

prime \'prīm\ n : earliest or best part or period ~ adj : standing first (as in significance or quality) ~ vb primed; prim·ing 1 : fill or load 2 : lay a preparatory coating on

prime minister n : chief executive of a parliamentary government

¹prim·er \'primər\ n : small introductory book

²prim·er \'prīmər\ n 1 : device for igniting an explosive 2 : material for priming a surface

prime·val \prī'mēvəl\ adj : relating to the earliest ages

prim·i·tive \'primətiv\ adj 1 : relating to or characteristic of an early stage of development 2 : of or relating to a tribal people or culture ~ n : one that is primitive —prim·i·tive·ly adv —prim·i·tive·ness n

pri·mor·di·al \prī'mordēəl\ adj : primeval

primp \'primp\ vb : dress or groom in a finicky manner

prim·rose \'prim,rōz\ n : low herb with clusters of showy flowers

prince \'prins\ n 1 : ruler 2 : son of a king or queen —prince·ly adj

prin·cess \'prinsəs, -,ses\ n 1 : daughter of a king or queen 2 : wife of a prince

prin·ci·pal \'prinsəpəl\ adj : most important ~ n 1 : leading person 2 : head of a school 3 : sum lent at interest —prin·ci·pal·ly adv

prin·ci·pal·i·ty \,prinsə'palətē\ n, pl -ties : territory of a prince

prin·ci·ple \'prinsəpəl\ n 1 : general or fundamental law 2 : rule or code of conduct or devotion to such a code

print \'print\ n 1 : mark or impression made by pressure 2 : printed state or form 3 : printed matter 4 : copy made by printing 5 : cloth with a figure stamped on it ~ vb 1 : produce impressions of (as from type) 2 : write in letters like those of printer's type —print·able adj —print·er n

print·ing \'printiŋ\ n : art or business of a printer

print·out \'print,aut\ n : printed output produced by a computer —print out vb

¹pri·or \'prīər\ n : head of a religious house —pri·o·ry \'prīərē\ n

²prior adj : coming before in time, order, or importance —pri·or·i·ty \prī'orətē\ n

pri·or·ess \'prīərəs\ n : nun who is head of a religious house

prism \'prizəm\ n : transparent 3-sided object that separates light into colors —pris·mat·ic \priz'matik\ adj

pris·on \'priz°n\ n : place where criminals are confined

pris·on·er \'priz°nər\ n : person on trial or in prison

pris·sy \'prisē\ adj -si·er; -est : overly prim —pris·si·ness n

pris·tine \'pris,tēn, pris'-\ adj : pure

pri·va·cy \'prīvəsē\ n, pl -cies : quality or state of being apart from others

pri·vate \'prīvət\ adj 1 : belonging to a particular individual or group 2 : carried on independently 3 : withdrawn from company or observation ~ n : enlisted person of the lowest rank in the marine corps or of one of the two lowest ranks in the army —pri·vate·ly adv

pri·va·teer \,prīvə'tir\ n : private ship armed to attack enemy ships and commerce

private first class n : enlisted person ranking next below a corporal in the army and next below a lance corporal in the marine corps

pri·va·tion \prī'vāshən\ n : lack of what is needed for existence

priv·i·lege \'privəlij\ n : right granted as an advantage or favor —priv·i·leged adj

privy \'privē\ adj 1 : private or secret 2 : having access to private or secret information ~ n, pl priv·ies : outdoor toilet —priv·i·ly \'privəlē\ adv

¹prize \'prīz\ n 1 : something offered or striven for in competition or in contests of chance 2 : something very desirable —prize adj —prize·win·ner n —prize·win·ning adj

²prize vb prized; priz·ing : value highly

³prize vb prized; priz·ing : pry

prize·fight·er n —prize·fight·ing n : professional boxing match —prize·fight·er n —prize·fight·ing n

¹pro \'prō\ n : favorable argument or person ~ adv : in favor

²pro n or adj : professional

prob·a·ble \'präbəbəl\ adj : seeming true or real or to have a good chance of happening —prob·a·bil·i·ty \,präbə'bilətē\ n —prob·a·bly \'präbəblē\ adv

pro·bate \'prō,bāt\ n : judicial determination of the validity of a will ~ vb -bat·ed; -bat·ing : establish by probate

pro·ba·tion \prō'bāshən\ n 1 : period of testing and trial 2 : freedom for a convict during good behavior under supervision —pro·ba·tion·ary \-shə,nerē\ adj —pro·ba·tion·er n

probe \'prōb\ n 1 : slender instrument for examining a cavity 2 : investigation ~ vb probed; prob·ing 1 : examine with a probe 2 : investigate

pro·bi·ty \'prōbətē\ n : honest behavior

prob·lem \'präbləm\ n 1 : question to be solved 2 : source of perplexity or vexation —problem adj —prob·lem·at·ic \,präblə'matik\ adj —prob·lem·at·i·cal \-ikəl\ adj

pro·bos·cis \prə'bäsəs\ n, pl -cis·es also -ci·des \-ə,dēz\ : long flexible snout

pro·ce·dure \prə'sējər\ n 1 : way of doing something 2 : series of steps in regular order —pro·ce·dur·al \-'sējərəl\ adj

pro·ceed \prō'sēd\ vb 1 : come forth 2 : go on in an orderly way 3 : begin and carry on an action 4 : advance

pro·ceed·ing n 1 : procedure 2 pl : something said or done or its official record

pro·ceeds \'prō,sēdz\ n pl : total money taken in

pro·cess \'präs,es, 'prōs-\ n, pl -cess·es \-,esəz, -əsəz, -ə,sēz\ 1 : something going on 2 : natural phenomenon marked by gradual changes 3 : series of actions or operations directed toward a result 4 : summons 5 : projecting part ~ vb : subject to a process —pro·ces·sor \-ər\ n

pro·ces·sion \prə'seshən\ n : group moving along in an orderly way

pro·ces·sion·al \-'seshənəl\ n : music for a procession

pro·claim \prō'klām\ vb : announce publicly or with conviction —proc·la·ma·tion \,präklə'māshən\ n

pro·cliv·i·ty \prō'klivətē\ n, pl -ties : inclination

pro·cras·ti·nate \prə'krastə,nāt\ vb -nat·ed; -nat·ing : put something off until later —pro·cras·ti·na·tion \-,krastə'nāshən\ n —pro·cras·ti·na·tor \-'krastə,nātər\ n

pro·cre·ate \'prōkrē,āt\ vb -at·ed; -at·ing : produce offspring —pro·cre·ation \,prōkrē'āshən\ n —pro·cre·ative \'prō,krē,ātiv\ adj —pro·cre·a·tor \-,ātər\ n

proc·tor \'präktər\ n : supervisor of students (as at an examination) —proctor vb

pro·cure \prō'kyur\ vb -cured; -cur·ing : get possession of —pro·cur·able \-'kyurəbəl\ adj —pro·cure·ment n —pro·cur·er n

prod \'präd\ vb -dd- : push with or as if with a pointed instrument —prod n

prod·i·gal \'prädigəl\ adj : recklessly extravagant or wasteful —prodigal n —prod·i·gal·i·ty \,prädə'galətē\ n

pro·di·gious \prə'dijəs\ adj : extraordinary in size or degree —pro·di·gious·ly adv

prod·i·gy \'prädəjē\ n, pl -gies : extraordinary person or thing

pro·duce \prə'düs, -'dyüs\ vb -duced; -duc·ing 1 : present to view 2 : give birth to 3 : bring into existence ~ \'präd,üs, 'prōd-, -,yüs\ n 1 : product 2 : agricultural products —pro·duc·er \prə'düsər, -'dyü-\ n

prod·uct \'präd,əkt\ n 1 : number resulting from multiplication 2 : something produced

pro·duc·tion \prə'dəkshən\ n : act, process, or result of producing —pro·duc·tive \-'dəktiv\ adj —pro·duc·tive·ness n —pro·duc·tiv·i·ty \prō,dək'tivətē, ,prädək-\ n

pro·fane \prō'fān\ vb -faned; -fan·ing : treat with irreverence ~ adj 1 : not concerned with religion 2 : serving to debase what is holy —pro·fane·ly adv —pro·fane·ness n —pro·fan·i·ty \prō'fanətē\ n

pro·fess \prə'fes\ vb 1 : declare openly 2 : confess one's faith in —pro·fessed·ly \-ədlē\ adv

pro·fes·sion \prə'feshən\ n 1 : open declaration of belief 2 : occupation requiring specialized knowledge and academic training

pro·fes·sion·al \prə'feshənəl\ adj 1 : of, relating to, or engaged in a profession 2 : playing sport for pay —professional n

—pro·fes·sion·al·ism n —pro·fes·sion·al·ize vb —pro·fes·sion·al·ly adv

pro·fes·sor \prə'fesər\ n : university or college teacher —pro·fes·so·ri·al \,prōfə'sōrēəl, ,präfə-\ adj —pro·fes·sor·ship n

prof·fer \'präfər\ vb -fered; -fer·ing : offer —proffer n

pro·fi·cient \prə'fishənt\ adj : very good at something —pro·fi·cien·cy \-ənsē\ n —proficient n —pro·fi·cient·ly adv

pro·file \'prō,fīl\ n : picture in outline —profile vb

prof·it \'präfət\ n 1 : valuable return 2 : excess of the selling price of goods over cost ~ vb : gain a profit —prof·it·able \'präfətəbəl\ adj —prof·it·ably adv —prof·it·less adj

prof·i·teer \,präfə'tir\ n : one who makes an unreasonable profit —profiteer vb

prof·li·gate \'präfligət, -lə,gāt\ adj 1 : shamelessly immoral 2 : wildly extravagant —prof·li·ga·cy \-gəsē\ n —profligate n —prof·li·gate·ly adv

pro·found \prə'faund\ adj 1 : marked by intellectual depth or insight 2 : deeply felt —pro·found·ly adv —pro·fun·di·ty \-'fəndətē\ n

pro·fuse \prə'fyüs\ adj : pouring forth liberally —pro·fuse·ly adv —pro·fu·sion \-'fyüzhən\ n

pro·gen·i·tor \prō'jenətər\ n : direct ancestor

prog·e·ny \'präjənē\ n, pl -nies : offspring

pro·ges·ter·one \prō'jestə,rōn\ n : female hormone

prog·no·sis \präg'nōsəs\ n, pl -no·ses \-,sēz\ : prospect of recovery from disease

prog·nos·ti·cate \präg'nästə,kāt\ vb -cat·ed; -cat·ing : predict from signs or symptoms —prog·nos·ti·ca·tion \-,nästə'kāshən\ n —prog·nos·ti·ca·tor \-'nästə,kātər\ n

pro·gram \'prō,gram, -grəm\ n 1 : outline of the order to be pursued or the subjects included (as in a performance) 2 : plan of procedure 3 : coded instructions for a computer ~ vb -grammed or -gramed; -gram·ming or -gram·ing 1 : enter in a program 2 : provide a computer with a program —pro·gram·ma·bil·i·ty \,prō,gramə'bilətē\ n —pro·gram·ma·ble \'prō,graməbəl\ adj —pro·gram·mer \'prō,gramər\ n

prog·ress \'prägrəs, -,res\ n : movement forward or to a better condition ~ \prə'gres\ vb 1 : move forward 2 : improve —pro·gres·sive \-'gresiv\ adj —pro·gres·sive·ly adv

pro·gres·sion \prə'greshən\ n 1 : act of progressing 2 : continuous connected series

pro·hib·it \prō'hibət\ vb : prevent by authority

pro·hi·bi·tion \,prōə'bishən\ n 1 : act of prohibiting 2 : legal restriction on sale or manufacture of alcoholic beverages —pro·hi·bi·tion·ist \-'bishənist\ n —pro·hib·i·tive \prō'hibətiv\ adj —pro·hib·i·tive·ly adv —pro·hib·i·to·ry \-'hibə,tōrē\ adj

proj·ect \'präj,ekt, -ikt\ n : planned undertaking ~ \prə'jekt\ vb 1 : design or plan 2 : protrude 3 : throw forward —pro·jec·tion \-'jekshən\ n

pro·jec·tile \prə'jekt°l\ n : missile hurled by external force

pro·jec·tor \-'jektər\ n : device for projecting pictures on a screen

pro·le·tar·i·an \,prōlə'terēən\ n : member of the proletariat —proletarian adj

pro·le·tar·i·at \-ēət\ n : laboring class

pro·lif·er·ate \prə'lifə,rāt\ vb -at·ed; -at·ing : grow or increase in number rapidly —pro·lif·er·a·tion \-,lifə'rāshən\ n

pro·lif·ic \prə'lifik\ adj : producing abundantly —pro·lif·i·cal·ly adv

pro·logue \'prō,lóg, -,läg\ n : preface

pro·long \prə'lóŋ\ vb : lengthen in time or extent —pro·lon·ga·tion \,prō,lóŋ'gāshən\ n

prom \'präm\ n : formal school dance

prom·e·nade \,prämə'nād, -'näd\ n 1 : leisurely walk 2 : place for strolling —promenade vb

prom·i·nence \'prämənəns\ n 1 : quality, state, or fact of being readily noticeable or distinguished 2 : something that stands out —prom·i·nent \-nənt\ adj —prom·i·nent·ly adv

pro·mis·cu·ous \prə'miskyəwəs\ adj : having a number of sexual partners —prom·is·cu·i·ty \prämis'kyüətē, ,prō,mis-\ n —pro·mis·cu·ous·ly adv —pro·mis·cu·ous·ness n

prom·ise \'präməs\ n 1 : statement that one will or do or not do something 2 : basis for expectation —promise vb —prom·is·so·ry \-ə,sōrē\ adj

prom·is·ing \'präməsiŋ\ adj : likely to succeed —prom·is·ing·ly adv

prom·on·to·ry \'prämən,tōrē\ n, pl -ries : point of land jutting into the sea

pro·mote \prə'mōt\ vb -mot·ed; -mot·ing 1 : advance in rank 2 : contribute to the growth, development, or prosperity of —

pro•mot•er *n* —**pro•motion** \-ˈmōshən\ *n* —**pro•mo•tion•al** \-ˈmōshənəl\ *adj*

[1]**prompt** \ˈprämpt\ *vb* **1** : incite **2** : give a cue to (an actor or singer) —**prompt•er** *n*

[2]**prompt** *adj* : ready and quick —**prompt•ly** *adv* —**prompt•ness** *n*

prone \ˈprōn\ *adj* **1** : having a tendency **2** : lying face downward —**prone•ness** \ˈprōnnəs\ *n*

prong \ˈproŋ\ *n* : sharp point of a fork —**pronged** \ˈproŋd\ *adj*

pro•noun \ˈprōˌnau̇n\ *n* : word used as a substitute for a noun

pro•nounce \prəˈnau̇ns\ *vb* **-nounced; -nounc•ing 1** : utter officially or as an opinion **2** : say or speak esp. correctly —**pro•nounce•able** *adj* —**pro•nounce•ment** *n* —**pro•nun•ci•a•tion** \-ˌnənsēˈāshən\ *n*

pro•nounced \-ˈnau̇nst\ *adj* : decided

[1]**proof** \ˈprüf\ *n* **1** : evidence of a truth or fact **2** : trial impression or print

[2]**proof** *adj* : designed for or successful in resisting or repelling

proof•read *vb* : read and mark corrections in —**proof•read•er** *n*

prop \ˈpräp\ *vb* **-pp- 1** : support **2** : sustain —**prop** *n*

pro•pa•gan•da \ˌpräpəˈgandə, ˌprōpə-\ *n* : the spreading of ideas or information to further or damage a cause —**pro•pa•gan•dist** \-dist\ *n* —**pro•pa•gan•dize** \-ˌdīz\ *vb*

prop•a•gate \ˈpräpəˌgāt\ *vb* **-gat•ed; -gat•ing 1** : reproduce biologically **2** : cause to spread —**prop•a•ga•tion** \ˌpräpəˈgāshən\ *n*

pro•pane \ˈprōˌpān\ *n* : heavy flammable gaseous fuel

pro•pel \prəˈpel\ *vb* **-ll-** : drive forward —**pro•pel•lant, pro•pel•lent** *n or adj*

pro•pel•ler \prəˈpelər\ *n* : hub with revolving blades that propels a craft

pro•pen•si•ty \prəˈpensətē\ *n, pl* **-ties** : particular interest or inclination

prop•er \ˈpräpər\ *adj* **1** : suitable or right **2** : limited to a specified thing **3** : correct **4** : strictly adhering to standards of social manners, dignity, or good taste —**prop•er•ly** *adv*

prop•er•ty \ˈpräpərtē\ *n, pl* **-ties 1** : quality peculiar to an individual **2** : something owned **3** : piece of real estate **4** : ownership

proph•e•cy \ˈpräfəsē\ *n, pl* **-cies** : prediction

proph•e•sy \-ˌsī\ *vb* **-sied; -sy•ing** : predict —**proph•e•si•er** \-ˌsīər\ *n*

proph•et \ˈpräfət\ *n* : one who utters revelations or predicts events —**proph•et•ess** \-əs\ *n* —**pro•phet•ic** \prəˈfetik\, **pro•phet•i•cal** \-ikəl\ *adj* —**pro•phet•i•cal•ly** *adv*

pro•pin•qui•ty \prəˈpiŋkwətē\ *n* : nearness

pro•pi•ti•ate \prōˈpishēˌāt\ *vb* **-at•ed; -at•ing** : gain or regain the favor of —**pro•pi•ti•a•tion** \-ˌpishēˈāshən\ *n* —**pro•pi•tia•to•ry** \-ˈpishēəˌtōrē\ *adj*

pro•pi•tious \prəˈpishəs\ *adj* : favorable

pro•po•nent \prəˈpōnənt\ *n* : one who argues in favor of something

pro•por•tion \prəˈpōrshən\ *n* **1** : relation of one part to another or to the whole with respect to magnitude, quantity, or degree **2** : symmetry **3** : share ~ *vb* : adjust in size in relation to others —**pro•por•tion•al** \-shənəl\ *adj* —**pro•por•tion•al•ly** *adv* —**pro•por•tion•ate** \-shənət\ *adj* —**pro•por•tion•ate•ly** *adv*

pro•pose \prəˈpōz\ *vb* **-posed; -pos•ing 1** : plan or intend **2** : make an offer of marriage **3** : present for consideration —**pro•pos•al** \-ˈpōzəl\ *n*

prop•o•si•tion \ˌpräpəˈzishən\ *n* : something proposed ~ *vb* : suggest sexual intercourse to

pro•pound \prəˈpau̇nd\ *vb* : set forth for consideration

pro•pri•e•tor \prəˈprīətər\ *n* : owner —**pro•pri•e•tary** \prəˈprīəˌterē\ *adj* —**pro•pri•e•tor•ship** *n* —**pro•pri•e•tress** \-ˈprīətrəs\ *n*

pro•pri•e•ty \prəˈprīətē\ *n, pl* **-ties** : standard of acceptability in social conduct

pro•pul•sion \prəˈpəlshən\ *n* **1** : action of propelling **2** : driving power —**pro•pul•sive** \-siv\ *adj*

pro•sa•ic \prōˈzāik\ *adj* : dull

pro•scribe \prōˈskrīb\ *vb* **-scribed; -scrib•ing** : prohibit —**pro•scrip•tion** \-ˈskripshən\ *n*

prose \ˈprōz\ *n* : ordinary language

pros•e•cute \ˈpräsiˌkyüt\ *vb* **-cut•ed; -cut•ing 1** : follow to the end **2** : seek legal punishment of —**pros•e•cu•tion** \ˌpräsiˈkyüshən\ *n* —**pros•e•cu•tor** \ˈpräsiˌkyütər\ *n*

pros•e•lyte \ˈpräsəˌlīt\ *n* : new convert —**pros•e•ly•tize** \ˈpräsələˌtīz\ *vb*

pros•pect \ˈpräsˌpekt\ *n* **1** : extensive view **2** : something awaited **3** : potential buyer ~ *vb* : look for mineral deposits —**pro•spec•tive** \prəˈspektiv, ˈpräsˌpek-\ *adj* —**pro•spec•tive•ly** *adv* —**pros•pec•tor** \-ˌpektər, -ˈpek-\ *n*

pro•spec•tus \prəˈspektəs\ *n* : introductory description of an enterprise

pros•per \ˈpräspər\ *vb* : thrive or succeed —**pros•per•ous** \-pərəs\ *adj*

pros•per•i•ty \präsˈperətē\ *n* : economic well-being

pros•tate \ˈpräsˌtāt\ *n* : glandular body about the base of the male urethra —**prostate** *adj*

pros•the•sis \präsˈthēsəs, ˈprästhə-\ *n, pl* **-the•ses** \-ˌsēz\ : artificial replacement for a body part —**pros•thet•ic** \präsˈthetik\ *adj*

pros•ti•tute \ˈprästəˌtüt, -ˌtyüt\ *vb* **-tut•ed; -tut•ing 1** : offer sexual activity for money **2** : put to corrupt or unworthy purposes ~ *n* : one who engages in sexual activities for money —**pros•ti•tu•tion** \ˌprästəˈtüshən, -ˈtyü-\ *n*

pros•trate \ˈpräsˌtrāt\ *adj* : stretched out with face on the ground ~ *vb* **-trat•ed; -trat•ing 1** : fall or throw (oneself) into a prostrate position **2** : reduce to helplessness —**pros•tra•tion** \präsˈtrāshən\ *n*

pro•tag•o•nist \prōˈtagənist\ *n* : main character in a drama or story

pro•tect \prəˈtekt\ *vb* : shield from injury —**pro•tec•tor** \-tər\ *n*

pro•tec•tion \prəˈtekshən\ *n* **1** : act of protecting **2** : one that protects —**pro•tec•tive** \-ˈtektiv\ *adj*

pro•tec•tor•ate \-tərət\ *n* : state dependent upon the authority of another state

pro•té•gé \ˈprōtəˌzhā\ *n* : one under the care and protection of an influential person

pro•tein \ˈprōˌtēn\ *n* : complex combination of amino acids present in living matter

pro•test \ˈprōˌtest\ *n* **1** : organized public demonstration of disapproval **2** : strong objection ~ \prəˈtest\ *vb* **1** : assert positively **2** : object strongly —**pro•tes•ta•tion** \ˌprätəsˈtāshən\ *n* —**pro•test•er, pro•tes•tor** \ˈprōˌtestər\ *n*

Prot•es•tant \ˈprätəstənt\ *n* : Christian not of a Catholic or Orthodox church —**Prot•es•tant•ism** \ˈprätəstəntˌizəm\ *n*

pro•to•col \ˈprōtəˌkol\ *n* : diplomatic etiquette

pro•ton \ˈprōˌtän\ *n* : positively charged atomic particle

pro•to•plasm \ˈprōtəˌplazəm\ *n* : complex colloidal living substance of plant and animal cells —**pro•to•plas•mic** \ˌprōtəˈplazmik\ *adj*

pro•to•type \ˈprōtəˌtīp\ *n* : original model

pro•to•zo•an \ˌprōtəˈzōən\ *n* : single-celled lower invertebrate animal

pro•tract \prōˈtrakt\ *vb* : prolong

pro•trac•tor \-ˈtraktər\ *n* : instrument for drawing and measuring angles

pro•trude \prōˈtrüd\ *vb* **-trud•ed; -trud•ing** : stick out or cause to stick out —**pro•tru•sion** \-ˈtrüzhən\ *n*

pro•tu•ber•ance \prōˈtübərəns, -ˈtyü-\ *n* : something that protrudes —**pro•tu•ber•ant** *adj*

proud \ˈprau̇d\ *adj* **1** : having or showing excessive self-esteem **2** : highly pleased **3** : having proper self-respect **4** : glorious —**proud•ly** *adv*

prove \ˈprüv\ *vb* **proved; proved** *or* **prov•en** \ˈprüvən\; **prov•ing 1** : test by experiment or by a standard **2** : establish the truth of by argument or evidence **3** : turn out esp. after trial or test —**prov•able** \ˈprüvəbəl\ *adj*

prov•en•der \ˈprävəndər\ *n* : dry food for domestic animals

prov•erb \ˈprävˌərb\ *n* : short meaningful popular saying —**pro•ver•bi•al** \prəˈvərbēəl\ *adj*

pro•vide \prəˈvīd\ *vb* **-vid•ed; -vid•ing 1** : take measures beforehand **2** : make a stipulation **3** : supply what is needed —**pro•vid•er** *n*

pro•vid•ed *conj* : if

prov•i•dence \ˈprävədəns\ *n* **1** *often cap* : divine guidance **2** *cap* : God **3** : quality of being provident

prov•i•dent \-ədənt\ *adj* **1** : making provision for the future **2** : thrifty —**prov•i•dent•ly** *adv*

prov•i•den•tial \ˌprävəˈdenchəl\ *adj* **1** : relating to Providence **2** : opportune

pro•vid•ing *conj* : provided

prov•ince \ˈprävəns\ *n* **1** : administrative district **2** *pl* : all of a country outside the metropolis **3** : sphere

pro•vin•cial \prəˈvinchəl\ *adj* **1** : relating to a province **2** : limited in outlook —**pro•vin•cial•ism** \-ˌizəm\ *n*

pro•vi•sion \prəˈvizhən\ *n* **1** : act of providing **2** : stock of food —usu. in pl. **3** : stipulation ~ *vb* : supply with provisions

pro•vi•sion•al \-ˈvizhənəl\ *adj* : provided for a temporary need —**pro•vi•sion•al•ly** *adv*

pro•vi•so \prəˈvīzō\ *n, pl* **-sos** *or* **-soes** : stipulation

pro•voke \prəˈvōk\ *vb* **-voked; -vok•ing 1** : incite to anger **2** : stir up on purpose —**prov•o•ca•tion** \ˌprävəˈkāshən\ *n* —**pro•voc•a•tive** \prəˈväkətiv\ *adj*

prow \ˈprau̇\ *n* : bow of a ship

prow•ess \ˈprau̇əs\ *n* **1** : valor **2** : extraordinary ability

prowl \ˈprau̇l\ *vb* : roam about stealthily —**prowl** *n* —**prowl•er** *n*

prox•i•mate \ˈpräksəmət\ *adj* : very near

prox•im•i•ty \präkˈsimətē\ *n* : nearness

proxy \ˈpräksē\ *n, pl* **prox•ies** : authority to act for another —**proxy** *adj*

prude \ˈprüd\ *n* : one who shows extreme modesty —**prud•ery** \ˈprüdərē\ *n* —**prud•ish** \ˈprüdish\ *adj*

pru•dent \ˈprüdᵊnt\ *adj* **1** : shrewd **2** : cautious **3** : thrifty —**pru•dence** \-ᵊns\ *n* —**pru•den•tial** \prüˈdenchəl\ *adj* —**pru•dent•ly** *adv*

[1]**prune** \ˈprün\ *n* : dried plum

[2]**prune** *vb* **pruned; prun•ing** : cut off unwanted parts

pru•ri•ent \ˈpru̇rēənt\ *adj* : lewd —**pru•ri•ence** \-ēəns\ *n*

[1]**pry** \ˈprī\ *vb* **pried; pry•ing** : look closely or inquisitively

[2]**pry** *vb* **pried; pry•ing** : raise, move, or pull apart with a lever

psalm \ˈsäm, ˈsälm\ *n* : sacred song or poem —**psalm•ist** *n*

pseu•do•nym \ˈsüdᵊnˌim\ *n* : fictitious name —**pseu•don•y•mous** \süˈdänəməs\ *adj*

pso•ri•a•sis \səˈrīəsəs\ *n* : chronic skin disease

psy•che \ˈsīkē\ *n* : soul or mind

psy•chi•a•try \səˈkīətrē, sī-\ *n* : branch of medicine dealing with mental, emotional, and behavioral disorders —**psy•chi•at•ric** \ˌsīkēˈatrik\ *adj* —**psy•chi•a•trist** \səˈkīətrist, sī-\ *n*

psy•chic \ˈsīkik\ *adj* **1** : relating to the psyche **2** : sensitive to supernatural forces ~ *n* : person sensitive to supernatural forces —**psy•chi•cal•ly** *adv*

psy•cho•anal•y•sis \ˌsīkōəˈnaləsəs\ *n* : study of the normally hidden content of the mind esp. to resolve conflicts —**psy•cho•an•a•lyst** \-ˈanᵊlist\ *n* —**psy•cho•an•al•yt•ic** \-ˌanᵊlˈitik\ *adj* —**psy•cho•an•a•lyze** \-ˈanᵊlˌīz\ *vb*

psy•chol•o•gy \sīˈkäləjē\ *n, pl* **-gies 1** : science of mind and behavior **2** : mental and behavioral aspect (as of an individual) —**psy•cho•log•i•cal** \ˌsīkəˈläjikəl\ *adj* —**psy•cho•log•i•cal•ly** *adv* —**psy•chol•o•gist** \sīˈkäləjist\ *n*

psy•cho•path \ˈsīkəˌpath\ *n* : mentally ill or unstable person —**psy•cho•path•ic** \ˌsīkəˈpathik\ *adj*

psy•cho•sis \sīˈkōsəs\ *n, pl* **-cho•ses** \-ˌsēz\ : mental derangement (as paranoia) —**psy•chot•ic** \-ˈkätik\ *adj or n*

psy•cho•so•mat•ic \ˌsīkəsəˈmatik\ *adj* : relating to bodily symptoms caused by mental or emotional disturbance

psy•cho•ther•a•py \ˌsīkōˈtherəpē\ *n* : treatment of mental disorder by psychological means —**psy•cho•ther•a•pist** \-pist\ *n*

pto•maine \ˈtōˌmān\ *n* : bacterial decay product

pu•ber•ty \ˈpyübərtē\ *n* : time of sexual maturity

pu•bic \ˈpyübik\ *adj* : relating to the lower abdominal region

pub•lic \ˈpəblik\ *adj* **1** : relating to the people as a whole **2** : civic **3** : not private **4** : open to all **5** : well-known ~ *n* : people as a whole —**pub•lic•ly** *adv*

pub•li•ca•tion \ˌpəbləˈkāshən\ *n* **1** : process of publishing **2** : published work

pub•lic•i•ty \pəˈblisətē\ *n* **1** : news information given out to gain public attention **2** : public attention

pub•li•cize \ˈpəbləˌsīz\ *vb* **-cized; -ciz•ing** : bring to public attention —**pub•li•cist** \-sist\ *n*

pub•lish \ˈpəblish\ *vb* **1** : announce publicly **2** : reproduce for sale esp. by printing —**pub•lish•er** *n*

puck•er \ˈpəkər\ *vb* : pull together into folds or wrinkles ~ *n* : wrinkle

pud•ding \ˈpu̇diŋ\ *n* : creamy dessert

pud•dle \ˈpədᵊl\ *n* : very small pool of water

pudgy \ˈpəjē\ *adj* **pudg•i•er; -est** : short and plump

pu•er•ile \ˈpyu̇rəl\ *adj* : childish

puff \ˈpəf\ *vb* **1** : blow in short gusts **2** : pant **3** : enlarge ~ *n* **1** : short discharge (as of air) **2** : slight swelling **3** : something light and fluffy —**puffy** *adj*

pug \ˈpəg\ *n* : small stocky dog

pu•gi•lism \ˈpyüjəˌlizəm\ *n* : boxing —**pu•gi•list** \-list\ *n* —**pu•gi•lis•tic** \ˌpyüjəˈlistik\ *adj*

pug•na•cious \ˌpəgˈnāshəs\ *adj* : prone to fighting —**pug•nac•i•ty** \-ˈnasətē\ *n*

puke \ˈpyük\ *vb* **puked; puk•ing** : vomit —**puke** *n*

pul•chri•tude \ˈpəlkrəˌtüd, -ˌtyüd\ *n* : beauty —**pul•chri•tu•di•nous** \ˌpəlkrəˈtüdᵊnəs, -ˈtyüd-\ *adj*

pull \ˈpu̇l\ *vb* **1** : exert force so as to draw (something) toward or out **2** : move **3** : stretch or tear ~ *n* **1** : act of pulling **2** : influence **3** : device for pulling something —**pull•er** *n*

pul•let \ˈpu̇lət\ *n* : young hen

pul•ley \ˈpu̇lē\ *n, pl* **-leys** : wheel with a grooved rim

Pull•man \ˈpu̇lmən\ *n* : railroad car with berths

pull•over \ˈpu̇lˌōvər\ *adj* : put on by being pulled over the head —**pullover** *n*

pul•mo•nary \ˈpu̇lməˌnerē, ˈpəl-\ *adj* : relating to the lungs

pulp \ˈpəlp\ *n* **1** : soft part of a fruit or vegetable **2** : soft moist mass (as of mashed wood) —**pulpy** *adj*

pul•pit \ˈpu̇lˌpit\ *n* : raised desk used in preaching

pul•sate \ˈpəlˌsāt\ *vb* **-sat•ed; -sat•ing** : expand and contract rhythmically —**pul•sa•tion** \ˌpəlˈsāshən\ *n*

pulse \ˈpəls\ *n* : arterial throbbing caused by heart contractions —**pulse** *vb*

pul•ver•ize \ˈpəlvəˌrīz\ *vb* **-ized; -iz•ing** : beat or grind into a powder

pu•ma \ˈpümə, ˈpyü-\ *n* : cougar

pum•ice \ˈpəməs\ *n* : light porous volcanic glass used in polishing

pum•mel \ˈpəməl\ *vb* **-meled; -mel•ing** : beat

[1]**pump** \ˈpəmp\ *n* : device for moving or compressing fluids ~ *vb* **1** : raise (as water) with a pump **2** : fill by means of a pump —with *up* **3** : move like a pump —**pump•er** *n*

[2]**pump** *n* : woman's low shoe

pum•per•nick•el \ˈpəmpərˌnikəl\ *n* : dark rye bread

pump•kin \ˈpəŋkən, ˈpəmpkən\ *n* : large usu. orange fruit of a vine related to the gourd

pun \ˈpən\ *n* : humorous use of a word in a way that suggests two or more interpretations —**pun** *vb*

[1]**punch** \ˈpənch\ *vb* **1** : strike with the fist **2** : perforate with a punch ~ *n* : quick blow with the fist —**punch•er** *n*

[2]**punch** *n* : tool for piercing or stamping

[3]**punch** *n* : mixed beverage often including fruit juice

punc•til•i•ous \pəŋkˈtilēəs\ *adj* : marked by precise accordance with conventions

punc•tu•al \ˈpəŋkchəwəl\ *adj* : prompt —**punc•tu•al•i•ty** \ˌpəŋkchəˈwalətē\ *n* —**punc•tu•al•ly** *adv*

punc•tu•ate \ˈpəŋkchəˌwāt\ *vb* **-at•ed; -at•ing** : mark with punctuation

punc•tu•a•tion \ˌpəŋkchəˈwāshən\ *n* : standardized marks in written matter to clarify the meaning and separate parts

punc•ture \ˈpəŋkchər\ *n* : act or result of puncturing ~ *vb* **-tured; -tur•ing** : make a hole in

pun•dit \ˈpəndət\ *n* **1** : learned person **2** : expert or critic

pun•gent \ˈpənjənt\ *adj* : having a sharp or stinging odor or taste —**pun•gen•cy** \-jənsē\ *n* —**pun•gent•ly** *adv*

pun•ish \ˈpənish\ *vb* : impose a penalty on or for —**pun•ish•able** *adj* —**pun•ish•ment** *n*

pu•ni•tive \ˈpyünətiv\ *adj* : inflicting punishment

pun•kin *var of* PUMPKIN

[1]**punt** \ˈpənt\ *n* : long narrow flat-bottomed boat ~ *vb* : propel (a boat) by pushing with a pole

[2]**punt** *vb* : kick a ball dropped from the hands ~ *n* : act of punting a ball

pu•ny \ˈpyünē\ *adj* **-ni•er; -est** : slight in power or size

pup \ˈpəp\ *n* : young dog

pu•pa \ˈpyüpə\ *n, pl* **-pae** \-ˌpē, -ˌpī\ *or* **-pas** : insect (as a moth) when it is in a cocoon —**pu•pal** \-pəl\ *adj*

[1]**pu•pil** \ˈpyüpəl\ *n* : young person in school

[2]**pupil** *n* : dark central opening of the iris of the eye

pup•pet \ˈpəpət\ *n* : small doll moved by hand or by strings —**pup•pe•teer** \ˌpəpəˈtir\ *n*

pup•py \ˈpəpē\ *n, pl* **-pies** : young dog

pur•chase \ˈpərchəs\ *vb* **-chased; -chas•ing** : obtain in exchange for money ~ *n* **1** : act of purchasing **2** : something purchased **3** : secure grasp —**purchas•er** *n*

pure \ˈpyu̇r\ *adj* **pur•er; pur•est** : free of foreign matter, contamination, or corruption —**pure•ly** *adv*

pu•ree \pyu̇ˈrā, -ˈrē\ *n* : thick liquid mass of food —**puree** *vb*

pur•ga•to•ry \ˈpərgəˌtōrē\ *n, pl* **-ries** : intermediate state after death for purification by expiating sins —**pur•ga•to•ri•al** \ˌpərgəˈtōrēəl\ *adj*

purge \ˈpərj\ *vb* **purged; purg•ing 1** : purify esp. from sin **2** : have or cause emptying of the bowels **3** : to get rid of ~ *n* **1** : act or result of purging **2** : something that purges —**pur•ga•tive** \ˈpərgətiv\ *adj or n*

pu•ri•fy \ˈpyu̇rəˌfī\ *vb* **-fied; -fy•ing** : make or become pure —**pu•ri•fi•ca•tion** \ˌpyu̇rəfəˈkāshən\ *n* —**pu•ri•fi•er** \-ˌfīər\ *n*

Pu•rim \ˈpu̇rim\ *n* : Jewish holiday celebrated in February or March in commemoration of the deliverance of the Jews from the massacre plotted by Haman

pu•ri•tan \'pyu̇rətᵊn\ *n* : one who practices or preaches a very strict moral code —**pu•ri•tan•i•cal** \ˌpyu̇rə'tanikəl\ *adj* —**pu•ri•tan•i•cal•ly** *adv*

pu•ri•ty \'pyu̇rətē\ *n* : quality or state of being pure

purl \'pərl\ *n* : stitch in knitting ~ *vb* : knit in purl stitch

pur•loin \pər'lȯin, 'pərˌlȯin\ *vb* : steal

pur•ple \'pərpəl\ *n* : bluish red color —**pur•plish** \'pərpəlish\ *adj*

pur•port \pər'pōrt\ *vb* : convey outwardly as the meaning ~ \'pərˌpōrt\ *n* : meaning —**pur•port•ed•ly** \-ədlē\ *adv*

pur•pose \'pərpəs\ *n* **1** : something (as a result) aimed at **2** : resolution ~ *vb* **-posed; -pos•ing** : intend —**pur•pose•ful** \-fəl\ *adj* —**pur•pose•ful•ly** *adv* —**pur•pose•less** *adj* —**pur•pose•ly** *adv*

purr \'pər\ *n* : low murmur typical of a contented cat —**purr** *vb*

1purse \'pərs\ *n* **1** : bag or pouch for money and small objects **2** : financial resource **3** : prize money

2purse *vb* **pursed; purs•ing** : pucker

pur•su•ance \pər'süəns\ *n* : act of carrying out or into effect

pursuant to \-'süənt-\ *prep* : according to

pur•sue \pər'sü\ *vb* **-sued; -su•ing 1** : follow in order to overtake **2** : seek to accomplish **3** : proceed along **4** : engage in —**pur•su•er** *n*

pur•suit \pər'süt\ *n* **1** : act of pursuing **2** : occupation

pur•vey \pər'vā\ *vb* **-veyed; -vey•ing** : supply (as provisions) usu. as a business —**pur•vey•or** \-ər\ *n*

pus \'pəs\ *n* : thick yellowish fluid (as in a boil)

push \'pu̇sh\ *vb* **1** : press against to move forward **2** : urge on or provoke ~ *n* **1** : vigorous effort **2** : act of pushing —**push•cart** *n* —**push•er** \'pu̇shər\ *n*

pushy \'pu̇shē\ *adj* **push•i•er; -est** : objectionably aggressive

pu•sil•lan•i•mous \ˌpyüsə'lanəməs\ *adj* : cowardly

pussy \'pu̇sē\ *n, pl* **puss•ies** : cat

pus•tule \'pəschül\ *n* : pus-filled pimple

put \'pu̇t\ *vb* **put; put•ting 1** : bring to a specified position or condition **2** : subject to pain, suffering, or death **3** : impose or cause to exist **4** : express **5** : cause to be used or employed —**put off** *vb* : postpone or delay —**put out** *vb* : bother or inconvenience —**put up** *vb* **1** : prepare for storage **2** : lodge **3** : contribute or pay —**put up with** : endure

pu•tre•fy \'pyütrəˌfī\ *vb* **-fied; -fy•ing** : make or become putrid —**pu•tre•fac•tion** \ˌpyütrə'fakshən\ *n*

pu•trid \'pyütrəd\ *adj* : rotten —**pu•trid•i•ty** \pyü'tridətē\ *n*

put•ty \'pətē\ *n, pl* **-ties** : doughlike cement —**putty** *vb*

puz•zle \'pəzəl\ *vb* **-zled; -zling 1** : confuse **2** : attempt to solve —with *out* or *over* ~ *n* : something that confuses or tests ingenuity —**puz•zle•ment** *n* —**puz•zler** \-ələr\ *n*

pyg•my \'pigmē\ *n, pl* **-mies** : dwarf —**pygmy** *adj*

py•lon \'pīˌlän, -lən\ *n* : tower or tall post

pyr•a•mid \'pirəˌmid\ *n* : structure with a square base and 4 triangular sides meeting at a point

pyre \'pīr\ *n* : material heaped for a funeral fire

py•ro•ma•nia \ˌpīrō'mānēə\ *n* : irresistible impulse to start fires —**py•ro•ma•ni•ac** \-nēˌak\ *n*

py•ro•tech•nics \ˌpīrə'tekniks\ *n pl* : spectacular display (as of fireworks) —**py•ro•tech•nic** \-nik\ *adj*

Pyr•rhic \'pirik\ *adj* : achieved at excessive cost

py•thon \'pīˌthän, -thən\ *n* : very large constricting snake

Q

q \'kyü\ *n, pl* **q's** *or* **qs** \'kyüz\ : 17th letter of the alphabet

1quack \'kwak\ *vb* : make a cry like that of a duck —**quack** *n*

2quack *n* : one who pretends to have medical or healing skill —**quack** *adj* —**quack•ery** \-ərē\ *n* —**quack•ish** *adj*

quad•ran•gle \'kwädˌraŋgəl\ *n* : rectangular courtyard

quad•rant \'kwädrənt\ *n* : 1/4 of a circle

quad•ri•lat•er•al \ˌkwädrə'latərəl\ *n* : 4-sided polygon

qua•drille \kwä'dril, kə-\ *n* : square dance for 4 couples

quad•ru•ped \'kwädrəˌped\ *n* : animal having 4 feet

qua•dru•ple \kwä'drüpəl, -'drəp-; 'kwädrəp-\ *vb* **-pled; -pling** \-pliŋ\ : multiply by 4 ~ *adj* : being 4 times as great or as many

qua•dru•plet \kwä'drəplət, -'drüp-; 'kwädrəp-\ *n* : one of 4 offspring born at one birth

quaff \'kwäf, 'kwaf\ *vb* : drink deeply or repeatedly —**quaff** *n*

quag•mire \'kwagˌmīr, 'kwäg-\ *n* : soft land or bog

qua•hog \'kōˌhȯg, 'kwȯ-, 'kwō-, -ˌhäg\ *n* : thick-shelled clam

1quail \'kwāl\ *n, pl* **quail** *or* **quails** : short-winged plump game bird

2quail *vb* : cower in fear

quaint \'kwānt\ *adj* : pleasingly old-fashioned or odd —**quaint•ly** *adv* —**quaint•ness** *n*

quake \'kwāk\ *vb* **quaked; quak•ing** : shake or tremble ~ *n* : earthquake

qual•i•fi•ca•tion \ˌkwäləfə'kāshən\ *n* **1** : limitation or stipulation **2** : special skill or experience for a job

qual•i•fy \'kwäləˌfī\ *vb* **-fied; -fy•ing 1** : modify or limit **2** : fit by skill or training for some purpose **3** : become eligible —**qual•i•fied** *adj* —**qual•i•fi•er** \-ˌfīər\ *n*

qual•i•ty \'kwälətē\ *n, pl* **-ties 1** : peculiar and essential character, nature, or feature **2** : excellence or distinction

qualm \'kwäm, 'kwälm, 'kwȯm\ *n* : sudden feeling of doubt or uneasiness

quan•da•ry \'kwändrē\ *n, pl* **-ries** : state of perplexity or doubt

quan•ti•ty \'kwäntətē\ *n, pl* **-ties 1** : something that can be measured or numbered **2** : considerable amount

quan•tum theory \'kwäntəm-\ *n* : theory in physics that radiant energy (as light) is composed of separate packets of energy

quar•an•tine \'kwȯrənˌtēn\ *n* **1** : restraint on the movements of persons or goods to prevent the spread of pests or disease **2** : place or period of quarantine —**quarantine** *vb*

quar•rel \'kwȯrəl\ *n* : basis of conflict —**quarrel** *vb* —**quar•rel•some** \-səm\ *adj*

1quar•ry \'kwȯrē\ *n, pl* **quarries** : prey

2quarry *n, pl* **-ries** : excavation for obtaining stone —**quarry** *vb*

quart \'kwȯrt\ *n* : unit of liquid measure equal to .95 liter or of dry measure equal to 1.10 liters

quar•ter \'kwȯrtər\ *n* **1** : 1/4 part **2** : 1/4 of a dollar **3** : city district **4** *pl* : place to live esp. for a time **5** : mercy ~ *vb* : divide into 4 equal parts

quar•ter•ly \'kwȯrtərlē\ *adv or adj* : at 3-month intervals ~ *n, pl* **-lies** : periodical published 4 times a year

quar•ter•mas•ter *n* **1** : ship's helmsman **2** : army supply officer

quar•tet \kwȯr'tet\ *n* **1** : music for 4 performers **2** : group of 4

quar•to \'kwȯrtō\ *n, pl* **-tos** : book printed on pages cut 4 from a sheet

quartz \'kwȯrts\ *n* : transparent crystalline mineral

quash \'kwäsh, 'kwȯsh\ *vb* **1** : set aside by judicial action **2** : suppress summarily and completely

qua•si \'kwāˌzī, -sī; 'kwäzē, 'kwäs-; 'kwāzē\ *adj* : similar or nearly identical

qua•train \'kwäˌtrān\ *n* : unit of 4 lines of verse

qua•ver \'kwāvər\ *vb* : tremble or trill —**quaver** *n*

quay \'kē, 'kā, 'kwā\ *n* : wharf

quea•sy \'kwēzē\ *adj* **-si•er; -est** : nauseated —**quea•si•ly** \-zəlē\ *adv* —**quea•si•ness** \-zēnəs\ *n*

queen \'kwēn\ *n* **1** : wife or widow of a king **2** : female monarch **3** : woman of rank, power, or attractiveness **4** : fertile female of a social insect —**queen•ly** *adj*

queer \'kwir\ *adj* : differing from the usual or normal —**queer•ly** *adv* —**queer•ness** *n*

quell \'kwel\ *vb* : put down by force

quench \'kwench\ *vb* **1** : put out **2** : satisfy (a thirst) —**quench•able** *adj* —**quench•er** *n*

quer•u•lous \'kwerələs, -yələs\ *adj* : fretful or whining —**quer•u•lous•ly** *adv* —**quer•u•lous•ness** *n*

que•ry \'kwirē, 'kwer-\ *n, pl* **-ries** : question —**query** *vb*

quest \'kwest\ *n or vb* : search

ques•tion \'kweschən\ *n* **1** : something asked **2** : subject for debate **3** : dispute ~ *vb* **1** : ask questions **2** : doubt or dispute **3** : subject to analysis —**ques•tion•er** *n*

ques•tion•able \'kweschənəbəl\ *adj* **1** : not certain **2** : of doubtful truth or morality —**ques•tion•ably** \-blē\ *adv*

question mark *n* : a punctuation mark ? used esp. at the end of a sentence to indicate a direct question

ques•tion•naire \ˌkweschə'nar\ *n* : set of questions

queue \'kyü\ *n* **1** : braid of hair **2** : a waiting line ~ *vb* **queued; queu•ing** *or* **queue•ing** : line up

quib•ble \'kwibəl\ *n* : minor objection —**quibble** *vb* —**quib•bler** *n*

quick \'kwik\ *adj* **1** : rapid **2** : alert or perceptive ~ *n* : sensitive area of living flesh —**quick** *adv* —**quick•ly** *adv* —**quick•ness** *n*

quick•en \'kwikən\ *vb* **1** : come to life **2** : increase in speed

quick•sand *n* : deep mass of sand and water

quick•sil•ver *n* : mercury

qui•es•cent \kwī'esᵊnt\ *adj* : being at rest —**qui•es•cence** \-əns\ *n*

qui•et \'kwīət\ *adj* **1** : marked by little motion or activity **2** : gentle **3** : free from noise **4** : not showy **5** : secluded ~ *vb* : pacify —**quiet** *adv or n* —**qui•et•ly** *adv* —**qui•et•ness** *n*

qui•etude \'kwīəˌtüd, -ˌtyüd\ *n* : quietness or repose

quill \'kwil\ *n* **1** : a large stiff feather **2** : porcupine's spine

quilt \'kwilt\ *n* : padded bedspread ~ *vb* : stitch or sew in layers with padding in between

quince \'kwins\ *n* : hard yellow applelike fruit

qui•nine \'kwīˌnīn\ *n* : bitter drug used against malaria

quin•tes•sence \kwin'tesᵊns\ *n* **1** : purest essence of something **2** : most typical example —**quin•tes•sen•tial** \ˌkwintə'senchəl\ *adj* —**quin•tes•sen•tial•ly** *adv*

quin•tet \kwin'tet\ *n* **1** : music for 5 performers **2** : group of 5

quin•tu•ple \kwin'tüpəl, -'tyüp-, -'təp-; 'kwintəp-\ *adj* **1** : having 5 units or members **2** : being 5 times as great or as many —**quintuple** *n or vb*

quin•tu•plet \-plət\ *n* : one of 5 offspring at one birth

quip \'kwip\ *vb* **-pp-** : make a clever remark —**quip** *n*

quire \'kwīr\ *n* : 24 or 25 sheets of paper of the same size and quality

quirk \'kwərk\ *n* : peculiarity of action or behavior —**quirky** *adj*

quit \'kwit\ *vb* **quit; quit•ting 1** : stop **2** : leave —**quit•ter** *n*

quite \'kwīt\ *adv* **1** : completely **2** : to a considerable extent

quits \'kwits\ *adj* : even or equal with another (as by repaying a debt)

1quiv•er \'kwivər\ *n* : case for arrows

2quiver *vb* : shake or tremble —**quiver** *n*

quix•ot•ic \kwik'sätik\ *adj* : idealistic to an impractical degree —**quix•ot•i•cal•ly** \-tiklē\ *adv*

quiz \'kwiz\ *n, pl* **quiz•zes** : short test ~ *vb* **-zz-** : question closely

quiz•zi•cal \'kwizikəl\ *adj* **1** : teasing **2** : curious

quoit \'kȯit, 'kwȯit, 'kwāt\ *n* : ring thrown at a peg in a game **(quoits)**

quon•dam \'kwändəm, -ˌdam\ *adj* : former

quo•rum \'kwōrəm\ *n* : required number of members present

quo•ta \'kwōtə\ *n* : proportional part or share

quotation mark *n* : one of a pair of punctuation marks " " or ' ' used esp. to indicate the beginning and the end of a quotation

quote \'kwōt\ *vb* **quot•ed; quot•ing 1** : repeat (another's words) exactly **2** : state (a price) —**quot•able** *adj* —**quo•ta•tion** \kwō'tāshən\ *n* —**quote** *n*

quo•tient \'kwōshənt\ *n* : number obtained from division

R

r \'är\ *n, pl* **r's** *or* **rs** \'ärz\ : 18th letter of the alphabet

rab•bet \'rabət\ *n* : groove in a board

rab•bi \'rabˌī\ *n* : Jewish religious leader —**rab•bin•ic** \rə'binik\, **rab•bin•i•cal** \-ikəl\ *adj*

rab•bin•ate \'rabənət, -ˌnāt\ *n* : office of a rabbi

rab•bit \'rabət\ *n, pl* **-bit** *or* **-bits** : long-eared burrowing mammal

rab•ble \'rabəl\ *n* : mob

ra•bid \'rabəd\ *adj* **1** : violent **2** : fanatical **3** : affected with rabies —**ra•bid•ly** *adv*

ra•bies \'rābēz\ *n, pl* **rabies** : acute deadly virus disease

rac•coon \ra'kün\ *n, pl* **-coon** *or* **-coons** : tree-dwelling mammal with a black mask and a bushy ringed tail

1race \'rās\ *n* **1** : strong current of water **2** : contest of speed **3** : election campaign ~ *vb* **raced; rac•ing 1** : run in a race **2** : rush —**race•course** *n* —**rac•er** *n* —**race•track** *n*

2race *n* **1** : family, tribe, people, or nation of the same stock **2** : division of mankind based on hereditary traits —**ra•cial** \'rāshəl\ *adj* —**ra•cial•ly** *adv*

race•horse *n* : horse used for racing

rac•ism \'rāsˌizəm\ *n* : discrimination based on the belief that some races are by nature superior —**rac•ist** \-ist\ *n*

rack \'rak\ *n* **1** : framework for display or storage **2** : instrument that stretches the body for torture ~ *vb* : torture with or as if with a rack

1rack•et \'rakət\ *n* : bat with a tight netting across an open frame

2racket *n* **1** : confused noise **2** : fraudulent scheme —**rack•e•teer** \ˌrakə'tir\ *n* —**rack•e•teer•ing** *n*

ra•con•teur \ˌrakˌän'tər\ *n* : storyteller

racy \'rāsē\ *adj* **rac•i•er; -est** : risqué —**rac•i•ly** *adv* —**rac•i•ness** *n*

ra•dar \'rāˌdär\ *n* : radio device for determining distance and direction of distant objects

ra•di•al \'rādēəl\ *adj* : having parts arranged like rays coming from a common center —**ra•di•al•ly** *adv*

ra•di•ant \'rādēənt\ *adj* **1** : glowing **2** : beaming with happiness **3** : transmitted by radiation —**ra•di•ance** \-əns\ *n* —**ra•di•ant•ly** *adv*

ra•di•ate \'rādēˌāt\ *vb* **-at•ed; -at•ing 1** : issue rays or in rays **2** : spread from a center —**ra•di•a•tion** \ˌrādē'āshən\ *n*

ra•di•a•tor \'rādēˌātər\ *n* : cooling or heating device

rad•i•cal \'radikəl\ *adj* **1** : fundamental **2** : extreme ~ *n* : person favoring extreme changes —**rad•i•cal•ism** \-ˌizəm\ *n* —**rad•i•cal•ly** *adv*

radii *pl of* RADIUS

ra•dio \'rādēˌō\ *n, pl* **-di•os 1** : wireless transmission or reception of sound by means of electric waves **2** : radio receiving set ~ *vb* : send a message to by radio —**radio** *adj*

ra•dio•ac•tiv•i•ty \ˌrādēōˌak'tivətē\ *n* : property of an element that emits energy through nuclear disintegration —**ra•dio•ac•tive** \-'aktiv\ *adj*

ra•di•ol•o•gy \ˌrādē'äləjē\ *n* : medical use of radiation —**ra•di•ol•o•gist** \-jist\ *n*

rad•ish \'radish\ *n* : pungent fleshy root usu. eaten raw

ra•di•um \'rādēəm\ *n* : metallic radioactive chemical element

ra•di•us \'rādēəs\ *n, pl* **-dii** \-ēˌī\ **1** : line from the center of a circle or sphere to the circumference or surface **2** : area defined by a radius

ra•don \'rāˌdän\ *n* : gaseous radioactive chemical element

raff•ish \'rafish\ *adj* : flashily vulgar —**raff•ish•ly** *adv* —**raff•ish•ness** *n*

raf•fle \'rafəl\ *n* : lottery among people who have bought tickets ~ *vb* **-fled; -fling** : offer in a raffle

1raft \'raft\ *n* : flat floating platform ~ *vb* : travel or transport by raft

2raft *n* : large amount or number

raf•ter \'raftər\ *n* : beam supporting a roof

1rag \'rag\ *n* : waste piece of cloth

2rag *n* : composition in ragtime

rag•a•muf•fin \'ragəˌməfən\ *n* : ragged dirty person

rage \'rāj\ *n* **1** : violent anger **2** : vogue ~ *vb* **raged; rag•ing 1** : be extremely angry or violent **2** : be out of control

rag•ged \'ragəd\ *adj* : torn —**rag•ged•ly** *adv* —**rag•ged•ness** *n*

ra•gout \ra'gü\ *n* : meat stew

rag•time *n* : syncopated music

rag•weed *n* : coarse weedy herb with allergenic pollen

raid \'rād\ *n* : sudden usu. surprise attack —**raid** *vb* —**raid•er** *n*

1rail \'rāl\ *n* **1** : bar serving as a guard or barrier **2** : bar forming a track for wheeled vehicles **3** : railroad

2rail *vb* : scold someone vehemently —**rail•er** *n*

rail•ing \'rāliŋ\ *n* : rail or a barrier of rails

rail•lery \'rālərē\ *n, pl* **-ler•ies** : good-natured ridicule

rail•road \'rālˌrōd\ *n* : road for a train laid with iron rails and wooden ties ~ *vb*

: force something hastily —**rail•road•er** *n* —**rail•road•ing** *n*
rail•way \-ˌwā\ *n* : railroad
rai•ment \'rāmənt\ *n* : clothing
rain \'rān\ **1** : water falling in drops from the clouds **2** : shower of objects ~ *vb* : fall as or like rain —**rain•coat** *n* —**rain•drop** *n* —**rain•fall** *n* —**rain•mak•er** *n* —**rain•mak•ing** *n* —**rain•storm** *n* —**rain•wa•ter** *n* —**rainy** *adj*
rain•bow \-ˌbō\ *n* : arc of colors formed by the sun shining through moisture
raise \'rāz\ *vb* **raised; rais•ing 1** : lift **2** : arouse **3** : erect **4** : collect **5** : breed, grow, or bring up **6** : increase **7** : make light ~ *n* : increase esp. in pay —**rais•er** *n*
rai•sin \'rāzᵊn\ *n* : dried grape
ra•ja, ra•jah \'räjə\ *n* : Indian prince
[1]**rake** \'rāk\ *n* : garden tool for smoothing or sweeping ~ *vb* **raked; rak•ing 1** : gather, loosen, or smooth with or as if with a rake **2** : sweep with gunfire
[2]**rake** *n* : dissolute man
rak•ish \'rākish\ *adj* : smart or jaunty —**rak•ish•ly** *adv* —**rak•ish•ness** *n*
ral•ly \'ralē\ *vb* **-lied; -ly•ing 1** : bring or come together **2** : revive or recover **3** : make a comeback ~ *n, pl* **-lies 1** : act of rallying **2** : mass meeting
ram \'ram\ *n* **1** : male sheep **2** : beam used in battering down walls or doors ~ *vb* **-mm- 1** : force or drive in or through **2** : strike against violently
RAM \'ram\ *n* : main internal storage area in a computer
ram•ble \'rambəl\ *vb* **-bled; -bling** : wander —**ramble** *n* —**ram•bler** \-blər\ *n*
ram•bunc•tious \ram'bəŋkshəs\ *adj* : unruly
ram•i•fi•ca•tion \ˌraməfə'kāshən\ *n* : consequence
ram•i•fy \'raməˌfī\ *vb* **-fied; -fy•ing** : branch out
ramp \'ramp\ *n* : sloping passage or connecting roadway
ram•page \'ramˌpāj, ram'pāj\ *vb* **-paged; -pag•ing** : rush about wildly ~ \'ramˌ-\ *n* : violent or riotous action or behavior
ram•pant \'rampənt\ *adj* : widespread —**ram•pant•ly** *adv*
ram•part \'ramˌpärt\ *n* : embankment of a fortification
ram•rod *n* : rod used to load or clean a gun ~ *adj* : strict or inflexible
ram•shack•le \'ramˌshakəl\ *adj* : shaky
ran *past of* RUN
ranch \'ranch\ *n* **1** : establishment for the raising of cattle, sheep, or horses **2** : specialized farm ~ *vb* : operate a ranch —**ranch•er** *n*
ran•cid \'ransəd\ *adj* : smelling or tasting as if spoiled —**ran•cid•i•ty** \ran'sidətē\ *n*
ran•cor \'raŋkər\ *n* : bitter deep-seated ill will —**ran•cor•ous** *adj*
ran•dom \'randəm\ *adj* : occurring by chance —**ran•dom•ly** *adv* —**random•ness** *n* —**at random** : without definite aim or method
ran•dom•ize \'randəˌmīz\ *vb* **-ized; -iz•ing** : select, assign, or arrange in a random way
rang *past of* RING
range \'rānj\ *n* **1** : series of things in a row **2** : open land for grazing **3** : cooking stove **4** : variation within limits **5** : place for target practice **6** : extent ~ *vb* **ranged; rang•ing 1** : arrange **2** : roam at large, freely, or over **3** : vary within limits
rang•er \'rānjər\ *n* : officer who manages and protects public lands
rangy \'rānjē\ *adj* **rang•i•er; -est** : being slender with long limbs —**rang•i•ness** *n*
[1]**rank** \'raŋk\ *adj* **1** : vigorous in growth **2** : unpleasantly strong-smelling —**rank•ly** *adv* —**rank•ness** *n*
[2]**rank** *n* **1** : line of soldiers **2** : orderly arrangement **3** : grade of official standing **4** : position within a group ~ *vb* **1** : arrange in formation or according to class **2** : take or have a relative position
rank and file *n* : general membership
ran•kle \'raŋkəl\ *vb* **-kled; -kling** : cause anger, irritation, or bitterness
ran•sack \'ranˌsak\ *vb* : search through and rob
ran•som \'ransəm\ *n* : something demanded for the freedom of a captive ~ *vb* : gain the freedom of by paying a price —**ran•som•er** *n*
rant \'rant\ *vb* : talk or scold violently —**rant•er** *n* —**rant•ing•ly** *adv*
[1]**rap** \'rap\ *n* : sharp blow or rebuke ~ *vb* **-pp-** : strike or criticize sharply
[2]**rap** *vb* **-pp-** : talk freely
ra•pa•cious \rə'pāshəs\ *adj* **1** : excessively greedy **2** : ravenous —**ra•pa•cious•ly** *adv* —**ra•pa•cious•ness** *n* —**ra•pac•i•ty** \-'pasətē\ *n*
[1]**rape** \'rāp\ *n* : herb grown as a forage crop and for its seeds (**rape•seed**)
[2]**rape** *vb* **raped; rap•ing** : force to have sexual intercourse —**rape** *n* —**rap•er** *n* —**rap•ist** \'rāpist\ *n*
rap•id \'rapəd\ *adj* : very fast —**ra•pid•i•ty** \rə'pidətē\ *n* —**rap•id•ly** *adv*
rap•ids \-ədz\ *n pl* : place in a stream where the current is swift
ra•pi•er \'rāpēər\ *n* : narrow 2-edged sword
rap•ine \'rapən, -ˌīn\ *n* : plunder
rap•port \ra'pōr\ *n* : harmonious relationship
rapt \'rapt\ *adj* : engrossed —**rapt•ly** *adv* —**rapt•ness** *n*
rap•ture \'rapchər\ *n* : spiritual or emotional ecstasy —**rap•tur•ous** \-chərəs\ *adj* —**rap•tur•ous•ly** *adv*
[1]**rare** \'rar\ *adj* **rar•er; rar•est** : having a portion relatively uncooked
[2]**rare** *adj* **rar•er; rar•est 1** : not dense **2** : unusually fine **3** : seldom met with —**rare•ly** *adv* —**rare•ness** *n* —**rar•i•ty** \'rarətē\ *n*
rar•e•fy \'rarəˌfī\ *vb* **-fied; -fy•ing** : make or become rare, thin, or less dense —**rar•e•fac•tion** \ˌrarə'fakshən\ *n*
rar•ing \'rarən, -iŋ\ *adj* : full of enthusiasm
ras•cal \'raskəl\ *n* : mean, dishonest, or mischievous person —**ras•cal•i•ty** \ras'kalətē\ *n* —**ras•cal•ly** \'raskəlē\ *adj*
[1]**rash** \'rash\ *adj* : too hasty in decision or action —**rash•ly** *adv* —**rash•ness** *n*
[2]**rash** *n* : a breaking out of the skin with red spots
rasp \'rasp\ *vb* **1** : rub with or as if with a rough file **2** : to speak in a grating tone ~ *n* : coarse file
rasp•ber•ry \'razˌberē\ *n* : edible red or black berry
rat \'rat\ *n* : destructive rodent larger than the mouse ~ *vb* : betray or inform on
ratch•et \'rachət\ *n* : notched device for allowing motion in one direction
rate \'rāt\ *n* **1** : quantity, amount, or degree measured in relation to some other quantity **2** : rank ~ *vb* **rat•ed; rat•ing 1** : estimate or determine the rank or quality of **2** : deserve
rath•er \'rathər, 'rət͟h-, 'rät͟h-\ *adv* **1** : preferably **2** : on the other hand **3** : more properly **4** : somewhat
rat•i•fy \'ratəˌfī\ *vb* **-fied; -fy•ing** : approve and accept formally —**rat•i•fi•ca•tion** \ˌratəfə'kāshən\ *n*
rat•ing \'rātiŋ\ *n* : classification according to grade
ra•tio \'rāshēō\ *n, pl* **-tios** : relation in number, quantity, or degree between things
ra•tion \'rashən, 'rāshən\ *n* : share or allotment (as of food) ~ *vb* : use or allot sparingly
ra•tio•nal \'rashənəl\ *adj* **1** : having reason or sanity **2** : relating to reason —**ra•tio•nal•ly** *adv*
ra•tio•nale \ˌrashə'nal\ *n* **1** : explanation of principles of belief or practice **2** : underlying reason
ra•tio•nal•ize \'rashənəˌlīz\ *vb* **-ized; -iz•ing** : justify (as one's behavior or weaknesses) esp. to oneself —**ra•tio•nal•i•za•tion** \ˌrashənələ'zāshən\ *n*
rat•tan \ra'tan, rə-\ *n* : palm with long stems used esp. for canes and wickerwork
rat•tle \'ratᵊl\ *vb* **-tled; -tling 1** : make a series of clattering sounds **2** : say briskly **3** : confuse or upset ~ *n* **1** : series of clattering sounds **2** : something (as a toy) that rattles
rat•tler \'ratlər\ *n* : rattlesnake
rat•tle•snake *n* : American venomous snake with a rattle at the end of the tail
rat•ty \'ratē\ *adj* **rat•ti•er; -est** : shabby
rau•cous \'rȯkəs\ *adj* : harsh or boisterous —**rau•cous•ly** *adv* —**rau•cous•ness** *n*
rav•age \'ravij\ *n* : destructive effect ~ *vb* **-aged; -ag•ing** : lay waste —**rav•ag•er** *n*
rave \'rāv\ *vb* **raved; rav•ing 1** : talk wildly in or as if in delirium **2** : talk with extreme enthusiasm ~ *n* **1** : act of raving **2** : enthusiastic praise
rav•el \'ravəl\ *vb* **-eled** *or* **-elled; -el•ing** *or* **-el•ling 1** : unravel **2** : tangle ~ *n* **1** : something tangled **2** : loose thread
ra•ven \'rāvən\ *n* : large black bird ~ *adj* : black and shiny
rav•en•ous \'ravənəs\ *adj* : very hungry —**rav•en•ous•ly** *adv* —**rav•en•ousness** *n*
ra•vine \rə'vēn\ *n* : narrow steep-sided valley
rav•ish \'ravish\ *vb* **1** : seize and take away by violence **2** : overcome with joy or delight **3** : rape —**rav•ish•er** *n* —**rav•ish•ment** *n*
raw \'rȯ\ *adj* **raw•er** \'rȯər\; **raw•est** \'rȯəst\ **1** : not cooked **2** : not processed **3** : not trained **4** : having the surface rubbed off **5** : cold and damp **6** : vulgar —**raw•ness** *n*
raw•hide \'rȯˌhīd\ *n* : untanned skin of cattle
ray \'rā\ *n* **1** : thin beam of radiant energy (as light) **2** : tiny bit
ray•on \'rāˌän\ *n* : fabric made from cellulose fiber
raze \'rāz\ *vb* **razed; raz•ing** : destroy or tear down
ra•zor \'rāzər\ *n* : sharp cutting instrument used to shave off hair
re- \rē, ˌrē, 'rē\ *prefix* **1** : again or anew **2** : back or backward

reaccelerate	**refocus**
reaccept	**refold**
reacclimatize	**reformulate**
reaccredit	**refreeze**
reacquaint	**refuel**
reacquire	**regain**
reactivate	**regrow**
reactivation	**regrowth**
readdress	**rehear**
readjust	**reheat**
readjustment	**rehire**
readmit	**rehospitalization**
readopt	**rehospitalize**
reaffirm	**reidentify**
realign	**reignite**
realignment	**reimplant**
reallocate	**reimpose**
reanalysis	**reincorporate**
reanalyze	**reindict**
reappear	**reinfection**
reappearance	**reinflate**
reapply	**reinject**
reappoint	**reinjection**
reapportion	**reinoculate**
reappraisal	**reinsert**
reappraise	**reinsertion**
reapprove	**reinspect**
reargue	**reinstall**
rearrange	**reinstitute**
rearrest	**reintegrate**
reassemble	**reintegration**
reassert	**reinter**
reassess	**reintroduce**
reassessment	**reinvent**
reassign	**reinvestigate**
reassignment	**reinvestigation**
reattach	**reinvigorate**
reattain	**rejudge**
reawaken	**rekindle**
rebalance	**reknit**
rebaptize	**relabel**
rebid	**relandscape**
rebind	**relaunch**
reborn	**relearn**
rebroadcast	**relight**
rebuild	**reline**
rebury	**reload**
recalculate	**remarriage**
recapture	**remarry**
recast	**rematch**
recertification	**remelt**
recertify	**remobilize**
rechannel	**remoisten**
recharge	**remold**
rechargeable	**remotivate**
recheck	**rename**
rechristen	**renegotiate**
recirculate	**reoccupy**
recirculation	**reoccur**
reclassification	**reoccurrence**
reclassify	**reoperate**
recolonize	**reorchestrate**
recombine	**reorganization**
recompute	**reorganize**
reconceive	**reorient**
reconnect	**repack**
reconquer	**repave**
reconquest	**rephotograph**
reconsider	**replan**
reconsideration	**replaster**
reconsolidate	**replay**
reconstruct	**replot**
recontaminate	**repolish**
reconvene	**repopulate**
reconvict	**repressurize**
recopy	**reprice**
re-create	**reprint**
recross	**reprocess**
redecorate	**reprogram**
rededicate	**reread**
rededication	**rereading**
redefine	**rerecord**
redeposit	**reregister**
redesign	**reroof**
redevelop	**reroute**
rediscover	**resalable**
rediscovery	**resale**
redissolve	**reschedule**
redistribute	**reseal**
redraft	**resegregate**
redraw	**resell**
reemerge	**resentence**
reemergence	**reset**
reemphasize	**resettle**
reenergize	**resew**
reengage	**reshoot**
reenlist	**reshow**
reenlistment	**resocialization**
reenroll	**resod**
reenter	**resolidify**
reequip	**restage**
reestablish	**restart**
reestablishment	**restate**
reestimate	**restatement**
reevaluate	**restimulate**
reevaluation	**restock**
reexamination	**restructure**
reexamine	**restudy**
refinance	**restyle**
refire	**resubmit**
refloat	**resupply**
resurface	**retune**
resurvey	**retype**
resynthesis	**reupholster**
resynthesize	**reusable**
retarget	**reuse**
reteach	**reutilize**
retell	**revaccinate**
retest	**revaccination**
rethink	**revisit**
retighten	**rewash**
retrain	**reweave**
retranslate	**rewind**
retransmit	**rewire**
retry	**rewrap**

reach \'rēch\ *vb* **1** : stretch out **2** : touch or try to touch or grasp **3** : extend to or arrive at **4** : communicate with ~ *n* **1** : act of reaching **2** : distance one can reach **3** : ability to reach —**reach•able** *adj* —**reach•er** *n*
re•act \rē'akt\ *vb* **1** : act in response to some influence or stimulus **2** : undergo chemical change —**re•ac•tive** \-'aktiv\ *adj*
re•ac•tion \rē'akshən\ *n* **1** : action or emotion caused by and directly related or counter to another action **2** : chemical change
re•ac•tion•ary \-shəˌnerē\ *adj* : relating to or favoring return to an earlier political order or policy —**reactionary** *n*
re•ac•tor \rē'aktər\ *n* **1** : one that reacts **2** : device for the controlled release of nuclear energy
read \'rēd\ *vb* **read** \'red\; **read•ing** \'rēdiŋ\ **1** : understand written language **2** : utter aloud printed words **3** : interpret **4** : study **5** : indicate ~ *adj* \'red\ : informed by reading —**read•a•bil•i•ty** \ˌrēdə'bilətē\ *n* —**read•able** *adj* —**read•ably** *adv* —**read•er** *n* —**read•er•ship** *n*
read•ing \'rēdiŋ\ *n* **1** : something read or for reading **2** : particular version, interpretation, or performance **3** : data indicated by an instrument
ready \'redē\ *adj* **read•i•er; -est 1** : prepared or available for use or action **2** : willing to do something ~ *vb* **read•ied; ready•ing** : make ready ~ *n* : state of being ready —**read•i•ly** *adv* —**read•i•ness** *n*
re•al \'rēl\ *adj* **1** : relating to fixed or immovable things (as land) **2** : genuine **3** : not imaginary ~ *adv* : very —**re•al•ness** *n* —**for real 1** : in earnest **2** : genuine
real estate *n* : property in houses and land
re•al•ism \'rēəˌlizəm\ *n* **1** : disposition to deal with facts practically **2** : faithful portrayal of reality —**re•al•ist** \-list\ *adj or n* —**re•al•is•tic** \ˌrēə'listik\ *adj* —**re•al•is•ti•cal•ly** \-tiklē\ *adv*
re•al•i•ty \rē'alətē\ *n, pl* **-ties 1** : quality or state of being real **2** : something real
re•al•ize \'rēəˌlīz\ *vb* **-ized; -iz•ing 1** : make actual **2** : obtain **3** : be aware of —**re•al•iz•able** *adj* —**re•al•i•za•tion** \ˌrēələ'zāshən\ *n*
re•al•ly \'rēlē, 'ril-\ *adv* : in truth
realm \'relm\ *n* **1** : kingdom **2** : sphere
[1]**ream** \'rēm\ *n* : quantity of paper that is 480, 500, or 516 sheets
[2]**ream** *vb* : enlarge, shape, or clean with a specially shaped tool (**ream•er**)
reap \'rēp\ *vb* : cut or clear (as a crop) with a scythe or machine —**reap•er** *n*
[1]**rear** \'rir\ *vb* **1** : raise upright **2** : breed or bring up **3** : rise on the hind legs
[2]**rear** *n* **1** : back **2** : position at the back of something ~ *adj* : being at the back —**rear•ward** \-wərd\ *adj or adv*
rear admiral *n* : commissioned officer in the navy or coast guard ranking next below a vice admiral
rea•son \'rēzᵊn\ *n* **1** : explanation or justification **2** : motive for action or belief **3** : power or process of thinking ~ *vb* **1** : use the faculty of reason **2** : try to persuade another —**rea•son•er** *n* —**rea•son•ing** \'rēzᵊniŋ\ *n*
rea•son•able \'rēzᵊnəbəl\ *adj* **1** : being within the bounds of reason **2** : inexpensive —**rea•son•able•ness** *n* —**rea•son•ably** \-blē\ *adv*
re•as•sure \ˌrēə'shu̇r\ *vb* : restore one's confidence —**re•as•sur•ance** \-'shu̇rəns\ *n* —**re•as•sur•ing•ly** *adv*
re•bate \'rēˌbāt\ *n* : return of part of a payment —**rebate** *vb*
reb•el \'rebəl\ *n* : one that resists authority ~ \ri'bel\ *vb* **-belled; -bel•ling 1** : resist authority **2** : feel or exhibit anger —**rebel** \'rebəl\ *adj*
re•bel•lion \ri'belyən\ *n* : resistance to authority and esp. to one's government
re•bel•lious \-yəs\ *adj* **1** : engaged in rebellion **2** : inclined to resist authority —**re•bel•lious•ly** *adv* —**re•bel•lious•ness** *n*
re•birth \'rē'bərth\ *n* **1** : new or second birth **2** : revival
re•bound \'rē'bau̇nd, ri-\ *vb* **1** : spring back on striking something **2** : recover from a reverse ~ \'rēˌ-\ *n* **1** : action of rebounding **2** : reaction to a reverse

re•buff \ri'bəf\ *vb* : refuse or repulse rudely **—rebuff** *n*
re•buke \-'byük\ *vb* **-buked; -buk•ing** : reprimand sharply **—rebuke** *n*
re•bus \'rēbəs\ *n* : riddle representing syllables or words with pictures
re•but \ri'bət\ *vb* **-but•ted; -but•ting** : refute **—re•but•ter** *n*
re•but•tal \-ᵊl\ *n* : opposing argument
re•cal•ci•trant \ri'kalsətrənt\ *adj* **1** : stubbornly resisting authority **2** : resistant to handling or treatment **—re•cal•ci•trance** \-trəns\ *n*
re•call \ri'kȯl\ *vb* **1** : call back **2** : remember **3** : revoke ~ \ri'-, 'rē,-\ *n* **1** : a summons to return **2** : remembrance **3** : act of revoking
re•cant \ri'kant\ *vb* : take back (something said) publicly
re•ca•pit•u•late \,rēkə'pichə,lāt\ *vb* **-lat•ed; -lat•ing** : summarize **—re•ca•pit•u•la•tion** \-,pichə'lāshən\ *n*
re•cede \ri'sēd\ *vb* **-ced•ed; -ced•ing 1** : move back or away **2** : slant backward
re•ceipt \-'sēt\ *n* **1** : act of receiving **2** : something (as payment) received —usu. in pl. **3** : writing acknowledging something received
re•ceive \ri'sēv\ *vb* **-ceived; -ceiv•ing 1** : take in or accept **2** : greet or entertain (visitors) **3** : pick up radio waves and convert into sounds or pictures **—re•ceiv•able** *adj*
re•ceiv•er \ri'sēvər\ *n* **1** : one that receives **2** : one having charge of property or money involved in a lawsuit **3** : apparatus for receiving radio waves **—re•ceiv•er•ship** *n*
re•cent \'rēsᵊnt\ *adj* **1** : having lately come into existence **2** : of the present time or time just past **—re•cent•ly** *adv* **—re•cent•ness** *n*
re•cep•ta•cle \ri'septikəl\ *n* : container
re•cep•tion \ri'sepshən\ *n* **1** : act of receiving **2** : social gathering at which guests are formally welcomed
re•cep•tion•ist \-shənist\ *n* : person employed to greet callers
re•cep•tive \ri'septiv\ *adj* : open and responsive to ideas, impressions, or suggestions **—re•cep•tive•ly** *adv* **—re•cep•tive•ness** *n* **—re•cep•tiv•i•ty** \,rē,sep'tivətē\ *n*
re•cess \'rē,ses, ri'ses\ *n* **1** : indentation in a line or surface **2** : suspension of a session for rest ~ *vb* **1** : make a recess in or put into a recess **2** : interrupt a session for a recess
re•ces•sion \ri'seshən\ *n* **1** : departing procession **2** : period of reduced economic activity
rec•i•pe \'resə,pē\ *n* : instructions for making something
re•cip•i•ent \ri'sipēənt\ *n* : one that receives
re•cip•ro•cal \ri'siprəkəl\ *adj* **1** : affecting each in the same way **2** : so related that one is equivalent to the other **—re•cip•ro•cal•ly** *adv* **—re•ci•proc•i•ty** \,resə'präsətē\ *n*
re•cip•ro•cate \-,kāt\ *vb* **-cat•ed; -cat•ing** : make a return for something done or given **—re•cip•ro•ca•tion** \-,siprə'kāshən\ *n*
re•cit•al \ri'sītᵊl\ *n* **1** : public reading or recitation **2** : music or dance concert or exhibition by pupils **—re•cit•al•ist** \-ᵊlist\ *n*
rec•i•ta•tion \,resə'tāshən\ *n* : a reciting or recital
re•cite \ri'sīt\ *vb* **-cit•ed; -cit•ing 1** : repeat verbatim **2** : recount **—re•cit•er** *n*
reck•less \'rekləs\ *adj* : lacking caution **—reck•less•ly** *adv* **—reck•less•ness** *n*
reck•on \'rekən\ *vb* **1** : count or calculate **2** : consider
reck•on•ing *n* **1** : act or instance of reckoning **2** : settling of accounts
re•claim \ri'klām\ *vb* **1** : change to a desirable condition **2** : obtain from a waste product or by-product **3** : demand or obtain the return of **—re•claim•able** *adj* **—rec•la•ma•tion** \,reklə'māshən\ *n*
re•cline \ri'klīn\ *vb* **-clined; -clin•ing** : lean backward or lie down
rec•luse \'rek,lüs, ri'klüs\ *n* : one who leads a secluded or solitary life
rec•og•ni•tion \,rekig'nishən\ *n* : act of recognizing or state of being recognized
re•cog•ni•zance \ri'känəzəns, -'käg-\ *n* : promise recorded before a court
rec•og•nize \'rekig,nīz\ *vb* **-nized; -niz•ing 1** : identify as previously known **2** : take notice of **3** : acknowledge esp. with appreciation **—rec•og•niz•able** \'rekəg,nīzəbəl\ *adj* **—rec•og•niz•ably** \-blē\ *adv*
re•coil \ri'kȯil\ *vb* : draw or spring back ~ \'rē,-, ri'-\ *n* : action of recoiling
rec•ol•lect \,rekə'lekt\ *vb* : remember
rec•ol•lec•tion \,rekə'lekshən\ *n* **1** : act or power of recollecting **2** : something recollected
rec•om•mend \,rekə'mend\ *vb* **1** : present as deserving of acceptance or trial **2** : advise **—rec•om•mend•able** \-'mendəbəl\ *adj*
rec•om•men•da•tion \,rekəmən'dāshən\ *n* **1** : act of recommending **2** : something recommended or that recommends
rec•om•pense \'rekəm,pens\ *n* : compensation **—recompense** *vb*
rec•on•cile \'rekən,sīl\ *vb* **-ciled; -cil•ing 1** : cause to be friendly again **2** : adjust or settle **3** : bring to acceptance **—rec•on•cil•able** *adj* **—rec•on•cile•ment** *n* **—rec•on•cil•er** *n* **—rec•on•cil•i•a•tion** \,rekən,silē'āshən\ *n*
re•con•dite \'rekən,dīt, ri'kän-\ *adj* **1** : hard to understand **2** : little known
re•con•di•tion \,rēkən'dishən\ *vb* : restore to good condition
re•con•nais•sance \ri'känəzəns, -səns\ *n* : exploratory survey of enemy territory
re•con•noi•ter, re•con•noi•tre \,rēkə'nȯitər, ,rekə-\ *vb* **-tered** *or* **-tred; -ter•ing** *or* **-tring** : make a reconnaissance of
re•cord \ri'kȯrd\ *vb* **1** : set down in writing **2** : register permanently **3** : indicate **4** : preserve (as sound or images) for later reproduction ~ \'rekərd\ *n* **1** : something recorded **2** : best performance
re•cord•er \ri'kȯrdər\ *n* **1** : person or device that records **2** : wind instrument with finger holes
[1]**re•count** \ri'kaůnt\ *vb* : relate in detail
[2]**re•count** \rē'-\ *vb* : count again **—recount** \'rē,-, ,rē'-\ *n*
re•coup \ri'küp\ *vb* : make up for (an expense or loss)
re•course \'rē,kōrs, ri'-\ *n* : source of aid or a turning to such a source
re•cov•er \ri'kəvər\ *vb* **1** : regain position, poise, or health **2** : recoup **—re•cov•er•able** *adj* **—re•cov•ery** \-'kəvərē\ *n*
rec•re•a•tion \,rekrē'āshən\ *n* : a refreshing of strength or spirits as a change from work or study **—rec•re•a•tion•al** \-shənəl\ *adj*
re•crim•i•na•tion \ri,krimə'nāshən\ *n* : retaliatory accusation **—re•crim•i•nate** *vb*
re•cruit \ri'krüt\ *n* : newly enlisted member ~ *vb* : enlist the membership or services of **—re•cruit•er** *n* **—re•cruit•ment** *n*
rect•an•gle \'rek,taŋgəl\ *n* : 4-sided figure with 4 right angles **—rect•an•gu•lar** \rek'taŋgyələr\ *adj*
rec•ti•fy \'rektə,fī\ *vb* **-fied; -fy•ing** : make or set right **—rec•ti•fi•ca•tion** \,rektəfə'kāshən\ *n*
rec•ti•tude \'rektə,tüd, -,tyüd\ *n* : moral integrity
rec•tor \'rektər\ *n* : pastor
rec•to•ry \'rektərē\ *n, pl* **-ries** : rector's residence
rec•tum \'rektəm\ *n, pl* **-tums** *or* **-ta** \-tə\ : last part of the intestine joining the colon and anus **—rec•tal** \-tᵊl\ *adj*
re•cum•bent \ri'kəmbənt\ *adj* : lying down
re•cu•per•ate \ri'küpə,rāt, -'kyü-\ *vb* **-at•ed; -at•ing** : recover (as from illness) **—re•cu•per•a•tion** \-,küpə'rāshən, -,kyü-\ *n* **—re•cu•per•a•tive** \-'küpərātiv, -'kyü-\ *adj*
re•cur \ri'kər\ *vb* **-rr- 1** : return in thought or talk **2** : occur again **—re•cur•rence** \-'kərəns\ *n* **—re•cur•rent** \-ənt\ *adj*
re•cy•cle \rē'sīkəl\ *vb* : process (as glass or cans) in order to regain a material for human use **—re•cy•cla•ble** \-kələbəl\ *adj*
red \'red\ *n* **1** : color of blood or of the ruby **2** *cap* : communist **—red** *adj* **—red•dish** *adj* **—red•ness** *n*
red•den \'redᵊn\ *vb* : make or become red or reddish
re•deem \ri'dēm\ *vb* **1** : regain, free, or rescue by paying a price **2** : atone for **3** : free from sin **4** : convert into something of value **—re•deem•able** *adj* **—re•deem•er** *n*
re•demp•tion \-'dempshən\ *n* : act of redeeming **—re•demp•tive** \-tiv\ *adj* **—re•demp•to•ry** \-tərē\ *adj*
red•head \-,hed\ *n* : one having red hair **—red•head•ed** \-'hedəd\ *adj*
red•o•lent \'redᵊlənt\ *adj* **1** : having a fragrance **2** : suggestive **—red•o•lence** \-əns\ *n* **—red•o•lent•ly** *adv*
re•dou•ble \ri'dəbəl\ *vb* **1** : make twice as great in size or amount **2** : intensify
re•doubt \ri'daůt\ *n* : small fortification
re•doubt•able \-əbəl\ *adj* : arousing dread
re•dound \ri'daůnd\ *vb* : have an effect
re•dress \ri'dres\ *vb* : set right ~ *n* **1** : relief or remedy **2** : compensation
red tape *n* : complex obstructive official routine
re•duce \ri'düs, -'dyüs\ *vb* **-duced; -duc•ing 1** : lessen **2** : put in a lower rank **3** : lose weight **—re•duc•er** *n* **—re•duc•ible** \-'düsəbəl, -'dyü-\ *adj*
re•duc•tion \ri'dəkshən\ *n* **1** : act of reducing **2** : amount lost in reducing **3** : something made by reducing
re•dun•dant \ri'dəndənt\ *adj* : using more words than necessary **—re•dun•dan•cy** \-dənsē\ *n* **—re•dun•dant•ly** *adv*
red•wood *n* : tall coniferous timber tree
reed \'rēd\ *n* **1** : tall slender grass of wet areas **2** : elastic strip that vibrates to produce tones in certain wind instruments **—reedy** *adj*
reef \'rēf\ *n* : ridge of rocks or sand at or near the surface of the water
reek \'rēk\ *n* : strong or disagreeable fume or odor ~ *vb* : give off a reek
[1]**reel** \'rēl\ *n* : revolvable device on which something flexible is wound or a quantity of something wound on it ~ *vb* **1** : wind on a reel **2** : pull in by reeling **—reel•able** *adj* **—reel•er** *n*
[2]**reel** *vb* **1** : whirl or waver as from a blow **2** : walk or move unsteadily ~ *n* : reeling motion
[3]**reel** *n* : lively dance
re•fer \ri'fər\ *vb* **-rr- 1** : direct or send to some person or place **2** : submit for consideration or action **3** : have connection **4** : mention or allude to something **—re•fer•able** \'refərəbəl, ri'fərə-\ *adj* **—re•fer•ral** \ri'fərəl\ *n*
ref•er•ee \,refə'rē\ *n* **1** : one to whom an issue is referred for settlement **2** : sports official ~ *vb* **-eed; -ee•ing** : act as referee
ref•er•ence \'refərəns\ *n* **1** : act of referring **2** : a bearing on a matter **3** : consultation for information **4** : person who can speak for one's character or ability or a recommendation given by such a person
ref•er•en•dum \,refə'rendəm\ *n, pl* **-da** \-də\ *or* **-dums** : a submitting of legislative measures for voters' approval or rejection
re•fill \,rē'fil\ *vb* : fill again **—re•fill** \'rē,-\ *n* **—re•fill•able** *adj*
re•fine \ri'fīn\ *vb* **-fined; -fin•ing 1** : free from impurities or waste matter **2** : improve or perfect **3** : free or become free of what is coarse or uncouth **—re•fine•ment** \-mənt\ *n* **—re•fin•er** *n*
re•fin•ery \ri'fīnərē\ *n, pl* **-er•ies** : place for refining (as of oil or sugar)
re•flect \ri'flekt\ *vb* **1** : bend or cast back (as light or heat) **2** : bring as a result **3** : cast reproach or blame **4** : ponder **—re•flec•tion** \-'flekshən\ *n* **—re•flec•tive** \-tiv\ *adj* **—re•flec•tor** \ri'flektər\ *n*
re•flex \'rē,fleks\ *n* : automatic response to a stimulus ~ *adj* **1** : bent back **2** : relating to a reflex **—re•flex•ly** *adv*
re•flex•ive \ri'fleksiv\ *adj* : of or relating to an action directed back upon the doer or the grammatical subject **—reflexive** *n* **—re•flex•ive•ly** *adv* **—re•flex•ive•ness** *n*
re•form \ri'fȯrm\ *vb* : make or become better esp. by correcting bad habits **—reform** *n* **—re•form•able** *adj* **—re•for•ma•tive** \-'fȯrmətiv\ *adj* **—re•form•er** *n*
re•for•ma•to•ry \ri'fȯrmə,tōrē\ *n, pl* **-ries** : penal institution for reforming young offenders
re•fract \ri'frakt\ *vb* : subject to refraction
re•frac•tion \-'frakshən\ *n* : the bending of a ray (as of light) when it passes from one medium into another **—re•frac•tive** \-tiv\ *adj*
re•frac•to•ry \ri'fraktərē\ *adj* : obstinate or unmanageable
re•frain \ri'frān\ *vb* : hold oneself back ~ *n* : verse recurring regularly in a song **—re•frain•ment** *n*
re•fresh \ri'fresh\ *vb* **1** : make or become fresh or fresher **2** : supply or take refreshment **—re•fresh•er** *n* **—re•fresh•ing•ly** *adv*
re•fresh•ment \-mənt\ *n* **1** : act of refreshing **2** *pl* : light meal
re•frig•er•ate \ri'frijə,rāt\ *vb* **-at•ed; -at•ing** : chill or freeze (food) for preservation **—re•frig•er•ant** \-ərənt\ *adj or n* **—re•frig•er•a•tion** \-,frijə'rāshən\ *n* **—re•frig•er•a•tor** \-'frijə,rātər\ *n*
ref•uge \'ref,yüj\ *n* **1** : protection from danger **2** : place that provides protection
ref•u•gee \,refyů'jē\ *n* : person who flees for safety
re•fund \ri'fənd, 'rē,fənd\ *vb* : give or put back (money) ~ \'rē,-\ *n* **1** : act of refunding **2** : sum refunded **—re•fund•able** *adj*
re•fur•bish \ri'fərbish\ *vb* : renovate
[1]**re•fuse** \ri'fyüz\ *vb* **-fused; -fus•ing** : decline to accept, do, or give **— re•fus•al** \-'fyüzəl\ *n*
[2]**ref•use** \'ref,yüs, -,yüz\ *n* : worthless matter
re•fute \ri'fyüt\ *vb* **-fut•ed; -fut•ing** : prove to be false **—ref•u•ta•tion** \,refyů'tāshən\ *n* **—re•fut•er** \ri'fyütər\ *n*
re•gal \'rēgəl\ *adj* **1** : befitting a king **2** : stately **—re•gal•ly** *adv*
re•gale \ri'gāl\ *vb* **-galed; -gal•ing 1** : entertain richly or agreeably **2** : delight
re•ga•lia \ri'gālyə\ *n pl* **1** : symbols of royalty **2** : insignia of an office or order **3** : finery
re•gard \ri'gärd\ *n* **1** : consideration **2** : feeling of approval and liking **3** *pl* : friendly greetings **4** : relation ~ *vb* **1** : pay attention to **2** : show respect for **3** : have an opinion of **4** : look at **5** : relate to **—re•gard•ful** *adj* **—re•gard•less** *adj*
re•gard•ing *prep* : concerning
regardless of \ri'gärdləs-\ *prep* : in spite of
re•gen•er•ate \ri'jenərət\ *adj* **1** : formed or created again **2** : spiritually reborn ~ \-'jenə,rāt\ *vb* **1** : reform completely **2** : replace (a lost body part) by new tissue growth **3** : give new life to **—re•gen•er•a•tion** \-,jenə'rāshən\ *n* **—re•gen•er•a•tive** \-'jenə,rātiv\ *adj* **—re•gen•er•a•tor** \-,rātər\ *n*
re•gent \'rējənt\ *n* **1** : person who rules during the childhood, absence, or incapacity of the sovereign **2** : member of a governing board **—re•gen•cy** \-jənsē\ *n*
re•gime \rā'zhēm, ri-\ *n* : government in power
reg•i•men \'rejəmən\ *n* : systematic course of treatment or training
reg•i•ment \'rejəmənt\ *n* : military unit ~ \-,ment\ *vb* **1** : organize rigidly for control **2** : make orderly **—reg•i•men•tal** \,rejə'mentᵊl\ *adj* **—reg•i•men•ta•tion** \-mən'tāshən\ *n*
re•gion \'rējən\ *n* : indefinitely defined area **—re•gion•al** \'rējənəl\ *adj* **—re•gion•al•ly** *adv*
reg•is•ter \'rejəstər\ *n* **1** : record of items or details or a book for keeping such a record **2** : device to regulate ventilation **3** : counting or recording device **4** : range of a voice or instrument ~ *vb* **1** : enter in a register **2** : record automatically **3** : get special care for mail by paying more postage
reg•is•trar \-,strär\ *n* : official keeper of records
reg•is•tra•tion \,rejə'strāshən\ *n* **1** : act of registering **2** : entry in a register
reg•is•try \'rejəstrē\ *n, pl* **-tries 1** : enrollment **2** : place of registration **3** : official record book
re•gress \ri'gres\ *vb* : go or cause to go back or to a lower level **—re•gres•sion** \-'greshən\ *n* **—re•gres•sive** *adj*
re•gret \ri'gret\ *vb* **-tt- 1** : mourn the loss or death of **2** : be very sorry for ~ *n* **1** : sorrow or the expression of sorrow **2** *pl* : message declining an invitation **—re•gret•ful** \-fəl\ *adj* **—re•gret•ful•ly** *adv* **—re•gret•ta•ble** \-əbəl\ *adj* **—re•gret•ta•bly** \-blē\ *adv* **—re•gret•ter** *n*
reg•u•lar \'regyələr\ *adj* **1** : conforming to what is usual, normal, or average **2** : steady, uniform, or unvarying **—regular** *n* **—reg•u•lar•i•ty** \,regyə'larətē\ *n* **—reg•u•lar•ize** \'regyələ,rīz\ *vb* **—reg•u•lar•ly** *adv*
reg•u•late \'regyə,lāt\ *vb* **-lat•ed; -lat•ing 1** : govern according to rule **2** : adjust to a standard **—reg•u•la•tive** \-,lātiv\ *adj* **—reg•u•la•tor** \-,lātər\ *n* **—reg•u•la•to•ry** \-lə,tōrē\ *adj*
reg•u•la•tion \,regyə'lāshən\ *n* **1** : act of regulating **2** : rule dealing with details of procedure
re•gur•gi•tate \rē'gərjə,tāt\ *vb* **-tat•ed; -tat•ing** : vomit **—re•gur•gi•ta•tion** \-,gərjə'tāshən\ *n*
re•ha•bil•i•tate \,rēhə'bilə,tāt\ *vb* **-tat•ed; -tat•ing 1** : reinstate **2** : make good or usable again **—re•ha•bil•i•ta•tion** \-,bilə'tāshən\ *n*
re•hears•al \ri'hərsəl\ *n* : practice session or performance
re•hearse \-'hərs\ *vb* **-hearsed; -hears•ing 1** : repeat or recount **2** : engage in a rehearsal of **—re•hears•er** *n*
reign \'rān\ *n* : sovereign's authority or rule ~ *vb* : rule as a sovereign
re•im•burse \,rēəm'bərs\ *vb* **-bursed; -burs•ing** : repay **—re•im•burs•able** *adj* **—re•im•burse•ment** *n*
rein \'rān\ *n* **1** : strap fastened to a bit to control an animal **2** : restraining influence ~ *vb* : direct by reins
re•in•car•na•tion \,rē,in,kär'nāshən\ *n* : rebirth of the soul **—re•in•car•nate** \,rēin'kär,nāt\ *vb*
rein•deer \'rān,dir\ *n* : caribou
re•in•force \,rēən'fōrs\ *vb* : strengthen or support **—re•in•force•ment** *n* **—re•in•forc•er** *n*
re•in•state \,rēən'stāt\ *vb* : restore to a former position **—re•in•state•ment** *n*
re•it•er•ate \rē'itə,rāt\ *vb* : say again **—re•it•er•a•tion** \-,itə'rāshən\ *n*
re•ject \ri'jekt\ *vb* **1** : refuse to grant or consider **2** : refuse to admit, believe, or receive **3** : throw out as useless or unsatisfactory ~ \'rē,-\ *n* : rejected person or thing **—re•jec•tion** \-'jekshən\ *n*
re•joice \ri'jȯis\ *vb* **-joiced; -joic•ing** : feel joy **—re•joic•er** *n*
re•join *vb* **1** \,rē'jȯin\ : join again **2** \ri'-\ : say in answer
re•join•der \ri'jȯindər\ *n* : answer
re•ju•ve•nate \ri'jüvə,nāt\ *vb* **-nat•ed; -nat•ing** : make young again **—re•ju•ve•na•tion** \-,jüvə'nāshən\ *n*
re•lapse \ri'laps, 'rē,laps\ *n* : recurrence of illness after a period of improvement ~ \ri'-\ *vb* : suffer a relapse
re•late \ri'lāt\ *vb* **-lat•ed; -lat•ing 1** : give a report of **2** : show a connection between **3** : have a relationship **—re•lat•able** *adj* **—re•lat•er, re•la•tor** *n*
re•la•tion \-'lāshən\ *n* **1** : account **2** : connection **3** : relationship **4** : reference **5** *pl* : dealings

re·la·tion·ship \-,ship\ *n* : the state of being related or interrelated

rel·a·tive \'relətiv\ *n* : person connected with another by blood or marriage ~ *adj* : considered in comparison with something else —**rel·a·tive·ly** *adv* —**rel·a·tive·ness** *n*

re·lax \ri'laks\ *vb* 1 : make or become less tense or rigid 2 : make less severe 3 : seek rest or recreation —**re·lax·er** *n*

re·lax·a·tion \,rē,lak'sāshən\ *n* 1 : lessening of tension 2 : recreation

re·lay \'rē,lā\ *n* : fresh supply (as of horses or people) arranged to relieve others ~ \'rē,-, ri'-\ *vb* **-layed; -lay·ing** : pass along in stages

re·lease \ri'lēs\ *vb* **-leased; -leas·ing** 1 : free from confinement or oppression 2 : relinquish 3 : permit publication, performance, exhibition, or sale ~ *n* 1 : relief from trouble 2 : discharge from an obligation 3 : act of releasing or what is released

rel·e·gate \'relə,gāt\ *vb* **-gat·ed; -gat·ing** 1 : remove to some less prominent position 2 : assign to a particular class or sphere —**rel·e·ga·tion** \relə'gāshən\ *n*

re·lent \ri'lent\ *vb* : become less severe

re·lent·less \-ləs\ *adj* : mercilessly severe or persistent —**re·lent·less·ly** *adv* —**re·lent·less·ness** *n*

rel·e·vance \'reləvəns\ *n* : relation to the matter at hand —**rel·e·vant** \-vənt\ *adj* —**rel·e·vant·ly** *adv*

re·li·able \ri'līəbəl\ *adj* : fit to be trusted —**re·li·abil·i·ty** \-,līə'bilətē\ *n* —**re·li·able·ness** *n* —**re·li·ably** \'līəblē\ *adv*

re·li·ance \ri'līəns\ *n* : act or result of relying

re·li·ant \ri'līənt\ *adj* : dependent

rel·ic \relik\ *n* 1 : object venerated because of its association with a saint or martyr 2 : remaining trace

re·lief \ri'lēf\ *n* 1 : lightening of something oppressive 2 : welfare

re·lieve \ri'lēv\ *vb* **-lieved; -liev·ing** 1 : free from a burden or distress 2 : release from a post or duty 3 : break the monotony of —**re·liev·er** *n*

re·li·gion \ri'lijən\ *n* 1 : service and worship of God 2 : set or system of religious beliefs —**re·li·gion·ist** *n*

re·li·gious \-'lijəs\ *adj* 1 : relating or devoted to an ultimate reality or deity 2 : relating to religious beliefs or observances 3 : faithful, fervent, or zealous —**re·li·gious·ly** *adv*

re·lin·quish \-'liŋkwish, -'lin-\ *vb* 1 : renounce 2 : let go of —**re·lin·quish·ment** *n*

rel·ish \'relish\ *n* 1 : keen enjoyment 2 : highly seasoned sauce (as of pickles) ~ *vb* : enjoy —**rel·ish·able** *adj*

re·live \rē'liv\ *vb* : live over again (as in the imagination)

re·lo·cate \rē'lō,kāt, ,rēlō'kāt\ *vb* : move to a new location —**re·lo·ca·tion** \,rēlō'kāshən\ *n*

re·luc·tant \ri'ləktənt\ *adj* : feeling or showing doubt or unwillingness —**re·luc·tance** \ri'ləktəns\ *n* —**re·luc·tant·ly** *adv*

re·ly \ri'lī\ *vb* **-lied; -ly·ing** : place faith or confidence—often with *on*

re·main \ri'mān\ *vb* 1 : be left after others have been removed 2 : be something yet to be done 3 : stay behind 4 : continue unchanged

re·main·der \-'māndər\ *n* : that which is left over

re·mains \-'mānz\ *n pl* 1 : remaining part or trace 2 : dead body

re·mark \ri'märk\ *vb* : express as an observation ~ *n* : passing comment

re·mark·able \-'märkəbəl\ *adj* : extraordinary —**re·mark·able·ness** *n* —**re·mark·ably** \-blē\ *adv*

re·me·di·al \ri'mēdēəl\ *adj* : intended to remedy or improve

rem·e·dy \'remədē\ *n, pl* **-dies** 1 : medicine that cures 2 : something that corrects an evil or compensates for a loss ~ *vb* **-died; -dy·ing** : provide or serve as a remedy for

re·mem·ber \ri'membər\ *vb* 1 : think of again 2 : keep from forgetting 3 : convey greetings from

re·mem·brance \-brəns\ *n* 1 : act of remembering 2 : something that serves to bring to mind

re·mind \ri'mīnd\ *vb* : cause to remember —**re·mind·er** *n*

rem·i·nisce \,remə'nis\ *vb* **-nisced; -nisc·ing** : indulge in reminiscence

rem·i·nis·cence \-'nis°ns\ *n* 1 : recalling of a past experience 2 : account of a memorable experience

rem·i·nis·cent \-°nt\ *adj* 1 : relating to reminiscence 2 : serving to remind —**rem·i·nis·cent·ly** *adv*

re·miss \ri'mis\ *adj* : negligent or careless in performance of duty —**re·miss·ly** *adv* —**re·miss·ness** *n*

re·mis·sion \ri'mishən\ *n* 1 : act of forgiving 2 : a period of relief from or easing of symptoms of a disease

re·mit \ri'mit\ *vb* **-tt-** 1 : pardon 2 : send money in payment

re·mit·tance \ri'mit°ns\ *n* : sum of money remitted

rem·nant \'remnənt\ *n* : small part or trace remaining

re·mod·el \rē'mäd°l\ *vb* : alter the structure of

re·mon·strance \ri'mänstrəns\ *n* : act or instance of remonstrating

re·mon·strate \ri'män,strāt\ *vb* **-strat·ed; -strat·ing** : speak in protest, reproof, or opposition —**re·mon·stra·tion** \ri-,män'strāshən, ,remən-\ *n*

re·morse \ri'mòrs\ *n* : distress arising from a sense of guilt —**re·morse·ful** *adj* —**re·morse·less** *adj*

re·mote \ri'mōt\ *adj* **-mot·er; -est** 1 : far off in place or time 2 : hard to reach or find 3 : acting, acted on, or controlled indirectly or from afar 4 : slight 5 : distant in manner —**re·mote·ly** *adv* —**re·mote·ness** *n*

re·move \ri'müv\ *vb* **-moved; -mov·ing** 1 : move by lifting or taking off or away 2 : get rid of —**re·mov·able** *adj* —**re·mov·al** \-vəl\ *n* —**re·mov·er** *n*

re·mu·ner·ate \ri'myünə,rāt\ *vb* **-at·ed; -at·ing** : pay —**re·mu·ner·a·tion** \-,myünə'rāshən\ *n* —**re·mu·ner·a·tor** \-,rātər\ *n*

re·mu·ner·a·tive \ri'myünərətiv, -,rāt-\ *adj* : gainful

re·nais·sance \,renə'säns, -'zäns\ *n* : rebirth or revival

re·nal \'rēn°l\ *adj* : relating to the kidneys

rend \'rend\ *vb* **rent** \'rent\; **rend·ing** : tear apart forcibly

ren·der \'rendər\ *vb* 1 : extract by heating 2 : hand over or give up 3 : do (a service) for another 4 : cause to be or become

ren·dez·vous \'rändi,vü, -dā-\ *n, pl* **ren·dez·vous** \-,vüz\ 1 : place appointed for a meeting 2 : meeting at an appointed place ~ *vb* **-voused; -vous·ing** : meet at a rendezvous

ren·di·tion \ren'dishən\ *n* : version

ren·e·gade \'reni,gād\ *n* : deserter of one faith or cause for another

re·nege \ri'nü, -'neg, -'nēg, -'nāg\ *vb* **-neged; -neg·ing** : go back on a promise —**re·neg·er** *n*

re·new \ri'nü, -'nyü\ *vb* 1 : make or become new, fresh, or strong again 2 : begin again 3 : grant or obtain an extension of —**re·new·able** *adj* —**re·new·al** *n* —**re·new·er** *n*

re·nounce \ri'nauns\ *vb* **-nounced; -nounc·ing** : give up, refuse, or resign —**re·nounce·ment** *n*

ren·o·vate \'renə,vāt\ *vb* **-vat·ed; -vat·ing** : make like new again —**ren·o·va·tion** \,renə'vāshən\ *n* —**ren·o·va·tor** \'renə,vātər\ *n*

re·nown \ri'naun\ *n* : state of being widely known and honored —**re·nowned** \-'naund\ *adj*

¹rent \'rent\ *n* : money paid or due periodically for the use of another's property ~ *vb* : hold or give possession and use of for rent —**rent·al** *n or adj* —**rent·er** *n*

²rent *n* : a tear in cloth

re·nun·ci·a·tion \ri,nənsē'āshən\ *n* : act of renouncing

¹re·pair \ri'par\ *vb* : go

²repair *vb* : restore to good condition ~ *n* 1 : act or instance of repairing 2 : condition —**re·pair·er** *n* —**re·pair·man** \-,man\ *n*

rep·a·ra·tion \,repə'rāshən\ *n* : money paid for redress—usu. pl.

rep·ar·tee \,repər'tē\ *n* : clever replies

re·past \ri'past, 'rē,past\ *n* : meal

re·pa·tri·ate \rē'pātrē,āt\ *vb* **-at·ed; -at·ing** : send back to one's own country —**re·pa·tri·ate** \-trēət, -trē,āt\ *n* —**re·pa·tri·a·tion** \-,pātrē'āshən\ *n*

re·pay \rē'pā\ *vb* **-paid; -pay·ing** : pay back —**re·pay·able** *adj* —**re·pay·ment** *n*

re·peal \ri'pēl\ *vb* : annul by legislative action —**repeal** *n* —**re·peal·er** *n*

re·peat \ri'pēt\ *vb* : say or do again ~ *n* 1 : act of repeating 2 : something repeated —**re·peat·able** *adj* —**re·peat·ed·ly** *adv* —**re·peat·er** *n*

re·pel \ri'pel\ *vb* **-pelled; -pel·ling** : drive away 2 : disgust —**re·pel·lent** \'pelənt\ *adj or n*

re·pent \ri'pent\ *vb* 1 : turn from sin 2 : regret —**re·pen·tance** \ri'pent°ns\ *n* —**re·pen·tant** \-°nt\ *adj*

re·per·cus·sion \,rēpər'kəshən, ,rep-\ *n* : effect of something done or said

rep·er·toire \'repər,twär\ *n* : pieces a company or performer can present

rep·er·to·ry \'repər,tōrē\ *n, pl* **-ries** 1 : repertoire 2 : theater with a resident company doing several plays

rep·e·ti·tion \,repə'tishən\ *n* : act or instance of repeating

rep·e·ti·tious \-'tishəs\ *adj* : tediously repeating —**rep·e·ti·tious·ly** *adv* —**rep·e·ti·tious·ness** *n*

re·pet·i·tive \ri'petətiv\ *adj* : repetitious —**re·pet·i·tive·ly** *adv* —**re·pet·i·tive·ness** *n*

re·pine \ri'pīn\ *vb* **re·pined; re·pin·ing** : feel or express discontent

re·place \ri'plās\ *vb* 1 : restore to a former position 2 : take the place of 3 : put something new in the place of —**re·place·able** *adj* —**re·place·ment** *n* —**re·plac·er** *n*

re·plen·ish \ri'plenish\ *vb* : stock or supply anew —**re·plen·ish·ment** *n*

re·plete \ri'plēt\ *adj* : full —**re·plete·ness** *n* —**re·ple·tion** \-'plēshən\ *n*

rep·li·ca \'replikə\ *n* : exact copy

rep·li·cate \'replə,kāt\ *vb* **-cat·ed; -cat·ing** : duplicate or repeat —**rep·li·cate** \-likət\ *n* —**rep·li·ca·tion** \-lə'kāshən\ *n*

re·ply \ri'plī\ *vb* **-plied; -ply·ing** : say or do in answer ~ *n, pl* **-plies** : answer

re·port \ri'pōrt\ *n* 1 : rumor 2 : statement of information (as events or causes) 3 : explosive noise ~ *vb* 1 : give an account of 2 : present an account of (an event) as news 3 : present oneself 4 : make known to authorities —**re·port·age** \ri'pōrtij, ,repər'täzh, ,rep,ȯr'-\ *n* —**re·port·ed·ly** *adv* —**re·port·er** *n* —**re·por·to·ri·al** \,repər'tōrēəl\ *adj*

re·pose \ri'pōz\ *vb* **-posed; -pos·ing** : lay or lie at rest ~ *n* 1 : state of resting 2 : calm or peace —**re·pose·ful** *adj*

re·pos·i·to·ry \ri'päzə,tōrē\ *n, pl* **-ries** : place where something is stored

re·pos·sess \,rēpə'zes\ *vb* : regain possession and legal ownership of —**re·pos·ses·sion** \-'zeshən\ *n*

rep·re·hend \,repri'hend\ *vb* : censure —**rep·re·hen·sion** \-'henchən\ *n*

rep·re·hen·si·ble \-'hensəbəl\ *adj* : deserving condemnation —**rep·re·hen·si·bly** *adv*

rep·re·sent \,repri'zent\ *vb* 1 : serve as a sign or symbol of 2 : act or speak for 3 : describe as having a specified quality or character —**rep·re·sen·ta·tion** \,repri-,zen'tāshən\ *n*

rep·re·sen·ta·tive \,repri'zentətiv\ *adj* 1 : standing or acting for another 2 : carried on by elected representatives ~ *n* 1 : typical example 2 : one that represents another 3 : member of usu. the lower house of a legislature —**rep·re·sen·ta·tive·ly** *adv* —**rep·re·sen·ta·tive·ness** *n*

re·press \ri'pres\ *vb* : restrain or suppress —**re·pres·sion** \-'preshən\ *n* —**re·pres·sive** \-'presiv\ *adj*

re·prieve \ri'prēv\ *n* 1 : a delay in punishment 2 : temporary respite —**reprieve** *vb*

rep·ri·mand \'reprə,mand\ *n* : formal or severe criticism —**reprimand** *vb*

re·pri·sal \ri'prīzəl\ *n* : act in retaliation

re·prise \ri'prēz\ *n* : musical repetition

re·proach \ri'prōch\ *n* 1 : disgrace 2 : rebuke ~ *vb* : express disapproval to —**re·proach·ful** *adj* —**re·proach·ful·ly** *adv* —**re·proach·ful·ness** *n*

rep·ro·bate \'reprə,bāt\ *n* : scoundrel —**reprobate** *adj*

rep·ro·ba·tion \,reprə'bāshən\ *n* : strong disapproval

re·pro·duce \,rēprə'düs, -'dyüs\ *vb* 1 : produce again or anew 2 : produce offspring —**re·pro·duc·ible** \-'düsəbəl, -'dyü-\ *adj* —**re·pro·duc·tion** \-'dək-shən\ *n* —**re·pro·duc·tive** \-'dəktiv\ *adj*

re·proof \ri'prüf\ *n* : blame or censure for a fault

re·prove \ri'prüv\ *vb* **-proved; -prov·ing** : express disapproval to or of

rep·tile \'rept°l, -,tīl\ *n* : air-breathing scaly vertebrate —**rep·til·ian** \rep'tilēən\ *adj or n*

re·pub·lic \ri'pəblik\ *n* : country with representative government

re·pub·li·can \-likən\ *adj* 1 : relating to or resembling a republic 2 : supporting a republic —**republican** *n* —**re·pub·li·can·ism** *n*

re·pu·di·ate \ri'pyüdē,āt\ *vb* **-at·ed; -at·ing** : refuse to have anything to do with —**re·pu·di·a·tion** \-,pyüdē'āshən\ *n*

re·pug·nant \ri'pəgnənt\ *adj* : contrary to one's tastes or principles —**re·pug·nance** \-nəns\ *n* —**re·pug·nant·ly** *adv*

re·pulse \ri'pəls\ *vb* **-pulsed; -puls·ing** 1 : drive or beat back 2 : rebuff 3 : be repugnant to —**repulse** *n* —**re·pul·sion** \-'pəlshən\ *n*

re·pul·sive \-siv\ *adj* : arousing aversion or disgust —**re·pul·sive·ly** *adv* —**re·pul·sive·ness** *n*

re·pu·ta·ble \'repyətəbəl\ *adj* : having a good reputation —**re·pu·ta·bly** \-blē\ *adv*

rep·u·ta·tion \,repyə'tāshən\ *n* : one's character or public esteem

re·pute \ri'pyüt\ *vb* **-put·ed; -put·ing** : think of as being ~ *n* : reputation —**re·put·ed** *adj* —**re·put·ed·ly** *adv*

re·quest \ri'kwest\ *n* : act or instance of asking for something or a thing asked for ~ *vb* 1 : make a request of 2 : ask for —**re·quest·er** *n*

re·qui·em \'rekwēəm, 'rāk-\ *n* : Mass for a dead person or a musical setting for this

re·quire \ri'kwīr\ *vb* **-quired; -quir·ing** 1 : insist on 2 : call for as essential —**re·quire·ment** *n*

req·ui·site \'rekwəzət\ *adj* : necessary —**requisite** *n*

req·ui·si·tion \,rekwə'zishən\ *n* : formal application or demand —**requisition** *vb*

re·quite \ri'kwīt\ *vb* **-quit·ed; -quit·ing** : make return for or to —**re·quit·al** \-'kwīt°l\ *n*

re·scind \ri'sind\ *vb* : repeal or cancel —**re·scis·sion** \-'sizhən\ *n*

res·cue \'reskyü\ *vb* **-cued; -cu·ing** : set free from danger or confinement —**rescue** *n* —**res·cu·er** *n*

re·search \ri'sərch, 'rē,sərch\ *n* : careful or diligent search esp. for new knowledge —**research** *vb* —**re·search·er** *n*

re·sem·ble \ri'zembəl\ *vb* **-sem·bled; -sem·bling** : be like or similar to —**re·sem·blance** \-'zembləns\ *n*

re·sent \ri'zent\ *vb* : feel or show annoyance at —**re·sent·ful** *adj* —**re·sent·ful·ly** *adv* —**re·sent·ment** *n*

res·er·va·tion \,rezər'vāshən\ *n* 1 : act of reserving or something reserved 2 : limiting condition

re·serve \ri'zərv\ *vb* **-served; -serv·ing** 1 : store for future use 2 : set aside for special use ~ *n* 1 : something reserved 2 : restraint in words or bearing 3 : military forces withheld from action or not part of the regular services —**re·served** *adj*

res·er·voir \'rezər,vwär, -,vwȯr, -,vȯr, -,vȯi\ *n* : place where something (as water) is kept in store

re·side \ri'zīd\ *vb* **-sid·ed; -sid·ing** 1 : make one's home 2 : be present

res·i·dence \'rezədəns\ *n* 1 : act or fact of residing in a place 2 : place where one lives —**res·i·dent** \-ənt\ *adj or n* —**res·i·den·tial** \,rezə'denchəl\ *adj*

res·i·due \'rezə,dü, -,dyü\ *n* : part remaining —**re·sid·u·al** \ri'zijəwəl\ *adj*

re·sign \ri'zīn\ *vb* 1 : give up deliberately 2 : give (oneself) over without resistance —**res·ig·na·tion** \,rezig'nāshən\ *n* —**re·sign·ed·ly** \-'zīnədlē\ *adv*

re·sil·ience \ri'zilyəns\ *n* : ability to recover or adjust easily

re·sil·ien·cy \-yənsē\ *n* : resilience

re·sil·ient \-yənt\ *adj* : elastic

res·in \'rez°n\ *n* : substance from the gum or sap of trees —**res·in·ous** *adj*

re·sist \ri'zist\ *vb* 1 : withstand the force or effect of 2 : fight against —**re·sist·ible** \-'zistəbəl\ *adj* —**re·sist·less** *adj*

re·sis·tance \ri'zistəns\ *n* 1 : act of resisting 2 : ability of an organism to resist disease 3 : opposition to electric current

re·sis·tant \-tənt\ *adj* : giving resistance

res·o·lute \'rezə,lüt\ *adj* : having a fixed purpose —**res·o·lute·ly** *adv* —**res·o·lute·ness** *n*

res·o·lu·tion \,rezə'lüshən\ *n* 1 : process of resolving 2 : firmness of purpose 3 : statement of the opinion, will, or intent of a body

re·solve \ri'zälv\ *vb* **-solved; -solv·ing** 1 : find an answer to 2 : make a formal resolution ~ *n* 1 : something resolved 2 : steadfast purpose —**re·solv·able** *adj*

res·o·nant \'rez°nənt\ *adj* 1 : continuing to sound 2 : relating to intensification or prolongation of sound (as by a vibrating body) —**res·o·nance** \-əns\ *n* —**res·o·nant·ly** *adv*

re·sort \ri'zȯrt\ *n* 1 : source of help 2 : place to go for vacation ~ *vb* 1 : go often or habitually 2 : have recourse

re·sound \ri'zaund\ *vb* : become filled with sound

re·sound·ing \-iŋ\ *adj* : impressive —**re·sound·ing·ly** *adv*

re·source \'rē,sȯrs, ri'sȯrs\ *n* 1 : new or reserve source 2 *pl* : available funds 3 : ability to handle situations —**re·source·ful** *adj* —**re·source·ful·ness** *n*

re·spect \ri'spekt\ *n* 1 : relation to something 2 : high or special regard 3 : detail ~ *vb* : consider deserving of high regard —**re·spect·er** *n* —**re·spect·ful** *adj* —**re·spect·ful·ly** *adv* —**re·spect·ful·ness** *n*

re·spect·able \ri'spektəbəl\ *adj* 1 : worthy of respect 2 : fair in size, quantity, or quality —**re·spect·abil·i·ty** \-,spektə'bi-lətē\ *n* —**re·spect·ably** \-'spektəblē\ *adv*

re·spec·tive \-tiv\ *adj* : individual and specific

re·spec·tive·ly \-lē\ *adv* 1 : as relating to each 2 : each in the order given

res·pi·ra·tion \,respə'rāshən\ *n* : act or process of breathing —**re·spi·ra·to·ry** \'respərə,tōrē, ri'spīrə-\ *adj* —**re·spire** \ri'spīr\ *vb*

res·pi·ra·tor \'respə,rātər\ *n* : device for artificial respiration

re·spite \'respət\ *n* : temporary delay or rest

re·splen·dent \ri'splendənt\ *adj* : shining brilliantly —**re·splen·dence** \-dəns\ *n* —**re·splen·dent·ly** *adv*

re·spond \ri'spänd\ *vb* 1 : answer 2 : react —**re·spon·dent** \-'spändənt\ *n or adj* —**re·spond·er** *n*

re·sponse \ri'späns\ *n* 1 : act of responding 2 : answer

re·spon·si·ble \ri'spänsəbəl\ *adj* 1 : an-

swerable for acts or decisions **2 :** able to fulfill obligations **3 :** having important duties **—re•spon•si•bil•i•ty** \ri͵spänsə'bilətē\ *n* **—re•spon•si•ble•ness** *n* **—re•spon•si•bly** \-blē\ *adv*

re•spon•sive \-siv\ *adj* **:** quick to respond **—re•spon•sive•ly** *adv* **—re•spon•sive•ness** *n*

1rest \'rest\ *n* **1 :** sleep **2 :** freedom from work or activity **3 :** state of inactivity **4 :** something used as a support ~ *vb* **1 :** get rest **2 :** cease action or motion **3 :** give rest to **4 :** sit or lie fixed or supported **5 :** depend **—rest•ful** *adj* **—rest•ful•ly** *adv*

2rest *n* **:** remainder

res•tau•rant \'restərənt, -tə͵ränt\ *n* **:** public eating place

res•ti•tu•tion \͵restə'tüshən, -'tyü-\ *n* **:** act or fact of restoring something or repaying someone

res•tive \'restiv\ *adj* **:** uneasy or fidgety **—res•tive•ly** *adv* **—res•tive•ness** *n*

rest•less \'restləs\ *adj* **1 :** lacking or giving no rest **2 :** always moving **3 :** uneasy **—rest•less•ly** *adv* **—rest•less•ness** *n*

re•store \ri'stōr\ *vb* **-stored; -stor•ing 1 :** give back **2 :** put back into use or into a former state **—re•stor•able** *adj* **—res•to•ra•tion** \͵restə'rāshən\ *n* **—re•stor•ative** \ri'stōrətiv\ *n or adj* **—re•stor•er** *n*

re•strain \ri'strān\ *vb* **:** limit or keep under control **—re•strain•able** *adj* **—re•strained** \-'strānd\ *adj* **—re•strain•ed•ly** \-'strānədlē\ *adv* **—re•strain•er** *n*

restraining order *n* **:** legal order directing one person to stay away from another

re•straint \-'strānt\ *n* **1 :** act of restraining **2 :** restraining force **3 :** control over feelings

re•strict \ri'strikt\ *vb* **1 :** confine within bounds **2 :** limit use of **—re•stric•tion** \-'strikshən\ *n* **—re•stric•tive** *adj* **—re•stric•tive•ly** *adv*

re•sult \ri'zəlt\ *vb* **:** come about because of something else ~ *n* **1 :** thing that results **2 :** something obtained by calculation or investigation **—re•sul•tant** \-'zəltᵊnt\ *adj or n*

re•sume \ri'züm\ *vb* **-sumed; -sum•ing :** return to or take up again after interruption **—re•sump•tion** \-'zəmpshən\ *n*

ré•su•mé, re•su•me, re•su•mé \'rezə͵mā, ͵rezə'-\ *n* **:** summary of one's career and qualifications

re•sur•gence \ri'sərjəns\ *n* **:** a rising again **—re•sur•gent** \-jənt\ *adj*

res•ur•rect \͵rezə'rekt\ *vb* **1 :** raise from the dead **2 :** bring to attention or use again **—res•ur•rec•tion** \-'rekshən\ *n*

re•sus•ci•tate \ri'səsə͵tāt\ *vb* **-tat•ed; -tat•ing :** bring back from apparent death **—re•sus•ci•ta•tion** \ri͵səsə'tāshən, ͵rē-\ *n* **—re•sus•ci•ta•tor** \-͵tātər\ *n*

re•tail \'rē͵tāl\ *vb* **:** sell in small quantities directly to the consumer ~ *n* **:** business of selling to consumers **—retail** *adj or adv* **—re•tail•er** *n*

re•tain \ri'tān\ *vb* **1 :** keep or hold onto **2 :** engage the services of

re•tain•er *n* **1 :** household servant **2 :** retaining fee

re•tal•i•ate \ri'talē͵āt\ *vb* **-at•ed; -at•ing :** return (as an injury) in kind **—re•tal•i•a•tion** \-͵talē'āshən\ *n* **—re•tal•ia•to•ry** \-'talyə͵tōrē\ *adj*

re•tard \ri'tärd\ *vb* **:** hold back **—re•tar•da•tion** \͵rē͵tär'dāshən, ri-\ *n*

re•tard•ed \ri'tärdəd\ *adj* **:** slow or limited in intellectual development

retch \'rech\ *vb* **:** try to vomit

re•ten•tion \ri'tenchən\ *n* **1 :** state of being retained **2 :** ability to retain **—re•ten•tive** \-'tentiv\ *adj*

ret•i•cent \'retəsənt\ *adj* **:** tending not to talk **—ret•i•cence** \-səns\ *n* **—ret•i•cent•ly** *adv*

ret•i•na \'retᵊnə\ *n, pl* **-nas** *or* **-nae** \-ᵊn͵ē\ **:** sensory membrane lining the eye **—ret•i•nal** \'retᵊnəl\ *adj*

ret•i•nue \'retᵊn͵ü, -͵yü\ *n* **:** attendants or followers of a distinguished person

re•tire \ri'tīr\ *vb* **-tired; -tir•ing 1 :** withdraw for privacy **2 :** end a career **3 :** go to bed **—re•tir•ee** \ri͵tī'rē\ *n* **—re•tire•ment** *n*

re•tir•ing \ri'tīriŋ\ *adj* **:** shy

re•tort \ri'tȯrt\ *vb* **:** say in reply ~ *n* **:** quick, witty, or cutting answer

re•trace \͵rē'trās\ *vb* **:** go over again or in reverse

re•tract \ri'trakt\ *vb* **1 :** draw back or in **2 :** withdraw a charge or promise **—re•tract•able** *adj* **—re•trac•tion** \-'trakshən\ *n*

re•treat \ri'trēt\ *n* **1 :** act of withdrawing **2 :** place of privacy or safety or meditation and study ~ *vb* **:** make a retreat

re•trench \ri'trench\ *vb* **:** cut down (as expenses) **—re•trench•ment** *n*

ret•ri•bu•tion \͵retrə'byüshən\ *n* **:** retaliation **—re•trib•u•tive** \ri'tribyətiv\ *adj* **—re•trib•u•to•ry** \-yə͵tōrē\ *adj*

re•trieve \ri'trēv\ *vb* **-trieved; -triev•ing 1 :** search for and bring in game **2 :** recover **—re•triev•able** *adj* **—re•triev•al** \-'trēvəl\ *n*

re•triev•er \-'trēvər\ *n* **:** dog for retrieving game

ret•ro•ac•tive \͵retrō'aktiv\ *adj* **:** made effective as of a prior date **—ret•ro•ac•tive•ly** *adv*

ret•ro•grade \'retrə͵grād\ *adj* **1 :** moving backward **2 :** becoming worse

ret•ro•gress \͵retrə'gres\ *vb* **:** move backward **—ret•ro•gres•sion** \-'greshən\ *n*

ret•ro•spect \'retrə͵spekt\ *n* **:** review of past events **—ret•ro•spec•tion** \͵retrə'spekshən\ *n* **—ret•ro•spec•tive** \-'spektiv\ *adj* **—ret•ro•spec•tive•ly** *adv*

re•turn \ri'tərn\ *vb* **1 :** go or come back **2 :** pass, give, or send back to an earlier possessor **3 :** answer **4 :** bring in as a profit **5 :** give or do in return ~ *n* **1 :** act of returning or something returned **2** *pl* **:** report of balloting results **3 :** statement of taxable income **4 :** profit **—return** *adj* **—re•turn•able** *adj or n* **—re•turn•er** *n*

re•union \rē'yünyən\ *n* **1 :** act of reuniting **2 :** a meeting of persons after a separation

re•vamp \͵rē'vamp\ *vb* **:** renovate or revise

re•veal \ri'vēl\ *vb* **1 :** make known **2 :** show plainly

rev•eil•le \'revəlē\ *n* **:** military signal sounded about sunrise

rev•el \'revəl\ *vb* **-eled** *or* **-elled; -el•ing** *or* **-el•ling 1 :** take part in a revel **2 :** take great pleasure ~ *n* **:** wild party or celebration **—rev•el•er, rev•el•ler** \-ər\ *n* **—rev•el•ry** \-rē\ *n*

rev•e•la•tion \͵revə'lāshən\ *n* **1 :** act of revealing **2 :** something enlightening or astonishing

re•venge \ri'venj\ *vb* **-venged; -veng•ing :** avenge ~ *n* **1 :** desire for retaliation **2 :** act of retaliation **—re•venge•ful** *adj* **—re•veng•er** *n*

rev•e•nue \'revə͵nü, -͵nyü\ *n* **:** money collected by a government

re•ver•ber•ate \ri'vərbə͵rāt\ *vb* **-at•ed; -at•ing :** resound in a series of echoes **—re•ver•ber•a•tion** \-͵vərbə'rāshən\ *n*

re•vere \ri'vir\ *vb* **-vered; -ver•ing :** show honor and devotion to **—rev•er•ence** \'revərəns\ *n* **—rev•er•ent** \-rənt\ *adj* **—rev•er•ent•ly** *adv*

rev•er•end \'revərənd\ *adj* **:** worthy of reverence ~ *n* **:** clergy member

rev•er•ie \'revərē\ *n, pl* **-er•ies :** daydream

re•verse \ri'vərs\ *adj* **1 :** opposite to a previous or normal condition **2 :** acting in an opposite way ~ *vb* **-versed; -vers•ing 1 :** turn upside down or completely around **2 :** change to the contrary or in the opposite direction ~ *n* **1 :** something contrary **2 :** change for the worse **3 :** back of something **—re•ver•sal** \-səl\ *n* **—re•verse•ly** *adv* **—re•vers•ible** \-'vərsəbəl\ *adj*

re•vert \ri'vərt\ *vb* **:** return to an original type or condition **—re•ver•sion** \-'vərzhᵊn\ *n*

re•view \ri'vyü\ *n* **1 :** formal inspection **2 :** general survey **3 :** critical evaluation **4 :** second or repeated study or examination ~ *vb* **1 :** examine or study again **2 :** reexamine judicially **3 :** look back over **4 :** examine critically **5 :** inspect **—re•view•er** *n*

re•vile \ri'vīl\ *vb* **-viled; -vil•ing :** abuse verbally **—re•vile•ment** *n* **—re•vil•er** *n*

re•vise \-'vīz\ *vb* **-vised; -vis•ing 1 :** look over something written to correct or improve **2 :** make a new version of **—re•vis•able** *adj* **—revise** *n* **—re•vis•er, re•vi•sor** \-'vīzər\ *n* **—re•vi•sion** \-'vizhən\ *n*

re•viv•al \-'vīvəl\ *n* **1 :** act of reviving or state of being revived **2 :** evangelistic meeting

re•vive \-'vīv\ *vb* **-vived; -viv•ing :** bring back to life or consciousness or into use **—re•viv•er** *n*

re•vo•ca•tion \͵revə'kāshən\ *n* **:** act or instance of revoking

re•voke \ri'vōk\ *vb* **-voked; -vok•ing :** annul by recalling **—re•vok•er** *n*

re•volt \-'vōlt\ *vb* **1 :** throw off allegiance **2 :** cause or experience disgust or shock ~ *n* **:** rebellion or revolution **—re•volt•er** *n*

re•volt•ing \-iŋ\ *adj* **:** extremely offensive **—re•volt•ing•ly** *adv*

rev•o•lu•tion \͵revə'lüshən\ *n* **1 :** rotation **2 :** progress in an orbit **3 :** sudden, radical, or complete change (as overthrow of a government) **—rev•o•lu•tion•ary** \-shə͵nerē\ *adj or n*

rev•o•lu•tion•ize \-shə͵nīz\ *vb* **-ized; -iz•ing :** change radically **—rev•o•lu•tion•iz•er** *n*

re•volve \ri'välv\ *vb* **-volved; -volv•ing 1 :** ponder **2 :** move in an orbit **3 :** rotate **—re•volv•able** *adj*

re•volv•er \ri'välvər\ *n* **:** pistol with a revolving cylinder

re•vue \ri'vyü\ *n* **:** theatrical production of brief numbers

re•vul•sion \ri'vəlshən\ *n* **:** complete dislike or repugnance

re•ward \ri'wȯrd\ *vb* **:** give a reward to or for ~ *n* **:** something offered for service or achievement

re•write \͵rē'rīt\ *vb* **-wrote; -writ•ten; -writ•ing :** revise **—rewrite** *n*

rhap•so•dy \'rapsədē\ *n, pl* **-dies 1 :** expression of extravagant praise **2 :** flowing free-form musical composition **—rhap•sod•ic** \rap'sädik\ *adj* **—rhap•sod•i•cal•ly** \-iklē\ *adv* **—rhap•so•dize** \'rapsə͵dīz\ *vb*

rhet•o•ric \'retərik\ *n* **:** art of speaking or writing effectively **—rhe•tor•i•cal** \ri'tȯrikəl\ *adj* **—rhet•o•ri•cian** \͵retə'rishən\ *n*

rheu•ma•tism \'rümə͵tizəm, 'rům-\ *n* **:** disorder marked by inflammation or pain in muscles or joints **—rheu•mat•ic** \rů'matik\ *adj*

rhine•stone \'rīn͵stōn\ *n* **:** a colorless imitation gem

rhi•no \'rīnō\ *n, pl* **-no** *or* **-nos :** rhinoceros

rhi•noc•er•os \rī'näsərəs\ *n, pl* **-noc•er•os•es** *or* **-noc•er•os** *or* **-noc•eri** \-'näsə͵rī\ **:** large thick-skinned mammal with 1 or 2 horns on the snout

rho•do•den•dron \͵rōdə'dendrən\ *n* **:** flowering evergreen shrub

rhom•bus \'rämbəs\ *n, pl* **-bus•es** *or* **-bi** \-͵bī\ **:** parallelogram with equal sides

rhu•barb \'rü͵bärb\ *n* **:** garden plant with edible stalks

rhyme \'rīm\ *n* **1 :** correspondence in terminal sounds **2 :** verse that rhymes ~ *vb* **rhymed; rhym•ing :** make or have rhymes

rhythm \'rithəm\ *n* **:** regular succession of sounds or motions **—rhyth•mic** \'rithmik\, **rhyth•mi•cal** \-mikəl\ *adj* **—rhyth•mi•cal•ly** *adv*

rhythm and blues *n* **:** popular music based on blues and black folk music

rib \'rib\ *n* **1 :** curved bone joined to the spine **2 :** riblike thing ~ *vb* **-bb- 1 :** furnish or mark with ribs **2 :** tease **—rib•ber** *n*

rib•ald \'ribəld\ *adj* **:** coarse or vulgar **—rib•ald•ry** \-əldrē\ *n*

rib•bon \'ribən\ *n* **1 :** narrow strip of fabric used esp. for decoration **2 :** strip of inked cloth (as in a typewriter)

ri•bo•fla•vin \͵rībə'flāvən, 'rībə͵-\ *n* **:** growth-promoting vitamin

rice \'rīs\ *n, pl* **rice :** starchy edible seeds of an annual cereal grass

rich \'rich\ *adj* **1 :** having a lot of money or possessions **2 :** valuable **3 :** containing much sugar, fat, or seasoning **4 :** abundant **5 :** deep and pleasing in color or tone **6 :** fertile **—rich•ly** *adv* **—rich•ness** *n*

rich•es \'richəz\ *n pl* **:** wealth

rick•ets \'rikəts\ *n* **:** childhood bone disease

rick•ety \'rikətē\ *adj* **:** shaky

rick•sha, rick•shaw \'rik͵shȯ\ *n* **:** small covered 2-wheeled carriage pulled by one person

ric•o•chet \'rikə͵shā, *Brit also* -͵shet\ *vb* **-cheted** \-͵shād\ *or* **-chet•ted** \-͵shetəd\; **-chet•ing** \-͵shāiŋ\ *or* **-chet•ting** \-͵shetiŋ\ **:** bounce off at an angle **—ricochet** *n*

rid \'rid\ *vb* **rid; rid•ding :** make free of something unwanted **—rid•dance** \'ridᵊns\ *n*

rid•den \'ridᵊn\ *adj* **:** overburdened with—used in combination

1rid•dle \'ridᵊl\ *n* **:** puzzling question ~ *vb* **-dled; -dling :** speak in riddles

2riddle *vb* **-dled; -dling :** fill full of holes

ride \'rīd\ *vb* **rode** \'rōd\; **rid•den** \'ridᵊn\; **rid•ing** \'rīdiŋ\ **1 :** be carried along **2 :** sit on and cause to move **3 :** travel over a surface **4 :** tease or nag ~ *n* **1 :** trip on an animal or in a vehicle **2 :** mechanical device ridden for amusement

rid•er *n* **1 :** one that rides **2 :** attached clause or document **—rid•er•less** *adj*

ridge \'rij\ *n* **1 :** range of hills **2 :** raised line or strip **3 :** line of intersection of 2 sloping surfaces **—ridgy** *adj*

rid•i•cule \'ridə͵kyül\ *vb* **-culed; -cul•ing :** laugh at or make fun of **—ridicule** *n*

ri•dic•u•lous \rə'dikyələs\ *adj* **:** arousing ridicule **—ri•dic•u•lous•ly** *adv* **—ri•dic•u•lous•ness** *n*

rife \'rīf\ *adj* **:** abounding **—rife** *adv*

riff•raff \'rif͵raf\ *n* **:** mob

1ri•fle \'rīfəl\ *vb* **-fled; -fling :** ransack esp. with intent to steal **—ri•fler** \-flər\ *n*

2rifle *n* **:** long shoulder weapon with spiral grooves in the bore **—ri•fle•man** \-mən\ *n* **—ri•fling** *n*

rift \'rift\ *n* **:** separation **—rift** *vb*

1rig \'rig\ *vb* **-gg- 1 :** fit out with rigging **2 :** set up esp. as a makeshift ~ *n* **1 :** distinctive shape, number, and arrangement of sails and masts of a sailing ship **2 :** equipment **3 :** carriage with its horse

2rig *vb* **-gg- :** manipulate esp. by deceptive or dishonest means

rig•ging \'rigiŋ, -ən\ *n* **:** lines that hold and move the masts, sails, and spars of a sailing ship

right \'rīt\ *adj* **1 :** meeting a standard of conduct **2 :** correct **3 :** genuine **4 :** normal **5 :** opposite of left ~ *n* **1 :** something that is correct, just, proper, or honorable **2 :** something to which one has a just claim **3 :** something that is on the right side ~ *adv* **1 :** according to what is right **2 :** immediately **3 :** completely **4 :** on or to the right ~ *vb* **1 :** restore to a proper state **2 :** bring or become upright again **—right•er** *n* **—right•ness** *n* **—right•ward** \-wərd\ *adj*

right angle *n* **:** angle whose sides are perpendicular to each other **—right–an•gled** \'rīt'aŋgəld\ *or* **right–an•gle** \-gəl\ *adj*

righ•teous \'rīchəs\ *adj* **:** acting or being in accordance with what is just or moral **—righ•teous•ly** *adv* **—righ•teous•ness** *n*

right•ful \'rītfəl\ *adj* **:** lawful **—right•ful•ly** \-ē\ *adv* **—right•ful•ness** *n*

right•ly \'rītlē\ *adv* **1 :** justly **2 :** properly **3 :** correctly

rig•id \'rijəd\ *adj* **:** lacking flexibility **—ri•gid•i•ty** \rə'jidətē\ *n* **—rig•id•ly** *adv*

rig•ma•role \'rigmə͵rōl, 'rigə-\ *n* **1 :** meaningless talk **2 :** complicated often unnecessary procedure

rig•or \'rigər\ *n* **:** severity **—rig•or•ous** *adj* **—rig•or•ous•ly** *adv*

rig•or mor•tis \͵rigər'mȯrtəs\ *n* **:** temporary stiffness of muscles occurring after death

rile \'rīl\ *vb* **riled; ril•ing :** anger

rill \'ril\ *n* **:** small brook

rim \'rim\ *n* **:** edge esp. of something curved ~ *vb* **-mm- :** border

1rime \'rīm\ *n* **:** frost **—rimy** \'rīmē\ *adj*

2rime *var of* RHYME

rind \'rīnd\ *n* **:** usu. hard or tough outer layer

1ring \'riŋ\ *n* **1 :** circular band used as an ornament or for holding or fastening **2 :** something circular **3 :** place for contest or display **4 :** group with a selfish or dishonest aim ~ *vb* **:** surround **—ringed** \'riŋd\ *adj* **—ring•like** *adj*

2ring *vb* **rang** \'raŋ\; **rung** \'rəŋ\; **ring•ing 1 :** sound resonantly when struck **2 :** cause to make a metallic sound by striking **3 :** resound **4 :** call esp. by a bell ~ *n* **1 :** resonant sound or tone **2 :** act or instance of ringing

ring•er \'riŋər\ *n* **1 :** one that sounds by ringing **2 :** illegal substitute **3 :** one that closely resembles another

ring•lead•er \'riŋ͵lēdər\ *n* **:** leader esp. of troublemakers

ring•let *n* **:** long curl

ring•worm *n* **:** contagious skin disease caused by fungi

rink \'riŋk\ *n* **:** enclosed place for skating

rinse \'rins\ *vb* **rinsed; rins•ing 1 :** cleanse usu. with water only **2 :** treat (hair) with a rinse ~ *n* **:** liquid used for rinsing **—rins•er** *n*

ri•ot \'rīət\ *n* **1 :** violent public disorder **2 :** random or disorderly profusion **—riot** *vb* **—ri•ot•er** *n* **—ri•ot•ous** *adj*

rip \'rip\ *vb* **-pp- :** cut or tear open ~ *n* **:** rent made by ripping **—rip•per** *n*

ripe \'rīp\ *adj* **rip•er; rip•est :** fully grown, developed, or prepared **—ripe•ly** *adv* **—rip•en** \'rīpən\ *vb* **—ripe•ness** *n*

rip–off *n* **:** theft **—rip off** *vb*

rip•ple \'ripəl\ *vb* **-pled; -pling 1 :** become lightly ruffled on the surface **2 :** sound like rippling water **—ripple** *n*

rise \'rīz\ *vb* **rose** \'rōz\; **ris•en** \'rizᵊn\; **ris•ing** \'rīziŋ\ **1 :** get up from sitting, kneeling, or lying **2 :** take arms **3 :** appear above the horizon **4 :** ascend **5 :** gain a higher position or rank **6 :** increase ~ *n* **1 :** act of rising **2 :** origin **3 :** elevation **4 :** increase **5 :** upward slope **6 :** area of high ground **—ris•er** \'rīzər\ *n*

risk \'risk\ *n* **:** exposure to loss or injury **—risk** *vb* **—risk•i•ness** *n* **—risky** *adj*

ris•qué \ris'kā\ *adj* **:** nearly indecent

rite \'rīt\ *n* **1 :** set form for conducting a ceremony **2 :** liturgy of a church **3 :** ceremonial action

rit•u•al \'richəwəl\ *n* **:** rite **—ritual** *adj* **—rit•u•al•ism** \-͵izəm\ *n* **—rit•u•al•is•tic** \͵richəwəl'istik\ *adj* **—rit•u•al•is•ti•cal•ly** \-tiklē\ *adv* **—rit•u•al•ly** \'richəwəlē\ *adv*

ri•val \'rīvəl\ *n* **1 :** competitor **2 :** peer ~ *vb* **-valed** *or* **-valled; -val•ing** *or* **-val•ling 1 :** be in competition with **2 :** equal **—rival** *adj* **—ri•val•ry** \-rē\ *n*

riv•er \'rivər\ *n* **:** large natural stream of water **—riv•er•bank** *n* **—riv•er•bed** *n* **—riv•er•boat** *n* **—riv•er•side** *n*

riv•et \'rivət\ *n* **:** headed metal bolt ~ *vb* **:** fasten with a rivet **—riv•et•er** *n*

riv•u•let \'rivyələt\ *n* **:** small stream

roach \'rōch\ *n* **:** cockroach

road \'rōd\ *n* **:** open way for vehicles, persons, and animals **—road•bed** *n* **—road•side** *n or adj* **—road•way** *n*

road•block *n* **:** obstruction on a road

road•run•ner *n* **:** large fast-running bird

roam \'rōm\ *vb* **:** wander

roan \'rōn\ *adj* **:** of a dark color sprinkled with white ~ *n* **:** animal with a roan coat

roar \'rōr\ *vb* **:** utter a full loud prolonged sound **—roar** *n* **—roar•er** *n*

roast \'rōst\ *vb* **1 :** cook by dry heat **2 :** criticize severely ~ *n* **:** piece of meat suitable for roasting **—roast** *adj* **—roast·er** *n*

rob \'räb\ *vb* **-bb- 1 :** steal from **2 :** commit robbery **—rob·ber** *n*

rob·bery \'räbərē\ *n, pl* **-ber·ies :** theft of something from a person by use of violence or threat

robe \'rōb\ *n* **1 :** long flowing outer garment **2 :** covering for the lower body ~ *vb* **robed; rob·ing :** clothe with or as if with a robe

rob·in \'räbən\ *n* **:** No. American thrush with a reddish breast

ro·bot \'rō,bät, -bət\ *n* **1 :** machine that looks and acts like a human being **2 :** efficient but insensitive person **—ro·bot·ic** \rō'bätik\ *adj*

ro·bust \rō'bəst, 'rō,bəst\ *adj* **:** strong and vigorously healthy **— ro·bust·ly** *adv* **— ro·bust·ness** *n*

1rock \'räk\ *vb* **:** sway or cause to sway back and forth ~ *n* **1 :** rocking movement **2 :** popular music marked by repetition and a strong beat

2rock *n* **:** mass of hard mineral material **— rock** *adj* **—rocky** *adj*

rock·er *n* **1 :** curved piece on which a chair rocks **2 :** chair that rocks

rock·et \'räkət\ *n* **1 :** self-propelled firework or missile **2 :** jet engine that carries its own oxygen ~ *vb* **:** rise abruptly and rapidly **—rock·et·ry** \-ətrē\ *n*

rod \'räd\ *n* **1 :** straight slender stick **2 :** unit of length equal to 5 yards

rode *past of* RIDE

ro·dent \'rōdᵊnt\ *n* **:** usu. small gnawing mammal

ro·deo \'rōdē,ō, rō'dāō\ *n, pl* **-de·os :** contest of cowboy skills

roe \'rō\ *n* **:** fish eggs

rogue \'rōg\ *n* **:** dishonest or mischievous person **—rogu·ery** \'rōgərē\ *n* **—rogu·ish** \'rōgish\ *adj* **—rogu·ish·ly** *adv* **—rogu·ish·ness** *n*

roil \'rȯil\ *vb* **1 :** make cloudy or muddy by stirring up **2 :** make angry

role \'rōl\ *n* **1 :** part to play **2 :** function

roll \'rōl\ *n* **1 :** official record or list of names **2 :** something rolled up or rounded **3 :** bread baked in a small rounded mass **4 :** sound of rapid drum strokes **5 :** heavy reverberating sound **6 :** rolling movement ~ *vb* **1 :** move by turning over **2 :** move on wheels **3 :** flow in a continuous stream **4 :** swing from side to side **5 :** shape or be shaped in rounded form **6 :** press with a roller

roll·er *n* **1 :** revolving cylinder **2 :** rod on which something is rolled up **3 :** long heavy ocean wave

roller skate *n* **:** a skate with wheels instead of a runner **—roller–skate** *vb*

rol·lick·ing \'rälikiŋ\ *adj* **:** full of good spirits

Ro·man Catholic \'rōmən-\ *n* **:** member of a Christian church led by a pope **—Roman Catholic** *adj* **—Roman Catholicism** *n*

ro·mance \rō'mans, 'rō,mans\ *n* **1 :** medieval tale of knightly adventure **2 :** love story **3 :** love affair ~ *vb* **-manced; -manc·ing 1 :** have romantic fancies **2 :** have a love affair with **—ro·manc·er** *n*

ro·man·tic \rō'mantik\ *adj* **1 :** visionary or imaginative **2 :** appealing to one's emotions **—ro·man·ti·cal·ly** \-iklē\ *adv*

romp \'rämp\ *vb* **:** play actively and noisily **—romp** *n*

roof \'rüf, 'rüf\ *n, pl* **roofs** \'rüfs, 'rüfs; 'rüvz, 'rüvz\ **:** upper covering part of a building ~ *vb* **:** cover with a roof **—roofed** \'rüft, 'rüft\ *adj* **—roof·ing** *n* **—roof·less** *adj* **—roof·top** *n*

1rook \'rük\ *n* **:** crowlike bird

2rook *vb* **:** cheat

rook·ie \'rükē\ *n* **:** novice

room \'rüm, 'rüm\ *n* **1 :** sufficient space **2 :** partitioned part of a building ~ *vb* **:** occupy lodgings **—room·er** *n* **—room·ful** *n* **—roomy** *adj*

room·mate *n* **:** one sharing the same lodgings

roost \'rüst\ *n* **:** support on which birds perch ~ *vb* **:** settle on a roost

roost·er \'rüstər, 'rüs-\ *n* **:** adult male domestic chicken

1root \'rüt, 'rüt\ *n* **1 :** leafless underground part of a seed plant **2 :** rootlike thing or part **3 :** source **4 :** essential core ~ *vb* **:** form, fix, or become fixed by roots **—root·less** *adj* **—root·let** \-lət\ *n* **—root·like** *adj*

2root *vb* **:** turn up with the snout

3root \'rüt, 'rüt\ *vb* **:** applaud or encourage noisily **—root·er** *n*

rope \'rōp\ *n* **:** large strong cord of strands of fiber ~ *vb* **roped; rop·ing 1 :** tie with a rope **2 :** lasso

ro·sa·ry \'rōzərē\ *n, pl* **-ries 1 :** string of beads used in praying **2 :** Roman Catholic devotion

1rose *past of* RISE

2rose \'rōz\ *n* **1 :** prickly shrub with bright flowers **2 :** purplish red **—rose** *adj* **—rose·bud** *n* **—rose·bush** *n*

rose·mary \'rōz,merē\ *n, pl* **-mar·ies :** fragrant shrubby mint

ro·sette \rō'zet\ *n* **:** rose-shaped ornament

Rosh Ha·sha·nah \,räshhä'shänə, ,rōsh-\ *n* **:** Jewish New Year observed as a religious holiday in September or October

ros·in \'räzᵊn\ *n* **:** brittle resin

ros·ter \'rästər\ *n* **:** list of names

ros·trum \'rästrəm\ *n, pl* **-trums** *or* **-tra** \-trə\ **:** speaker's platform

rosy \'rōzē\ *adj* **ros·i·er; -est 1 :** of the color rose **2 :** hopeful **—ros·i·ly** *adv* **—ros·i·ness** *n*

rot \'rät\ *vb* **-tt- :** undergo decomposition ~ *n* **1 :** decay **2 :** disease in which tissue breaks down

ro·ta·ry \'rōtərē\ *adj* **1 :** turning on an axis **2 :** having a rotating part

ro·tate \'rō,tāt\ *vb* **-tat·ed; -tat·ing 1 :** turn about an axis or a center **2 :** alternate in a series **—ro·ta·tion** \rō'tāshən\ *n* **—ro·ta·tor** \'rō,tātər\ *n*

rote \'rōt\ *n* **:** repetition from memory

ro·tor \'rōtər\ *n* **1 :** part that rotates **2 :** system of rotating horizontal blades for supporting a helicopter

rot·ten \'rätᵊn\ *adj* **1 :** having rotted **2 :** corrupt **3 :** extremely unpleasant or inferior **—rot·ten·ness** *n*

ro·tund \rō'tənd\ *adj* **:** rounded **—ro·tun·di·ty** \-'təndətē\ *n*

ro·tun·da \rō'təndə\ *n* **:** building or room with a dome

roué \rù'ā\ *n* **:** man given to debauched living

rouge \'rüzh, 'rüj\ *n* **:** cosmetic for the cheeks **—rouge** *vb*

rough \'rəf\ *adj* **1 :** not smooth **2 :** not calm **3 :** harsh, violent, or rugged **4 :** crudely or hastily done ~ *n* **:** rough state or something in that state ~ *vb* **1 :** roughen **2 :** manhandle **3 :** make roughly **—rough·ly** *adv* **—rough·ness** *n*

rough·age \'rəfij\ *n* **:** coarse bulky food

rough·en \'rəfən\ *vb* **:** make or become rough

rough·neck \'rəf,nek\ *n* **:** rowdy

rou·lette \rü'let\ *n* **:** gambling game using a whirling numbered wheel

1round \'raùnd\ *adj* **1 :** having every part the same distance from the center **2 :** cylindrical **3 :** complete **4 :** approximate **5 :** blunt **6 :** moving in or forming a circle ~ *n* **1 :** round or curved thing **2 :** series of recurring actions or events **3 :** period of time or a unit of action **4 :** fired shot **5 :** cut of beef ~ *vb* **1 :** make or become round **2 :** go around **3 :** finish **4 :** express as an approximation **—round·ish** *adj* **—round·ly** *adv* **—round·ness** *n*

2round *prep or adv* **:** around

round·about *adj* **:** indirect

round·up \'raùnd,əp\ *n* **1 :** gathering together of range cattle **2 :** summary **—round up** *vb*

rouse \'raùz\ *vb* **roused; rous·ing 1 :** wake from sleep **2 :** stir up

rout \'raùt\ *n* **1 :** state of wild confusion **2 :** disastrous defeat ~ *vb* **:** defeat decisively

route \'rüt, 'raùt\ *n* **:** line of travel ~ *vb* **rout·ed; rout·ing :** send by a selected route

rou·tine \rü'tēn\ *n* **1 :** regular course of procedure **2 :** an often repeated speech, formula, or part **—routine** *adj* **—rou·tine·ly** *adv*

rove \'rōv\ *vb* **roved; rov·ing :** wander or roam **—rov·er** *n*

1row \'rō\ *vb* **1 :** propel a boat with oars **2 :** carry in a rowboat ~ *n* **:** act of rowing **—row·boat** *n* **—row·er** \'rōər\ *n*

2row *n* **:** number of objects in a line

3row \'raù\ *n* **:** noisy quarrel **—row** *vb*

row·dy \'raùdē\ *adj* **-di·er; -est :** coarse or boisterous in behavior **—row·di·ness** *n* **—rowdy** *n*

roy·al \'rȯiəl\ *adj* **:** relating to or befitting a king ~ *n* **:** person of royal blood **—roy·al·ly** *adv*

roy·al·ty \'rȯiəltē\ *n, pl* **-ties 1 :** state of being royal **2 :** royal persons **3 :** payment for use of property

rub \'rəb\ *vb* **-bb- 1 :** use pressure and friction on a body **2 :** scour, polish, erase, or smear by pressure and friction **3 :** chafe with friction ~ *n* **:** difficulty

rub·ber \'rəbər\ *n* **1 :** one that rubs **2 :** waterproof elastic substance or something made of it **—rubber** *adj* **—rub·ber·ize** \-,īz\ *vb* **—rub·bery** *adj*

rub·bish \'rəbish\ *n* **:** waste or trash

rub·ble \'rəbəl\ *n* **:** broken fragments esp. of a destroyed building

ru·ble \'rübəl\ *n* **:** monetary unit of Russia

ru·by \'rübē\ *n, pl* **-bies :** precious red stone or its color **—ruby** *adj*

rud·der \'rədər\ *n* **:** steering device at the rear of a ship or aircraft

rud·dy \'rədē\ *adj* **-di·er; -est :** reddish **— rud·di·ness** *n*

rude \'rüd\ *adj* **rud·er; rud·est 1 :** roughly made **2 :** impolite **—rude·ly** *adv* **—rude·ness** *n*

ru·di·ment \'rüdəmənt\ *n* **1 :** something not fully developed **2 :** elementary principle **—ru·di·men·ta·ry** \,rüdə'mentərē\ *adj*

rue \'rü\ *vb* **rued; ru·ing :** feel regret for ~ *n* **:** regret **—rue·ful** \-fəl\ *adj* **—rue·ful·ly** *adv* **—rue·ful·ness** *n*

ruf·fi·an \'rəfēən\ *n* **:** brutal person

ruf·fle \'rəfəl\ *vb* **-fled; -fling 1 :** draw into or provide with pleats **2 :** roughen the surface of **3 :** irritate ~ *n* **:** strip of fabric pleated on one edge **—ruf·fly** \'rəfəlē, -flē\ *adj*

rug \'rəg\ *n* **:** piece of heavy fabric used as a floor covering

rug·ged \'rəgəd\ *adj* **1 :** having a rough uneven surface **2 :** severe **3 :** strong **—rug·ged·ly** *adv* **—rug·ged·ness** *n*

ru·in \'rüən\ *n* **1 :** complete collapse or destruction **2 :** remains of something destroyed —usu. in pl. **3 :** cause of destruction ~ *vb* **1 :** destroy **2 :** damage beyond repair **3 :** bankrupt

ru·in·ous \'rüənəs\ *adj* **:** causing ruin **— ruin·ous·ly** *adv*

rule \'rül\ *n* **1 :** guide or principle for governing action **2 :** usual way of doing something **3 :** government **4 :** straight strip (as of wood or metal) marked off in units for measuring ~ *vb* **ruled; rul·ing 1 :** govern **2 :** give as a decision **—rul·er** *n*

rum \'rəm\ *n* **:** liquor made from molasses or sugarcane

rum·ble \'rəmbəl\ *vb* **-bled; -bling :** make a low heavy rolling sound **—rumble** *n*

ru·mi·nant \'rümənənt\ *n* **:** hoofed mammal (as a cow or deer) that chews the cud **— ruminant** *adj*

ru·mi·nate \'rümə,nāt\ *vb* **-nat·ed; -nat·ing :** contemplate **—ru·mi·na·tion** \,rümə'nāshən\ *n*

rum·mage \'rəmij\ *vb* **-maged; -mag·ing :** search thoroughly

rum·my \'rəmē\ *n* **:** card game

ru·mor \'rümər\ *n* **1 :** common talk **2 :** widespread statement not authenticated **—rumor** *vb*

rump \'rəmp\ *n* **:** rear part of an animal

rum·ple \'rəmpəl\ *vb* **-pled; -pling :** tousle or wrinkle **—rumple** *n*

rum·pus \'rəmpəs\ *n* **:** disturbance

run \'rən\ *vb* **ran** \'ran\; **run; run·ning 1 :** go rapidly or hurriedly **2 :** enter a race or election **3 :** operate **4 :** continue in force **5 :** flow rapidly **6 :** take a certain direction **7 :** manage **8 :** incur ~ *n* **1 :** act of running **2 :** brook **3 :** continuous series **4 :** usual kind **5 :** freedom of movement **6 :** lengthwise ravel

run·around *n* **:** evasive or delaying action esp. in response to a request

run·away \'rənə,wā\ *n* **:** fugitive ~ *adj* **1 :** fugitive **2 :** out of control

run–down *adj* **:** being in poor condition

1rung *past part of* RING

2rung \'rəŋ\ *n* **:** horizontal piece of a chair or ladder

run·ner \'rənər\ *n* **1 :** one that runs **2 :** thin piece or part on which something slides **3 :** slender creeping branch of a plant

run·ner–up *n, pl* **run·ners–up :** competitor who finishes second

run·ning \'rəniŋ\ *adj* **1 :** flowing **2 :** continuous

runt \'rənt\ *n* **:** small person or animal **— runty** *adj*

run·way \'rən,wā\ *n* **:** strip on which aircraft land and take off

ru·pee \rü'pē, 'rü,-\ *n* **:** monetary unit (as of India)

rup·ture \'rəpchər\ *n* **1 :** breaking or tearing apart **2 :** hernia ~ *vb* **-tured; -tur·ing :** cause or undergo rupture

ru·ral \'rùrəl\ *adj* **:** relating to the country or agriculture

ruse \'rüs, 'rüz\ *n* **:** trick

1rush \'rəsh\ *n* **:** grasslike marsh plant

2rush *vb* **1 :** move forward or act with too great haste **2 :** perform in a short time ~ *n* **:** violent forward motion ~ *adj* **:** requiring speed **—rush·er** *n*

rus·set \'rəsət\ *n* **1 :** reddish brown color **2 :** a baking potato **—russet** *adj*

rust \'rəst\ *n* **1 :** reddish coating on exposed iron **2 :** reddish brown color **—rust** *vb* **— rusty** *adj*

rus·tic \'rəstik\ *adj* **:** relating to or suitable for the country or country dwellers ~ *n* **:** rustic person **—rus·ti·cal·ly** *adv*

rus·tle \'rəsəl\ *vb* **-tled; -tling 1 :** make or cause a rustle **2 :** forage food **3 :** steal cattle from the range ~ *n* **:** series of small sounds **—rus·tler** \-ələr\ *n*

rut \'rət\ *n* **1 :** track worn by wheels or feet **2 :** set routine **—rut·ted** *adj*

ruth·less \'rüthləs\ *adj* **:** having no pity **— ruth·less·ly** *adv* **—ruth·less·ness** *n*

-ry \rē\ *n suffix* **:** -ery

rye \'rī\ *n* **1 :** cereal grass grown for grain **2 :** whiskey from rye

S

s \'es\ *n, pl* **s's** *or* **ss** \'esəz\ **:** 19th letter of the alphabet

1-s \s *after sounds* f, k, k̲, p, t, th; əz *after sounds* ch, j, s, sh, z, zh; z *after other sounds*\ —used to form the plural of most nouns

2-s *vb suffix* —used to form the 3d person singular present of most verbs

Sab·bath \'sabəth\ *n* **1 :** Saturday observed as a day of worship by Jews and some Christians **2 :** Sunday observed as a day of worship by Christians

sa·ber, sa·bre \'sābər\ *n* **:** curved cavalry sword

sa·ble \'sābəl\ *n* **1 :** black **2 :** dark brown mammal or its fur

sab·o·tage \'sabə,täzh\ *n* **:** deliberate destruction or hampering ~ *vb* **-taged; -tag·ing :** wreck through sabotage

sab·o·teur \,sabə'tər\ *n* **:** person who sabotages

sac \'sak\ *n* **:** anatomical pouch

sac·cha·rin \'sakərən\ *n* **:** low-calorie artificial sweetener

sac·cha·rine \-ərən\ *adj* **:** nauseatingly sweet

sa·chet \sa'shā\ *n* **:** small bag with perfumed powder (**sachet powder**)

1sack \'sak\ *n* **:** bag ~ *vb* **:** fire

2sack *vb* **:** plunder a captured place

sack·cloth *n* **:** rough garment worn as a sign of penitence

sac·ra·ment \'sakrəmənt\ *n* **:** formal religious act or rite **—sac·ra·men·tal** \,sakrə'mentᵊl\ *adj*

sa·cred \'sākrəd\ *adj* **1 :** set apart for or worthy of worship **2 :** worthy of reverence **3 :** relating to religion **—sa·cred·ly** *adv* **— sa·cred·ness** *n*

sac·ri·fice \'sakrə,fīs\ *n* **1 :** the offering of something precious to a deity or the thing offered **2 :** loss or deprivation ~ *vb* **-ficed; -fic·ing :** offer or give up as a sacrifice **—sac·ri·fi·cial** \,sakrə'fishəl\ *adj*

sac·ri·lege \'sakrəlij\ *n* **:** violation of something sacred **—sac·ri·le·gious** \,sakrə'lijəs, -'lējəs\ *adj*

sac·ro·sanct \'sakrō,saŋkt\ *adj* **:** sacred

sad \'sad\ *adj* **-dd- 1 :** affected with grief or sorrow **2 :** causing sorrow **—sad·den** \'sadᵊn\ *vb* **—sad·ly** *adv* **—sad·ness** *n*

sad·dle \'sadᵊl\ *n* **:** seat for riding on horseback ~ *vb* **-dled; -dling :** put a saddle on

sa·dism \'sā,dizəm, 'sad,iz-\ *n* **:** delight in cruelty **—sa·dist** \'sādist, 'sad-\ *n* **—sa·dis·tic** \sə'distik\ *adj* **—sa·dis·ti·cal·ly** *adv*

sa·fa·ri \sə'färē, -'far-\ *n* **:** hunting expedition in Africa

safe \'sāf\ *adj* **saf·er; saf·est 1 :** free from harm **2 :** providing safety ~ *n* **:** container to keep valuables safe **—safe·keep·ing** *n* **—safe·ly** *adv*

safe·guard *n* **:** measure or device for preventing accidents **—safeguard** *vb*

safe·ty \'sāftē\ *n, pl* **-ties 1 :** freedom from danger **2 :** protective device

saf·flow·er \'saf,laùər\ *n* **:** herb with seeds rich in edible oil

saf·fron \'safrən\ *n* **:** orange powder from a crocus flower used in cooking

sag \'sag\ *vb* **-gg- :** droop, sink, or settle **— sag** *n*

sa·ga \'sägə\ *n* **:** story of heroic deeds

sa·ga·cious \sə'gāshəs\ *adj* **:** shrewd **—sa·gac·i·ty** \-'gasətē\ *n*

1sage \'sāj\ *adj* **:** wise or prudent ~ *n* **:** wise man **—sage·ly** *adv*

2sage *n* **:** mint used in flavoring

sage·brush *n* **:** low shrub of the western U.S.

said *past of* SAY

sail \'sāl\ *n* **1 :** fabric used to catch the wind and move a boat or ship **2 :** trip on a sailboat ~ *vb* **1 :** travel on a ship or sailboat **2 :** move with ease or grace **—sail·boat** *n* **—sail·or** \'sālər\ *n*

sail·fish *n* **:** large fish with a very large dorsal fin

saint \'sānt, *before a name* ,sānt *or* sənt\ *n* **:** holy or godly person **—saint·ed** \-əd\ *adj* **—saint·hood** \-,hùd\ *n* **—saint·li·ness** *n* **—saint·ly** *adj*

¹sake \'sāk\ n 1 : purpose or reason 2 : one's good or benefit

²sa•ke, sa•ki \'sākē\ n : Japanese rice wine

sa•la•cious \sə'lāshəs\ adj : sexually suggestive —sa•la•cious•ly adv

sal•ad \'saləd\ n : dish usu. of raw lettuce, vegetables, or fruit

sal•a•man•der \salə,mandər\ n : lizardlike amphibian

sa•la•mi \sə'lämē\ n : highly seasoned dried sausage

sal•a•ry \'salərē\ n, pl -ries : regular payment for services

sale \'sāl\ n 1 : transfer of ownership of property for money 2 : selling at bargain prices 3 sales pl : activities involved in selling —sal•able, sale•able \'sāləbəl\ adj —sales•man \-mən\ n —sales•per•son n —sales•wom•an n

sa•lient \'sālyənt\ adj : standing out conspicuously

sa•line \'sā,lēn, -,līn\ adj : containing salt —sa•lin•i•ty \sā'linətē\ n

sa•li•va \sə'līvə\ n : liquid secreted into the mouth —sal•i•vary \'salə,verē\ adj —sal•i•vate \-,vāt\ vb —sal•i•va•tion \salə-'vāshən\ n

sal•low \'salō\ adj : of a yellowish sickly color

sal•ly \'salē\ n, pl -lies 1 : quick attack on besiegers 2 : witty remark —sally vb

salm•on \'samən\ n, pl salmon 1 : food fish with pink or red flesh 2 : deep yellowish pink color

sa•lon \sə'län, 'sal,än, sa'lō̇m\ n : elegant room or shop

sa•loon \sə'lün\ n 1 : public cabin on a passenger ship 2 : barroom

sal•sa \'sȯlsə, 'sal-\ n : spicy sauce of tomatoes, onions, and hot peppers

salt \'sȯlt\ n 1 : white crystalline substance that consists of sodium and chlorine 2 : compound formed usu. from acid and metal —salt vb or adj —salt•i•ness n —salty adj

salt•wa•ter adj : relating to or living in salt water

sa•lu•bri•ous \sə'lübrēəs\ adj : good for health

sal•u•tary \'salyə,terē\ adj : health-giving or beneficial

sal•u•ta•tion \salyə'tāshən\ n : greeting

sa•lute \sə'lüt\ vb -lut•ed; -lut•ing : honor by ceremony or formal movement —salute n

sal•vage \'salvij\ n : something saved from destruction ~ vb -vaged; -vag•ing : rescue or save

sal•va•tion \sal'vāshən\ n : saving of a person from sin or danger

salve \'sav, 'sȧv\ n : medicinal ointment ~ vb salved; salv•ing : soothe

sal•ver \'salvər\ n : small tray

sal•vo \'salvō\ n, pl -vos or -voes : simultaneous discharge of guns

same \'sām\ adj : being the one referred to ~ pron : the same one or ones ~ adv : in the same manner —same•ness n

sam•ple \'sampəl\ n : piece or part that shows the quality of a whole ~ vb -pled; -pling : judge by a sample

sam•pler \'samplər\ n : piece of needlework testing skill in embroidering

san•a•to•ri•um \sanə'tōrēəm\ n, pl -riums or -ria \-ēə\ : hospital for the chronically ill

sanc•ti•fy \'saŋktə,fī\ vb -fied; -fy•ing : make holy —sanc•ti•fi•ca•tion \,saŋk-təfə'kāshən\ n

sanc•ti•mo•nious \saŋktə'mōnēəs\ adj : hypocritically pious —sanc•ti•mo•nious•ly adv

sanc•tion \'saŋkshən\ n 1 : authoritative approval 2 : coercive measure —usu. pl ~ vb : approve

sanc•ti•ty \'saŋktətē\ n, pl -ties : quality or state of being holy or sacred

sanc•tu•ary \'saŋkchə,werē\ n, pl -ar•ies 1 : consecrated place 2 : place of refuge

sand \'sand\ n : loose granular particles of rock ~ vb : smooth with an abrasive —sand•bank n —sand•er n —sand•storm n —sandy adj

san•dal \'sand²l\ n : shoe consisting of a sole strapped to the foot

sand•pa•per n : abrasive paper —sandpaper vb

sand•pip•er \-,pīpər\ n : long-billed shorebird

sand•stone n : rock made of naturally cemented sand

sand•wich \'sand,wich\ n : 2 or more slices of bread with a filling between them ~ vb : squeeze or crowd in

sane \'sān\ adj san•er; san•est 1 : mentally healthy 2 : sensible —sane•ly adv

sang past of SING

san•gui•nary \'saŋgwə,nerē\ adj : bloody

san•guine \'saŋgwən\ adj 1 : reddish 2 : cheerful

san•i•tar•i•um \sanə'terēəm\ n, pl -i•ums or -ia \-ēə\ : sanatorium

san•i•tary \'sanə,terē\ adj 1 : relating to health 2 : free from filth or infective matter

san•i•ta•tion \sanə'tāshən\ n : protection of health by maintenance of sanitary conditions

san•i•ty \'sanətē\ n : soundness of mind

sank past of SINK

¹sap \'sap\ n 1 : fluid that circulates through a plant 2 : gullible person

²sap vb -pp- 1 : undermine 2 : weaken or exhaust gradually

sa•pi•ent \'sāpēənt, 'sapē-\ adj : wise —sa•pi•ence \-əns\ n

sap•ling \'saplin\ n : young tree

sap•phire \'saf,īr\ n : hard transparent blue gem

sap•py \'sapē\ adj -pi•er; -est 1 : full of sap 2 : overly sentimental

sap•suck•er \'sap,səkər\ n : small No. American woodpecker

sar•casm \'sär,kazəm\ n 1 : cutting remark 2 : ironical criticism or reproach —sar•cas•tic \sär'kastik\ adj —sar•cas•ti•cal•ly adv

sar•coph•a•gus \sär'käfəgəs\ n, pl -gi \-,gī, -,jī\ : large stone coffin

sar•dine \sär'dēn\ n : small fish preserved for use as food

sar•don•ic \sär'dänik\ adj : disdainfully humorous —sar•don•i•cal•ly adv

sa•rong \sə'rȯn, -'rän\ n : loose garment worn esp. by Pacific islanders

sar•sa•pa•ril•la \saspə'rilə, ,särs-\ n : dried roots of a tropical American plant used esp. for flavoring or a carbonated drink flavored with this

sar•to•ri•al \sär'tōrēəl\ adj : relating to a tailor or men's clothes

¹sash \'sash\ n : broad band worn around the waist or over the shoulder

²sash, n pl sash 1 : frame for a pane of glass in a door or window 2 : movable part of a window

sas•sa•fras \'sasə,fras\ n : No. American tree or its dried root bark

sassy \'sasē\ adj sass•i•er; -est : saucy

sat past of SIT

Sa•tan \'sāt²n\ n : devil —sa•tan•ic \sə'tanik, sā-\ adj —sa•tan•i•cal•ly adv

satch•el \'sachəl\ n : small bag

sate \'sāt\ vb sat•ed; sat•ing : satisfy fully

sat•el•lite \'sat²l,īt\ n 1 : toady 2 : body or object that revolves around a larger celestial body

sa•ti•ate \'sāshē,āt\ vb -at•ed; -at•ing : sate —sa•ti•ety \sa'tīətē\ n

sat•in \'sat²n\ n : glossy fabric —sat•iny adj

sat•ire \'sa,tīr\ n : literary ridicule done with humor —sa•tir•ic \sə'tirik\, sa•tir•i•cal \-ikəl\ adj —sa•tir•i•cal•ly adv —sat•i•rist \'satərist\ n —sat•i•rize \-ə,rīz\ vb

sat•is•fac•tion \satəs'fakshən\ n : state of being satisfied —sat•is•fac•to•ri•ly \-'faktərəlē\ adv —sat•is•fac•to•ry \-'faktərē\ adj

sat•is•fy \'satəs,fī\ vb -fied; -fy•ing 1 : make happy 2 : pay what is due to or on —sat•is•fy•ing•ly adv

sat•u•rate \'sachə,rāt\ vb -rat•ed; -rat•ing : soak or charge thoroughly —sat•u•ra•tion \sachə'rāshən\ n

Sat•ur•day \'satərdā, -dē\ n : 7th day of the week

sat•ur•nine \'satər,nīn\ adj : sullen

sa•tyr \'sātər, 'sat-\ n : pleasure-loving forest god of ancient Greece

sauce \'sȯs\ n : fluid dressing or topping for food —sauce•pan n

sau•cer \'sȯsər\ n : small shallow dish under a cup

saucy \'sasē, 'sȯsē\ adj sauc•i•er; -est : insolent —sauc•i•ly adv —sauc•i•ness n

sau•er•kraut \'sau̇ər,krau̇t\ n : finely cut and fermented cabbage

sau•na \'saunə\ n : steam or dry heat bath or a room or cabinet used for such a bath

saun•ter \'sȯntər, 'sänt-\ vb : stroll

sau•sage \'sȯsij\ n : minced and highly seasoned meat

sau•té \sȯ'tā, sō-\ vb -téed or -téd; -té•ing : fry in a little fat —sauté n

sav•age \'savij\ adj 1 : wild 2 : cruel ~ n : person belonging to a primitive society —sav•age•ly adv —sav•age•ness n —sav•age•ry n

¹save \'sāv\ vb saved; sav•ing 1 : rescue from danger 2 : guard from destruction 3 : redeem from sin 4 : put aside as a reserve —sav•er n

²save prep : except

sav•ior, sav•iour \'sāvyər\ n 1 : one who saves 2 cap : Jesus Christ

sa•vor \'sāvər\ n : special flavor ~ vb : taste with pleasure —sa•vory adj

¹saw past of SEE

²saw \'sȯ\ n : cutting tool with teeth ~ vb sawed; sawed or sawn; saw•ing : cut with a saw —saw•dust \-,dəst\ n —saw•mill n —saw•yer \-yər\ n

saw•horse n : support for wood being sawed

sax•o•phone \'saksə,fōn\ n : wind instrument with a reed mouthpiece and usu. a bent metal body

say \'sā\ vb said \'sed\; say•ing \'sāin\; says \'sez\ 1 : express in words 2 : state positively ~ n, pl says \'sāz\ 1 : expression of opinion 2 : power of decision

say•ing \'sāin\ n : commonly repeated statement

scab \'skab\ n 1 : protective crust over a sore or wound 2 : worker taking a striker's job ~ vb -bb- 1 : become covered with a scab 2 : work as a scab —scab•by adj

scab•bard \'skabərd\ n : sheath for the blade of a weapon

scaf•fold \'skafəld, -,ōld\ n 1 : raised platform for workmen 2 : platform on which a criminal is executed

¹scald \'skȯld\ vb 1 : burn with hot liquid or steam 2 : heat to the boiling point

¹scale \'skāl\ n : weighing device ~ vb scaled; scal•ing : weigh

²scale n 1 : thin plate esp. on the body of a fish or reptile 2 : thin coating or layer ~ vb scaled; scal•ing : strip of scales —scaled \'skāld\ adj —scale•less adj —scaly adj

³scale n 1 : graduated series 2 : size of a sample (as a model) in proportion to the size of the actual thing 3 : standard of estimation or judgment 4 : series of musical tones ~ vb scaled; scal•ing 1 : climb by a ladder 2 : arrange in a graded series

scal•lion \'skalyən\ n : bulbless onion

scal•lop \'skäləp, 'skal-\ n 1 : marine mollusk 2 : rounded projection on a border

scalp \'skalp\ n : skin and flesh of the head ~ vb 1 : remove the scalp from 2 : resell at a greatly increased price —scalp•er n

scal•pel \'skalpəl\ n : surgical knife

scamp \'skamp\ n : rascal

scam•per \'skampər\ vb : run nimbly —scamper n

scan \'skan\ vb -nn- 1 : read (verses) so as to show meter 2 : examine closely or hastily 3 : examine with a sensing device —scan n —scan•ner n

scan•dal \'skand²l\ n 1 : disgraceful situation 2 : malicious gossip —scan•dal•ize vb —scan•dal•ous adj

scant \'skant\ adj : barely sufficient ~ vb : stint —scant•i•ly adv —scanty adj

scape•goat \'skāp,gōt\ n : one that bears the blame for others

scap•u•la \'skapyələ\ n, pl -lae \-,lē\ or -las : shoulder blade

scar \'skär\ n : mark where a wound has healed —scar vb

scar•ab \'skarəb\ n : large dark beetle or an ornament representing one

scarce \'skers\ adj scarc•er; scarc•est : lacking in quantity or number —scar•ci•ty \'skersətē\ n

scarce•ly \'skerslē\ adv 1 : barely 2 : almost not

scare \'sker\ vb scared; scar•ing : frighten ~ n : fright —scary adj

scare•crow \'sker,krō\ n : figure for scaring birds from crops

scarf \'skärf\ n, pl scarves \'skärvz\ or scarfs : cloth worn about the shoulders or the neck

scar•let \'skärlət\ n : bright red color —scarlet adj

scarlet fever n : acute contagious disease marked by fever, sore throat, and red rash

scath•ing \'skāthin\ adj : bitterly severe

scat•ter \'skatər\ vb 1 : spread about irregularly 2 : disperse

scav•en•ger \'skavənjər\ n 1 : person that collects refuse or waste 2 : animal that feeds on decayed matter —scav•enge \'skavənj\ vb

sce•nar•io \sə'narē,ō, -'när-\ n, pl -i•os 1 : plot of a play or movie 2 : possible sequence of events

scene \'sēn\ n 1 : single situation in a play or movie 2 : stage setting 3 : view 4 : display of emotion —sce•nic \'sēnik\ adj

scen•ery \'sēnərē\ n, pl -er•ies 1 : painted setting for a stage 2 : picturesque view

scent \'sent\ vb 1 : smell 2 : fill with odor ~ n 1 : odor 2 : sense of smell 3 : perfume —scent•ed \'sentəd\ adj

scep•ter \'septər\ n : staff signifying authority

scep•tic \'skeptik\ var of SKEPTIC

sched•ule \'skejül, esp Brit 'shedyül\ n : list showing sequence of events ~ vb -uled; -ul•ing : make a schedule of

scheme \'skēm\ n 1 : crafty plot 2 : systematic design ~ vb schemed; schem•ing : form a plot —sche•mat•ic \ski'matik\ adj —schem•er n

schism \'sizəm, 'skiz-\ n : split —schis•mat•ic \siz'matik, skiz-\ n or adj

schizo•phre•nia \skitsə'frēnēə\ n : severe mental illness —schiz•oid \'skit,sȯid\ adj or n —schizo•phren•ic \skitsə'frenik\ adj

schol•ar \'skälər\ n : student or learned person —schol•ar•ly adj

schol•ar•ship \-,ship\ n 1 : qualities or learning of a scholar 2 : money given to a student to pay for education

scho•las•tic \skə'lastik\ adj : relating to schools, scholars, or scholarship

¹school \'skül\ n 1 : institution for learning 2 : pupils in a school 3 : group with shared beliefs ~ vb : teach —school•boy n —school•girl n —school•house n —school•mate n —school•room n —school•teach•er n

²school n : large number of fish swimming together

schoo•ner \'skünər\ n : sailing ship

sci•ence \'sīəns\ n : branch of systematic study esp. of the physical world —sci•en•tif•ic \,sīən'tifik\ adj —sci•en•tif•i•cal•ly adv —sci•en•tist \'sīəntist\ n

scin•til•late \'sint²l,āt\ vb -lat•ed; -lat•ing : flash —scin•til•la•tion \,sint²l'āshən\ n

scin•til•lat•ing adj : brilliantly lively or witty

sci•on \'sīən\ n : descendant

scis•sors \'sizərz\ n pl : small shears

scoff \'skäf\ vb : mock —scoff•er n

scold \'skōld\ n : person who scolds ~ vb : criticize severely

scoop \'küp\ n : shovellike utensil ~ vb 1 : take out with a scoop 2 : dig out

scoot \'sküt\ vb : move swiftly

scoot•er \'skütər\ n : child's foot-propelled vehicle

¹scope \'skōp\ n 1 : extent 2 : room for development

²scope n : viewing device (as a microscope)

scorch \'skȯrch\ vb : burn the surface of

score \'skōr\ n, pl scores 1 or pl score : twenty 2 : cut 3 : record of points made (as in a game) 4 : debt 5 : music of a composition ~ vb scored; scor•ing 1 : record 2 : mark with lines 3 : gain in a game 4 : assign a grade to 5 : compose a score for —score•less adj —scor•er n

scorn \'skȯrn\ n : emotion involving both anger and disgust ~ vb : hold in contempt —scorn•er n —scorn•ful \-fəl\ adj —scorn•ful•ly adv

scor•pi•on \'skȯrpēən\ n : poisonous long-tailed animal

scoun•drel \'skaundrəl\ n : villain

¹scour \'skau̇ər\ vb : examine thoroughly

²scour vb : rub in order to clean

scourge \'skərj\ n 1 : whip 2 : punishment ~ vb scourged; scourg•ing 1 : lash 2 : punish severely

scout \'skau̇t\ vb : inspect or observe to get information ~ n : person sent out to get information

scow \'skau̇\ n : large flat-bottomed boat with square ends

scowl \'skau̇l\ vb : make a frowning expression of displeasure —scowl n

scrag•gly \'skraglē\ adj : irregular or unkempt

scram \'skram\ vb -mm- : go away at once

scram•ble \'skrambəl\ vb -bled; -bling 1 : clamber clumsily around 2 : struggle for possession of something 3 : mix together 4 : cook (eggs) by stirring during frying —scramble n

¹scrap \'skrap\ n 1 : fragment 2 : discarded material ~ vb -pp- : get rid of as useless

²scrap vb -pp- : fight —scrap n —scrap•per n

scrap•book n : blank book in which mementos are kept

scrape \'skrāp\ vb scraped; scrap•ing 1 : remove by drawing a knife over 2 : clean or smooth by rubbing 3 : draw across a surface with a grating sound 4 : damage by contact with a rough surface 5 : gather or proceed with difficulty ~ n 1 : act of scraping 2 : predicament —scrap•er n

scratch \'skrach\ vb 1 : scrape or dig with or as if with claws or nails 2 : cause to move gratingly 3 : delete by or as if by drawing a line through ~ n : mark or sound made in scratching —scratchy adj

scrawl \'skrȯl\ vb : write hastily and carelessly —scrawl n

scraw•ny \'skrȯnē\ adj -ni•er; -est : very thin

scream \'skrēm\ vb : cry out loudly and shrilly ~ n : loud shrill cry

screech \'skrēch\ vb n : shriek

screen \'skrēn\ n 1 : device or partition used to protect or decorate 2 : surface on which pictures appear (as in movies) ~ vb : shield or separate with or as if with a screen

screw \'skrü\ n 1 : grooved fastening device 2 : propeller ~ vb 1 : fasten by means of a screw 2 : move spirally

screw•driv•er \'skrü,drīvər\ n : tool for turning screws

scrib•ble \'skribəl\ vb -bled; -bling : write hastily or carelessly —scribble n —scrib•bler \-ələr\ n

scribe \'skrīb\ n : one who writes or copies writing

scrimp \'skrimp\ vb : economize greatly

scrip \'skrip\ n 1 : paper money for less than a dollar 2 : certificate entitling one to something (as stock)

script \'skript\ n : text (as of a play)

scrip•ture \'skripchər\ n : sacred writings of a religion —scrip•tur•al \'skripchərəl\ adj

scroll \'skrōl\ *n* **1 :** roll of paper for writing a document **2 :** spiral or coiled design
scro•tum \'skrōtəm\ *n, pl* **-ta** \-ə\ *or* **-tums :** pouch containing the testes
scrounge \'skraủnj\ *vb* **scrounged; scroung•ing :** collect by or as if by foraging
[1]**scrub** \'skrəb\ *n* **:** stunted tree or shrub or a growth of these **—scrub** *adj* **—scrub•by** *adj*
[2]**scrub** *vb* **-bb- :** clean or wash by rubbing **—scrub** *n*
scruff \'skrəf\ *n* **:** loose skin of the back of the neck
scrump•tious \'skrəmpshəs\ *adj* **:** delicious
scru•ple \'skrüpəl\ *n* **:** reluctance due to ethical considerations **—scruple** *vb* **—scru•pu•lous** \-pyələs\ *adj* **—scru•pu•lous•ly** *adv*
scru•ti•ny \'skrütᵊnē\ *n, pl* **-nies :** careful inspection **—scru•ti•nize** \-ᵊn,īz\ *vb*
scud \'skəd\ *vb* **-dd- :** move speedily
scuff \'skəf\ *vb* **:** scratch, scrape, or wear away **—scuff** *n*
scuf•fle \'skəfəl\ *vb* **-fled; -fling 1 :** struggle at close quarters **2 :** shuffle one's feet **—scuffle** *n*
scull \'skəl\ *n* **1 :** oar **2 :** racing shell propelled with sculls ~ *vb* **:** propel a boat by an oar over the stern
scul•lery \'skələrē\ *n, pl* **-ler•ies :** room for cleaning dishes and cookware
sculpt \'skəlpt\ *vb* **:** sculpture
sculp•ture \'skəlpchər\ *n* **:** work of art carved or molded ~ *vb* **-tured; -tur•ing :** form as sculpture **—sculp•tor** \-tər\ *n* **—sculp•tur•al** \-chərəl\ *adj*
scum \'skəm\ *n* **:** slimy film on a liquid
scur•ri•lous \'skərələs\ *adj* **:** vulgar or abusive
scur•ry \'skərē\ *vb* **-ried; -ry•ing :** scamper
scur•vy \'skərvē\ *n* **:** vitamin-deficiency disease
[1]**scut•tle** \'skətᵊl\ *n* **:** pail for coal
[2]**scuttle** *vb* **-tled; -tling :** sink (a ship) by cutting holes in its bottom
[3]**scuttle** *vb* **-tled; -tling :** scamper
scythe \'sīth\ *n* **:** tool for mowing by hand **—scythe** *vb*
sea \'sē\ *n* **1 :** large body of salt water **2 :** ocean **3 :** rough water **—sea** *adj* **—sea•coast** *n* **—sea•food** *n* **—sea•port** *n* **—sea•shore** *n* **—sea•wa•ter** *n*
sea•bird *n* **:** bird frequenting the open ocean
sea•board *n* **:** country's seacoast
sea•far•er \-,farər\ *n* **:** seaman **—sea•far•ing** \-,fariŋ\ *adj or n*
sea horse *n* **:** small fish with a horselike head
[1]**seal** \'sēl\ *n* **:** large sea mammal of cold regions **—seal•skin** *n*
[2]**seal** *n* **1 :** device for stamping a design **2 :** something that closes ~ *vb* **1 :** affix a seal to **2 :** close up securely **3 :** determine finally **—seal•ant** \-ənt\ *n* **—seal•er** *n*
sea lion *n* **:** large Pacific seal with external ears
seam \'sēm\ *n* **1 :** line of junction of 2 edges **2 :** layer of a mineral ~ *vb* **:** join by sewing **—seam•less** *adj*
sea•man \'sēmən\ *n* **1 :** one who helps to handle a ship **2 :** naval enlisted man ranking next below a petty officer third class **—sea•man•ship** *n*
seaman apprentice *n* **:** naval enlisted man ranking next below a seaman
seaman recruit *n* **:** naval enlisted man of the lowest rank
seam•stress \'sēmstrəs\ *n* **:** woman who sews
seamy \'sēmē\ *adj* **seam•i•er; -est :** unpleasant or sordid
sé•ance \'sā,äns\ *n* **:** meeting for communicating with spirits
sea•plane *n* **:** airplane that can take off from and land on the water
sear \'sir\ *vb* **:** scorch **—sear** *n*
search \'sərch\ *vb* **1 :** look through **2 :** seek **—search** *n* **—search•er** *n* **—search•light** *n*
sea•sick *adj* **:** nauseated by the motion of a ship **—sea•sick•ness** *n*
[1]**sea•son** \'sēzᵊn\ *n* **1 :** division of the year **2 :** customary time for something **—sea•son•al** \'sēzᵊnəl\ *adj* **—sea•son•al•ly** *adv*
[2]**season** *vb* **1 :** add spice to (food) **2 :** make strong or fit for use **—sea•son•ing** \-ᵊniŋ\ *n*
sea•son•able \'sēznəbəl\ *adj* **:** occurring at a suitable time **—sea•son•ably** \-blē\ *adv*
seat \'sēt\ *n* **1 :** place to sit **2 :** chair, bench, or stool for sitting on **3 :** place that serves as a capital or center ~ *vb* **1 :** place in or on a seat **2 :** provide seats for
sea•weed *n* **:** marine alga
sea•wor•thy *adj* **:** strong enough to hold up to a sea voyage
se•cede \si'sēd\ *vb* **-ced•ed; -ced•ing :** withdraw from a body (as a nation)
se•clude \si'klüd\ *vb* **-clud•ed; -clud•ing :** shut off alone **—se•clu•sion** \si'klüzhən\ *n*
[1]**sec•ond** \'sekənd\ *adj* **:** next after the 1st ~ *n* **1 :** one that is second **2 :** one who assists (as in a duel) **—second, sec•ond•ly** *adv*
[2]**second** *n* **1 :** 60th part of a minute **2 :** moment
sec•ond•ary \'sekən,derē\ *adj* **1 :** second in rank or importance **2 :** coming after the primary or elementary
sec•ond•hand *adj* **1 :** not original **2 :** used before
second lieutenant *n* **:** lowest ranking commissioned officer of the army, air force, or marines
se•cret \'sēkrət\ *adj* **1 :** hidden **2 :** kept from general knowledge **—se•cre•cy** \-krəsē\ *n* **—secret** *n* **—se•cre•tive** \'sēkrətiv, si'krēt-\ *adj* **—se•cret•ly** *adv*
sec•re•tar•i•at \,sekrə'terēət\ *n* **:** administrative department
sec•re•tary \'sekrə,terē\ *n, pl* **-tar•ies 1 :** one hired to handle correspondence and other tasks for a superior **2 :** official in charge of correspondence or records **3 :** head of a government department **—sec•re•tari•al** \,sekrə'terēəl\ *adj*
[1]**se•crete** \si'krēt\ *vb* **-cret•ed; -cret•ing :** produce as a secretion
[2]**se•crete** \si'krēt, 'sēkrət\ *vb* **-cret•ed; -cret•ing :** hide
se•cre•tion \si'krēshən\ *n* **1 :** process of secreting **2 :** product of glandular activity
sect \'sekt\ *n* **:** religious group
sec•tar•i•an \sek'terēən\ *adj* **1 :** relating to a sect **2 :** limited in character or scope ~ *n* **:** member of a sect
sec•tion \'sekshən\ *n* **:** distinct part **—sec•tion•al** \-shənəl\ *adj*
sec•tor \'sektər\ *n* **1 :** part of a circle between 2 radii **2 :** distinctive part
sec•u•lar \'sekyələr\ *adj* **1 :** not sacred **2 :** not monastic
se•cure \si'kyủr\ *adj* **-cur•er; -est :** free from danger or loss ~ *vb* **1 :** fasten safely **2 :** get **—se•cure•ly** *adv*
se•cu•ri•ty \si'kyủrətē\ *n, pl* **-ties 1 :** safety **2 :** something given to guarantee payment **3** *pl* **:** bond or stock certificates
se•dan \si'dan\ *n* **1 :** chair carried by 2 men **2 :** enclosed automobile
[1]**se•date** \si'dāt\ *adj* **:** quiet and dignified **—se•date•ly** *adv*
[2]**sedate** *vb* **-dat•ed; -dat•ing :** dose with sedatives **—se•da•tion** \si'dāshən\ *n*
sed•a•tive \'sedətiv\ *adj* **:** serving to relieve tension ~ *n* **:** sedative drug
sed•en•tary \'sedᵊn,terē\ *adj* **:** characterized by much sitting
sedge \'sej\ *n* **:** grasslike marsh plant
sed•i•ment \'sedəmənt\ *n* **:** material that settles to the bottom of a liquid or is deposited by water or a glacier **—sed•i•men•ta•ry** \,sedə'mentərē\ *adj* **—sed•i•men•ta•tion** \-mən'tāshən, -,men-\ *n*
se•di•tion \si'dishən\ *n* **:** revolution against a government **—se•di•tious** \-əs\ *adj*
se•duce \si'düs, -'dyüs\ *vb* **-duced; -duc•ing 1 :** lead astray **2 :** entice to sexual intercourse **—se•duc•er** *n* **—se•duc•tion** \-'dəkshən\ *n* **—se•duc•tive** \-tiv\ *adj*
sed•u•lous \'sejələs\ *adj* **:** diligent
[1]**see** \'sē\ *vb* **saw** \'sȯ\; **seen** \'sēn\; **see•ing 1 :** perceive by the eye **2 :** have experience of **3 :** understand **4 :** make sure **5 :** meet with or escort
[2]**see** *n* **:** jurisdiction of a bishop
seed \'sēd\ *n, pl* **seed** *or* **seeds 1 :** part by which a plant is propagated **2 :** source ~ *vb* **1 :** sow **2 :** remove seeds from **—seed•less** *adj*
seed•ling \-liŋ\ *n* **:** young plant grown from seed
seedy \-ē\ *adj* **seed•i•er; -est 1 :** full of seeds **2 :** shabby
seek \'sēk\ *vb* **sought** \'sȯt\; **seek•ing 1 :** search for **2 :** try to reach or obtain **—seek•er** *n*
seem \'sēm\ *vb* **:** give the impression of being **—seem•ing•ly** *adv*
seem•ly \-lē\ *adj* **seem•li•er; -est :** proper or fit
seep \'sēp\ *vb* **:** leak through fine pores or cracks **—seep•age** \'sēpij\ *n*
seer \'sēər\ *n* **:** one who foresees or predicts events
seer•suck•er \'sir,səkər\ *n* **:** light puckered fabric
see•saw \'sē,sȯ\ *n* **:** board balanced in the middle **—seesaw** *vb*
seethe \'sēth\ *vb* **seethed; seeth•ing :** become violently agitated
seg•ment \'segmənt\ *n* **:** division of a thing **—seg•ment•ed** \-,mentəd\ *adj*
seg•re•gate \'segri,gāt\ *vb* **-gat•ed; -gat•ing 1 :** cut off from others **2 :** separate by races **—seg•re•ga•tion** \,segri'gāshən\ *n*
seine \'sān\ *n* **:** large weighted fishing net ~ *vb* **:** fish with a seine
seis•mic \'sīzmik, 'sīs-\ *adj* **:** relating to an earthquake
seis•mo•graph \-mə,graf\ *n* **:** apparatus for detecting earthquakes
seize \'sēz\ *vb* **seized; seiz•ing :** take by force **—sei•zure** \'sēzhər\ *n*
sel•dom \'seldəm\ *adv* **:** not often
se•lect \sə'lekt\ *adj* **1 :** favored **2 :** discriminating ~ *vb* **:** take by preference **—se•lec•tive** \-'lektiv\ *adj*
se•lec•tion \sə'lekshən\ *n* **:** act of selecting or thing selected
se•lect•man \si'lekt,man, -mən\ *n* **:** New England town official
self \'self\ *n, pl* **selves** \'selvz\ **:** essential person distinct from others
self- *comb form* **1 :** oneself or itself **2 :** of oneself or itself **3 :** by oneself or automatic **4 :** to, for, or toward oneself

self-addressed
self-administered
self-analysis
self-appointed
self-assertive
self-assurance
self-assured
self-awareness
self-cleaning
self-closing
self-complacent
self-conceit
self-confessed
self-confidence
self-confident
self-contained
self-contempt
self-contradiction
self-contradictory
self-control
self-created
self-criticism
self-defeating
self-defense
self-denial
self-denying
self-destruction
self-destructive
self-determination
self-determined
self-discipline
self-doubt
self-educated
self-employed
self-employment
self-esteem
self-evident
self-explanatory
self-expression
self-fulfilling
self-fulfillment
self-governing
self-government
self-help
self-image
self-importance
self-important
self-imposed
self-improvement
self-indulgence
self-indulgent
self-inflicted
self-interest
self-love
self-operating
self-pity
self-portrait
self-possessed
self-possession
self-preservation
self-proclaimed
self-propelled
self-propelling
self-protection
self-reliance
self-reliant
self-respect
self-respecting
self-restraint
self-sacrifice
self-satisfaction
self-satisfied
self-service
self-serving
self-starting
self-styled
self-sufficiency
self-sufficient
self-supporting
self-taught
self-winding

self–cen•tered *adj* **:** concerned only with one's own self
self–con•scious *adj* **:** uncomfortably aware of oneself as an object of observation **—self–con•scious•ly** *adv* **—self–con•scious•ness** *n*
self•ish \'selfish\ *adj* **:** excessively or exclusively concerned with one's own well-being **—self•ish•ly** *adv* **—self•ish•ness** *n*
self•less \'selfləs\ *adj* **:** unselfish **—self•less•ness** *n*
self–made *adj* **:** having succeeded by one's own efforts
self–righ•teous *adj* **:** strongly convinced of one's own righteousness
self•same \'self,sām\ *adj* **:** precisely the same
sell \'sel\ *vb* **sold** \'sōld\; **sell•ing 1 :** transfer (property) esp. for money **2 :** deal in as a business **3 :** be sold **—sell•er** *n*
selves *pl of* SELF
se•man•tic \si'mantik\ *adj* **:** relating to meaning in language **—se•man•tics** \-iks\ *n sing or pl*
sem•a•phore \'semə,fōr\ *n* **1 :** visual signaling apparatus **2 :** signaling by flags
sem•blance \'sembləns\ *n* **:** appearance
se•men \'sēmən\ *n* **:** male reproductive fluid
se•mes•ter \sə'mestər\ *n* **:** half a school year
semi- \,semi, 'sem-, -,ī\ *prefix* **1 :** half **2 :** partial
semi•co•lon \'semi,kōlən\ *n* **:** punctuation mark ;
semi•con•duc•tor *n* **:** substance between a conductor and a nonconductor in ability to conduct electricity **—semi•con•duct•ing** *adj*
semi•fi•nal *adj* **:** being next to the final **—semifinal** *n*
semi•for•mal *adj* **:** being or suitable for an occasion of moderate formality
sem•i•nal \'semənᵊl\ *adj* **1 :** relating to seed or semen **2 :** causing or influencing later development
sem•i•nar \'semə,när\ *n* **:** conference or conferencelike study
sem•i•nary \'semə,nerē\ *n, pl* **-nar•ies :** school and esp. a theological school **—sem•i•nar•i•an** \,semə'nerēən\ *n*
sen•ate \'senət\ *n* **:** upper branch of a legislature **—sen•a•tor** \-ər\ *n* **—sen•a•to•rial** \,senə'tōrēəl\ *adj*
send \'send\ *vb* **sent** \'sent\; **send•ing 1 :** cause to go **2 :** propel **—send•er** *n*
se•nile \'sēn,īl, 'sen-\ *adj* **:** mentally deficient through old age **—se•nil•i•ty** \si'nilətē\ *n*
se•nior \'sēnyər\ *adj* **:** older or higher ranking **—senior** *n* **—se•nior•i•ty** \,sēn'yȯrətē\ *n*
senior chief petty officer *n* **:** petty officer in the navy or coast guard ranking next below a master chief petty officer
senior master sergeant *n* **:** noncommissioned officer in the air force ranking next below a chief master sergeant
sen•sa•tion \sen'sāshən\ *n* **1 :** bodily feeling **2 :** condition of excitement or the cause of it **—sen•sa•tion•al** \-shənəl\ *adj*
sense \'sens\ *n* **1 :** meaning **2 :** faculty of perceiving something physical **3 :** sound mental capacity ~ *vb* **sensed; sens•ing 1 :** perceive by the senses **2 :** detect automatically **—sense•less** *adj* **—sense•less•ly** *adv*
sen•si•bil•i•ty \,sensə'bilətē\ *n, pl* **-ties :** delicacy of feeling
sen•si•ble \'sensəbəl\ *adj* **1 :** capable of sensing or being sensed **2 :** aware or conscious **3 :** reasonable **—sen•si•bly** \-blē\ *adv*
sen•si•tive \'sensətiv\ *adj* **1 :** subject to excitation by or responsive to stimuli **2 :** having power of feeling **3 :** easily affected **—sen•si•tive•ness** *n* **—sen•si•tiv•i•ty** \,sensə'tivətē\ *n*
sen•si•tize \'sensə,tīz\ *vb* **-tized; -tiz•ing :** make or become sensitive
sen•sor \'sen,sȯr, -sər\ *n* **:** device that responds to a physical stimulus
sen•so•ry \'sensərē\ *adj* **:** relating to sensation or the senses
sen•su•al \'senchəwəl, -shəwəl\ *adj* **1 :** pleasing the senses **2 :** devoted to the pleasures of the senses **—sen•su•al•ist** *n* **—sen•su•al•i•ty** \,senchə'walətē\ *n* **—sen•su•al•ly** *adv*
sen•su•ous \'senchəwəs\ *adj* **:** having strong appeal to the senses
sent *past of* SEND
sen•tence \'sentᵊns, -ᵊnz\ *n* **1 :** judgment of a court **2 :** grammatically self-contained speech unit ~ *vb* **-tenced; -tenc•ing :** impose a sentence on
sen•ten•tious \sen'tenchəs\ *adj* **:** using pompous language
sen•tient \'senchēənt\ *adj* **:** capable of feeling
sen•ti•ment \'sentəmənt\ *n* **1 :** belief **2 :** feeling
sen•ti•men•tal \,sentə'mentᵊl\ *adj* **:** influenced by tender feelings **—sen•ti•men•tal•ism** *n* **—sen•ti•men•tal•ist** *n* **—sen•ti•men•tal•i•ty** \-,men'talətē, -mən-\ *n* **—sen•ti•men•tal•ize** \-'mentᵊl,īz\ *vb* **—sen•ti•men•tal•ly** *adv*
sen•ti•nel \'sentᵊnəl\ *n* **:** sentry
sen•try \'sentrē\ *n, pl* **-tries :** one who stands guard
se•pal \'sēpəl, 'sep-\ *n* **:** modified leaf in a flower calyx
sep•a•rate \'sepə,rāt\ *vb* **-rat•ed; -rat•ing 1 :** set or keep apart **2 :** become divided or detached ~ \'seprət, 'sepə-\ *adj* **1 :** not connected or shared **2 :** distinct from each other **—sep•a•ra•ble** \'sepərəbəl\ *adj* **—sep•a•rate•ly** *adv* **—sep•a•ra•tion** \,sepə'rāshən\ *n* **—sep•a•ra•tor** \'sepə,rātər\ *n*
se•pia \'sēpēə\ *n* **:** brownish gray
Sep•tem•ber \sep'tembər\ *n* **:** 9th month of the year having 30 days
sep•ul•chre, sep•ul•cher \'sepəlkər\ *n* **:** burial vault **—se•pul•chral** \sə'pəlkrəl\ *adj*
se•quel \'sēkwəl\ *n* **1 :** consequence or result **2 :** continuation of a story
se•quence \'sēkwəns\ *n* **:** continuous or connected series **—se•quen•tial** \si'kwenchəl\ *adj* **—se•quen•tial•ly** *adv*
se•ques•ter \si'kwestər\ *vb* **:** segregate
se•quin \'sēkwən\ *n* **:** spangle
se•quoia \si'kwȯiə\ *n* **:** huge California coniferous tree
sera *pl of* SERUM
ser•aph \'serəf\ *n, pl* **-a•phim** \-ə,fim\ *or* **-aphs :** angel **—se•raph•ic** \sə'rafik\ *adj*
sere \'sir\ *adj* **:** dried up or withered
ser•e•nade \,serə'nād\ *n* **:** music sung or played esp. to a woman being courted **—serenade** *vb*
ser•en•dip•i•ty \,serən'dipətē\ *n* **:** good luck in finding things not sought for **—ser•en•dip•i•tous** \-əs\ *adj*
se•rene \sə'rēn\ *adj* **:** tranquil **—se•rene•ly** *adv* **—se•ren•i•ty** \sə'renətē\ *n*
serf \'sərf\ *n* **:** peasant obligated to work the land **—serf•dom** \-dəm\ *n*
serge \'sərj\ *n* **:** twilled woolen cloth
ser•geant \'särjənt\ *n* **:** noncommissioned officer (as in the army) ranking next below a staff sergeant
sergeant first class *n* **:** noncommissioned officer in the army ranking next below a master sergeant
sergeant major *n, pl* **sergeants major** *or* **sergeant majors 1 :** noncommissioned officer serving as an enlisted adviser in a headquarters **2 :** noncommissioned officer in the marine corps ranking above a first sergeant
se•ri•al \'sirēəl\ *adj* **:** being or relating to a series or sequence ~ *n* **:** story appearing in parts **—se•ri•al•ly** *adv*

se•ries \ˈsirēz\ *n, pl* **series** : number of things in order
se•ri•ous \ˈsirēəs\ *adj* **1** : subdued in appearance or manner **2** : sincere **3** : of great importance —**se•ri•ous•ly** *adv* —**se•ri•ous•ness** *n*
ser•mon \ˈsərmən\ *n* : lecture on religion or behavior
ser•pent \ˈsərpənt\ *n* : snake —**ser•pen•tine** \-pənˌtēn, -ˌtīn\ *adj*
ser•rat•ed \ˈserˌātəd\ *adj* : saw-toothed
se•rum \ˈsirəm\ *n, pl* **-rums** *or* **-ra** \-ə\ : watery part of blood
ser•vant \ˈsərvənt\ *n* : person employed for domestic work
serve \ˈsərv\ *vb* **served; serv•ing 1** : work through or perform a term of service **2** : be of use **3** : prove adequate **4** : hand out (food or drink) **5** : be of service to —**serv•er** *n*
ser•vice \ˈsərvəs\ *n* **1** : act or means of serving **2** : meeting for worship **3** : branch of public employment or the persons in it **4** : set of dishes or silverware **5** : benefit ~ *vb* **-viced; -vic•ing** : repair —**ser•vice•able** *adj* —**ser•vice•man** \-ˌman, -mən\ *n* —**ser•vice•wom•an** *n*
ser•vile \ˈsərvəl, -ˌvīl\ *adj* : behaving like a slave —**ser•vil•i•ty** \ˌsərˈvilətē\ *n*
serv•ing \ˈsərviŋ\ *n* : helping
ser•vi•tude \ˈsərvəˌtüd, -ˌtyüd\ *n* : slavery
ses•a•me \ˈsesəmē\ *n* : annual herb or its seeds that are used in flavoring
ses•sion \ˈseshən\ *n* : meeting
set \ˈset\ *vb* **set; set•ting 1** : cause to sit **2** : place **3** : settle, arrange, or adjust **4** : cause to be or do **5** : become fixed or solid **6** : sink below the horizon ~ *adj* : settled ~ *n* **1** : group classed together **2** : setting for the scene of a play or film **3** : electronic apparatus **4** : collection of mathematical elements —**set forth** : begin a trip —**set off** *vb* : set forth —**set out** *vb* : begin a trip or undertaking —**set up** *vb* **1** : assemble or erect **2** : cause
set•back *n* : reverse
set•tee \seˈtē\ *n* : bench or sofa
set•ter \ˈsetər\ *n* : large long-coated hunting dog
set•ting \ˈsetiŋ\ *n* : the time, place, and circumstances in which something occurs
set•tle \ˈsetᵊl\ *vb* **-tled; -tling 1** : come to rest **2** : sink gradually **3** : establish in residence **4** : adjust or arrange **5** : calm **6** : dispose of (as by paying) **7** : decide or agree on —**set•tle•ment** \-mənt\ *n* —**set•tler** \ˈsetᵊlər\ *n*
sev•en \ˈsevən\ *n* : one more than 6 —**seven** *adj or pron* —**sev•enth** \-ənth\ *adj or adv or n*
sev•en•teen \ˌsevənˈtēn\ *n* : one more than 16 —**seventeen** *adj or pron* —**sev•en•teenth** \-ˈtēnth\ *adj or n*
sev•en•ty \ˈsevəntē\ *n, pl* **-ties** : 7 times 10 —**sev•en•ti•eth** \-tēəth\ *adj or n* —**seventy** *adj or pron*
sev•er \ˈsevər\ *vb* **-ered; -er•ing** : cut off or apart —**sev•er•ance** \ˈsevrəns, -vərəns\ *n*
sev•er•al \ˈsevrəl, ˈsevə-\ *adj* **1** : distinct **2** : consisting of an indefinite but not large number —**sev•er•al•ly** *adv*
se•vere \səˈvir\ *adj* **-ver•er; -est 1** : strict **2** : restrained or unadorned **3** : painful or distressing **4** : hard to endure —**se•vere•ly** *adv* —**se•ver•i•ty** \-ˈverətē\ *n*
sew \ˈsō\ *vb* **sewed; sewn** \ˈsōn\ *or* **sewed; sew•ing** : join or fasten by stitches —**sew•ing** *n*
sew•age \ˈsüij\ *n* : liquid household waste
[1]**sew•er** \ˈsōər\ *n* : one that sews
[2]**sew•er** \ˈsüər\ *n* : pipe or channel to carry off waste matter
sex \ˈseks\ *n* **1** : either of 2 divisions into which organisms are grouped according to their reproductive roles or the qualities which differentiate them **2** : copulation —**sexed** \ˈsekst\ *adj* —**sex•less** *adj* —**sex•u•al** \ˈsekshəwəl\ *adj* —**sex•u•al•i•ty** \ˌsekshəˈwalətē\ *n* —**sex•u•al•ly** *adv* —**sexy** *adj*
sex•ism \ˈsekˌsizəm\ *n* : discrimination based on sex and esp. against women —**sex•ist** \ˈseksist\ *adj or n*
sex•tant \ˈsekstənt\ *n* : instrument for navigation
sex•tet \sekˈstet\ *n* **1** : music for 6 performers **2** : group of 6
sex•ton \ˈsekstən\ *n* : church caretaker
shab•by \ˈshabē\ *adj* **-bi•er; -est 1** : worn and faded **2** : dressed in worn clothes **3** : not generous or fair —**shab•bi•ly** *adv* —**shab•bi•ness** *n*
shack \ˈshak\ *n* : hut
shack•le \ˈshakəl\ *n* : metal device to bind legs or arms ~ *vb* **-led; -ling** : bind or fasten with shackles
shad \ˈshad\ *n* : Atlantic food fish
shade \ˈshād\ *n* **1** : space sheltered from the light esp. of the sun **2** : gradation of color **3** : small difference **4** : something that shades ~ *vb* **shad•ed; shad•ing 1** : shelter from light and heat **2** : add shades of color to **3** : show slight differences esp. in color or meaning
shad•ow \ˈshadō\ *n* **1** : shade cast upon a surface by something blocking light **2** : trace **3** : gloomy influence ~ *vb* **1** : cast a shadow **2** : follow closely —**shad•owy** *adj*
shady \ˈshādē\ *adj* **shad•i•er; -est 1** : giving shade **2** : of dubious honesty
shaft \ˈshaft\ *n* **1** : long slender cylindrical part **2** : deep vertical opening (as of a mine)
shag \ˈshag\ *n* : shaggy tangled mat
shag•gy \ˈshagē\ *adj* **-gi•er; -est 1** : covered with long hair or wool **2** : not neat and combed
shake \ˈshāk\ *vb* **shook** \ˈshu̇k\; **shak•en** \ˈshākən\; **shak•ing 1** : move or cause to move quickly back and forth **2** : distress **3** : clasp (hands) as friendly gesture —**shake** *n* —**shak•er** \-ər\ *n*
shake–up *n* : reorganization
shaky \ˈshākē\ *adj* **shak•i•er; -est** : not sound, stable, or reliable —**shak•i•ly** *adv* —**shak•i•ness** *n*
shale \ˈshāl\ *n* : stratified rock
shall \ˈshal\ *vb, past* **should** \ˈshu̇d\; *pres sing & pl* **shall** —used as an auxiliary to express a command, futurity, or determination
shal•low \ˈshalō\ *adj* **1** : not deep **2** : not intellectually profound
shal•lows \-ōz\ *n pl* : area of shallow water
sham \ˈsham\ *adj or n or vb* : fake
sham•ble \ˈshambəl\ *vb* **-bled; -bling** : shuffle along —**sham•ble** *n*
sham•bles \ˈshambəlz\ *n* : state of disorder
shame \ˈshām\ *n* **1** : distress over guilt or disgrace **2** : cause of shame or regret ~ *vb* **shamed; sham•ing 1** : make ashamed **2** : disgrace —**shame•ful** \-fəl\ *adj* —**shame•ful•ly** \-ē\ *adv* —**shame•less** *adj* —**shame•less•ly** *adv*
shame•faced \ˈshāmˈfāst\ *adj* : ashamed
sham•poo \shamˈpü\ *vb* : wash one's hair ~ *n, pl* **-poos** : act of or preparation used in shampooing
sham•rock \ˈshamˌräk\ *n* : plant of legend with 3-lobed leaves
shank \ˈshaŋk\ *n* : part of the leg between the knee and ankle
shan•ty \ˈshantē\ *n, pl* **-ties** : hut
shape \ˈshāp\ *vb* **shaped; shap•ing** : form esp. in a particular structure or appearance ~ *n* **1** : distinctive appearance or arrangement of parts **2** : condition —**shape•less** \-ləs\ *adj* —**shape•li•ness** *n* —**shape•ly** *adj*
shard \ˈshärd\ *n* : broken piece
share \ˈsher\ *n* **1** : portion belonging to one **2** : interest in a company's stock ~ *vb* **shared; shar•ing** : divide or use with others —**share•hold•er** *n* —**shar•er** *n*
share•crop•per \-ˌkräpər\ *n* : farmer who works another's land in return for a share of the crop —**share•crop** *vb*
shark \ˈshärk\ *n* : voracious sea fish
sharp \ˈshärp\ *adj* **1** : having a good point or cutting edge **2** : alert, clever, or sarcastic **3** : vigorous or fierce **4** : having prominent angles or a sudden change in direction **5** : distinct **6** : higher than the true pitch ~ *adv* : exactly ~ *n* : sharp note —**sharp•ly** *adv* —**sharp•ness** *n*
sharp•en \ˈshärpən\ *vb* : make sharp —**sharp•en•er** \-ənər\ *n*
sharp•shoot•er *n* : expert marksman —**sharp•shoot•ing** *n*
shat•ter \ˈshatər\ *vb* : smash or burst into fragments —**shat•ter•proof** \-ˌprüf\ *adj*
shave \ˈshāv\ *vb* **shaved; shaved** *or* **shav•en** \ˈshāvən\; **shav•ing 1** : cut off with a razor **2** : make bare by cutting the hair from **3** : slice very thin ~ *n* : act or instance of shaving —**shav•er** *n*
shawl \ˈshȯl\ *n* : loose covering for the head or shoulders
she \ˈshē\ *pron* : that female one
sheaf \ˈshēf\ *n, pl* **sheaves** \ˈshēvz\ : bundle esp. of grain stalks
shear \ˈshir\ *vb* **sheared; sheared** *or* **shorn** \ˈshōrn\; **shear•ing 1** : trim wool from **2** : cut off with scissorlike action
shears \ˈshirz\ *n pl* : cutting tool with 2 blades fastened so that the edges slide by each other
sheath \ˈshēth\ *n, pl* **sheaths** \ˈshēt͟hz, ˈshēths\ : covering (as for a blade)
sheathe \ˈshēt͟h\ *vb* **sheathed; sheath•ing** : put into a sheath
shed \ˈshed\ *vb* **shed; shed•ding 1** : give off (as tears or hair) **2** : cause to flow or diffuse ~ *n* : small storage building
sheen \ˈshēn\ *n* : subdued luster
sheep \ˈshēp\ *n, pl* **sheep** : domesticated mammal covered with wool —**sheep•skin** *n*
sheep•ish \ˈshēpish\ *adj* : embarrassed by awareness of a fault
sheer \ˈshir\ *adj* **1** : pure **2** : very steep **3** : very thin or transparent —**sheer** *adv*
sheet \ˈshēt\ *n* : broad flat piece (as of cloth or paper)
sheikh, sheik \ˈshēk, ˈshāk\ *n* : Arab chief —**sheikh•dom, sheik•dom** \-dəm\ *n*
shelf \ˈshelf\ *n, pl* **shelves** \ˈshelvz\ **1** : flat narrow structure used for storage or display **2** : sandbank or rock ledge
shell \ˈshel\ *n* **1** : hard or tough outer covering **2** : case holding explosive powder and projectile for a weapon **3** : light racing boat with oars ~ *vb* **1** : remove the shell of **2** : bombard —**shelled** \ˈsheld\ *adj* —**shell•er** *n*
shel•lac \shəˈlak\ *n* : varnish ~ *vb* **-lacked; -lack•ing 1** : coat with shellac **2** : defeat —**shel•lack•ing** *n*
shell•fish *n* : water animal with a shell
shel•ter \ˈsheltər\ *n* : something that gives protection ~ *vb* : give refuge to
shelve \ˈshelv\ *vb* **shelved; shelv•ing 1** : place or store on shelves **2** : dismiss or put aside
she•nan•i•gans \shəˈnanigənz\ *n pl* : mischievous or deceitful conduct
shep•herd \ˈshepərd\ *n* : one that tends sheep ~ *vb* : act as a shepherd or guardian
shep•herd•ess \ˈshepərdəs\ *n* : woman who tends sheep
sher•bet \ˈshərbət\, **sher•bert** \-bərt\ *n* : fruit-flavored frozen dessert
sher•iff \ˈsherəf\ *n* : county law officer
sher•ry \ˈsherē\ *n, pl* **-ries** : type of wine
shield \ˈshēld\ *n* **1** : broad piece of armor carried on the arm **2** : something that protects —**shield** *vb*
shier *comparative of* SHY
shiest *superlative of* SHY
shift \ˈshift\ *vb* **1** : change place, position, or direction **2** : get by ~ *n* **1** : loose-fitting dress **2** : an act or instance of shifting **3** : scheduled work period
shift•less \-ləs\ *adj* : lazy
shifty \ˈshiftē\ *adj* **shift•i•er; -est** : tricky or untrustworthy
shil•le•lagh \shəˈlālē\ *n* : club or stick
shil•ling \ˈshiliŋ\ *n* : former British coin
shilly–shally \ˈshilēˌshalē\ *vb* **–shall•ied; –shally•ing 1** : hesitate **2** : dawdle
shim•mer \ˈshimər\ *vb or n* : glimmer
shin \ˈshin\ *n* : front part of the leg below the knee ~ *vb* **-nn-** : climb by sliding the body close along
shine \ˈshīn\ *vb* **shone** \-shōn\ *or* **shined; shin•ing 1** : give off or cause to give off light **2** : be outstanding **3** : polish ~ *n* : brilliance
shin•gle \ˈshiŋgəl\ *n* **1** : small thin piece used in covering roofs or exterior walls —**shingle** *vb*
shin•gles \ˈshiŋgəlz\ *n pl* : acute inflammation of spinal nerves
shin•ny \ˈshinē\ *vb* **-nied; -ny•ing** : shin
shiny \ˈshīnē\ *adj* **shin•i•er; -est** : bright or polished
ship \ˈship\ *n* **1** : large oceangoing vessel **2** : aircraft or spacecraft ~ *vb* **-pp- 1** : put on a ship **2** : transport by carrier —**ship•board** *n* —**ship•build•er** *n* —**ship•per** *n* —**ship•wreck** *n or vb* —**ship•yard** *n*
-ship \ˌship\ *n suffix* **1** : state, condition, or quality **2** : rank or profession **3** : skill **4** : something showing a state or quality
ship•ment \-mənt\ *n* : an act of shipping or the goods shipped
ship•ping \ˈshipiŋ\ *n* **1** : ships **2** : transportation of goods
ship•shape *adj* : tidy
shire \ˈshīr, *in place-name compounds* ˌshir, shər\ *n* : British county
shirk \ˈshərk\ *vb* : evade —**shirk•er** *n*
shirr \ˈshər\ *vb* **1** : gather (cloth) by drawing up parallel lines of stitches **2** : bake (eggs) in a dish
shirt \ˈshərt\ *n* : garment for covering the torso —**shirt•less** *adj*
shiv•er \ˈshivər\ *vb* : tremble —**shiver** *n* —**shiv•ery** *adj*
shoal \ˈshōl\ *n* : shallow place (as in a river)
[1]**shock** \ˈshäk\ *n* : pile of sheaves set up in a field
[2]**shock** *n* **1** : forceful impact **2** : violent mental or emotional disturbance **3** : effect of a charge of electricity **4** : depression of the vital bodily processes ~ *vb* **1** : strike with surprise, horror, or disgust **2** : subject to an electrical shock —**shock•proof** *adj*
[3]**shock** *n* : bushy mass (as of hair)
shod•dy \ˈshädē\ *adj* **-di•er; -est** : poorly made or done —**shod•di•ly** \ˈshädᵊlē\ *adv* —**shod•di•ness** *n*
shoe \ˈshü\ *n* **1** : covering for the human foot **2** : horseshoe ~ *vb* **shod** \ˈshäd\; **shoe•ing** : put horseshoes on —**shoe•lace** *n* —**shoe•ma•ker** *n*
shone *past of* SHINE
shook *past of* SHAKE
shoot \ˈshüt\ *vb* **shot** \ˈshät\; **shoot•ing 1** : propel (as an arrow or bullet) **2** : wound or kill with a missile **3** : discharge (a weapon) **4** : drive (as a ball) at a goal **5** : photograph **6** : move swiftly ~ *n* : new plant growth —**shoot•er** *n*
shop \ˈshäp\ *n* : place where things are made or sold ~ *vb* **-pp-** : visit stores —**shop•keep•er** *n* —**shop•per** *n*
shop•lift *vb* : steal goods from a store —**shop•lift•er** \-ˌliftər\ *n*
[1]**shore** \ˈshōr\ *n* : land along the edge of water —**shore•line** *n*
[2]**shore** *vb* **shored; shor•ing** : prop up ~ *n* : something that props
shore•bird *n* : bird of the seashore
shorn *past part of* SHEAR
short \ˈshȯrt\ *adj* **1** : not long or tall or extending far **2** : brief in time **3** : curt **4** : not having or being enough ~ *adv* : curtly ~ *n* **1** *pl* : short drawers or trousers **2** : short circuit —**short•en** \-ᵊn\ *vb* —**short•ly** *adv* —**short•ness** *n*
short•age \ˈshȯrtij\ *n* : deficiency
short•cake *n* : dessert of biscuit with sweetened fruit
short•change *vb* : cheat esp. by giving too little change
short circuit *n* : abnormal electric connection —**short–circuit** *vb*
short•com•ing *n* : fault or failing
short•cut \-ˌkət\ *n* **1** : more direct route than that usu. taken **2** : quicker way of doing something
short•hand *n* : method of speed writing
short–lived \ˈshȯrtˈlīvd, -ˌlivd\ *adj* : of short life or duration
short•sight•ed *adj* : lacking foresight
shot \ˈshät\ *n* **1** : act of shooting **2** : attempt (as at making a goal) **3** : small pellets forming a charge **4** : range or reach **5** : photograph **6** : injection of medicine **7** : small serving of liquor —**shot•gun** *n*
should \ˈshu̇d\ *past of* SHALL —used as an auxiliary to express condition, obligation, or probability
shoul•der \ˈshōldər\ *n* **1** : part of the body where the arm joins the trunk **2** : part that projects or lies to the side ~ *vb* : push with or bear on the shoulder
shoulder blade *n* : flat triangular bone at the back of the shoulder
shout \ˈshau̇t\ *vb* : give voice loudly —**shout** *n*
shove \ˈshəv\ *vb* **shoved; shov•ing** : push along or away —**shove** *n*
shov•el \ˈshəvəl\ *n* : broad tool for digging or lifting ~ *vb* **-eled** *or* **-elled; -el•ing** *or* **-el•ling** : take up or dig with a shovel
show \ˈshō\ *vb* **showed** \ˈshōd\; **shown** \ˈshōn\ *or* **showed; show•ing 1** : present to view **2** : reveal or demonstrate **3** : teach **4** : prove **5** : conduct or escort **6** : appear or be noticeable ~ *n* **1** : demonstrative display **2** : spectacle **3** : theatrical, radio, or television program —**show•case** *n* —**show off** *vb* **1** : display proudly **2** : act so as to attract attention —**show up** *vb* : arrive
show•down *n* : decisive confrontation
show•er \ˈshau̇ər\ *n* **1** : brief fall of rain **2** : bath in which water sprinkles down on the person or a facility for such a bath **3** : party at which someone gets gifts ~ *vb* **1** : rain or fall in a shower **2** : bathe in a shower —**show•ery** *adj*
showy \ˈshōē\ *adj* **show•i•er; -est** : very noticeable or overly elaborate —**show•i•ly** *adv* —**show•i•ness** *n*
shrap•nel \ˈshrapnᵊl\ *n, pl* **shrapnel** : metal fragments of a bomb
shred \ˈshred\ *n* : narrow strip cut or torn off ~ *vb* **-dd-** : cut or tear into shreds
shrew \ˈshrü\ *n* **1** : scolding woman **2** : mouselike mammal —**shrew•ish** \-ish\ *adj*
shrewd \ˈshrüd\ *adj* : clever —**shrewd•ly** *adv* —**shrewd•ness** *n*
shriek \ˈshrēk\ *n* : shrill cry —**shriek** *vb*
shrill \ˈshril\ *adj* : piercing and high-pitched —**shril•ly** *adv*
shrimp \ˈshrimp\ *n* : small sea crustacean
shrine \ˈshrīn\ *n* **1** : tomb of a saint **2** : hallowed place
shrink \ˈshriŋk\ *vb* **shrank** \ˈshraŋk\; **shrunk** \ˈshrəŋk\ *or* **shrunk•en** \ˈshrəŋkən\; **shrink•ing 1** : draw back or away **2** : become smaller —**shrink•able** *adj*
shrink•age \ˈshriŋkij\ *n* : amount lost by shrinking
shriv•el \ˈshrivəl\ *vb* **-eled** *or* **-elled; -el•ing** *or* **-el•ling** : shrink or wither into wrinkles
shroud \ˈshrau̇d\ *n* **1** : cloth put over a corpse **2** : cover or screen ~ *vb* : veil or screen from view
shrub \ˈshrəb\ *n* : low woody plant —**shrub•by** *adj*
shrub•bery \ˈshrəbərē\ *n, pl* **-ber•ies** : growth of shrubs
shrug \ˈshrəg\ *vb* **-gg-** : hunch the shoulders up in doubt, indifference, or uncertainty —**shrug** *n*
shuck \ˈshək\ *vb* : strip of a shell or husk —**shuck** *n*
shud•der \ˈshədər\ *vb* : tremble —**shudder** *n*
shuf•fle \ˈshəfəl\ *vb* **-fled; -fling 1** : mix together **2** : walk with a sliding movement —**shuffle** *n*
shuf•fle•board \ˈshəfəlˌbōrd\ *n* : game of sliding disks into a scoring area
shun \ˈshən\ *vb* **-nn-** : keep away from
shunt \ˈshənt\ *vb* : turn off to one side
shut \ˈshət\ *vb* **shut; shut•ting 1** : bar passage into or through (as by moving a lid

or door) 2 : suspend activity —shut out *vb* : exclude —shut up *vb* : stop or cause to stop talking

shut–in *n* : invalid

shut·ter \'shətər\ *n* 1 : movable cover for a window 2 : camera part that exposes film

shut·tle \'shətᵊl\ *n* 1 : part of a weaving machine that carries thread back and forth 2 : vehicle traveling back and forth over a short route ~ *vb* -tled; -tling : move back and forth frequently

shut·tle·cock \'shətᵊl,käk\ *n* : light conical object used in badminton

shy \'shī\ *adj* shi·er *or* shy·er \'shīər\; shi·est *or* shy·est \'shīəst\ 1 : sensitive and hesitant in dealing with others 2 : wary 3 : lacking ~ *vb* shied; shy·ing : draw back (as in fright) —shy·ly *adv* —shy·ness *n*

sib·i·lant \'sibələnt\ *adj* : having the sound of the *s* or the *sh* in *sash* —sibilant *n*

sib·ling \'sibliŋ\ *n* : brother or sister

sick \'sik\ *adj* 1 : not in good health 2 : nauseated 3 : relating to or meant for the sick —sick·bed *n* —sick·en \-ən\ *vb* —sick·ly *adj* —sick·ness *n*

sick·le \'sikəl\ *n* : curved short-handled blade

side \'sīd\ *n* 1 : part to left or right of an object or the torso 2 : edge or surface away from the center or at an angle to top and bottom or ends 3 : contrasting or opposing position or group —sid·ed *adj*

side·board *n* : piece of dining-room furniture for table service

side·burns \-,bərnz\ *n pl* : whiskers in front of the ears

side·long \'sīd,lȯŋ\ *adv or adj* : to or along the side

side·show *n* : minor show at a circus

side·step *vb* 1 : step aside 2 : avoid

side·swipe \-,swīp\ *vb* : strike with a glancing blow —sideswipe *n*

side·track *vb* : lead aside or astray

side·walk *n* : paved walk at the side of a road

side·ways \-,wāz\ *adv or adj* 1 : to or from the side 2 : with one side to the front

sid·ing \'sīdiŋ\ *n* 1 : short railroad track 2 : material for covering the outside of a building

si·dle \'sīdᵊl\ *vb* -dled; -dling : move sideways or unobtrusively

siege \'sēj\ *n* : persistent attack (as on a fortified place)

si·es·ta \sē'estə\ *n* : midday nap

sieve \'siv\ *n* : utensil with holes to separate particles

sift \'sift\ *vb* 1 : pass through a sieve 2 : examine carefully —sift·er *n*

sigh \'sī\ *n* : audible release of the breath (as to express weariness) —sigh *vb*

sight \'sīt\ *n* 1 : something seen or worth seeing 2 : process, power, or range of seeing 3 : device used in aiming 4 : view or glimpse ~ *vb* : get sight of —sight·ed *adj* —sight·less *adj* —sight–see·ing *adj* —sight·seer \-,sēər\ *n*

sign \'sīn\ *n* 1 : symbol 2 : gesture expressing a command or thought 3 : public notice to advertise or warn 4 : trace ~ *vb* 1 : mark with or make a sign 2 : write one's name on —sign·er *n*

sig·nal \'signᵊl\ *n* 1 : sign of command or warning 2 : electronic transmission ~ *vb* -naled *or* -nalled; -nal·ing *or* -nal·ling : communicate or notify by signals ~ *adj* : distinguished

sig·na·to·ry \'signə,tōrē\ *n, pl* -ries : person or government that signs jointly with others

sig·na·ture \'signə,chu̇r\ *n* : one's name written by oneself

sig·net \'signət\ *n* : small seal

sig·nif·i·cance \sig'nifikəns\ *n* 1 : meaning 2 : importance —sig·nif·i·cant \-kənt\ *adj* —sig·nif·i·cant·ly *adv*

sig·ni·fy \'signə,fī\ *vb* -fied; -fy·ing 1 : show by a sign 2 : mean —sig·ni·fi·ca·tion \,signəfə'kāshən\ *n*

si·lence \'sīləns\ *n* : state of being without sound ~ *vb* -lenced; -lenc·ing : keep from making noise or sound —si·lenc·er *n*

si·lent \'sīlənt\ *adj* : having or producing no sound —si·lent·ly *adv*

sil·hou·ette \,silə'wet\ *n* : outline filled in usu. with black ~ *vb* -ett·ed; -ett·ing : represent by a silhouette

sil·i·ca \'silikə\ *n* : mineral found as quartz and opal

sil·i·con \'silikən, -,kän\ *n* : nonmetallic chemical element

silk \'silk\ *n* 1 : fine strong lustrous protein fiber from moth larvae (silk·worms \-,wərmz\) 2 : thread or cloth made from silk —silk·en \'silkən\ *adj* —silky *adj*

sill \'sil\ *n* : bottom part of a window frame or a doorway

sil·ly \'silē\ *adj* sil·li·er; -est : foolish or stupid —sil·li·ness *n*

si·lo \'sīlō\ *n, pl* -los : tall building for storing animal feed

silt \'silt\ *n* : fine earth carried by rivers ~ *vb* : obstruct or cover with silt

sil·ver \'silvər\ *n* 1 : white ductile metallic chemical element 2 : silverware ~ *adj* : having the color of silver —sil·very *adj*

sil·ver·ware \-,war\ *n* : eating and serving utensils esp. of silver

sim·i·lar \'simələr\ *adj* : resembling each other in some ways —sim·i·lar·i·ty \,simə'larətē\ *n* —sim·i·lar·ly \'simələrlē\ *adv*

sim·i·le \'simə,lē\ *n* : comparison of unlike things using *like* or *as*

sim·mer \'simər\ *vb* : stew gently

sim·per \'simpər\ *vb* : give a silly smile —simper *n*

sim·ple \'simpəl\ *adj* -pler; -plest 1 : free from dishonesty, vanity, or pretense 2 : of humble origin or modest position 3 : not complex 4 : lacking education, experience, or intelligence —sim·ple·ness *n* —sim·ply \-plē\ *adv*

sim·ple·ton \'simpəltən\ *n* : fool

sim·plic·i·ty \sim'plisətē\ *n* : state or fact of being simple

sim·pli·fy \'simplə,fī\ *vb* -fied; -fy·ing : make easier —sim·pli·fi·ca·tion \,simpləfə'kāshən\ *n*

sim·u·late \'simyə,lāt\ *vb* -lat·ed; -lat·ing : create the effect or appearance of —sim·u·la·tion \,simyə'lāshən\ *n* —sim·u·la·tor \'simyə,lātər\ *n*

si·mul·ta·ne·ous \,sīməl'tānēəs\ *adj* : occurring or operating at the same time —si·mul·ta·ne·ous·ly *adv* —si·mul·ta·ne·ous·ness *n*

sin \'sin\ *n* : offense against God ~ *vb* -nn- : commit a sin —sin·ful \-fəl\ *adj* —sin·less *adj* —sin·ner *n*

since \'sins\ *adv* 1 : from a past time until now 2 : backward in time ~ *prep* 1 : in the period after 2 : continuously from ~ *conj* 1 : from the time when 2 : because

sin·cere \sin'sir\ *adj* -cer·er; -cer·est : genuine or honest —sin·cere·ly *adv* —sin·cer·i·ty \-'serətē\ *n*

si·ne·cure \'sīni,kyu̇r, 'sini-\ *n* : well-paid job that requires little work

sin·ew \'sinyü\ *n* 1 : tendon 2 : physical strength —sin·ewy *adj*

sing \'siŋ\ *vb* sang \'saŋ\ *or* sung \'səŋ\; sung; sing·ing : produce musical tones with the voice —sing·er *n*

singe \'sinj\ *vb* singed; singe·ing : scorch lightly

sin·gle \'siŋgəl\ *adj* 1 : one only 2 : unmarried ~ *n* : separate one —single·ness *n* —sin·gly \-glē\ *adv* —single out *vb* : select or set aside

sin·gu·lar \'siŋgyələr\ *adj* 1 : relating to a word form denoting one 2 : outstanding or superior 3 : queer —singular *n* —sin·gu·lar·i·ty \,siŋgyə'larətē\ *n* —sin·gu·lar·ly \'siŋgyələrlē\ *adv*

sin·is·ter \'sinəstər\ *adj* : threatening evil

sink \'siŋk\ *vb* sank \'saŋk\ *or* sunk \'səŋk\; sunk; sink·ing 1 : submerge or descend 2 : grow worse 3 : make by digging or boring 4 : invest ~ *n* : basin with a drain

sink·er \'siŋkər\ *n* : weight to sink a fishing line

sin·u·ous \'sinyəwəs\ *adj* : winding in and out —sin·u·os·i·ty \,sinyə'wäsətē\ *n* —sin·u·ous·ly *adv*

si·nus \'sīnəs\ *n* : skull cavity usu. connecting with the nostrils

sip \'sip\ *vb* -pp- : drink in small quantities —sip *n*

si·phon \'sīfən\ *n* : tube that draws liquid by suction —siphon *vb*

sir \'sər\ *n* 1 —used before the first name of a knight or baronet 2 —used as a respectful form of address

sire \'sīr\ *n* : father ~ *vb* sired; sir·ing : beget

si·ren \'sīrən\ *n* 1 : seductive woman 2 : wailing warning whistle

sir·loin \'sər,lȯin\ *n* : cut of beef

sirup *var of* SYRUP

si·sal \'sīsəl, -zəl\ *n* : strong rope fiber

sis·sy \'sisē\ *n, pl* -sies : timid or effeminate boy

sis·ter \'sistər\ *n* : female sharing one or both parents with another person —sis·ter·hood \-,hu̇d\ *n* —sis·ter·ly *adj*

sis·ter–in–law *n, pl* sis·ters–in–law : sister of one's spouse or wife of one's brother

sit \'sit\ *vb* sat \'sat\; sit·ting 1 : rest on the buttocks or haunches 2 : roost 3 : hold a session 4 : pose for a portrait 5 : have a location 6 : rest or fix in place —sit·ter *n*

site \'sīt\ *n* : place

sit·u·at·ed \'sichə,wātəd\ *adj* : located

sit·u·a·tion \,sichə'wāshən\ *n* 1 : location 2 : condition 3 : job

six \'siks\ *n* : one more than 5 —six *adj or pron* —sixth \'siksth\ *adj or adv or n*

six·teen \siks'tēn\ *n* : one more than 15 —sixteen *adj or pron* —six·teenth \-'tēnth\ *adj or n*

six·ty \'sikstē\ *n, pl* -ties : 6 times 10 —six·ti·eth \-əth\ *adj or n* —sixty *adj or pron*

siz·able, size·able \'sīzəbəl\ *adj* : quite large —siz·ably \-blē\ *adv*

size \'sīz\ *n* : measurement of the amount of space something takes up ~ *vb* : grade according to size

siz·zle \'sizəl\ *vb* -zled; -zling : fry with a hissing sound —sizzle *n*

skate \'skāt\ *n* 1 : metal runner on a shoe for gliding over ice 2 : roller skate —skate *vb* —skat·er *n*

skein \'skān\ *n* : loosely twisted quantity of yarn or thread

skel·e·ton \'skelətᵊn\ *n* : bony framework —skel·e·tal \-ətᵊl\ *adj*

skep·tic \'skeptik\ *n* : one who is critical or doubting —skep·ti·cal \-tikəl\ *adj* —skep·ti·cism \-tə,sizəm\ *n*

sketch \'skech\ *n* 1 : rough drawing 2 : short story or essay —sketch *vb* —sketchy *adj*

skew·er \'skyüər\ *n* : long pin for holding roasting meat —skewer *vb*

ski \'skē\ *n, pl* skis : long strip for gliding over snow or water —ski *vb* —ski·er *n*

skid \'skid\ *n* 1 : plank for supporting something or on which it slides 2 : act of skidding ~ *vb* -dd- : slide sideways

skiff \'skif\ *n* : small boat

skill \'skil\ *n* : developed or learned ability —skilled \'skild\ *adj* —skill·ful \-fəl\ *adj* —skill·ful·ly *adv*

skil·let \'skilət\ *n* : pan for frying

skim \'skim\ *vb* -mm- 1 : take off from the top of a liquid 2 : read or move over swiftly ~ *adj* : having the cream removed —skim·mer *n*

skimp \'skimp\ *vb* : give too little of something —skimpy *adj*

skin \'skin\ *n* 1 : outer layer of an animal body 2 : rind ~ *vb* -nn- : take the skin from —skin·less *adj* —skinned *adj* —skin·tight *adj*

skin diving *n* : sport of swimming under water with a face mask and flippers

skin·flint \'skin,flint\ *n* : stingy person

skin·ny \'skinē\ *adj* -ni·er; -est : very thin

skip \'skip\ *vb* -pp- 1 : move with leaps 2 : read past or ignore —skip *n*

skip·per \'skipər\ *n* : ship's master —skipper *vb*

skir·mish \'skərmish\ *n* : minor combat —skirmish *vb*

skirt \'skərt\ *n* : garment or part of a garment that hangs below the waist ~ *vb* : pass around the edge of

skit \'skit\ *n* : brief usu. humorous play

skit·tish \'skitish\ *adj* : easily frightened

skulk \'skəlk\ *vb* : move furtively

skull \'skəl\ *n* : bony case that protects the brain

skunk \'skəŋk\ *n* : mammal that can forcibly eject an ill-smelling fluid

sky \'skī\ *n, pl* skies 1 : upper air 2 : heaven —sky·line *n* —sky·ward \-wərd\ *adv or adj*

sky·lark \'skī,lärk\ *n* : European lark noted for its song

sky·light *n* : window in a roof or ceiling

sky·rock·et *n* : shooting firework ~ *vb* : rise suddenly

sky·scrap·er \-,skrāpər\ *n* : very tall building

slab \'slab\ *n* : thick slice

slack \'slak\ *adj* 1 : careless 2 : not taut 3 : not busy ~ *n* 1 : part hanging loose 2 *pl* : casual trousers —slack·en *vb* —slack·ly *adv* —slack·ness *n*

slag \'slag\ *n* : waste from melting of ores

slain *past part of* SLAY

slake \'slāk\ *vb* slaked; slak·ing : quench

slam \'slam\ *n* : heavy jarring impact ~ *vb* -mm- : shut, strike, or throw violently and loudly

slan·der \'slandər\ *n* : malicious gossip ~ *vb* : hurt (someone) with slander —slan·der·er *n* —slan·der·ous *adj*

slang \'slaŋ\ *n* : informal nonstandard vocabulary —slangy *adj*

slant \'slant\ *vb* 1 : slope 2 : present with a special viewpoint ~ *n* : sloping direction, line, or plane

slap \'slap\ *vb* -pp- : strike sharply with the open hand —slap *n*

slash \'slash\ *vb* 1 : cut with sweeping strokes 2 : reduce sharply ~ *n* : gash

slat \'slat\ *n* : thin narrow flat strip

slate \'slāt\ *n* 1 : dense fine-grained layered rock 2 : roofing tile or writing tablet of slate 3 : list of candidates ~ *vb* slat·ed; slat·ing : designate

slat·tern \'slatərn \ *n* : untidy woman —slat·tern·ly *adj*

slaugh·ter \'slȯtər\ *n* 1 : butchering of livestock for market 2 : great and cruel destruction of lives ~ *vb* : commit slaughter upon —slaugh·ter·house *n*

slave \'slāv\ *n* : one owned and forced into service by another ~ *vb* slaved; slav·ing : work as or like a slave —slave *adj* —slav·ery \'slāvərē\ *n*

sla·ver \'slavər, 'slāv-\ *vb or n* : slobber

slav·ish \'slāvish\ *adj* : of or like a slave —slav·ish·ly *adv*

slay \'slā\ *vb* slew \'slü\; slain \'slān\; slay·ing : kill —slay·er *n*

slea·zy \'slēzē, 'slā-\ *adj* -zi·er; -est : shabby or shoddy

sled \'sled\ *n* : vehicle on runners —sled *vb*

[1]sledge \'slej\ *n* : sledgehammer

[2]sledge *n* : heavy sled

sledge·ham·mer *n* : heavy long-handled hammer —sledgehammer *adj or vb*

sleek \'slēk\ *adj* : smooth or glossy —sleek *vb*

sleep \'slēp\ *n* : natural suspension of consciousness ~ *vb* slept \'slept\; sleep·ing : rest in a state of sleep —sleep·er *n* —sleep·less *adj* —sleep·walk·er *n*

sleepy \'slēpē\ *adj* sleep·i·er; -est 1 : ready for sleep 2 : quietly inactive —sleep·i·ly \'slēpəlē\ *adv* —sleep·i·ness \-pēnəs\ *n*

sleet \'slēt\ *n* : frozen rain —sleet *vb* —sleety *adj*

sleeve \'slēv\ *n* : part of a garment for the arm —sleeve·less *adj*

sleigh \'slā\ *n* : horse-drawn sled with seats ~ *vb* : drive or ride in a sleigh

sleight of hand \'slīt-\ : skillful manual manipulation or a trick requiring it

slen·der \'slendər\ *adj* 1 : thin esp. in physique 2 : scanty

sleuth \'slüth\ *n* : detective

slew \'slü\ *past of* SLAY

slice \'slīs\ *n* : thin flat piece ~ *vb* sliced; slic·ing : cut a slice from

slick \'slik\ *adj* 1 : very smooth 2 : clever —slick *vb*

slick·er \'slikər\ *n* : raincoat

slide \'slīd\ *vb* slid \'slid\; slid·ing \'slīdiŋ\ : move smoothly along a surface ~ *n* 1 : act of sliding 2 : surface on which something slides 3 : transparent picture for projection

slier *comparative of* SLY

sliest *superlative of* SLY

slight \'slīt\ *adj* 1 : slender 2 : frail 3 : small in degree ~ *vb* 1 : ignore or treat as unimportant —slight *n* —slight·ly *adv*

slim \'slim\ *adj* -mm- 1 : slender 2 : scanty ~ *vb* -mm- : make or become slender

slime \'slīm\ *n* : dirty slippery film (as on water) —slimy *adj*

sling \'sliŋ\ *vb* slung \'sləŋ\; sling·ing : hurl with or as if with a sling ~ *n* 1 : strap for swinging and hurling stones 2 : looped strap or bandage to lift or support

sling·shot *n* : forked stick with elastic bands for shooting pebbles

slink \'sliŋk\ *vb* slunk \'sləŋk\; slink·ing : move stealthily or sinuously —slinky *adj*

[1]slip \'slip\ *vb* -pp- 1 : escape quietly or secretly 2 : slide along smoothly 3 : make a mistake 4 : to pass without being noticed or done 5 : fall off from a standard ~ *n* 1 : ship's berth 2 : sudden mishap 3 : mistake 4 : woman's undergarment

[2]slip *n* 1 : plant shoot 2 : small strip (as of paper)

slip·per \'slipər\ *n* : shoe that slips on easily

slip·pery \'slipərē\ *adj* -peri·er; -est 1 : slick enough to slide on 2 : tricky —slip·peri·ness *n*

slip·shod \'slip,shäd\ *adj* : careless

slit \'slit\ *vb* slit; slit·ting : make a slit in ~ *n* : long narrow cut

slith·er \'slithər\ *vb* : glide along like a snake —slith·ery *adj*

sliv·er \'slivər\ *n* : splinter

slob \'släb\ *n* : untidy person

slob·ber \'släbər\ *vb* : dribble saliva —slobber *n*

slo·gan \'slōgən\ *n* : word or phrase expressing the aim of a cause

sloop \'slüp\ *n* : one-masted sailboat

slop \'släp\ *n* : food waste for animal feed ~ *vb* -pp- : spill

slope \'slōp\ *vb* sloped; slop·ing : deviate from the vertical or horizontal ~ *n* : upward or downward slant

slop·py \'släpē\ *adj* -pi·er; -est 1 : muddy 2 : untidy

slot \'slät\ *n* : narrow opening

sloth \'slȯth, 'slōth\ *n, pl* sloths *with* ths *or* thz\ 1 : laziness 2 : slow-moving mammal —sloth·ful *adj*

slouch \'slau̇ch\ *n* 1 : drooping posture 2 : lazy or incompetent person ~ *vb* : walk or stand with a slouch

[1]slough \'slü, 'slau̇\ *n* : swamp

[2]slough \'sləf\, **sluff** *vb* : cast off (old skin)

slov·en·ly \'sləvənlē\ *adj* : untidy

slow \'slō\ *adj* 1 : sluggish or stupid 2 : moving, working, or happening at less than the usual speed ~ *vb* 1 : make slow 2 : go slower —slow *adv* —slow·ly *adv* —slow·ness *n*

sludge \'sləj\ *n* : slushy mass (as of treated sewage)

slug \'sləg\ *n* 1 : mollusk related to the snails 2 : bullet 3 : metal disk ~ *vb* -gg- : strike forcibly —slug·ger *n*

slug·gish \'sləgish\ *adj* : slow in movement or flow —slug·gish·ly *adv* —slug·gish·ness *n*

sluice \'slüs\ *n* : channel for water ~ *vb* sluiced; sluic·ing : wash in running water

slum \'sləm\ *n* : thickly populated area marked by poverty

slum·ber \'sləmbər\ *vb or n* : sleep

slump \'sləmp\ *vb* 1 : sink suddenly 2 : slouch —slump *n*

slung *past of* SLING
slunk *past of* SLINK
1slur \ˈslər\ *vb* **-rr-** : run (words or notes) together **—slur** *n*
2slur *n* : malicious or insulting remark
slurp \ˈslərp\ *vb* : eat or drink noisily **—slurp** *n*
slush \ˈsləsh\ *n* : partly melted snow **—slushy** *adj*
slut \ˈslət\ *n* **1** : untidy woman **2** : lewd woman **—slut•tish** *adj*
sly \ˈslī\ *adj* **sli•er** \ˈslīər\; **sli•est** \ˈslīəst\ : given to or showing secrecy and deception **—sly•ly** *adv* **—sly•ness** *n*
1smack \ˈsmak\ *n* : characteristic flavor ~ *vb* : have a taste or hint
2smack *vb* **1** : move (the lips) so as to make a sharp noise **2** : kiss or slap with a loud noise ~ *n* **1** : sharp noise made by the lips **2** : noisy slap
3smack *adv* : squarely and sharply
4smack *n* : fishing boat
small \ˈsmȯl\ *adj* **1** : little in size or amount **2** : few in number **3** : trivial **—small•ish** *adj* **—small•ness** *n*
small•pox \ˈsmȯlˌpäks\ *n* : contagious virus disease
smart \ˈsmärt\ *vb* **1** : cause or feel stinging pain **2** : endure distress ~ *adj* **1** : intelligent or resourceful **2** : stylish **—smart** *n* **—smart•ly** *adv* **—smart•ness** *n*
smash \ˈsmash\ *vb* : break or be broken into pieces ~ *n* **1** : smashing blow **2** : act or sound of smashing
smat•ter•ing \ˈsmatəriŋ\ *n* **1** : superficial knowledge **2** : small scattered number or amount
smear \ˈsmir\ *n* : greasy stain ~ *vb* **1** : spread (something sticky) **2** : smudge **3** : slander
smell \ˈsmel\ *vb* **smelled** \ˈsmeld\ *or* **smelt** \ˈsmelt\; **smell•ing 1** : perceive the odor of **2** : have or give off an odor ~ *n* **1** : sense by which one perceives odor **2** : odor **—smelly** *adj*
1smelt \ˈsmelt\ *n, pl* **smelts** *or* **smelt** : small food fish
2smelt *vb* : melt or fuse (ore) in order to separate the metal **—smelt•er** *n*
smile \ˈsmīl\ *n* : facial expression with the mouth turned up usu. to show pleasure **—smile** *vb*
smirk \ˈsmərk\ *vb* : wear a conceited smile **—smirk** *n*
smite \ˈsmīt\ *vb* **smote** \ˈsmōt\; **smit•ten** \ˈsmitᵊn\ *or* **smote; smit•ing** \ˈsmītiŋ\ **1** : strike heavily or kill **2** : affect strongly
smith \ˈsmith\ *n* : worker in metals and esp. a blacksmith
smithy \ˈsmithē\ *n, pl* **smith•ies** : a smith's workshop
smock \ˈsmäk\ *n* : loose dress or protective coat
smog \ˈsmäg, ˈsmȯg\ *n* : fog and smoke **—smog•gy** *adj*
smoke \ˈsmōk\ *n* : sooty gas from burning ~ *vb* **smoked; smok•ing 1** : give off smoke **2** : inhale the fumes of burning tobacco **3** : cure (as meat) with smoke **—smoke•less** *adj* **—smok•er** *n* **—smoky** *adj*
smoke•stack *n* : chimney through which smoke is discharged
smol•der, smoul•der \ˈsmōldər\ *vb* **1** : burn and smoke without flame **2** : be suppressed but active **—smolder** *n*
smooth \ˈsmüth\ *adj* **1** : having a surface without irregularities **2** : not jarring or jolting ~ *vb* : make smooth **—smooth•ly** *adv* **—smooth•ness** *n*
smor•gas•bord \ˈsmȯrgəsˌbōrd\ *n* : buffet consisting of many foods
smoth•er \ˈsməthər\ *vb* **1** : kill by depriving of air **2** : cover thickly
smudge \ˈsməj\ *vb* **smudged; smudg•ing** : soil or blur by rubbing ~ *n* **1** : thick smoke **2** : dirty spot
smug \ˈsməg\ *adj* **-gg-** : content in one's own virtue or accomplishment **—smug•ly** *adv* **—smug•ness** *n*
smug•gle \ˈsməgəl\ *vb* **-gled; -gling** : import or export secretly or illegally **—smug•gler** \ˈsməglər\ *n*
smut \ˈsmət\ *n* **1** : something that soils **2** : indecent language or matter **3** : disease of plants caused by fungi **—smut•ty** *adj*
snack \ˈsnak\ *n* : light meal
snag \ˈsnag\ *n* : unexpected difficulty ~ *vb* **-gg-** : become caught on something that sticks out
snail \ˈsnāl\ *n* : small mollusk with a spiral shell
snake \ˈsnāk\ *n* : long-bodied limbless reptile **—snake•bite** *n*
snap \ˈsnap\ *vb* **-pp- 1** : bite at something **2** : utter angry words **3** : break suddenly with a sharp sound ~ *n* **1** : act or sound of snapping **2** : fastening that closes with a click **3** : something easy to do **—snap•per** *n* **—snap•pish** *adj* **—snap•py** *adj*
snap•drag•on *n* : garden plant with spikes of showy flowers
snap•shot \ˈsnapˌshät\ *n* : casual photograph
snare \ˈsnar\ *n* : trap for catching game ~ *vb* : capture or hold with or as if with a snare
1snarl \ˈsnärl\ *n* : tangle ~ *vb* : cause to become knotted
2snarl *vb or n* : growl
snatch \ˈsnach\ *vb* **1** : try to grab something suddenly **2** : seize or take away suddenly ~ *n* **1** : act of snatching **2** : something brief or fragmentary
sneak \ˈsnēk\ *vb* : move or take in a furtive manner ~ *n* : one who acts in a furtive manner **—sneak•i•ly** \ˈsnēkəlē\ *adv* **—sneak•ing•ly** *adv* **—sneaky** *adj*
sneak•er \ˈsnēkər\ *n* : sports shoe
sneer \ˈsnir\ *vb* : smile scornfully **—sneer** *n*
sneeze \ˈsnēz\ *vb* **sneezed; sneez•ing** : force the breath out with sudden and involuntary violence **—sneeze** *n*
snick•er \ˈsnikər\ *n* : partly suppressed laugh **—snicker** *vb*
snide \ˈsnīd\ *adj* : subtly ridiculing
sniff \ˈsnif\ *vb* **1** : draw air audibly up the nose **2** : detect by smelling **—sniff** *n*
snip \ˈsnip\ *n* : fragment snipped off ~ *vb* **-pp-** : cut off by bits
1snipe \ˈsnīp\ *n, pl* **snipes** *or* **snipe** : game bird of marshy areas
2snipe *vb* **sniped; snip•ing** : shoot at an enemy from a concealed position **—snip•er** *n*
snips \ˈsnips\ *n pl* : scissorslike tool
sniv•el \ˈsnivəl\ *vb* **-eled** *or* **-elled; -el•ing** *or* **-el•ling 1** : have a running nose **2** : whine
snob \ˈsnäb\ *n* : one who acts superior to others **—snob•bery** \-ərē\ *n* **—snob•bish** *adj* **—snob•bish•ly** *adv* **—snob•bish•ness** *n*
snoop \ˈsnüp\ *vb* : pry in a furtive way ~ *n* : prying person
snooze \ˈsnüz\ *vb* **snoozed; snooz•ing** : take a nap **—snooze** *n*
snore \ˈsnōr\ *vb* **snored; snor•ing** : breathe with a hoarse noise while sleeping **—snore** *n*
snort \ˈsnȯrt\ *vb* : force air noisily through the nose **—snort** *n*
snout \ˈsnaůt\ *n* : long projecting muzzle (as of a swine)
snow \ˈsnō\ *n* : crystals formed from water vapor ~ *vb* : fall as snow **—snow•ball** *n* **—snow•bank** *n* **—snow•drift** *n* **—snow•fall** *n* **—snow•plow** *n* **—snow•storm** *n* **—snowy** *adj*
snow•shoe *n* : frame of wood strung with thongs for walking on snow
snub \ˈsnəb\ *vb* **-bb-** : ignore or avoid through disdain **—snub** *n*
1snuff \ˈsnəf\ *vb* : put out (a candle) **—snuff•er** *n*
2snuff *vb* : draw forcibly into the nose ~ *n* : pulverized tobacco
snug \ˈsnəg\ *adj* **-gg- 1** : warm, secure, and comfortable **2** : fitting closely **—snug•ly** *adv* **—snug•ness** *n*
snug•gle \ˈsnəgəl\ *vb* **-gled; -gling** : curl up comfortably
so \ˈsō\ *adv* **1** : in the manner or to the extent indicated **2** : in the same way **3** : therefore **4** : finally **5** : thus ~ *conj* : for that reason
soak \ˈsōk\ *vb* **1** : lie in a liquid **2** : absorb ~ *n* : act of soaking
soap \ˈsōp\ *n* : cleaning substance **—soap** *vb* **—soapy** *adj*
soar \ˈsōr\ *vb* : fly upward on or as if on wings
sob \ˈsäb\ *vb* **-bb-** : weep with convulsive heavings of the chest **—sob** *n*
so•ber \ˈsōbər\ *adj* **1** : not drunk **2** : serious or solemn **—so•ber•ly** *adv*
so•bri•ety \səˈbrīətē, sō-\ *n* : quality or state of being sober
soc•cer \ˈsäkər\ *n* : game played by kicking a ball
so•cia•ble \ˈsōshəbəl\ *adj* : friendly **—so•cia•bil•i•ty** \ˌsōshəˈbilətē\ *n* **—so•cia•bly** \ˈsōshəblē\ *adv*
so•cial \ˈsōshəl\ *adj* **1** : relating to pleasant companionship **2** : naturally living or growing in groups **3** : relating to human society ~ *n* : social gathering **—so•cial•ly** *adv*
so•cial•ism \ˈsōshəˌlizəm\ *n* : social system based on government control of the production and distribution of goods **—so•cial•ist** \ˈsōshəlist\ *n or adj* **—so•cial•is•tic** \ˌsōshəˈlistik\ *adj*
so•cial•ize \ˈsōshəˌlīz\ *vb* **-ized; -iz•ing 1** : regulate by socialism **2** : adapt to social needs **3** : participate in a social gathering **—so•cial•i•za•tion** \ˌsōshələˈzāshən\ *n*
social work *n* : services concerned with aiding the poor and socially maladjusted **—social worker** *n*
so•ci•ety \səˈsīətē\ *n, pl* **-et•ies 1** : companionship **2** : community life **3** : rich or fashionable class **4** : voluntary group
so•ci•ol•o•gy \ˌsōsēˈäləjē\ *n* : study of social relationships **—so•ci•o•log•i•cal** \-əˈläjikəl\ *adj* **—so•ci•ol•o•gist** \-ˈäləjist\ *n*
1sock \ˈsäk\ *n, pl* **socks** *or* **sox** : short stocking
2sock *vb or n* : punch
sock•et \ˈsäkət\ *n* : hollow part that holds something
sod \ˈsäd\ *n* : turf ~ *vb* **-dd-** : cover with sod
so•da \ˈsōdə\ *n* **1** : carbonated water or a soft drink **2** : ice cream drink made with soda
sod•den \ˈsädᵊn\ *adj* **1** : lacking spirit **2** : soaked or soggy
so•di•um \ˈsōdēəm\ *n* : soft waxy silver white metallic chemical element
so•fa \ˈsōfə\ *n* : wide padded chair
soft \ˈsȯft\ *adj* **1** : not hard, rough, or harsh **2** : nonalcoholic **—soft•en** \ˈsȯfən\ *vb* **—soft•en•er** \-ənər\ *n* **—soft•ly** *adv* **—soft•ness** *n*
soft•ball *n* : game like baseball
soft•ware \ˈsȯftˌwar\ *n* : computer programs
sog•gy \ˈsägē\ *adj* **-gi•er; -est** : heavy with moisture **—sog•gi•ness** \-ēnəs\ *n*
1soil \ˈsȯil\ *vb* : make or become dirty ~ *n* : embedded dirt
2soil *n* : loose surface material of the earth
so•journ \ˈsōˌjərn, sōˈjərn\ *n* : temporary stay ~ *vb* : reside temporarily
so•lace \ˈsäləs\ *n or vb* : comfort
so•lar \ˈsōlər\ *adj* : relating to the sun or the energy in sunlight
sold *past of* SELL
sol•der \ˈsädər, ˈsȯd-\ *n* : metallic alloy melted to join metallic surfaces ~ *vb* : cement with solder
sol•dier \ˈsōljər\ *n* : person in military service ~ *vb* : serve as a soldier **—sol•dier•ly** *adj or adv*
1sole \ˈsōl\ *n* : bottom of the foot or a shoe **—soled** *adj*
2sole *n* : flatfish caught for food
3sole *adj* : single or only **—sole•ly** *adv*
sol•emn \ˈsäləm\ *adj* **1** : dignified and ceremonial **2** : highly serious **—so•lem•ni•ty** \səˈlemnətē\ *n* **—sol•emn•ly** *adv*
so•lic•it \səˈlisət\ *vb* : ask for **—so•lic•i•ta•tion** \-ˌlisəˈtāshən\ *n*
so•lic•i•tor \səˈlisətər\ *n* **1** : one that solicits **2** : lawyer
so•lic•i•tous \səˈlisətəs\ *adj* : showing or expressing concern **—so•lic•i•tous•ly** *adv* **—so•lic•i•tude** \səˈlisəˌtüd, -ˌtyüd\ *n*
sol•id \ˈsäləd\ *adj* **1** : not hollow **2** : having 3 dimensions **3** : hard **4** : of good quality **5** : of one character ~ *n* **1** : 3-dimensional figure **2** : substance in solid form **—solid** *adv* **—so•lid•i•ty** \səˈlidətē\ *n* **—sol•id•ly** *adv* **—sol•id•ness** *n*
sol•i•dar•i•ty \ˌsäləˈdarətē\ *n* : unity of purpose
so•lid•i•fy \səˈlidəˌfī\ *vb* **-fied; -fy•ing** : make or become solid **—so•lid•i•fi•ca•tion** \-ˌlidəfəˈkāshən\ *n*
so•lil•o•quy \səˈliləkwē\ *n, pl* **-quies** : dramatic monologue **—so•lil•o•quize** \-ˌkwīz\ *vb*
sol•i•taire \ˈsäləˌtar\ *n* **1** : solitary gem **2** : card game for one person
sol•i•tary \-ˌterē\ *adj* **1** : alone **2** : secluded **3** : single
sol•i•tude \-ˌtüd, -ˌtyüd\ *n* : state of being alone
so•lo \ˈsōlō\ *n, pl* **-los** : performance by only one person ~ *adv* : alone **—solo** *adj or vb* **—so•lo•ist** *n*
sol•stice \ˈsälstəs\ *n* : time of the year when the sun is farthest north or south of the equator
sol•u•ble \ˈsälyəbəl\ *adj* **1** : capable of being dissolved **2** : capable of being solved **—sol•u•bil•i•ty** \ˌsälyəˈbilətē\ *n*
so•lu•tion \səˈlüshən\ *n* **1** : answer to a problem **2** : homogeneous liquid mixture
solve \ˈsälv\ *vb* **solved; solv•ing** : find a solution for **—solv•able** *adj*
sol•vent \ˈsälvənt\ *adj* **1** : able to pay all debts **2** : dissolving or able to dissolve ~ *n* : substance that dissolves or disperses another substance **—sol•ven•cy** \-vənsē\ *n*
som•ber, som•bre \ˈsämbər\ *adj* **1** : dark **2** : grave **—som•ber•ly** *adv*
som•bre•ro \səmˈbrerō\ *n, pl* **-ros** : broad-brimmed hat
some \ˈsəm\ *adj* **1** : one unspecified **2** : unspecified or indefinite number of **3** : at least a few or a little ~ *pron* : a certain number or amount
-some \səm\ *adj suffix* : characterized by a thing, quality, state, or action
some•body \ˈsəmbədē, -ˌbäd-\ *pron* : some person
some•day \ˈsəmˌdā\ *adv* : at some future time
some•how \-ˌhaů\ *adv* : by some means
some•one \-ˌwən\ *pron* : some person
som•er•sault \ˈsəmərˌsȯlt\ *n* : body flip **—somersault** *vb*
some•thing \ˈsəmthiŋ\ *pron* : some undetermined or unspecified thing
some•time \ˈsəmˌtīm\ *adv* : at a future, unknown, or unnamed time
some•times \-ˌtīmz\ *adv* : occasionally
some•what \-ˌhwət, -ˌhwät\ *adv* : in some degree
some•where \-ˌhwer\ *adv* : in, at, or to an unknown or unnamed place
som•no•lent \ˈsämnələnt\ *adj* : sleepy **—som•no•lence** \-ləns\ *n*
son \ˈsən\ *n* : male offspring
so•nar \ˈsōˌnär\ *n* : device that detects and locates underwater objects using sound waves
so•na•ta \səˈnätə\ *n* : instrumental composition
song \ˈsȯŋ\ *n* : music and words to be sung
song•bird *n* : bird with musical tones
son•ic \ˈsänik\ *adj* : relating to sound waves or the speed of sound
son–in–law *n, pl* **sons–in–law** : husband of one's daughter
son•net \ˈsänət\ *n* : poem of 14 lines
so•no•rous \səˈnōrəs, ˈsänərəs\ *adj* **1** : loud, deep, or rich in sound **2** : impressive **—so•nor•i•ty** \səˈnȯrətē\ *n*
soon \ˈsün\ *adv* **1** : before long **2** : promptly **3** : early
soot \ˈsůt, ˈsət, ˈsüt\ *n* : fine black substance formed by combustion **—sooty** *adj*
soothe \ˈsüth\ *vb* **soothed; sooth•ing** : calm or comfort **—sooth•er** *n*
sooth•say•er \ˈsüthˌsāər\ *n* : prophet **—sooth•say•ing** \-iŋ\ *n*
sop \ˈsäp\ *n* : conciliatory bribe, gift, or concession ~ *vb* **-pp- 1** : dip in a liquid **2** : soak **3** : mop up
so•phis•ti•cat•ed \səˈfistəˌkātəd\ *adj* **1** : complex **2** : wise, cultured, or shrewd in human affairs **—so•phis•ti•ca•tion** \-ˌfistəˈkāshən\ *n*
soph•ist•ry \ˈsäfəstrē\ *n* : subtly fallacious reasoning or argument **—soph•ist** \ˈsäfist\ *n*
soph•o•more \ˈsäfᵊmˌōr, ˈsäfˌmōr\ *n* : 2d-year student
so•po•rif•ic \ˌsäpəˈrifik, ˌsōp-\ *adj* : causing sleep or drowsiness
so•pra•no \səˈpranō\ *n, pl* **-nos** : highest singing voice
sor•cery \ˈsȯrsərē\ *n* : witchcraft **—sor•cer•er** \-rər\ *n* **—sor•cer•ess** \-rəs\ *n*
sor•did \ˈsȯrdəd\ *adj* : filthy or vile **—sor•did•ly** *adv* **—sor•did•ness** *n*
sore \ˈsōr\ *adj* **sor•er; sor•est 1** : causing pain or distress **2** : severe or intense **3** : angry ~ *n* : sore usu. infected spot on the body **—sore•ly** *adv* **—sore•ness** *n*
sor•ghum \ˈsȯrgəm\ *n* : forage grass
so•ror•i•ty \səˈrȯrətē\ *n, pl* **-ties** : women's student social group
1sor•rel \ˈsȯrəl\ *n* : brownish orange to light brown color or an animal of this color
2sorrel *n* : herb with sour juice
sor•row \ˈsärō\ *n* : deep distress, sadness, or regret or a cause of this **—sor•row•ful** \-fəl\ *adj* **—sor•row•ful•ly** *adv*
sor•ry \ˈsärē\ *adj* **-ri•er; -est 1** : feeling sorrow, regret, or penitence **2** : dismal
sort \ˈsȯrt\ *n* **1** : kind **2** : nature ~ *vb* : classify **—out of sorts** : grouchy
sor•tie \ˈsȯrtē, sȯrˈtē\ *n* : military attack esp. against besiegers
SOS \ˌesˌōˈes\ *n* : call for help
so–so \ˈsōˈsō\ *adj or adv* : barely acceptable
sot \ˈsät\ *n* : drunkard **—sot•tish** *adj*
souf•flé \süˈflā\ *n* : baked dish made light with beaten egg whites
sought *past of* SEEK
soul \ˈsōl\ *n* **1** : immaterial essence of an individual life **2** : essential part **3** : person
soul•ful \ˈsōlfəl\ *adj* : full of or expressing deep feeling **—soul•ful•ly** *adv*
1sound \ˈsaůnd\ *adj* **1** : free from fault, error, or illness **2** : firm or hard **3** : showing good judgment **—sound•ly** *adv* **—sound•ness** *n*
2sound *n* **1** : sensation of hearing **2** : energy of vibration sensed in hearing **3** : something heard ~ *vb* **1** : make or cause to make a sound **2** : seem **—sound•less** *adj* **—sound•less•ly** *adv* **—sound•proof** *adj or vb*
3sound *n* : wide strait ~ *vb* **1** : measure the depth of (water) **2** : investigate
soup \ˈsüp\ *n* : broth usu. containing pieces of solid food **—soupy** *adj*
sour \ˈsaůər\ *adj* **1** : having an acid or tart taste **2** : disagreeable ~ *vb* : become or make sour **—sour•ish** *adj* **—sour•ly** *adv* **—sour•ness** *n*
source \ˈsōrs\ *n* **1** : point of origin **2** : one that provides something needed
souse \ˈsaůs\ *vb* **soused; sous•ing 1** : pickle **2** : immerse **3** : intoxicate ~ *n* **1** : something pickled **2** : drunkard
south \ˈsaůth\ *adv* : to or toward the south ~ *adj* : situated toward, at, or coming from the south ~ *n* **1** : direction to the right of sunrise **2** *cap* : regions to the south **—south•er•ly** \ˈsəthərlē\ *adv or adj* **—south•ern** \ˈsəthərn\ *adj* **—South•ern•er** *n* **—south•ern•most** \-ˌmōst\ *adj* **—south•ward** \ˈsaůthwərd\ *adv or adj* **—south•wards** \-wərdz\ *adv*
south•east \saůthˈēst, *naut* saůˈēst\ *n* **1** : direction between south and east **2** *cap* : regions to the southeast **—southeast** *adj or adv* **—south•east•er•ly** *adv or adj* **—south•east•ern** \-ərn\ *adj*
south pole *n* : the southernmost point of the earth
south•west \saůthˈwest, *naut* saůˈwest\ *n* **1** : direction between south and west **2** *cap*

: regions to the southwest **—southwest** *adj or adv* **—south•west•er•ly** *adv or adj* **—south•west•ern** \-ərn\ *adj*

sou•ve•nir \ˈsüvəˌnir\ *n* : something that is a reminder of a place or event

sov•er•eign \ˈsävərən\ *n* **1** : supreme ruler **2** : gold coin of the United Kingdom ~ *adj* **1** : supreme **2** : independent **—sov•er•eign•ty** \-tē\ *n*

[1]sow \ˈsau̇\ *n* : female swine

[2]sow \ˈsō\ *vb* **sowed; sown** \ˈsōn\ *or* **sowed, sow•ing 1** : plant or strew with seed **2** : scatter abroad **—sow•er** \ˈsōər\ *n*

sox *pl of* SOCK

soy•bean \ˈsȯiˌbēn\ *n* : legume with edible seeds

spa \ˈspä\ *n* : resort at a mineral spring

space \ˈspās\ *n* **1** : period of time **2** : area in, around, or between **3** : region beyond earth's atmosphere **4** : accommodations ~ *vb* **spaced; spac•ing** : place at intervals **—space•craft** *n* **—space•flight** *n* **—space•man** *n* **—space•ship** *n*

spa•cious \ˈspāshəs\ *adj* : large or roomy **—spa•cious•ly** *adv* **—spa•cious•ness** *n*

[1]spade \ˈspād\ *n or vb* : shovel **—spade•ful** *n*

[2]spade *n* : playing card marked with a black figure like an inverted heart

spa•ghet•ti \spəˈgetē\ *n* : pasta strings

span \ˈspan\ *n* **1** : amount of time **2** : distance between supports ~ *vb* **-nn-** : extend across

span•gle \ˈspaŋgəl\ *n* : small disk of shining metal or plastic **—spangle** *vb*

span•iel \ˈspanyəl\ *n* : small or medium-sized dog with drooping ears and long wavy hair

spank \ˈspaŋk\ *vb* : hit on the buttocks with an open hand

[1]spar \ˈspär\ *n* : pole or boom

[2]spar *vb* **-rr-** : practice boxing

spare \ˈspar\ *adj* **1** : held in reserve **2** : thin or scanty ~ *vb* **spared; spar•ing 1** : reserve or avoid using **2** : avoid punishing or killing **—spare** *n*

spar•ing \ˈspariŋ\ *adj* : thrifty **—spar•ing•ly** *adv*

spark \ˈspärk\ *n* **1** : tiny hot and glowing particle **2** : smallest beginning or germ **3** : visible electrical discharge ~ *vb* **1** : emit or produce sparks **2** : stir to activity

spar•kle \ˈspärkəl\ *vb* **-kled; -kling 1** : flash **2** : effervesce ~ *n* : gleam **—spark•ler** \-klər\ *n*

spar•row \ˈsparō\ *n* : small singing bird

sparse \ˈspärs\ *adj* **spars•er; spars•est** : thinly scattered **—sparse•ly** *adv*

spasm \ˈspazəm\ *n* **1** : involuntary muscular contraction **2** : sudden, violent, and temporary effort or feeling **—spas•mod•ic** \spazˈmädik\ *adj* **—spas•mod•i•cal•ly** *adv*

spas•tic \ˈspastik\ *adj* : relating to, marked by, or affected with muscular spasm **—spastic** *n*

[1]spat \ˈspat\ *past of* SPIT

[2]spat *n* : petty dispute

spa•tial \ˈspāshəl\ *adj* : relating to space **—spa•tial•ly** *adv*

spat•ter \ˈspatər\ *vb* : splash with drops of liquid **—spatter** *n*

spat•u•la \ˈspachələ\ *n* : flexible knifelike utensil

spawn \ˈspȯn\ *vb* **1** : produce eggs or offspring **2** : bring forth ~ *n* : egg cluster **—spawn•er** *n*

spay \ˈspā\ *vb* : remove the ovaries of (a female)

speak \ˈspēk\ *vb* **spoke** \ˈspōk\; **spo•ken** \ˈspōkən\; **speak•ing 1** : utter words **2** : express orally **3** : address an audience **4** : use (a language) in talking **—speak•er** *n*

spear \ˈspir\ *n* : long pointed weapon ~ *vb* : strike or pierce with a spear

spear•head *n* : leading force, element, or influence **—spearhead** *vb*

spear•mint *n* : aromatic garden mint

spe•cial \ˈspeshəl\ *adj* **1** : unusual or unique **2** : particularly favored **3** : set aside for a particular use **—special** *n* **—spe•cial•ly** *adv*

spe•cial•ist \ˈspeshəlist\ *n* **1** : person who specializes in a particular branch of learning or activity **2** : any of four enlisted ranks in the army corresponding to the grades of corporal through sergeant first class

spe•cial•ize \ˈspeshəˌlīz\ *vb* **-ized; -iz•ing** : concentrate one's efforts **—spe•cial•i•za•tion** \ˌspeshələˈzāshən\ *n*

spe•cial•ty \ˈspeshəltē\ *n, pl* **-ties** : area or field in which one specializes

spe•cie \ˈspēshē, -sē\ *n* : money in coin

spe•cies \ˈspēshēz, -sēz\ *n, pl* **spe•cies** : biological grouping of closely related organisms

spe•cif•ic \spiˈsifik\ *adj* : definite or exact **—spe•cif•i•cal•ly** *adv*

spec•i•fi•ca•tion \ˌspesəfəˈkāshən\ *n* **1** : act or process of specifying **2** : detailed description of work to be done —usu. pl.

spec•i•fy \ˈspesəˌfī\ *vb* **-fied; -fy•ing** : mention precisely or by name

spec•i•men \-əmən\ *n* : typical example

spe•cious \ˈspēshəs\ *adj* : apparently but not really genuine or correct

speck \ˈspek\ *n* : tiny particle or blemish **—speck** *vb*

speck•led \ˈspekəld\ *adj* : marked with spots

spec•ta•cle \ˈspektikəl\ *n* **1** : impressive public display **2** *pl* : eyeglasses

spec•tac•u•lar \spekˈtakyələr\ *adj* : sensational or showy

spec•ta•tor \ˈspekˌtātər\ *n* : person who looks on

spec•ter, spec•tre \ˈspektər\ *n* **1** : ghost **2** : haunting vision

spec•tral \ˈspektrəl\ *adj* : relating to or resembling a specter or spectrum

spec•trum \ˈspektrəm\ *n, pl* **-tra** \-trə\ *or* **-trums** : series of colors formed when white light is dispersed into its components

spec•u•late \ˈspekyəˌlāt\ *vb* **-lat•ed; -lat•ing 1** : think about things yet unknown **2** : risk money in a business deal in hope of high profit **—spec•u•la•tion** \ˌspekyəˈlāshən\ *n* **—spec•u•la•tive** \ˈspekyəˌlātiv\ *adj* **—spec•u•la•tor** \-ˌlātər\ *n*

speech \ˈspēch\ *n* **1** : power, act, or manner of speaking **2** : talk given to an audience **—speech•less** *adj*

speed \ˈspēd\ *n* **1** : quality of being fast **2** : rate of motion or performance ~ *vb* **sped** \ˈsped\ *or* **speed•ed; speed•ing** : go at a great or excessive rate of speed **—speed•boat** *n* **—speed•er** *n* **—speed•i•ly** \ˈspēdᵊlē\ *adv* **—speed•up** \-ˌəp\ *n* **—speedy** *adj*

speed•om•e•ter \spiˈdämətər\ *n* : instrument for indicating speed

[1]spell \ˈspel\ *n* : influence of or like magic

[2]spell *vb* **1** : name, write, or print the letters of **2** : mean **—spell•er** *n*

[3]spell *vb* : substitute for or relieve (someone) ~ *n* **1** : turn at work **2** : period of time

spell•bound *adj* : held by a spell

spend \ˈspend\ *vb* **spent** \ˈspent\; **spend•ing 1** : pay out **2** : cause or allow to pass **—spend•er** *n*

spend•thrift \ˈspendˌthrift\ *n* : wasteful person

sperm \ˈspərm\ *n, pl* **sperm** *or* **sperms** : semen or a germ cell in it

spew \ˈspyü\ *vb* : gush out in a stream

sphere \ˈsfir\ *n* **1** : figure with every point on its surface at an equal distance from the center **2** : round body **3** : range of action or influence **—spher•i•cal** \ˈsfirikəl, ˈsfer-\ *adj*

spher•oid \ˈsfir-\ *n* : spherelike figure

spice \ˈspīs\ *n* **1** : aromatic plant product for seasoning food **2** : interesting quality **—spice** *vb* **—spicy** *adj*

spi•der \ˈspīdər\ *n* : small insectlike animal with 8 legs **—spi•dery** *adj*

spig•ot \ˈspigət, ˈspikət\ *n* : faucet

spike \ˈspīk\ *n* : very large nail ~ *vb* **spiked; spik•ing** : fasten or pierce with a spike **—spiked** \ˈspīkt\ *adj*

spill \ˈspil\ *vb* **1** : fall, flow, or run out unintentionally **2** : divulge ~ *n* **1** : act of spilling **2** : something spilled **—spill•able** *adj*

spill•way *n* : passage for surplus water

spin \ˈspin\ *vb* **spun** \ˈspən\; **spin•ning 1** : draw out fiber and twist into thread **2** : form thread from a sticky body fluid **3** : revolve or cause to revolve extremely fast ~ *n* : rapid rotating motion **—spin•ner** *n*

spin•ach \ˈspinich\ *n* : garden herb with edible leaves

spi•nal \ˈspīnᵊl\ *adj* : relating to the backbone **—spi•nal•ly** *adv*

spinal cord *n* : thick strand of nervous tissue that extends from the brain along the back within the backbone

spin•dle \ˈspindᵊl\ *n* **1** : stick used for spinning thread **2** : shaft around which something turns

spin•dly \ˈspindlē\ *adj* : tall and slender

spine \ˈspīn\ *n* **1** : backbone **2** : stiff sharp projection on a plant or animal **—spine•less** *adj* **—spiny** *adj*

spin•et \ˈspinət\ *n* : small piano

spin•ster \ˈspinstər\ *n* : woman who has never married

spi•ral \ˈspīrəl\ *adj* : circling or winding around a single point or line **—spiral** *n or vb* **—spi•ral•ly** *adv*

spire \ˈspīr\ *n* : steeple **—spiry** *adj*

spir•it \ˈspirət\ *n* **1** : life-giving force **2** *cap* : presence of God **3** : ghost **4** : mood **5** : vivacity or enthusiasm **6** *pl* : alcoholic liquor ~ *vb* : carry off secretly **—spir•it•ed** *adj* **—spir•it•less** *adj*

spir•i•tu•al \ˈspirichəwəl\ *adj* **1** : relating to the spirit or sacred matters **2** : deeply religious ~ *n* : religious folk song **—spir•i•tu•al•i•ty** \ˌspirichəˈwalətē\ *n* **—spir•i•tu•al•ly** *adv*

spir•i•tu•al•ism \ˈspirichəwəˌlizəm\ *n* : belief that spirits communicate with the living **—spir•i•tu•al•ist** \-list\ *n or adj*

[1]spit \ˈspit\ *n* **1** : rod for holding and turning meat over a fire **2** : point of land that runs into the water

[2]spit *vb* **spit** *or* **spat** \ˈspat\; **spit•ting** : eject saliva from the mouth ~ *n* **1** : saliva **2** : perfect likeness

spite \ˈspīt\ *n* : petty ill will ~ *vb* **spit•ed; spit•ing** : annoy or offend **—spite•ful** \-fəl\ *adj* **—spite•ful•ly** *adv* **—in spite of** : in defiance or contempt of

spit•tle \ˈspitᵊl\ *n* : saliva

spit•toon \spiˈtün\ *n* : receptacle for spit

splash \ˈsplash\ *vb* : scatter a liquid on **—splash** *n*

splat•ter \ˈsplatər\ *vb* : spatter **—splatter** *n*

splay \ˈsplā\ *vb* : spread out or apart **—splay** *n or adj*

spleen \ˈsplēn\ *n* **1** : organ for maintenance of the blood **2** : spite or anger

splen•did \ˈsplendəd\ *adj* **1** : impressive in beauty or brilliance **2** : outstanding **—splen•did•ly** *adv*

splen•dor \ˈsplendər\ *n* **1** : brilliance **2** : magnificence

splice \ˈsplīs\ *vb* **spliced; splic•ing** : join (2 things) end to end **—splice** *n*

splint \ˈsplint\ *n* **1** : thin strip of wood **2** : something that keeps an injured body part in place

splin•ter \ˈsplintər\ *n* : thin needlelike piece ~ *vb* : break into splinters

split \ˈsplit\ *vb* **split; split•ting** : divide lengthwise or along a grain **—split** *n*

splotch \ˈspläch\ *n* : blotch

splurge \ˈsplərj\ *vb* **splurged; splurg•ing** : indulge oneself **—splurge** *n*

splut•ter \ˈsplətər\ *n* : sputter **—splutter** *vb*

spoil \ˈspȯil\ *n* : plunder ~ *vb* **spoiled** \ˈspȯild, ˈspȯilt\ *or* **spoilt** \ˈspȯilt\; **spoil•ing 1** : pillage **2** : ruin **3** : rot **—spoil•age** \ˈspȯilij\ *n* **—spoil•er** *n*

[1]spoke \ˈspōk\ *past of* SPEAK

[2]spoke *n* : rod from the hub to the rim of a wheel

spo•ken *past part of* SPEAK

spokes•man \spōksmən\ *n* : person who speaks for others

spokes•wom•an \-ˌwu̇mən\ *n* : woman who speaks for others

sponge \ˈspənj\ *n* **1** : porous water-absorbing mass that forms the skeleton of some marine animals **2** : spongelike material used for wiping ~ *vb* **sponged; spong•ing 1** : wipe with a sponge **2** : live at another's expense **—spongy** \ˈspənjē\ *adj*

spon•sor \ˈspänsər\ *n* : one who assumes responsibility for another or who provides financial support **—sponsor** *vb* **—spon•sor•ship** *n*

spon•ta•ne•ous \spänˈtānēəs\ *adj* : done, produced, or occurring naturally or without planning **— spon•ta•ne•i•ty** \ˌspäntənˈēətē\ *n* **— spon•ta•ne•ous•ly** \spänˈtānēəslē\ *adv*

spoof \ˈspüf\ *vb* : make good-natured fun of **—spoof** *n*

spook \ˈspük\ *n* : ghost ~ *vb* : frighten **—spooky** *adj*

spool \ˈspül\ *n* : cylinder on which something is wound

spoon \ˈspün\ *n* : utensil consisting of a small shallow bowl with a handle **—spoon** *vb* **—spoon•ful** \-ˌfu̇l\ *n*

spoor \ˈspu̇r, ˈspōr\ *n* : track or trail esp. of a wild animal

spo•rad•ic \spəˈradik\ *adj* : occasional **—spo•rad•i•cal•ly** *adv*

spore \ˈspōr\ *n* : primitive usu. one-celled reproductive body

sport \ˈspōrt\ *vb* **1** : frolic **2** : show off ~ *n* **1** : physical activity engaged in for pleasure **2** : jest **3** : person who shows good sportsmanship **—sport•ive** \-iv\ *adj* **—sporty** *adj*

sports•cast \ˈspōrtsˌkast\ *n* : broadcast of a sports event **—sports•cast•er** \-ˌkastər\ *n*

sports•man \-mən\ *n* : one who enjoys hunting and fishing

sports•man•ship \-mənˌship\ *n* : ability to be gracious in winning or losing

spot \ˈspät\ *n* **1** : blemish **2** : distinctive small part **3** : location ~ *vb* **-tt- 1** : mark with spots **2** : see or recognize ~ *adj* : made at random or in limited numbers **—spot•less** *adj* **— spot•less•ly** *adv*

spot•light *n* **1** : intense beam of light **2** : center of public interest **—spotlight** *vb*

spot•ty \ˈspätē\ *adj* **-ti•er; -est** : uneven in quality

spouse \ˈspau̇s\ *n* : one's husband or wife

spout \ˈspau̇t\ *vb* **1** : shoot forth in a stream **2** : say pompously ~ *n* **1** : opening through which liquid spouts **2** : jet of liquid

sprain \ˈsprān\ *n* : twisting injury to a joint ~ *vb* : injure with a sprain

sprat \ˈsprat\ *n* : small or young herring

sprawl \ˈsprȯl\ *vb* : lie or sit with limbs spread out **—sprawl** *n*

[1]spray \ˈsprā\ *n* : branch or arrangement of flowers

[2]spray *n* **1** : mist **2** : device that discharges liquid as a mist **—spray** *vb* **—spray•er** *n*

spread \ˈspred\ *vb* **spread; spread•ing 1** : open up or unfold **2** : scatter or smear over a surface **3** : cause to be known or to exist over a wide area ~ *n* **1** : extent to which something is spread **2** : cloth cover **3** : something intended to be spread **—spread•er** *n*

spread•sheet \ˈspredˌshēt\ *n* : accounting program for a computer

spree \ˈsprē\ *n* : burst of indulging in something

sprig \ˈsprig\ *n* : small shoot or twig

spright•ly \ˈsprītlē\ *adj* **-li•er; -est** : lively **—spright•li•ness** *n*

spring \ˈspriŋ\ *vb* **sprang** \ˈspraŋ\ *or* **sprung** \ˈsprəŋ\; **sprung; spring•ing 1** : move or grow quickly or by elastic force **2** : come from by descent **3** : make known suddenly ~ *n* **1** : source **2** : flow of water from underground **3** : season between winter and summer **4** : elastic body or device (as a coil of wire) **5** : leap **6** : elastic power **—springy** *adj*

sprin•kle \ˈspriŋkəl\ *vb* **-kled; -kling** : scatter in small drops or particles ~ *n* : light rainfall **—sprin•kler** *n*

sprint \ˈsprint\ *n* : short run at top speed **—sprint** *vb* **—sprint•er** *n*

sprite \ˈsprīt\ *n* : elf or elfish person

sprock•et \ˈspräkət\ *n* : toothed wheel whose teeth engage the links of a chain

sprout \ˈsprau̇t\ *vb* : send out new growth ~ *n* : plant shoot

[1]spruce \ˈsprüs\ *n* : conical evergreen tree

[2]spruce *adj* **spruc•er; spruc•est** : neat and stylish in appearance ~ *vb* **spruced; spruc•ing** : make or become neat

spry \ˈsprī\ *adj* **spri•er** *or* **spry•er** \ˈsprīər\; **spri•est** *or* **spry•est** \ˈsprīəst\ : agile and active

spume \ˈspyüm\ *n* : froth

spun *past of* SPIN

spunk \ˈspəŋk\ *n* : courage **—spunky** *adj*

spur \ˈspər\ *n* **1** : pointed device used to urge on a horse **2** : something that urges to action **3** : projecting part ~ *vb* **-rr-** : urge on **—spurred** *adj*

spu•ri•ous \ˈspyu̇rēəs\ *adj* : not genuine

spurn \ˈspərn\ *vb* : reject

[1]spurt \ˈspərt\ *n* : burst of effort, speed, or activity ~ *vb* : make a spurt

[2]spurt *vb* : gush out~ *n* : sudden gush

sput•ter \ˈspətər\ *vb* **1** : talk hastily and indistinctly in excitement **2** : make popping sounds **—sputter** *n*

spy \ˈspī\ *vb* **spied; spy•ing** : watch or try to gather information secretly **—spy** *n*

squab \ˈskwäb\ *n, pl* **squabs** *or* **squab** : young pigeon

squab•ble \ˈskwäbəl\ *n or vb* : dispute

squad \ˈskwäd\ *n* : small group

squad•ron \ˈskwädrən\ *n* : small military unit

squal•id \ˈskwäləd\ *adj* : filthy or wretched

squall \ˈskwȯl\ *n* : sudden violent brief storm **—squally** *adj*

squa•lor \ˈskwälər\ *n* : quality or state of being squalid

squan•der \ˈskwändər\ *vb* : waste

square \ˈskwar\ *n* **1** : instrument for measuring right angles **2** : flat figure that has 4 equal sides and 4 right angles **3** : open area in a city **4** : product of number multiplied by itself ~ *adj* **squar•er; squar•est 1** : being a square in form **2** : having sides meet at right angles **3** : multiplied by itself **4** : being a square unit of area **5** : honest ~ *vb* **squared; squar•ing 1** : form into a square **2** : multiply (a number) by itself **3** : conform **4** : settle **—square•ly** *adv*

[1]squash \ˈskwäsh, ˈskwȯsh\ *vb* **1** : press flat **2** : suppress

[2]squash *n, pl* **squash•es** *or* **squash** : garden vegetable

squat \ˈskwät\ *vb* **-tt- 1** : stoop or sit on one's heels **2** : settle on land one does not own ~ *n* : act or posture of squatting ~ *adj* **squat•ter; squat•test** : short and thick **—squat•ter** *n*

squaw \ˈskwȯ\ *n* : American Indian woman

squawk \ˈskwȯk\ *n* : harsh loud cry **—squawk** *vb*

squeak \ˈskwēk\ *vb* : make a thin high-pitched sound **—squeak** *n* **—squeaky** *adj*

squeal \ˈskwēl\ *vb* **1** : make a shrill sound or cry **2** : protest **—squeal** *n*

squea•mish \ˈskwēmish\ *adj* : easily nauseated or disgusted

squeeze \ˈskwēz\ *vb* **squeezed; squeez•ing 1** : apply pressure to **2** : extract by pressure **—squeeze** *n* **—squeez•er** *n*

squelch \ˈskwelch\ *vb* : suppress (as with a retort) **—squelch** *n*

squid \ˈskwid\ *n, pl* **squid** *or* **squids** : 10-armed long-bodied sea mollusk

squint \ˈskwint\ *vb* : look with the eyes partly closed **—squint** *n or adj*

squire \ˈskwīr\ *n* **1** : knight's aide **2** : country landholder **3** : lady's devoted escort ~ *vb* **squired; squir•ing** : escort

squirm \ˈskwərm\ *vb* : wriggle

squir•rel \ˈskwərəl\ *n* : rodent with a long bushy tail

squirt \'skwərt\ *vb* : eject liquid in a spurt —**squirt** *n*

stab \'stab\ *n* 1 : wound made by a pointed weapon 2 : quick thrust 3 : attempt ~ *vb* -**bb**- : pierce or wound with or as if with a pointed weapon

¹sta•ble \'stābəl\ *n* : building for domestic animals ~ *vb* -**bled**; -**bling** : keep in a stable

²stable *adj* **sta•bler**; **sta•blest** 1 : firmly established 2 : mentally and emotionally healthy 3 : steady —**sta•bil•i•ty** \stə'bi-lətē\ *n* —**sta•bil•i•za•tion** \,stābələ'zā-shən\ *n* —**sta•bi•lize** \stābə,līz\ *vb* —**sta•bi•liz•er** *n*

stac•ca•to \stə'kätō\ *adj* : disconnected

stack \'stak\ *n* : large pile ~ *vb* : pile up

sta•di•um \'stādēəm\ *n* : outdoor sports arena

staff \'staf\ *n, pl* **staffs** \'stafs, stavz\ *or* **staves** \stavz, 'stāvz\ 1 : rod or supporting cane 2 : people assisting a leader 3 : 5 horizontal lines on which music is written ~ *vb* : supply with workers —**staff•er** *n*

staff sergeant *n* : noncommissioned officer ranking next above a sergeant in the army, air force, or marine corps

stag \'stag\ *n, pl* **stags** *or* **stag** : male deer ~ *adj* : only for men ~ *adv* : without a date

stage \'stāj\ *n* 1 : raised platform for a speaker or performers 2 : theater 3 : step in a process ~ *vb* **staged**; **stag•ing** : produce (a play)

stage•coach *n* : passenger coach

stag•ger \'stagər\ *vb* 1 : reel or cause to reel from side to side 2 : overlap or alternate —**stagger** *n* —**stag•ger•ing•ly** *adv*

stag•nant \'stagnənt\ *adj* : not moving or active —**stag•nate** \-,nāt\ *vb* —**stag•na•tion** \stag'nāshən\ *n*

¹staid \'stād\ *adj* : sedate

²staid *past of* STAY

stain \'stān\ *vb* 1 : discolor 2 : dye (as wood) 3 : disgrace ~ *n* 1 : discolored area 2 : mark of guilt 3 : coloring preparation —**stain•less** *adj*

stair \'star\ *n* 1 : step in a series for going from one level to another 2 *pl* : flight of steps —**stair•way** *n*

stair•case *n* : series of steps with their framework

stake \'stāk\ *n* 1 : usu. small post driven into the ground 2 : bet 3 : prize in a contest ~ *vb* **staked**; **stak•ing** 1 : mark or secure with a stake 2 : bet

sta•lac•tite \stə'lak,tīt\ *n* : icicle-shaped deposit hanging in a cavern

sta•lag•mite \stə'lag,mīt\ *n* : icicle-shaped deposit on a cavern floor

stale \'stāl\ *adj* **stal•er**; **stal•est** 1 : having lost good taste and quality from age 2 : no longer new, strong, or effective —**stale•ness** *n*

stale•mate \'stāl,māt\ *n* : deadlock —**stalemate** *vb*

¹stalk \'stȯk\ *vb* 1 : walk stiffly or proudly 2 : pursue stealthily

²stalk *n* : plant stem —**stalked** \'stȯkt\ *adj*

¹stall \'stȯl\ *n* 1 : compartment in a stable 2 : booth where articles are sold

²stall *vb* : bring or come to a standstill unintentionally

³stall *vb* : delay, evade, or keep a situation going to gain advantage or time

stal•lion \'stalyən\ *n* : male horse

stal•wart \'stȯlwərt\ *adj* : strong or brave

sta•men \'stāmən\ *n* : flower organ that produces pollen

stam•i•na \'stamənə\ *n* : endurance

stam•mer \'stamər\ *vb* : hesitate in speaking —**stammer** *n*

stamp \'stamp\ *vb* 1 : pound with the sole of the foot or a heavy implement 2 : impress or imprint 3 : cut out with a die 4 : attach a postage stamp to ~ *n* 1 : device for stamping 2 : act of stamping 3 : government seal showing a tax or fee has been paid

stam•pede \stam'pēd\ *n* : headlong rush of frightened animals ~ *vb* -**ped•ed**; -**ped•ing** : flee in panic

stance \'stans\ *n* : way of standing

¹stanch \'stȯnch, 'stänch\ *vb* : stop the flow of (as blood)

²stanch *var of* STAUNCH

stan•chion \'stanchən\ *n* : upright support

stand \'stand\ *vb* **stood** \'stu̇d\ **stand•ing** 1 : be at rest in or assume an upright position 2 : remain unchanged 3 : be steadfast 4 : maintain a relative position or rank 5 : set upright 6 : undergo or endure ~ *n* 1 : act or place of standing, staying, or resisting 2 : sales booth 3 : structure for holding something upright 4 : group of plants growing together 5 *pl* : tiered seats 6 : opinion or viewpoint

stan•dard \'standərd\ *n* 1 : symbolic figure or flag 2 : model, rule, or guide 3 : upright support —**standard** *adj* —**stan•dard•i•za•tion** \,standərdə'zāshən\ *n* —**stan•dard•ize** \'standərd,īz\ *vb*

standard time *n* : time established over a region or country

stand•ing \'standiŋ\ *n* 1 : relative position or rank 2 : duration

stand•still *n* : state of rest

stank *past of* STINK

¹stan•za \'stanzə\ *n* : division of a poem

¹sta•ple \'stāpəl\ *n* : U-shaped wire fastener —**staple** *vb* —**sta•pler** \-plər\ *n*

²staple *n* : chief commodity or item —**staple** *adj*

star \'stär\ *n* 1 : celestial body visible as a point of light 2 : 5- or 6-pointed figure representing a star 3 : leading performer ~ *vb* -**rr**- 1 : mark with a star 2 : play the leading role —**star•dom** \stärdəm\ *n* —**star•less** *adj* —**star•light** *n* —**star•ry** *adj*

star•board \'stärbərd\ *n* : right side of a ship or airplane looking forward —**starboard** *adj*

starch \'stärch\ *n* : nourishing carbohydrate from plants also used in adhesives and laundering ~ *vb* : stiffen with starch —**starchy** *adj*

stare \'star\ *vb* **stared**; **star•ing** : look intently with wide-open eyes —**stare** *n* —**star•er** *n*

stark \'stärk\ *adj* 1 : absolute 2 : severe or bleak ~ *adv* : completely —**stark•ly** *adv*

star•ling \'stärliŋ\ *n* : bird related to the crows

start \'stärt\ *vb* 1 : twitch or jerk (as from surprise) 2 : perform or show performance of the first part of an action or process ~ *n* 1 : sudden involuntary motion 2 : beginning —**start•er** *n*

star•tle \'stärt³l\ *vb* -**tled**; -**tling** : frighten or surprise suddenly

starve \'stärv\ *vb* **starved**; **starv•ing** 1 : suffer or die from hunger 2 : kill with hunger —**star•va•tion** \stär'vāshən\ *n*

stash \'stash\ *vb* : store in a secret place for future use —**stash** *n*

state \'stāt\ *n* 1 : condition of being 2 : condition of mind 3 : nation or a political unit within it ~ *vb* **stat•ed**; **stat•ing** 1 : express in words 2 : establish —**state•hood** \-,hu̇d\ *n*

state•ly \'stātlē\ *adj* -**li•er**; -**est** : having impressive dignity —**state•li•ness** *n*

state•ment \'stātmənt\ *n* 1 : something stated 2 : financial summary

state•room *n* : private room on a ship

states•man \'stātsmən\ *n* : one skilled in government or diplomacy —**states•man•like** *adj* —**states•man•ship** *n*

stat•ic \'statik\ *adj* 1 : relating to bodies at rest or forces in equilibrium 2 : not moving 3 : relating to stationary charges of electricity ~ *n* : noise on radio or television from electrical disturbances

sta•tion \'stāshən\ *n* 1 : place of duty 2 : regular stop on a bus or train route 3 : social standing 4 : place where radio or television programs originate ~ *vb* : assign to a station

sta•tion•ary \'stāshə,nerē\ *adj* 1 : not moving or not movable 2 : not changing

sta•tio•nery \'stāshə,nerē\ *n* : letter paper with envelopes

sta•tis•tic \stə'tistik\ *n* : single item of statistics

sta•tis•tics \-tiks\ *n pl* : numerical facts collected for study —**sta•tis•ti•cal** \-tikəl\ *adj* —**sta•tis•ti•cal•ly** *adv* —**stat•is•ti•cian** \statə'stishən\ *n*

stat•u•ary \'stachə,werē\ *n, pl* -**ar•ies** : collection of statues

stat•ue \'stachü\ *n* : solid 3-dimensional likeness —**stat•u•ette** \stachə'wet\ *n*

stat•u•esque \stachə'wesk\ *adj* : tall and shapely

stat•ure \'stachər\ *n* 1 : height 2 : status gained by achievement

sta•tus \'stātəs, 'stat-\ *n* : relative situation or condition

sta•tus quo \-'kwō\ *n* : existing state of affairs

stat•ute \'stachüt\ *n* : law —**stat•u•to•ry** \'stachə,tōrē\ *adj*

staunch \'stȯnch\ *adj* : steadfast —**staunch•ly** *adv*

stave \'stāv\ *n* : narrow strip of wood ~ *vb* **staved** *or* **stove** \'stōv\ **stav•ing** 1 : break a hole in 2 : drive away

staves *pl of* STAFF

¹stay \'stā\ *n* : support ~ *vb* **stayed**; **stay•ing** : prop up

²stay *vb* **stayed** \'stād\ *or* **staid** \'stād\ **stay•ing** 1 : pause 2 : remain 3 : reside 4 : stop or postpone 5 : satisfy for a time ~ *n* : staying

stead \'sted\ *n* : one's place, job, or function —**in good stead** : to advantage

stead•fast \-,fast\ *adj* : faithful or determined —**stead•fast•ly** *adv*

steady \'stedē\ *adj* **stead•i•er**; -**est** 1 : firm in position or sure in movement 2 : calm or reliable 3 : constant 4 : regular ~ *vb* **stead•ied**; **steady•ing** : make or become steady —**steadi•ly** \'sted³lē\ *adv* —**steadi•ness** *n* —**steady** *adv*

steak \'stāk\ *n* : thick slice of meat

steal \'stēl\ *vb* **stole** \'stōl\ **sto•len** \'stōlən\ **steal•ing** 1 : take and carry away wrong-

fully and with intent to keep 2 : move secretly or slowly

stealth \'stelth\ *n* : secret or unobtrusive procedure —**stealth•i•ly** \-thəlē\ *adv* —**stealthy** *adj*

steam \'stēm\ *n* : vapor of boiling water ~ *vb* : give off steam —**steam•boat** *n* —**steam•ship** *n* —**steamy** *adj*

steed \'stēd\ *n* : horse

steel \'stēl\ *n* : tough carbon-containing iron ~ *vb* : fill with courage —**steel** *adj* —**steely** *adj*

¹steep \'stēp\ *adj* : having a very sharp slope or great elevation —**steep•ly** *adv* —**steep•ness** *n*

²steep *vb* : soak in a liquid

stee•ple \'stēpəl\ *n* : usu. tapering church tower

stee•ple•chase *n* : race over hurdles

¹steer \'stir\ *n* : castrated ox

²steer *vb* 1 : direct the course of (as a ship or car) 2 : guide

steer•age \'stirij\ *n* : section in a ship for people paying the lowest fares

stein \'stīn\ *n* : mug

stel•lar \'stelər\ *adj* : relating to stars or resembling a star

¹stem \'stem\ *n* : main upright part of a plant ~ *vb* -**mm**- 1 : derive 2 : make progress against —**stem•less** *adj* —**stemmed** *adj*

²stem *vb* -**mm**- : stop the flow of

stench \'stench\ *n* : stink

sten•cil \'stensəl\ *n* : printing sheet cut with letters to let ink pass through —**stencil** *vb*

ste•nog•ra•phy \stə'nägrəfē\ *n* : art or process of writing in shorthand —**ste•nog•ra•pher** \-fər\ *n* —**steno•graph•ic** \stenə'grafik\ *adj*

sten•to•ri•an \sten'tōrēən\ *adj* : extremely loud and powerful

step \'step\ *n* 1 : single action of a leg in walking or running 2 : rest for the foot in going up or down 3 : degree, rank, or stage 4 : way of walking ~ *vb* -**pp**- 1 : move by steps 2 : press with the foot

step- \'step-\ *comb form* : related by a remarriage and not by blood

step•lad•der *n* : light portable set of steps in a hinged frame

steppe \'step\ *n* : dry grassy treeless land esp. of Asia

-ster \stər\ *n suffix* 1 : one that does, makes, or uses 2 : one that is associated with or takes part in 3 : one that is

ste•reo \'sterē,ō, 'stir-\ *n, pl* -**reos** : stereophonic sound system —**stereo** *adj*

ste•reo•phon•ic \sterēə'fänik, ,stir-\ *adj* : relating to a 3-dimensional effect of reproduced sound

ste•reo•type \'sterēə,tīp, 'stir-\ *n* : gross often mistaken generalization —**stereotype** *vb* —**ste•reo•typ•i•cal** \sterēə'tipikəl\ *adj* —**ste•reo•typ•i•cal•ly** *adv*

ste•reo•typed \'sterēə,tīpt, 'stir-\ *adj* : lacking originality or individuality

ster•ile \'sterəl\ *adj* 1 : unable to bear fruit, crops, or offspring 2 : free from disease germs —**ster•il•i•ty** \stə'rilətē\ *n* —**ster•il•i•za•tion** \sterələ'zāshən\ *n* —**ster•il•ize** \-ə,līz\ *vb* —**ster•il•iz•er** *n*

ster•ling \'stərliŋ\ *adj* 1 : being or made of an alloy of 925 parts of silver with 75 parts of copper 2 : excellent

¹stern \'stərn\ *adj* 1 : severe —**stern•ly** *adv* —**stern•ness** *n*

²stern *n* : back end of a boat

ster•num \'stərnəm\ *n, pl* -**nums** *or* -**na** \-nə\ : long flat chest bone joining the 2 sets of ribs

stetho•scope \'stethə,skōp\ *n* : instrument used for listening to sounds in the chest

ste•ve•dore \'stēvə,dōr\ *n* : worker who loads and unloads ships

stew \'stü, 'styü\ *n* 1 : dish of boiled meat and vegetables 2 : state of worry or agitation —**stew** *vb*

stew•ard \'stüərd, 'styü-\ *n* 1 : manager of an estate or an organization 2 : person on a ship or airliner who looks after passenger comfort —**stew•ard•ship** *n*

stew•ard•ess \-əs\ *n* : woman who is a steward (as on an airplane)

¹stick \'stik\ *n* 1 : cut or broken branch 2 : long thin piece of wood or something resembling it

²stick *vb* **stuck** \'stək\ **stick•ing** 1 : stab 2 : thrust or project 3 : hold fast to something 4 : attach 5 : become jammed or fixed

stick•er \'stikər\ *n* : adhesive label

stick•ler \'stiklər\ *n* : one who insists on exactness or completeness

sticky \'stikē\ *adj* **stick•i•er**; -**est** 1 : adhesive or gluey 2 : muggy 3 : difficult

stiff \'stif\ *adj* 1 : not bending easily 2 : tense 3 : formal 4 : strong 5 : severe —**stiff•en** \'stifən\ *vb* —**stiff•en•er** \-ənər\ *n* —**stiff•ly** *adv* —**stiff•ness** *n*

sti•fle \'stīfəl\ *vb* -**fled**; -**fling** 1 : smother or suffocate 2 : suppress

stig•ma \'stigmə\ *n, pl* -**ma•ta** \stig'mätə, 'stigmətə\ *or* -**mas** : mark of disgrace —**stig•ma•tize** \'stigmə,tīz\ *vb*

stile \'stīl\ *n* : steps for crossing a fence

sti•let•to \stə'letō\ *n, pl* -**tos** *or* -**toes** : slender dagger

¹still \'stil\ *adj* 1 : motionless 2 : silent ~ *vb* : make or become still ~ *adv* 1 : without motion 2 : up to and during this time 3 : in spite of that ~ *n* : silence —**still•ness** *n*

²still *n* : apparatus used in distillation

still•born *adj* : born dead —**still•birth** *n*

stilt \'stilt\ *n* : one of a pair of poles for walking

stilt•ed \'stiltəd\ *adj* : not easy and natural

stim•u•lant \'stimyələnt\ *n* : substance that temporarily increases the activity of an organism —**stimulant** *adj*

stim•u•late \-,lāt\ *vb* -**lat•ed**; -**lat•ing** : make active —**stim•u•la•tion** \stimyə'lāshən\ *n*

stim•u•lus \'stimyələs\ *n, pl* -**li** \-,lī\ : something that stimulates

sting \'stiŋ\ *vb* **stung** \'stəŋ\ **sting•ing** 1 : prick painfully 2 : cause to suffer acutely ~ *n* 1 : act of stinging or a resulting wound —**sting•er** *n*

stin•gy \'stinjē\ *adj* **stin•gi•er**; -**est** : not generous —**stin•gi•ness** *n*

stink \'stiŋk\ *vb* **stank** \'staŋk\ *or* **stunk** \'stəŋk\ **stink•ing** : have a strong offensive odor —**stink** *n* —**stink•er** *n*

stint \'stint\ *vb* : be sparing or stingy ~ *n* 1 : restraint 2 : quantity or period of work

sti•pend \'stī,pend, -pənd\ *n* : money paid periodically

stip•ple \'stipəl\ *vb* -**pled**; -**pling** : engrave, paint, or draw with dots instead of lines —**stipple** *n*

stip•u•late \'stipyə,lāt\ *vb* -**lat•ed**; -**lat•ing** : demand as a condition —**stip•u•la•tion** \stipyə'lāshən\ *n*

stir \'stər\ *vb* -**rr**- 1 : move slightly 2 : prod or push into activity 3 : mix by continued circular movement ~ *n* : act or result of stirring

stir•rup \'stərəp\ *n* : saddle loop for the foot

stitch \'stich\ *n* 1 : loop formed by a needle in sewing 2 : sudden sharp pain ~ *vb* 1 : fasten or decorate with stitches 2 : sew

stock \'stäk\ *n* 1 : block or part of wood 2 : original from which others derive 3 : farm animals 4 : supply of goods 5 : money invested in a large business 6 *pl* : instrument of punishment like a pillory with holes for the feet or feet and hands ~ *vb* : provide with stock

stock•ade \stä'kād\ *n* : defensive or confining enclosure

stock•ing \'stäkiŋ\ *n* : close-fitting covering for the foot and leg

stock•pile *n* : reserve supply —**stockpile** *vb*

stocky \'stäkē\ *adj* **stock•i•er**; -**est** : short and relatively thick

stock•yard *n* : yard for livestock to be slaughtered or shipped

stodgy \'stäjē\ *adj* **stodg•i•er**, -**est** 1 : dull 2 : old-fashioned

sto•ic \'stōik\, **sto•i•cal** \-ikəl\ *adj* : showing indifference to pain —**stoic** *n* —**sto•i•cal•ly** *adv* —**sto•i•cism** \stōə,sizəm\ *n*

stoke \'stōk\ *vb* **stoked**; **stok•ing** : stir up a fire or supply fuel to a furnace —**stok•er** *n*

¹stole \'stōl\ *past of* STEAL

²stole *n* : long wide scarf

stolen *past part of* STEAL

stol•id \'stäləd\ *adj* : having or showing little or no emotion —**stol•id•ly** \'stälədlē\ *adv*

stom•ach \'stəmək, -ik\ *n* 1 : saclike digestive organ 2 : abdomen 3 : appetite or desire ~ *vb* : put up with —**stom•ach•ache** *n*

stomp \'stämp, 'stȯmp\ *vb* : stamp

stone \'stōn\ *n* 1 : hardened earth or mineral matter 2 : small piece of rock 3 : seed that is hard or has a hard covering ~ *vb* **stoned**; **ston•ing** : pelt or kill with stones —**stony** *adj*

stood *past of* STAND

stool \'stül\ *n* 1 : seat usu. without back or arms 2 : footstool 3 : discharge of feces

¹stoop \'stüp\ *vb* 1 : bend over 2 : lower oneself ~ *n* 1 : act of bending over 2 : bent position of shoulders

²stoop *n* : small porch at a house door

stop \'stäp\ *vb* -**pp**- 1 : block an opening 2 : end or cause to end 3 : pause for rest or a visit in a journey ~ *n* 1 : plug 2 : act or place of stopping 3 : delay in a journey —**stop•light** *n* —**stop•page** \-ij\ *n* —**stop•per** *n*

stop•gap *n* : temporary measure or thing

stor•age \'stōrij\ *n* : safekeeping of goods (as in a warehouse)

store \'stōr\ *vb* **stored**; **stor•ing** : put aside for future use ~ *n* 1 : something stored 2 : retail business establishment —**store•house** *n* —**store•keep•er** *n* —**store•room** *n*

stork \'stȯrk\ *n* : large wading bird

storm \'stȯrm\ *n* 1 : heavy fall of rain or snow 2 : violent outbreak ~ *vb* 1 : rain or snow heavily 2 : rage 3 : make an attack against —**stormy** *adj*

¹sto•ry \'stōrē\ *n, pl* -**ries** 1 : narrative 2 : report —**sto•ry•tell•er** *n*

2story *n, pl* **-ries :** floor of a building
stout \'stau̇t\ *adj* **1 :** firm or strong **2 :** thick or bulky **—stout•ly** *adv* **— stout•ness** *n*
1stove \'stōv\ *n* **:** apparatus for providing heat (as for cooking or heating)
2stove *past of* STAVE
stow \'stō\ *vb* **1 :** pack in a compact mass **2 :** put or hide away
strad•dle \'stradᵊl\ *vb* **-dled; -dling :** stand over or sit on with legs on opposite sides **—straddle** *n*
strafe \'strāf\ *vb* **strafed; straf•ing :** fire upon with machine guns from a low-flying airplane
strag•gle \'stragəl\ *vb* **-gled; -gling :** wander or become separated from others **—strag•gler** \-ələr\ *n*
straight \'strāt\ *adj* **1 :** having no bends, turns, or twists **2 :** just, proper, or honest **3 :** neat and orderly ∼ *adv* **:** in a straight manner **—straight•en** \'strātᵊn\ *vb*
straight•for•ward \strāt'fȯrwərd\ *adj* **:** frank or honest
straight•way *adv* **:** immediately
1strain \'strān\ *n* **1 :** lineage **2 :** trace
2strain *vb* **1 :** exert to the utmost **2 :** filter or remove by filtering **3 :** injure by improper use ∼ *n* **1 :** excessive tension or exertion **2 :** bodily injury from excessive effort **—strain•er** *n*
strait \'strāt\ *n* **1 :** narrow channel connecting 2 bodies of water **2** *pl* **:** distress
strait•en \'strātᵊn\ *vb* **1 :** hem in **2 :** make distressing or difficult
1strand \'strand\ *vb* **1 :** drive or cast upon the shore **2 :** leave helpless
2strand *n* **1 :** twisted fiber of a rope **2 :** length of something ropelike
strange \'strānj\ *adj* **strang•er; strang•est 1 :** unusual or queer **2 :** new **—strange•ly** *adv* **—strange•ness** *n*
strang•er \'strānjər\ *n* **:** person with whom one is not acquainted
stran•gle \'straŋgəl\ *vb* **-gled; -gling :** choke to death **—stran•gler** \-glər\ *n*
stran•gu•la•tion \,straŋgyə'lāshən\ *n* **:** act or process of strangling
strap \'strap\ *n* **:** narrow strip of flexible material used esp. for fastening ∼ *vb* **1 :** secure with a strap **2 :** beat with a strap **—strap•less** *n*
strap•ping \'strapiŋ\ *adj* **:** robust
strat•a•gem \'stratəjəm, -,jem\ *n* **:** deceptive scheme or maneuver
strat•e•gy \'stratəjē\ *n, pl* **-gies :** carefully worked out plan of action **—stra•te•gic** \strə'tējik\ *adj* **—strat•e•gist** \'stratəjist\ *n*
strat•i•fy \'stratə,fī\ *vb* **-fied; -fy•ing :** form or arrange in layers **—strat•i•fi•ca•tion** \,stratəfə'kāshən\ *n*
strato•sphere \'stratə,sfir\ *n* **:** earth's atmosphere from about 7 to 31 miles above the surface
stra•tum \'strātəm, 'strat-\ *n, pl* **-ta** \'strātə, 'strat-\ **:** layer
straw \'strȯ\ *n* **1 :** grass stems after grain is removed **2 :** tube for drinking ∼ *adj* **:** made of straw
straw•ber•ry \'strȯ,berē\ *n* **:** juicy red pulpy fruit
stray \'strā\ *vb* **:** wander or deviate ∼ *n* **:** person or animal that strays ∼ *adj* **:** separated from or not related to anything close by
streak \'strēk\ *n* **1 :** mark of a different color **2 :** narrow band of light **3 :** trace **4 :** run (as of luck) or series ∼ *vb* **1 :** form streaks in or on **2 :** move fast
stream \'strēm\ *n* **1 :** flow of water on land **2 :** steady flow (as of water or air) ∼ *vb* **1 :** flow in a stream **2 :** pour out streams
stream•er \'strēmər\ *n* **:** long ribbon or ribbonlike flag
stream•lined \-,līnd, -'līnd\ *adj* **1 :** made with contours to reduce air or water resistance **2 :** simplified **3 :** modernized **—streamline** *vb*
street \'strēt\ *n* **:** thoroughfare esp. in a city or town
street•car *n* **:** passenger vehicle running on rails in the streets
strength \'streŋth\ *n* **1 :** quality of being strong **2 :** toughness **3 :** intensity
strength•en \'streŋthən\ *vb* **:** make, grow, or become stronger **—strength•en•er** \'streŋthənər\ *n*
stren•u•ous \'strenyəwəs\ *adj* **1 :** vigorous **2 :** requiring or showing energy **—stren•u•ous•ly** *adv*
stress \'stres\ *n* **1 :** pressure or strain that tends to distort a body **2 :** relative prominence given to one thing among others **3 :** state of physical or mental tension or something inducing it ∼ *vb* **:** put stress on **—stress•ful** \'stresfəl\ *adj*
stretch \'strech\ *vb* **1 :** spread or reach out **2 :** draw out in length or breadth **3 :** make taut **4 :** exaggerate **5 :** become extended without breaking ∼ *n* **:** act of extending beyond normal limits
stretch•er \'strechər\ *n* **:** device for carrying a sick or injured person
strew \'strü\ *vb* **strewed; strewed** *or* **strewn** \'strün\; **strew•ing 1 :** scatter **2 :** cover by scattering something over
strick•en \'strikən\ *adj* **:** afflicted with disease
strict \'strikt\ *adj* **1 :** allowing no escape or evasion **2 :** precise **—strict•ly** *adv* **—strict•ness** *n*
stric•ture \'strikchər\ *n* **:** hostile criticism
stride \'strīd\ *vb* **strode** \'strōd\; **strid•den** \'stridᵊn\; **strid•ing :** walk or run with long steps ∼ *n* **1 :** long step **2 :** manner of striding
stri•dent \'strīdᵊnt\ *adj* **:** loud and harsh
strife \'strīf\ *n* **:** conflict
strike \'strīk\ *vb* **struck** \'strək\; **struck; strik•ing** \'strīkiŋ\ **1 :** hit sharply **2 :** delete **3 :** produce by impressing **4 :** cause to sound **5 :** afflict **6 :** occur to or impress **7 :** cause (a match) to ignite by rubbing **8 :** refrain from working **9 :** find **10 :** take on (as a pose) ∼ *n* **1 :** act or instance of striking **2 :** work stoppage **3 :** military attack **—strik•er** *n* **—strike out** *vb* **:** start out vigorously **—strike up** *vb* **:** start
strik•ing \'strīkiŋ\ *adj* **:** very noticeable **—strik•ing•ly** *adv*
string \'striŋ\ *n* **1 :** line usu. of twisted threads **2 :** series **3** *pl* **:** stringed instruments ∼ *vb* **strung** \'strəŋ\; **string•ing 1 :** thread on or with a string **2 :** hang or fasten by a string
stringed \'striŋd\ *adj* **:** having strings
strin•gent \'strinjənt\ *adj* **:** severe
stringy \'striŋē\ *adj* **string•i•er; -est :** tough or fibrous
1strip \'strip\ *vb* **-pp- 1 :** take the covering or clothing from **2 :** undress **—strip•per** *n*
2strip *n* **:** long narrow flat piece
stripe \'strīp\ *n* **:** distinctive line or long narrow section ∼ *vb* **striped** \'strīpt\; **strip•ing :** make stripes on **—striped** \'strīpt, 'strīpəd\ *adj*
strive \'strīv\ *vb* **strove** \'strōv\; **stri•ven** \'strivən\ *or* **strived; striv•ing** \'strīviŋ\ **1 :** struggle **2 :** try hard
strode *past of* STRIDE
stroke \'strōk\ *vb* **stroked; strok•ing :** rub gently ∼ *n* **1 :** act of swinging or striking **2 :** sudden action
stroll \'strōl\ *vb* **:** walk leisurely **—stroll** *n* **—stroll•er** *n*
strong \'strȯŋ\ *adj* **1 :** capable of exerting great force or of withstanding stress or violence **2 :** healthy **3 :** zealous **—strong•ly** *adv*
strong•hold *n* **:** fortified place
struck *past of* STRIKE
struc•ture \'strəkchər\ *n* **1 :** building **2 :** arrangement of elements ∼ *vb* **-tured; -tur•ing :** make into a structure **—struc•tur•al** \-chərəl\ *adj*
strug•gle \'strəgəl\ *vb* **-gled; -gling 1 :** make strenuous efforts to overcome an adversary **2 :** proceed with great effort ∼ *n* **1 :** strenuous effort **2 :** intense competition for superiority
strum \'strəm\ *vb* **-mm- :** play (a musical instrument) by brushing the strings with the fingers
strum•pet \'strəmpət\ *n* **:** prostitute
strung *past of* STRING
strut \'strət\ *vb* **-tt- :** walk in a proud or showy manner ∼ *n* **1 :** proud walk **2 :** supporting bar or rod
strych•nine \'strik,nīn, -nən, -,nēn\ *n* **:** bitter poisonous substance
stub \'stəb\ *n* **:** short end or section ∼ *vb* **-bb- :** strike against something
stub•ble \'stəbəl\ *n* **:** short growth left after cutting **—stub•bly** *adj*
stub•born \'stəbərn\ *adj* **1 :** determined not to yield **2 :** hard to control **—stub•born•ly** *adv* **—stub•born•ness** *n*
stub•by \'stəbē\ *adj* **:** short, blunt, and thick
stuc•co \'stəkō\ *n, pl* **-cos** *or* **-coes :** plaster for coating outside walls **—stuc•coed** \'stəkōd\ *adj*
stuck *past of* STICK
stuck–up \'stək'əp\ *adj* **:** conceited
1stud \'stəd\ *n* **:** male horse kept for breeding
2stud *n* **1 :** upright beam for holding wall material **2 :** projecting nail, pin, or rod ∼ *vb* **-dd- :** supply or dot with studs
stu•dent \'stüdᵊnt, 'styü-\ *n* **:** one who studies
stud•ied \'stədēd\ *adj* **:** premeditated
stu•dio \'stüdē,ō, 'styü-\ *n, pl* **-dios 1 :** artist's workroom **2 :** place where movies are made or television or radio shows are broadcast
stu•di•ous \'stüdēəs, 'styü-\ *adj* **:** devoted to study **—stu•di•ous•ly** *adv*
study \'stədē\ *n, pl* **stud•ies 1 :** act or process of learning about something **2 :** branch of learning **3 :** careful examination **4 :** room for reading or studying ∼ *vb* **stud•ied; study•ing :** apply the attention and mind to a subject
stuff \'stəf\ *n* **1 :** personal property **2 :** raw or fundamental material **3 :** unspecified material or things ∼ *vb* **:** fill by packing things in **—stuff•ing** *n*
stuffy \'stəfē\ *adj* **stuff•i•er; -est 1 :** lacking fresh air **2 :** unimaginative or pompous
stul•ti•fy \'stəltə,fī\ *vb* **-fied; -fy•ing 1 :** cause to appear foolish **2 :** impair or make ineffective **3 :** have a dulling effect on
stum•ble \'stəmbəl\ *vb* **-bled; -bling 1 :** lose one's balance or fall in walking or running **2 :** speak or act clumsily **3 :** happen by chance **—stumble** *n*
stump \'stəmp\ *n* **:** part left when something is cut off ∼ *vb* **:** confuse **—stumpy** *adj*
stun \'stən\ *vb* **-nn- 1 :** make senseless or dizzy by or as if by a blow **2 :** bewilder
stung *past of* STING
stunk *past of* STINK
stun•ning \'stəniŋ\ *adj* **1 :** astonishing or incredible **2 :** strikingly beautiful **—stun•ning•ly** *adv*
1stunt \'stənt\ *vb* **:** hinder the normal growth or progress of
2stunt *n* **:** spectacular feat
stu•pe•fy \'stüpə,fī, 'styü-\ *vb* **-fied; -fy•ing 1 :** make insensible by or as if by drugs **2 :** amaze
stu•pen•dous \stu̇'pendəs, styu̇-\ *adj* **:** very big or impressive **—stu•pen•dous•ly** *adv*
stu•pid \'stüpəd, 'styü-\ *adj* **:** not sensible or intelligent **—stu•pid•i•ty** \stu̇'pidətē, styu̇-\ *n* **—stu•pid•ly** *adv*
stu•por \'stüpər, 'styü-\ *n* **:** state of being conscious but not aware or sensible
stur•dy \'stərdē\ *adj* **-di•er; -est :** strong **—stur•di•ly** \'stərdᵊlē\ *adv* **—stur•di•ness** *n*
stur•geon \'stərjən\ *n* **:** fish whose roe is caviar
stut•ter \'stətər\ *vb or n* **:** stammer
1sty \'stī\ *n, pl* **sties :** pig pen
2sty, stye \'stī\ *n, pl* **sties** *or* **styes :** inflamed swelling on the edge of an eyelid
style \'stīl\ *n* **1 :** distinctive way of speaking, writing, or acting **2 :** elegant or fashionable way of living ∼ *vb* **styled; styl•ing 1 :** name **2 :** give a particular design or style to **—styl•ish** \'stīlish\ *adj* **—styl•ish•ly** *adv* **—styl•ish•ness** *n* **—styl•ist** \-ist\ *n* **—styl•ize** \'stīəl,īz\ *vb*
sty•lus \'stīləs\ *n, pl* **-li** \'stīl,ī\ **1 :** pointed writing tool **2 :** phonograph needle
sty•mie \'stīmē\ *vb* **-mied; -mie•ing :** block or frustrate
suave \'swäv\ *adj* **:** well-mannered and gracious **—suave•ly** *adv*
1sub \'səb\ *n or vb* **:** substitute
2sub *n* **:** submarine
sub- \,səb, 'səb\ *prefix* **1 :** under or beneath **2 :** subordinate or secondary **3 :** subordinate portion of **4 :** with repetition of a process so as to form, stress, or deal with subordinate parts or relations **5 :** somewhat **6 :** nearly

subacute
subagency
subagent
subarctic
subarea
subatmospheric
subaverage
subbase
subbasement
subbranch
subcabinet
subcategory
subclass
subclassification
subclassify
subcommission
subcommittee
subcommunity
subcomponent
subcontract
subcontractor
subculture
subdean
subdepartment
subdistrict
subentry
subfamily
subfreezing
subgroup
subhead
subheading
subhuman
subindex
subindustry
sublease
sublethal
sublevel
subliterate
subnetwork
suboceanic
suborder
subpar
subpart
subplot
subpolar
subprincipal
subprocess
subprogram
subproject
subregion
subsea
subsection
subsense
subspecialty
subspecies
substage
subsurface
subsystem
subtemperate
subtheme
subtopic
subtotal
subtreasury
subtype
subunit
subvariety

sub•con•scious \,səb'känchəs\ *adj* **:** existing without conscious awareness ∼ *n* **:** part of the mind concerned with subconscious activities **—sub•con•scious•ly** *adv*
sub•di•vide \,səbdə'vīd, 'səbdə,vīd\ *vb* **1 :** divide into several parts **2 :** divide (land) into building lots **—sub•di•vi•sion** \-'vizhən, -,vizh-\ *n*
sub•due \səb'dü, -'dyü\ *vb* **-dued; -du•ing 1 :** bring under control **2 :** reduce the intensity of
sub•ject \'səbjikt\ *n* **1 :** person under the authority of another **2 :** something being discussed or studied **3 :** word or word group about which something is said in a sentence ∼ *adj* **1 :** being under one's authority **2 :** prone **3 :** dependent on some condition or act ∼ \səb'jekt\ *vb* **1 :** bring under control **2 :** cause to undergo **—sub•jec•tion** \-'jekshən\ *n*
sub•jec•tive \,səb'jektiv\ *adj* **:** deriving from an individual viewpoint or bias **—sub•jec•tive•ly** *adv* **—sub•jec•tiv•i•ty** \-,jek'tivətē\ *n*
sub•ju•gate \'səbji,gāt\ *vb* **-gat•ed; -gat•ing :** bring under one's control **—sub•ju•ga•tion** \,səbji'gāshən\ *n*
sub•junc•tive \səb'jəŋktiv\ *adj* **:** relating to a verb form which expresses possibility or contingency **—subjunctive** *n*
sub•let \'səb,let\ *vb* **-let; -let•ting :** rent (a property) from a lessee
sub•lime \sə'blīm\ *adj* **:** splendid **—sub•lime•ly** *adv*
sub•ma•rine \'səbmə,rēn, ,səbmə'-\ *adj* **:** existing, acting, or growing under the sea ∼ *n* **:** underwater boat
sub•merge \səb'mərj\ *vb* **-merged; -merg•ing :** put or plunge under the surface of water **—sub•mer•gence** \-'mərjəns\ *n* **—sub•mers•ible** \səb'mərsəbəl\ *adj or n* **—sub•mer•sion** \-'mərzhən\ *n*
sub•mit \səb'mit\ *vb* **-tt- 1 :** yield **2 :** give or offer **—sub•mis•sion** \-'mishən\ *n* **—sub•mis•sive** \-'misiv\ *adj*
sub•nor•mal \,səb'nȯrməl\ *adj* **:** falling below what is normal
sub•or•di•nate \sə'bȯrdᵊnət\ *adj* **:** lower in rank ∼ *n* **:** one that is subordinate ∼ \sə'bȯrdᵊn,āt\ *vb* **-nat•ed; -nat•ing :** place in a lower rank or class **—sub•or•di•na•tion** \-,bȯrdᵊn'āshən\ *n*
sub•poe•na \sə'pēnə\ *n* **:** summons to appear in court ∼ *vb* **-naed; -na•ing :** summon with a subpoena
sub•scribe \səb'skrīb\ *vb* **-scribed; -scrib•ing 1 :** give consent or approval **2 :** agree to support or to receive and pay for **—sub•scrib•er** *n*
sub•scrip•tion \səb'skripshən\ *n* **:** order for regular receipt of a publication
sub•se•quent \'səbsikwənt, -sə,kwent\ *adj* **:** following after **—sub•se•quent•ly** \-,kwentlē, -kwənt-\ *adv*
sub•ser•vi•ence \səb'sərvēəns\ *n* **:** obsequious submission **—sub•ser•vi•en•cy** \-ənsē\ *n* **—sub•ser•vi•ent** \-ənt\ *adj*
sub•side \səb'sīd\ *vb* **-sid•ed; -sid•ing :** die down in intensity
sub•sid•iary \səb'sidē,erē\ *adj* **1 :** furnishing support **2 :** of secondary importance ∼ *n* **:** company controlled by another company
sub•si•dize \'səbsə,dīz\ *vb* **-dized; -diz•ing :** aid with a subsidy
sub•si•dy \'səbsədē\ *n, pl* **-dies :** gift of supporting funds
sub•sist \səb'sist\ *vb* **:** acquire the necessities of life **—sub•sis•tence** \-'sistəns\ *n*
sub•stance \'səbstəns\ *n* **1 :** essence or essential part **2 :** physical material **3 :** wealth
sub•stan•dard \,səb'standərd\ *adj* **:** falling short of a standard or norm
sub•stan•tial \səb'stanchəl\ *adj* **1 :** plentiful **2 :** considerable **—sub•stan•tial•ly** *adv*
sub•stan•ti•ate \səb'stanchē,āt\ *vb* **-at•ed; -at•ing :** verify **—sub•stan•ti•a•tion** \-,stanchē'āshən\ *n*
sub•sti•tute \'səbstə,tüt, -,tyüt\ *n* **:** replacement ∼ *vb* **-tut•ed; -tut•ing :** put or serve in place of another **—substitute** *adj* **—sub•sti•tu•tion** \,səbstə'tüshən, -'tyü-\ *n*
sub•ter•fuge \'səbtər,fyüj\ *n* **:** deceptive trick
sub•ter•ra•nean \,səbtə'rānēən\ *adj* **:** lying or being underground
sub•ti•tle \'səb,tītᵊl\ *n* **:** movie caption
sub•tle \'sətᵊl\ *adj* **-tler** \-ər\; **-tlest** \-ist\ **1 :** hardly noticeable **2 :** clever **—sub•tle•ty** \-tē\ *n* **—sub•tly** \-ᵊlē\ *adv*
sub•tract \səb'trakt\ *vb* **:** take away (as one number from another) **—sub•trac•tion** \-'trakshən\ *n*
sub•urb \'səb,ərb\ *n* **:** residential area adjacent to a city **—sub•ur•ban** \sə'bərbən\ *adj or n* **—sub•ur•ban•ite** \-bə,nīt\ *n*
sub•vert \səb'vərt\ *vb* **:** overthrow or ruin **—sub•ver•sion** \-'vərzhən\ *n* **—sub•ver•sive** \-'vərsiv\ *adj*
sub•way \'səb,wā\ *n* **:** underground electric railway
suc•ceed \sək'sēd\ *vb* **1 :** follow (someone) in a job, role, or title **2 :** attain a desired object or end
suc•cess \-'ses\ *n* **1 :** favorable outcome **2 :** gaining of wealth and fame **3 :** one that succeeds **—suc•cess•ful** \-fəl\ *adj* **—suc•cess•ful•ly** *adv*
suc•ces•sion \sək'seshən\ *n* **1 :** order, act, or right of succeeding **2 :** series
suc•ces•sive \-'sesiv\ *adj* **:** following in order **—suc•ces•sive•ly** *adv*
suc•ces•sor \-'sesər\ *n* **:** one that succeeds another
suc•cinct \sək'siŋkt, sə'siŋkt\ *adj* **:** brief **—suc•cinct•ly** *adv* **—suc•cinct•ness** *n*
suc•cor \'səkər\ *n or vb* **:** help
suc•co•tash \'səkə,tash\ *n* **:** beans and corn cooked together

suc•cu•lent \\'səkyələnt\ *adj* : juicy —**suc•cu•lence** \-ləns\ *n* —**succulent** *n*

suc•cumb \sə'kəm\ *vb* 1 : yield 2 : die

such \\'səch\ *adj* 1 : of this or that kind 2 : having a specified quality —**such** *pron or adv*

suck \\'sək\ *vb* 1 : draw in liquid with the mouth 2 : draw liquid from by or as if by mouth —**suck** *n*

suck•er \\'səkər\ *n* 1 : one that sucks or clings 2 : easily deceived person

suck•le \\'səkəl\ *vb* **-led; -ling** : give or draw milk from the breast or udder

suck•ling \\'səkliŋ\ *n* : young unweaned mammal

su•crose \\'sü,krōs, -,krōz\ *n* : cane or beet sugar

suc•tion \\'səkshən\ *n* 1 : act of sucking 2 : act or process of drawing in by partially exhausting the air

sud•den \\'səd⁰n\ *adj* 1 : happening unexpectedly 2 : steep 3 : hasty —**sud•den•ly** *adv* —**sud•den•ness** *n*

suds \\'sədz\ *n pl* : soapy water esp. when frothy —**sudsy** \\'sədzē\ *adj*

sue \\'sü\ *vb* **sued; su•ing** 1 : petition 2 : bring legal action against

suede, suède \\'swād\ *n* : leather with a napped surface

su•et \\'süət\ *n* : hard beef fat

suf•fer \\'səfər\ *vb* 1 : experience pain, loss, or hardship 2 : permit —**suf•fer•er** *n*

suf•fer•ing \-əriŋ\ *n* : pain or hardship

suf•fice \sə'fīs\ *vb* **-ficed; -fic•ing** : be sufficient

suf•fi•cient \sə'fishənt\ *adj* : adequate —**suf•fi•cien•cy** \-ənsē\ *n* —**suf•fi•cient•ly** *adv*

suf•fix \\'səf,iks\ *n* : letters added at the end of a word —**suffix** \\'səfiks, ,sə'fiks\ *vb* —**suf•fix•a•tion** \,səf,ik'sāshən\ *n*

suf•fo•cate \\'səfə,kāt\ *vb* **-cat•ed; -cat•ing** : suffer or die or cause to die from lack of air —**suf•fo•cat•ing•ly** *adv* —**suf•fo•ca•tion** \,səfə'kāshən\ *n*

suf•frage \\'səfrij\ *n* : right to vote

suf•fuse \sə'fyüz\ *vb* **-fused; -fus•ing** : spread over or through

sug•ar \\'shügər\ *n* : sweet substance ~ *vb* : mix, cover, or sprinkle with sugar —**sug•ar•cane** *n* —**sug•ary** *adj*

sug•gest \səg'jest, sag-\ *vb* 1 : put into someone's mind 2 : remind one by association of ideas —**sug•gest•ible** \-'jestəbəl\ *adj* —**sug•ges•tion** \'jeschən\ *n*

sug•ges•tive \-'jestiv\ *adj* : suggesting something improper —**sug•ges•tive•ly** *adv* —**sug•ges•tive•ness** *n*

sui•cide \\'süə,sīd\ *n* 1 : act of killing oneself purposely 2 : one who commits suicide —**sui•cid•al** \,süə'sīd⁰l\ *adj*

suit \\'süt\ *n* 1 : action in court to recover a right or claim 2 : number of things used or worn together 3 : one of the 4 sets of playing cards ~ *vb* 1 : be appropriate or becoming to 2 : meet the needs of —**suit•abil•i•ty** \,sütə'bilətē\ *n* —**suit•able** \\'sütəbəl\ *adj* —**suit•ably** *adv*

suit•case *n* : case for a traveler's clothing

suite \\'swēt, *for 2 also* 'süt\ *n* 1 : group of rooms 2 : set of matched furniture

suit•or \\'sütər\ *n* : one who seeks to marry a woman

sul•fur \\'səlfər\ *n* : nonmetallic yellow chemical element —**sul•fu•ric** \,səl'fyùrik\ *adj* —**sul•fu•rous** \-'fyùrəs, ,səlfərəs, 'səlfyə-\ *adj*

sulk \\'səlk\ *vb* : be moodily silent or irritable —**sulk** *n*

sulky \\'səlkē\ *adj* : inclined to sulk ~ *n* : light 2-wheeled horse-drawn cart —**sulk•i•ly** \\'səlkəlē\ *adv* —**sulk•i•ness** \-kēnəs\ *n*

sul•len \\'sələn\ *adj* 1 : gloomily silent 2 : dismal —**sul•len•ly** *adv* —**sul•len•ness** *n*

sul•ly \\'səlē\ *vb* **-lied; -ly•ing** : cast doubt or disgrace on

sul•tan \\'səlt⁰n\ *n* : sovereign of a Muslim state —**sul•tan•ate** \-,āt\ *n*

sul•try \\'səltrē\ *adj* **-tri•er; -est** 1 : very hot and moist 2 : sexually arousing

sum \\'səm\ *n* 1 : amount 2 : gist 3 : result of addition ~ *vb* **-mm-** : find the sum of

su•mac \\'shü,mak, 'sü-\ *n* : shrub with spikes of berries

sum•ma•ry \\'səmərē\ *adj* 1 : concise 2 : done without delay or formality ~ *n, pl* **-ries** : concise statement —**sum•mar•i•ly** \sə'merəlē, 'səmərəlē\ *adv* —**sum•ma•rize** \səmə,rīz\ *vb*

sum•ma•tion \sə'māshən\ *n* : a summing up esp. in court

sum•mer \\'səmər\ *n* : season in which the sun shines most directly —**sum•mery** *adj*

sum•mit \\'səmət\ *n* 1 : highest point 2 : high-level conference

sum•mon \\'səmən\ *vb* 1 : send for or call together 2 : order to appear in court —**sum•mon•er** *n*

sum•mons \\'səmənz\ *n, pl* **sum•mons•es** : an order to answer charges in court

sump•tu•ous \\'səmpchəwəs\ *adj* : lavish

sun \\'sən\ *n* 1 : shining celestial body around which the planets revolve 2 : light of the sun ~ *vb* **-nn-** : expose to the sun —**sun•beam** *n* —**sun•block** *n* —**sun•burn** *n or vb* —**sun•glass•es** *n pl* —**sun•light** *n* —**sun•ny** *adj* —**sun•rise** *n* —**sun•set** *n* —**sun•shine** *n* —**sun•tan** *n*

sun•dae \\'səndē\ *n* : ice cream with topping

Sun•day \\'səndā, -dē\ *n* : 1st day of the week

sun•di•al \-,dīəl\ *n* : device for showing time by the sun's shadow

sun•dries \\'səndrēz\ *n, pl* : various small articles

sun•dry \-drē\ *adj* : several

sun•fish *n* : perchlike freshwater fish

sun•flow•er *n* : tall plant grown for its oil-rich seeds

sung *past of* SING

sunk *past of* SINK

sunk•en \\'səŋkən\ *adj* 1 : submerged 2 : fallen in

sun•spot *n* : dark spot on the sun

sun•stroke *n* : heatstroke from the sun

sup \\'səp\ *vb* **-pp-** : eat the evening meal

super \\'süpər\ *adj* : very fine

super- \,süpər, 'sü-\ *prefix* 1 : higher in quantity, quality, or degree than 2 : in addition 3 : exceeding a norm 4 : in excessive degree or intensity 5 : surpassing others of its kind 6 : situated above, on, or at the top of 7 : more inclusive than 8 : superior in status or position

superabundance	superpolite
superabundant	superport
superambitious	superpowerful
superathlete	superrich
superbomb	supersalesman
superclean	superscout
supercolossal	supersecrecy
superconvenient	supersecret
supercop	supersensitive
superdense	supersize
supereffective	supersized
superefficiency	superslick
superefficient	supersmooth
superfast	supersoft
supergood	superspecial
supergovernment	superspecialist
supergroup	superspy
superhero	superstar
superheroine	superstate
superhuman	superstrength
superintellectual	superstrong
superintelligence	supersystem
superintelligent	supertanker
superman	superthick
supermodern	superthin
superpatriot	supertight
superpatriotic	superweapon
superpatriotism	superwoman
superplane	

su•perb \sù'pərb\ *adj* : outstanding —**su•perb•ly** *adv*

su•per•cil•ious \,süpər'silēəs\ *adj* : haughtily contemptuous

su•per•fi•cial \,süpər'fishəl\ *adj* : relating to what is only apparent —**su•per•fi•ci•al•i•ty** \-,fishē'alətē\ *n* —**su•per•fi•cial•ly** *adv*

su•per•flu•ous \sù'pərfləwəs\ *adj* : more than necessary —**su•per•flu•i•ty** \,süpər'flüətē\ *n*

su•per•im•pose \,süpərim'pōz\ *vb* : lay over or above something

su•per•in•tend \,süpərin'tend\ *vb* : have charge and oversight of —**su•per•in•ten•dence** \-'tendəns\ *n* —**su•per•in•ten•den•cy** \-dənsē\ *n* —**su•per•in•ten•dent** \-dənt\ *n*

su•pe•ri•or \sù'pirēər\ *adj* 1 : higher, better, or more important 2 : haughty —**superior** *n* —**su•pe•ri•or•i•ty** \-,pirē'orətē\ *n*

su•per•la•tive \sù'pərlətiv\ *adj* 1 : relating to or being an adjective or adverb form that denotes an extreme level 2 : surpassing others —**superlative** *n* —**su•per•la•tive•ly** *adv*

su•per•mar•ket \\'süpər,märkət\ *n* : self-service grocery store

su•per•nat•u•ral \,süpər'nachərəl\ *adj* : beyond the observable physical world —**su•per•nat•u•ral•ly** *adv*

su•per•pow•er \\'süpər,paùər\ *n* : politically and militarily dominant nation

su•per•sede \,süpər'sēd\ *vb* **-sed•ed; -sed•ing** : take the place of

su•per•son•ic \-'sänik\ *adj* : faster than the speed of sound

su•per•sti•tion \,süpər'stishən\ *n* : beliefs based on ignorance, fear of the unknown, or trust in magic —**su•per•sti•tious** \-əs\ *adj*

su•per•struc•ture \\'süpər,strəkchər\ *n* : something built on a base or as a vertical extension

su•per•vise \\'süpər,vīz\ *vb* **-vised; -vis•ing** : have charge of —**su•per•vi•sion** \,süpər'vizhən\ *n* —**su•per•vi•sor** \\'süpər,vīzər\ *n* —**su•per•vi•so•ry** \,süpər'vīzə-rē\ *adj*

su•pine \sù'pīn\ *adj* 1 : lying on the back 2 : indifferent or abject

sup•per \\'səpər\ *n* : evening meal

sup•plant \sə'plant\ *vb* : take the place of

sup•ple \\'səpəl\ *adj* **-pler; -plest** : able to bend easily

sup•ple•ment \\'səpləmənt\ *n* : something that adds to or makes up for a lack —**supplement** *vb* —**sup•ple•men•tal** \,səplə'ment⁰l\ *adj* —**sup•ple•men•ta•ry** \-'mentərē\ *adj*

sup•pli•ant \\'səplēənt\ *n* : one who supplicates

sup•pli•cate \\'səplə,kāt\ *vb* **-cat•ed; -cat•ing** 1 : pray to God 2 : ask earnestly and humbly —**sup•pli•cant** \-likənt\ *n* —**sup•pli•ca•tion** \,səplə'kāshən\ *n*

sup•ply \sə'plī\ *vb* **-plied; -ply•ing** : furnish ~ *n, pl* **-plies** 1 : amount needed or available 2 *pl* : provisions —**sup•pli•er** \-'plīər\ *n*

sup•port \sə'pōrt\ *vb* 1 : take sides with 2 : provide with food, clothing, and shelter 3 : hold up or serve as a foundation for —**support** *n* —**sup•port•able** *adj* —**sup•port•er** *n*

sup•pose \sə'pōz\ *vb* **-posed; -pos•ing** 1 : assume to be true 2 : expect 3 : think probable —**sup•po•si•tion** \,səpə'zishən\ *n*

sup•pos•i•to•ry \sə'päzə,tōrē\ *n, pl* **-ries** : medicated material for insertion (as into the rectum)

sup•press \sə'pres\ *vb* 1 : put an end to by authority 2 : keep from being known 3 : hold back —**sup•pres•sant** \sə'pres⁰nt\ *n* —**sup•pres•sion** \-'preshən\ *n*

su•prem•a•cy \sù'preməsē\ *n, pl* **-cies** : supreme power or authority

su•preme \sù'prēm\ *adj* 1 : highest in rank or authority 2 : greatest possible —**su•preme•ly** *adv*

Supreme Being *n* : God

sur•charge \\'sər,chärj\ *n* 1 : excessive load or burden 2 : extra fee or cost

sure \\'shùr\ *adj* **sur•er; sur•est** 1 : confident 2 : reliable 3 : not to be disputed 4 : bound to happen ~ *adv* : surely —**sure•ness** *n*

sure•ly \\'shùrlē\ *adv* 1 : in a sure manner 2 : without doubt 3 : indeed

sure•ty \\'shùrətē\ *n, pl* **-ties** 1 : guarantee 2 : one who gives a guarantee for another person

surf \\'sərf\ *n* : waves that break on the shore ~ *vb* : ride the surf —**surf•board** *n* —**surf•er** *n* —**surf•ing** *n*

sur•face \\'sərfəs\ *n* 1 : the outside of an object 2 : outward aspect ~ *vb* **-faced; -fac•ing** : rise to the surface

sur•feit \\'sərfət\ *n* 1 : excess 2 : excessive indulgence (as in food or drink) 3 : disgust caused by excess ~ *vb* : feed, supply, or indulge to the point of surfeit

surge \\'sərj\ *vb* **surged; surg•ing** : rise and fall in or as if in waves ~ *n* : sudden increase

sur•geon \\'sərjən\ *n* : physician who specializes in surgery

sur•gery \\'sərjərē\ *n, pl* **-ger•ies** : medical treatment involving cutting open the body

sur•gi•cal \\'sərjikəl\ *adj* : relating to surgeons or surgery —**sur•gi•cal•ly** *adv*

sur•ly \\'sərlē\ *adj* **-li•er; -est** : having a rude nature —**sur•li•ness** *n*

sur•mise \sər'mīz\ *vb* **-mised; -mis•ing** : guess —**surmise** *n*

sur•mount \-'maùnt\ *vb* 1 : prevail over 2 : get to or be the top of

sur•name \\'sər,nām\ *n* : family name

sur•pass \sər'pas\ *vb* : go beyond or exceed —**sur•pass•ing•ly** *adv*

sur•plice \\'sərpləs\ *n* : loose white outer ecclesiastical vestment

sur•plus \\'sər,pləs\ *n* : quantity left over

sur•prise \sə'prīz, sər-\ *vb* **-prised; -pris•ing** 1 : come upon or affect unexpectedly 2 : amaze —**surprise** *n* —**sur•pris•ing** *adj* —**sur•pris•ing•ly** *adv*

sur•ren•der \sə'rendər\ *vb* : give up oneself or a possession to another ~ *n* : act of surrendering

sur•rep•ti•tious \,sərəp'tishəs\ *adj* : done, made, or acquired by stealth —**sur•rep•ti•tious•ly** *adv*

sur•rey \\'sərē\ *n, pl* **-reys** : horse-drawn carriage

sur•ro•gate \\'sərəgāt, -gət\ *n* : substitute

sur•round \sə'raùnd\ *vb* : enclose on all sides

sur•round•ings \sə'raùndiŋz\ *n pl* : objects, conditions, or area around something

sur•veil•lance \sər'vāləns, -'vālyəns, -'vā-əns\ *n* : careful watch

sur•vey \sər'vā\ *vb* **-veyed; -vey•ing** 1 : look over and examine closely 2 : make a survey of (as a tract of land) ~ \'sər,-\ *n, pl* **-veys** 1 : inspection 2 : process of measuring (as land) —**sur•vey•or** \-ər\ *n*

sur•vive \sər'vīv\ *vb* **-vived; -viv•ing** 1 : remain alive or in existence 2 : outlive or outlast —**sur•viv•al** *n* —**sur•vi•vor** \-'vīvər\ *n*

sus•cep•ti•ble \sə'septəbəl\ *adj* : likely to allow or be affected by something —**sus•cep•ti•bil•i•ty** \-,septə'bilətē\ *n*

sus•pect \'səs,pekt, sə'spekt\ *adj* 1 : regarded with suspicion 2 : questionable

~ \'səs,pekt\ *n* : one who is suspected (as of a crime) ~ \sə'spekt\ *vb* 1 : have doubts of 2 : believe guilty without proof 3 : guess

sus•pend \sə'spend\ *vb* 1 : temporarily stop or keep from a function or job 2 : withhold (judgment) temporarily 3 : hang

sus•pend•er \sə'spendər\ *n* : one of 2 supporting straps holding up trousers and passing over the shoulders

sus•pense \sə'spens\ *n* : excitement and uncertainty as to outcome —**sus•pense•ful** *adj*

sus•pen•sion \sə'spenchən\ *n* : act of suspending or the state or period of being suspended

sus•pi•cion \sə'spishən\ *n* 1 : act of suspecting something 2 : trace

sus•pi•cious \sə'spishəs\ *adj* 1 : arousing suspicion 2 : inclined to suspect —**sus•pi•cious•ly** *adv*

sus•tain \sə'stān\ *vb* 1 : provide with nourishment 2 : keep going 3 : hold up 4 : suffer 5 : support or prove

sus•te•nance \\'səstənəns\ *n* 1 : nourishment 2 : something that sustains or supports

svelte \\'sfelt\ *adj* : slender and graceful

swab \\'swäb\ *n* 1 : mop 2 : wad of absorbent material for applying medicine ~ *vb* **-bb-** : use a swab on

swad•dle \\'swäd⁰l\ *vb* **-dled; -dling** \\'swäd⁰liŋ\ : bind (an infant) in bands of cloth

swag•ger \\'swagər\ *vb* **-gered; -ger•ing** 1 : walk with a conceited swing 2 : boast —**swagger** *n*

¹**swal•low** \\'swälō\ *n* : small migratory bird

²**swallow** *vb* 1 : take into the stomach through the throat 2 : envelop or take in 3 : accept too easily —**swallow** *n*

swam *past of* SWIM

swamp \\'swämp\ *n* : wet spongy land ~ *vb* : deluge (as with water) —**swampy** *adj*

swan \\'swän\ *n* : white long-necked swimming bird

swap \\'swäp\ *vb* **-pp-** : trade —**swap** *n*

swarm \\'swórm\ *n* 1 : mass of honeybees leaving a hive to start a new colony 2 : large crowd ~ *vb* : gather in a swarm

swar•thy \\'swórthē, -thē\ *adj* **-thi•er; -est** : dark in complexion

swash•buck•ler \\'swäsh,bəklər\ *n* : swaggering or daring soldier or adventurer —**swash•buck•ling** \-,bəkliŋ\ *adj*

swat \\'swät\ *vb* **-tt-** : hit sharply —**swat** *n* —**swat•ter** *n*

swatch \\'swäch\ *n* : sample piece (as of fabric)

swath \\'swäth, 'swóth\, **swathe** \\'swäth, 'swóth, 'swáth\ *n* : row or path cut (as through grass)

swathe \\'swäth, 'swóth, 'swáth\ *vb* **swathed; swath•ing** : wrap with or as if with a bandage

sway \\'swā\ *vb* 1 : swing gently from side to side 2 : influence ~ *n* 1 : gentle swinging from side to side 2 : controlling power or influence

swear \\'swar\ *vb* **swore** \\'swōr\, **sworn** \\'swōrn\; **swear•ing** 1 : make or cause to make a solemn statement under oath 2 : use profane language —**swear•er** *n* —**swear•ing** *n*

sweat \\'swet\ *vb* **sweat** *or* **sweat•ed; sweat•ing** 1 : excrete salty moisture from skin glands 2 : form drops of moisture on the surface 3 : work or cause to work hard —**sweat** *n* —**sweaty** *adj*

sweat•er \\'swetər\ *n* : knitted jacket or pullover

sweat•shirt \\'swet,shərt\ *n* : loose collarless heavy cotton jersey pullover

sweep \\'swēp\ *vb* **swept** \\'swept\; **sweep•ing** 1 : remove or clean by a brush or a single forceful wipe (as of the hand) 2 : move over with speed and force (as of the hand) 3 : move or extend in a wide curve ~ *n* 1 : a clearing off or away 2 : single forceful wipe or swinging movement 3 : scope —**sweep•er** *n* —**sweep•ing** *adj*

sweep•stakes \\'swēp,stāks\ *n, pl* **sweepstakes** : contest in which the entire prize may go to the winner

sweet \\'swēt\ *adj* 1 : being or causing the pleasing taste typical of sugar 2 : not stale or spoiled 3 : not salted 4 : pleasant 5 : much loved ~ *n* : something sweet —**sweet•en** \\'swēt⁰n\ *vb* —**sweet•ly** *adv* —**sweet•ness** *n* —**sweet•en•er** \-⁰nər\ *n*

sweet•heart *n* : person one loves

sweet potato *n* : sweet yellow edible root of a tropical vine

swell \\'swel\ *vb* **swelled; swelled** *or* **swol•len** \\'swōlən\; **swell•ing** 1 : enlarge 2 : bulge 3 : fill or be filled with emotion ~ *n* 1 : long rolling ocean wave 2 : condition of bulging —**swell•ing** *n*

swel•ter \\'sweltər\ *vb* : be uncomfortable from excessive heat

swept *past of* SWEEP

swerve \\'swərv\ *vb* **swerved; swerv•ing** : move abruptly aside from a course —**swerve** *n*

1swift \'swift\ *adj* **1 :** moving with great speed **2 :** occurring suddenly **—swift•ly** *adv* **—swift•ness** *n*
2swift *n* **:** small insect-eating bird
swig \'swig\ *vb* **-gg- :** drink in gulps **—swig** *n*
swill \'swil\ *vb* **:** swallow greedily ~ *n* **1 :** animal food of refuse and liquid **2 :** garbage
swim \'swim\ *vb* **swam** \'swam\; **swum** \'swəm\; **swim•ming 1 :** propel oneself in water **2 :** float in or be surrounded with a liquid **3 :** be dizzy ~ *n* **:** act or period of swimming **—swim•mer** *n*
swin•dle \'swindəl\ *vb* **-dled; -dling** \-iŋ\ **:** cheat (someone) of money or property **—swindle** *n* **—swin•dler** \-ər\ *n*
swine \'swīn\ *n, pl* **swine :** short-legged hoofed mammal with a snout **—swin•ish** \'swīnish\ *adj*
swing \'swiŋ\ *vb* **swung** \'swəŋ\; **swing•ing 1 :** move or cause to move rapidly in an arc **2 :** sway or cause to sway back and forth **3 :** hang so as to sway or sag **4 :** turn on a hinge or pivot **5 :** manage or handle successfully ~ *n* **1 :** act or instance of swinging **2 :** swinging movement (as in trying to hit something) **3 :** suspended seat for swinging **—swing** *adj* **—swing•er** *n*
swipe \'swīp\ *n* **:** strong sweeping blow ~ *vb* **swiped; swip•ing 1 :** strike or wipe with a sweeping motion **2 :** steal esp. with a quick movement
swirl \'swərl\ *vb* **:** move or cause to move in a circle **—swirl** *n*
swish \'swish\ *n* **:** hissing, sweeping, or brushing sound **—swish** *vb*
switch \'swich\ *n* **1 :** slender flexible whip or twig **2 :** blow with a switch **3 :** shift, change, or reversal **4 :** device that opens or closes an electrical circuit ~ *vb* **1 :** punish or urge on with a switch **2 :** change or reverse roles, positions, or subjects **3 :** operate a switch of
switch•board *n* **:** panel of switches to make and break telephone connections
swiv•el \'swivəl\ *vb* **-eled** *or* **-elled; -el•ing** *or* **-el•ling :** swing or turn on a pivot **—swivel** *n*
swollen *past part of* SWELL
swoon \'swün\ *n* **:** faint **—swoon** *vb*
swoop \'swüp\ *vb* **:** make a swift diving attack **—swoop** *n*
sword \'sōrd\ *n* **:** thrusting or cutting weapon with a long blade
sword•fish *n* **:** large ocean fish with a long swordlike projection
swore *past of* SWEAR
sworn *past part of* SWEAR
swum *past part of* SWIM
swung *past of* SWING
syc•a•more \'sikə,mōr\ *n* **:** shade tree
sy•co•phant \'sikəfənt\ *n* **:** servile flatterer **—syc•o•phan•tic** \,sikə'fantik\ *adj*
syl•la•ble \'siləbəl\ *n* **:** unit of a spoken word **—syl•lab•ic** \sə'labik\ *adj*
syl•la•bus \'siləbəs\ *n, pl* **-bi** \-,bī\ *or* **-bus•es :** summary of main topics (as of a course of study)
syl•van \'silvən\ *adj* **1 :** living or located in a wooded area **2 :** abounding in woods
sym•bol \'simbəl\ *n* **:** something that represents or suggests another thing **—sym•bol•ic** \sim'bälik\ *adj* **—sym•bol•i•cal•ly** *adv*
sym•bol•ism \'simbə,lizəm\ *n* **:** representation of meanings with symbols
sym•bol•ize \'simbə,līz\ *vb* **-ized; -iz•ing :** serve as a symbol of **—sym•bol•i•za•tion** \,simbələ'zāshən\ *n*
sym•me•try \'simətrē\ *n, pl* **-tries :** regularity and balance in the arrangement of parts **—sym•met•ri•cal** \sə'metrikəl\ *adj* **—sym•met•ri•cal•ly** *adv*
sym•pa•thize \'simpə,thīz\ *vb* **-thized; -thiz•ing :** feel or show sympathy **—sym•pa•thiz•er** *n*
sym•pa•thy \'simpəthē\ *n, pl* **-thies 1 :** ability to understand or share the feelings of another **2 :** expression of sorrow for another's misfortune **—sym•pa•thet•ic** \,simpə'thetik\ *adj* **—sym•pa•thet•i•cal•ly** *adv*
sym•pho•ny \'simfənē\ *n, pl* **-nies :** composition for an orchestra or the orchestra itself **—sym•phon•ic** \sim'fänik\ *adj*
sym•po•sium \sim'pōzēəm\ *n, pl* **-sia** \-zēə\ *or* **-siums :** conference at which a topic is discussed
symp•tom \'simptəm\ *n* **:** unusual feeling or reaction that is a sign of disease **—symp•tom•at•ic** \,simptə'matik\ *adj*
syn•a•gogue, syn•a•gog \'sinə,gäg, -,gōg\ *n* **:** Jewish house of worship
syn•chro•nize \'siŋkrə,nīz, 'sin-\ *vb* **-nized; -niz•ing 1 :** occur or cause to occur at the same instant **2 :** cause to agree in time **—syn•chro•ni•za•tion** \,siŋkrənə'zāshən, ,sin-\ *n*
syn•co•pa•tion \,siŋkə'pāshən, ,sin-\ *n* **:** shifting of the regular musical accent to the weak beat **—syn•co•pate** \'siŋkə,pāt, 'sin-\ *vb*
syn•di•cate \'sindikət\ *n* **:** business association ~ \-də,kāt\ *vb* **-cat•ed; -cat•ing 1 :** form a syndicate **2 :** publish through a syndicate **—syn•di•ca•tion** \,sində'kāshən\ *n*
syn•drome \'sin,drōm\ *n* **:** particular group of symptoms
syn•onym \'sinə,nim\ *n* **:** word with the same meaning as another **—syn•on•y•mous** \sə'nänəməs\ *adj* **—syn•on•y•my** \-mē\ *n*
syn•op•sis \sə'näpsəs\ *n, pl* **-op•ses** \-,sēz\ **:** condensed statement or outline
syn•tax \'sin,taks\ *n* **:** way in which words are put together **—syn•tac•tic** \sin'taktik\ *or* **syn•tac•ti•cal** \-tikəl\ *adj*
syn•the•sis \'sinthəsəs\ *n, pl* **-the•ses** \-,sēz\ **:** combination of parts or elements into a whole **—syn•the•size** \-,sīz\ *vb*
syn•thet•ic \sin'thetik\ *adj* **:** artificially made **—synthetic** *n* **—syn•thet•i•cal•ly** *adv*
syph•i•lis \'sifələs\ *n* **:** venereal disease
sy•ringe \sə'rinj, 'sirinj\ *n* **:** plunger device for injecting or withdrawing liquids
syr•up \'sərəp, 'sirəp\ *n* **:** thick sticky sweet liquid **—syr•upy** *adj*
sys•tem \'sistəm\ *n* **1 :** arrangement of units that function together **2 :** regular order **—sys•tem•at•ic** \,sistə'matik\ *adj* **—sys•tem•at•i•cal•ly** *adv* **—sys•tem•a•tize** \'sistəmə,tīz\ *vb*
sys•tem•ic \sis'temik\ *adj* **:** relating to the whole body

T

t \'tē\ *n, pl* **t's** *or* **ts** \'tēz\ **:** 20th letter of the alphabet
tab \'tab\ *n* **1 :** short projecting flap **2** *pl* **:** careful watch
tab•by \'tabē\ *n, pl* **-bies :** domestic cat
tab•er•na•cle \'tabər,nakəl\ *n* **:** house of worship
ta•ble \'tābəl\ *n* **1 :** piece of furniture having a smooth slab fixed on legs **2 :** supply of food **3 :** arrangement of data in columns **4 :** short list **—ta•ble•cloth** *n* **—ta•ble•top** *n* **—ta•ble•ware** *n* **—tab•u•lar** \'tabyələr\ *adj*
tab•leau \'tab,lō\ *n, pl* **-leaux** \-,lōz\ **1 :** graphic description **2 :** depiction of a scene by people in costume
ta•ble•spoon *n* **1 :** large serving spoon **2 :** measuring spoon holding ½ fluid ounce **—ta•ble•spoon•ful** \-,fu̇l\ *n*
tab•let \'tablət\ *n* **1 :** flat slab suited for an inscription **2 :** collection of sheets of paper glued together at one edge **3 :** disk-shaped pill
tab•loid \'tab,lōid\ *n* **:** newspaper of small page size
ta•boo \tə'bü, ta-\ *adj* **:** banned esp. as immoral or dangerous **—taboo** *n or vb*
tab•u•late \'tabyə,lāt\ *vb* **-lat•ed; -lat•ing :** put in the form of a table **—tab•u•la•tion** \,tabyə'lāshən\ *n* **—tab•u•la•tor** \'tabyə,lātər\ *n*
tac•it \'tasət\ *adj* **:** implied but not expressed **—tac•it•ly** *adv* **—tac•it•ness** *n*
tac•i•turn \'tasə,tərn\ *adj* **:** not inclined to talk
tack \'tak\ *n* **1 :** small sharp nail **2 :** course of action ~ *vb* **1 :** fasten with tacks **2 :** add on
tack•le \'takəl, *naut often* 'tāk-\ *n* **1 :** equipment **2 :** arrangement of ropes and pulleys **3 :** act of tackling ~ *vb* **-led; -ling 1 :** seize or throw down **2 :** start dealing with
1tacky \'takē\ *adj* **tack•i•er; -est :** sticky to the touch
2tacky *adj* **tack•i•er; -est :** cheap or gaudy
tact \'takt\ *n* **:** sense of the proper thing to say or do **—tact•ful** \-fəl\ *adj* **—tact•ful•ly** *adv* **—tact•less** *adj* **—tact•less•ly** *adv*
tac•tic \'taktik\ *n* **:** action as part of a plan
tac•tics \'taktiks\ *n sing or pl* **1 :** science of maneuvering forces in combat **2 :** skill of using available means to reach an end **—tac•ti•cal** \-tikəl\ *adj* **—tac•ti•cian** \tak'tishən\ *n*
tac•tile \'taktəl, -,tīl\ *adj* **:** relating to or perceptible through the sense of touch
tad•pole \'tad,pōl\ *n* **:** larval frog or toad with tail and gills
taf•fe•ta \'tafətə\ *n* **:** crisp lustrous fabric (as of silk)
taf•fy \'tafē\ *n, pl* **-fies :** candy stretched until porous
1tag \'tag\ *n* **:** piece of hanging or attached material ~ *vb* **-gg- 1 :** provide or mark with a tag **2 :** follow closely
2tag *n* **:** children's game of trying to catch one another ~ *vb* **:** touch a person in tag
tail \'tāl\ *n* **1 :** rear end or a growth extending from the rear end of an animal **2 :** back or last part **3 :** the reverse of a coin ~ *vb* **:** follow **—tailed** \'tāld\ *adj* **—tail•less** *adj*
tail•gate \-,gāt\ *n* **:** hinged gate on the back of a vehicle that can be lowered for loading ~ *vb* **-gat•ed; -gat•ing :** drive too close behind another vehicle
tail•light *n* **:** red warning light at the back of a vehicle
tai•lor \'tālər\ *n* **:** one who makes or alters garments ~ *vb* **1 :** fashion or alter (clothes) **2 :** make or adapt for a special purpose
tail•spin *n* **:** spiral dive by an airplane
taint \'tānt\ *vb* **:** affect or become affected with something bad and esp. decay ~ *n* **:** trace of decay or corruption
take \'tāk\ *vb* **took** \'tu̇k\; **tak•en** \'tākən\; **tak•ing 1 :** get into one's possession **2 :** become affected by **3 :** receive into one's body (as by eating) **4 :** pick out or remove **5 :** use for transportation **6 :** need or make use of **7 :** lead, carry, or cause to go to another place **8 :** undertake and do, make, or perform ~ *n* **:** amount taken **—take•over** *n* **—tak•er** *n* **—take advantage of :** profit by **—take exception :** object **—take off** *vb* **1 :** remove **2 :** go away **3 :** mimic **4 :** begin flight **—take over** *vb* **:** assume control or possession of or responsibility for **—take place :** happen
take•off *n* **:** act or instance of taking off
talc \'talk\ *n* **:** soft mineral used in making toilet powder (**tal•cum powder** \'talkəm-\)
tale \'tāl\ *n* **1 :** story or anecdote **2 :** falsehood
tal•ent \'talənt\ *n* **:** natural mental or creative ability **—tal•ent•ed** *adj*
tal•is•man \'taləsmən, -əz-\ *n, pl* **-mans :** object thought to act as a charm
talk \'tȯk\ *vb* **1 :** express one's thoughts in speech **2 :** discuss **3 :** influence to a position or course of action by talking ~ *n* **1 :** act of talking **2 :** formal discussion **3 :** rumor **4 :** informal lecture **—talk•a•tive** \-ətiv\ *adj* **—talk•er** *n*
tall \'tȯl\ *adj* **:** extending to a great or specified height **—tall•ness** *n*
tal•low \'talō\ *n* **:** hard white animal fat used esp. in candles
tal•ly \'talē\ *n, pl* **-lies :** recorded amount ~ *vb* **-lied; -ly•ing 1 :** add or count up **2 :** match
tal•on \'talən\ *n* **:** bird's claw
tam \'tam\ *n* **:** tam-o'-shanter
tam•bou•rine \,tambə'rēn\ *n* **:** small drum with loose disks at the sides
tame \'tām\ *adj* **tam•er; tam•est 1 :** changed from being wild to being controllable by man **2 :** docile **3 :** dull ~ *vb* **tamed; tam•ing :** make or become tame **—tam•able, tame•able** *adj* **—tame•ly** *adv* **—tam•er** *n*
tam–o'–shan•ter \'tamə,shantər\ *n* **:** Scottish woolen cap with a wide flat circular crown
tamp \'tamp\ *vb* **:** drive down or in by a series of light blows
tam•per \'tampər\ *vb* **:** interfere so as to change for the worse
tan \'tan\ *vb* **-nn- 1 :** change (hide) into leather esp. by soaking in a liquid containing tannin **2 :** make or become brown (as by exposure to the sun) ~ *n* **1 :** brown skin color induced by the sun **2 :** light yellowish brown **—tan•ner** *n* **—tan•nery** \'tanərē\ *n*
tan•dem \'tandəm\ *adv* **:** one behind another
tang \'taŋ\ *n* **:** sharp distinctive flavor **—tangy** *adj*
tan•gent \'tanjənt\ *adj* **:** touching a curve or surface at only one point ~ *n* **1 :** tangent line, curve, or surface **2 :** abrupt change of course **—tan•gen•tial** \tan'jenchəl\ *adj*
tan•ger•ine \'tanjə,rēn, ,tanjə'-\ *n* **:** deep orange citrus fruit
tan•gi•ble \'tanjəbəl\ *adj* **1 :** able to be touched **2 :** substantially real **—tan•gi•bly** *adv*
tan•gle \'taŋgəl\ *vb* **-gled; -gling :** unite in intricate confusion ~ *n* **:** tangled twisted mass
tan•go \'taŋgō\ *n, pl* **-gos :** dance of Latin-American origin **—tango** *vb*
tank \'taŋk\ *n* **1 :** large artificial receptacle for liquids **2 :** armored military vehicle **—tank•ful** *n*
tan•kard \'taŋkərd\ *n* **:** tall one-handled drinking vessel
tank•er \'taŋkər\ *n* **:** vehicle or vessel with tanks for transporting a liquid
tan•nin \'tanən\ *n* **:** substance of plant origin used in tanning and dyeing
tan•ta•lize \'tantəl,īz\ *vb* **-lized; -liz•ing :** tease or torment by keeping something desirable just out of reach **—tan•ta•liz•er** *n* **—tan•ta•liz•ing•ly** *adv*
tan•ta•mount \'tantə,mau̇nt\ *adj* **:** equivalent in value or meaning
tan•trum \'tantrəm\ *n* **:** fit of bad temper
1tap \'tap\ *n* **1 :** faucet **2 :** act of tapping ~ *vb* **-pp- 1 :** pierce so as to draw off fluid **2 :** connect into **—tap•per** *n*
2tap *vb* **-pp- :** rap lightly ~ *n* **:** light stroke or its sound
tape \'tāp\ *n* **1 :** narrow flexible strip (as of cloth, plastic, or metal) **2 :** tape measure ~ *vb* **taped; tap•ing 1 :** fasten with tape **2 :** record on tape
tape measure *n* **:** strip of tape marked in units for use in measuring
ta•per \'tāpər\ *n* **1 :** slender wax candle **2 :** gradual lessening of width in a long object ~ *vb* **1 :** make or become smaller toward one end **2 :** diminish gradually
tap•es•try \'tapəstrē\ *n, pl* **-tries :** heavy handwoven ruglike wall hanging
tape•worm *n* **:** long flat intestinal worm
tap•i•o•ca \,tapē'ōkə\ *n* **:** a granular starch used esp. in puddings
tar \'tär\ *n* **:** thick dark sticky liquid distilled (as from coal) ~ *vb* **-rr- :** treat or smear with tar
ta•ran•tu•la \tə'ranchələ, -'rantələ\ *n* **:** large hairy usu. harmless spider
tar•dy \'tärdē\ *adj* **-di•er; -est :** late **—tar•di•ly** \'tärdəlē\ *adv* **—tar•di•ness** *n*
tar•get \'tärgət\ *n* **1 :** mark to shoot at **2 :** goal to be achieved ~ *vb* **1 :** make a target of **2 :** establish as a goal
tar•iff \'tarəf\ *n* **1 :** duty or rate of duty imposed on imported goods **2 :** schedule of tariffs, rates, or charges
tar•nish \'tärnish\ *vb* **:** make or become dull or discolored **—tarnish** *n*
tar•pau•lin \tär'pȯlən, 'tärpə-\ *n* **:** waterproof protective covering
1tar•ry \'tarē\ *vb* **-ried; -ry•ing :** be slow in leaving
2tar•ry \'tärē\ *adj* **:** resembling or covered with tar
1tart \'tärt\ *adj* **1 :** pleasantly sharp to the taste **2 :** caustic **—tart•ly** *adv* **—tart•ness** *n*
2tart *n* **:** small pie
tar•tan \'tärtən\ *n* **:** woolen fabric with a plaid design
tar•tar \'tärtər\ *n* **:** hard crust on the teeth
task \'task\ *n* **:** assigned work
task•mas•ter *n* **:** one that burdens another with labor
tas•sel \'tasəl, 'täs-\ *n* **:** hanging ornament made of a bunch of cords fastened at one end
taste \'tāst\ *vb* **tast•ed; tast•ing 1 :** test or determine the flavor of **2 :** eat or drink in small quantities **3 :** have a specific flavor ~ *n* **1 :** small amount tasted **2 :** bit **3 :** special sense that identifies sweet, sour, bitter, or salty qualities **4 :** individual preference **5 :** critical appreciation of quality **—taste•ful** \-fəl\ *adj* **—taste•ful•ly** *adv* **—taste•less** *adj* **—taste•less•ly** *adv* **—tast•er** *n*
tasty \'tāstē\ *adj* **tast•i•er; -est :** pleasing to the sense of taste **—tast•i•ness** *n*
tat•ter \'tatər\ *n* **1 :** part torn and left hanging **2** *pl* **:** tattered clothing ~ *vb* **:** make or become ragged
tat•tle \'tatəl\ *vb* **-tled; -tling :** inform on someone **—tat•tler** *n*
tat•tle•tale *n* **:** one that tattles
tat•too \ta'tü\ *vb* **:** mark the skin with indelible designs or figures **—tattoo** *n*
taught *past of* TEACH
taunt \'tȯnt\ *n* **:** sarcastic challenge or insult **—taunt** *vb* **—taunt•er** *n*
taut \'tȯt\ *adj* **:** tightly drawn **—taut•ly** *adv* **—taut•ness** *n*
tav•ern \'tavərn\ *n* **:** establishment where liquors are sold to be drunk on the premises
taw•dry \'tȯdrē\ *adj* **-dri•er; -est :** cheap and gaudy **—taw•dri•ly** \'tȯdrəlē\ *adv*
taw•ny \'tȯnē\ *adj* **-ni•er; -est :** brownish orange
tax \'taks\ *vb* **1 :** impose a tax on **2 :** charge **3 :** put under stress ~ *n* **1 :** charge by authority for public purposes **2 :** strain **—tax•able** *adj* **—taxa•tion** \tak'sāshən\ *n* **—tax•pay•er** *n* **—tax•pay•ing** *adj*
taxi \'taksē\ *n, pl* **tax•is** \-sēz\ **:** automobile transporting passengers for a fare ~ *vb* **tax•ied; taxi•ing** *or* **taxy•ing; tax•is** *or* **tax•ies 1 :** transport or go by taxi **2 :** move along the ground before takeoff or after landing
taxi•cab \'taksē,kab\ *n* **:** taxi
taxi•der•my \'taksə,dərmē\ *n* **:** skill or job of stuffing and mounting animal skins **—taxi•der•mist** \-mist\ *n*
tea \'tē\ *n* **:** cured leaves of an oriental shrub or a drink made from these **—tea•cup** *n* **—tea•pot** *n*
teach \'tēch\ *vb* **taught** \'tȯt\; **teach•ing 1 :** tell or show the fundamentals or skills of something **2 :** cause to know the consequences **3 :** impart knowledge of —

teach•able adj —**teach•er** n —**teaching** n
teak \'tēk\ n : East Indian timber tree or its wood
tea•ket•tle \'tē,ketᵊl\ n : covered kettle with a handle and spout for boiling water
teal \'tēl\ n, pl **teal** or **teals** : small short-necked wild duck
team \'tēm\ n 1 : draft animals harnessed together 2 : number of people organized for a game or work ~ vb : form or work together as a team —**team** adj —**team•mate** n —**team•work** n
team•ster \'tēmstər\ n 1 : one that drives a team of animals 2 : one that drives a truck
¹**tear** \'tir\ n : drop of salty liquid that moistens the eye —**tear•ful** \-fəl\ adj —**tear•ful•ly** adv
²**tear** \'tar\ vb **tore** \'tōr\; **torn** \'tōrn\; **tear•ing** 1 : separate or pull apart by force 2 : move or act with violence or haste ~ n : act or result of tearing
tease \'tēz\ vb **teased; teas•ing** : annoy by goading, coaxing, or tantalizing ~ n 1 : act of teasing or state of being teased 2 : one that teases
tea•spoon \'tē,spün\ n 1 : small spoon for stirring or sipping 2 : measuring spoon holding ⅙ fluid ounce —**tea•spoon•ful** \-,fu̇l\ n
teat \'tēt\ n : protuberance through which milk is drawn from an udder or breast
tech•ni•cal \'teknikəl\ adj 1 : having or relating to special mechanical or scientific knowledge 2 : by strict interpretation of rules —**tech•ni•cal•ly** adv
tech•ni•cal•i•ty \,teknə'kalətē\ n, pl **-ties** : detail meaningful only to a specialist
technical sergeant n : noncommissioned officer in the air force ranking next below a master sergeant
tech•ni•cian \tek'nishən\ n : person with the technique of a specialized skill
tech•nique \tek'nēk\ n : manner of accomplishing something
tech•nol•o•gy \tek'näləjē\ n, pl **-gies** : applied science —**tech•no•log•i•cal** \,teknə'läjikəl\ adj
te•dious \'tēdēəs\ adj : wearisome from length or dullness —**te•dious•ly** adv —**te•dious•ness** n
te•di•um \'tēdēəm\ n : tedious state or quality
tee \'tē\ n : mound or peg on which a golf ball is placed before beginning play —**tee** vb
teem \'tēm\ vb : become filled to overflowing
teen•age \'tēn,āj\, **teen•aged** \-,ājd\ adj : relating to people in their teens —**teen•ag•er** \-,ājər\ n
teens \'tēnz\ n pl : years 13 to 19 in a person's life
tee•pee var of TEPEE
tee•ter \'tētər\ vb 1 : move unsteadily 2 : seesaw —**teeter** n
teeth pl of TOOTH
teethe \'tēth\ vb **teethed; teeth•ing** : grow teeth
tele•cast \'teli,kast\ vb **-cast; -cast•ing** : broadcast by television —**telecast** n —**tele•cast•er** n
tele•com•mu•ni•ca•tion \'teləkəmyünə'kāshən\ n : communication at a distance (as by radio or telephone)
tele•gram \'telə,gram\ n : message sent by telegraph
tele•graph \-,graf\ n : system for communication by electrical transmission of coded signals ~ vb : send by telegraph —**te•leg•ra•pher** \tə'legrəfər\ n —**tele•graph•ic** \,telə'grafik\ adj
te•lep•a•thy \tə'lepəthē\ n : apparent communication without known sensory means —**tele•path•ic** \,telə'pathik\ adj —**tele•path•i•cal•ly** adv
tele•phone \'telə,fōn\ n : instrument or system for electrical transmission of spoken words ~ vb **-phoned; -phon•ing** : communicate with by telephone —**tele•phon•er** n
tele•scope \-,skōp\ n : tube-shaped optical instrument for viewing distant objects ~ vb **-scoped; -scop•ing** : slide or cause to slide inside another similar section —**tele•scop•ic** \,telə'skäpik\ adj
tele•vise \'telə,vīz\ vb **-vised; -vis•ing** : broadcast by television
tele•vi•sion \-,vizhən\ n : transmission and reproduction of images by radio waves
tell \'tel\ vb **told** \'tōld\; **tell•ing** 1 : count 2 : relate in detail 3 : reveal 4 : give information or an order to 5 : find out by observing
tell•er \'telər\ n 1 : one that relates or counts 2 : bank employee handling money
te•mer•i•ty \tə'merətē\ n, pl **-ties** : boldness
temp \'temp\ n 1 : temperature 2 : temporary worker
tem•per \'tempər\ vb 1 : dilute or soften 2 : toughen ~ n 1 : characteristic attitude or feeling 2 : toughness 3 : disposition or control over one's emotions
tem•per•a•ment \'tempərəmənt\ n : characteristic frame of mind — **tem•per•a•men•tal** \,temprə'mentᵊl\ adj
tem•per•ance \'temprəns\ n : moderation in or abstinence from indulgence and esp. the use of intoxicating drink
tem•per•ate \'tempərət\ adj : moderate
tem•per•a•ture \'tempər,chu̇r, -prə,chu̇r, -chər\ n 1 : degree of hotness or coldness 2 : fever
tem•pest \'tempəst\ n : violent storm —**tem•pes•tu•ous** \tem'peschəwəs\ adj
¹**tem•ple** \'tempəl\ n : place of worship
²**temple** n : flattened space on each side of the forehead
tem•po \'tempō\ n, pl **-pi** \-,pē\ or **-pos** : rate of speed
tem•po•ral \'tempərəl\ adj : relating to time or to secular concerns
tem•po•rary \'tempə,rerē\ adj : lasting for a short time only —**tem•po•rar•i•ly** \,tempə'rerəlē\ adv
tempt \'tempt\ vb 1 : coax or persuade to do wrong 2 : attract or provoke —**tempt•er** n —**tempt•ing•ly** adv —**tempt•ress** \'temptrəs\ n
temp•ta•tion \temp'tāshən\ n 1 : act of tempting 2 : something that tempts
ten \'ten\ n 1 : one more than 9 2 : 10th in a set or series 3 : thing having 10 units —**ten** adj or pron —**tenth** \'tenth\ adj or adv or n
ten•a•ble \'tenəbəl\ adj : capable of being held or defended —**ten•a•bil•i•ty** \,tenə'bilətē\ n
te•na•cious \tə'nāshəs\ adj 1 : holding fast 2 : retentive —**te•na•cious•ly** adv —**te•nac•i•ty** \tə'nasətē\ n
ten•ant \'tenənt\ n : one who occupies a rented dwelling —**ten•an•cy** \-ənsē\ n
¹**tend** \'tend\ vb : take care of or supervise something
²**tend** vb 1 : move in a particular direction 2 : show a tendency
ten•den•cy \'tendənsē\ n, pl **-cies** : likelihood to move, think, or act in a particular way
¹**ten•der** \'tendər\ adj 1 : soft or delicate 2 : expressing or responsive to love or sympathy 3 : sensitive (as to touch) —**ten•der•ly** adv —**ten•der•ness** n
²**tend•er** \'tendər\ n 1 : one that tends 2 : boat providing transport to a larger ship 3 : vehicle attached to a steam locomotive for carrying fuel and water
³**ten•der** n 1 : offer of a bid for a contract 2 : something that may be offered in payment —**tender** vb
ten•der•ize \'tendə,rīz\ vb **-ized; -iz•ing** : make (meat) tender —**ten•der•iz•er** \'tendə,rīzər\ n
ten•der•loin \'tender,lȯin\ n : tender beef or pork strip from near the backbone
ten•don \'tendən\ n : cord of tissue attaching muscle to bone —**ten•di•nous** \-dənəs\ adj
ten•dril \'tendrəl\ n : slender coiling growth of some climbing plants
ten•e•ment \'tenəmənt\ n 1 : house divided into apartments 2 : shabby dwelling
te•net \'tenət\ n : principle of belief
ten•nis \'tenəs\ n : racket-and-ball game played across a net
ten•or \'tenər\ n 1 : general drift or meaning 2 : highest natural adult male voice
ten•pin \'ten,pin\ n : bottle-shaped pin bowled at in a game (**tenpins**)
¹**tense** \'tens\ n : distinct verb form that indicates time
²**tense** adj **tens•er; tens•est** 1 : stretched tight 2 : marked by nervous tension —**tense** vb —**tense•ly** adv —**tense•ness** n —**ten•si•ty** \'tensətē\ n
ten•sile \'tensəl, -,sīl\ adj : relating to tension
ten•sion \'tenchən\ n 1 : tense condition 2 : state of mental unrest or of potential hostility or opposition
tent \'tent\ n : collapsible shelter
ten•ta•cle \'tentikəl\ n : long flexible projection of an insect or mollusk —**ten•ta•cled** \-kəld\ adj —**ten•tac•u•lar** \ten'takyələr\ adj
ten•ta•tive \'tentətiv\ adj : subject to change or discussion —**ten•ta•tive•ly** adv
ten•u•ous \'tenyəwəs\ adj 1 : not dense or thick 2 : flimsy or weak —**ten•u•ous•ly** adv —**ten•u•ous•ness** n
ten•ure \'tenyər\ n : act, right, manner, or period of holding something —**ten•ured** \-yərd\ adj
te•pee \'tē,pē\ n : conical tent
tep•id \'tepəd\ adj : moderately warm
term \'tərm\ n 1 : period of time 2 : mathematical expression 3 : special word or phrase 4 pl : conditions 5 pl : relations ~ vb : name
ter•mi•nal \'tərmənᵊl\ n 1 : end 2 : device for making an electrical connection 3 : station at end of a transportation line —**terminal** adj
ter•mi•nate \'tərmə,nāt\ vb **-nat•ed; -nat•ing** : bring or come to an end —**ter•mi•na•ble** \-nəbəl\ adj —**ter•mi•na•tion** \,tərmə'nāshən\ n
ter•mi•nol•o•gy \,tərmə'näləjē\ n : terms used in a particular subject
ter•mi•nus \'tərmənəs\ n, pl **-ni** \-,nī\ or **-nus•es** 1 : end 2 : end of a transportation line
ter•mite \'tər,mīt\ n : wood-eating insect
tern \'tərn\ n : small sea bird
ter•race \'terəs\ n 1 : balcony or patio 2 : bank with a flat top ~ vb **-raced; -rac•ing** : landscape in a series of banks
ter•ra–cot•ta \,terə'kätə\ n : reddish brown earthenware
ter•rain \tə'rān\ n : features of the land
ter•ra•pin \'terəpən\ n : No. American turtle
ter•rar•i•um \tə'rarēəm\ n, pl **-ia** \-ēə\ or **-i•ums** : container for keeping plants or animals
ter•res•tri•al \tə'restrēəl\ adj 1 : relating to the earth or its inhabitants 2 : living or growing on land
ter•ri•ble \'terəbəl\ adj 1 : exciting terror 2 : distressing 3 : intense 4 : of very poor quality —**ter•ri•bly** \-blē\ adv
ter•ri•er \'terēər\ n : small dog
ter•rif•ic \tə'rifik\ adj 1 : exciting terror 2 : extraordinary
ter•ri•fy \'terə,fī\ vb **-fied; -fy•ing** : fill with terror —**ter•ri•fy•ing•ly** adv
ter•ri•to•ry \'terə,tōrē\ n, pl **-ries** : particular geographical region —**ter•ri•to•ri•al** \,terə'tōrēəl\ adj
ter•ror \'terər\ n : intense fear and panic or a cause of it
ter•ror•ism \-,izəm\ n : systematic covert warfare to produce terror for political coercion —**ter•ror•ist** \-ist\ adj or n
ter•ror•ize \-,īz\ vb **-ized; -iz•ing** 1 : fill with terror 2 : coerce by threat or violence
ter•ry \'terē\ n, pl **-ries** : absorbent fabric with a loose pile
terse \'tərs\ adj **ters•er; ters•est** : concise —**terse•ly** adv —**terse•ness** n
ter•tia•ry \'tərshē,erē\ adj : of 3d rank, importance, or value
test \'test\ n : examination or evaluation ~ vb : examine by a test —**test•er** n
tes•ta•ment \'testəmənt\ n 1 cap : division of the Bible 2 : will —**tes•ta•men•ta•ry** \,testə'mentərē\ adj
tes•ti•cle \'testikəl\ n : testis
tes•ti•fy \'testə,fī\ vb **-fied; -fy•ing** 1 : give testimony 2 : serve as evidence
tes•ti•mo•ni•al \,testə'mōnēəl\ n 1 : favorable recommendation 2 : tribute —**testimonial** adj
tes•ti•mo•ny \'testə,mōnē\ n, pl **-nies** : statement given as evidence in court
tes•tis \'testəs\ n, pl **-tes** \-,tēz\ : male reproductive gland
tes•ty \'testē\ adj **-ti•er; -est** : easily annoyed
tet•a•nus \'tetᵊnəs\ n : bacterial disease producing violent spasms
tête–à–tête \,tātə'tāt\ adv : privately ~ n : private conversation ~ adj : private
teth•er \'tethər\ n : leash ~ vb : restrain with a leash
text \'tekst\ n 1 : author's words 2 : main body of printed or written matter on a page 3 : textbook 4 : scriptural passage used as the theme of a sermon 5 : topic —**tex•tu•al** \'tekschəwəl\ adj
text•book \-,bu̇k\ n : book on a school subject
tex•tile \'tek,stīl, 'tekstᵊl\ n : fabric
tex•ture \'tekschər\ n 1 : feel and appearance of something 2 : structure
than \'than\ conj or prep —used in comparisons
thank \'thaŋk\ vb : express gratitude to
thank•ful \-fəl\ adj : giving thanks —**thank•ful•ly** adv —**thank•ful•ness** n
thank•less adj : not appreciated
thanks \'thaŋks\ n pl : expression of gratitude
Thanks•giv•ing \thaŋks'giviŋ\ n : 4th Thursday in November observed as a legal holiday for giving thanks for divine goodness
that \'that\ pron, pl **those** \thōz\ 1 : something indicated or understood 2 : the one farther away ~ adj, pl **those** : being the one mentioned or understood or farther away ~ conj or pron —used to introduce a clause ~ adv : to such an extent
thatch \'thach\ vb : cover with thatch ~ n : covering of matted straw
thaw \'thȯ\ vb : melt or cause to melt —**thaw** n
the \thə, before vowel sounds usu thē\ definite article : that particular one ~ adv —used before a comparative or superlative
the•ater, the•atre \'thēətər\ n 1 : building or room for viewing a play or movie 2 : dramatic arts
the•at•ri•cal \thē'atrikəl\ adj 1 : relating to the theater 2 : involving exaggerated emotion
thee \thē\ pron, archaic objective case of THOU
theft \'theft\ n : act of stealing
their \ther\ adj : relating to them
theirs \'therz\ pron : their one or ones
the•ism \'thē,izəm\ n : belief in the existence of a god or gods —**the•ist** \-ist\ n or adj —**the•is•tic** \thē'istik\ adj
them \them\ pron, objective case of THEY
theme \'thēm\ n 1 : subject matter 2 : essay 3 : melody developed in a piece of music —**the•mat•ic** \thi'matik\ adj
them•selves \thəm'selvz, them-\ pron pl : they, them —used reflexively or for emphasis
then \'then\ adv 1 : at that time 2 : soon after that 3 : in addition 4 : in that case 5 : consequently ~ n : that time ~ adj : existing at that time
thence \'thens, 'thens\ adv : from that place or fact
the•oc•ra•cy \thē'äkrəsē\ n, pl **-cies** : government by officials regarded as divinely inspired —**the•o•crat•ic** \,thēə'kratik\ adj
the•ol•o•gy \thē'äləjē\ n, pl **-gies** : study of religion —**the•o•lo•gian** \,thēə'lōjən\ n —**the•o•log•i•cal** \-'läjikəl\ adj
the•o•rem \'thēərəm, 'thirəm\ n : provable statement of truth
the•o•ret•i•cal \,thēə'retikəl\ adj : relating to or being theory —**the•o•ret•i•cal•ly** adv
the•o•rize \'thēə,rīz\ vb **-rized; -riz•ing** : put forth theories —**the•o•rist** n
the•o•ry \'thēərē, 'thirē\ n, pl **-ries** 1 : general principles of a subject 2 : plausible or scientifically acceptable explanation 3 : judgment, guess, or opinion
ther•a•peu•tic \,therə'pyütik\ adj : offering or relating to remedy —**ther•a•peu•ti•cal•ly** adv
ther•a•py \'therəpē\ n, pl **-pies** : treatment for mental or physical disorder —**ther•a•pist** \-pist\ n
there \'thar\ adv 1 : in, at, or to that place 2 : in that respect ~ pron —used to introduce a sentence or clause ~ n : that place or point
there•abouts, there•about \,tharə'bau̇ts, 'tharə,-, -'bau̇t\ adv : near that place, time, number, or quantity
there•af•ter \thar'aftər\ adv : after that
there•by \thar'bī, 'thar,bī\ adv 1 : by that 2 : connected with or with reference to that
there•fore \'thar,fōr\ adv : for that reason
there•in \thar'in\ adv 1 : in or into that place, time, or thing 2 : in that respect
there•of \-'əv, -'äv\ adv 1 : of that or it 2 : from that
there•upon \'tharə,pȯn, -,pän; ,tharə'pȯn, -'pän\ adv 1 : on that matter 2 : therefore 3 : immediately after that
there•with \thar'with, -'with\ adv : with that
ther•mal \'thərməl\ adj : relating to, caused by, or conserving heat —**ther•mal•ly** adv
ther•mo•dy•nam•ics \,thərmədī'namiks\ n : physics of heat
ther•mom•e•ter \thər'mämətər\ n : instrument for measuring temperature —**ther•mo•met•ric** \,thərmə'metrik\ adj —**ther•mo•met•rical•ly** adv
ther•mos \'thərməs\ n : double-walled bottle used to keep liquids hot or cold
ther•mo•stat \'thərmə,stat\ n : automatic temperature control —**ther•mo•stat•ic** \,thərmə'statik\ adj —**ther•mo•stat•i•cal•ly** adv
the•sau•rus \thi'sȯrəs\ n, pl **-sau•ri** \-'sȯr,ī\ or **-sau•rus•es** \-'sȯrəsəz\ : book of words and esp. synonyms
these pl of THIS
the•sis \'thēsəs\ n, pl **the•ses** \'thē,sēz\ 1 : proposition to be argued for 2 : essay embodying results of original research
thes•pi•an \'thespēən\ adj : dramatic ~ n : actor
they \'thā\ pron 1 : those ones 2 : people in general
thi•a•mine \'thīəmən, -,mēn\ n : essential vitamin
thick \'thik\ adj 1 : having relatively great mass from front to back or top to bottom 2 : viscous ~ n : most crowded or thickest part —**thick•ly** adv —**thick•ness** n
thick•en \'thikən\ vb : make or become thick —**thick•en•er** \-ənər\ n
thick•et \'thikət\ n : dense growth of bushes or small trees
thick–skinned \-'skind\ adj : insensitive to criticism
thief \'thēf\ n, pl **thieves** \'thēvz\ : one that steals
thieve \'thēv\ vb **thieved; thiev•ing** : steal —**thiev•ery** n
thigh \'thī\ n : upper part of the leg
thigh•bone \'thī,bōn\ n : femur
thim•ble \'thimbəl\ n : protective cap for the finger in sewing —**thim•ble•ful** n
thin \'thin\ adj **-nn-** 1 : having relatively little mass from front to back or top to bottom 2 : not closely set or placed 3 : relatively free flowing 4 : lacking substance, fullness, or strength ~ vb **-nn-** : make or become thin —**thin•ly** adv —**thin•ness** n
thing \'thiŋ\ n 1 : matter of concern 2 : event or act 3 : object 4 pl : possessions
think \'thiŋk\ vb **thought** \'thȯt\; **think•ing** 1 : form or have in the mind 2 : have as

an opinion **3** : ponder **4** : devise by thinking **5** : imagine **—think•er** *n*

thin–skinned *adj* : extremely sensitive to criticism

third \ˈthərd\ *adj* : being number 3 in a countable series ~ *n* **1** : one that is third **2** : one of 3 equal parts **—third, third•ly** *adv*

third dimension *n* : thickness or depth **—third–dimensional** *adj*

third world *n* : less developed nations of the world

thirst \ˈthərst\ *n* **1** : dryness in mouth and throat **2** : intense desire ~ *vb* : feel thirst **—thirsty** *adj*

thir•teen \ˌthərˈtēn\ *n* : one more than 12 **—thirteen** *adj or pron* **—thir•teenth** \-ˈtēnth\ *adj or n*

thir•ty \ˈthərtē\ *n, pl* **thirties** : 3 times 10 **—thir•ti•eth** \-ēəth\ *adj or n* **—thirty** *adj or pron*

this \ˈt͟his\ *pron, pl* **these** \ˈt͟hēz\ : something close or under immediate discussion ~ *adj, pl* **these** : being the one near, present, just mentioned, or more immediately under observation ~ *adv* : to such an extent or degree

this•tle \ˈthisəl\ *n* : tall prickly herb

thith•er \ˈthit͟hər\ *adv* : to that place

thong \ˈthȯŋ\ *n* : strip of leather or hide

tho•rax \ˈthōrˌaks\ *n, pl* **-rax•es** *or* **-ra•ces** \ˈthōrəˌsēz\ **1** : part of the body between neck and abdomen **2** : middle of 3 divisions of an insect body **—tho•rac•ic** \thəˈrasik\ *adj*

thorn \ˈthȯrn\ *n* : sharp spike on a plant or a plant bearing these **—thorny** *adj*

thor•ough \ˈthərō\ *adj* : omitting or overlooking nothing **—thor•ough•ly** *adv* **—thor•ough•ness** *n*

thor•ough•bred \ˈthərəˌbred\ *n* **1** *cap* : light speedy racing horse **2** : one of excellent quality**—thoroughbred** *adj*

thor•ough•fare \ˈthərəˌfar\ *n* : public road

those *pl of* THAT

thou \ˈthau̇\ *pron, archaic* : you

though \ˈt͟hō\ *adv* : however ~ *conj* **1** : despite the fact that **2** : granting that

thought \ˈthȯt\ *past of* THINK ~ *n* **1** : process of thinking **2** : serious consideration **3** : idea

thought•ful \-fəl\ *adj* **1** : absorbed in or showing thought **2** : considerate of others **—thought•ful•ly** *adv* **—thought•ful•ness** *n*

thought•less \-ləs\ *adj* **1** : careless or reckless **2** : lacking concern for others **—thought•less•ly** *adv*

thou•sand \ˈthau̇zᵊnd\ *n, pl* **-sands** *or* **-sand** : 10 times 100 **—thousand** *adj* **—thousandth** \-ᵊnth\ *adj or n*

thrash \ˈthrash\ *vb* **1** : thresh **2** : beat **3** : move about violently **—thrash•er** *n*

thread \ˈthred\ *n* **1** : fine line of fibers **2** : train of thought **3** : ridge around a screw ~ *vb* **1** : pass thread through **2** : put together on a thread **3** : make one's way through or between

thread•bare *adj* **1** : worn so that the thread shows **2** : trite

threat \ˈthret\ *n* **1** : expression of intention to harm **2** : thing that threatens

threat•en \ˈthretᵊn\ *vb* **1** : utter threats **2** : show signs of being near or impending **—threat•en•ing•ly** *adv*

three \ˈthrē\ *n* **1** : one more than 2 **2** : 3d in a set or series**—three** *adj or pron*

three•fold \ˈthrēˌfōld\ *adj* : triple **—three-fold** \-ˈfōld\ *adv*

three•score *adj* : being 3 times 20

thresh \ˈthresh, ˈthrash\ *vb* : beat to separate grain **—thresh•er** *n*

thresh•old \ˈthreshˌōld\ *n* **1** : sill of a door **2** : beginning stage

threw *past of* THROW

thrice \ˈthrīs\ *adv* : 3 times

thrift \ˈthrift\ *n* : careful management or saving of money **—thrift•i•ly** \ˈthriftəlē\ *adv* **—thrift•less** *adj* **—thrifty** *adj*

thrill \ˈthril\ *vb* **1** : have or cause to have a sudden sharp feeling of excitement **2** : tremble **—thrill** *n* **—thrill•er** *n* **—thrill•ing•ly** *adv*

thrive \ˈthrīv\ *vb* **throve** \ˈthrōv\ *or* **thrived; thriv•en** \ˈthrivən\ **1** : grow vigorously **2** : prosper

throat \ˈthrōt\ *n* **1** : front part of the neck **2** : passage to the stomach **—throat•ed** *adj* **—throaty** *adj*

throb \ˈthräb\ *vb* **-bb-** : pulsate **—throb** *n*

throe \ˈthrō\ *n* **1** : pang or spasm **2** *pl* : hard or painful struggle

throne \ˈthrōn\ *n* : chair representing power or sovereignty

throng \ˈthrȯŋ\ *n or vb* : crowd

throt•tle \ˈthrätᵊl\ *vb* **-tled; -tling** : choke ~ *n* : valve regulating volume of fuel and air delivered to engine cylinders

through \ˈthrü\ *prep* **1** : into at one side and out at the other side of **2** : by way of **3** : among, between, or all around **4** : because of **5** : throughout the time of ~ \ˈthrü\ *adv* **1** : from one end or side to the other **2** : from beginning to end **3** : to the core **4** : into the open ~ *adj* **1** : going directly from origin to destination **2** : finished

through•out \thrüˈau̇t\ *adv* **1** : everywhere **2** : from beginning to end ~ *prep* **1** : in or to every part of **2** : during the whole of

throve *past of* THRIVE

throw \ˈthrō\ *vb* **threw** \ˈthrü\; **thrown** \ˈthrōn\; **throw•ing 1** : propel through the air **2** : cause to fall or fall off **3** : put suddenly in a certain position or condition **4** : move quickly as if throwing **5** : put on or off hastily **—throw** *n* **—throw•er** \ˈthrōər\ *n* **—throw up** *vb* : vomit

thrush \ˈthrəsh\ *n* : songbird

thrust \ˈthrəst\ *vb* **thrust; thrust•ing 1** : shove forward **2** : stab or pierce **—thrust** *n*

thud \ˈthəd\ *n* : dull sound of something falling **—thud** *vb*

thug \ˈthəg\ *n* : ruffian or gangster

thumb \ˈthəm\ *n* **1** : short thick division of the hand opposing the fingers **2** : glove part for the thumb ~ *vb* : leaf through with the thumb **—thumb•nail** *n*

thump \ˈthəmp\ *vb* : strike with something thick or heavy causing a dull sound **—thump** *n*

thun•der \ˈthəndər\ *n* : sound following lightning **—thunder** *vb* **—thun•der•clap** *n* **—thun•der•ous** \ˈthəndərəs\ *adj* **—thun•der•ous•ly** *adv*

thun•der•bolt \-ˌbōlt\ *n* : discharge of lightning with thunder

thun•der•show•er \ˈthəndərˌshau̇ər\ *n* : shower with thunder and lightning

thun•der•storm *n* : storm with thunder and lightning

Thurs•day \ˈthərzdā, -dē\ *n* : 5th day of the week

thus \ˈt͟həs\ *adv* **1** : in this or that way **2** : to this degree or extent **3** : because of this or that

thwart \ˈthwȯrt\ *vb* : block or defeat

thy \ˈt͟hī\ *adj, archaic* : your

thyme \ˈtīm, ˈthīm\ *n* : cooking herb

thy•roid \ˈthīˌrȯid\ *adj* : relating to a large endocrine gland **(thyroid gland)**

thy•self \t͟hīˈself\ *pron, archaic* : yourself

ti•ara \tēˈarə, -ˈär-\ *n* : decorative formal headband

tib•ia \ˈtibēə\ *n, pl* **-i•ae** \-ēˌē\ : bone between the knee and ankle

tic \ˈtik\ *n* : twitching of facial muscles

1tick \ˈtik\ *n* : small 8-legged blood-sucking animal

2tick *n* **1** : light rhythmic tap or beat **2** : check mark ~ *vb* **1** : make ticks **2** : mark with a tick **3** : operate

tick•er \ˈtikər\ *n* **1** : something (as a watch) that ticks **2** : telegraph instrument that prints on paper tape

tick•et \ˈtikət\ *n* **1** : tag showing price, payment of a fee or fare, or a traffic offense **2** : list of candidates ~ *vb* : put a ticket on

tick•ing \ˈtikiŋ\ *n* : fabric covering of a mattress

tick•le \ˈtikəl\ *vb* **-led; -ling 1** : please or amuse **2** : touch lightly causing uneasiness, laughter, or spasmodic movements **—tickle** *n*

tick•lish \ˈtiklish\ *adj* **1** : sensitive to tickling **2** : requiring delicate handling **—tick•lish•ly** *adv* **—tick•lish•ness** *n*

tid•al wave \ˈtīdᵊl-\ *n* : high sea wave following an earthquake

tid•bit \ˈtidˌbit\ *n* : choice morsel

tide \ˈtīd\ *n* : alternate rising and falling of the sea ~ *vb* **tid•ed; tid•ing** : be enough to allow (one) to get by for a time **—tid•al** \ˈtīdᵊl\ *adj* **—tide•wa•ter** *n*

tid•ings \ˈtīdiŋz\ *n pl* : news or message

ti•dy \ˈtīdē\ *adj* **-di•er; -est 1** : well ordered and cared for **2** : large or substantial **—ti•di•ness** *n* **—tidy** *vb*

tie \ˈtī\ *n* **1** : line or ribbon for fastening, uniting, or closing **2** : cross support to which railroad rails are fastened **3** : uniting force **4** : equality in score or tally or a deadlocked contest **5** : necktie ~ *vb* **tied; ty•ing** *or* **tie•ing 1** : fasten or close by wrapping and knotting a tie **2** : form a knot in **3** : gain the same score or tally as an opponent

tier \ˈtir\ *n* : one of a steplike series of rows

tiff \ˈtif\ *n* : petty quarrel **—tiff** *vb*

ti•ger \ˈtīgər\ *n* : very large black-striped cat **—ti•ger•ish** \-gərish\ *adj* **—ti•gress** \-grəs\ *n*

tight \ˈtīt\ *adj* **1** : fitting close together esp. so as not to allow air or water in **2** : held very firmly **3** : taut **4** : fitting too snugly **5** : difficult **6** : stingy **7** : evenly contested **8** : low in supply **—tight** *adv* **—tight•en** \-ᵊn\ *vb* **—tight•ly** *adv* **—tight•ness** *n*

tights \ˈtīts\ *n pl* : skintight garments

tight•wad \ˈtītˌwäd\ *n* : stingy person

tile \ˈtīl\ *n* : thin piece of stone or fired clay used on roofs, floors, or walls ~ *vb* : cover with tiles

1till \ˈtil\ *prep or conj* : until

2till *vb* : cultivate (soil) **—till•able** *adj*

3till *n* : money drawer

1till•er \ˈtilər\ *n* : one that cultivates soil

2til•ler \ˈtilər\ *n* : lever for turning a boat's rudder

tilt \ˈtilt\ *vb* : cause to incline ~ *n* : slant

tim•ber \ˈtimbər\ *n* **1** : cut wood for building **2** : large squared piece of wood **3** : wooded land or trees for timber ~ *vb* : cover, frame, or support with timbers **—tim•bered** *adj* **—tim•ber•land** \-ˌland\ *n*

tim•bre \ˈtambər, ˈtim-\ *n* : sound quality

time \ˈtīm\ *n* **1** : period during which something exists or continues or can be accomplished **2** : point at which something happens **3** : customary hour **4** : age **5** : tempo **6** : moment, hour, day, or year as indicated by a clock or calendar **7** : one's experience during a particular period ~ *vb* **timed; tim•ing 1** : arrange or set the time of **2** : determine or record the time, duration, or rate of **—time•keep•er** *n* **—time•less** *adj* **—time•less•ness** *n* **—time•li•ness** *n* **—time•ly** *adv* **—tim•er** *n*

time•piece *n* : device to show time

times \ˈtīmz\ *prep* : multiplied by

time•ta•ble \ˈtīmˌtābəl\ *n* : table of departure and arrival times

tim•id \ˈtiməd\ *adj* : lacking in courage or self-confidence **—ti•mid•i•ty** \təˈmidətē\ *n* **—tim•id•ly** *adv*

tim•o•rous \ˈtimərəs\ *adj* : fearful **—tim•o•rous•ly** *adv* **—tim•o•rous•ness** *n*

tim•pa•ni \ˈtimpənē\ *n pl* : set of kettledrums **—tim•pa•nist** \-nist\ *n*

tin \ˈtin\ *n* **1** : soft white metallic chemical element **2** : metal food can

tinc•ture \ˈtiŋkchər\ *n* : alcoholic solution of a medicine

tin•der \ˈtindər\ *n* : substance used to kindle a fire

tine \ˈtīn\ *n* : one of the points of a fork

tin•foil \ˈtinˌfȯil\ *n* : thin metal sheeting

tinge \ˈtinj\ *vb* **tinged; tinge•ing** *or* **ting•ing** \ˈtinjiŋ\ **1** : color slightly **2** : affect with a slight odor ~ *n* : slight coloring or flavor

tin•gle \ˈtiŋgəl\ *vb* **-gled; -gling** : feel a ringing, stinging, or thrilling sensation **—tingle** *n*

tin•ker \ˈtiŋkər\ *vb* : experiment in repairing something **—tin•ker•er** *n*

tin•kle \ˈtiŋkəl\ *vb* **-kled; -kling** : make or cause to make a high ringing sound **—tinkle** *n*

tin•sel \ˈtinsəl\ *n* : decorative thread or strip of glittering metal or paper

tint \ˈtint\ *n* **1** : slight or pale coloration **2** : color shade ~ *vb* : give a tint to

ti•ny \ˈtīnē\ *adj* **-ni•er; -est** : very small

1tip \ˈtip\ *vb* **-pp- 1** : overturn **2** : lean ~ *n* : act or state of tipping

2tip *n* : pointed end of something ~ *vb* **-pp- 1** : furnish with a tip **2** : cover the tip of

3tip *n* : small sum given for a service performed ~ *vb* : give a tip to

4tip *n* : piece of confidential information ~ *vb* **-pp-** : give confidential information to

tip–off \ˈtipˌȯf\ *n* : indication

tip•ple \ˈtipəl\ *vb* **-pled; -pling** : drink intoxicating liquor esp. habitually or excessively **—tip•pler** *n*

tip•sy \ˈtipsē\ *adj* **-si•er; -est** : unsteady or foolish from alcohol

tip•toe \ˈtipˌtō\ *n* : the toes of the feet ~ *adv or adj* : supported on tiptoe ~ *vb* **-toed; -toe•ing** : walk quietly or on tiptoe

tip–top *n* : highest point ~ *adj* : excellent

ti•rade \tīˈrād, ˈtīˌ-\ *n* : prolonged speech of abuse

1tire \ˈtīr\ *vb* **tired; tir•ing 1** : make or become weary **2** : wear out the patience of **—tire•less** *adj* **—tire•less•ly** *adv* **—tire•less•ness** *n* **—tire•some** \-səm\ *adj* **—tire•some•ly** *adv* **—tire•some•ness** *n*

2tire *n* : rubber cushion encircling a car wheel

tired \ˈtīrd\ *adj* : weary

tis•sue \ˈtishü\ *n* **1** : soft absorbent paper **2** : layer of cells forming a basic structural element of an animal or plant body

ti•tan•ic \tīˈtanik, tə-\ *adj* : gigantic

ti•ta•ni•um \tīˈtānēəm, tə-\ *n* : gray light strong metallic chemical element

tithe \ˈtīt͟h\ *n* : tenth part paid or given esp. for the support of a church **—tithe** *vb* **—tith•er** *n*

tit•il•late \ˈtitᵊlˌāt\ *vb* **-lat•ed; -lat•ing** : excite pleasurably **—tit•il•la•tion** \ˌtitᵊlˈāshən\ *n*

ti•tle \ˈtītᵊl\ *n* **1** : legal ownership **2** : distinguishing name **3** : designation of honor, rank, or office **4** : championship **—ti•tled** *adj*

tit•ter \ˈtitər\ *n* : nervous or affected laugh **—titter** *vb*

tit•u•lar \ˈtichələr\ *adj* **1** : existing in title only **2** : relating to or bearing a title

tiz•zy \ˈtizē\ *n, pl* **tizzies** : state of agitation or worry

TNT \ˌtēˌenˈtē\ *n* : high explosive

to \ˈtü\ *prep* **1** : in the direction of **2** : at, on, or near **3** : resulting in **4** : before or until **5** —used to show a relationship or object of a verb **6** —used with an infinitive ~ *adv* **1** : forward **2** : to a state of consciousness

toad \ˈtōd\ *n* : tailless leaping amphibian

toad•stool \-ˌstül\ *n* : mushroom esp. when inedible or poisonous

toady \ˈtōdē\ *n, pl* **toad•ies** : one who flatters to gain favors **—toady** *vb*

toast \ˈtōst\ *vb* **1** : make (as a slice of bread) crisp and brown **2** : drink in honor of someone or something **3** : warm ~ *n* **1** : toasted sliced bread **2** : act of drinking in honor of someone **—toast•er** *n*

to•bac•co \təˈbakō\ *n, pl* **-cos** : broad-leaved herb or its leaves prepared for smoking or chewing

to•bog•gan \təˈbägən\ *n* : long flat-bottomed light sled ~ *vb* : coast on a toboggan

to•day \təˈdā\ *adv* **1** : on or for this day **2** : at the present time ~ *n* : present day or time

tod•dle \ˈtädᵊl\ *vb* **-dled; -dling** : walk with tottering steps like a young child **—toddle** *n* **—tod•dler** \ˈtädᵊlər\ *n*

to–do \təˈdü\ *n, pl* **to–dos** \-ˈdüz\ : disturbance or fuss

toe \ˈtō\ *n* : one of the 5 end divisions of the foot **—toe•nail** *n*

tof•fee, tof•fy \ˈtȯfē, ˈtä-\ *n, pl* **toffees** *or* **toffies** : candy made of boiled sugar and butter

to•ga \ˈtōgə\ *n* : loose outer garment of ancient Rome

to•geth•er \təˈget͟hər\ *adv* **1** : in or into one place or group **2** : in or into contact or association **3** : at one time **4** : as a group **—to•geth•er•ness** *n*

togs \ˈtägz, ˈtȯgz\ *n pl* : clothing

toil \ˈtȯil\ *vb* : work hard and long **—toil** *n* **—toil•er** *n* **—toil•some** *adj*

toi•let \ˈtȯilət\ *n* **1** : dressing and grooming oneself **2** : bathroom **3** : water basin to urinate and defecate in

to•ken \ˈtōkən\ *n* **1** : outward sign or expression of something **2** : small part representing the whole **3** : piece resembling a coin

told *past of* TELL

tol•er•a•ble \ˈtälərəbəl\ *adj* **1** : capable of being endured **2** : moderately good **—tol•er•a•bly** \-blē\ *adv*

tol•er•ance \ˈtälərəns\ *n* **1** : lack of opposition for beliefs or practices differing from one's own **2** : capacity for enduring **3** : allowable deviation **—tol•er•ant** *adj* **—tol•er•ant•ly** *adv*

tol•er•ate \ˈtäləˌrāt\ *vb* **-at•ed; -at•ing 1** : allow to be or to be done without opposition **2** : endure or resist the action of **—tol•er•a•tion** \ˌtäləˈrāshən\ *n*

1toll \ˈtōl\ *n* **1** : fee paid for a privilege or service **2** : cost of achievement in loss or suffering **—toll•booth** *n* **—toll•gate** *n*

2toll *vb* **1** : cause the sounding of (a bell) **2** : sound with slow measured strokes ~ *n* : sound of a tolling bell

tom•a•hawk \ˈtäməˌhȯk\ *n* : light ax used as a weapon by American Indians

to•ma•to \təˈmātō, -ˈmät-\ *n, pl* **-toes** : tropical American herb or its fruit

tomb \ˈtüm\ *n* : house, vault, or grave for burial

tom•boy \ˈtämˌbȯi\ *n* : girl who behaves in a manner usu. considered boyish

tomb•stone *n* : stone marking a grave

tom•cat \ˈtämˌkat\ *n* : male cat

tome \ˈtōm\ *n* : large or weighty book

to•mor•row \təˈmärō\ *adv* : on or for the day after today **—tomorrow** *n*

tom–tom \ˈtämˌtäm\ *n* : small-headed drum beaten with the hands

ton \ˈtən\ *n* : unit of weight equal to 2000 pounds

tone \ˈtōn\ *n* **1** : vocal or musical sound **2** : sound of definite pitch **3** : manner of speaking that expresses an emotion or attitude **4** : color quality **5** : healthy condition **6** : general character or quality ~ *vb* : soften or muffle —often used with *down* **—ton•al** \-ᵊl\ *adj* **—to•nal•i•ty** \tōˈnalətē\ *n*

tongs \ˈtäŋz, ˈtȯŋz\ *n pl* : grasping device of 2 joined or hinged pieces

tongue \ˈtəŋ\ *n* **1** : fleshy movable organ of the mouth **2** : language **3** : something long and flat and fastened at one end **—tongued** \ˈtəŋd\ *adj* **—tongue•less** *adj*

ton•ic \ˈtänik\ *n* : something (as a drug) that invigorates or restores health **—tonic** *adj*

to•night \təˈnīt\ *adv* : on this night ~ *n* : present or coming night

ton•sil \ˈtänsəl\ *n* : either of a pair of oval masses in the throat **—ton•sil•lec•to•my** \ˌtänsəˈlektəmē\ *n* **—ton•sil•li•tis** \-ˈlītəs\ *n*

too \ˈtü\ *adv* **1** : in addition **2** : excessively

took *past of* TAKE

tool \ˈtül\ *n* : device worked by hand ~ *vb* : shape or finish with a tool

toot \ˈtüt\ *vb* : sound or cause to sound esp. in short blasts **—toot** *n*

tooth \ˈtüth\ *n, pl* **teeth** \ˈtēth\ **1** : one of the hard structures in the jaws for chewing **2** : one of the projections on the edge of a

gear wheel **—tooth•ache** *n* **—tooth•brush** *n* **—toothed** \'tütht\ *adj* **—tooth•less** *adj* **—tooth•paste** *n* **—tooth•pick** *n*
tooth•some \'tüthsəm\ *adj* **1 :** delicious **2 :** attractive
1top \'täp\ *n* **1 :** highest part or level of something **2 :** lid or covering ~ *vb* **-pp- 1 :** cover with a top **2 :** surpass **3 :** go over the top of ~ *adj* **:** being at the top **—topped** *adj*
2top *n* **:** spinning toy
to•paz \'tō,paz\ *n* **:** hard gem
top•coat *n* **:** lightweight overcoat
top•ic \'täpik\ *n* **:** subject for discussion or study
top•i•cal \-ikəl\ *adj* **1 :** relating to or arranged by topics **2 :** relating to current or local events **—top•i•cal•ly** *adv*
top•most \'täp,mōst\ *adj* **:** highest of all
top–notch \-'näch\ *adj* **:** of the highest quality
to•pog•ra•phy \tə'pägrəfē\ *n* **1 :** art of mapping the physical features of a place **2 :** outline of the form of a place **—to•pog•ra•pher** \-fər\ *n* **—top•o•graph•ic** \,täpə'grafik\, **top•o•graph•i•cal** \-ikəl\ *adj*
top•ple \'täpəl\ *vb* **-pled; -pling :** fall or cause to fall
top•sy–tur•vy \,täpsē'tərvē\ *adv or adj* **1 :** upside down **2 :** in utter confusion
torch \'tȯrch\ *n* **:** flaming light **—torch•bear•er** *n* **—torch•light** *n*
tore *past of* TEAR
tor•ment \'tȯr,ment\ *n* **:** extreme pain or anguish or a source of this ~ *vb* **1 :** cause severe anguish to **2 :** harass **—tor•men•tor** \-ər\ *n*
torn *past part of* TEAR
tor•na•do \tȯr'nādō\ *n, pl* **-does** *or* **-dos :** violent destructive whirling wind
tor•pe•do \tȯr'pēdō\ *n, pl* **-does :** self-propelled explosive submarine missile ~ *vb* **:** hit with a torpedo
tor•pid \'tȯrpəd\ *adj* **1 :** having lost motion or the power of exertion **2 :** lacking vigor **—tor•pid•i•ty** \tȯr'pidətē\ *n*
tor•por \'tȯrpər\ *n* **:** extreme sluggishness or lethargy
torque \'tȯrk\ *n* **:** turning force
tor•rent \'tȯrənt\ *n* **1 :** rushing stream **2 :** tumultuous outburst **—tor•ren•tial** \tȯ'renchəl, tə-\ *adj*
tor•rid \'tȯrəd\ *adj* **1 :** parched with heat **2 :** impassioned
tor•sion \'tȯrshən\ *n* **:** a twisting or being twisted **—tor•sion•al** \'tȯrshənəl\ *adj* **—tor•sion•al•ly** *adv*
tor•so \'tȯrsō\ *n, pl* **-sos** *or* **-si** \-,sē\ **:** trunk of the human body
tor•til•la \tȯr'tēyə\ *n* **:** round flat cornmeal or wheat flour bread
tor•toise \'tȯrtəs\ *n* **:** land turtle
tor•tu•ous \'tȯrchəwəs\ *adj* **1 :** winding **2 :** tricky
tor•ture \'tȯrchər\ *n* **1 :** use of pain to punish or force **2 :** agony ~ *vb* **-tured; -tur•ing :** inflict torture on **—tor•tur•er** *n*
toss \'tȯs, 'täs\ *vb* **1 :** move to and fro or up and down violently **2 :** throw with a quick light motion **3 :** move restlessly **—toss** *n*
toss–up *n* **1 :** a deciding by flipping a coin **2 :** even chance
tot \'tät\ *n* **:** small child
to•tal \'tōtᵊl\ *n* **:** entire amount ~ *vb* **-taled** *or* **-talled; -tal•ing** *or* **-tal•ling 1 :** add up **2 :** amount to **—total** *adj* **—to•tal•ly** *adv*
to•tal•i•tar•i•an \tō,talə'terēən\ *adj* **:** relating to a political system in which the government has complete control over the people **—totalitarian** *n* **—to•tal•i•tar•i•an•ism** \-ēə,nizəm\ *n*
to•tal•i•ty \tō'talətē\ *n, pl* **-ties :** whole amount or entirety
tote \'tōt\ *vb* **tot•ed; tot•ing :** carry
to•tem \'tōtəm\ *n* **:** often carved figure used as a family or tribe emblem
tot•ter \'tätər\ *vb* **1 :** sway as if about to fall **2 :** stagger
touch \'təch\ *vb* **1 :** make contact with so as to feel **2 :** be or cause to be in contact **3 :** take into the hands or mouth **4 :** treat or mention a subject **5 :** relate or concern **6 :** move to sympathetic feeling ~ *n* **1 :** light stroke **2 :** act or fact of touching or being touched **3 :** sense of feeling **4 :** trace **5 :** state of being in contact **—touch up** *vb* **:** improve with minor changes
touch•down \'təch,daún\ *n* **:** scoring of 6 points in football
touch•stone *n* **:** test or criterion of genuineness or quality
touchy \'təchē\ *adj* **touch•i•er; -est 1 :** easily offended **2 :** requiring tact
tough \'təf\ *adj* **1 :** strong but elastic **2 :** not easily chewed **3 :** severe or disciplined **4 :** stubborn ~ *n* **:** rowdy **—tough•ly** *adv* **—tough•ness** *n*
tough•en \'təfən\ *vb* **:** make or become tough
tou•pee \tü'pā\ *n* **:** small wig for a bald spot
tour \'túr\ *n* **1 :** period of time spent at work or on an assignment **2 :** journey with a return to the starting point ~ *vb* **:** travel over to see the sights **—tour•ist** \'túrist\ *n*
tour•na•ment \'túrnəmənt, 'tər-\ *n* **1 :** medieval jousting competition **2 :** championship series of games
tour•ney \-nē\ *n, pl* **-neys :** tournament
tour•ni•quet \'túrnikət, 'tər-\ *n* **:** tight bandage for stopping blood flow
tou•sle \'taúzəl\ *vb* **-sled; -sling :** dishevel (as someone's hair)
tout \'taút, 'tüt\ *vb* **:** praise or publicize loudly
tow \'tō\ *vb* **:** pull along behind **—tow** *n*
to•ward, to•wards \'tōrd, tə'wȯrd, 'tōrdz, tə'wȯrdz\ *prep* **1 :** in the direction of **2 :** with respect to **3 :** in part payment on
tow•el \'taúəl\ *n* **:** absorbent cloth or paper for wiping or drying
tow•er \'taúər\ *n* **:** tall structure ~ *vb* **:** rise to a great height **—tow•ered** \'taúərd\ *adj* **—tow•er•ing** *adj*
tow•head \'tō,hed\ *n* **:** person having whitish blond hair **—tow•head•ed** \-,hedəd\ *adj*
town \'taún\ *n* **1 :** small residential area **2 :** city **—towns•peo•ple** \'taúnz,pēpəl\ *n pl*
town•ship \'taún,ship\ *n* **1 :** unit of local government **2 :** 36 square miles of U.S. public land
tox•ic \'täksik\ *adj* **:** poisonous **—tox•ic•i•ty** \täk'sisətē\ *n*
tox•in \'täksən\ *n* **:** poison produced by an organism
toy \'tȯi\ *n* **:** something for a child to play with ~ *vb* **:** amuse oneself or play with something ~ *adj* **1 :** designed as a toy **2 :** very small
1trace \'trās\ *vb* **traced; trac•ing 1 :** mark over the lines of (a drawing) **2 :** follow the trail or the development of ~ *n* **1 :** track **2 :** tiny amount or residue **—trace•able** *adj* **—trac•er** *n*
2trace *n* **:** line of a harness
tra•chea \'trākēə\ *n, pl* **-che•ae** \-kē,ē\ **:** windpipe **—tra•che•al** \-kēəl\ *adj*
track \'trak\ *n* **1 :** trail left by wheels or footprints **2 :** racing course **3 :** train rails **4 :** awareness of a progression **5 :** looped belts propelling a vehicle ~ *vb* **1 :** follow the trail of **2 :** make tracks on **—track•er** *n*
track–and–field *adj* **:** relating to athletic contests of running, jumping, and throwing events
1tract \'trakt\ *n* **1 :** stretch of land **2 :** system of body organs
2tract *n* **:** pamphlet of propaganda
trac•ta•ble \'traktəbəl\ *adj* **:** easily controlled
trac•tion \'trakshən\ *n* **:** gripping power to permit movement **—trac•tion•al** \-shənəl\ *adj* **—trac•tive** \'traktiv\ *adj*
trac•tor \'traktər\ *n* **1 :** farm vehicle used esp. for pulling **2 :** truck for hauling a trailer
trade \'trād\ *n* **1 :** one's regular business **2 :** occupation requiring skill **3 :** the buying and selling of goods **4 :** act of trading ~ *vb* **trad•ed; trad•ing 1 :** give in exchange for something **2 :** buy and sell goods **3 :** be a regular customer **—trades•peo•ple** \'trādz,pēpəl\ *n pl*
trade–in \'trād,in\ *n* **:** an item traded to a merchant at the time of a purchase
trade•mark \'trād,märk\ *n* **:** word or mark identifying a manufacturer **—trademark** *vb*
trades•man \'trādzmən\ *n* **:** shopkeeper
tra•di•tion \trə'dishən\ *n* **:** belief or custom passed from generation to generation **—tra•di•tion•al** \-'dishənəl\ *adj* **—tra•di•tion•al•ly** *adv*
tra•duce \trə'düs, -'dyüs\ *vb* **-duced; -duc•ing :** lower the reputation of **—tra•duc•er** *n*
traf•fic \'trafik\ *n* **1 :** business dealings **2 :** movement along a route ~ *vb* **:** do business **—traf•fick•er** *n* **—traffic light** *n*
trag•e•dy \'trajədē\ *n, pl* **-dies 1 :** serious drama describing a conflict and having a sad end **2 :** disastrous event
trag•ic \'trajik\ *adj* **:** being a tragedy **—trag•i•cal•ly** *adv*
trail \'trāl\ *vb* **1 :** hang down and drag along the ground **2 :** draw along behind **3 :** follow the track of **4 :** dwindle ~ *n* **1 :** something that trails **2 :** path or evidence left by something
trail•er \'trālər\ *n* **1 :** vehicle intended to be hauled **2 :** dwelling designed to be towed to a site
train \'trān\ *n* **1 :** trailing part of a gown **2 :** retinue or procession **3 :** connected series **4 :** group of linked railroad cars ~ *vb* **1 :** cause to grow as desired **2 :** make or become prepared or skilled **3 :** point **—train•ee** *n* **—train•er** *n* **—train•load** *n*
traipse \'trāps\ *vb* **traipsed; traips•ing :** walk
trait \'trāt\ *n* **:** distinguishing quality
trai•tor \'trātər\ *n* **:** one who betrays a trust or commits treason **—trai•tor•ous** *adj*
tra•jec•to•ry \trə'jektərē\ *n, pl* **-ries :** path of something moving through air or space
tram•mel \'traməl\ *vb* **-meled** *or* **-melled; -mel•ing** *or* **-mel•ling :** impede **—trammel** *n*
tramp \'tramp\ *vb* **1 :** walk or hike **2 :** tread on ~ *n* **:** beggar or vagrant
tram•ple \'trampəl\ *vb* **-pled; -pling :** walk or step on so as to bruise or crush **—trample** *n* **—tram•pler** \-plər\ *n*
tram•po•line \,trampə'lēn, 'trampə,-\ *n* **:** resilient sheet or web supported by springs and used for bouncing **—tram•po•lin•ist** \-ist\ *n*
trance \'trans\ *n* **1 :** sleeplike condition **2 :** state of mystical absorption
tran•quil \'traŋkwəl, 'tran-\ *adj* **:** quiet and undisturbed **—tran•quil•ize** \-kwə,līz\ *vb* **—tran•quil•iz•er** *n* **—tran•quil•li•ty** *or* **tran•quil•i•ty** \tran'kwilətē, traŋ-\ *n* **—tran•quil•ly** *adv*
trans•act \trans'akt, tranz-\ *vb* **:** conduct (business)
trans•ac•tion \-'akshən\ *n* **1 :** business deal **2** *pl* **:** records of proceedings
tran•scend \trans'end\ *vb* **:** rise above or surpass **—tran•scen•dent** \-'endənt\ *adj* **—tran•scen•den•tal** \,trans,en'dentᵊl, -ən-\ *adj*
tran•scribe \trans'krīb\ *vb* **-scribed; -scrib•ing :** make a copy, arrangement, or recording of **—tran•scrip•tion** \trans'kripshən\ *n*
tran•script \'trans,kript\ *n* **:** official copy
tran•sept \'trans,ept\ *n* **:** part of a church that crosses the nave at right angles
trans•fer \trans'fər, 'trans,fər\ *vb* **-rr- 1 :** move from one person, place, or situation to another **2 :** convey ownership of **3 :** print or copy by contact **4 :** change to another vehicle or transportation line ~ \'trans,fər\ *n* **1 :** act or process of transferring **2 :** one that transfers or is transferred **3 :** ticket permitting one to transfer **—trans•fer•able** \trans'fərəbəl\ *adj* **—trans•fer•al** \-əl\ *n* **—trans•fer•ence** \-əns\ *n*
trans•fig•ure \trans'figyər\ *vb* **-ured; -ur•ing 1 :** change the form or appearance of **2 :** glorify **—trans•fig•u•ra•tion** \,trans,figyə'rāshən\ *n*
trans•fix \trans'fiks\ *vb* **1 :** pierce through **2 :** hold motionless
trans•form \-'fȯrm\ *vb* **1 :** change in structure, appearance, or character **2 :** change (an electric current) in potential or type **—trans•for•ma•tion** \,transfər'māshən\ *n* **—trans•form•er** \trans'fȯrmər\ *n*
trans•fuse \trans'fyüz\ *vb* **-fused; -fus•ing 1 :** diffuse into or through **2 :** transfer (as blood) into a vein **—trans•fu•sion** \-'fyüzhən\ *n*
trans•gress \trans'gres, tranz-\ *vb* **:** sin **—trans•gres•sion** \-'greshən\ *n* **—trans•gres•sor** \-'gresər\ *n*
tran•sient \'tranchənt\ *adj* **:** not lasting or staying long **—transient** *n* **—tran•sient•ly** *adv*
tran•sis•tor \tranz'istər, trans-\ *n* **:** small electronic device used in electronic equipment **—tran•sis•tor•ize** \-tə,rīz\ *vb*
tran•sit \'transət, 'tranz-\ *n* **1 :** movement over, across, or through **2 :** local and esp. public transportation **3 :** surveyor's instrument
tran•si•tion \trans'ishən, tranz-\ *n* **:** passage from one state, stage, or subject to another **—tran•si•tion•al** \-'ishənəl\ *adj*
tran•si•to•ry \'transə,tōrē, 'tranz-\ *adj* **:** of brief duration
trans•late \trans'lāt, tranz-\ *vb* **-lat•ed; -lat•ing :** change into another language **—trans•lat•able** *adj* **—trans•la•tion** \-'lāshən\ *n* **—trans•la•tor** \-'lātər\ *n*
trans•lu•cent \trans'lüsᵊnt, tranz-\ *adj* **:** not transparent but clear enough to allow light to pass through **—trans•lu•cence** \-ᵊns\ *n* **—trans•lu•cen•cy** \-ᵊnsē\ *n* **—trans•lu•cent•ly** *adv*
trans•mis•sion \-'mishən\ *n* **1 :** act or process of transmitting **2 :** system of gears between a car engine and drive wheels
trans•mit \-'mit\ *vb* **-tt- 1 :** transfer from one person or place to another **2 :** pass on by inheritance **3 :** broadcast **—trans•mis•si•ble** \-'misəbəl\ *adj* **—trans•mit•ta•ble** \-'mitəbəl\ *adj* **—trans•mit•tal** \-'mitᵊl\ *n* **—trans•mit•ter** *n*
tran•som \'transəm\ *n* **:** often hinged window above a door
trans•par•ent \trans'parənt\ *adj* **1 :** clear enough to see through **2 :** obvious **—trans•par•en•cy** \-ənsē\ *n* **—trans•par•ent•ly** *adv*
tran•spire \trans'pīr\ *vb* **-spired; -spir•ing :** take place **—tran•spi•ra•tion** \,transpə'rāshən\ *n*
trans•plant \trans'plant\ *vb* **1 :** dig up and move to another place **2 :** transfer from one body part or person to another **—transplant** \'trans,-\ *n* **—trans•plan•ta•tion** \,trans,plan'tāshən\ *n*
trans•port \trans'pōrt\ *vb* **1 :** carry or deliver to another place **2 :** carry away by emotion ~ \'trans,-\ *n* **1 :** act of transporting **2 :** rapture **3 :** ship or plane for carrying troops or supplies **—trans•por•ta•tion** \,transpər'tāshən\ *n* **—trans•port•er** *n*
trans•pose \trans'pōz\ *vb* **-posed; -pos•ing :** change the position, sequence, or key **—trans•po•si•tion** \,transpə'zishən\ *n*
trans•ship \tran'ship, trans-\ *vb* **:** transfer from one mode of transportation to another **—trans•ship•ment** *n*
trans•verse \trans'vərs, tranz-\ *adj* **:** lying across **—trans•verse** \'trans,vərs, 'tranz-\ *n* **—trans•verse•ly** *adv*
trap \'trap\ *n* **1 :** device for catching animals **2 :** something by which one is caught unawares **3 :** device to allow one thing to pass through while keeping other things out ~ *vb* **-pp- :** catch in a trap **—trap•per** *n*
trap•door *n* **:** door in a floor or roof
tra•peze \tra'pēz\ *n* **:** suspended bar used by acrobats
trap•e•zoid \'trapə,zȯid\ *n* **:** plane 4-sided figure with 2 parallel sides **—trap•e•zoi•dal** \,trapə'zȯidᵊl\ *adj*
trap•pings \'trapiŋz\ *n pl* **1 :** ornamental covering **2 :** outward decoration or dress
trash \'trash\ *n* **:** something that is no good **—trashy** *adj*
trau•ma \'traumə, 'trȯ-\ *n* **:** bodily or mental injury **—trau•mat•ic** \trə'matik, trȯ-, trau-\ *adj*
tra•vail \trə'vāl, 'trav,āl\ *n* **:** painful work or exertion ~ *vb* **:** labor hard
trav•el \'travəl\ *vb* **-eled** *or* **-elled; -el•ing** *or* **-el•ling 1 :** take a trip or tour **2 :** move or be carried from point to point ~ *n* **:** journey —often pl. **—trav•el•er, trav•el•ler** *n*
tra•verse \trə'vərs, tra'vərs, 'travərs\ *vb* **-versed; -vers•ing :** go or extend across **—tra•verse** \'travərs\ *n*
trav•es•ty \'travəstē\ *n, pl* **-ties :** imitation that makes crude fun of something **—travesty** *vb*
trawl \'trȯl\ *vb* **:** fish or catch with a trawl ~ *n* **:** large cone-shaped net **—trawl•er** *n*
tray \'trā\ *n* **:** shallow flat-bottomed receptacle for holding or carrying something
treach•er•ous \'trechərəs\ *adj* **:** disloyal or dangerous **—treach•er•ous•ly** *adv*
treach•ery \'trechərē\ *n, pl* **-er•ies :** betrayal of a trust
tread \'tred\ *vb* **trod** \'träd\; **trod•den** \'trädᵊn\ *or* **trod; tread•ing 1 :** step on or over **2 :** walk **3 :** press or crush with the feet ~ *n* **1 :** way of walking **2 :** sound made in walking **3 :** part on which a thing runs
trea•dle \'tredᵊl\ *n* **:** foot pedal operating a machine **—treadle** *vb*
tread•mill *n* **1 :** mill worked by walking persons or animals **2 :** wearisome routine
trea•son \'trēzᵊn\ *n* **:** attempt to overthrow the government **—trea•son•able** \'trēzᵊnəbəl\ *adj* **—trea•son•ous** \-ᵊnəs\ *adj*
trea•sure \'trezhər, 'trāzh-\ *n* **1 :** wealth stored up **2 :** something of great value ~ *vb* **-sured; -sur•ing :** keep as precious
trea•sur•er \'trezhərər, 'trāzh-\ *n* **:** officer who handles funds
trea•sury \'trezhərē, 'trāzh-\ *n, pl* **-sur•ies :** place or office for keeping and distributing funds
treat \'trēt\ *vb* **1 :** have as a topic **2 :** pay for the food or entertainment of **3 :** act toward or regard in a certain way **4 :** give medical care to ~ *n* **1 :** food or entertainment paid for by another **2 :** something special and enjoyable **—treat•ment** \-mənt\ *n*
trea•tise \'trētəs\ *n* **:** systematic written exposition or argument
trea•ty \'trētē\ *n, pl* **-ties :** agreement between governments
tre•ble \'trebəl\ *n* **1 :** highest part in music **2 :** upper half of the musical range ~ *adj* **:** triple in number or amount ~ *vb* **-bled; -bling :** make triple **—tre•bly** *adv*
tree \'trē\ *n* **:** tall woody plant ~ *vb* **treed; tree•ing :** force up a tree **—tree•less** *adj*
trek \'trek\ *n* **:** difficult trip ~ *vb* **-kk- :** make a trek
trel•lis \'treləs\ *n* **:** structure of crossed strips
trem•ble \'trembəl\ *vb* **-bled; -bling 1 :** shake from fear or cold **2 :** move or sound as if shaken
tre•men•dous \tri'mendəs\ *adj* **:** amazingly large, powerful, or excellent **—tre•men•dous•ly** *adv*
trem•or \'tremər\ *n* **:** a trembling
trem•u•lous \'tremyələs\ *adj* **:** trembling or quaking
trench \'trench\ *n* **:** long narrow cut in land
tren•chant \'trenchənt\ *adj* **:** sharply perceptive
trend \'trend\ *n* **:** prevailing tendency, direction, or style ~ *vb* **:** move in a particular direction **—trendy** \'trendē\ *adj*
trep•i•da•tion \,trepə'dāshən\ *n* **:** nervous apprehension
tres•pass \'trespəs, -,pas\ *n* **1 :** sin **2 :** unauthorized entry onto someone's property ~ *vb* **1 :** sin **2 :** enter illegally **—tres•pass•er** *n*
tress \'tres\ *n* **:** long lock of hair
tres•tle \'tresəl\ *n* **1 :** support with a hori-

zontal piece and spreading legs **2** : framework bridge

tri•ad \'trī,ad, -əd\ *n* : union of 3

tri•age \trē'äzh, 'trē,äzh\ *n* : system of dealing with cases (as patients) according to priority guidelines intended to maximize success

tri•al \'trīəl\ *n* **1** : hearing and judgment of a matter in court **2** : source of great annoyance **3** : test use or experimental effort **—trial** *adj*

tri•an•gle \'trī,aŋgəl\ *n* : plane figure with 3 sides and 3 angles **—tri•an•gu•lar** \trī-'aŋgyələr\ *adj*

tribe \'trīb\ *n* : social group of numerous families **—trib•al** \'trībəl\ *adj* **—tribes•man** \'trībzmən\ *n*

trib•u•la•tion \,tribyə'lāshən\ *n* : suffering from oppression

tri•bu•nal \trī'byünəl, tri-\ *n* **1** : court **2** : something that decides

trib•u•tary \'tribyə,terē\ *n, pl* **-tar•ies** : stream that flows into a river or lake

trib•ute \'trib,yüt\ *n* **1** : payment to acknowledge submission **2** : tax **3** : gift or act showing respect

trick \'trik\ *n* **1** : scheme to deceive **2** : prank **3** : deceptive or ingenious feat **4** : mannerism **5** : knack **6** : tour of duty ~ *vb* : deceive by cunning **—trick•ery** \-ərē\ *n* **—trick•ster** \-stər\ *n*

trick•le \'trikəl\ *vb* **-led; -ling** : run in drops or a thin stream **—trickle** *n*

tricky \'trikē\ *adj* **trick•i•er; -est 1** : inclined to trickery **2** : requiring skill or caution

tri•cy•cle \'trī,sikəl\ *n* : 3-wheeled bicycle

tri•dent \'trīdənt\ *n* : 3-pronged spear

tri•en•ni•al \'trī'enēəl\ *adj* : lasting, occurring, or done every 3 years **—triennial** *n*

tri•fle \'trīfəl\ *n* : something of little value or importance ~ *vb* **-fled; -fling 1** : speak or act in a playful or flirting way **2** : toy **—tri•fler** *n*

tri•fling \'trīfliŋ\ *adj* : trivial

trig•ger \'trigər\ *n* : finger-piece of a firearm lock that fires the gun ~ *vb* : set into motion **—trigger** *adj* **—trig•gered** \-ərd\ *adj*

trig•o•nom•e•try \,trigə'nämətrē\ *n* : mathematics dealing with triangular measurement **—trig•o•no•met•ric** \-nə-'metrik\ *adj*

trill \'tril\ *n* **1** : rapid alternation between 2 adjacent tones **2** : rapid vibration in speaking ~ *vb* : utter in or with a trill

tril•lion \'trilyən\ *n* : 1000 billions **—trillion** *adj* **—tril•lionth** \-yənth\ *adj or n*

tril•o•gy \'triləjē\ *n, pl* **-gies** : 3-part literary or musical composition

trim \'trim\ *vb* **-mm- 1** : decorate **2** : make neat or reduce by cutting ~ *adj* **-mm-** : neat and compact ~ *n* **1** : state or condition **2** : ornaments **—trim•ly** *adv* **—trim•mer** *n*

trim•ming \'trimiŋ\ *n* : something that ornaments or completes

Trin•i•ty \'trinətē\ *n* : divine unity of Father, Son, and Holy Spirit

trin•ket \'triŋkət\ *n* : small ornament

trio \'trēō\ *n, pl* **tri•os 1** : music for 3 performers **2** : group of 3

trip \'trip\ *vb* **-pp- 1** : step lightly **2** : stumble or cause to stumble **3** : make or cause to make a mistake **4** : release (as a spring or switch) ~ *n* **1** : journey **2** : stumble **3** : drug-induced experience

tri•par•tite \trī'pär,tīt\ *adj* : having 3 parts or parties

tripe \'trīp\ *n* **1** : animal's stomach used as food **2** : trash

tri•ple \'tripəl\ *vb* **-pled; -pling** : make 3 times as great ~ *n* : group of 3 ~ *adj* **1** : having 3 units **2** : being 3 times as great or as many

trip•let \'triplət\ *n* **1** : group of 3 **2** : one of 3 offspring born together

trip•li•cate \'triplikət\ *adj* : made in 3 identical copies ~ *n* : one of 3 copies

tri•pod \'trī,päd\ *n* : a stand with 3 legs **—tripod, tri•po•dal** \'tripədəl, 'trī,päd-\ *adj*

tri•sect \'trī,sekt, trī'-\ *vb* : divide into 3 usu. equal parts **—tri•sec•tion** \'trī,sekshən\ *n*

trite \'trīt\ *adj* **trit•er; trit•est** : commonplace

tri•umph \'trīəmf\ *n, pl* **-umphs** : victory or great success ~ *vb* : obtain or celebrate victory **—tri•um•phal** \trī'əmfəl\ *adj* **—tri•um•phant** \-fənt\ *adj* **—tri•um•phant•ly** *adv*

tri•um•vi•rate \trī'əmvərət\ *n* : ruling body of 3 persons

triv•et \'trivət\ *n* **1** : 3-legged stand **2** : stand to hold a hot dish

triv•ia \'trivēə\ *n sing or pl* : unimportant details

triv•i•al \'trivēəl\ *adj* : of little importance **—triv•i•al•i•ty** \,trivē'alətē\ *n*

trod *past of* TREAD

trodden *past part of* TREAD

troll \'trōl\ *n* : dwarf or giant of folklore inhabiting caves or hills

trol•ley \'trälē\ *n, pl* **-leys** : streetcar run by overhead electric wires

trol•lop \'träləp\ *n* : untidy or immoral woman

trom•bone \träm'bōn, 'träm,-\ *n* : musical instrument with a long sliding tube **—trom•bon•ist** \-'bōnist, -,bō-\ *n*

troop \'trüp\ *n* **1** : cavalry unit **2** *pl* : soldiers **3** : collection of people or things ~ *vb* : move or gather in crowds

troop•er \'trüpər\ *n* **1** : cavalry soldier **2** : police officer on horseback or state police officer

tro•phy \'trōfē\ *n, pl* **-phies** : prize gained by a victory

trop•ic \'träpik\ *n* **1** : either of the 2 parallels of latitude one 23½ degrees north of the equator (**tropic of Cancer** \-'kansər\) and one 23½ degrees south of the equator (**tropic of Cap•ri•corn** \-'kaprə,kȯrn\) **2** *pl* : region lying between the tropics **—tropic, trop•i•cal** \-ikəl\ *adj*

trot \'trät\ *n* : moderately fast gait esp. of a horse with diagonally paired legs moving together ~ *vb* **-tt-** : go at a trot **—trot•ter** *n*

troth \'träth, 'trȯth, 'trōth\ *n* **1** : pledged faithfulness **2** : betrothal

trou•ba•dour \'trübə,dōr\ *n* : medieval lyric poet

trou•ble \'trəbəl\ *vb* **-bled; -bling 1** : disturb **2** : afflict **3** : make an effort ~ *n* **1** : cause of mental or physical distress **2** : effort **—trou•ble•mak•er** *n* **—trou•ble•some** *adj* **—trou•ble•some•ly** *adv*

trough \'trȯf\ *n, pl* **troughs** \'trȯfs, 'trȯvz\ **1** : narrow container for animal feed or water **2** : long channel or depression (as between waves)

trounce \'trau̇ns\ *vb* **trounced; trounc•ing** : thrash, punish, or defeat severely

troupe \'trüp\ *n* : group of stage performers **—troup•er** *n*

trou•sers \'trau̇zərz\ *n pl* : long pants **—trouser** *adj*

trous•seau \'trüsō, trü'sō\ *n, pl* **-seaux** \-sōz, -'sōz\ *or* **-seaus** : bride's collection of clothing and personal items

trout \'trau̇t\ *n, pl* **trout** : freshwater food and game fish

trow•el \'trau̇əl\ *n* **1** : tool for spreading or smoothing **2** : garden scoop **—trowel** *vb*

troy \'trȯi\ *n* : system of weights based on a pound of 12 ounces

tru•ant \'trüənt\ *n* : student absent from school without permission **—tru•an•cy** \-ənsē\ *n* **—truant** *adj*

truce \'trüs\ *n* : agreement to halt fighting

truck \'trək\ *n* **1** : wheeled frame for moving heavy objects **2** : automotive vehicle for transporting heavy loads ~ *vb* : transport on a truck **—truck•er** *n* **—truck•load** *n*

truck•le \'trəkəl\ *vb* **-led; -ling** : yield slavishly to another

tru•cu•lent \'trəkyələnt\ *adj* : aggressively self-assertive **—truc•u•lence** \-ləns\ *n* **—truc•u•len•cy** \-lənsē\ *n* **—tru•cu•lent•ly** *adv*

trudge \'trəj\ *vb* **trudged; trudg•ing** : walk or march steadily and with difficulty

true \'trü\ *adj* **tru•er; tru•est 1** : loyal **2** : in agreement with fact or reality **3** : genuine ~ *adv* **1** : truthfully **2** : accurately ~ *vb* **trued; true•ing** : make balanced or even **—tru•ly** *adv*

true–blue *adj* : loyal

truf•fle \'trəfəl\ *n* **1** : edible fruit of an underground fungus **2** : ball-shaped chocolate candy

tru•ism \'trü,izəm\ *n* : obvious truth

trump \'trəmp\ *n* : card of a designated suit any of whose cards will win over other cards ~ *vb* : take with a trump

trumped–up \'trəmpt'əp\ *adj* : made-up

trum•pet \'trəmpət\ *n* : tubular brass wind instrument with a flaring end ~*vb* **1** : blow a trumpet **2** : proclaim loudly **—trum•pet•er** *n*

trun•cate \'trəŋ,kāt, 'trən-\ *vb* **-cat•ed; -cat•ing** : cut short **—trun•ca•tion** \,trəŋ-'kāshən\ *n*

trun•dle \'trəndəl\ *vb* **-dled; -dling** : roll along

trunk \'trəŋk\ *n* **1** : main part (as of a body or tree) **2** : long muscular nose of an elephant **3** : storage chest **4** : storage space in a car **5** *pl* : shorts

truss \'trəs\ *vb* : bind tightly ~ *n* **1** : set of structural parts forming a framework **2** : appliance worn to hold a hernia in place

trust \'trəst\ *n* **1** : reliance on another **2** : assured hope **3** : credit **4** : property held or managed in behalf of another **5** : combination of firms that reduces competition **6** : something entrusted to another's care **7** : custody ~ *vb* **1** : depend **2** : hope **3** : entrust **4** : have faith in **—trust•ful** \-fəl\ *adj* **—trust•ful•ly** *adv* **—trust•ful•ness** *n* **—trust•worth•i•ness** *n* **—trust•wor•thy** *adj*

trust•ee \,trəs'tē\ *n* : person holding property in trust **—trust•ee•ship** *n*

trusty \'trəstē\ *adj* **trust•i•er; -est** : dependable

truth \'trüth\ *n, pl* **truths** \'trüthz, 'trüths\ **1** : real state of things **2** : true or accepted statement **3** : agreement with fact or reality **—truth•ful** \-fəl\ *adj* **—truth•ful•ly** *adv* **—truth•ful•ness** *n*

try \'trī\ *vb* **tried; try•ing 1** : conduct the trial of **2** : put to a test **3** : strain **4** : make an effort at ~ *n, pl* **tries** : act of trying

try•out *n* : competitive test of performance esp. for athletes or actors **—try out** *vb*

tryst \'trist, 'trīst\ *n* : secret rendezvous of lovers

tsar \'zär, 'tsär, 'sär\ *var of* CZAR

T–shirt \'tē,shərt\ *n* : collarless pullover shirt with short sleeves

tub \'təb\ *n* **1** : wide bucketlike vessel **2** : bathtub

tu•ba \'tübə, 'tyü-\ *n* : large low-pitched brass wind instrument

tube \'tüb, 'tyüb\ *n* **1** : hollow cylinder **2** : round container from which a substance can be squeezed **3** : airtight circular tube of rubber inside a tire **4** : electronic device consisting of a sealed usu. glass container with electrodes inside **—tubed** \'tübd, 'tyübd\ *adj* **—tube•less** *adj*

tu•ber \'tübər, 'tyü-\ *n* : fleshy underground growth (as of a potato) **—tu•ber•ous** \-rəs\ *adj*

tu•ber•cu•lo•sis \tu̇,bərkyə'lōsəs, tyu̇-\ *n, pl* **-lo•ses** \-,sēz\ : bacterial disease esp. of the lungs **—tu•ber•cu•lar** \-'bərkyələr\ *adj* **—tu•ber•cu•lous** \-ləs\ *adj*

tub•ing \'tübiŋ, 'tyü-\ *n* : series or arrangement of tubes

tu•bu•lar \'tübyələr, 'tyü-\ *adj* : of or like a tube

tuck \'tək\ *vb* **1** : pull up into a fold **2** : put into a snug often concealing place **3** : make snug in bed —with *in* ~ *n* : fold in a cloth

tuck•er \'təkər\ *vb* : fatigue

Tues•day \'tüzdā, 'tyüz-, -dē\ *n* : 3d day of the week

tuft \'təft\ *n* : clump (as of hair or feathers) **—tuft•ed** \'təftəd\ *adj*

tug \'təg\ *vb* **-gg- 1** : pull hard **2** : move by pulling ~ *n* **1** : act of tugging **2** : tugboat

tug•boat *n* : boat for towing or pushing ships through a harbor

tug–of–war \,təgə'wȯr\ *n, pl* **tugs–of–war** : pulling contest between 2 teams

tu•ition \tu̇'ishən, 'tyü-\ *n* : cost of instruction

tu•lip \'tüləp, 'tyü-\ *n* : herb with cup-shaped flowers

tum•ble \'təmbəl\ *vb* **-bled; -bling 1** : perform gymnastic feats of rolling and turning **2** : fall or cause to fall suddenly **3** : toss ~ *n* : act of tumbling

tum•bler \'təmblər\ *n* **1** : acrobat **2** : drinking glass **3** : obstruction in a lock that can be moved (as by a key)

tu•mid \'tüməd, 'tyü-\ *adj* : turgid

tum•my \'təmē\ *n, pl* **-mies** : belly

tu•mor \'tümər 'tyü-\ *n* : abnormal and useless growth of tissue **—tu•mor•ous** *adj*

tu•mult \'tü,məlt 'tyü-\ *n* **1** : uproar **2** : violent agitation of mind or feelings **—tu•mul•tu•ous** \tu̇'məlchəwəs, tyü-\ *adj*

tun \'tən\ *n* : large cask

tu•na \'tünə 'tyü-\ *n, pl* **-na** *or* **-nas** : large sea food fish

tun•dra \'təndrə\ *n* : treeless arctic plain

tune \'tün, 'tyün\ *n* **1** : melody **2** : correct musical pitch **3** : harmonious relationship ~ *vb* **tuned; tun•ing 1** : bring or come into harmony **2** : adjust in musical pitch **3** : adjust a receiver so as to receive a broadcast **4** : put in first-class working order **—tun•able** *adj* **—tune•ful** \-fəl\ *adj* **—tun•er** *n*

tung•sten \'təŋstən\ *n* : metallic element used for electrical purposes and in hardening alloys (as steel)

tu•nic \'tünik, 'tyü-\ *n* **1** : ancient knee-length garment **2** : hip-length blouse or jacket

tun•nel \'tənəl\ *n* : underground passageway ~ *vb* **-neled** *or* **-nelled; -nel•ing** *or* **-nel•ling** : make a tunnel through or under something

tur•ban \'tərbən\ *n* : wound headdress worn esp. by Muslims

tur•bid \'tərbəd\ *adj* **1** : dark with stirred-up sediment **2** : confused **—tur•bid•i•ty** \,tər'bidətē\ *n*

tur•bine \'tərbən, -,bīn\ *n* : engine turned by the force of gas or water on fan blades

tur•bo•jet \'tərbō,jet\ *n* : airplane powered by a jet engine having a turbine-driven air compressor or the engine itself

tur•bo•prop \'tərbō,präp\ *n* : airplane powered by a propeller turned by a jet engine-driven turbine

tur•bu•lent \'tərbyələnt\ *adj* **1** : causing violence or disturbance **2** : marked by agitation or tumult **—tur•bu•lence** \-ləns\ *n* **—tur•bu•lent•ly** *adv*

tu•reen \tə'rēn, tyu̇-\ *n* : deep bowl for serving soup

turf \'tərf\ *n* : upper layer of soil bound by grass and roots

tur•gid \'tərjəd\ *adj* **1** : swollen **2** : too highly embellished in style **—tur•gid•i•ty** \,tər'jidətē\ *n*

tur•key \'tərkē\ *n, pl* **-keys** : large American bird raised for food

tur•moil \'tər,mȯil\ *n* : extremely agitated condition

turn \'tərn\ *vb* **1** : move or cause to move around an axis **2** : twist (a mechanical part) to operate **3** : wrench **4** : cause to face or move in a different direction **5** : reverse the sides or surfaces of **6** : upset **7** : go around **8** : become or cause to become **9** : seek aid from a source ~ *n* **1** : act or instance of turning **2** : change **3** : place at which something turns **4** : place, time, or opportunity to do something in order **—turn•er** *n* **—turn down** *vb* : decline to accept **— turn in** *vb* **1** : deliver or report to authorities **2** : go to bed **—turn off** *vb* : stop the functioning of **—turn out** *vb* **1** : expel **2** : produce **3** : come together **4** : prove to be in the end **—turn over** *vb* : transfer **—turn up** *vb* **1** : discover or appear **2** : happen unexpectedly

turn•coat *n* : traitor

tur•nip \'tərnəp\ *n* : edible root of an herb

turn•out \'tərn,au̇t\ *n* **1** : gathering of people for a special purpose **2** : size of a gathering

turn•over *n* **1** : upset or reversal **2** : filled pastry **3** : volume of business **4** : movement (as of goods or people) into, through, and out of a place

turn•pike \'tərn,pīk\ *n* : expressway on which tolls are charged

turn•stile \-,stīl\ *n* : post with arms pivoted on the top that allows people to pass one by one

turn•ta•ble *n* : platform that turns a phonograph record

tur•pen•tine \'tərpən,tīn\ *n* : oil distilled from pine-tree resin and used as a solvent

tur•pi•tude \'tərpə,tüd, -,tyüd\ *n* : inherent baseness

tur•quoise \'tər,kȯiz, -,kwȯiz\ *n* : blue or greenish gray gemstone

tur•ret \'tərət\ *n* **1** : little tower on a building **2** : revolving tool holder or gun housing

tur•tle \'tərtəl\ *n* : reptile with the trunk enclosed in a bony shell

tur•tle•dove *n* : wild pigeon

tur•tle•neck *n* : high close-fitting collar that can be turned over or a sweater or shirt with this collar

tusk \'təsk\ *n* : long protruding tooth (as of an elephant) **—tusked** \'təskt\ *adj*

tus•sle \'təsəl\ *n or vb* : struggle

tu•te•lage \'tütəlij, 'tyüt-\ *n* **1** : act of protecting **2** : instruction esp. of an individual

tu•tor \'tütər, 'tyü-\ *n* : private teacher ~ *vb* : teach usu. individually

tux•e•do \,tək'sēdō\ *n, pl* **-dos** *or* **-does** : semiformal evening clothes for a man

TV \,tē'vē, 'tē,vē\ *n* : television

twain \'twān\ *n* : two

twang \'twaŋ\ *n* **1** : harsh sound like that of a plucked bowstring **2** : nasal speech or resonance ~ *vb* : sound or speak with a twang

tweak \'twēk\ *vb* : pinch and pull playfully **—tweak** *n*

tweed \'twēd\ *n* **1** : rough woolen fabric **2** *pl* : tweed clothing **—tweedy** *adj*

tweet \'twēt\ *n* : chirping note **—tweet** *vb*

twee•zers \'twēzərz\ *n pl* : small pincerlike tool

twelve \'twelv\ *n* **1** : one more than 11 **2** : 12th in a set or series **3** : something having 12 units **—twelfth** \'twelfth\ *adj or n* **—twelve** *adj or pron*

twen•ty \'twentē\ *n, pl* **-ties** : 2 times 10 **—twen•ti•eth** \-ēəth\ *adj or n* **—twenty** *adj or pron*

twen•ty–twen•ty, 20–20 *adj* : being vision of normal sharpness

twice \'twīs\ *adv* **1** : on 2 occasions **2** : 2 times

twig \'twig\ *n* : small branch **—twig•gy** *adj*

twi•light \'twī,līt\ *n* : light from the sky at dusk or dawn **—twilight** *adj*

twill \'twil\ *n* : fabric with a weave that gives an appearance of diagonal lines in the fabric

twilled \'twild\ *adj* : made with a twill weave

twin \'twin\ *n* : either of 2 offspring born together ~ *adj* **1** : born with one another or as a pair at one birth **2** : made up of 2 similar parts

twine \'twīn\ *n* : strong twisted thread ~ *vb* **twined; twin•ing 1** : twist together **2** : coil about a support **—twin•er** *n* **—twiny** *adj*

twinge \'twinj\ *vb* **twinged; twing•ing** *or* **twinge•ing** : affect with or feel a sudden sharp pain ~ *n* : sudden sharp stab (as of pain)

twin•kle \'twiŋkəl\ *vb* **-kled; -kling** : shine with a flickering light ~ *n* **1** : wink **2** : intermittent shining **— twin•kler** \-klər\ *n*

twirl \'twərl\ *vb* : whirl round ~ *n* **1** : act of twirling **2** : coil **—twirl•er** *n*

twist \'twist\ *vb* **1 :** unite by winding (threads) together **2 :** wrench **3 :** move in or have a spiral shape **4 :** follow a winding course ~ *n* **1 :** act or result of twisting **2 :** unexpected development

twist·er \'twistər\ *n* **:** tornado

[1]twit \'twit\ *n* **:** fool

[2]twit *vb* **-tt- :** taunt

twitch \'twich\ *vb* **:** move or pull with a sudden motion ~ *n* **:** act of twitching

twit·ter \'twitər\ *vb* **:** make chirping noises ~ *n* **:** small intermittent noise

two \'tü\ *n, pl* **twos 1 :** one more than one **2 :** the 2d in a set or series **3 :** something having 2 units **—two** *adj or pron*

two·fold \'tü,fōld\ *adj* **:** double **—two·fold** \-'fōld\ *adv*

two·some \'tüsəm\ *n* **:** couple

-ty *n suffix* **:** quality, condition, or degree

ty·coon \tī'kün\ *n* **:** powerful and successful businessman

tying *pres part of* TIE

tyke \'tīk\ *n* **:** small child

tym·pa·num \'timpənəm\ *n, pl* **-na** \-nə\ **:** eardrum or the cavity which it closes externally **—tym·pan·ic** \tim'panik\ *adj*

type \'tīp\ *n* **1 :** class, kind, or group set apart by common characteristics **2 :** special design of printed letters ~ *vb* **typed; typ·ing 1 :** write with a typewriter **2 :** identify or classify as a particular type

type·writ·er *n* **:** keyboard machine that produces printed material by striking a ribbon with raised letters **—type·write** *vb*

ty·phoid \'tī,fȯid, tī'-\ *adj* **:** relating to or being a communicable bacterial disease (**typhoid fever**)

ty·phoon \tī'fün\ *n* **:** hurricane of the western Pacific ocean

ty·phus \'tīfəs\ *n* **:** severe disease with fever, delirium, and rash

typ·i·cal \'tipikəl\ *adj* **:** having the essential characteristics of a group **—typ·i·cal·i·ty** \,tipə'kalətē\ *n* **—typ·i·cal·ly** *adv* **—typ·i·cal·ness** *n*

typ·i·fy \'tipə,fī\ *vb* **-fied; -fy·ing :** be typical of

typ·ist \'tīpist\ *n* **:** one who operates a typewriter

ty·pog·ra·phy \tī'pägrəfē\ *n* **1 :** art of printing with type **2 :** style, arrangement, or appearance of printed matter **—ty·po·graph·ic** \,tīpə'grafik\, **ty·po·graph·i·cal** \-ikəl\ *adj* **—ty·po·graph·i·cal·ly** *adv*

ty·ran·ni·cal \tə'ranikəl, tī-\ *adj* **:** relating to a tyrant **—ty·ran·ni·cal·ly** *adv*

tyr·an·nize \'tirə,nīz\ *vb* **-nized; -niz·ing :** rule or deal with in the manner of a tyrant **—tyr·an·niz·er** *n*

tyr·an·ny \'tirənē\ *n, pl* **-nies :** unjust use of absolute governmental power

ty·rant \'tīrənt\ *n* **:** harsh ruler having absolute power

ty·ro \'tīrō\ *n, pl* **-ros :** beginner

tzar \'zär, 'tsär, 'sär\ *var of* CZAR

U

u \'yü\ *n, pl* **u's** *or* **us** \'yüz\ **:** 21st letter of the alphabet

ubiq·ui·tous \yü'bikwətəs\ *adj* **:** omnipresent **—ubiq·ui·tous·ly** *adv* **—ubiq·ui·ty** \-wətē\ *n*

ud·der \'ədər\ *n* **:** animal sac containing milk glands and nipples

ug·ly \'əglē\ *adj* **ug·li·er; -est 1 :** offensive to look at **2 :** mean or quarrelsome **—ug·li·ness** *n*

uku·le·le \,yükə'lālē\ *n* **:** small 4-string guitar

ul·cer \'əlsər\ *n* **:** eroded sore **—ul·cer·ous** *adj*

ul·cer·ate \'əlsə,rāt\ *vb* **-at·ed; -at·ing :** become affected with an ulcer **—ul·cer·a·tion** \,əlsə'rāshən\ *n* **—ul·cer·a·tive** \'əlsə,rātiv\ *adj*

ul·na \'əlnə\ *n* **:** bone of the forearm opposite the thumb

ul·te·ri·or \,əl'tirēər\ *adj* **:** not revealed

ul·ti·mate \'əltəmət\ *adj* **:** final, maximum, or extreme **—ultimate** *n* **—ul·ti·mate·ly** *adv*

ul·ti·ma·tum \,əltə'mātəm, -'mät-\ *n, pl* **-tums** *or* **-ta** \-ə\ **:** final proposition or demand carrying or implying a threat

ul·tra·vi·o·let \,əltrə'vīələt\ *adj* **:** having a wavelength shorter than visible light

um·bi·li·cus \,əmbə'līkəs, ,əm'bili-\ *n, pl* **-li·ci** \-bə'lī,kī, -,sī; -'bilə,kī, -,kē\ *or* **-li·cus·es :** small depression on the abdominal wall marking the site of the cord (**umbilical cord**) that joins the unborn fetus to its mother **—um·bil·i·cal** \,əm'bilikəl\ *adj*

um·brage \'əmbrij\ *n* **:** resentment

um·brel·la \,əm'brelə\ *n* **:** collapsible fabric device to protect from sun or rain

um·pire \'əm,pīr\ *n* **1 :** arbitrator **2 :** sport official **—umpire** *vb*

ump·teen \'əmp'tēn\ *adj* **:** very numerous **—ump·teenth** \-'tēnth\ *adj*

un- \,ən, 'ən\ *prefix* **1 :** not **2 :** opposite of

unable
unabridged
unacceptable
unaccompanied
unaccounted
unacquainted
unaddressed
unadorned
unadulterated
unafraid
unaided
unalike
unambiguous
unambitious
unannounced
unanswered
unanticipated
unappetizing
unappreciated
unapproved
unarguable
unarguably
unassisted
unattended
unattractive
unauthorized
unavailable
unavoidable
unbearable
unbiased
unbranded
unbreakable
uncensored
unchallenged
unchangeable
unchanged
unchanging
uncharacteristic
uncharged
unchaste
uncivilized
unclaimed
unclear
uncleared
unclothed
uncluttered
uncombed
uncomfortable
uncomfortably
uncomplimentary
unconfirmed
unconsummated
uncontested
uncontrolled
uncontroversial
unconventional
unconventionally
unconverted
uncooked
uncooperative
uncoordinated
uncovered
uncultivated
undamaged
undated
undecided
undeclared
undefeated
undemocratic
undependable
undeserving
undesirable
undetected
undetermined
undeveloped
undeviating
undignified
undisturbed
undivided
undomesticated
undrinkable
unearned
uneducated
unemotional
unending
unendurable
unenforceable
unenlightened
unethical
unexcitable
unexciting
unexplainable
unexplored
unfair
unfairly
unfairness
unfavorable
unfavorably
unfeigned
unfilled
unfinished
unflattering
unforeseeable
unforeseen
unforgivable
unforgiving
unfulfilled
unfurnished
ungenerous
ungentlemanly
ungraceful
ungrammatical
unharmed
unhealthful
unheated
unhurt
unidentified
unimaginable
unimaginative
unimportant
unimpressed
uninformed
uninhabited
uninjured
uninsured
unintelligent
unintelligible
unintelligibly
unintended
unintentional
unintentionally
uninterested
uninteresting
uninterrupted
uninvited
unjust
unjustifiable
unjustified
unjustly
unknowing
unknowingly
unknown
unleavened
unlicensed
unlikable
unlimited
unlovable
unmanageable
unmarked
unmarried
unmerciful
unmercifully
unmerited
unmolested
unmotivated
unmoving
unnamed
unnecessarily
unnecessary
unneeded
unnoticeable
unnoticed
unobjectionable
unobservable
unobservant
unobtainable
unobtrusive
unobtrusively
unofficial
unopened
unopposed
unorganized
unoriginal
unorthodox
unorthodoxy
unpaid
unpardonable
unpatriotic
unpaved
unpleasant
unpleasantly
unpleasantness
unpopular
unpopularity
unposed
unpredictability
unpredictable
unpredictably
unprejudiced
unprepared
unpretentious
unproductive
unprofitable
unprotected
unproved
unproven
unprovoked
unpunished
unqualified
unquenchable
unquestioning
unreachable
unreadable
unready
unrealistic
unreasonable
unreasonably
unrefined
unrelated
unreliable
unremembered
unrepentant
unrepresented
unrequited
unresolved
unresponsive
unrestrained
unrestricted
unrewarding
unripe
unsafe
unsalted
unsanitary
unsatisfactory
unsatisfied
unscented
unscheduled
unseasoned
unseen
unselfish
unselfishly
unselfishness
unshaped
unshaven
unskillful
unskillfully
unsolicited
unsolved
unsophisticated
unsound
unsoundly
unsoundness
unspecified
unspoiled
unsteadily
unsteadiness
unsteady
unstructured
unsubstantiated
unsuccessful
unsuitable
unsuitably
unsuited
unsupervised
unsupported
unsure
unsurprising
unsuspecting
unsweetened
unsympathetic
untamed
untanned
untidy
untouched
untrained
untreated
untrue
untrustworthy
untruthful
unusable
unusual
unvarying
unverified
unwanted
unwarranted
unwary
unwavering
unweaned
unwed
unwelcome
unwholesome
unwilling
unwillingly
unwillingness
unwise
unwisely
unworkable
unworthily
unworthiness
unworthy
unyielding

un·ac·cus·tomed *adj* **1 :** not customary **2 :** not accustomed

un·af·fect·ed *adj* **1 :** not influenced or changed by something **2 :** natural and sincere **—un·af·fect·ed·ly** *adv*

unan·i·mous \yù'nanəməs\ *adj* **1 :** showing no disagreement **2 :** formed with the agreement of all **—una·nim·i·ty** \,yünə'nimətē\ *n* **—unan·i·mous·ly** *adv*

un·armed *adj* **:** not armed or armored

un·as·sum·ing *adj* **:** not bold or arrogant

un·at·tached *adj* **1 :** not attached **2 :** not married or engaged

un·aware *adv* **:** unawares ~ *adj* **:** not aware

un·awares \,ənə'warz\ *adv* **1 :** without warning **2 :** unintentionally

un·bal·anced *adj* **1 :** not balanced **2 :** mentally unstable

un·beat·en *adj* **:** not beaten

un·be·com·ing *adj* **:** not proper or suitable **—un·be·com·ing·ly** *adv*

un·be·liev·able *adj* **1 :** improbable **2 :** superlative **—un·be·liev·ably** *adv*

un·bend *vb* **-bent; -bend·ing :** make or become more relaxed and friendly

un·bend·ing *adj* **:** formal and inflexible

un·bind *vb* **-bound; -bind·ing 1 :** remove bindings from **2 :** release

un·bolt *vb* **:** open or unfasten by withdrawing a bolt

un·born *adj* **:** not yet born

un·bo·som *vb* **:** disclose thoughts or feelings

un·bowed \,ən'baủd\ *adj* **:** not defeated or subdued

un·bri·dled \,ən'brīdᵊld\ *adj* **:** unrestrained

un·bro·ken *adj* **1 :** not damaged **2 :** not interrupted

un·buck·le *vb* **:** unfasten the buckle of

un·bur·den *vb* **:** relieve (oneself) of anxieties

un·but·ton *vb* **:** unfasten the buttons of

un·called–for *adj* **:** too harsh or rude for the occasion

un·can·ny \ən'kanē\ *adj* **1 :** weird **2 :** suggesting superhuman powers **—un·can·ni·ly** \-'kanᵊlē\ *adv*

un·ceas·ing *adj* **:** never ceasing **—un·ceas·ing·ly** *adv*

un·cer·e·mo·ni·ous *adj* **:** acting without ordinary courtesy **—un·cer·e·mo·ni·ous·ly** *adv*

un·cer·tain *adj* **1 :** not determined, sure, or definitely known **2 :** subject to chance or change **—un·cer·tain·ly** *adv* **—un·cer·tain·ty** *n*

un·chris·tian *adj* **:** not consistent with Christian teachings

un·cle \'əŋkəl\ *n* **1 :** brother of one's father or mother **2 :** husband of one's aunt

un·clean *adj* **:** not clean or pure **—un·clean·ness** *n*

un·clog *vb* **:** remove an obstruction from

un·coil *vb* **:** release or become released from a coiled state

un·com·mit·ted *adj* **:** not pledged to a particular allegiance or course of action

un·com·mon *adj* **1 :** rare **2 :** superior **—un·com·mon·ly** *adv*

un·com·pro·mis·ing *adj* **:** not making or accepting a compromise

un·con·cerned *adj* **1 :** disinterested **2 :** not anxious or upset **—un·con·cerned·ly** *adv*

un·con·di·tion·al *adj* **:** not limited in any way **—un·con·di·tion·al·ly** *adv*

un·con·scio·na·ble *adj* **:** shockingly unjust or unscrupulous **—un·con·scio·na·bly** *adv*

un·con·scious *adj* **1 :** not awake or aware of one's surroundings **2 :** not consciously done ~ *n* **:** part of one's mental life that one is not aware of **—un·con·scious·ly** *adv* **—un·con·scious·ness** *n*

un·con·sti·tu·tion·al *adj* **:** not according to or consistent with a constitution

un·con·trol·la·ble *adj* **:** incapable of being controlled **—un·con·trol·la·bly** *adv*

un·count·ed *adj* **:** countless

un·couth \,ən'küth\ *adj* **:** rude and vulgar

un·cov·er *vb* **1 :** reveal **2 :** expose by removing a covering

unc·tion \'əŋkshən\ *n* **1 :** rite of anointing **2 :** exaggerated or insincere earnestness

unc·tu·ous \'əŋkchəwəs\ *adj* **1 :** oily **2 :** insincerely smooth in speech or manner **—unc·tu·ous·ly** *adv*

un·cut *adj* **1 :** not cut down, into, off, or apart **2 :** not shaped by cutting **3 :** not abridged

un·daunt·ed *adj* **:** not discouraged **—un·daunt·ed·ly** *adv*

un·de·ni·able *adj* **:** plainly true **—un·de·ni·ably** *adv*

un·der \'əndər\ *adv* **:** below or beneath something ~ *prep* **1 :** lower than and sheltered by **2 :** below the surface of **3 :** covered or concealed by **4 :** subject to the authority of **5 :** less than ~ *adj* **1 :** lying below or beneath **2 :** subordinate **3 :** less than usual, proper, or desired

un·der·age \,əndər'āj\ *adj* **:** of less than legal age

un·der·brush \'əndər,brəsh\ *n* **:** shrubs and small trees growing beneath large trees

un·der·clothes \'əndər,klōz, -,klōthz\ *n pl* **:** underwear

un·der·cloth·ing \-,klōthiŋ\ *n* **:** underwear

un·der·cov·er \,əndər'kəvər\ *adj* **:** employed or engaged in secret investigation

un·der·cur·rent \'əndər,kərənt\ *n* **:** hidden tendency or opinion

un·der·cut \,əndər'kət\ *vb* **-cut; -cut·ting :** offer to sell or to work at a lower rate than

un·der·de·vel·oped \,əndərdi'veləpt\ *adj* **:** not normally or adequately developed esp. economically

un·der·dog \'əndər,dȯg\ *n* **:** contestant given least chance of winning

un·der·done \,əndər'dən\ *adj* **:** not thoroughly done or cooked

un·der·es·ti·mate \,əndər'estə,māt\ *vb* **:** estimate too low

un·der·ex·pose \,əndərik'spōz\ *vb* **:** give less than normal exposure to **—un·der·ex·po·sure** *n*

un·der·feed \,əndər'fēd\ *vb* **-fed; -feed·ing :** feed inadequately

un·der·foot \,əndər'fủt\ *adv* **1 :** under the feet **2 :** in the way of another

un·der·gar·ment \'əndər,gärmənt\ *n* **:** garment to be worn under another

un·der·go \,əndər'gō\ *vb* **-went** \-'went\; **-gone; -go·ing 1 :** endure **2 :** go through (as an experience)

un·der·grad·u·ate \,əndər'grajəwət\ *n* **:** university or college student

un·der·ground \,əndər'graủnd\ *adv* **1 :** beneath the surface of the earth **2 :** in secret ~ \'əndər,-\ *adj* **1 :** being or growing under the surface of the ground **2 :** secret ~ \'əndər,-\ *n* **:** secret political movement or group

un·der·growth \'əndər'grōth\ *n* **:** low growth on the floor of a forest

un·der·hand \'əndər,hand\ *adv or adj* **1 :** with secrecy and deception **2 :** with the hand kept below the waist

un·der·hand·ed \,əndər'handəd\ *adj or adv* **:** underhand **—un·der·hand·ed·ly** *adv* **—un·der·hand·ed·ness** *n*

un·der·line \'əndər,līn\ *vb* **1 :** draw a line under **2 :** stress **—underline** *n*

un·der·ling \'əndərliŋ\ *n* **:** inferior

un·der·ly·ing \,əndər,līiŋ\ *adj* **:** basic

un·der·mine \,əndər'mīn\ *vb* **1 :** excavate beneath **2 :** weaken or wear away secretly or gradually

un·der·neath \,əndər'nēth\ *prep* **:** directly under ~ *adv* **1 :** below a surface or object **2 :** on the lower side

un·der·nour·ished \,əndər'nərisht\ *adj* **:** insufficiently nourished **—un·der·nour·ish·ment** *n*

un·der·pants \'əndər,pants\ *n pl* **:** short undergarment for the lower trunk

un·der·pass \-,pas\ *n* **:** passageway crossing underneath another

un·der·pin·ning \'əndər,piniŋ\ *n* **:** support

un·der·priv·i·leged *adj* **:** poor

un•der•rate \ˌəndər'rāt\ *vb* : rate or value too low

un•der•score \'əndərˌskōr\ *vb* **1** : underline **2** : emphasize **—underscore** *n*

un•der•sea \ˌəndər'sē\ *adj* : being, carried on, or used beneath the surface of the sea ~ \ˌəndər'sē\, **un•der•seas** \-'sēz\ *adv* : beneath the surface of the sea

un•der•sec•re•tary *n* : deputy secretary

un•der•sell \ˌəndər'sel\ *vb* **-sold; -sell•ing** : sell articles cheaper than

un•der•shirt \'əndərˌshərt\ *n* : shirt worn as underwear

un•der•shorts \'əndərˌshȯrts\ *n pl* : short underpants

un•der•side \'əndərˌsīd, ˌəndər'sīd\ *n* : side or surface lying underneath

un•der•sized \ˌəndər'sīzd\ *adj* : unusually small

un•der•stand \ˌəndər'stand\ *vb* **-stood** \-'stu̇d\; **-stand•ing 1** : be aware of the meaning of **2** : deduce **3** : have a sympathetic attitude **—un•der•stand•able** \-'standəbəl\ *adj* **—un•der•stand•ably** \-blē\ *adv*

un•der•stand•ing \ˌəndər'standiŋ\ *n* **1** : intelligence **2** : ability to comprehend and judge **3** : mutual agreement ~ *adj* : sympathetic

un•der•state \ˌəndər'stāt\ *vb* **1** : represent as less than is the case **2** : state with restraint **—un•der•state•ment** *n*

un•der•stood \ˌəndər'stu̇d\ *adj* **1** : agreed upon **2** : implicit

un•der•study \'əndərˌstədē, ˌəndər'-\ *vb* : study another actor's part in order to substitute **—understudy** \'əndərˌ-\ *n*

un•der•take \ˌəndər'tāk\ *vb* **-took; -tak•en; -tak•ing 1** : attempt (a task) or assume (a responsibility) **2** : guarantee

un•der•tak•er \'əndərˌtākər\ *n* : one in the funeral business

un•der•tak•ing \'əndərˌtākiŋ, ˌəndər'-\ *n* **1** : something (as work) that is undertaken **2** : promise

under–the–counter *adj* : illicit

un•der•tone \'əndərˌtōn\ *n* : low or subdued tone or utterance

un•der•tow \-ˌtō\ *n* : current beneath the waves that flows seaward

un•der•val•ue \ˌəndər'valyü\ *vb* : value too low

un•der•wa•ter \-'wȯtər, -'wät-\ *adj* : being or used below the surface of the water **—underwater** *adv*

under way *adv* : in motion or in progress

un•der•wear \'əndərˌwar\ *n* : clothing worn next to the skin and under ordinary clothes

un•der•world \'əndərˌwərld\ *n* **1** : place of departed souls **2** : world of organized crime

un•der•write \'əndərˌrīt, ˌəndərˌ-\ *vb* **-wrote; -writ•ten; -writ•ing 1** : provide insurance for **2** : guarantee financial support of **—un•der•writ•er** *n*

un•dies \'əndēz\ *n pl* : underwear

un•do *vb* **-did; -done; -do•ing 1** : unfasten **2** : reverse **3** : ruin **—un•do•ing** *n*

un•doubt•ed *adj* : certain **—un•doubt•ed•ly** *adv*

un•dress *vb* : remove one's clothes ~ *n* : state of being naked

un•due *adj* : excessive **—un•du•ly** *adv*

un•du•late \'ənjəˌlāt\ *vb* **-lat•ed; -lat•ing** : rise and fall regularly **—un•du•la•tion** \ˌənjə'lāshən\ *n*

un•dy•ing *adj* : immortal or perpetual

un•earth *vb* : dig up or discover

un•earth•ly *adj* : supernatural

un•easy *adj* **1** : awkward or embarrassed **2** : disturbed or worried **—un•eas•i•ly** *adv* **—un•eas•i•ness** *n*

un•em•ployed *adj* : not having a job **—un•em•ploy•ment** *n*

un•equal *adj* : not equal or uniform **—un•equal•ly** *adv*

un•equaled, un•equalled *adj* : having no equal

un•equiv•o•cal *adj* : leaving no doubt **—un•equiv•o•cal•ly** *adv*

un•err•ing *adj* : infallible **—un•err•ing•ly** *adv*

un•even *adj* **1** : not smooth **2** : not regular or consistent **—un•even•ly** *adv* **—un•even•ness** *n*

un•event•ful *adj* : lacking interesting or noteworthy incidents **—un•event•ful•ly** *adv*

un•ex•pect•ed \ˌənik'spektəd\ *adj* : not expected **—un•ex•pect•ed•ly** *adv*

un•fail•ing *adj* : steadfast **—un•fail•ing•ly** *adv*

un•faith•ful *adj* : not loyal **—un•faith•ful•ly** *adv* **—un•faith•ful•ness** *n*

un•fa•mil•iar *adj* **1** : not well known **2** : not acquainted **—un•fa•mil•iar•i•ty** *n*

un•fas•ten *vb* : release a catch or lock

un•feel•ing *adj* : lacking feeling or compassion **—un•feel•ing•ly** *adv*

un•fit *adj* : not suitable **—un•fit•ness** *n*

un•flap•pa•ble \ˌən'flapəbəl\ *adj* : not easily upset or panicked **—un•flap•pa•bly** *adv*

un•fold *vb* **1** : open the folds of **2** : reveal **3** : develop

un•for•get•ta•ble *adj* : memorable **—un•for•get•ta•bly** *adv*

un•for•tu•nate *adj* **1** : not lucky or successful **2** : deplorable **—unfortunate** *n* **—un•for•tu•nate•ly** *adv*

un•found•ed *adj* : lacking a sound basis

un•freeze *vb* **-froze; -fro•zen; -freez•ing** : thaw

un•friend•ly *adj* : not friendly or kind **—un•friend•li•ness** *n*

un•furl *vb* : unfold or unroll

un•gain•ly *adj* : clumsy **—un•gain•li•ness** *n*

un•god•ly *adj* : wicked **—un•god•li•ness** *n*

un•grate•ful *adj* : not thankful for favors **—un•grate•ful•ly** *adv* **—un•grate•ful•ness** *n*

un•guent \'əŋgwənt, 'ən-\ *n* : ointment

un•hand *vb* : let go

un•hap•py *adj* **1** : unfortunate **2** : sad **—un•hap•pi•ly** *adv* **—un•hap•pi•ness** *n*

un•healthy *adj* **1** : not wholesome **2** : not well

un•heard–of \ˌən'hərdəv, -ˌäv\ *adj* : unprecedented

un•hinge \ˌən'hinj\ *vb* **1** : take from the hinges **2** : make unstable esp. mentally

un•hitch *vb* : unfasten

un•ho•ly *adj* : sinister or shocking **—un•ho•li•ness** *n*

un•hook *vb* : release from a hook

uni•cel•lu•lar \ˌyüni'selyələr\ *adj* : having or consisting of a single cell

uni•corn \'yünəˌkȯrn\ *n* : legendary animal with one horn in the middle of the forehead

uni•cy•cle \'yüniˌsīkəl\ *n* : pedal-powered vehicle with only a single wheel

uni•di•rec•tion•al \ˌyünidə'rekshənəl, -dī-\ *adj* : working in only a single direction

uni•form \'yünəˌfȯrm\ *adj* : not changing or showing any variation ~ *n* : distinctive dress worn by members of a particular group **—uni•for•mi•ty** \ˌyünə'fȯrmətē\ *n* **—uni•form•ly** *adv*

uni•fy \'yünəˌfī\ *vb* **-fied; -fy•ing** : make into a coherent whole **—uni•fi•ca•tion** \ˌyünəfə'kāshən\ *n*

uni•lat•er•al \ˌyünə'latərəl\ *adj* : having, affecting, or done by one side only **—uni•lat•er•al•ly** *adv*

un•im•peach•able *adj* : blameless

un•in•hib•it•ed *adj* : free of restraint **—un•in•hib•it•ed•ly** *adv*

union \'yünyən\ *n* **1** : act or instance of joining **2** or more things into one or the state of being so joined **2** : confederation of nations or states **3** : organization of workers (**labor union, trade union**)

union•ize \'yünyəˌnīz\ *vb* **-ized; -iz•ing** : form into a labor union **—union•i•za•tion** \ˌyünyənə'zāshən\ *n*

unique \yu̇'nēk\ *adj* **1** : being the only one of its kind **2** : very unusual **—unique•ly** *adv* **—unique•ness** *n*

uni•son \'yünəsən, -nəzən\ *n* **1** : sameness in pitch **2** : exact agreement

unit \'yünət\ *n* **1** : smallest whole number **2** : definite amount or quantity used as a standard of measurement **3** : single part of a whole **—unit** *adj*

unite \yu̇'nīt\ *vb* **unit•ed; unit•ing** : put or join together

uni•ty \'yünətē\ *n, pl* **-ties 1** : quality or state of being united or a unit **2** : harmony

uni•ver•sal \ˌyünə'vərsəl\ *adj* **1** : relating to or affecting everyone or everything **2** : present or occurring everywhere **—uni•ver•sal•ly** *adv*

uni•verse \'yünəˌvərs\ *n* : the complete system of all things that exist

uni•ver•si•ty \ˌyünə'vərsətē\ *n, pl* **-ties** : institution of higher learning

un•kempt \ˌən'kempt\ *adj* : not neat or combed

un•kind *adj* : not kind or sympathetic **—un•kind•li•ness** *n* **—un•kind•ly** *adv* **—un•kind•ness** *n*

un•law•ful *adj* : illegal **—un•law•ful•ly** *adv*

un•leash *vb* : free from control or restraint

un•less \ən'les\ *conj* : except on condition that

un•like \ən'līk, 'ənˌlīk\ *adj* **1** : not similar **2** : not equal ~ *prep* : different from **—un•like•ly** \ən'līklē\ *adv* **—un•like•ness** \-nəs\ *n* **—un•like•li•hood** \-lēhu̇d\ *n*

un•load *vb* **1** : take (cargo) from a vehicle, vessel, or plane **2** : take a load from **3** : discard

un•lock *vb* **1** : unfasten through release of a lock **2** : release or reveal

un•lucky *adj* **1** : experiencing bad luck **2** : likely to bring misfortune **—un•luck•i•ly** *adv*

un•mis•tak•able *adj* : not capable of being mistaken or misunderstood **—un•mis•tak•ably** *adv*

un•moved *adj* **1** : not emotionally affected **2** : remaining in the same place or position

un•nat•u•ral *adj* **1** : not natural or spontaneous **2** : abnormal **—un•nat•u•ral•ly** *adv* **—un•nat•u•ral•ness** *n*

un•nerve *vb* : deprive of courage, strength, or steadiness

un•oc•cu•pied *adj* **1** : not busy **2** : not occupied

un•pack *vb* **1** : remove (things packed) from a container **2** : remove the contents of (a package)

un•par•al•leled *adj* : having no equal

un•plug *vb* **1** : unclog **2** : disconnect from an electric circuit by removing a plug

un•prec•e•dent•ed *adj* : unlike or superior to anything known before

un•prin•ci•pled *adj* : unscrupulous

un•ques•tion•able *adj* : acknowledged as beyond doubt **—un•ques•tion•ably** *adv*

un•rav•el *vb* **1** : separate the threads of **2** : solve

un•re•al *adj* : not real or genuine **—un•re•al•i•ty** *n*

un•rea•son•ing *adj* : not using or being guided by reason

un•re•lent•ing *adj* : not yielding or easing **—un•re•lent•ing•ly** *adv*

un•rest *n* : turmoil

un•ri•valed, un•ri•valled *adj* : having no rival

un•roll *vb* **1** : unwind a roll of **2** : become unrolled

un•ruf•fled *adj* : not agitated or upset

un•ruly \ˌən'rülē\ *adj* : not readily controlled or disciplined **—un•rul•i•ness** *n*

un•scathed \ˌən'skāt͟hd\ *adj* : unharmed

un•sci•en•tif•ic *adj* : not in accord with the principles and methods of science

un•screw *vb* : loosen or remove by withdrawing screws or by turning

un•scru•pu•lous *adj* : being or acting in total disregard of conscience, ethical principles, or rights of others **—un•scru•pu•lous•ly** *adv* **—un•scru•pu•lous•ness** *n*

un•seal *vb* : break or remove the seal of

un•sea•son•able *adj* : not appropriate or usual for the season **—un•sea•son•ably** *adv*

un•seem•ly \ˌən'sēmlē\ *adj* : not polite or in good taste **—un•seem•li•ness** *n*

un•set•tle *vb* : disturb **—un•set•tled** *adj*

un•sight•ly \ˌən'sītlē\ *adj* : not attractive

un•skilled *adj* : not having or requiring a particular skill

un•snap *vb* : loosen by undoing a snap

un•speak•able \ˌən'spēkəbəl\ *adj* : extremely bad **—un•speak•ably** \-blē\ *adv*

un•sta•ble *adj* **1** : not mentally or physically balanced **2** : tending to change

un•stop *vb* **1** : unclog **2** : remove a stopper from

un•stop•pa•ble \ˌən'stäpəbəl\ *adj* : not capable of being stopped

un•strung \ˌən'strəŋ\ *adj* : nervously tired or anxious

un•sung \ˌən'səŋ\ *adj* : not celebrated in song or verse

un•tan•gle *vb* **1** : free from a state of being tangled **2** : find a solution to

un•think•able \ˌən'thiŋkəbəl\ *adj* : not to be thought of or considered possible

un•think•ing *adj* : careless **—un•think•ing•ly** *adv*

un•tie *vb* **-tied; -ty•ing** *or* **-tie•ing** : open by releasing ties

un•til \ˌən'til\ *prep* : up to the time of ~ *conj* : to the time that

un•time•ly *adj* **1** : premature **2** : coming at an unfortunate time

un•to \ˌən'tü, 'ənˌ-\ *prep* : to

un•told *adj* **1** : not told **2** : too numerous to count

un•tow•ard \ˌən'tōrd\ *adj* **1** : difficult to manage **2** : inconvenient

un•truth *n* **1** : lack of truthfulness **2** : lie

un•used *adj* **1** \ˌən'yüst, -'yüzd\ : not accustomed **2** \-'yüzd\ : not used

un•well *adj* : sick

un•wieldy \ˌən'wēldē\ *adj* : too big or awkward to manage easily

un•wind *vb* **-wound; -wind•ing 1** : undo something that is wound **2** : become unwound **3** : relax

un•wit•ting *adj* **1** : not knowing **2** : not intended **—un•wit•ting•ly** *adv*

un•wont•ed *adj* **1** : unusual **2** : not accustomed by experience

un•wrap *vb* : remove the wrappings from

un•writ•ten *adj* : made or passed on only in speech or through tradition

un•zip *vb* : zip open

up \'əp\ *adv* **1** : in or to a higher position or level **2** : from beneath a surface or level **3** : in or into an upright position **4** : out of bed **5** : to or with greater intensity **6** : into existence, evidence, or knowledge **7** : away **8**—used to indicate a degree of success, completion, or finality **9** : in or into parts ~ *adj* **1** : in the state of having risen **2** : raised to or at a higher level **3** : moving, inclining, or directed upward **4** : in a state of greater intensity **5** : at an end ~ *vb* **upped** *or in 1* **up; upped; up•ping; ups** *or in 1* **up 1** : act abruptly **2** : move or cause to move upward ~ *prep* **1** : to, toward, or at a higher point of **2** : along or toward the beginning of

up•braid \ˌəp'brād\ *vb* : criticize or scold

up•bring•ing \'əpˌbriŋiŋ\ *n* : process of bringing up and training

up•com•ing \ˌəp'kəmiŋ\ *adj* : approaching

up•date \ˌəp'dāt\ *vb* : bring up to date **—update** \'əpˌdāt\ *n*

up•end \ˌəp'end\ *vb* **1** : stand or rise on end **2** : overturn

up•grade \'əpˌgrād\ *n* **1** : upward slope **2** : increase ~ \'əpˌ-, ˌəp'-\ *vb* : raise to a higher position

up•heav•al \ˌəp'hēvəl\ *n* **1** : a heaving up (as of part of the earth's crust) **2** : violent change

up•hill \ˌəp'hil\ *adv* : upward on a hill or incline ~ \'əpˌ-\ *adj* **1** : going up **2** : difficult

up•hold \ˌəp'hōld\ *vb* **-held; -hold•ing** : support or defend **—up•hold•er** *n*

up•hol•ster \ˌəp'hōlstər\ *vb* : cover (furniture) with padding and fabric (**up•hol•stery** \-stərē\) **—up•hol•ster•er** *n*

up•keep \'əpˌkēp\ *n* : act or cost of keeping up or maintaining

up•land \'əplənd, -ˌland\ *n* : high land **—upland** *adj*

up•lift \ˌəp'lift\ *vb* **1** : lift up **2** : improve the condition or spirits of **—up•lift** \'əpˌ-\ *n*

up•on \ə'pȯn, -'pän\ *prep* : on

up•per \'əpər\ *adj* : higher in position, rank, or order ~ *n* : top part of a shoe

upper hand *n* : advantage

up•per•most \'əpərˌmōst\ *adv* : in or into the highest or most prominent position **—uppermost** *adj*

up•pi•ty \'əpətē\ *adj* : acting with a manner of undue importance

up•right \'əpˌrīt\ *adj* **1** : vertical **2** : erect in posture **3** : morally correct ~ *n* : something that stands upright **—upright** *adv* **—up•right•ly** *adv* **—up•right•ness** *n*

up•ris•ing \'əpˌrīziŋ\ *n* : revolt

up•roar \'əpˌrōr\ *n* : state of commotion or violent disturbance

up•roar•i•ous \ˌəp'rōrēəs\ *adj* **1** : marked by uproar **2** : extremely funny **—up•roar•i•ous•ly** *adv*

up•root \ˌəp'rüt, -'ru̇t\ *vb* : remove by or as if by pulling up by the roots

up•set \ˌəp'set\ *vb* **-set; -set•ting 1** : force or be forced out of the usual position **2** : disturb emotionally or physically ~ \'əpˌ-\ *n* **1** : act of throwing into disorder **2** : minor physical disorder ~ *adj* : emotionally disturbed or agitated

up•shot \'əpˌshät\ *n* : final result

up•side down \ˌəpˌsīd'dau̇n\ *adv* **1** : turned so that the upper and lower parts are reversed **2** : in or into confusion or disorder **—upside–down** *adj*

up•stairs \'əpˌstarz, ˌəp'-\ *adv* : up the stairs or to the next floor ~ *adj* : situated on the floor above ~ *n sing or pl* : part of a building above the ground floor

up•stand•ing \ˌəp'standiŋ, 'əpˌ-\ *adj* : honest

up•start \'əpˌstärt\ *n* : one who claims more personal importance than is warranted **—up•start** *adj*

up•swing \'əpˌswiŋ\ *n* : marked increase (as in activity)

up•tight \ˌəp'tīt\ *adj* **1** : tense **2** : angry **3** : rigidly conventional

up–to–date *adj* : current **—up–to–date•ness** *n*

up•town \'əpˌtau̇n\ *n* : upper part of a town or city **—uptown** *adj or adv*

up•turn \'əpˌtərn\ *n* : improvement or increase

up•ward \'əpwərd\, **up•wards** \-wərdz\ *adv* **1** : in a direction from lower to higher **2** : toward a higher or greater state or number ~ *adj* : directed toward or situated in a higher place **—up•ward•ly** *adv*

up•wind \ˌəp'wind\ *adv or adj* : in the direction from which the wind is blowing

ura•ni•um \yu̇'rānēəm\ *n* : metallic radioactive chemical element

ur•ban \'ərbən\ *adj* : characteristic of a city

ur•bane \ˌər'bān\ *adj* : polished in manner **—ur•ban•i•ty** \ˌər'banətē\ *n*

ur•ban•ite \'ərbəˌnīt\ *n* : city dweller

ur•chin \'ərchən\ *n* : mischievous youngster

-ure *n suffix* : act or process

ure•thra \yu̇'rēthrə\ *n, pl* **-thras** *or* **-thrae** \-ˌthrē\ : canal that carries off urine from the bladder **—ure•thral** \-thrəl\ *adj*

urge \'ərj\ *vb* **urged; urg•ing 1** : earnestly plead for or insist on (an action) **2** : try to persuade **3** : impel to a course of activity ~ *n* : force or impulse that moves one to action

ur•gent \'ərjənt\ *adj* **1** : calling for immediate attention **2** : urging insistently **—ur•gen•cy** \-jənsē\ *n* **—ur•gent•ly** *adv*

uri•nal \'yu̇rənᵊl\ *n* : receptacle to urinate in

uri•nate \'yu̇rəˌnāt\ *vb* **-nat•ed; -nat•ing** : discharge urine **—uri•na•tion** \ˌyu̇rə'nāshən\ *n*

urine \'yu̇rən\ *n* : liquid waste material from the kidneys **—uri•nary** \-əˌnerē\ *adj*

urn \'ərn\ *n* **1** : vaselike or cuplike vessel on a pedestal **2** : large coffee pot

us \ˈəs\ *pron, objective case of* WE
us•able \ˈyüzəbəl\ *adj* : suitable or fit for use —**us•abil•i•ty** \ˌyüzəˈbilətē\ *n*
us•age \ˈyüsij, -zij\ *n* **1** : customary practice **2** : way of doing or of using something
use \ˈyüs\ *n* **1** : act or practice of putting something into action **2** : state of being used **3** : way of using **4** : privilege, ability, or power to use something **5** : utility or function **6** : occasion or need to use ~ \ˈyüz\ *vb* **used** \ˈyüzd; *"used to" usu* ˈyüstə\; **us•ing** \ˈyüziŋ\ **1** : put into action or service **2** : consume **3** : behave toward **4** : to make use of **5** —used in the past tense with *to* to indicate a former practice —**use•ful** \ˈyüsfəl\ *adj* —**use•ful•ly** *adv* —**use•ful•ness** *n* —**use•less** \ˈyüsləs\ *adj* —**use•less•ly** *adv* —**use•less•ness** *n* —**us•er** *n*
used \ˈyüzd\ *adj* : not new
ush•er \ˈəshər\ *n* : one who escorts people to their seats ~ *vb* : conduct to a place
ush•er•ette \ˌəshəˈret\ *n* : woman or girl who is an usher
usu•al \ˈyüzhəwəl\ *adj* : being what is expected according to custom or habit —**usu•al•ly** \ˈyüzhəwəlē\ *adv*
usurp \yüˈsərp, -ˈzərp\ *vb* : seize and hold by force or without right —**usur•pa•tion** \ˌyüsərˈpāshən, -zər-\ *n* —**usurp•er** *n*
usu•ry \ˈyüzhərē\ *n, pl* **-ries 1** : lending of money at excessive interest or the rate or amount of such interest —**usu•rer** \-zhərər\ *n* —**usu•ri•ous** \yüˈzhurēəs\ *adj*
uten•sil \yüˈtensəl\ *n* **1** : eating or cooking tool **2** : useful tool
uter•us \ˈyütərəs\ *n, pl* **uteri** \-ˌrī\ : organ for containing and nourishing an unborn offspring —**uter•ine** \-ˌrīn, -rən\ *adj*
util•i•tar•i•an \yüˌtiləˈterēən\ *adj* : being or meant to be useful rather than beautiful
util•i•ty \yüˈtilətē\ *n, pl* **-ties 1** : usefulness **2** : regulated business providing a public service (as electricity)
uti•lize \ˈyütᵊlˌīz\ *vb* **-lized; -liz•ing** : make use of —**uti•li•za•tion** \ˌyütᵊləˈzāshən\ *n*
ut•most \ˈətˌmōst\ *adj* **1** : most distant **2** : of the greatest or highest degree or amount —**utmost** *n*
uto•pia \yüˈtōpēə\ *n* : place of ideal perfection —**uto•pi•an** \-pēən\ *adj or n*
ut•ter \ˈətər\ *adj* : absolute ~ *vb* : express with the voice —**ut•ter•er** \-ərər\ *n* —**ut•ter•ly** *adv*
ut•ter•ance \ˈətərəns\ *n* : what one says

V

v \ˈvē\ *n, pl* **v's** *or* **vs** \ˈvēz\ : 22d letter of the alphabet
va•can•cy \ˈvākənsē\ *n, pl* **-cies 1** : state of being vacant **2** : unused or unoccupied place or office
va•cant \-kənt\ *adj* **1** : not occupied, filled, or in use **2** : devoid of thought or expression —**va•cant•ly** *adv*
va•cate \-ˌkāt\ *vb* **-cat•ed; -cat•ing 1** : annul **2** : leave unfilled or unoccupied
va•ca•tion \vāˈkāshən, və-\ *n* : period of rest from routine —**vacation** *vb* —**va•ca•tion•er** *n*
vac•ci•nate \ˈvaksəˌnāt\ *vb* **-nat•ed; -nat•ing** : administer a vaccine usu. by injection
vac•ci•na•tion \ˌvaksəˈnāshən\ *n* : act of or the scar left by vaccinating
vac•cine \vakˈsēn, ˈvakˌ-\ *n* : substance to induce immunity to a disease
vac•il•late \ˈvasəˌlāt\ *vb* **-lat•ed; -lat•ing** : waver between courses or opinions —**vac•il•la•tion** \ˌvasəˈlāshən\ *n*
vac•u•ous \ˈvakyəwəs\ *adj* **1** : empty **2** : dull or inane —**va•cu•ity** \vaˈkyüətē, və-\ *n* —**vac•u•ous•ly** *adv* —**vac•u•ous•ness** *n*
vac•u•um \ˈvakˌyüm, -yəm\ *n, pl* **vac•u•ums** *or* **vac•ua** \-yəwə\ : empty space with no air ~ *vb* : clean with a vacuum cleaner
vacuum cleaner *n* : appliance that cleans by suction
vag•a•bond \ˈvagəˌbänd\ *n* : wanderer with no home —**vagabond** *adj*
va•ga•ry \ˈvāgərē, vəˈgerē\ *n, pl* **-ries** : whim
va•gi•na \vəˈjīnə\ *n, pl* **-nae** \-ˌnē\ *or* **-nas** : canal that leads out from the uterus —**vag•i•nal** \ˈvajənᵊl\ *adj*
va•grant \ˈvāgrənt\ *n* : person with no home and no job —**va•gran•cy** \-grənsē\ *n* —**vagrant** *adj*
vague \ˈvāg\ *adj* **vagu•er; vagu•est** : not clear, definite, or distinct —**vague•ly** *adv* —**vague•ness** *n*
vain \ˈvān\ *adj* **1** : of no value **2** : unsuccessful **3** : conceited —**vain•ly** *adv*
va•lance \ˈvaləns, ˈvāl-\ *n* : border drapery
vale \ˈvāl\ *n* : valley
vale•dic•to•ri•an \ˌvaləˌdikˈtōrēən\ *n* : student giving the farewell address at commencement
vale•dic•to•ry \-ˈdiktərē\ *adj* : bidding farewell —**valedictory** *n*
va•lence \ˈvāləns\ *n* : degree of combining power of a chemical element
val•en•tine \ˈvalənˌtīn\ *n* : sweetheart or a card sent to a sweetheart or friend on St. Valentine's Day
va•let \ˈvalət, ˈvalˌā, vaˈlā\ *n* : male personal servant
val•iant \ˈvalyənt\ *adj* : brave or heroic —**val•iant•ly** *adv*
val•id \ˈvaləd\ *adj* **1** : proper and legally binding **2** : founded on truth or fact —**va•lid•i•ty** \vəˈlidətē, va-\ *n* —**val•id•ly** *adv*
val•i•date \ˈvaləˌdāt\ *vb* **-dat•ed; -dat•ing** : establish as valid —**val•i•da•tion** \ˌvaləˈdāshən\ *n*
va•lise \vəˈlēs\ *n* : suitcase
val•ley \ˈvalē\ *n, pl* **-leys** : long depression between ranges of hills
val•or \ˈvalər\ *n* : bravery or heroism —**val•or•ous** \ˈvalərəs\ *adj*
valu•able \ˈvalyəwəbəl\ *adj* **1** : worth a lot of money **2** : being of great importance or use —**valuable** *n*
val•u•a•tion \ˌvalyəˈwāshən\ *n* **1** : act or process of valuing **2** : market value of a thing
val•ue \ˈvalyü\ *n* **1** : fair return or equivalent for something exchanged **2** : how much something is worth **3** : distinctive quality (as of a color or sound) **4** : guiding principle or ideal—usu. pl. ~ *vb* **val•ued; val•u•ing 1** : estimate the worth of **2** : appreciate the importance of —**val•ue•less** *adj* —**val•u•er** *n*
valve \ˈvalv\ *n* : structure or device to control flow of a liquid or gas —**valved** \ˈvalvd\ *adj* —**valve•less** *adj*
vam•pire \ˈvamˌpīr\ *n* **1** : legendary night-wandering dead body that sucks human blood **2** : bat that feeds on the blood of animals
1**van** \ˈvan\ *n* : vanguard
2**van** *n* : enclosed truck
va•na•di•um \vəˈnādēəm\ *n* : soft ductile metallic chemical element
van•dal \ˈvandᵊl\ *n* : person who willfully defaces or destroys property —**van•dal•ism** \-ˌizəm\ *n* —**van•dal•ize** \-ˌīz\ *vb*
vane \ˈvān\ *n* : bladelike device designed to be moved by force of the air or water
van•guard \ˈvanˌgärd\ *n* **1** : troops moving at the front of an army **2** : forefront of an action or movement
va•nil•la \vəˈnilə\ *n* : a flavoring made from the pods of a tropical orchid or this orchid
van•ish \ˈvanish\ *vb* : disappear suddenly
van•i•ty \ˈvanətē\ *n, pl* **-ties 1** : futility or something that is futile **2** : undue pride in oneself **3** : makeup case or table
van•quish \ˈvaŋkwish, ˈvan-\ *vb* **1** : overcome in battle or in a contest **2** : gain mastery over
van•tage \ˈvantij\ *n* : position of advantage or perspective
va•pid \ˈvapəd, ˈvāpəd\ *adj* : lacking spirit, liveliness, or zest —**va•pid•i•ty** \vaˈpidətē\ *n* —**vap•id•ly** \ˈvapədlē\ *adv* —**vap•id•ness** *n*
va•por \ˈvāpər\ *n* **1** : fine separated particles floating in and clouding the air **2** : gaseous form of an ordinarily liquid substance —**va•por•ous** \-pərəs\ *adj*
va•por•ize \ˈvāpəˌrīz\ *vb* **-ized; -iz•ing** : convert into vapor —**va•por•i•za•tion** \ˌvāpərəˈzāshən\ *n* —**va•por•iz•er** *n*
vari•able \ˈverēəbəl\ *adj* : apt to vary —**vari•abil•i•ty** \ˌverēəˈbilətē\ *n* —**vari•able** *n* —**vari•ably** *adv*
vari•ance \ˈverēəns\ *n* **1** : instance or degree of variation **2** : disagreement or dispute **3** : legal permission to build contrary to a zoning law
vari•ant \-ənt\ *n* : something that differs from others of its kind —**variant** *adj*
vari•a•tion \ˌverēˈāshən\ *n* : instance or extent of varying
vari•cose \ˈvarəˌkōs\ *adj* : abnormally swollen and dilated
var•ied \ˈverēd\ *adj* : showing variety —**var•ied•ly** *adv*
var•ie•gat•ed \ˈverēəˌgātəd\ *adj* : having patches, stripes, or marks of different colors —**var•ie•gate** \-ˌgāt\ *vb* —**var•ie•ga•tion** \ˌverēəˈgāshən\ *n*
va•ri•ety \vəˈrīətē\ *n, pl* **-et•ies 1** : state of being different **2** : collection of different things **3** : something that differs from others of its kind
var•i•ous \ˈverēəs\ *adj* : being many and unlike —**var•i•ous•ly** *adv*
var•nish \ˈvärnish\ *n* : liquid that dries to a hard glossy protective coating ~ *vb* : cover with varnish
var•si•ty \ˈvärsətē\ *n, pl* **-ties** : principal team representing a school
vary \ˈverē\ *vb* **var•ied; vary•ing 1** : alter **2** : make or be of different kinds
vas•cu•lar \ˈvaskyələr\ *adj* : relating to a channel for the conveyance of a body fluid (as blood or sap)
vase \ˈvās, ˈvāz\ *n* : tall usu. ornamental container to hold flowers
vas•sal \ˈvasəl\ *n* **1** : one acknowledging another as feudal lord **2** : one in a dependent position —**vas•sal•age** \-əlij\ *n*
vast \ˈvast\ *adj* : very great in size, extent, or amount —**vast•ly** *adv* —**vast•ness** *n*
vat \ˈvat\ *n* : large tub- or barrel-shaped container
vaude•ville \ˈvödvəl, ˈväd-, ˈvōd-, -ˌvil, -əvəl, -əˌvil\ *n* : stage entertainment of unrelated acts
1**vault** \ˈvölt\ *n* **1** : masonry arch **2** : usu. underground storage or burial room ~ *vb* : form or cover with a vault —**vault•ed** *adj* —**vaulty** *adj*
2**vault** *vb* : spring over esp. with the help of the hands or a pole ~ *n* : act of vaulting —**vault•er** *n*
vaunt \ˈvónt\ *vb* : boast —**vaunt** *n*
veal \ˈvēl\ *n* : flesh of a young calf
veer \ˈvir\ *vb* : change course esp. gradually —**veer** *n*
veg•e•ta•ble \ˈvejtəbəl, ˈvejə-\ *adj* **1** : relating to or obtained from plants **2** : like that of a plant ~ *n* **1** : plant **2** : plant grown for food
veg•e•tar•i•an \ˌvejəˈterēən\ *n* : person who eats no meat —**vegetarian** *adj* —**veg•e•tar•i•an•ism** \-ēəˌnizəm\ *n*
veg•e•tate \ˈvejəˌtāt\ *vb* **-tat•ed; -tat•ing** : lead a dull inert life
veg•e•ta•tion \ˌvejəˈtāshən\ *n* : plant life —**veg•e•ta•tion•al** \-shənəl\ *adj* —**veg•e•ta•tive** \ˈvejəˌtātiv\ *adj*
ve•he•ment \ˈvēəmənt\ *adj* : showing strong esp. violent feeling —**ve•he•mence** \-məns\ *n* —**ve•he•ment•ly** *adv*
ve•hi•cle \ˈvēˌhikəl, ˈvēəkəl\ *n* **1** : medium through which something is expressed, applied, or administered **2** : structure for transporting something esp. on wheels —**ve•hic•u•lar** \vēˈhikyələr\ *adj*
veil \ˈvāl\ *n* **1** : sheer material to hide something or to cover the face and head **2** : something that hides ~ *vb* : cover with a veil
vein \ˈvān\ *n* **1** : rock fissure filled with deposited mineral matter **2** : vessel that carries blood toward the heart **3** : sap-carrying tube in a leaf **4** : distinctive element or style of expression —**veined** \ˈvānd\ *adj*
ve•loc•i•ty \vəˈläsətē\ *n, pl* **-ties** : speed
ve•lour, ve•lours \vəˈlür\ *n, pl* **velours** \-ˈlürz\ : fabric with a velvetlike pile
vel•vet \ˈvelvət\ *n* : fabric with a short soft pile —**velvet** *adj* —**vel•vety** *adj*
ve•nal \ˈvēnᵊl\ *adj* : capable of being corrupted esp. by money —**ve•nal•i•ty** \viˈnalətē\ *n* —**ve•nal•ly** *adv*
vend \ˈvend\ *vb* : sell —**vend•ible** *adj* —**ven•dor** \ˈvendər\ *n*
ven•det•ta \venˈdetə\ *n* : feud marked by acts of revenge
ve•neer \vəˈnir\ *n* **1** : thin layer of fine wood glued over a cheaper wood **2** : superficial display ~ *vb* : overlay with a veneer
ven•er•a•ble \ˈvenərəbəl\ *adj* : deserving of respect
ven•er•ate \ˈvenəˌrāt\ *vb* **-at•ed; -at•ing** : respect esp. with reverence —**ven•er•a•tion** \ˌvenəˈrāshən\ *n*
venereal disease \vəˈnirēəl-\ *n* : contagious disease spread through copulation
ven•geance \ˈvenjəns\ *n* : punishment in retaliation for an injury or offense
venge•ful \ˈvenjfəl\ *adj* : filled with a desire for revenge —**venge•ful•ly** *adv*
ve•nial \ˈvēnēəl\ *adj* : capable of being forgiven
ven•i•son \ˈvenəsən, -əzən\ *n* : deer meat
ven•om \ˈvenəm\ *n* **1** : poison secreted by certain animals **2** : ill will —**ven•om•ous** \-əməs\ *adj*
vent \ˈvent\ *vb* **1** : provide with or let out at a vent **2** : give expression to ~ *n* : opening for passage or for relieving pressure
ven•ti•late \ˈventᵊlˌāt\ *vb* **-lat•ed; -lat•ing** : allow fresh air to circulate through —**ven•ti•la•tion** \ˌventᵊlˈāshən\ *n* —**ven•ti•la•tor** \ˈventᵊlˌātər\ *n*
ven•tri•cle \ˈventrikəl\ *n* : heart chamber that pumps blood into the arteries
ven•tril•o•quist \venˈtriləˌkwist\ *n* : one who can make the voice appear to come from another source —**ven•tril•o•quism** \-ˌkwizəm\ *n* —**ven•tril•o•quy** \-kwē\ *n*
ven•ture \ˈvenchər\ *vb* **-tured; -tur•ing 1** : risk or take a chance on **2** : put forward (an opinion) ~ *n* : speculative business enterprise
ven•ture•some \-səm\ *adj* : brave or daring —**ven•ture•some•ly** *adv* —**ven•ture•some•ness** *n*
ven•ue \ˈvenyü\ *n* : scene of an action or event
ve•rac•i•ty \vəˈrasətē\ *n, pl* **-ties** : truthfulness or accuracy —**ve•ra•cious** \vəˈrāshəs\ *adj*
ve•ran•da, ve•ran•dah \vəˈrandə\ *n* : large open porch
verb \ˈvərb\ *n* : word that expresses action or existence
ver•bal \ˈvərbəl\ *adj* **1** : having to do with or expressed in words **2** : oral **3** : relating to or formed from a verb —**ver•bal•i•za•tion** \ˌvərbələˈzāshən\ *n* —**ver•bal•ize** \ˈvərbəˌlīz\ *vb* —**ver•bal•ly** \-ē\ *adv*
verbal auxiliary *n* : auxiliary verb
ver•ba•tim \vərˈbātəm\ *adv or adj* : using the same words
ver•biage \ˈvərbēij\ *n* : excess of words
ver•bose \vərˈbōs\ *adj* : using more words than are needed —**ver•bos•i•ty** \-ˈbäsətē\ *n*
ver•dant \ˈvərdᵊnt\ *adj* : green with growing plants —**ver•dant•ly** *adv*
ver•dict \ˈvərdikt\ *n* : decision of a jury
ver•dure \ˈvərjər\ *n* : green growing vegetation or its color
verge \ˈvərj\ *vb* **verged; verg•ing** : be almost on the point of happening or doing something ~ *n* **1** : edge **2** : threshold
ver•i•fy \ˈverəˌfī\ *vb* **-fied; -fy•ing** : establish the truth, accuracy, or reality of —**ver•i•fi•able** *adj* —**ver•i•fi•ca•tion** \ˌverəfəˈkāshən\ *n*
ver•i•ly \ˈverəlē\ *adv* : truly or confidently
veri•si•mil•i•tude \ˌverəsəˈmiləˌtüd\ *n* : appearance of being true
ver•i•ta•ble \ˈverətəbəl\ *adj* : actual or true —**ver•i•ta•bly** *adv*
ver•i•ty \ˈverətē\ *n, pl* **-ties** : truth
ver•mi•cel•li \ˌvərməˈchelē, -ˈsel-\ *n* : thin spaghetti
ver•min \ˈvərmən\ *n, pl* **vermin** : small animal pest
ver•mouth \vərˈmüth\ *n* : dry or sweet wine flavored with herbs
ver•nac•u•lar \vərˈnakyələr\ *adj* : relating to a native language or dialect and esp. its normal spoken form ~ *n* : vernacular language
ver•nal \ˈvərnᵊl\ *adj* : relating to spring
ver•sa•tile \ˈvərsətᵊl\ *adj* : having many abilities or uses —**ver•sa•til•i•ty** \ˌvərsəˈtilətē\ *n*
1**verse** \ˈvərs\ *n* **1** : line or stanza of poetry **2** : poetry **3** : short division of a chapter in the Bible
2**verse** *vb* **versed; vers•ing** : make familiar by experience, study, or practice
ver•sion \ˈvərzhən\ *n* **1** : translation of the Bible **2** : account or description from a particular point of view
ver•sus \ˈvərsəs\ *prep* : opposed to or against
ver•te•bra \ˈvərtəbrə\ *n, pl* **-brae** \-ˌbrā, -ˌbrē\ *or* **-bras** : segment of the backbone —**ver•te•bral** \vərˈtēbrəl, ˈvərtə-\ *adj*
ver•te•brate \ˈvərtəbrət, -ˌbrāt\ *n* : animal with a backbone —**vertebrate** *adj*
ver•tex \ˈvərˌteks\ *n, pl* **ver•ti•ces** \ˈvərtəˌsēz\ **1** : point of intersection of lines or surfaces **2** : highest point
ver•ti•cal \ˈvərtikəl\ *adj* : rising straight up from a level surface —**vertical** *n* —**ver•ti•cal•i•ty** \ˌvərtəˈkalətē\ *n* —**ver•ti•cal•ly** *adv*
ver•ti•go \ˈvərtiˌgō\ *n, pl* **-goes** *or* **-gos** : dizziness
verve \ˈvərv\ *n* : liveliness or vividness
very \ˈverē\ *adj* **veri•er; -est 1** : exact **2** : exactly suitable **3** : mere or bare **4** : precisely the same ~ *adv* **1** : to a high degree **2** : in actual fact
ves•i•cle \ˈvesikəl\ *n* : membranous cavity —**ve•sic•u•lar** \vəˈsikyələr\ *adj*
ves•pers \ˈvespərz\ *n pl* : late afternoon or evening worship service
ves•sel \ˈvesəl\ *n* **1** : a container (as a barrel, bottle, bowl, or cup) for a liquid **2** : craft for navigation esp. on water **3** : tube in which a body fluid is circulated
1**vest** \ˈvest\ *vb* **1** : give a particular authority, right, or property to **2** : clothe with or as if with a garment
2**vest** *n* : sleeveless garment usu. worn under a suit coat
ves•ti•bule \ˈvestəˌbyül\ *n* : enclosed entrance —**ves•tib•u•lar** \veˈstibyələr\ *adj*
ves•tige \ˈvestij\ *n* : visible trace or remains —**ves•ti•gial** \veˈstijēəl\ *adj* —**ves•ti•gial•ly** *adv*
vest•ment \ˈvestmənt\ *n* : clergy member's garment
ves•try \ˈvestrē\ *n, pl* **-tries** : church storage room for garments and articles
vet•er•an \ˈvetərən\ *n* **1** : former member of the armed forces **2** : person with long experience —**veteran** *adj*

Veterans Day *n* : 4th Monday in October or formerly November 11 observed as a legal holiday in commemoration of the end of war in 1918 and 1945

vet·er·i·nar·i·an \ˌvetərən'erēən\ *n* : doctor of animals —**vet·er·i·nary** \'vetərənˌerē\ *adj*

ve·to \'vētō\ *n, pl* **-toes 1** : power to forbid and esp. the power of a chief executive to prevent a bill from becoming law **2** : exercise of the veto ~ *vb* **1** : forbid **2** : reject a legislative bill

vex \'veks\ *vb* **vexed; vex·ing** : trouble, distress, or annoy —**vex·a·tion** \vek'sāshən\ *n* —**vex·a·tious** \-shəs\ *adj*

via \'vīə, 'vēə\ *prep* : by way of

vi·a·ble \'vīəbəl\ *adj* **1** : capable of surviving or growing **2** : practical or workable —**vi·a·bil·i·ty** \ˌvīə'bilətē\ *n* —**vi·a·bly** \'vīəblē\ *adv*

via·duct \'vīəˌdəkt\ *n* : elevated roadway or railway bridge

vi·al \'vīəl\ *n* : small bottle

vi·brant \'vībrənt\ *adj* **1** : vibrating **2** : pulsing with vigor or activity **3** : sounding from vibration —**vi·bran·cy** \-brənsē\ *n*

vi·brate \'vīˌbrāt\ *vb* **-brat·ed; -brat·ing 1** : move or cause to move quickly back and forth or side to side **2** : respond sympathetically —**vi·bra·tion** \vī'brāshən\ *n* —**vi·bra·tor** \'vīˌbrātər\ *n* —**vi·bra·tory** \'vībrəˌtōrē\ *adj*

vic·ar \'vikər\ *n* : parish clergy member —**vi·car·iate** \-ēət\ *n*

vi·car·i·ous \vī'karēəs\ *adj* : sharing in someone else's experience through imagination or sympathetic feelings —**vi·car·i·ous·ly** *adv* —**vi·car·i·ous·ness** *n*

vice \'vīs\ *n* **1** : immoral habit **2** : depravity

vice- \ˌvīs\ *prefix* : one that takes the place of

vice-chancellor	**vice president**
vice-consul	**vice presidential**
vice presidency	**vice-regent**

vice admiral *n* : commissioned officer in the navy or coast guard ranking above a rear admiral

vice·roy \'vīsˌrȯi\ *n* : provincial governor who represents the sovereign

vice ver·sa \ˌvīsi'vərsə, ˌvīs'vər-\ *adv* : with the order reversed

vi·cin·i·ty \və'sinətē\ *n, pl* **-ties** : surrounding area

vi·cious \'vishəs\ *adj* **1** : wicked **2** : savage **3** : malicious —**vi·cious·ly** *adv* —**vi·cious·ness** *n*

vi·cis·si·tude \və'sisəˌtüd, vī-, -ˌtyüd\ *n* : irregular, unexpected, or surprising change —usu. used in pl.

vic·tim \'viktəm\ *n* : person killed, hurt, or abused

vic·tim·ize \'viktəˌmīz\ *vb* **-ized; -iz·ing** : make a victim of —**vic·tim·i·za·tion** \ˌviktəmə'zāshən\ *n* —**vic·tim·iz·er** \'viktəˌmīzər\ *n*

vic·tor \'viktər\ *n* : winner

Vic·to·ri·an \vik'tōrēən\ *adj* : relating to the reign of Queen Victoria of England or the art, taste, or standards of her time ~ *n* : one of the Victorian period

vic·to·ri·ous \vik'tōrēəs\ *adj* : having won a victory —**vic·to·ri·ous·ly** *adv*

vic·to·ry \'viktərē\ *n, pl* **-ries** : success in defeating an enemy or opponent or in overcoming difficulties

vict·uals \'vitᵊlz\ *n pl* : food

vid·eo \'vidēˌō\ *adj* : relating to the television image

vid·eo·cas·sette \ˌvidēˌōkə'set\ *n* : cassette containing videotape

vid·eo·tape \'vidēōˌtāp\ *vb* : make a recording of (a television production) on special tape —**videotape** *n*

vie \'vī\ *vb* **vied; vy·ing** : contend —**vi·er** \'vīər\ *n*

view \'vyü\ *n* **1** : process of seeing or examining **2** : opinion **3** : area of landscape that can be seen **4** : range of vision **5** : purpose or object ~ *vb* **1** : look at **2** : think about or consider —**view·er** *n*

view·point *n* : position from which something is considered

vig·il \'vijəl\ *n* **1** : day of devotion before a religious feast **2** : act or time of keeping awake **3** : long period of keeping watch (as over a sick or dying person)

vig·i·lant \'vijələnt\ *adj* : alert esp. to avoid danger —**vig·i·lance** \-ləns\ *n* —**vig·i·lant·ly** *adv*

vig·i·lan·te \ˌvijə'lantē\ *n* : one of a group independent of the law working to suppress crime

vi·gnette \vin'yet\ *n* : short descriptive literary piece

vig·or \'vigər\ *n* **1** : energy or strength **2** : intensity or force —**vig·or·ous** \'vigərəs\ *adj* —**vig·or·ous·ly** *adv* —**vig·or·ous·ness** *n*

vile \'vīl\ *adj* **vil·er; vil·est** : thoroughly bad or contemptible —**vile·ly** *adv* —**vile·ness** *n*

vil·i·fy \'viləˌfī\ *vb* **-fied; -fy·ing** : speak evil of —**vil·i·fi·ca·tion** \ˌviləfə'kāshən\ *n* —**vil·i·fi·er** \'viləˌfīər\ *n*

vil·la \'vilə\ *n* : country estate

vil·lage \'vilij\ *n* : small country town —**vil·lag·er** *n*

vil·lain \'vilən\ *n* : bad person —**vil·lain·ess** \-ənəs\ *n* —**vil·lainy** *n*

vil·lain·ous \-ənəs\ *adj* : evil or corrupt —**vil·lain·ous·ly** *adv* —**vil·lain·ous·ness** *n*

vim \'vim\ *n* : energy

vin·di·cate \'vindəˌkāt\ *vb* **-cat·ed; -cat·ing 1** : avenge **2** : exonerate **3** : justify —**vin·di·ca·tion** \ˌvində'kāshən\ *n* —**vin·di·ca·tor** \'vindəˌkātər\ *n*

vin·dic·tive \vin'diktiv\ *adj* : seeking or meant for revenge —**vin·dic·tive·ly** *adv* —**vin·dic·tive·ness** *n*

vine \'vīn\ *n* : climbing or trailing plant

vin·e·gar \'vinigər\ *n* : acidic liquid obtained by fermentation —**vin·e·gary** \-gərē\ *adj*

vine·yard \'vinyərd\ *n* : plantation of grapevines

vin·tage \'vintij\ *n* **1** : season's yield of grapes or wine **2** : period of origin ~ *adj* : of enduring interest

vi·nyl \'vīnᵊl\ *n* : strong plastic

vi·o·la \vē'ōlə\ *n* : instrument of the violin family tuned lower than the violin —**vi·o·list** \-list\ *n*

vi·o·late \'vīəˌlāt\ *vb* **-lat·ed; -lat·ing 1** : act with disrespect or disregard of **2** : rape **3** : desecrate —**vi·o·la·tion** \ˌvīə'lāshən\ *n* —**vi·o·la·tor** \'vīəˌlātər\ *n*

vi·o·lence \'vīələns\ *n* : intense physical force that causes or is intended to cause injury or destruction —**vi·o·lent** \-lənt\ *adj* —**vi·o·lent·ly** *adv*

vi·o·let \'vīələt\ *n* **1** : small flowering plant **2** : reddish blue

vi·o·lin \ˌvīə'lin\ *n* : bowed stringed instrument —**vi·o·lin·ist** \-nist\ *n*

VIP \ˌvēˌī'pē\ *n, pl* **VIPs** \-'pēz\ : very important person

vi·per \'vīpər\ *n* **1** : venomous snake **2** : treacherous or malignant person

vi·ra·go \və'rägō, -'rā-; 'virəˌgō\ *n, pl* **-goes** *or* **-gos** : shrew

vi·ral \'vīrəl\ *adj* : relating to or caused by a virus

vir·gin \'vərjən\ *n* **1** : unmarried woman **2** : a person who has never had sexual intercourse ~ *adj* **1** : chaste **2** : natural and unspoiled —**vir·gin·al** \-əl\ *adj* —**vir·gin·al·ly** *adv* —**vir·gin·i·ty** \vər'jinətē\ *n*

vir·gule \'vərgyül\ *n* : mark / used esp. to denote "or" or "per"

vir·ile \'virəl\ *adj* : masculine —**vi·ril·i·ty** \və'rilətē\ *n*

vir·tu·al \'vərchəwəl\ *adj* : being in effect but not in fact or name —**vir·tu·al·ly** *adv*

vir·tue \'vərchü\ *n* **1** : moral excellence **2** : effective or commendable quality **3** : chastity

vir·tu·os·i·ty \ˌvərchə'wäsətē\ *n, pl* **-ties** : great skill (as in music)

vir·tu·o·so \ˌvərchə'wōsō, -zō\ *n, pl* **-sos** *or* **-si** \-ˌsē, -ˌzē\ : highly skilled performer esp. of music —**virtuoso** *adj*

vir·tu·ous \'vərchəwəs\ *adj* **1** : morally good **2** : chaste —**vir·tu·ous·ly** *adv*

vir·u·lent \'virələnt, -yələnt\ *adj* **1** : extremely severe or infectious **2** : full of malice —**vir·u·lence** \-ləns\ *n* —**vir·u·lent·ly** *adv*

vi·rus \'vīrəs\ *n* **1** : tiny disease-causing agent **2** : a computer program that performs a malicious action (as destroying data)

vi·sa \'vēzə, -sə\ *n* : authorization to enter a foreign country

vis·age \'vizij\ *n* : face

vis·cera \'visərə\ *n pl* : internal bodily organs esp. of the trunk

vis·cer·al \'visərəl\ *adj* **1** : bodily **2** : instinctive **3** : deeply or crudely emotional —**vis·cer·al·ly** *adv*

vis·cid \'visəd\ *adj* : viscous —**vis·cid·i·ty** \vis'idətē\ *n*

vis·count \'vīˌkau̇nt\ *n* : British nobleman ranking below an earl and above a baron

vis·count·ess \-əs\ *n* **1** : wife of a viscount **2** : woman with rank of a viscount

vis·cous \'viskəs\ *adj* : having a thick or sticky consistency —**vis·cos·i·ty** \vis'käsətē\ *n*

vise \'vīs\ *n* : device for clamping something being worked on

vis·i·bil·i·ty \ˌvizə'bilətē\ *n, pl* **-ties** : degree or range to which something can be seen

vis·i·ble \'vizəbəl\ *adj* **1** : capable of being seen **2** : manifest or apparent —**vis·i·bly** *adv*

vi·sion \'vizhən\ *n* **1** : vivid picture seen in a dream or trance or in the imagination **2** : foresight **3** : power of seeing ~ *vb* : imagine

vi·sion·ary \'vizhəˌnerē\ *adj* **1** : given to dreaming or imagining **2** : illusory **3** : not practical ~ *n* : one with great dreams or projects

vis·it \'vizət\ *vb* **1** : go or come to see **2** : stay with for a time as a guest **3** : cause or be a reward, affliction, or punishment ~ *n* : short stay as a guest —**vis·it·able** *adj* —**vis·i·tor** \-ər\ *n*

vis·i·ta·tion \ˌvizə'tāshən\ *n* **1** : official visit **2** : divine punishment or favor **3** : severe trial

vi·sor \'vīzər\ *n* **1** : front piece of a helmet **2** : part (as on a cap or car windshield) that shades the eyes

vis·ta \'vistə\ *n* : distant view

vi·su·al \'vizhəwəl\ *adj* **1** : relating to sight **2** : visible —**vi·su·al·ly** *adv*

vi·su·al·ize \'vizhəwəˌlīz\ *vb* **-ized; -iz·ing** : form a mental image of —**vi·su·al·i·za·tion** \ˌvizhəwələ'zāshən\ *n* —**vi·su·al·iz·er** \'vizhəwəˌlīzər\ *n*

vi·tal \'vītᵊl\ *adj* **1** : relating to, necessary for, or characteristic of life **2** : full of life and vigor **3** : fatal **4** : very important —**vi·tal·ly** *adv*

vi·tal·i·ty \vī'talətē\ *n, pl* **-ties 1** : life force **2** : energy

vital signs *n pl* : body's pulse rate, respiration, temperature, and usu. blood pressure

vi·ta·min \'vītəmən\ *n* : natural organic substance essential to health

vi·ti·ate \'vishēˌāt\ *vb* **-at·ed; -at·ing 1** : spoil or impair **2** : invalidate —**vi·ti·a·tion** \ˌvishē'āshən\ *n* —**vi·ti·a·tor** \'vishēˌātər\ *n*

vit·re·ous \'vitrēəs\ *adj* : relating to or resembling glass

vit·ri·ol \'vitrēəl\ *n* : something caustic, corrosive, or biting —**vit·ri·ol·ic** \ˌvitrē'älik\ *adj*

vi·tu·per·ate \vī'tüpəˌrāt, və-, -'tyü-\ *vb* **-at·ed; -at·ing** : abuse in words —**vi·tu·per·a·tion** \-ˌtüpə'rāshən, -ˌtyü-\ *n* —**vi·tu·per·a·tive** \-'tüpərətiv, -'tyü-, -pəˌrāt-\ *adj* —**vi·tu·per·a·tive·ly** *adv*

vi·va·cious \vəvāshəs, vī-\ *adj* : lively —**vi·va·cious·ly** *adv* —**vi·va·ciousness** *n* —**vi·vac·i·ty** \-'vasətē\ *n*

viv·id \'vivəd\ *adj* **1** : lively **2** : brilliant **3** : intense or sharp —**viv·id·ly** *adv* —**viv·id·ness** *n*

viv·i·fy \'vivəˌfī\ *vb* **-fied; -fy·ing** : give life or vividness to

vivi·sec·tion \ˌvivə'sekshən, 'vivəˌ-\ *n* : experimental operation on a living animal

vix·en \'viksən\ *n* **1** : scolding woman **2** : female fox

vo·cab·u·lary \vō'kabyəˌlerē\ *n, pl* **-lar·ies 1** : list or collection of words **2** : stock of words used by a person or about a subject

vo·cal \'vōkəl\ *adj* **1** : relating to or produced by or for the voice **2** : speaking out freely and usu. emphatically

vocal cords *n pl* : membranous folds in the larynx that are important in making vocal sounds

vo·cal·ist \'vōkəlist\ *n* : singer

vo·cal·ize \-ˌlīz\ *vb* **-ized; -iz·ing** : give vocal expression to

vo·ca·tion \vō'kāshən\ *n* : regular employment —**vo·ca·tion·al** \-shənəl\ *adj*

vo·cif·er·ous \vō'sifərəs\ *adj* : noisy and insistent —**vo·cif·er·ous·ly** *adv*

vod·ka \'vädkə\ *n* : colorless distilled grain liquor

vogue \'vōg\ *n* : brief but intense popularity —**vogu·ish** \'vōgish\ *adj*

voice \'vȯis\ *n* **1** : sound produced through the mouth by humans and many animals **2** : power of speaking **3** : right of choice or opinion ~ *vb* **voiced; voic·ing** : express in words —**voiced** \'vȯist\ *adj*

void \'vȯid\ *adj* **1** : containing nothing **2** : lacking —with *of* **3** : not legally binding ~ *n* **1** : empty space **2** : feeling of hollowness ~ *vb* **1** : discharge (as body waste) **2** : make (as a contract) void —**void·able** *adj* —**void·er** *n*

vol·a·tile \'välətᵊl\ *adj* **1** : readily vaporizing at a relatively low temperature **2** : likely to change suddenly —**vol·a·til·i·ty** \ˌvälə'tilətē\ *n* —**vol·a·til·ize** \'välətᵊlˌīz\ *vb*

vol·ca·no \väl'kānō\ *n, pl* **-noes** *or* **-nos** : opening in the earth's crust from which molten rock and steam come out —**vol·ca·nic** \-'kanik\ *adj*

vo·li·tion \vō'lishən\ *n* : free will —**vo·li·tion·al** \-'lishənəl\ *adj*

vol·ley \'välē\ *n, pl* **-leys 1** : flight of missiles (as arrows) **2** : simultaneous shooting of many weapons

vol·ley·ball *n* : game of batting a large ball over a net

volt \'vōlt\ *n* : unit for measuring the force that moves an electric current

volt·age \'vōltij\ *n* : quantity of volts

vol·u·ble \'välyəbəl\ *adj* : fluent and smooth in speech —**vol·u·bil·i·ty** \ˌvälyə'bilətē\ *n* —**vol·u·bly** \'välyəblē\ *adv*

vol·ume \'välyəm\ *n* **1** : book **2** : space occupied as measured by cubic units **3** : amount **4** : loudness of a sound

vo·lu·mi·nous \və'lümənəs\ *adj* : large or bulky

vol·un·tary \'välənˌterē\ *adj* **1** : done, made, or given freely and without expecting compensation **2** : relating to or controlled by the will —**vol·un·tar·i·ly** *adv*

vol·un·teer \ˌvälən'tir\ *n* : person who offers to help or work without expecting payment or reward ~ *vb* **1** : offer or give voluntarily **2** : offer oneself as a volunteer

vo·lup·tuous \və'ləpchəwəs\ *adj* **1** : luxurious **2** : having a full and sexually attractive figure —**vo·lup·tuous·ly** *adv* —**vo·lup·tuous·ness** *n*

vom·it \'vämət\ *vb* : throw up the contents of the stomach —**vomit** *n*

voo·doo \'vüdü\ *n, pl* **voodoos 1** : religion derived from African polytheism and involving sorcery **2** : one who practices voodoo **3** : charm or fetish used in voodoo —**voodoo** *adj* —**voo·doo·ism** \-ˌizəm\ *n*

vo·ra·cious \vȯ'rāshəs, və-\ *adj* : greedy or exceedingly hungry —**vo·ra·cious·ly** *adv* —**vo·ra·cious·ness** *n* —**vo·rac·i·ty** \-'rasətē\ *n*

vor·tex \'vȯrˌteks\ *n, pl* **vor·ti·ces** \'vȯrtəˌsēz\ : whirling liquid

vo·ta·ry \'vōtərē\ *n, pl* **-ries 1** : devoted participant, adherent, admirer, or worshiper

vote \'vōt\ *n* **1** : individual expression of preference in choosing or reaching a decision **2** : right to indicate one's preference or the preference expressed ~ *vb* **vot·ed; vot·ing 1** : cast a vote **2** : choose or defeat by vote —**vote·less** *adj* —**vot·er** *n*

vo·tive \'vōtiv\ *adj* : consisting of or expressing a vow, wish, or desire

vouch \'vau̇ch\ *vb* : give a guarantee or personal assurance

vouch·er \'vau̇chər\ *n* : written record or receipt that serves as proof of a transaction

vouch·safe \vau̇ch'sāf\ *vb* **-safed; -saf·ing** : grant as a special favor

vow \'vau̇\ *n* : solemn promise to do something or to live or act a certain way —**vow** *vb*

vow·el \'vau̇əl\ *n* **1** : speech sound produced without obstruction or friction in the mouth **2** : letter representing such a sound

voy·age \'vȯiij\ *n* : long journey esp. by water or through space ~ *vb* **-aged; -ag·ing** : make a voyage —**voy·ag·er** *n*

vul·ca·nize \'vəlkəˌnīz\ *vb* **-nized; -niz·ing** : treat (as rubber) to make more elastic or stronger

vul·gar \'vəlgər\ *adj* **1** : relating to the common people **2** : lacking refinement **3** : offensive in manner or language —**vul·gar·ism** \-ˌrizəm\ *n* —**vul·gar·ize** \-ˌrīz\ *vb* —**vul·gar·ly** *adv*

vul·gar·i·ty \ˌvəl'garətē\ *n, pl* **-ties 1** : state of being vulgar **2** : vulgar language or act

vul·ner·a·ble \'vəlnərəbəl\ *adj* : susceptible to attack or damage —**vul·ner·a·bil·i·ty** \ˌvəlnərə'bilətē\ *n* —**vul·ner·a·bly** *adv*

vul·ture \'vəlchər\ *n* : large flesh-eating bird

vul·va \'vəlvə\ *n, pl* **-vae** \-ˌvē, -ˌvī\ : external genital parts of the female

vying *pres part of* VIE

W

w \'dəbəlˌyü\ *n, pl* **w's** *or* **ws** \-ˌyüz\ : 23d letter of the alphabet

wad \'wäd\ *n* **1** : little mass **2** : soft mass of fibrous material **3** : pliable plug to retain a powder charge **4** : considerable amount ~ *vb* **1** : form into a wad **2** : stuff with a wad

wad·dle \'wädᵊl\ *vb* **-dled; -dling** : walk with short steps swaying from side to side —**waddle** *n*

wade \'wād\ *vb* **wad·ed; wad·ing 1** : step in or through (as water) **2** : move with difficulty —**wade** *n* —**wad·er** *n*

wa·fer \'wāfər\ *n* **1** : thin crisp cake or cracker **2** : waferlike thing

waf·fle \'wäfəl\ *n* : crisped cake of batter cooked in a hinged utensil (**waffle iron**) ~ *vb* : vacillate

waft \'wäft, 'waft\ *vb* : cause to move lightly by wind or waves —**waft** *n*

^{1}**wag** \'wag\ *vb* **-gg-** : sway or swing from side to side or to and fro —**wag** *n*

^{2}**wag** *n* : wit —**wag·gish** *adj*

wage \'wāj\ *vb* **waged; wag·ing** : engage in ~ *n* **1** : payment for labor or services **2** : compensation

wa·ger \'wājər\ *n or vb* : bet

wag•gle \'wagəl\ *vb* **-gled; -gling :** wag —**waggle** *n*

wag•on \'wagən\ *n* **1 :** 4-wheeled vehicle drawn by animals **2 :** child's 4-wheeled cart

waif \'wāf\ *n* **:** homeless child

wail \'wāl\ *vb* **1 :** mourn **2 :** make a sound like a mournful cry —**wail** *n*

wain•scot \'wānskət, -ˌskōt, -ˌskät\ *n* **:** usu. paneled wooden lining of an interior wall —**wainscot** *vb*

waist \'wāst\ *n* **1 :** narrowed part of the body between chest and hips **2 :** waistlike part —**waist•line** *n*

wait \'wāt\ *vb* **1 :** remain in readiness or expectation **2 :** delay **3 :** attend as a waiter ~ *n* **1 :** concealment **2 :** act or period of waiting

wait•er \'wātər\ *n* **:** person who serves others at tables

wait•per•son \'wāt,pərsən\ *n* **:** a waiter or waitress

wait•ress \'wātrəs\ *n* **:** woman who serves others at tables

waive \'wāv\ *vb* **waived; waiv•ing :** give up claim to

waiv•er \'wāvər\ *n* **:** act of waiving right, claim, or privilege

1wake \'wāk\ *vb* **woke** \'wōk\; **wo•ken** \'wōkən\; **wak•ing 1 :** keep watch **2 :** bring or come back to consciousness after sleep ~ *n* **1 :** state of being awake **2 :** watch held over a dead body

2wake *n* **:** track left by a ship

wake•ful \'wākfəl\ *adj* **:** not sleeping or able to sleep —**wake•ful•ness** *n*

wak•en \'wākən\ *vb* **:** wake

wale \'wāl\ *n* **:** ridge on cloth

walk \'wók\ *vb* **1 :** move or cause to move on foot **2 :** pass over, through, or along by walking ~ *n* **1 :** a going on foot **2 :** place or path for walking **3 :** distance to be walked **4 :** way of living **5 :** way of walking **6 :** slow 4-beat gait of a horse —**walk•er** *n*

wall \'wól\ *n* **1 :** structure for defense or for enclosing something **2 :** upright enclosing part of a building or room **3 :** something like a wall ~ *vb* **:** provide, separate, surround, or close with a wall —**walled** \'wóld\ *adj*

wal•la•by \'wäləbē\ *n, pl* **-bies :** small or medium-sized kangaroo

wal•let \'wälət\ *n* **:** pocketbook with compartments

wall•flow•er *n* **1 :** mustardlike plant with showy fragrant flowers **2 :** one who remains on the sidelines of social activity

wal•lop \'wäləp\ *n* **1 :** powerful blow **2 :** ability to hit hard ~ *vb* **1 :** beat soundly **2 :** hit hard

wal•low \'wälō\ *vb* **1 :** roll about in deep mud **2 :** indulge oneself excessively ~ *n* **:** place for wallowing

wall•pa•per *n* **:** decorative paper for walls —**wallpaper** *vb*

wal•nut \'wól,nət\ *n* **1 :** nut with a furrowed shell and adherent husk **2 :** tree on which this nut grows or its brown wood

wal•rus \'wólrəs, 'wäl-\ *n, pl* **-rus** *or* **-rus•es :** large seallike mammal of northern seas having ivory tusks

waltz \'wólts\ *n* **:** gliding dance to music having 3 beats to the measure or the music —**waltz** *vb*

wam•pum \'wämpəm\ *n* **:** strung shell beads used by No. American Indians as money

wan \'wän\ *adj* **-nn- :** sickly or pale —**wan•ly** *adv* —**wan•ness** *n*

wand \'wänd\ *n* **:** slender staff

wan•der \'wändər\ *vb* **1 :** move about aimlessly **2 :** stray **3 :** become delirious —**wan•der•er** *n*

wan•der•lust \'wändər,ləst\ *n* **:** strong urge to wander

wane \'wān\ *vb* **waned; wan•ing 1 :** grow smaller or less **2 :** lose power, prosperity, or influence —**wane** *n*

wan•gle \'waŋgəl\ *vb* **-gled; -gling :** obtain by sly or devious means

want \'wónt\ *vb* **1 :** lack **2 :** need **3 :** desire earnestly ~ *n* **1 :** deficiency **2 :** dire need **3 :** something wanted

want•ing \-iŋ\ *adj* **1 :** not present or in evidence **2 :** falling below standards **3 :** lacking in ability ~ *prep* **1 :** less or minus **2 :** without

wan•ton \'wóntᵊn\ *adj* **1 :** lewd **2 :** having no regard for justice or for others' feelings, rights, or safety ~ *n* **:** lewd or immoral person ~ *vb* **:** be wanton —**wan•ton•ly** *adv* —**wan•ton•ness** *n*

wa•pi•ti \'wäpətē\ *n, pl* **-ti** *or* **-tis :** elk

war \'wór\ *n* **1 :** armed fighting between nations **2 :** state of hostility or conflict **3 :** struggle between opposing forces or for a particular end ~ *vb* **-rr- :** engage in warfare —**war•less** \-ləs\ *adj* —**war•time** *n*

war•ble \'wórbəl\ *n* **1 :** melodious succession of low pleasing sounds **2 :** musical trill ~ *vb* **-bled; -bling :** sing or utter in a trilling way

war•bler \'wórblər\ *n* **1 :** small thrushlike singing bird **2 :** small bright-colored insect-eating bird

ward \'wórd\ *n* **1 :** a guarding or being under guard or guardianship **2 :** division of a prison or hospital **3 :** electoral or administrative division of a city **4 :** person under protection of a guardian or a law court ~ *vb* **:** turn aside —**ward•ship** *n*

1-ward \wərd\ *adj suffix* **1 :** that moves, tends, faces, or is directed toward **2 :** that occurs or is situated in the direction of

2-ward, -wards *adv suffix* **1 :** in a (specified) direction **2 :** toward a (specified) point, position, or area

war•den \'wórdᵊn\ *n* **1 :** guardian **2 :** official charged with supervisory duties or enforcement of laws **3 :** official in charge of a prison

ward•er \'wórdər\ *n* **:** watchman or warden

ward•robe \'wórd,rōb\ *n* **1 :** clothes closet **2 :** collection of wearing apparel

ware \'war\ *n* **1 :** articles for sale —often pl. **2 :** items of fired clay

ware•house \-,haùs\ *n* **:** place for storage of merchandise —**warehouse** *vb* —**ware•house•man** \-mən\ *n* —**ware•hous•er** \-,haùzər, -sər\ *n*

war•fare \'wór,far\ *n* **1 :** military operations between enemies **2 :** struggle

war•head \-,hed\ *n* **:** part of a missile holding the explosive material

war•like *adj* **:** fond of, relating to, or used in war

warm \'wórm\ *adj* **1 :** having or giving out moderate or adequate heat **2 :** serving to retain heat **3 :** showing strong feeling **4 :** giving a pleasant impression of warmth, cheerfulness, or friendliness ~ *vb* **1 :** make or become warm **2 :** give warmth or energy to **3 :** experience feelings of affection **4 :** become increasingly ardent, interested, or competent —**warm•er** *n* —**warm•ly** *adv* —**warm up** *vb* **:** make ready by preliminary activity

war•mon•ger \'wór,məŋgər, -,mäŋ-\ *n* **:** one who attempts to stir up war

warmth \'wórmth\ *n* **1 :** quality or state of being warm **2 :** enthusiasm

warn \'wórn\ *vb* **1 :** put on guard **2 :** notify in advance —**warn•ing** \-iŋ\ *n or adj*

warp \'wórp\ *n* **1 :** lengthwise threads in a woven fabric **2 :** twist ~ *vb* **1 :** twist out of shape **2 :** lead astray **3 :** distort

war•rant \'wórənt, 'wär-\ *n* **1 :** authorization **2 :** legal writ authorizing action ~ *vb* **1 :** declare or maintain positively **2 :** guarantee **3 :** approve **4 :** justify

warrant officer *n* **1 :** officer in the armed forces ranking next below a commissioned officer **2 :** commissioned officer in the navy or coast guard ranking below an ensign

war•ran•ty \'wórəntē, 'wär-\ *n, pl* **-ties :** guarantee of the integrity of a product

war•ren \'wórən, 'wär-\ *n* **:** area where rabbits are bred and kept

war•rior \'wóryər, 'wórēər; 'wärē-, 'wäryər\ *n* **:** man engaged or experienced in warfare

war•ship \'wór,ship\ *n* **:** naval vessel

wart \'wórt\ *n* **1 :** small projection on the skin caused by a virus **2 :** wartlike protuberance —**warty** *adj*

wary \'warē\ *adj* **war•i•er; -est :** careful in guarding against danger or deception

was *past 1st & 3d sing of* BE

wash \'wósh, 'wäsh\ *vb* **1 :** cleanse with or as if with a liquid (as water) **2 :** wet thoroughly with liquid **3 :** flow along the border of **4 :** flow in a stream **5 :** move or remove by or as if by the action of water **6 :** cover or daub lightly with a liquid **7 :** undergo laundering ~ *n* **1 :** act of washing or being washed **2 :** articles to be washed **3 :** surging action of water or disturbed air —**wash•able** \-əbəl\ *adj*

wash•board *n* **:** grooved board to scrub clothes on

wash•bowl *n* **:** large bowl for water for washing hands and face

wash•cloth *n* **:** cloth used for washing one's face and body

washed–up \'wósht'əp, 'wäsht-\ *adj* **:** no longer capable or usable

wash•er \'wóshər, 'wäsh-\ *n* **1 :** machine for washing **2 :** ring used around a bolt or screw to ensure tightness or relieve friction

wash•ing \'wóshiŋ, 'wäsh-\ *n* **:** articles to be washed

Washington's Birthday *n* **:** the 3d Monday in February or formerly February 22 observed as a legal holiday

wash•out *n* **1 :** washing out or away of earth **2 :** failure

wash•room *n* **:** bathroom

wasp \'wäsp, 'wósp\ *n* **:** slender-bodied winged insect related to the bees and having a formidable sting

wasp•ish \'wäspish, 'wós-\ *adj* **:** irritable

was•sail \'wäsəl, wä'sāl\ *n* **1 :** toast to someone's health **2 :** liquor drunk on festive occasions **3 :** riotous drinking —**was•sail** *vb*

waste \'wāst\ *n* **1 :** sparsely settled or barren region **2 :** act or an instance of wasting **3 :** refuse (as garbage or rubbish) **4 :** material (as feces) produced but not used by a living body ~ *vb* **wast•ed; wast•ing 1 :** ruin **2 :** spend or use carelessly **3 :** lose substance or energy ~ *adj* **1 :** wild and uninhabited **2 :** being of no further use —**wast•er** *n* —**waste•ful** \-fəl\ *adj* —**waste•ful•ly** *adv* —**waste•ful•ness** *n*

waste•bas•ket \-,baskət\ *n* **:** receptacle for refuse

waste•land \-,land, -lənd\ *n* **:** barren uncultivated land

wast•rel \'wāstrəl, 'wästrəl\ *n* **:** one who wastes

watch \'wäch, 'wóch\ *vb* **1 :** be or stay awake intentionally **2 :** be on the lookout for danger **3 :** observe **4 :** keep oneself informed about ~ *n* **1 :** act of keeping awake to guard **2 :** close observation **3 :** one that watches **4 :** period of duty on a ship or those on duty during this period **5 :** timepiece carried on the person —**watch•er** *n*

watch•dog *n* **1 :** dog kept to guard property **2 :** one that protects

watch•ful \-fəl\ *adj* **:** steadily attentive —**watch•ful•ly** *adv* —**watch•ful•ness** *n*

watch•man \-mən\ *n* **:** person assigned to watch

watch•word *n* **1 :** secret word used as a signal **2 :** slogan

wa•ter \'wótər, 'wät-\ *n* **1 :** liquid that descends as rain and forms rivers, lakes, and seas **2 :** liquid containing or resembling water ~ *vb* **1 :** supply with or get water **2 :** dilute with or as if with water **3 :** form or secrete watery matter

water buffalo *n* **:** common oxlike often domesticated Asian buffalo

wa•ter•col•or *n* **1 :** paint whose liquid part is water **2 :** picture made with watercolors

wa•ter•course *n* **:** stream of water

wa•ter•cress \-,kres\ *n* **:** perennial salad plant with white flowers

wa•ter•fall *n* **:** steep descent of the water of a stream

wa•ter•fowl *n* **1 :** bird that frequents the water **2 waterfowl** *pl* **:** swimming game birds

wa•ter•front *n* **:** land fronting a body of water

water lily *n* **:** aquatic plant with floating leaves and showy flowers

wa•ter•logged \-,lógd, -,lägd\ *adj* **:** filled or soaked with water

wa•ter•mark *n* **1 :** mark showing how high water has risen **2 :** a marking in paper visible under light ~ *vb* **:** mark (paper) with a watermark

wa•ter•mel•on *n* **:** large fruit with sweet juicy usu. red pulp

water moccasin *n* **:** venomous snake of the southeastern U.S.

wa•ter•pow•er *n* **:** power of moving water used to run machinery

wa•ter•proof *adj* **:** not letting water through ~ *vb* **:** make waterproof —**wa•ter•proof•ing** *n*

wa•ter•shed \-,shed\ *n* **:** dividing ridge between two drainage areas or one of these areas

water ski *n* **:** ski used on water when the wearer is towed —**wa•ter–ski** *vb* —**wa•ter–ski•er** *n*

wa•ter•spout *n* **1 :** pipe from which water is spouted **2 :** tornado over a body of water

wa•ter•tight *adj* **1 :** so tight as not to let water in **2 :** allowing no possibility for doubt or uncertainty

wa•ter•way *n* **:** navigable body of water

wa•ter•works *n pl* **:** system by which water is supplied (as to a city)

wa•tery \'wótərē, 'wät-\ *adj* **1 :** containing, full of, or giving out water **2 :** being like water **3 :** soft and soggy

watt \'wät\ *n* **:** unit of electric power —**watt•age** \'wätij\ *n*

wat•tle \'wätᵊl\ *n* **1 :** framework of flexible branches used in building **2 :** fleshy process hanging usu. about the head or neck (as of a bird) —**wat•tled** \-ᵊld\ *adj*

wave \'wāv\ *vb* **waved; wav•ing 1 :** flutter **2 :** signal with the hands **3 :** wave to and fro with the hand **4 :** curve up and down like a wave ~ *n* **1 :** moving swell on the surface of water **2 :** wave-like shape **3 :** waving motion **4 :** surge **5 :** disturbance that transfers energy from point to point —**wave•let** \-lət\ *n* —**wave•like** *adj* —**wavy** *adj*

wave•length \'wāv,leŋth\ *n* **1 :** distance from crest to crest in the line of advance of a wave **2 :** line of thought that reveals a common understanding

wa•ver \'wāvər\ *vb* **1 :** fluctuate in opinion, allegiance, or direction **2 :** flicker **3 :** falter —**waver** *n* —**wa•ver•er** *n* —**wa•ver•ing•ly** *adv*

1wax \'waks\ *n* **1 :** yellowish plastic substance secreted by bees **2 :** substance like beeswax ~ *vb* **:** treat or rub with wax esp. for polishing

2wax *vb* **1 :** grow larger **2 :** become

wax•en \'waksən\ *adj* **:** made of or resembling wax

waxy \'waksē\ *adj* **wax•i•er; -est :** made of, full of, or resembling wax

way \'wā\ *n* **1 :** thoroughfare for travel or passage **2 :** route **3 :** course of action **4 :** method **5 :** detail **6 :** usual or characteristic state of affairs **7 :** condition **8 :** distance **9 :** progress along a course —**by the way :** in a digression —**by way of 1 :** for the purpose of **2 :** by the route through —**out of the way :** remote

way•bill *n* **:** paper that accompanies a shipment and gives details of goods, route, and charges

way•far•er \'wā,farər\ *n* **:** traveler esp. on foot —**way•far•ing** \-,fariŋ\ *adj*

way•lay \'wā,lā\ *vb* **-laid** \-,lād\; **-lay•ing :** lie in wait for

way•side *n* **:** side of a road

way•ward \'wāwərd\ *adj* **1 :** following one's own capricious inclinations **2 :** unpredictable

we \'wē\ *pron* —used of a group that includes the speaker or writer

weak \'wēk\ *adj* **1 :** lacking strength or vigor **2 :** deficient in vigor of mind or character **3 :** of less than usual strength **4 :** not having or exerting authority —**weak•en** \'wēkən\ *vb* —**weak•ly** *adv*

weak•ling \-liŋ\ *n* **:** person who is physically, mentally, or morally weak

weak•ly \'wēklē\ *adj* **:** feeble

weak•ness \-nəs\ *n* **1 :** quality or state of being weak **2 :** fault **3 :** object of special liking

wealth \'welth\ *n* **1 :** abundant possessions or resources **2 :** profusion

wealthy \'welthē\ *adj* **wealth•i•er; -est :** having wealth

wean \'wēn\ *vb* **1 :** accustom (a young mammal) to take food by means other than nursing **2 :** free from dependence

weap•on \'wepən\ *n* **1 :** something (as a gun) that may be used to fight with **2 :** means by which one contends against another —**weap•on•less** *adj*

wear \'war\ *vb* **wore** \'wōr\; **worn** \'wōrn\; **wear•ing 1 :** use as an article of clothing or adornment **2 :** carry on the person **3 :** show an appearance of **4 :** decay by use or by scraping **5 :** lessen the strength of **6 :** endure use ~ *n* **1 :** act of wearing **2 :** clothing **3 :** lasting quality **4 :** result of use —**wear•able** \'warəbəl\ *adj* —**wear•er** *n* —**wear out** *vb* **1 :** make or become useless by wear **2 :** tire

wea•ri•some \'wirēsəm\ *adj* **:** causing weariness —**wea•ri•some•ly** *adv* —**wea•ri•some•ness** *n*

wea•ry \'wirē\ *adj* **-ri•er; -est 1 :** worn out in strength, freshness, or patience **2 :** expressing or characteristic of weariness ~ *vb* **-ried; -ry•ing :** make or become weary —**wea•ri•ly** *adv* —**wea•ri•ness** *n*

wea•sel \'wēzəl\ *n* **:** small slender flesh-eating mammal

weath•er \'wethər\ *n* **:** state of the atmosphere ~ *vb* **1 :** expose to or endure the action of weather **2 :** endure

weath•er–beat•en *adj* **:** worn or damaged by exposure to the weather

weath•er•man \-,man\ *n* **:** one who forecasts and reports the weather

weath•er•proof *adj* **:** able to withstand exposure to weather —**weatherproof** *vb*

weather vane *n* **:** movable device that shows the way the wind blows

weave \'wēv\ *vb* **wove** \'wōv\ *or* **weaved; wo•ven** \'wōvən\ *or* **weaved; weav•ing 1 :** form by interlacing strands of material **2 :** to make as if by weaving together parts **3 :** follow a winding course ~ *n* **:** pattern or method of weaving —**weav•er** *n*

web \'web\ *n* **1 :** cobweb **2 :** animal or plant membrane **3 :** network ~ *vb* **-bb- :** cover or provide with a web —**webbed** \'webd\ *adj*

web•bing \'webiŋ\ *n* **:** strong closely woven tape

wed \'wed\ *vb* **-dd- 1 :** marry **2 :** unite

wed•ding \'wediŋ\ *n* **:** marriage ceremony and celebration

wedge \'wej\ *n* **:** V-shaped object used for splitting, raising, forcing open, or tightening ~ *vb* **wedged; wedg•ing 1 :** tighten or split with a wedge **2 :** force into a narrow space

wed•lock \'wed,läk\ *n* **:** marriage

Wednes•day \'wenzdā, -dē\ *n* **:** 4th day of the week

wee \'wē\ *adj* **:** very small

weed \'wēd\ *n* **:** unwanted plant ~ *vb* **1 :** remove weeds **2 :** get rid of —**weed•er** *n* —**weedy** *adj*

weeds *n pl* **:** mourning clothes

week \'wēk\ *n* **1 :** 7 successive days **2 :** calendar period of 7 days beginning with Sunday and ending with Saturday **3 :** the working or school days of the calendar week

week·day \'wēk,dā\ *n* : any day except Sunday and often Saturday

week·end \-,end\ *n* : Saturday and Sunday ~ *vb* : spend the weekend

week·ly \'wēklē\ *adj* : occurring, appearing, or done every week ~ *n, pl* **-lies** : weekly publication —**weekly** *adv*

weep \'wēp\ *vb* **wept** \'wept\; **weep·ing** : shed tears —**weep·er** *n* —**weepy** *adj*

wee·vil \'wēvəl\ *n* : small injurious beetle with a long head usu. curved into a snout —**wee·vily, wee·vil·ly** \'wēvəlē\ *adj*

weft \'weft\ *n* : crosswise threads or yarn in weaving

weigh \'wā\ *vb* **1** : determine the heaviness of **2** : have a specified weight **3** : consider carefully **4** : raise (an anchor) off the sea floor **5** : press down or burden

weight \'wāt\ *n* **1** : amount that something weighs **2** : relative heaviness **3** : heavy object **4** : burden or pressure **5** : importance ~ *vb* **1** : load with a weight **2** : oppress —**weight·less** \-ləs\ *adj* —**weight·less·ness** *n* —**weighty** \'wātē\ *adj*

weird \'wird\ *adj* **1** : unearthly or mysterious **2** : strange —**weird·ly** *adv* —**weird·ness** *n*

wel·come \'welkəm\ *vb* **-comed; -com·ing** : accept or greet cordially ~ *adj* : received or permitted gladly ~ *n* : cordial greeting or reception

weld \'weld\ *vb* : unite by heating, hammering, or pressing ~ *n* : union by welding —**weld·er** *n*

wel·fare \'wel,far\ *n* **1** : prosperity **2** : government aid for those in need

[1]well \'wel\ *n* **1** : spring **2** : hole sunk in the earth to obtain a natural deposit (as of oil) **3** : source of supply **4** : open space extending vertically through floors ~ *vb* : flow forth

[2]well *adv* **bet·ter** \'betər\; **best** \'best\ **1** : in a good or proper manner **2** : satisfactorily **3** : fully **4** : intimately **5** : considerably ~ *adj* **1** : satisfactory **2** : prosperous **3** : desirable **4** : healthy

well-adjusted \,welə'jəstəd\ *adj* : well-balanced

well-ad·vised \,weləd'vīzd\ *adj* : prudent

well-balanced \'wel'balənst\ *adj* **1** : evenly balanced **2** : emotionally or psychologically sound

well-be·ing \'wel'bēiŋ\ *n* : state of being happy, healthy, or prosperous

well-bred \-'bred\ *adj* : having good manners

well-done *adj* **1** : properly performed **2** : cooked thoroughly

well-heeled \-'hēld\ *adj* : financially well-off

well-mean·ing *adj* : having good intentions

well-nigh *adv* : nearly

well-off *adj* : being in good condition esp. financially

well-read \-'red\ *adj* : well informed through reading

well-round·ed \-'raùndəd\ *adj* : broadly developed

well·spring *n* : source

well-to-do \,weltə'dü\ *adj* : prosperous

welsh \'welsh, 'welch\ *vb* **1** : avoid payment **2** : break one's word

Welsh rabbit *n* : melted often seasoned cheese poured over toast or crackers

Welsh rare·bit \-'rarbət\ *n* : Welsh rabbit

welt \'welt\ *n* **1** : narrow strip of leather between a shoe upper and sole **2** : ridge raised on the skin usu. by a blow ~ *vb* : hit hard

wel·ter \'weltər\ *vb* **1** : toss about **2** : wallow ~ *n* : confused jumble

wen \'wen\ *n* : abnormal growth or cyst

wench \'wench\ *n* : young woman

wend \'wend\ *vb* : direct one's course

went *past of* GO

wept *past of* WEEP

were *past 2d sing, past pl,* or *past subjunctive of* BE

were·wolf \'wer,wùlf, 'wir-, 'wər-\ *n, pl* **-wolves** \-,wùlvz\ : person held to be able to change into a wolf

west \'west\ *adv* : to or toward the west ~ *adj* : situated toward or at or coming from the west ~ *n* **1** : direction of sunset **2** *cap* : regions to the west —**west·er·ly** \'westərlē\ *adv or adj* —**west·ward** \-wərd\ *adv or adj* —**west·wards** \-wərdz\ *adv*

west·ern \'westərn\ *adj* **1** *cap* : of a region designated West **2** : lying toward or coming from the west —**West·ern·er** *n*

wet \'wet\ *adj* **-tt-** **1** : consisting of or covered or soaked with liquid **2** : not dry ~ *n* : moisture ~ *vb* **-tt-** : make or become moist —**wet·ly** *adv* —**wet·ness** *n*

whack \'hwak\ *vb* : strike sharply ~ *n* **1** : sharp blow **2** : proper working order **3** : chance **4** : try

[1]whale \'hwāl\ *n, pl* **whales** *or* **whale** : large marine mammal ~ *vb* **whaled; whal·ing** : hunt for whales —**whale·boat** *n* —**whal·er** *n*

[2]whale *vb* **whaled; whal·ing** : strike or hit vigorously

whale·bone *n* : horny substance attached to the upper jaw of some large whales (**whalebone whales**)

wharf \'hwórf\ *n, pl* **wharves** \'hwórvz\ : structure alongside which boats lie to load or unload

what \'hwät\ *pron* **1** —used to inquire the identity or nature of something **2** : that which **3** : whatever ~ *adv* : in what respect ~ *adj* **1** —used to inquire about the identity or nature of something **2** : how remarkable or surprising **3** : whatever

what·ev·er \hwät'evər\ *pron* **1** : anything or everything that **2** : no matter what ~ *adj* : of any kind at all

what·not \'hwät,nät\ *pron* : any of various other things that might be mentioned

what·so·ev·er \,hwätsō'evər\ *pron or adj* : whatever

wheal \'hwēl\ *n* : a welt on the skin

wheat \'hwēt\ *n* : cereal grain that yields flour —**wheat·en** *adj*

whee·dle \'hwēdᵊl\ *vb* **-dled; -dling** : coax or tempt by flattery

wheel \'hwēl\ *n* **1** : disk or circular frame capable of turning on a central axis **2** : device of which the main part is a wheel ~ *vb* **1** : convey or move on wheels or a wheeled vehicle **2** : rotate **3** : turn so as to change direction —**wheeled** *adj* —**wheel·er** *n* —**wheel·less** *adj*

wheel·bar·row \-,barō\ *n* : one-wheeled vehicle for carrying small loads

wheel·base *n* : distance in inches between the front and rear axles of an automotive vehicle

wheel·chair *n* : chair mounted on wheels esp. for the use of disabled persons

wheeze \'hwēz\ *vb* **wheezed; wheez·ing** : breathe with difficulty and with a whistling sound —**wheeze** *n* —**wheezy** *adj*

whelk \'hwelk\ *n* : large sea snail

whelp \'hwelp\ *n* : one of the young of various carnivorous mammals (as a dog) ~ *vb* : bring forth whelps

when \'hwen\ *adv* —used to inquire about or designate a particular time ~ *conj* **1** : at or during the time that **2** : every time that **3** : if **4** : although ~ *pron* : what time

whence \'hwens\ *adv or conj* : from what place, source, or cause

when·ev·er \hwen'evər\ *conj or adv* : at whatever time

where \'hwer\ *adv* **1** : at, in, or to what place **2** : at, in, or to what situation, position, direction, circumstances, or respect ~ *conj* **1** : at, in, or to what place, position, or circumstance **2** : at, in, or to which place ~ *n* : place

where·abouts \-ə,baùts\ *adv* : about where ~ *n sing or pl* : place where a person or thing is

where·as \hwer'az\ *conj* **1** : while on the contrary **2** : since

where·by *conj* : by, through, or in accordance with which

where·fore \'hwer,fōr\ *adv* **1** : why **2** : therefore ~ *n* : reason

where·in \hwer'in\ *adv* : in what respect

where·of \-'əv, -äv\ *conj* : of what, which, or whom

where·up·on \'hwerə,pón, -,pän\ *conj* **1** : on which **2** : and then

wher·ev·er \hwer'evər\ *adv* : where ~ *conj* : at, in, or to whatever place or circumstance

where·with·al \'hwerwith,ól, -with-\ *n* : resources and esp. money

whet \'hwet\ *vb* **-tt-** **1** : sharpen by rubbing (as with a stone) **2** : stimulate —**whet·stone** *n*

whether \'hwethər\ *conj* **1** : if it is or was true that **2** : if it is or was better **3** : whichever is the case

whey \'hwā\ *n* : watery part of sour milk

which \'hwich\ *adj* **1** : being what one or ones out of a group **2** : whichever ~ *pron* **1** : which one or ones **2** : whichever

which·ev·er \hwich'evər\ *pron or adj* : no matter what one

whiff \'hwif\ *n* **1** : slight gust **2** : inhalation of odor, gas, or smoke **3** : slight trace ~ *vb* : inhale an odor

while \'hwīl\ *n* **1** : period of time **2** : time and effort used ~ *conj* **1** : during the time that **2** : as long as **3** : although ~ *vb* **whiled; whil·ing** : cause to pass esp. pleasantly

whim \'hwim\ *n* : sudden wish, desire, or change of mind

whim·per \'hwimpər\ *vb* : cry softly —**whimper** *n*

whim·si·cal \'hwimzikəl\ *adj* **1** : full of whims **2** : erratic —**whim·si·cal·i·ty** \,hwimzə'kalətē\ *n* —**whim·si·cal·ly** *adv*

whim·sy, whim·sey \'hwimzē\ *n, pl* **-sies** *or* **-seys** **1** : whim **2** : fanciful creation

whine \'hwīn\ *vb* **whined; whin·ing** **1** : utter a usu. high-pitched plaintive cry **2** : complain —**whine** *n* —**whin·er** *n* —**whiny** *adj*

whin·ny \'hwinē\ *vb* **-nied; -ny·ing** : neigh —**whinny** *n*

whip \'hwip\ *vb* **-pp-** **1** : move quickly **2** : strike with something slender and flexible **3** : defeat **4** : incite **5** : beat into a froth ~ *n* **1** : flexible device used for whipping **2** : party leader responsible for discipline **3** : thrashing motion —**whip·per** *n*

whip·cord *n* **1** : thin tough cord **2** : cloth made of hard-twisted yarns

whip·lash *n* : injury from a sudden sharp movement of the neck and head

whip·per·snap·per \'hwipər,snapər\ *n* : small, insignificant, or presumptuous person

whip·pet \'hwipət\ *n* : small swift dog often used for racing

whip·poor·will \'hwipər,wil\ *n* : American nocturnal bird

whir \'hwər\ *vb* **-rr-** : move, fly, or revolve with a whir ~ *n* : continuous fluttering or vibratory sound

whirl \'hwərl\ *vb* **1** : move or drive in a circle **2** : spin **3** : move or turn quickly **4** : reel ~ *n* **1** : rapid circular movement **2** : state of commotion or confusion **3** : try

whirl·pool *n* : whirling mass of water having a depression in the center

whirl·wind *n* : whirling wind storm

whisk \'hwisk\ *n* **1** : quick light sweeping or brushing motion **2** : usu. wire kitchen implement for beating ~ *vb* **1** : move or convey briskly **2** : beat **3** : brush lightly

whisk broom *n* : small broom

whis·ker \'hwiskər\ *n* **1** *pl* : beard **2** : long bristle or hair near an animal's mouth —**whis·kered** \-kərd\ *adj*

whis·key, whis·ky \'hwiskē\ *n, pl* **-keys** *or* **-kies** : liquor distilled from a fermented mash of grain

whis·per \'hwispər\ *vb* **1** : speak softly **2** : tell by whispering ~ *n* **1** : soft low sound **2** : rumor

whist \'hwist\ *n* : card game

whis·tle \'hwisəl\ *n* **1** : device by which a shrill sound is produced **2** : shrill clear sound made by a whistle or through the lips ~ *vb* **-tled; -tling** **1** : make or utter a whistle **2** : signal or call by a whistle **3** : produce by whistling —**whis·tler** *n*

whis·tle-blow·er \'hwisəl,blōər\ *n* : informer

whis·tle-stop *n* : brief political appearance

whit \'hwit\ *n* : bit

white \'hwīt\ *adj* **whit·er; -est** **1** : free from color **2** : of the color of new snow or milk **3** : having light skin ~ *n* **1** : color of maximum lightness **2** : white part or thing **3** : person who is light-skinned —**white·ness** *n* —**whit·ish** *adj*

white blood cell *n* : blood cell that does not contain hemoglobin

white·cap \'hwīt,kap\ *n* : wave crest breaking into white foam

white-col·lar *adj* : relating to salaried employees with duties not requiring protective or work clothing

white elephant *n* : something costly but of little use or value

white·fish \'hwīt,fish\ *n* : freshwater food fish

whit·en \'hwītᵊn\ *vb* : make or become white —**whit·en·er** \'hwītᵊnər\ *n*

white slave *n* : woman or girl held unwillingly for purposes of prostitution —**white slavery** *n*

white·tail \'hwīt,tāl\ *n* : No. American deer

white·wash *vb* **1** : whiten with a composition (as of lime and water) **2** : gloss over or cover up faults or wrongdoing —**whitewash** *n*

whith·er \'hwithər\ *adv* **1** : to what place **2** : to what situation, position, degree, or end

[1]whit·ing \'hwītiŋ\ *n* : usu. light or silvery food fish

[2]whiting *n* : pulverized chalk or limestone

whit·tle \'hwitᵊl\ *vb* **-tled; -tling** **1** : pare **2** : shape by paring **3** : reduce gradually

whiz, whizz \'hwiz\ *vb* **-zz-** : make a sound like a speeding object —**whiz, whizz** *n*

who \'hü\ *pron* **1** what or which person or persons **2** : person or persons that **3** : —used to introduce a relative clause

who·dun·it \hü'dənət\ *n* : detective or mystery story

who·ev·er \hü'evər\ *pron* : no matter who

whole \'hōl\ *adj* **1** : being in healthy or sound condition **2** : having all its parts or elements **3** : constituting the total sum of ~ *n* **1** : complete amount or sum **2** : something whole or entire —**on the whole 1** : considering all circumstances **2** : in general —**whole·ness** *n*

whole·heart·ed \'hōl'härtəd\ *adj* : sincere

whole number *n* : integer

whole·sale *n* : sale of goods in quantity usu. for resale by a retail merchant ~ *adj* **1** : of or relating to wholesaling **2** : performed on a large scale ~ *vb* **-saled; -sal·ing** : sell at wholesale —**wholesale** *adv* —**whole·sal·er** *n*

whole·some \-səm\ *adj* **1** : promoting mental, spiritual, or bodily health **2** : healthy —**whole·some·ness** *n*

whole wheat *adj* : made of ground entire wheat kernels

whol·ly \'hōlē\ *adv* **1** : totally **2** : solely

whom \'hüm\ *pron, objective case of* WHO

whom·ev·er \hüm'evər\ *pron, objective case of* WHOEVER

whoop \'hwüp, 'hüp, 'hwùp, 'hùp\ *vb* : shout loudly ~ *n* : shout

whooping cough *n* : infectious disease marked by convulsive coughing fits

whop·per \'hwäpər\ *n* **1** : something unusually large or extreme of its kind **2** : monstrous lie

whop·ping \'hwäpiŋ\ *adj* : extremely large

whore \'hōr\ *n* : prostitute

whorl \'hwórl, 'hwərl\ *n* : spiral —**whorled** *adj*

whose \'hüz\ *adj* : of or relating to whom or which ~ *pron* : whose one or ones

who·so·ev·er \,hüsō'evər\ *pron* : whoever

why \'hwī\ *adv* : for what reason, cause, or purpose ~ *conj* **1** : reason for which **2** : for which ~ *n, pl* **whys** : reason ~ *interj* —used esp. to express surprise

wick \'wik\ *n* : cord that draws up oil, tallow, or wax to be burned

wick·ed \'wikəd\ *adj* **1** : morally bad **2** : harmful or troublesome **3** : very unpleasant **4** : very impressive —**wick·ed·ly** *adv* —**wick·ed·ness** *n*

wick·er \'wikər\ *n* **1** : small pliant branch **2** : wickerwork —**wicker** *adj*

wick·er·work *n* : work made of wickers

wick·et \'wikət\ *n* **1** : small gate, door, or window **2** : frame in cricket or arch in croquet

wide \'wīd\ *adj* **wid·er; wid·est** **1** : covering a vast area **2** : measured at right angles to the length **3** : having a great measure across **4** : opened fully **5** : far from the thing in question ~ *adv* **wid·er; wid·est** **1** : over a great distance **2** : so as to leave considerable space between **3** : fully —**wide·ly** *adv* —**wid·en** \'wīdᵊn\ *vb*

wide-awake *adj* : alert

wide-eyed *adj* **1** : having the eyes wide open **2** : amazed **3** : naive

wide·spread *adj* : widely extended

wid·ow \'widō\ *n* : woman who has lost her husband by death and has not married again ~ *vb* : cause to become a widow —**wid·ow·hood** *n*

wid·ow·er \'widəwər\ *n* : man who has lost his wife by death and has not married again

width \'width\ *n* **1** : distance from side to side **2** : largeness of extent **3** : measured and cut piece of material

wield \'wēld\ *vb* **1** : use or handle esp. effectively **2** : exert —**wield·er** *n*

wie·ner \'wēnər\ *n* : frankfurter

wife \'wīf\ *n, pl* **wives** \'wīvz\ : married woman —**wife·hood** *n* —**wife·less** *adj* —**wife·ly** *adj*

wig \'wig\ *n* : manufactured covering of hair for the head

wig·gle \'wigəl\ *vb* **-gled; -gling** **1** : move with quick jerky or shaking movements **2** : wriggle —**wiggle** *n* —**wig·gler** *n*

wig·gly \-əlē\ *adj* **1** : tending to wiggle **2** : wavy

wig·wag \'wig,wag\ *vb* : signal by a flag or light waved according to a code

wig·wam \'wig,wäm\ *n* : American Indian hut consisting of a framework of poles overlaid with bark, rush mats, or hides

wild \'wīld\ *adj* **1** : living or being in a state of nature and not domesticated or cultivated **2** : unrestrained **3** : turbulent **4** : crazy **5** : uncivilized **6** : erratic ~ *n* **1** : wilderness **2** : undomesticated state ~ *adv* : without control —**wild·ly** *adv* —**wild·ness** *n*

wild·cat \-,kat\ *n* : any of various undomesticated cats (as a lynx) ~ *adj* **1** : not sound or safe **2** : unauthorized

wil·der·ness \'wildərnəs\ *n* : uncultivated and uninhabited region

wild·fire \'wīld,fīr\ *n* : sweeping and destructive fire

wild·fowl *n* : game waterfowl

wild·life \'wīld,līf\ *n* : undomesticated animals

wile \'wīl\ *n* : trick to snare or deceive ~ *vb* **wiled; wil·ing** : lure

will \'wil\ *vb, past* **would** \'wùd\; *pres sing & pl* **will** **1** : wish **2** —used as an auxiliary verb to express (1) desire or willingness (2) customary action (3) simple future time (4) capability (5) determination (6) probability (7) inevitability or (8) a command **3** : dispose of by a will ~ *n* **1** : often determined wish **2** : act, process, or experience of willing **3** : power of controlling one's actions or emotions **4** : legal document disposing of property after death

will·ful, wil·ful \'wilfəl\ *adj* **1** : governed by will without regard to reason **2** : intentional —**will·ful·ly** *adv*

will·ing \'wiliŋ\ *adj* **1** : inclined or favorably disposed in mind **2** : prompt to act **3** : done, borne, or accepted voluntarily or

without reluctance **—will•ing•ly** *adv* **—will•ing•ness** *n*

will–o'–the–wisp \ˌwiləthə'wisp\ *n* **1 :** light that appears at night over marshy grounds **2 :** misleading or elusive goal or hope

wil•low \'wilō\ *n* **:** quick-growing shrub or tree with flexible shoots

wil•lowy \'wiləwē\ *adj* **:** gracefully tall and slender

will•pow•er \'wilˌpau̇ər\ *n* **:** energetic determination

wil•ly–nil•ly \ˌwilē'nilē\ *adv or adj* **:** without regard for one's choice

wilt \'wilt\ *vb* **1 :** lose or cause to lose freshness and become limp esp. from lack of water **2 :** grow weak

wily \'wīlē\ *adj* **wil•i•er; -est :** full of craftiness **—wil•i•ness** *n*

win \'win\ *vb* **won** \'wən\; **win•ning 1 :** get possession of esp. by effort **2 :** gain victory in battle or a contest **3 :** make friendly or favorable ~ *n* **:** victory

wince \'wins\ *vb* **winced; winc•ing :** shrink back involuntarily **—wince** *n*

winch \'winch\ *n* **:** machine for hoisting or pulling with a drum around which rope is wound **—winch** *vb*

1wind \'wind\ *n* **1 :** movement of the air **2 :** breath **3 :** gas in the stomach or intestines **4 :** air carrying a scent **5 :** intimation ~ *vb* **1 :** get a scent of **2 :** cause to be out of breath

2wind \'wīnd\ *vb* **wound** \'wau̇nd\; **wind•ing 1 :** have or follow a curving course **2 :** move or lie to encircle **3 :** encircle or cover with something pliable **4 :** tighten the spring of ~ *n* **:** turn or coil **—wind•er** *n*

wind•break \-ˌbrāk\ *n* **:** trees and shrubs to break the force of the wind

wind•break•er \-ˌbrākər\ *n* **:** light wind-resistant jacket

wind•fall \'windˌfȯl\ *n* **1 :** thing blown down by wind **2 :** unexpected benefit

wind instrument *n* **:** musical instrument (as a flute or horn) sounded by wind and esp. by the breath

wind•lass \'windləs\ *n* **:** winch esp. for hoisting anchor

wind•mill \'windˌmil\ *n* **:** machine worked by the wind turning vanes

win•dow \'windō\ *n* **1 :** opening in the wall of a building to let in light and air **2 :** pane in a window **3 :** span of time for something **4 :** area of a computer display **—win•dow•less** *adj*

win•dow–shop *vb* **:** look at the displays in store windows **—win•dow–shop•per** *n*

wind•pipe \'windˌpīp\ *n* **:** passage for the breath from the larynx to the lungs

wind•shield \-ˌshēld\ *n* **:** transparent screen in front of the occupants of a vehicle

wind•up \'wīndˌəp\ *n* **:** end **—wind up** *vb*

wind•ward \'windwərd\ *adj* **:** being in or facing the direction from which the wind is blowing ~ *n* **:** direction from which the wind is blowing

windy \'windē\ *adj* **wind•i•er; -est 1 :** having wind **2 :** indulging in useless talk

wine \'wīn\ *n* **1 :** fermented grape juice **2 :** usu. fermented juice of a plant product (as fruit) used as a beverage ~ *vb* **:** treat to or drink wine

wing \'wiŋ\ *n* **1 :** movable paired appendage for flying **2 :** winglike thing **3** *pl* **:** area at the side of the stage out of sight **4 :** faction ~ *vb* **1 :** fly **2 :** propel through the air **—winged** *adj* **—wing•less** *adj* **—on the wing :** in flight **—under one's wing :** in one's charge or care

wink \'wiŋk\ *vb* **1 :** close and open the eyes quickly **2 :** avoid seeing or noticing something **3 :** twinkle **4 :** close and open one eye quickly as a signal or hint ~ *n* **1 :** brief sleep **2 :** act of winking **3 :** instant **—wink•er** *n*

win•ner \'winər\ *n* **:** one that wins

win•ning \-iŋ\ *n* **1 :** victory **2 :** money won at gambling ~ *adj* **1 :** victorious **2 :** charming

win•now \'winō\ *vb* **1 :** remove (as chaff) by a current of air **2 :** sort or separate something

win•some \'winsəm\ *adj* **1 :** causing joy **2 :** cheerful or gay **—win•some•ly** *adv* **—win•some•ness** *n*

win•ter \'wintər\ *n* **:** season between autumn and spring ~ *adj* **:** sown in autumn for harvest the next spring or summer **—win•ter•time** *n*

win•ter•green \'wintərˌgrēn\ *n* **:** low heathlike evergreen plant with red berries

win•try \'wintrē\ *adj* **win•tri•er; -est 1 :** characteristic of winter **2 :** cold in feeling

wipe \'wīp\ *vb* **wiped; wip•ing 1 :** clean or dry by rubbing **2 :** remove by rubbing **3 :** erase completely **4 :** destroy **5 :** pass over a surface ~ *n* **:** act or instance of wiping **—wip•er** *n*

wire \'wīr\ *n* **1 :** thread of metal **2 :** work made of wire **3 :** telegram or cablegram ~ *vb* **1 :** provide with wire **2 :** bind or mount with wire **3 :** telegraph **—wire•less** *adj*

wire•less \-ləs\ *n, chiefly Brit* **:** radio

wire•tap *vb* **:** connect into a telephone or telegraph wire to get information **—wire•tap** *n* **—wire•tap•per** *n*

wir•ing \'wīriŋ\ *n* **:** system of wires

wiry \'wīrē\ *adj* **wir•i•er** \'wīrēər\; **-est 1 :** resembling wire **2 :** slender yet strong and sinewy **—wir•i•ness** *n*

wis•dom \'wizdəm\ *n* **1 :** accumulated learning **2 :** good sense

wisdom tooth *n* **:** last tooth on each half of each human jaw

1wise \'wīz\ *n* **:** manner

2wise *adj* **wis•er; wis•est 1 :** having or showing wisdom, good sense, or good judgment **2 :** aware of what is going on **—wise•ly** *adv*

wise•crack *n* **:** clever, smart, or flippant remark ~ *vb* **:** make a wisecrack

wish \'wish\ *vb* **1 :** have a desire **2 :** express a wish concerning **3 :** request ~ *n* **1 :** a wishing or desire **2 :** expressed will or desire

wish•bone *n* **:** forked bone in front of the breastbone in most birds

wish•ful \-fəl\ *adj* **1 :** expressive of a wish **2 :** according with wishes rather than fact

wishy–washy \'wishēˌwȯshē, -ˌwäsh-\ *adj* **:** weak or insipid

wisp \'wisp\ *n* **1 :** small bunch of hay or straw **2 :** thin strand, strip, fragment, or streak **3 :** something frail, slight, or fleeting **—wispy** *adj*

wis•te•ria \wis'tirēə\ *n* **:** pealike woody vine with long clusters of flowers

wist•ful \'wistfəl\ *adj* **:** full of longing **—wist•ful•ly** *adv* **—wist•ful•ness** *n*

wit \'wit\ *n* **1 :** reasoning power **2 :** mental soundness —usu. pl. **3 :** quickness and cleverness in handling words and ideas **4 :** talent for clever remarks or one noted for witty remarks **—wit•less** *adj* **—wit•less•ly** *adv* **—wit•less•ness** *n* **—wit•ted** *adj*

witch \'wich\ *n* **1 :** person believed to have magic power **2 :** ugly old woman ~ *vb* **:** bewitch

witch•craft \'wichˌkraft\ *n* **:** power or practices of a witch

witch•ery \'wichərē\ *n, pl* **-er•ies 1 :** witchcraft **2 :** charm

witch ha•zel \'wichˌhāzəl\ *n* **1 :** shrub having small yellow flowers in fall **2 :** alcoholic lotion made from witch hazel bark

witch–hunt *n* **1 :** searching out and persecution of supposed witches **2 :** harassment esp. of political opponents

with \'with, 'with\ *prep* **1 :** against, to, or toward **2 :** in support of **3 :** because of **4 :** in the company of **5 :** having **6 :** despite **7 :** containing **8 :** by means of

with•draw \with'drȯ, with-\ *vb* **-drew** \-'drü\; **-drawn** \-'drȯn\; **-draw•ing** \-'drȯiŋ\ **1 :** take back or away **2 :** call back or retract **3 :** go away **4 :** terminate one's participation in or use of **—with•draw•al** \-'drȯəl\ *n*

with•drawn \with'drȯn\ *adj* **:** socially detached and unresponsive

with•er \'withər\ *vb* **1 :** shrivel **2 :** lose or cause to lose energy, force, or freshness

with•ers \'witharz\ *n pl* **:** ridge between the shoulder bones of a horse

with•hold \with'hōld, with-\ *vb* **-held** \-'held\; **-hold•ing 1 :** hold back **2 :** refrain from giving

with•in \with'in, with-\ *adv* **1 :** in or into the interior **2 :** inside oneself ~ *prep* **1 :** in or to the inner part of **2 :** in the limits or compass of

with•out \with'au̇t, with-\ *prep* **1 :** outside **2 :** lacking **3 :** unaccompanied or unmarked by **—without** *adv*

with•stand \with'stand, with-\ *vb* **-stood** \-'stu̇d\; **-stand•ing :** oppose successfully

wit•ness \'witnəs\ *n* **1 :** testimony **2 :** one who testifies **3 :** one present at a transaction to testify that it has taken place **4 :** one who has personal knowledge or experience **5 :** something serving as proof ~ *vb* **1 :** bear witness **2 :** act as legal witness of **3 :** furnish proof of **4 :** be a witness of **5 :** be the scene of

wit•ti•cism \'witəˌsizəm\ *n* **:** witty saying or phrase

wit•ting \'witiŋ\ *adj* **:** intentional **—witting•ly** *adv*

wit•ty \'witē\ *adj* **-ti•er; -est :** marked by or full of wit **—wit•ti•ly** \'witᵊlē\ *adv* **—wit•ti•ness** *n*

wives *pl of* WIFE

wiz•ard \'wizərd\ *n* **1 :** magician **2 :** very clever person **—wiz•ard•ry** \-ərdrē\ *n*

wiz•ened \'wizᵊnd\ *adj* **:** dried up

wob•ble \'wäbəl\ *vb* **-bled; -bling 1 :** move or cause to move with an irregular rocking motion **2 :** tremble **3 :** waver **—wob•ble** *n* **—wob•bly** \'wäbəlē\ *adj*

woe \'wō\ *n* **1 :** deep suffering **2 :** misfortune

woe•be•gone \'wōbiˌgȯn\ *adj* **:** exhibiting woe, sorrow, or misery

woe•ful \'wōfəl\ *adj* **1 :** full of woe **2 :** bringing woe **—woe•ful•ly** *adv*

woke *past of* WAKE

woken *past part of* WAKE

wolf \'wu̇lf\ *n, pl* **wolves** \'wu̇lvz\ **:** large doglike predatory mammal ~ *vb* **:** eat greedily **—wolf•ish** *adj*

wol•fram \'wu̇lfrəm\ *n* **:** tungsten

wol•ver•ine \ˌwu̇lvə'rēn\ *n, pl* **-ines :** flesh-eating mammal related to the weasels

wom•an \'wu̇mən\ *n, pl* **wom•en** \'wimən\ **1 :** adult female person **2 :** womankind **3 :** feminine nature **—wom•an•hood** \-ˌhu̇d\ *n* **—wom•an•ish** *adj*

wom•an•kind \-ˌkīnd\ *n* **:** females of the human race

wom•an•ly \-lē\ *adj* **:** having qualities characteristic of a woman **—wom•an•li•ness** \-lēnəs\ *n*

womb \'wüm\ *n* **:** uterus

won *past of* WIN

won•der \'wəndər\ *n* **1 :** cause of astonishment or surprise **2 :** feeling (as of astonishment) aroused by something extraordinary ~ *vb* **1 :** feel surprise **2 :** feel curiosity or doubt

won•der•ful \'wəndərfəl\ *adj* **1 :** exciting wonder **2 :** unusually good **—won•der•ful•ly** *adv* **—won•der•ful•ness** *n*

won•der•land \-ˌland, -lənd\ *n* **1 :** fairylike imaginary realm **2 :** place that excites admiration or wonder

won•der•ment \-mənt\ *n* **:** wonder

won•drous \'wəndrəs\ *adj* **:** wonderful **—won•drous•ly** *adv* **—won•drous•ness** *n*

wont \'wȯnt, 'wōnt\ *adj* **:** accustomed ~ *n* **:** habit **—wont•ed** *adj*

woo \'wü\ *vb* **:** try to gain the love or favor of **—woo•er** *n*

wood \'wu̇d\ *n* **1 :** dense growth of trees usu. smaller than a forest —often pl. **2 :** hard fibrous substance of trees and shrubs beneath the bark **3 :** wood prepared for some use (as burning) ~ *adj* **1 :** wooden **2 :** suitable for working with wood **3** *or* **woods** \'wu̇dz\ **:** living or growing in woods **—wood•chop•per** *n* **—wood•pile** *n* **—wood•shed** *n*

wood•bine \'wu̇dˌbīn\ *n* **:** climbing vine

wood•chuck \-ˌchək\ *n* **:** thick-bodied grizzled animal of No. America

wood•craft *n* **1 :** skill and practice in matters relating to the woods **2 :** skill in making articles from wood

wood•cut \-ˌkət\ *n* **1 :** relief printing surface engraved on wood **2 :** print from a woodcut

wood•ed \'wu̇dəd\ *adj* **:** covered with woods

wood•en \'wu̇dᵊn\ *adj* **1 :** made of wood **2 :** lacking resilience **3 :** lacking ease, liveliness or interest **—wood•en•ly** *adv* **—wood•en•ness** *n*

wood•land \-lənd, -ˌland\ *n* **:** land covered with trees

wood•peck•er \'wu̇dˌpekər\ *n* **:** brightly marked bird with a hard bill for drilling into trees

woods•man \'wu̇dzmən\ *n* **:** person who works in the woods

wood•wind \'wu̇dˌwind\ *n* **:** one of a group of wind instruments (as a flute or oboe)

wood•work *n* **:** work (as interior house fittings) made of wood

woody \'wu̇dē\ *adj* **wood•i•er; -est 1 :** abounding with woods **2 :** of, containing, or like wood fibers **—wood•i•ness** *n*

woof \'wu̇f\ *n* **:** weft

wool \'wu̇l\ *n* **1 :** soft hair of some mammals and esp. the sheep **2 :** something (as a textile) made of wool **—wooled** \'wu̇ld\ *adj*

wool•en, wool•len \'wu̇lən\ *adj* **1 :** made of wool **2 :** relating to the manufacture of woolen products ~ *n* **1 :** woolen fabric **2 :** woolen garments —usu. pl.

wool•gath•er•ing *n* **:** idle daydreaming

wool•ly \'wu̇lē\ *adj* **-li•er; -est 1 :** of, relating to, or bearing wool **2 :** consisting of or resembling wool **3 :** confused or turbulent

woo•zy \'wüzē\ *adj* **-zi•er; -est 1 :** confused **2 :** somewhat dizzy, nauseated, or weak **—woo•zi•ness** *n*

word \'wərd\ *n* **1 :** brief remark **2 :** speech sound or series of speech sounds that communicates a meaning **3 :** written representation of a word **4 :** order **5 :** news **6 :** promise **7** *pl* **:** dispute ~ *vb* **:** express in words **—word•less** *adj*

word•ing \'wərdiŋ\ *n* **:** verbal expression

word processing *n* **:** production of structured and printed documents through a computer program **(word processor) —word process** *vb*

wordy \'wərdē\ *adj* **word•i•er; -est :** using many words **—word•i•ness** *n*

wore *past of* WEAR

work \'wərk\ *n* **1 :** labor **2 :** employment **3 :** task **4 :** something (as an artistic production) produced by mental effort or physical labor **5** *pl* **:** place where industrial labor is done **6** *pl* **:** moving parts of a mechanism **7 :** workmanship ~ *adj* **1 :** suitable for wear while working **2 :** used for work ~ *vb* **worked** \'wərkt\ *or* **wrought** \'rȯt\, **work•ing 1 :** bring to pass **2 :** create by expending labor upon **3 :** bring or get into a form or condition **4 :** set or keep in operation **5 :** solve **6 :** cause to labor **7 :** arrange **8 :** excite **9 :** labor **10 :** perform work regularly for wages **11 :** function according to plan or design **12 :** produce a desired effect **—work•bench** *n* **—work•man** \-mən\ *n* **—work•room** *n* **—in the works :** in preparation

work•able \'wərkəbəl\ *adj* **1 :** capable of being worked **2 :** feasible **—work•able•ness** *n*

work•a•day \'wərkəˌdā\ *adj* **1 :** relating to or suited for working days **2 :** ordinary

work•a•hol•ic \ˌwərkə'hȯlik, -'häl-\ *n* **:** compulsive worker

work•day \'wərkˌdā\ *n* **1 :** day on which work is done **2 :** period of time during which one is working

work•er \'wərkər\ *n* **:** person who works esp. for wages

work•horse *n* **1 :** horse used for hard work **2 :** person who does most of the work of a group task

work•house *n* **:** place of confinement for persons who have committed minor offenses

work•ing \'wərkiŋ\ *adj* **1 :** adequate to allow work to be done **2 :** adopted or assumed to help further work or activity ~ *n* **:** operation —usu. used in pl.

work•ing•man \'wərkiŋˌman\ *n* **:** worker

work•man•like \-ˌlīk\ *adj* **:** worthy of a good workman

work•man•ship \-ˌship\ *n* **1 :** art or skill of a workman **2 :** quality of a piece of work

work•out \'wərkˌau̇t\ *n* **:** exercise to improve one's fitness

work out *vb* **1 :** bring about by effort **2 :** solve **3 :** develop **4 :** to be successful **5 :** perform exercises

work•shop *n* **1 :** small establishment for manufacturing or handicrafts **2 :** seminar emphasizing exchange of ideas and practical methods

world \'wərld\ *n* **1 :** universe **2 :** earth with its inhabitants and all things upon it **3 :** people in general **4 :** great number or quantity **5 :** class of persons or their sphere of interest

world•ly \'wərldlē\ *adj* **1 :** devoted to this world and its pursuits rather than to religion **2 :** sophisticated **—world•li•ness** *n*

world•ly–wise *adj* **:** possessing understanding of human affairs

world•wide *adj* **:** extended throughout the entire world **—worldwide** *adv*

worm \'wərm\ *n* **1 :** earthworm or a similar animal **2** *pl* **:** disorder caused by parasitic worms ~ *vb* **1 :** move or cause to move in a slow and indirect way **2 :** to free from worms **—wormy** *adj*

worm•wood \'wərmˌwu̇d\ *n* **1 :** aromatic woody herb (as sagebrush) **2 :** something bitter or grievous

worn *past part of* WEAR

worn–out \'wōrn'au̇t\ *adj* **:** exhausted or used up by or as if by wear

wor•ri•some \'wərēsəm\ *adj* **1 :** causing worry **2 :** inclined to worry

wor•ry \'wərē\ *vb* **-ried; -ry•ing 1 :** shake and mangle with the teeth **2 :** disturb **3 :** feel or express anxiety ~ *n, pl* **-ries 1 :** anxiety **2 :** cause of anxiety **—wor•ri•er** *n*

worse \'wərs\ *adj, comparative of* BAD *or of* ILL **1 :** bad or evil in a greater degree **2 :** more unwell ~ *n* **1 :** one that is worse **2 :** greater degree of badness ~ *adv, comparative of* BAD *or of* ILL **:** in a worse manner

wors•en \'wərsᵊn\ *vb* **:** make or become worse

wor•ship \'wərshəp\ *n* **1 :** reverence toward a divine being or supernatural power **2 :** expression of reverence **3 :** extravagant respect or devotion ~ *vb* **-shiped** *or* **-shipped; -ship•ing** *or* **-ship•ping 1 :** honor or reverence **2 :** perform or take part in worship **—wor•ship•er, wor•ship•per** *n*

worst \'wərst\ *adj, superlative of* BAD *or of* ILL **1 :** most bad, evil, ill, or corrupt **2 :** most unfavorable, unpleasant, or painful ~ *n* **:** one that is worst ~ *adv, superlative of* ILL *or of* BAD *or* BADLY **:** to the extreme degree of badness ~ *vb* **:** defeat

wor•sted \'wu̇stəd, 'wərstəd\ *n* **:** smooth compact wool yarn or fabric made from such yarn

worth \'wərth\ *prep* **1 :** equal in value to **2 :** deserving of ~ *n* **1 :** monetary value **2 :** value of something measured by its qualities **3 :** moral or personal merit

worth•less \-ləs\ *adj* **1 :** lacking worth **2 :** useless **—worth•less•ness** *n*

worth•while \-'hwīl\ *adj* **:** being worth the time or effort spent

wor•thy \'wərthē\ *adj* **-thi•er; -est 1 :** having worth or value **2 :** having sufficient worth ~ *n, pl* **-thies :** worthy person **—wor•thi•ly** *adv* **—wor•thi•ness** *n*

would \'wu̇d\ *past of* WILL —used to express (1) preference (2) intent (3) habitual action (4) contingency (5) probability or (6) a request

would–be \'wu̇d'bē\ *adj* **:** desiring or pretending to be

1wound \'wünd\ *n* **1 :** injury in which the skin is broken **2 :** mental hurt ~ *vb* **:** inflict a wound to or in

2wound \'waund\ *past of* WIND

wove *past of* WEAVE

woven *past part of* WEAVE

wrack \'rak\ *n* **:** ruin

wraith \'rāth\ *n, pl* **wraiths** \'rāths, 'rāthz\ **1 :** ghost **2 :** insubstantial appearance

wran•gle \'raŋgəl\ *vb or n* **:** quarrel **—wran•gler** *n*

wrap \'rap\ *vb* **-pp- 1 :** cover esp. by winding or folding **2 :** envelop and secure for transportation or storage **3 :** enclose, surround, or conceal wholly **4 :** coil, fold, draw, or twine about something ~ *n* **1 :** wrapper or wrapping **2 :** outer garment (as a shawl)

wrap•per \'rapər\ *n* **1 :** that in which something is wrapped **2 :** one that wraps

wrap•ping *n* **:** something used to wrap an object

wrath \'rath\ *n* **:** violent anger **—wrath•ful** \-fəl\ *adj*

wreak \'rēk\ *vb* **1 :** inflict **2 :** bring about

wreath \'rēth\ *n, pl* **wreaths** \'rēthz, 'rēths\ **:** something (as boughs) intertwined into a circular shape

wreathe \'rēth\ *vb* **wreathed; wreathing 1 :** shape into or take on the shape of a wreath **2 :** decorate or cover with a wreath

wreck \'rek\ *n* **1 :** broken remains (as of a ship or vehicle) after heavy damage **2 :** something disabled or in a state of ruin **3 :** an individual who has become weak or infirm **4 :** action of breaking up or destroying something ~ *vb* **:** ruin or damage by breaking up

wreck•age \'rekij\ *n* **1 :** act of wrecking **2 :** remains of a wreck

wreck•er \-ər\ *n* **1 :** automotive vehicle for removing disabled cars **2 :** one that wrecks or tears down and removes buildings

wren \'ren\ *n* **:** small mostly brown singing bird

wrench \'rench\ *vb* **1 :** pull with violent twisting or force **2 :** injure or disable by a violent twisting or straining ~ *n* **1 :** forcible twisting **2 :** tool for exerting a twisting force

wrest \'rest\ *vb* **1 :** pull or move by a forcible twisting movement **2 :** gain with difficulty ~ *n* **:** forcible twist

wres•tle \'resəl, 'ras-\ *vb* **-tled; -tling 1 :** scuffle with and attempt to throw and pin an opponent **2 :** compete against in wrestling **3 :** struggle (as with a problem) ~ *n* **:** action or an instance of wrestling **—wres•tler** \'reslər, 'ras-\ *n*

wres•tling \'resliŋ\ *n* **:** sport in which 2 opponents try to throw and pin each other

wretch \'rech\ *n* **1 :** miserable unhappy person **2 :** vile person

wretch•ed \'rechəd\ *adj* **1 :** deeply afflicted, dejected, or distressed **2 :** grievous **3 :** inferior **—wretch•ed•ly** *adv* **—wretch•ed•ness** *n*

wrig•gle \'rigəl\ *vb* **-gled; -gling 1 :** twist and turn restlessly **2 :** move along by twisting and turning **—wriggle** *n* **—wrig•gler** \'rigələr\ *n*

wring \'riŋ\ *vb* **wrung** \'rəŋ\; **wring•ing 1 :** squeeze or twist out moisture **2 :** get by or as if by twisting or pressing **3 :** twist together in anguish **4 :** pain **—wring•er** *n*

wrin•kle \'riŋkəl\ *n* **:** crease or small fold on a surface (as in the skin or in cloth) ~ *vb* **-kled; -kling :** develop or cause to develop wrinkles **—wrin•kly** \-kəlē\ *adj*

wrist \'rist\ *n* **:** joint or region between the hand and the arm

writ \'rit\ *n* **1 :** something written **2 :** legal order in writing

write \'rīt\ *vb* **wrote** \'rōt\; **writ•ten** \'ritᵊn\; **writ•ing** \'rītiŋ\ **1 :** form letters or words on a surface **2 :** form the letters or the words of (as on paper) **3 :** make up and set down for others to read **4 :** write a letter to **—write off** *vb* **:** cancel

writ•er \'rītər\ *n* **:** one that writes esp. as a business or occupation

writhe \'rīth\ *vb* **writhed; writh•ing :** twist and turn this way and that

writ•ing \'rītiŋ\ *n* **1 :** act of one that writes **2 :** handwriting **3 :** something written or printed

wrong \'rȯŋ\ *n* **1 :** unfair or unjust act **2 :** something that is contrary to justice **3 :** state of being or doing wrong ~ *adj* **wrong•er** \'rȯŋər\; **wrong•est** \'rȯŋəst\ **1 :** sinful **2 :** not right according to a standard **3 :** unsuitable **4 :** incorrect ~ *adv* **1 :** in a wrong direction or manner **2 :** incorrectly ~ *vb* **wronged; wrong•ing 1 :** do wrong to **2 :** treat unjustly **—wrong•ly** *adv*

wrong•do•er \-'düər\ *n* **:** one who does wrong **—wrong•do•ing** \-'düiŋ\ *n*

wrong•ful \-fəl\ *adj* **1 :** wrong **2 :** illegal **—wrong•ful•ly** *adv* **—wrong•ful•ness** *n*

wrong•head•ed \'rȯŋ'hedəd\ *adj* **:** stubborn in clinging to wrong opinion or principles **—wrong•head•ed•ly** *adv* **—wrong•head•ed•ness** *n*

wrote *past of* WRITE

wrought \'rȯt\ *adj* **1 :** formed **2 :** hammered into shape **3 :** deeply stirred

wrung *past of* WRING

wry \'rī\ *adj* **wri•er** \'rīər\; **wri•est** \'rīəst\ **1 :** turned abnormally to one side **2 :** twisted **3 :** cleverly and often ironically humorous **—wry•ly** *adv* **—wry•ness** *n*

X

x \'eks\ *n, pl* **x's** *or* **xs** \'eksəz\ **1 :** 24th letter of the alphabet **2 :** unknown quantity ~ *vb* **x-ed; x-ing** *or* **x'ing :** cancel with a series of *x*'s—usu. with *out*

xe•non \'zē,nän, 'zen,än\ *n* **:** heavy gaseous chemical element

xe•no•pho•bia \,zenə'fōbēə, ,zēn-\ *n* **:** fear and hatred of foreign people and things **—xe•no•phobe** \'zenə,fōb, 'zēn-\ *n*

Xmas \'krisməs\ *n* **:** Christmas

x–ra•di•a•tion *n* **1 :** exposure to X rays **2 :** radiation consisting of X rays

x–ray \'eks,rā\ *vb* **:** examine, treat, or photograph with X rays

X ray *n* **1 :** radiation of short wavelength that is able to penetrate solids **2 :** photograph taken with X rays **—X–ray** *adj*

xy•lo•phone \'zīlə,fōn\ *n* **:** musical instrument with wooden bars that are struck **—xy•lo•phon•ist** \-,fōnist\ *n*

Y

y \'wī\ *n, pl* **y's** *or* **ys** \'wīz\ **:** 25th letter of the alphabet

1-y \ē\ *adj suffix* **1 :** composed or full of **2 :** like **3 :** performing or apt to perform an action

2-y \ē\ *n suffix, pl* **-ies 1 :** state, condition, or quality **2 :** activity, place of business, or goods dealt with **3 :** whole group

yacht \'yät\ *n* **:** luxurious pleasure boat ~ *vb* **:** race or cruise in a yacht

ya•hoo \'yāhü, 'yä-\ *n, pl* **-hoos :** uncouth or stupid person

yak \'yak\ *n* **:** big hairy Asian ox

yam \'yam\ *n* **1 :** edible root of a tropical vine **2 :** deep orange sweet potato

yam•mer \'yamər\ *vb* **1 :** whimper **2 :** chatter **—yammer** *n*

yank \'yaŋk\ *n* **:** strong sudden pull **—yank** *vb*

Yank \'yaŋk\ *n* **:** Yankee

Yan•kee \'yaŋkē\ *n* **:** native or inhabitant of New England, the northern U.S., or the U.S.

yap \'yap\ *vb* **-pp- 1 :** yelp **2 :** chatter **—yap** *n*

1yard \'yärd\ *n* **1 :** 3 feet **2 :** long spar for supporting and spreading a sail **—yard•age** \-ij\ *n*

2yard *n* **1 :** enclosed roofless area **2 :** grounds of a building **3 :** work area

yard•arm \'yärd,ärm\ *n* **:** end of the yard of a square-rigged ship

yard•stick *n* **1 :** measuring stick 3 feet long **2 :** standard for judging

yar•mul•ke \'yäməkə, 'yär-, -məl-\ *n* **:** a small brimless cap worn by Jewish males in a synagogue

yarn \'yärn\ *n* **1 :** spun fiber for weaving or knitting **2 :** tale

yaw \'yȯ\ *vb* **:** deviate erratically from a course **—yaw** *n*

yawl \'yȯl\ *n* **:** sailboat with 2 masts

yawn \'yȯn\ *vb* **:** open the mouth wide ~ *n* **:** deep breath through a wide-open mouth **—yawn•er** *n*

ye \'yē\ *pron* **:** you

yea \'yā\ *adv* **1 :** yes **2 :** truly ~ *n* **:** affirmative vote

year \'yir\ *n* **1 :** period of about 365 days **2** *pl* **:** age

year•book *n* **:** annual report of the year's events

year•ling \'yirliŋ, 'yərlən\ *n* **:** one that is or is rated as a year old

year•ly \'yirlē\ *adj* **:** annual **—yearly** *adv*

yearn \'yərn\ *vb* **1 :** feel desire esp. for what one cannot have **2 :** feel tenderness or compassion

yearn•ing \-iŋ\ *n* **:** tender or urgent desire

yeast \'yēst\ *n* **:** froth or sediment in sugary liquids containing a tiny fungus and used in making alcoholic liquors and as a leaven in baking **—yeasty** *adj*

yell \'yel\ *vb* **:** utter a loud cry **—yell** *n*

yel•low \'yelō\ *adj* **1 :** of the color yellow **2 :** sensational **3 :** cowardly ~ *vb* **:** make or turn yellow ~ *n* **1 :** color of lemons **2 :** yolk of an egg **—yel•low•ish** \'yeləwish\ *adj*

yellow fever *n* **:** virus disease marked by prostration, jaundice, fever, and often hemorrhage

yellow jacket *n* **:** wasp with yellow stripes

yelp \'yelp\ *vb* **:** utter a sharp quick shrill cry **—yelp** *n*

yen \'yen\ *n* **:** strong desire

yeo•man \'yōmən\ *n* **1 :** attendant or officer in a royal or noble household **2 :** small farmer **3 :** naval petty officer with clerical duties **—yeo•man•ry** \-rē\ *n*

-yer —see -ER

yes \'yes\ *adv* —used to express consent or agreement ~ *n* **:** affirmative answer

ye•shi•va, ye•shi•vah \yə'shēvə\ *n, pl* **ye•shivas** *or* **ye•shi•voth** \-,shē'vōt, -'vōth\ **:** Jewish school

yes–man \'yes,man\ *n* **:** person who agrees with every opinion or suggestion of a boss

yes•ter•day \'yestərdē\ *adv* **1 :** on the day preceding today **2 :** only a short time ago ~ *n* **1 :** day last past **2 :** time not long past

yet \'yet\ *adv* **1 :** in addition **2 :** up to now **3 :** so soon as now **4 :** nevertheless ~ *conj* **:** but

yew \'yü\ *n* **:** evergreen tree or shrubs with dark stiff poisonous needles

yield \'yēld\ *vb* **1 :** surrender **2 :** grant **3 :** bear as a crop **4 :** produce **5 :** cease opposition or resistance ~ *n* **:** quantity produced or returned

yo•del \'yōdᵊl\ *vb* **-deled** *or* **-delled; -del•ing** *or* **-del•ling :** sing by abruptly alternating between chest voice and falsetto **—yodel** *n* **—yo•del•er** \'yōdᵊlər\ *n*

yo•ga \'yōgə\ *n* **:** system of exercises for attaining bodily or mental control and well-being

yo•gi \'yōgē\ *n* **:** person who practices yoga

yo•gurt \'yōgərt\ *n* **:** fermented slightly acid soft food made from milk

yoke \'yōk\ *n* **1 :** neck frame for coupling draft animals or for carrying loads **2 :** clamp **3 :** slavery **4 :** tie or link **5 :** piece of a garment esp. at the shoulder ~ *vb* **yoked; yok•ing 1 :** couple with a yoke **2 :** join

yo•kel \'yōkəl\ *n* **:** naive and gullible country person

yolk \'yōk\ *n* **:** yellow part of an egg **—yolked** \'yōkt\ *adj*

Yom Kip•pur \,yōmki'pu̇r, ,yäm-, -'kipər\ *n* **:** Jewish holiday observed in September or October with fasting and prayer as a day of atonement

yon \'yän\ *adj or adv* **:** YONDER

yon•der \'yändər\ *adv* **:** at or to that place ~ *adj* **:** distant

yore \'yōr\ *n* **:** time long past

you \'yü\ *pron* **1 :** person or persons addressed **2 :** person in general

young \'yəŋ\ *adj* **youn•ger** \'yəŋgər\; **youn•gest** \'yəŋgəst\ **1 :** being in the first or an early stage of life, growth, or development **2 :** recently come into being **3 :** youthful ~ *n, pl* **young :** persons or animals that are young **—young•ish** \-ish\ *adj*

young•ster \-stər\ *n* **1 :** young person **2 :** child

your \yər, 'yu̇r, 'yōr\ *adj* **:** relating to you or yourself

yours \'yu̇rz, 'yōrz\ *pron* **:** the ones belonging to you

your•self \yər'self\ *pron, pl* **your•selves** \-'selvz\ **:** you —used reflexively or for emphasis

youth \'yüth\ *n, pl* **youths** \'yüthz, 'yüths\ **1 :** period between childhood and maturity **2 :** young man **3 :** young persons **4 :** state or quality of being young, fresh, or vigorous

youth•ful \'yüthfəl\ *adj* **1 :** relating to or appropriate to youth **2 :** young **3 :** vigorous and fresh **—youth•ful•ly** *adv* **—youth•ful•ness** *n*

yowl \'yau̇l\ *vb* **:** utter a loud long mournful cry **—yowl** *n*

yo–yo \'yō,yō\ *n, pl* **-yos :** toy that falls from or rises to the hand as it unwinds and rewinds on a string

yuc•ca \'yəkə\ *n* **:** any of several plants related to the lilies that grow in dry regions

yule \'yül\ *n* **:** Christmas **—yule•tide** \-,tīd\ *n*

yum•my \'yəmē\ *adj* **-mi•er; -est :** highly attractive or pleasing

Z

z \'zē\ *n, pl* **z's** *or* **zs :** 26th letter of the alphabet

za•ny \'zānē\ *n, pl* **-nies 1 :** clown **2 :** silly person ~ *adj* **-ni•er; -est :** crazy or foolish **—za•ni•ly** *adv* **—za•ni•ness** *n*

zeal \'zēl\ *n* **:** enthusiasm

zeal•ot \'zelət\ *n* **:** fanatical partisan

zeal•ous \'zeləs\ *adj* **:** filled with zeal **—zeal•ous•ly** *adv* **—zeal•ous•ness** *n*

ze•bra \'zēbrə\ *n* **:** horselike African mammal marked with light and dark stripes

zeit•geist \'tsīt,gīst, 'zīt-\ *n* **:** general spirit of an era

ze•nith \'zēnəth\ *n* **:** highest point

zeph•yr \'zefər\ *n* **:** gentle breeze

zep•pe•lin \'zepələn\ *n* **:** rigid airship like a blimp

ze•ro \'zērō\ *n, pl* **-ros 1 :** number represented by the symbol 0 or the symbol itself **2 :** starting point **3 :** lowest point ~ *adj* **:** having no size or quantity

zest \'zest\ *n* **1 :** quality of enhancing enjoyment **2 :** keen enjoyment **—zest•ful** \-fəl\ *adj* **—zest•ful•ly** *adv* **—zest•ful•ness** *n*

zig•zag \'zig,zag\ *n* **:** one of a series of short sharp turns or angles ~ *adj* **:** having zigzags ~ *adv* **:** in or by a zigzag path ~ *vb* **-gg- :** proceed along a zigzag path

zil•lion \'zilyən\ *n* **:** large indeterminate number

zinc \'ziŋk\ *n* **:** bluish white crystaline metallic chemical element

zing \'ziŋ\ *n* **1 :** shrill humming noise **2 :** energy **—zing** *vb*

zin•nia \'zinēə, 'zēnyə\ *n* **:** American herb widely grown for its showy flowers

1zip \'zip\ *vb* **-pp- :** move or act with speed ~ *n* **:** energy

2zip *vb* **-pp- :** close or open with a zipper

zip code *n* **:** number that identifies a U.S. postal delivery area

zip•per \'zipər\ *n* **:** fastener consisting of 2 rows of interlocking teeth

zip•py \'zipē\ *adj* **-pi•er; -est :** brisk

zir•con \'zər,kän\ *n* **:** zirconium-containing mineral sometimes used in jewelry

zir•co•ni•um \,zər'kōnēəm\ *n* **:** corrosion-resistant gray metallic element

zith•er \'zithər, 'zith-\ *n* **:** stringed musical instrument played by plucking

zi•ti \'zētē\ *n, pl* **ziti :** short tubular pasta

zo•di•ac \'zōdē,ak\ *n* **:** imaginary belt in the heavens encompassing the paths of the planets and divided into 12 signs used in astrology **—zo•di•a•cal** \zō'dīəkəl\ *adj*

zom•bie \'zämbē\ *n* **:** person thought to have died and been brought back to life without free will

zon•al \'zōnᵊl\ *adj* **:** of, relating to, or having the form of a zone **—zon•al•ly** *adv*

zone \'zōn\ *n* **1 :** division of the earth's surface based on latitude and climate **2 :** distinctive area ~ *vb* **zoned; zon•ing 1 :** mark off into zones **2 :** reserve for special purposes **—zo•na•tion** \zō'nāshən\ *n*

zoo \'zü\ *n, pl* **zoos :** collection of living animals usu. for public display **—zoo•keep•er** *n*

zo•ol•o•gy \zō'äləjē\ *n* **:** science of animals **—zo•o•log•i•cal** \,zōə'läjikəl\ *adj* **—zo•ol•o•gist** \zō'äləjist\ *n*

zoom \'züm\ *vb* **1 :** move with a loud hum or buzz **2 :** move or increase with great speed **—zoom** *n*

zuc•chi•ni \zu̇'kēnē\ *n, pl* **-ni** *or* **-nis :** summer squash with smooth cylindrical dark green fruits

zwie•back \'swēbak, 'swī-, 'zwē-, 'zwī-\ *n* **:** biscuit of baked, sliced, and toasted bread

zy•gote \'zī,gōt\ *n* **:** cell formed by the union of 2 sexual cells **—zy•got•ic** \zī'gätik\ *adj*

Abbreviations

Most of these abbreviations have been given in one form. Variation in use of periods, in type, and in capitalization is frequent and widespread (as *mph, MPH, m.p.h., Mph*).

abbr abbreviation
AC alternating current
acad academic, academy
AD in the year of our Lord
adj adjective
adv adverb, advertisement
advt advertisement
AF air force, audio frequency
agric agricultural, agriculture
AK Alaska
aka also known as
AL, Ala Alabama
alg algebra
Alta Alberta
a.m., AM before noon
Am, Amer America, American
amp ampere
amt amount
anc ancient
anon anonymous
ans answer
ant antonym
APO army post office
approx approximate, approximately
Apr April
apt apartment, aptitude
AR Arkansas
arith arithmetic
Ariz Arizona
Ark Arkansas
art article, artificial
assn association
assoc associate, associated, association
asst assistant
ATM automated teller machine
att attached, attention, attorney
attn attention
atty attorney
Aug August
auth authentic, author, authorized
aux, auxil auxiliary
av avoirdupois
AV audiovisual
ave avenue
avg average
AZ Arizona
BA bachelor of arts
bal balance
bar barometer, barrel
bbl barrel, barrels
BC before Christ, British Columbia
BCE before the Christian Era, before the Common Era
bet between
biog biographer, biographical, biography
biol biologic, biological, biologist, biology
bldg building
blvd boulevard
BO backorder, best offer, body odor, box office, branch office
Brit Britain, British
bro brother, brothers
bros brothers
BS bachelor of science
Btu British thermal unit
bu bureau, bushel
c carat, cent, centimeter, century, chapter, circa, cup
C Celsius, centigrade
ca circa
CA, Cal, Calif California
cal calendar, caliber, calorie
Can, Canad Canada, Canadian
cap capacity, capital, capitalize, capitalized
Capt captain
CB citizens band
CDT central daylight time
cen central
cert certificate, certification, certified, certify
cf compare
chap chapter
chem chemistry
cir circle, circuit, circular, circumference
civ civil, civilian
cm centimeter
co company, county
CO Colorado
c/o care of
COD cash on delivery, collect on delivery
col colonial, colony, color, colored, column, counsel
Col colonel, Colorado
Colo Colorado

comp comparative, compensation, compiled, compiler, composition, compound, comprehensive, comptroller
cong congress, congressional
conj conjunction
Conn Connecticut
cont continued
contr contract, contraction
corp corporal, corporation
corr corrected, correction
cp compare, coupon
CPR cardiopulmonary resuscitation
cr credit, creditor
CSA Confederate States of America
CST Central standard time
ct carat, cent, count, court
CT central time, certified teacher, Connecticut
cu cubic
cur currency, current
CZ Canal Zone
d penny
DA district attorney
dag dekagram
dal dekaliter
dam dekameter
dbl double
DC direct current, District of Columbia
DDS doctor of dental science, doctor of dental surgery
DE Delaware
dec deceased, decrease
Dec December
deg degree
Del Delaware
Dem Democrat, Democratic
dept department
det detached, detachment, detail, determine
dg decigram
dia, diam diameter
diag diagonal, diagram
dict dictionary
dif, diff difference
dim dimension, diminished
dir director
disc discount
dist distance, district
div divided, dividend, division, divorced
dl deciliter
dm decimeter
DMD doctor of dental medicine
DOB date of birth
doz dozen
DP data processing
dr dram, drive, drum
Dr doctor
DST daylight saving time
DUI driving under the influence
DWI driving while intoxicated
dz dozen
e east, eastern, excellent
ea each
ecol ecological, ecology
econ economics, economist, economy
EDT Eastern daylight time
e.g. for example
EKG electrocardiogram, electrocardiograph
elec electric, electrical, electricity
elem elementary
eng engine, engineer, engineering
Eng England, English
esp especially
EST Eastern standard time
ET eastern time
et al and others
etc et cetera
ex example, express, extra
exec executive
f false, female, feminine
F, Fah, Fahr Fahrenheit
Feb February
fed federal, federation
fem female, feminine
FL, Fla Florida
fl oz fluid ounce
FPO fleet post office
fr father, friar, from
Fri Friday
ft feet, foot, fort
fut future
FYI for your information
g gram

Ga, GA Georgia
gal gallery, gallon
gen general
geog geographic, geographical, geography
geol geologic, geological, geology
geom geometric, geometrical, geometry
gm gram
GMT Greenwich mean time
GOP Grand Old Party (Republican)
gov government, governor
govt government
GP general practice, general practitioner
gr grade, grain, gram
gram grammar, grammatical
gt great
GU Guam
hd head
hf half
hgt height
hgwy highway
HI Hawaii
hist historian, historical, history
hon honor, honorable, honorary
hr here, hour
HS high school
ht height
HT Hawaiian time
hwy highway
i intransitive, island, isle
Ia, IA Iowa
ICU intensive care unit
ID Idaho, identification
i.e. that is
IL, Ill Illinois
imp imperative, imperfect
in inch
IN Indiana
inc incomplete, incorporated
ind independent
Ind Indian, Indiana
inf infinitive
int interest
interj interjection
intl, intnl international
ital italic, italicized
Jan January
JD juvenile delinquent
jour journal, journeyman
JP justice of the peace
jr, jun junior
JV junior varsity
Kans Kansas
kg kilogram
km kilometer
KS Kansas
kW kilowatt
Ky, KY Kentucky
l late, left, liter, long
L large
La Louisiana
LA Los Angeles, Louisiana
lat latitude
lb pound
lg large, long
lib liberal, librarian, library
long longitude
m male, masculine, meter, mile
M medium
MA Massachusetts
Man Manitoba
Mar March
masc masculine
Mass Massachusetts
math mathematical, mathematician
max maximum
Md Maryland
MD doctor of medicine, Maryland
MDT mountain daylight time
Me, ME Maine
med medium
mg milligram
mgr manager
MI, Mich Michigan
mid middle
min minimum, minor, minute
Minn Minnesota
misc miscellaneous
Miss Mississippi
ml milliliter
mm millimeter
MN Minnesota
mo month
Mo, MO Missouri
Mon Monday
Mont Montana
mpg miles per gallon

mph miles per hour
MRI magnetic resonance imaging
MS Mississippi
MST Mountain standard time
mt mount, mountain
MT Montana, Mountain time
n neuter, noun
N north, northern
NA North America, not applicable
nat national, native, natural
natl national
naut nautical
NB New Brunswick
NC North Carolina
ND, N Dak North Dakota
NE, Neb, Nebr Nebraska
neg negative
neut neuter
Nev Nevada
Nfld Newfoundland
NH New Hampshire
NJ New Jersey
NM, N Mex New Mexico
no north, number
Nov November
NR not rated
NS Nova Scotia
NV Nevada
NWT Northwest Territories
NY New York
NYC New York City
O Ohio
obj object, objective
occas occasionally
Oct October
off office, officer, official
OH Ohio
OJ orange juice
OK, Okla Oklahoma
Ont Ontario
opp opposite
OR, Ore, Oreg Oregon
orig original, originally
oz ounce, ounces
p page
Pa Pennsylvania
PA Pennsylvania, public address
PAC political action committee
par paragraph, parallel
part participle, particular
pass passenger, passive
pat patent
PC percent, politically correct, postcard
pd paid
PD police department
PDT Pacific daylight time
PE physical education
PEI Prince Edward Island
Penn, Penna Pennsylvania
pg page
PIN personal identification number
pk park, peak, peck
pkg package
pl place, plural
p.m., PM afternoon
PMS premenstrual syndrome
PO post office
Port Portugal, Portuguese
pos position, positive
poss possessive
pp pages
PQ Province of Quebec
pr pair, price, printed
PR public relations, Puerto Rico
prep preposition
pres present, president
prob probable, probably, problem
prof professor
pron pronoun
prov province
PS postscript, public school
PST Pacific standard time
psych psychology
pt part, payment, pint, point
PT Pacific time, physical therapy
pvt private
qr quarter
qt quantity, quart
Que Quebec
quot quotation
r right, river
rd road, rod, round
RDA recommended daily allowance, recommended dietary allowance

recd received
reg region, register, registered, regular
rel relating, relative, religion
rep report, reporter, representative, republic
Rep Republican
res residence
rev reverse, review, revised, revision, revolution
Rev reverend
RFD rural free delivery
RI Rhode Island
rm room
rpm revolutions per minute
RR railroad, rural route
RSVP please reply
rt right
rte route
s small, south, southern
SA South America
SASE self-addressed stamped envelope
Sask Saskatchewan
Sat Saturday
SC South Carolina
sci science, scientific
SD, S Dak South Dakota
secy secretary
sen senate, senator, senior
Sept, Sep September
sing singular
sm small
so south, southern
soph sophomore
sp spelling
spec special, specifically
specif specific, specifically
SPF sun protection factor
sq square
sr senior
Sr sister
SSN Social Security number
SSR Soviet Socialist Republic
st street
St saint
std standard
subj subject
Sun Sunday
supt superintendent
SWAT Special Weapons and Tactics
syn synonym
t teaspoon, temperature, ton, transitive, troy, true
T tablespoon
tbs, tbsp tablespoon
TD touchdown
tech technical, technician, technology
Tenn Tennessee
terr territory
Tex Texas
Th, Thu, Thur, Thurs Thursday
TN Tennessee
trans translated, translation, translator
tsp teaspoon
Tu, Tue, Tues Tuesday
TX Texas
UK United Kingdom
UN United Nations
univ universal, university
US United States
USA United States of America
USSR Union of Soviet Socialist Republics
usu usual, usually
UT Utah
UV ultraviolet
v verb, versus
Va, VA Virginia
var variant, variety
vb verb
VG very good
VI Virgin Islands
vol volume, volunteer
VP vice-president
vs versus
Vt, VT Vermont
W west, western
WA, Wash Washington
Wed Wednesday
WI, Wis, Wisc Wisconsin
wk week, work
wt weight
WV, W Va West Virginia
WY, Wyo Wyoming
XL extra large, extra long
yd yard
yr year, younger, your
YT Yukon Territory

A Brief Guide to Punctuation

APOSTROPHE '

1. **indicates the possessive case of nouns and indefinite pronouns** 〈the boy's mother〉 〈the boys' mothers〉 〈It is anyone's guess.〉
2. **marks omissions in contracted words** 〈didn't〉 〈o'clock〉
3. **often forms plurals of letters, figures, and words referred to as words** 〈You should dot your *i*'s and cross your *t*'s.〉 〈several 8's〉 〈She has trouble pronouncing her *the*'s.〉

BRACKETS [ ]

1. **set off extraneous data such as editorial additions esp. within quoted material** 〈wrote that the author was "trying to dazzle his readers with phrases like *jeu de mots* [play on words]"〉
2. **function as parentheses within parentheses** 〈Bowman Act (22 Stat., ch. 4, § [or sec.] 4, p. 50)〉

COLON :

1. **introduces word, clause, or phrase that explains, illustrates, amplifies, or restates what has gone before** 〈The sentence was poorly constructed: it lacked both unity and coherence.〉
2. **introduces a series** 〈Three countries were represented: England, France, and Belgium.〉
3. **introduces lengthy quoted material set off from the rest of a text by indentation but not by quotation marks** 〈I quote from the text of Chapter One:〉
4. **separates data in time-telling and data in bibliographic and biblical references** 〈8:30 a.m.〉 〈New York: Smith Publishing Co.〉 〈John 4:10〉
5. **separates titles and subtitles (as of books)** 〈*The Tragic Dynasty: A History of the Romanovs*〉
6. **follows the salutation in formal correspondence** 〈Dear Sir:〉 〈Gentlemen:〉

COMMA ,

1. **separates main clauses joined by a coordinating conjunction (as *and, but, or, nor,* or *for*) and very short clauses not so joined** 〈She knew very little about him, and he volunteered nothing.〉 〈I came, I saw, I conquered.〉
2. **sets off an adverbial clause (or a long phrase) that precedes the main clause** 〈When she found that her friends had deserted her, she sat down and cried.〉
3. **sets off from the rest of the sentence transitional words and expressions (as *on the contrary, on the other hand*), conjunctive adverbs (as *consequently, furthermore, however*), and expressions that introduce an illustration or example (as *namely, for example*)** 〈Your second question, on the other hand, remains open.〉 〈The mystery, however, remains unsolved.〉 〈She expects to travel through two countries, namely, France and England.〉
4. **separates words, phrases, or clauses in series and coordinate adjectives modifying a noun** 〈Men, women, and children crowded into the square.〉 〈The harsh, cold wind was strong.〉
5. **sets off from the rest of the sentence parenthetic elements (as nonrestrictive modifiers)** 〈Our guide, who wore a blue beret, was an experienced traveler.〉 〈We visited Gettysburg, the site of a famous battle.〉
6. **introduces a direct quotation, terminates a direct quotation that is neither a question nor an exclamation, and encloses split quotations** 〈John said, "I am leaving."〉 〈"I am leaving," John said.〉 〈"I am leaving," John said with determination, "even if you want me to stay."〉
7. **sets off words in direct address, absolute phrases, and mild interjections** 〈You may go, Mary, if you wish.〉 〈I fear the encounter, his temper being what it is.〉 〈Ah, that's my idea of an excellent dinner.〉
8. **separates a question from the rest of the sentence which it ends** 〈It's a fine day, isn't it?〉
9. **indicates the omission of a word or words, and esp. a word or words used earlier in the sentence** 〈Common stocks are preferred by some investors; bonds, by others.〉
10. **is used to avoid ambiguity** 〈To Mary, Jane was someone special.〉
11. **sets off geographical names (as state or country from city), items in dates, and addresses from the rest of a text** 〈Shreveport, Louisiana, is the site of a large air base.〉 〈On Sunday, June 23, 1940, he was wounded.〉 〈Number 10 Downing Street, London, is a famous address.〉
12. **follows the salutation in informal correspondence and follows the closing line of a formal or informal letter** 〈Dear Mary,〉 〈Affectionately,〉 〈Very truly yours,〉

DASH —

1. **usu. marks an abrupt change or break in the continuity of a sentence** 〈When in 1960 the stockpile was sold off—indeed, dumped as surplus—natural-rubber sales were hard hit.—Barry Commoner〉
2. **introduces a summary statement after a series** 〈Oil, steel, and wheat—these are the sinews of industrialization.〉
3. **often precedes the attribution of a quotation** 〈My foot is on my native heath . . . .—Sir Walter Scott〉

ELLIPSIS . . . .

1. **indicates the omission of one or more words within a quoted passage** 〈The head is not more native to the heart . . . than is the throne of Denmark to thy father.—Shakespeare〉 **four dots indicates the omission of one or more sentences within the passage or the omission of words at the end of a sentence** 〈Avoiding danger is no safer in the long run than outright exposure. . . . Life is either a daring adventure or nothing.—Helen Keller〉
2. **indicates halting speech or an unfinished sentence in dialogue** 〈"I'd like to . . . that is . . . if you don't mind. . . ." He faltered and then stopped speaking.〉

EXCLAMATION POINT !

1. **terminates an emphatic phrase or sentence** 〈Get out of here!〉
2. **terminates an emphatic interjection** 〈Encore!〉

HYPHEN -

1. **marks separation or division of a word at the end of a line** 〈mill-[end of line]stone〉
2. **is used between some prefix and word combinations, as prefix + proper name;** 〈pre-Renaissance〉 **prefix ending with a vowel + word beginning often with the same vowel** 〈co-opted〉 〈re-ink〉; **stressed prefix + word, esp. when this combination is similar to a different one** 〈re-cover a sofa〉 *but* 〈recover from an illness〉
3. **is used in some compounds, esp. those containing prepositions** 〈president-elect〉 〈sister-in-law〉
4. **is often used between elements of a unit modifier in attributive position in order to avoid ambiguity** 〈He is a small-business man.〉 〈She has gray-green eyes.〉
5. **suspends the first part of a hyphenated compound when used with another hyphenated compound** 〈a six- or eight-cylinder engine〉
6. **is used in writing out compound numbers between 21 and 99** 〈thirty-four〉 〈one hundred twenty-eight〉
7. **is used between the numerator and the denominator in writing out fractions esp. when they are used as modifiers** 〈a two-thirds majority of the vote〉
8. **serves instead of the phrase "(up) to and including" between numbers and dates** 〈pages 40-98〉 〈the decade 1960-69〉

HYPHEN, DOUBLE =

is used in the end-of-line division of a hyphenated compound to indicate that the compound is hyphenated and not closed 〈self-[end of line]seeker〉 *but* 〈self-[end of line]same〉

PARENTHESES ( )

1. **set off supplementary, parenthetic, or explanatory material when the interruption is more marked than that usu. indicated by commas** 〈Three old destroyers (all now out of commission) will be scrapped.〉 〈He is hoping (as we all are) that this time he will succeed.〉
2. **enclose numerals which confirm a written number in a text** 〈Delivery will be made in thirty (30) days.〉
3. **enclose numbers or letters in a series** 〈We must set forth (1) our long-term goals, (2) our immediate objectives, and (3) the means at our disposal.〉

PERIOD .

1. **terminates sentences or sentence fragments that are neither interrogatory nor exclamatory** 〈Obey the law.〉 〈He obeyed the law.〉
2. **follows some abbreviations and contractions** 〈Dr.〉 〈Jr.〉 〈etc.〉 〈cont.〉

QUESTION MARK ?

1. **terminates a direct question** 〈Who threw the bomb?〉 〈"Who threw the bomb?" he asked.〉 〈To ask the question Who threw the bomb? is unnecessary.〉
2. **indicates the writer's ignorance or uncertainty** 〈Omar Khayyám, Persian poet (1048?-1122)〉

QUOTATION MARKS, DOUBLE " "

1. **enclose direct quotations in conventional usage** 〈He said, "I am leaving."〉
2. **enclose words or phrases borrowed from others, words used in a special way, and often slang when it is introduced into formal writing** 〈He called himself "emperor," but he was really just a dictator.〉 〈He was arrested for smuggling "smack."〉
3. **enclose titles of short poems, short stories, articles, lectures, chapters of books, songs, short musical compositions, and radio and TV programs** 〈Robert Frost's "Dust of Snow"〉 〈Pushkin's "Queen of Spades"〉 〈The third chapter of *Treasure Island* is entitled "The Black Spot."〉 〈Ravel's "Bolero"〉 〈NBC's "Today Show"〉
4. **are used with other punctuation marks in the following ways: the period and the comma fall *within* the quotation marks** 〈"I am leaving," he said.〉 〈His camera was described as "waterproof," but "moisture-resistant" would have been a better description.〉 **the semicolon falls *outside* the quotation marks** 〈He spoke of his "little cottage in the country"; he might have called it a mansion.〉 **the dash, the question mark, and the exclamation point fall *within* the quotation marks when they refer to the quoted matter only; they fall *outside* when they refer to the whole sentence** 〈He asked, "When did you leave?"〉 〈What is the meaning of "the open door"?〉 〈The sergeant shouted, "Halt!"〉 〈Save us from his "mercy"!〉

QUOTATION MARKS, SINGLE ' '

enclose a quotation within a quotation in conventional usage 〈The witness said, "I distinctly heard him say, 'Don't be late,' and then I heard the door close."〉

SEMICOLON ;

1. **links main clauses not joined by coordinating conjunctions** 〈Some people have the ability to write well; others do not.〉
2. **links main clauses joined by conjunctive adverbs (as *consequently, furthermore, however*)** 〈Speeding is illegal; furthermore, it is very dangerous.〉
3. **links clauses which themselves contain commas even when such clauses are joined by coordinating conjunctions** 〈Mr. King, whom you met yesterday, will represent us on the committee; but you should follow the proceedings yourself, because they are vitally important to us.〉

SLASH /

1. **separates alternatives** 〈. . . designs intended for high-heat and/or high-speed applications—F. S. Badger, Jr.〉
2. **separates successive divisions (as months or years) of an extended period of time** 〈the fiscal year 1972/73〉
3. **serves as a dividing line between run-in lines of poetry** 〈Say, sages, what's the charm on earth/Can turn death's dart aside?—Robert Burns〉
4. **often represents *per* in abbreviations** 〈9 ft/sec〉 〈20 km/hr〉

Webster's
Concise
Atlas
of the World

Preface

Webster's Concise Atlas of the World provides a concise and up-to-date picture of the political and physical forces that shape our world today. It enables readers to locate features of the Earth's surface, measure distances, plan trips, and trace routes, but most importantly visualize a world in transition.

In today's political environment, transitions are characterized by the formation of new countries, changes in borders between countries, and the adoption of new place names within countries. Today's maps are changed by many other forces as well. Advances in technology, for instance, are reshaping the way we measure the world, the way we see the world, and, consequently, the way we think about creating the maps that represent the world. Simply applying computer technology, of course, does not guarantee that an atlas will be accurate or current. That is the mapmaker's responsibility. New technology can, however, provide the tools to create an atlas of much improved clarity, legibility, and design.

With features such as these, an atlas becomes a unique tool for discovering the political and physical patterns, distributions, and relationships that are an inherent part of any regional or global landscape. The information within it graphically defines the world and helps the reader to comprehend the complexity of the changing world in which we live.

Contents

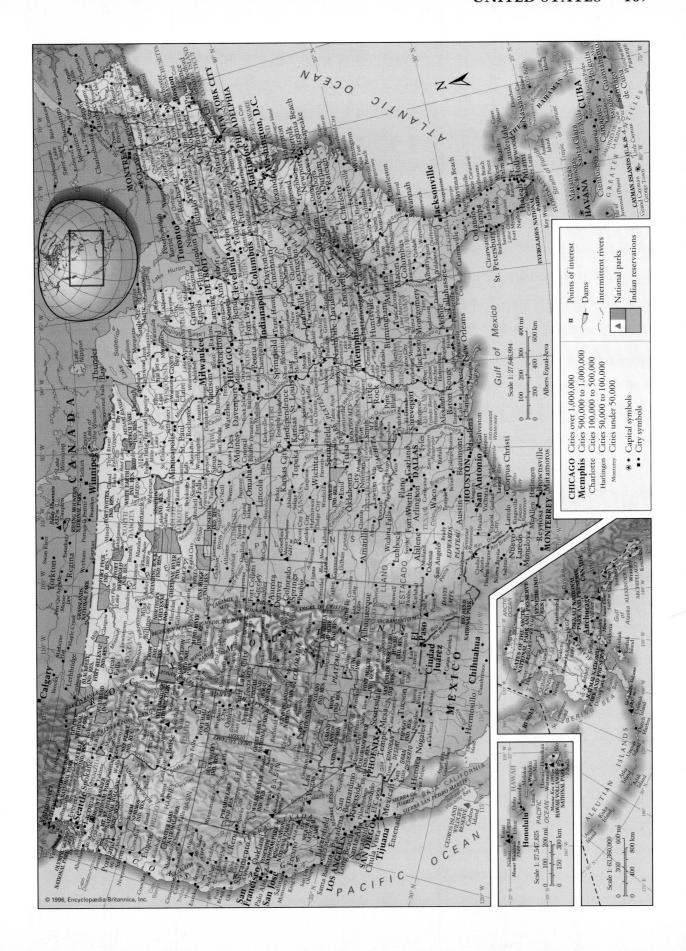

CHICAGO Cities over 1,000,000
Memphis Cities 500,000 to 1,000,000
Charlotte Cities 100,000 to 500,000
Hartlingen Cities 50,000 to 100,000
Monterey Cities under 50,000

⊛ ★ Capital symbols
□ • City symbols

▣ Points of interest
⚒ Dams
Intermittent rivers
National parks
Indian reservations

Scale 1: 27,646,994

Albers Equal-Area

Scale 1:27,547,825

Scale 1: 63,360,000

ARCTIC

QUEEN ELIZABETH ISLANDS

BEAUFORT SEA

Baffin
Bay

Greenland
(Denmark)

GREENLAND SEA

CHUKCHI
SEA

BROOKS RANGE
Arctic Circle
Alaska (U.S.)
Fairbanks
ALASKA RANGE
Mt. Denali
Anchorage

Victoria
I.

Baffin I.

Reykjavik
ICELAND

BERING
SEA

Gulf of
Alaska

Great
Bear L.

Hudson
Bay

Great Slave L.

LABRADOR
SEA

IRELAND   U.K.
Dublin   London

ALEUTIAN
ISLANDS

Vancouver
Seattle
Portland

C A N A D A

Edmonton
Calgary   Saskatoon
Winnipeg

L. Superior

Island of
Newfoundland
St. Johns

FRANCE

ROCKY MOUNTAINS

Minneapolis
Chicago
Detroit

Quebec
Montréal
Ottawa
Toronto
Boston
Halifax

Gulf of St.
Lawrence

PORTUGAL
Lisbon

Madrid
SPAIN

San Francisco
Los Angeles
San Diego
Phoenix

UNITED STATES
Denver
Las
Vegas
Kansas City
St. Louis
Memphis

New York City
Philadelphia
Washington, D.C.

ATLANTIC
OCEAN

AZORES
(Portugal)

MADEIRA IS.
(Portugal)   Rabat
Casablanca   MOROCCO   ATLAS

Oklahoma
City   Dallas
Houston

Atlanta

Bermuda (U.K.)

Tropic of Cancer

HAWAIIAN IS.
(U.S.)

SIERRA MADRE OCCIDENTAL
Juárez
MEXICO

Monterrey

Gulf of
Mexico

Miami
Nassau   THE
BAHAMAS

TURKS AND CAICOS (U.K.)

CANARY IS.
(Spain)
El Aaiún
Western
Sahara
(Morocco)

MAURITANIA   MALI

Nouakchott

Guadalajara

Mexico City

Bay of
Campeche

Havana   CUBA

Santo Domingo

PUERTO RICO (U.S.)
VIRGIN IS. (U.S.-U.K.)

CAPE
VERDE
Praia

THE GAMBIA
Dakar   SENEGAL   BURKINA
FASO

N

PACIFIC
OCEAN

Guatemala City
GUATEMALA
San Salvador
EL SALVADOR
NICARAGUA

Kingston
Belmopan
BELIZE JAMAICA
Tegucigalpa
HONDURAS
Managua

Port-au-
Prince
HAITI

ANTIGUA AND BARBUDA
ST. KITTS AND NEVIS
Guadeloupe (Fr.)
DOMINICA
Martinique (Fr.)
ST. LUCIA
BARBADOS
ST. VINCENT AND THE GRENADINES

Banjul
Bissau
GUINEA-
BISSAU   Conakry
Freetown
SIERRA LEONE

Bamako
Ouagadougou
GUINEA
CÔTE
D'IVOIRE   GHANA

DOMINICAN
REPUBLIC

Palmyra Atoll (U.S.)

San José
COSTA RICA

Barranquilla
Maracaibo

CARIBBEAN SEA

GRENADA
TRINIDAD AND TOBAGO

Monrovia
LIBERIA   Abidjan
Accra

Equator

PANAMÁ   Panama
City   Caracas
LLANOS

VENEZUELA
Bogotá   GUYANA
Georgetown   SURINAME
Paramaribo

French
Guiana
(FR.)

Gulf of
Guinea

GALÁPAGOS IS.
(Ecuador)   Cali
COLOMBIA   GUIANA HIGHLANDS   Cayenne

KIRIBATI

Quito
ECUADOR
Guayaquil   Iquitos
Manaus   Belém

Amazon
Fortaleza

WESTERN
SAMOA
AMERICAN SAMOA
(U.S.)

COOK IS. (N.Z.)

FRENCH
POLYNESIA
(France)

Lima

ANDES
PERU

BRAZIL

Recife

São Francisco

Bahia

TONGA

Tropic of Capricorn

Arequipa

Titicaca
La Paz
BOLIVIA
Sucre

BRAZILIAN
HIGHLANDS
Brasília

Belo Horizonte
Rio de Janeiro
São Paulo

30° S

San Félix I.
San Ambrosia I.

Antofagasta

GRAN
CHACO
Asunción
PARAGUAY

ATACAMA DESERT

Córdoba

PAMPAS
URUGUAY
Rosario
Montevideo
Buenos
Aires

Pôrto Alegre

ATLANTIC
OCEAN

Scale at equator
1: 119,240,000

0   500   1000   1500   2000 mi

0   1000   2000   3000 km

Robinson

JUAN FERNÁNDEZ
ISLANDS

Mt. Aconcagua
Santiago
Concepción

ANDES
ARGENTINA
CHILE

Chiloé I.

60° S

PATAGONIA

FALKLAND IS.
(U.K.)

SOUTH GEORGIA (U.K.)

Tierra del
Fuego   Cape Horn

Antarctic Circle

Alexander I.

ANTARCTIC
PEN.

WEDDELL SEA

Berkner I.

MARIE BYRD LAND

T R A N S A N T A R C T I C   M O U N T A I N S

OCEAN   30° E   60° E   90° E   120° E   150° E

SVALBARD (Norway)
NORWEGIAN
SEA
FRANZ JOSEF
LAND
NOVAYA
ZEMLYA
KARA SEA
NEW SIBERIAN
IS.
EAST
SIBERIAN
SEA
Arctic Circle
60° N
BERING
SEA
KAMCHATKA
PEN.

NORWAY SWEDEN FINLAND
Helsinki
Arkhangelsk
WEST
SIBERIAN
PLAIN
R U S S I A
VERKHOYANSK MTS.
KOLYMA MTS.

Oslo Stockholm St. Petersburg
EST.
Tallinn
LAT.
LITH. Vilnius
Perm
Yekaterinburg
Omsk
Lena
Yakutsk
STANOVOY MTS.

NORTH
SEA DEN.
Copenhagen
BALTIC
BELARUS
Minsk
Moscow
Nizhy
Novgorod
Kazan
Ufa
Chelyabinsk
Novosibirsk
Novokuznetsk
Barnaul
Lake
Baikal
Irkutsk
Chita
Amur
Khabarovsk
Sakhalin

NETH.
GER.
Berlin
CZ. REP.
Warsaw
Samara
Volgograd
Yenisey

Paris
BEL.
LUX.
SW. AUS. HUN.
SL. CR.
MOL.
UKRAINE
Kiev
L. Balkhash
KAZAKHSTAN
Alma-Ata
Bishkek
TIAN SHAN
Ulaanbaatar
MONGOLIA
Shenyang
Harbin
Vladivostok
Hokkaido

FR.
ITALY
B.-H.
YUGO.
ROM.
Bucharest
BLACK SEA
GEORGIA
Tbilisi
ARAL
SEA
UZBEKISTAN
Tashkent
KYRGYZSTAN
GOBI DESERT
Huang
Beijing
NORTH
KOREA
Pyongyang
JAPAN
Honshu
Tokyo

Rome
ALB.
MAC.
BUL.
GREECE
ARMENIA
AZERBAIJAN
TURKMENISTAN
TAJIKISTAN
KUNLUN MTS.
C H I N A
Tianjin
Xi'an
Seoul
SOUTH
KOREA
Pusan
Osaka
Shikoku
PACIFIC
OCEAN

Athens
TURKEY
Ankara
CYPRUS
SYRIA
Damascus
ZAGROS
MTNS.
Ashkhabad
Tehran
AFGHANISTAN
Kabul
PLATEAU OF
TIBET
Lhasa
Chongqing
Nanjing
Wuhan
Kyushu
Shanghai
MIDWAY IS.
(U.S.)
30° N

Algiers
MEDI
TUNISIA
Tunis
Tripoli
MTNS.
LEBANON
ISRAEL
Jerusalem
IRAQ
Baghdad
IRAN
Islamabad
Delhi
Lahore
NEPAL
Kathmandu
Mount
Everest
BHUTAN
Thimphu
Xi
Guangzhou
TAIWAN
Taipei
Kaohsiung
Tropic of Cancer

SAHARA
ALGERIA
LIBYA
EGYPT
Alexandria
Cairo
JORDAN
KUWAIT
Kuwait
Riyadh
BAHRAIN
QATAR U.A.E.
Muscat
Karachi
New Delhi
PAKISTAN
Ahmadabad
I N D I A
Calcutta
Dhaka
BANGLADESH
MYANMAR
LAOS
Hanoi
HONG
KONG (U.K.)
SOUTH
CHINA
SEA
PHILIPPINE
SEA
NORTHERN
MARIANA
IS. (U.S.)

AHAGGAR
MTS.
TIBESTI
MTS.
NIGER
L. Nasser
NILE
SAUDI
ARABIA
Jiddah
RUB AL KHALI
DESERT
OMAN
ARABIAN
SEA
Bombay
Nagpur
Hyderabad
Bay of
Bengal
Yangon
Vientiane
THAILAND
VIETNAM
Phnom Penh
Luzon
Manila
Guam
(U.S.)
MARSHALL IS.

CHAD
L. Chad
SUDAN
Khartoum
Asmara
ERITREA
YEMEN
Gulf of
Aden
Socotra
(Yemen)
Bangalore
Madras
ANDAMAN IS.
(India)
Bangkok
Ho Chi Minh City
CAMBODIA
PHILIPPINES
Mindanao
Koror
PALAU
Palikir
Majuro

NIGER
NIGERIA
Niamey
Abuja
N'Djamena
Addis
Ababa
DJIBOUTI
Djibouti
Cape
Gwardafuy
ETHIOPIA
ETHIOPIAN
PLATEAU
SOMALIA
Colombo
SRI
LANKA
NICOBAR IS.
(India)
Kuala
Lumpur
BRUNEI
Bandar Seri Begawan
FEDERATED STATES OF MICRONESIA
Bairiki

BENIN
TOGO
Porto-Novo
CAMEROON
Yaounde
C.A.R.
Bangui
UGANDA
Kampala
Mogadishu
MALDIVES
Male
MALAYSIA
SINGAPORE
Medan
Borneo
Celebes
New Guinea
KIRIBATI

EQ.
GUINEA
Malabo
Libreville
CONGO
GABON
RWANDA
Kigali
Nairobi
KENYA
Victoria
Sumatra
I N D O N E S I A
Equator

Brazzaville
Cabinda
(ANGOLA)
Kinshasa
BURUNDI
Bujumbura
ZAIRE
Congo
Lake
Victoria
Kilimanjaro
TANZANIA
Dar es Salaam
Lake
Tanganyika
SEYCHELLES
BRITISH
INDIAN
OCEAN
TERRITORY
(U.K.)
Palembang
Jakarta
Bandung
Semarang
Surabaya
Java
PAPUA
NEW GUINEA
Port Moresby
SOLOMON
ISLANDS
Honiara
TUVALU
Funafuti

Luanda
ANGOLA
MALAWI
Lake
Malawi
Moroni
COMOROS
INDIAN
OCEAN
KEELING IS.
(Austl.)
Timor
ARAFURA
SEA
ARNHE
M LAND
CORAL
SEA
VANUATU
Port-Vila
Efate
FIJI
Suva

ZAMBIA
Lusaka
ZIMBABWE
Harare
Lilongwe
MOZAMBIQUE
Mozambique Channel
Antananarivo
MAURITIUS
Port Louis
Reunion (Fr.)
GREAT SANDY
DESERT
GREAT
ARTESIAN
BASIN
New Caledonia
(Fr.)
Tropic of Capricorn

NAMIBIA
Windhoek
BOTSWANA
Gaborone
Pretoria
MADAGASCAR
A U S T R A L I A
Brisbane
30° S

NAMIB DESERT
Orange
Johannesburg
Maputo
Mbabane
SWAZILAND
Maseru
LESOTHO
GREAT VICTORIA
DESERT
Darling
Sydney
Auckland

SOUTH
AFRICA
Cape Town
Cape of Good Hope
Perth
Great Australian
Bight
Adelaide
Canberra
Melbourne
NEW
ZEALAND
Wellington

Saint Paul I. (Fr.)
Amsterdam I. (Fr.)
Tasmania
Hobart
TASMAN
SEA

CROZET IS.
(Fr.)
PRINCE EDWARD IS.
(South Africa)
Kerguelen I.
(Fr.)
AUCKLAND IS.
(N.Z.)

60° S

Antarctic Circle

ENDERBY
LAND
WILKES LAND
VICTORIA
LAND

QUEEN MAUD LAND
A N T A R C T I C A
ROSS SEA

30° E   60° E   90° E

© 1996, Encyclopædia Britannica, Inc.

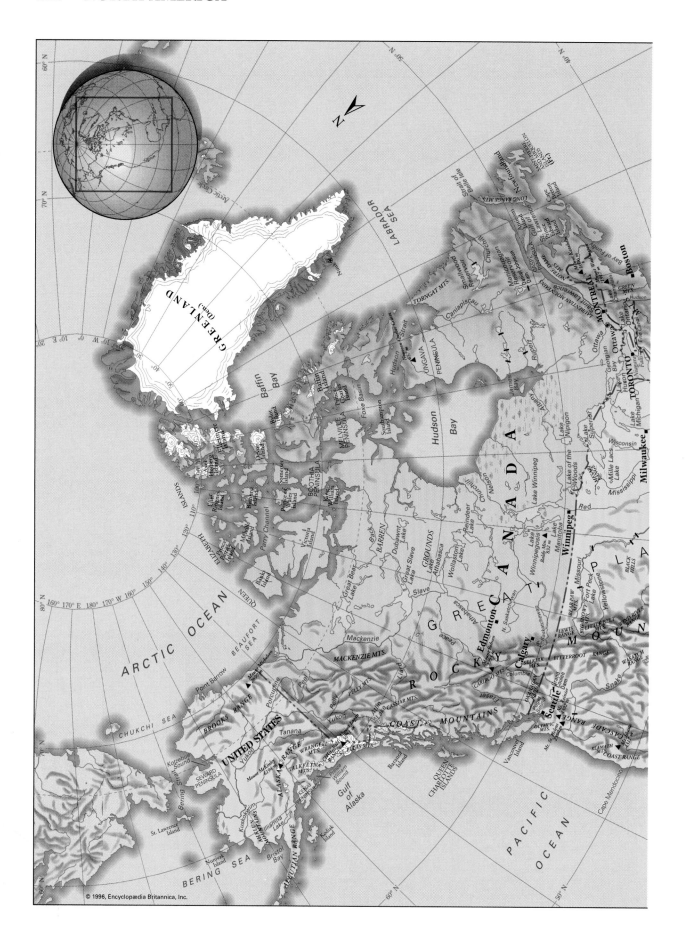

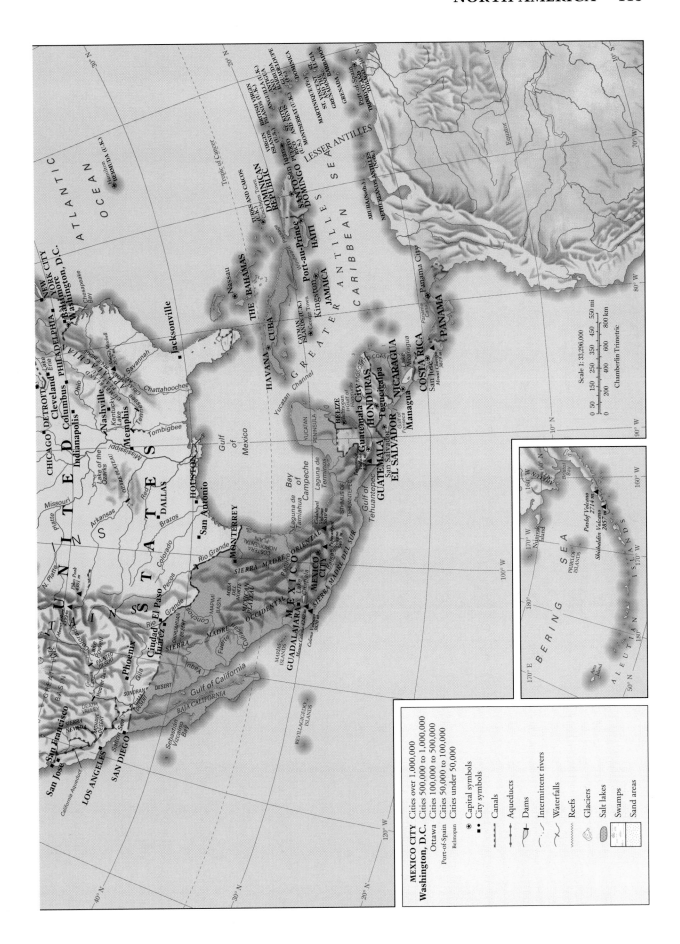

ATLANTIC

OCEAN

Hamilton (U.K.)

⊕ BERMUDA (U.K.)

Tropic of Cancer

Equator

VIRGIN BRITISH VIRGIN (U.K.)
ISLANDS (U.S.)   ANGUILLA (U.K.)
ST. KITTS   ANTIGUA AND BARBUDA
AND NEVIS   GUADELOUPE (Fr.)
San Juan   DOMINICA
PUERTO   MARTINIQUE (Fr.)
RICO (U.S.)   ST. LUCIA
MONTSERRAT (U.K.)   BARBADOS
ST. VINCENT   Port-of-Spain
GRENADA   TRINIDAD AND
TOBAGO

TURKS AND CAICOS

LESSER ANTILLES

Cockburn Town

DOMINICAN
REPUBLIC   SANTO
DOMINGO

Port-au-Prince

HAITI

ARUBA (Neth.)   NETHERLANDS ANTILLES (Neth.)

NEW YORK CITY

PHILADELPHIA   Baltimore

Washington, D.C.

Chesapeake
Bay

Nassau

THE BAHAMAS

HAVANA   CUBA

Yucatan Channel

Old Bahama Ch.

HAVANA

CUBA

CAYMAN
ISLANDS (U.K.)
George Town

Kingston

JAMAICA

G R E A T E R   A N T I L L E S

C A R I B B E A N   S E A

Panama City

Panama
Canal   PANAMA

COSTA RICA

San José

Mount Chirripó
3819 m

MOSQUITO COAST

NICARAGUA   Lake
Nicaragua

Managua

Tegucigalpa

HONDURAS

Gulf of
Fonseca

Guatemala City   San Salvador

BELIZE   Belmopan

GUATEMALA   EL SALVADOR

Gulf of
Honduras

Jacksonville

Savannah

Chattahoochee

CHICAGO   DETROIT   Cleveland   Columbus

Lake
Erie

Ohio

Indianapolis   Nashville   Kentucky Lake   Tennessee

Memphis

Tombigbee

Lake of the
Ozarks

OZARK PLATEAU

Arkansas

Red

DALLAS

Brazos

HOUSTON

San Antonio

Gulf
of
Mexico

YUCATAN

YUCATAN
PENINSULA

Bay
of
Campeche

Laguna de
Terminos

Gulf of
Tehuantepec

ISTHMUS OF
TEHUANTEPEC

MONTERREY

Laguna de
Tamiahua

COSTERA
NOROESTE
PLAIN

Rio Grande

S I E R R A M A D R E O R I E N T A L

SIERRA MADRE DEL SUR

MEXICO
CITY

GUADALAJARA

Lake Chapala

MEXICAN
PLATEAU

MESA DEL
NORTE

MAPIMI
BASIN

Conchos

Ciudad
Juárez   El Paso

Pecos

Colorado

S I E R R A   M A D R E

SIERRA   OCCIDENTAL

Fuerte

Culican

MARIAS
ISLANDS

REVILLAGIGEDO
ISLANDS

M E X I C O

N. Platte   Pikes Peak
4301 m

UNITED   STATES

Missouri

Platte

Mississippi

Phoenix

Gila

Salton Sea

SONORAN

DESERT

MOHAVE
DESERT

DEATH
VALLEY

SIERRA
NEVADA

GREAT   BASIN

Lake
Mead

Hoover Dam

PAINTED
DESERT

Gulf of California

BAJA CALIFORNIA

Sebastian
Vizcaino Bay

San Francisco

San José

LOS ANGELES

SAN DIEGO

California Aqueduct

BERING   SEA

ALEUTIAN   ISLANDS

PRIBILOF
ISLANDS

Nunivak
Island

Bristol
Bay

Pavlof Volcano
2714 m

Shishaldin Volcano
2857 m

Amu
Island

160° W

170° W

180°

170° E

60° N

50° N

Scale 1:33,296,000

Chamberlin Trimetric

0   150   250   350   450   550 mi

0   200   400   600   800 km

MEXICO CITY   Cities over 1,000,000
Washington, D.C.   Cities 500,000 to 1,000,000
Ottawa   Cities 100,000 to 500,000
Port-of-Spain   Cities 50,000 to 100,000
Belmopan   Cities under 50,000

⊛   Capital symbols
∷   City symbols
        Canals
        Aqueducts
        Dams
        Intermittent rivers
        Waterfalls
        Reefs
        Glaciers
        Salt lakes
        Swamps
        Sand areas

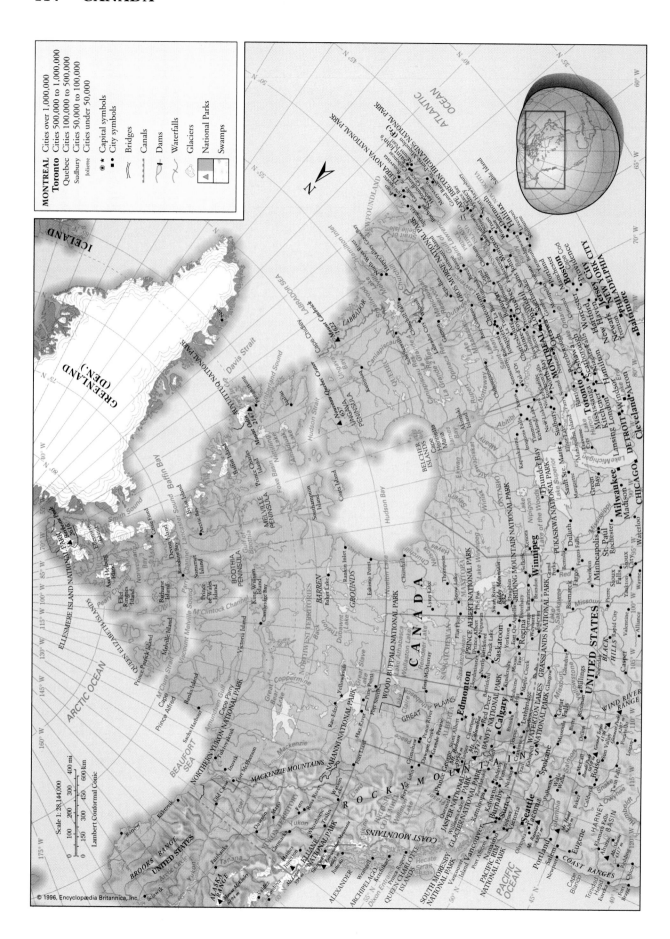

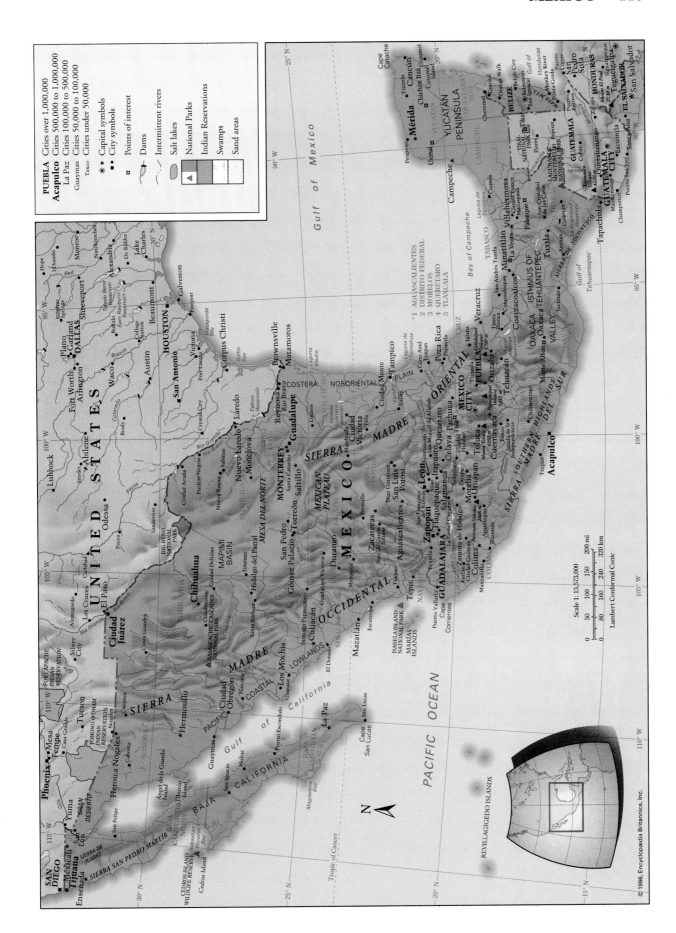

PUEBLA   Cities over 1,000,000
Acapulco   Cities 500,000 to 1,000,000
La Paz   Cities 100,000 to 500,000
Guaymas   Cities 50,000 to 100,000
Taxco   Cities under 50,000

⊛ ★   Capital symbols
■ •   City symbols
▪   Points of interest
╤   Dams
〰   Intermittent rivers
     Salt lakes
     National Parks
     Indian Reservations
     Swamps
     Sand areas

*1 AGUASCALIENTES
 2 DISTRITO FEDERAL
 3 MORELOS
 4 QUERÉTARO
 5 TLAXCALA

Scale 1: 13,573,000

0   50   100   150   200 mi
0   80 160 240 320 km
Lambert Conformal Conic

© 1996, Encyclopædia Britannica, Inc.

N

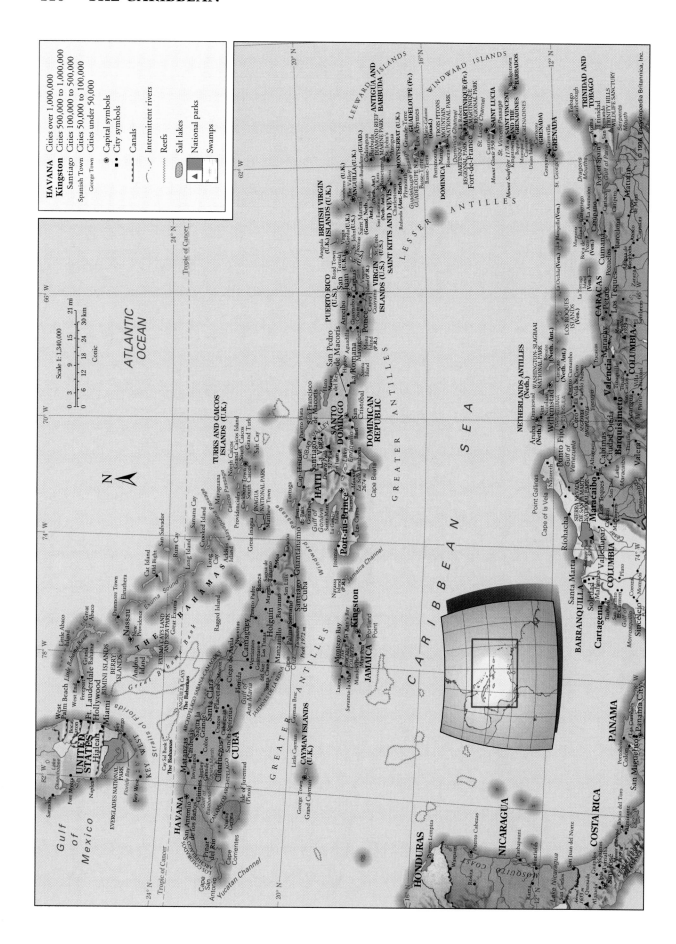

Scale 1:1,340,000

Conic

ATLANTIC OCEAN

CARIBBEAN SEA

GREATER ANTILLES

LESSER ANTILLES

WINDWARD ISLANDS

LEEWARD ISLANDS

Gulf of Mexico

HAVANA
CUBA
HAITI
DOMINICAN REPUBLIC
SANTO DOMINGO
Port-au-Prince
JAMAICA
Kingston
PUERTO RICO (U.S.)
San Juan
BAHAMAS
Nassau
TURKS AND CAICOS ISLANDS (U.K.)
CAYMAN ISLANDS (U.K.)
George Town

UNITED STATES
Miami

BRITISH VIRGIN ISLANDS (U.K.)
VIRGIN ISLANDS (U.S.)
ANGUILLA (U.K.)
SAINT KITTS AND NEVIS
ANTIGUA AND BARBUDA
MONTSERRAT (U.K.)
GUADELOUPE (Fr.)
DOMINICA
MARTINIQUE (Fr.)
SAINT LUCIA
SAINT VINCENT AND THE GRENADINES
BARBADOS
GRENADA
TRINIDAD AND TOBAGO

NETHERLANDS ANTILLES (Neth.)
Aruba (Neth.)
Curaçao (Neth. Ant.)
Willemstad

VENEZUELA
CARACAS
Maracaibo
Valencia
Barquisimeto
COLUMBIA
BARRANQUILLA
Cartagena
Santa Marta

PANAMA
COSTA RICA
NICARAGUA
HONDURAS

© 1996, Encyclopaedia Britannica, Inc.

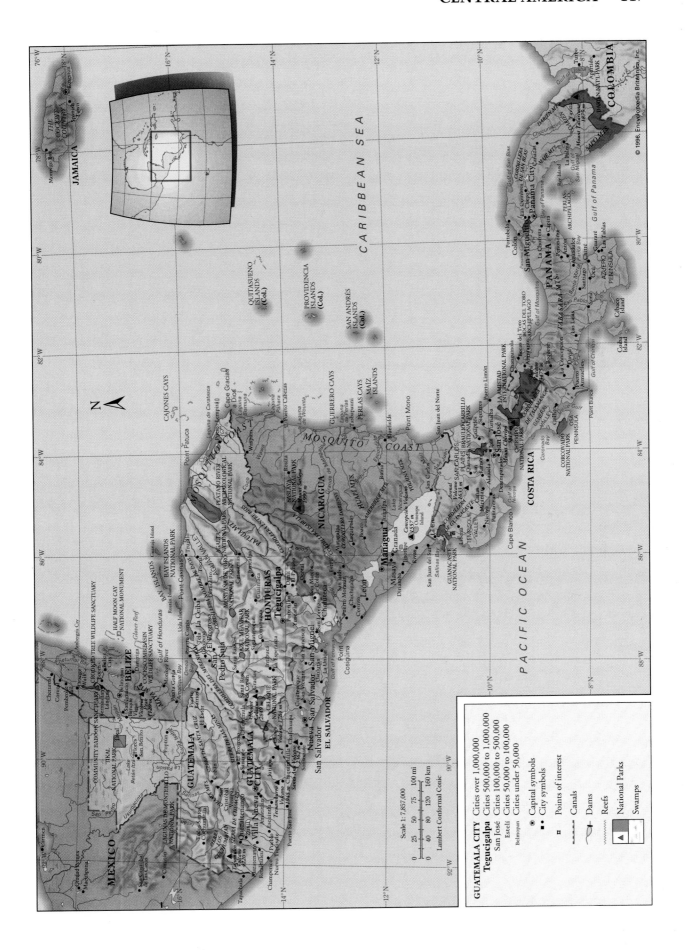

© 1996, Encyclopædia Britannica, Inc.

COLOMBIA

CARIBBEAN SEA

JAMAICA

THE COCKPIT COUNTRY

Montego Bay
Spanish Town
Kingston

Gulf of Urabá
LOS KATIOS NAT'L PARK
Turbo
Acandi
Gulf of San Blas
CORDILLERA DE SAN BLAS
Las Cumbres
Chepo
Colón
Portobelo
Panama City
PANAMA
MATA MTS.
Chitré
Gulf of Panama
PERLAS ARCHIPELAGO
DARIEN MTS.
SERRANÍA DEL DARIÉN
Mount Tacarcuna
1875 m
Chucunaque

QUITASUEÑO ISLANDS (Col.)

PROVIDENCIA ISLANDS (Col.)

SAN ANDRÉS ISLANDS (Col.)

MAIZ ISLANDS

PERLAS CAYS

GUERRERO CAYS

CAJONES CAYS

N

MOSQUITO COAST

Cape Gracias a Dios
Point Patuca
Laguna de Caratasca

Puerto Cabezas
Laguna Pahara

BAY ISLANDS NATIONAL PARK
BAY ISLANDS
Guanaja Island
Roatán Island
Utila Island
Trujillo
Point Castilla

Bluefields
Point Mono
San Juan del Norte

COSTA RICA
LA AMISTAD INTERNATIONAL PARK
Puerto Limón
Gulf of Mosquito
BOCAS DEL TORO
Changuinola
Almirante
Bocas del Toro
TABASARÁ MTS.
BRAULIO CARRILLO NATIONAL PARK
San José
Alajuela
Cartago
CORDILLERA DE TALAMANCA
Mount Chirripó
3820 m
GOLFO DULCE
Golfito
Puerto Armuelles
CORCOVADO NATIONAL PARK
OSA PENINSULA
Gulf of Chiriquí
Coiba Island
Cébaco Island
AZUERO PENINSULA

NICARAGUA
HONDURAS
Tegucigalpa
SASLAYA NATIONAL PARK
Waspán
Coco
HUAPI MTS.
YOLAINA MTS.
Lake Nicaragua
Ometepe Island
Concepción Volcano
1557 m
Managua
Masaya
Granada
León

MOSQUITIA
RÍO PLÁTANO ARCHAEOLOGICAL NATIONAL PARK
Mount Sallalá
AGALTA VALLEY
La Ceiba
San Pedro Sula
MONTAÑA DE YORO NATIONAL PARK
PICO BONITO NATIONAL PARK
Comayagua
Gulf of Honduras

BELIZE
Belize City
Belmopan
COCKSCOMB BASIN WILDLIFE SANCTUARY
CROOKED TREE WILDLIFE SANCTUARY
HALF MOON CAY NATIONAL MONUMENT
Half Moon Cay
Glover Reef
Ambergris Cay

MEXICO
Chetumal
Chetumal Bay

GUATEMALA
TIKAL NATIONAL PARK
Lake Petén Itzá
LAGUNAS DE MONTEBELLO NATIONAL PARK

GUATEMALA CITY
Villa Nueva
Quetzaltenango

EL SALVADOR
San Salvador
Santa Ana
San Miguel
MONTECRISTO NATIONAL PARK
EL IMPOSIBLE NATIONAL PARK
Gulf of Fonseca

PACIFIC OCEAN

Cape Blanco
GUANACASTE NATIONAL PARK
NICOYA PENINSULA
Gulf of Nicoya
TEMPISQUE VALLEY

Scale 1:7,857,000

0   25   50   75   100 mi
0 40 80 120 160 km

Lambert Conformal Conic

GUATEMALA CITY Cities over 1,000,000
Tegucigalpa Cities 500,000 to 1,000,000
San José Cities 100,000 to 500,000
Estelí Cities 50,000 to 100,000
Belmopan Cities under 50,000

✪ Capital symbols
•• City symbols
▫ Points of interest
       Canals
⊟ Dams
〰 Reefs
▲ National Parks
       Swamps

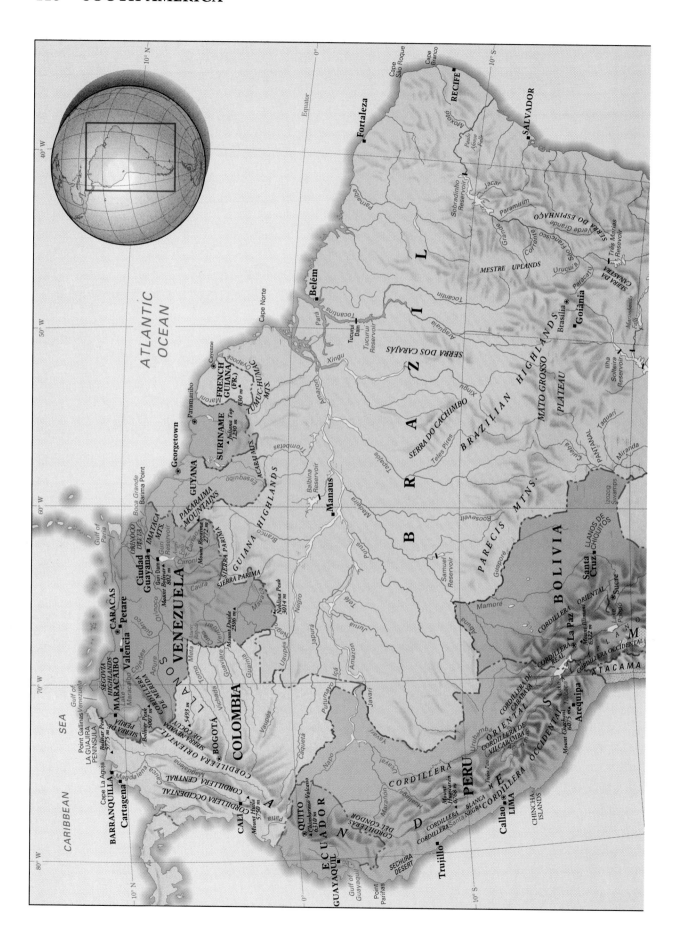

ATLANTIC OCEAN

CARIBBEAN SEA

RECIFE

SALVADOR

Fortaleza

Belém

Cape São Roque

Cape Branco

Equator

MESTRE UPLANDS

B R A Z I L

SERRA DO ESPINHAÇO

SERRA DA CANASTRA

Brasília

Goiânia

SERRA DOS CARAJÁS

SERRA DO CACHIMBO

BRAZILIAN HIGHLANDS

MATO GROSSO PLATEAU

PANTANAL

P A R E C I S   M T N S.

Cape Norte

Cayenne

FRENCH GUIANA (FR.)
Juliana Top
1230 m

SURINAME

TUMUC-HUMAC MTS.
850 m

Paramaribo

Georgetown

ACARAÍ MTS.

PAKARAIMA MOUNTAINS

Mount Roraima
2772 m

GUYANA

GUIANA HIGHLANDS

SIERRA PARIMA

SIERRA PARIMA

Guri Dam
Mount Bolívar
802 m

Ciudad Guayana

ORINOCO DELTA

IMATACA MTS.

Boca Grande

Barima Point

Gulf of Paria

CARACAS

Petare

Valencia

MARACAIBO

Lake Maracaibo

SEGOVIA HIGHLANDS

Venezuela

VENEZUELA

SIERRA DE PERIJÁ

Bolívar Peak
5007 m

CORDILLERA DE MÉRIDA

L L A N O S

BARRANQUILLA

Cartagena

Point Gallinas
LA GUAJIRA PENINSULA

Cape La Aguja

Bolívar Peak
5775 m
SIERRA NEVADA DE SANTA MARTA

Magdalena

Cauca

CORDILLERA OCCIDENTAL

CORDILLERA CENTRAL

CORDILLERA ORIENTAL

BOGOTÁ

COLOMBIA

5493 m

Mount Huila
5750 m

Orinoco

Meta

Guaviare

Vichada

Tomo

Vaupés

Caquetá

Putumayo

Japurá

Içá

Napo

Nebina Peak
3014 m
Mount Duida
2396 m

Caura

Caroní

NEGRO

Branco

Essequibo

Trombetas

Amazon

Xingu

Tapajós

Teles Pires

Madeira

Guaporé

Mamoré

Beni

Manaus

Balbina Reservoir

Roosevelt

Samuel Reservoir

Pará

Tocantins

Tucuruí Dam
Tucuruí Reservoir

Araguaia

Tocantins

São Francisco

Grande

Corrente

Uruçuí

Paranã

Paracatu

Parnaíba

Jacaré

Itaparica Reservoir

Sobradinho Reservoir

Ilha Solteira Reservoir

Três Marias Reservoir

Paraná

Verde

Cuiabá

Taquari

Miranda

Paraguay

LLANOS DE CHIQUITOS

Izozog Swamps

BOLIVIA

Santa Cruz

Sucre

La Paz

Lake Poopó

Lake Titicaca

Mount Illimani
6322 m

CORDILLERA REAL

CORDILLERA OCCIDENTAL

A L T I P L A N O

ATACAMA

Arequipa

CORDILLERA DE CARABAYA

CORDILLERA DE VILCABAMBA

CORDILLERA ORIENTAL

PERU

A N D E S

CORDILLERA BLANCA
Santa
CORDILLERA NEGRA

LIMA

Callao

CHINCHA ISLANDS

Mount Huascarán
6768 m

Mount Coropuna
6425 m

Mount Ausangate
6372 m

Trujillo

SECHURA DESERT

Marañón

Ucayali

Urubamba

Apurímac

Huallaga

Amazon

Javari

Juruá

Purús

Ucayali

Yavarí

QUITO

Chimborazo Volcano
6310 m

ECUADOR

GUAYAQUIL

Gulf of Guayaquil

Point Pariñas

CORDILLERAS DEL CONDOR

A N D E S

CORDILLERA

Pastaza

CAMPUANA

Patía

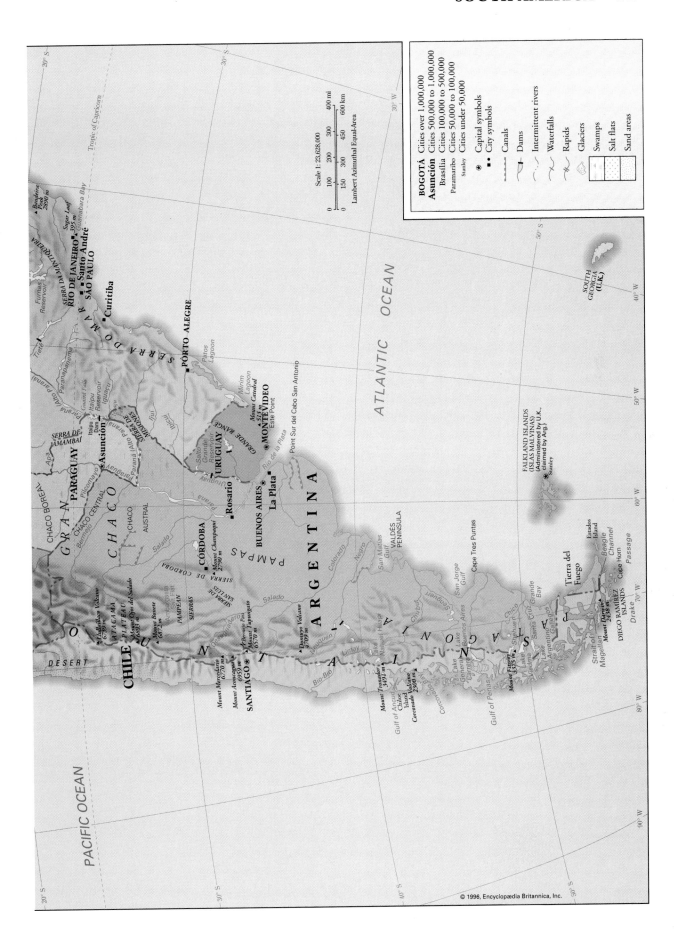

PACIFIC OCEAN

ATLANTIC OCEAN

CHILE

ARGENTINA

PARAGUAY

URUGUAY

BOLIVIA

PAMPAS

PATAGONIA

GRAN CHACO

CHACO BOREAL

CHACO CENTRAL

CHACO AUSTRAL

ATACAMA PLATEAU

DESERT

SANTIAGO

Mount Aconcagua 6959 m
Mount Mercedario 6770 m
Mount Bonete 6872 m
Mount Ojos del Salado 6893 m
Llullaillaco Volcano 6739 m
Mount Tupungato 6570 m
Mount Champaquí 2790 m
Domuyo Volcano 4709 m
Cerro El Nevado
Mount Tronador 3491 m
Corcovado Volcano 2300 m

CÓRDOBA
Rosario
BUENOS AIRES
La Plata
MONTEVIDEO
Mount Catedral 513 m
Asunción
PORTO ALEGRE
Curitiba
SÃO PAULO
Santo André
RIO DE JANEIRO
Sugar Loaf 395 m
Bandeira Peak 2890 m

SERRA DO MAR
SERRA DA MANTIQUEIRA
SERRA DE AMAMBAÍ
SERRA DE MARACAJU
MISIONES
GRANDE RANGE
SIERRA DE CÓRDOBA
SIERRA DE SAN LUIS
SIERRAS PAMPEANAS

Tropic of Capricorn

Furnas Reservoir
Guanabara Bay
Tietê
Paranapanema
Paranaíba
Paraná
Alto Paraná
Iguaçu
Iguaçu Falls
Itaipu Reservoir
Itaipu Dam
Uruguay
Ijuí
Guaíba
Patos Lagoon
Mirim Lagoon
Río de la Plata
Point Sur del Cabo San Antonio
Este Point
Salto Grande Reservoir
Apa
Pilcomayo
Bermejo
Salado
Salado
Dulce
Carcarañá
Desaguadero
Colorado
Negro
Limay
Neuquén
Río Negro
Bío-Bío
Chubut
Senguerr
Chico
Deseado
Santa Cruz
Gallegos
San Matías Gulf
San Jorge Gulf
Gulf of Penas
Gulf of Ancud
VALDÉS PENINSULA
Cape Tres Puntas
Lake Nahuel Huapí
Lake Buenos Aires
Lake General Carrera
Lake Viedma
Lake Argentino
Chiloé Island
Mount Fitzroy 3375 m

Tierra del Fuego
Estados Island
Beagle Channel
Cape Horn
Drake Passage
Strait of Magellan
DIEGO RAMÍREZ ISLANDS
Mount Darwin 2438 m

FALKLAND ISLANDS
(ISLAS MALVINAS)
(Administered by U.K.,
claimed by Arg.)
Stanley

SOUTH GEORGIA
(U.K.)

20° S
30° S
40° S
50° S
90° W
80° W
70° W
60° W
50° W
40° W
30° W

Scale 1:23,628,000
Lambert Azimuthal Equal-Area

0 100 200 300 400 mi
0 150 300 450 600 km

BOGOTÁ   Cities over 1,000,000
Asunción   Cities 500,000 to 1,000,000
Brasilia   Cities 100,000 to 500,000
Paramaribo Cities 50,000 to 100,000
Stanley   Cities under 50,000

⊛ Capital symbols
■ • City symbols

Canals
Dams
Intermittent rivers
Waterfalls
Rapids
Glaciers
Swamps
Salt flats
Sand areas

© 1996, Encyclopædia Britannica, Inc.

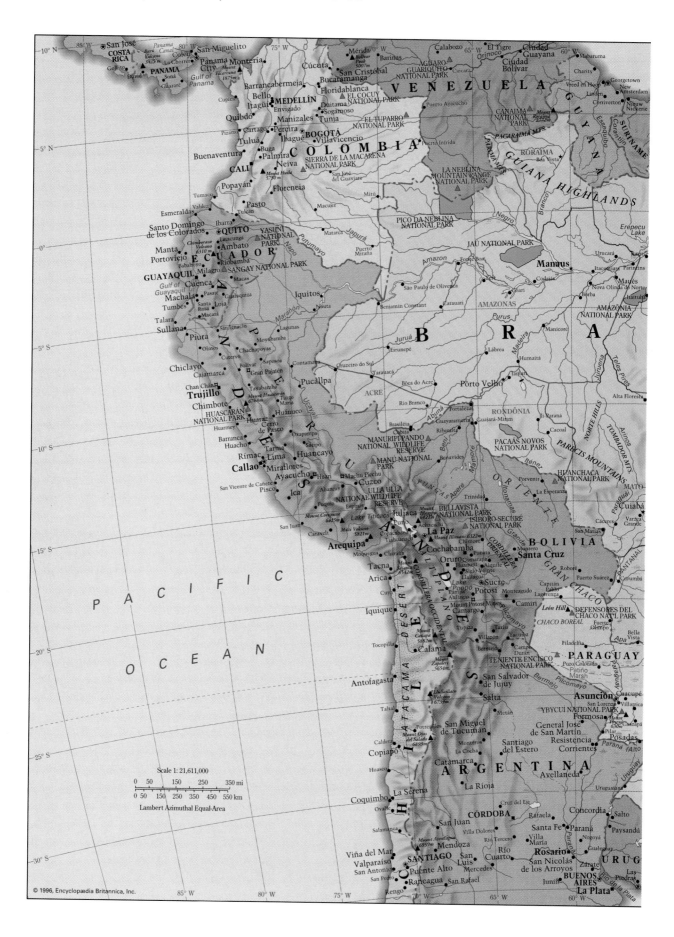

San José
COSTA
RICA
Golfito
David
Panama
Canal
Barú
Volcano
3425 m
La Chorrera
PANAMA
Soná
Mount
Chirripó
3820 m
Gáarare
Gulf of
Panama
San Miguelito
Panama
City
Monteria
Cupica
Quibdó
Bello
Itagüí
MEDELLÍN
Envigado
Manizales
Pizarro
Cartago
Pereira
Tuluá
Buga
Palmira
CALI
Mount Huila
5750 m
Popayán
Tumaco
Esmeraldas
Valdez
Santo Domingo
de los Colorados
Ibarra
Manta
Portoviejo
Chimborazo
Volcano
6310 m
Latacunga
Ambato
QUITO
Riobamba
ECUADOR
Babahoyo
GUAYAQUIL
Milagro
SANGAY NATIONAL PARK
Gulf of
Guayaquil
Cuenca
Machala
Pasaje
Guaiaquiza
Santa
Rosa
Loja
Tumbes
Macará
Talara
Sullana
Piura
Chiclayo
Olmos
Cajamarca
Bolívar
Cuervo
Chachapoyas
Chan Chán
Trujillo
Tayabamba
Mount Huascarán
6768 m
Chimbote
HUASCARÁN
NATIONAL PARK
Huarmey
Huaraz
Cerro
de Pasco
Barranca
Huacho
Rímac
Lima
Tarma
Callao
Miraflores
San Vicente de Cañete
Ica
Puquio
Pisco
Mount Coropuna
6425 m
San Juan
Mount Solimana
6323 m
Caravelí
Mt Vilcota
5821 m
Arequipa
Moquegua
Tacna
Arica
Iquique

Cúcuta
Mérida
Bolívar
Peak
5007 m
Barinas
Bucaramanga
Floridablanca
Barrancabermeja
Duitama
Tunja
Sogamoso
BOGOTÁ
Villavicencio
COLOMBIA
SIERRA DE LA MACARENA
NATIONAL PARK
Neiva
Florencia
San José
del Guaviare
Puerto Inírida
Pasto
Tulcán
Macuer
Mitú
Macjer
YASUNÍ
NATIONAL
PARK
Putumayo
Puerto
Miraña
Iquitos
Marañón
Moyobamba
Saposoa
Contamana
Pucallpa
Huánuco
Oxapampa
Satipo
Huancayo
Ayacucho
Abancay
Machu Picchu
Cuzco
Espinar
ULLA ULLA
NATIONAL WILDLIFE
RESERVE

VENEZUELA
Calabozo
El Tigre
Orinoco
Ciudad
Guayana
Ciudad
Bolívar
Maburuma
Charity
AGUARO
GUARIQUITO
NATIONAL PARK
Caicara
Puerto Ayacucho
CANAIMA
NATIONAL
PARK
Mount
Roraima
2772 m
EL TUPARRO
NATIONAL PARK
PACARAIMA MTS.
RORAIMA
Boa Vista
Georgetown
New
Amsterdam
Corriverton
Linden
Nieuw
Nickerie
SURINAME
GUYANA
GUIANA HIGHLANDS
LA NEBLINA
MOUNTAIN RANGE
NATIONAL PARK
PICO DA NEBLINA
NATIONAL PARK
Negro
Branco
Urucara
Erepecu
Lake
JAÚ NATIONAL PARK
Manaus
Fonte Boa
Amazon
São Paulo de Olivença
Benjamin Constant
Carauari
AMAZONAS
Itacoatiara
Parintins
Codajás
Maués
Nova Olinda do Norte
Itaituba
AMAZÔNIA
NATIONAL PARK
Coari
Purus
Juruá
Manicoré
Eirunepé
B R A Z I L
Lábrea
Humaitá
Madeira
Cruzeiro do Sul
Tarauacá
Boca do Acre
ACRE
Rio Branco
Brasiléia
Porto Velho
Fortaleza
Guajará-Mirim
RONDÔNIA
Ji-Paraná
Alta Floresta
Cacoal
NORTE HILLS
Arinos
TOMBADOR MTS.
MANURIPI-PANDO
NATIONAL WILDLIFE
RESERVE
Riberalta
PACAÁS NOVOS
NATIONAL PARK
PARECIS MOUNTAINS
Benavides
MANU NATIONAL
PARK
Porvenir
La Esperanza
HUANCHACA
NATIONAL PARK
MATO
Trinidad
BELLAVISTA
NATIONAL PARK
ISIBORO-SECURÉ
NATIONAL PARK
O R I E N T E
San José
Cuiabá
Várzea
Grande
Cáceres
San Matías
La Paz
Cochabamba
Oruro
BOLIVIA
Santa Cruz
Montero
Robore
Puerto Suárez
Corumbá
PANTANAL
Achacachi
Lake Titicaca
Juliaca
Puno
Copacabana
Tiahuanaco
Mount Illimani
6323 m
CORDILLERA
ORIENTAL
GRAN CHACO
Potosí
Sucre
Monteagudo
Capitán
Pablo
Lagerenza
Camiri
DEFENSORES DEL
CHACO NAT'L PARK
León Hill
CHACO BOREAL
Fuerte
Olimpo
Bella
Vista
Apa
PARAGUAY
Filadelfia
TENIENTE ENCISO
NATIONAL PARK
Pozo
Colorado
Patiño
Marsh
ALTIPLANO
Siglo Veinte
Huanuni
Aiquile
Comarapa
CORDILLERA
OCCIDENTAL
Lake
Poopó
Lake
Uyuni
Camargo
Tupiza
Villazón
Tarija
Yacuiba
Bermejo
Pilcomayo
ATACAMA DESERT
Mount
Sajama
6542 m
Mount
Cápac
5882 m
Calama
Mount
Zapaleri
5654 m
San Salvador
de Jujuy
Salta
Tocopilla
Antofagasta
Taltal
Mount
Llullaillaco
Volcano
6739 m
Potrerillos
Mount Ojos
del Salado
6893 m
Metán
YBYCUÍ NATIONAL PARK
San Lorenzo
ASUNCIÓN
Villarrica
Caacupé
San Miguel
de Tucumán
Santiago
del Estero
Formosa
General José
de San Martín
Resistencia
Corrientes
Pilar
Posadas
Campo
Durán
Embarcación
Mount
630 m
Copiapó
Caldera
Monteros
La Cocha
Catamarca
Avellaneda
La Rioja
ARGENTINA
Huasco
Coquimbo
La Serena
Ovalle
Salamanca
San Juan
Villa Dolores
Villa María
Mendoza
Mount Aconcagua
6959 m
Viña del Mar
Valparaíso
San Antonio
SANTIAGO
Puente Alto
San Pedro
Rengo
Rancagua
San Rafael
San Luis
Río
Cuarto
Mercedes
Junín
CÓRDOBA
Cruz del Eje
Rafaela
Santa Fe
Río Tercero
Paraná
Nogoyá
Rosario
San Nicolás
de los Arroyos
Gualeguay
Gualeguaychú
BUENOS
AIRES
La Plata
Uruguaiana
Uruguay
Concordia
Salto
Paysandú
URUG
Zárate
Las
Piedras
Río de la Plata

PACIFIC

OCEAN

Scale 1: 21,611,000

0   50   150   250   350 mi
0 50 150 250 350 450 550 km

Lambert Azimuthal Equal-Area

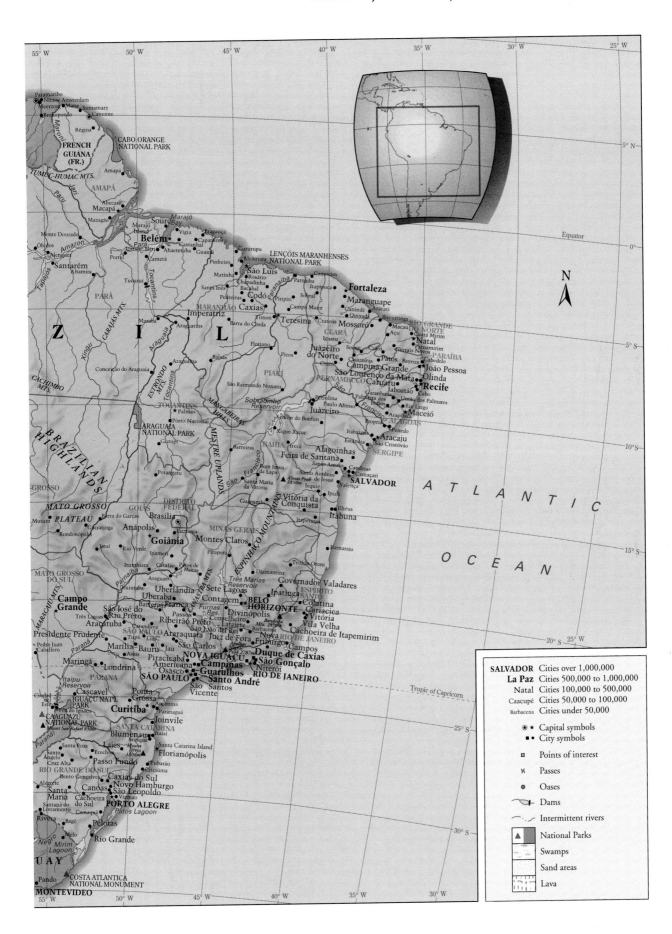

55° W   50° W   45° W   40° W   35° W   30° W   25° W

Paramaribo
Nieuw Amsterdam   Mana   Sinnamary
Meerzorg   Cayenne
Brokopondo   Régina

FRENCH
GUIANA
(FR.)

CABO ORANGE
NATIONAL PARK

TUMUC-HUMAC MTS.

AMAPÁ

Abecatuaia
Macapá
Mazagão   Amapá

Monte Dourado
Óbidos   Alenquer
Santarém   Altamira

Marajó
Island   Marajó
Bay
Soure   Vigia   Bragança
Belém   Pará   Castanhal   Capanema   Cururupu   LENÇÓIS MARANHENSES
NATIONAL PARK
Abaetetuba   Guamá   Alcântara   Camocim
Portel   Cametá   Pinheiro   São Luís   Parnaíba   Itapipoca   Fortaleza
Matinha   Rosário   Maranguape
Santa Inês   Chapadinha   Sobral   Acaraú   Canindé
Codó   Bacabal   Quixadá   Ibicuitinga   RIO GRANDE
Caxias   Timon   Campo Maior   Macau   DO NORTE
Teresina   Crateús   Ceará Mirim   Açu
Imperatriz   Mossoró   Natal
Marabá   Araguatins   Barra do Corda   Picos   CEARÁ   Iguatu   Sousa   Patos   Parnamirim
Araguaína   Balsas   Floriano   Juázeiro   Caicó   Bayeux   PARAÍBA
do Norte   Guazeiras   Cabedelo
Conceição do Araguaia   PIAUÍ   Crato   Campina Grande   João Pessoa
São Raimundo Nonato   São Lourenço da Mata   Olinda
PERNAMBUCO   Caruaru   Recife
Palmas   Petrolina   Garanhuns   Jaboatão   Cabo
Pôrto Nacional   Sobradinho   Paulo Afonso   Palmeira dos   União dos Palmares
Reservoir   Juázeiro   Índios   Rio Largo
ARAGUAIA   Senhor do Bonfim   Propriá   Maceió
NATIONAL PARK   ALAGOAS
Gurupi   Xique-Xique   Itabaiana   Aracaju
Estância   São Cristóvão
Barreiras   Irecê   SERGIPE
Alagoinhas
Feira de Santana   Santo Amaro   Candeias
Porangatu   Bom Jesus   BAHIA   Camaçari
da Lapa   Santa Maria   Santo Antônio   SALVADOR
da Vitória   de Jesus   Valença
Barra do Garças   Almas Peak   Jequié   Ipiaú
1851m   Ilhéus
Brasília   Vitória da   Itabuna
Anápolis   Luziânia   Conquista
DISTRITO
FEDERAL   Guanambi   Itapetinga
Cairatinga   GOIÁS   Itamaraju
Rondonópolis   Goiânia   Montes Claros
Itaí   MINAS GERAIS
Rio Verde   Ipameri   Pirapora   Teófilo Otoni
Ituiutaba   Catalão   Patos de   Diamantina
Minas   Governador Valadares
Araguari   ESPÍRITO
Uberlândia   Três Marias   Ipatinga   SANTO
Uberaba   Reservoir   Sete Lagoas   Colatina
Contagem   BELO   Cariacica
Barretos   Franca   HORIZONTE   Vitória
São José do   Furnas   Divinópolis   Vila Velha
Rio Prêto   Res.   Conselheiro   Cachoeira de Itapemirim
Araçatuba   Ribeirão Prêto   Lafaiete   Bandeira
Sarandira   Mtn 2890m
Presidente Prudente   Tupã   São João del Rei   Juiz de Fora   Barbacena
Pedro Juan   São Carlos   Nova   RIO DE JANEIRO
Caballero   Marília   Bauru   Itu   Friburgo   Campos
Assis   Araraquara   Agulha   Niterói
Maringá   Piracicaba   Peak 2787m   Campos
Londrina   Americana   NOVA IGUAÇU   Duque de Caxias
Osasco   Campinas   São Gonçalo
Itaipu   PARANÁ   São Paulo   Guarulhos   RIO DE JANEIRO
Reservoir   Santo André   Niterói
Ponta   São
Ciudad del   Cascavel   Grossa   Vicente   Santos
Este   Foz do Iguaçu   Antonina
IGUAÇU NAT'L   Curitiba   Paranaguá
PARK   CAAGUAZU   Joinvile
NATIONAL PARK   Mount San Rafael 850m
SANTA CATARINA
Blumenau   Itajaí
Santa Rosa   Lajes   Brusque
Santo   Erechim   Mount   Santa Catarina Island
Ângelo   Itajaí   Florianópolis
Cruz Alta   Passo Fundo   1808m   Tubarão
RIO GRANDE DO SUL   Criciúma
Bento Gonçalves   Caxias do Sul
Alegrete   Canoas   Novo Hamburgo
Santa   Cachoeira   São Leopoldo
Maria   do Sul   Viamão
Santana do   PORTO ALEGRE
Livramento   Patos Lagoon
Rivera   Bagé   Pelotas
Melo   Negro   Rio Grande
Mirim
Lagoon
UAY
Pando   COSTA ATLANTICA
NATIONAL MONUMENT
MONTEVIDEO

BRAZILIAN HIGHLANDS
MATO GROSSO
CARAJÁS MTS.
CÁCHIMBO MTS.
ESTRONDO MTS.
MARANHÃO MTS.
MESTRE ORLANDS
ESPINHAÇO MOUNTAINS
MANTIQUEIRA MTS.
MARACAJU MTS.
MATO GROSSO PLATEAU
MATO GROSSO DO SUL
Campo Grande
Três Lagoas

ATLANTIC

OCEAN

Equator
5° N
0°
5° S
10° S
15° S
20° S   25° W
25° S
Tropic of Capricorn
30° S

N

SALVADOR	Cities over 1,000,000
La Paz	Cities 500,000 to 1,000,000
Natal	Cities 100,000 to 500,000
Caacupé	Cities 50,000 to 100,000
Barbacena	Cities under 50,000

⊛ ★ Capital symbols
• • City symbols

⊡   Points of interest
)(Passes
⊙   Oases
⌐   Dams
⌒⌒ Intermittent rivers
▲   National Parks
     Swamps
     Sand areas
     Lava

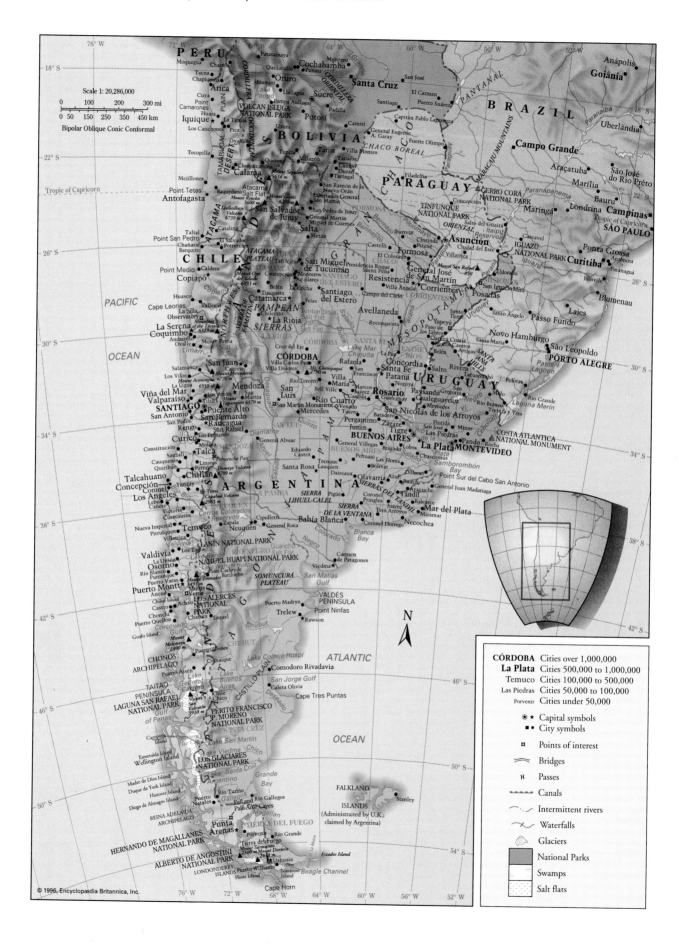

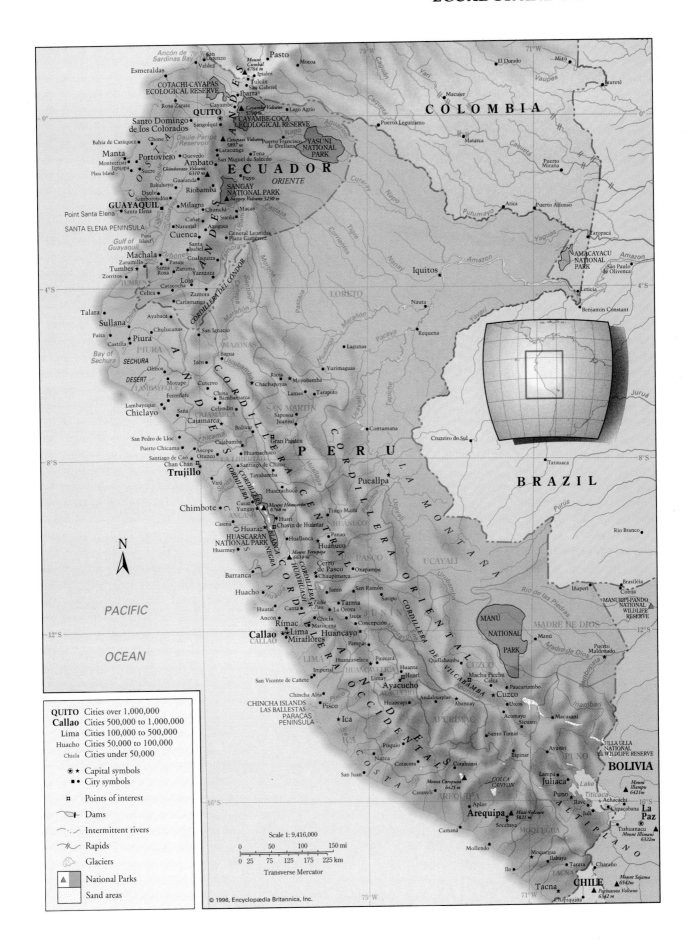

Ancón de
Sardinas Bay
San Lorenzo
Valdez
Esmeraldas
Mount
Cumbal
4764 m
Pasto
Mocoa
El Dorado
Mitú
Isuretê

Ipiales
Tulcán
San Gabriel
COTACHI-CAYAPAS
ECOLOGICAL RESERVE
Ibarra
Rosa Zárate
Cayambe
Cayambe Volcano
5790 m
Lago Agrio
CAYAMBE-COCA
ECOLOGICAL RESERVE
Macujer
COLOMBIA
Mitú

QUITO
Santo Domingo
de los Colorados
Sangolquí
Puerto Leguizamo
Matarca

Bahía de Caráquez
Chone
Daule-Peripa
Reservoir
Catopaxi Volcano
5897 m
Latacunga
Tena
Puerto Francisco
de Orellana
YASUNI
NATIONAL
PARK
Caquetá
Puerto
Miraña

Manta
Montecristi
Jipijapa
Portoviejo
Quevedo
San Miguel de Salcedo
Ambato
Guaranda
ECUADOR
Puyo
ORIENTE
Aguarico
Sucre
Plata Island
Babahoyo
Chimborazo Volcano
6310 m
Riobamba
SANGAY
NATIONAL PARK
Sangay Volcano 5230 m
Macas
Napo
Arica
Puerto Alfonso

Daule
Samborondón
GUAYAQUIL
Milagro
Chunchi
Cañar
Sucúa
Curaray
Putumayo
Yaguas
Taropacá

Point Santa Elena
Santa Elena
SANTA ELENA PENINSULA
Naranjal
Azogues
General Leonidas
Plaza Gutiérrez
AMACAYACU
NATIONAL
PARK
Amazon
São Paulo
de Olivença

Puná
Island
Cuenca
Gulf of
Guayaquil
Santa
Isabel
Morona
Iquitos
Leticia

Machala
Zarumilla
Pasaje
Pastaza
Benjamín Constant

Tumbes
Zorritos
Santa
Rosa
Zaruma
Yantzaza
Loja
LORETO
Nauta
Yavarí

Talara
Celica
Catacocha
Zamora
Cariamanga
Marañón
Pacaya
Requena

Sullana
Ayabaca
Chulucanas
San Ignacio
AMAZONAS
Nanay
Juruá

Paita
Castilla
Piura
PIURA
Jaén
Utcubamba
Lagunas
Yurimaguas

Bay of
Sechura
SECHURA
Olmos
Cutervo
Rioja
Chachapoyas
Moyobamba
Tapiche

DESERT
LAMBAYEQUE
Motupe
Chota
Bambamarca
Lamas
Tarapoto

Lambayeque
Ferreñafe
Celendín
CAJAMARCA
Saña
SAN MARTÍN
Saposoa
Juanjuí
Contamana
Cruzeiro do Sul
Tarauacá
BRAZIL
Río Branco

Chiclayo
Cajamarca
Bolívar
Gran Pajatén
Ucayali

San Pedro de Lloc
Cajabamba
Chicama
Puerto Chicama
Ascope
Huamachuco
LA LIBERTAD
Santiago de Cao
Otuzco
PERU
LA MONTAÑA

Chan Chán
Santiago de Chuco
Trujillo
Tayabamba

Virú
Huacrachuco
Pucallpa
Purús
Brasiléia
Iñapari
Cobija
MANURIPI-PANDO
NATIONAL
WILDLIFE
RESERVE

Chimbote
Caraz
Yungay
Mount Huascarán
6768 m
Huari
Chavín de Huántar
Tingo María
ANCASH
Río de las Piedras

Casma
Huaraz
HUASCARAN
NATIONAL PARK
Huallanca
Panao
HUANUCO
UCAYALI

Huarmey
Mount Yerupajá
6634 m
CORDILLERA
BLANCA
CORDILLERA
NEGRA
Huánuco
Urubamba
MADRE DE DIOS

Barranca
Cerro
de Pasco
Oxapampa
PASCO
San Ramón
CORDILLERA
ORIENTAL
Manú

Huacho
Huaral
Huatal
Canta
Tarma
La Oroya
Junín
Satipo
Inambari

Ancón
Ticlio
Pass
Chicla
Jauja
Concepción
MANÚ
NATIONAL
PARK
Manú
Puerto
Maldonado

Rímac
Lima
Callao
CALLAO
Miraflores
Matucana
Huancayo
Pampas
Huancavelica
Paucará
Huanta
Huari
Quillabamba
Calca
CUZCO
Paucartambo

LIMA
San Vicente de Cañete
Imperial
HUANCAVELICA
Lircay
Machu Picchu
VILCABAMBA
Urcos
Cuzco
Acomayo
Sicuani

Chincha Alta
CHINCHA ISLANDS
LAS BALLESTAS
PARACAS
PENINSULA
Pisco
Huancapi
Ayacucho
Andahuaylas
Abancay
APURIMAC
Santo Tomás
Macusani

Ica
ICA
Puquio
Espinar
Ayaviri
Lampa
ULLA ULLA
NATIONAL
WILDLIFE RESERVE
BOLIVIA

Nazca
Coracora
Cotahuasi
PUNO
Juliaca
Lake
Titicaca
Mount
Illampu
6421m

San Juan
Caravelí
Mount Coropuna
6425 m
COLCA
CANYON
Puno
Ilave
Juli
Copacabana
Achacachi
La
Paz

AREQUIPA
Aplao
Arequipa
Misti Volcano
5821 m
Socabaya
MOQUEGUA
Tiahuanaco
Mount Illimani
6322m

Camaná
Moquegua
Ilabaya
Tarata
Charaña
Mount Sajama
6542m

Mollendo
Ilo
TACNA
Tacna
CHILE
Chapiquiña
Pariacaca Volcano
6342 m

N

PACIFIC

OCEAN

Legend:

QUITO	Cities over 1,000,000
Callao	Cities 500,000 to 1,000,000
Lima	Cities 100,000 to 500,000
Huacho	Cities 50,000 to 100,000
Chicla	Cities under 50,000

⊛ ★   Capital symbols
■ •   City symbols

⊡   Points of interest

↿   Dams

Intermittent rivers

Rapids

Glaciers

▲   National Parks

Sand areas

Scale 1: 9,416,000

0   50   100   150 mi
0   25   75   125   175   225 km
Transverse Mercator

© 1996, Encyclopædia Britannica, Inc.

71°W
75°W
71°W
75°W
0°
4°S
8°S
12°S
16°S

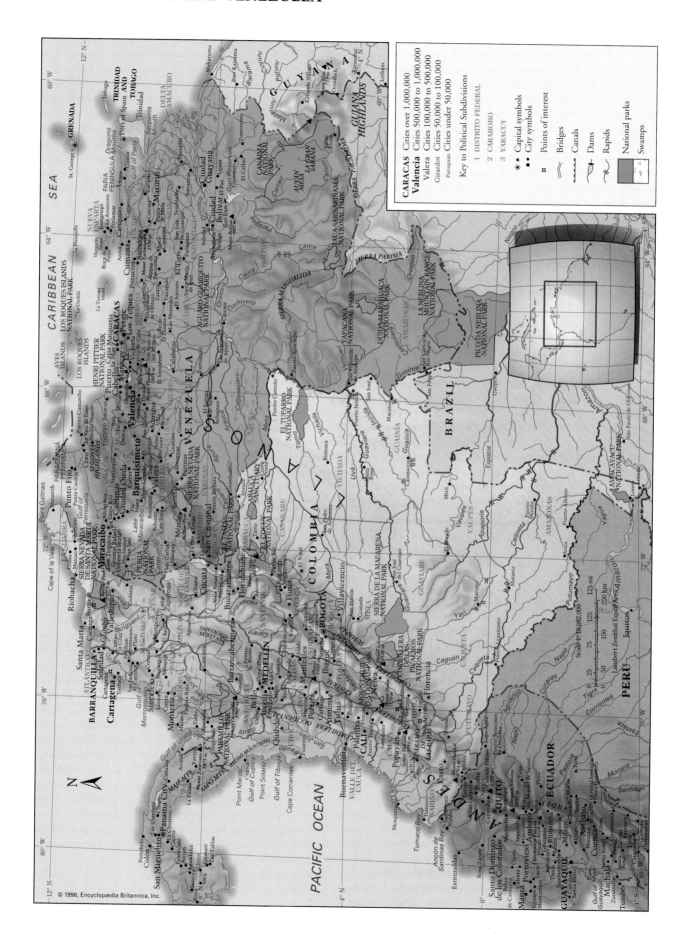

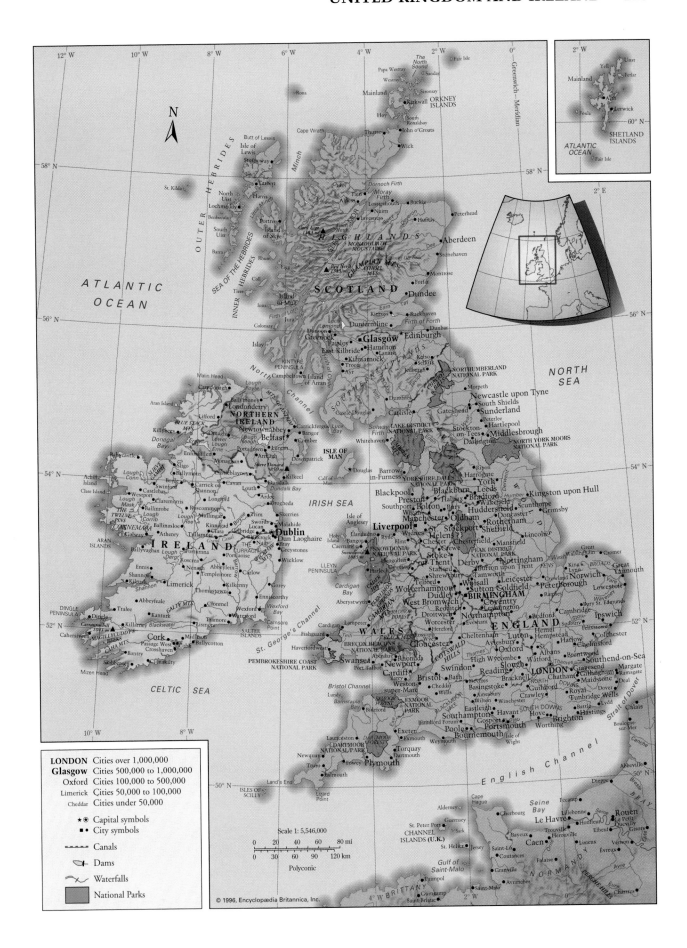

NORTH
SEA

ATLANTIC
OCEAN

OUTER HEBRIDES

SEA OF THE HEBRIDES

INNER HEBRIDES

HIGHLANDS

SCOTLAND

GRAMPIAN MTS

ATHOLL MTS

MONADHLIATH MOUNTAINS

Ben Nevis 1343 m

Glasgow   Edinburgh

NORTHERN IRELAND

Belfast

BLUE STACK MTS

SPERRIN MTS

ISLE OF MAN

NORTHUMBERLAND NATIONAL PARK

Newcastle upon Tyne

LAKE DISTRICT NATIONAL PARK

NORTH YORK MOORS NATIONAL PARK

IRELAND

Dublin

IRISH SEA

YORKSHIRE DALES NATIONAL PARK

PEAK DISTRICT NATIONAL PARK

THE TWELVE PINS

CONNEMARA

ARAN ISLANDS

THE CURRAGH

WICKLOW MTS

SNOWDONIA NATIONAL PARK

Snowdon 1085 m

LLEYN PENINSULA

Liverpool

BIRMINGHAM

ENGLAND

Cardigan Bay

CAMBRIAN MTS

CADER IDRIS

RADNOR FOREST

GALTY MTS

DINGLE PENINSULA

Carrantuohill 1041 m

MAGILLYCUDDY'S REEKS

CAHA MTS

SALTEE ISLANDS

St. George's Channel

WALES

BRECON BEACONS NATIONAL PARK

COTSWOLD HILLS

LONDON

PEMBROKESHIRE COAST NATIONAL PARK

Bristol Channel

EXMOOR NATIONAL PARK

BLACKDOWN HILLS

SOUTH DOWNS

CELTIC SEA

DARTMOOR NATIONAL PARK

Isle of Wight

English Channel

Strait of Dover

ISLES OF SCILLY

Land's End

Lizard Point

CHANNEL ISLANDS (U.K.)

Gulf of Saint-Malo

NORMANDY

BRITTANY

Seine Bay

Rouen

Le Havre

Caen

Scale 1: 5,546,000

0   20   40   60   80 mi

0   30   60   90   120 km

Polyconic

© 1996, Encyclopædia Britannica, Inc.

LONDON   Cities over 1,000,000
Glasgow   Cities 500,000 to 1,000,000
Oxford   Cities 100,000 to 500,000
Limerick   Cities 50,000 to 100,000
Cheddar   Cities under 50,000

★ ⊛   Capital symbols
• ■   City symbols
------   Canals
⌐ᴢ   Dams
∿   Waterfalls
▨   National Parks

LONDON	Cities over 1,000,000
Stockholm	Cities 500,000 to 1,000,000
Oslo	Cities 100,000 to 500,000
Luxembourg	Cities 50,000 to 100,000
Vaduz	Cities under 50,000

⊛ National capital symbols
★ Country capital symbols
■ City symbols
┄┄ Canals
     Dams
     Glaciers
     Salt lakes
     Swamps
     Salt flats

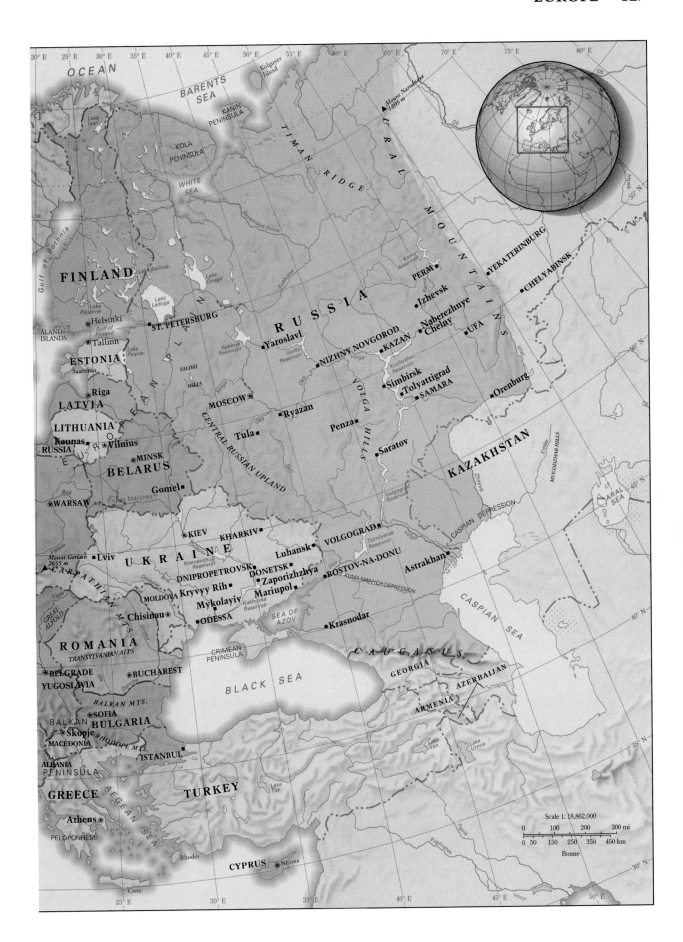

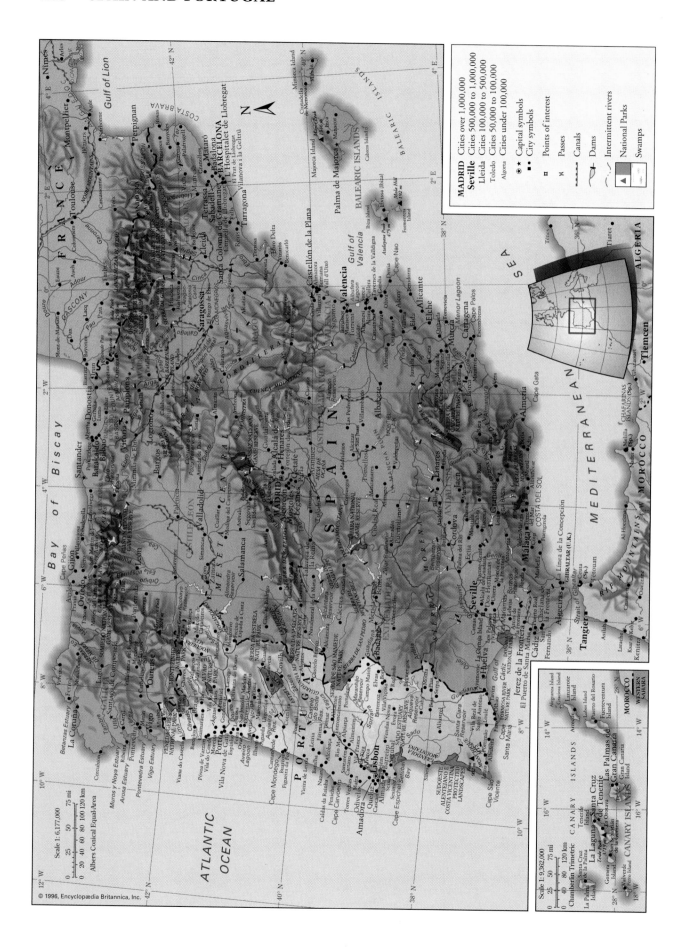

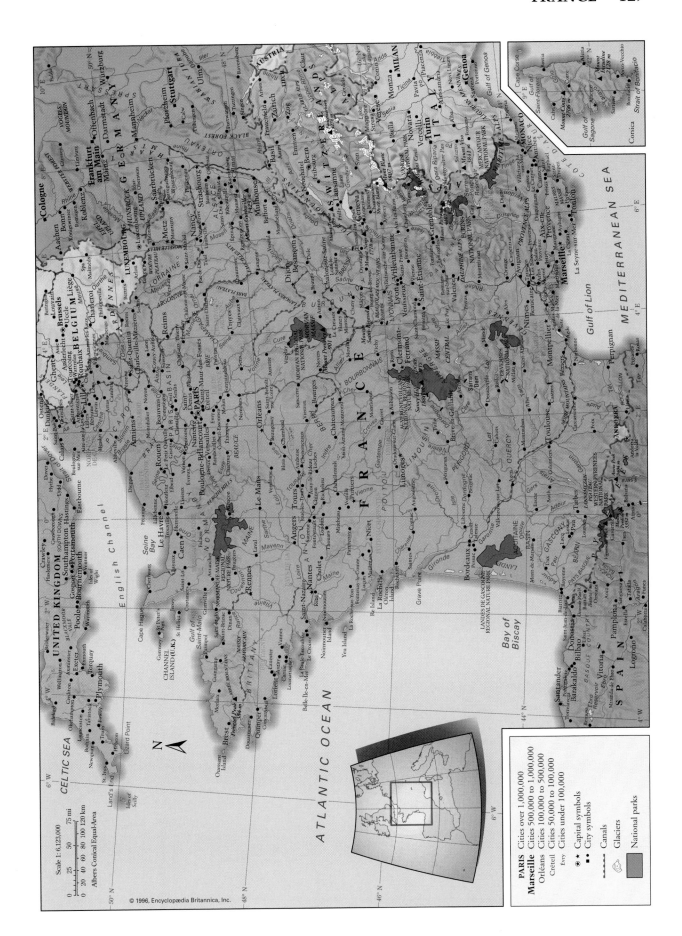

© 1996, Encyclopædia Britannica, Inc.

ROME   Cities over 1,000,000
Venice Cities 500,000 to 1,000,000
Verona Cities 100,000 to 500,000
Pisa   Cities 50,000 to 100,000
Assiso Cities under 50,000

⊛ ★   Capital symbols
● ■   City symbols

▫   Points of interest

〕(Passes

---   Canals

〜   Dams

〜   Intermittent rivers

🐾   Glaciers

     National parks

     Swamps

     Salt flats

Scale 1: 6,208,000

0   25   50   75   100 mi
0   40   80   120   160 km

Secant Conic

© 1996, Encyclopædia Britannica, Inc.

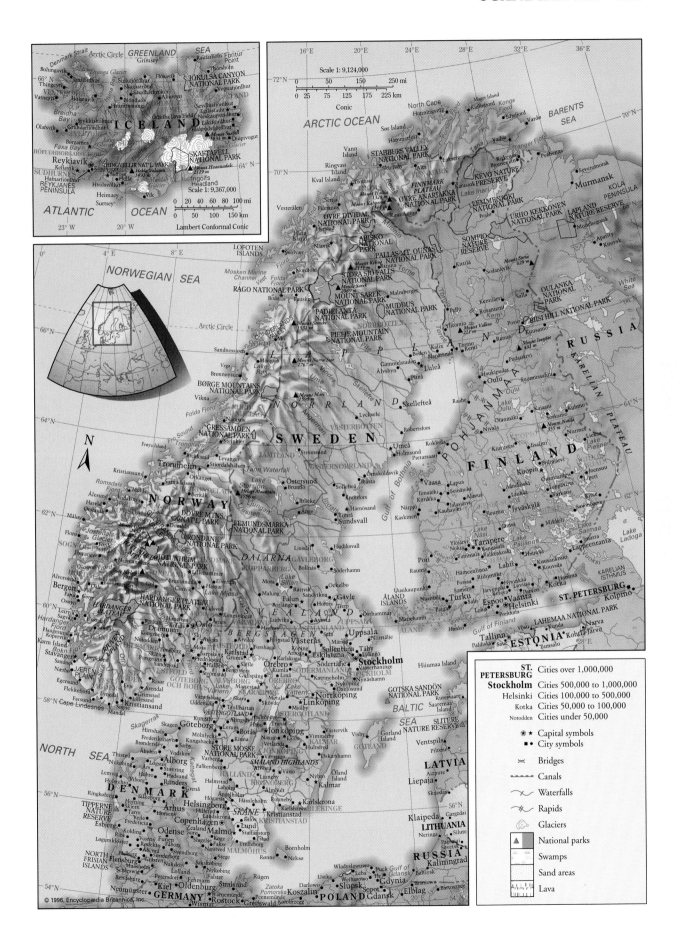

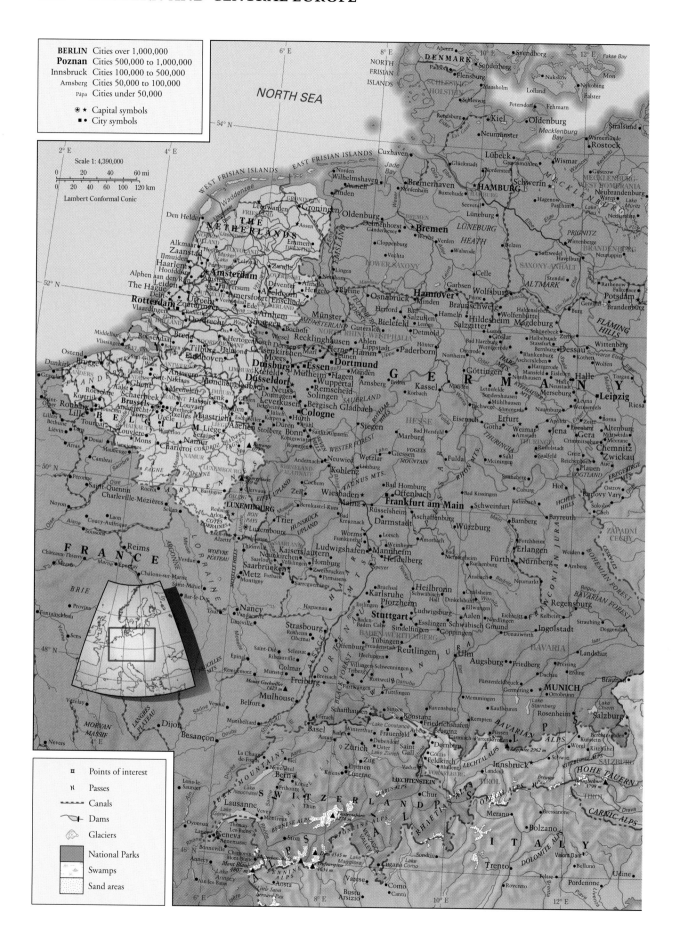

BERLIN Cities over 1,000,000
Poznan Cities 500,000 to 1,000,000
Innsbruck Cities 100,000 to 500,000
Arnsberg Cities 50,000 to 100,000
Pápa Cities under 50,000

⊛ ★ Capital symbols
■ • City symbols

Scale 1: 4,390,000

0   20   40   60 mi
0 20 40 60 100 120 km

Lambert Conformal Conic

⊡ Points of interest
⋊ Passes
----- Canals
⟋ Dams
⊜ Glaciers
National Parks
Swamps
Sand areas

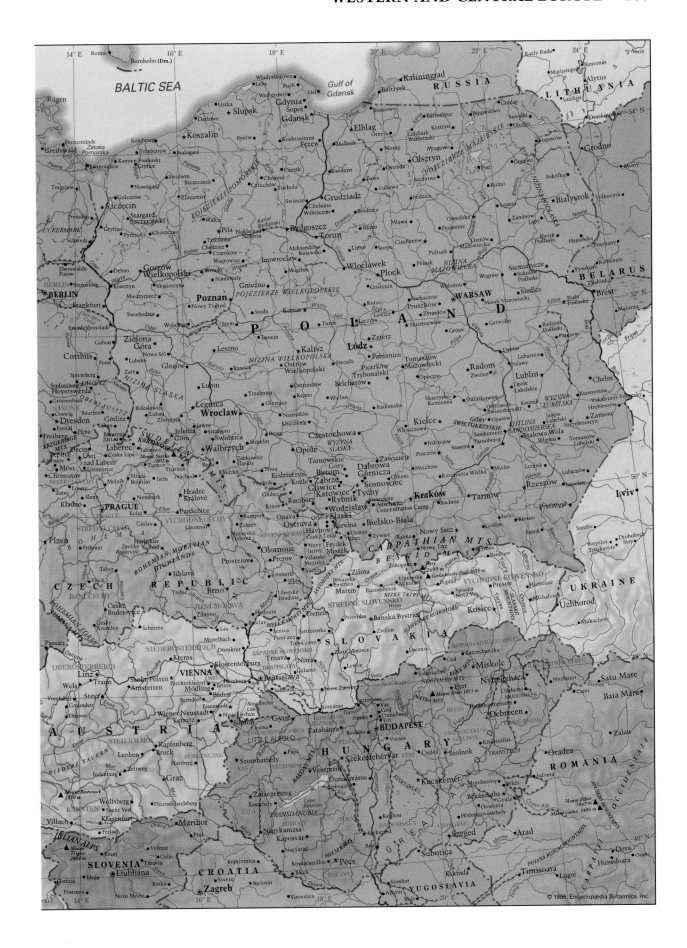

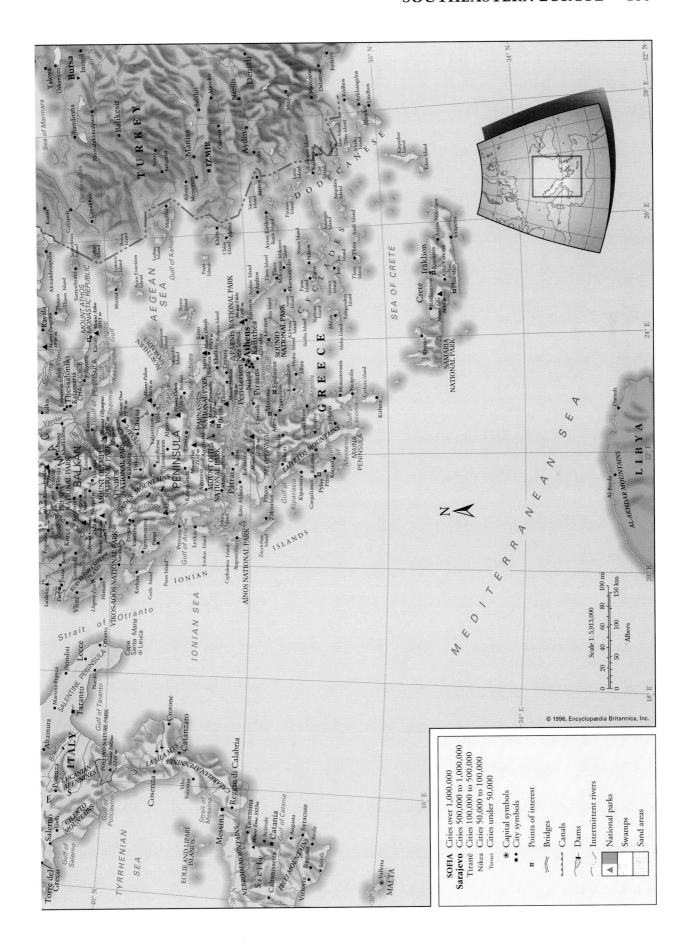

© 1996, Encyclopædia Britannica, Inc.

Scale 1:5,913,000
Albers

SOFIA Cities over 1,000,000
Sarajevo Cities 500,000 to 1,000,000
Tiranë Cities 100,000 to 500,000
Nikea Cities 50,000 to 100,000
Tecuci Cities under 50,000

✪ Capital symbols
▪• City symbols
⊡ Points of interest

) Bridges
⋯ Canals
⌐ Dams
∿ Intermittent rivers

National parks
Swamps
Sand areas

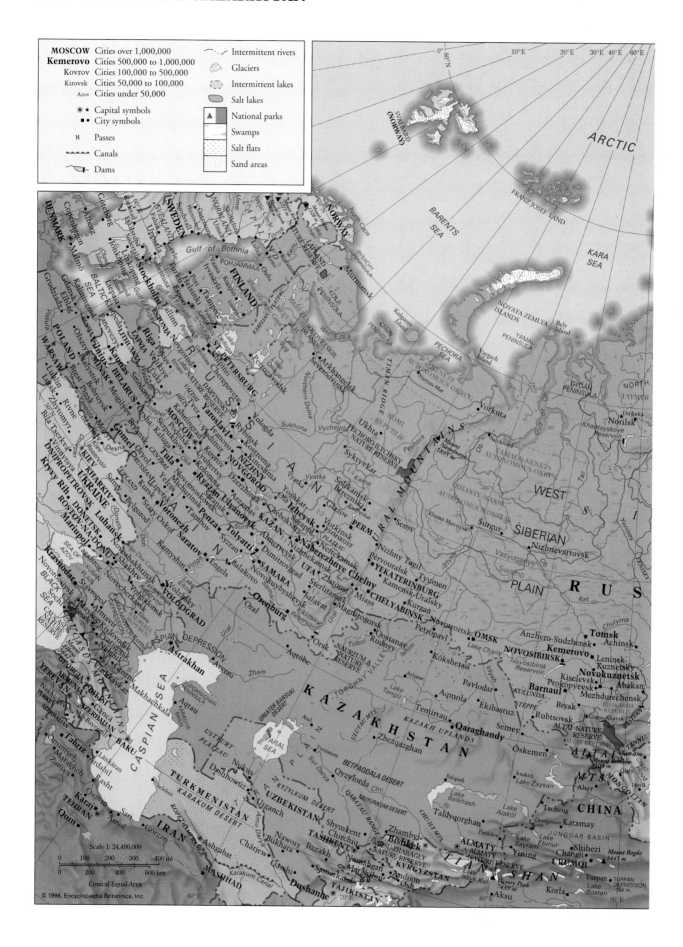

MOSCOW	Cities over 1,000,000
Kemerovo	Cities 500,000 to 1,000,000
Kovrov	Cities 100,000 to 500,000
Kirovsk	Cities 50,000 to 100,000
Azov	Cities under 50,000

⊛ ★ Capital symbols
▪ City symbols

ⴴ Passes
------ Canals
⌇┼ Dams

〜 Intermittent rivers
🌀 Glaciers
🌀 Intermittent lakes
🌀 Salt lakes
▲ National parks
  Swamps
  Salt flats
  Sand areas

Scale 1: 24,490,000

0 100 200 300 400 mi

0 200 400 600 km

Conical Equal-Area

© 1996, Encyclopaedia Britannica, Inc.

Key to Political subdivision names (shown by number on map):

1 ADYGEA REPUBLIC
2 KARACHAY-CHERKESSIA REPUBLIC
3 KABARDINO-BALKARIA REPUBLIC
4 NORTH OSSETIA (ALANIA) REPUBLIC
5 CHECHNIA REPUBLIC
6 DAGESTAN REPUBLIC
7 INGUSHETIA REPUBLIC
8 MORDVINIA REPUBLIC

9   CHUVASHIA REPUBLIC
10 MARI EL REPUBLIC
11 TATARSTAN REPUBLIC
12 UDMURTIA REPUBLIC
13 BASHKORTOSTAN REPUBLIC
14 KOMI-PERMYAK AUTONOMOUS OKRUG
15 UST-ORDA BURYAT AUTONOMOUS OKRUG
16 AGA-BURYAT AUTONOMOUS OKRUG

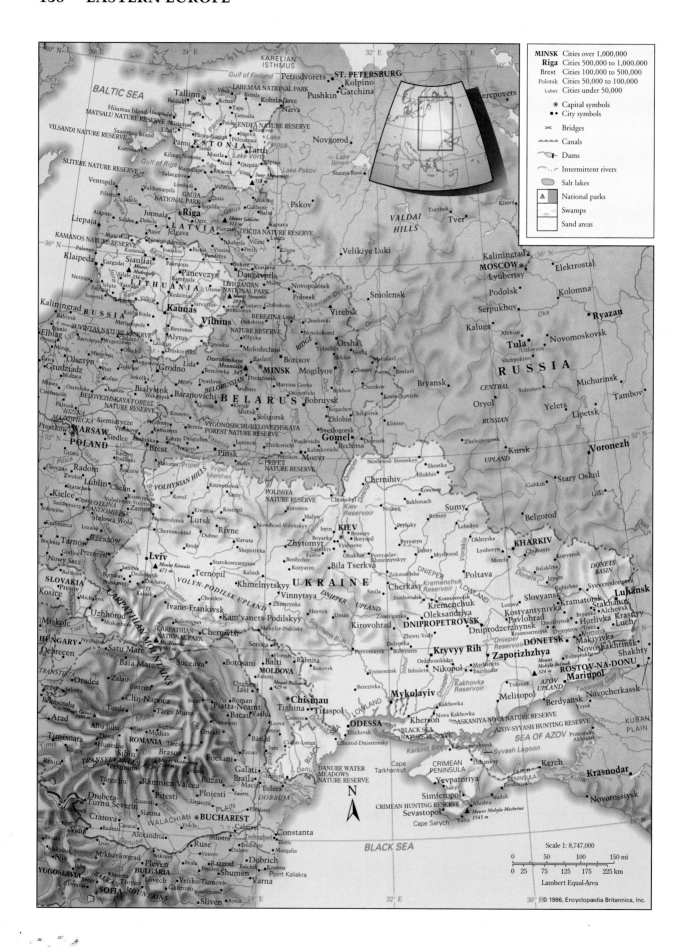

MINSK Cities over 1,000,000
Riga Cities 500,000 to 1,000,000
Brest Cities 100,000 to 500,000
Polotsk Cities 50,000 to 100,000
Lubny Cities under 50,000

⊛ Capital symbols
■ • City symbols

⤨ Bridges
     Canals
     Dams
     Intermittent rivers
     Salt lakes
▲ National parks
     Swamps
     Sand areas

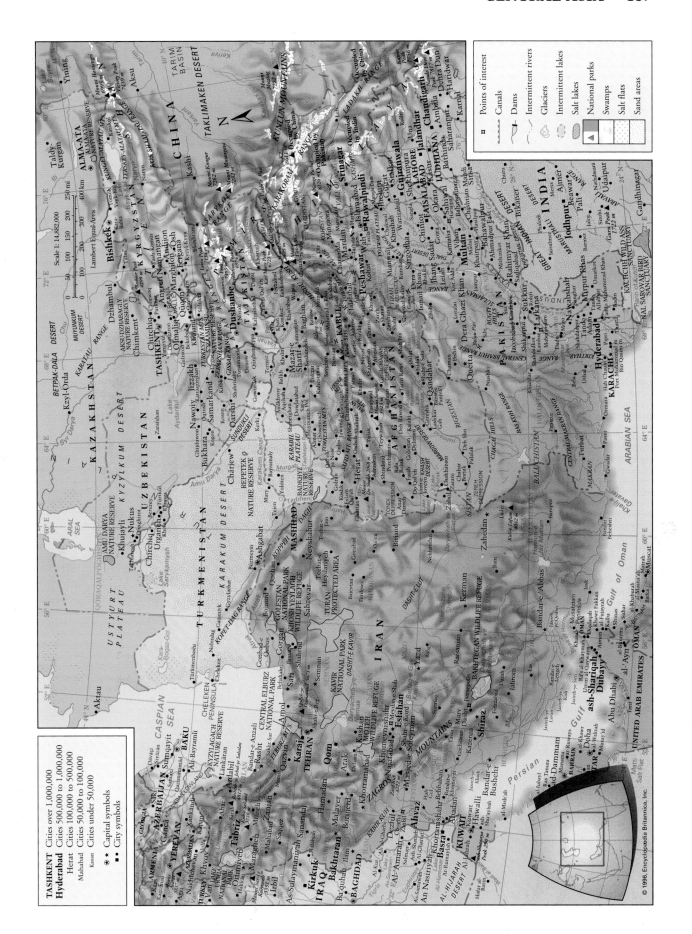

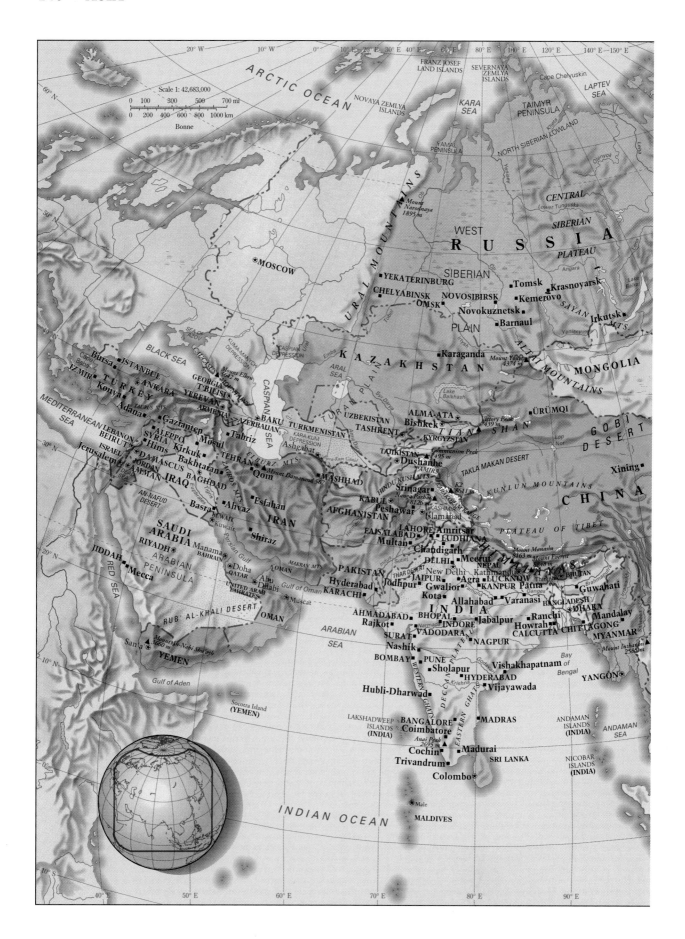

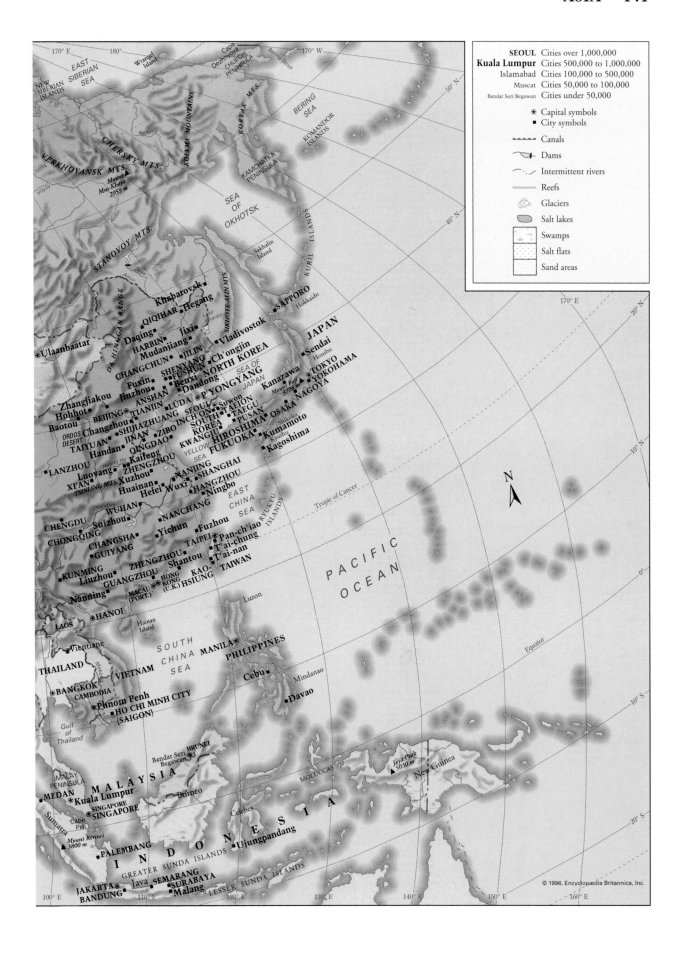

Legend:

SEOUL — Cities over 1,000,000
Kuala Lumpur — Cities 500,000 to 1,000,000
Islamabad — Cities 100,000 to 500,000
Muscat — Cities 50,000 to 100,000
Bandar Seri Begawan — Cities under 50,000

⊛ Capital symbols
■ City symbols

------ Canals
Dams
Intermittent rivers
Reefs
Glaciers
Salt lakes
Swamps
Salt flats
Sand areas

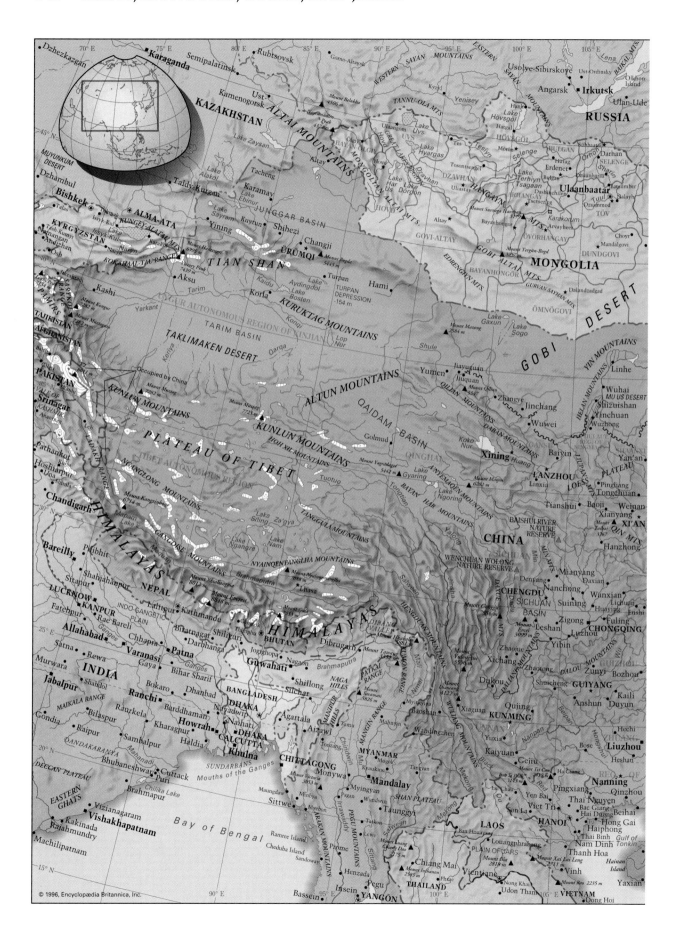

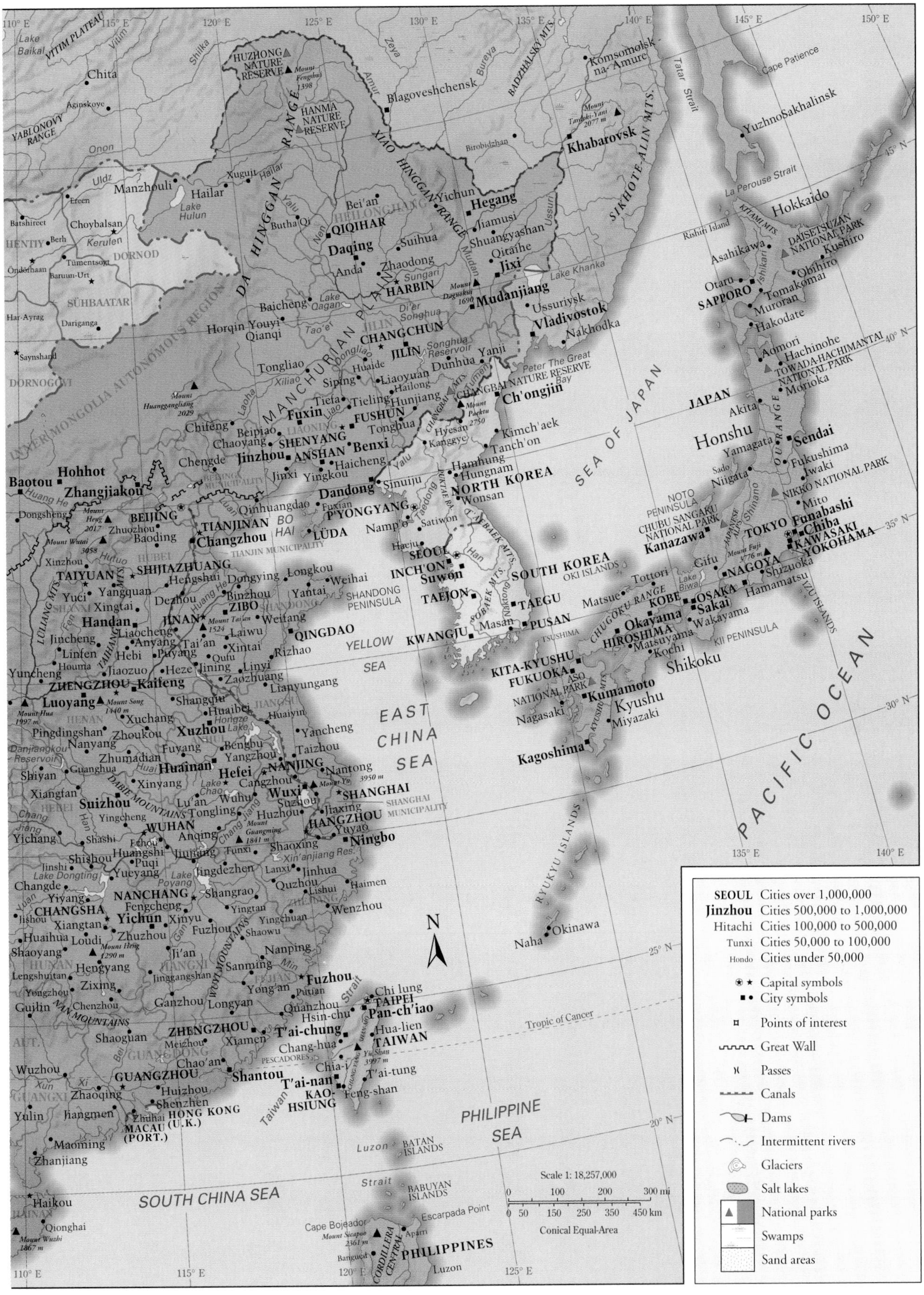
SEOUL Cities over 1,000,000
Jinzhou Cities 500,000 to 1,000,000
Hitachi Cities 100,000 to 500,000
Tunxi Cities 50,000 to 100,000
Hondo Cities under 50,000
Capital symbols
City symbols
Points of interest
Great Wall
Passes
Canals
Dams
Intermittent rivers
Glaciers
Salt lakes
National parks
Swamps
Sand areas
Scale 1: 18,257,000
0 100 200 300 mi
0 50 150 250 350 450 km
Conical Equal-Area
N
SEA OF JAPAN
PACIFIC OCEAN
EAST CHINA SEA
YELLOW SEA
SOUTH CHINA SEA
PHILIPPINE SEA
BO HAI
JAPAN
NORTH KOREA
SOUTH KOREA
TAIWAN
PHILIPPINES
HONG KONG (U.K.)
MACAU (PORT.)
Hokkaido
Honshu
Shikoku
Kyushu
Luzon
RYUKYU ISLANDS
Tropic of Cancer
BEIJING
TIANJIN
SHANGHAI
SEOUL
P'YONGYANG
TOKYO
TAIPEI
HARBIN
CHANGCHUN
SHENYANG
WUHAN
NANJING
HANGZHOU
GUANGZHOU
OSAKA
YOKOHAMA
SAPPORO
Vladivostok
Khabarovsk
DA HINGGAN RANGE
XIAO HINGGAN RANGE
SIKHOTE-ALIN MTS.
MANCHURIAN PLAIN
INNER MONGOLIA AUTONOMOUS REGION
SHANDONG PENINSULA
La Perouse Strait
Tatar Strait
Lake Baikal
Chita
Okinawa
Naha
Hainan
Haikou

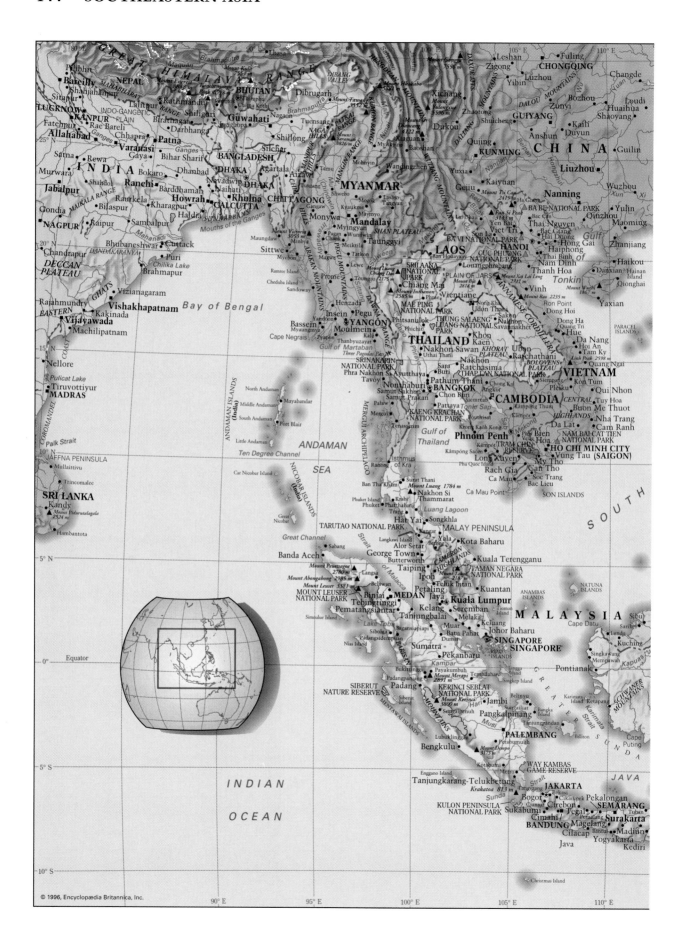

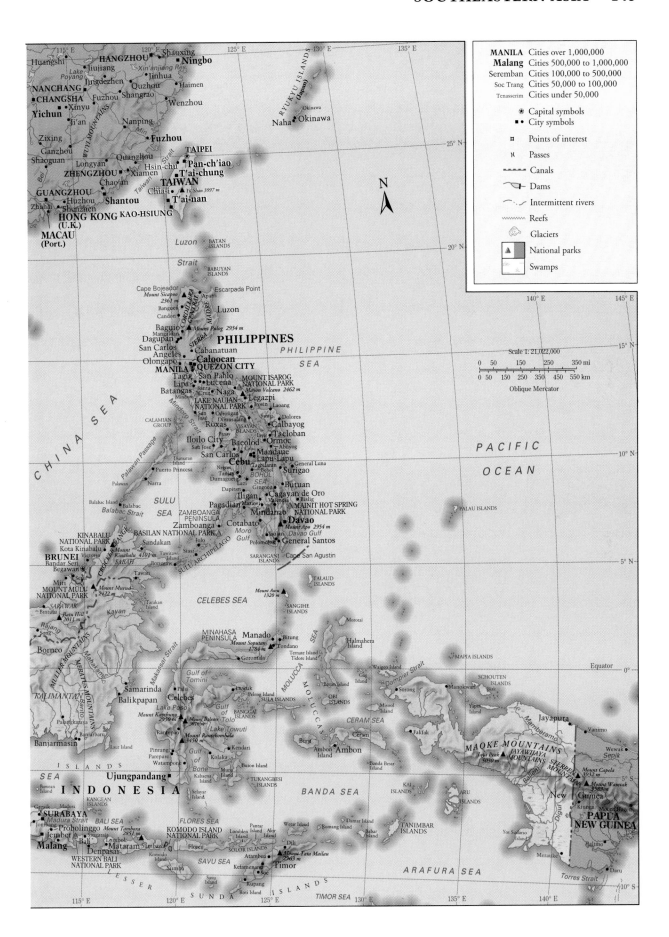

Legend:

MANILA	Cities over 1,000,000
Malang	Cities 500,000 to 1,000,000
Seremban	Cities 100,000 to 500,000
Soc Trang	Cities 50,000 to 100,000
Tenasserim	Cities under 50,000
⊛	Capital symbols
▪	City symbols
⊡	Points of interest
⋈	Passes
-----	Canals
	Dams
	Intermittent rivers
wwwww	Reefs
	Glaciers
▲	National parks
	Swamps

Scale 1: 21,022,000

0 50   150   250   350 mi
0 50 150 250 350 450 550 km

Oblique Mercator

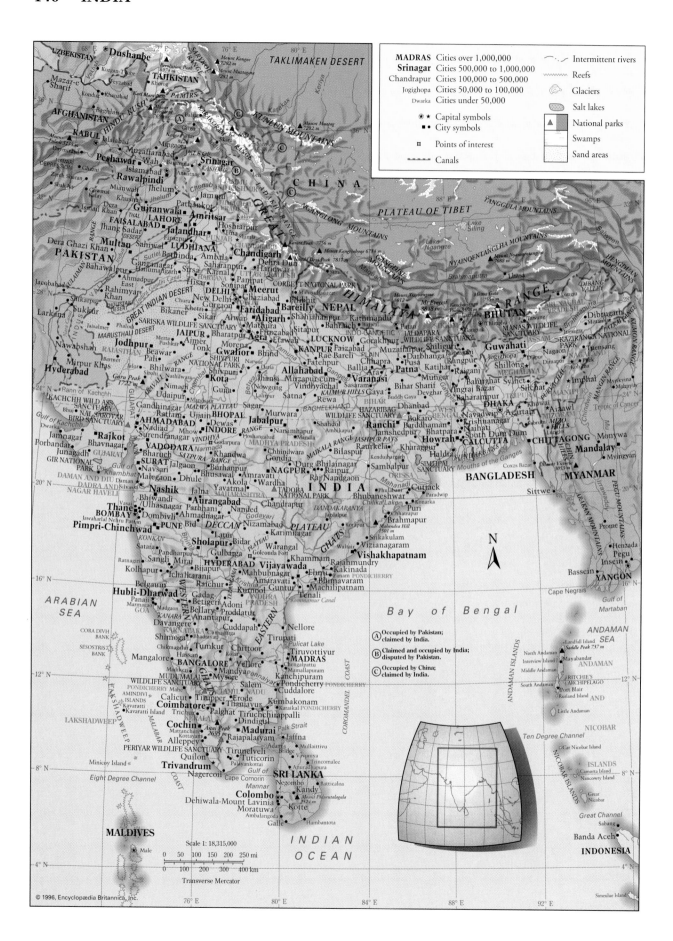

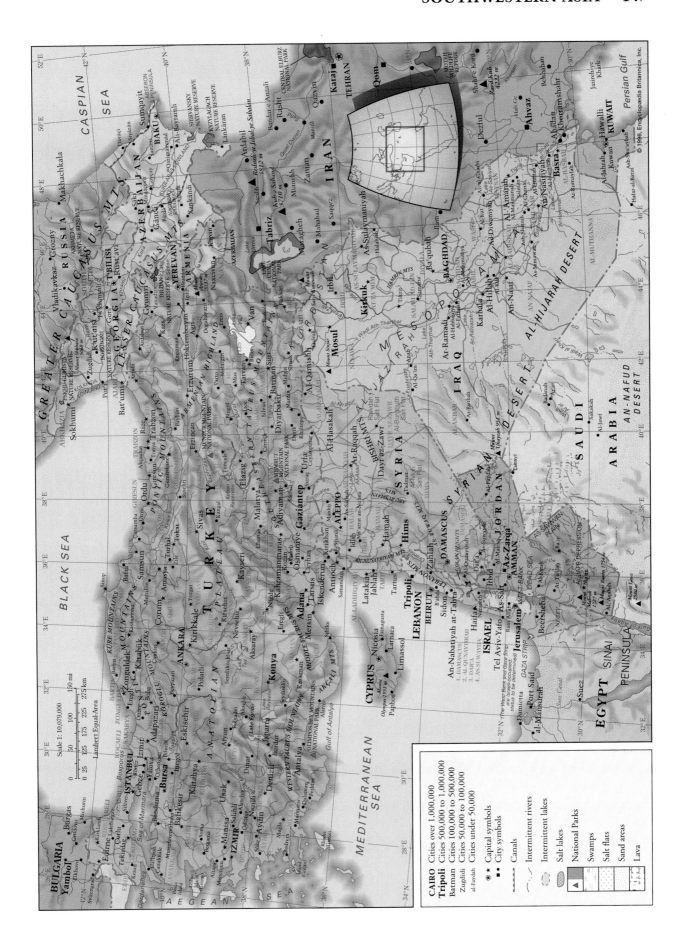

© 1996, Encyclopædia Britannica, Inc.

Map legend:

CAIRO	Cities over 1,000,000
Tripoli	Cities 500,000 to 1,000,000
Batman	Cities 100,000 to 500,000
Zugdidi	Cities 50,000 to 100,000
al-Faydah	Cities under 50,000

- ✴ ★ Capital symbols
- ✴ ■ City symbols
- Canals
- Intermittent rivers
- Intermittent lakes
- Salt lakes
- ▲ National Parks
- Swamps
- Salt flats
- Sand areas
- Lava

Scale 1: 10,079,000

Lambert Equal-Area

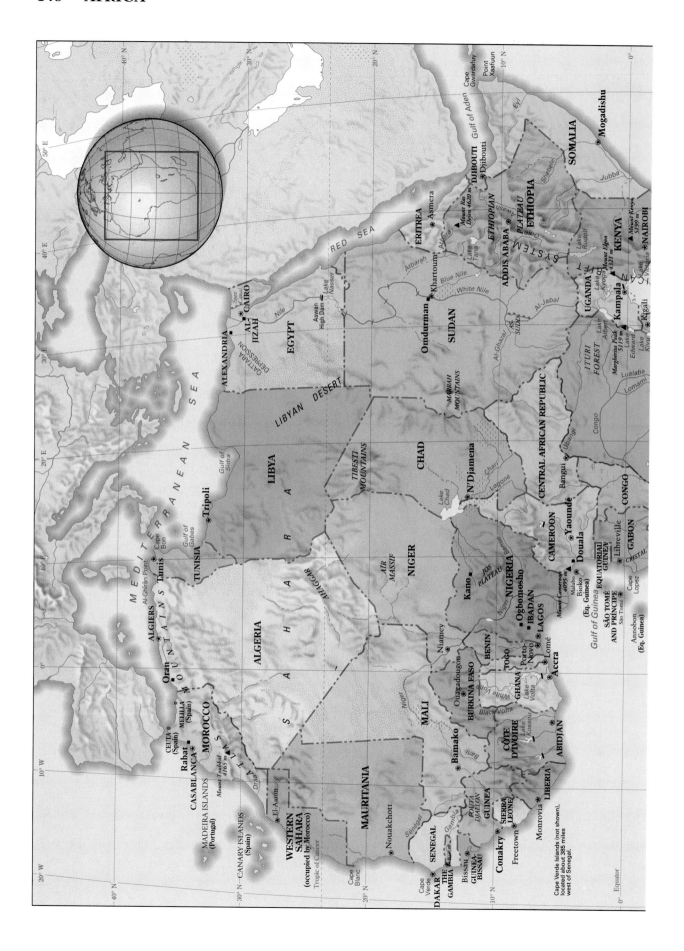

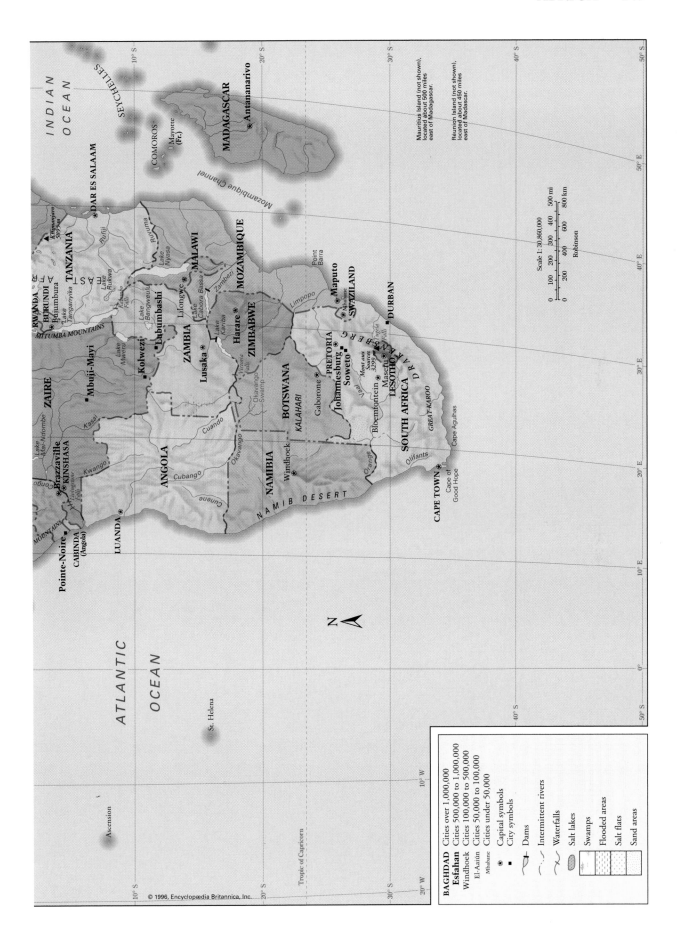

Mauritius Island (not shown), located about 500 miles east of Madagascar.

Reunion Island (not shown), located about 450 miles east of Madagascar.

Scale 1: 30,860,000

Robinson

BAGHDAD Cities over 1,000,000
Esfahan Cities 500,000 to 1,000,000
Windhoek Cities 100,000 to 500,000
El-Aaiún Cities 50,000 to 100,000
Mbabane Cities under 50,000

⊛ Capital symbols
■ City symbols

▬ Dams
Intermittent rivers
Waterfalls
Salt lakes
Swamps
Flooded areas
Salt flats
Sand areas

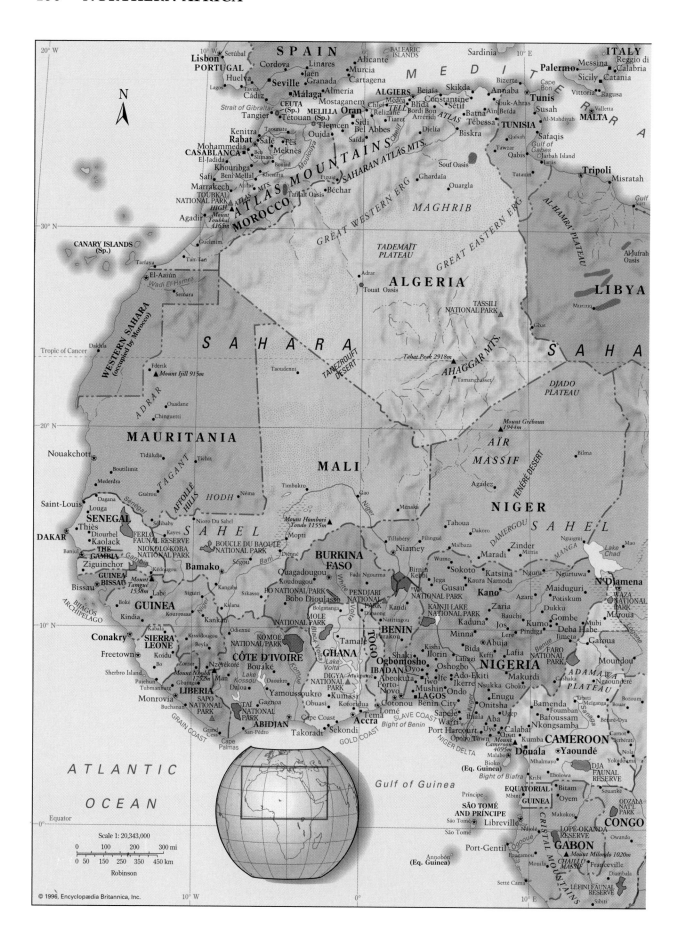

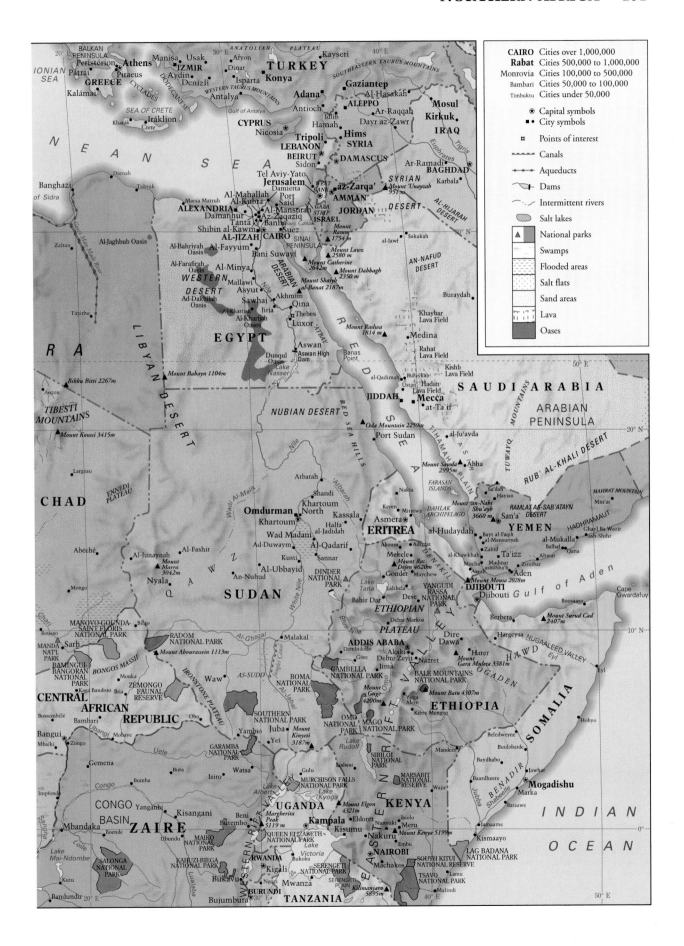

Map legend:

CAIRO	Cities over 1,000,000
Rabat	Cities 500,000 to 1,000,000
Monrovia	Cities 100,000 to 500,000
Bambari	Cities 50,000 to 100,000
Timbuktu	Cities under 50,000
⊛	Capital symbols
∙	City symbols
□	Points of interest
⊷	Canals
⊶	Aqueducts
⊨	Dams
⌇	Intermittent rivers
◠	Salt lakes
▲	National parks
	Swamps
	Flooded areas
	Salt flats
	Sand areas
	Lava
	Oases

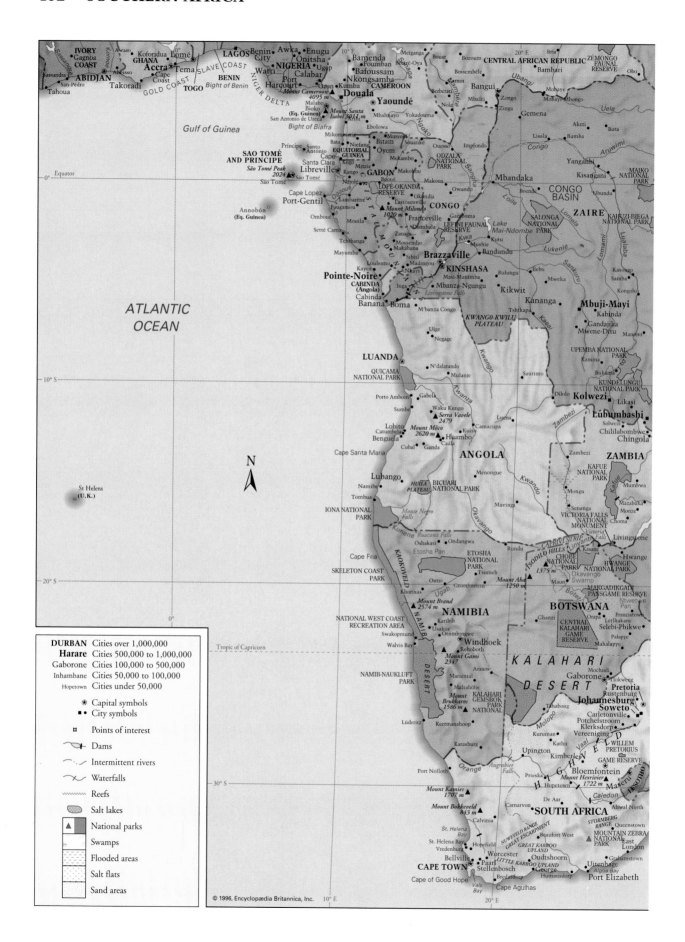

Legend:

DURBAN	Cities over 1,000,000
Harare	Cities 500,000 to 1,000,000
Gaborone	Cities 100,000 to 500,000
Inhambane	Cities 50,000 to 100,000
Hopetown	Cities under 50,000

⊛ Capital symbols

▪ City symbols

⊡ Points of interest

⊱ Dams

Intermittent rivers

Waterfalls

Reefs

Salt lakes

▲ National parks

Swamps

Flooded areas

Salt flats

Sand areas

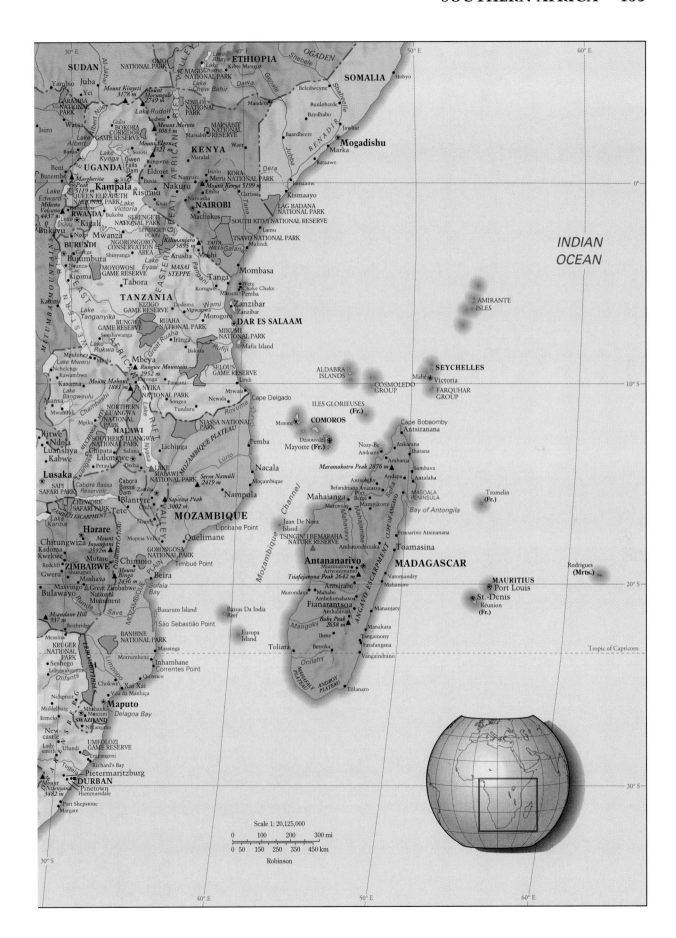

30° E

SUDAN

Yambio • Juba
• Yei

GARAMBA NATIONAL PARK

Mount Kinyeti 3178 m
Mount Morungole 2749 m

OMO NATIONAL PARK

Lake Abaya
Lake Chamo   Kibre Mengist
• Chew Bahir

ETHIOPIA

Dawa

MAGO NATIONAL PARK

Shebele

OGADEN

Genale

Beledweyne

SOMALIA

Hobyo

40° E

50° E

60° E

• Isiro
• Watsa

Gulu •
BOKORA CORRIDOR GAME RESERVE
Kidwal
Mount Moroto 3083 m

SIBILOI NATIONAL PARK

Mandera

Mount Eldon 4321 m

MARSABIT NATIONAL RESERVE

Marsabit •

• Buulobarde

Baydhabo

BENADIR

• Burao
Lake Albert
Lake Kyoga
Soroti •
Bungoma

Wajir •

• Baardheere

Jawhar •

• Baraawe

• Beni
Butembo •

UGANDA

Margherita Peak 5119 m
QUEEN ELIZABETH NATIONAL PARK

Kampala
Owen Falls Dam

Iliki
Busia

Maralal •

Isiolo •
Meru
KORA NATIONAL PARK

Dera

Mogadishu

Marka •

Lake Edward
Mikeno Volcano 4437 m

Kisumu
Nakuru

Eldoret •
Nanyuki •

KENYA

Mount Kenya 5199 m

Lake Victoria

RWANDA
Kigali •

Kisii •
Naivasha •

Embu •

Garissa •

Jamaame •

0°

Bukavu •
Lake Kivu

Ngozi •

Bukoba •

NAIROBI
Machakos •

SOUTH KITUI NATIONAL RESERVE

Kismaayo •

BURUNDI
Bujumbura •

Mwanza •

SERENGETI NATIONAL PARK
SERENGETI PLAIN

Lamu •

LAG BADANA NATIONAL PARK

Gitega •
Nyanza-Lac •
Kigoma •

Shinyanga •
NGORONGORO CONSERVATION AREA

Kilimanjaro 5895 m

Arusha •

TSAVO NATIONAL PARK

Tabora •

MOYOWOSI GAME RESERVE
Lake Eyasi

Moshi •

MASAI STEPPE

Galana

Malindi •

Kalemie •

TANZANIA

Dodoma •
KIZIGO GAME RESERVE

Pangani

Korogwe •

Tanga •

Mombasa •

Lake Tanganyika

Mpulungu •
Lake Rukwa

RUAHA NATIONAL PARK
Mpwapwa •
RUNGWA GAME RESERVE

Wete •
Chake Chake •
Mkoani •

Pemba

Morogoro •

Zanzibar •
Zanzibar

INDIAN
OCEAN

AMIRANTE ISLES

Lake Mweru
Nchelenge •
Kawambwa •

Mbala •

Mbeya •

Rungwe Mountain 2952 m

Iringa •

DAR ES SALAAM

MIKUMI NATIONAL PARK

Kasama •
Lake Bangweulu

Mount Mahoni 1881 m

NYIKA NATIONAL PARK

Panhani

Ifakata •

Mafia Island

Mansa •
Mwinilunga •

Karonga •

Songea •

SELOUS GAME RESERVE

SEYCHELLES

Mpika •

NORTHERN LUANGWA NATIONAL PARK

Tunduru •

Lindi •

Newala •

Cape Delgado

ALDABRA ISLANDS

Mahé •
Victoria •

Kitwe •
Ndola •

Chambeshi

MALAWI

Lichinga •

NIASSA NATIONAL PARK

Rovuma

Mtwara •

ILES GLORIEUSES (Fr.)

COSMOLEDO GROUP

FARQUHAR GROUP

10° S

Luanshya •
Kabwe •

SOUTHERN LUANGWA NATIONAL PARK
Chipata •
Salima •

Lilongwe •

Pemba •

Moroni •

COMOROS

Cape Bobaomby
Antsiranana •

Lusaka •
SAPI SAFARI PARK

Petauke •
Dedza •

LAKE MALAWI NATIONAL PARK

Nacala •

Dzaouvdzi •
Mayotte (Fr.)

Nosy-Be •
Andoany •

Ankarana
Iharana •

Cabora Bassa Reservoir

CHEWORE SAFARI PARK

Serra Namúli 2419 m

Zomba •

Moçambique •

Maromokotro Peak 2876 m

Ambanja •

Sambava •

ZAMBEZI ESCARPMENT
Lake Kariba

Cabora Bassa Dam
Tete •

Sapitwa Peak 3002 m
Blantyre •

Chiri

Nampula •

Antsohihy •

Andapa •

Antalaha •

MASOALA PENINSULA

Tromelin (Fr.)

Harare •
Chitungwiza •
Kadoma •

Mount Inyangani 2592 m

GORONGOSA NATIONAL PARK

Lipobane Point

Quelimane •

Juan De Nova Island

TSINGIN'I BEMARAHA NATURE RESERVE

Befandriana Avaratra •
Port-Bergé •

Mahajanga •

Sofia

Maevatanana •

Bay of Antongila

Fenoarivo Atsinanana •

Kwekwe •
Redcliff •
Gweru •
Shurugwi •
Mashava •

ZIMBABWE

Mutare •
Chimoio •

Mount Nyangani 2436 m

ZAMBEZI PLAIN

Timbuè Point

Beira •

Ambatondrazaka •

Mahavavy

Mampikony •

ANGAVO ESCARPMENT
CLIFF OF ANGAVO

Toamasina •

Bulawayo •
Masvingo •

Great Zimbabwe National Monument

Sofala Bay

Antananarivo
Marinarivo •
Arivonimamo •

MADAGASCAR

Vatomandry •

MAURITIUS

Rodrigues (Mrts.)

20° S

Msandane Hill 937 m
Beitbridge •

Bazaruto Island

Tsiafajavona Peak 2642 m

Antsirabe •

Mahanoro •

Port Louis •

Messina •

Save

Bassas Da India Reef

São Sebastião Point

Mahabo •
Morondava •
Ambohimahasoa •

Fianarantsoa •
Ambalavao •

Mananjary •

St.-Denis •
Réunion (Fr.)

KRUGER NATIONAL PARK

Seshego •
Lebowakgomo •

BANHINE NATIONAL PARK

Massinga •

Europa Island

Boby Peak 2658 m

Manakara •

Olifants
Limpopo

Morrumbene •

Ihosy •

Manakara •
Tangainony •

Nelspruit •

Inhambane •
Correntes Point

Toliara •

Betroka •

Tarafangana •

Chokwe •
Xai Xai •

Quissico •

Vangaindrano •

Tropic of Capricorn

Vila da Manhiça •

MAHAFALY PLATEAU

Middelburg •

Maputo
Delagoa Bay

Onilahy

Ermelo •

SWAZILAND
Nhlangano •

ANDROY PLATEAU
Tôlanaro •

Newcastle •
Ladysmith •

UMFOLOZI GAME RESERVE
Empangeni •

Ulundi •

Mbabane •

Richard's Bay •

Mount Ntlenyana 3482 m

Pietermaritzburg •

DURBAN
Pinetown •

Hammarsdale •

30° S

Port Shepstone •
Margate •

Scale 1: 20,125,000

0   100   200   300 mi

0 50 150 250 350 450 km

Robinson

30° S

40° E

50° E

60° E

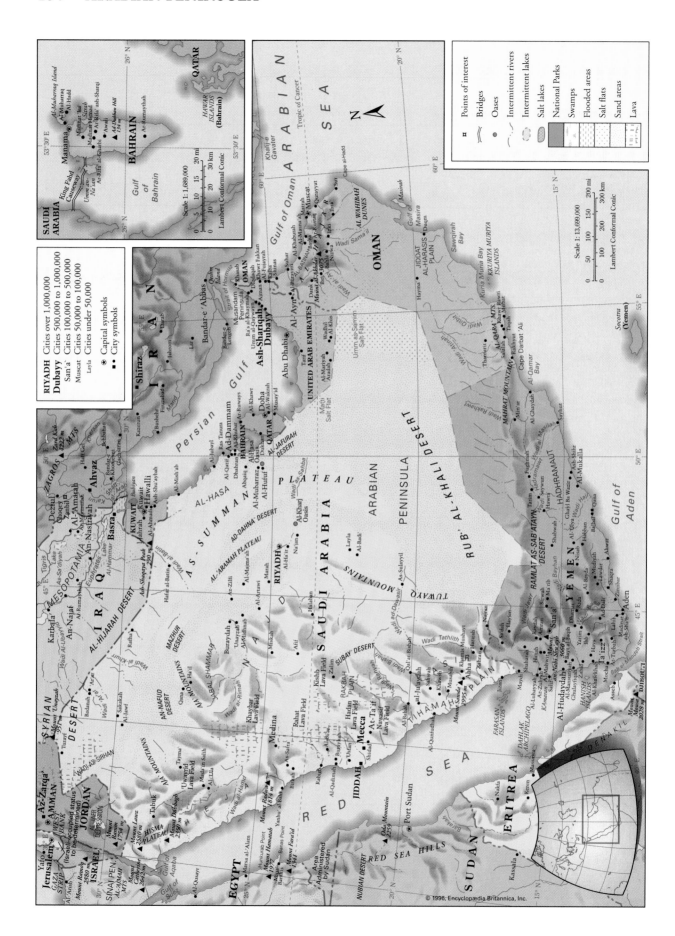

© 1996, Encyclopædia Britannica, Inc.

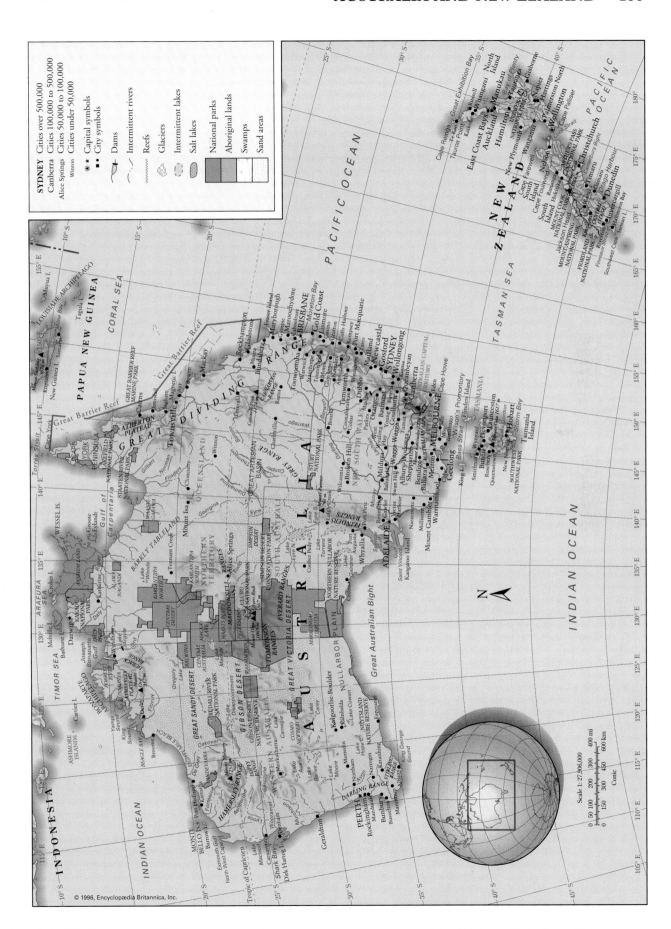

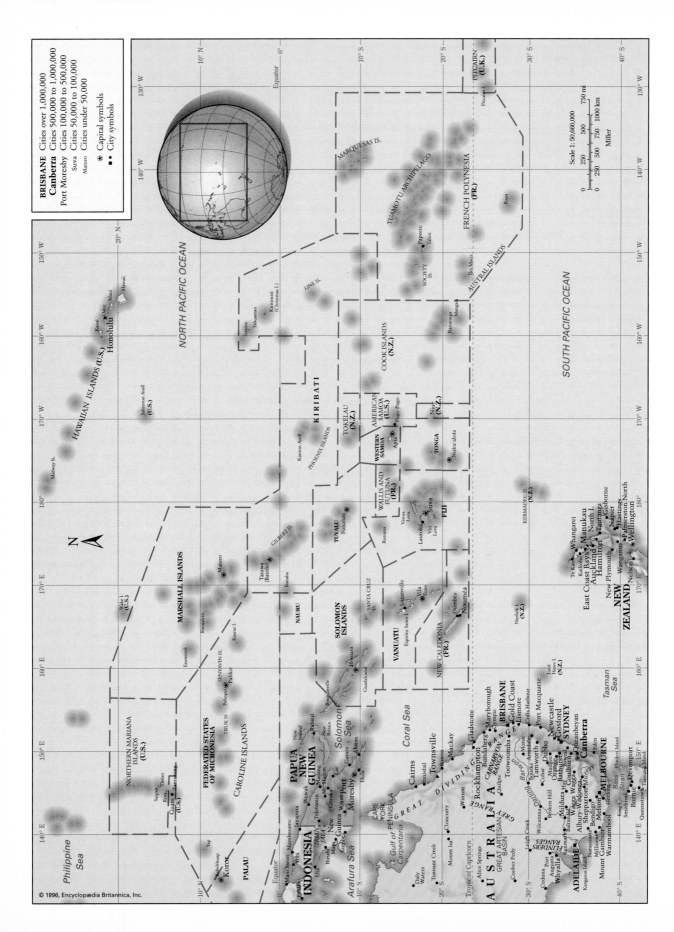

BRISBANE   Cities over 1,000,000
Canberra   Cities 500,000 to 1,000,000
Port Moresby   Cities 100,000 to 500,000
Suva   Cities 50,000 to 100,000
Majuro   Cities under 50,000

⊛ Capital symbols
■ • City symbols

Scale 1:50,660,000

N

NORTH PACIFIC OCEAN

SOUTH PACIFIC OCEAN

Philippine Sea

HAWAIIAN ISLANDS (U.S.)
Honolulu
Hawaii
Oahu
Maui
Kauai

Midway Ik.

Johnston Atoll (U.S.)

Wake I. (U.S.)

MARSHALL ISLANDS
Majuro

Enewetak
Kwajalein
Kosrae I.
Ponape I.

NORTHERN MARIANA ISLANDS (U.S.)
Saipan
Rota
Tinian
Guam (U.S.)

FEDERATED STATES OF MICRONESIA
CAROLINE ISLANDS
TRUK IS.
SENYAVIN IS.
Palikir
Yap

PALAU
Koror

INDONESIA

MARQUESAS IS.

TUAMOTU ARCHIPELAGO

FRENCH POLYNESIA (FR.)

Rapa

SOCIETY IS.
Papeete
Tahiti
Ile Maiao

AUSTRAL ISLANDS
Rurutu
Tubuai
Raivavae
Mangaia

LINE IS.
Teraina
Tabuaeran
Kiritimati (Christmas I.)

KIRIBATI
Kanton Atoll
PHOENIX ISLANDS

COOK ISLANDS (N.Z.)

TOKELAU (N.Z.)
AMERICAN SAMOA (U.S.)
Pago Pago

WESTERN SAMOA
Apia

Niue (N.Z.)

TONGA
Nuku'alofa

WALLIS AND FUTUNA (FR.)

TUVALU
Funafuti

GILBERT IS.
Tarawa (Bairiki)
Banaba

NAURU

SANTA CRUZ IS.

SOLOMON ISLANDS
Guadalcanal
Honiara
Bougainville

FIJI
Suva
Viti Levu
Vanua Levu
Lautoka
Rotuma

VANUATU
Luganville
Vila (Efate)

NEW CALEDONIA (FR.)
Noumea
Dumbea
Espiritu Santo I.

KERMADEC IS. (N.Z.)

Norfolk I. (N.Z.)

Lord Howe I. (N.Z.)

PITCAIRN (U.K.)
Pitcairn I.

NEW ZEALAND
Whangarei
Te Kao
Kaikohe
East Coast Bays
Auckland
Manukau
North I.
Hamilton
Tauranga
Gisborne
Napier
Hastings
Palmerston North
Wanganui
New Plymouth
Nelson
Wellington

Coral Sea

Solomon Sea

Arafura Sea

Tasman Sea

Bass Strait

Tropic of Capricorn

Equator

PAPUA NEW GUINEA
Port Moresby
Lae
Madang
Wewak
Goroka
Mt. Hagen
Popondetta
Rabaul
New Britain
New Ireland
Jayapura
Manokwari
Merauke
Sorong
New Guinea
Hula

CAPE YORK PENINSULA

Gulf of Carpentaria

GREAT DIVIDING RANGE

GREAT ARTESIAN BASIN

GREY RANGE

FLINDERS RANGES

AUSTRALIA

Cairns
Innisfail
Townsville
Mackay
Rockhampton
Gladstone
Bundaberg
Maryborough
BRISBANE
Gold Coast
Lismore
Toowoomba
Coffs Harbour
Port Macquarie
Newcastle
Gosford
SYDNEY
Wollongong
Canberra
Queanbeyan
MELBOURNE
Geelong
Warrnambool
Portland
Mount Gambier
ADELAIDE
Whyalla
Port Augusta
Kangaroo Island
Ceduna
Coober Pedy
Alice Springs
Tennant Creek
Daly Waters
Mount Isa
Cloncurry
Winton
Longreach
Charleville
Quilpie
Leigh Creek
Broken Hill
Wilcannia
Bourke
Dubbo
Orange
Bathurst
Goulburn
Wagga Wagga
Albury-Wodonga
Shepparton
Bendigo
Ballarat
Mildura
Cobar
Tamworth
Armidale
Moree
Narrabri
Griffith
Naracoorte
Millicent
Melton
Launceston
Burnie
Devonport
Smithton
Queenstown
TASMANIA
Flinders Island
King Island

© 1996, Encyclopædia Britannica, Inc.

AFGHANISTAN ....pg. 139

Capital: ....Kabul
Area: ....652,225 sq km; 251,825 sq mi
Highest Elev.: .....Mt. Nowshak 7,490 m; 24,580 ft
Longest River: ....Amu 2,540 km; 1,580 mi
Avg. Temperature: . .Jan = -3°C; Jul = 25°C
Currency: ....Afghani
Official Language: . .Pashto, Dari (Persian)

Name	Lat./Long.
Adraskan	33°39' N, 062°16' E
Ajrestan	33°31' N, 067°11' E
Almar	35°50' N, 064°32' E
Anar Darreh	32°46' N, 061°39' E
Andkhvoy	36°56' N, 065°08' E
Aqchah	36°56' N, 066°11' E
Asadabad	34°52' N, 071°09' E
Baghlan	36°13' N, 068°46' E
Baghran	33°04' N, 065°05' E
Balkh (Bactra)	36°46' N, 066°54' E
Bala Boluk	32°38' N, 062°28' E
Bamian (Bamyan)	34°50' N, 067°50' E
Banow	35°38' N, 069°15' E
Baraki	33°58' N, 068°58' E
Bazar-e Panjva'i	31°32' N, 065°28' E
Chahar Borjak	30°17' N, 062°03' E
Chaghcharan	34°31' N, 065°15' E
Chakhansur	31°10' N, 062°04' E
Deh Rawod	32°37' N, 065°27' E
Deh Shu	30°26' N, 063°19' E
Delaram	32°11' N, 063°25' E
Do Qal'eh	32°08' N, 061°27' E
Dowlatabad	36°26' N, 064°55' E
Duraj	37°56' N, 070°43' E
Eshkashem	36°42' N, 071°34' E
Eslam Qal'eh	34°40' N, 061°04' E
Farah (Farrah, Ferah)	32°22' N, 062°07' E
Feyzabad (Faizabad)	37°06' N, 070°34' E
Gardeyz (Gardez)	33°37' N, 069°07' E
Gereshk	31°48' N, 064°34' E
Ghazni	33°33' N, 068°26' E
Ghowrmach	35°44' N, 063°47' E
Ghurian	34°21' N, 061°30' E
Gizab	33°23' N, 066°16' E
Golestan	32°37' N, 063°39' E
Golran	35°06' N, 061°41' E
Gowmal Kalay	32°31' N, 068°51' E
Herat (Harat)	34°20' N, 062°12' E
Jalalabad	34°26' N, 070°28' E
Jaldak	31°58' N, 066°43' E
Jawand	35°04' N, 064°09' E
Kabul	34°31' N, 069°12' E
Kajaki	32°16' N, 065°03' E
Keshendeh (Aq Kopruk)	36°05' N, 066°51' E
Khadir	33°55' N, 065°56' E
Khanabad	36°41' N, 069°07' E
Kholm	36°42' N, 067°41' E
Khowst	33°22' N, 069°57' E
Konduz (Qonduz)	36°45' N, 068°51' E
Koshk	34°57' N, 062°15' E
Kowt-e 'Ashrow (Maidanshar)	34°27' N, 068°48' E
Kuhestanat	35°49' N, 065°52' E
Khwazagak	34°53' N, 065°18' E
Lash-e Joveyn	31°43' N, 061°37' E
Lashkar Gah (Bust)	31°35' N, 064°21' E
Mahmud-e Raqi	35°01' N, 069°20' E
Mazar-e Sharif	36°42' N, 067°06' E
Meymaneh (Maimana)	35°55' N, 064°47' E
Mundul	35°17' N, 070°10' E
Navor	33°53' N, 067°57' E
Owbeh	34°22' N, 063°10' E
Palalak	30°14' N, 062°54' E
Panjab	34°22' N, 067°01' E
Pasaband	33°41' N, 064°51' E
Qades	34°48' N, 063°26' E
Qal'eh-ye Now	34°59' N, 063°08' E
Qalat	32°07' N, 066°54' E
Qandahar (Kandahar)	31°35' N, 065°45' E
Samangan (Aybak)	36°16' N, 068°01' E
Sar-e Pol	36°14' N, 065°55' E
Sayghan	35°11' N, 067°42' E
Shah Juy	32°31' N, 067°25' E
Shahr-e Safa	31°50' N, 066°22' E
Shahrak	34°06' N, 064°18' E
Shahrestan	33°41'N, 066°33' E
Sheberghan (Shebirghan, Shibarghan)	36°41' N, 065°45' E
Shindand (Sabzevar)	33°18' N, 062°08' E
Shir Khan	37°11' N, 068°36' E
Tarin Kowt	32°38' N, 065°52' E
Teywarah	33°21' N, 064°25' E
Tokzar	35°52' N, 066°26' E
Tulak	33°58' N, 063°44' E
Warsaj	36°12' N, 070°02' E
Yangi Qal'eh	37°28' N, 069°36' E
Zareh Sharan	33°08' N, 068°47' E
Zarghun Shahr	32°51' N, 068°25' E

ALBANIA ....pg. 134

Capital: ....Tiranë
Area: ....28,748 sq km; 11,100 sq mi
Highest Elev.: .....Mt. Korab 2,750 m; 9,030 ft
Longest River: .....Drin 280 km; 170 mi
Avg. Temperature: . .Jan = 7°C; Jul = 25°C
Currency: ....lek
Official Language: . .Albanian

Name	Lat./Long.
Berat	40°42' N, 019°57' E
Cerrik	41°02' N, 019°57' E
Çorovodë	40°30' N, 020°13' E
Durres	41°19' N, 019°26' E
Elbasan	41°06' N, 020°05' E
Fier	40°43' N, 019°34' E
Himare	40°07' N, 019°44' E
Kavajë	41°11' N, 019°33' E
Korce (Koritsa)	40°37' N, 020°46' E
Laç	41°38' N, 019°43' E
Patos	40°38' N, 019°39' E
Pogradec	40°54' N, 020°39' E
Puke	42°03' N, 019°54' E
Sarandë	39°52' N, 020°00' E
Shkoder (Scutari)	42°05' N, 019°30' E
Tiranë (Tirana)	41°20' N, 019°50' E
Vlore	40°27' N, 019°30' E
Vorë	41°23' N, 019°40' E

ALGERIA ....pg. 150

Capital: ....Algiers
Area: ....2,381,741 sq km; 919,595 sq mi
Highest Elev.: .....Mt. Tahat 2,920 m; 9,570 ft
Longest River: .....Chelif 730 km; 450 mi
Avg. Temperature: . .Jan = 12°C; Jul = 24°C
Currency: ....Algerian dinar
Official Language: . .Arabic

Name	Lat./Long.
Aïn Beïda (Daoud)	35°48' N, 007°24' E
Algiers (or Al-Jaza'ir)	36°47' N, 003°03' E
Annaba (Bone)	36°54' N, 007°46' E
Batna	35°34' N, 006°11' E
Béchar (Colomb-Bechar)	31°37' N, 002°13' W
Bejaïa (Bougie)	36°45' N, 005°05' E
Biskra (Beskra)	34°51' N, 005°44' E
Bordj Bou Arréridj	36°04' N, 004°47' E
Chlef (El-Asnam or Orleansville)	36°10' N, 001°20' E
Constantine (Qacentina)	36°22' N, 006°37' E
Ghardaïa	32°29' N, 003°40' E
Mostaganem (Mestghanem)	35°56' N, 000°05' E
Orleansville, *see* Chlef	
Oran (Wahran)	35°42' N, 000°38' W
Ouargla (Warqla)	31°57' N, 005°20' E
Qacentina, *see* Constantine	
Saïda	34°50' N, 000°09' E
Sétif (Stif)	36°12' N, 005°24' E
Sidi Bel Abbes	35°12' N, 000°38' W
Skikda (Philippeville)	36°52' N, 006°54' E
Souk-Ahras	36°17' N, 007°57' E
Stif, *see* Sétif	
Tébessa (Tbessa or Theveste)	35°24' N, 008°07' E
Tiaret (Tihert or Tagdempt)	35°22' N, 001°19' E
Tlemcen (Tilimsen)	34°52' N, 001°19' W
Wahran, *see* Oran	
Wargla, *see* Ouargla	

ANDORRA ....pg. 128

Capital: ....Andorra la Vella
Area: ....468 sq km; 181 sq mi
Highest Elev.: .....Coma Pedrosa 2,950 m; 9,680 ft
Longest River: .....Valira d'Orient 20 km; 10 mi
Avg. Temperature: . .Jan = 2.3°C; Jul = 19.3°C
Currency: ....French franc, Spanish Peseta
Official Language: . .Catalan

Name	Lat./Long.
Andorra la Vella	42°30' N, 001°30' E

ANGOLA ....pg. 152

Capital: ....Luanda
Area: ....1,246,700 sq km; 481,354 sq mi
Highest Elev.: .....Mt. Moca 2,620 m; 8,600 ft
Longest River: .....Kwanza 960 km; 600 mi
Avg. Temperature: . .Jan = 26°C; Jul = 20°C
Currency: ....new kwanza
Official Language: . .Portuguese

Name	Lat./Long.
Benguela (São Félipe de Benguela)	12°35' S, 013°24' E
Cabinda	05°33' S, 012°12' E
Caála (Robert Williams)	12°51' S, 015°34' E
Camacupa (General Machado)	12°01' S, 017°29' E
Catumbela	12°26' S, 013°33' E
Cubal	13°02' S, 014°15' E
Dalatando, *see* N'dalatando	
Gabela	10°51' S, 014°22' E
Ganda (Mariano Machado)	13°01' S, 014°38' E
General Machado, *see* Camacupa	
Henrique de Carvalho, *see* Saurimo	
Huambo (Nova Lisboa)	12°46' S, 015°44' E
Kuito (Silva Porto)	12°23' S, 016°56' E
Lobito	12°21' S, 013°33' E
Luanda (São Paulo de Luanda)	08°49' S, 013°15' E
Lubango (Sá da Bandeira)	14°55' S, 013°30' E
Luena (Vila Luso)	11°47' S, 019°55' E
Mariano Machado, *see* Ganda	
Mavinga	15°48' S, 020°21' E
M'banza Congo (São Salvador)	06°16' S, 014°15' E
Menongue (Serpa Pinto)	14°40' S, 017°42' E
Moçâmedes, *see* Namibe	
Mossamedes, *see* Namibe	
Namibe (Moçâmedes, or Mossamedes)	15°10' S, 012°09' E
N'dalatando (Dalatando, or Salazar)	09°18' S, 014°55' E
Negage	07°46' S, 015°16' E
Nova Lisboa, *see* Huambo	
Novo Redondo, *see* Sumbe	
Porto Alexandre, *see* Tombua	
Porto Amboin	10°44' S, 013°45' E
Robert Williams, *see* Caála	
Sá da Bandeira, *see* Lubango	
Salazar, *see* N'dalatando	
Santa Comba, *see* Waku Kungo	
São Félipe de Benguela, *see* Benguela	
São Paulo de Luanda, *see* Luanda	
São Salvador, *see* M'banza Congo	
Saurimo (Henrique de Carvalho)	09°39' S, 020°24' E
Serpa Pinto, *see* Menongue	
Silva Porto, *see* Kuito	
Soyo	06°08' S, 012°22' E
Sumbe (Novo Redondo)	11°12' S, 013°50' E
Tombua (Porto Alexandre)	15°48' S, 011°51' E
Uige (Carmona)	07°37' S, 015°03' E
Vila Luso, *see* Luena	
Waku Kungo (Santa Comba)	11°21' S, 015°07' E

ANTIGUA & BARBUDA pg. 116

Capital: ....Saint John's
Area: ....441.6 sq km; 170.5 sq mi
Highest Elev.: .....Boggy Pk. 410 m; 1,330 ft
Avg. Temperature: . .Jan = 25.5°C; Jul = 25.5°C
Currency: ....East Caribbean dollar
Official Language: . .English

Name	Lat./Long.
Codrington	17°38' N, 061°50' W
St. John's	17°06' N, 061°51' W

ARGENTINA ....pg. 122

Capital: ....Buenos Aires
Area: ....2,780,400 sq km; 1,073,518 sq mi
Highest Elev.: ....Mt. Aconcagua 6,960 m; 22,830 ft
Longest River: . . .Parana 4,880 km; 3,030 mi
Avg. Temperature: Jan = 24°C; Jul = 10°C
Currency: ....peso
Official Language: Spanish

Name	Lat./Long.
Aguilares	27°26' N, 065°37' E
Avellaneda	29°07' S, 059°40' W
Ayacucho	37°09' S, 058°29' W
Azul	36°47' S, 059°51' W
Bahía Blanca	38°43' S, 062°17' W
Balcarce	37°50' S, 058°15' W
Baradero	33°48' S, 059°30' W
Belén	27°39' S, 067°02' W
Bell Ville	32°37' S, 062°42' W
Bolívar	36°15' S, 061°06' W
Bragado	35°08' S, 060°30' W
Buenos Aires	34°36' S, 058°27' W
Caleta Olivia	46°26' S, 067°32' W
Campo del Cielo	27°35' S, 062°00' W
Campo Durán	22°14' S, 063°42' W
Carmen de Patagones	40°48' S, 062°59' W
Casilda	33°03' S, 061°10' W
Castelli	25°57' S, 060°37' W
Catamarca	28°28' S, 065°47' W
Caucete	31°39' S, 068°17' W
Chacabuco	34°38' S, 060°29' W
Chascomus	35°34' S, 058°01' W
Chilecito	29°10' S, 067°30' W
Cipolletti	38°56' S, 067°59' W
Clorinda	25°17' S, 057°43' W
Comodoro Rivadavia	45°52' S, 067°30' W
Concepción	27°20' S, 065°35' W
Concordia	31°24' S, 058°02' W
Cordoba	31°24' S, 064°11' W
Coronel Dorrego	38°42' S, 061°17' W
Coronel Pringles	37°58' S, 061°22' W
Corrientes	27°28' S, 058°50' W
Cruz Del Eje	30°44' S, 064°48' W
Curuzú Cuatiá	29°47' S, 058°03' W
Daireaux	36°36' S, 061°45' W
Dean Funes	30°26' S, 064°21' W
Dolores	36°20' S, 057°40' W
Eduardo Castex	35°54' S, 064°18' W
El Colorado	26°18' S, 059°22' W
Esquel	42°54' S, 071°19' W
Formosa	26°11' S, 058°11' W
Frías	28°39' S, 065°09' W
General Alvear	34°58' S, 067°42' W
General José de San Martín	26°33' S, 059°21' W
General Juan Madariaga	37°00' S, 057°09' W
General Martín Miguel de Güemes	24°40' S, 065°03' W
General Roca	39°02' S, 067°35' W
General Villegas	35°02' S, 063°01' W
Gualeguay	33°09' S, 059°20' W
Gualeguaychu	33°01' S, 058°31' W
Ibarreta	25°13' S, 059°51' W
Juárez	37°40' S, 059°48' W
Junín	34°35' S, 060°57' W
La Cocha	27°47' S, 065°34' W
La Paz	30°45' S, 059°39' W
La Plata	34°55' S, 057°57' W
La Rioja	29°26' S, 066°51' W
Las Flores	36°03' S, 059°07' W
Libertador General San Martín	23°48' S, 064°48' W
Lobos	35°11' S, 059°06' W
Mar del Plata	38°00' S, 057°33' W
Marcos Juárez	32°42' S, 062°06' W
Mendoza	32°53' S, 068°49' W
Mercedes	33°40' S, 065°28' W
Metán	25°29' S, 064°57' W
Miramar	38°16' S, 057°51' W
Monteros	27°10' S, 065°30' W
Necochea	38°33' S, 058°45' W
Neuquén	38°57' S, 068°04' W
Nogoyá	32°24' S, 059°48' W
Olavarria	36°54' S, 060°17' W
Paraná	31°44' S, 060°32' W
Paso de los Libres	29°43' S, 057°05' W
Pehuajó	35°48' S, 061°53' W
Pergamino	33°53' S, 060°35' W
Pigüé	37°37' S, 062°25' W
Pirané	25°43' S, 059°06' W
Posadas	27°23' S, 055°53' W
Presidencia Roque Saenz Pena	26°47' S, 060°27' W
Puerto Madryn	42°46' S, 065°03' W
Rafaela	31°16' S, 061°29' W
Rauch	36°46' S, 059°06' W
Rawson	43°18' S, 065°06' W
Reconquista	29°09' S, 059°39' W
Resistencia	27°27' S, 058°59' W
Río Cuarto	33°08' S, 064°21' W
Río Gallegos	51°38' S, 069°13' W
Río Grande	53°47' S, 067°42' W
Río Tercero	32°11' S, 064°06' W
Río Turbio	51°32' S, 072°18' W
Rosario	32°57' S, 060°40' W
Salta	24°47' S, 065°25' W
San Carlos de Bariloche	41°09' S, 071°18' W
San Francisco	31°26' S, 062°05' W
San Juan	31°32' S, 068°31' W
San Luis	33°18' S, 066°21' W
San Martín	33°04' S, 068°28' W
San Miguel de Tucumán	26°49' S, 065°13' W
San Nicolás de los Arroyos	33°20' S, 060°13' W
San Pedro de Jujuy	24°14' S, 064°52' W
San Rafael	34°36' S, 068°20' W
San Ramón de la Nueva Orán	23°08' S, 064°20' W
San Salvador de Jujuy	24°11' S, 065°18' W
Santa Fe	31°38' S, 060°42' W
Santa Rosa	36°37' S, 064°17' W
Santiago del Estero	27°47' S, 064°16' W
Santo Tomé	28°33' S, 056°03' W
Tafí Viejo	26°44' S, 065°16' W
Tandil	37°19' S, 059°09' W
Tartagal	22°32' S, 063°49' W
Tigre	34°25' S, 058°34' W
Tinogasta	28°04' S, 067°34' W
Trelew	43°15' S, 065°18' W
Trenque Lauquen	35°58' S, 062°42' W
Tres Arroyos	38°23' S, 060°17' W
Ushuaia	54°48' S, 068°18' W
Venado Tuerto	33°45' S, 061°58' W
Viedma	40°48' S, 063°00' W
Villa Ángela	27°35' S, 060°43' W
Villa Carlos Paz	31°24' S, 000°31' W
Villa Dolores	31°56' S, 065°12' W
Villa María	32°25' S, 063°15' W
Zapala	38°54' S, 070°04' W
Zárate	34°06' S, 059°02' W

ARMENIA ....pg. 147

Capital: ....Yerevan
Area: ....29,800 sq km; 11,500 sq mi
Highest Elev.: .....Mt. Aragats 4,090 m; 13,420 ft
Longest River: .....Aras 1,070 km; 670 mi
Avg. Temperature: . .Jan = -5°C; Jul = 25°C
Currency: ....dram
Official Language: . .Armenian

Name	Lat./Long.
Ejmiadzin (Echmiadzin)	40°10' N, 044°18' E
Gyumri (Kumayri, Alexandropol, or Leninakan)	40°48' N, 043°50' E
Hoktemberyan (Oktemberyan)	40°09' N, 044°02' E
Hrazdan (Razdan)	40°29' N, 044°46' E
Sevan	40°32' N, 044°56' E
Vanadzor	40°48' N, 044°30' E

AUSTRALIA ....pg. 155

Capital: ....Canberra
Area: ....7,682,300 sq km; 2,966,200 sq mi
Highest Elev.: ....Mt. Kosciusko 2,330 m; 7,310 ft
Longest River: . . .Murray 2,590 km; 1,610 mi
Avg. Temperature: .Jan = 22°C; Jul = 12°C
Currency: ....Australian dollar
Official Language: .English

Name	Lat./Long.
Adelaide	34°56' S, 138°36' E
Albany	35°02' S, 117°53' E
Albury-Wodonga	36°05' S, 146°55' E
Alice Springs	23°42' S, 133°53' E
Armidale	30°31' S, 151°39' E
Ayr	19°35' S, 147°24' E
Ballarat	37°33' S, 143°51' E
Balranald	34°38' S, 143°34' E
Bathurst	33°25' S, 149°34' E
Bendigo	36°46' S, 144°16' E
Bourke	30°06' S, 145°56' E
Bowen	20°01' S, 148°14' E
Bowral	34°28' S, 150°25' E
Brisbane	27°30' S, 153°01' E
Broken Hill	31°57' S, 141°26' E
Broome	17°58' S, 122°14' E
Bunbury	33°20' S, 115°38' E
Bundaberg	24°51' S, 152°21' E
Burnie	41°04' S, 145°55' E
Busselton	33°39' S, 115°20' E
Caboolture	27°05' S, 152°57' E
Cairns	16°55' S, 145°46' E
Canberra	35°20' S, 149°10' E
Carnarvon	24°52' S, 113°38' E
Casino	28°52' S, 153°03' E
Ceduna	32°07' S, 133°40' E
Charleville	26°24' S, 146°15' E
Cloncurry	20°42' S, 140°30' E
Cobar	31°30' S, 145°49' E
Coffs Harbour	30°18' S, 153°08' E
Colac	38°20' S, 143°35' E
Coober Pedy	29°01' S, 134°43' E
Cooma	36°14' S, 149°08' E
Coonabarabran	31°16' S, 149°17' E
Copley, *see* Leigh Creek	
Darwin	12°28' S, 130°50' E
Denham	25°55' S, 113°32' E
Derby	17°18' S, 123°38' E
Devonport	41°10' S, 146°21' E
Dubbo	32°15' S, 148°37' E
Eden	37°04' S, 149°54' E
Esperance	33°51' S, 121°53' E
Gawler	34°36' S, 138°44' E
Geelong	38°09' S, 144°21' E
Geraldton	28°46' S, 114°36' E
Gladstone	23°51' S, 151°15' E
Glen Innes	29°44' S, 151°44' E
Gold Coast	28°06' S, 153°27' E
Goondiwindi	28°33' S, 150°19' E
Gosford	33°26' S, 151°21' E
Goulburn	34°45' S, 149°43' E
Grafton	29°41' S, 152°56' E
Gympie	26°11' S, 152°40' E
Hay	34°30' S, 144°51' E
Hobart	42°55' S, 147°20' E
Ingham	18°39' S, 146°10' E
Innisfail	17°32' S, 146°02' E
Kalgoorlie-Boulder	30°45' S, 121°28' E
Kambalda	31°12' S, 121°40' E
Karratha	20°53' S, 116°40' E
Katanning	33°42' S, 117°33' E
Katherine	14°28' S, 132°16' E
Kempsey	31°05' S, 152°50' E
Kiama	34°41' S, 150°52' E
Launceston	41°25' S, 147°08' E
Leigh Creek (Copley)	30°32' S, 138°26' E
Lismore	28°48' S, 153°16' E
Mackay	21°09' S, 149°12' E
Maitland	32°44' S, 151°33' E
Mandurah	32°33' S, 115°42' E
Manjimup	34°14' S, 116°09' E
Maroochydore	26°39' S, 153°06' E
Maryborough	25°32' S, 152°42' E
Meekatharra	26°36' S, 118°29' E
Melbourne	37°50' S, 145°00' E
Melton	37°41' S, 144°35' E
Merredin	31°29' S, 118°16' E
Mildura	34°12' S, 142°09' E
Millicent	37°36' S, 140°21' E
Moe	38°10' S, 146°16' E
Moree	29°28' S, 149°51' E
Mount Gambier	37°50' S, 140°46' E
Mount Isa	20°44' S, 139°30' E
Mudgee	32°36' S, 149°35' E
Naracoorte	36°58' S, 140°44' E
Narrabri	30°19' S, 149°47' E
Narrogin	32°56' S, 117°10' E
New Norfolk	42°47' S, 147°04' E
Newcastle	32°55' S, 151°45' E

Name	Lat./Long.
Northam	31°40' S, 116°40' E
Orange	33°17' S, 149°06' E
Parkes	33°08' S, 148°11' E
Perth	31°56' S, 115°50' E
Port Augusta	32°30' S, 137°46' E
Port Hedland	20°19' S, 118°34' E
Port Macquarie	31°26' S, 152°55' E
Port Pirie	33°11' S, 138°01' E
Queanbeyan	35°21' S, 149°14' E
Queenscliff (Shortland Bluff, Whale Head)	38°16' S, 144°39' E
Queenstown	42°05' S, 145°33' E
Renmark	34°10' S, 140°45' E
Rockhampton	23°23' S, 150°30' E
Rockingham	32°17' S, 115°43' E
Roma	26°35' S, 148°47' E
Sale	38°06' S, 147°04' E
Shepparton	36°23' S, 145°24' E
Shortland Bluff, *see* Queenscliff	
Smithton	40°50' S, 145°07' E
Stanthorpe	28°40' S, 151°57' E
Swan Hill	35°21' S, 143°34' E
Sydney	33°53' S, 151°12' E
Tamworth	31°06' S, 150°56' E
Taree	31°54' S, 152°28' E
Tennant Creek	19°39' S, 134°12' E
Tenterfield	29°03' S, 152°01' E
Toowoomba	27°33' S, 151°58' E
Townsville	19°15' S, 146°48' E
Tumut	35°18' S, 148°13' E
Victor Harbour	35°34' S, 138°37' E
Wagga Wagga	35°07' S, 147°22' E
Warrnambool	38°23' S, 142°29' E
Warwick	28°14' S, 152°01' E
Wauchope	31°27' S, 152°44' E
West Wyalong	33°55' S, 147°13' E
Whale Head, *see* Queenscliff	
Whyalla	33°02' S, 137°35' E
Wilcannia	31°34' S, 143°23' E
Winton	22°24' S, 143°02' E
Wollongong	34°25' S, 150°54' E
Wonthaggi	38°37' S, 145°32' E
Wyndham	15°28' S, 128°06' E
Wynyard	41°00' S, 145°43' E
Young	34°19' S, 148°18'E

AUSTRIA ....pg. 133

Capital: ....Vienna
Area: ....83,859 sq km; 32,378 sq mi
Highest Elev.: .....Grossglockner 3,800 m; 12,460 ft
Longest River: ....Danube 2,850 km; 1770 mi
Avg. Temperature: .Jan = -2°C; Jul = 20°C
Currency: ....Austrian schilling
Official Language: .German

Name	Lat./Long.
Bruck	47°25' N, 015°17' E
Graz	47°04' N, 015°27' E
Innsbruck	47°16' N, 011°24' E
Klagenfurt	46°38' N, 014°18' E
Leoben (Donawitz)	47°23' N, 015°06' E
Linz	48°18' N, 014°18' E
Neunkirchen	47°43' N, 016°05' E
Trofaiach	47°25' N, 015°00' E
Salzburg	47°48' N, 013°02' E
Sankt Pölten	48°12' N, 015°38' E
Steyr	48°03' N, 014°25' E
Villach	46°36' N, 013°50' E
Vienna (Bécs, Viden, Wien))	48°12' N, 016°22' E
Wien, *see* Vienna	

AZERBAIJAN ....pg. 147

Capital: ....Baku
Area: ....86,600 sq km; 33,400 sq mi
Highest Elev.: .....Mt. Bazardyuzyu 4,470m; 14,650 ft
Longest River: ....Kura 1,360 km; 850 mi
Avg. Temperature: .Jan = -4°C; Jul = 26°C
Currency: ....manat
Official Language: .Azerbaijani

Name	Lat./Long.
Äli-Bayramli	39°55' N, 048°56' E
Baku (Baky)	40°23' N, 049°51' E
Gäncä (Gyandzha, Gandzha, Kirovabad,or Yelizavetpol)	40°41' N, 046°22' E
Mingäçevir (Mingechaur)	40°45' N, 047°03' E
Naxcivan (Nakhichevan)	39°12' N, 045°24' E
Säki (Sheki, Nukha)	41°12' N, 047°12' E
Xankändi (Stepanakert)	39°50' N, 046°46' E
Sumqait (Sumgait)	40°36' N, 049°38' E
Yelizavetpol, *see* Gäncä	

BAHAMAS, THE ....pg. 116

Capital: ....Nassau
Area: ....13,939 sq km; 5,382 sq mi
Highest Elev.: .....Mt. Alvernia 60 m; 210 ft
Avg. Temperature: .Jan = 22.1°C; Jul = 20.9°C
Currency: ....Bahamian dollar
Official Language: .English

Name	Lat./Long.
Dunmore Town	25°30' N,076°39' W
Freeport	26°32' N,078°42' W
Matthew Town	20°57' N,073°40' W
Nassau	25°05' N,077°21' W
West End	26°41' N,078°58' W

BAHRAIN ....pg. 154

Capital: ....Manama
Area: ....694.2 sq km; 268.0 sq mi
Highest Elev.: .....ad-Dukhan Hill 130 m; 440 ft
Avg. Temperature: .Jan = 17.4°C; Jul = 33.8°C
Currency: ....Bahrain dinar
Official Language: .Arabic

Name	Lat./Long.
Manama	26°13' N, 050°35' E
Muharraq, al-	26°16' N, 050°37' E
Rifa' ash-Sharqi, ar-	26°07' N, 050°34' E
Rumaythah, ar-	25°55' N, 050°33' E

BANGLADESH ....pg. 146

Capital: ....Dhaka
Area: ....148,393 sq km; 57,295 sq mi
Highest Elev.: ....Keokradong 930 m; 3,040 ft
Longest River: ....Brahmaputra 2,900 km; 1,800 mi
Avg. Temperature: .Jan = 19°C; Jul = 29°C
Currency: ....Bangladesh taka
Official Language: .Bengali

Name	Lat./Long.
Azmiriganj	24°33' N, 091°14' E
Bagerhat (Bagherhat)	22°40' N, 089°48' E
Bajitpur	24°13' N, 090°57' E
Barisal	22°42' N, 090°22' E
Bhairab Bazar	24°04' N, 090°58' E
Bogra	24°51' N, 089°22' E
Brahmanbaria	23°59' N, 091°07' E
Chandpur	23°13' N, 090°39' E
Chittagong	22°20' N, 091°50' E
Chuadanga	23°38' N, 088°51' E
Comilla (Kumilla)	23°27' N, 091°12' E
Dhaka (Dacca or Dhakal)	23°43' N, 090°25' E
Dinajpur	25°38' N, 088°38' E
Faridpur	23°36' N, 089°50' E
Gopalpur	24°50' N, 090°06' E
Jamalpur	24°55' N, 089°56' E
Jessore	23°10' N, 089°13' E
Jhenida	23°33' N, 089°10' E
Khulna	22°48' N, 089°33' E
Kishorganj	24°26' N, 090°46' E
Kurigram	25°49' N, 089°39' E
Kushtia	23°55' N, 089°07' E
Laksham	23°14' N, 091°08' E
Lakshmipur	22°57' N, 090°50' E
Lalmanir Hat (Lalmonirhat)	25°54' N, 089°27' E
Madaripur	23°10' N, 090°12' E
Mymensingh (Nasirabad)	24°45' N, 090°24' E
Naogaon	24°47' N, 088°56' E
Narayanganj	23°37' N, 090°30' E
Narsinghdi (Narsingdi)	23°55' N, 090°43' E
Noakhali (Sudharam)	22°49' N, 091°06' E
Pabna (Pubna)	24°00' N, 089°15' E
Patuakhali	22°21' N, 090°21' E
Rajshahi	24°22' N, 088°36' E
Rangpur	25°45' N, 089°15' E
Saidpur	25°47' N, 088°54' E
Satkhira	22°43' N, 089°06' E
Sherpur	24°41' N, 089°25' E
Sherpur	25°01' N, 090°01' E
Siraganj (Seraganj)	24°27' N, 089°43' E
Sylhet	24°54' N, 091°52' E
Tangail	24°15' N, 089°55' E

BARBADOS ....pg. 116

Capital: ....Bridgetown
Area: ....430 sq km; 166 sq mi
Highest Elev.: .....Mt. Hillaby 340 m; 1,110 ft
Avg. Temperature: .Jan = 24.5°C; Jul = 27.0°C
Currency: ....Barbados dollar
Official Language: .English

Name	Lat./Long.
Bridgetown	13°06' N,059°37' W

BELARUS ....pg. 138

Capital: ....Minsk
Area: ....207,600 sq km; 80,200 sq mi
Highest Elev.: .....Dzerzhinskaya Mtn. 350 m; 1,140 ft
Longest River: ....Dnieper 2,200 km; 1,370 mi
Avg. Temperature: .Jan = -6°C; Jul = 17°C
Currency: ....Belarusian rubel
Official Language: .Belarusian

Name	Lat./Long.
Baranovichi	53°08' N, 026°02' E
Bereza (Beryoza)	52°32' N, 024°59' E
Berezovka (Beryozovka)	53°43' N, 025°30' E
Bobruysk	53°09' N, 029°14' E
Borisov	54°15' N, 028°30' E
Brest (Brest-Litovsk)	52°06' N, 023°42' E
Bykhov	53°31' N, 030°15' E
Chashniki	54°52' N, 029°10' E
Chausy	53°48' N, 030°58' E
Chechersk (Chechyorsk)	52°55' N, 030°55' E
Cherikov	53°34' N, 031°23' E
Dokshitsy	54°54' N, 027°46' E
Dobrush	52°25' N, 031°19' E
Drogichin	52°11' N, 025°09' E
Dzerzhinsk	53°41' N, 027°08' E
Glubokoye	55°08' N, 027°41' E
Gorki	54°17' N, 030°59' E
Gomel	52°25' N, 031°00' E
Grodno (Hrodna)	53°41' N, 023°50' E
Ivanovo	52°09' N, 025°32' E
Kalinkovichi	52°08' N, 029°19' E
Kamenets	52°24' N, 023°49' E
Kletsk	53°04' N, 026°38' E
Kobrin	52°13' N, 024°21' E
Kossovo	52°45' N, 025°09' E
Kostyukovichi	53°20' N, 032°03' E
Lepel	54°53' N, 028°42' E
Lida	53°53' N, 025°18' E
Luninets	52°15' N, 026°48' E
Malorita	51°47' N, 024°05' E
Maryina Gorka	53°31' N, 028°09' E
Minsk (Mensk)	53°54' N, 027°34' E
Miory	55°37' N, 027°38' E
Mogilyov (Mogilev or Mahilyou)	53°54' N, 030°21' E
Molodechno	54°19' N, 026°51' E
Mosty	53°25' N, 024°32' E
Mozyr (Mazyr)	52°03' S, 029°16' E
Novolukomi	54°39' N, 029°13' E
Novopolotsk (Navapolatsk)	55°32' N, 028°39' E
Orsha	54°31' N, 030°26' E
Osipovichi	53°18' N, 028°38' E
Petrikov	52°08' N, 028°30' E
Pinsk	52°07' N, 026°07' E
Polotsk (Polatsk)	55°29' N, 028°47' E
Postavy	55°07' N, 026°50' E
Pruzhany	52°33' N, 024°28' E
Rechitsa (Rechytsa)	52°22' N, 030°23' E
Rogachev (Rogachyov)	53°05' N, 030°03' E
Slonim	53°06' N, 025°19' E
Slutsk	53°01' N, 027°33' E
Stolbtsy	53°29' N, 026°44' E
Soligorsk (Salihorsk)	52°48' N, 027°32' E
Stolin	51°53' N, 026°51' E
Svetlogorsk (Svetlahorsk)	52°38' N, 029°46' E
Tolochin	54°25' N, 029°42' E
Vasilevichi	52°15' N, 029°50' E
Vileyka	54°30' N, 026°55' E
Vitebsk	55°12' N, 030°11' E
Volkovysk	53°10' N, 024°28' E
Vysokoye	52°22' N, 023°22' E
Zaslavl	54°00' N, 027°17' E
Zhabinka	52°12' N, 024°01' E
Zhitkovichi	52°14' N, 027°52' E
Zhlobin	52°54' N, 030°03' E
Zhodino	54°06' N, 028°21' E

BELGIUM ....pg. 132

Capital: ....Brussels
Area: ....30,518 sq km; 11,783 sq mi
Highest Elev.: .....Botrange 690 m; 2,280 ft
Longest River: .....Meuse (Maas) 950 km; 590 mi
Avg. Temperature: .Jan = 2°C; Jul = 17°C
Currency: ....Belgian franc
Official Language: .Dutch, French, German

Name	Lat./Long.
Aalst (Alost)	50°56' N, 004°02' E
Anderlecht	50°50' N, 004°18' E
Antwerp (Antwerpen, Anvers)	51°13' N, 004°25' E
Bastogne	50°00' N, 005°43' E
Brugge (Bruges)	51°13' N, 003°14' E
Brussels (Brussel, Bruxelles)	50°50' N, 004°20' E
Charleroi	50°25' N, 004°26' E
Doornik, *see* Tournai	
Etterbeek	50°50' N, 004°23' E
Forest (Vorst)	50°48' N, 004°19' E
Genk (Genck)	50°58' N, 005°30' E
Ghent (Gand, Gent)	51°03' N, 003°43' E
Hasselt	50°56' N, 005°20' E
Ixelles (Elsene)	50°50' N, 004°22' E
Jemappes	50°27' N, 003°53' E
Kapellen	51°19' N, 004°26' E
Kortrijk (Courtrai)	50°50' N, 003°16' E
La Louviere	50°28' N, 004°11' E
Liege (Luttich)	50°38' N, 005°34' E
Louvain (Leuven)	50°53' N, 004°42' E
Mechelen (Malines)	51°02' N, 004°28' E
Mons (Bergen)	50°27' N, 003°56' E
Mouscron (Moeskroen)	50°44' N, 003°13' E
Namur (Namen)	50°28' N, 004°52' E
Ostend (Oostende)	51°13' N, 002°55' E
Roeselare (Roulers)	50°57' N, 003°08' E
Schaerbeek (Schaarbeek)	50°51' N, 004°23' E
Seraing	50°36' N, 005°29' E
Sint-Gillis-Waas	51°13' N, 004°08' E
Sint-Niklaas	51°10' N, 004°08' E
Spa	50°30' N, 005°52' E
Tournai (Doornik)	50°36' N, 003°23' E
Uccle (Ukkel)	50°48' N, 004°19' E
Waterloo	50°43' N, 004°23' E

BELIZE ....pg. 117

Capital: ....Belmopan
Area: ....22,965 sq km; 8,867 sq mi
Highest Elev.: .....Victoria Pk. 1,120 m; 3,680 ft
Longest River: .....Belize 290 km; 180 mi
Avg. Temperature: .Jan = 24°C; Jul = 28°C
Currency: ....Belize dollar
Official Language: .English

Name	Lat./Long.
Belize City (Belice)	17°30' N,088°12' W
Belmopan	17°15' N,088°46' W
Corozal	18°24' N,088°24' W
Dangriga (Stann Creek)	16°58' N,088°13' W
Monkey River	16°22' N,088°29' W
Orange Walk	18°06' N,088°33' W
Pembroke Hall	18°17' N, 088°27' W

BENIN ....pg. 150

Capital: ....Porto-Novo
Area: ....112,680 sq km; 43,500 sq mi
Highest Elev.: .....Atakora Mts. 640 m; 2,100 ft
Longest River: .....Ouémé 450 km; 280 mi
Avg. Temperature: .Jan = 28°C; Jul = 26°C
Currency: ....CFA franc
Official Language: .French

Name	Lat./Long.
Cotonou	06°21' N, 002°26' E
Parakou	09°21' N, 002°37' E
Porto-Novo	06°29' N, 002°37' E

BHUTAN ....pg. 146

Capital: ....Thimphu
Area: ....47,000 sq km; 18,150 sq mi
Highest Elev.: .....Mt. Kula 7,550 m; 24,780 ft
Longest River: .....Wong 370 km; 230 mi
Avg. Temperature: .Jan = 0°C; Jul = 15°C
Currency: ....ngultrum
Official Language: .Dzongkha

Name	Lat./Long.
Thimphu	27°28' N 089°38' E

BOLIVIA ....pg. 120

Capital: ....La Paz
Area: ....1,098,581 sq km; 424,164 sq mi
Highest Elev.: .....Mt. Sajama 6,540 m; 21,460 ft
Longest River: .....Mamoré 1,900 km; 1,200 mi
Avg. Temperature: .Jan = 18°C; Jul = 10°C
Currency: ....boliviano
Official Language: .Spanish, Aymara, Quechua

Name	Lat./Long.
Cochabamba	17°24' S,066°09' W
La Paz	16°30' S,068°09' W
Monteagudo	19°49' S,063°59' W
Montero	17°20' S,063°15' W
Oruro	17°59' S,067°09' W
Porvenir	11°15' S,068°41' W
Potosi	19°35' S,065°45' W
Sucre	19°02' S,065°17' W
Tarija	21°31' S,064°45' W
Tiahuanacu (Tiwanacu)	16°33' S,068°42' W
Trinidad	14°47' S,064°47' W

BOSNIA & HERZEGOVINA pg. 134

Capital: ....Sarajevo
Area: ....51,129 sq km; 19,741 sq mi
Highest Elev.: .....Mt. Maglic 2,390 m; 7,830 ft
Longest River: .....Sava 940 km; 580 mi
Avg. Temperature: .Jan = -1.4°C; Jul = 19.6°C
Currency: ....Bosnian dinar
Official Language: .Serbo-Croatian

Name	Lat./Long.
Brcko	44°52' N, 018°49' E
Gorazde	43°40' N, 018°59' E
Jablanica	43°39' N, 017°45' E
Jajce	44°21' N, 017°17' E
Kladanj	44°14' N, 018°42' E
Kljuc	44°32' N, 016°47' E
Konjic	43°39' N, 017°58' E
Prijedor	44°59' N, 016°42' E
Sanski Most	44°46' N, 016°40' E
Sarajevo	43°50' N, 018°25' E
Srebrenica	44°06' N, 019°18' E
Titov Vrbas, *see* Vrbas	
Travnik	44°14' N, 017°40' E
Tuzla	44°33' N, 018°41' E
Vares	44°10' N, 018°20' E
Vrbas (Titov Vrbas)	45°34' N, 019°39' E
Zenica	44°13' N, 017°55' E

BOTSWANA ....pg. 152

Capital: ....Gaborone
Area: ....581,730 sq km; 224,607 sq mi
Highest Elev.: .....Otse Mtn. 1,490 m; 4,890 ft
Longest River: .....Limpopo 1,610 km; 1,000 mi
Avg. Temperature: .Jan = 25°C; Jul = 15°C
Currency: ....pula
Official Language: .English

Name	Lat./Long.
Francistown	21°13' S, 027°31' E
Gaborone	24°40' S, 025°54' E
Ghanzi	21°34' S, 021°47' E
Kasane	17°49' S, 025°09' E
Letlhakane	21°25' S, 025°35' E
Mahalapye	23°04' S, 026°50' E
Maun	19°59' S, 023°25' E
Mochudi	24°25' S, 026°09' E
Orapa	21°17' S, 025°22' E
Palapye (Palapye Road)	22°33' S, 027°08' E
Selebi-Phikwe	22°01' S, 027°50' E
Shashe	21°26' S, 027°27' E
Tlokweng	24°32' S, 025°58' E
Tshabong	26°03' S, 022°27' E

BRAZIL ....pg. 121

Capital: ....Brasília
Area: ....8,547,404 sq km; 3,300,171 sq mi
Highest Elev.: ....Neblina Pk, 3,010 m; 9,890 ft
Longest River: ....Amazon 6,570 km; 4,080 mi
Avg. Temperature: .Jan = 25°C; Jul = 20°C
Currency: ....real
Official Language: .Portuguese

Name	Lat./Long.
Abacate	00°19' N, 050°53' W
Abaetetuba	01°42' S,048°54' W
Alagoinhas	12°07' S,038°26' W
Alcântara	02°24' S,044°24' W
Alegrete	29°46' S,055°46' W
Altamira	03°12' S,052°12' W
Americana	22°45' S,047°20' W
Amapá	02°03' N,050°48' W
Anápolis	16°20' S,048°58' W
Aracaju	10°55' S,037°04' W
Araçatuba	21°12' S,050°25' W
Araguaína	07°12' S,048°12' W
Araguari	18°38' S,048°11' W
Arapiraca	09°45' S,036°39' W
Araraquara	21°47' S,048°10' W
Assis	22°40' S,050°25' W
Bacabal	04°14' S,044°47' W
Bagé	31°20' S,054°06' W
Balsas	07°31' S,046°02' W
Barreiras	12°08' S,045°00' W
Barretos	20°33' S,048°33' W
Bauru	22°19' S,049°04' W
Bayeux	07°08' S,034°56' W
Belém (Para)	01°27' S,048°29' W
Belo Horizonte	19°55' S,043°56' W
Blumenau	26°56' S,049°03' W
Boa Vista	02°49' N,060°30' W
Bom Jesus da Lapa	13°15' S,043°25' W
Braganca	01°03' S,046°46' W
Brasília	15°47' S,047°55' W
Brusque	27°06' S,048°56' W
Cabo	08°17' S,035°02' W
Caceres	16°04' S,057°41' W
Cachoeira do Sul	30°02' S,052°54' W
Cachoeiro de Itapemirim	20°51' S,041°06' W
Camaçari	12°41' S,038°18' W
Campina Grande	07°13' S,035°53' W
Campinas	22°54' S,047°05' W
Campo Grande	20°27' S,054°37' W
Campos	21°45' S,041°18' W
Candeias	12°40' S,038°33' W
Canoas	29°56' S,051°11' W
Cariacica	20°16' S,040°25' W
Caruaru	08°17' S,035°58' W
Cascavel	24°57' S,053°28' W
Castanhal	01°18' S,047°55' W
Catanduva	21°08' S,048°58' W
Caxias	04°50' S,043°21' W
Caxias do Sul	29°10' S,051°11' W
Coari	04°05' S,063°08' W
Codo	04°29' S,043°53' W

Name	Lat./Long.
Colatina	19°32' S, 040°37' W
Conselheiro Lafaiete	20°40' S, 043°48' W
Contagem	19°55' S, 044°06' W
Corumbá	19°01' S, 057°39' W
Crato	07°14' S, 039°23' W
Criciúma	28°40' S, 049°23' W
Cruz Alta	28°39' S, 053°36' W
Cruzeiro do Sul	07°38' S, 072°36' W
Cuiaba	15°35' S, 056°05' W
Curitiba	25°25' S, 049°15' W
Diamantina	18°15' S, 043°36' W
Divinópolis	20°09' S, 044°54' W
Duque de Caxias	22°47' S, 043°18' W
Erechim	27°38' S, 052°17' W
Feira de Santana	12°15' S, 038°57' W
Florianópolis	27°35' S, 048°34' W
Fonte Boa	02°32' S, 066°01' W
Fortaleza	03°43' S, 038°30' W
Foz do Iguacu	25°33' S, 054°35' W
Franca	20°32' S, 047°24' W
Garanhuns	08°54' S, 036°29' W
Goiânia	16°40' S, 049°16' W
Governador Valadares	18°51' S, 041°56' W
Guarulhos	23°28' S, 046°32' W
Gurupi	11°43' S, 049°04' W
Ilhéus	14°49' S, 039°02' W
Imperatriz	05°32' S, 047°29' W
Itabuna	14°48' S, 039°16' W
Itaituba	04°17' S, 055°59' W
Itajai	26°53' S, 048°39' W
Itamaraju	17°04' S, 039°32' W
Itapetinga	15°15' S, 040°15' W
Itapipoca	03°30' S, 039°35' W
Ituiutaba	18°58' S, 049°28' W
Itumbiara	18°25' S, 049°13' W
Jaboatão	08°07' S, 035°01' W
Jatai	17°53' S, 051°43' W
Jau	22°18' S, 048°33' W
Jequié	13°51' S, 040°05' W
Ji-Páraná	10°55' S, 061°59' W
João Pessoa	07°07' S, 034°52' W
Joinvile	26°18' S, 048°50' W
Juazeiro	09°25' S, 040°30' W
Juàzeiro do Norte	07°12' S, 039°20' W
Juiz de Fora	21°45' S, 043°20' W
Lajes	27°48' S, 050°19' W
Limeira	22°34' S, 047°24' W
Lins	21°40' S, 049°45' W
Londrina	23°18' S, 051°09' W
Luziânia	16°15' S, 047°56' W
Macapá	00°02' N, 051°03' W
Maceió	09°40' S, 035°43' W
Manaus	03°08' S, 060°01' W
Marabá	05°21' S, 049°07' W
Maranguape	03°53' S, 038°40' W
Marília	22°13' S, 049°56' W
Maringá	23°25' S, 051°55' W
Maues	03°24' S, 057°42' W
Monte Dourado	00°52' S, 052°31' W
Montes Claros	16°43' S, 043°52' W
Mossoró	05°11' S, 037°20' W
Natal	05°47' S, 035°13' W
Niteroi	22°53' S, 043°07' W
Nova Friburgo	22°16' S, 042°32' W
Nova Iguaçu	22°45' S, 043°27' W
Novo Hamburgo	29°41' S, 051°08' W
Olinda	08°01' S, 034°51' W
Osasco	23°32' S, 046°46' W
Paranaguá	25°31' S, 048°30' W
Parnaiba	02°54' S, 041°47' W
Parnamirim	05°55' S, 035°15' W
Passo Fundo	28°15' S, 052°24' W
Passos	20°43' S, 046°37' W
Patos	07°01' S, 037°16' W
Patos de Minas	18°35' S, 046°32' W
Paulo Afonso	09°21' S, 038°14' W
Pelotas	31°46' S, 052°20' W
Petrolina	09°24' S, 040°30' W
Piracicaba	22°43' S, 047°38' W
Pocos de Caldas	21°48' S, 046°34' W
Ponta Grossa	25°05' S, 050°09' W
Pôrto Alegre	30°04' S, 051°11' W
Pôrto Velho	08°46' S, 063°54' W
Presidente Prudente	22°07' S, 051°22' W
Recife	08°03' S, 034°54' W
Ribeirão Prêto	21°10' N, 047°48' W
Rio Branco	09°58' S, 067°48' W
Rio de Janeiro	22°54' S, 043°14' W
Rio Grande	32°02' S, 052°05' W
Rio Largo	09°29' S, 035°51' W
Rio Verde	17°43' S, 050°56' W
Rondonópolis	16°28' S, 054°38' W
Salvador	12°59' S, 038°31' W
Santa Inês	03°39' S, 045°22' W
Santa Maria	29°41' S, 053°48' W
Santa Maria da Vitoria	13°24' S, 044°12' W
Santa Rosa	27°52' S, 054°29' W
Santana do Livramento	30°53' S, 055°31' W
Santarém	02°26' S, 054°42' W
Santo Andre	23°40' S, 046°31' W
Santo Antônio de Jesus	12°58' S, 039°16' W
Santos	23°57' S, 046°20' W
São Carlos	22°01' S, 047°54' W
São Cristóvão	11°01' S, 037°12' W
São Gonçalo	22°51' S, 043°04' W
São Joao del Rei	21°09' S, 044°16' W
São José do Rio Prêto	20°48' S, 049°23' W
São Leopoldo	29°46' S, 051°09' W
São Lourenco da Mata	08°00' S, 035°03' W
São Luís	02°31' S, 044°16' W
São Paulo	23°32' S, 046°37' W
São Raimundo Nonato	09°01' S, 042°42' W
São Vicente	23°58' S, 046°23' W
Sete Lagoas	19°27' S, 044°14' W
Sobral	03°42' S, 040°21' W
Tefé	03°22' S, 064°42' W
Teófilo Otoni	17°51' S, 041°30' W
Teresina	05°05' S, 042°49' W
Timon	05°06' S, 042°49' W
Três Lagoas	20°48' S, 051°43' W
Tubarão	28°30' S, 049°01' W
Tucurui	03°42' S, 049°27' W
Tupã	21°56' S, 050°30' W
Uberaba	19°45' S, 047°55' W
Uruguaiana	29°45' S, 057°05' W
Varzea Grande	15°39' S, 056°08' W
Viamao	30°05' S, 051°02' W
Vila Velha (Espírito Santo)	20°20' S, 040°17' W

Name	Lat./Long.
Vitoria	20°19' S, 040°21' W
Vitória da Conquista	14°51' S, 040°51' W

BRUNEI ....pg. 145

Capital:	Bandar Seri Begawan
Area:	5,765 sq km; 2,226 sq mi
Highest Elev.:	Pagon Pk. 1,850 m; 6,070 ft
Avg. Temperature:	Jan = 26.7°C; Jul = 27.8°C
Currency:	Brunei dollar
Official Language:	Malay

Bandar Seri Begawan (Brunei)	04°53' N, 114°56' E
Seria	04°37' N, 114°19' E

BULGARIA ....pg. 134

Capital:	Sofia
Area:	110,994 sq km; 42,855 sq mi
Highest Elev.:	Musala Pk. 2,930 m; 9,600 ft
Longest River:	Danube 2,850 km; 1770 mi
Avg. Temperature:	Jan = -2°C; Jul = 21°C
Currency:	lev
Official Language:	Bulgarian

Balchik	43°25' N, 028°10' E
Berkovitsa	43°14' N, 023°07' E
Blagoevgrad	42°01' N, 023°06' E
Burgas	42°30' N, 027°28' E
Gabrovo	42°52' N, 025°19' E
Kazanluk	42°37' N, 025°24' E
Khaskovo	41°56' N, 025°33' E
Kurdzhali	41°39' N, 025°22' E
Kyustendil	42°17' N, 022°41' E
Lovech	43°08' N, 024°43' E
Mikhaylovgrad	43°25' N, 023°13' E
Nikopol	43°42' N, 024°54' E
Pazardzhik	42°12' N, 024°20' E
Pernik (Dimitrovo)	42°36' N, 023°02' E
Petrich	41°24' N, 023°13' E
Pleven	43°25' N, 024°37' E
Plovdiv	42°09' N, 024°45' E
Razgrad	43°32' N, 026°31' E
Ruse	43°50' N, 025°57' E
Silistra	44°07' N, 027°16' E
Sliven	42°40' N, 026°19' E
Sofia	42°41' N, 023°19' E
Stara Zagora	42°25' N, 025°38' E
Troyan	42°53' N, 024°43' E
Varna	43°13' N, 027°55' E
Veliko Turnovo	43°04' N, 025°39' E
Velingrad	42°01' N, 024°00' E
Vidin	43°59' N, 022°52' E
Vratsa (Vraca)	43°12' N, 023°33' E
Yambol	42°29' N, 026°30' E

BURKINA FASO ....pg. 150

Capital:	Ouagadougou
Area:	274,400 sq km; 105,946 sq mi
Highest Elev.:	Tena Kourou 750 m; 2,460 ft
Longest River:	Black Volta 1,160 km; 720 mi
Avg. Temperature:	Jan = 25°C; Jul = 28°C
Currency:	CFA franc
Official Language:	French

Bobo Dioulasso	11°12' N, 004°18' W
Koudougou	12°15' N, 002°22' W
Ouagadougou	12°22' N, 001°31' W

BURUNDI ....pg. 153

Capital:	Bujumbura
Area:	27,816 sq km; 10,740 sq mi
Highest Elev.:	Mt. Heha 2,670 m; 8,760 ft
Longest River:	Ruvubu 480 km; 300 mi
Avg. Temperature:	Jan = 23°C; Jul = 23°C
Currency:	Burundi franc
Official Language:	Rundi; French

Bujumbura	03°23' S, 029°22' E
Gitega	03°26' S, 029°56' E
Ngozi	02°54' S, 029°50' E
Nyanza-Lac	04°21' S, 029°36' E

CAMBODIA ....pg. 144

Capital:	Phnom Penh
Area:	181,916 sq km; 70,238 sq mi
Highest Elev.:	Mt. Aôral 1,810 m; 5,950 ft
Longest River:	Mekong 4,350 km; 2,700 mi
Avg. Temperature:	Jan = 26°C; Jul = 28°C
Currency:	riel
Official Language:	Khmer

Batdambang (Battambang)	13°06' N, 103°12' E
Chong Kal	13°57' N, 103°35' E
Kâmpóng Saôm (Sihanoukville)	10°38' N, 103°30' E
Kâmpôt	10°37' N, 104°11' E
Krong Kaôh Kong	11°37' N, 102°59' E
Phnom Penh (Phnum Penh or Pnom Penh)	11°33' N, 104°55' E
Phnum Tbeng Meanchey	13°49' N, 104°58' E
Pouthisat (Pursat)	12°32' N, 103°55' E
Prey Veng	11°29' N, 105°19' E
Siempang	14°07' N, 106°23' E
Siemreab	13°22' N, 103°51' E

CAMEROON ....pg. 150

Capital:	Yaoundé
Area:	475,442 sq km; 183,569 sq mi
Highest Elev.:	Mt. Cameroon 4,100 m; 13,440 ft
Longest River:	Sanaga 530 km; 330 mi
Avg. Temperature:	Jan = 24°C; Jul = 23°C
Currency:	CFA franc
Official Language:	French, English

Bafoussam	05°28' N, 010°25' E
Bamenda	05°56' N, 010°10' E

Name	Lat./Long.
Douala	04°03' N, 009°42' E
Foumban	05°43' N, 010°55' E
Kumba	04°38' N, 009°25' E
Nkongsamba	04°57' N, 009°56' E
Yaoundé	03°52' N, 011°31' E

CANADA ....pg. 114

Capital:	Ottawa
Area:	9,970,610 sq km; 3,849,674 sq mi
Highest Elev.:	Mt. Logan 5,950 m; 19,520 ft
Longest River:	Mackenzie 4,240 km; 2,640 mi
Avg. Temperature:	Jan = -11°C; Jul = 21°C
Currency:	Canadian dollar
Official Language:	English, French

Amos	48°35' N, 078°07' W
Arctic Bay	73°02' N, 085°11' W
Baie-Comeau	49°13' N, 068°09' W
Baker Lake	64°15' N, 096°00' W
Banff	51°10' N, 115°34' W
Barrie	44°24' N, 079°40' W
Battleford	52°44' N, 108°19' W
Beauport	46°52' N, 071°11' W
Bonavista	48°39' N, 053°07' W
Brandon	49°50' N, 099°57' W
Bridgewater	44°23' N, 064°31' W
Brooks	50°35' N, 111°53' W
Buchans	48°49' N, 056°52' W
Burlington	43°19' N, 079°47' W
Burnaby	49°16' N, 122°57' W
Calgary	51°03' N, 114°05' W
Cambridge Bay	69°03' N, 105°05' W
Camrose	53°01' N, 112°50' W
Carbonear	47°44' N, 053°13' W
Carmacks	62°05' N, 136°17' W
Charlesbourg	46°51' N, 071°16' W
Charlottetown	46°14' N, 063°08' W
Chatham	42°24' N, 082°11' W
Chibougamau	49°55' N, 074°22' W
Chicoutimi	48°26' N, 071°04' W
Churchill	58°46' N, 094°10' W
Churchill Falls	53°33' N, 064°01' W
Cranbrook	49°30' N, 115°46' W
Dartmouth	44°40' N, 063°34' W
Dauphin	51°09' N, 100°03' W
Dawson	64°04' N, 139°26' W
Dawson Creek	55°46' N, 120°14' W
Duck Lake	52°49' N, 106°14' W
Edmonton	53°33' N, 113°28' W
Elliot Lake	46°23' N, 082°42' W
Enderby	50°33' N, 119°09' W
Eskimo Point	61°07' N, 094°03' W
Esterhazy	50°39' N, 102°05' W
Estevan	49°08' N, 102°59' W
Faro	62°14' N, 133°20' W
Fernie	49°30' N, 115°04' W
Flin Flon	54°46' N, 101°53' W
Fogo	49°43' N, 054°17' W
Fort Liard	60°15' N, 123°28' W
Fort MacLeod	49°43' N, 113°25' W
Fort McMurray	56°44' N, 111°23' W
Fort McPherson	67°27' N, 134°53' W
Fort Qu'Appelle	50°46' N, 103°48' W
Fort Smith	60°00' N, 111°53' W
Fort St. John	56°15' N, 120°51' W
Fredericton	45°58' N, 066°39' W
Gagnon	51°53' N, 068°10' W
Gander	48°57' N, 054°37' W
Gaspe	48°50' N, 064°29' W
Glace Bay	46°12' N, 059°57' W
Granby	45°24' N, 072°43' W
Grand Bank	47°06' N, 055°46' W
Grand Falls	48°56' N, 055°40' W
Grande Prairie	55°10' N, 118°48' W
Grimshaw	56°11' N, 117°36' W
Grise Fiord	76°25' N, 082°55' W
Haines Junction	60°45' N, 137°30' W
Halifax	44°39' N, 063°36' W
Hamilton	43°15' N, 079°51' W
Happy Valley-Goose Bay	53°19' N, 060°20' W
Harbour Grace	47°42' N, 053°13' W
Hay River	60°49' N, 115°47' W
Inuvik	68°21' N, 133°43' W
Iqaluit (Frobisher Bay)	63°45' N, 068°31' W
Iroquois Falls	48°46' N, 080°41' W
Jasper	52°53' N, 118°05' W
Joliette	46°01' N, 073°27' W
Jonquiere	48°25' N, 071°13' W
Kamloops	50°40' N, 120°19' W
Kapuskasing	49°25' N, 082°26' W
Kelowna	49°53' N, 119°29' W
Kenora	49°47' N, 094°29' W
Kindersley	51°28' N, 109°10' W
Kirkland Lake	48°09' N, 080°02' W
Kitchener	43°27' N, 080°29' W
La Baie	48°20' N, 070°52' W
La Tuque	47°26' N, 072°47' W
Labrador City	52°57' N, 066°55' W
Lethbridge	49°42' N, 112°49' W
Lewisporte	49°14' N, 055°03' W
Liverpool	44°02' N, 064°43' W
Lloydminster	53°17' N, 110°00' W
London	42°59' N, 081°14' W
Longueuil	45°32' N, 073°30' W
Lynn Lake	56°51' N, 101°03' W
Maple Creek	49°55' N, 109°29' W
Marystown	47°10' N, 055°09' W
Mayo	63°36' N, 135°54' W
Medicine Hat	50°03' N, 110°40' W
Mississauga	43°35' N, 079°39' W
Moncton	46°07' N, 064°48' W
Montmagny	46°59' N, 070°33' W
Montreal	45°30' N, 073°36' W
Moose Jaw	50°24' N, 105°32' W
Mount Pearl	47°31' N, 052°47' W
Nanaimo	49°10' N, 123°56' W
Nelson	49°30' N, 117°17' W
Nepean	45°16' N, 075°46' W
New Liskeard	47°30' N, 079°40' W
Niagara Falls	43°06' N, 079°04' W
Nickel Centre	46°34' N, 080°49' W
Nipawin	53°22' N, 104°00' W
North Battleford	52°47' N, 108°17' W
North Bay	46°19' N, 079°28' W
North West River	53°32' N, 060°08' W
Old Crow	67°34' N, 139°50' W
Oshawa	43°54' N, 078°51' W

Name	Lat./Long.
Ottawa	45°25' N, 075°42' W
Pangnirtung	66°08' N, 065°43' W
Parry Sound	45°21' N, 080°02' W
Peace River	56°14' N, 117°17' W
Perce	48°32' N, 064°13' W
Peterborough	44°18' N, 078°19' W
Pine Point	60°50' N, 114°28' W
Port Alberni	49°14' N, 124°48' W
Port Hawkesbury	45°37' N, 061°21' W
Portage la Prairie	49°59' N, 098°18' W
Prince Albert	53°12' N, 105°46' W
Prince George	53°55' N, 122°45' W
Prince Rupert	54°19' N, 130°19' W
Quebec	46°49' N, 071°14' W
Quesnel	53°00' N, 122°30' W
Rae-Edzo	62°50' N, 116°03' W
Rankin Inlet	62°49' N, 092°05' W
Red Deer	52°16' N, 113°48' W
Regina	50°27' N, 104°37' W
Resolute Bay	74°41' N, 094°54' W
Revelstoke	50°59' N, 118°12' W
Rimouski	48°26' N, 068°33' W
Roberval	48°31' N, 072°13' W
Ross River	61°59' N, 132°26' W
Sachs Harbour	72°00' N, 125°13' W
Saint Albert	53°38' N, 113°38' W
Saint John	45°16' N, 066°03' W
Saint John's	47°34' N, 052°43' W
Sainte-Foy	46°47' N, 071°17' W
Saskatoon	52°07' N, 106°38' W
Sault Ste. Marie	46°31' N, 084°20' W
Scarborough	43°47' N, 079°15' W
Schefferville	54°48' N, 066°50' W
Selkirk	50°09' N, 096°52' W
Senneterre	48°23' N, 077°14' W
Sept-Iles	50°12' N, 066°23' W
Shawinigan	46°33' N, 072°45' W
Shelburne	43°46' N, 065°19' W
Sherbrooke	45°25' N, 071°54' W
Snow Lake	54°53' N, 100°02' W
Springdale	49°30' N, 056°04' W
Sturgeon Falls	46°22' N, 079°55' W
Sudbury	46°30' N, 081°00' W
Surrey	49°06' N, 122°47' W
Swan River	52°07' N, 101°16' W
Sydney	46°09' N, 060°11' W
Teslin	60°10' N, 132°43' W
The Pas	53°50' N, 101°15' W
Thompson	55°45' N, 097°52' W
Thunder Bay	48°24' N, 089°19' W
Timmins	48°28' N, 081°20' W
Toronto	43°39' N, 079°23' W
Trois-Rivieres	46°21' N, 072°33' W
Truro	45°22' N, 063°16' W
Tuktoyaktuk	69°27' N, 133°02' W
Val-d'Or	48°06' N, 077°47' W
Vancouver	49°15' N, 123°07' W
Vernon	50°16' N, 119°16' W
Wabush	52°55' N, 066°52' W
Watson Lake	60°04' N, 128°42' W
Weyburn	49°40' N, 103°51' W
Whitehorse	60°43' N, 135°03' W
Williams Lake	52°08' N, 122°09' W
Windsor	42°18' N, 083°01' W
Windsor	44°59' N, 064°08' W
Winnipeg	49°53' N, 097°09' W
Yarmouth	43°50' N, 066°07' W
Yellowknife	62°27' N, 114°22' W
Yorkton	51°13' N, 102°28' W

CAPE VERDE ....pg. 148

Capital:	Praia
Area:	4,033 sq km; 1,557 sq mi
Highest Elev.:	Mt. Cano 2,830 m; 9,280 ft
Avg. Temperature:	Jan = 22°C; Jul = 27°C
Currency:	escudo
Official Language:	Portuguese

Mindelo	16°53' N, 025°00' W
Praia	14°55' N, 023°31' W

CENTRAL AFRICAN REP. ....pg. 151

Capital:	Bangui
Area:	622,436 sq km; 240,324 sq mi
Highest Elev.:	Mt. Gaou 1,420 m; 4,660 ft
Longest River:	Ubangi-Uele 2,250 km; 1,400 mi
Avg. Temperature:	Jan = 26°C; Jul = 25°C
Currency:	CFA franc
Official Language:	French, Sango

Bangui	04°22' N 018°35' E

CHAD ....pg. 151

Capital:	N'Djamena
Area:	1,284,000 sq km; 495,755 sq mi
Highest Elev.:	Mt. Koussi 3,410 m; 11,200 ft
Longest River:	Chari 1,400 km; 870 mi
Avg. Temperature:	Jan = 24°C; Jul = 28°C
Currency:	CFA franc
Official Language:	Arabic, French

Abéché	13°49' N, 020°49' E
Moundou	08°34' N, 016°05' E
N'Djamena (Fort Lamy)	12°07' N, 015°03' E
Sarh (Fort-Archambault)	09°09' N, 018°23' E

CHILE ....pg. 122

Capital:	Santiago
Area:	756,626 sq km; 292,135 sq mi
Highest Elev.:	Ojos del Salado 6,890 m; 22,610 ft
Longest River:	Loa 440 km; 280 mi
Avg. Temperature:	Jan = 21°C; Jul = 9°C
Currency:	peso
Official Language:	Spanish

Achao	42°28' S, 073°30' W
Ancud	41°52' S, 073°50' W

Name	Lat./Long.
Andacollo	30°14' S, 071°06' W
Antofagasta	23°39' S, 070°24' W
Arica	18°29' S, 070°20' W
Baquedano	23°20' S, 069°51' W
Calama	22°28' S, 068°56' W
Caldera	27°04' S, 070°50' W
Cañete	37°48' S, 073°24' W
Castro	42°29' S, 073°46' W
Catalina	25°13' S, 069°43' W
Cauquenes	35°58' S, 072°21' W
Chaitén	42°55' S, 072°43' W
Chile Chico	46°33' S, 071°44' W
Chillán	36°36' S, 072°07' W
Chonchi	42°38' S, 073°47' W
Chuquicamata	22°19' S, 068°56' W
Coihaique	45°34' S, 072°04' W
Concepción	36°50' S, 073°03' W
Constitución	35°20' S, 072°25' W
Copiapo	27°22' S, 070°20' W
Coquimbo	29°58' S, 071°21' W
Coronel	37°01' S, 073°08' W
Curacautín	38°26' S, 071°53' W
Curico	34°59' S, 071°14' W
Cuya	19°07' S, 070°08' W
El Salvador	26°14' S, 069°37' W
El Toro	37°17' S, 071°28' W
Huara	19°59' S, 069°47' W
Huasco	28°28' S, 071°14' W
Iquique	20°13' S, 070°10' W
La Serena	29°54' S, 071°16' W
La Tirana	20°21' S, 069°40' W
La Unión	40°17' S, 073°05' W
Lebu	37°37' S, 073°39' W
Linares	35°51' S, 071°36' W
Los Andes	32°50' S, 070°37' W
Los Angeles	37°28' S, 072°21' W
Los Canchones	20°27' S, 069°37' W
Los Lagos	39°51' S, 072°50' W
Los Vilos	31°55' S, 071°31' W
Mejillones	23°06' S, 070°27' W
Molina	35°07' S, 071°17' W
Monte Patria	30°42' S, 070°58' W
Nueva Imperial	38°44' S, 072°57' W
Osorno	40°34' S, 073°09' W
Ovalle	30°36' S, 071°12' W
Oyahue	21°14' S, 068°16' W
Parral	36°09' S, 071°50' W
Pica	20°30' S, 069°21' W
Pitrufquén	38°59' S, 072°39' W
Porvenir	53°18' S, 070°22' W
Potrerillos	26°26' S, 069°29' W
Puente Alto	33°37' S, 070°35' W
Puerto Aisén	45°24' S, 072°42' W
Puerto Cisnes	44°45' S, 072°42' W
Puerto Montt	41°28' S, 072°57' W
Puerto Natales	51°44' S, 072°31' W
Puerto Quellon	43°07' S, 073°37' W
Puerto Varas	41°19' S, 072°59' W
Punta Arenas	53°09' S, 070°55' W
Purranque	40°55' S, 073°10' W
Quirihue	36°17' S, 072°32' W
Rancagua	34°10' S, 070°45' W
Rengo	34°25' S, 070°52' W
Río Blanco	40°50' S, 073°32' W
Salamanca	31°47' S, 070°58' W
San Antonio	33°35' S, 071°38' W
San Bernardo	33°36' S, 070°43' W
San Fernando	34°35' S, 071°00' W
San Pedro	33°54' S, 071°28' W
Santiago	33°27' S, 070°40' W
Sauzal	35°45' S, 072°07' W
Talca	35°26' S, 071°40' W
Talcahuano	36°43' S, 073°07' W
Taltal	25°24' S, 070°29' W
Temuco	38°44' S, 072°36' W
Tierra Amarilla	27°29' S, 070°17' W
Tiltil	33°05' S, 070°56' W
Tocopilla	22°05' S, 070°12' W
Tome	36°37' S, 072°57' W
Valdivia	39°48' S, 073°14' W
Vallenar	28°35' S, 070°46' W
Valparaíso	33°02' S, 071°38' W
Victoria	38°13' S, 072°20' W
Vicuna	30°02' S, 070°44' W
Villarrica	39°16' S, 072°13' W
Viña del Mar	33°02' S, 071°34' W
Yungay	37°07' S, 072°01' W

CHINA

pg. 142

Capital: Peking
Area: 9,572,900 sq km; 3,696,100 sq mi
Highest Elev.: Mt. Everest 8,850 m; 29,020 ft
Longest River: Yangtze 6,300 km; 3,920 mi
Avg. Temperature: Jan = -5°C; Jul = 26°C
Currency: Renminbi
Official Language: Mandarin Chinese

Name	Lat./Long.
Aksu	41°09' N, 080°15' E
Altay	47°52' N, 088°07' E
Anda (locally Sartu)	46°24' N, 125°19' E
Anqing	30°31' N, 117°02' E
Anshan	41°07' N, 122°57' E
Anshun	26°15' N, 105°56' E
Anyang (locally Zhangde)	36°05' N, 114°21' E
Baicheng	45°37' N, 122°49' E
Baiyin	36°32' N, 104°12' E
Baoding	38°52' N, 115°29' E
Baoji	34°23' N, 107°09' E
Baoshan	25°07' N, 099°09' E
Baotou	40°36' N, 109°59' E
Bei'an	48°16' N, 126°36' E
Beihai	21°29' N, 109°06' E
Beijing	39°56' N, 116°24' E
Beipiao	41°48' N, 120°44' E
Bengbu	32°57' N, 117°20' E
Benxi	41°20' N, 123°45' E
Bose	23°54' N, 106°37' E
Bozhou	27°23' N, 109°18' E
Butha Qi (locally Zalantun)	48°00' N, 123°43' E
Cangzhou	31°47' N, 119°58' E
Changchun	43°52' N, 125°21' E
Changde	29°02' N, 111°14' E
Changji	44°01' N, 087°19' E
Changsha	28°12' N, 112°58' E
Changzhi	36°11' N, 113°06' E
Changzhou	38°19' N, 116°52' E
Chaoyang	41°33' N, 122°25' E
Chengde	40°58' N, 117°53' E
Chengdu	30°40' N, 104°04' E
Chenzhou	25°48' N, 113°02' E
Chifeng	42°17' N, 118°53' E
Chongqing (locally Yuzhou)	29°34' N, 106°35' E
Dandong	40°08' N, 124°24' E
Daqing	46°36' N, 125°00' E
Daxian	31°16' N, 107°31' E
Denyang	31°08' N, 104°24' E
Dezhou	37°27' N, 116°18' E
Dongsheng	39°49' N, 109°59' E
Dongying	37°30' N, 118°31' E
Dukou	26°33' N, 101°44' E
Dunhua	43°21' N, 128°13' E
Duyun	26°16' N, 107°31' E
Enshi	30°18' N, 109°29' E
Fengcheng	28°12' N, 115°46' E
Fuling	29°43' N, 107°24' E
Fushun	41°52' N, 123°53' E
Fuxian (locally Wafangdian)	39°38' N, 122°00' E
Fuxin	42°06' N, 121°46' E
Fuyang	32°54' N, 115°49' E
Fuzhou	26°05' N, 119°18' E
Fuzhou	28°01' N, 116°20' E
Ganzhou	25°51' N, 114°56' E
Gejiu	23°23' N, 103°09' E
Golmud	36°22' N, 094°55' E
Guanghua (locally Laohekou)	32°22' N, 111°40' E
Guangzhou	23°07' N, 113°15' E
Guilin	25°17' N, 110°17' E
Guiyang	26°35' N, 106°43' E
Haicheng	40°52' N, 123°00' E
Haikou	20°03' N, 110°19' E
Hailar	49°12' N, 119°42' E
Hailong (locally Meichekou)	42°32' N, 125°38' E
Hami	42°48' N, 093°27' E
Handan	36°35' N, 114°29' E
Hanzhong	33°08' N, 107°02' E
Harbin	45°45' N, 126°39' E
Hebi	35°57' N, 114°13' E
Hechi (locally Jinchengjiang)	24°42' N, 108°02' E
Hefei	31°51' N, 117°17' E
Hegang	47°24' N, 130°22' E
Hengshui	37°43' N, 115°42' E
Hengyang	26°54' N, 112°36' E
Heshan	23°42' N, 108°48' E
Heze (locally Caozhou)	35°14' N, 115°27' E
Hohhot	40°47' N, 111°37' E
Horqin Youyi Qianqi (locally Ulan Hot)	46°05' N, 122°05' E
Houma	35°36' N, 111°21' E
Huaibei	33°57' N, 116°45' E
Huaide (locally Gongzhuling)	43°30' N, 124°49' E
Huaihua (locally Yushuwan)	27°33' N, 109°57' E
Huainan	32°40' N, 117°00' E
Huaiyin (locally Wangying)	33°35' N, 119°02' E
Huangshi	30°13' N, 115°06' E
Huizhou	23°05' N, 114°24' E
Hunjiang (locally Badaojiang)	41°54' N, 126°26' E
Huzhou (locally Wuxing)	30°52' N, 120°06' E
Jiamusi	46°50' N, 130°21' E
Jiangmen	22°35' N, 113°05' E
Jiaozuo	35°15' N, 113°13' E
Jiaxing	30°46' N, 120°45' E
Jiayuguan	39°49' N, 098°18' E
Jilin	43°51' N, 126°33' E
Jinan	36°40' N, 117°00' E
Jinchang	38°24' N, 102°06' E
Jincheng	35°30' N, 112°50' E
Jingdezhen	29°16' N, 117°11' E
Jinggangshan	26°37' N, 114°05' E
Jinhua	29°07' N, 119°39' E
Jining	35°24' N, 116°33' E
Jinshi	29°40' N, 111°45' E
Jinxi	40°45' N, 120°50' E
Jinzhou	41°07' N, 121°06' E
Jishou	28°19' N, 109°43' E
Jiujiang	29°44' N, 115°59' E
Jiuquan (locally Suzhou)	39°46' N, 098°34' E
Jixi	45°18' N, 130°58' E
Kaifeng	34°51' N, 114°21' E
Kaili	26°35' N, 107°55' E
Kaiyuan	23°42' N, 103°14' E
Karamay	45°30' N, 084°55' E
Kashi	39°29' N, 075°58' E
Korla	41°44' N, 086°09' E
Kunming	25°04' N, 102°41' E
Kuytun	44°25' N, 085°00' E
Laiwu	36°41' N, 118°28' E
Lanxi	29°13' N, 119°28' E
Lanzhou	36°03' N, 103°41' E
Lengshuitan	26°27' N, 111°35' E
Leshan	29°34' N, 103°44' E
Lhasa	29°39' N, 091°06' E
Lianyungang (locally Xinpu)	34°36' N, 119°13' E
Liaocheng	36°26' N, 115°58' E
Liaoyang	41°17' N, 123°11' E
Liaoyuan	42°55' N, 125°09' E
Linfen	36°05' N, 111°31' E
Linhe	40°50' N, 107°30' E
Linxia	35°28' N, 102°55' E
Linyi	37°05' N, 118°20' E
Liuzhou	24°19' N, 109°24' E
Longyan	25°11' N, 117°00' E
Loudi	27°45' N, 111°59' E
Lu'an	31°45' N, 116°29' E
Luoyang	34°41' N, 112°28' E
Luzhou	28°53' N, 105°23' E
Maoming	21°39' N, 110°54' E
Mianyang	31°28' N, 104°46' E
Mudanjiang	44°35' N, 129°36' E
Nanchang	28°41' N, 115°53' E
Nanchong	30°48' N, 106°04' E
Nanjing	32°03' N, 118°47' E
Nanning	22°49' N, 108°19' E
Nanping	26°38' N, 118°10' E
Nantong	32°02' N, 120°53' E
Nanyang	33°00' N, 112°32' E
Ningbo	29°53' N, 121°33' E
Pingdingshan	33°44' N, 113°18' E
Pingliang	35°32' N, 106°41' E
Pingxiang	22°06' N, 106°44' E
Puqi	29°43' N, 113°53' E
Putian	25°26' N, 119°01' E
Puyang	35°42' N, 114°59' E
Qingdao	36°04' N, 120°19' E
Qinzhou	21°57' N, 108°37' E
Qiqihar	47°22' N, 123°57' E
Qitaihe	45°48' N, 130°53' E
Quanzhou	24°54' N, 118°35' E
Qujing	25°36' N, 103°49' E
Sanming	26°14' N, 117°35' E
Shanghai	31°14' N, 121°28' E
Shangqiu (locally Zhuji)	34°27' N, 115°39' E
Shangrao	28°26' N, 117°58' E
Shantou	23°22' N, 116°40' E
Shaoguan	24°48' N, 113°35' E
Shaowu	27°18' N, 117°30' E
Shaoxing	30°00' N, 120°35' E
Shashi	30°19' N, 112°14' E
Shenyang	41°48' N, 123°27' E
Shenzhen	22°32' N, 114°08' E
Shihezi	44°18' N, 086°02' E
Shijiazhuang	38°03' N, 114°29' E
Shiyan	32°34' N, 110°47' E
Shuangyashan	46°40' N, 131°21' E
Shuicheng	26°36' N, 104°51' E
Siping	43°10' N, 124°20' E
Suining	30°32' N, 105°32' E
Suizhou	31°36' N, 113°03' E
Tacheng	46°45' N, 082°57' E
Tai'an	36°12' N, 117°07' E
Taiyuan	37°52' N, 112°33' E
Taizhou	32°29' N, 119°55' E
Tianshui	34°35' N, 105°43' E
Tiefa	42°30' N, 123°25' E
Tieling	42°18' N, 123°49' E
Tongchuan	35°05' N, 109°05' E
Tonghua	41°41' N, 125°55' E
Tongliao	43°37' N, 122°16' E
Tunxi	29°43' N, 118°19' E
Turpan	42°56' N, 089°10' E
Urumqi	43°48' N, 087°35' E
Wanxian	30°49' N, 108°24' E
Weifang	36°43' N, 119°06' E
Weihai	37°30' N, 122°06' E
Weinan	34°30' N, 109°30' E
Wenzhou	28°01' N, 120°39' E
Wuhai	39°47' N, 106°52' E
Wuhan	30°35' N, 114°16' E
Wuhu	31°21' N, 118°22' E
Wuwei (locally Liangzhou)	37°58' N, 102°48' E
Wuxi	31°35' N, 120°18' E
Wuzhong	38°00' N, 106°10' E
Wuzhou	23°29' N, 111°19' E
Xi'an	34°16' N, 108°54' E
Xiangfan	32°03' N, 112°05' E
Xiangtan	27°51' N, 112°54' E
Xianyang	34°22' N, 108°42' E
Xichang	27°53' N, 102°18' E
Xingtai	37°03' N, 114°30' E
Xining	36°37' N, 101°46' E
Xintai	35°54' N, 117°44' E
Xinyang (locally Pingqiao)	32°03' N, 114°05' E
Xinyu	27°48' N, 114°56' E
Yan'an	36°36' N, 109°28' E
Yancheng	33°23' N, 120°08' E
Yangquan	37°54' N, 113°36' E
Yangzhou	32°24' N, 119°26' E
Yanji	42°53' N, 129°31' E
Yantai	37°32' N, 121°24' E
Yibin	28°46' N, 104°34' E
Yichang	30°42' N, 111°17' E
Yichun	27°50' N, 114°24' E
Yichun	47°42' N, 128°54' E
Yinchuan	38°28' N, 106°19' E
Yingkou	40°40' N, 122°17' E
Yingtan	28°14' N, 117°00' E
Yining	43°54' N, 081°21' E
Yiyang	28°36' N, 112°20' E
Yongzhou	26°14' N, 111°37' E
Yuci	37°42' N, 112°44' E
Yueyang	29°23' N, 113°06' E
Yulin	22°38' N, 110°09' E
Yumen (locally Laojunmiao)	39°50' N, 097°44' E
Yuncheng	35°01' N, 110°59' E
Yuyao	30°03' N, 121°09' E
Zaozhuang	34°53' N, 117°34' E
Zhangjiakou	40°50' N, 114°56' E
Zhangye	38°56' N, 100°27' E
Zhaoqing	23°03' N, 112°27' E
Zhaotong	27°19' N, 103°43' E
Zhumadian	32°58' N, 114°03' E
Zhuozhou	39°30' N, 115°58' E
Zibo (locally Zhangdian)	36°48' N, 118°03' E
Zixing	25°58' N, 113°24' E
Zunyi	27°42' N, 106°55' E

COLOMBIA

pg. 124

Capital: Bogotá
Area: 1,141,748 sq km; 440,831 sq mi
Highest Elev.: Sierra Nevada de Santa Marta 5,780 m; 18,950 ft
Longest River: Magdalena 1,500 km; 930 mi
Avg. Temperature: Jan = 14°C; Jul = 13°C
Currency: peso
Official Language: Spanish

Name	Lat./Long.
Acandí	08°32' N, 077°14' W
Aguachica	08°19' N, 073°38' W
Andes	05°40' N, 075°53' W
Anserma	05°13' N, 075°48' W
Apartadó	07°54' N, 076°39' W
Arauca	07°05' N, 070°45' W
Arica	02°08' S, 071°47' W
Armenia	04°31' N, 075°41' W
Barrancabermeja	07°03' N, 073°52' W
Barranquilla	10°59' N, 074°48' W
Bello	06°20' N, 075°33'W
Bisinaca	04°30' N, 069°40' W
Bogotá	04°36' N, 074°05' W
Bolivar	01°50' N, 076°58' W
Bucaramanga	07°08' N, 073°09' W
Buenaventura	03°53' N, 077°04' W
Buga	03°54' N, 076°17' W
Caldas	06°05' N, 075°38' W
Cali	03°27' N, 076°31'W
Campo de la Cruz	10°23' N, 074°53' W
Caranacoa	02°25' N, 068°57' W
Cartagena	10°25' N, 075°32' W
Cartago	04°45' N, 075°55' W
Caucasia	08°00' N, 075°12' W
Cereté	08°53' N, 075°48' W
Cerrejón	11°02' N, 072°39' W
Chigorodó	07°41' N, 076°42' W
Chiquinquirá	05°37' N, 073°50' W
Ciénaga	11°01' N, 074°15' W
Codazzi	10°02' N, 073°14' W
Copacabana	06°21' N, 075°30' W
Corozal	09°19' N, 075°18' W
Cravo Norte	06°18' N, 070°12' W
Cúcuta	07°54' N, 072°31' W
Cupica	06°41' N, 077°30' W
Duitama	05°50' N, 073°02' W
El Banco	09°00' N, 073°58' W
El Carmen	09°43' N, 075°08' W
El Dorado	01°11' N, 071°52' W
El Yopal	05°21' N, 072°23' W
Envigado	06°10' N, 075°35' W
Facatativá	04°49' N, 074°22' W
Florencia	01°36' N, 075°36' W
Florida	03°21' N, 076°15' W
Floridablanca	07°04' N, 073°06' W
Garzón	02°12' N, 075°38' W
Girardot	04°18' N, 074°48' W
Granada	03°34' N, 073°45' W
Honda	05°12' N, 074°45' W
Ibagué	04°27' N, 075°14' W
Ipiales	00°50' N, 077°37' W
Itagüí	06°10' N, 075°36' W
La Ceja	06°02' N, 075°26' W
La Dorada	05°27' N, 074°40' W
Leticia	04°09' S, 069°57' W
Loreto	03°48' N, 070°15' W
Lorica	09°14' N, 075°49' W
Macujer	00°24' N, 073°07' W
Magangué	09°14' N, 074°45' W
Maicao	11°23' N, 072°13' W
Malambo	10°52' N, 074°47' W
Matarca	00°30' S, 072°38' W
Macanal	02°45' N, 067°58' W
Manizales	05°05' N, 075°32' W
Medellín	06°15' N, 075°35' W
Mitú	01°08' N, 070°03' W
Mocoa	01°09' N, 076°37' W
Mompós	09°14' N, 074°26' W
Montería	08°46' N, 075°53' W
Mosquera	02°30' N, 078°29' W
Mulatos	08°39' N, 076°44' W
Nazareth	12°11' N, 071°17' W
Neiva	02°56' N, 075°18' W
Ocana	08°15' N, 073°20' W
Palmira	03°32' N, 076°16' W
Pamplona	07°23' N, 072°39' W
Pasto	01°13' N, 077°17' W
Paz de Rio	05°59' N, 072°47' W
Pereira	04°49' N, 075°43' W
Pitalito	01°51' N, 076°02' W
Pizarro	04°58' N, 077°22' W
Planeta Rica	08°25' N, 075°36' W
Plato	09°47' N, 074°47' W
Popayán	02°27' N, 076°36' W
Puerto Alfonso	02°11' S, 070°59' W
Puerto Berrío	06°29' N, 074°24' W
Puerto Carreño	06°12' N, 067°22' W
Puerto Inírida	03°51' N, 067°55' W
Puerto Leguízamo	00°12' S, 074°46' W
Puerto Miraña	01°20' S, 070°19' W
Puerto Tejada	03°14' N, 076°24' W
Quibdó	05°42' N, 076°40' W
Ráquira	05°33' N, 073°38' W
Ríohacha	11°33' N, 072°55' W
Sahagún	08°57' N, 075°27' W
San Felipe	01°52' N, 067°06' W
San Jacinto	09°50' N, 075°08' W
San José	03°15' N, 067°20' W
San José de Guaviare	02°35' N, 072°38' W
San Juan Nepomuceno	09°57' N, 075°05' W
San Martín	03°42' N, 073°42' W
San Pedro de Arimena	04°37' N, 071°42' W
Santa Marta	11°15' N, 074°13' W
Santa Rosa	03°32' N, 069°48' W
Santander	03°01' N, 076°28' W
Sincelejo	09°18' N, 075°24' W
Soacha	04°35' N, 074°13' W
Socorro	06°29' N, 073°16' W
Sogamoso	05°43' N, 072°56' W
Soledad	10°55' N, 074°46' W
Sonsón	05°42' N, 075°18' W
Tame	06°28' N, 071°44' W
Tuluá	04°06' N, 076°11' W
Turbaco	10°20' N, 075°25' W
Turbo	08°06' N, 076°43' W
Tumaco	01°49' N, 078°46' W
Tunja	05°31' N, 073°22' W
Uribia	11°43' N, 072°16' W
Urrao	06°20' N, 076°11' W
Valledupar	10°29' N, 073°15' W
Villa Rosario	07°50' N, 072°28' W
Villavicencio	04°09' N, 073°37' W
Yarumal	06°58' N, 075°24' W
Zipaquirá	05°02' N, 074°00' W

COMOROS

pg. 153

Capital: Moroni
Area: 1,862 sq km; 719 sq mi
Highest Elev.: Mt. Karthala 2,360 m; 7,750 ft
Avg. Temperature: Jan = 19°C; Jul = 30°C
Currency: Comorian franc
Official Language: Comorian, Arabic, French

Name	Lat./Long.
Moroni	11°41' S, 043°16' E

CONGO

pg. 152

Capital: Brazzaville
Area: 342,000 sq km; 132,047 sq mi
Longest River: Congo 4,700 km; 2,900 mi
Avg. Temperature: Jan = 25°C; Jul = 25°C
Currency: CFA franc
Official Language: French

Name	Lat./Long.
Brazzaville	04°16' S, 015°17' E
Djambala	02°33' S, 014°45' E
Gamboma	01°53' S, 015°51' E
Impfondo	01°37' N, 018°04' E
Kayes	04°25' S, 011°41' E
Loubomo	04°12' N, 012°41' E
Madingou	04°09' S, 013°34' E
Makabana	02°48' S, 012°29' E

Name	Lat./Long.
Makoua	00°01' N, 015°39' E
Mossendjo	02°57' S, 012°44' E
Nkayi	04°11' S, 013°18' E
Ouesso	01°37' N, 016°04' E
Owando	00°29' S, 015°55' E
Pointe-Noire	04°48' S, 011°51' E
Sibiti	03°41' S, 013°21' E
Souanke	02°05' N, 014°03' E
Zanaga	02°15' S, 013°50' E

COSTA RICA ....pg. 117

Capital: ....San José
Area: ....51,100 sq km; 19,730 sq mi
Highest Elev.: .....Mt. Chirripó 3,820 m; 12,530 ft
Longest River: .....San Juan 200 km; 120 mi
Avg. Temperature: ..Jan = 19°C; Jul = 21°C
Currency: ....Costa Rican colón
Official Language: ..Spanish

Name	Lat./Long.
Alajuela	10°01' N, 084°13' W
Desamparados	09°54' N, 084°05' W
Puerto Limon (Limón)	10°00' N, 083°02' W
Puntarenas	09°58' N, 084°50' W
San José	09°56' N, 084°05' W

CÔTE D'IVOIRE ....pg. 150

Capital: ....Abidjan
Area: ....320,763 sq km; 123,847 sq mi
Highest Elev.: .....Mt. Nimba 1,750 m; 5,750 ft
Longest River: .....Bandama 800 km; 500 mi
Avg. Temperature: ..Jan = 27°C; Jul = 26°C
Currency: ....CFA franc
Official Language: ..French

Name	Lat./Long.
Abidjan	05°19' N, 004°02' W
Bouaké	07°41' N, 005°02' W
Daloa	06°53' N, 006°27' W
Gagnoa	06°08' N, 005°56' W
Man	07°24' N, 007°33' W
San-Pédro	04°44' N, 006°37' W
Yamoussoukro	06°49' N, 005°17' W

CROATIA ....pg. 130

Capital: ....Zagreb
Area: ....56,538 sq km; 21,829 sq mi
Highest Elev.: .....Mt. Troglav 1,910 m; 6,280 ft
Longest River: .....Sava 940 km; 580 mi
Avg. Temperature: ..Jan = 0°C; Jul = 22°C
Currency: ....kuna
Official Language: ..Croatian

Name	Lat./Long.
Karlovac	45°29' N, 015°33' E
Knin	44°02' N, 016°12' E
Nin	44°14' N, 015°11' E
Opatija	45°20' N, 014°19' E
Osijek	45°33' N, 018°42' E
Ploce	43°04' N, 017°26' E
Pozega (Slavonska Pozega)	45°20' N, 017°41' E
Pula	44°52' N, 013°50' E
Rijeka	45°21' N, 014°24' E
Sisak	45°29' N, 016°22' E
Slavonski Brod	45°09' N, 018°02' E
Split	43°31' N, 016°26' E
Trogir	43°32' N, 016°15' E
Vukovar	45°21' N, 019°00' E
Zadar	44°07' N 015°15' E
Zagreb	45°48' S, 016°00' E

CUBA ....pg. 116

Capital: ....Havana
Area: ....110,861 sq km; 42,804 sq mi
Highest Elev.: .....Turquino Pk. 1,970 m; 6,480 ft
Longest River: .....Cauto 370 km; 230 mi
Avg. Temperature: ..Jan = 22°C; Jul = 28°C
Currency: ....Cuban peso
Official Language: ..Spanish

Name	Lat./Long.
Banes	20°58' N, 075°43' W
Bayamo	20°23' N, 076°39' W
Camaguey	21°23' N, 077°55' W
Cárdenas	23°02' N, 081°12' W
Ciego de Avila	21°51' N, 078°46' W
Cienfuegos	22°09' N, 080°27' W
Colón	22°43' N, 080°54' W
Florida	21°32' N, 078°14' W
Guantánamo	20°08' N, 075°12' W
Guines	22°50' N, 082°02' W
Havana (La Habana)	23°08' N, 082°22' W
Holguín	20°53' N, 076°15' W
Jovellanos	22°48' N, 081°12' W
Las Tunas	20°58' N, 076°57' W
Manzanillo	20°21' N, 077°07' W
Matanzas	23°03' N, 081°35' W
Morón	22°06' N, 078°38' W
Palma Soriano	20°13' N, 076°00' W
Pinar del Rio	22°25' N, 083°42' W
Placetas	22°19' N, 079°40' W
Sagua la Grande	22°49' N, 080°05' W
San Antonio de los Baños	22°53' N, 082°30' W
Sancti Spíritus	21°56' N, 079°27' W
Santa Clara	22°24' N, 079°58' W
Santiago de Cuba	20°01' N, 075°49' W

CYPRUS ....pg. 147

Capital: ....Nicosia
Area: ....9,251 sq km; 3,572 sq mi
Highest Elev.: .....Mt. Olympus 1,950 m; 6,400 ft
Longest River: .....Pedieos 100 km; 60 mi
Avg. Temperature: ..Jan = 10°C; Jul = 28°C
Currency: ....Cyprus pound
Official Language: ..Greek, Turkish

Name	Lat./Long.
Larnaca	34°55' N, 033°38' E
Limassol	34°40' N, 033°02' E
Nicosia	35°10' N, 033°22' E

CZECH REPUBLIC ......pg. 133

Capital: ....Prague
Area: ....78,864 sq km; 30,450 sq mi
Highest Elev.: .....Mt. Snezka 1,600 m; 5,260 ft
Longest River: .....Elbe 1,160 km; 720 mi
Avg. Temperature: ..Jan = -1.5°C; Jul = 19.4°C
Currency: ....Czech koruna
Official Language: ..Czech

Name	Lat./Long.
Brno	49°12' N, 016°38' E
Ceská Lípa	50°41' N, 014°33' E
Ceské Budejovice	48°59' N, 014°28' E
Cesky Tesin	49°45' N, 018°37' E
Cheb	50°04' N, 012°22' E
Chomutov	50°27' N, 013°26' E
Decín	50°47' N, 014°13' E
Frydek-Mistek	49°41' N, 018°21' E
Havírov	49°47' N, 018°22' E
Hodonín	48°52' N, 017°08' E
Hradec Králové	50°13' N, 015°50' E
Jablonec	50°43' N, 015°11' E
Jihlava	49°24' N, 015°35' E
Karlovy Vary	50°13' N, 012°54' E
Karvina	49°52' N, 018°33' E
Kladno	50°09' N, 014°06' E
Kolín	50°02' N, 015°12' E
Kromeríz	49°18' N, 017°24' E
Liberec	50°47' N, 015°03' E
Litvinov	50°36' N, 013°37' E
Mladá Boleslav	50°25' N, 014°54' E
Most	50°32' N, 013°39' E
Novy Jicín	49°36' N, 018°01' E
Olomouc	49°35' N, 017°15' E
Opava	49°57' N, 017°55' E
Orlova	49°51' N, 018°25' E
Ostrava	49°50' N, 018°17' E
Písek	49°18' N, 014°09' E
Plzen	49°45' N, 013°22' E
Prague (Praha)	50°05' N, 014°28' E
Príbram	49°42' N, 014°01' E
Prostejov	49°28' N, 017°07' E
Sumperk	49°58' N, 016°58' E
Tábor	49°25' N, 014°40' E
Teplice	50°38' N, 013°50' E
Trebic	49°13' N, 015°53' E
Trinec	49°41' N, 018°39' E
Trutnov	50°34' N, 015°54' E
Ústí nad Labem	50°40' N, 014°02' E
Valasské Mezirící	49°28' N, 017°58' E
Vsetín	49°20' N, 018°00' E
Znojmo	48°51' N, 016°03' E

DENMARK ....pg. 131

Capital: ....Copenhagen
Area: ....43,094 sq km; 16,639 sq mi
Highest Elev.: .....Yding Forest Hill 170 m; 570 ft
Longest River: .....Gudena 160 km; 100 mi
Avg. Temperature: ..Jan = 0°C; Jul = 18°C
Currency: ....Danish krone
Official Language: ..Danish

Name	Lat./Long.
Alborg (Aalborg)	57°03' N, 009°56' E
Arhus (Aarhus)	56°09' N, 010°13' E
Copenhagen (Kobenhavn)	55°40' N, 012°35' E
Esbjerg	55°28' N, 008°27' E
Fredericia	55°35' N, 009°46' E
Frederiksberg	55°41' N, 012°32' E
Helsingor	56°02' N, 012°37' E
Horsens	55°52' N, 009°52' E
Kolding	55°29' N, 009°29' E
Odense	55°24' N, 010°23' E
Randers	56°28' N, 010°03' E
Ronne	55°06' N, 014°42' E
Roskilde	55°39' N, 012°05' E
Vejle	55°42' N, 009°32' E

DJIBOUTI ....pg. 151

Capital: ....Djibouti
Area: ....23,200 sq km; 8,950 sq mi
Highest Elev.: .....Mt. Mousa 2,060 m; 6,770 ft
Avg. Temperature: ..Jan = 25°C; Jul = 36°C
Currency: ....Djibouti franc
Official Language: ..Arabic, French

Name	Lat./Long.
Djibouti	11°36' N, 043°09' E

DOMINICA ....pg. 116

Capital: ....Roseau
Area: ....750 sq km; 290 sq mi
Highest Elev.: .....Mt. Diablotin 1,450 m; 4,750 ft
Avg. Temperature: ..Jan = 27°C; Jul = 32°C
Currency: ....East Caribbean dollar
Official Language: ..English

Name	Lat./Long.
Marigot	15°32' N, 061°18' W
Portsmouth	15°35' N, 061°28' W
Roseau	15°18' N, 061°24' W

DOMINICAN REP. ......pg. 116

Capital: ....Santo Domingo
Area: ....48,443sq km; 18,704 sq mi
Highest Elev.: .....Duarta Pk. 3,180 m; 10,420 ft
Longest River: .....Yaque del Norte 390 km; 240 mi
Avg. Temperature: ..Jan = 24°C; Jul = 27°C
Currency: ....Dominican peso
Official Language: ..Spanish

Name	Lat./Long.
Barahona	18°12' N, 071°06' W
La Romana	18°25' N, 068°58' W
La Vega	19°13' N, 070°31' W
Mao	19°34' N, 071°05' W
Puerto Plata	19°48' N, 070°41' W
San Cristóbal	18°25' N, 070°06' W
San Francisco De Macoris	19°18' N, 070°15' W
San Juan	18°48' N, 071°14' W
San Pedro De Macoris	18°27' N, 069°18' W
Santiago	19°27' N, 070°42' W
Santo Domingo	18°28' N, 069°54' W

ECUADOR ....pg. 123

Capital: ....Quito
Area: ....272,045 sq km; 105,037 sq mi
Highest Elev.: .....Chimborazo 6,310 m; 20,700 ft
Longest River: .....Napo 890 km; 550 mi
Avg. Temperature: ..Jan = 13°C; Jul = 13°C
Currency: ....Sucre
Official Language: ..Spanish

Name	Lat./Long.
Ambato	01°15' S, 078°37' W
Babahoyo	01°49' S, 079°31' W
Bahia de Caraquez	00°36' S, 080°25' W
Catacocha	04°04' S, 079°38' W
Celica	04°07' S, 079°57' W
Chone	00°41' S, 080°06' W
Cuenca	02°53' S, 078°59' W
Daule	01°52' S, 079°58' W
Esmeraldas	00°59' N, 079°42' W
General Leonidas Plaza Gutierrez	02°58' S, 078°25' W
Gualaquiza	03°24' S, 078°33' W
Guaranda	01°36' S, 079°00' W
Guayaquil	02°10' S, 079°54' W
Ibarra	00°21' N, 078°07' W
Jipijapa	01°20' S, 080°35' W
Lago Agrio (Nueva Loja)	00°06' N, 076°52' W
Latacunga	00°56' S, 078°37' W
Loja	04°00' S, 079°13' W
Macas	02°19' S, 078°07' W
Machala	03°16' S, 079°58' W
Manta	00°57' S, 080°44' W
Milagro	02°07' S, 079°36' W
Montecristi	01°03' S, 080°40' W
Naranjal	02°40' S, 079°37' W
Pasaje	03°20' S, 079°49' W
Portoviejo	01°03' S, 080°27' W
Puerto Francisco de Orellana (Coca)	00°28' S, 076°58' W
Puyo	01°28' S, 077°59' W
Quevedo	01°02' S, 079°27' W
Quito	00°13' S, 078°30' W
Riobamba	01°40' S, 078°38' W
Rosa Zarate	00°20' N, 079°28' W
Samborondon	01°57' S, 079°44' W
San Gabriel	00°36' N, 077°49' W
San Lorenzo	01°17' N, 078°50' W
Sangolqui	00°19' S, 078°27' W
San Miguel de Salcedo (San Miguel)	01°02' S, 078°34' W
Santa Elena	02°14' S, 080°51' W
Santa Isabel	03°16' S, 079°19' W
Santa Rosa	03°27' S, 079°58' W
Santo Domingo de los Colorados (Santo Domingo)	00°15' S, 079°09' W
Sucre	01°16' S, 080°26' W
Sucua	02°28' S, 078°10' W
Tena	00°59' S, 077°49' W
Tulcan	00°48' N, 077°43' W
Valdez	01°15' N, 079°00' W
Yantzaza	03°51' S, 078°45' W
Zamora	04°04' S, 078°58' W
Zaruma	03°41' S, 079°37' W

EGYPT ....pg. 151

Capital: ....Cairo
Area: ....997,739 sq km; 385,229 sq mi
Highest Elev.: .....Mt. Catherine 2,640 m; 8,670 ft
Longest River: .....Nile 6,650 km; 4,130 mi
Avg. Temperature: ..Jan = 13°C; Jul = 28°C
Currency: ....Egyptian pound
Official Language: ..Arabic

Name	Lat./Long.
Al-Fayyum	29°19' N, 030°50' E
Al-Jizah	30°01' N, 031°13' E
Al-Minya	28°06' N, 030°45' E
Akhmim	26°34' N, 031°44' E
Alexandria (al-Iskandariyah)	31°12' N, 029°54' E
Aswan	24°05' N, 032°53' E
Asyut	27°11' N, 031°11' E
Az-Zaqaziq	30°35' N, 031°31' E
Banha	30°28' N, 031°11' E
Bani Suwayf	29°05' N, 031°05' E
Bur Sa'id, *see* Port Said	
Cairo (Al-Qahirah)	30°03' N, 031°15' E
Damanhur	31°02' N, 030°28' E
Jirja	26°20' N, 031°53' E
Luxor (al-Uqsur)	25°41' N, 032°39' E
Mallawi	27°44' N, 030°50' E
Marsa Matruh	31°21' N, 027°14' E
Port Said (Bur Sa'id)	31°16' N, 032°18' E
Qina	26°10' N, 032°43' E
Sawhaj	26°33' N, 031°42' E
Shibin al-Kawm	30°33' N, 031°01' E
Suez (as-Suways)	29°58' N, 032°33' E
Tanta	30°47' N, 031°00' E

EL SALVADOR ....pg. 117

Capital: ....San Salvador
Area: ....21,041 sq km; 8,124 sq mi
Highest Elev.: .....Santa Ana Volc. 2,360 m; 7,750 ft
Longest River: .....Lempa 320 km; 200 mi
Avg. Temperature: ..Jan = 22°C; Jul = 23°C
Currency: ....colón
Official Language: ..Spanish

Name	Lat./Long.
San Miguel	13°29' N, 088°11' W
San Salvador	13°42' N, 089°12' W

EQUATORIAL GUINEA .pg. 152

Capital: ....Malabo
Area: ....28,051 sq km; 10,831 sq mi
Highest Elev.: .....Mt. Santa Isabel 3,010 m; 9,880 ft
Longest River: .....Benito 3200 km; 200 mi
Avg. Temperature: ..Jan = 25°C; Jul = 24°C
Currency: ....CFA franc
Official Language: ..Spanish

Name	Lat./Long.
Malabo (Santa Isabel)	03°21' N, 008°40' E

ERITREA ....pg. 151

Capital: ....Asmara
Area: ....117,400 sq km; 45,300 sq mi
Highest Elev.: .....Mt. Soira 3,010 m; 9,890 ft
Avg. Temperature: ..Jan = 21.1°C; Jul = 25.6°C
Currency: ....Ethiopian birr
Official Language: ..Tigrinya, Arabic

Name	Lat./Long.
Asmera (Asmara)	15°20' N, 038°56' E
Mitsiwa (Massawa)	15°36' N, 039°28' E

ESTONIA ....pg. 138

Capital: ....Tallinn
Area: ....45,227 sq km; 17,462 sq mi
Highest Elev.: .....Suur Munamägi 320 m; 1,040 ft
Longest River: .....Pärnu 140 km; 90 mi
Avg. Temperature: ..Jan = -6°C; Jul = 17°C
Currency: ....kroon
Official Language: ..Estonian

Name	Lat./Long.
Jõgeva	58°45' N, 026°24' E
Kehra	59°20' N, 025°20' E
Kilingi-Nõmme	58°09' N, 024°58' E
Kohtla-Järve	59°24' N, 027°15' E
Kuressaare (Kingissepa)	58°15' N, 022°28' E
Lihula (Lihula)	58°41' N, 023°50' E
Marjamaa	58°54' N, 024°26' E
Mustla	58°14' N, 025°52' E
Narva	59°23' N, 028°12' E
Nuia	58°06' N, 025°33' E
Otepaa	58°03' N, 026°30' E
Paldiski	59°20' N, 024°06' E
Paide	58°54' N, 025°33' E
Pärnu	58°24' N, 024°32' E
Parnu-Jaagupi	58°37' N, 024°30' E
Rapla	59°01' N, 024°47' E
Rapina	58°06' N, 027°27' E
Saue	59°18' N, 024°34' E
Tallinn	59°25' N, 024°45' E
Tamsalu	59°10' N, 026°06' E
Tapa	59°16' N, 025°58' E
Tartu	58°23' N, 026°43' E
Voru	57°50' N, 027°03' E

ETHIOPIA ....pg. 151

Capital: ....Addis Ababa
Area: ....1,133,882 sq km; 437,794 sq mi
Highest Elev.: ....Mt. Ras Dejen 4,620 m; 15,160 ft
Avg. Temperature: .Jan = 16°C; Jul = 15°C
Currency: ....Ethiopian birr
Official Language: .Amharic

Name	Lat./Long.
Addis Ababa (Adis Abeba)	09°02' N, 038°42' E
Bahir Dar	11°36' N, 037°23' E
Debre Zeyit	08°45' N, 038°59' E
Dese (Dase)	11°08' N, 039°38' E
Dire Dawa	09°35' N, 041°52' E
Gonder	12°36' N, 037°28' E
Harer (Harar)	09°19' N, 042°07' E
Jima (Jimma)	07°40' N, 036°50' E
Mekele	13°30' N, 039°28' E
Nazret	08°33' N, 039°16' E

FIJI ....pg. 156

Capital: ....Suva
Area: ....18,274 sq km; 7,056 sq mi
Highest Elev.: .....Mt. Tomaniivi 1,320 m; 4,340 ft
Longest River: .....Rewa 150 km; 95 mi
Avg. Temperature: ..Jan = 27°C; Jul = 24°C
Currency: ....Fiji dollar
Official Language: ..English

Name	Lat./Long.
Lautoka	17°37' S, 177°28' E
Suva	18°08' S, 178°25' E

FINLAND ....pg. 131

Capital: ....Helsinki
Area: ....338,145 sq km; 130,559 sq mi
Highest Elev.: .....Mt. Haltia 1,330 m; 4,360 ft
Longest River: .....Kemi 550 km; 340 mi
Avg. Temperature: ..Jan = -6°C; Jul = 17°C
Currency: ....markka
Official Language: ..Finnish, Swedish

Name	Lat./Long.
Espoo (Esbo)	60°13' N, 024°40' E
Forssa	60°49' N, 023°38' E
Hameenlinna (Tavastehus)	61°00' N, 024°27' E
Hanko	59°50' N, 022°57' E
Heinola	61°13' N, 026°02' E
Helsinki	60°10' N, 024°58' E
Ivalo	68°39' N, 027°36' E
Joensuu	62°36' N, 029°46' E
Jyväskylä	62°14' N, 025°44' E
Kangasala	61°28' N, 024°05' E
Kotka	60°28' N, 026°55' E
Kouvola	60°52' N, 026°42' E
Kuhmo	64°08' N, 029°31' E
Kuopio	62°54' N, 027°41' E
Lahti	60°58' N, 025°40' E
Lappeenranta (Villmanstrand)	61°04' N, 028°11' E
Lapua	62°57' N, 023°00' E
Lohja	60°15' N, 024°05' E
Mikkeli (Sankt Michel)	61°41' N, 027°15' E
Nivala	63°55' N, 024°58' E
Nurmes	63°33' N, 029°07' E
Oulu (Uleåborg)	65°01' N, 025°28' E
Pello	66°47' N, 023°55' E
Pori (Björneborg)	61°29' N, 021°47' E
Posio	66°06' N, 028°09' E
Raahe	64°41' N, 024°29' E
Rauma	61°08' N, 021°30' E
Salla	66°50' N, 028°40' E
Salo	60°23' N, 023°08' E
Sotkamo	64°08' N, 028°25' E

Name	Lat./Long.
Tampere (Tammerfors)	61°30' N, 023°45' E
Turku (Åbo)	60°27' N, 022°17' E
Vaasa (Vasa)	63°06' N, 021°36' E
Vantaa (Vanda)	60°18' N, 024°51' E

FRANCE ....pg. 129

Capital: Paris
Area: 543,965 sq km; 210,026 sq mi
Highest Elev.: Mont Blanc 4,810 m; 15,770 ft
Longest River: Loire 1,020 km; 630 mi
Avg. Temperature: Jan = 19°C; Jul = 27°C
Currency: franc
Official Language: French

Name	Lat./Long.
Abbeville	50°06' N, 001°50' E
Agde	43°19' N, 003°28' E
Agen	44°12' N, 000°38' E
Aigues-Mortes	43°34' N, 004°11' E
Aire-sur-la-Lys	50°38' N, 002°24' E
Aix-en-Provence	43°32' N, 005°26' E
Aix-les-Bains	45°42' N, 005°55' E
Ajaccio	41°55' N, 008°44' E
Albi	43°56' N, 002°09' E
Alençon	48°26' N, 000°05' E
Aleria	42°06' N, 009°31' E
Alès	44°08' N, 004°05' E
Amboise	47°25' N, 000°59' E
Amiens	49°54' N, 002°18' E
Angers	47°28' N, 000°33' W
Angoulême	45°39' N, 000°09' E
Annecy	45°54' N, 006°07' E
Annemasse	46°12' N, 006°15' E
Antibes	43°35' N, 007°07' E
Arles	43°40' N, 004°38' E
Armentières	50°41' N, 002°53' E
Arras	50°17' N, 002°47' E
Aubagne	43°17' N, 005°34' E
Aubusson	45°57' N, 002°10' E
Auch	43°39' N, 000°35' E
Auray	47°40' N, 002°59' W
Aurillac	44°55' N, 002°27' E
Autun	46°57' N, 004°18' E
Auxerre	47°48' N, 003°34' E
Avignon	43°57' N, 004°49' E
Avranches	48°41' N, 001°22' W
Azay-le-Rideau	47°16' N, 000°28' E
Bar-le-Duc	48°47' N, 005°10' E
Bastia	42°42' N, 009°27' E
Bayeux	49°16' N, 000°42' W
Bayonne	43°29' N, 001°29' W
Beaucaire	43°48' N, 004°38' E
Beaugency	47°47' N, 001°38' E
Beaune	47°02' N, 004°50' E
Beauvais	49°26' N, 002°05' E
Belfort	47°38' N, 006°52' E
Bergerac	44°51' N, 000°29' E
Besançon	47°15' N, 006°02' E
Bèthune	50°32' N, 002°38' E
Bèziers	43°21' N, 003°15' E
Biarritz	43°29' N, 001°34' W
Blanzy	46°42' N, 004°23' E
Blois	47°35' N, 001°20' E
Bobigny	48°54' N, 002°27' E
Bonifacio	41°23' N, 009°09' E
Bonneville	46°05' N, 006°25' E
Bordeaux	44°50' N, 000°34' W
Boulogne-Billancourt	48°50' N, 002°15' E
Boulogne-sur-Mer	50°43' N, 001°37' E
Bourg-en-Bresse	46°12' N, 005°13' E
Bourges	47°05' N, 002°24' E
Bourgoin	45°35' N, 005°17' E
Brest	48°24' N, 004°29' W
Briançon	44°54' N, 006°39' E
Brive-la-Gaillarde	45°09' N, 001°32' E
Caen	49°11' N, 000°21' W
Cahors	44°26' N, 001°26' E
Calais	50°57' N, 001°50' E
Calvi	42°34' N, 008°45' E
Cambrai	50°10' N, 003°14' E
Cannes	43°33' N, 007°01' E
Carcassonne	43°13' N, 002°21' E
Carnac	47°35' N, 003°05' W
Carpentras	44°03' N, 005°03' E
Castres	43°36' N, 002°15' E
Cenon	44°51' N, 000°32' W
Chalon-sur-Saône	46°47' N, 004°51' E
Châlons-Sur-Marne	48°57' N, 004°22' E
Chambéry	45°34' N, 005°56' E
Chambord	47°37' N, 001°31' E
Chamonix-Mont-Blanc	45°55' N, 006°52' E
Chantilly	49°12' N, 002°28' E
Charleville-Mézières	49°46' N, 004°43' E
Chartres	48°27' N, 001°30' E
Châteauroux	46°49' N, 001°42' E
Château-Thierry	49°03' N, 003°24' E
Châtellerault	46°48' N, 000°32' E
Chaumont	48°07' N, 005°08' E
Chenonceaux	47°20' N, 001°04' E
Cherbourg	49°39' N, 001°39' W
Chinon	47°10' N, 000°15' E
Cholet	47°04' N, 000°53' W
Clairvaux	48°09' N, 004°47' E
Clermont-Ferrand	45°47' N, 003°05' E
Cluny	46°26' N, 004°39' E
Cognac	45°42' N, 000°20' W
Colmar	48°05' N, 007°22' E
Colomiers	43°37' N, 001°21' E
Compiègne	49°25' N, 002°50' E
Concarneau	47°52' N, 003°55' W
Corbeil-Essonnes	48°36' N, 002°29' E
Corte	42°18' N, 009°09' E
Coucy-Auffrique	49°31' N, 003°19' E
Coutances	49°03' N, 001°26' W
Creil	49°16' N, 002°29' E
Crèteil	48°47' N, 002°28' E
Croix	50°40' N, 003°09' E
Dax	43°43' N, 001°03' W
Decazeville	44°33' N, 002°15' E
Dieppe	49°56' N, 001°05' E
Digne	44°06' N, 006°14' E
Dijon	47°19' N, 005°01' E
Dinan	48°27' N, 002°02' W
Dole	47°06' N, 005°30' E
Douai	50°22' N, 003°04' E
Douarnenez	48°06' N, 004°20' W
Draguignan	43°32' N, 006°28' E
Dreux	48°44' N, 001°22' E
Dunkirk (Dunkerque)	51°03' N, 002°22' E
Eauze	43°52' N, 000°06' E
Falaise	48°54' N, 000°12' W
Fécamp	49°45' N, 000°22' E
Firminy	45°23' N, 004°18' E
Foix	42°58' N, 001°36' E
Fontaine	45°11' N, 005°40' E
Fontainebleau	48°24' N, 002°42' E
Fontenay-le-Comte	46°28' N, 000°49' W
Fontevrault	47°11' N, 000°03' E
Forbach	49°11' N, 006°54' E
Fougéres	48°21' N, 001°12' W
Fréjus	43°26' N, 006°44' E
Gap	44°34' N, 006°05' E
Gavarnie	42°44' N, 000°00' E
Gisors	49°17' N, 001°47' E
Granville	48°50' N, 001°36' W
Grasse	43°40' N, 006°55' E
Gravelines	50°59' N, 002°07' E
Grenoble	45°10' N, 005°43' E
Guéret	46°10' N, 001°52' E
Guingamp	48°33' N, 003°09' W
Haguenau	48°49' N, 007°47' E
Herouville	49°12' N, 000°19' W
Hesdin	50°22' N, 002°02' E
Honfleur	49°25' N, 000°14' E
Hyères	43°07' N, 006°07' E
Istres	43°31' N, 004°59' E
Joué-lès-Tours	47°21' N, 000°40' E
Kaysersberg	48°08' N, 007°15' E
La Baule-Escoublac	47°17' N, 002°24' W
La Ciotat	43°10' N, 005°36' E
La Roche-sur-Yon	46°40' N, 001°26' W
La Rochelle	46°10' N, 001°09' W
La Seyne-sur-Mer	43°06' N, 005°53' E
Lacq	43°25' N, 000°38' W
Lanester	47°45' N, 003°21' W
Langres	47°52' N, 005°20' E
Laon	49°34' N, 003°37' E
Laval	48°04' N, 000°46' W
Le Cannet	43°34' N, 007°01' E
Le Creusot	46°48' N, 004°26' E
Le Croisic	47°18' N, 002°31' W
Le Havre	49°30' N, 000°08' E
Le Mans	48°00' N, 000°12' E
Le Petit Quevilly	49°26' N, 001°02' E
Le Puy	45°02' N, 003°53' E
Lens	50°26' N, 002°50' E
Les Baux-de-Provence	43°45' N, 004°48' E
Lescar	43°20' N, 000°25' W
Libourne	44°55' N, 000°14' W
Liévin	50°25' N, 002°46' E
Lille	50°38' N, 003°04' E
Lillebonne	49°31' N, 000°33' E
Lillers	50°34' N, 002°29' E
Limoges	45°45' N, 001°20' E
Lisieux	49°09' N, 000°14' E
Loches	47°08' N, 001°00' E
Locmariaquer	47°34' N, 002°57' W
Longwy	49°31' N, 005°46' E
Lons-le-Saunier	46°40' N, 005°33' E
Lorient	47°45' N, 003°22' W
Loudun	47°00' N, 000°04' E
Lourdes	43°06' N, 000°03' W
Luçon	46°27' N, 001°10' W
Lunéville	48°36' N, 006°30' E
Lyon	45°45' N, 004°51' E
Mâcon	46°18' N, 004°50' E
Maillezais	46°22' N, 000°44' W
Marignane	43°25' N, 005°13' E
Marseille	43°18' N, 005°24' E
Martigues	43°24' N, 005°03' E
Maubeuge	50°17' N, 003°58' E
Meaux	48°57' N, 002°52' E
Melun	48°32' N, 002°40' E
Mende	44°31' N, 003°30' E
Menton	43°47' N, 007°30' E
Metz	49°08' N, 006°10' E
Millau	44°06' N, 003°05' E
Mirebeau	46°47' N, 000°11' E
Mont-de-Marsan	43°53' N, 000°30' W
Montauban	44°01' N, 001°21' E
Montbéliard	47°31' N, 006°48' E
Montceau	46°40' N, 004°22' E
Montdidier	49°39' N, 002°34' E
Montélimar	44°34' N, 004°45' E
Montigny	49°06' N, 006°09' E
Montluçon	46°20' N, 002°36' E
Montpellier	43°36' N, 003°53' E
Morlaix	48°35' N, 003°50' W
Moulins	46°34' N, 003°20' E
Mulhouse	47°45' N, 007°20' E
Munster	48°03' N, 007°08' E
Nancy	48°41' N, 006°12' E
Nanterre	48°54' N, 002°12' E
Nantes	47°13' N, 001°33' W
Narbonne	43°11' N, 003°00' E
Nemours	48°16' N, 002°42' E
Nevers	46°59' N, 003°10' E
Nice	43°42' N, 007°15' E
Nîmes	43°50' N, 004°21' E
Niort	46°19' N, 000°28' W
Noirmoutier	47°00' N, 002°15' W
Noyon	49°35' N, 003°00' E
Obernai	48°28' N, 007°29' E
Oradour-sur-Glane	45°56' N, 001°02' E
Orange	44°08' N, 004°48' E
Orléans	47°55' N, 001°54' E
Oyonnax	46°15' N, 005°40' E
Paimpol	48°46' N, 003°03' W
Paris	48°52' N, 002°20' E
Parthenay	46°39' N, 000°15' W
Pau	43°18' N, 000°22' W
Périgueux	45°11' N, 000°43' E
Péronne	49°56' N, 002°56' E
Perpignan	42°41' N, 002°53' E
Pessac	44°48' N, 000°37' W
Poitiers	46°35' N, 000°20' E
Pontoise	49°03' N, 002°06' E
Porto-Vecchio	41°35' N, 009°17' E
Privas	44°44' N, 004°36' E
Provins	48°33' N, 003°18' E
Quimper	48°00' N, 004°06' W
Rambouillet	48°39' N, 001°50' E
Reims	49°15' N, 004°02' E
Remiremont	48°01' N, 006°35' E
Rennes	48°05' N, 001°41' W
Rezé	47°12' N, 001°34' W
Ribeauvillé	48°12' N, 007°19' E
Richelieu	47°01' N, 000°19' E
Riom	45°54' N, 003°07' E
Roanne	46°02' N, 004°04' E
Rochefort	45°56' N, 000°59' W
Rocroi	49°55' N, 004°31' E
Rodez	44°20' N, 002°34' E
Romans-sur-Isère	45°03' N, 005°03' E
Rosheim	48°30' N, 007°28' E
Roubaix	50°42' N, 003°10' E
Rouen	49°26' N, 001°05' E
Saint-Affrique	43°57' N, 002°53' E
Saint-Amand-les-Eaux	50°26' N, 003°26' E
Saint-Amand-Montrond	46°43' N, 002°31' E
Saint-Benoît-sur-Loire	47°49' N, 002°18' E
Saint-Brieuc	48°31' N, 002°47' W
Saint-Chamond	45°28' N, 004°30' E
Saint-Denis	48°56' N, 002°22' E
Saint-Dié	48°17' N, 006°57' E
Saint-Dizier	48°38' N, 004°57' E
Saint-Étienne	45°26' N, 004°24' E
Saint-Jean-de-Luz	43°23' N, 001°40' W
Saint-Lô	49°07' N, 001°05' W
Saint-Malo	48°39' N, 002°01' W
Saint-Maur-des-Fossés	48°48' N, 002°30' E
Saint-Mihiel	48°54' N, 005°33' E
Saint-Nazaire	47°17' N, 002°12' W
Saint-Omer	50°45' N, 002°15' E
Saint-Pol	51°02' N, 002°21' E
Saint-Priest	45°42' N, 004°57' E
Saint-Quentin	49°51' N, 003°17' E
Saint-Raphaël	43°25' N, 006°46' E
Saint-Tropez	43°16' N, 006°38' E
Saintes	45°45' N, 000°38' W
Saintes-Maries-de-la-Mer	43°27' N, 004°26' E
Salon-de-Provence	43°38' N, 005°06' E
Sancerre	47°20' N, 002°50' E
Sarreguemines	49°06' N, 007°03' E
Sartène	41°37' N, 008°59' E
Saumur	47°16' N, 000°05' W
Sedan	49°42' N, 004°57' E
Sélestat	48°16' N, 007°27' E
Senlis	49°12' N, 002°35' E
Sens	48°12' N, 003°17' E
Sète	43°24' N, 003°41' E
Soissons	49°22' N, 003°20' E
Strasbourg	48°35' N, 007°45' E
Talence	44°49' N, 000°36' W
Tarascon	43°48' N, 004°40' E
Tarbes	43°14' N, 000°05' E
Thionville	49°22' N, 006°10' E
Thonon-les-Bains	46°22' N, 006°29' E
Thouars	46°58' N, 000°13' W
Tignes	45°30' N, 006°55' E
Toul	48°41' N, 005°54' E
Toulon	43°07' N, 005°56' E
Toulouse	43°36' N, 001°26' E
Tourcoing	50°43' N, 003°09' E
Tours	47°23' N, 000°41' E
Trouville	49°22' N, 000°05' E
Troyes	48°18' N, 004°05' E
Tulle	45°16' N, 001°46' E
Valence	44°56' N, 004°54' E
Valenciennes	50°21' N, 003°32' E
Vandoeuvre	48°39' N, 006°11' E
Vannes	47°40' N, 002°45' W
Vaulx-en-Velin	45°47' N, 004°56' E
Vendôme	47°48' N, 001°04' E
Vénissieux	45°41' N, 004°53' E
Verdun	49°10' N, 005°23' E
Vernon	49°05' N, 001°29' E
Versailles	48°48' N, 002°08' E
Vesoul	47°38' N, 006°10' E
Vézelay	47°28' N, 003°44' E
Vichy	46°07' N, 003°25' E
Vienne	45°31' N, 004°52' E
Vierzon	47°13' N, 002°05' E
Villefranche-sur-Mer	43°42' N, 007°19' E
Villefranche-sur-Saône	45°59' N, 004°43' E
Villeneuve-sur-Lot	44°24 'N, 000°43' E
Villeurbanne	45°46' N, 004°53' E
Vouillé	46°38' N, 000°10' E
Wattrelos	50°42' N, 003°13' E
Wissembourg	49°02' N, 007°57' E

GABON ....pg. 152

Capital: Libreville
Area: 267,667 sq km; 103,347 sq mi
Highest Elev.: Mt. Iboundji 980 m; 3,220 ft
Longest River: Ogooué 1,200 km; 750 mi
Avg. Temperature: Jan = 27°C; Jul = 24°C
Currency: CFA franc
Official Language: French

Name	Lat./Long.
Bitam	02°05' N, 011°29' E
Booué	00°06' S, 011°56' E
Fougamou	01°13' S, 010°36' E
Franceville	01°38' N, 013°35' E
Kango	00°09' S, 010°08' E
Lambaréné	00°42' S, 010°13' E
Lastoursville	00°49' S, 012°42' E
Libreville	00°23' S, 009°27' E
Makokou	00°34' N, 012°52' E
Mayumba	03°25' S, 010°39' E
Mekambo	01°01' N, 013°56' E
Minvoul	02°09' S, 012°08' E
Mitzic	00°47' N, 011°34' E
Mouila	01°52' S, 011°01' E
Ndjolé	00°11' S, 010°45' E
Okondja	00°41' S, 013°47' E
Omboue	01°34' S, 009°15' E
Oyem	01°37' N, 011°35' E
Port-Gentil	00°43' S, 008°47' E
Setté Cama	02°32' S, 009°45' E
Tchibanga	02°51' S, 011°02' E

GAMBIA, THE ....pg. 150

Capital: Banjul
Area: 10,689sq km; 4,127 sq mi
Longest River: Gambia 1,130 km; 700 mi
Avg. Temperature: Jan = 23°C; Jul = 28°C
Currency: dalasi
Official Language: English

Name	Lat./Long.
Banjul	13°27' N, 016°35' W

GEORGIA ....pg. 147

Capital: Tbilisi
Area: 69,700 sq km; 26,900 sq mi
Highest Elev.: Mt. Shkhara 5,070 m; 16,630 ft
Longest River: Kura 1,360 km; 850 mi
Avg. Temperature: Jan = 0°C; Jul = 39°C
Currency: Georgian coupon
Official Language: Georgian

Name	Lat./Long.
Batumi	41°38' N, 041°38' E
Gori	41°58' N, 044°07' E
Kutaisi	42°15' N, 042°40' E
Poti	42°09' N, 041°40' E
Sokhumi	43°00' N, 041°02' E
Tbilisi (Tiflis)	41°42' N, 044°45' E
Zugdidi	42°30' N, 041°53' E

GERMANY ....pg. 132

Capital: Berlin
Area: 356,733 sq km; 137,735sq mi
Highest Elev.: Zugspitze 2,960 m; 9,720 ft
Longest River: Rhine 1,390 km; 870 mi
Avg. Temperature: Jan = -0.5°C; Jul = 17.4°C
Currency: Deutsche mark
Official Language: German

Name	Lat./Long.
Aachen	50°46' N, 006°06' E
Aalen	48°50' N, 010°06' E
Ahlen	51°45' N, 007°55' E
Altenburg	50°59' N, 012°27' E
Amberg	49°27' N, 011°52' E
Amorbach	49°39' N, 009°14' E
Andernach	50°26' N, 007°24' E
Ansbach	49°18' N, 010°35' E
Apolda	51°01' N, 011°30' E
Arnsberg	51°23' N, 008°05' E
Arnstadt	50°50' N, 010°57' E
Aschaffenburg	49°59' N, 009°09' E
Aschersleben	51°45' N, 011°28' E
Aue	50°35' N, 012°42' E
Augsburg	48°22' N, 010°53' E
Aurich	53°28' N, 007°29' E
Bad Harzburg	51°53' N, 010°34' E
Bad Hersfeld	50°52' N, 009°42' E
Bad Homburg	50°13' N, 008°37' E
Bad Kissingen	50°12' N, 010°05' E
Bad Kreuznach	49°50' N, 007°52' E
Bad Mergentheim	49°29' N, 009°46' E
Bad Salzuflen	52°05' N, 008°46' E
Baden-Baden	48°45' N, 008°15' E
Bamberg	49°52' N, 010°52' E
Bautzen	51°11' N, 014°26' E
Bayreuth	49°57' N, 011°35' E
Berchtesgaden	47°38' N, 013°00' E
Bergheim	50°58' N, 006°39' E
Bergisch Gladbach	50°59' N, 007°08' E
Berlin	52°30' N, 013°22' E
Bernburg	51°48' N, 011°44' E
Bernkastel-Kues	49°55' N, 007°04' E
Bielefeld	52°02' N, 008°32' E
Blankenburg	51°47' N, 010°57' E
Bocholt	51°50' N, 006°36' E
Bonn	50°44' N, 007°06' E
Borna	51°07' N, 012°30' E
Brandenburg	52°25' N, 012°33' E
Braunschweig (Brunswick)	52°16' N, 010°32' E
Breisach	48°02' N, 007°35' E
Bremen	53°05' N, 008°48' E
Bremerhaven	53°33' N, 008°35' E
Brilon	51°24' N, 008°34' E
Bruchsal	49°08' N, 008°36' E
Brühl	50°50' N, 006°54' E
Brunswick, *see* Braunschweig	
Burg	52°16' N, 011°51' E
Buxtehude	53°27' N, 009°42' E
Calw	48°43' N, 008°44' E
Celle	52°37' N, 010°05' E
Chemnitz (Karl-Marx-Stadt)	50°50' N, 012°55' E
Cloppenburg	52°51' N, 008°02' E
Coburg	50°15' N, 010°58' E
Cochem	50°08' N, 007°09' E
Cologne (Köln)	50°56' N, 006°57' E
Coswig	51°08' N, 013°35' E
Cottbus	51°46' N, 014°20' E
Crailsheim	49°09' N, 010°05' E
Crimmitschau	50°49' N, 012°23' E
Cuxhaven	53°53' N, 008°42' E
Dachau	48°16' N, 011°26' E
Darmstadt	49°52' N, 008°39' E
Deggendorf	48°50' N, 012°58' E
Delmenhorst	53°03' N, 008°37' E
Dessau	51°50' N, 012°15' E
Detmold	51°56' N, 008°53' E
Dinkelsbühl	49°04' N, 010°19' E
Donauwörth	48°42' N, 010°48' E
Dormagen	51°06' N, 006°50' E
Dorsten	51°40' N, 006°58' E
Dortmund	51°31' N, 007°27' E
Dresden	51°03' N, 013°45' E
Duisburg	51°26' N, 006°45' E
Düren	50°48' N, 006°29' E
Düsseldorf	51°13' N, 006°46' E
Eberswalde-Finow	52°50' N, 013°47' E
Eichstätt	48°53' N, 011°11' E
Eisenach	50°59' N, 010°19' E
Eisenberg	50°58' N, 011°54' E
Eisenhüttenstadt	52°09' N, 014°39' E
Eisleben	51°32' N, 011°33' E
Ellwangen	48°57' N, 010°08' E

Name	Lat./Long.
Elmshorn	53°45' N, 009°39' E
Emden	53°22' N, 007°13' E
Erding	48°18' N, 011°56' E
Erfurt	50°59' N, 011°02' E
Erlangen	49°36' N, 011°01' E
Eschwege	51°11' N, 010°04' E
Eschweiler	50°49' N, 006°17' E
Essen	51°27' N, 007°01' E
Esslingen	48°45' N, 009°18' E
Ettlingen	48°57' N, 008°24' E
Falkensee	52°34' N, 013°05' E
Flensburg	54°47' N, 009°26' E
Forchheim	49°43' N, 011°04' E
Forst	51°44' N, 014°38' E
Frankenthal	49°32' N, 008°21' E
Frankfurt	52°21' N, 014°33' E
Frankfurt am Main	50°07' N, 008°41' E
Freiberg	50°55' N, 013°22' E
Freiburg	48°00' N, 007°51' E
Freising	48°24' N, 011°44' E
Freital	51°01' N, 013°39' E
Freudenstadt	48°26' N, 008°25' E
Friedberg	48°21' N, 010°59' E
Friedrichshafen	47°39' N, 009°29' E
Fulda	50°33' N, 009°40' E
Fürstenfeldbruck	48°11' N, 011°15' E
Fürth	49°28' N, 011°00' E
Furtwangen	48°03' N, 008°12' E
Füssen	47°34' N, 010°42' E
Ganderkesee	53°02' N, 008°32' E
Garbsen	52°25' N, 009°36' E
Garmisch-Partenkirchen	47°30' N, 011°06' E
Gelsenkirchen	51°31' N, 007°06' E
Genthin	52°24' N, 012°10' E
Gera	50°52' N, 012°05' E
Germering	48°08' N, 011°22' E
Giessen	50°35' N, 008°39' E
Glückstadt	53°47' N, 009°25' E
Göppingen	48°42' N, 009°40' E
Görlitz	51°10' N, 015°00' E
Goslar	51°54' N, 010°26' E
Gotha	50°57' N, 010°43' E
Göttingen	51°32' N, 009°56' E
Greifswald	54°06' N, 013°23' E
Greiz	50°39' N, 012°12' E
Grevesmühlen	53°52' N, 011°11' E
Grossenhain	51°17' N, 013°33' E
Guben (Wilhelm-Pieck Stadt Guben)	51°57' N, 014°43' E
Güstrow	53°48' N, 012°10' E
Gutersloh	51°54' N, 008°23' E
Hagen	51°21' N, 007°28' E
Hagenow	53°26' N, 011°11' E
Halberstadt	51°54' N, 011°03' E
Haldensleben	52°18' N, 011°25' E
Halle	51°30' N, 012°00' E
Halle-Neustadt	51°29' N, 011°56' E
Hamburg	53°33' N, 010°00' E
Hameln	52°06' N, 009°21' E
Hamm	51°41' N, 007°48' E
Hannover	52°22' N, 009°43' E
Harzgerode	51°38' N, 011°09' E
Havelburg	52°49' N, 012°05' E
Hechingen	48°21' N, 008°59' E
Heidelberg	49°25' N, 008°42' E
Heidenheim	48°41' N, 010°09' E
Heilbronn	49°08' N, 009°13' E
Herford	52°08' N, 008°41' E
Herne	51°33' N, 007°13' E
Hildesheim	52°09' N, 009°58' E
Hof	50°19' N, 011°55' E
Homburg	49°19' N, 007°20' E
Höxter	51°46' N, 009°23' E
Hoyerswerda	51°26' N, 014°15' E
Hürth	50°52' N, 006°52' E
Ingolstadt	48°46' N, 011°26' E
Jena	50°56' N, 011°35' E
Jülich	50°56' N, 006°22' E
Kaiserslautern	49°27' N, 007°45' E
Karl-Marx-Stadt, *see* Chemnitz	
Karlsruhe	49°01' N, 008°24' E
Kassel	51°19' N, 009°30' E
Kaufbeuren	47°53' N, 010°37' E
Kelheim	48°55' N, 011°52' E
Kempten	47°43' N, 010°19' E
Kerpen	50°52' N, 006°41' E
Kiel	54°20' N, 010°08' E
Kleve	51°47' N, 006°09' E
Koblenz	50°21' N, 007°36' E
Köln, *see* Cologne	
Königswinter	50°41' N, 007°11' E
Konstanz	47°40' N, 009°11' E
Korbach	51°17' N, 008°52' E
Köthen	51°45' N, 011°58' E
Krefeld	51°20' N, 006°34' E
Kulmbach	50°06' N, 011°27' E
Landshut	48°32' N, 012°09' E
Leinefelde	51°23' N, 010°20' E
Leipzig	51°18' N, 012°20' E
Lemgo	52°02' N, 008°54' E
Leuna	51°19' N, 012°01' E
Leverkusen	51°01' N, 006°59' E
Limburg	50°23' N, 008°03' E
Lingen	52°31' N, 007°19' E
Lippstadt	51°40' N, 008°21' E
Löbau	51°06' N, 014°40' E
Lörrach	47°37' N, 007°40' E
Lorsch	49°39' N, 008°34' E
Lübeck	53°52' N, 010°42' E
Ludwigsburg	48°54' N, 009°11' E
Ludwigshafen	49°29' N, 008°27' E
Lüneburg	53°15' N, 010°24' E
Lünen	51°37' N, 007°31' E
Lutter	51°59' N, 010°16' E
Maasholm	54°41' N, 009°59' E
Magdeburg	52°10' N, 011°40' E
Mainz	50°00' N, 008°15' E
Mannheim	49°29' N, 008°28' E
Mansfeld	51°35' N, 011°28' E
Marburg	50°49' N, 008°46' E
Marl	51°39' N, 007°05' E
Meerane	50°51' N, 012°28' E
Meiningen	50°33' N, 010°25' E
Memmingen	47°59' N, 010°10' E
Menden	51°26' N, 007°48' E
Merseburg	51°22' N, 012°00' E
Minden	52°17' N, 008°55' E

Name	Lat./Long.
Mittenwald	47°26' N, 011°15' E
Moers	51°27' N, 006°39' E
Molln	53°38' N, 010°41' E
Monchengladbach	51°12' N, 006°26' E
Mühlhausen	51°13' N, 010°27' E
Mülheim	51°26' N, 006°53' E
Münden	51°25' N, 009°41' E
Munich	48°09' N, 011°35' E
Münster	51°58' N, 007°38' E
Naumburg	51°09' N, 011°49' E
Neubrandenburg	53°34' N, 013°16' E
Neumarkt	49°17' N, 011°28' E
Neumünster	54°04' N, 009°59' E
Neunkirchen	49°21' N, 007°11' E
Neuruppin	52°56' N, 012°48' E
Neuss	51°12' N, 006°42' E
Neustrelitz	53°22' N, 013°05' E
Neuwied	50°26' N, 007°28' E
Norden	53°36' N, 007°12' E
Nordenham	53°30' N, 008°29' E
Norderstedt	53°42' N, 010°01' E
Nordhausen	51°31' N, 010°48' E
Nordhorn	52°26' N, 007°05' E
Nördlingen	48°51' N, 010°30' E
Northeim	51°42' N, 010°00' E
Nürnberg (Nuremberg)	49°27' N, 011°05' E
Offenbach	50°06' N, 008°46' E
Offenburg	48°29' N, 007°56' E
Oldenburg	54°18' N, 010°53' E
Oldenburg	53°10' N, 008°12' E
Osnabrück	52°16' N, 008°03' E
Osterode	51°44' N, 010°11' E
Ottobrunn	48°04' N, 011°41' E
Paderborn	51°43' N, 008°46' E
Parchim	53°26' N, 011°51' E
Passau	48°35' N, 013°29' E
Peenemünde	54°08' N, 013°47' E
Peine	52°19' N, 010°14' E
Petersdorf	54°29' N, 011°04' E
Pforzheim	48°53' N, 008°42' E
Pirmasens	49°12' N, 007°36' E
Pirna	50°58' N, 013°56' E
Plauen	50°30' N, 012°08' E
Potsdam	52°24' N, 013°04' E
Prenzlau	53°19' N, 013°52' E
Quedlinburg	51°47' N, 011°09' E
Rathenow	52°36' N, 012°20' E
Ravensburg	47°47' N, 009°37' E
Recklinghausen	51°37' N, 007°12' E
Regensburg	49°01' N, 012°06' E
Reichenbach	50°37' N, 012°18' E
Remagen	50°34' N, 007°14' E
Remscheid	51°11' N, 007°12' E
Rendsburg	54°18' N, 009°40' E
Reutlingen	48°29' N, 009°13' E
Rheine	52°17' N, 007°27' E
Riesa	51°18' N, 013°18' E
Rosenheim	47°51' N, 012°08' E
Rostock	54°05' N, 012°08' E
Rothenburg	49°23' N, 010°11' E
Rottweil	48°10' N, 008°37' E
Rudolstadt	50°43' N, 011°20' E
Rüsselsheim	50°00' N, 008°25' E
Saalfeld	50°39' N, 011°22' E
Saarbrücken	49°14' N, 007°00' E
Saarlouis	49°19' N, 006°45' E
Salzgitter	52°05' N, 010°20' E
Salzwedel	52°51' N, 011°09' E
Sankt Augustin	50°46' N, 007°11' E
Schleswig	54°31' N, 009°33' E
Schönebeck	52°01' N, 011°45' E
Schwäbisch Gmünd	48°48' N, 009°47' E
Schwäbisch Hall	49°06' N, 009°44' E
Schwedt	53°04' N, 014°18' E
Schweinfurt	50°03' N, 010°14' E
Schwerin	53°38' N, 011°23' E
Seevetal	53°24' N, 009°58' E
Senftenberg	51°31' N, 014°01' E
Siegen	50°52' N, 008°02' E
Sikéai (Sikies)	37°31' N, 021°53' E
Sindelfingen	48°42' N, 009°01' E
Singen	47°46' N, 008°50' E
Solingen	51°11' N, 007°05' E
Sömmerda	51°09' N, 011°06' E
Sondershausen	51°22' N, 010°52' E
Sonneberg	50°21' N, 011°10' E
Speyer	49°19' N, 008°26' E
Spremberg	51°33' N, 014°22' E
Stassfurt	51°52' N, 011°35' E
Stendal	52°36' N, 011°51' E
Stolberg	50°46' N, 006°14' E
Stralsund	54°18' N, 013°06' E
Straubing	48°53' N, 012°34' E
Strausberg	52°35' N, 013°53' E
Stuttgart	48°46' N, 009°11' E
Suhl	50°36' N, 010°42' E
Torgau	51°34' N, 013°00' E
Torgelow	53°38' N, 014°01' E
Triberg	48°08' N, 008°14' E
Trier	49°45' N, 006°38' E
Tübingen	48°32' N, 009°03' E
Tuttlingen	47°59' N, 008°49' E
Uelzen	52°58' N, 010°34' E
Ulm	48°24' N, 010°00' E
Vechta	52°43' N, 008°17' E
Velzen	52°58' N, 010°34' E
Verden	52°55' N, 009°14' E
Villingen-Schwenningen	48°04' N, 008°27' E
Völklingen	49°15' N, 006°51' E
Walsrode	52°54' N, 009°40' E
Waren	53°31' N, 012°41' E
Warnemünde	54°10' N, 012°05' E
Weiden	49°41' N, 012°10' E
Weimar	50°59' N, 011°19' E
Weinheim	49°33' N, 008°40' E
Weissenfels	51°12' N, 011°58' E
Wernigerode	51°50' N, 010°47' E
Wesel	51°40' N, 006°37' E
Wetzlar	50°33' N, 008°30' E
Weyhe	52°58' N, 008°48' E
Wiesbaden	50°05' N, 008°15' E
Wilhelm-Pieck-Stadt Guben, *see* Guben	
Wilhelmshaven	53°31' N, 008°08' E
Wismar	53°54' N, 011°28' E
Wittenberg	51°52' N, 012°39' E
Wittenberge	53°00' N, 011°45' E

Name	Lat./Long.
Wolfen	51°40' N, 012°17' E
Wolfenbüttel	52°10' N, 010°33' E
Wolfsburg	52°26' N, 010°48' E
Worms	49°38' N, 008°21' E
Wuppertal	51°16' N, 007°11' E
Würzburg	49°48' N, 009°56' E
Zeitz	51°03' N, 012°09' E
Zell	50°02' N, 007°11' E
Zerbst	51°58' N, 012°05' E
Zittau	50°54' N, 014°50' E
Zweibrucken	49°15' N, 007°22' E
Zwickau	50°44' N, 012°30'E

GHANA ....pg. 150

Capital: ....Accra
Area: ....238,533 sq km; 92,098 sq mi
Highest Elev.: .....Mt. Afadjato 890 m; 2,900 ft
Longest River: .....Black Volta 1,160 km; 720 mi
Avg. Temperature: . .Jan = 28°C; Jul = 25°C
Currency: ....cedi
Official Language: . .English

Name	Lat./Long.
Accra	05°33' N, 000°13' W
Cape Coast	05°06' N, 001°15' W
Koforidua	05°14' N, 001°20' W
Kumasi	06°41' N, 001°37' W
Obuasi	06°12' N, 001°40' W
Sekondi	04°56' N, 001°42' W
Takoradi	04°53' N, 001°45' W
Tamale	09°24' N, 000°50' W
Tema	05°37' N, 000°01' W

GREECE ....pg. 135

Capital: ....Athens
Area: ....131,957 sq km; 50,949 sq mi
Highest Elev.: .....Mt. Olympus 2,920 m; 9,570 ft
Longest River: .....Aliákmon 300 km; 190 mi
Avg. Temperature: . .Jan = 9°C; Jul = 28°C
Currency: ....drachma
Official Language: . .Greek

Name	Lat./Long.
Alexandroúpolis (Alexandhroupolis)	40°51' N, 025°52' E
Almirós	39°11' N, 022°46' E
Amphissa (Amfissa)	38°32' N, 022°23' E
Ándros	37°50' N, 024°56' E
Athens (Athínai)	37°59' N, 023°44' E
Árgos	37°38' N, 022°44' E
Argostólion	38°11' N, 020°29' E
Argos Orestikón	40°28' N, 021°16' E
Arkhángelos	36°12' N, 028°08' E
Áyios Kírikos	37°35' N, 026°14' E
Corinth (Korinthos)	37°56' N, 022°56' E
Dráma	41°09' N, 024°09' E
Elassón	39°54' N, 022°11' E
Ermoupolis, *see* Hermoupolis	
Flórina	40°47' N, 021°24' E
Glifadha (Glyphada)	37°52' N, 023°45' E
Idhra	37°21' N, 023°28' E
Igoumenitsa	39°30' N, 020°16' E
Ioannina (Yannina)	39°40' N, 020°50' E
Ios	36°44' N, 025°17' E
Iraklion (Candia or Herakleion)	35°20' N, 025°08' E
Kalabáka	39°42' N, 021°38' E
Kalamai (Kalamata)	37°02' N, 022°07' E
Kalamaria	40°35' N, 022°58' E
Kallithea	37°57' N, 023°42' E
Kardhitsa	39°22' N, 021°55' E
Karpenísion	38°55' N, 021°47' E
Katerini	40°16' N, 022°30' E
Kavala (Kavalla or Neapolis)	40°56' N, 024°25' E
Kariaí	40°15' N, 024°15' E
Kérkira	39°36' N, 019°55' E
Khalkidhón (Nea Khalkidhon)	40°44' N, 022°36' E
Kilkís	41°00' N, 022°52' E
Kími	38°38' N, 024°06' E
Kíthira	36°09' N, 022°59' E
Khalkis (Chalcis)	38°28' N, 023°36' E
Khania (Canea)	35°31' N, 024°02' E
Khios (Chios)	38°22' N, 026°08' E
Komotiní	41°07' N, 025°24' E
Korinthos, *see* Corinth	
Kos	36°53' N, 027°18' E
Kozáni	40°18' N, 021°47' E
Kranídhion	37°23' N, 023°09' E
Lágos	41°01' N, 025°07' E
Larisa (Larissa)	39°38' N, 022°25' E
Lávrion (Laurium)	37°43' N, 024°03' E
Leondárion	39°11' N, 022°08' E
Leonídhion	37°10' N, 022°52' E
Levkás	38°50' N, 020°42' E
Lindhos (Lindos)	36°06' N, 028°04' E
Mestá	38°16' N, 025°55' E
Monemvasía	36°41' N, 023°03' E
Navplion (Nauplia)	37°34' N, 022°48' E
Nea Ionia	38°02' N, 023°45' E
Neapolis	40°19' N, 021°23' E
Nikea (Nikaia)	37°58' N, 023°39' E
Orestiás	41°30' N, 026°31' E
Párga	39°17' N, 020°24' E
Patrai	38°15' N, 021°44' E
Páros	37°05' N, 025°09' E
Pérama	39°42' N, 020°51' E
Peristerion	38°01' N, 023°42' E
Pílos	36°55' N, 021°42' E
Piraeus (Piraievs)	37°57' N, 028°38 'E
Políyiros	40°23' N, 023°27' E
Pyrgos (Pirgos)	37°41' N, 021°27' E
Rodhos (Rhodes)	36°26' N, 028°13' E
Sámos	37°45' N, 026°58' E
Serrai	41°05' N, 023°33' E
Siátista	40°16' N, 021°33' E
Souflíon	41°12' N, 026°18' E
Sparta (Sparti)	37°05' N, 022°26' E
Thásos	40°47' N, 024°43' E
Thebes (Thivai)	38°19' N, 023°19' E
Thessaloniki (Salonika)	40°38' N, 022°56' E
Thíra	36°25' N, 025°26' E
Tinos	37°32' N, 025°10' E
Trikala	39°33' N, 021°46' E
Tripolis	37°31' N, 022°22' E
Valestínon	39°23' N, 022°45' E
Veroia	40°31' N, 022°12' E
Xánthi	41°08' N, 024°53' E

GRENADA ....pg. 116

Capital: ....St. George's
Area: ....344 sq km; 133 sq mi
Highest Elev.: .....Mt. St. Catherine 840 m; 2,7600 ft
Avg. Temperature: . .Jan = 28°C; Jul = 28°C
Currency: ....East Caribbean dollar
Official Language: . .English

Name	Lat./Long.
St. George's	12°03' N, 061°45' W

GUATEMALA ....pg. 117

Capital: ....Guatemala City
Area: ....108,889 sq km; 42,042 sq mi
Highest Elev.: . . .Tajumulco Volc. 4,220 m; 13,850 ft
Longest River: . . .Motagua 400 km; 250 mi
Avg. Temperature: Jan = 16°C; Jul = 19°C
Currency: ......Guatemalan quetzal
Official Language: Spanish

Name	Lat./Long.
Escuintla	14°18' N, 090°47' W
Guatemala City (Guatemala)	14°38' N, 090°31' W
Puerto San Jose (San Jose)	13°55' N, 090°49' W
Quezaltenango	14°50' N, 091°31' W

GUINEA ....pg. 150

Capital: ....Conakry
Area: ....245,857 sq km; 94,926 sq mi
Highest Elev.: .....Mt. Nimba 1,750 m; 5,750 ft
Longest River: .....Niger 4,200 km; 2,600 mi
Avg. Temperature: . .Jan = 26°C; Jul = 26°C
Currency: ....Guinean franc
Official Language: . .French

Name	Lat./Long.
Conakry	09°31' N, 013°43' W
Kankan	10°23' N, 009°18' W
Kindia	10°04' N, 012°51' W
Labé	11°19' N, 012°17' W
Nzérékoré	07°45' N, 008°49' W

GUINEA-BISSAU ....pg. 150

Capital: ....Bissau
Area: ....36,125 sq km; 13,948 sq mi
Avg. Temperature: . .Jan = 25°C; Jul = 27°C
Currency: ....Guinea-Bissau peso
Official Language: . .Portuguese

Name	Lat./Long.
Bissau	11°51' N, 015°35' W

GUYANA ....pg. 120

Capital: ....Georgetown
Area: ....215,083 sq km; 83,044 sq mi
Highest Elev.: .....Mt. Roraima 2,770 m; 9,090 ft
Longest River: .....Essequibo 1,010 km; 630 mi
Avg. Temperature: . .Jan = 26°C; Jul = 27°C
Currency: ....Guyana dollar
Official Language: . .English

Name	Lat./Long.
Charity	07°24' N, 058°36' W
Corriverton	05°52' N, 057°10' W
Georgetown	06°48' N, 058°10' W
Mabaruma	08°12' N, 059°47' W
New Amsterdam	06°15' N, 057°31' W
Vreed en Hoop	06°48' N, 058°11' W

HAITI ....pg. 116

Capital: ....Port-au-Prince
Area: ....27,700 sq km; 10,695 sq mi
Highest Elev.: .....Mt. la Selle 2,700 m; 8,770 ft
Longest River: .....Artibonite 280 km; 170 mi
Avg. Temperature: . .Jan = 31°C; Jul = 35°C
Currency: ....gourde
Official Language: . .Haitian Creole, French

Name	Lat./Long.
Cap-Haïtien	19°45' N, 072°12' W
Gonaives	19°27' N, 072°41' W
Port-au-Prince	18°32' N, 072°20' W

HONDURAS ....pg. 117

Capital: ....Tegucigalpa
Area: ....112,088 sq km; 43,277 sq mi
Highest Elev.: .....Mt. Celaque 2,850 m; 9,350 ft
Longest River: .....Coco 780 km; 4900 mi
Avg. Temperature: . .Jan = 19°C; Jul = 23°C
Currency: ....Honduran lempira
Official Language: . .Spanish

Name	Lat./Long.
Choluteca	13°18' N, 087°12' W
El Progreso	15°24' N, 087°48' W
La Ceiba	15°47' N, 086°48' W
San Marcos de Colón	13°26' N, 086°48' W
San Pedro Sula	15°30' N, 088°02' W
Tegucigalpa	14°06' N, 087°13' W

HUNGARY ....pg. 134

Capital: ....Budapest
Area: ....93,033 sq km; 35,920 sq mi
Highest Elev.: .....Mt. Kekes 1,010 m; 3,330 ft
Longest River: .....Danube 2,850 km; 1,770 mi
Avg. Temperature: . .Jan = -1°C; Jul = 22°C
Currency: ....forint
Official Language: . .Hungarian

Name	Lat./Long.
Békéscsaba	46°41' N, 021°06' E
Budapest	47°30' N, 019°05' E
Debrecen	47°32' N, 021°38' E
Dunakeszi	47°38' N, 019°08' E
Dunaújváros (Sztálinváros)	46°59' N, 018°56' E

Name	Lat./Long.
Eger	47°54' N, 020°23' E
Gyor	47°41' N, 017°38' E
Hódmezovásárhely	46°25' N, 020°20' E
Kaposvár	46°22' N, 017°48' E
Kecskemét	46°54' N, 019°42' E
Miskolc	48°06' N, 020°47' E
Nagyatád	46°13' N, 017°22' E
Nagykanizsa	46°27' N, 016°59' E
Nyíregyháza	47°57' N, 021°43' E
Ózd	48°13' N, 020°18' E
Pécs	46°05' N, 018°14' E
Salgótarján	48°07' N, 019°49' E
Sopron	47°41' N, 016°36' E
Szeged	46°15' N, 020°10' E
Székesfehérvár	47°12' N, 018°25' E
Szolnok	47°11' N, 020°12' E
Szombathely	47°14' N, 016°37' E
Tatabánya	47°34' N, 018°25' E
Vác	47°47' N, 019°08' E
Veszprém	47°06' N, 017°55' E
Zalaegerszeg	46°50' N, 016°51' E

ICELAND

pg. 131

Capital: Reykjavík
Area: 102,819 sq km; 39,699 sq mi
Highest Elev.: Mt. Hvannadals 2,120 m; 6,950 ft
Longest River: Thjorsa 230 km; 140 mi
Avg. Temperature: Jan = 1°C; Jul = 11°C
Currency: króna
Official Language: Icelandic

Name	Lat./Long.
Akureyri	65°40' N, 018°06' W
Reykjavík	64°09' N, 021°57' W

INDIA

pg. 146

Capital: New Delhi
Area: 3,165,596 sq km; 1,222,243sq mi
Highest Elev.: KanchenjungaPk. 8,590 m; 28,210 ft
Longest River: Ganges 2,510 km; 1,560 mi
Avg. Temperature: Jan = 13.9°C; Jul = 31.1°C
Currency: Indian rupee
Official Language: Hindi, English

Name	Lat./Long.
Adoni	15°38' N, 077°17' E
Agartala	23°49' N, 091°16' E
Agra	27°11' N, 078°01' E
Ahmadabad (Ahmedabad)	23°02' N, 072°37' E
Ahmadnagar (Ahmednagar)	19°05' N, 074°44' E
Ajmer	26°27' N, 074°38' E
Akola	20°44' N, 077°00' E
Aligarh	27°53' N, 078°05' E
Allahabad	25°27' N, 081°51' E
Alleppey	09°29' N, 076°19' E
Alwar	27°34' N, 076°36' E
Amaravati (Amaravathi)	16°35' N, 080°22' E
Amritsar	31°35' N, 074°53' E
Anantapur	14°41' N, 077°36' E
Ara (Arrah)	25°34' N, 084°40' E
Aurangabad	19°53' N, 075°20' E
Baharampur (Berhampore)	24°06' N, 088°15' E
Bahraich	27°35' N, 081°36' E
Ballia	25°45' N, 084°10' E
Balurghat	25°13' N, 088°46' E
Bangalore	12°59' N, 077°35' E
Barddhaman (Burdwan)	23°15' N, 087°51' E
Bareilly	28°21' N, 079°25' E
Barmer	25°45' N, 071°23' E
Batala	31°48' N, 075°12' E
Bathinda (Bhatinda)	30°12' N, 074°57' E
Beawar	26°06' N, 074°19' E
Belgaum	15°52' N, 074°30' E
Bellary	15°09' N, 076°56' E
Bettiah	26°48' N, 084°30' E
Bhadravati	13°52' N, 075°43' E
Bharatpur	27°13' N, 077°29' E
Bharuch (Broach)	21°42' N, 072°58' E
Bhatpara	22°52' N, 088°24' E
Bhavnagar (Bhaunagar)	21°46' N, 072°09' E
Bhilainagar	21°13' N, 081°26' E
Bhilwara	25°21' N, 074°38' E
Bhimavaram	16°32' N, 081°32' E
Bhind	26°34' N, 078°48' E
Bhiwandi	19°18' N, 073°04' E
Bhopal	23°16' N, 077°24' E
Bhubaneshwar	20°14' N, 085°50' E
Bhuj	23°16' N, 069°40' E
Bhusawal	21°03' N, 075°46' E
Bid (Bhir)	18°59' N, 075°46' E
Bidar	17°54' N, 077°33' E
Bihar Sharif	25°11' N, 085°31' E
Bijapur	16°50' N, 075°42' E
Bikaner	28°01' N, 073°18' E
Bilaspur	31°20' N, 076°45' E
Bilaspur	22°05' N, 082°09' E
Bombay (Mumbai)	18°58' N, 072°50' E
Brahmapur (Berhampur)	19°19' N, 084°47' E
Burhanpur	21°18' N, 076°14' E
Calcutta	22°32' N, 088°22' E
Calicut (Kozhikode)	11°15' N, 075°46' E
Chandigarh	30°44' N, 076°55' E
Chandrapur (Chanda)	19°57' N, 079°18' E
Chatrapur, *see* Chhatrapur	
Chengalpattu (Chingleput)	12°42' N, 079°59' E
Chhapra	25°46' N, 084°45' E
Chhatrapur (Chatrapur)	19°21' N, 084°59' E
Chhindwara	22°04' N, 078°56' E
Chikmagalur	13°19' N, 075°47' E
Chitradurga (Chitaldrug)	14°14' N, 076°24' E
Chittoor	13°12' N, 079°07' E
Churu	28°18' N, 074°57' E
Cochin	09°58' N, 076°14' E
Coimbatore	11°00' N, 076°58' E
Cuddalore	11°45' N, 079°45' E
Cuddapah	14°28' N, 078°49' E
Cuttack	20°30' N, 085°50' E
Darbhanga	26°10' N, 085°54' E
Datia	25°40' N, 078°28' E
Davangere	14°28' N, 075°55' E
Dehra Dun	30°19' N, 078°02' E
Delhi	28°40' N, 077°13' E
Devghar (Deoghar)	24°29' N, 086°42' E
Dewas	22°58' N, 076°04' E
Dhanbad	23°48' N, 086°27' E
Dhule (Dhulia)	20°54' N, 074°47' E
Dibrugarh	27°29' N, 094°54' E
Dimapur	25°54' N, 093°44' E
Dindigul	10°21' N, 077°57' E
Durg	21°11' N, 081°17' E
Eluru (Ellore)	16°42' N, 081°06' E
Erode	11°21' N, 077°44' E
Etawah	26°46' N, 079°02' E
Faizabad (Fyzabad)	26°47' N, 082°08' E
Faridabad	28°26' N, 077°19' E
Fatehpur	25°56' N, 080°48' E
Firozabad	27°09' N, 078°25' E
Firozpur (Ferozepore)	30°55' N, 074°36' E
Gadag-Betigeri	15°25' N, 075°37' E
Gandhinagar	23°12' N, 072°40' E
Gangtok	27°20' N, 088°37' E
Gauhati, *see* Guwahati	
Gaya	24°47' N, 085°00' E
Ghaziabad	28°40' N, 077°26' E
Gorakhpur	26°45' N, 083°22' E
Gulbarga	17°20' N, 076°50' E
Guna	24°39' N, 077°19' E
Guntur	16°18' N, 080°27' E
Gurgaon	28°28' N, 077°02' E
Guwahati (Gauhati)	26°11' N, 091°44' E
Gwalior	26°13' N, 078°10' E
Hanumangarh (Sadulgarh)	29°35' N, 074°19' E
Haridwar (Hardwar)	29°58' N, 078°10' E
Hassan	13°00' N, 076°05' E
Hisar (Hissar)	29°10' N, 075°43' E
Hoshangabad	22°45' N, 077°43' E
Hoshiarpur	31°32' N, 075°54' E
Howrah (Haora)	22°35' N, 088°20' E
Hubli-Dharwad	15°21' N, 075°10' E
Hugli-Chunchura	22°54' N, 088°24' E
Hyderabad	17°23' N, 078°28' E
Ichalkaranji	16°42' N, 074°28' E
Imphal	24°49' N, 093°57' E
Indore	22°43' N, 075°50' E
Itanagar	27°09' N, 093°33' E
Jabalpur (Jubbulpore)	23°10' N, 079°57' E
Jaipur	26°55' N, 075°49' E
Jalandhar (Jullundur)	31°19' N, 075°34' E
Jalgaon	21°01' N, 075°34' E
Jalna	19°50' N, 075°53' E
Jamalpur	25°18' N, 086°30' E
Jammu	32°44' N, 074°52' E
Jamnagar	22°28' N, 070°04' E
Jamshedpur	22°48' N, 086°11' E
Jhansi	25°26' N, 078°35' E
Jodhpur	26°17' N, 073°02' E
Kakinada (Cocanada)	16°56' N, 082°13' E
Kanchipuram (Conjeeveram)	12°50' N, 079°43' E
Kanpur (Cawnpore)	26°28' N, 080°21' E
Karimnagar	18°26' N, 079°09' E
Karnal	29°41' N, 076°59' E
Katihar	25°32' N, 087°35' E
Khammam (Khammamett)	17°15' N, 080°09' E
Khandwa	21°50' N, 076°20' E
Kharagpur	22°20' N, 087°20' E
Kohima	25°40' N, 094°07' E
Kolar	13°08' N, 078°08' E
Kolhapur	16°42' N, 074°13' E
Kota (Kotah)	25°11' N, 075°50' E
Kottayam	09°35' N, 076°31' E
Krishnanagar	23°24' N, 088°30' E
Kumbakonam	10°58' N, 079°23' E
Lalitpur	24°41' N, 078°25' E
Latur	18°24' N, 076°35' E
Lucknow	26°51' N, 080°55' E
Ludhiana	30°54' N, 075°51' E
Machilipatnam (Bandar, Masulipatam)	16°10' N, 081°08' E
Madgaon (Margao)	15°18' N, 073°57' E
Madras	13°05' N, 080°17' E
Madurai (Madura)	09°56' N, 078°07' E
Mahbubnagar	16°44' N, 077°59' E
Malegaon	20°33' N, 074°32' E
Mandsaur (Mandasor)	24°04' N, 075°04' E
Mandya	12°33' N, 076°54' E
Mangalore	12°52' N, 074°53' E
Marmagao (Mormugao)	15°24' N, 073°48' E
Mathura (Muttra)	27°30' N, 077°41' E
Meerut	28°59' N, 077°42' E
Mhow	22°33' N, 075°46' E
Miraj	16°50' N, 074°38' E
Morena (Pech Morena)	26°29' N, 078°01' E
Munger (Monghyr)	25°23' N, 086°28' E
Murwara	23°51' N, 080°24' E
Muzaffarpur	26°07' N, 085°24' E
Mysore	12°18' N, 076°39' E
Nadiad	22°42' N, 072°52' E
Nagaon (Nowgong)	26°21' N, 092°40' E
Nagercoil	08°10' N, 077°26' E
Nagpur	21°09' N, 079°06' E
Naihati	22°54' N, 088°25' E
Nanded (Nander)	19°09' N, 077°20' E
Nashik (Nasik)	19°59' N, 073°48' E
Nathdwara	24°56' N, 073°49' E
Navadwip (Nabadwip)	23°25' N, 088°22' E
Navsari	20°51' N, 072°55' E
Nellore	14°26' N, 079°58' E
New Delhi	28°36' N, 077°12' E
Nizamabad	18°40' N, 078°07' E
Palghat	10°47' N, 076°39' E
Pali	25°46' N, 073°20' E
Pandharpur	17°40' N, 075°20' E
Parbhani	19°16' N, 076°47' E
Pathankot	32°17' N, 075°39' E
Patna	25°36' N, 085°07' E
Pilibhit	28°38' N, 079°48' E
Pimpri-Chinchwad	18°36' N, 073°43' E
Pondicherry (Pondichery, Puduchcheri)	11°56' N, 079°53' E
Porbandar	21°38' N, 069°36' E
Port Blair	11°40' N, 092°45' E
Proddatur	14°44' N, 078°33' E
Pune (Poona)	18°32' N, 073°52' E
Quilon	08°53' N, 076°36' E
Rae Bareli	26°13' N, 081°14' E
Raichur	16°12' N, 077°22' E
Raiganj	25°37' N, 088°07' E
Raipur	21°14' N, 081°38' E
Rajapalaiyam	09°27' N, 077°34' E
Rajkot	22°18' N, 070°47' E
Ranchi	23°21' N, 085°20' E
Ratlam	23°19' N, 075°04' E
Ratnagiri	16°59' N, 073°18' E
Rewa (Rewah)	24°32' N, 081°18' E
Sagar (Saugor)	23°50' N, 078°43' E
Saharanpur	29°58' N, 077°33' E
Salem	11°39' N, 078°10' E
Sambalpur	21°27' N, 083°58' E
Sangli	16°52' N, 074°34' E
Sasaram	24°57' N, 084°02' E
Satara	17°41' N, 073°59' E
Satna	24°35' N, 080°50' E
Shahdol (Sahdol)	23°17' N, 081°21' E
Shahjahanpur	27°53' N, 079°55' E
Shiliguri (Siliguri)	26°42' N, 088°26' E
Shillong	25°34' N, 091°53' E
Shimla (Simla)	31°06' N, 077°10' E
Shimoga	13°55' N, 075°34' E
Shivpuri	25°26' N, 077°39' E
Sholapur (Solapur)	17°41' N, 075°55' E
Sikar	27°37' N, 075°09' E
Silchar	24°49' N, 092°48' E
Silvassa	20°15' N, 073°00' E
Simla, *see* Shimla	
Sirsa	29°32' N, 075°01' E
Sitapur	27°34' N, 080°41' E
Sonipat (Sonepat)	28°59' N, 077°01' E
South Dum Dum	22°34' N, 088°23' E
Srikakulam (Chicacole)	18°18' N, 083°54' E
Srinagar	34°05' N, 074°49' E
Surat	21°10' N, 072°50' E
Surendranagar (Wadhwan)	22°42' N, 071°41' E
Tenali	16°15' N, 080°35' E
Thanjavur (Tanjore)	10°48' N, 079°09' E
Tiruchchirappalli (Tiruchirappalli, Trichinopoly)	10°49' N, 078°41' E
Tirunelveli (Tinnevelly)	08°44' N, 077°42' E
Tirupati	13°39' N, 079°25' E
Tirupper (Tiruppur)	11°06' N, 077°21' E
Tiruvottiyur	13°09' N, 080°18' E
Tonk	26°10' N, 075°47' E
Trichur	10°31' N, 076°13' E
Trivandrum	08°29' N, 076°55' E
Tumkur	13°21' N, 077°05' E
Tuticorin	08°47' N, 078°08' E
Udaipur	24°35' N, 073°41' E
Ujjain	23°11' N, 075°46' E
Ulhasnagar	19°12' N, 072°58' E
Vasai (Bassein)	19°21' N, 072°48' E
Valsad (Bulsar)	20°38' N, 072°56' E
Vellore	12°56' N, 079°08' E
Vijayawada (Vijayavada, Bezwada)	16°31' N, 080°37' E
Vizianagaram (Vizianagram)	18°07' N, 083°25' E
Wadhwan, *see* Surendranagar	
Wardha	20°45' N, 078°37' E
Yavatmal (Yeotmal)	20°24' N, 078°08' E

INDONESIA

pg. 144

Capital: Jakarta
Area: 1,919,317 sq km; 741,052 sq mi
Highest Elev.: Jaya Pk. 5,030 m; 16,500 ft
Longest River: Kapuas 1,140 km; 710 mi
Avg. Temperature: Jan = 26°C; Jul = 27°C
Currency: Indonesian rupiah
Official Language: Bahasa Indonesia

Name	Lat./Long.
Ambon	03°43' S, 128°12' E
Atambua	09°07' S, 124°54' E
Balikpapan	01°17' S, 116°50' E
Banda Aceh (Kuta Raja)	05°34' N, 095°20' E
Bandung	06°54' S, 107°36' E
Bagansiapiapi	02°09' N, 100°49' E
Banjarbaru	03°25' S, 114°50' E
Banjarmasin	03°20' S, 114°35' E
Bantul	07°54' S, 110°20' E
Batang	06°55' S, 109°45' E
Bekasi	06°14' S, 106°59' E
Belinyu	01°38' S, 105°46' E
Binjai	03°36' N, 098°30' E
Bitung	01°27' N, 125°11' E
Blitar	08°06' S, 112°09' E
Bogor	06°35' S, 106°47' E
Brebes	06°53' S, 109°03' E
Bukittinggi	00°19' S, 100°22' E
Cianjur	06°49' S, 107°08' E
Cikampek	06°24' S, 107°27' E
Cilacap	07°44' S, 109°00' E
Cimahi	06°53' S, 107°32' E
Cirebon	06°44' S, 108°34' E
Denpasar	08°39' S, 115°13' E
Depok	06°24' S, 106°50' E
Dili	08°33' S, 125°34' E
Dumai	01°41' N, 101°27' E
Garut	07°13' S, 107°54' E
Gresik	07°09' S, 112°38' E
Indramayu	06°20' S, 108°19' E
Jakarta	06°10' S, 106°48' E
Jambi	01°36' S, 103°37' E
Jayapura	02°32' S, 140°42' E
Jember	08°10' S, 113°42' E
Jepara (Japara)	06°35' S, 110°39' E
Jombang	07°33' S, 112°14' E
Karawang	06°19' S, 107°17' E
Kediri	07°49' S, 112°01' E
Kefamenanu	09°27' S, 124°29' E
Kendari	03°57' S, 122°35' E
Ketapang	01°52' S, 109°59' E
Klaten	07°42' S, 110°35' E
Kolaka	04°03' S, 121°36' E
Kotabumi	04°50' S, 104°54' E
Kudus	06°48' S, 110°50' E
Kuningan	06°59' S, 108°29' E
Kupang	10°10' S, 123°35' E
Langsa	04°28' N, 097°58' E
Lubuklinggau	03°10' S, 102°52' E
Lumajang	08°08' S, 113°13' E
Madiun	07°37' S, 111°31' E
Magelang	07°28' S, 110°13' E
Malang	07°59' S, 112°37' E
Mampawah, *see* Mempawah	
Manado	01°29' N, 124°51' E
Manokwari	00°52' S, 134°05' E
Mataram	08°35' S, 116°07' E
Medan	03°35' N, 098°40' E
Mempawah (Mampawah)	00°22' N, 108°58' E
Metro	05°05' S, 105°20' E
Mojokerto	07°28' S, 112°26' E
Muncar	08°26' S, 114°20' E
Padang	00°57' S, 100°21' E
Padangpanjang	00°27' S, 100°25' E
Padangsidempuan	01°22' N, 099°16' E
Palangkaraya	02°16' S, 113°56' E
Palembang	02°55' S, 104°45' E
Palu	00°53' S, 119°53' E
Pangkalpinang	02°08' S, 106°08' E
Pare	07°46' S, 112°11' E
Parepare	04°01' S, 119°38' E
Pasuruan	07°38' S, 112°54' E
Pati	06°45' S, 111°01' E
Payakumbuh	00°14' S, 100°38' E
Pekalongan	06°53' S, 109°40' E
Pekanbaru (Pakanbaru)	00°32' N, 101°27' E
Pemalang	06°54' S, 109°22' E
Pematangsiantar	02°57' N, 099°03' E
Perabumulih	03°27' S, 104°15' E
Pinrang	03°48' S, 119°38' E
Ponorogo	07°52' S, 111°27' E
Pontianak	00°02' S, 109°20' E
Probolinggo	07°45' S, 113°13' E
Purwakarta	06°34' S, 107°26' E
Purwokerto	07°25' S, 109°14' E
Purworejo	07°43' S, 110°01' E
Rantepao	02°59' S, 119°54' E
Salatiga	07°19' S, 110°30' E
Samarinda	00°30' S, 117°09' E
Semarang	06°58' S, 110°25' E
Serang	06°07' S, 106°09' E
Sibolga	01°45' N, 098°48' E
Sidoarjo	07°27' S, 112°43' E
Singaraja	08°07' S, 115°06' E
Singkawang	00°54' N, 109°00' E
Situbondo	07°42' S, 114°00' E
Soe	09°52' S, 124°17' E
Sorong	00°53' S, 131°15' E
Subang	06°34' S, 107°45' E
Sukabumi	06°55' S, 106°56' E
Sumedang	06°52' S, 107°55' E
Sumenep	07°01' S, 113°52' E
Sungailiat	01°51' S, 106°08' E
Surabaya	07°15' S, 112°45' E
Surakarta	07°35' S, 110°50' E
Tangerang	06°11' S, 106°37' E
Tanggul	08°10' S, 113°26' E
Tanjungbalai	02°58' N, 099°48' E
Tanjungpandan	02°45' S, 107°39' E
Tanjungkarang-Telukbetung	05°27' S, 105°16' E
Tasikmalaya	07°20' S, 108°12' E
Tebingtinggi	03°20' N, 099°09' E
Tegal	06°52' S, 109°08' E
Tembilahan	00°19' S, 103°09' E
Tondano	01°19' N, 124°54' E
Tuban	06°54' S, 112°03' E
Tulungagung	08°04' S, 111°54' E
Ujungpandang	05°07' S, 119°24' E
Watampone	04°32' S, 120°20' E
Yogyakarta	07°48' S, 110°22' E

IRAN

pg. 139

Capital: Tehran
Area: 1,638,057 sq km; 632,457 sq mi
Highest Elev.: Mt. Demavend 5,610 m; 18,400 ft
Longest River: Karun 830 km; 520 mi
Avg. Temperature: Jan = 2°C; Jul = 30°C
Currency: rial
Official Language: Farsi

Name	Lat./Long.
Abadan	30°20' N, 048°16' E
Ahar	38°28' N, 047°04' E
Ahvaz	31°19' N, 048°42' E
Amol	36°28' N, 052°21' E
Arak	34°05' N, 049°41' E
Ardabil	38°15' N, 048°18' E
Bafq	31°36' N, 055°24' E
Bajestan	34°31' N, 058°10' E
Bakhtaran	34°19' N, 047°04' E
Bam	29°06' N, 058°21' E
Bampur	27°12' N, 060°27' E
Bandar Beheshti	25°18' N, 060°37' E
Bandar-e 'Abbas	27°11' N, 056°17' E
Bandar-e Anzali	37°28' N, 049°27' E
Bandar-e Bushehr	28°59' N, 050°50' E
Bandar-e Khomeyni	30°25' N, 049°05' E
Bandar-e Lengeh	26°33' N, 054°53' E
Bastam	36°29' N, 055°00' E
Behbahan	30°35' N, 050°14' E
Behshahr	36°43' N, 053°34' E
Birjand	32°53' N, 059°13' E
Bojnurd	37°28' N, 057°19' E
Borujerd	33°54' N, 048°46' E
Darab	28°45' N, 054°34' E
Delijan	33°59' N, 050°40' E
Dezful	32°23' N, 048°24' E
Esfahan	32°40' N, 051°38' E
Ferdows	34°00' N, 058°09' E
Firuzabad	28°50' N, 052°36' E
Gachsaran	30°12' N, 050°47' E
Gonabad	34°20' N, 058°42' E
Gonbad-e Qabus	37°15' N, 055°09' E
Gorgan	36°50' N, 054°29' E
Haft Gel	31°27' N, 049°32' E
Hamadan	34°48' N, 048°30' E
Ilam	33°38' N, 046°26' E
Jahrom	28°31' N, 053°33' E
Jask	25°38' N, 057°46' E
Jolfa	38°57' N, 045°38' E
Karaj	35°48' N, 050°59' E
Kashan	33°59' N, 051°29' E
Kazerun	29°37' N, 051°38' E
Kerman	30°17' N, 057°05' E
Khomeynishahr	32°41' N, 051°31' E
Khorramabad	33°30' N, 048°20' E
Khorramshahr	30°25' N, 048°11' E
Khvoy	38°33' N, 044°58' E
Ladiz	28°56' N, 061°19' E
Lar	27°41' N, 054°17' E
Mahabad	36°45' N, 045°43' E
Malayer	34°18' N, 048°50' E
Manjil	36°44' N, 049°24' E
Maragheh	37°23' N, 046°14' E
Marv Dasht	29°52' N, 052°48' E
Mashhad	36°18' N, 059°36' E
Masjed-e Soleyman	31°58' N, 049°18' E
Mianeh	37°26' N, 047°42' E
Najafabad	32°37' N, 051°21' E
Nehbandan	31°32' N, 060°02' E
Neyshabur	36°12' N, 058°50' E
Orumiyeh	37°33' N, 045°04' E
Qa'en	33°44' N, 059°11' E

Name	Lat./Long.
Qazvin	36°16' N, 050°00' E
Qom	34°39' N, 050°54' E
Quchan	37°06' N, 058°30' E
Rafsanjan	30°24' N, 056°00' E
Rasht	37°16' N, 049°36' E
Sabzevar	36°13' N, 057°42' E
Sakht Sar	36°53' N, 050°41' E
Sanandaj	35°19' N, 047°00' E
Saqqez	36°14' N, 046°16' E
Sarab	37°56' N, 047°32' E
Sari	36°34' N, 053°04' E
Semnan	35°33' N, 053°24' E
Shahr-e Kord	32°19' N, 050°50' E
Shahr-e Rey	35°35' N, 051°25' E
Shahrud	36°25' N, 054°58' E
Shiraz	29°36' N, 052°32' E
Surmaq	31°03' N, 052°48' E
Tabriz	38°05' N, 046°18' E
Tehran	35°40' N, 051°26' E
Torbat-e Heydariyeh	35°16' N, 059°13' E
Torbat-e Jam	35°14' N, 060°36' E
Yasuj	30°40' N, 051°36' E
Yazd	31°53' N, 054°22' E
Zabol	31°02' N, 061°30' E
Zahedan	29°30' N, 060°52' E
Zanjan	36°40' N, 048°29' E

IRAQ .... pg. 147

Capital: ....Baghdad
Area: ....435,052 sq km; 167,975 sq mi
Longest River: .....Tigris 1,900 km; 1,180 mi
Avg. Temperature: . .Jan = 10°C; Jul = 34°C
Currency: ....Iraqi dinar
Official Language: . .Arabic

Name	Lat./Long.
Ad-Diwaniyah	31°59' N, 044°56' E
Al-'Amarah	31°50' N, 047°09' E
Al-Basrah, *see* Basra	
Al-Hillah	32°29' N, 044°25' E
Al-Kut	32°30' N, 045°49' E
Al-Mawsil, *see* Mosul	
An-Najaf	31°59' N, 044°20' E
An-Nasiriyah	31°02' N, 046°16' E
Ar-Ramadi	33°25' N, 043°17' E
As-Samawah	31°18' N, 045°17' E
As-Sulaymaniyah	35°33' N, 045°26' E
Ba'qubah	33°45' N, 044°38' E
Baghdad	33°21' N, 044°25' E
Basra (Al-Basrah)	30°30' N, 047°47' E
Irbil (Arbela, Arbil, or Erbil)	36°11' N, 044°01' E
Karbala'	32°36' N, 044°02' E
Kirkuk	35°28' N, 044°23' E
Mosul (Al-Mawsil)	36°20' N, 043°08' E

IRELAND .... pg. 125

Capital: ....Dublin
Area: ....70,285 sq km; 27,137 sq mi
Highest Elev.: .....Carrantuohill 1,040 m; 3,410 ft
Longest River: .....Shannon 260 km; 160 mi
Avg. Temperature: . .Jan = 5°C; Jul = 15°C
Currency: ....Irish pound
Official Language: . .Irish, English

Name	Lat./Long.
Abbeyfeale	52°23' N, 009°18' W
Abbeyleix	52°54' N, 007°21' W
Athenry	53°18' N, 008°45' W
Ardee	53°51' N, 006°32' W
Ballinasloe	53°20' N, 008°13' W
Ballinrobe	53°38' N, 009°14' W
Ballycotton	51°50' N, 008°01' W
Ballymote	54°05' N, 008°31' W
Ballyvaghan	53°07' N, 009°09' W
Bantry	51°41' N, 009°27' W
Boyle	53°58' N, 008°18' W
Blackrock (Carraig Dubh)	53°18' N, 006°10' W
Bray (Bre)	53°12' N, 006°06' W
Cahersiveen	51°58' N, 010°13' W
Carrick on Shannon	53°57' N, 008°05' W
Castlebar	53°51' N, 009°18' W
Castleblayney	54°07' N, 006°44' W
Cavan (Cabhan, An)	54°00' N, 007°22' W
Celbridge	53°20' N, 006°33' W
Clara	53°20' N, 007°37' W
Claremorris	53°43' N, 009°00' W
Clonakilty	51°37' N, 008°53' W
Clonmel (Cluain Meala)	52°21' N, 007°42' W
Cobh	51°51' N, 008°17' W
Cork (Corcaigh)	51°54' N, 008°28' W
Crosshaven	51°48' N, 008°18' W
Dingle	52°08' N, 010°15' W
Drogheda (Droichead Atha)	53°43' N, 006°21' W
Dublin	53°20' N, 006°15' W
Dundalk (Dun Dealgan)	54°00' N, 006°25' W
Dun Laoghaire	53°17' N, 006°07' W
Ennis (Inis)	52°51' N, 008°59' W
Enniscorthy	52°30' N, 006°34' W
Fermoy	52°08' N, 008°17' W
Galway (Gaillimh)	53°17' N, 009°03' W
Gorey	52°40' N, 006°18' W
Greystones	53°09' N, 006°04' W
Kanturk	52°10' N, 008°54' W
Kilkenny (Cill Chainnigh)	52°39' N, 007°15' W
Killarney (Cill Airne)	52°03' N, 009°31' W
Kilrush	52°38' N, 009°29' W
Limerick (Luimneach)	52°40' N, 008°37' W
Lismore (Lios Mor)	52°08' N, 007°55' W
Longford	53°44' N, 007°48' W
Louth (Lu)	53°57' N, 006°32' W
Lucan	53°21' N, 006°27' W
Malahide	53°27' N, 006°09' W
Midleton	51°55' N, 008°10' W
Monaghan	54°15' N, 006°58' W
Mullingar	53°32' N, 007°21' W
Naas (Nas, An)	53°13' N, 006°40' W
Nenagh	52°52' N, 008°12' W
Portlaoise (Maryborough, Portlaoighise)	53°02' N, 007°18' W
Portumna	53°05' N, 008°13' W
Roscommon	53°38' N, 008°11' W
Roscrea	52°57' N, 007°48' W
Shannon	52°42' N, 008°52' W
Skerries	53°35' N, 006°07' W
Skibbereen	51°33' N, 009°16' W
Sligo	54°16' N, 008°29' W
Swinford	53°57' N, 008°57' W
Swords	53°27' N, 006°13' W
Templemore	52°47' N, 007°50' W
Thomastown	52°31' N, 007°08' W
Tralee	52°16' N, 009°43' W
Tramore	52°09' N, 007°09' W
Trim	53°33' N, 006°48' W
Tullamore	53°16' N, 007°29' W
Waterford (Port Lairge)	52°15' N, 007°06' W
Westport	53°48' N, 009°31' W
Wexford (Loch Garman)	52°20' N, 006°28' W
Wicklow (Cill Mhantain)	52°59' N, 006°03' W

ISRAEL .... pg. 147

Capital: ....Jerusalem
Area: ....20,700 sq km; 7,992 sq mi
Highest Elev.: .....Mt. Meron 1,210 m; 3,960 ft
Longest River: .....Jordan 360 km; 220 mi
Avg. Temperature: . .Jan = 9°C; Jul = 24°C
Currency: ....New (Israeli) sheqel
Official Language: . .Hebrew, Arabic

Name	Lat./Long.
Beersheba (Be'er Sheva')	31°14' N, 034°47' E
Haifa (Hefa)	32°50' N, 035°00' E
Jerusalem (Yerushalayim)	31°46' N, 035°14' E
Nazareth (Nazerat)	32°42' N, 035°18' E
Tel Aviv-Yafo	32°04' N, 034°46' E

ITALY .... pg. 130

Capital: ....Rome
Area: ....301,277 sq km; 116,324 sq mi
Highest Elev.: .....Mont Blanc 4,810 m; 15,770 ft
Longest River: .....Po 650 km; 400 mi
Avg. Temperature: . .Jan = 7°C; Jul = 25°C
Currency: ....lira
Official Language: . .Italian

Name	Lat./Long.
Acireale	37°37' N, 015°10' E
Adrano (Aderno)	37°40' N, 014°50' E
Adria	45°03' N, 012°03' E
Agrigento (Girgenti)	37°19' N, 013°34' E
Alba	44°42' N, 008°02' E
Alcamo	37°59' N, 012°58' E
Alessandria	44°54' N, 008°37' E
Alghero	40°33' N, 008°19' E
Altamura	40°49' N, 016°33' E
Ancona	43°38' N, 013°30' E
Andria	41°13' N, 016°17' E
Anzio (Antium)	41°27' N, 012°37' E
Aosta	45°44' N, 007°20' E
Aquileia	45°46' N, 013°22' E
Arezzo	43°25' N, 011°53' E
Argenta	44°37' N, 011°50' E
Ascoli Piceno	42°51' N, 013°34' E
Assisi	43°04' N, 012°37' E
Asti	44°54' N, 008°12' E
Atri	42°35' N, 013°58' E
Augusta	37°13' N, 015°13' E
Avellino	40°54' N, 014°47' E
Aversa	40°58' N, 014°12' E
Avezzano	42°02' N, 013°25' E
Avola	36°54' N, 015°08' E
Bardonecchia	45°05' N, 006°42' E
Bari	41°08' N, 016°51' E
Barletta	41°19' N, 016°17' E
Belluno	46°09' N, 012°13' E
Benevento	41°08' N, 014°45' E
Bergamo	45°41' N, 009°43' E
Biella	45°34' N, 008°03' E
Bitonto	41°06' N, 016°41' E
Bobbio	44°46' N, 009°23' E
Bologna	44°29' N, 011°20' E
Bolzano	46°31' N, 011°22' E
Bordighera	43°46' N, 007°39' E
Brescia	45°33' N, 010°15' E
Bressanone (Brixen)	46°43' N, 011°39' E
Brindisi	40°38' N, 017°56' E
Bronte	37°47' N, 014°50' E
Busto Arsizio	45°37' N, 008°51' E
Cagliari	39°13' N, 009°07' E
Caltanissetta	37°29' N, 014°04' E
Campobasso	41°34' N, 014°39' E
Canosa di Puglia	41°13' N, 016°04' E
Cantù	45°44' N, 009°08' E
Carbonia	39°10' N, 008°31' E
Carpi	44°47' N, 010°53' E
Carrara	44°05' N, 010°06' E
Cascina	43°41' N, 010°33' E
Caserta	41°04' N, 014°20' E
Castellammare di Stabia	40°42' N, 014°29' E
Castelvetrano	37°41' N, 012°47' E
Catania	37°30' N, 015°06' E
Catanzaro	38°54' N, 016°35' E
Cerignola	41°16' N, 015°54' E
Cesena	44°08' N, 012°15' E
Chianciano Terme	43°02' N, 011°49' E
Chiavari	44°19' N, 009°19' E
Chieti	42°21' N, 014°10' E
Chioggia	45°13' N, 012°17' E
Civitavecchia	42°06' N, 011°48' E
Como	45°47' N, 009°05' E
Coni, *see* Cuneo	
Corleone	37°49' N, 013°18' E
Corneto, *see* Tarquinia	
Cosenza	39°18' N, 016°15' E
Cremona	45°07' N, 010°02' E
Crotone	39°05' N, 017°08' E
Cuneo (Coni)	44°23' N, 007°32' E
Eboli	40°36' N, 015°04' E
Empoli	43°43' N, 010°57' E
Enna	37°34' N, 014°16' E
Erice (Monte San Giuliano)	38°02' N, 012°35' E
Este	45°14' N, 011°39' E
Fabriano	43°20' N, 012°54' E
Fano	43°50' N, 013°01' E
Feltre	46°01' N, 011°54' E
Fermo	43°09' N, 013°43' E
Ferrara	44°50' N, 011°35' E
Florence (Firenze or Florentia)	43°46' N, 011°15' E
Foggia	41°27' N, 015°34' E
Foligno	42°57' N, 012°42' E
Fondi	41°21' N, 013°25' E
Forlì	44°13' N, 012°03' E
Formia	41°15' N, 013°37' E
Fossano	44°33' N, 007°43' E
Frascati	41°48' N, 012°41' E
Frosinone	41°38' N, 013°19' E
Gela	37°04' N, 014°15' E
Genoa (Genova)	44°25' N, 008°57' E
Gorizia (Gorz)	45°57' N, 013°38' E
Grosseto	42°46' N, 011°08' E
Guastalla	44°55' N, 010°39' E
Iesi, *see* Jesi	
Iglesias	39°19' N, 008°32' E
Imola	44°21' N, 011°42' E
Imperia	43°53' N, 008°03' E
Jesi (Iesi)	43°31' N, 013°14' E
L'Aquila	42°22' N, 013°22' E
La Spezia	44°07' N, 009°50' E
Lanciano	42°14' N, 014°23' E
Larderello	43°14' N, 010°53' E
Latina	41°28' N, 012°52' E
Lecce	40°23' N, 018°11' E
Lecco	45°51' N, 009°23' E
Leghorn (Livorno)	43°33' N, 010°19' E
Legnano	45°36' N, 008°54' E
Lucca	43°50' N, 010°29' E
Lucera	41°30' N, 015°20' E
Lugo	44°25' N, 011°54' E
Macerata	43°18' N, 013°27' E
Manfredonia	41°38' N, 015°55' E
Mantua (Mantova)	45°09' N, 010°48' E
Marsala	37°48' N, 012°26' E
Martina Franca	40°42' N, 017°20' E
Massa	44°01' N, 010°09' E
Matera	40°40' N, 016°36' E
Mazara del Vallo	37°39' N, 012°35' E
Melfi	41°00' N, 015°39' E
Merano	46°40' N, 011°09' E
Messina (Messana)	38°11' N, 015°34' E
Mestre	45°29' N, 012°15' E
Milan (Milano)	45°28' N, 009°12' E
Modena	44°40' N, 010°55' E
Mola di Bari	41°04' N, 017°05' E
Molfetta	41°12' N, 016°36' E
Moncalieri	45°00' N, 007°41' E
Monreale	38°05' N, 013°17' E
Monte San Giuliano, *see* Erice	
Monza	45°35' N, 009°16' E
Naples (Napoli or Neapolis)	40°50' N, 014°15' E
Nardò	40°11' N, 018°02' E
Nola	40°55' N, 014°33' E
Novara	45°28' N, 008°38' E
Nuoro	40°19' N, 009°20' E
Olbia	40°55' N, 009°31' E
Oristano	39°54' N, 008°36' E
Orosei	40°23' N, 009°42' E
Ortona	42°21' N, 014°24' E
Orvieto	42°43' N, 012°07' E
Otranto	40°09' N, 018°30' E
Padua (Padova)	45°25' N, 011°53' E
Palazzolo Acreide	37°04' N, 014°54' E
Palermo	38°07' N, 013°22' E
Parma	44°48' N, 010°20' E
Pavia	45°10' N, 009°10' E
Perugia (Perusia)	43°08' N, 012°22' E
Pesaro (Pisaurum)	43°54' N, 012°55' E
Pescara	42°28' N, 014°13' E
Peschiera del Garda	45°26' N, 010°42' E
Piacenza	45°01' N, 009°40' E
Piombino	42°55' N, 010°32' E
Pisa	43°43' N, 010°23' E
Pisaurum, *see* Pesaro	
Pistoia	43°55' N, 010°54' E
Pordenone	45°57' N, 012°39' E
Portici	40°49' N, 014°20' E
Porto Torres	40°50' N, 008°24' E
Potenza	40°38' N, 015°48' E
Pozzuoli	40°49' N, 014°07' E
Prato	43°53' N, 011°06' E
Ragusa	36°55' N, 014°44' E
Ravenna	44°25' N, 012°12' E
Recanati	43°24' N, 013°32' E
Reggio di Calabria	38°06' N, 015°39' E
Reggio nell'Emilia	44°43' N, 010°36' E
Rimini	44°04' N, 012°34' E
Rivoli	45°04' N, 007°31' E
Rome (Roma)	41°54' N, 012°29' E
Rovereto	45°53' N, 011°02' E
Rovigo	45°04' N, 011°47' E
Ruvo di Puglia	41°07' N, 016°29' E
Salerno	40°41' N, 014°47' E
San Giovanni Rotondo	41°42' N, 015°44' E
San Remo	43°49' N, 007°46' E
San Severo	41°41' N, 015°23' E
Sansepolcro	43°34' N, 012°08' E
Sarroch	39°04' N, 009°00' E
Sassari	40°43' N, 008°34' E
Savona	44°17' N, 008°30' E
Schio	45°43' N, 011°21' E
Sciacca	37°31' N, 013°03' E
Scicli	36°47' N, 014°42' E
Sesto San Giovanni	45°32' N, 009°14' E
Siena	43°19' N, 011°21' E
Siracusa, *see* Syracuse	
Sondrio	46°10' N, 009°52' E
Sora	41°43' N, 013°37' E
Spezia, *see* La Spezia	
Spoleto	42°44' N, 012°44' E
Sulmona	42°03' N, 013°55' E
Syracuse (Siracusa)	37°04' N, 015°18' E
Taormina	37°51' N, 015°17' E
Taranto (Taras or Tarentum)	40°28' N, 017°14' E
Tarquinia (Corneto)	42°15' N, 011°45' E
Tempio Pausania	40°54' N, 009°06' E
Teramo	42°39' N, 013°42' E
Terni	42°34' N, 012°37' E
Terracina	41°17' N, 013°15' E
Tivoli (Tibur)	41°58' N, 012°48' E
Todi	42°47' N, 012°24' E
Torino, *see* Turin	
Torre Annunziata	40°45' N, 014°27' E
Torre del Greco	40°47' N, 014°22' E
Tortona	44°54' N, 008°52' E
Trapani	38°01' N, 012°29' E
Trento	46°04' N, 011°08' E
Treviso	45°40' N, 012°15' E
Trieste	45°40' N, 013°46' E
Turin (Torino)	45°03' N, 007°40' E
Udine	46°03' N, 013°14' E
Umbertide	43°18' N, 012°20' E
Urbino	43°43' N, 012°38' E
Varese	45°48' N, 008°50' E
Vasto	42°07' N, 014°42' E
Venice (Venezia)	45°27' N, 012°21' E
Vercelli	45°19' N, 008°25' E
Verona	45°27' N, 011°00' E
Viareggio	43°52' N, 010°14' E
Vibo Valentia	38°40' N, 016°06' E
Vicenza	45°33' N, 011°33' E
Vigevano	45°19' N, 008°51' E
Viterbo	42°25' N, 012°06' E
Vittoria	36°57' N, 014°32' E
Volterra	43°24' N, 010°51' E

JAMAICA .... pg. 116

Capital: ....Kingston
Area: ....10,991 sq km; 4,244 sq mi
Highest Elev.: .....Blue Mountain Pk. 2,260 m; 7,400 ft
Longest River: .....Black 70 km; 40 mi
Avg. Temperature: . .Jan = 25°C; Jul = 28°C
Currency: ....Jamaica dollar
Official Language: . .English

Name	Lat./Long.
Kingston	17°58' N, 076°48' W
Montego Bay	18°28' N, 077°55' W

JAPAN .... pg. 143

Capital: ....Tokyo
Area: ....337,835 sq km; 145,883 sq mi
Highest Elev.: .....Mt. Fuji 3,780 m; 12,390 ft
Longest River: .....Shinano 370 km; 230 mi
Avg. Temperature: . .Jan = 4°C; Jul = 25°C
Currency: ....yen
Official Language: . .Japanese

Name	Lat./Long.
Akita	39°43' N, 140°07' E
Aomori	40°49' N, 140°45' E
Asahikawa	43°46' N, 142°22' E
Chiba	35°36' N, 140°07' E
Fukuoka	33°35' N, 130°24' E
Fukushima	37°45' N, 140°28' E
Funabashi	35°42' N, 139°59' E
Gifu	35°25' N, 136°45' E
Hachinohe	40°30' N, 141°29' E
Hakodate	41°45' N, 140°43' E
Hiroshima	34°24' N, 132°27' E
Hofu	34°03' N, 131°34' E
Iwaki	37°05' N, 140°50' E
Kagoshima	31°36' N, 130°33' E
Kanazawa	36°34' N, 136°39' E
Kawasaki	35°32' N, 139°43' E
Kita-Kyushu	33°50' N, 130°50' E
Kobe	34°41' N, 135°10' E
Kochi	33°33' N, 133°33' E
Kumamoto	32°48' N, 130°43' E
Kushiro	42°58' N, 144°23' E
Kutchan	42°54' N, 140°45' E
Matsue	35°28' N, 133°04' E
Matsuyama	33°50' N, 132°45' E
Mito	36°22' N, 140°28' E
Miyazaki	31°52' N, 131°25' E
Morioka	39°42' N, 141°09' E
Muroran	42°18' N, 140°59' E
Nagasaki	32°48' N, 129°55' E
Nagoya	35°10' N, 136°55' E
Niigata	37°55' N, 139°03' E
Obihiro	42°55' N, 143°12' E
Okayama	34°39' N, 133°55' E
Osaka	34°40' N, 135°30' E
Otaru	43°13' N, 141°00' E
Sakai	34°35' N, 135°28' E
Sapporo	43°03' N, 141°21' E
Sendai	31°49' N, 130°18' E
Shizuoka	34°58' N, 138°23' E
Tokyo	35°42' N, 139°46' E
Tomakomai	42°38' N, 141°36' E
Tottori	35°30' N, 134°14' E
Wakayama	34°13' N, 135°11' E
Wakkanai	45°25' N, 141°40' E
Yaizu	34°52' N, 138°20' E
Yamagata	38°15' N, 140°20' E
Yokohama	35°27' N, 139°39' E

JORDAN .... pg. 147

Capital: ....Amman
Area: ....88,946 sq km; 34,342 sq mi
Highest Elev.: .....Mt. Ramm 1,750 m; 5,760 ft
Longest River: .....Jordan 360 km; 220 mi
Avg. Temperature: . .Jan = 8°C; Jul = 25°C
Currency: ....Jordan dinar
Official Language: . .Arabic

Name	Lat./Long.
Amman ('Amman)	31°57' N, 035°56' E
As Salt	32°03' N, 035°44' E
Az Zarqa'	32°05' N, 036°06' E
Irbid	32°33' N, 035°51' E

KAZAKHSTAN .... pg. 136

Capital: ....Almaty
Area: ....2,717,300 sq km; 1,049,200 sq mi
Highest Elev.: ....Mt. Khan-Tengri 7,000 m; 22,950 ft
Longest River: ....Irtysh 4,250 km; 2,640 mi
Avg. Temperature: Jan = -10°C; Jul = 24°C
Currency: ....tenge
Official Language: Kazakh

Name	Lat./Long.
Almaty (Alma-Ata)	43°15' N, 076°57' E
Atyrau (Atenau, Gurjev, or Guryev)	47°07' N, 051°53' E
Aqmola (Akmola, Akmolinsk, Celinograd, or Tselinograd)	51°10' N, 071°30' E
Aqtau (Aktau, or Shevchenko)	43°39' N, 051°12' E
Aqtöbe (Aktyubinsk)	50°17' N, 057°10' E
Balqhas (Balkhash or Balchas)	46°49' N, 075°00' E
Celinograd, *see* Aqmola	
Dzhezkazgan	47°47' N, 067°46' E
Kökshetau (Kokchetav)	53°17' N, 069°30' E
Leningor(Leninogorsk or Ridder)	50°22' N, 083°32' E
Leninsk, *see* Tyrutam	
Oral (Uralsk)	51°14' N, 051°22' E
Öskemen (Ust-Kamenogorsk)	49°58' N, 082°40' E
Pavlodar	52°18' N, 076°57' E
Petropavl (Petropavlovsk)	54°52' N, 069°06' E

Name	Lat./Long.
Qaraghandy (Karaganda)	49°50' N, 073°10' E
Qostanay (Kustanay)	53°10' N, 063°35' E
Qyzylorda(Kzyl-Orda)	44°48' N, 065°28' E
Rudnyy (Rudny)	52°57' N, 063°07' E
Semey (Semipalatinsk	50°28' N, 080°13' E
Shchuchinsk (Scucinsk)	52°56' N, 070°12' E
Shymkent (Chimkent or Cimkent)	42°18' N, 069°36' E
Taldyqorghan (Taldy-Kurgan)	45°00' N, 078°24' E
Termirtau (Samarkand)	50°05' N, 072°56' E
Tyrutam (Turaram or Leninsk)	45°40' N, 063°20' E
Zhezqazghan (Ekibastuz)	51°40' N, 075°22' E
Zhmbyl (Dzhambul)	42°54' N, 071°22' E

KENYA ... pg. 153

Capital: Nairobi
Area: 582,646 sq km; 224,961 sq mi
Highest Elev.: Mt. Kenya 5,200 m; 17,0600 ft
Longest River: Tana 710 km; 440 mi
Avg. Temperature: Jan = 18°C; Jul = 15°C
Currency: Kenya shilling
Official Language: Swahili, English

Name	Lat./Long.
Bungoma	00°34' N, 034°34' E
Busia	00°28' N, 034°06' E
Eldoret	00°31' N, 035°17' E
Embu	00°32' S, 037°27' E
Garissa	00°28' S, 039°38' E
Isiolo	00°21' N, 037°35' E
Kisii	00°41' S, 034°46' E
Kisumu	00°06' S, 034°45' E
Lamu	02°16' S, 040°54' E
Lodwar	03°07' N, 035°36' E
Machakos	01°31' S, 037°16' E
Malindi	03°13' S, 040°07' E
Mandera	03°56' N, 041°52' E
Maralal	01°06' N, 036°42' E
Marsabit	02°20' N, 037°59' E
Meru	00°03' N, 037°39' E
Nairobi	01°17' S, 036°49' E
Nakuru	00°17' S, 036°04' E
Nanyuki	00°01' N, 037°04' E
Wajir	01°45' N, 040°04' E

KIRIBATI ... pg. 156

Capital: Bairiki
Area: 811 sq km; 313 sq mi
Highest Elev.: Banaba 80 m; 270 ft
Avg. Temperature: Jan = 28°C; Jul = 28°C
Currency: Australian dollar
Official Language: English

Name	Lat./Long.
Bairiki	01°20' N, 173°01' E

KOREA, NORTH ... pg. 143

Capital: P'yongyang
Area: 122,762 sq km; 47,399 sq mi
Highest Elev.: Mt. Paektu 2,740 m; 9,000 ft
Longest River: Yalu 810 km; 500 mi
Avg. Temperature: Jan = -8°C; Jul = 24°C
Currency: won
Official Language: Korean

Name	Lat./Long.
Ch'ongjin	41°46' N, 129°49' E
Haeju	38°02' N, 125°42' E
Kanggye	40°58' N, 126°36' E
Kimch'aek (Songjin)	40°41' N, 129°12' E
Namp'o	38°44' N, 125°24' E
P'yongyang	39°01' N, 125°45' E
Sinuiju	40°06' N, 124°24' E
Wonsan	39°10' N, 127°26' E

KOREA, SOUTH ... pg. 143

Capital: Seoul
Area: 99,274 sq km; 38,330 sq mi
Highest Elev.: Mt. Halla 1,950 m; 6,400 ft
Longest River: Naktong 520 km; 330 mi
Avg. Temperature: Jan = 2°C; Jul = 24°C
Currency: won
Official Language: Korean

Name	Lat./Long.
Inch'on	37°28' N, 126°38' E
Kwangju	35°09' N, 126°55' E
Masan	35°11' N, 128°34' E
Pusan	35°06' N, 129°03' E
Seoul (Soul)	37°34' N, 127°00' E
Suwon	37°16' N, 127°01' E
Taegu (Daegu or Taiku)	35°52' N, 128°36' E
Taejon	36°20' N, 127°26' E

KUWAIT ... pg. 154

Capital: Kuwait
Area: 17,818 sq km; 6,880 sq mi
Highest Elev.: Ash-Shaqaya Pk. 290 m; 950 ft
Avg. Temperature: Jan = 13°C; Jul = 35°C
Currency: Kuwaiti dinar
Official Language: Arabic

Name	Lat./Long.
Ahmadi, al-	29°05' N, 048°04' E
Hawalli	29°19' N, 048°02' E
Jahrah, al-	29°20' N, 047°40' E
Kuwait	29°20' N, 047°59' E
Shu'aybah, ash-	29°03' N, 048°08' E

KYRGYZSTAN ... pg. 139

Capital: Bishkek
Area: 198,500 sq km; 76,600 sq mi
Highest Elev.: Victory Pk. 7,440 m; 24,410 ft
Longest River: Naryn 700 km; 430 mi
Avg. Temperature: Jan = -13°C; Jul = 21°C
Currency: som
Official Language: Kyrgyz, Russian

Name	Lat./Long.
Bishkek (Frunze)	42°54' N, 074°36' E
Kara-Balta	42°50' N, 073°52' E
Karakol (Przhevalsk)	42°33' N, 078°18' E
Osh	40°32' N, 072°48' E
Tokmok	42°52' N, 075°18' E
Ysyk-Köl (Rybachye)	42°26' N, 076°12' E

LAOS ... pg. 144

Capital: Vientiane
Area: 236,800 sq km; 91,429 sq mi
Highest Elev.: Mt. Bia 2,820 m; 9,250 ft
Longest River: Mekong 4,350 km; 2,700 mi
Avg. Temperature: Jan = 21°C; Jul = 27°C
Currency: kip
Official Language: Lao

Name	Lat./Long.
Savannakhet	16°33' N, 104°45' E
Vientiane (Viangchan)	17°58' N, 102°36' E

LATVIA ... pg. 138

Capital: Riga
Area: 64,610 sq km; 24,946 sq mi
Highest Elev.: Mt. Gaizins 310 m; 1,020 ft
Longest River: Daugava 1,020 km; 630 mi
Avg. Temperature: Jan = -4°C; Jul = 17°C
Currency: lats
Official Language: Latvian

Name	Lat./Long.
Aluksne	57°25' N, 027°03' E
Aizpute	56°43' N, 021°36' E
Auce	56°28' N, 022°53' E
Balvi	57°08' N, 027°15' E
Cesis	57°18' N, 025°15' E
Daugavpils	55°53' N, 026°32' E
Dobele	56°37' N, 023°16' E
Gulbene	57°11' N, 026°45' E
Ilukste	55°58' N, 026°18' E
Jekabpils	56°29' N, 025°51' E
Jelgava	56°39' N, 023°42' E
Jurmala	56°58' N, 023°34' E
Karsava	56°47' N, 027°40' E
Liepaja	56°31' N, 021°01' E
Limbazi	57°31' N, 024°42' E
Ludza	56°33' N, 027°43' E
Mazsalace	57°52' N, 025°03' E
Ogre	56°49' N, 024°36' E
Piltene	57°13' N, 021°40' E
Preili	56°18' N, 026°43' E
Riga (Riga)	56°57' N, 024°06' E
Rujiena	57°54' N, 025°19' E
Sabile	57°03' N, 022°35' E
Salacgriva	57°45' N, 024°21' E
Saldus	56°40' N, 022°30' E
Sigulda	57°09' N, 024°51' E
Valmiera	57°33' N, 025°24' E
Ventspils	57°24' N, 021°31' E
Viesite	56°21' N, 025°33' E
Vilani	56°33' N, 026°57' E
Zilupe	56°23' N, 028°07' E

LEBANON ... pg. 147

Capital: Beirut
Area: 10,230 sq km; 3,950 sq mi
Highest Elev.: Qurnet as-Sawda 3,090 m; 10,140 ft
Longest River: Litani 150 km; 90 mi
Avg. Temperature: Jan = 14°C; Jul = 26°C
Currency: Lebanese pound
Official Language: Arabic

Name	Lat./Long.
Beirut (Bayrut)	33°53' N, 035°30' E
Sayda, *see* Sidon	
Sidon (Sayda)	33°33' N, 035°22' E
Tripoli (Tarabulus)	34°26' N, 035°51' E

LESOTHO ... pg. 152

Capital: Maseru
Area: 30,355 sq km; 11,720 sq mi
Highest Elev: Mt. Ntlenyana 3,480 m; 11,420 ft
Longest River: Orange 2,100 km; 1,300 mi
Avg. Temperature: Jan = 21.1°C; Jul = 7.7°C
Currency: loti
Official Language: Sotho, English

Name	Lat./Long.
Maseru	29°19' S, 027°29' E

LIBERIA ... pg. 150

Capital: Monrovia
Area: 99,067 sq km; 38,250 sq mi
Highest Elev.: Mt. Nimba 1,750 m; 5,750 ft
Longest River: Cavalla 510 km; 320 mi
Avg. Temperature: Jan = 26°C; Jul = 24°C
Currency: Liberian dollar
Official Language: English

Name	Lat./Long.
Monrovia	06°19' N, 010°48' E

LIBYA ... pg. 150

Capital: Tripoli
Area: 1,757,000 sq km; 678,400 sq mi
Highest Elev.: Bikku Bitti. 2,290 m; 7,500 ft
Avg. Temperature: Jan = 12°C; Jul = 26°C
Currency: Libyan dinar
Official Language: Arabic

Name	Lat./Long.
Banghazi (Bengasi or Benghazi)	32°07' N, 020°04' E
Darnah (Derna)	32°46' N, 022°39' E
Misratah (Misurata)	32°23' N, 015°06' E
Tarabulus, *see* Tripoli	
Tazirbu	25°45' N, 021°00' E
Tobruk (Tubruq)	32°05' N, 023°59' E
Tripoli (Tarabulus)	32°54' N, 013°11' E

LIECHTENSTEIN ... pg. 132

Capital: Vaduz
Area: 160 sq km; 618 sq mi
Highest Elev.: Grauspitz 2,600 m; 8,530 ft
Longest River: Rhine 1,390 km; 870 mi
Avg. Temperature: Jan = -1°C; Jul = 17°C
Currency: Swiss franc
Official Language: German

Name	Lat./Long.
Vaduz	47°09' N, 009°31' E

LITHUANIA ... pg. 138

Capital: Vilnius
Area: 65,301 sq km; 25,213 sq mi
Highest Elev.: Mt. Juozapine 290 m; 960 ft
Longest River: Neman 940 km; 580 mi
Avg. Temperature: Jan = -5°C; Jul = 17°C
Currency: litas
Official Language: Lithuanian

Name	Lat./Long.
Alytus	54°24' N, 024°03' E
Birstonas	54°37' N, 024°02' E
Birzai	56°12' N, 024°45' E
Druskininkai	54°01' N, 023°58' E
Gargzdai	55°43' N, 021°24' E
Joniskis	56°14' N, 023°37' E
Jurbarkas	55°04' N, 022°46' E
Kaunas	54°54' N, 023°54' E
Kazly Ruda	54°46' N, 023°30' E
Kedainiai	55°17' N, 023°58' E
Klaipeda	55°43' N, 021°07' E
Kursenai	56°00' N, 022°56' E
Lazdijai	54°14' N, 023°31' E
Marijampole (Kapsukas)	54°34' N, 023°21' E
Mazeikiai	56°19' N, 022°20' E
Naujoji Akmene	56°19' N, 022°54' E
Neringa	55°22' N, 021°04' E
Pagegiai	55°09' N, 021°54' E
Pakruojis	58°58' N, 023°52' E
Palanga	55°55' N, 021°03' E
Pandelys	56°01' N, 025°13' E
Panevezys	55°44' N, 024°21' E
Ramygala	55°31' N, 024°18' E
Salcininkai	54°18' N, 025°23' E
Siauliai	55°56' N, 023°19' E
Silale	55°28' N, 022°12' E
Silute	55°21' N, 021°29' E
Sirvintos	55°03' N, 024°57' E
Taurage	55°15' N, 022°17' E
Utena	55°30' N, 025°36' E
Vilkija	55°03' N, 023°35' E
Vilnius	54°41' N, 025°19' E

LUXEMBOURG ... pg. 132

Capital: Luxembourg
Area: 2,586 sq km; 999 sq mi
Highest Elev.: Buurgplaatz 560 m; 1,840 ft
Longest River: Sûre 170 km; 110 mi
Temperature: Jan = 0°C; Jul = 17°C
Currency: Luxembourg franc
Official Language: none

Name	Lat./Long.
Esch-sur-Alzette	49°30' N, 005°59' E
Luxembourg	49°36' N, 006°08' E

MACEDONIA ... pg. 135

Capital: Skopje
Area: 25,713 sq km; 9,928 sq mi
Highest Elev.: Mt. Korab 2,750 m; 9,030 ft
Longest River: Vardar 420 km; 260 mi
Avg. Temperature: Jan = 4°C; Jul = 31°C
Currency: denar
Official Language: Macedonian

Name	Lat./Long.
Gostivar	41°48' N, 020°54' E
Krusevo	41°22' N, 021°15' E
Kumanovo	42°08' N, 021°43' E
Ohrid	41°07' N, 020°48' E
Prilep	41°21' N, 021°34' E
Skopje (Skoplje)	42°00' N, 021°29' E
Stip	41°44' N, 022°12' E
Strumica	41°26' N, 022°39' E
Tetovo	42°01' N, 020°59' E

MADAGASCAR ... pg. 153

Capital: Antananarivo
Area: 587,041 sq km; 226,658 sq mi
Highest Elev.: Maromokotro Pk. 2,880 m; 9,440 ft
Longest River: Mangoky 560 km; 350 mi
Avg. Temperature: Jan = 20°C; Jul = 13°C
Currency: Malagasy franc
Official Language: Malagasy, French

Name	Lat./Long.
Ambalavao	21°50' S, 046°56' E
Ambanja	13°41' S, 048°27' E
Ambatondrazaka	17°50' S, 048°25' E
Ambohimahasoa	21°07' S, 047°13' E
Andapa	14°39' S, 049°39' E
Andoany (Hell-Ville, Helville, or Nosy-Be)	13°24' S, 048°16' E
Ankarana (Sosumav)	13°05' S, 048°55' E
Antananarivo (Tananarive)	18°55' S, 047°31' E
Antsirabe	19°51' S, 047°02' E
Antsiranana (Diego-Suarez)	12°16' S, 049°17' E
Antsohihy	14°52' S, 047°59' E
Arivonimamo	19°01' S, 047°11' E
Befandriana Avaratra (Befandriana-Nord)	15°16' S, 048°32' E
Betroka	23°16' S, 046°05' E
Diego-Suarez, *see* Antsiranana	
Farafangana	22°49' S, 047°50' E
Fianarantsoa	21°26' S, 047°05' E
Hell-Ville, *see* Andoany	
Iharana (Vohemar or Vohimarina)	13°21' S, 050°00' E
Ihosy	22°24' S, 046°07' E
Mahabo	20°23' S, 044°40' E
Mahajanga (Majunga)	15°43' S, 046°19' E
Mahanoro	19°54' S, 048°48' E
Mampikony	16°06' S, 047°38' E
Manakara	22°08' S, 048°01' E
Mananjary	21°13' S, 048°20' E
Marovoay	16°06' S, 046°38' E
Miarinarivo	18°57' S, 046°55' E
Morondava	20°17' S, 044°17' E
Nosy-Be, *see* Andoany	
Port-Bergé (Boriziny)	15°33' S, 047°40' E
Sosumav, *see* Ankarana	
Tangainony	22°42' S, 047°45' E
Taolanaro, *see* Tolanaro	
Toamasina (Tamatave)	18°10' S, 049°23' E
Tôlanaro (Faradofay, Fort-Dauphin or Taolanaro)	25°02' S, 047°00' E
Toliara (Toliary or Tulear)	23°21' S, 043°40' E
Vangaindrano	23°21' S, 047°36' E
Vatomandry	19°20' S, 048°59' E
Vohemar, *see* Iharana	
Vohimarina, *see* Iharana	

MALAWI ... pg. 153

Capital: Lilongwe
Area: 118,484 sq km; 45,747 sq mi
Highest Elev.: Mlanje 3,000 m; 9,850 ft
Longest River: Shire 400 km; 250 mi
Avg. Temperature: Jan = 22°C; Jul = 16°C
Currency: Malawi kwacha
Official Language: English

Name	Lat./Long.
Blantyre	15°47' S, 035°00' E
Dedza	14°22' S, 034°20' E
Karonga	09°56' S, 033°56' E
Lilongwe	13°59' S, 033°47' E
Mzuzu	11°27' S, 033°55' E
Nsanje (Port Herald)	16°55' S, 035°16' E
Port Herald, *see* Nsanje	
Salima	13°47' S, 034°26' E
Zomba	15°23' S, 035°20' E

MALAYSIA ... pg. 144

Capital: Kuala Lumpur
Area: 330,442 sq km; 127,584 sq mi
Highest Elev.: Mt. Kinabalu 4,100 m; 13,450 ft
Longest River: Pahang 430 km; 270 mi
Avg. Temperature: Jan = 28°C; Jul = 28°C
Currency: ringgit
Official Language: Malay

Name	Lat./Long.
Alor Setar	06°07' N, 100°22' E
Batu Pahat	01°51' N, 102°56' E
Bintulu	03°10' N, 113°02' E
Butterworth	05°25' N, 100°24' E
George Town (Pinang)	05°25' N, 100°20' E
Ipoh	04°35' N, 101°05' E
Johor Baharu	01°28' N, 103°45' E
Kangar	06°26' N, 100°12' E
Kelang (Klang)	03°02' N, 101°27' E
Keluang	02°02' N, 103°19' E
Kota Baharu	06°08' N, 102°15' E
Kota Kinabalu (Jesselton)	05°59' N, 116°04' E
Kuala Lumpur	03°10' N, 101°42' E
Kuala Terengganu	05°20' N, 103°08' E
Kuantan	03°48' N, 103°20' E
Kuching	01°33' N, 110°20' E
Melaka (Malacca)	02°12' N, 102°15' E
Miri	04°23' N, 113°59' E
Muar (Bandar Maharani)	02°02' N, 102°34' E
Petaling Jaya	03°05' N, 101°39' E
Sandakan	05°50' N, 118°07' E
Seremban	02°43' N, 101°56' E
Song	02°01' N, 112°33' E
Sibu	02°18' N, 111°49' E
Taiping	04°51' N, 100°44' E
Teluk Intan (Telok Anson)	04°02' N, 101°01' E
Victoria (Labuan)	05°17' N, 115°15' E

MALDIVES ... pg. 146

Capital: Male
Area: 298 sq km; 115 sq mi
Temperature: Jan = 30°C; Jul = 30°C
Currency: Maldivian rufiyaa
Official Language: Divehi

Name	Lat./Long.
Male	04°10' N, 073°30' E

MALI ... pg. 150

Capital: Bamako
Area: 1,248,574 sq km; 482,077 sq mi
Highest Elev.: Hombori Tondo 1,160 m; 3,770 ft
Longest River: Niger 4,200 km; 2,600 mi
Avg. Temperature: Jan =23°C; Jul = 29°C
Currency: CFA franc
Official Language: French

Name	Lat./Long.
Bamako	12°39' N,008°00' W
Gao	16°16' N,000°03' W
Kayes	14°27' N,011°26' W
Mopti	14°30' N,004°12' W
Ségou	13°27' N,006°16' W
Sikasso	11°19' N,005°40' W
Timbuktu	16°46' N,003°01' W

MALTA ... pg. 133

Capital: Valletta
Area: 316 sq km; 122 sq mi
Highest Elev.: Ta' Zuta 250 m; 830 ft
Avg. Temperature: Jan = 13°C; Jul = 26°C
Currency: Maltese lira
Official Language: Maltese, English

Name	Lat./Long.
Valletta (Valetta)	35°54' N, 014°31' E

MARSHALL ISLANDS . . pg. 156

Capital: . . . . .Majuro
Area: . . . . .181.5 sq km; 70.1 sq mi
Avg. Temperature: . .Jan = 28°C; Jul = 28°C
Currency: . . . . .U.S. dollar
Official Language: . .Marshallese, English

Name	Lat./Long.
Majuro	07°09' N,171°12' E

MAURITANIA . . . . .pg. 150

Capital: . . . . .Nouakchott
Area: . . . . .1,030,700 sq km; 398,000 sq mi
Highest Elev: . . . . .Ijill 910 m; 3,000 ft
Longest River: . . . . .Senegal 1,080 km; 670 mi
Avg. Temperature: . .Jan = 21°C; Jul = 28°C
Currency: . . . . .ouguiya
Official Language: . .Arabic

Name	Lat./Long.
Nouakchott	18°06' N,015°57' W

MAURITIUS . . . . .pg. 153

Capital: . . . . .Port Louis
Area: . . . . .2,040 sq km; 788 sq mi
Highest Elev.: . . . .Petite Rivière-Noire Pk 830 m; 2,710 ft
Longest River: . . . .Grand River South East 40 km; 25 mi
Avg. Temperature: .Jan = 23°C; Jul = 23°C
Currency: . . . . . . .Mauritian rupee
Official Language: .English

Name	Lat./Long.
Port Louis	20°10' S, 057°30'E

MEXICO . . . . .pg. 115

Capital: . . . . .Mexico City
Area: . . . . .1,958,201 sq km; 756,066 sq mi
Highest Elev.: . . . . .Citlaltepetl 5,700 m; 18,700 ft
Longest River: . . . . .Rio Grande 2,830 km; 1,760 mi
Avg. Temperature: . .Jan = 12°C; Jul = 17°C
Currency: . . . . .new peso
Official Language: . .Spanish

Name	Lat./Long.
Acámbaro	20°02' N, 100°44' W
Acapulco	16°51' N, 099°55' W
Aguascalientes	21°53' N, 102°18' W
Apatzingán	19°05' N, 102°21' W
Arriaga	16°14' N, 093°54' W
Autlán	19°46' N, 104°22' W
Caborca	30°37' N, 112°06' W
Campeche	19°51' N, 090°32' W
Cananea	30°57' N, 110°18' W
Cancún	21°05' N, 086°46' W
Casas Grandes	30°22' N, 107°57' W
Celaya	20°31' N, 100°49' W
Cerro Azul	21°12' N, 097°44' W
Chetumal	18°30' N, 088°18' W
Chihuahua	28°38' N, 106°05' W
Chilpancingo	17°33' N, 099°30' W
Ciudad Acuña (Las Vacas)	29°18' N, 100°55' W
Ciudad de Mexico, *see* Mexico City	
Ciudad Delicias	28°13' N, 105°28' W
Ciudad Guzmán	19°41' N, 103°29' W
Ciudad Hidalgo	19°41' N, 100°34' W
Ciudad Juárez	31°44' N, 106°29' W
Ciudad Mante	22°44' N, 098°57' W
Ciudad Obregón	27°29' N, 109°56' W
Ciudad Pemex	17°54' N, 092°30' W
Ciudad Victoria	23°44' N, 099°08' W
Coatzacoalcos	18°09' N, 094°25' W
Colima	19°14' N, 103°43' W
Comitán	16°15' N, 092°08' W
Cozumel	20°31' N, 086°55' W
Cuauhtémoc	28°25' N, 106°52' W
Cuernavaca	18°55' N, 099°15' W
Culiacán	24°48' N, 107°24' W
Díaz Gutiérrez	22°12' N, 100°57' W
Durango	24°02' N, 104°40' W
El Dorado	24°17' N, 107°21' W
Ensenada	31°52' N, 116°37' W
Escuinapa	22°51' N, 105°48' W
Fresnillo	23°10' N, 102°53' W
Gómez Palacio	25°34' N, 103°30' W
Guadalajara	20°40' N, 103°20' W
Guadalupe	25°41' N, 100°15' W
Guadalupe Victoria	24°27' N, 104°07' W
Guanajuato	21°01' N, 101°15' W
Guasave	25°34' N, 108°27' W
Guaymas	27°56' N, 110°54' W
Hermosillo	29°04' N, 110°58' W
Heroica Nogales	31°20' N, 110°56' W
Hidalgo del Parral (Parral)	26°56' N, 105°40' W
Iguala de la Independencia	18°21' N, 099°32' W
Irapuato	20°41' N, 101°21' W
Jalapa	19°32' N, 096°55' W
Jerez de Garcia Salinas	22°39' N, 103°00' W
Jiménez	27°08' N, 104°55' W
Juchitan	16°26' N, 095°01' W
La Paz	24°10' N, 110°18' W
La Piedad Cavadas	20°21' N, 102°00' W
Las Penas, *see* Puerto Vallarta	
Las Vacas, *see* Ciudad Acuña	
León	21°07' N, 101°40' W
Linares	24°52' N, 099°34' W
Los Mochis	25°45' N, 108°57' W
Los Tuxtlas, *see* San Andres Tuxtla	
Macuspana	17°46' N, 092°36' W
Manzanillo	19°03' N, 104°20' W
Matamoros	18°36' N, 098°28' W
Matamoros	25°53' N, 097°30' W
Matehuala	23°39' N, 100°39' W
Mazatlán	23°13' N, 106°25' W
Mérida	20°58' N, 089°37' W
Mexicali	32°40' N, 115°29' W
Mexico City (Ciudad de Mexico)	19°24' N, 099°09' W
Minatitlán	17°59' N, 094°31' W
Monclova	26°54' N, 101°25' W
Monterrey	25°40' N, 100°19' W
Morelia	19°42' N, 101°07' W
Muleje	26°53' N, 112°01' W
Navojoa	27°06' N, 109°26' W
Nueva Rosita	27°57' N, 101°13' W
Nuevo Laredo	27°30' N, 099°31' W
Oaxaca	17°03' N, 096°43' W
Orizaba	18°51' N, 097°06' W
Pachuca	20°07' N, 098°44' W
Papantla	20°27' N, 097°19' W
Parral, *see* Hidalgo del Parral	
Piedras Negras	28°42' N, 100°31' W
Poza Rica	20°33' N, 097°27' W
Progreso	21°17' N, 089°40' W
Puebla	19°03' N, 098°12' W
Puerto Escondido	25°48' N, 111°20' W
Puerto Vallarta (Las Penas)	20°37' N, 105°15' W
Querétaro	20°36' N, 100°23' W
Reynosa	26°07' N, 098°18' W
Río Bravo	25°59' N, 098°06' W
Sabinas	27°51' N, 101°07' W
Salamanca	20°34' N, 101°12' W
Saltillo	25°25' N, 101°00' W
San Andrés Tuxtla (Los Tuxtlas)	18°27' N, 095°13' W
San Cristóbal de las Casas	16°45' N, 092°38' W
San Felipe	31°00' N, 114°52' W
San Francisco del Rincon	21°01' N, 101°51' W
San Ignacio	27°27' N, 112°51' W
San Lucas	22°53' N, 109°54' W
San Luis	32°29' N, 114°48' W
San Luis Potosí	22°09' N, 100°59' W
San Miguel de Allende	20°55' N, 100°45' W
San Pedro	25°45' N, 102°59' W
Sánta Barbara	26°48' N, 105°49' W
Santa Catarina	25°41' N, 100°28' W
Santiago Papasquiaro	25°03' N, 105°25' W
Silao	20°56' N, 101°26' W
Tampico	22°13' N, 097°51' W
Tapachula	14°54' N, 092°17' W
Taxco	18°33' N, 099°36' W
Tecoman	18°55' N, 103°53' W
Tecpan	17°15' N, 100°41' W
Tehuacán	18°27' N, 097°23' W
Tepic	21°30' N, 104°54' W
Tequila	20°54' N, 103°47' W
Tierra Blanca	18°27' N, 096°21' W
Tijuana	32°32' N, 117°01' W
Tizimin	21°09' N, 088°09' W
Tlaquepaque	20°39' N, 103°19' W
Tlaxcala	19°19' N, 098°14' W
Toluca	19°17' N, 099°40' W
Torreón	25°33' N, 103°26' W
Tula	23°00' N, 099°43' W
Tuxpan	20°57' N, 097°24' W
Tuxpan	21°57' N, 105°18' W
Tuxtla	16°45' N, 093°07' W
Uruapan	19°25' N, 102°04' W
Valles	21°59' N, 099°01' W
Veracruz	19°12' N, 096°08' W
Villahermosa	17°59' N, 092°55' W
Zacapu	19°50' N, 101°43' W
Zacatecas	22°47' N, 102°35' W
Zamora de Hidalgo	19°59' N, 102°16' W
Zapopan	20°43' N, 103°24' W

MICRONESIA . . . . .pg. 156

Capital: . . . . .Palikir, on Pohnpei
Area: . . . . .701.4 sq km; 270.8 sq mi
Highest Elev.: . . . . .Mt. Totolom 790 m; 2,590 ft
Avg. Temperature: . .Jan = 27°C; Jul = 26°C
Currency: . . . . .U.S. dollar
Official Language: . .none

Name	Lat./Long.
Palikir	06°59' N, 158°08' E

MOLDOVA . . . . .pg. 134

Capital: . . . . .Chisinau
Area: . . . . .33,700 sq km; 13,000 sq mi
Highest Elev.: . . . . .Mt. Balanesti 430 m; 1,410 ft
Longest River: . . . . .Dniester 1,350 km; 840 mi
Avg. Temperature: . .Jan = -4°C; Jul = 20°C
Currency: . . . . .Moldovan leu
Official Language: . .Romanian

Name	Lat./Long.
Calaras	47°16' N, 028°19' E
Causeni	46°38' N, 029°25' E
Comrat (Komrat)	46°18' N, 028°39' E
Chisinau	47°00' N, 028°50' E
Drochia	48°02' N, 027°48' E
Dubasari	47°07' N, 029°10' E
Falesti (Faleshty)	47°34' N, 027°42' E
Jura (Kagul)	45°54' N, 028°11' E
Leova (Leovo)	46°28' N, 028°15' E
Orhei (Orgeyev)	47°22' N, 028°49' E
Rabnita	47°45' N, 029°00' E
Rezina	47°45' N, 028°58' E
Soroca (Soroki)	48°09' N, 028°18' E
Tiraspol	46°50' N, 029°37' E
Ungheni	47°12' N, 027°48' E

MONGOLIA . . . . .pg. 142

Capital: . . . . .Ulaanbaatar
Area: . . . . .1,566,500 sq km; 604,800 sq mi
Highest Elev.: . . .Nayramadlin Pk. 4,370 m; 14,350 ft
Longest River: . . .Selenga 1,480 km; 920 mi
Temperature: . . . .Jan = -26°C; Jul = 16°C
Currency: . . . . . .tugrik
Official Language: Khalkha Mongolian

Name	Lat./Long.
Darhan	49°29' N, 105°55' E
Ulaanbaatar	47°55' N, 106°53' E

MOROCCO . . . . .pg. 150

Capital: . . . . .Rabat
Area: . . . . .458,730 sq km; 177,117 sq mi
Highest Elev.: . . . . .Mt. Toubkal 4,170 m; 13,670 ft
Longest River: . . . . .Oum er-Rbia 560 km; 350 mi
Avg. Temperature: . .Jan =13°C; Jul = 33°C
Currency: . . . . .Moroccan dirham
Official Language: . .Arabic

Name	Lat./Long.
Agadir	30°24' N,009°36' W
Beni Mellal	32°20' N,006°21' W
Casablanca (Ad-Dar al-Bayda' or Dar el-Beida)	33°37' N,007°35' W
El-Jadida (Mazagan)	33°15' N,008°30' W
Fès (Fez)	34°02' N,004°59' W
Kenitra (Mina Hassan Tani or Port-Lyautey)	34°16' N,006°36' W
Khouribga	32°53' N,006°54' W
Marrakech	31°38' N,008°00' W
Meknès	33°54' N,005°33' W
Mohammedia (Fedala)	33°42' N,007°24' W
Oujda	34°40' N,001°54' W
Rabat (Ribat)	34°02' N,006°50' W
Safi (Asfi)	32°18' N,009°14' W
Salé (Sla)	34°04' N,006°48' W
Tan-Tan	28°26' N,011°06' W
Tangier (Tanger)	35°48' N,005°48' W
Tétouan (Tetuan)	35°34' N,005°22' W

MOZAMBIQUE . . . . .pg. 153

Capital: . . . . .Maputo
Area: . . . . .812,379 sq km; 313,661 sq mi
Highest Elev.: . . . . .Mt. Binga 2,440 m; 7,990 ft
Longest River: . . . . .Zambezi 3,500 km; 2,200 mi
Avg. Temperature: . .Jan = 25°C; Jul = 18°C
Currency: . . . . .metical
Official Language: . .Portuguese

Name	Lat./Long.
Beira	19°50' S, 034°52' E
Chimoio (Vila Pery)	19°08' S, 033°29' E
Chokwe	24°32' S, 032°59' E
Inhambane	23°52' S, 035°23' E
Lichinga	13°18' S, 035°14' E
Maputo (Lourenco Marques)	25°58' S, 032°34' E
Massinga	23°20' S, 035°22' E
Moçambique (Mozambique)	15°03' S, 040°45' E
Mopeia Velha	17°59' S, 035°43' E
Morrumbene	23°39' S, 035°20' E
Nacala	14°33' S, 040°40' E
Nampula	15°09' S, 039°18' E
Pemba	12°57' S, 040°30' E
Quelimane	17°51' S, 036°52' E
Quissico	24°43' S, 034°45' E
Tete	16°10' S, 033°36' E
Vila da Manhiça	25°24' S, 032°48' E
Xai Xai (Joao Belo)	25°04' S, 033°39' E

MYANMAR . . . . .pg. 144

Capital: . . . . .Yangôn
Area: . . . . .676,577 sq km; 261,228 sq mi
Highest Elev.: . . . . .Mt. Hkakabo 5,880 m; 19,300 ft
Longest River: . . . .Irrawaddy 2,170 km; 1,350 mi
Avg. Temperature: . .Jan = 25°C; Jul = 27°C
Currency: . . . . .Myanmar kyat
Official Language: . .Burmese

Name	Lat./Long.
Bassein (Pathein)	16°47' N, 094°44' E
Chauk	20°53' N, 094°49' E
Gangaw	22°10' N, 094°08' E
Henzada	17°38' N, 095°28' E
Kale	16°05' N, 097°54' E
Kyaukme	22°32' N, 097°02' E
Lashio	22°56' N, 097°45' E
Lewe	19°38' N, 096°07' E
Magwe (Magway)	20°09' N, 094°55' E
Mandalay	22°00' N, 096°05' E
Maungdaw	20°49' N, 092°22' E
Mawlamyine, *see* Moulmein	
Maymyo	22°02' N, 096°28' E
Meiktila	20°52' N, 095°52' E
Mergui	12°26' N, 098°36' E
Mogok	22°55' N, 096°30' E
Mohnyin	24°47' N, 096°22' E
Monywa	22°07' N, 095°08' E
Moulmein (Mawlamyine)	16°30' N, 097°38' E
Myaungmya	16°36' N, 094°56' E
Myingyan	21°28' N, 095°23' E
Myitkyina	25°23' N, 097°24' E
Nyaunglebin	17°57' N, 096°44' E
Pakokku	21°20' N, 095°06' E
Palaw	12°58' N, 098°39' E
Pegu (Bago)	17°20' N, 096°29' E
Prome (Pye)	18°49' N, 095°13' E
Pyapon	16°17' N, 095°41' E
Pyinmana	19°44' N, 096°13' E
Rangoon, *see* Yangôn	
Sagaing	21°52' N, 095°59' E
Shwebo	22°34' N, 095°42' E
Sittwe (Akyab)	20°09' N, 092°54' E
Tangyan	22°29' N, 098°24' E
Tatkon	20°07' N, 096°13' E
Tamu	24°13' N, 094°19' E
Taunggyi	20°47' N, 097°02' E
Tavoy (Dawei)	14°05' N, 098°12' E
Tenasserim	12°05' N, 099°01' E
Thaton	16°55' N, 097°22' E
Thanbyuzayat	15°58' N, 097°44' E
Toungoo	18°56' N, 096°26' E
Yangôn (Rangoon)	16°47' N, 096°10' E

NAMIBIA . . . . .pg. 152

Capital: . . . . .Windhoek
Area: . . . . .825,118 sq km; 318,580 sq mi
Highest Elev: . . . . . .Mt. Brand 2,570 m; 8,440 ft
Longest River: . . . . .Orange 2,100 km; 1,300 mi
Avg. Temperature: . .Jan = 23.3°C; Jul = 12.9°C
Currency: . . . . .Namibian dollar
Official Language: . .English

Name	Lat./Long.
Aranos	24°08' S, 019°07' E
Grootfontein	19°34' S, 018°07' E
Karasburg	28°01' S, 018°45' E
Karibib	21°56' S, 015°50' E
Keetmanshoop	26°35' S, 018°08' E
Khorixas	20°22' S, 014°58' E
Lüderitz	26°38' S, 015°09' E
Maltahöhe	24°50' S, 016°59' E
Mariental	24°38' S, 017°58' E
Ondangwa (Ondangua)	17°55' S, 015°57' E
Oshakati	17°47' S, 015°41' E
Otjimbingwe	22°21' S, 016°08' E
Outjo	20°07' S, 016°09' E
Rehoboth	23°19' S, 017°05' E
Rundu	17°56' S, 019°46' E
Swakopmund	22°41' S, 014°32' E
Tsumeb	19°14' S, 017°43' E
Usakos	22°00' S, 015°36' E
Walvis Bay	22°57' S, 014°30' E
Windhoek	22°35' S, 017°05' E

NEPAL .pg. 146

Capital: . . . . .Kathmandu
Area: . . . . .147,181 sq km; 56,827 sq mi
Highest Elev.: . . . . .Mt. Everest 8,850 m; 29,020 ft
Longest River: . . . . .Karnali 510 km; 320 mi
Avg. Temperature: . .Jan = 10°C; Jul = 24°C
Currency: . . . . .Nepalese rupee
Official Language: . .Nepali

Name	Lat./Long.
Bhaktpur (Bhadgaon)	27°41' N, 085°25' E
Kathmandu	27°43' N, 085°19' E
Lalitpur, *see* Patan	
Patan (Lalitpur)	27°40' N, 085°20' E

NETHERLANDS . . . . .pg. 132

Capital: . . . . .Amsterdam
Area: . . . . .41,526 sq km; 16,033 sq mi
Highest Elev.: . . . . .Vaalser Hill 320 m; 1,050 ft
Longest River: . . . . .Rhine 1,390 km; 870 mi
Avg. Temperature: . .Jan = 2.3°C; Jul = 16.5°C
Currency: . . . . .Netherlands guilder
Official Language: . .Dutch

Name	Lat./Long.
Alkmaar	52°38' N, 004°45' E
Almelo	52°21' N, 006°40' E
Amersfoort	52°09' N, 005°23' E
Amstelveen	52°18' N, 004°52' E
Amsterdam	52°21' N, 004°55' E
Apeldoorn	52°13' N, 005°58' E
Arnhem	51°59' N, 005°55' E
Assen	53°00' N, 006°33' E
Bergen op Zoom	51°30' N, 004°18' E
Breda	51°34' N, 004°48' E
Delft	52°00' N, 004°22' E
Den Helder	52°58' N, 004°46' E
Deventer	52°15' N, 006°12' E
Dordrecht (Dort or Dordt)	51°48' N, 004°40' E
Ede	52°02' N, 005°40' E
Eindhoven	51°27' N, 005°28' E
Emmen	52°47' N, 006°54' E
Enschede	52°13' N, 006°54' E
Geleen	50°58' N, 005°50' E
Groningen	53°13' N, 006°33' E
Haarlem	52°22' N, 004°39' E
Haarlemmermeer, *see* Hoofddorp	
Heerlen	50°54' N, 005°59' E
Helmond	51°29' N, 005°40' E
Hengelo	52°16' N, 006°48' E
Hilversum	52°14' N, 005°11' E
Hoofddorp (Haarlemmermeer)	52°18' N, 004°42' E
Hoorn	52°39' N, 005°04' E
Ijmuiden	52°28' N, 004°36' E
Lelystad	52°31' N, 005°29' E
Leeuwarden (Ljouwert)	53°12' N, 005°47' E
Leiden (Leyden)	52°09' N, 004°30' E
Maastricht	50°51' N, 005°41' E
Middelburg	51°30' N, 003°37' E
Nieuwegein	52°02' N, 005°06' E
Nijmegen (Nimwegen)	51°50' N, 005°52' E
Oss	51°46' N, 005°32' E
Purmerend	52°31' N, 004°57' E
Ridderkerk	51°52' N, 004°36' E
Roosendaal	51°32' N, 004°28' E
Rosmalen	51°43' N, 005°22' E
Rotterdam	51°55' N, 004°30' E
's-Gravenhage, *see* The Hague	
's-Hertogenbosch (Den Bosch or Bois-le-Duc)	51°42' N, 005°19' E
Schiedam	51°55' N, 004°24' E
Soest	52°11' N, 005°18' E
The Hague ('s-Gravenhage, Den Haag, or La Haye)	52°05' N, 004°18'E
Tilburg	51°33' N, 005°07' E
Utrecht	52°05' N, 005°08' E
Veenendaal	52°02' N, 005°33' E
Vlaardingen	51°55' N, 004°21' E
Vlissingen (Flushing)	51°27' N, 003°35' E
Zaanstad	52°27' N, 004°50' E
Zoetermeer	52°03' N, 004°30' E
Zwolle	52°30' N, 006°05' E

NEW ZEALAND . . . . .pg. 155

Capital: . . . . .Wellington
Area: . . . . .270,534 sq km; 104,454 sq mi
Highest Elev.: . . . . .Mt. Cook 3,760 m; 12,350 ft
Longest River: . . . . .Waikato 420 km; 260 mi
Avg. Temperature: . .Jan = 16°C; Jul = 8°C
Currency: . . . . .New Zealand dollar
Official Language: . .English, Maori

Name	Lat./Long.
Auckland	36°52' S, 174°46' E
Cheviot	42°49' S, 173°16' E
Christchurch	43°32' S, 172°39' E
Dunedin	45°53' S, 170°29' E
Hamilton	37°47' S, 175°16' E
Invercargill	46°25' S, 168°22' E
Lower Hutt	41°13' S, 174°56' E
Manukau	36°57' S, 174°56' E
Napier	39°31' S, 176°54' E
Palmerston North	40°21' S, 175°37' E
Rotorua	38°10' S, 176°14' E
Takapuna	36°47' S, 174°45' E
Tauranga	37°42' S, 176°08' E
Waihi Beach	37°24' S, 175°56' E
Wellington	41°18' S, 174°47' E
Whangarei	35°43' S, 174°20' E

NICARAGUA ....pg. 117

Capital: ....Managua
Area: ....131,670 sq km; 50,838 sq mi
Highest Elev.: .....Mogoton Pk. 2,100 m; 6,900 ft
Longest River: .....Coco 780 km; 490 mi
Avg. Temperature: . .Jan = 26°C; Jul = 27°C
Currency: ....córdoba oro
Official Language: . .Spanish

Name	Lat./Long.
Esteli	13°05' N, 086°21' W
Granada	11°56' N, 085°57' W
León	12°26' N, 086°53' W
Managua	12°09' N, 086°17' W
Masaya	11°58' N, 086°06' W
Matagalpa	12°55' N, 085°55' W

NIGER ....pg. 150

Capital: ....Niamey
Area: ....1,186,408 sq km; 458,075 sq mi
Highest Elev.: .....Mt. Gréboun 1,940 m; 6,380 ft
Longest River: .....Niger 4,200 km; 2,600 mi
Temperature: ......Jan = 24°C; Jul = 29°C
Currency: ....CFA franc
Official Language: . .French

Name	Lat./Long.
Agadez	16°58' N, 007°59' E
Maradi	13°29' N, 007°06' E
Niamey	13°31' N, 002°07' E
Tahoua	14°54' N, 005°16' E
Zinder	13°48' N, 008°59' E

NIGERIA ....pg. 150

Capital: ....Abuja
Area: ....923,768 sq km; 356,669 sq mi
Longest River: .....Niger 4,200 km; 2,600 mi
Avg. Temperature: . .Jan =27°C; Jul = 25°C
Currency: ....Nigerian nairo
Official Language: . .English

Name	Lat./Long.
Abuja	09°15' N, 006°56' E
Azare	11°41' N, 010°12' E
Bauchi	10°19' N, 009°50' E
Benin City	06°20' N, 005°38' E
Bida	09°05' N, 006°01' E
Calabar	04°57' N, 008°19' E
Deba Habe	10°13' N, 011°23' E
Dukku	10°49' N, 010°46' E
Enugu	06°26' N, 007°29' E
Gboko	07°19' N, 009°00' E
Gombe	10°17' N, 011°10' E
Gusau	12°10' N, 006°40' E
Ife	07°28' N, 004°34' E
Ihiala	05°51' N, 006°51' E
Ikerre	07°30' N, 005°14' E
Ilorin	08°30' N, 004°33' E
Iwo	07°38' N, 004°11' E
Jega	12°13' N, 004°23' E
Jimeta	09°17' N, 012°28' E
Jos	09°55' N, 008°54' E
Kaduna	10°31' N, 007°26' E
Kano	12°00' N, 008°31' E
Katsina	13°00' N, 007°36' E
Kaura Namoda	12°36' N, 006°35' E
Keffi	08°51' N, 007°52' E
Kishi	09°05' N, 003°51' E
Kumo	10°03' N, 011°13' E
Lafia	08°29' N, 008°31' E
Lafiagi	08°52' N, 005°25' E
Lagos	06°27' N, 003°23' E
Lere	09°43' N, 009°21' E
Maiduguri	11°51' N, 013°09' E
Makurdi	07°44' N, 008°32' E
Minna	09°37' N, 006°33' E
Mubi	10°16' N, 013°16' E
Mushin	06°32' N, 003°22' E
Nguru	12°53' N, 010°28' E
Nsukka	06°52' N, 007°23' E
Ogbomosho	08°08' N, 004°16' E
Ondo	07°06' N, 004°50' E
Onitsha	06°10' N, 006°47' E
Opobo Town	04°31' N, 007°32' E
Oron	04°50' N, 008°14' E
Oshogbo	07°46' N, 004°34' E
Oyo	07°51' N, 003°56' E
Pindiga	09°59' N, 010°54' E
Port Harcourt	04°46' N, 007°01' E
Potiskum	11°43' N, 011°04' E
Sapele	05°55' N, 005°42' E
Shaki	08°40' N, 003°23' E
Sokoto	13°04' N, 005°15' E
Ugep	05°48' N, 008°05' E
Uyo	05°03' N, 007°56' E
Warri	05°31' N, 005°45' E
Zaria	11°04' N, 007°42' E

NORWAY ....pg. 131

Capital: ....Oslo
Area: ....323,878 sq km; 125,050 sq mi
Highest Elev.: .....Galdho Pk. 2,470 m; 8,100 ft
Longest River: .....Glomma 600 km; 370 mi
Avg. Temperature: . .Jan = 5°C; Jul = 17°C
Currency: ....Norwegian krone
Official Language: . .Norwegian

Name	Lat./Long.
Alta	69°58' N, 023°15' E
Arendal	58°27' N, 008°48' E
Årnes	60°09' N, 011°28' E
Batsfjord	70°38' N, 029°44' E
Bergen	60°23' N, 005°20' E
Berkåk	62°50' N, 010°00' E
Bodø	67°17' N, 014°23' E
Brumunddal	60°53' N, 010°56' E
Drammen	59°44' N, 010°15' E
Dombås	62°05' N, 009°08' E
Eidsvoll	60°19' N, 011°14' E
Elverum	60°53' N, 011°34' E
Fauske	67°15' N, 015°24' E
Fredrikstad	59°13' N, 010°57' E
Gjovik	60°48' N, 010°42' E
Gol	60°42' N, 008°57' E
Hamar	60°48' N, 011°06' E
Hammerfest	70°40' N, 023°42' E
Hermansverk	61°11' N, 006°51' E
Hønefoss	60°10' N, 010°18' E
Honningsvag	70°59' N, 025°59' E
Kautokeino	68°59' N, 023°08' E
Kjøllefjord	70°56' N, 027°21' E
Kolsås	59°55' N, 010°31' E
Kongsberg	59°39' N, 009°39' E
Kongsvinger	60°12' N, 012°00' E
Kristiansand	58°10' N, 008°00' E
Lakselv	70°03' N, 024°56' E
Levanger	63°45' N, 011°18' E
Lillehammer	61°08' N, 010°30' E
Mandal	58°02' N, 007°27' E
Mo	66°19' N, 014°10' E
Molde	62°44' N, 007°11' E
Mosjøen	65°50' N, 013°12' E
Namsos	64°29' N, 011°30' E
Narvik	68°26' N, 017°25' E
Notodden	59°34' N, 009°17' E
Oslo (Christiania, Kristiania)	59°55' N, 010°45' E
Skien	59°12' N, 009°36' E
Stavanger	58°58' N, 005°45' E
Steinkjer	64°01' N, 011°30' E
Tønsberg	59°17' N, 010°25' E
Tromsø	69°40' N, 018°58' E
Trondheim	63°25' N, 010°25' E
Vadsø	70°05' N, 029°46' E
Vardø	70°22' N, 031°06' E

OMAN ....pg. 154

Capital: ....Muscat
Area: ....306,000 sq km; 118,150 sq mi
Highest Elev.: .....Mt. Al-Jabal al-Akhdar 3000 m; 14,350 ft
Avg. Temperature: . .Jan = 22°C; Jul = 34°C
Currency: ....rial Omani
Official Language: . .Arabic

Name	Lat./Long.
Bahla' (Bahlah)	22°58' N, 057°18' E
Barka'	23°43' N, 057°53' E
Dank	23°33' N, 056°16' E
Duqm	19°39' N, 057°42' E
Hayma'	19°56' N, 056°19' E
Izki	22°56' N, 057°46' E
Ibra'	22°43' N, 058°32' E
Khaburah, al-	23°59' N, 057°08' E
Khasab	26°12' N, 056°15' E
Khawr Rawri (Khor Rori)	17°02' N, 054°27' E
Masna'ah, al-	23°47' N, 057°38' E
Masqat, *see* Muscat	
Matrah	23°37' N, 058°34' E
Mirbat	17°00' N, 054°41' E
Muscat (Masqat)	23°37' N, 058°35' E
Nizwa (Nazwah)	22°56' N, 057°32' E
Qurayyat	23°15' N, 058°54' E
Rakhyut	16°44' N, 053°20' E
Rustaq, ar-	23°24' N, 057°26' E
Salalah	17°00' N, 054°06' E
Shinas	24°46' N, 056°28' E
Suhar	24°22' N, 056°45' E
Sur	22°34' N, 059°32' E
Taqah	17°02' N, 054°24' E
Thamarit	17°39' N, 054°02' E

PAKISTAN ....pg. 139

Capital: ....Islamabad
Area: ....796,095 sq km; 307,374 sq mi
Highest Elev.: .....K2 8,610 m; 28,250 ft
Longest River: .....Indus 2,900 km; 1,800 mi
Avg. Temperature: . .Jan = 13°C; Jul = 32°C
Currency: ....Pakistan rupee
Official Language: . .Urdu

Name	Lat./Long.
Ahmadpur East	29°09' N, 071°16' E
Badin	24°39' N, 068°50' E
Bahawalnagar	29°59' N, 073°16' E
Bahawalpur	29°24' N, 071°41' E
Bela	26°14' N, 066°19' E
Bhakkar	31°38' N, 071°04' E
Chakwal	32°56' N, 072°52' E
Chaman	30°55' N, 066°27' E
Charsadda	34°09' N, 071°44' E
Chiniot	31°43' N, 072°59' E
Chishtian Mandi	29°48' N, 072°52' E
Chitral	35°51' N, 071°47' E
Dadu	26°44' N, 067°47' E
Dera Ghazi Khan	30°03' N, 070°38' E
Dera Ismail Khan	31°50' N, 070°54' E
Dir	35°12' N, 071°53' E
Faisalabad (Lyallpur)	31°25' N, 073°05' E
Gojra	31°09' N, 072°41' E
Gujranwala	32°09' N, 074°11' E
Gujrat	32°34' N, 074°05' E
Gwadar	25°07' N, 062°19' E
Hab Chauki	25°01' N, 066°53' E
Haripur	33°59' N, 072°56' E
Hasilpur	29°43' N, 072°33' E
Hyderabad	25°22' N, 068°22' E
Islamabad	33°42' N, 073°10' E
Jacobabad	28°17' N, 068°26' E
Jampur	29°39' N, 070°36' E
Jhang Sadar (Jhang-Maghiana)	31°16' N, 072°19' E
Jhelum	32°56' N, 073°44' E
Kamalia	30°44' N, 072°39' E
Kambar	27°36' N, 068°00' E
Kandhkot	28°14' N, 069°11' E
Karachi	24°52' N, 067°03' E
Kasur	31°07' N, 074°27' E
Khairpur	29°35' N, 072°14' E
Khushab	32°18' N, 072°21' E
Khuzdar	27°48' N, 066°37' E
Kohat	33°35' N, 071°26' E
Kot Addu	30°28' N, 070°58' E
Kundian	32°27' N, 071°28' E
Lahore	31°35' N, 074°18' E
Larkana	27°33' N, 068°13' E
Leiah	30°58' N, 070°56' E
Mailsi	29°48' N, 072°11' E
Mansehra	34°20' N, 073°12' E
Mardan	34°12' N, 072°02' E
Mianwali	32°35' N, 071°33' E
Mingaora	34°47' N, 072°22' E
Mirpur Khas	25°32' N, 069°00' E
Mithankot	28°57' N, 070°22' E
Moro	26°40' N, 068°00' E
Multan	30°11' N, 071°29' E
Nawabshah	26°15' N, 068°25' E
Nushki	29°33' N, 066°01' E
Okara	30°49' N, 073°27' E
Ormara	25°12' N, 064°38' E
Panjgur	26°58' N, 064°06' E
Pasni	25°16' N, 063°28' E
Peshawar	34°01' N, 071°33' E
Pipri	24°52' N, 067°23' E
Pishin	30°35' N, 067°00' E
Port Muhammad Bin Qasim	24°46' N, 067°20' E
Quetta	30°12' N, 067°00' E
Rahimyar Khan	28°25' N, 070°18' E
Rawalpindi	33°36' N, 073°04' E
Sadiqabad	28°18' N, 070°08' E
Sahiwal (Montgomery)	30°40' N, 073°06' E
Sanghar	26°02' N, 068°57' E
Sangla (Sangla Hill)	31°43' N, 073°23' E
Sargodha	32°05' N, 072°40' E
Shahdadkot	27°51' N, 067°54' E
Shahdadpur	25°56' N, 068°37' E
Shekhupura	31°42' N, 073°59' E
Shikarpur	27°57' N, 068°38' E
Sialkot	32°30' N, 074°31' E
Sui	28°37' N, 069°19' E
Sukkur	27°42' N, 068°52' E
Tando Adam	25°46' N, 068°40' E
Tando Allahyar	25°28' N, 068°43' E
Tando Muhammad Khan	25°08' N, 068°32' E
Thatta	24°45' N, 067°55' E
Turbat	25°59' N, 063°04' E
Uthal	25°48' N, 066°37' E
Vihari	30°02' N, 072°21' E
Wah	33°48' N, 072°42' E
Wazirabad	32°27' N, 074°07' E
Zhob (Fort Sandeman)	31°20' N, 069°27' E

PALAU ....pg. 156

Capital: ....Koror
Area: ....487 sq km; 181 sq mi
Highest Elev.: .....Koror 630 m; 2,060 ft
Avg. Temperature: . .Jan =27°C; Jul = 28°C
Currency: ....U. S. dollar
Official Language: . .Palauan, English

Name	Lat./Long.
Koror	07°20' N, 134°29' E

PANAMA ....pg. 117

Capital: ....Panama City
Area: ....75,517 sq km; 29,157 sq mi
Highest Elev.: .....Baru Volc. 3,480 m; 11,400 ft
Longest River: .....Tuira 170 km; 110 mi
Avg. Temperature: . .Jan = 27°C; Jul = 27°C
Currency: ....balboa
Official Language: . .Spanish

Name	Lat./Long.
Aguadulce	08°15' N, 080°33' W
Almirante	09°18' N, 082°24' W
Antón	08°24' N, 080°16' W
Boquete	08°47' N, 082°26' W
Cañazas	09°06' N, 078°10' W
Capira	08°45' N, 079°53' W
Changuinola	09°26' N, 082°31' W
Chepo	09°10' N, 079°06' W
Chitré	07°58' N, 080°26' W
Colón	09°22' N, 079°54' W
David	08°26' N, 082°26' W
Guararé	07°49' N, 080°17' W
La Chorrera	08°53' N, 079°47' W
La Concepción	08°31' N, 082°37' W
La Palma	08°25' N, 078°09' W
Las Cumbres	09°05' N, 079°32' W
Las Lajas	08°15' N, 081°52' W
Las Tablas	07°46' N, 080°17' W
Ocú	07°57' N, 080°47' W
Panama City (Panamá)	08°58' N, 079°32' W
Penonomé	08°31' N, 080°22' W
Portobelo (Puerto Bello)	09°33' N, 079°39' W
Puerto Armuelles	08°17' N, 082°52' W
Puerto Bello, *see* Portobelo	
San Miguelito	09°02' N, 079°30' E
Santiago	08°06' N, 080°59' W
Soná	08°01' N, 081°19' W
Yaviza (Yavisa)	08°11' N, 077°41' W

PAPUA NEW GUINEA . .pg. 156

Capital: ....Port Moresby
Area: ....462,840 sq km; 104,454 sq mi
Highest Elev.: .....Mt. Whilhem 4,510 m; 700 ft
Longest River: .....Sepic 1,100 km; 78 mi
Avg. Temperature: . .Jan = 28°C; Jul = 27°C
Currency: ....Papua New Guinea kina
Official Language: . .English, Maori

Name	Lat./Long.
Alotau	10°20' S, 150°25' E
Goroka	06°05' S, 145°23' E
Lae	06°44' S, 147°00' E
Madang	05°13' S, 145°48' E
Mt. Hagen	05°52' S, 144°13' E
Port Moresby	09°29' S, 147°11' E
Rabaul	04°12' S, 152°11' E
Telefomin	05°08' S, 141°35' E
Wewak	03°33' S, 143°38' E

PARAGUAY ....pg. 122

Capital: ....Asuncion
Area: ....406,752 sq km; 157,048 sq mi
Highest Elev: .....Mt. San Rafael 850 m; 2,790 ft
Longest River: .....Paraguay 2,550 km; 1,580 mi
Avg. Temperature: . .Jan = 29°C; Jul = 18°C
Currency: ....Paraguayan Guaraní
Official Language: . .Spanish, Guaraní

Name	Lat./Long.
Asuncion	25°16' S, 057°40' W
Caaguazu	25°26' S, 056°02' W
Ciudad del Este (Puerto Presidente Stroessner)	25°31' S, 054°37' W
Encarnacion	27°20' S, 055°54' W
Pedro Juan Caballero	22°34' S, 055°37' W
San Lazaro	22°10' S, 057°58' W

PERU ....pg. 123

Capital: ....Lima
Area: ....1,285,216 sq km; 496,225 sq mi
Highest Elev.: . . .Mt. Huascarán 6,770 m; 22,210 ft
Longest River: . . .Ucayali 1,470 km; 910 mi
Avg. Temperature: .Jan = 22°C; Jul = 15°C
Currency: ....nuevo sol
Official Language: .Spanish, Quechua, Aymara

Name	Lat./Long.
Ancon	11°47' S, 077°11' W
Acomayo	13°55' S, 071°41' W
Andahuaylas	13°39' S, 073°23' W
Ascope	07°43' S, 079°07' W
Arequipa	16°24' S, 071°33' W
Ayacucho	13°07' S, 074°13' W
Ayabaca	04°38' S, 079°43' W
Ayaviri	14°52' S, 070°35' W
Bolívar	07°18' S, 077°48' W
Barranca	10°45' S, 077°46' W
Cajabamba	07°37' S, 078°03' W
Cajamarca	07°10' S, 078°31' W
Callao	12°04' S, 077°09' W
Camana	16°37' S, 072°42' W
Canta	11°25' S, 076°38' W
Caraveli	15°46' S, 073°22' W
Casma	09°28' S, 078°19' W
Castilla	05°12' S, 080°38' W
Cerro de Pasco	10°41' S, 076°16' W
Chiclayo	06°46' S, 079°51' W
Chicla	11°45' S, 076°18' W
Chimbote	09°05' S, 078°36' W
Chachapoyas	06°12' S, 077°51' W
Chaupimarca	10°26' S, 076°32' W
Chincha Alta	13°27' S, 076°08' W
Chulucanas	05°06' S, 080°10' W
Contamana	07°15' S, 074°54' W
Coracora	15°02' S, 073°47' W
Cotahuasi	15°12' S, 072°56' W
Cuzco	13°31' S, 071°59' W
Ferreñafe	06°38' S, 079°48' W
Espinar	14°47' S, 071°29' W
Huacho	11°07' S, 077°37' W
Huallanca	09°51' S, 076°56' W
Huamachuco	07°48' S, 078°04' W
Huancavelica	12°46' S, 075°02' W
Huancayo	12°04' S, 075°14' W
Huanta	12°56' S, 074°15' W
Huánuco	09°55' S, 076°14' W
Huari	09°20' S, 077°14' W
Huarmey	10°04' S, 078°10' W
Ica	14°04' S, 075°42' W
Ilave	16°05' S, 069°40' W
Ilo	17°38' S, 071°20' W
Imperial	13°04' S, 076°21' W
Iquitos	03°46' S, 073°15' W
Jaén	05°42' S, 078°47' W
Juli	16°13' S, 069°27' W
Juliaca	15°30' S, 070°08' W
Junín	11°10' S, 076°00' W
La Oroya	11°32' S, 075°54' W
Lagunas	05°14' S, 075°38' W
Lambayeque	06°42' S, 079°55' W
Lampa	15°21' S, 070°22' W
Lima	12°03' S, 077°03' W
Macusani	14°05' S, 070°26' W
Miraflores	12°07' S, 077°02' W
Moquegua	17°12' S, 070°56' W
Moyobamba	06°03' S, 076°58' W
Mollendo	17°02' S, 072°01' W
Nauta	04°32' S, 073°33' W
Nazca	14°50' S, 074°57' W
Olmos	05°59' S, 079°46' W
Otuzco	07°54' S, 078°35' W
Oxapampa	10°34' S, 075°24' W
Pampas	12°24' S, 074°54' W
Paita	05°06' S, 081°07' W
Paucara	12°42' S, 074°41' W
Paucartambo	13°18' S, 071°40' W
Pisco	13°42' S, 076°13' W
Piura	05°12' S, 080°38' W
Pucallpa	08°23' S, 074°32' W
Puerto Chicama	07°42' S, 079°27' W
Puno	15°50' S, 070°02' W
Rioja	06°05' S, 077°09' W
Requena	04°58' S, 073°50' W
Rímac	12°03' S, 077°03' W
San Ignacio	05°08' S, 078°59' W
San Juan	15°21' S, 075°10' W
San Pedro de Lloc	07°26' S, 079°31' W
San Ramón	11°08' S, 075°20' W
San Vicente de Canete	13°05' S, 076°24' W
Saña	06°55' S, 079°35' W
Santo Tomás	14°29' S, 072°06' W
Sicuani	14°16' S, 071°13' W
Socabaya	16°28' S, 071°31' W
Sullana	04°53' S, 080°41' W
Tacna	18°01' S, 070°15' W
Talara	04°34' S, 081°17' W
Tarapoto	06°30' S, 076°25' W
Tarata	17°28' S, 070°02' W
Tayabamba	08°17' S, 077°18' W
Tingo Maria	09°09' S, 075°56' W
Trujillo	08°07' S, 079°02' W
Tumbes	03°34' S, 080°28' W
Urcos	13°42' S, 071°38' W
Viru	08°25' S, 078°45' W
Yurimaguas	05°54' S, 076°05' W

PHILIPPINES ....pg. 145

Capital: ....Manila
Area: ....300,076 sq km; 115,860 sq mi
Highest Elev.: .....Mt. Apo 2,950 m; 9,690 ft
Longest River: .....Agusan 390 km; 240 mi
Avg. Temperature: . .Jan = 25°C; Jul = 27°C
Currency: ....Philippine peso
Official Language: . .Filipino, English

Name	Lat./Long.
Angeles	15°09' N, 120°35' E
Antipolo	14°35' N, 121°10' E

Name	Lat./Long.
Bacolod	10°40' N, 122°56' E
Baguio	16°25' N, 120°36' E
Balabac	07°59' N, 117°04' E
Baliuag	14°57' N, 120°54' E
Bangued	17°36' N, 120°37' E
Bislig	08°13' N, 126°19' E
Butuan	08°54' N, 125°35' E
Cabanatuan	15°29' N, 120°58' E
Cagayan de Oro	08°29' N, 124°39' E
Caloocan	14°39' N, 120°58' E
Candon	17°12' N, 120°27' E
Cavite	14°29' N, 120°55' E
Cebu	10°18' N, 123°54' E
Cotabato	07°13' N, 124°15' E
Dagupan	16°03' N, 120°20' E
Dapitan	08°39' N, 123°25' E
Davao	07°04' N, 125°36' E
Dumaguete	09°18' N, 123°18' E
General Luna	09°47' N, 126°09' E
General Santos	06°07' N, 125°10' E
Gingoog	08°50' N, 125°07' E
Iligan	08°14' N, 124°14' E
Iloilo City	10°42' N, 122°33' E
Isabela	06°42' N, 121°58' E
Isulan	06°37' N, 124°40' E
Jolo	06°03' N, 121°00' E
Lapu-Lapu (Opon)	10°19' N, 123°57' E
Laoang	12°34' N, 125°00' E
Lazi	09°08' N, 123°38' E
Legazpi	13°08' N, 123°44' E
Lucena	13°56' N, 121°37' E
Malolos	14°51' N, 120°49' E
Mandaue	10°20' N, 123°56' E
Mangaldan	16°04' N, 120°24' E
Manila	14°35' N, 121°00' E
Marawi (Dansalan)	08°01' N, 124°18' E
Naga (Nueva Caceres)	13°37' N, 123°11' E
Narra	09°16' N, 118°25' E
Olongapo	14°50' N, 120°16' E
Ormoc	11°00' N, 124°37' E
Pagadian	07°49' N, 123°25' E
Polomolok	06°13' N, 125°04' E
Puerto Princesa	09°44' N, 118°44' E
Quezon City	14°38' N, 121°00' E
San Fernando	16°37' N, 120°19' E
San Jose	12°21' N, 121°04' E
San Pablo	14°04' N, 121°19' E
Santa Cruz	13°29' N, 122°02' E
Tacloban	11°15' N, 125°00' E
Tagbilaran	09°39' N, 123°51' E
Tagig	14°32' N, 121°04' E
Tanjay	09°31' N, 123°09' E
Valencia	07°57' N, 125°03' E
Zamboanga	06°54' N, 122°04' E

POLAND ....pg. 133

Capital: ....Warsaw
Area: ....312,685 sq km; 120,728 sq mi
Highest Elev.: .....Rysy 2,500 m; 8,200 ft
Longest River: .....Vistula 1,050 km; 650 mi
Avg. Temperature: . .Jan = -4°C; Jul = 19°C
Currency: ....zloty
Official Language: . .Polish

Name	Lat./Long.
Belchatów	51°22' N, 019°23' E
Biala Podlaska	52°02' N, 023°08' E
Bialystok	53°08' N, 023°09' E
Bielsko-Biala	49°49' N, 019°02' E
Bydgoszcz	53°09' N, 018°00' E
Bytom	50°21' N, 018°58' E
Chelm	51°08' N, 023°30' E
Czestochowa	50°48' N, 019°07' E
Dabrowa Górnicza	50°20' N, 019°12' E
Elblag	54°10' N, 019°23' E
Gdansk (Danzig)	54°21' N, 018°40' E
Gdynia	54°30' N, 018°33' E
Gliwice	50°17' N, 018°40' E
Glogów	51°40' N, 016°06' E
Gniezno	52°33' N, 017°36' E
Gorzów Wielkopolski	52°44' N, 015°14' E
Grudziadz	53°29' N, 018°46' E
Inowroclaw	52°48' N, 018°16' E
Jelenia Góra	50°54' N, 015°44' E
Kalisz	51°45' N, 018°05' E
Katowice	50°16' N, 019°01' E
Kedzierzyn-Kozle	50°21' N, 018°12' E
Kielce	50°50' N, 020°40' E
Konin	52°13' N, 018°16' E
Koszalin	54°12' N, 016°11' E
Kraków	50°05' N, 019°55' E
Krosno	49°41' N, 021°47' E
Kutno	52°14' N, 019°22' E
Legnica	51°12' N, 016°12' E
Leszno	51°51' N, 016°35' E
Lódz	51°45' N, 019°28' E
Lomza	53°11' N, 022°05' E
Lubin	51°24' N, 016°12' E
Lublin	51°15' N, 022°34' E
Mielec	50°17' N, 021°25' E
Nowy Sacz	49°38' N, 020°43' E
Olsztyn	53°47' N, 020°29' E
Opole	50°40' N, 017°57' E
Ostroleka	53°05' N, 021°34' E
Ostrow Wielkopolski	51°39' N, 017°49' E
Ostrowiec Shwietokrzyski	50°56' N, 021°24' E
Pabianice	51°40' N, 019°22' E
Pila	53°09' N, 016°45' E
Piotrków Trybunalski	51°24' N, 019°41' E
Plock	52°33' N, 019°42' E
Poznan	52°25' N, 016°58' E
Pruszków	52°10' N, 020°50' E
Przemysl	49°47' N, 022°47' E
Pulawy	51°25' N, 021°58' E
Racibórz	50°05' N, 018°12' E
Radom	51°25' N, 021°09' E
Radomsko	51°04' N, 019°27' E
Rybnik	50°07' N, 018°32' E
Rzeszów	50°03' N, 022°00' E
Siedlce	52°10' N, 022°18' E
Skarzysko-Kamienna	51°07' N, 020°54' E
Slupsk	54°27' N, 017°02' E
Sopot	54°27' N, 018°34' E
Sosnowiec	50°18' N, 019°10' E
Stalowa Wola	50°34' N, 022°03' E
Starachowice	51°04' N, 021°04' E
Stargard Szczecinski	53°20' N, 015°03' E
Suwalki	54°06' N, 022°56' E
Szczecin (Stettin)	53°25' N, 014°35' E
Tarnów	50°01' N, 020°59' E
Tarnowskie Góry	50°27' N, 018°52' E
Tczew	54°06' N, 018°48' E
Tomaszow Mazowiecki	51°32' N, 020°01' E
Torun	53°02' N, 018°36' E
Tychy	50°08' N, 018°59' E
Walbrzych	50°46' N, 016°17' E
Warsaw (Warszawa)	52°15' N, 021°00' E
Wloclawek	52°39' N, 019°05' E
Wodzislaw Slaski	50°00' N, 018°28' E
Wroclaw (Breslau)	51°06' N, 017°02' E
Zabrze	50°19' N, 018°47' E
Zamosc	50°43' N, 023°15' E
Zawiercie	50°30' N, 019°26' E
Zgierz	51°51' N, 019°25' E
Zielona Góra	51°56' N, 015°30' E

PORTUGAL ....pg. 128

Capital: ....Lisbon
Area: ....91,831 sq km; 35,456 sq mi
Highest Elev.: .....Serra da Estrela 1,990 m; 6,530 ft
Longest River: ....Douro 900 km; 560 mi
Avg. Temperature: .Jan = 11°C; Jul = 22°C
Currency: ....escudo
Official Language: .Portuguese

Name	Lat./Long.
Amadora	38°45' N, 009°14' W
Barreiro	38°40' N, 009°04' W
Braga	41°33' N, 008°26' W
Coimbra	40°12' N, 008°25' W
Lisbon (Lisboa)	38°43' N, 009°08' W
Ponta Delgada	37°44' N, 025°40' W
Porto (Oporto)	41°09' N, 008°37' W
Setúbal	38°32' N, 008°54' W
Vila Franca de Xira	38°57' N, 008°59' W

QATAR ....pg. 154

Capital: ....Doha
Area: ....11,427 sq km; 4,412 sq mi
Avg. Temperature: . .Jan = 21°C; Jul = 40°C
Currency: ....riyal
Official Language: . .Arabic

Name	Lat./Long.
Doha (ad-Dawhah)	25°17' N, 051°32' E
Dukhan	25°25' N, 050°47' E
Musay'id	25°00' N, 051°33' E
Ruways, ar-	26°08' N, 051°13' E
Wakrah, al-	25°10' N, 051°36' E

ROMANIA ....pg. 134

Capital: ....Bucharest
Area: ....237,500 sq km; 91,699 sq mi
Highest Elev.: .....Mt. Moldoveanu 2,540 m; 8,350 ft
Longest River: .....Danube 2,850 km; 1,770 mi
Avg. Temperature: . .Jan = -3°C; Jul = 23°C
Currency: ....Romanian leu
Official Language: . .Romanian

Name	Lat./Long.
Alba Iulia (Gyulafehervar)	46°04' N, 023°35' E
Alexandria	43°59' N, 025°20' E
Arad	46°11' N, 021°19' E
Bacau	46°34' N, 026°54' E
Baia Mare	47°40' N, 023°35' E
Barlad	46°14' N, 027°40' E
Bistrita	47°08' N, 024°29' E
Botosani	47°45' N, 026°40' E
Braila	45°16' N, 027°59' E
Brasov (Orasul Stalin)	45°38' N, 025°35' E
Bucharest	44°26' N, 026°06' E
Buzau	45°09' N, 026°50' E
Calafat	43°59' N, 022°56' E
Calarasi	44°12' N, 027°20' E
Campia Turzii	46°33' N, 023°53' E
Câmpulung	45°16' N, 025°03' E
Câmpulung Moldovenesc	47°32' N, 025°34' E
Cluj-Napoca	46°46' N, 023°36' E
Constanta	44°11' N, 028°39' E
Costesti	44°40' N, 024°53' E
Craiova	44°19' N, 023°48' E
Curtea De Arges	45°08' N, 024°41' E
Dej	47°09' N, 023°52' E
Deva	45°53' N, 022°54' E
Drobeta-Turnu Severin	44°38' N, 022°40' E
Eforie (Eforia)	44°06' N, 028°38' E
Faurei	45°04' N, 027°14' E
Fetesti	44°23' N, 027°50' E
Focsani	45°42' N, 027°11' E
Gaesti	44°43' N, 025°19' E
Galati (Galatz)	45°27' N, 028°03' E
Gheorghe Gheorghiu Dej, *see* Onesti	
Giurgiu	43°53' N, 025°58' E
Hunedoara	45°45' N, 022°54' E
Iasi (Jassy)	47°10' N, 027°36' E
Lugoj	45°41' N, 021°55' E
Mangalia	43°48' N, 028°35' E
Medgidia	44°15' N, 028°17' E
Medias	46°10' N, 024°21' E
Miercurea-Ciuc	46°21' N, 025°48' E
Mizil	45°01' N, 026°27' E
Odorheíul Secuíesc	46°18' N, 025°18' E
Onesti (Gheorghe Gheorghiu Dej)	46°15' N, 026°45' E
Oradea (Nagyvarad)	47°04' N, 021°56' E
Pascani	47°15' N, 026°44' E
Petrosani	45°25' N, 023°22' E
Piatra-Neamt	46°55' N, 026°20' E
Pitesti	44°51' N, 024°52' E
Ploiesti (Ploesti)	44°57' N, 026°01' E
Râmnicu Sarat	45°23' N, 027°03' E
Reghin	46°46' N, 024°42' E
Resita	45°18' N, 021°55' E
Roman	46°55' N, 026°55' E
Satu Mare	47°48' N, 022°53' E
Sebes	45°58' N, 023°34' E
Sfantu Gheorghe	45°52' N, 025°47' E
Sibiu (Nagyszeben)	45°48' N, 024°09' E
Sighisoara	46°13' N, 024°48' E
Sinaia	45°21' N, 025°33' E
Slatina	44°26' N, 024°22' E
Slobozia	44°34' N, 027°22' E
Suceava	47°38' N, 026°15' E
Tandarei	44°39' N, 027°40' E
Targoviste	44°56' N, 025°27' E
Târgu Secuesc	46°00' N, 026°08' E
Targu Jiu	45°03' N, 023°17' E
Targu Mures	46°33' N, 024°34' E
Tecuci	45°52' N, 027°25' E
Techirghiol	44°03' N, 028°36' E
Timisoara	45°45' N, 021°13' E
Titu-Targ	44°39' N, 025°32' E
Topoloveni	44°49' N, 025°05' E
Tulcea	45°10' N, 028°48' E
Turda	46°34' N, 023°47' E
Urziceni	44°43' N, 026°38' E
Vaslui	46°38' N, 027°44' E
Videle	44°17' N, 025°31' E
Zalau	47°12' N, 023°03' E

RUSSIA ....pg. 136

Capital: ......Moscow
Area: ....17,075,400 sq km; 6,592,800 sq mi
Highest Elev.: . .Mt. Elbrus 5,640 m; 18,510 ft
Longest River: . .Lena 4,400 km; 2,730 mi
Avg. Temperature:Jan = -10°C; Jul = 18°C
Currency: .....ruble
Official Language:Russian

Name	Lat./Long.
Abakan	53°43' N, 091°26' E
Achinsk	56°17' N, 090°30' E
Aginskoye	51°06' N, 114°32' E
Akademgorodok	54°49' N, 083°09' E
Aldan	58°37' N, 125°24' E
Aleksandrovsk-Grushevsky, *see* Shakhty	
Aleksandrovsk-Sakhalinsky	50°54' N, 142°10' E
Aleksin	54°31' N, 037°05' E
Almetyevsk	54°53' N, 052°20' E
Anadyr (Novo-Mariinsk)	64°45' N, 177°29' E
Andropov, *see* Rybinsk	
Angarsk	52°34' N, 103°54' E
Anzhero-Sudzhensk	56°07' N, 086°00' E
Arkhangelsk (Archangel)	64°34' N, 040°32' E
Armavir	45°00' N, 041°08' E
Arzamas	55°23' N, 043°50' E
Astrakhan	46°21' N, 048°03' E
Balakovo	52°02' N, 047°47' E
Barnaul	53°22' N, 083°45' E
Belgorod	50°36' N, 036°34' E
Berezniki	59°24' N, 056°46' E
Birobidzhan	48°48' N, 132°57' E
Biysk (Biisk)	52°34' N, 085°15' E
Blagoveshchensk	50°16' N, 127°32' E
Bobriki, *see* Novomoskovsk	
Bratsk	56°21' N, 101°55' E
Brezhnev, *see* Naberezhnye Chelny	
Bryansk	53°15' N, 034°22' E
Cheboksary	56°09' N, 047°15' E
Chelyabinsk	55°10' N, 061°24' E
Cherepovets	59°08' N, 037°54' E
Cherkessk	44°14' N, 042°03' E
Chita	52°03' N, 113°30' E
Chkalov, *see* Orenburg	
Dimitrovgrad (Melekess)	54°15' N, 049°33' E
Dudinka	69°25' N, 086°15' E
Dzaudzhikau, *see* Vladikavkaz	
Dzerzhinsk	56°15' N, 043°24' E
Ekaterinodar, *see* Krasnodar	
Elektrostal	55°47' N, 038°28' E
Elista	46°16' N, 044°14' E
Engels	51°30' N, 046°07' E
Gatchina (Krasnogvardeysk)	59°34' N, 030°08' E
Glazov	58°09' N, 052°40' E
Gorky, *see* Nizhny Novgorod	
Gorno-Altaysk (Ulala, or Oyrot-Tura)	51°58' N, 085°58' E
Grozny	43°20' N, 045°42' E
Ioshkar-Ola, *see* Yoshkar-Ola	
Irkutsk	52°16' N, 104°20' E
Ivanovo	57°00' N, 040°59' E
Izhevsk (Ustinov)	56°51' N, 053°14' E
Kalinin, *see* Tver	
Kaliningrad (Königsberg)	54°43' N, 020°30' E
Kaluga	54°31' N, 036°16' E
Kamensk-Uralsky	56°25' N, 061°54' E
Kamyshin	50°06' N, 045°24' E
Kansk	56°13' N, 095°41' E
Kazan	55°45' N, 049°08' E
Kemerovo	55°20' N, 086°05' E
Khabarovsk	48°30' N, 135°06' E
Khanty-Mansiysk (Ostyako-Vogulsk)	61°00' N, 069°06' E
Kineshma	57°28' N, 042°07' E
Kirov, *see* Vyatka	
Kiselevsk (Kiselyovsk)	54°00' N, 086°39' E
Kislovodsk	43°55' N, 042°43' E
Kolchugino, *see* Leninsk-Kuznetsky	
Kolomna	55°05' N, 038°47' E
Kolpino	59°45' N, 030°36' E
Komsomolsk-na-Amure	50°35' N, 137°02' E
Königsberg, *see* Kaliningrad	
Kostroma	57°46' N, 040°55' E
Kovrov	56°25' N, 041°18' E
Kozlov, *see* Michurinsk	
Krasnodar (Ekaterinodar, or Yekaterinodar)	45°02' N, 039°00' E
Krasnogvardeysk, *see* Gatchina	
Krasnoyarsk	56°01' N, 092°50' E
Kudymkar	59°01' N, 054°39' E
Kurgan	55°26' N, 065°18' E
Kursk	51°42' N, 036°12' E
Kuybyshev, *see* Samara	
Kuznetsk, *see* Novokuznetsk	
Kyzyl (Khem-Beldyr)	51°42' N, 094°27' E
Leningrad, *see* St. Petersburg	
Leninsk-Kuznetsky (Kolchugino)	54°38' N, 086°10' E
Lensk	60°43' N, 114°55' E
Lipetsk	52°37' N, 039°35' E
Lyubertsy	55°41' N, 037°53' E
Magadan	59°34' N, 150°48' E
Magnitogorsk	53°27' N, 059°04' E
Makhachkala	42°58' N, 047°30' E
Maykop (Maikop)	44°35' N, 040°10' E
Melekess, *see* Dimitrovgrad	
Mezhdurechensk	53°42' N, 088°03' E
Miass	54°59' N, 060°06' E
Michurinsk (Kozlov)	52°54' N, 040°30' E
Mikhaylovka (Mikhailovka)	50°04' N, 043°15' E
Mirny	62°33' N, 113°53' E
Molotov, *see* Perm	
Molotovsk, *see* Severodvinsk	
Moscow (Moskva)	55°45' N, 037°35' E
Murmansk	68°58' N, 033°05' E
Naberezhnye Chelny (Brezhnev)	55°42' N, 052°19' E
Nadezhdinsk, *see* Serov	
Nakhodka	42°47' N, 132°52' E
Nalchik	43°29' N, 043°37' E
Naryan-Mar	67°39' N, 053°00' E
Nizhnekamsk	55°36' N, 051°47' E
Nizhnevartovsk	60°56' N, 076°38' E
Nizhny Novgorod (Gorky)	56°20' N, 044°00' E
Nizhny Tagil	57°55' N, 059°57' E
Norilsk	69°20' N, 088°06' E
Novgorod	58°31' N, 031°17' E
Novo-Mariinsk, *see* Anadyr	
Novocherkassk	47°25' N, 040°06' E
Novokuybyshevsk	53°07' N, 049°58' E
Novokuznetsk (Kuznetsk, or Stalinsk)	53°45' N, 087°06' E
Novomoskovsk (Bobriki, or Stalinogorsk)	54°05' N, 038°13' E
Novorossiysk	44°43' N, 037°47' E
Novoshakhtinsk	47°47' N, 039°56' E
Novosibirsk	55°02' N, 082°55' E
Novotroitsk	51°12' N, 058°20' E
Omsk	55°00' N, 073°24' E
Ordzhonikidze, *see* Vladikavkaz	
Orenburg (Chkalov)	51°45' N, 055°06' E
Orsk	51°12' N, 058°34' E
Oryol	52°55' N, 036°05' E
Ostyako-Vogulsk, *see* Khanty-Mansiysk	
Oyrot-Tura, *see* Gorno-Altaysk	
Palana	59°07' N, 159°58' E
Penza	53°13' N, 045°00' E
Perm (Molotov)	58°00' N, 056°15' E
Pervouralsk	56°54' N, 059°58' E
Petropavlovsk-Kamchatsky	53°01' N, 158°39' E
Petrozavodsk	61°49' N, 034°20' E
Pevek	69°42' N, 170°17' E
Podolsk	55°26' N, 037°33' E
Prokopyevsk	53°53' N, 086°45' E
Pskov	57°50' N, 028°20' E
Pyatigorsk	44°01' N, 043°05' E
Rostov-na-Donu (Rostov-on-Don)	47°14' N, 039°42' E
Rubtsovsk	51°30' N, 081°15' E
Ryazan (Riazan)	54°38' N, 039°44' E
Rybinsk (Andropov, or Shcherbakov)	58°03' N, 038°50' E
Salavat	53°21' N, 055°55' E
Salekhard	66°33' N, 066°40' E
Samara (Kuybyshev)	53°12' N, 050°09' E
Sankt Peterburg, *see* St. Petersburg	
Saransk	54°11' N, 045°11' E
Sarapul	56°28' N, 053°48' E
Saratov	51°34' N, 046°02' E
Serov (Nadezhdinsk)	59°36' N, 060°35' E
Serpukhov	54°55' N, 037°25' E
Severodvinsk (Molotovsk)	64°34' N, 039°50' E
Shakhty (Aleksandrovsk-Grushevsky)	47°42' N, 040°13' E
Shcherbakov, *see* Rybinsk	
Simbirsk *see* Ulyanovsk	
Smolensk	54°47' N, 032°03' E
Sochi	43°35' N, 039°45' E
Solikamsk	59°39' N, 056°47' E
Srednekolymsk	67°27' N, 153°41' E
St. Petersburg (Leningrad, or Sankt Peterburg)	59°55' N, 030°15' E
Stalingrad, *see* Volgograd	
Stalinogorsk, *see* Novomoskovsk	
Stalinsk, *see* Novokuznetsk	
Stary Oskol	51°17' N, 037°51' E
Stavropol (Voroshilovsk)	45°03' N, 041°58' E
Sterlitamak	53°37' N, 055°58' E
Surgut	61°14' N, 073°20' E
Susuman	62°47' N, 148°10' E
Sverdlovsk, *see* Yekaterinburg	
Syktyvkar	61°40' N, 050°48' E
Syzran	53°11' N, 048°27' E
Taganrog	47°12' N, 038°56' E
Tambov	52°43' N, 041°27' E
Tolyatti (Stavropal, or Tolyattigrad)	53°31' N, 049°26' E
Tomsk	56°30' N, 084°58' E
Tsaritsyn, *see* Volgograd	
Tula	54°12' N, 037°37' E
Tura	64°17' N, 100°15' E
Tver (Kalinin)	56°52' N, 035°55' E
Tyumen	57°09' N, 065°26' E
Udachny	62°33' N, 113°53' E
Ufa	55°45' N, 055°56' E
Ukhta	63°33' N, 053°40' E
Ulala, *see* Gorno-Altaysk	
Ulan-Ude	51°50' N, 107°37' E
Ulyanovsk (Simbirsk)	54°20' N, 048°24' E
Usolye-Sibirskoye	52°45' N, 103°41' E
Ussuriysk	43°48' N, 131°59' E
Ust-Ordinsky	52°48' N, 104°45' E
Ustinov, *see* Izhevsk	
Velikiye Luki	56°20' N, 030°32' E
Verkhoyansk	67°35' N, 133°27' E
Viipuri, *see* Vyborg	
Vladikavkaz (Dzaudzhikau, or Ordzhonikidze)	43°40' N, 044°40' E
Vladimir	56°10' N, 040°25' E
Vladivostok	43°08' N, 131°54' E
Volgodonsk	47°32' N, 042°09' E
Volgograd (Stalingrad, or Tsaritsyn)	48°45' N, 044°25' E
Vologda	59°13' N, 039°54' E
Volzhsky	48°49' N, 044°44' E
Vorkuta	67°30' N, 064°00' E
Voronezh	51°38' N, 039°12' E
Voroshilovsk, *see* Stavropol	
Votkinsk	57°03' N, 053°39' E
Vyatka (Viatka, or Kirov)	58°33' N, 049°42' E
Vyborg (Viipuri)	60°42' N, 028°45' E
Yakutsk	62°00' N, 129°40' E
Yaroslavl	57°37' N, 039°52' E
Yekaterinburg (Sverdlovsk)	56°51' N, 060°36' E
Yekaterinodar, *see* Krasnodar	
Yelets	52°37' N, 038°30' E
Yoshkar-Ola (Ioshkar-Ola)	56°40' N, 047°55' E
Yuzhno-Sakhalinsk	46°57' N, 142°44' E
Zlatoust	55°10' N, 059°40' E

RWANDA ....pg. 153

Capital: ....Kigali
Area: ....25,271 sq km; 9,757 sq mi
Highest Elev.: .....Karisimbi 4,510 m; 14,790 ft
Longest River: .....Kagura 400 km; 250 mi
Avg. Temperature: . .Jan = 20.8°C; Jul = 20.2°C
Currency: ....Rwanda franc
Official Language: . .Rwanda, French

Name	Lat./Long.
Kigali	01°57' S, 030°04' E
Ruhengeri	01°30' S, 029°38' E

SAINT KITTS AND NEVIS pg. 116

Capital: ....Basseterre
Area: ....269.4 sq km; 104 sq mi
Highest Elev: ......Mt. Liamuiga 1,160 m; 3,790 ft
Avg. Temperature: . .Jan = 27°C; Jul = 27°C
Currency: ....East Caribbean dollar
Official Language: . .English

Name	Lat./Long.
Basseterre	17°18' N, 062°43' W
Charlestown	17°08' N, 062°37' W

SAINT LUCIA ....pg. 116

Capital: ....Castries
Area: ....617 sq km; 238 sq mi
Highest Elev: ......Mt. Gimie 960 m; 3,150 ft
Avg. Temperature: . .Jan = 24.2°C; Jul = 27.0°C
Currency: ....East Caribbean dollar
Official Language: . .English

Name	Lat./Long.
Castries	14°01' N, 061°00' W

SAINT VINCENT AND THE GRENADINES ....pg. 116

Capital: ....Kingstown
Area: ....389.3 sq km; 150.3 sq mi
Highest Elev.: ....Soufrière 1,230 m; 4,080 ft
Avg. Temperature: . .Jan = 25°C; Jul = 27°C
Currency: ....East Caribbean dollar
Official Language: . .English

Name	Lat./Long.
Kingstown	13°09' N, 061°14' W

SAN MARINO ....pg. 130

Capital: ....San Marino
Area: ....61.2 sq km; 23.6 sq mi
Highest Elev.: .....Mt. Titano 740 m; 2,420 ft
Avg. Temperature: . .Jan = 26°C; Jul = -7°C
Currency: ....Italian lira
Official Language: . .Italian

Name	Lat./Long.
San Marino	43°56' N, 012°25' E

SÃO TOMÉ AND PRÍNCIPE. pg. 150

Capital: ....São Tomé
Area: ....1,001 sq km; 386 sq mi
Highest Elev.: .....São Tomé Peak 2,020 m; 6,640 ft
Avg. Temperature: .Jan = 26°C; Jul = 26°C
Currency: ....dobra
Official Language: .Portuguese

Name	Lat./Long.
São Tomé	00°20' N, 006°44' E

SAUDI ARABIA ....pg. 154

Capital: ....Riyadh
Area: ....2,240,000 sq km; 865,000 sq mi
Avg. Temperature: . .Jan = 15°C; Jul = 34°C
Currency: ....Saudi riyal
Official Language: . .Arabic

Name	Lat./Long.
Abha	18°13' N, 042°30' E
Abqaiq (Buqayq)	25°56' N, 049°40' E
Afif	23°55' N, 042°56' E
Ar'ar	30°59' N, 041°02' E
Badanah	30°59' N, 040°58' E
Bahah, al-	20°01' N, 041°28' E
Badi', al-	22°02' N, 046°34' E
Bi'ar, al-	22°39' N, 039°40' E
Birkah	23°48' N, 038°50' E
Buraydah	26°20' N, 043°59' E
Buraykah	22°21' N, 039°20' E
Dammam, ad-	26°26' N, 050°07' E
Hafar al-Batin	28°27' N, 045°58' E
Ha'il	27°33' N, 041°42' E
Halaban	23°29' N, 044°23' E
Harajah	17°56' N, 043°21' E
Ha'ir, al-	24°23' N, 046°50' E
Hufuf, al-	25°22' N, 049°34' E
Ju'aydah, al-	19°40' N, 041°34' E
Jubayl, al-	27°01' N, 049°40' E
Jiddah	21°29' N, 039°12' E
Khamis Mushayt	18°18' N, 042°44' E
Khawsh	18°59' N, 041°53' E
Khubar, al-	26°17' N, 050°12' E
Layla	22°17' N, 046°45' E
Mada'in Salih	26°48' N, 037°57' E
Madinah, al-, *see* Medina	
Mecca (Makkah)	21°27' N, 39°49' E
Medina (al-Madinah; Yathrib)	24°28' N, 039°36' E
Mish'ab, al-	28°12' N, 048°36' E
Miskah	24°49' N, 042°56' E
Mubarraz, al-	25°25' N, 049°35' E
Musabih	18°42' N, 042°01' E
Na'jan	24°05' N, 047°10' E
Najran	17°26' N, 044°15' E
Qana	27°47' N, 041°25' E
Qatif, al-	26°33' N, 050°00' E
Qunfudhah, al-	19°08' N, 041°05' E
Rabigh	22°48' N, 039°02' E
Rafha'	29°38' N, 043°30' E
Ras Tanura	26°42' N, 050°06' E
Riyadh (ar-Riyad)	24°38' N, 046°43' E
Tabuk	28°23' N, 036°35' E
Safra', as-	24°02' N, 038°56' E
Sahwah	19°19' N, 042°06' E
Sakakah	29°59' N, 040°12' E
Shidad	21°19' N, 040°03' E
Ta'if, at-	21°16' N, 040°25' E
Tayma'	27°38' N, 038°29' E
Turayf	31°41' N, 038°39' E
Ula, al-	26°38' N, 037°55' E
'Usfan	21°55' N, 039°22' E
Yathrib, *see* Medina	
Zalim	22°43' N, 042°10' E
Zahran	17°40' N, 043°30' E
Zilfi, az-	26°18' N, 044°48' E

SENEGAL ....pg. 150

Capital: ....Dakar
Area: ....196,712 sq km; 75,951 sq mi
Highest Elev.: .....Fouta Djallon 500 m; 1,640 ft
Longest River: .....Senegal 1,080 km; 670 mi
Avg. Temperature: . .Jan =21°C; Jul = 28°C
Currency: ....CFA franc
Official Language: . .French

Name	Lat./Long.
Dakar	14°40' N, 017°26' W
Diourbel	14°40' N, 016°15' W
Kaolack	14°09' N, 016°04' W
Louga	15°37' N, 016°13' W
Thiès	14°48' N, 016°56' W
Saint Louis	16°02' N, 016°30' W
Ziguinchor	12°35' N, 016°16' W

SEYCHELLES ....pg. 153

Capital: ....Victoria
Area: ....455 sq km; 176 sq mi
Highest Elev.: .....Morne Seychelles 910 m; 2,970 ft
Avg. Temperature: .Jan = 30°C; Jul = 24°C
Currency: ....Seychelles rupee
Official Language: .Seselwa

Name	Lat./Long.
Victoria	04°37' S, 055°27' E

SIERRA LEONE ....pg. 150

Capital: ....Freetown
Area: ....71,740 sq km; 27,699 sq mi
Highest Elev.: . . .Mt. Loma Mansa 1,940 m; 6,390 ft
Longest River: . . .Rokel 400 km; 250 mi
Avg. Temperature: Jan = 27°C; Jul = 26°C
Currency: ....leone
Official Language: English

Name	Lat./Long.
Freetown	08°30' N, 013°15' W
Koidu	08°38' N, 010°59' W

SINGAPORE ....pg. 144

Capital: ....Singapore
Area: ....641.0 sq km; 247.5 sq mi
Highest Elev: ......Timah Hill 160 m; 530 ft
Avg. Temperature: . .Jan = 25.6°C; Jul = 27.1°C
Currency: ....Singapore dollar
Official Language: . .Chinese, Malay, Tamil, English

Name	Lat./Long.
Singapore	01°16' N, 103°50' E

SLOVAKIA ....pg. 134

Capital: ....Bratislava
Area: ....49,036 sq km; 18,933 sq mi
Highest Elev.: .....Gerlachovsky Pk. 2,660 m; 8,710 ft
Longest River: .....Vah 390 km; 240 mi
Avg. Temperature: . .Jan = 0.7°C; Jul = 19.1°C
Currency: ....Slovak koruna
Official Language: . .Slovak

Name	Lat./Long.
Banská Bystrica	48°44' N, 019°09' E
Bratislava	48°09' N, 017°07' E
Komárno	47°46' N, 018°08' E
Kosice	48°42' N, 021°15' E
Martin	49°04' N, 018°56' E
Michalovce	48°45' N, 021°56' E
Nitra	48°19' N, 018°05' E
Nové Zámky	47°59' N, 018°10' E
Poprad	49°03' N, 020°18' E
Povazská Bystrica	49°07' N, 018°27' E
Presov	49°00' N, 021°15' E
Spisská Nová Ves	48°57' N, 020°34' E
Trencín	48°54' N, 018°02' E
Trnava	48°22' N, 017°36' E
Zilina	49°13' N, 018°44' E
Zvolen	48°35' N, 019°08' E

SLOVENIA ....pg. 134

Capital: ....Ljubljana
Area: ....20,256 sq km; 7,821 sq mi
Highest Elev.: .....Mt. Triglav 2,860 m; 9,400 ft
Longest River: .....Sava 580 km; 940 mi
Avg. Temperature: . .Jan = 0°C; Jul = 21°C
Currency: ....Yugoslav dinar
Official Language: . .Slovene

Name	Lat./Long.
Idrija	46°00' N, 014°02' E
Kocevje	45°39' N, 014°51' E
Kranj	46°14' N, 014°22' E
Ljubljana	46°02' N, 014°30' E
Novo Mesto	45°48' N, 015°10' E
Postojna	45°47' N, 014°14' E
Ptuj	46°25' N, 015°52' E
Trbovlje	46°10' N, 015°03' E
Velenje	46°22' N, 015°07' E

SOLOMON ISLANDS . . .pg. 156

Capital: ....Honiara
Area: ....28,370 sq km; 10,954 sq mi
Highest Elev.: .....Makarakombou 2,450 m; 8,030 ft
Avg. Temperature: . .Jan = 28.9°C; Jul = 27.8°C
Currency: ....Soloman Islands dollar
Official Language: . .English

Name	Lat./Long.
Honiara	09°26' S, 159°57' E

SOMALIA ....pg. 151

Capital: ....Mogadishu
Area: ....637,00 sq km; 246,00 sq mi
Highest Elev.: .....Mt. Surud Cad 2,410 m; 7,900 ft
Longest River: ....Shabeelle 1,820 km; 1,130 mi
Avg. Temperature: .Jan = 26°C; Jul = 26°C
Currency: ....Somali shilling
Official Language: .Somali, Arabic

Name	Lat./Long.
Berbera	10°25' N, 045°02' E
Hargeysa	09°35' N, 044°04' E
Kismaayo (Chisimayu)	00°22' S, 042°32' E
Marka (Merca)	01°43' N, 044°53' E
Merca, *see* Marka	
Mogadishu (Mogadiscio or Muqdisho)	02°04' N, 045°22' E

SOUTH AFRICA ....pg. 153

Capital: ....Pretoria, Bloemfontein, Cape Town
Area: ....1,223,201 sq km; 472,281 sq mi
Highest Elev: . . .Mt. Aux Sources 3,300 m; 10,820 ft
Avg. Temperature:Jan = 21°C; Jul = 13°C
Currency: .....rand
Official Language:Afrikaans, English, Ndebele, Pedi, Sotho, Swazi, Tsonga, Tswana, Venda, Xhosa, Zulu,

Name	Lat./Long.
Aliwal North	30°42' S, 026°42' E
Beaufort West	32°21' S, 022°35' E
Bellville	33°54' S, 018°38' E
Bloemfontein	29°08' S, 026°10' E
Boksburg	26°13' S, 028°15' E
Bredasdorp	34°32' S, 020°02' E
Calvinia	31°28' S, 019°47' E
Cape Town (Kaapstad)	33°55' S, 018°25' E
Carletonville	26°22' S, 027°24' E
Carnarvon	30°57' S, 022°08' E
De Aar	30°39' S, 024°01' E
Durban (Port Natal)	29°51' S, 031°01' E
East London	33°02' S, 027°55' E
Empangeni	28°45' S, 031°54' E
Ermelo	26°32' S, 029°59' E
George	33°58' S, 022°27' E
Germiston	26°13' S, 028°11' E
Grahamstown	33°18' S, 026°32' E
Hammarsdale	29°48' S, 030°39' E
Hopefield	33°04' S, 018°21' E
Hopetown	29°37' S, 024°05' E
Humansdorp	34°02' S, 024°46' E
Johannesburg	26°12' S, 028°05' E
Kaapstad, *see* Cape Town	
Kathu (Sishen)	27°40' S, 023°01' E
Kimberley	28°45' S, 024°46' E
Klerksdorp	26°52' S, 026°40' E
Krugersdorp	26°06' S, 027°46' E
Kuruman	27°28' S, 023°26' E
Ladysmith	28°33' S, 029°47' E
Lebowakgomo	24°12' S, 029°30' E
Margate	30°51' S, 030°22' E
Messina	22°21' S, 030°03' E
Middelburg	25°47' S, 029°28' E
Nelspruit	25°28' S, 030°58' E
Newcastle	27°45' S, 029°56' E
Oudtshoorn	33°35' S, 022°12' E
Paarl	33°44' S, 018°58' E
Pietermaritzburg	29°37' S, 030°23' E
Pinetown	29°49' S, 030°51' E
Port Elizabeth	33°58' S, 025°35' E
Port Shepstone	30°45' S, 030°27' E
Potchefstroom	26°43' S, 027°06' E
Pretoria	25°45' S, 028°10' E
Prieska	29°40' S, 022°45' E
Queenstown	31°54' S, 026°53' E
Richard's Bay	28°48' S, 032°05' E
Rustenburg	25°40' S, 027°15' E
Seshego	23°51' S, 029°23' E
Soweto	26°16' S, 027°52' E
Stellenbosch	33°56' S, 018°51' E
Tembisa	25°59' S, 028°13' E
Uitenhage	33°46' S, 025°24' E
Ulundi	28°17' S, 031°25' E
Umlazi	29°49' S, 029°59' E
Upington	28°27' S, 021°15' E
Vanderbijlpark	26°42' S, 027°49' E
Vereeniging	26°40' S, 027°56' E
Vredenburg	32°54' S, 017°59' E
Welkom	27°59' S, 026°42' E
Worcester	33°39' S, 019°26' E

SPAIN ....pg. 128

Capital: ....Madrid
Area: ....504,783 sq km; 194,898 sq mi
Highest Elev.: .....Mulhacén Pk. 3,480 m; 11,420 ft
Longest River: ....Ebro 920 km; 570 mi
Avg. Temperature: .Jan = 5°C; Jul = 24°C
Currency: ....peseta
Official Language: .Castilian Spanish

Name	Lat./Long.
Albacete	38°59' N, 001°51' W
Alcalá de Guadaira	37°20' N, 005°50' W
Alcalá de Henares	40°29' N, 003°22' W
Alcoy	38°42' N, 000°28' W
Algeciras	36°08' N, 005°30' W
Almeria	36°50' N, 002°27' W
Avilés	43°33' N, 005°55' W
Badajoz	38°53' N, 006°58' W
Badalona	41°27' N, 002°15' E
Barcelona	41°23' N, 002°11' E
Bilbao	43°15' N, 002°58' W
Burgos	42°21' N, 003°42' W
Cáceres	39°29' N, 006°22' W
Cádiz (Cadiz)	36°32' N, 006°18' W
Cartagena	37°36' N, 000°59' W
Castellón de la Plana	39°59' N, 000°02' W
Ciudad Real	38°59' N, 003°56' W
Cornella de Llobregat	41°21' N, 002°05' E
Coslada	40°26' N, 003°34' W
Donostia (San Sebastian)	43°19' N, 001°59' W
Dos Hermanas	37°17' N, 005°55' W
El Prat de Llobregat	41°20' N, 002°06' E
El Puerto de Santa Maria	36°36' N, 006°13' W
Elda	38°29' N, 000°47' W
Elx, *see* Elche	
Gernika-Lumo (Guernica y Luno)	43°19' N, 002°41' W
Getafe	40°18' N, 003°43' W
Gijón	43°32' N, 005°40' W
Granada	37°11' N, 003°36' W
Granollers	41°37' N, 002°18' E
Guadalajara	40°38' N, 003°10' W
Huelva	37°16' N, 006°57' W
Irun	43°21' N, 001°47' W
Jaén	37°46' N, 003°47' W
Jerez de la Frontera	36°41' N, 006°08' W
La Coruña (A Coruna)	43°22' N, 008°23' W
Las Palmas de Gran Canaria	28°06' N, 015°24' W
Leganés	40°19' N, 003°45' W
León	42°36' N, 005°34' W
Linares	38°05' N, 003°38' W
Lleida (Lerida)	41°37' N, 000°37' E
Logroño	42°28' N, 002°27' W
Lugo	43°00' N, 007°34' W
Madrid	40°24' N, 003°41' W
Málaga	36°43' N, 004°25' W
Manresa	41°44' N, 001°50' E
Mataró	41°32' N, 002°27' E
Mérida	38°55' N, 006°20' W
Móstoles	40°19' N, 003°51' W
Murcia	37°59' N, 001°07' W
Oviedo	43°22' N, 005°50' W
Palencia	42°01' N, 004°32' W
Pamplona (Iruna)	42°49' N, 001°38' W
Parla	40°14' N, 003°46' W
Portugalete	43°19' N, 003°01' W
Puertollano	38°41' N, 004°07' W
Reus	41°09' N, 001°07' E
Sabadell	41°33' N, 002°06' E
Salamanca	40°58' N, 005°39' W
San Fernando	36°28' N, 006°12' W
San Sebastian, *see* Donostia	
Santa Coloma de Gramanet	41°27' N, 002°13' E
Santa Cruz de Tenerife	28°27' N, 016°14' W
Santander	43°28' N, 003°48' W
Santiago de Compostela	42°53' N, 008°33' W
Saragossa (Zaragoza)	41°38' N, 000°53' W
Segovia	40°57' N, 004°07' W
Seville (Sevilla)	37°23' N, 005°59' W
Talavera de la Reina	39°57' N, 004°50' W
Tarragona	41°07' N, 001°15' E
Toledo	39°52' N, 004°01' W
Torrent	39°26' N, 000°28' W
Valencia	39°28' N, 000°22' W
Valladolid	41°39' N, 004°43' W
Vigo	42°14' N, 008°43' W
Vitoria (Gasteiz)	42°51' N, 002°40' W
Zamora	41°30' N, 005°45' W
Zaragoza, *see* Saragossa	

SRI LANKA ....pg. 146

Capital: ....Colombo
Area: ....65,610 sq km; 25,332 sq mi
Highest Elev.: .....Mt. Pidurutalagala 2,520 m; 8,280 ft
Longest River: .....Mahaweli 330 km; 210 mi
Avg. Temperature: . .Jan = 26°C; Jul = 27°C
Currency: ....Sri Lankan rupee
Official Language: . .Sinhala, Timil

Name	Lat./Long.
Batticaloa	07°43' N, 081°42' E
Colombo	06°56' N, 079°51' E
Dehiwala-Mount Lavinia	06°51' N, 079°52' E
Galle	06°02' N, 080°13' E
Jaffna	09°40' N, 080°00' E
Kandy	07°18' N, 080°38' E
Kotte (Sri Jayewardenepura Kotte)	06°54' N, 079°54' E
Moratuwa	06°46' N, 079°53' E
Negombo	07°13' N, 079°50' E
Trincomalee	08°34' N, 081°14' E

SUDAN ....pg. 151

Capital: ....Khartoum
Area: ....2,503,890 sq km; 966,757 sq mi
Highest Elev.: .....Mt. Kinyeti 3,190 m; 10,460 ft
Longest River: .....Nile 6,650 km; 4,130 mi
Avg. Temperature: . .Jan =23°C; Jul = 31°C
Currency: ....Sudanese dinar
Official Language: . .Arabic

Name	Lat./Long.
Al-Fashir	13°38' N, 025°21' E
Al-Khartum Bahri, *see* Khartoum North	
Al-Qadarif (Gedaref)	14°02' N, 035°24' E
Al-Ubbayid (El-Obeid)	13°11' N, 030°13' E
Bur Sudan, *see* Port Sudan	
Juba	04°51' N, 031°37' E
Kassala	15°28' N, 036°24' E
Khartoum (Al-Khartum)	15°36' N, 032°32' E
Khartoum North (Al-Khartum Bahri)	15°38' N, 032°33' E
Kusti	13°10' N, 032°40' E
Nyala	12°03' N, 024°53' E
Omdurman (Umm Durman)	15°38' N, 032°30' E
Port Sudan (Bur Sudan)	19°37' N, 037°14' E
Umm Durman, *see* Omdurman	
Wad Madani	14°24' N, 033°32' E
Waw	07°42' N, 028°00' E

SURINAME .pg. 121

Capital: Paramaribo
Area: 163,820 sq km; 63,251sq mi
Highest Elev.: Juliana Top 1,230 m; 4,040 ft
Longest River: Courantyne 700 km; 450 mi
Avg. Temperature: Jan = 26°C; Jul = 27°C
Currency: Suriname guilder
Official Language: Dutch

Name	Lat./Long.
Brownsweg	05°01' N, 055°10' W
Paramaribo	05°50' N, 055°10' W
Zanderij	05°27' N, 055°12' W

SWAZILAND .pg. 153

Capital: Mbabane
Area: 17,364 sq km; 6,704 sq mi
Highest Elev.: Mt. Emlembe 1,860 m; 6,110 ft
Avg. Temperature: Jan = 20.0°C; Jul = 12.2°C
Currency: lilangeni
Official Language: Swazi, English

Name	Lat./Long.
Manzini (Bremersdorp)	26°29' S, 031°22' E
Mbabane	26°19' S, 031°08' E
Nhlangano	27°07' S, 031°12' E

SWEDEN .pg. 131

Capital: Stockholm
Area: 449,964 sq km; 173,732 sq mi
Highest Elev.: Mt. Kebne 2,110 m; 6,930 ft
Longest River: Klar 720 km; 450 mi
Avg. Temperature: Jan = -3°C; Jul = 18°C
Currency: Swedish krona
Official Language: Swedish

Name	Lat./Long.
Alingsås	57°56' N, 012°31' E
Ålmhult	56°33' N, 014°08' E
Alvesta	56°54' N, 014°33' E
Älvsbyn	65°40' N, 021°00' E
Ånge	62°31' N, 015°37' E
Ängelholm	56°15' N, 012°51' E
Arboga	59°24' N, 015°50' E
Arvika	59°40' N, 012°34' E
Avesta	60°09' N, 016°12' E
Bengtsfors	59°02' N, 012°13' E
Bjästa	63°12' N, 018°30' E
Boden	65°50' N, 021°42' E
Bollnäs	61°21' N, 016°22' E
Borås	57°43' N, 012°55' E
Borlänge	60°29' N, 015°25' E
Bräcke	62°45' N, 015°25' E
Brunflo	63°05' N, 014°49' E
Eksjö	57°40' N, 014°57' E
Eskilstuna	59°22' N, 016°30' E
Eslöv	55°50' N, 013°20' E
Falkenberg	56°54' N, 012°28' E
Falköping	58°10' N, 013°31' E
Falun	60°36' N, 015°38' E
Filipstad	59°43' N, 014°10' E
Forshaga	59°32' N, 013°28' E
Gammelstaden	65°38' N, 022°01' E
Gävle	60°40' N, 017°10' E
Göteborg	57°43' N, 011°58' E
Gullspång	58°59' N, 014°06' E
Habo	57°55' N, 014°04' E
Hagfors	60°02' N, 013°39' E
Halmstad	56°39' N, 012°50' E
Haparanda	65°50' N, 024°10' E
Härnösand	62°38' N, 017°56' E
Hässleholm	56°09' N, 013°46' E
Helsingborg	56°03' N, 012°42' E
Hofors	60°33' N, 016°17' E
Höganas	56°12' N, 012°33' E
Holmsund	63°42' N, 020°21' E
Hudiksvall	61°44' N, 017°07' E
Hultsfred	57°29' N, 015°50' E
Jönköping	57°47' N, 014°11' E
Kalix	65°51' N, 023°08' E
Kalmar	56°40' N, 016°22' E
Karlshamn	56°10' N, 014°51' E
Karlskoga	59°20' N, 014°31' E
Karlskrona	56°10' N, 015°35' E
Karlstad	59°22' N, 013°30' E
Katrineholm	59°00' N, 016°12' E
Kinna	57°30' N, 012°41' E
Kiruna	67°51' N, 020°13' E
Köping	59°31' N, 016°00' E
Kramfors	62°56' N, 017°47' E
Kristianstad	56°02' N, 014°08' E
Kumla	59°08' N, 015°08' E
Kungälv	57°52' N, 011°58' E
Kungsbacka	57°29' N, 012°04' E
Laholm	56°31' N, 013°02' E
Landskrona	55°52' N, 012°50' E
Laxå	58°59' N, 014°37' E
Lerum	57°46' N, 012°16' E
Lidingö	59°22' N, 018°08' E
Linköping	58°25' N, 015°37' E
Ljungby	56°50' N, 013°56' E
Ljusdal	61°50' N, 016°06' E
Ludvika	60°09' N, 015°11' E
Luleå	65°34' N, 022°10' E
Lund	55°42' N, 013°11' E
Lycksele	64°36' N, 018°40' E
Malmberget	67°10' N, 020°40' E
Malmö	55°36' N, 013°00' E
Malung	60°40' N, 013°42' E
Mariestad	58°43' N, 013°51' E
Märsta	59°37' N, 017°51' E
Mjölby	58°19' N, 015°08' E
Mölnlycke	57°39' N, 012°09' E
Mora	61°00' N, 014°33' E
Motala	58°33' N, 015°03' E
Nassjö	57°39' N, 014°41' E
Norrköping	58°36' N, 016°11' E
Norrtälje	59°46' N, 018°42' E
Nybro	56°45' N, 015°54' E
Nyköping	58°45' N, 017°00' E
Nynäshamn	58°54' N, 017°57' E
Ockelbo	60°53' N, 016°43' E
Örebro	59°17' N, 015°13' E
Örnsköldsvik	63°18' N, 018°43' E
Øskarshamn	57°16' N, 016°26' E
Östersund	63°11' N, 014°39' E
Östhammar	60°16' N, 018°22' E
Oxelösund	58°40' N, 017°06' E
Piteå	65°20' N, 021°30' E
Rättvik	60°53' N, 015°06' E
Robertsfors	64°11' N, 020°51' E
Ronneby	56°12' N, 015°18' E
Säffle	59°08' N, 012°54' E
Sala	59°55' N, 016°36' E
Sandviken	60°37' N, 016°46' E
Skara	58°22' N, 013°25' E
Skellefteå	64°46' N, 020°57' E
Skövde	58°24' N, 013°50' E
Soderhamn	61°18' N, 017°03' E
Sodertalje	59°12' N, 017°37' E
Solleftea	63°10' N, 017°16' E
Sollentuna	59°25' N, 017°57' E
Staffanstorp	55°38' N, 013°13' E
Stenungsund	58°05' N, 011°49' E
Stockholm	59°20' N, 018°03' E
Strömstad	58°56' N, 011°10' E
Strömsund	63°51' N, 015°35' E
Sundsvall	62°23' N, 017°18' E
Svenljunga	57°30' N, 013°07' E
Täby	59°30' N, 018°03' E
Tierp	60°20' N, 017°30' E
Timrå	62°29' N, 017°18' E
Tranås	58°03' N, 014°59' E
Trelleborg	55°22' N, 013°10' E
Trollhättan	58°16' N, 012°18' E
Uddevalla	58°21' N, 011°55' E
Umea	63°50' N, 020°15' E
Uppsala	59°52' N, 017°38' E
Vänersborg	58°22' N, 012°19' E
Varberg	57°06' N, 012°15' E
Värnamo	57°11' N, 014°02' E
Västerås	59°37' N, 016°33' E
Västerhaninge	59°07' N, 018°06' E
Västervik	57°45' N, 016°38' E
Växjö	56°53' N, 014°49' E
Vetlanda	57°26' N, 015°04' E
Vimmerby	57°40' N, 015°51' E
Visby	57°38' N, 018°18' E
Ystad	55°25' N, 013°49' E

SWITZERLAND .pg. 132

Capital: Bern
Area: 41,284 sq km; 15,940 sq mi
Highest Elev.: Dufourspitze 4,630 m; 15,200 ft
Longest River: Rhine 1,390 km; 870 mi
Avg. Temperature: Jan = -1°C; Jul = 18°C
Currency: Swiss franc
Official Language: French, German, Italian

Name	Lat./Long.
Aarau	47°23' N, 008°03' E
Arbon	47°31' N, 009°26' E
Baden	47°28' N, 008°18' E
Basel (Bale)	47°35' N, 007°32' E
Bern	46°55' N, 007°28' E
Biel (Bienne)	47°10' N, 007°15' E
Chur (Coire)	46°51' N, 009°30' E
Frauenfeld	47°33' N, 008°54' E
Fribourg (Freiburg)	46°48' N, 007°09' E
Geneva (Geneve, Genf, Ginevra)	46°12' N, 006°10' E
Lausanne	46°32' N, 006°40' E
Lucerne (Luzern)	47°05' N, 008°16' E
Lugano (Lauis)	46°00' N, 008°58' E
Neuchatel (Neuenburg)	47°00' N, 006°58' E
Saint Gall (Sankt Gallen)	47°28' N, 009°24' E
Schaffhausen	47°42' N, 008°38' E
Thun (Thoune)	46°45' N, 007°37' E
Vevey	46°27' N, 006°51' E
Winterthur	47°30' N, 008°45' E
Zug	47°10' N, 008°31' E
Zürich	47°22' N, 008°33' E

SYRIA .pg. 154

Capital: Damascus
Area: 185,180 sq km; 71,498 sq mi
Highest Elev.: Mt. Hermon 2,810 m; 9,230 ft
Longest River: Euphrates 2,700 km; 1,700 mi
Avg. Temperature: Jan = 7°C; Jul = 27°C
Currency: Syrian pound
Official Language: Arabic

Name	Lat./Long.
Al-Hasakah	36°29' N, 040°45' E
Al-Ladhiqiyah, *see* Latakia	
Al-Qamishli (Al-Kamishly)	37°02' N, 041°14' E
Ar-Raqqah (Rakka)	35°57' N, 039°01' E
As-Suwayda`	32°42' N, 036°34' E
Damascus	33°30' N, 036°18' E
Dar'a	32°37' N, 036°06' E
Dayr az-Zawr	35°20' N, 040°09' E
Halab, *see* Aleppo	
Hamah (Hama)	35°08' N, 036°45' E
Hims (Homs)	34°44' N, 036°43' E
Idlib	35°55' N, 036°38' E
Latakia (Al-Ladhiqiyah)	35°31' N, 035°47' E
Tartus	34°53' N, 035°53' E

TAIWAN .pg. 143

Capital: Taipei
Area: 36,179 sq km; 13,969 sq mi
Highest Elev.: Yü Shan 13,110 m; 4,000 ft
Longest River: Choshui 190 km; 120 mi
Avg. Temperature: Jan = 15°C; Jul = 28°C
Currency: New Taiwan dollar
Official Language: Mandarin Chinese

Name	Lat./Long.
Chang-hua	24°05' N, 120°32' E
Chi-lung	25°08' N, 121°44' E
Chia-i	23°29' N, 120°27' E
Chu-tung	24°44' N, 121°05' E
Feng-shan	22°38' N, 120°21' E
Feng-yuan	24°15' N, 120°43' E
Hsin-chu	24°48' N, 120°58' E
Hua-lien	23°59' N, 121°36' E
I-lan	24°46' N, 121°45' E
Kang-shan	22°48' N, 120°17' E
Kao-hsiung	22°38' N, 120°17' E
Lo-tung	24°41' N, 121°46' E
Lu-kang	24°03' N, 120°25' E
Miao-li	24°34' N, 120°49' E
Nan-t'ou	23°55' N, 120°41' E
San-ch'ung	25°04' N, 121°30' E
T'ai-chung	24°09' N, 120°41' E
T'ai-nan	23°00' N, 120°12' E
T'ai-tung	22°45' N, 121°09' E
T'ao-yuan	25°00' N, 121°18' E
Taipei (T'ai-pei)	25°03' N, 121°30' E
Yuan-lin	23°58' N, 120°34' E
Yung-k'ang	23°02' N, 120°15' E

TAJIKISTAN .pg. 139

Capital: Dushanbe
Area: 143,100 sq km; 55,300 sq mi
Highest Elev: Communism Pk. 7,500 m; 24,590 ft
Longest River: Pyandzh 1,130 km; 700 mi
Avg. Temperature: Jan = 1°C; Jul = 28°C
Currency: Russian ruble
Official Language: Tajik

Name	Lat./Long.
Dushanbe	38°33' N, 068°48' E
Khujand (Leninabad, or Khojand)	40°17' N, 069°37' E
Qurghonteppa	37°50' N, 068°47' E

TANZANIA .pg. 153

Capital: Dodoma
Area: 942,799 sq km; 364,017 sq mi
Highest Elev.: Kilimanjaro 5,890 m; 19,340 ft
Longest River: Rufiji 280 km; 175 mi
Avg. Temperature: Jan = 28°C; Jul = 24°C
Currency: Tanznian shilling
Official Language: Swahili, English

Name	Lat./Long.
Arusha	03°22' S, 036°41' E
Bukoba	01°20' S, 031°49' E
Chake Chake	05°15' S, 039°46' E
Dar es Salaam	06°48' S, 039°17' E
Dodoma	06°11' S, 035°45' E
Ifakara	08°08' S, 036°41' E
Iringa	07°46' S, 035°42' E
Kigoma	04°52' S, 029°38' E
Korogwe	05°09' S, 038°29' E
Lindi	10°00' S, 039°43' E
Mbeya	08°54' S, 033°27' E
Mkoani	05°22' S, 039°39' E
Morogoro	06°49' S, 037°40' E
Moshi	03°21' S, 037°20' E
Mpwapwa	06°21' S, 036°29' E
Mtwara	10°16' S, 040°11' E
Mwanza	02°31' S, 032°54' E
Pangani	09°32' S, 035°31' E
Songea	10°41' S, 035°39' E
Sumbawanga	07°58' S, 031°37' E
Tabora	05°01' S, 032°48' E
Tanga	05°04' S, 039°06' E
Tunduru	11°07' S, 037°21' E
Wete	05°04' S, 039°43' E
Zanzibar	06°10' S, 039°11' E

THAILAND .pg. 144

Capital: Bangkok
Area: 513,115 sq km; 198,115 sq mi
Highest Elev.: Mt. Inthanon 2,590 m; 8,480 ft
Longest River: Chao Phraya 370 km; 230 mi
Avg. Temperature: Jan = 26°C; Jul = 29°C
Currency: Thai baht
Official Language: Thai

Name	Lat./Long.
Bangkok (Krung Thep)	13°45' N, 100°31' E
Chiang Mai (Chiengmai)	18°47' N, 098°59' E
Chon Buri	13°22' N, 100°59' E
Hat Yai (Haad Yai)	07°01' N, 100°28' E
Khon Kaen	16°26' N, 102°50' E
Krung Thep, *see* Bangkok	
Nakhon Ratchasima (Khorat)	14°58' N, 102°07' E
Nakhon Sawan	15°41' N, 100°07' E
Nakhon Si Thammarat	08°26' N, 099°58' E
Nong Khai	17°52' N, 102°44' E
Nonthaburi	13°50' N, 100°29' E
Pattaya	12°54' N, 100°51' E
Phra Nakhon Si Ayutthaya (Ayutthaya)	14°21' N, 100°33' E
Phichit	16°26' N, 100°22' E
Phitsanulok	16°50' N, 100°15' E
Phuket	07°53' N, 098°24' E
Sakon Nakhon	17°10' N, 104°09' E
Samut Prakan	13°36' N, 100°36' E
Samut Sakhon (Samut Sakorn)	13°32' N, 100°17' E
Sara Buri	14°32' N, 100°55' E
Trang	07°33' N, 099°36' E
Ubon Ratchathani	15°14' N, 104°54' E
Udon Thani	17°26' N, 102°46' E
Uthai Thani	15°22' N, 100°03' E
Yala	06°33' N, 101°18' E

TOGO .pg. 150

Capital: Lomé
Area: 56,785 sq km; 21,925 sq mi
Highest Elev.: Mt. Baumann 990 m; 3,240 ft
Longest River: Oti 520 km; 320 mi
Avg. Temperature: Jan =28°C; Jul = 27°C
Currency: CFA franc
Official Language: French

Name	Lat./Long.
Lomé	06°08' N, 001°13' E

TONGA .pg. 156

Capital: Nuku'alofa
Area: 749.9 sq km; 289.5 sq mi
Highest Elev.: Kao 1,030 m; 3,380 ft
Avg. Temperature: Jan = 30°C; Jul = 25°C
Currency: pan'anga
Official Language: Tongan, English

Name	Lat./Long.
Nuku'alofa	21°08' N, 175°12' E

TRINIDAD & TOBAGO .pg. 116

Capital: Port of Spain
Area: 5,128 sq km; 1,980 sq mi
Highest Elev.: Aripo Mtn. 940 m; 3,080 ft
Longest River: Ortoire 50 km; 30 mi
Avg. Temperature: Jan = 24°C; Jul = 26°C
Currency: Trinadad & Tobago dollar
Official Language: English

Name	Lat./Long.
Port of Spain	10°39' N, 061°31' W
San Fernando	10°17' N, 061°28' W

TUNISIA .pg. 150

Capital: Tunis
Area: 164,150 sq km; 63,378 sq mi
Highest Elev.: Mt. ash-Sha'nabi 1,540 m; 5,070 ft
Longest River: Marjardah 460 km; 290 mi
Avg. Temperature: Jan = 10°C; Jul = 26°C
Currency: dinar
Official Language: Arabic

Name	Lat./Long.
Bizerte (Banzart)	37°17' N, 009°52' E
Gabes, *see* Qabis	
Gafsa, *see* Qafsah	
Jarjis (Zarzis)	33°30' N, 011°07' E
Safaqis (Sfax)	34°44' N, 010°46' E
Susah (Sousa or Sousse)	35°49' N, 010°38' E
Tunis (Tunis)	36°48' N, 010°11' E
Qabis (Gabes or Tacape)	33°53' N, 010°07' E
Qafsah (Gafsa)	34°25' N, 008°48' E
Zarzis, *see* Jarjis	

TURKEY .pg. 147

Capital: Ankara
Area: 779,452 sq km; 300,948 sq mi
Highest Elev.: Mt. Ararat 5,140 m; 16,850 ft
Longest River: Kizil 1,180 km; 730 mi
Avg. Temperature: Jan = 0°C; Jul = 23°C
Currency: Turkish lira
Official Language: Turkish

Name	Lat./Long.
Adana	37°01' N, 035°18' E
Adapazari	40°46' N, 030°24' E
Adiyaman (Husnumansur)	37°46' N, 038°17' E
Afyon	38°45' N, 030°33' E
Agri (Karakose)	39°44' N, 043°03' E
Akhisar (Thyatira)	38°55' N, 027°51' E
Aksaray	38°23' N, 034°03' E
Aksehir	38°21' N, 031°25' E
Amasya	40°39' N, 035°51' E
Ankara (Angora)	39°56' N, 032°52' E
Antalya (Attalia or Hatay)	36°53' N, 030°42' E
Antioch (Antakya)	36°14' N, 036°07' E
Aydin	37°51' N, 027°51' E
Bafra	41°34' N, 035°56' E
Balikesir	39°39' N, 027°53' E
Bandirma (Panderma)	40°20' N, 027°58' E
Batman	37°52' N, 041°07' E
Bilecik	40°09' N, 029°59' E
Bolu	40°44' N, 031°37' E
Burdur (Buldur)	37°43' N, 030°17' E
Bursa (Brusa)	40°11' N, 029°04' E
Çanakkale	40°09' N, 026°24' E
Ceyhan	37°04' N, 035°47' E
Çorlu	41°09' N, 027°48' E
Çorum	40°33' N, 034°58' E
Denizli	37°46' N, 029°06' E
Diyarbakir (Amida)	37°55' N, 040°14' E
Düzce	40°50' N, 031°10' E
Edirne (Adrianople or Hadrianople)	41°40' N, 026°34' E
Elazig	38°41' N, 039°14' E
Elbistan	38°13' N, 037°12' E
Eregli	37°31' N, 034°04' E
Eregli (Bender-Eregli or Karadenizereglisi)	41°17' N, 031°25' E
Erzincan	39°44' N, 039°29' E
Erzurum	39°55' N, 041°17' E
Eskisehir	39°46' N, 030°32' E
Gaziantep	37°05' N, 037°22' E
Gebze	40°48' N, 029°25' E
Giresun	40°55' N, 038°24' E
Gümüshane	40°27' N, 039°29' E
Hakkâri (Colemerik)	37°34' N, 043°44' E
Igdir	39°56' N, 044°02' E
Inegöl	40°05' N, 029°31' E
Iskenderun (Alexandretta)	36°35' N, 036°10' E
Isparta (Hamid-Abad)	37°46' N, 030°33' E
Istanbul (Constantinople)	41°01' N, 028°58' E
Izmir (Smyrna)	38°25' N, 027°09' E
Izmit	40°46' N, 029°55' E
Kadirli	37°23' N, 036°05' E
Kahramanmaras (Maras)	37°36' N, 036°55' E
Karabük	41°12' N, 032°37' E
Karaman	37°11' N, 033°14' E
Kars	40°37' N, 043°05' E
Kastamonu (Castamoni)	41°22' N, 033°47' E
Kayseri (Caesarea)	38°43' N, 035°30' E
Kherson	46°38' N, 032°36' E
Kirikkale	39°50' N, 033°31' E
Kirsehir	39°09' N, 034°10' E
Kiziltepe	37°12' N, 040°36' E
Konya (Iconium)	37°52' N, 032°31' E
Körfez	40°46' N, 029°45' E
Kozan	37°27' N, 035°49' E
Kütahya	39°25' N, 029°59' E
Malatya	38°21' N, 038°19' E
Manisa	38°36' N, 027°26' E
Mardin	37°18' N, 040°44' E
Mersin	36°48' N, 034°38' E
Nazilli	37°55' N, 028°21' E
Nevsehir	38°38' N, 034°43' E
Nigde	37°59' N, 034°42' E
Ödemis	38°13' N, 027°59' E
Oleksandriya	48°40' N, 033°07' E
Ordu	41°00' N, 037°53' E
Osmaniye	37°05' N, 036°14' E
Polatli	39°36' N, 032°09' E
Rize	41°02' N, 040°31' E
Salihli	38°29' N, 028°09' E

Name	Lat./Long.
Samsun (Amisus)	41°17' N, 036°20' E
Slovyansk	48°52' N, 037°37' E
Siirt	37°56' N, 041°57' E
Silvan	38°08' N, 041°01' E
Sinop	42°01' N, 035°09' E
Sivas (Sebastia)	39°45' N, 037°02' E
Siverek	37°45' N, 039°19' E
Söke	37°45' N, 027°24' E
Soma	39°10' N, 027°36' E
Tarsus	36°55' N, 034°53' E
Tatvan	38°30' N, 042°16' E
Tekirdag (Rodosto)	40°59' N, 027°31' E
Tokat	40°19' N, 036°34' E
Trabzon (Trapezus or Trebizond)	41°00' N, 039°43' E
Tunceli (Kalan)	39°07' N, 039°32' E
Turhal	40°24' N, 036°06' E
Urfa	37°08' N, 038°46' E
Usak (Ushak)	38°41' N, 029°25' E
Van	38°30' N, 043°23' E
Yalova	40°39' N, 029°15' E
Yozgat	39°50' N, 034°48' E
Zonguldak	41°27' N, 031°49' E

TURKMENISTAN ....pg. 139

Capital: ....Ashgabat
Area: ....488,100 sq km; 188,500 sq mi
Longest River: .....Amu Darya 2,540 km; 1,580 mi
Avg. Temperature: ..Jan = -1°C; Jul = 29°C
Currency: ....manat
Official Language: ..Turkmen

Name	Lat./Long.
Ashgabat (Ashgabat, or Poltoratsk)	37°57' N, 058°23' E
Cheleken	39°26' N, 053°07' E
Chirchiq	41°50' N, 059°58' E
Mary (Merv)	37°36' N, 061°50' E
Nebitdag	39°30' N, 054°22' E
Turkmenbashi (Krasnovodsk)	40°00' N, 053°00' E

TUVALU ....pg. 156

Capital: ....Fangafale on Funafuti atoll
Area: ....23.9 sq km; 9.3 sq mi
Avg. Temperature: ..Jan = 26°C; Jul = 26°C
Currency: ....Tuvalu dollar
Official Language: ..none

Name	Lat./Long.
Funafuti	22°14' N, 138°45' E

UGANDA ....pg. 153

Capital: ....Kampala
Area: ....241,040 sq km; 93,070 sq mi
Highest Elev.: ....Margherita Pk. 5,110 m; 16,760 ft
Longest River: ...Victoria Nile 420 km; 260 mi
Avg. Temperature: .Jan = 22°C; Jul = 21°C
Currency: ......Uganda shilling
Official Language: .English, Swahili

Name	Lat./Long.
Gulu	02°47' N, 032°18' E
Kampala	00°19' N, 032°35' E
Soroti	01°43' N, 033°37' E

UKRAINE ....pg. 138

Capital: ....Kiev
Area: ....603,700 sq km; 233,100 sq mi
Highest Elev.: .....Mt. Hoverlya 2,060 m; 6,760 ft
Longest River: .....Dnieper 2,200 km; 1,370 mi
Avg. Temperature: ..Jan = -6.1°C; Jul = 20.4°C
Currency: ....karbovanets
Official Language: ..Ukrainian

Name	Lat./Long.
Alchevsk	48°30' N, 038°47' E
Berdyansk	46°45' N, 036°47' E
Berdychiv	49°54' N, 028°35' E
Bila Tserkva	49°47' N, 030°07' E
Bilhorod-Dnistrovsky	46°12' N, 030°21' E
Boryspil	50°21' N, 030°57' E
Brody	50°05' N, 025°09' E
Bryanka	48°30' N, 038°40' E
Cherkasy	49°26' N, 032°04' E
Chernihiv	51°30' N, 031°18' E
Chernivtsi	48°18' N, 025°56' E
Chervonohrad	50°23' N, 024°14' E
Chornobyl (Chernobyl)	51°16' N, 030°14' E
Chortkiv	49°01' N, 025°48' E
Dniprodzerzhynsk	48°30' N, 034°37' E
Dnipropetrovsk	48°27' N, 034°59' E
Donetsk	48°00' N, 037°48' E
Drohobych	49°21' N, 023°30' E
Dymytrov	48°16' N, 037°17' E
Dzerzhynsk	48°26' N, 037°50' E
Dzhankoy	45°43' N, 034°24' E
Enerhodar	47°29' N, 034°47' E
Fastiv	50°05' N, 029°55' E
Feodosiya	45°02' N, 035°23' E
Illichivsk	46°18' N, 030°40' E
Inhulets	47°44' N, 033°15' E
Ivano-Frankivsk	48°56' N, 024°43' E
Izmayil	45°21' N, 028°50' E
Izyum	49°12' N, 037°19' E
Kalush	49°01' N, 024°22' E
Kamyanets	48°40' N, 026°34' E
Kerch	45°21' N, 036°28' E
Kharkiv	50°00' N, 036°15' E
Kiev (Kyyiv)	50°26' N, 030°31' E
Kirovohrad	48°30' N, 032°18' E
Kolomyya	48°32' N, 025°02' E
Komsomolsk	49°02' N, 033°40' E
Konotop	51°14' N, 033°12' E
Korosten	50°57' N, 028°39' E
Kostyantynivka	48°32' N, 037°43' E
Kotovsk	47°45' N, 029°32' E
Kovel	51°13' N, 024°43' E
Kramatorsk	48°43' N, 037°32' E
Krasnoarmiysk	48°17' N, 037°11' E
Krasnyy Luch	48°08' N, 038°56' E
Kremenchuk	49°04' N, 033°25' E
Kryvyy Rih	47°55' N, 033°21' E
Lozova	48°54' N, 036°20' E
Lubny	50°01' N, 033°00' E
Luhansk	48°34' N, 039°20' E
Lutsk	50°45' N, 025°20' E
Lviv	49°50' N, 024°00' E
Lysychansk	48°55' N, 038°26' E
Makiyivka	48°02' N, 037°58' E
Marhanets	47°38' N, 034°38' E
Mariupol	47°06' N, 037°33' E
Melitopol	46°50' N, 035°22' E
Merefa	49°48' N, 036°03' E
Mukacheve	48°27' N, 022°43' E
Mykolayiv	46°58' N, 032°00' E
Nikopol	47°34' N, 034°24' E
Nizhyn	51°03' N, 031°53' E
Nova Kakhovka	46°46' N, 033°22' E
Novohrad-Volynskyy	50°36' N, 027°37' E
Novovolynsk	50°44' N, 024°10' E
Odessa	46°28' N, 030°44' E
Pavlohrad	48°31' N, 035°52' E
Pervomaysk	48°03' N, 030°52' E
Poltava	49°35' N, 034°34' E
Pryluky	50°36' N, 032°24' E
Rivne	50°37' N, 026°15' E
Romny	50°45' N, 033°28' E
Sevastopol	44°36' N, 033°32' E
Shepetivka	50°11' N, 027°04' E
Shostka	51°52' N, 033°29' E
Simferopol	44°57' N, 034°06' E
Smila	49°14' N, 031°53' E
Snizhne	48°01' N, 038°46' E
Stakhanov	48°34' N, 038°40' E
Stryy	49°15' N, 023°51' E
Sumy	50°54' N, 034°48' E
Sverdlovsk	48°05' N, 039°40' E
Svitlovodsk	49°05' N, 033°15' E
Ternopil	49°33' N, 025°35' E
Torez	48°02' N, 038°35' E
Uman	48°45' N, 030°13' E
Uzhhorod	48°37' N, 022°18' E
Vinnytsya	49°14' N, 028°29' E
Zaporizhzhya	47°49' N, 035°11' E
Zhovti Vody	48°21' N, 033°32' E
Zhytomyr	50°15' N, 028°40' E

UNITED ARAB EMIRATES pg. 154

Capital: ....Abu Dhabi
Area: ....83,600 sq km; 32,280 sq mi
Avg. Temperature: ..Jan = 18°C; Jul = 34°C
Currency: ........U.A.E. dirham
Official Language: .Arabic

Name	Lat./Long.
Abu Dhabi	24°28' N, 054°22' E
'Ajman	25°25' N, 055°27' E
'Aradah	22°59' N, 053°26' E
'Ayn, al-	24°13' N, 055°46' E
Diqdaqah	25°40' N, 055°58' E
Dubayy	25°16' N, 055°18' E
Fujayrah, al-	25°08' N, 056°21' E
Khawr Fakkan	25°21' N, 056°22' E
Khis, al-	23°00' N, 054°12' E
Ra's al-Khaymah	25°47' N, 055°57' E
Shariqah, ash-	25°22' N, 055°23' E
Tarif	24°03' N, 053°46' E
Wadhil	23°03' N, 054°08' E

UNITED KINGDOM ....pg. 125

Capital: ....London
Area: ....244,110 sq km; 94,251 sq mi
Highest Elev.: .....Ben Nevis 1,340 m; 4,410 ft
Longest River: .....Severn 290 km; 180 mi
Avg. Temperature: ..Jan = 4°C; Jul = 18°C
Currency: ....pound sterling
Official Language: ..English

Name	Lat./Long.
Aberdare (Aberdar)	51°43' N, 003°27' W
Aberdeen	57°09' N, 002°08' W
Aberystwyth	52°25' N, 004°05' W
Aith	60°17' N, 001°23' W
Alness	57°42' N, 004°15' W
Amesbury	51°10' N, 001°47' W
Armagh	54°21' N, 006°40' W
Aylesbury	51°49' N, 000°49' W
Ayr	55°28' N, 004°37' W
Ballymoney	55°05' N, 006°31' W
Bangor	53°13' N, 004°08' W
Bangor	54°39' N, 005°42' W
Barrow-in-Furness	54°07' N, 003°14' W
Barry	51°25' N, 003°16' W
Basingstoke	51°16' N, 001°05' W
Bath	51°23' N, 002°22' W
Battle	50°55' N, 000°29' E
Bedford	52°08' N, 000°28' W
Belfast	54°35' N, 005°56' W
Bideford	51°01' N, 004°12' W
Birmingham	52°29' N, 001°51' W
Blackburn	53°45' N, 002°29' W
Blackpool	53°49' N, 003°03' W
Blandford Forum	50°51' N, 002°10' W
Bolton	53°34' N, 002°26' W
Bournemouth	50°43' N, 001°53' W
Bracknell	51°25' N, 000°45' W
Bradford	53°47' N, 001°45' W
Brentwood	51°37' N, 000°19' E
Brighton	50°51' N, 000°08' W
Bristol	51°26' N, 002°35' W
Buckhaven	56°11' N, 003°02' W
Buckie	57°41' N, 002°59' W
Burton upon Trent	52°48' N, 001°38' W
Bury	53°35' N, 002°19' W
Bury St. Edmunds	52°15' N, 000°43' E
Caernarfon	53°08' N, 004°16' W
Cambridge	52°12' N, 000°09' E
Campbeltown	55°26' N, 005°37' W
Cardiff	51°29' N, 003°11' W
Cardigan	52°05' N, 004°40' W
Carlisle	54°53' N, 002°57' W
Carrickfergus	54°43' N, 005°44' W
Castle Douglas	54°57' N, 003°56' W
Chatham	51°22' N, 000°32' E
Cheddar	51°17' N, 002°47' W
Chelmsford	51°44' N, 000°28' E
Cheltenham	51°54' N, 002°05' W
Chester	53°12' N, 002°54' W
Chesterfield	53°14' N, 001°25' W
Colchester	51°54' N, 000°54' E
Comber	54°33' N, 005°42' W
Coventry	52°24' N, 001°31' W
Crawley	51°07' N, 000°11' W
Crewe	53°06' N, 002°27' W
Cromer	52°56' N, 001°18' E
Crowland	52°41' N, 000°10' W
Cwmbran	51°39' N, 003°01' W
Darlington	54°32' N, 001°34' W
Dartmouth	50°21' N, 003°35' W
Deal	51°13' N, 001°24' E
Derby	52°55' N, 001°28' W
Devizes	51°21' N, 002°00' W
Doncaster	53°31' N, 001°08' W
Douglas	54°09' N, 004°28' W
Dover	51°08' N, 001°19' E
Downpatrick	54°19' N, 005°42' W
Droitwich	52°16' N, 002°09' W
Dudley	52°31' N, 002°06' W
Dumfries	55°04' N, 003°36' W
Dunbar	56°00' N, 002°31' W
Dundee	56°29' N, 003°02' W
Dunfermline	56°04' N, 003°26' W
Dunoon	55°57' N, 004°55' W
East Kilbride	55°46' N, 004°11' W
Eastleigh	50°58' N, 001°21' W
Edinburgh	55°57' N, 003°10' W
Enniskillen	54°22' N, 007°38' W
Evesham	52°05' N, 001°57' W
Exeter	50°43' N, 003°31' W
Exmouth	50°37' N, 003°24' W
Falmouth	50°09' N, 005°04' W
Felixstowe	51°58' N, 001°21' E
Fishguard	52°00' N, 004°59' W
Flint	53°15' N, 003°08' W
Forfar	56°39' N, 002°53' W
Fowey	50°20' N, 004°38' W
Gateshead	54°56' N, 001°37' W
Gillingham	51°23' N, 000°33' E
Glasgow	55°52' N, 004°15' W
Gloucester	51°52' N, 002°14' W
Gosport	50°48' N, 001°09' W
Gravesend	51°27' N, 000°23' E
Great Walsingham	52°54' N, 000°54' E
Great Yarmouth	52°36' N, 001°44' E
Greenock	55°57' N, 004°46' W
Grimsby	53°34' N, 000°05' W
Guildford	51°14' N, 000°35' W
Halifax	53°44' N, 001°51' W
Hamilton	55°47' N, 004°02' W
Harlech	52°52' N, 004°06' W
Harlow	51°46' N, 000°07' E
Harrogate	54°00' N, 001°32' W
Hartlepool	54°41' N, 001°13' W
Hastings	50°52' N, 000°35' E
Havant	50°51' N, 000°59' W
Haverfordwest	51°48' N, 004°58' W
Hemel Hempstead	51°45' N, 000°28' W
Hereford	52°04' N, 002°43' W
High Wycombe	51°38' N, 000°45' W
Hove	50°50' N, 000°11' W
Huddersfield	53°39' N, 001°47' W
Huntly	57°27' N, 002°48' W
Inverness	57°29' N, 004°14' W
Ipswich	52°03' N, 001°09' E
Jedburgh	55°28' N, 002°33' W
John o'Groats	58°38' N, 003°04' W
Kelso	55°36' N, 002°26' W
Kilmarnock	55°36' N, 004°30' W
King's Lynn	52°45' N, 000°24' E
Kingston upon Hull	53°45' N, 000°20' W
Kinross	56°12' N, 003°25' W
Kirkwall	58°59' N, 002°57' W
Lampeter	52°07' N, 004°05' W
Lanark	55°40' N, 003°46' W
Launceston	50°38' N, 004°21' W
Leamington	52°15' N, 001°33' W
Leeds	53°48' N, 001°32' W
Leicester	52°38' N, 001°08' W
Lincoln	53°14' N, 000°32' W
Liverpool	53°25' N, 002°57' W
Llandudno	53°19' N, 003°50' W
Llangollen	52°58' N, 003°10' W
Lochmaddy	57°36' N, 007°10' W
London	51°30' N, 000°07' W
Lossiemouth	57°43' N, 003°17' W
Lowestoft	52°28' N, 001°45' E
Lurgan	54°28' N, 006°20' W
Luton	51°53' N, 000°25' W
Lydd	50°57' N, 000°55' E
Maidstone	51°16' N, 000°32' E
Manchester	53°29' N, 002°15' W
Mansfield	53°09' N, 001°12' W
Margate	51°23' N, 001°23' E
Middlesbrough	54°34' N, 001°12' W
Montrose	56°43' N, 002°28' W
Morpeth	55°10' N, 001°41' W
Nairn	57°35' N, 003°52' W
Newcastle upon Tyne	54°58' N, 001°36' W
Newport	51°35' N, 002°59' W
Newquay	50°25' N, 005°05' W
Newtownabbey	54°40' N, 005°57' W
Northampton	52°15' N, 000°54' W
Norwich	52°38' N, 001°18' E
Nottingham	52°58' N, 001°10' W
Oldham	53°32' N, 002°07' W
Omagh	54°36' N, 007°18' W
Oswestry	52°52' N, 003°03' W
Oxford	51°45' N, 001°15' W
Paisley	55°50' N, 004°25' W
Peterborough	52°35' N, 000°14' W
Peterhead	57°31' N, 001°47' W
Peterlee	54°45' N, 001°20' W
Plymouth	50°23' N, 004°09' W
Poole	50°43' N, 001°59' W
Port Talbot	51°35' N, 003°48' W
Portadown	54°26' N, 006°27' W
Portree	57°25' N, 006°11' W
Portsmouth	50°49' N, 001°04' W
Preston	53°46' N, 002°42' W
Ramsey	54°19' N, 004°23' W
Ramsgate	51°20' N, 001°25' E
Reading	51°27' N, 000°58' W
Redditch	52°18' N, 001°56' W
Rhondda	51°39' N, 003°29' W
Ripon	54°08' N, 001°31' W
Ross-on-Wye	51°55' N, 002°35' W
Rotherham	53°26' N, 001°21' W
Royal Tunbridge Wells	51°08' N, 000°16' E
Ryde	50°44' N, 001°10' W
St. Albans	51°45' N, 000°20' W
St. Helens	53°27' N, 002°45' W
Scunthorpe	53°35' N, 000°39' W
Selkirk	55°33' N, 002°50' W
Sheffield	53°23' N, 001°28' W
Shrewsbury	52°42' N, 002°45' W
Slough	51°30' N, 000°34' W
South Shields	54°59' N, 001°26' W
Southampton	50°55' N, 001°24' W
Southend-on-Sea	51°33' N, 000°42' E
Southport	53°39' N, 003°00' W
Stafford	52°49' N, 002°07' W
Stockport	53°25' N, 002°10' W
Stockton-on-Tees	54°35' N, 001°20' W
Stoke-on-Trent	53°01' N, 002°11' W
Stonehaven	56°58' N, 002°12' W
Stornoway	58°12' N, 006°23' W
Sudbury	52°02' N, 000°44' E
Sunderland	54°55' N, 001°23' W
Sutton Coldfield	52°33' N, 001°48' W
Swansea	51°38' N, 003°58' W
Swindon	51°34' N, 001°46' W
Tain	57°48' N, 004°03' W
Tamworth	52°38' N, 001°40' W
Tarbert	57°54' N, 006°48' W
Telford	52°41' N, 002°28' W
Thurso	58°36' N, 003°31' W
Torquay	50°29' N, 003°32' W
Troon	55°32' N, 004°39' W
Truro	50°16' N, 005°03' W
Wakefield	53°41' N, 001°30' W
Walsall	52°35' N, 001°59' W
Watford	51°40' N, 000°24' W
Wells	51°12' N, 002°39' W
West Bromwich	52°32' N, 002°01' W
Weston-super-Mare	51°21' N, 002°58' W
Weymouth	50°37' N, 002°28' W
Whitehaven	54°33' N, 003°35' W
Wick	58°26' N, 003°06' W
Widnes	53°22' N, 002°44' W
Wigan	53°33' N, 002°38' W
Wilton	51°05' N, 001°52' W
Winchester	51°04' N, 001°19' W
Wolverhampton	52°35' N, 002°08' W
Worcester	52°12' N, 002°13' W
Worthing	50°49' N, 000°23' W
York	53°57' N, 001°06' W

UNITED STATES ....pg. 109

Capital: ....Washington, D.C.
Area: ....9,529,063 sq km; 3,679,192 sq mi
Highest Elev.: ....Mt. McKinley 6,190 m; 20,320 ft
Longest River: ...Missouri 3,730 km; 2,320 mi
Avg. Temperature: .Jan = 3°C; Jul = 26°C
Currency: ....dollar
Official Language: .none

Name	Lat./Long.
Aberdeen, S.D.	45°28' N, 098°29' W
Aberdeen, Wash.	46°59' N, 123°50' W
Abilene, Kan.	38°55' N, 097°13' W
Abilene, Tex.	32°28' N, 099°43' W
Ada, Okla.	34°46' N, 096°41' W
Akron, Ohio	41°05' N, 081°31' W
Alamogordo, N.M.	32°54' N, 105°57' W
Alamosa, Colo.	37°28' N, 105°52' W
Albany, Ga.	31°35' N, 084°10' W
Albany, N.Y.	42°39' N, 073°45' W
Albuquerque, N.M.	35°05' N, 106°39' W
Alexandria, La.	31°18' N, 092°27' W
Alexandria, Va.	38°48' N, 077°03' W
Alliance, Neb.	42°06' N, 102°52' W
Alpena, Mich.	45°04' N, 083°27' W
Alton, Ill.	38°53' N, 090°11' W
Alturas, Calif.	41°29' N, 120°32' W
Altus, Okla.	34°38' N, 099°20' W
Amarillo, Tex.	35°13' N, 101°50' W
Americus, Ga.	32°04' N, 084°14' W
Anaconda, Mont.	46°08' N, 112°57' W
Anchorage, Alaska	61°13' N, 149°54' W
Andalusia, Ala.	31°18' N, 086°29' W
Ann Arbor, Mich.	42°17' N, 083°45' W
Annapolis, Md.	38°59' N, 076°30' W
Appleton, Wis.	44°16' N, 088°25' W
Arcata, Calif.	40°52' N, 124°05' W
Arlington, Tex.	32°44' N, 097°07' W
Arlington, Va.	38°53' N, 077°07' W
Asheville, N.C.	35°36' N, 082°33' W
Ashland, Ky.	38°28' N, 082°38' W
Ashland, Wis.	46°35' N, 090°53' W
Aspen, Colo.	39°11' N, 106°49' W
Astoria, Ore.	46°11' N, 123°50' W
Athens, Ga.	33°57' N, 083°23' W
Atlanta, Ga.	33°45' N, 084°23' W
Atlantic City, N.J.	39°21' N, 074°27' W
Augusta, Ga.	33°28' N, 081°58' W
Augusta, Me.	44°19' N, 069°47' W
Aurora, Colo.	39°43' N, 104°49' W
Austin, Minn.	43°40' N, 092°58' W
Austin, Tex.	30°17' N, 097°45' W
Baker, Mont.	46°22' N, 104°17' W
Baker, Ore.	44°47' N, 117°50' W
Bakersfield, Calif.	35°23' N, 119°01' W
Baltimore, Md.	39°17' N, 076°37' W
Bangor, Me.	44°48' N, 068°46' W
Bar Harbor, Me.	44°23' N, 068°13' W
Barrow, Alaska	71°18' N, 156°47' W
Bartlesville, Okla.	36°45' N, 095°59' W
Baton Rouge, La.	30°27' N, 091°11' W
Bay City, Mich.	43°36' N, 083°54' W
Beaumont, Tex.	30°05' N, 094°06' W
Bellingham, Wash.	48°46' N, 122°29' W
Beloit, Wis.	42°31' N, 089°01' W
Bemidji, Minn.	47°28' N, 094°52' W
Bend, Ore.	44°04' N, 121°19' W
Berlin, N.H.	44°28' N, 071°11' W
Bethel, Alaska	60°48' N, 161°45' W
Beulah, N.D.	47°15' N, 101°46' W
Billings, Mont.	45°47' N, 108°30' W
Biloxi, Miss.	30°24' N, 088°53' W
Birmingham, Ala.	33°31' N, 086°48' W
Bismarck, N.D.	46°48' N, 100°47' W
Bloomington, Ind.	39°10' N, 086°32' W
Blythe, Calif.	33°37' N, 114°36' W
Boca Raton, Fla.	26°21' N, 080°05' W
Bogalusa, La.	30°47' N, 089°52' W
Boise, Idaho	43°37' N, 116°13' W
Boston, Mass.	42°22' N, 071°04' W

Name	Lat./Long.
Boulder, Colo.	40°01' N, 105°17' W
Bowling Green, Ky.	36°59' N, 086°27' W
Bozeman, Mont.	45°41' N, 111°02' W
Bradenton, Fla.	27°30' N, 082°34' W
Brady, Tex.	31°09' N, 099°20' W
Brainerd, Minn.	46°22' N, 094°12' W
Bremerton, Wash.	47°34' N, 122°38' W
Brigham City, Utah	41°31' N, 112°01' W
Brookings, S.D.	44°19' N, 096°48' W
Brownsville, Tex.	25°54' N, 097°30' W
Brunswick, Ga.	31°10' N, 081°30' W
Bryan, Tex.	30°40' N, 096°22' W
Buffalo, N.Y.	42°53' N, 078°53' W
Buffalo, Tex.	31°28' N, 096°04' W
Burlington, Ia.	40°48' N, 091°06' W
Burlington, Vt.	44°29' N, 073°12' W
Burns, Ore.	43°35' N, 119°03' W
Butte, Mont.	46°00' N, 112°32' W
Cairo, Ill.	37°00' N, 089°11' W
Caldwell, Idaho	43°40' N, 116°41' W
Canton, Ohio	40°48' N, 081°23' W
Cape Girardeau, Mo.	37°19' N, 089°32' W
Carbondale, Ill.	37°44' N, 089°13' W
Carlsbad, N.M.	32°25' N, 104°14' W
Carson City, Nev.	39°10' N, 119°46' W
Casa Grande, Ariz.	32°53' N, 111°45' W
Casper, Wyo.	42°51' N, 106°19' W
Cedar City, Utah	37°41' N, 113°04' W
Chadron, Neb.	42°50' N, 103°00' W
Champaign, Ill.	40°07' N, 088°15' W
Charleston, S.C.	32°46' N, 079°56' W
Charleston, W.Va.	38°21' N, 081°39' W
Charlotte, N.C.	35°13' N, 080°51' W
Chattanooga, Tenn.	35°03' N, 085°19' W
Chesapeake, Va.	36°50' N, 076°17' W
Cheyenne, Wyo.	41°08' N, 104°49' W
Chicago, Ill.	41°53' N, 087°38' W
Chico, Calif.	39°44' N, 121°50' W
Chula Vista, Calif.	32°38' N, 117°05' W
Cincinnati, Ohio	39°06' N, 084°31' W
Clarksdale, Miss.	34°12' N, 090°35' W
Clayton, N.M.	36°27' N, 103°11' W
Clearwater, Fla.	27°58' N, 082°48' W
Cleveland, Ohio	41°30' N, 081°42' W
Clinton, Okla.	35°31' N, 098°58' W
Clovis, N.M.	34°24' N, 103°12' W
Cody, Wyo.	44°32' N, 109°03' W
Coeur d'Alene, Idaho	47°41' N, 116°46' W
College Station, Tex.	30°37' N, 096°21' W
Colorado Springs, Colo.	38°50' N, 104°49' W
Columbia, S.C.	34°00' N, 081°03' W
Columbus, Ga.	32°29' N, 084°59' W
Columbus, Miss.	33°30' N, 088°25' W
Columbus, Ohio	39°58' N, 083°00' W
Concord, N.H.	43°12' N, 071°32' W
Coos Bay, Ore.	43°22' N, 124°12' W
Coral Gables, Fla.	25°45' N, 080°16' W
Cordele, Ga.	31°58' N, 083°47' W
Cordova, Alaska	60°33' N, 145°45' W
Corinth, Miss.	34°56' N, 088°31' W
Corpus Christi, Tex.	27°47' N, 097°24' W
Corsicana, Tex.	32°06' N, 096°28' W
Corvallis, Ore.	44°34' N, 123°16' W
Council Bluffs, Ia.	41°16' N, 095°52' W
Covington, Ky.	39°05' N, 084°31' W
Crescent City, Calif.	41°45' N, 124°12' W
Crystal City, Tex.	28°41' N, 099°50' W
Dalhart, Tex.	36°04' N, 102°31' W
Dallas, Tex.	32°47' N, 096°49' W
Dalton, Ga.	34°46' N, 084°58' W
Danville, Va.	36°36' N, 079°23' W
Davenport, Ia.	41°32' N, 090°35' W
Davis, Calif.	38°33' N, 121°44' W
Dayton, Ohio	39°45' N, 084°12' W
Daytona Beach, Fla.	29°13' N, 081°01' W
Decorah, Ia.	43°18' N, 091°48' W
Denver, Colo.	39°44' N, 104°59' W
Des Moines, Ia.	41°35' N, 093°37' W
Detroit, Mich.	42°20' N, 083°03' W
Dickinson, N.D.	46°53' N, 102°47' W
Dillingham, Alaska	59°03' N, 158°28' W
Dillon, Mont.	45°13' N, 112°38' W
Dodge City, Kan.	37°45' N, 100°0' W
Dothan, Ala.	31°13' N, 085°24' W
Dover, Del.	39°10' N, 075°32' W
Dover, N.H.	43°12' N, 070°53' W
Dubuque, Ia.	42°30' N, 090°41' W
Duluth, Minn.	46°47' N, 092°07' W
Duncan, Okla.	34°30' N, 097°57' W
Durango, Colo.	37°17' N, 107°53' W
Durham, N.C.	36°00' N, 078°54' W
Dutch Harbor, Alaska	53°53' N, 166°32' W
East St. Louis, Ill.	38°37' N, 090°09' W
Eau Claire, Wis.	44°49' N, 091°30' W
El Cajon, Calif.	32°48' N, 116°58' W
El Dorado, Ark.	33°12' N, 092°40' W
El Paso, Tex.	31°45' N, 106°29' W
Elko, Nev.	40°50' N, 115°46' W
Ely, Minn.	47°55' N, 091°51' W
Ely, Nev.	39°15' N, 114°54' W
Emporia, Kan.	38°25' N, 096°11' W
Enid, Okla.	36°24' N, 097°53' W
Erie, Pa.	42°08' N, 080°05' W
Escanaba, Mich.	45°45' N, 087°04' W
Escondido, Calif.	33°07' N, 117°05' W
Eugene, Ore.	44°05' N, 123°04' W
Eunice, La.	30°30' N, 092°25' W
Eureka, Calif.	40°47' N, 124°09' W
Eustis, Fla.	28°51' N, 081°41' W
Evanston, Wyo.	41°16' N, 110°58' W
Everett, Wash.	47°59' N, 122°12' W
Fairbanks, Alaska,	64°51' N, 147°45' W
Falls City, Neb.	40°03' N, 095°36' W
Fargo, N.D.	46°53' N, 096°48' W
Farmington, N.M.	36°44' N, 108°12' W
Fayetteville, Ark.	36°03' N, 094°09' W
Fayetteville, N.C.	35°03' N, 078°53' W
Fergus Falls, Minn.	46°17' N, 096°04' W
Flagstaff, Ariz.	35°12' N, 111°39' W
Flint, Mich.	43°01' N, 083°41' W
Florence, S.C.	34°12' N, 079°46' W
Fort Bragg, Calif.	39°26' N, 123°48' W
Fort Collins, Colo.	40°35' N, 105°05' W
Fort Dodge, Ia.	42°30' N, 094°11' W
Fort Lauderdale, Fla.	26°07' N, 080°08' W
Fort Madison, Ia.	40°38' N, 091°27' W
Fort Myers, Fla.	26°39' N, 081°53' W
Fort Pierce, Fla.	27°26' N, 080°19' W
Fort Smith, Ark.	35°23' N, 094°25' W

Name	Lat./Long.
Fort Wayne, Ind.	41°04' N, 085°09' W
Fort Worth, Tex.	32°45' N, 097°18' W
Frankfort, Ky.	38°12' N, 084°52' W
Freeport, Ill.	42°17' N, 089°36' W
Freeport, Tex.	28°57' N, 095°21' W
Fremont, Neb.	41°26' N, 096°30' W
Fresno, Calif.	36°44' N, 119°47' W
Gadsden, Ala.	34°01' N, 086°01' W
Gainesville, Fla.	29°40' N, 082°20' W
Gainesville, Ga.	34°17' N, 083°49' W
Galena, Alaska	64°44' N, 156°56' W
Gallup, N.M.	35°31' N, 108°45' W
Galveston, Tex.	29°18' N, 094°48' W
Garden City, Kan.	37°58' N, 100°52' W
Garland, Tex.	32°54' N, 096°38' W
Gary, Ind.	41°36' N, 087°20' W
Georgetown, S.C.	33°23' N, 079°17' W
Gillette, Wyo.	44°18' N, 105°30' W
Glasgow, Ky.	37°00' N, 085°55' W
Glasgow, Mont.	48°12' N, 106°38' W
Glendive, Mont.	47°07' N, 104°43' W
Glenwood Springs, Colo.	39°33' N, 107°19' W
Goliad, Tex.	28°40' N, 097°23' W
Goodland, Kan.	39°21' N, 101°43' W
Grand Forks, N.D.	47°55' N, 097°03' W
Grand Island, Neb.	40°55' N, 098°21' W
Grand Junction, Colo.	39°04' N, 108°33' W
Grand Rapids, Mich.	42°58' N, 085°40' W
Granite Falls, Minn.	44°49' N, 095°33' W
Great Falls, Mont.	47°30' N, 111°17' W
Greeley, Colo.	40°25' N, 104°42' W
Green Bay, Wis.	44°31' N, 088°00' W
Greensboro, N.C.	36°04' N, 079°48' W
Greenville, Ala.	31°50' N, 086°38' W
Greenville, Miss.	33°24' N, 091°04' W
Greenwood, S.C.	34°12' N, 082°10' W
Griffin, Ga.	33°15' N, 084°16' W
Gulfport, Miss.	30°22' N, 089°06' W
Guymon, Okla.	36°41' N, 101°29' W
Hampton, Va.	37°02' N, 076°21' W
Hannibal, Mo.	39°42' N, 091°22' W
Harlingen, Tex.	26°12' N, 097°42' W
Harrisburg, Pa.	40°16' N, 076°53' W
Hartford, Conn.	41°46' N, 072°41' W
Hattiesburg, Miss.	31°20' N, 089°17' W
Helena, Mont.	46°36' N, 112°02' W
Henderson, Nev.	36°02' N, 114°59' W
Hialeah, Fla.	25°51' N, 080°16' W
Hilo, Hawaii	19°44' N, 155°05' W
Hobbs, N.M.	32°42' N, 103°08' W
Hollywood, Fla.	26°01' N, 080°09' W
Honokaa, Hawaii	20°05' N, 155°28' W
Honolulu, Hawaii	21°19' N, 157°52' W
Hope, Ark.	33°40' N, 093°36' W
Hot Springs, Ark.	34°31' N, 093°03' W
Houghton, Mich.	47°07' N, 088°34' W
Houston, Tex.	29°46' N, 095°22' W
Hugo, Okla.	34°01' N, 095°31' W
Huntsville, Ala.	34°44' N, 086°35' W
Hutchinson, Kan.	38°05' N, 097°56' W
Idaho Falls, Idaho	43°30' N, 112°02' W
Independence, Mo.	39°05' N, 094°24' W
Indianapolis, Ind.	39°46' N, 086°09' W
International Falls, Minn.	48°36' N, 093°25' W
Iron Mountain, Mich.	45°49' N, 088°04' W
Ironwood, Mich.	46°27' N, 090°09' W
Ithaca, N.Y.	42°26' N, 076°30' W
Jackson, Miss.	32°18' N, 090°12' W
Jackson, Tenn.	35°37' N, 088°49' W
Jacksonville, Fla.	30°20' N, 081°39' W
Jacksonville, N.C.	34°45' N, 077°26' W
Jamestown, N.Y.	42°06' N, 079°14' W
Jefferson City, Mo.	38°34' N, 092°10' W
Jersey City, N.J.	40°44' N, 074°04' W
Joliet, Ill.	41°32' N, 088°05' W
Jonesboro, Ark.	35°50' N, 090°42' W
Jonesboro, Ga.	33°31' N, 084°22' W
Juneau, Alaska	58°20' N, 134°27' W
Kaktovik, Alaska	70°08' N, 143°38' W
Kalamazoo, Mich.	42°17' N, 085°35' W
Kalispell, Mont.	48°12' N, 114°19' W
Kansas City, Kan.	39°07' N, 094°38' W
Kansas City, Mo.	39°06' N, 094°35' W
Kapaa, Hawaii	22°05' N, 159°19' W
Kearney, Neb.	40°42' N, 099°05' W
Kenai, Alaska	60°33' N, 151°16' W
Ketchikan, Alaska	55°21' N, 131°39' W
Key Largo, Fla.	25°06' N, 080°27' W
Key West, Fla.	24°33' N, 081°49' W
King City, Calif.	36°13' N, 121°08' W
Kingman, Ariz.	35°12' N, 114°04' W
Kingsville, Tex.	27°31' N, 097°52' W
Kirksville, Mo.	40°12' N, 092°35' W
Klamath Falls, Ore.	42°12' N, 121°46' W
Knoxville, Tenn.	35°58' N, 083°55' W
Kodiak, Alaska	57°47' N, 152°24' W
Kokomo, Ind.	40°30' N, 086°08' W
La Crosse, Wis.	43°48' N, 091°15' W
La Junta, Colo.	37°59' N, 103°33' W
Lafayette, La.	30°14' N, 092°01' W
Lake Charles, La.	30°14' N, 093°13' W
Lake Havasu City, Ariz.	34°29' N, 114°19' W
Lakeland, Fla.	28°03' N, 081°57' W
Lansing, Mich.	42°44' N, 084°33' W
Laramie, Wyo.	41°19' N, 105°35' W
Laredo, Tex.	27°30' N, 099°30' W
Las Cruces, N.M.	32°19' N, 106°47' W
Las Vegas, N.M.	35°36' N, 105°13' W
Las Vegas, Nev.	36°01' N, 115°09' W
Laurel, Miss.	31°41' N, 089°08' W
Lawton, Okla.	34°37' N, 098°25' W
Lebanon, N.H.	43°39' N, 072°15' W
Lewiston, Idaho	46°25' N, 117°01' W
Lewiston, Me.	44°06' N, 070°13' W
Lewiston, Mont.	47°03' N, 109°25' W
Lexington, Ky.	38°01' N, 084°30' W
Liberal, Kan.	37°02' N, 100°55' W
Lihue, Hawaii	21°59' N, 159°23' W
Lima, Ohio	40°44' N, 084°06' W
Lincoln, Me.	45°22' N, 068°30' W
Lincoln, Neb.	40°50' N, 096°41' W
Little Rock, Ark.	34°45' N, 092°17' W
Logan, Utah	41°44' N, 111°50' W
Long Beach, Calif.	33°47' N, 118°11' W
Los Alamos, N.M.	35°53' N, 106°19' W
Los Angeles, Calif.	34°04' N, 118°15' W
Louisville, Ky.	38°15' N, 085°46' W
Lowell, Mass.	42°38' N, 071°19' W
Lubbock, Tex.	33°35' N, 101°51' W

Name	Lat./Long.
Lynchburg, Va.	37°25' N, 079°09' W
Macomb, Ill.	40°27' N, 090°40' W
Macon, Ga.	32°51' N, 083°38' W
Madison, Wis.	43°04' N, 089°24' W
Manchester, N.H.	43°00' N, 071°28' W
Mandan, N.D.	46°50' N, 100°54' W
Mankato, Minn.	44°10' N, 094°00' W
Marietta, Ohio	39°25' N, 081°27' W
Marinette, Wis.	45°06' N, 087°38' W
Marion, Ind.	40°32' N, 085°40' W
Marquette, Mich.	46°33' N, 087°24' W
Massillon, Ohio	40°48' N, 081°32' W
McAllen, Tex.	26°12' N, 098°14' W
McCall, Idaho	44°55' N, 116°06' W
McCook, Neb.	40°12' N, 100°38' W
Medford, Ore.	42°19' N, 122°52' W
Meeker, Colo.	40°02' N, 107°55' W
Melbourne, Fla.	28°05' N, 080°37' W
Memphis, Tenn.	35°08' N, 090°03' W
Meridian, Miss.	32°22' N, 088°42' W
Mesa, Ariz.	33°25' N, 111°49' W
Miami, Fla.	25°47' N, 080°11' W
Midland, Mich.	43°36' N, 084°14' W
Midland, Tex.	32°00' N, 102°05' W
Miles City, Mont.	46°25' N, 105°51' W
Milledgeville, Ga.	33°05' N, 083°14' W
Milwaukee, Wis.	43°02' N, 087°55' W
Minneapolis, Minn.	44°59' N, 093°16' W
Minot, N.D.	48°14' N, 101°18' W
Missoula, Mont.	46°52' N, 114°01' W
Mitchell, S.D.	43°43' N, 098°02' W
Moab, Utah	38°35' N, 109°33' W
Mobile, Ala.	30°41' N, 088°03' W
Moline, Ill.	41°30' N, 090°31' W
Monterey, Calif.	36°37' N, 121°55' W
Montgomery, Ala.	32°23' N, 086°19' W
Montpelier, Vt.	44°16' N, 072°35' W
Montrose, Colo.	38°29' N, 107°53' W
Morehead City, N.C.	34°43' N, 076°43' W
Morgan City, La.	29°42' N, 091°12' W
Morgantown, W.Va.	39°38' N, 079°57' W
Moscow, Idaho	46°44' N, 117°00' W
Mount Vernon, Ill.	38°19' N, 088°55' W
Murfreesboro, Ark.	34°04' N, 093°41' W
Murfreesboro, Tenn.	35°50' N, 086°23' W
Muskogee, Okla.	35°45' N, 095°22' W
Myrtle Beach, S.C.	33°42' N, 078°53' W
Naples, Fla.	26°08' N, 081°48' W
Nashville-Davidson, Tenn.	36°10' N, 086°47' W
Natchez, Miss.	31°34' N, 091°24' W
Needles, Calif.	34°51' N, 114°37' W
Nevada, Mo.	37°51' N, 094°22' W
New Albany, Ind.	38°18' N, 085°49' W
New Bedford, Mass.	41°38' N, 070°56' W
New Bern, N.C.	35°07' N, 077°03' W
New Haven, Conn.	41°18' N, 072°55' W
New Madrid, Mo.	36°36' N, 089°32' W
New Orleans, La.	29°58' N, 090°04' W
New York City, N.Y.	40°43' N, 074°00' W
Newark, N.J.	40°44' N, 074°10' W
Newcastle, Wyo.	43°50' N, 104°11' W
Newport News, Va.	36°59' N, 076°25' W
Newport, Ore.	44°39' N, 124°03' W
Newport, R.I.	41°29' N, 071°18' W
Niagara Falls, N.Y.	43°06' N, 079°03' W
Nogales, Ariz.	31°20' N, 110°56' W
Nome, Alaska	64°30' N, 165°25' W
Norfolk, Va.	36°51' N, 076°17' W
Norman, Okla.	35°13' N, 097°26' W
North Augusta, S.C.	33°30' N, 081°59' W
North Platte, Neb.	41°08' N, 100°46' W
O'neill, Neb.	42°27' N, 098°39' W
Oakland, Calif.	37°49' N, 122°16' W
Ocala, Fla.	29°11' N, 082°08' W
Oceanside, Calif.	33°12' N, 117°23' W
Odessa, Tex.	31°52' N, 102°23' W
Ogallala, Neb.	41°08' N, 101°43' W
Ogden, Utah	41°13' N, 111°58' W
Oklahoma City, Okla.	35°30' N, 097°30' W
Omaha, Neb.	41°17' N, 096°01' W
Orem, Utah	40°18' N, 111°42' W
Orlando, Fla.	28°33' N, 081°23' W
Oshkosh, Wis.	44°01' N, 088°33' W
Ottawa, Ill.	41°20' N, 088°50' W
Ottumwa, Ia.	41°01' N, 092°25' W
Overton, Nev.	36°33' N, 114°27' W
Owensboro, Ky.	37°46' N, 087°07' W
Paducah, Ky.	37°05' N, 088°37' W
Pahala, Hawaii	19°12' N, 155°29' W
Palm Springs, Calif.	33°50' N, 116°33' W
Palo Alto, Calif.	37°27' N, 122°10' W
Panama City, Fla.	30°10' N, 085°40' W
Paris, Tex.	33°40' N, 095°33' W
Parsons, Kan.	37°20' N, 095°16' W
Pasadena, Calif.	34°09' N, 118°09' W
Pasadena, Tex.	29°43' N, 095°13' W
Pascagoula, Miss.	30°21' N, 088°33' W
Paterson, N.J.	40°55' N, 074°11' W
Pecos, Tex.	31°26' N, 103°30' W
Pendleton, Ore.	45°40' N, 118°47' W
Pensacola, Fla.	30°25' N, 087°13' W
Peoria, Ill.	40°42' N, 089°36' W
Petoskey, Mich.	45°22' N, 084°57' W
Philadelphia, Pa.	39°57' N, 075°10' W
Phoenix, Ariz.	33°27' N, 112°04' W
Pierre, S.D.	44°22' N, 100°21' W
Pine Bluff, Ark.	34°13' N, 092°01' W
Pittsburgh, Pa.	40°26' N, 080°01' W
Plano, Tex.	33°01' N, 096°41' W
Plattsburgh, N.Y.	44°42' N, 073°27' W
Pocatello, Idaho	42°52' N, 112°27' W
Point Hope, Alaska	68°21' N, 166°41' W
Port Gibson, Miss.	31°58' N, 090°59' W
Port Lavaca, Tex.	28°37' N, 096°38' W
Port Royal, S.C.	32°23' N, 080°42' W
Portland, Me.	43°39' N, 070°16' W
Portland, Ore.	45°32' N, 122°37' W
Prescott, Ariz.	34°33' N, 112°28' W
Presque Isle, Me.	46°41' N, 068°01' W
Providence, R.I.	41°49' N, 071°24' W
Provo, Utah	40°14' N, 111°39' W
Pueblo, Colo.	38°15' N, 104°36' W
Pullman, Wash.	46°44' N, 117°10' W
Racine, Wis.	42°44' N, 087°48' W
Raleigh, N.C.	35°46' N, 078°38' W
Rapid City, S.D.	44°05' N, 103°14' W
Red Bluff, Calif.	40°11' N, 122°15' W
Redding, Calif.	40°35' N, 122°24' W
Redfield, S.D.	44°53' N, 098°31' W

Name	Lat./Long.
Reno, Nev.	39°31' N, 119°48' W
Rice Lake, Wis.	45°30' N, 091°44' W
Richfield, Utah	38°46' N, 112°05' W
Richmond, Ind.	39°50' N, 084°54' W
Richmond, Va.	37°33' N, 077°27' W
Riverside, Calif.	33°59' N, 117°22' W
Riverton, Wyo.	43°02' N, 108°23' W
Roanoke, Va.	37°16' N, 079°56' W
Rochester, Minn.	44°01' N, 092°28' W
Rochester, N.Y.	43°10' N, 077°37' W
Rock Hill, S.C.	34°56' N, 081°01' W
Rock Island, Ill.	41°30' N, 090°34' W
Rock Springs, Wyo.	41°35' N, 109°12' W
Rockford, Ill.	42°16' N, 089°06' W
Rolla, Mo.	37°57' N, 091°46' W
Rome, Ga.	34°15' N, 085°09' W
Roseburg, Ore.	43°13' N, 123°20' W
Roswell, N.M.	33°24' N, 104°32' W
Sacramento, Calif.	38°35' N, 121°29' W
Saginaw, Mich.	43°26' N, 083°56' W
Salem, Ore.	44°56' N, 123°02' W
Salina, Kan.	38°50' N, 097°37' W
Salinas, Calif.	36°40' N, 121°39' W
Salmon, Idaho	45°11' N, 113°54' W
Salt Lake City, Utah	40°45' N, 111°53' W
San Angelo, Tex.	31°28' N, 100°26' W
San Antonio, Tex.	29°25' N, 098°30' W
San Bernardino, Calif.	34°07' N, 117°19' W
San Diego, Calif.	32°43' N, 117°09' W
San Francisco, Calif.	37°47' N, 122°25' W
San Jose, Calif.	37°20' N, 121°53' W
San Luis Obispo, Calif.	35°17' N, 120°40' W
Sanderson, Tex.	30°09' N, 102°24' W
Santa Ana, Calif.	33°46' N, 117°52' W
Santa Barbara, Calif.	34°25' N, 119°42' W
Santa Fe, N.M.	35°41' N, 105°57' W
Santa Maria, Calif.	34°57' N, 120°26' W
Sarasota, Fla.	27°20' N, 082°32' W
Sault Ste. Marie, Mich.	46°30' N, 084°21' W
Savannah, Ga.	32°05' N, 081°06' W
Scott City, Kan.	38°29' N, 100°54' W
Scottsbluff, Neb.	41°52' N, 103°40' W
Scottsdale, Ariz.	33°29' N, 111°56' W
Searcy, Ark.	35°15' N, 091°44' W
Seattle, Wash.	47°36' N, 122°20' W
Sebring, Fla.	27°30' N, 081°27' W
Seguin, Tex.	29°34' N, 097°58' W
Selawik, Alaska	66°36' N, 160°00' W
Seldovia, Alaska	59°26' N, 151°43' W
Selma, Ala.	32°25' N, 087°01' W
Sharpsburg, Md.	39°28' N, 077°45' W
Sheboygan, Wis.	43°45' N, 087°42' W
Sheridan, Wyo.	44°48' N, 106°58' W
Show Low, Ariz.	34°15' N, 110°02' W
Shreveport, La.	32°31' N, 093°45' W
Sierra Vista, Ariz.	31°33' N, 110°18' W
Silver City, N.M.	32°46' N, 108°17' W
Sioux City, Ia.	42°30' N, 096°24' W
Sioux Falls, S.D.	43°33' N, 096°44' W
Skagway, Alaska	59°28' N, 135°19' W
Snyder, Tex.	32°44' N, 100°55' W
Socorro, N.M.	34°04' N, 106°54' W
Somerset, Ky.	37°05' N, 084°36' W
South Bend, Ind.	41°41' N, 086°15' W
Sparks, Nev.	39°32' N, 119°45' W
Spencer, Ia.	43°09' N, 095°10' W
Spokane, Wash.	47°40' N, 117°24' W
Springfield, Ill.	39°48' N, 089°38' W
Springfield, Mo.	37°13' N, 093°17' W
St. Augustine, Fla.	29°54' N, 081°19' W
St. Cloud, Minn.	45°34' N, 094°10' W
St. George, Utah	37°06' N, 113°35' W
St. Joseph, Mo.	39°46' N, 094°50' W
St. Louis, Mo.	38°37' N, 090°11' W
St. Maries, Idaho	47°19' N, 116°35' W
St. Paul, Minn.	44°57' N, 093°06' W
St. Petersburg, Fla.	27°46' N, 082°39' W
State College, Pa.	40°48' N, 077°52' W
Ste. Genevieve, Mo.	37°59' N, 090°03' W
Steamboat Springs, Colo.	40°29' N, 106°50' W
Stillwater, Minn.	45°03' N, 092°49' W
Sumter, S.C.	33°55' N, 080°21' W
Sun Valley, Idaho	43°42' N, 114°21' W
Superior, Wis.	46°44' N, 092°06' W
Syracuse, N.Y.	43°03' N, 076°09' W
Tacoma, Wash.	47°14' N, 122°26' W
Tallahassee, Fla.	30°27' N, 084°17' W
Tampa, Fla.	27°57' N, 082°27' W
Tempe, Ariz.	33°25' N, 111°56' W
Temple, Tex.	31°06' N, 097°21' W
Terre Haute, Ind.	39°28' N, 087°25' W
Texarkana, Ark.	33°26' N, 094°03' W
Thief River Falls, Minn.	48°07' N, 096°10' W
Tifton, Ga.	31°27' N, 083°31' W
Titusville, Fla.	28°37' N, 080°49' W
Toledo, Ohio	41°39' N, 083°33' W
Tonopah, Nev.	38°04' N, 117°14' W
Topeka, Kan.	39°03' N, 095°40' W
Traverse City, Mich.	44°46' N, 085°38' W
Trenton, N.J.	40°14' N, 074°46' W
Trinidad, Colo.	37°10' N, 104°31' W
Troy, Ala.	31°48' N, 085°58' W
Troy, N.Y.	42°44' N, 073°41' W
Tucson, Ariz.	32°13' N, 110°58' W
Tulsa, Okla.	36°10' N, 095°55' W
Tupelo, Miss.	34°16' N, 088°43' W
Tuscaloosa, Ala.	33°12' N, 087°34' W
Twin Falls, Idaho	42°34' N, 114°28' W
Tyler, Tex.	32°21' N, 095°18' W
Ukiah, Calif.	39°09' N, 123°12' W
Utica, N.Y.	43°06' N, 075°14' W
Uvalde, Tex.	29°13' N, 099°47' W
Valdez, Alaska	61°07' N, 146°16' W
Valdosta, Ga.	30°50' N, 083°17' W
Valentine, Neb.	42°52' N, 100°33' W
Vero Beach, Fla.	27°38' N, 080°24' W
Vicksburg, Miss.	32°21' N, 090°53' W
Victoria, Tex.	28°48' N, 097°00' W
Vincennes, Ind.	38°41' N, 087°32' W
Virginia Beach, Va.	36°51' N, 075°59' W
Waco, Tex.	31°33' N, 097°09' W
Wahpeton, N.D.	46°15' N, 096°36' W
Wailuku, Hawaii	20°53' N, 156°30' W
Walla Walla, Wash.	46°04' N, 118°20' W
Warren, Pa.	41°51' N, 079°08' W
Washington, D.C.	38°54' N, 077°02' W
Waterloo, Ia.	42°30' N, 092°21' W
Watertown, N.Y.	43°59' N, 075°55' W
Waycross, Ga.	31°13' N, 082°21' W

Name	Lat./Long.
Wayne, Neb.	42°14' N, 097°01' W
Weiser, Idaho	44°45' N, 116°58' W
West Palm Beach, Fla.	26°43' N, 080°03' W
Wheeling, W.Va.	40°04' N, 080°43' W
Wichita Falls, Tex.	33°54' N, 098°30' W
Wichita, Kan.	37°42' N, 097°20' W
Williamsport, Pa.	41°15' N, 077°00' W
Wilmington, N.C.	34°14' N, 077°55' W
Winfield, Kan.	37°15' N, 096°59' W
Winnemucca, Nev.	40°58' N, 117°44' W
Winslow, Ariz.	35°02' N, 110°42' W
Winston-Salem, N.C.	36°06' N, 080°14' W
Worcester, Mass.	42°16' N, 071°48' W
Worthington, Minn.	43°37' N, 095°36' W
Wrangell, Alaska	56°28' N, 132°23' W
Yakima, Wash.	46°36' N, 120°31' W
Yankton, S.D.	42°53' N, 097°23' W
Yazoo City, Miss.	32°51' N, 090°25' W
Youngstown, Ohio	41°06' N, 080°39' W
Yuba City, Calif.	39°08' N, 121°37' W
Yuma, Ariz.	32°43' N, 114°37' W
Zanesville, Ohio	39°56' N, 082°01' W

URUGUAY ....pg. 122

Capital: ....Montevideo
Area: ....176,215 sq km; 68,037 sq mi
Highest Elev.: .....Mt. Mirador 500 m; 1,640 ft
Longest River: ....Negro 800 km; 500 mi
Avg. Temperature: . .Jan = 23°C; Jul = 11°C
Currency: ....peso uruguayo
Official Language: .Spanish

Name	Lat./Long.
Las Piedras	34°44' S, 056°13' W
Melo	32°22' S, 054°11' W
Mercedes	33°16' S, 058°01' W
Minas	34°23' S, 055°14' W
Montevideo	34°53' S, 056°11' W
Paysandu	32°19' S, 058°05' W
Rivera	30°54' S, 055°31' W
Salto	31°23' S, 057°58' W

UZBEKISTAN ....pg. 139

Capital: ....Tashkent
Area: ....447,400 sq km; 172,700 sq mi
Highest Elev.: .....Beshtor Pk. 4,300 m; 14,400 ft
Longest River: .....Amu Darya 2,540 km; 1,580 mi
Avg. Temperature: . .Jan = 0°C; Jul = 29°C
Currency: ....sum
Official Language: . .Uzbek

Name	Lat./Long.
Andijon	40°45' N, 072°22' E
Angren	41°01' N, 070°12' E
Bekobod	40°13' N, 069°14' E
Beruniy(Biruni)	41°42' N, 060°44' E
Bukhara (Bokhara)	39°48' N, 064°25' E
Denow	38°16' N, 067°54' E
Fergana (Skobelev)	40°23' N, 071°46' E
Guliston(Mirzachul)	40°29' N, 068°46' E
Jizzakh	40°06' N, 067°50' E
Kattaqurghan	39°55' N, 066°15' E
Kogon	39°43' N, 064°33' E
Marghilon	40°27' N, 071°42' E
Namangan	41°00' N, 071°40' E
Nawoiy	40°09' N, 065°22' E
Nukus	42°29' N, 059°38' E
Olmaliq	40°50' N, 069°35' E
Qarshi	38°53' N, 065°48' E
Quqon	40°30' N, 070°57' E
Samarkand	39°40' N, 066°58' E
Tashkent (Toshkent)	41°20' N, 069°18' E
Turmiz	37°14' N, 067°16' E
Urganch	41°33' N, 060°38' E

VANUATU ....pg. 156

Capital: ....Vila
Area: ....12,190 sq km; 4,707 sq mi
Highest Elev.: .....Mt. Tabwémasana 1,880 m; 6,170 ft
Avg. Temperature: . .Jan = 22.6°C; Jul = 27.6°C
Currency: ....vatu
Official Language: . .Bislama, French, English

Name	Lat./Long.
Port-Vila, *see* Vila	
Vila (Port-Vila)	17°44' S, 168°18' E

VENEZUELA.............pg. 124

Capital: ....Caracas
Area: ....912,050 sq km; 352,144 sq mi
Highest Elev.: .....Mt. Bolívar 5,010 m; 16,430 ft
Longest River: .....Orinoco 2,740 km; 1,700 mi
Avg. Temperature: . .Jan = 19°C; Jul = 21°C
Currency: ....bolívar
Official Language: . .Spanish

Name	Lat./Long.
Acarigua	09°33' N, 069°12' W
Achaguas	07°46' N, 068°14' W
Altagracia	10°07' N, 071°14' W
Altagracia de Orituco	09°52' N, 066°23' W
Anaco	09°27' N, 064°28' W
Aragua de Barcelona	09°28' N, 064°49' W
Araya	10°34' N, 064°15' W
Barcelona	10°08' N, 064°42' W
Barinas	08°38' N, 070°12' W
Barinitas	08°45' N, 070°25' W
Barquisimeto	10°04' N, 069°19' W
Barrancas	08°46' N, 070°06' W
Betijoque	09°23' N, 070°44' W
Biscucuy	09°22' N, 069°59' W
Bobures	09°15' N, 071°11' W
Boca de Pozo	11°00' N, 064°23' W
Cabimas	10°23' N, 071°28' W
Caicara (Caicara de Orinoco)	07°37' N, 066°10' W
Caicara	09°49' N, 063°36' W
Caja Seca	09°09' N, 071°05' W
Calabozo	08°56' N, 067°26' W
Camaguán	08°06' N, 067°36' W
Cantaura	09°19' N, 064°21' W
Caracas	10°30' N, 066°55' W
Cariaco	10°29' N, 063°33' W
Caripito	10°08' N, 063°06' W
Carora	10°11' N, 070°05' W
Carúpano	10°40' N, 063°14' W
Casigua	08°46' N, 072°30' W
Catia la Mar	10°36' N, 067°02' W
Ciudad Bolívar	08°08' N, 063°33' W
Ciudad Guayana (San Felix)	08°23' N, 062°40' W
Ciudad Ojeda	10°12' N, 071°19' W
Clarines	09°56' N, 065°10' W
Coro	11°25' N, 069°41' W
Cumana	10°28' N, 064°10' W
Duaca	10°18' N, 069°10' W
El Callao	07°21' N, 061°49' W
El Pao	08°01' N, 062°38' W
El Samán de Apure	07°55' N, 068°44' W
El Socorro	08°59' N, 065°44' W
El Sombrero	09°23' N, 067°03' W
El Tigre	08°55' N, 064°15' W
El Tocuyo	09°47' N, 069°48' W
Guacara	10°14' N, 067°53' W
Guanare	09°03' N, 069°45' W
Guanarito	08°42' N, 069°12' W
Guasdualito	07°15' N, 070°44' W
Guasipati	07°28' N, 061°54' W
Güiria	10°34' N, 062°18' W
Irapa	10°34' N, 062°35' W
Juangriego	11°05' N, 063°57' W
La Asunción	11°02' N, 063°53' W
La Fría	08°13' N, 072°15' W
La Grita	08°08' N, 071°59' W
La Vela de Coro	11°27' N, 069°34' W
La Victoria	10°14' N, 067°20' W
Las Mercedes	09°07' N, 066°24' W
Los Teques	10°21' N, 067°02' W
Machiques	10°04' N, 072°34' W
Maiquetia	10°36' N, 066°57' W
Maracaibo	10°40' N, 071°37' W
Maracay	10°15' N, 067°36' W
Maturín	09°45' N, 063°11' W
Mene Grande	09°49' N, 070°56' W
Mérida	08°36' N, 071°08' W
Morón	10°29' N, 068°11' W
Pariaguán	08°51' N, 064°43' W
Petare	10°29' N, 066°49' W
Píritu	09°23' N, 069°12' W
Porlamar	10°57' N, 063°51' W
Pozuelos	10°11' N, 064°39' W
Pueblo Nuevo	11°07' N, 069°28' W
Puerto Ayacucho	05°40' N, 067°35' W
Puerto Cabello	10°28' N, 068°01' W
Puerto Cumarebo	11°29' N, 069°21' W
Punta Cardón	11°38' N, 070°14' W
Punta de Mata	09°43' N, 063°38' W
Punto Fijo	11°42' N, 070°13' W
San Carlos	09°40' N, 068°36' W
San Carlos	09°01' N, 071°55' W
San Carlos de Río Negro	01°55' N, 067°04' W
San Cristóbal	07°46' N, 072°14' W
San Felipe	10°20' N, 068°44' W
San Felix, *see* Ciudad Guayana	
San Fernando de Apure	07°54' N, 067°28' W
San Fernando de Atabapo	04°03' N, 067°42' W
San José	10°01' N, 072°23' W
San José de Guanipa (El Tigrito)	08°54' N, 064°09' W
San Juan de los Morros	09°55' N, 067°21' W
Santa Bárbara	07°47' N, 071°10' W
Santa Elena	04°37' N, 061°08' W
Santa María de Ipire	08°49' N, 065°19' W
Santa Rita	10°32' N, 071°32' W
Siquisique	10°34' N, 069°42' W
Soledad	08°10' N, 063°34' W
Temblador	08°59' N, 062°44' W
Tía Juana	10°16' N, 071°22' W
Tinaco	09°42' N, 068°26' W
Tinaquillo	09°55' N, 068°18' W
Tovar	08°20' N, 071°46' W
Trujillo	09°22' N, 070°26' W
Tucacas	10°48' N, 068°19' W
Tucupido	09°17' N, 065°47' W
Tucupita	09°04' N, 062°03' W
Tumeremo	07°18' N, 061°30' W
Turmero	10°14' N, 067°29' W
Upata	08°01' N, 062°24' W
Valencia	10°11' N, 068°00' W
Valera	09°19' N, 070°37' W
Valle de la Pascua	09°13' N, 066°00' W
Villa Bruzual	09°20' N, 069°06' W
Villa de Cura	10°02' N, 067°29' W
Zaraza	09°21' N, 065°19' W

VIETNAM ....pg. 144

Capital: ....Hanoi
Area: ....331,041 sq km; 127,816 sq mi
Highest Elev.: .....Fan Si Pk. 3,140 m; 10,310 ft
Longest River: .....Red 1,200 km; 750 mi
Avg. Temperature: . .Jan = 17°C; Jul = 29°C
Currency: ....dong
Official Language: . .Vietnamese

Name	Lat./Long.
Bac Giang	21°16' N, 106°12' E
Bac Can	22°08' N, 105°50' E
Bac Lieu	09°17' N, 105°43' E
Bien Hoa	10°57' N, 106°49' E
Buon Me Thuot (Lac Giao)	12°40' N, 108°03' E
Ca Mau	09°11' N, 105°08' E
Cam Pha	21°01' N, 107°19' E
Cam Ranh	11°54' N, 109°13' E
Can Tho	10°02' N, 105°47' E
Chau Doc	10°42' N, 105°07' E
Da Lat	11°56' N, 108°25' E
Da Nang (Tourane)	16°04' N, 108°13' E
Dong Ha	16°49' N, 107°08' E
Dong Hoi	17°29' N, 106°36' E
Ha Giang	22°50' N, 104°59' E
Hai Duong	20°56' N, 106°19' E
Haiphong (Hai Phong)	20°52' N, 106°41' E
Hanoi (Ha Noi)	21°02' N, 105°51' E
Ho Chi Minh City (Saigon)	10°45' N, 106°40' E
Hoa Binh	20°50' N, 105°20' E
Hoi An	15°52' N, 108°19' E
Hong Gai (Hon Gai)	20°57' N, 107°05' E
Hue	16°28' N, 107°36' E
Kon Tum (Cong Tum or Kontun)	14°21' N, 108°00' E
Lai Chau	22°04' N, 103°10' E
Long Xuyen	10°23' N, 105°25' E
Minh Hoa	17°47' N, 106°01' E
My Tho	10°21' N, 106°21' E
Nam Dinh	20°25' N, 106°10' E
Nha Trang	12°15' N, 109°11' E
Phan Rang	11°34' N, 108°59' E
Phan Thiet	10°56' N, 108°06' E
Pleiku (Play Cu)	13°59' N, 108°00' E
Qui Nhon	13°46' N, 109°14' E
Rach Gia	10°01' N, 105°05' E
Sa Dec	10°18' N, 105°46' E
Soc Trang	09°36' N, 105°58' E
Son La	21°19' N, 103°54' E
Tam Ky	15°34' N, 108°29' E
Tan An	10°32' N, 106°25' E
Thai Binh	20°27' N, 106°20' E
Thai Nguyen	21°36' N, 105°50' E
Thanh Hoa	19°48' N, 105°46' E
Tuy Hoa	13°05' N, 109°18' E
Viet Tri	21°18' N, 105°26' E
Vinh	18°40' N, 105°40' E
Vung Tau	10°21' N, 107°04' E
Yen Bai	21°42' N, 104°52' E

WESTERN SAMOA ......pg. 156

Capital: ....Apia
Area: ....2,831 sq km; 1,093 sq mi
Highest Elev.: .....Mt. Silisili 1,860 m; 6,100 ft
Avg. Temperature: . .Jan = 26.3°C; Jul = 25.1°C
Currency: ....tala
Official Language: . .Samoan, English

Name	Lat./Long.
Apia	13°50' S, 171°44' W

YEMEN ....pg. 154

Capital: ....Sana'
Area: ....472,099 sq km; 182,278 sq mi
Highest Elev: ......Mt. An-Nabi Shu'ayb 3,660 m; 12,010 ft
Avg. Temperature: . .Jan = 25°C; Jul = 32°C
Currency: ....Yemen rial
Official Language: . .Arabic

Name	Lat./Long.
Aden ('Adan)	12°46' N, 045°02' E
'Amran	15°41' N, 043°55' E
Balhaf	13°58' N, 048°11' E
Dhamar	14°33' N, 044°24' E
Ghaydah, al-	16°13' N, 052°11' E
Habban	14°21' N, 047°05' E
Hayjan	16°40' N, 044°05' E
Hays	13°56' N, 043°29' E
Hudaydah, al-	14°48' N, 042°57' E
Ibb	13°58' N, 044°11' E
Madinat ash-Sha'b	12°50' N, 044°56' E
Ma'rib	15°25' N, 045°21' E
Maydi	16°19' N, 042°48' E
Min'ar	16°43' N, 051°18' E
Mocha (al-Mukha)	13°19' N, 043°15' E
Mukalla, al-	14°32' N, 049°08' E
Qana	14°00' N, 048°20' E
Raydah	15°50' N, 044°03' E
Rida'	14°25' N, 044°50' E
Sa'dah	16°57' N, 043°46' E
San'a'	15°21' N, 044°12' E
Sayhut	15°12' N, 051°14' E
Shaharah	16°11' N, 043°42' E
Sirwah	15°27' N, 045°01' E
Ta'izz	13°34' N, 044°02' E
Yarim	14°18' N, 044°23' E
Zabid	14°12' N, 043°19' E

YUGOSLAVIA ....pg. 134

Capital: ....Belgrade
Area: ....102,173 sq km; 39,449 sq mi
Highest Elev.: .....Titov Vrb 2,750 m; 9,010 ft
Longest River: .....Danube 2,850 km; 1,770 mi
Avg. Temperature: . .Jan = 0°C; Jul = 23°C
Currency: ....new dinar
Official Language: . .Serbo-Croatian

Name	Lat./Long.
Belgrade	44°50' N, 020°30' E
Cacak	43°54' N, 020°21' E
Kragujevac	44°01' N, 020°55' E
Kraljevo	43°44' N, 020°43' E
Krusevac	43°35' N, 021°20' E
Leskovac	42°59' N, 021°57' E
Nis	43°19' N, 021°54' E
Novi Pazar	43°08' N, 020°31' E
Novi Sad	45°15' N, 019°50' E
Pancevo	44°52' N, 020°39' E
Podgorica (Titograd)	42°26' N, 019°16' E
Pristina	42°40' N, 021°10' E
Sabac	44°45' N, 019°43' E
Smederevo	44°39' N, 020°56' E
Sombor	45°46' N, 019°07' E
Subotica	46°06' N, 019°40' E
Uzice (Titovo Uzice)	43°52' N, 019°51' E
Valjevo	44°16' N, 019°53' E
Vranje	42°33' N, 021°54' E
Zrenjanin	45°23' N, 020°23' E

ZAIRE ....pg. 152

Capital: ....Kinshasa
Area: ....2,344,858 sq km; 905,354 sq mi
Highest Elev.: ....Margherita Pk. 5,120 m; 16,800 ft
Longest River: ...Congo 4,630 km; 2,880 mi
Avg. Temperature: .Jan = 27°C; Jul = 22°C
Currency: ....new zaïre
Official Language: .French

Name	Lat./Long.
Aketi	02°44' N, 023°46' E
Banana	06°01' S, 012°24' E
Bandundu	03°19' S, 017°22' E
Beni	00°30' N, 029°28' E
Boende	00°13' S, 020°52' E
Boma	05°51' S, 013°03' E
Bukama	09°12' S, 025°51' E
Bukavu	02°30' S, 028°52' E
Bulungu	04°33' S, 018°36' E
Bumba	02°11' N, 022°28' E
Bunia	01°34' N, 030°15' E
Buta	02°48' N, 024°44' E
Butembo	00°09' N, 029°17' E
Dilolo	10°42' S, 022°20' E
Gandajika	06°45' S, 023°57' E
Gemena	03°15' N, 019°46' E
Ilebo	04°19' S, 020°35' E
Inga	05°39' S, 013°39' E
Isiro	02°46' N, 027°37' E
Kabinda	06°08' S, 024°29' E
Kalemi (Albertville)	05°56' S, 029°12' E
Kamina	08°44' S, 025°00' E
Kananga (Luluabourg)	05°54' S, 022°25' E
Kasongo	04°27' S, 026°40' E
Kikwit	05°02' S, 018°49' E
Kinshasa (Leopoldville)	04°18' S, 015°18' E
Kisangani (Stanleyville)	00°30' N, 025°12' E
Kolwezi	10°43' S, 025°28' E
Kongolo	05°23' S, 027°00' E
Kutu	02°44' S, 018°09' E
Likasi	10°59' S, 026°44' E
Lisala	02°09' N, 021°31' E
Lubumbashi (Elisabethville)	11°40' N, 027°28' E
Manono	07°18' S, 027°25' E
Masi-Manimba	04°46' S, 017°55' E
Mbandaka	00°04' N, 018°16' E
Mbanza-Ngungu	05°15' S, 014°52' E
Mbuji-Mayi	06°09' S, 023°36' E
Mobayi-Mbongo	04°18' N, 021°11' E
Mushie	03°01' S, 016°54' E
Mweka	04°51' S, 021°34' E
Mwene-Ditu	07°03' S, 023°27' E
Samba	04°38' S, 026°22' E
Tshikapa	06°25' S, 020°48' E
Ubundu	00°21' S, 025°29' E
Watsa	03°03' N, 029°32' E
Yangambi	00°47' N, 024°28' E
Zongo	04°21' N, 018°36' E

ZAMBIA ....pg. 153

Capital: ....Lusaka
Area: ....752,614 sq km; 290,586 sq mi
Highest Elev.: .....Mt. Mahoni 2,150 m; 7,100 ft
Longest River: .....Zambezi 3,500 km; 2,200 mi
Avg. Temperature: . .Jan =21°C; Jul = 16°C
Currency: ....Zambian kwacha
Official Language: . .English

Name	Lat./Long.
Chililabombwe (Bancroft)	12°22' S, 027°50' E
Chingola	12°32' S, 027°52' E
Chipata (Fort Jameson)	13°39' S, 032°40' E
Choma	16°49' S, 026°59' E
Fort Jameson, *see* Chipata	
Kabwe (Broken Hill)	14°27' S, 028°27' E
Kasama	10°13' S, 031°12' E
Kawambwa	09°47' S, 029°05' E
Kitwe	12°49' S, 028°13' E
Livingstone (Maramba)	17°51' S, 025°52' E
Luanshya	13°08' S, 028°25' E
Lusaka	15°25' S, 028°17' E
Mansa (Fort Rosebery)	11°12' S, 028°53' E
Mazabuka	15°51' S, 027°46' E
Mbala	08°50' S, 031°22' E
Mongu	15°17' S, 023°08' E
Monze	16°16' S, 027°29' E
Mpika	11°50' S, 031°27' E
Mpulungu	08°46' S, 031°07' E
Mumbwa	14°59' S, 027°04' E
Mwamfuli (Samfya)	11°21' S, 029°33' E
Nchelenge	09°21' S, 029°44' E
Ndola	12°58' S, 028°38' E
Petauke	14°15' S, 031°20' E
Samfya, *see* Mwamfuli	
Senanga	16°07' S, 023°16' E
Solwezi	12°11' S, 026°24' E
Zambezi	13°33' S, 023°07' E

ZIMBABWE ....pg. 153

Capital: ....Harare
Area: ....390,757 sq km; 150,872 sq mi
Highest Elev.: .....Mt. Inyangani 2,590 m; 8,500 ft
Longest River: ....Zambezi 3,500 km; 2,200 mi
Avg. Temperature: . .Jan = 21°C; Jul = 14°C
Currency: ....Zimbabwe dollar
Official Language: . .English

Name	Lat./Long.
Beitbridge	22°13' S, 030°00' E
Bulawayo	20°09' S, 028°35' E
Chitungwiza	18°47' S, 032°37' E
Fort Victoria, *see* Masvingo	
Gatooma, *see* Kadoma	
Gweru (Gwelo)	19°27' S, 029°49' E
Harare (Salisbury)	17°50' S, 031°03' E
Hwange (Wankie)	18°22' S, 026°29' E
Kadoma (Gatooma)	18°21' S, 029°55' E
Kwekwe (Que Que)	18°55' S, 029°49' E
Mashava	20°03' S, 030°29' E
Masvingo (Fort Victoria, or Nyanda)	20°05' S, 030°50' E
Mutare (Umtali)	18°58' S, 032°40' E
Nyanda, *see* Masvingo	
Que Que, *see* Kwekwe	
Redcliff	19°02' S, 029°47' E
Salisbury, *see* Harare	
Selulwe, *see* Shurugwi	
Shurugwi (Selukwe)	19°40' S, 030°00' E
Umtali, *see* Mutare	
Wankie, *see* Hwange	

Webster's
Concise Guide
to Punctuation
and Style

Contents

1 Punctuation

Punctuation marks are used to help clarify the structure and meaning of sentences. They separate groups of words for meaning and emphasis; they convey an idea of the variations in pitch, volume, pauses, and intonation of the spoken language; and they help avoid ambiguity. The choice of what punctuation to use, if any, will often be clear and unambiguous. In other cases, a sentence may allow for several punctuation patterns. In cases like these, varying notions of correctness have developed, and two writers might, with equal correctness, punctuate the same sentence quite differently, relying on their individual judgment and taste.

Apostrophe

The apostrophe is used to form most possessives and contractions as well as some plurals and inflections.

1. The apostrophe is used to indicate the possessive of nouns and indefinite pronouns. (For details, see the section beginning on page 203.)

   the girl's shoe
   the boys' fathers
   Simmons's role
   children's laughter
   anyone's guess
   the Browns' house
   Arkansas's capital

2. Apostrophes are sometimes used to form plurals of letters, numerals, abbreviations, symbols, and words referred to as words. (For details, see the section beginning on page 201.)

   cross your *t*'s
   three 8's *or* three 8s
   two L.H.D.'s *or* two L.H.D.s
   used &'s instead of *and*'s

3. Apostrophes mark omissions in contractions made of two or more words and in contractions of single words.

   wasn't
   they're

   she'd rather not
   Jake's had it
   ass'n
   dep't

4. The apostrophe is used to indicate that letters have been intentionally omitted from a word in order to imitate informal speech.

   "Singin' in the Rain," the popular song and movie
   "Snap 'em up" was his response.

   Sometimes such words are so consistently spelled with an apostrophe that the spelling becomes an accepted variant.

   rock 'n' roll [*for* rock and roll]
   ma'am [*for* madam]
   sou'wester [*for* southwester]

5. Apostrophes mark the omission of digits in numerals.

   class of '98
   fashion in the '90s

   If the apostrophe is used when writing the plurals of numerals, either the apostrophe that stands for the missing figures is omitted or the word is spelled out.

   90's *or* nineties *but not* '90's

6. In informal writing, apostrophes are used to produce forms of verbs that are made of individually pronounced letters. An apostrophe or a hyphen is also sometimes used to add an *-er* ending to an abbreviation; if no confusion would result, the apostrophe is usually omitted.

   OK'd the budget
   X'ing out the mistakes
   4-H'er
   49er

Brackets

Outside of mathematics and chemistry texts, brackets are primarily used for insertions into carefully handled quoted matter. They are rarely seen in general writing but are common in historical and scholarly contexts.

1. Brackets enclose editorial comments, corrections, and clarifications inserted into quoted matter.

   Surely that should have peaked [sic] the curiosity of a serious researcher.
   Here they much favour the tiorba [theorbo], the arclute [archlute], and the cittarone [chitarrone], while we at home must content ourselves with the lute alone.
   In Blaine's words, "All the vocal aristocracy showed up—Nat [Cole], Billy [Eckstine], Ella [Fitzgerald], Mabel Mercer— 'cause nobody wanted to miss that date."

2. Brackets enclose insertions that take the place of words or phrases.

   And on the next page: "Their assumption is plainly that [Durocher] would be the agent in any such negotiation."

3. Brackets enclose insertions that supply missing letters.

   A postscript to a December 17 letter to Waugh notes, "If D[eutsch] won't take the manuscript, perhaps someone at Faber will."

4. Brackets enclose insertions that alter the form of a word used in an original text.

> He dryly observes (p. 78) that the Gravely investors had bought stocks because "they want[ed] to see themselves getting richer."

5. Brackets are used to indicate that capitalization has been altered. This is generally optional; it is standard practice only where meticulous handling of original source material is crucial (particularly legal and scholarly contexts).

> As Chief Justice Warren held for the Court, "[T]he Attorney General may bring an injunctive action . . ."
> *or in general contexts*
> "The Attorney General may bring . . ."

Brackets also enclose editorial notes when text has been italicized for emphasis.

> But tucked away on page 11 we find this fascinating note: "In addition, we anticipate that *siting these new plants in marginal neighborhoods will decrease the risk of organized community opposition*" [italics added].

6. Brackets function as parentheses within parentheses, especially where two sets of parentheses could be confusing.

> Posner's recent essays (including the earlier *Law and Literature* [1988]) bear this out.

7. In mathematical copy, brackets are used with parentheses to indicate units contained within larger units. They are also used with various meanings in chemical names and formulas.

> $x + 5[(x + y)(2x - y)]$
> $Ag[Pt(NO_2)_4]$

With Other Punctuation

8. Punctuation that marks the end of a phrase, clause, item in a series, or sentence follows any bracketed material appended to that passage.

> The report stated, "if we fail to find additional sources of supply [of oil and gas], our long-term growth will be limited."

When brackets enclose a complete sentence, closing punctuation is placed within the brackets.

> [Since this article was written, new archival evidence of document falsification has come to light.]

Colon

The colon is usually a mark of introduction, indicating that what follows it—generally a clause, a phrase, or a list—has been pointed to or described in what precedes it. (For the use of capitals following a colon, see paragraphs 7–8 on page 192.)

With Phrases and Clauses

1. A colon introduces a clause or phrase that explains, illustrates, amplifies, or restates what has gone before.

> An umbrella is a foolish extravagance: if you don't leave it in the first restaurant, a gust of wind will destroy it on the way home.
> Dawn was breaking: the distant peaks were already glowing with the sun's first rays.

2. A colon introduces an appositive.

> The issue comes down to this: Will we offer a reduced curriculum, or will we simply cancel the program?
> That year Handley's old obsession was replaced with a new one: jazz.

3. A colon introduces a list or series, often following a phrase such as *the following* or *as follows*.

> She has trial experience on three judicial levels: county, state, and federal.
> Anyone planning to participate should be prepared to do the following: hike five miles with a backpack, sleep on the ground without a tent, and paddle a canoe through rough water.

It is occasionally used like a dash to introduce a summary statement following a series.

> Baseball, soccer, skiing, track: he excelled in every sport he took up.

4. Although the colon usually follows a full independent clause, it also often interrupts a sentence before the clause is complete.

> The nine proposed program topics are: offshore supply, vessel traffic, ferry services, ship repair, . . .
> Information on each participant includes: name, date of birth, mailing address, . . .
> For example: 58 percent of union members voted, but only 44 percent of blue-collar workers as a whole.
> The association will:
> Act with trust, integrity, and professionalism.
> Operate in an open and effective manner.
> Take the initiative in seeking diversity.

With Quotations

5. A colon usually introduces lengthy quoted material that is set off from the rest of a text by indentation but not by quotation marks.

> The *Rumpole* series has been nicely encapsulated as follows: Rumpled, disreputable, curmudgeonly barrister Horace Rumpole often wins cases despite the disdain of his more aristocratic colleagues. Fond of cheap wine ("Château Thames Embankment") and Keats's poetry, he refers to his wife as "She Who Must Be Obeyed" (an allusion to the title character of H. Rider Haggard's *She*).

6. A colon is often used before a quotation in running text, especially when (1) the quotation is lengthy, (2) the quotation is a formal statement or is being given special emphasis, or (3) a full independent clause precedes the colon.

> Said Murdoch: "The key to the success of this project is good planning. We need to know precisely what steps we will need to take, what kind of staff we will require, what the project will cost, and when we can expect completion."
> The inscription reads: "Here lies one whose name was writ in water."
> This was his verbatim response: "At this time Mr. Wilentz is still in the company's employ, and no change in his status is anticipated imminently."

Other Uses

7. A colon separates elements in bibliographic publication data and page references, in biblical citations, and in formulas used to express time and ratios. No space precedes or follows a colon between numerals.

Stendhal, *Love* (New York: Penguin, 1975)
Paleobiology 3:121
John 4:10
8:30 a.m.
a winning time of 3:43:02
a ration of 3:5

8. A colon separates titles and subtitles.

Southwest Stories: Tales from the Desert

9. A colon follows the salutation in formal correspondence.

Dear Judge Wright:
Dear Laurence:
Dear Product Manager:
Ladies and Gentlemen:

10. A colon follows headings in memorandums, government correspondence, and general business letters.

TO:
SUBJECT:
VIA:
REFERENCE:

11. An unspaced colon separates the writer's and typist's initials in the identification lines of business letters.

WAL:jml

A colon also separates copy abbreviations from the initials of copy recipients. (The abbreviation *cc* stands for *carbon* or *courtesy copy; bcc* stands for *blind carbon* or *courtesy copy*.) A space follows a colon used with the fuller name of a recipient.

cc:RSP
    JES
bcc:MWK
bcc: Mr. Jones

With Other Punctuation

12. A colon is placed outside quotation marks and parentheses that punctuate the larger sentence.

The problem becomes most acute in "Black Rose and Destroying Angel": plot simply ceases to exist.
Wilson and Hölldobler remark on the same phenomenon in *The Ants* (1990):

Comma

The comma is the most frequently used punctuation mark in English and the one that provides the most difficulties to writers. Its most common uses are to separate items in a series and to set off or distinguish grammatical elements within sentences.

Between Main Clauses

1. A comma separates main clauses joined by a coordinating conjunction, such as *and, but, or, nor,* or *so.*

She knew very little about the new system, and he volunteered nothing.
The trial lasted for nine months, but the jury took only four hours to reach its verdict.
We will not respond to any more questions on that topic this afternoon, nor will we respond to similar questions in the future.

All the first-floor windows were barred, so he had clambered up onto the fire escape.

2. When one or both of the clauses are short or closely related in meaning, the comma is often omitted.

They said good-bye and everyone hugged.

If commas set off another phrase that modifies the whole sentence, the comma between main clauses is often omitted.

Six thousand years ago, the top of the volcano blew off in a series of powerful eruptions and the sides collapsed into the middle.

3. Commas are sometimes used to separate short and obviously parallel main clauses that are not joined by conjunctions.

One day you're a successful corporate lawyer, the next day you're out of work.

Use of a comma to join clauses that are neither short nor obviously parallel, called *comma fault* or *comma splice,* is avoided. Clauses not joined by conjunctions are normally separated by semicolons. For details, see paragraph 1 on page 190.

4. If a sentence is composed of three or more clauses that are short and free of commas, the clauses are occasionally all separated by commas even if the last two are not joined by a conjunction. If the clauses are long or punctuated, they are separated with semicolons; the last two clauses are sometimes separated by a comma if they are joined by a conjunction. (For more details, see paragraph 5 on page 191.)

Small fish fed among the marsh weed, ducks paddled along the surface, an occasional muskrat ate greens along the bank.
The kids were tired and whiny; Napoleon, usually so calm, was edgy; Tabitha seemed to be going into heat, and even the guinea pigs were agitated.

With Compound Predicates

5. Commas are not normally used to separate the parts of a compound predicate.

The firefighter tried to enter the burning building but was turned back by the thick smoke.

However, they are often used if the predicate is long and complicated, if one part is being stressed, or if the absence of a comma could cause a momentary misreading.

The board helps to develop the financing and marketing strategies for new corporate divisions, and issues periodic reports on expenditures, revenues, and personnel appointments.
This is an unworkable plan, and has been from the start.
I try to explain to him what I want him to do, and get nowhere.

With Subordinate Clauses and Phrases

6. Adverbial clauses and phrases that begin a sentence are usually set off with commas.

Having made that decision, we turned our attention to other matters.
In order to receive a high school diploma, a student must earn 16 credits from public or private secondary schools.

In addition, staff members respond to queries, take new orders, and initiate billing.

If the sentence can be easily read without a comma, the comma may be omitted. The phrase will usually be short—four words or less—but even after a longer phrase the comma is often omitted.

> As cars age, they depreciate. *or* As cars age they depreciate.
>
> In January the firm will introduce a new line of investigative services.
>
> On the map the town appeared as a small dot in the midst of vast emptiness.
>
> If nobody comes forward by Friday I will have to take further steps.

7. Adverbial clauses and phrases that introduce a main clause other than the first main clause are usually set off with commas. If the clause or phrase follows a conjunction, one comma often precedes the conjunction and one follows the clause or phrase. Alternatively, one comma precedes the conjunction and two more enclose the clause or phrase, or a single comma precedes the conjunction. Short phrases, and phrases in short sentences, tend not to be enclosed in commas.

> They have redecorated the entire store, but[,] to the delight of their customers, it retains much of its original flavor.
>
> We haven't left Springfield yet, but when we get to Boston we'll call you.

8. A comma is not used after an introductory phrase if the phrase immediately precedes the main verb.

> From the next room came a loud expletive.

9. A subordinate clause or phrase that modifies a noun is not set off by commas if it is *restrictive* (or *essential*)—that is, if its removal would alter the noun's meaning.

> The man who wrote this obviously had no firsthand knowledge of the situation.
>
> They entered through the first door that wasn't locked.

If the meaning would not be altered by its removal, the clause or phrase is considered *nonrestrictive* (or *nonessential*) and usually is set off by commas.

> The new approach, which was based on team teaching, was well received.
>
> Wechsler, who has done solid reporting from other battlefronts, is simply out of his depth here.
>
> They tried the first door, which led nowhere.

10. Commas set off an adverbial clause or phrase that falls between the subject and the verb.

> The Clapsaddle sisters, to keep up appearances, rode to the park every Sunday in their rented carriage.

11. Commas set off modifying phrases that do not immediately precede the word or phrase they modify.

> Scarbo, intent as usual on his next meal, was snuffling around the butcher's bins.
>
> The negotiators, tired and discouraged, headed back to the hotel.
>
> We could see the importance, both long-term and short-term, of her proposal.

12. An absolute phrase (a participial phrase with its own subject that is grammatically independent of the rest of the sentence) is set off with commas.

Our business being concluded, we adjourned for refreshments.

We headed southward, the wind freshening behind us, to meet the rest of the fleet in the morning.

I'm afraid of his reaction, his temper being what it is.

With Appositives

13. Commas set off a word, phrase, or clause that is in apposition to (that is, equivalent to) a preceding or following noun and that is nonrestrictive.

> It sat nursing its front paw, the injured one.
>
> Aleister Crowley, Britain's most infamous satanist, is the subject of a remarkable new biography.
>
> A cherished landmark in the city, the Hotel Sandburg has managed once again to escape the wrecking ball.
>
> The committee cochairs were a lawyer, John Larson, and an educator, Mary Conway.

14. Restrictive appositives are not set off by commas.

> He next had a walk-on role in the movie *The Firm.*
>
> Longfellow's poem *Evangeline* was a favorite of my grandmother's.
>
> The committee cochairs were the lawyer John Larson and the educator Mary Conway.
>
> Lord Castlereagh was that strange anomaly[,] a Labor-voting peer.

With Introductory and Interrupting Elements

15. Commas set off transitional words and phrases.

> Indeed, close coordination will be essential.
>
> Defeat may be inevitable; however, disgrace is not.
>
> The second report, on the other hand, shows a strong bias.

When such words and phrases fall in the middle of a clause, commas are sometimes unnecessary.

> They thus have no chips left to bargain with.
>
> The materials had indeed arrived.
>
> She would in fact see them that afternoon.

16. Commas set off parenthetic elements, such as authorial asides.

> All of us, to tell the truth, were completely amazed.
>
> It was, I should add, not the first time I'd seen him in this condition.

17. Commas are often used to set off words or phrases that introduce examples or explanations, such as *namely, for example,* and *that is.*

> He expects to visit three countries, namely, France, Spain, and Germany.
>
> I would like to develop a good, workable plan, that is, one that would outline our goals and set a timetable for accomplishing them.

Such introductory words and phrases may also often be preceded by a dash, parenthesis, or semicolon. Regardless of the punctuation that precedes the word or phrase, a comma usually follows it.

> Sports develop two valuable traits—namely, self-control and the ability to make quick decisions.
>
> In writing to the manufacturer, be as specific as possible (i.e., list the missing or defective parts, describe the malfunction, and identify the store where the unit was purchased).
>
> Most had traveled great distances to participate; for example, three had come from Australia, one from Japan, and two from China.

18. Commas set off words in direct address.

> This is our third and final notice, Mr. Sutton.
> The facts, my fellow Americans, are very different.

19. Commas set off mild interjections or exclamations.

> Ah, the mosaics in Ravenna are matchless.
> Uh-oh, His Eminence seems to be on the warpath this morning.

With Contrasting Expressions

20. A comma is sometimes used to set off contrasting expressions within a sentence.

> This project will take six months, not six weeks.

21. When two or more contrasting modifiers or prepositions, one of which is introduced by a conjunction or adverb, apply to a noun that follows immediately, the second is set off by two commas or a single comma, or not set off at all.

> A solid, if overly wordy, assessment
> *or* a solid, if overly wordy assessment
> *or* a solid if overly wordy assessment
> This street takes you away from, not toward, the capitol.
> *or* This street takes you away from, not toward, the capitol.
> grounds for a civil, and maybe a criminal, case
> *or* grounds for a civil, and maybe a criminal case
> *or* grounds for a civil and maybe a criminal case

Dashes or parentheses are often used instead of commas in such sentences.

> grounds for a civil (and maybe a criminal) case

22. A comma does not usually separate elements that are contrasted through the use of a pair of correlative conjunctions such as *either . . . or, neither . . . nor,* and *not only . . . but also.*

> Neither my brother nor I noticed the error.
> He was given the post not only because of his diplomatic connections but also because of his great tact and charm.

When correlative conjunctions join main clauses, a comma usually separates the clauses unless they are short.

> Not only did she have to see three salesmen and a visiting reporter, but she also had to prepare for next day's meeting.
> Either you do it my way or we don't do it at all.

23. Long parallel contrasting and comparing clauses are separated by commas; short parallel phrases are not.

> The more that comes to light about him, the less savory he seems.
> The less said the better.

With Items in a Series

24. Words, phrases, and clauses joined in a series are separated by commas.

> Men, women, and children crowded aboard the train.
> Her job required her to pack quickly, to travel often, and to have no personal life.
> He responded patiently while reporters shouted questions, flashbulbs popped, and the crowd pushed closer.

When the last two items in a series are joined by a conjunction, the final comma is often omitted, especially where this would not result in ambiguity. In individual publications, the final comma is usually consistently used, consistently omitted, or used only where a given sentence would otherwise be ambiguous or hard to read. It is consistently used in most nonfiction books; elsewhere it tends to be used or generally omitted equally often.

> We are looking for a house with a big yard, a view of the harbor[,] and beach and docking privileges.

25. A comma is not generally used to separate items in a series all of which are joined with conjunctions.

> I don't understand what this policy covers or doesn't cover or only partially covers.
> They left behind the fogs and the wood storks and the lonesome soughing of the wind.

26. When the elements in a series are long or complex or consist of clauses that themselves contain commas, the elements are usually separated by semicolons, not commas. See paragraph 7 on page 191.

With Coordinate Modifiers

27. A comma is generally used to separate two or more adjectives, adverbs, or phrases that modify the same word or phrase.

> She spoke in a calm, reflective manner.
> They set to their work again grimly, intently.

The comma is often omitted when the adjectives are short.

> one long thin strand
> a small white stone
> little nervous giggles
> skinny young waiters
> in this harsh new light

The comma is generally omitted where it is ambiguous whether the last modifier and the noun—or two of the modifiers—constitute a unit.

> the story's stark dramatic power
> a pink stucco nightclub

In some writing, especially works of fiction, commas may be omitted from most series of coordinate modifiers as a matter of style.

28. A comma is not used between two adjectives when the first modifies the combination of the second plus the noun it modifies.

> the last good man
> a good used car
> his protruding lower lip
> the only fresh water
> the only freshwater lake
> their black pickup truck

A comma is also not used to separate an adverb from the adjective or adverb that it modifies.

> this formidably difficult task

In Quotations

29. A comma usually separates a direct quotation from a phrase identifying its source or speaker. If the quotation is a question or an exclamation and the identifying phrase follows the quotation, the comma is replaced by a question mark or an exclamation point.

She answered, "I'm afraid it's all we've got."
"The comedy is over," he muttered.
"How about another round?" Elaine piped up.
"I suspect," said Mrs. Horowitz, "we haven't seen the last of her."
"You can sink the lousy thing for all I care!" Trumbull shouted back.
"And yet . . . ," she mused.
"We can't get the door op—" Captain Hunt is heard shouting before the tape goes dead.

In some cases, a colon can replace a comma preceding a quotation; see paragraph 6 on page 178.

30. When short or fragmentary quotations are used in a sentence that is not primarily dialogue, they are usually not set off by commas.

He glad-handed his way through the small crowd with a "Looking good, Joe" or "How's the wife" for every beaming face.
Just because he said he was "about to leave this minute" doesn't mean he actually left.

Sentences that fall within sentences and do not constitute actual dialogue are not usually set off with commas. These may be mottoes or maxims, unspoken or imaginary dialogue, or sentences referred to as sentences; and they may or may not be enclosed in quotation marks. Where quotation marks are not used, a comma is often inserted to mark the beginning of the shorter sentence clearly. (For the use of quotation marks with such sentences, see paragraph 6 on page 189.)

"The computer is down" was the response she dreaded.
He spoke with a candor that seemed to insist, This actually happened to me and in just this way.
The first rule is, When in doubt, spell it out.

When the shorter sentence functions as an appositive (the equivalent to an adjacent noun), it is set off with commas when nonrestrictive and not when restrictive.

We had the association's motto, "We make waves," printed on our T-shirts.
He was fond of the slogan "Every man a king, but no man wears a crown."

31. A comma introduces a directly stated question, regardless of whether it is enclosed in quotation marks or if its first word is capitalized. It is not used to set off indirect discourse or indirect questions introduced by a conjunction (such as *that* or *what*).

I wondered, what is going on here?
The question is, How do we get out of this situation?
but
Margot replied quietly that she'd never been happier.
I wondered what was going on here.
The question is how do we get out of this situation.

32. The comma is usually omitted before quotations that are very short exclamations or representations of sounds.

He jumped up suddenly and cried "I've got it!"

Replacing Omitted Words

33. A comma may indicate the omission of a word or phrase in parallel constructions where the omitted word or phrase appears earlier in the sentence. In short sentences, the comma is usually omitted.

The larger towns were peopled primarily by shopkeepers, artisans, and traders; the small villages, by peasant farmers.
Seven voted for the proposal, three against.
He critiqued my presentation and I his.

34. A comma sometimes replaces the conjunction *that.*

The smoke was so thick, they were forced to crawl.
Chances are, there are still some tickets left.

With Addresses, Dates, and Numbers

35. Commas set off the elements of an address except for zip codes.

Write to Bureau of the Census, Washington, DC 20233.
In Needles, California, their luck ran out.

When a city name and state (province, country, etc.) name are used together to modify a noun that follows, the second comma may be omitted but is more often retained.

We visited their Enid, Oklahoma plant.
but more commonly
We visited their Enid, Oklahoma, plant.

36. Commas set off the year in a full date.

On July 26, 1992, the court issued its opinion.
Construction for the project began on April 30, 1995.

When only the month and year are given, the first comma is usually omitted.

In December 1903, the Wright brothers finally succeeded in keeping an airplane aloft for a few seconds.
October 1929 brought an end to all that.

37. A comma groups numerals into units of three to separate thousands, millions, and so on.

2,000 case histories
15,000 units
a population of 3,450,000
a fee of $12,500

Certain types of numbers do not contain commas, including decimal fractions, street addresses, and page numbers. (For more on the use of the comma with numbers, see paragraphs 1–3 on page 216.)

2.5544
12537 Wilshire Blvd.
page 1415

With Names, Degrees, and Titles

38. A comma separates a surname from a following professional, academic, honorary, or religious degree or title, or an abbreviation for a branch of the armed forces.

Amelia P. Artandi, M.D.
Robert Hynes Menard, Ph.D., L.H.D.
John L. Farber, Esq.
Sister Mary Catherine, S.C.
Admiral Herman Washington, USN

39. A comma is often used between a surname and the abbreviations *Jr.* and *Sr.*

Douglas Fairbanks, Sr. *or* Douglas Fairbanks Sr.
Dr. Martin Luther King, Jr. *or* Dr. Martin Luther King Jr.

40. A comma is often used to set off corporate identifiers such as *Incorporated, Inc., Ltd., P.C.,* and *L.P.* However, many company names omit this comma.

> StarStage Productions, Incorporated
> Hart International Inc.
> Walsh, Brandon & Kaiser, P.C.
> The sales manager from Doyle Southern, Inc., spoke at Tuesday's meeting.

Other Uses

41. A comma follows the salutation in informal correspondence and usually follows the complimentary close in both informal and formal correspondence.

> Dear Rachel,
> Affectionately,
> Very truly yours,

42. The comma is used to avoid ambiguity when the juxtaposition of two words or expressions could cause confusion.

> Under Mr. Thomas, Jefferson High School has flourished.
> He scanned the landscape that opened out before him, and guided the horse gently down.

43. When normal sentence order is inverted, a comma often precedes the subject and verb. If the structure is clear without it, it is often omitted.

> That we would succeed, no one doubted.
> And a splendid occasion it was.

With Other Punctuation

44. Commas are used next to brackets, ellipsis points, parentheses, and quotation marks. Commas are not used next to colons, dashes, exclamation points, question marks, or semicolons. If one of the latter falls at the same point where a comma would fall, the comma is dropped. (For more on the use of commas with other punctuation, see the sections for each individual mark.)

> "If they find new sources [of oil and gas], their earnings will obviously rebound. . . ."
> "This book takes its place among the most serious, . . . comprehensive, and enlightened treatments of its great subject."
> There are only six small files (at least in this format), which take up very little disk space.
> According to Hartmann, the people are "savage," their dwellings are "squalid," and the landscape is "a pestilential swamp."

Dash

The dash can function like a comma, a colon, or a parenthesis. Like commas and parentheses, dashes set off parenthetic material such as examples, supplemental facts, and explanatory or descriptive phrases. Like a colon, a dash introduces clauses that explain or expand upon something that precedes them. Though sometimes considered a less formal equivalent of the colon and parenthesis, the dash may be found in all kinds of writing, including the most formal, and the choice of which mark to use is often a matter of personal preference.

The common dash (also called the *em dash,* since it is approximately the width of a capital M in typeset material) is usually represented by two hyphens in typed and keyboarded material. (Word-processing programs make it available as a special character.)

Spacing around the dash varies. Most newspapers insert a space before and after the dash; many popular magazines do the same; but most books and journals omit spacing.

The *en dash* and the *two-* and *three-em dashes* have more limited uses, which are explained in paragraphs 13–15 on page 184.

Abrupt Change or Suspension

1. The dash marks an abrupt change or break in the structure of a sentence.

> The students seemed happy enough with the new plan, but the alumni—there was the problem.

2. A dash is used to indicate interrupted speech or a speaker's confusion or hesitation.

> "The next point I'd like to bring up—" the speaker started to say.
> "Yes," he went on, "yes—that is—I guess I agree."

Parenthetic and Amplifying Elements

3. Dashes are used in place of commas or parentheses to emphasize or draw attention to parenthetic or amplifying material.

> With three expert witnesses in agreement, the defense can be expected to modify its strategy—somewhat.
> This amendment will finally prevent corporations—large and small—from buying influence through exorbitant campaign contributions.

When dashes are used to set off parenthetic elements, they often indicate that the material is more digressive than elements set off with commas but less digressive than elements set off by parentheses. For examples, see paragraph 16 on page 180 and paragraph 1 on page 186.

4. Dashes set off or introduce defining phrases and lists.

> The fund sought to acquire controlling positions—a minimum of 25% of outstanding voting securities—in other companies.
> Davis was a leading innovator in at least three styles—bebop, cool jazz, and jazz-rock fusion.

5. A dash is often used in place of a colon or semicolon to link clauses, especially when the clause that follows the dash explains, summarizes, or expands upon the preceding clause in a somewhat dramatic way.

> The results were in—it had been a triumphant success.

6. A dash or a pair of dashes often sets off illustrative or amplifying material introduced by such phrases as *for example, namely,* and *that is,* when the break in continuity is greater than that shown by a comma, or when the dash would clarify the sentence structure better than a comma. (For more details, see paragraph 17 on page 180.)

> After some discussion the motion was tabled—that is, it was removed indefinitely from the board's consideration.
> Lawyers should generally—in pleadings, for example—attempt to be as specific as possible.

7. A dash may introduce a summary statement that follows a series of words or phrases.

> Crafts, food booths, children's activities, cider-making demonstrations—there was something for everyone.
>
> Once into bankruptcy, the company would have to pay cash for its supplies, defer maintenance, and lay off workers—moves that could threaten its future.

8. A dash often precedes the name of an author or source at the end of a quoted passage—such as an epigraph, extract, or book or film blurb—that is not part of the main text. The attribution may appear immediately after the quotation or on the next line.

> Only the sign is for sale.
> —Søren Kierkegaard
>
> "I return to her stories with more pleasure, and await them with more anticipation, than those of any of her contemporaries."—William Logan, *Chicago Tribune*

With Other Punctuation

9. If a dash appears at a point where a comma could also appear, the comma is omitted.

> Our lawyer has read the transcript—all 1,200 pages of it—and he has decided that an appeal would not be useful.
>
> If we don't succeed—and the critics say we won't—then the whole project is in jeopardy.

In a series, dashes that would force a comma to be dropped are often replaced by parentheses.

> The holiday movie crowds were being entertained by street performers: break dancers, a juggler (who doubled as a sword swallower), a steel-drummer, even a three-card-monte dealer.

10. If the second of a pair of dashes would fall where a period should also appear, the dash is omitted.

> Instead, he hired his mother—an odd choice by any standard.

Much less frequently, the second dash will be dropped in favor of a colon or semicolon.

> Valley Health announced general improvements to its practice—two to start this week: evening office hours and a voice-mail message system.
>
> His conduct has always been exemplary—near-perfect attendance, excellent productivity, a good attitude; nevertheless, his termination cannot be avoided.

11. When a pair of dashes sets off material ending with an exclamation point or a question mark, the mark is placed inside the dashes.

> His hobby was getting on people's nerves—especially mine!—and he was extremely good at it.
>
> There would be a "distinguished guest speaker"—was there ever any other kind?—and plenty of wine afterwards.

12. Dashes are used inside parentheses, and vice versa, to indicate parenthetic material within parenthetic material. The second dash is omitted if it would immediately precede the closing parenthesis; a closing parenthesis is never omitted.

> We were looking for a narrator (or narrators—sometimes a script call for more than one) who could handle a variety of assignments.

The wall of the Old City contains several gates—particularly Herod's Gate, the Golden Gate, and Zion Gate (or "David's Gate")—with rich histories.

En Dash and Long Dashes

13. The *en dash* generally appears only in typeset material; in typed or keyboarded material the simple hyphen is usually used instead. (Word-processing programs provide the en dash as a special character.) Newspapers similarly use the hyphen in place of the en dash. The en dash is shorter than the em dash but longer than the hyphen. It is most frequently used between numbers, dates, or other notations to signify "(up) to and including."

> pages 128–34
> 1995–97
> September 24–October 5
> 8:30 a.m.–4:30 p.m.

The en dash replaces a hyphen in compound adjectives when at least one of the elements is a two-word compound. It replaces the word *to* between capitalized names, and is used to indicate linkages such as boundaries, treaties, and oppositions.

> post–Cold War era
> Boston–Washington train
> New Jersey–Pennsylvania border
> male–female differences   *or*   male-female differences

14. A *two-em dash* is used to indicate missing letters in a word and, less frequently, to indicate a missing word.

> The nearly illegible letter is addressed to a Mr. P—— of Baltimore.

15. A *three-em dash* indicates that a word has been left out or that an unknown word or figure is to be supplied.

> The study was carried out in ———, a fast-growing Sunbelt city.

Ellipsis Points

Ellipsis points (also known as *ellipses, points of ellipsis,* and *suspension points*) are periods, usually in groups of three, that signal an omission from quoted material or indicate a pause or trailing off of speech. A space usually precedes and follows each ellipsis point. (In newspaper style, spaces are usually omitted.)

1. Ellipsis points indicate the omission of one or more words within a quoted sentence.

> We the People of the United States . . . do ordain and establish this Constitution for the United States of America.

2. Ellipsis points are usually not used to indicate the omission of words that precede the quoted portion. However, in some formal contexts, especially when the quotation is introduced by a colon, ellipsis points are used.

> He ends with a stirring call for national resolve that "government of the people, by the people, for the people shall not perish from the earth."
>
> Its final words define the war's purpose in democratic terms: ". . . that government of the people, by the people, for the people shall not perish from the earth."

Ellipsis points following quoted material are omitted when it forms an integral part of a larger sentence.

> She maintained that it was inconsistent with "government of the people, by the people, for the people."

3. Punctuation used in the original that falls on either side of the ellipsis points is often omitted; however, it may be retained, especially if this helps clarify the sentence.

> Now we are engaged in a great civil war testing whether that nation . . . can long endure.
>
> But, in a larger sense, we can not dedicate, . . . we can not hallow this ground.
>
> We the People of the United States, in Order to . . . promote the general Welfare, and secure the Blessings of Liberty . . . , do ordain and establish this Constitution for the United States of America.

4. If an omission includes an entire sentence within a passage, the last part of a sentence within a passage, or the first part of a sentence other than the first quoted sentence, the period preceding or following the omission is retained (with no space preceding it) and is followed by three ellipsis points. When the first part of a sentence is omitted but the quoted portion acts as a sentence, the first quoted word is usually capitalized.

> We have come to dedicate a portion of that field, as a final resting place for those who here gave their lives that this nation might live. . . . But, in a larger sense, we can not dedicate—we can not consecrate—we can not hallow—this ground.
>
> Now we are engaged in a great civil war. . . . We are met on a great battlefield of that war.
>
> The brave men, living and dead, who struggled here, have consecrated it, far above our poor power to add or detract. . . . From these honored dead we take increased devotion to that cause for which they gave the last full measure of devotion. . . .

Alternatively, the period may be dropped and all omissions may be indicated simply by three ellipsis points.

5. If the last words of a quoted sentence are omitted and the original sentence ends with punctuation other than a period, the end punctuation often follows the ellipsis points, especially if it helps clarify the quotation.

> He always ends his harangues with some variation on the question, "What could you have been thinking when you . . . ?"

6. When ellipsis points are used to indicate that a quotation has been intentionally left unfinished, the terminal period is omitted.

> The paragraph beginning "Recent developments suggest . . . " should be deleted.

7. A line of ellipsis points indicates that one or more lines have been omitted from a poem.

> When I heard the learned astronomer,
> . . . .
> How soon unaccountable I became tired and sick,
> Til rising and gliding out I wandered off by myself,
> In the mystical moist night-air, and from time to time,
> Looked up in perfect silence at the stars.

8. Ellipsis points are used to indicate faltering speech, especially if the faltering involves a long pause or a sentence that trails off or is intentionally left unfinished. Generally no other terminal punctuation is used.

> The speaker seemed uncertain. "Well, that's true . . . but even so . . . I think we can do better."
>
> "Despite these uncertainties, we believe we can do it, but . . ."
>
> "I mean . . ." he said, "like . . . How?"

9. Ellipsis points are sometimes used informally as a stylistic device to catch a reader's attention, often replacing a dash or colon.

> They think that nothing can go wrong . . . but it does.

10. In newspaper and magazine columns consisting of social notes, local events listings, or short items of celebrity news, ellipsis points often take the place of paragraphing to separate the items. (Ellipsis points are also often used in informal personal correspondence in place of periods or paragraphing.)

> Congratulations to Debra Morricone, our up-and-coming singing star, for her full scholarship to the Juilliard School this fall! . . . And kudos to Paul Chartier for his winning All-State trumpet performance last Friday in Baltimore! . . . Look for wit and sparkling melody when the Lions mount their annual Gilbert & Sullivan show at Syms Auditorium. This year it's . . .

Exclamation Point

The exclamation point is used to mark a forceful comment or exclamation.

1. An exclamation point can punctuate a sentence, phrase, or interjection.

> There is no alternative!
> Without a trace!
> My God! It's monstrous!

2. The exclamation point may replace the question mark when an ironic, angry, or emphatic tone is more important than the actual question.

> Aren't you finished yet!
> Do you realize what you've done!
> Why me!

Occasionally it is used *with* the question mark to indicate a very forceful question.

> How much did you say?!
> You did what!?

3. The exclamation point falls within brackets, dashes, parentheses, and quotation marks when it punctuates only the enclosed material. It is placed outside them when it punctuates the entire sentence.

> All of this proves—at long last!—that we were right from the start.
>
> Somehow the dog got the gate open (for the third time!) and ran into the street.
>
> He sprang to his feet and shouted "Point of order!"
>
> At this rate the national anthem will soon be replaced by "You Are My Sunshine"!

4. If an exclamation point falls where a comma could also go, the comma is dropped.

> "Absolutely not!" he snapped.
> They wouldn't dare! she told herself over and over.

If the exclamation point is part of a title, it may be followed by a comma. If the title falls at the end of a sentence, no period follows it.

> *Hello Dolly!,* which opened in 1964, would become one of the ten longest-running shows in Broadway history.
> His favorite management book is still *Up the Organization!*

Hyphen

Hyphens have a variety of uses, the most significant of which is to join the elements of compound nouns and modifiers.

1. Hyphens are used to link elements in compound words. (For more on compound words, see the section beginning on page 204.)

> secretary-treasurer
> cost-effective
> fund-raiser
> spin-off

2. In some words, a hyphen separates a prefix, suffix, or medial element from the rest of the word. Consult a dictionary in doubtful cases. (For details on using a hyphen with a prefix or a suffix, see the section beginning on page 208.)

> anti-inflation
> umbrella-like
> jack-o'-lantern

3. In typed and keyboarded material, a hyphen is generally used between numbers and dates with the meaning "(up) to and including." In typeset material it is replaced by an en dash. (For details on the en dash, see paragraph 13 on page 184.)

> pages 128–34
> the years 1995–97

4. A hyphen marks an end-of-line division of a word.

> In 1975 smallpox, formerly a great scourge, was declared totally eradicated by the World Health Organization.

5. A hyphen divides letters or syllables to give the effect of stuttering, sobbing, or halting speech.

> "S-s-sammy, it's my t-toy!"

6. Hyphens indicate a word spelled out letter by letter.

> l-i-a-i-s-o-n

7. Hyphens are sometimes used to produce inflected forms of verbs made of individually pronounced letters or to add an *-er* ending to an abbreviation. However, apostrophes are more commonly used for these purposes. (For details on these uses of the apostrophe, see paragraph 6 on page 177.)

> DH-ing for the White Sox   *or*   DH'ing for the White Sox
> a dedicated UFO-er   *or*   a dedicated UFO'er

Parentheses

Parentheses generally enclose material that is inserted into a main statement but is not intended to be an essential part of it. For some of the cases described below, commas or dashes are frequently used instead. (For examples, see paragraph 16 on page 180 and paragraph 3 on page 183.) Parentheses are particularly used when the inserted material is only incidental. Unlike commas and dashes, an opening parenthesis is always followed by a closing one. Because parentheses are almost always used in pairs, and their shapes indicate their relative functions, they often clarify a sentence's structure better than commas or dashes.

Parenthetic Elements

1. Parentheses enclose phrases and clauses that provide examples, explanations, or supplementary facts or numerical data.

> Nominations for principal officers (president, vice president, treasurer, and secretary) were heard and approved.
> Four computers (all outdated models) will be replaced.
> First-quarter sales figures were good (up 8%), but total revenues showed a slight decline (down 1%).

2. Parentheses sometimes enclose phrases and clauses introduced by expressions such as *namely, that is, e.g.,* and *i.e.,* particularly where parentheses would clarify the sentence's structure better than commas. (For more details, see paragraph 17 on page 180.)

> In writing to the manufacturer, be as specific as possible (i.e., list the defective parts, describe the malfunction, and identify the store where the unit was purchased), but also as concise.

3. Parentheses enclose definitions or translations in the main part of a sentence.

> The company announced plans to sell off its housewares (small-appliances) business.
> The *grand monde* (literally, "great world") of prewar Parisian society consisted largely of titled aristocracy.

4. Parentheses enclose abbreviations that follow their spelled-out forms, or spelled-out forms that follow abbreviations.

> She cited a study by the Food and Drug Administration (FDA).
> They attended last year's convention of the ABA (American Booksellers Association).

5. Parentheses often enclose cross-references and bibliographic references.

> Specialized services are also available (see list of stores at end of brochure).
> The diagram (Fig. 3) illustrates the action of the pump.
> Subsequent studies (Braxton 1990; Roh and Weinglass 1993) have confirmed these findings.

6. Parentheses enclose numerals that confirm a spelled-out number in a business or legal context.

> Delivery will be made in thirty (30) days.
> The fee is Four Thousand Dollars ($4,000), payable to UNCO, Inc.

7. Parentheses enclose the name of a state that is inserted into a proper name for identification.

the Kalispell (Mont.) Regional Hospital
the *Sacramento* (Calif.) *Bee*

8. Parentheses may be used to enclose personal asides.

> Claims were made of its proven efficacy (some of us were skeptical).
> *or*
> Claims were made of its proven efficacy. (Some of us were skeptical.)

9. Parentheses are used to enclose quotations that illustrate or support a statement made in the main text.

> After he had a few brushes with the police, his stepfather had him sent to jail as an incorrigible ("It will do him good").

Other Uses

10. Parentheses enclose unpunctuated numbers or letters indicating individual elements or items in a series within a sentence.

> Sentences can be classified as (1) simple, (2) multiple or compound, and (3) complex.

11. Parentheses indicate alternative terms.

> Please sign and return the enclosed form(s).

12. Parentheses may be used to indicate losses in accounting.

> <table><tr><td colspan="2">Operating Profits
(in millions)</td></tr><tr><td>Cosmetics . . . .</td><td>26.2</td></tr><tr><td>Food products . . . . .</td><td>47.7</td></tr><tr><td>Food services . . . . . .</td><td>54.3</td></tr><tr><td>Transportation . . . .</td><td>(17.7)</td></tr><tr><td>Sporting goods . . . .</td><td>(11.2)</td></tr><tr><td>Total . . . .</td><td>99.3</td></tr></table>

With Other Punctuation

13. When an independent sentence is enclosed in parentheses, its first word is capitalized and a period (or other closing punctuation) is placed inside the parentheses.

> The discussion was held in the boardroom. (The results are still confidential.)

A parenthetic expression that occurs within a sentence—even if it could stand alone as a separate sentence—does not end with a period but may end with an exclamation point, a question mark, or quotation marks.

> Although several trade organizations opposed the legislation (there were at least three paid lobbyists working on Capitol Hill), the bill passed easily.
> The conference was held in Portland (Me., not Ore.).
> After waiting in line for an hour (why do we do these things?), we finally left.

A parenthetic expression within a sentence does not require capitalization unless it is a quoted sentence.

> He was totally confused ("What can we do?") and refused to see anyone.

14. If a parenthetic expression within a sentence is composed of two independent clauses, a semicolon rather than a period usually separates them. Independent sentences enclosed together in parentheses employ normal sentence capitalization and punctuation.

> We visited several showrooms, looked at the prices (it wasn't a pleasant experience; prices in this area have not gone down), and asked all the questions we could think of.
> We visited several showrooms and looked at the prices. (It wasn't a pleasant experience. Prices in this area have not gone down.)

Entire paragraphs are rarely enclosed in parentheses; instead, paragraphs of incidental material often appear as footnotes or endnotes.

15. No punctuation (other than a period after an abbreviation) is placed immediately before an opening parenthesis within a sentence; if punctuation is required, it follows the final parenthesis.

> I'll get back to you tomorrow (Friday), when I have more details.
> Tickets cost $14 in advance ($12 for seniors); the price at the door is $18.
> The relevant figures are shown below (in millions of dollars):

16. Parentheses sometimes appear within parentheses when no confusion would result; alternatively, the inner parentheses are replaced with brackets.

> Checks must be drawn in U.S. dollars. (*Please note:* We cannot accept checks drawn on Canadian banks for amounts less than four U.S. dollars ($4.00). The same regulation applies to Canadian money orders.)

17. Dashes and parentheses may be used together to set off parenthetic material. (For details, see paragraph 12 on page 184.)

> The orchestra is spirited, and the cast—an expert and enthusiastic crew of Savoyards (some of them British imports)—comes through famously.

Period

Periods almost always serve to mark the end of a sentence or abbreviation.

1. A period ends a sentence or a sentence fragment that is neither a question nor an exclamation.

> From the Format menu, choose Style.
> Robert decided to bring champagne.
> Unlikely. In fact, inconceivable.

Only one period ends a sentence.

> The jellied gasoline was traced to the Trenton-based Quality Products, Inc.
> Miss Toklas states categorically that "This is the best way to cook frogs' legs."

2. A period punctuates some abbreviations. No space follows an internal period within an abbreviation. (For details on punctuating abbreviations, see the section beginning on page 210.)

> | | |
> |---|---|
> | Assn. | e.g. |
> | Ph.D. | p.m. |
> | Dr. | etc. |

3. Periods are used with a person's initials, each followed by a space. (Newspaper style omits the space.) If the initials replace the name, they are unspaced and may also be written without periods.

J. B. S. Haldane
L.B.J. *or* LBJ

4. A period follows numerals and letters when they are used without parentheses in outlines and vertical lists.

    I. Objectives
      A. Economy
        1. Low initial cost
        2. Low maintenance cost
      B. Ease of operation
    Required skills are:
      1. Shorthand
      2. Typing
      3. Transcription

5. A period is placed within quotation marks, even when it did not punctuate the original quoted material. (In British practice, the period goes outside the quotation marks whenever it does not belong to the original quoted material.)

> The founder was known to his employees as "the old man."
> "I said I wanted to fire him," Henry went on, "but she said, 'I don't think you have the contractual privilege to do that.'"

6. When brackets or parentheses enclose an independent sentence, the period is placed inside them. When brackets or parentheses enclose a sentence that is part of a larger sentence, the period for the enclosed sentence is omitted.

> Arturo finally arrived on the 23rd with the terrible news that Katrina had been detained by the police. [This later proved to be false; see letter 255.]
> I took a good look at her (she was standing quite close to me).

Question Mark

The question mark always indicates a question or doubt.

1. A question mark ends a direct question.

> What went wrong?
> "When do they arrive?" she asked.

A question mark follows a period only when the period punctuates an abbreviation. No period follows a question mark.

> Is he even an M.D.?
> "Will you arrive by 10 p.m.?"
> A local professor would be giving a paper with the title "Economic Stagnation or Equilibrium?"

2. Polite requests that are worded as questions usually take periods, because they are not really questions. Conversely, a sentence that is intended as a question but whose word order is that of a statement is punctuated with a question mark.

> Could you please send the necessary forms.
> They flew in yesterday?

3. The question mark ends a question that forms part of a sentence. An indirect question is not followed by a question mark.

> What was her motive? you may be asking.
> I naturally wondered, Will it really work?
> I naturally wondered whether it would really work.
> He asked when the report was due.

4. The question mark punctuates each element of a series of questions that share a single beginning and are neither numbered nor lettered. When the series is numbered or lettered, only one question mark is generally used.

> Can you give us a reasonable forecast? Back up your predictions? Compare them with last year's earnings?
> Can you (1) give us a reasonable forecast, (2) back up your predictions, and (3) compare them with last year's earnings?

5. The question mark indicates uncertainty about a fact or the accuracy of a transcription.

> Homer, Greek epic poet (9th–8th? cent. B.C.)
> He would have it that Farjeon[?] is the onlie man for us.

6. The question mark is placed inside brackets, dashes, parentheses, or quotation marks when it punctuates only the material enclosed by them and not the sentence as a whole. It is placed outside them when it punctuates the entire sentence.

> I took a vacation in 1992 (was it really that long ago?), but I haven't had time for one since.
> What did Andrew mean when he called the project "a fiasco from the start"?
> Williams then asks, "Do you realize the extent of the problem [the housing shortage]?"

Quotation Marks

The following paragraphs describe the use of quotation marks to enclose quoted matter in regular text, and for other, less frequent uses. For the use of quotation marks to enclose titles, see paragraph 70 on page 199.

Basic Uses

1. Quotation marks enclose direct quotations but not indirect quotations or paraphrases.

> Dr. Mee added, "We'd be grateful for anything you could do."
> "We just got the lab results," he crowed, "and the blood types match!"
> "I'm leaving," she whispered. "This meeting could go on forever."
> "Mom, we *tried* that already!" they whined in unison.
> "Ssshh!" she hissed.
> She said she was leaving.
> Algren once said something like, Don't ever play poker with anyone named Doc, and never eat at a diner called Mom's.

2. Quotation marks enclose fragments of quoted matter.

> The agreement makes it clear that he "will be paid only upon receipt of an acceptable manuscript."
> As late as 1754, documents refer to him as "yeoman" and "husbandman."

3. Quotation marks enclose words or phrases borrowed from others, and words of obvious informality introduced into formal writing. Words introduced as specialized terminology are sometimes enclosed in quotation marks but more often italicized.

> Be sure to send a copy of your résumé—or as some folks would say, your "biodata summary."
> They were afraid the patient had "stroked out"—had had a cerebrovascular accident.

referred to as "closed" or "privately held" corporations
but more frequently
referred to as *closed* or *privately held* corporations
New Hampshire's only "green" B&B

4. Quotation marks are sometimes used to enclose words referred to as words. Italics are also frequently used for this purpose.

> changed every "he" to "she"
> *or*
> changed every *he* to *she*

5. Quotation marks may enclose representations of sounds, though these are also frequently italicized.

> If it sounds like "quank, quank" [*or* like *quank, quank*], it may be the green treefrog.

6. Quotation marks often enclose short sentences that fall within longer sentences, especially when the shorter sentence is meant to suggest spoken dialogue. Mottoes and maxims, unspoken or imaginary dialogue, and sentences referred to as sentences may all be treated in this way.

> On the gate was the inscription "Arbeit macht frei" [or *Arbeit macht frei*]—"Work will make you free."
> The fact was, the poor kid didn't know "C'mere" from "Sic 'em."
> In effect, the voters were saying "You blew it, and you don't get another chance."
> Their reaction could only be described as "Kill the messenger."
> She never got used to their "That's the way it goes" attitude.
> *or*
> She never got used to their that's-the-way-it-goes attitude.

Quotation marks are often omitted in sentences of this kind when the structure is clear without them. (For the use of commas in such sentences, see paragraphs 29–30 on page 181.)

> The first rule is, When in doubt, spell it out.

7. Direct questions are enclosed in quotation marks when they represent quoted dialogue, but usually not otherwise.

> She asked, "What went wrong?"
> The question is, What went wrong?
> We couldn't help wondering, Where's the plan?
> *or*
> We couldn't help wondering, "Where's the plan?"

8. Quotation marks enclose translations of foreign or borrowed terms.

> This is followed by the Dies Irae ("Day of Wrath"), a climactic movement in many settings of the Requiem.
> The term comes from the Latin *sesquipedalis,* meaning "a foot and a half long."

They also frequently enclose definitions.

> *Concupiscent* simply means "lustful."
> *or*
> *Concupiscent* simply means lustful.

9. Quotation marks sometimes enclose letters referred to as letters.

> The letter "m" is wider than the letter "i."
> Put an "x" in the right spot.

However, such letters are more frequently italicized (or underlined), or left undifferentiated from the surrounding text where no confusion would result.

> How many *e*'s are in her name?
> a V-shaped blade
> He was happy to get a B in the course.

With Longer Quotations

10. Quotation marks are not used with longer passages of prose or poetry that are indented as separate paragraphs, called *extracts* or *block quotations*. Quoted text is usually set as an extract when it is longer than a sentence or runs to at least four lines, but individual requirements of consistency, clarity, or emphasis may alter these limits. Extracts are set off from the normal text by (1) indenting the passage on the left, and often on the right as well, and (2) usually setting it in smaller type. Extracts are usually preceded by a sentence ending with a colon, and they usually begin with a capitalized first word. The first line of an extract has no added indention; however, if the extract consists of more than one paragraph, the subsequent paragraphs are indented. (For the use of ellipsis points to show omissions within extracts, see the section beginning on page 184.)

> The chapter begins with a general description of memos:
>> The interoffice memorandum or memo is a means of informal communication within a firm or organization. It replaces the salutation, complimentary close, and written signature of the letter with identifying headings.

If the extract continues the flow of an incomplete sentence, no punctuation is required and the extract begins with a lowercase letter.

> They describe the memo as
>> a means of informal communication within a firm or organization. It replaces the salutation, complimentary close, and written signature of the letter with identifying headings.

If the sentence preceding the extract does not refer directly to it, the sentence usually ends with a period, though a colon is also common.

> As of the end of April she believed that the product stood a good chance of success.
>> Unit sales are strong, revenues are better than forecast, shipments are being made on schedule, and inventory levels are stable.

11. When an extract itself includes quoted material, double quotation marks enclose the material.

> The authors recommend the following procedure:
>> The presiding officer will call for the appropriate report from an officer, board member, standing committee, or special committee by saying, "Will the chairperson of the Ways and Means Committee please present the committee's report?"

12. When poetry is set as an extract, the lines are divided exactly as in the original. A spaced slash separates lines of run-in poetry.

> The experience reminded them of Pope's observation:
>> A little learning is a dang'rous thing;
>> Drink deep, or taste not the Pierian spring:
>> There shallow draughts intoxicate the brain,
>> And drinking largely sobers us again.
>
> When Gerard Manley Hopkins wrote that "Nothing is so beautiful as spring— / When weeds, in wheels, shoot long and lovely and lush," he probably had my yard in mind.

13. Quotation marks are not used with epigraphs. However, they are generally used with advertising blurbs.

> The whole of science is nothing more than a refinement of everyday thinking.
> —Albert Einstein

> "A brutal irony, a slam-bang humor and a style of writing as balefully direct as a death sentence."—*Time*

With Other Punctuation

14. When a period or comma follows text enclosed in quotation marks, it is placed within the quotation marks, even if the original language quoted was not followed by a period or comma.

> He smiled and said, "I'm happy for you."
> But perhaps Pound's most perfect poem was "The Return."
> The cameras were described as "waterproof," but "moisture-resistant" would have been a better description.

In British usage, the period or comma goes outside the quoted matter whenever the original text did not include the punctuation.

15. When a colon or semicolon follows text enclosed in quotation marks, the colon or semicolon is placed outside the quotation marks.

> But they all chimed in on "O Sole Mio": raw adolescents, stately matrons, decrepit old pensioners, their voices soaring in passion together.
> She spoke of her "little cottage in the country"; she might better have called it a mansion.

16. The dash, question mark, and exclamation point are placed inside quotation marks when they punctuate the quoted matter only, but outside the quotation marks when they punctuate the whole sentence.

> "I can't see how—" he started to say.
> He thought he knew where he was going—he remembered her saying, "Take two lefts, then stay to the right"—but the streets didn't look familiar.
> He asked, "When did they leave?"
> What is the meaning of "the open door"?
> She collapsed in her seat with a stunned "Good God!"
> Save us from his "mercy"!

Single Quotation Marks

17. Single quotation marks replace double quotation marks when the quoted material occurs within quoted material.

> The witness said, "I distinctly heard him say, 'Don't be late,' and then I heard the door close."
> "We'd like to close tonight with that great Harold Arlen wee-hours standard, 'One for My Baby.'"
> This analysis is indebted to Del Banco's "Elizabeth Bishop's 'Insomnia': An Inverted View."

When both single and double quotation marks occur at the end of a sentence, the period falls within both sets of marks.

> The witness said, "I distinctly heard him say, 'Don't be late.'"

British usage often reverses American usage, enclosing quoted material in single quotation marks, and enclosing quotations within quotations in double quotation marks. In British usage, commas and periods following quoted material go inside only those quotation marks that enclose material that originally included the period or comma.

18. A quotation within a quotation within a quotation is usually enclosed in double quotation marks. (Such constructions are usually avoided by rewriting.)

> As the *Post* reported it, "Van Houten's voice can be clearly heard saying, 'She said "You wouldn't dare" and I said "I just did."'"
> *or*
> The *Post* reported that Van Houten's voice was clearly heard saying, "She said 'You wouldn't dare' and I said 'I just did.'"

Semicolon

The semicolon may be used much like the comma, period, or colon, depending on the context. Like a comma, it may separate elements in a series. Like a period or colon, it frequently marks the end of a complete clause, and like a colon it signals that the remainder of the sentence is closely related to the first part. However, in each case the semicolon is normally used in a distinctive way. It serves as a higher-level comma; it connects clauses, as a period does not; and it does not imply any following exemplification, amplification, or description, as a colon generally does.

Between Clauses

1. A semicolon separates related independent clauses joined without a coordinating conjunction.

> Cream the shortening and sugar; add the eggs and beat well.
> The river rose and overflowed its banks; roads became flooded and impassable; freshly plowed fields disappeared from sight.

2. A semicolon often replaces a comma between two clauses joined by a coordinating conjunction if the sentence might otherwise be confusing—for example, because of particularly long clauses or the presence of other commas.

> In a society that seeks to promote social goals, government will play a powerful role; and taxation, once simply a means of raising money, becomes, in addition, a way of furthering those goals.

3. A semicolon joins two clauses when the second includes a conjunctive adverb such as *accordingly, however, indeed,* or *thus,* or a phrase that acts like a conjunctive adverb such as *in that case, as a result,* or *on the other hand.*

> Most people are covered by insurance of some kind; indeed, many don't even see their medical bills.
> It won't be easy to sort out the facts; a decision must be made, however.
> The case could take years to work its way through the courts; as a result, many plaintiffs will accept settlements.

When *so* and *yet* are treated as conjunctive adverbs, they are often preceded by a semicolon and followed by a comma. When treated as coordinating conjunctions, as they usually are, they are generally only preceded by a comma.

> The new recruits were bright, diligent, and even enthusiastic; yet[,] the same problems persisted.
> His grades improved sharply, yet the high honor roll still eluded him.

4. A semicolon may join two statements when the second clause is elliptical, omitting essential words that are supplied by the first. In short sentences, a comma often replaces the semicolon.

> The conference sessions, designed to allow for full discussions, were much too long; the breaks between them, much too short.
> The aged Scotch was haunting, the Asiago piquant.

5. When a series of clauses are separated by semicolons and a coordinating conjunction precedes the final clause, the final semicolon is sometimes replaced with a comma.

> The bars had all closed hours ago; a couple of coffee shops were open but deserted[; *or* ,] and only a few lighted upper-story windows gave evidence of other victims of insomnia.

6. A semicolon is often used before introductory expressions such as *for example, that is,* and *namely,* in place of a colon, comma, dash, or parenthesis. (For more details, see paragraph 17 on page 180.)

> On one point only did everyone agree; namely, too much money had been spent already.
> We were fairly successful on that project; that is, we made our deadlines and met our budget.

In a Series

7. A semicolon is used in place of a comma to separate phrases or items in a series when the phrases or items themselves contain commas. A comma may replace the semicolon before a conjunction that precedes the last item in a series.

> The assets in question include $22 million in land, buildings, and equipment; $34 million in cash, investments, and accounts receivable; and $8 million in inventory.
> The votes against were: Precinct 1, 418; Precinct 2, 332; Precinct 3, 256.
> The debate about the nature of syntactic variation continues to this day (Labov 1991; Dines 1991, 1993; Romaine 1995).
> The Pissarro exhibition will travel to Washington, D.C.; Manchester, N.H.; Portland, Ore., and Oakland, Calif.

When the items in a series are long or are sentences themselves, they are usually separated by semicolons even if they lack internal commas.

> Among the committee's recommendations were the following: more hospital beds in urban areas where there are waiting lines for elective surgery; smaller staff size in half-empty rural hospitals; and review procedures for all major purchases.

With Other Punctuation

8. A semicolon that punctuates the larger sentence is placed outside quotation marks and parentheses.

> I heard the senator on yesterday's "All Things Considered"; his views on Medicare are encouraging.
> She found him urbane and entertaining (if somewhat overbearing); he found her charmingly ingenuous.

Slash

The slash (also known as the *virgule, diagonal, solidus, oblique,* and *slant*) is most commonly used in place of a short word or a hyphen or en dash, or to separate numbers or text elements. There is generally no space on either side of the slash.

1. A slash represents the words *per* or *to* when used between units of measure or the terms of a ratio.

> 40,000 tons/year
> 29 mi/gal
> price/earnings ratio   *or*   price–earnings ratio
> cost/benefit analysis   *or*   cost–benefit analysis
> a 50/50 split   *or*   a 50-50 split
> 20/20 vision

2. A slash separates alternatives, usually representing the words *or* or *and/or.*

> alumni/ae
> his/her
> the *affect/effect* problem   *or*   the *affect-effect* problem

3. A slash replaces the word *and* in some compound terms.

> air/sea cruise   *or*   air-sea cruise
> the May/June issue   *or*   the May-June issue
> 1996/97   *or*   1996–97
> travel/study trip   *or*   travel-study trip

4. A slash is sometimes used to replace certain prepositions such as *at, versus,* and *for.*

> U.C./Berkeley   *or*   U.C.–Berkeley
> parent/child issues   *or*   parent–child issues
> Vice President/Editorial   *or*   Vice President, Editorial

5. A slash punctuates a few abbreviations.

> w/o [*for* without]
> c/o [*for* care of]
> I/O [*for* input/output]
> d/b/a [*for* doing business as]
> w/w [*for* wall-to-wall]
> o/a [*for* on or about]

6. The slash separates the elements in a numerical date, and numerators and denominators in fractions.

> 11/29/95
> 2 3/16 inches wide   *or* $2\frac{3}{16}$ inches wide
> a 7/8-mile course   *or*   a $\frac{7}{8}$-mile course

7. The slash separates lines of poetry that are run in with the text around them. A space is usually inserted before and after the slash.

> Alexander Pope once observed: "'Tis with our judgments as our watches, none / Go just alike, yet each believes his own."

2 Capitals and Italics

Words and phrases are capitalized or italicized (underlining takes the place of italics in typed or handwritten text) to indicate that they have a special significance in particular contexts. (Quotation marks sometimes perform the same functions; see paragraphs 69–71 on page 199 and the section on quotation marks beginning on page 188.)

Beginnings

1. The first word of a sentence or sentence fragment is capitalized.

> They make a desert and call it peace.
> So many men, so many opinions.
> O times! O customs!

2. The first word of a sentence contained within parentheses is capitalized. However, a parenthetical sentence occurring inside another sentence is not capitalized unless it is a complete quoted sentence.

> No one answered the telephone. (They were probably on vacation.)
> The road remains almost impassable (the locals don't seem to care), and the journey is only for the intrepid.
> After waiting in line for an hour (what else could we do?), we finally left.
> In the primary election Evans placed third ("My campaign started late").

3. The first word of a direct quotation is capitalized. However, if the quotation is interrupted in mid-sentence, the second part does not begin with a capital.

> The department manager explained, "We have no budget for new computers."
> "We have no budget for new computers," explained the department manager, "but we may next year."

4. When a quotation, whether a sentence fragment or a complete sentence, is syntactically dependent on the sentence in which it occurs, the quotation does not begin with a capital.

> The brochure promised a tour of "the most exotic ancient sites."
> His first response was that "there is absolutely no truth to the reports."

5. The first word of a sentence within a sentence that is not a direct quotation is usually capitalized. Examples include mottoes and rules, unspoken or imaginary dialogue, sentences referred to as sentences, and direct questions. (For the use of commas and quotation marks with such sentences, see paragraphs 30–31 on page 182 and paragraphs 6–7 on page 189.)

> You know the saying "Fools rush in where angels fear to tread."
> The first rule is, When in doubt, spell it out.

> One ballot proposition sought to enforce the sentencing rule of "Three strikes and you're out."
> My question is, When can we go?

6. The first word of a line of poetry is traditionally capitalized. However, in the poetry of this century line beginnings are often lowercased. The poem's original capitalization is always reproduced.

> Death is the mother of beauty, mystical,
> Within whose burning bosom we devise
> Our earthly mothers waiting, sleeplessly.
> —Wallace Stevens

> If tributes cannot
> be implicit,
> give me diatribes and the fragrance of iodine,
> the cork oak acorn grown in Spain . . .
> —Marianne Moore

7. The first word following a colon is lowercased when it begins a list and usually lowercased when it begins a complete sentence. However, when the sentence introduced is lengthy and distinctly separate from the preceding clause, it is often capitalized.

> In the early morning they broadcast an urgent call for three necessities: bandages, antibiotics, and blood.
> The advantage of this system is clear: it's inexpensive.
> The situation is critical: This company cannot hope to recoup the fourth-quarter losses that were sustained in five operating divisions.

8. If a colon introduces a series of sentences, the first word of each sentence is capitalized.

> Consider the steps we have taken: A subcommittee has been formed to evaluate past performance. New sources of revenue are being explored. Several candidates have been interviewed for the new post of executive director.

9. The first words of items that form complete sentences in run-in lists are usually capitalized, as are the first words of items in vertical lists. However, numbered phrases within a sentence are lowercased. For details, see the section beginning on page 219.

10. The first word in an outline heading is capitalized.

> I. Editorial tasks
> II. Production responsibilities
>   A. Cost estimates
>   B. Bids

11. In minutes and legislation, the introductory words *Whereas* and *Resolved* are capitalized (and *Resolved* is also italicized). The word immediately following is also capitalized.

> Whereas, Substantial benefits . . .
> *Resolved,* That . . .

12. The first word and certain other words of the salutation of a letter and the first word of a complimentary close are capitalized.

> Dear Sir or Madam:
> Ladies and Gentlemen:
> To whom it may concern:
> Sincerely yours,
> Very truly yours,

13. The first word and each subsequent major word following a SUBJECT or TO heading in a memorandum are capitalized.

> SUBJECT: Pension Plans
> TO: All Department Heads and Editors

Proper Nouns and Adjectives

The following paragraphs describe the ways in which a broad range of proper nouns and adjectives are styled. Capitals are always employed, sometimes in conjunction with italics or quotation marks.

Abbreviations

1. Abbreviated forms of proper nouns and adjectives are capitalized, just as the spelled-out forms would be. (For details on capitalizing abbreviations, see the section beginning on page 210.)

> Jan. [*for* January]
> NATO [*for* North Atlantic Treaty Organization]

Abstractions and Personifications

2. Abstract concepts and qualities are sometimes capitalized when the concept or quality is being personified. If the term is simply used in conjunction with other words that allude to human characteristics or qualities, it is not capitalized.

> as Autumn paints each leaf in fiery colors
> the statue of Justice with her scales
> hoping that fate would lend a hand

Academic Degrees

3. The names of academic degrees are capitalized when they follow a person's name. The names of specific degrees used without a person's name are usually lowercased. More general names for degrees are lowercased.

> Lawton I. Byrne, Doctor of Laws
> earned his associate in science degree
> *or* earned his Associate in Science degree
> completed course work for his doctorate
> working for a master's degree

Abbreviations for academic degrees are always capitalized. (For details, see paragraphs 11–12 on page 212.)

> Susan L. Wycliff, M.S.W.
> received her Ph.D. in clinical psychology

Animals and Plants

4. The common names of animals and plants are not capitalized unless they contain a proper noun, in which case the proper noun is usually capitalized and any name element preceding (but not following) it is often capitalized. When in doubt, consult a dictionary. (For scientific names, see the section on page 198.)

> the springer spaniel   Queen Anne's lace
> Holstein cows   black-eyed Susan
> California condor   mayflower
> a Great Dane   jack-in-the-pulpit

Awards and Prizes

5. Names of awards and prizes are capitalized. Words and phrases that are not actually part of the award's name are lowercased.

> Academy Award
> Emmy
> Rhodes Scholarship
> Rhodes scholar
> Pulitzer Prize–winning novelist
> Nobel Prize winner
> Nobel Prize in medicine
> *but*
> Nobel Peace Prize

Derivatives of Proper Names

6. Derivatives of proper names are capitalized when used in their primary sense. If the derived term has taken on a specialized meaning, it is often lowercased. Consult a dictionary when in doubt.

> Roman sculpture
> Viennese culture
> Victorian prudery
> a Britishism
> Hodgkins disease
> chinaware
> pasteurized milk
> french fries
> *but*
> American cheese
> Dutch door

Geographical and Topographical References

7. Terms that identify divisions of the earth's surface and distinct areas, regions, places, or districts are capitalized, as are derivative nouns and adjectives.

> the Pacific Rim   Burgundy
> the Great Lakes   Burgundians
> Arnhem Land   the Highlands
> the Golan Heights   Highland attitudes

8. Popular names of localities are capitalized.

> Little Italy   the Sunbelt
> the Left Bank   the Big Easy

9. Compass points are capitalized when they refer to a geographical region or form part of a street name. They are lowercased when they refer to a simple direction.

> the Southwest   North Pole
> West Coast   north of the Rio Grande
> North Atlantic   born in the East
> East Pleasant Street   driving east on I-90

10. Nouns and adjectives that are derived from compass points and that designate or refer to a specific geographical region are usually capitalized.

> Southern hospitality
> Easterners
> Southwestern recipes
> Northern Europeans

11. Words designating global, national, regional, and local political divisions are capitalized when they are essential elements of specific names. They are usually lowercased

when they precede a proper name or are not part of a specific name.

>the Roman Empire
>British Commonwealth nations
>New York State
>the state of New York
>the Third Precinct
>voters in three precincts

In legal documents, such words are often capitalized regardless of position.

>the State of New York

12. Common geographical terms (such as *lake, mountain, river,* or *valley*) are capitalized if they are part of a proper name.

>Lake Tanganyika   Cape of Good Hope
>Great Salt Lake   Massachusetts Bay
>Atlas Mountains   Cayman Islands
>Mount Everest   Yosemite Valley

13. Common geographical terms preceding names are usually capitalized.

>Lakes Huron and Erie
>Mounts McKinley and Whitney

When *the* precedes the common term, the term is lowercased.

>the river Nile

14. Common geographical terms that are not used as part of a single proper name are not capitalized. These include plural terms that follow two or more proper names, and terms that are used descriptively or alone.

>the Indian and South Pacific oceans
>the Mississippi and Missouri rivers
>the Pacific coast of Mexico
>Caribbean islands
>the river delta

15. The names of streets, monuments, parks, landmarks, well-known buildings, and other public places are capitalized. However, common terms that are part of these names (such as *street, park,* or *bridge*) are lowercased when they occur after multiple names or are used alone.

>State Street   Golden Gate Bridge
>the Lincoln Memorial   Empire State Building
>Statue of Liberty   Beverly Hills Hotel
>the Pyramids   back to the hotel
>Grant Park   Main and Oak streets

Well-known shortened forms of place-names are capitalized.

>the Hill [*for* Capitol Hill]
>the Channel [*for* English Channel]
>the Street [*for* Wall Street]

Governmental, Judicial, and Political Bodies

16. Full names of legislative, deliberative, executive, and administrative bodies are capitalized, as are easily recognizable short forms of these names. However, nonspecific noun and adjective references to them are usually lowercased.

>United States Congress
>Congress
>the House
>the Fed
>congressional hearings
>a federal agency

When words such as *department, committee,* or *agency* are used in place of a full name, they are most often capitalized when the department or agency is referring to itself, but otherwise usually lowercased.

>This Department welcomes constructive criticism . . .
>The department claimed to welcome such criticism . . .

When such a word is used in the plural to describe more than one specific body, it is usually capitalized when it precedes the names and lowercased when it follows them.

>involving the Departments of State and Justice
>a briefing from the State and Justice departments

17. Full names of high courts are capitalized. Short forms of such names are often capitalized in legal documents but lowercased otherwise.

>. . . in the U.S. Court of Appeals for the Ninth Circuit
>International Court of Justice
>The court of appeals [*or* Court of Appeals] held . . .
>the Virginia Supreme Court
>a federal district court
>the state supreme court

However, both the full and short names of the U.S. Supreme Court are capitalized.

>the Supreme Court of the United States
>the Supreme Court
>the Court

18. Names of city and county courts are usually lowercased.

>the Springfield municipal court
>small-claims court
>the county court
>juvenile court

19. The noun *court,* when it applies to a specific judge or presiding officer, is capitalized in legal documents.

>It is the opinion of this Court that . . .
>The Court found that . . .

20. The terms *federal* and *national* are capitalized only when they are essential elements of a name or title. (*Federal* is also capitalized when it refers to a historical architectural style, to members of the original Federalist party, or to adherents of the Union in the Civil War.)

>Federal Election Commission
>a federal commission
>Federalist principles
>National Security Council
>national security

21. The word *administration* is sometimes capitalized when it refers to the administration of a specific U.S. president, but is more commonly lowercased. Otherwise, it is

lowercased except when it is a part of the official name of a government agency.

> the Reagan administration *or* the Reagan Administration
> the administration *or* the Administration
> from one administration to the next
> the Social Security Administration

22. Names of political organizations and their adherents are capitalized, but the word *party* is often lowercased.

> the Democratic National Committee
> the Republican platform
> the Christian Coalition
> most Republicans
> the Democratic party *or* the Democratic Party
> party politics

Names of less-distinct political groupings are usually lowercased, as are their derivative forms.

> the right wing
> the liberals
> the conservative agenda
> *but often*
> the Left
> the Right

23. Terms describing political and economic philosophies are usually lowercased; if derived from proper names, they are usually capitalized. Consult a dictionary for doubtful cases.

> authoritarianism   nationalism
> democracy   social Darwinist
> fascism *or* Fascism   Marxist

Historical Periods and Events

24. The names of some historical and cultural periods and movements are capitalized. When in doubt, consult a dictionary or encyclopedia.

> Bronze Age   Third Reich
> Middle Ages   the atomic age
> Prohibition   Victorian era
> the Renaissance   age of Pericles
> New Deal   the baby boom
> Fifth Republic

25. Century and decade designations are normally lowercased.

> the nineteenth century
> the twenties
> the turn of the century
> a 12th-century manuscript
> *but*
> Gay Nineties
> Roaring Twenties

26. The names of conferences, councils, expositions, and specific sporting, cultural, and historical events are capitalized.

> Fourth World Conference on Women
> Council of Trent
> New York World's Fair
> Super Bowl
> Cannes Film Festival

> Miss America Contest
> San Francisco Earthquake
> Johnstown Flood

27. Full names of specific treaties, laws, and acts are capitalized.

> Treaty of Versailles
> the Nineteenth Amendment
> the Bill of Rights
> Clean Air Act of 1990
> *but*
> gun-control laws
> an equal-rights amendment

28. The words *war, revolution,* and *battle* are capitalized when they are part of a full name. Official names of actions are capitalized. Descriptive terms such as *assault* and *siege* are usually lowercased even when used in conjunction with a place-name.

> War of the Roses
> World War II
> the French Revolution
> Battle of Gettysburg
> Operation Desert Storm
> between the two world wars
> the American and French revolutions
> the siege of Leningrad
> Washington's winter campaign

Hyphenated Compounds

29. The second (third, etc.) element of a hyphenated compound is generally capitalized only if it is itself a proper noun or adjective.

> Arab-Israeli negotiations
> East-West trade agreements
> French-speaking peoples
> Forty-second street
> twentieth-century architecture

30. When joined to a proper noun or adjective, common prefixes (such as *pre-* or *anti-*) are usually lowercased, but geographical and ethnic combining forms (such as *Anglo-* or *Sino-*) are capitalized. (For details, see paragraphs 45 and 52 on pages 208–209.)

> anti-Soviet forces
> Sino-Japanese relations

Legal Material

31. The names of the plaintiff and defendant in legal case titles are italicized. The *v.* (for *versus*) may be roman or italic. Cases that do not involve two opposing parties are also italicized. When the party involved rather than the case itself is being discussed, the reference is not italicized. In running text, a case name involving two opposing parties may be shortened.

> *Jones* v. *Massachusetts*
> *Smith et al. v. Jones*
> *In re Jones*
> She covered the Jones trial for the newspaper.
> The judge based his ruling on a precedent set in the *Jones* decision.

Medical Terms

32. Proper names that are elements in terms designating diseases, symptoms, syndromes, and tests are capitalized. Common nouns are lowercased; however, abbreviations of such nouns are all-capitalized.

Alzheimer's disease	black lung disease
Tourette's syndrome	mumps
Schick test	AIDS

33. Scientific names of disease-causing organisms follow the rules discussed in paragraph 58 on page 198. The names of diseases or conditions derived from scientific names of organisms are lowercased and not italicized.

   a neurotoxin produced by *Clostridium botulinum*
   nearly died of botulism

34. Generic names of drugs are lowercased; trade names should be capitalized.

   retinoic acid
   Retin-A

Military Terms

35. The full titles of branches of the U.S. armed forces are capitalized, as are standard short forms.

U.S. Marine Corps	the Marines
the Marine Corps	the Corps

Those of other countries are capitalized when the precise title is used; otherwise they are usually lowercased. The plurals of *army, navy, air force,* and *coast guard* are lowercased.

   Royal Air Force
   the Guatemalan army
   the tiny armies of both countries

The modifiers *army, navy, marine, coast guard,* and *air force* are usually lowercased; *naval* is lowercased unless it is part of an official name. The noun *marine* is usually lowercased.

an army helicopter	the first naval engagement
a career navy man	the Naval Reserves
the marine barracks	a former marine

Full or shortened names of specific units of a branch are usually capitalized.

   U.S. Army Corps of Engineers
   the Third Army
   the Eighty-second [*or* 82nd] Airborne
   the U.S. Special Forces, or Green Berets
   . . . of the First Battalion. The battalion commander . . .

36. Military ranks are capitalized when they precede the names of their holders, or replace the name in direct address. Otherwise they are lowercased.

   Major General Smedley Butler
   Please be seated, Admiral.
   The major arrived precisely on time.

37. The names of decorations, citations, and medals are capitalized.

   Medal of Honor
   Purple Heart

Numerical Designations

38. A noun introducing a reference number is usually capitalized. The abbreviation *No.* is usually omitted.

Order 704	Form 2E
Flight 409	Policy 118-4-Y

39. Nouns used with numbers or letters to refer to major reference entities or actual captions in books or periodicals are usually capitalized. Nouns that designate minor reference entities and do not appear in captions are lowercased.

Book II	Figure D.4
Volume 5	page 101
Chapter 2	line 8
Table 3	paragraph 6.1
Example 16.2	question 21

Organizations

40. Names of organizations, corporations, and institutions, and terms derived from those names to designate their members, are capitalized.

   the League of Women Voters
   General Motors Corporation
   the Smithsonian Institution
   the University of the South
   the Rotary Club
   all Rotarians

Common nouns used descriptively or occurring after the names of two or more organizations are lowercased.

   enrolled at the university
   Yale and Harvard universities
     but
   the Universities of Utah and Nevada

41. Words such as *agency, department, division, group,* or *office* that designate corporate and organizational units are capitalized only when used as part of a specific proper name. (For governmental units, see paragraph 16 on page 194.)

   head of the Sales Division of K2 Outfitters
   a memo to the sales divisions of both companies

42. Nicknames for organizations are capitalized.

   the Big Six accounting firms
   referred to IBM as Big Blue
   trading on the Big Board

People

43. The names and initials of persons are capitalized. If a name is hyphenated, both elements are capitalized. Particles forming the initial elements of surnames (such as *de, della, der, du, l', la, le, ten, ter, van,* and *von*) may or may not be capitalized, depending on the practice of the family or individual. However, the particle is always capitalized at the beginning of a sentence. The prefixes *Mac, Mc,* and *O'* are always capitalized.

   Cecil Day-Lewis
   Agnes de Mille
   Cecil B. DeMille
   Walter de la Mare

Mark deW. Howe
Martin Van Buren
. . . of van Gogh's life. Van Gogh's technique is . . .

44. A nickname or epithet that either is added to or replaces the name of a person or thing is capitalized.

Babe Ruth   the Sun King
Stonewall Jackson   Deep Throat
Billy the Kid   Big Mama Thornton

A nickname or epithet placed between a person's first and last name is enclosed in quotation marks or parentheses or both. If it precedes the first name, it is sometimes enclosed in quotation marks but more often not.

Charlie "Bird" [*or* ("Bird") *or* (Bird)] Parker
Mother Maybelle Carter

45. Words of family relationship preceding or used in place of a person's name are capitalized; otherwise, they are lowercased.

Uncle Fred   her uncle's book
Mother's birthday   my mother's legacy

46. Words designating languages, nationalities, peoples, races, religious groups, and tribes are capitalized. Designations based on color are usually lowercased.

Spanish   Muslims
Spaniards   Assiniboin
Chinese   both blacks and whites
Asians   white, black, and Hispanic
                       jurors

47. Corporate, professional, and governmental titles are capitalized when they immediately precede a person's name, unless the name is being used as an appositive.

President John Tyler
Professor Wendy Doniger of the University of Chicago
Senator William Fulbright of Arkansas
Arkansas's late former senator, William Fulbright

48. When corporate or governmental titles are used as part of a descriptive phrase to identify a person rather than as part of the name itself, the title is lowercased.

Marcia Ramirez, president of Logex Corp.
the president of Logex Corp., Marcia Ramirez
but
Logex Corp.'s prospects for the coming year were outlined by President Marcia Ramirez.

49. High governmental titles may be capitalized when used in place of individuals' names. In minutes and official records of proceedings, corporate or organizational titles are capitalized when used in place of individuals' names.

The Secretary of State objected.
The Judge will respond to questions in her chambers.
The Treasurer then stated his misgivings about the project.
but
The report reached the senator's desk yesterday.
The judge's rulings were widely criticized.
The co-op's treasurer, it turned out, had twice been convicted of embezzlement.

50. The word *president* may be capitalized whenever it refers to the U.S. presidency, but more commonly is capitalized only when it refers to a specific U.S. president.

It is the duty of the president [*or* President] to submit a budget to Congress.
The President's budget, due out on Wednesday, is being eagerly awaited.

51. Titles are capitalized when they are used in direct address.

Is it very contagious, Doctor?
You may call your next witness, Counselor.

Religious Terms

52. Words designating the supreme being are capitalized. Plural forms such as *gods, goddesses,* and *deities* are not.

Allah   the Almighty
Brahma   the Trinity
Jehovah   in the eyes of God
Yahweh   the angry gods

53. Personal pronouns referring to the supreme being are often capitalized, especially in religious writing. Relative pronouns (such as *who, whom,* and *whose*) usually are not.

God gave His [*or* his] Son
Allah, whose Prophet, Muhammad . . .

54. Traditional designations of apostles, prophets, and saints are capitalized.

the Madonna   the Twelve
the Prophet   St. John of the Cross
Moses the Lawgiver   John the Baptist

55. Names of religions, denominations, creeds and confessions, and religious orders are capitalized, as are adjectives and nouns derived from these names.

Judaism   Eastern Orthodox
Church of England   Islamic
Apostles' Creed   Jesuit teachers
Society of Jesus   a Buddhist

Full names of specific places of worship are capitalized, but terms such as *church, synagogue,* and *mosque* are lowercased when used alone. The word *church* is sometimes capitalized when it refers to the worldwide Catholic Church.

Hunt Memorial Church
the local Baptist church
Beth Israel Synagogue
services at the synagogue

56. Names of the Bible and other sacred works, their books and parts, and versions or editions of them are capitalized but not italicized. Adjectives derived from the names of sacred books are capitalized, except for the words *biblical* and *scriptural.*

Bible   biblical
the Scriptures   Talmud
Revised Standard Version Talmudic
Old Testament   Koran *or* Qur'an
Book of Revelation   Koranic *or* Qur'anic

57. The names of prayers and well-known passages of the Bible are capitalized.

> the Ave Maria   Ten Commandments
> Lord's Prayer   Sermon on the Mount
> the Our Father   the Beatitudes

Scientific Terms

58. Genus names in biological binomial nomenclature are capitalized; species names are lowercased, even when derived from a proper name. Both names are italicized.

> Both the wolf and the domestic dog are included in the genus *Canis.*
> The California condor *(Gymnogyps californianus)* is facing extinction.

The names of races, varieties, or subspecies are lowercased and italicized.

> *Hyla versicolor chrysoscelis*
> *Otis asio naevius*

59. The New Latin names of classes, families, and all groups above the genus level in zoology and botany are capitalized but not italicized. Their derivative nouns and adjectives are lowercased.

> Gastropoda   gastropod
> Thallophyta   thallophytic

60. The names, both scientific and informal, of planets and their satellites, stars, constellations, and other specific celestial objects are capitalized. However, except in technical writing, the words *sun, earth,* and *moon* are usually lowercased unless they occur with other astronomical names. A generic term that follows the name of a celestial object is usually lowercased.

> Jupiter   Mars, Venus, and Earth
> the North Star   life on earth
> Andromeda   a voyage to the moon
> Ursa Major   Halley's comet
> the Little Dipper

Names of meteorological phenomena are lowercased.

> aurora australis
> northern lights
> parhelic circle

61. Terms that identify geological eons, eras, periods, systems, epochs, and strata are capitalized. The generic terms that follow them are lowercased.

> Mesozoic era
> Upper Cretaceous epoch
> Quaternary period
> in the Middle Ordovician
> the Age of Reptiles

62. Proper names that are elements of the names of scientific laws, theorems, and principles are capitalized, but the common nouns *law, theorem, theory,* and the like are lowercased. In the names of popular or fanciful theories or observations, such words are usually capitalized as well.

> Mendel's law
> the Pythagorean theorem
> Occam's razor
> Einstein's theory of relativity
> Murphy's Law
> the Peter Principle

63. The names of computer services and databases are capitalized. Some names of computer languages are written with an initial capital letter, some with all letters capitalized, and some commonly both ways. When in doubt, consult a dictionary.

> America Online
> World Wide Web
> CompuServe
> Microsoft Word
> Pascal *or* PASCAL
> BASIC
> Internet *or* internet

Time Periods and Dates

64. The names of the days of the week, months of the year, and holidays and holy days are capitalized. Names of the seasons are lowercased.

> Tuesday   Ramadan
> June   Holy Week
> Yom Kippur   last winter's storm
> Veterans Day

Titles of Works

65. Words in titles of books, magazines, newspapers, plays, movies, long poems, and works of art such as paintings and sculpture are capitalized except for internal articles, coordinating conjunctions, prepositions, and the *to* of infinitives. Prepositions of four or more letters are often capitalized. The entire title is italicized. For sacred works, see paragraph 56 on page 197.

> *Far from* [or *From*] *the Madding Crowd*
> Wolfe's *Of Time and the River*
> *Publishers Weekly*
> *USA Today*
> the original play *A Streetcar Named Desire*
> *All about* [or *About*] *Eve,* with Bette Davis
> Monet's *Water-Lily Pool,* in the Louvre
> Rodin's *Thinker*

The elements of hyphenated compounds in titles are usually capitalized, but articles, coordinating conjunctions, and prepositions are lowercased.

> *The Post-Physician Era: Medicine in the Twenty-First Century*
> *Politics in Early Seventeenth-Century England*

66. The first word following a colon in a title is capitalized.

> *Jane Austen: A Literary Life*

67. An initial article that is part of a title is capitalized and italicized. It is often omitted if it would be awkward in context.

> *The Oxford English Dictionary*
> the 20-volume *Oxford English Dictionary*

68. In the titles of newspapers, the city or local name is usually italicized, but the preceding *the* is usually not italicized or capitalized.

> reported in the *New York Times*
> last Thursday's *Atlanta Constitution*

69. Many periodicals, especially newspapers, do not use italics for titles, but instead either simply capitalize the important words of the title or, more commonly, capitalize the words and enclose the title in quotation marks.

    the NB. column in the Times Literary Supplement
    The Nobel committee singled out Walcott's book-length epic "Omeros."

70. The titles of articles in periodicals, short poems, short stories, essays, lectures, dissertations, chapters of books, radio and television programs, and novellas published in a collection are capitalized and enclosed in quotation marks. The capitalization of articles, conjunctions, and prepositions follows the rules explained in paragraph 65 above.

    an article on Rwanda, "After the Genocide," in the *New Yorker*
    Robert Frost's "Death of the Hired Man"
    O'Connor's story "Good Country People"
    "The Literature of Exhaustion," John Barth's seminal essay
    last Friday's lecture, "Labor's Task: A View for the Nineties"
    The Jungle Book's ninth chapter is the well-known "Rikki-tikki-tavi."
    listening to "All Things Considered"
    watched "Good Morning America"

71. The titles of long musical compositions are generally capitalized and italicized; the titles of songs and other short compositions are capitalized and enclosed in quotation marks, as are the popular names of longer works. The titles of compositions identified primarily by their musical forms (such as *quartet, sonata,* or *mass*) are capitalized only, as are movements identified by their tempo markings.

    Mozart's *The Magic Flute*
    Frank Loesser's *Guys and Dolls*
    "The Lady Is a Tramp"
    Beethoven's "Für Elise"
    the Piano Sonata in C-sharp minor, Op. 27, No. 2, or "Moonlight" Sonata
    Symphony No. 104 in D major
    Brahms's Violin Concerto in D
    the Adagietto movement from Mahler's Fifth Symphony

72. Common titles of book sections (such as *preface, introduction,* or *index*) are usually capitalized when they refer to a section of the same book in which the reference is made. Otherwise, they are usually lowercased. (For numbered sections of books, see paragraph 39 on page 196.)

    See the Appendix for further information.
    In the introduction to her book, the author explains her goals.

Trademarks

73. Registered trademarks, service marks, collective marks, and brand names are capitalized. They do not normally require any further acknowledgment of their special status.

Frisbee	Jacuzzi	Levi's
Coke	Kleenex	Vaseline
College Board	Velcro	Dumpster
Realtor	Xerox	Scotch tape
Walkman	Band-Aid	Teflon

Transportation

74. The names of individual ships, submarines, airplanes, satellites, and space vehicles are capitalized and italicized. The designations *U.S.S., S.S., M.V.,* and *H.M.S.* are not italicized.

    Challenger
    Enola Gay
    H.M.S. *Bounty*

Other Styling Conventions

1. Foreign words and phrases that have not been fully adopted into English are italicized. In general, any word that appears in the main section of *Merriam-Webster's Collegiate Dictionary* does not need to be italicized.

    These accomplishments will serve as a monument, *aere perennius,* to the group's skill and dedication.
    "The cooking here is *wunderbar!*"
    The prix fixe lunch was $20.
    The committee meets on an ad hoc basis.

    A complete foreign-language sentence (such as a motto) can also be italicized. However, long sentences are usually treated as quotations; that is, they are set in roman type and enclosed in quotation marks. (For details, see paragraph 6 on page 189.)

    The inscription *Honi soit qui mal y pense* encircles the seal.

2. In nonfiction writing, unfamiliar words or words that have a specialized meaning are set in italics on their first appearance, especially when accompanied by a short definition. Once these words have been introduced and defined, they are not italicized in subsequent references.

    Vitiligo is a condition in which skin pigment cells stop making pigment. Vitiligo usually affects . . .
    Another method is the *direct-to-consumer* transaction, in which the publisher markets directly to the individual by mail or door-to-door.

3. Italics are often used to indicate words referred to as words. However, if the word was actually spoken, it is usually enclosed in quotation marks instead.

    Purists still insist that *data* is a plural noun.
    Only can also be an adverb, as in "I *only* tried to help."
    We heard his warning, but we weren't sure what "repercussions" meant in that context.

4. Italics are often used for letters referred to as letters, particularly when they are shown in lowercase.

    You should dot your *i*'s and cross your *t*'s.

    If the letter is being used to refer to its sound and not its printed form, slashes or brackets are used instead of italics in technical contexts.

    The pure /p/ sound is rarely heard in the mountain dialect.

    A letter used to indicate a shape is capitalized but not italicized. Such letters are often set in sans-serif type.

    an A-frame house
    the I beam
    Churchill's famous V sign
    forming a giant X

5. Italics are often used to show numerals referred to as numerals. However, if there is no chance of confusion, they are usually not italicized.

> The first *2* and the last *1* are barely legible.
> Anyone whose ticket number ends in 4 or 6 will win a door prize.

6. Italics are used to emphasize or draw attention to words in a sentence.

> Students must notify the dean's office *in writing* of any added or dropped courses.
> It was not *the* model for the project, but merely *a* model.

7. Italics are used to indicate a word created to suggest a sound.

> Its call is a harsh, drawn-out *kreee-awww*.

8. Individual letters are sometimes italicized when used for lists within sentences or for identifying elements in an illustration.

> providing information about *(a)* typing, *(b)* transcribing, *(c)* formatting, and *(d)* graphics
> located at point A on the diagram

9. Commas, colons, and semicolons that follow italicized words are usually italicized.

> the Rabbit tetralogy (*Rabbit Run, Rabbit Redux, Rabbit is Rich,* and *Rabbit at Rest*); *Bech: A Book; S;* and others

However, question marks, exclamation points, quotation marks, and apostrophes are not italicized unless they are part of an italicized title.

> Did you see the latest issue of *Newsweek*?
> Despite the greater success of *Oklahoma!* and *South Pacific,* Rodgers was fondest of *Carousel.*
> "Over Christmas vacation he finished *War and Peace.*"
> Students always mistake the old script *s*'s for *f*'s.

Parentheses and brackets may be italicized if most of the words they enclose are also italicized, or if both the first and last words are italicized.

> (*see also Limited Partnership*)
> [German, *wunderbar*]
> (*and* is replaced throughout by *&*)

10. Full capitalization is occasionally used for emphasis or to indicate that a speaker is talking very loudly. It is avoided in formal writing, where italics are far more often used for emphasis.

> Term papers received after Friday, May 18, WILL BE RETURNED UNREAD.
> Scalpers mingled in the noisy crowd yelling "SIXTY DOLLARS!"

11. The text of signs, labels, and inscriptions may be reproduced in various ways.

> a poster reading SPECIAL THRILLS COMING SOON
> a gate bearing the infamous motto "Arbeit macht frei"
> a Do Not Disturb sign
> a barn with an old CHEW MAIL POUCH ad on the side
> the stop sign

12. *Small capitals,* identical to large capitals but usually about the height of a lowercase *x,* are commonly used for era designations and computer commands. They may also be used for cross-references, for headings in constitutions and bylaws, and for speakers in a dramatic dialogue.

> The dwellings date from A.D. 200 or earlier.
> Press ALT+CTRL+PLUS SIGN on the numeric keyboard.
> (See LETTERS AS LETTERS, page 162.)
> SECTION IV. The authority for parliamentary procedure in meetings of the Board . . .
> LADY WISHFORT. O dear, has my Nephew made his Addresses to Millamant? I order'd him.
> FOIBLE. Sir Wilfull is set in to drinking, Madam, in the Parlour.

13. *Underlining* indicates italics in typed material. It is almost never seen in typeset text.

14. *Boldface* type has traditionally been used primarily for headings and captions. It is sometimes also used in place of italics for terminology introduced in the text, especially for terms that are accompanied by definitions; for cross-references; for headwords in listings such as glossaries, gazetteers, and bibliographies; and for page references in indexes that locate a specific kind of material, such as illustrations, tables, or the main discussions of a given topic. (In mathematical texts, arrays, tensors, vectors, and matrix notation are standardly set bold as well.)

> **Application Forms and Tests**   Many offices require applicants to fill out an employment form. Bring a copy . . .
> **Figure 4.2: The Electromagnetic Spectrum**
> The two axes intersect at a point called the **origin**.
> See **Medical Records**, page 123.
> **antecedent:** the noun to which a pronoun refers
> **appositive:** a word, phrase, or clause that is equivalent to a preceding noun
> Records, medical, **123–37**, 178, 243
> Referrals, **38–40**, 139

Punctuation that follows boldface type is set bold when it is part of a heading or heading-like text; otherwise it is generally set roman.

> **Table 9:** Metric Conversion
> **Warning:** This and similar medications . . .
> Excellent fourth-quarter earnings were reported by the pharmaceutical giants **Abbott Laboratories, Burroughs Wellcome,** and **Merck.**

3 Plurals, Possessives, and Compounds

This chapter describes the ways in which plurals, possessives, and compounds are most commonly formed.

In regard to plurals and compounds, consulting a dictionary will solve many of the problems discussed in this chapter. A good college dictionary, such as *Merriam-Webster's Collegiate Dictionary,* will provide plural forms for any common word, as well as a large number of permanent compounds. Any dictionary much smaller than the *Collegiate* will often be more frustrating in what it fails to show than helpful in what it shows.

Plurals

The basic rules for writing plurals of English words, stated in paragraph 1, apply in the vast majority of cases. The succeeding paragraphs treat the categories of words whose plurals are most apt to raise questions.

Most good dictionaries give thorough coverage to irregular and variant plurals, and many of the rules provided here are reflected in the dictionary entries.

The symbol → is used here to link the singular and plural forms.

1. The plurals of most English words are formed by adding -*s* to the singular. If the noun ends in -*s, -x, -z, -ch,* or -*sh,* so that an extra syllable must be added in order to pronounce the plural, -*es* is added. If the noun ends in a -*y* preceded by a consonant, the -*y* is changed to -*i* and -*es* is added.

   voter → voters
   anticlimax → anticlimaxes
   blitz → blitzes
   blowtorch → blowtorches
   calabash → calabashes
   allegory → allegories

Abbreviations
2. The plurals of abbreviations are commonly formed by adding -*s* or -*'s;* however, there are some significant exceptions. (For details, see paragraphs 1–5 on page 211.)

yr. → yrs.	M.B.A. → M.B.A.'s
TV → TVs	p. → pp.

Animals
3. The names of many fishes, birds, and mammals have both a plural formed with a suffix and one that is identical with the singular. Some have only one or the other.

   bass → bass *or* basses
   partridge → partridge *or* partridges
   sable → sables *or* sable
   lion → lions
   sheep → sheep

Many of the animals that have both plural forms are ones that are hunted, fished, or trapped; those who hunt, fish for, and trap them are most likely to use the unchanged form. The -*s* form is often used to emphasize diversity of kinds.

   caught three bass
     but
   basses of the Atlantic Ocean
   a place where antelope feed
     but
   antelopes of Africa and southwest Asia

Compounds and Phrases
4. Most compounds made up of two nouns—whether they appear as one word, two words, or a hyphenated word—form their plurals by pluralizing the final element only.

   courthouse → courthouses
   judge advocate → judge advocates
   player-manager → player-managers

5. The plural form of a compound consisting of an -*er* noun and an adverb is made by pluralizing the noun element only.

   runner-up → runners-up
   onlooker → onlookers
   diner-out → diners-out
   passerby → passersby

6. Nouns made up of words that are not nouns form their plurals on the last element.

   show-off → show-offs
   pushover → pushovers
   tie-in → tie-ins
   lineup → lineups

7. Plurals of compounds that consist of two nouns separated by a preposition are normally formed by pluralizing the first noun.

   sister-in-law → sisters-in-law
   attorney-at-law → attorneys-at-law
   power of attorney → powers of attorney
   chief of staff → chiefs of staff
   grant-in-aid → grants-in-aid

8. Compounds that consist of two nouns separated by a preposition and a modifier form their plurals in various ways.

   snake in the grass → snakes in the grass
   justice of the peace → justices of the peace
   jack-in-the-box → jack-in-the-boxes *or* jacks-in-the-box
   will-o'-the wisp → will-o'-the-wisps

9. Compounds consisting of a noun followed by an adjective are usually pluralized by adding -*s* to the noun. If the adjective tends to be understood as a noun, the compound may have more than one plural form.

   attorney general → attorneys general *or* attorney generals
   sergeant major → sergeants major *or* sergeant majors
   poet laureate → poets laureate *or* poet laureates
   heir apparent → heirs apparent
   knight-errant → knights-errant

Foreign Words and Phrases

10. Many nouns of foreign origin retain the foreign plural. However, most also have a regular English plural.

> alumnus → alumni
> genus → genera
> crisis → crises
> criterion → criteria
> appendix → appendixes *or* appendices
> concerto → concerti *or* concertos
> symposium → symposia *or* symposiums

11. Phrases of foreign origin may have a foreign plural, an English plural, or both.

> pièces de résistance → pièces de résistance
> hors d'oeuvre → hors d'oeuvres
> beau monde → beau mondes *or* beaux mondes

Irregular Plurals

12. A few English nouns form their plurals by changing one or more of their vowels, or by adding -en or -ren.

> foot → feet   woman → women
> goose → geese   tooth → teeth
> louse → lice   ox → oxen
> man → men   child → children
> mouse → mice

13. Some nouns do not change form in the plural. (See also paragraph 3 above.)

> series → series   corps → corps
> politics → politics   species → species

14. Some nouns ending in -f, -fe, and -ff have plurals that end in -ves. Some of these also have regularly formed plurals.

> elf → elves
> loaf → loaves
> scarf → scarves *or* scarfs
> wife → wives
> staff → staffs *or* staves

Italic Elements

15. Italicized words, phrases, abbreviations, and letters are usually pluralized by adding -s or -'s in roman type. (See also paragraphs 16, 21, and 26 below.)

> three *Fortune*s missing from the stack
> a couple of *Gravity's Rainbow*s in stock
> used too many *etc.*'s in the report
> a row of *x*'s

Letters

16. The plurals of letters are usually formed by adding -'s, although capital letters are often pluralized by adding -s alone.

> p's and q's
> V's of migrating geese *or* Vs of migrating geese
> dot your *i*'s
> straight As *or* straight A's

Numbers

17. Numerals are pluralized by adding -s or, less commonly, -'s.

> two par 5s *or* two par 5's
> 1990s *or* 1990's
> in the 80s *or* in the 80's *or* in the '80s
> the mid-$20,000s *or* the mid-$20,000's

18. Written-out numbers are pluralized by adding -s.

> all the fours and eights
> scored three tens

Proper Nouns

19. The plurals of proper nouns are usually formed with -s or -es.

> Clarence → Clarences
> Jones → Joneses
> Fernandez → Fernandezes

20. Plurals of proper nouns ending in -y usually retain the -y and add -s.

> Sunday → Sundays
> Timothy → Timothys
> Camry → Camrys

Words ending in -y that were originally proper nouns are usually pluralized by changing -y to -i and adding -es, but a few retain the -y.

> bobby → bobbies
> johnny → johnnies
> Tommy → Tommies
> Bloody Mary → Bloody Marys

Quoted Elements

21. The plural of words in quotation marks are formed by adding -s or -'s within the quotation marks, or -s outside the quotation marks.

> too many "probably's" [*or* "probablys"] in the statement
> one "you" among millions of "you"s
> a record number of "I can't recall"s

Symbols

22. When symbols are referred to as physical characters, the plural is formed by adding either -s or -'s.

> printed three *s
> used &'s instead of *and*'s
> his π's are hard to read

Words Ending in -ay, -ey, and -oy

23. Words that end in -ay, -ey, or -oy, unlike other words ending in -y, are pluralized by simply adding -s.

> castaways
> donkeys
> envoys

Words Ending in -ful

24. Any noun ending in -ful can be pluralized by adding -s, but most also have an alternative plural with -s preceding the suffix.

> handful → handfuls
> teaspoonful → teaspoonfuls
> armful → armfuls *or* armsful
> bucketful → bucketfuls *or* bucketsful

Words Ending in *-o*

25. Most words ending in *-o* are normally pluralized by adding *-s*. However, some words ending in *-o* preceded by a consonant take *-es* plurals.

> solo → solos
> photo → photos
> tomato → tomatoes
> potato → potatoes
> hobo → hoboes
> hero → heroes
> cargo → cargoes *or* cargos
> proviso → provisos *or* provisoes
> halo → haloes *or* halos
> echo → echoes
> motto → mottoes

Words Used as Words

26. Words referred to as words and italicized usually form their plurals by adding *-'s* in roman type. (See also paragraph 21 above.)

> five *and*'s in one sentence
> all those *wherefore*'s and *howsoever*'s

When a word referred to as a word has become part of a fixed phrase, the plural is usually formed by adding *-s* without the apostrophe.

> oohs and aahs
> dos and don'ts *or* do's and don'ts

Possessives

Common Nouns

1. The possessive of singular and plural common nouns that do not end in an *s* or *z* sound is formed by adding *-'s* to the end of the word.

> the child's skates
> women's voices
> the cat's dish
> this patois's range
> people's opinions
> the criteria's common theme

2. The possessive of singular nouns ending in an *s* or *z* sound is usually formed by adding *-'s*. A less common alternative is to add *-'s* only when it is easily pronounced; if it would create a word that is difficult to pronounce, only an apostrophe is added.

> the witness's testimony
> the disease's course
> the race's sponsors
> the prize's recipient
> rickets's symptoms *or* rickets' symptoms

A multisyllabic singular noun that ends in an *s* or *z* sound drops the *-s* if it is followed by a word beginning with an *s* or *z* sound.

> for appearance' sake
> for goodness' sake

3. The possessive of plural nouns ending in an *s* or *z* sound is formed by adding only an apostrophe. However, the possessive of one-syllable irregular plurals is usually formed by adding *-'s*.

> dogs' leashes   buyers' guarantees
> birds' migrations   lice's lifespans

Proper Names

4. The possessives of proper names are generally formed in the same way as those of common nouns. The possessive of singular proper names is formed by adding *-'s*.

> Jane's rules of behavior
> three books of Carla's
> Tom White's presentation
> Paris's cafes

The possessive of plural proper names, and of some singular proper names ending in an *s* or *z* sound, is made by adding just an apostrophe.

> the Stevenses' reception
> the Browns' driveway
> Massachusetts' capital
> New Orleans' annual festival
> the United States' trade deficit
> Protosystems' president

5. The possessive of singular proper names ending in an *s* or *z* sound may be formed by adding either *-'s* or just an apostrophe. Adding *-'s* to all such names, without regard for the pronunciation of the resulting word, is more common than adding just the apostrophe. (For exceptions see paragraph 6 below.)

> Jones's car *or* Jones' car
> Bliss's statue *or* Bliss' statue
> Dickens's novels *or* Dickens' novels

6. The possessive form of classical and biblical names of two or more syllables ending in *-s* or *-es* is usually made by adding just an apostrophe. If the name has only one syllable, the possessive form is made by adding *-'s*.

> Socrates' students   Elias' prophecy
> Claudius' reign   Zeus's warnings
> Ramses' kingdom   Cis's sons

The possessives of the names *Jesus* and *Moses* are always formed with just an apostrophe.

> Jesus' disciples
> Moses' law

7. The possessive of names ending in a silent *-s*, *-z*, or *-x* are usually formed with *-'s*.

> Des Moines's recreation department
> Josquin des Prez's music
> Delacroix's painting

8. When the possessive ending is added to an italicized name, it is not italicized.

> *East of Eden*'s main characters
> the *Spirit of St. Louis*'s historic flight
> *Brief Encounter*'s memorable ending

Pronouns

9. The possessive of indefinite pronouns is formed by adding *-'s*.

anyone's rights
everybody's money
someone's coat
somebody's wedding
one's own
either's preference

Some indefinite pronouns usually require an *of* phrase to indicate possession.

the rights of each
the inclination of many
the satisfaction of all

10. Possessive pronouns do not include apostrophes.

mine	hers
ours	his
yours	theirs
its	

Miscellaneous Styling Conventions

11. No apostrophe is generally used today with plural nouns that are more descriptive than possessive.

weapons systems
managers meeting
singles bar
steelworkers union
awards banquet

12. The possessive form of a phrase is made by adding an apostrophe or -*'s* to the last word in the phrase.

his father-in-law's assistance
board of directors' meeting
from the student of politics' point of view
after a moment or so's thought

Constructions such as these are often rephrased.

from the point of view of the student of politics
after thinking for a moment or so

13. The possessive form of words in quotation marks can be formed in two ways, with -*'s* placed either inside the quotation marks or outside them.

the "Marseillaise"'s [*or* "Marseillaise's"] stirring melody

Since both arrangements look awkward, this construction is usually avoided.

the stirring melody of the "Marseillaise"

14. Possessives of abbreviations are formed like those of nouns that are spelled out. The singular possessive is formed by adding -*'s;* the plural possessive, by adding an apostrophe only.

the IRS's ruling
AT&T's long-distance service
IBM Corp.'s annual report
Eli Lilly & Co.'s chairman
the HMOs' lobbyists

15. The possessive of nouns composed of numerals is formed in the same way as for other nouns. The possessive of singular nouns is formed by adding -*'s;* the possessive of plural nouns is formed by adding an apostrophe only.

1996's commencement speaker
the 1920s' greatest jazz musicians

16. Individual possession is indicated by adding -*'s* to each noun in a sequence. Joint possession may be indicated in the same way, but is most commonly indicated by adding an apostrophe or -*'s* to the last noun in the sequence.

Joan's and Emily's friends
Jim's, Ed's, and Susan's reports
her mother and father's anniversary
Peter and Jan's trip   *or*   Peter's and Jan's trip

Compounds

A compound is a word or word group that consists of two or more parts that work together as a unit to express a specific concept. Compounds can be formed by combining two or more words (as in *double-check, cost-effective, farmhouse, graphic equalizer, park bench, around-the-clock,* or *son of a gun*), by combining prefixes or suffixes with words (as in *ex-president, shoeless, presorted,* or *uninterruptedly*), or by combining two or more word elements (as in *macrophage* or *photochromism*). Compounds are written in one of three ways: solid (as in *cottonmouth*), hyphenated (*screenwriter-director*), or open (*health care*). Because of the variety of standard practice, the choice among these styles for a given compound represents one of the most common and vexing of all style issues that writers encounter.

A good dictionary will list many *permanent compounds,* compounds so commonly used that they have become permanent parts of the language. It will not list *temporary compounds,* those created to meet a writer's need at a particular moment. Most compounds whose meanings are self-evident from the meanings of their component words will not be listed, even if they are permanent and quite widely used. Writers thus cannot rely wholly on dictionaries to guide them in writing compounds.

One approach is to hyphenate all compounds not in the dictionary, since hyphenation immediately identifies them as compounds. But hyphenating all such compounds runs counter to some well-established American practice and can therefore call too much attention to the compound and momentarily distract the reader. Another approach (which applies only to compounds whose elements are complete words) is to leave open any compound not in the dictionary. Though this is widely done, it can result in the reader's failing to recognize a compound for what it is. A third approach is to pattern the compound after other similar ones. Though this approach is likely to be more complicated, it can make the compound look more familiar and thus less distracting or confusing. The paragraphs that follow are intended to help you use this approach.

As a general rule, writing meant for readers in specialized fields usually does not hyphenate compounds, especially technical terminology.

Compound Nouns

Compound nouns are combinations of words that function in a sentence as nouns. They may consist of two or more nouns, a noun and a modifier, or two or more elements that are not nouns.

Short compounds consisting of two nouns often begin as open compounds but tend to close up as they become familiar.

1. **noun + noun** Compounds composed of two nouns that are short and commonly used, of which the first is accented, are usually written solid.

farmhouse   paycheck
hairbrush   football
lifeboat   workplace

2. When a noun + noun compound is short and common but pronounced with nearly equal stress on both nouns, it is more likely to be open.

fuel oil   health care
park bench   desk lamp

3. Noun + noun compounds that consist of longer nouns and are self-evident or temporary are usually written open.

costume designer
computer terminal
billiard table

4. When a noun + noun compound describes a double title or double function, the compound is hyphenated.

hunter-gatherer
secretary-treasurer
bar-restaurant

Sometimes a slash is used in place of the hyphen.

bar/restaurant

5. Compounds formed from a noun or adjective followed by *man, woman, person,* or *people* and denoting an occupation are normally solid.

anchorman   spokesperson
congresswoman   salespeople

6. Compounds that are units of measurement are hyphenated.

foot-pound   column-inch
kilowatt-hour   light-year

7. **adjective + noun** Most adjective + noun compounds are written open.

municipal court   minor league
genetic code   nuclear medicine
hazardous waste   basic training

8. Adjective + noun compounds consisting of two short words are often written solid when the first word is accented. However, some are usually written open, and a few are hyphenated.

notebook   dry cleaner
bluebird   steel mill
shortcut   two-step

9. **participle + noun** Most participle + noun compounds are written open.

landing craft   barbed wire
frying pan   preferred stock
sounding board   informal consent

10. **noun's + noun** Compounds consisting of a possessive noun followed by another noun are usually written open; a few are hyphenated. Compounds of this type that have become solid have lost the apostrophe.

fool's gold   cat's-paw
hornet's nest   bull's-eye
seller's market   foolscap
Queen Anne's lace menswear

11. **noun + verb + -er or -ing** Compounds in which the first noun is the object of the verb or gerund to which the suffix has been added are most often written open but sometimes hyphenated. Permanent compounds like these are sometimes written solid.

problem solver   fund-raiser
deal making   gene-splicing
ticket-taker   air conditioner
street-sweeping   lifesaving

12. **object + verb** Noun compounds consisting of a verb preceded by a noun that is its object are written in various ways.

fish fry   bodyguard
eye-opener   roadblock

13. **verb + object** A few, mostly older compounds are formed from a verb followed by a noun that is its object; they are written solid.

cutthroat   carryall
breakwater   pickpocket

14. **noun + adjective** Compounds composed of a noun followed by an adjective are written open or hyphenated.

sum total   president-elect
consul general   secretary-general

15. **particle + noun** Compounds consisting of a particle (usually a preposition or adverb) and a noun are usually written solid, especially when they are short and the first syllable is accented.

downturn   undertone
outfield   upswing
input   afterthought
outpatient   onrush

A few particle + noun compounds, especially when composed of longer elements or having equal stress on both elements, are hyphenated or open.

on-ramp   off year
cross-reference   cross fire

16. **verb + particle; verb + adverb** These compounds may be hyphenated or solid. Compounds with particles such as *to, in,* and *on* are often hyphenated. Compounds with particles such as *up, off,* and *out* are hyphenated or solid with about equal frequency. Those with longer particles or adverbs are usually solid.

lean-to   spin-off
trade-in   payoff
add-on   time-out
start-up   turnout
backup   hideaway

17. **verb + -er + particle; verb + -ing + particle** Except for *passerby,* these compounds are hyphenated.

runner-up	carrying-on
diners-out	talking-to
listener-in	falling-out

18. **letter + noun**   Compounds formed from a single letter (or sometimes a combination of them) followed by a noun are either open or hyphenated.

T square	T-shirt
B vitamin	f-stop
V neck	H-bomb
Rh factor	A-frame
D major	E-mail *or* e-mail

19. **Compounds of three or four elements**   Compounds of three or four words may be either hyphenated or open. Those incorporating prepositional phrases are more often open; others are usually hyphenated.

editor in chief	right-of-way
power of attorney	jack-of-all-trades
flash in the pan	give-and-take
base on balls	rough-and-tumble

20. **Reduplication compounds**   Compounds that are formed by reduplication and so consist of two similar-sounding elements are hyphenated if each element has more than one syllable. If each element has only one syllable, the compound is often written solid. Very short words and newly coined words are more often hyphenated.

namby-pamby	singsong
razzle-dazzle	sci-fi
crisscross	hip-hop

Compound Adjectives

Compound adjectives are combinations of words that work together to modify a noun—that is, they work as *unit modifiers.* As unit modifiers they can be distinguished from other strings of adjectives that may also precede a noun.

For instance, in "a low, level tract of land" the two adjectives each modify the noun separately; the tract is both low and level. These are *coordinate* (i.e., equal) *modifiers.* In "a low monthly fee" the first adjective modifies the noun plus the second adjective; the phrase denotes a monthly fee that is low. It could not be revised to "a monthly and low fee" without altering or confusing its meaning. Thus, these are *noncoordinate modifiers.* However, "low-level radiation" does not mean radiation that is low and level or level radiation that is low, but rather radiation that is at a low level. Both words work as a unit to modify the noun.

Unit modifiers are usually hyphenated, in order to help readers grasp the relationship of the words and to avoid confusion. The hyphen in "a call for more-specialized controls" removes any ambiguity as to which word *more* modifies. By contrast, the lack of a hyphen in a phrase like "graphic arts exhibition" may give it an undesirable ambiguity.

21. **Before the noun (attributive position)**   Most two-word compound adjectives are hyphenated when placed before the noun.

   the fresh-cut grass
   its longer-lasting effects
   her lace-trimmed dress

   a made-up excuse
   his best-selling novel
   projected health-care costs

22. Compounds whose first word is an adverb ending in *-ly* are usually left open.

   a privately chartered boat
   politically correct opinions
   its weirdly skewed perspective
   a tumultuously cascading torrent

23. Compounds formed of an adverb not ending in *-ly* followed by a participle (or sometimes an adjective) are usually hyphenated when placed before a noun.

   the well-worded statement
   more-stringent measures
   his less-exciting prospects
   their still-awaited assignments
   her once-famous uncle

24. The combination of *very* + adjective is not a unit modifier. (See also paragraph 33 below.)

   a very happy baby

25. When a compound adjective is formed by using a compound noun to modify another noun, it is usually hyphenated.

   a hazardous-waste site
   the basic-training period
   a minor-league pitcher
   a roll-call vote
   their problem-solving abilities

   Some familiar open compound nouns are frequently left open when used as adjectives.

   a high school diploma   *or*   a high-school diploma
   a real estate license   *or*   a real-estate license
   an income tax refund   *or*   an income-tax refund

26. A proper name used as a modifier is not hyphenated. A word that modifies the proper name is attached by a hyphen (or an en dash in typeset material).

   the Civil War era
   a New England tradition
   a *New York Times* article
   the Supreme Court decision
   the splendid *Gone with the Wind* premiere
   a Los Angeles-based company
   a Pulitzer Prize–winning author
   pre–Bull Run skirmishes

27. Compound adjectives composed of foreign words are not hyphenated when placed before a noun unless they are hyphenated in the foreign language itself.

   per diem expenses
   an ad hoc committee
   her *faux-naïf* style
   a comme il faut arrangement
   the a cappella chorus
   a ci-devant professor

28. Compounds that are quoted, capitalized, or italicized are not hyphenated.

a "Springtime in Paris" theme
the book's "I'm OK, you're OK" tone
his AMERICA FIRST sign
the *No smoking* notice

29. Chemical names and most medical names used as modifiers are not hyphenated.

   a sodium hypochlorite bleach
   the amino acid sequence
   a new Parkinson's disease medication

30. Compound adjectives of three or more words are hyphenated when they precede the noun.

   step-by-step instructions
   state-of-the-art equipment
   a wait-and-see attitude
   a longer-than-expected list
   turn-of-the-century medicine

31. **Following the noun** When a compound adjective follows the noun it modifies, it usually ceases to be a unit modifier and is therefore no longer hyphenated.

   instructions that guide you step by step
   a list that was longer than expected

   However, a compound that follows the noun it modifies often keeps its hyphen if it continues to function as a unit modifier, especially if its first element is a noun.

   hikers who were ill-advised to cross the glacier
   an actor too high-strung to relax
   industries that could be called low-tech
   metals that are corrosion-resistant
   tends to be accident-prone

32. Permanent compound adjectives are usually written as they appear in the dictionary even when they follow the noun they modify.

   for reasons that are well-known
   a plan we regarded as half-baked
   The problems are mind-boggling.

   However, compound adjectives of three or more words are normally not hyphenated when they follow the noun they modify, since they usually cease to function as adjectives.

   These remarks are off the record.
   medical practice of the turn of the century

   When compounds of three or more words appear as hyphenated adjectives in dictionaries, the hyphens are retained as long as the phrase is being used as a unit modifier.

   The candidate's position was middle-of-the-road.

33. When an adverb modifies another adverb that is the first element of a compound modifier, the compound may lose its hyphen. If the first adverb modifies the whole compound, however, the hyphen is retained.

   a very well developed idea
      but
   a delightfully well-written book
   a most ill-timed event

34. Adjective compounds that are color names in which each element can function as a noun are almost always hyphenated.

   red-orange fabric
   The fabric was red-orange.

   Color names in which the first element can only be an adjective are often unhyphenated before a noun and usually unhyphenated after.

   a bright red tie
   the pale yellow-green chair
   reddish orange fabric   *or*   reddish-orange fabric
   The fabric was reddish orange.

35. Compound modifiers that include a number followed by a noun (except for the noun *percent*) are hyphenated when they precede the noun they modify, but usually not when they follow it. (For details on measurement, see paragraph 42 on page 221.)

   the four-color press
   a 12-foot-high fence
   a fence 12 feet high
   a 300-square-mile area
   an area of 300 square miles
      but
   a 10 percent raise

   If a currency symbol precedes the number, the hyphen is omitted.

   an $8.5 million deficit

36. An adjective composed of a number followed by a noun in the possessive is not hyphenated.

   a nine days' wonder
   a two weeks' wait
      but
   a two-week wait

Compound Adverbs

37. Adverb compounds consisting of preposition + noun are almost always written solid. However, there are a few important exceptions.

   downstairs
   uphill
   offshore
   overnight
      but
   in-house
   off-key
   on-line

38. Compound adverbs of more than two words are usually written open, and they usually follow the words they modify.

   here and there
   more or less
   head and shoulders
   hand in hand
   every which way
   once and for all
      but
   a more-or-less certain result

   A few three-word adverbs are usually hyphenated, but many are written open even if the corresponding adjective is hyphenated.

   placed back-to-back
   met face-to-face
      but

a word-for-word quotation
quoted word for word
software bought off the shelf

Compound Verbs

39. Two-word verbs consisting of a verb followed by an adverb or a preposition are written open.

follow up   take on
roll back   run across
strike out   set back

40. A compound composed of a particle followed by a verb is written solid.

overlook   undercut
outfit   download

41. A verb derived from an open or hyphenated compound noun is hyphenated.

double-space   water-ski
rubber-stamp   field-test

42. A verb derived from a solid noun is written solid.

mastermind   brainstorm
highlight   sideline

Compounds Formed with Word Elements

Many new and temporary compounds are formed by adding word elements to existing words or by combining word elements. There are three basic kinds of word elements: prefixes (such as *anti-, non-, pre-, post-, re-, super-*), suffixes (such as *-er, -fold, -ism, -ist, -less, -ness*), and combining forms (such as *mini-, macro-, pseudo-, -graphy, -logy*). Prefixes and suffixes are usually attached to existing words; combining forms are usually combined to form new words.

43. prefix + word Except as specified in the paragraphs below, compounds formed from a prefix and a word are usually written solid.

anticrime   subzero
nonaligned   superheroine
premedical   transnational
reorchestration   postdoctoral

44. If the prefix ends with a vowel and the word it is attached to begins with the same vowel, the compound is usually hyphenated.

anti-incumbent   semi-independent
de-escalate   intra-arterial
co-organizer   pre-engineered

However, there are many exceptions.

reelect
preestablished
cooperate

45. If the base word or compound to which a prefix is added is capitalized, the resulting compound is almost always hyphenated.

pre-Victorian
anti-Western
post-Darwinian
non-English-speaking
    but

transatlantic
transalpine

If the prefix and the base word together form a new proper name, the compound may be solid with the prefix capitalized.

Postimpressionists
Precambrian
    but
Pre-Raphaelite

46. Compounds made with *ex-*, in its "former" sense, and *self-* are hyphenated.

ex-mayor   self-control
ex-husband   self-sustaining

Compounds formed from *vice-* are usually hyphenated. Some permanent compounds are open.

vice-chair   vice president
vice-consul   vice admiral

A temporary compound with *quasi(-)* or *pseudo(-)* may be written open (if *quasi* or *pseudo* is being treated as a modifier) or hyphenated (if it is being treated as a combining form).

quasi intellectual *or* quasi-intellectual
pseudo liberal *or* pseudo-liberal

47. If a prefix is added to a hyphenated compound, it may be either followed by a hyphen or closed up solid to the next element. Permanent compounds of this kind should be checked in a dictionary.

unair-conditioned
ultra-up-to-date
non-self-governing
unself-confident

48. If a prefix is added to an open compound, the hyphen is often replaced by an en dash in typeset material.

ex–campaign treasurer
post–World War I era

49. A compound that would be identical with another word if written solid is usually hyphenated to prevent misreading.

a re-creation of the setting
shopped at the co-op
multi-ply fabric

50. Compounds that might otherwise be solid are often hyphenated in order to clarify their formation, meaning, or pronunciation.

tri-city   non-news
de-iced   anti-fur
re-oil   pro-choice

51. When prefixes are attached to numerals, the compounds are hyphenated.

pre-1995 models
post-1945 economy
non-19th-century architecture

52. Compounds created from proper ethnic or national combining forms are hyphenated when the second ele-

ment is an independent word, but solid when it is a combining form.

Anglo-Saxon   Anglophile
Judeo-Christian Francophone
Sino-Japanese   Sinophobe

53. Prefixes that are repeated in the same compound are separated by a hyphen.

re-refried
post-postmodern

54. Compounds consisting of different prefixes or adjectives with the same base word which are joined by *and* or *or* are shortened by pruning the first compound back to a hyphenated prefix.

pre- and postoperative care
anti- or pro-Revolutionary sympathies
over- and underachievers
early- and mid-20th-century painters
4-, 6-, and 8-foot lengths

55. word + suffix Except as noted in the paragraphs below, compounds formed by adding a suffix to a word are written solid.

Fourierism   characterless
benightedness custodianship
yellowish   easternmost

56. Compounds made with a suffix or a terminal combining form are often hyphenated if the base word is more than two syllables long, if it ends with the same letter the suffix begins with, or if it is a proper name.

industry-wide   jewel-like
recession-proof Hollywood-ish
American-ness   Europe-wide

57. Compounds made from a number + *-odd* are hyphenated. A number + *-fold* is written solid if the number is spelled out but hyphenated if it is in numerals.

fifty-odd   tenfold
50-odd   10-fold

58. Most compounds formed from an open or hyphenated compound + a suffix do not separate the suffix with a hyphen. But combining forms that also exist as independent words, such as *-like, -wide, -worthy,* and *-proof,* are attached by a hyphen.

self-righteousness
middle-of-the-roadism
bobby-soxer
a Red Cross-like approach
a New York-wide policy

Open compounds often become hyphenated when a suffix is added unless they are proper nouns.

flat-taxer
Ivy Leaguer
World Federalist

59. combining form + combining form New terms in technical fields created with one or more combining forms are normally written solid.

cyberworld
macrographic

4 Abbreviations

Abbreviations may be used to save space and time, to avoid repetition of long words and phrases, or simply to conform to conventional usage.

The contemporary styling of abbreviations is inconsistent and arbitrary, and no set of rules can hope to cover all the possible variations, exceptions, and peculiarities encountered in print. The form abbreviations take—capitalized vs. lowercased, punctuated vs. unpunctuated—often depends on a writer's preference or a publisher's or organization's policy. However, the following paragraphs provide a number of useful guidelines to contemporary practice. In doubtful cases, a good general dictionary or a dictionary of abbreviations will usually show standard forms for common abbreviations.

The present discussion deals largely with general, non-technical writing. In scientific writing, abbreviations are almost never punctuated.

An abbreviation is not divided at the end of a line.

Abbreviations are almost never italicized. An abbreviation consisting of single initial letters, whether punctuated or not, never standardly has spacing between the letters. (Initials of personal names, however, normally are separated by spaces.)

The first reference to any frequently abbreviated term or name that could be confusing or unfamiliar is commonly spelled out, often followed immediately by its abbreviation in parentheses. Later references employ the abbreviation alone.

Punctuation

1. A period follows most abbreviations that are formed by omitting all but the first few letters of a word.

   cont. [*for* continued]
   enc. [*for* enclosure]
   Oct. [*for* October]
   univ. [*for* university]

   Former abbreviations that are now considered words do not need a period.

   lab   photo
   gym   ad

2. A period follows most abbreviations that are formed by omitting letters from the middle of a word.

   govt. [*for* government]
   atty. [*for* attorney]
   bros. [*for* brothers]
   Dr. [*for* Doctor]

   Some abbreviations, usually called *contractions,* replace the omitted letters with an apostrophe. Such contractions do not end with a period. (In American usage, very few contractions other than two-word contractions involving verbs are in standard use.)

   ass'n   *or*   assn. [*for* association]
   dep't   *or*   dept. [*for* department]
   nat'l   *or*   natl. [*for* national]
   can't [*for* cannot]

3. Periods are usually omitted from abbreviations made up of single initial letters. However, for some of these abbreviations, especially uncapitalized ones, the periods are usually retained. No space follows an internal period.

   GOP [*for* Grand Old Party]
   PR [*for* public relations]
   CEO   *or*   C.E.O. [*for* chief executive officer]
   a.m. [*for* ante meridiem]

4. A few abbreviations are punctuated with one or more slashes in place of periods. (For details on the slash, see the section beginning on page 191.)

   c/o [*for* care of]
   d/b/a   *or*   d.b.a. [*for* doing business as]
   w/o [*for* without]
   w/w [*for* wall-to-wall]

5. Terms in which a suffix is added to a numeral are not genuine abbreviations and do not require a period. (For details on ordinal numbers, see the section on page 216.)

   1st   3d
   2nd   8vo

6. Isolated letters of the alphabet used to designate a shape or position in a sequence are not abbreviations and are not punctuated.

   T square
   A1
   F minor

7. When a punctuated abbreviation ends a sentence, its period becomes the terminal period.

   For years she claimed she was "the oldest living fossil at Briggs & Co."

Capitalization

1. Abbreviations are capitalized if the words they represent are proper nouns or adjectives.

   F [*for* Fahrenheit]
   IMF [*for* International Monetary Fund]
   Jan. [*for* January]
   Amer. [*for* American]
   LWV [*for* League of Women Voters]

2. Abbreviations are usually all-capitalized when they represent initial letters of lowercased words. However, some common abbreviations formed in this way are often lowercased.

   IQ [*for* intelligence quotient]
   U.S. [*for* United States]
   COLA [*for* cost-of-living allowance]
   FYI [*for* for your information]
   f.o.b.   *or*   FOB [*for* free on board]
   c/o [*for* care of]

3. Most abbreviations formed from single initial letters that are pronounced as words, rather than as a series of letters, are capitalized. Those that are not proper nouns and have been assimilated into the language as words in their own right are most often lowercased.

OSHA	snafu
NATO	laser
CARE	sonar
NAFTA	scuba

4. Abbreviations that are ordinarily capitalized are commonly used to begin sentences, but abbreviations that are ordinarily uncapitalized are not.

Dr. Smith strongly disagrees.
OSHA regulations require these new measures.
Page 22 [*not* P. 22] was missing.

Plurals, Possessives, and Compounds

1. Punctuated abbreviations of single words are pluralized by adding *-s* before the period.

yrs. [*for* years]
hwys. [*for* highways]
figs. [*for* figures]

2. Punctuated abbreviations that stand for phrases or compounds are usually pluralized by adding *-'s* after the last period.

M.D.'s *or* M.D.s
Ph.D.'s *or* Ph.D.s
LL.B.'s *or* LL.B.s
v.p.'s

3. All-capitalized, unpunctuated abbreviations are usually pluralized by adding a lowercase *-s*.

IRAs	CPAs
PCs	SATs

4. The plural form of a few lowercase one-letter abbreviations is made by repeating the letter.

ll. [*for* lines]
pp. [*for* pages]
nn. [*for* notes]
vv. [*for* verses]
ff. *or* ff [*for* and the following ones *or* folios]

5. The plural form of abbreviations of units of measurement (including one-letter abbreviations) is the same as the singular form. (For more on units of measurement, see the section on page 221.)

10 cc *or* cc. [*for* cubic centimeters]
30 m *or* m. [*for* meters]
15 mm *or* mm. [*for* millimeters]
24 h. [*for* hours]
10 min. [*for* minutes]
45 mi. [*for* miles]

However, in informal nontechnical text several such abbreviations are pluralized like other single-word abbreviations.

lbs.	qts.
gals.	hrs.

6. Possessives of abbreviations are formed like those of spelled-out nouns: the singular possessive is formed by adding *-'s*, the plural possessive simply by adding an apostrophe.

the CEO's speech
Apex Co.'s profits
the PACs' influence
Brown Bros.' ads

7. Compounds that consist of an abbreviation added to another word are formed in the same way as compounds that consist of spelled-out nouns.

an FDA-approved drug
an R&D-driven company
the Eau Claire, Wisc.–based publisher

Compounds formed by adding a prefix or suffix to an abbreviation are usually hyphenated.

pre-CD recordings
non-IRA deductions
a CIA-like operation
a PCB-free product

Specific Styling Conventions

A and *An*

1. The choice of the article *a* or *an* before abbreviations depends on the sound, rather than the actual letter, with which the abbreviation begins. If it begins with a consonant sound, *a* is normally used; if with a vowel sound, *an* is used.

a CD-ROM version
a YAF member
a U.S. Senator
an FDA-approved drug
an M.D. degree
an ABA convention

A.D. and *B.C.*

2. The abbreviations A.D. and B.C. and other abbreviated era designations usually appear in books and journals as small capitals; in newspapers and in typed or keyboarded material, they usually appear as full capitals. The abbreviation B.C. follows the date; A.D. usually precedes the date, though in many publications A.D. follows the date as well. In references to whole centuries, A.D. follows the century. (For more on era designations, see paragraph 12 on page 218.)

A.D. 185 *but also* 185 A.D.
41 B.C.
the fourth century A.D.

Agencies, Associations, Organizations, and Companies

3. The names of agencies, associations, and organizations are usually abbreviated after being spelled out on their first occurrence in a text. If a company is easily recognizable from its initials, the abbreviation is likewise usually employed after the first mention. The abbreviations are usually all-capitalized and unpunctuated. (In contexts

where the abbreviation will be recognized, it often replaces the full name throughout.)

> Next, the president of the Pioneer Valley Transit Authority presented the annual PVTA award.
> . . . at the American Bar Association (ABA) meeting in June. The ABA's new officers . . .
> International Business Machines released its first-quarter earnings figures today. An IBM spokesperson . . .

4. The words *Company, Corporation, Incorporated,* and *Limited* in company names are commonly abbreviated even at their first appearance, except in quite formal writing.

> Procter & Gamble Company   *or*   Procter & Gamble Co.
> Brandywine Corporation   *or*   Brandywine Corp.

Ampersand

5. The ampersand (&), representing the word *and,* is often used in the names of companies.

> H&R Block
> Standard & Poor's
> Ogilvy & Mather

It is not used in the names of federal agencies.

> U.S. Fish and Wildlife Service
> Office of Management and Budget

Even when a spelled-out *and* appears in a company's official name, it is often replaced by an ampersand in writing referring to the company, whether for the sake of consistency or because of the writer's inability to verify the official styling.

6. When an ampersand is used in an abbreviation, there is usually no space on either side of the ampersand.

> The Barkers welcome all guests to their B&B at 54 West Street.
> The S&P 500 showed gains in technology stocks.
> The Texas A&M Aggies prevailed again on Sunday.

7. When an ampersand is used between the last two elements in a series, the comma is omitted.

> Jones, Kuhn & Malloy, Attorneys at Law

Books of the Bible

8. Books of the Bible are spelled out in running text but generally abbreviated in references to chapter and verse.

> The minister based his first Advent sermon on Matthew.
> Ye cannot serve God and mammon.—Matt. 6:24

Compass Points

9. Compass points are normally abbreviated when they follow street names; these abbreviations may be punctuated and are usually preceded by a comma.

> 1600 Pennsylvania Avenue[,] NW [N.W.]

When a compass point precedes the word *Street, Avenue,* etc., or when it follows the word but forms an integral part of the street name, it is usually spelled out.

> 230 West 43rd Street
> 50 Park Avenue South

Dates

10. The names of days and months are spelled out in running text.

> at the Monday editorial meeting
> the December issue of *Scientific American*
> a meeting held on August 1, 1995

The names of months usually are not abbreviated in datelines of business letters, but they are often abbreviated in government and military correspondence.

business dateline: November 1, 1995
military dateline: 1 Nov 95

Degrees and Professional Ratings

11. Abbreviations of academic degrees are usually punctuated; abbreviations of professional ratings are slightly more commonly unpunctuated.

> Ph.D.
> B.Sc.
> M.B.A.
> PLS   *or*   P.L.S. [*for* Professional Legal Secretary]
> CMA   *or*   C.M.A. [*for* Certified Medical Assistant]
> FACP   *or*   F.A.C.P. [*for* Fellow of the American College of Physicians]

12. Only the first letter of each element in abbreviations of degrees and professional ratings is generally capitalized.

> D.Ch.E. [*for* Doctor of Chemical Engineering]
> Litt.D. [*for* Doctor of Letters]
> D.Th. [*for* Doctor of Theology]
> *but*
> LL.B. [*for* Bachelor of Laws]
> LL.M. [*for* Master of Laws]
> LL.D. [*for* Doctor of Laws]

Geographical Names

13. When abbreviations of state names are used in running text immediately following the name of a city or county, the traditional state abbreviations are often used.

> Ellen White of 49 Lyman St., Saginaw, Mich., has been chosen . . .
> the Dade County, Fla., public schools
> *but*
> Grand Rapids, in western Michigan, . . .

Official postal service abbreviations for states are used in mailing addresses.

> 6 Bay Rd.
> Gibson Island, MD 21056

14. Terms such as *Street, Road,* and *Boulevard* are often written as punctuated abbreviations in running text when they form part of a proper name.

> an accident on Windward Road [*or* Rd.]
> our office at 1234 Cross Blvd. [*or* Boulevard]

15. Names of countries are usually spelled in full in running text.

> South Africa's president urged the United States to impose meaningful sanctions.

Abbreviations for country names (in tables, for example), are usually punctuated. When formed from the single initial letters of two or more individual words, they are sometimes unpunctuated.

Mex.	Scot.
Can.	U.K. *or* UK
Ger.	U.S. *or* US

16. *United States* is normally abbreviated when used as an adjective or attributive. When used as a noun, it is generally spelled out.

> the U.S. Department of Justice
> U.S. foreign policy
> The United States has declined to participate.

17. *Saint* is usually abbreviated when it is part of a geographical or topographical name. *Mount, Point,* and *Fort* may be either spelled out or abbreviated. (For the abbreviation of *Saint* with personal names, see paragraph 25 below.)

> St. Paul, Minnesota *or* Saint Paul, Minnesota
> St. Thomas, U.S.V.I. *or* Saint Thomas
> Mount Vernon *or* Mt. Vernon
> Point Reyes *or* Pt. Reyes
> Fort Worth *or* Ft. Worth
> Mt. Kilimanjaro *or* Mount Kilimanjaro

Latin Words and Phrases

18. Several Latin words and phrases are almost always abbreviated. They are punctuated, lowercased, and usually not italicized.

etc.	ibid.
i.e.	op. cit.
e.g.	q.v.
cf.	c. *or* ca.
viz.	fl.
et al.	et seq.

Versus is usually abbreviated *v.* in legal writing, *vs.* otherwise.

> *Da Costa* v. *United States*
> good vs. evil
>   *or* good versus evil

Latitude and *Longitude*

19. The words *latitude* and *longitude* are abbreviated in tables and in technical contexts but often written out in running text.

> *in a table:* lat. 10°20′N *or* lat. 10-20N
> *in text:* from 10°20′ north latitude to 10°30′ south latitude
>   *or* from lat. 10°20′N to lat. 10°30′S

Military Ranks and Units

20. Official abbreviations for military ranks follow specific unpunctuated styles for each branch of the armed forces. Nonmilitary writing usually employs a punctuated and less concise style.

> *in the military:* BG Carter R. Stokes, USA
>   LCDR Dawn Wills-Craig, USN
>   Col S. J. Smith, USMC
>   LTJG Carlos Ramos, USCG
>   Sgt Bernard P. Brodkey, USAF

> *outside the military:* Brig. Gen. Carter R. Stokes
>   Lt. Comdr. Dawn Wills-Craig
>   Col. S. J. Smith
>   Lt. (j.g.) Carlos Ramos
>   Sgt. Bernard P. Brodkey

21. Outside the military, military ranks are usually given in full when used with a surname only but abbreviated when used with a full name.

> Major Mosby
> Maj. John S. Mosby

Number

22. The word *number,* when followed by a numeral, is usually abbreviated to *No.* or *no.*

> The No. 1 priority is to promote profitability.
> We recommend no. 6 thread.
> Policy No. 123-5-X
> Publ. Nos. 12 and 13

Personal Names

23. When initials are used with a surname, they are spaced and punctuated. Unspaced initials of a few famous persons, which may or may not be punctuated, are sometimes used in place of their full names.

> E. M. Forster
> C. P. E. Bach
> JFK *or* J.F.K.

24. The abbreviations *Jr.* and *Sr.* may or may not be preceded by a comma.

> Martin Luther King Jr.
>   *or* Martin Luther King, Jr.

Saint

25. The word *Saint* is often abbreviated when used before the name of a saint. When it forms part of a surname or an institution's name, it follows the style used by the person or institution. (For the styling of *Saint* in geographical names, see paragraph 17 above.)

> St. [*or* Saint] Teresa of Avila
> Augustus Saint-Gaudens
> Ruth St. Denis
> St. Martin's Press
> St. John's College

Scientific Terms

26. In binomial nomenclature, a genus name may be abbreviated to its initial letter after the first reference. The abbreviation is always capitalized, punctuated, and italicized.

> . . . its better-known relative *Atropa belladonna* (deadly nightshade).
> Only *A. belladonna* is commonly found in . . .

27. Abbreviations for the names of chemical compounds and the symbols for chemical elements and formulas are unpunctuated.

MSG	O
PCB	NaCl
Pb	FeS

28. Abbreviations in computer terms are usually unpunctuated.

PC	Esc
RAM	Alt
CD-ROM	Ctrl
I/O	ASCII
DOS	EBCDIC

Time

29. When time is expressed in figures, the abbreviations *a.m. (ante meridiem)* and *p.m. (post meridiem)* are most often written as punctuated lowercase letters, sometimes as punctuated small capital letters. In newspapers, they usually appear in full-size capitals. (For more on *a.m.* and *p.m.,* see paragraph 39 on page 221.)

8:30 a.m.   *or*   8:30 A.M.   *or*   8:30 A.M.
10:00 p.m.   *or*   10:00 P.M.   *or*   10:00 P.M.

Time-zone designations are usually capitalized and unpunctuated.

9:22 a.m. EST [*for* eastern standard time]
4:45 p.m. CDT [*for* central daylight time]

Titles and Degrees

30. The courtesy titles *Mr., Ms., Mrs.,* and *Messrs.* occur only as abbreviations today. The professional titles *Doctor, Professor, Representative,* and *Senator* are often abbreviated.

Ms. Lee A. Downs
Messrs. Lake, Mason, and Nambeth
Doctor Howe   *or*   Dr. Howe

31. Despite some traditional objections, the honorific titles *Honorable* and *Reverend* are often abbreviated, with and without *the* preceding the titles.

the Honorable Samuel I. O'Leary
or   [the] Hon. Samuel I. O'Leary

the Revered Samuel I. O'Leary
or   [the] Rev. Samuel I. O'Leary

32. When an abbreviation for an academic degree, professional certification, or association membership follows a name, no courtesy or professional title precedes it.

Dr. Jesse Smith   *or*   Jesse Smith, M.D.
but not   Dr. Jesse Smith, M.D.
Katherine Fox Derwinski, CLU
Carol W. Manning, M.D., FACPS
Michael B. Jones II, J.D.
Peter D. Cohn, Jr., CPA

33. The abbreviation *Esq.* (for *Esquire*) often follows attorneys' names in correspondence and in formal listings, and less often follows the names of certain other professionals, including architects, consuls, clerks of court, and justices of the peace. It is not used if a degree or professional rating follows the name, or if a courtesy title or honorific (*Mr., Ms., Hon., Dr.,* etc.) precedes the name.

Carolyn B. West, Esq.
not   Ms. Carolyn B. West, Esq.
and not   Carolyn B. West, J.D., Esq.

Units of Measurement

34. A unit of measurement that follows a figure is often abbreviated, especially in technical writing. The figure and abbreviation are separated by a space. If the numeral is written out, the unit should also be written out.

15 cu. ft.   *but*   fifteen cubic feet
What is its capacity in cubic feet?

35. Abbreviations for metric units are usually unpunctuated; those for traditional units are usually punctuated in nonscientific writing. (For more on units of measurement, see the section on page 221.)

14 ml	8 ft.
12 km	4 sec.
50 m	20 min.

5 Numbers

The treatment of numbers presents special difficulties because there are so many conventions to follow, some of which may conflict in a particular passage. The major issue is whether to spell out numbers or to express them in figures, and usage varies considerably on this point.

Numbers as Words or Figures

At one style extreme—usually limited to proclamations, legal documents, and some other types of very formal writing—all numbers (sometimes even including dates) are written out. At the other extreme, some types of technical writing may contain no written-out numbers. Figures are generally easier to read than spelled-out numbers; however, the spelled-out forms are helpful in certain circumstances, and are often felt to be less jarring than figures in nontechnical writing.

Basic Conventions

1. Two alternative basic conventions are in common use. The first and more widely used system requires that numbers up through nine be spelled out, and that figures be used for exact numbers greater than nine. (In a variation of this system, the number ten is spelled out.) Round numbers that consist of a whole number between one and nine followed by *hundred, thousand, million,* etc., may either be spelled out or expressed in figures.

   > The museum includes four rooms of early American tools and implements, 345 pieces in all.
   > He spoke for almost three hours, inspiring his audience of 19,000 devoted followers.
   > They sold more than 700 [*or* seven hundred] TVs during the 10-day sale.
   > She'd told him so a thousand times.

2. The second system requires that numbers from one through ninety-nine be spelled out, and that figures be used for all exact numbers above ninety-nine. (In a variation of this system, the number one hundred is spelled out.) Numbers that consist of a whole number between one and ninety-nine followed by *hundred, thousand, million,* etc., are also spelled out.

   > Audubon's engraver spent nearly twelve years completing these four volumes, which comprise 435 hand-colored plates.
   > In the course of four hours, she signed twenty-five hundred copies of her book.

3. Written-out numbers only use hyphens following words ending in *-ty*. The word *and* before such words is usually omitted.

   > twenty-two
   > five hundred ninety-seven
   > two thousand one hundred forty-nine

Sentence Beginnings

4. Numbers that begin a sentence are written out. An exception is occasionally made for dates. Spelled-out numbers that are lengthy and awkward are usually avoided by restructuring the sentence.

   > Sixty-two new bills will be brought before the committee.
   > *or* There will be 62 new bills brought before the committee.
   > Nineteen ninety-five was our best earnings year so far.
   > *or occasionally* 1995 was our best earnings year so far.
   > One hundred fifty-seven illustrations, including 86 color plates, are contained in the book.
   > *or* The book contains 157 illustrations, including 86 color plates.

Adjacent Numbers and Numbers in Series

5. Two separate figures are generally not written adjacent to one another in running text unless they form a series. Instead, either the sentence is rephrased or one of the figures is spelled out—usually the figure with the shorter written form.

   > sixteen ½-inch dowels
   > worked five 9-hour days in a row
   > won twenty 100-point games
   > lost 15 fifty-point matches
   > By 1997, thirty schools . . .

6. Numbers paired at the beginning of a sentence are usually written alike. If the first word of the sentence is a spelled-out number, the second number is also spelled out. However, each number may instead be styled independently, even if that results in an inconsistent pairing.

   > Sixty to seventy-five copies will be required.
   > *or* Sixty to 75 copies will be required.

7. Numbers that form a pair or a series within a sentence or a paragraph are often treated identically even when they would otherwise be styled differently. The style of the largest number usually determines that of the others. If one number is a mixed or simple fraction, figures are used for all the numbers in the series.

   > She wrote one composition for English and translated twelve [*or* 12] pages for French that night.
   > His total record sales came to a meager 8 [*or* eight] million; Bing Crosby's, he mused, may have surpassed 250 million.
   > The three jobs took 5, 12, and 4½ hours, respectively.

Round Numbers

8. Approximate or round numbers, particularly those that can be expressed in one or two words, are often spelled out in general writing. In technical and scientific writing, they are expressed as numerals.

   > seven hundred people   *or*   700 people
   > five thousand years   *or*   5,000 years
   > four hundred thousand volumes   *or*   400,000 volumes
   > *but not*   400 thousand volumes
   > *but in technical writing*
   > 200 species of fish
   > 50,000 people per year
   > 300,000 years

9. Round (and round-appearing) numbers of one million and above are often expressed as figures followed by the word *million, billion,* and so forth. The figure may in-

clude a one- or two-digit decimal fraction; more exact numbers are written entirely in figures.

> the last 600 million years
> about 4.6 billion years old
> 1.2 million metric tons of grain
> $7.25 million
> $3,456,000,000

Ordinal Numbers

10. Ordinal numbers generally follow the styling rules for cardinal numbers. In technical writing, ordinal numbers are usually written as figure-plus-suffix combinations. Certain ordinal numbers—for example, those for percentiles and latitudes—are usually set as figures even in nontechnical contexts.

> entered the seventh grade
> wrote the 9th [*or* ninth] and 12th [*or* twelfth] chapters
> in the 21st [*or* twenty-first] century
> the 7th percentile
> the 38th parallel

11. In figure-plus-suffix combinations where the figure ends in 2 or 3, either a one- or a two-letter suffix may be used. A period does not follow the suffix.

> 2d   *or*   2nd
> 33d   *or*   33rd
> 102d   *or*   102nd

Roman Numerals

12. Roman numerals are traditionally used to differentiate rulers and popes with identical names.

> King George III
> Henri IV
> Innocent X

13. When Roman numerals are used to differentiate related males with the same name, they are used only with the full name. Ordinals are sometimes used instead of Roman numerals. The possessive is formed in the usual way. (For the use of *Jr.* and *Sr.,* see paragraph 24 on page 213.)

> James R. Watson II
> James R. Watson 2nd *or* 2d
> James R. Watson II's [*or* 2nd's *or* 2d's] alumni gift

14. Lowercase Roman numerals are generally used to number book pages that precede the regular Arabic sequence (often including a table of contents, acknowledgments, foreword, or other material).

> on page iv of the preface
> See Introduction, pp. ix–xiii.

15. Roman numerals are used in outlines; see paragraph 23 on page 220.

16. Roman numerals are found as part of a few established scientific and technical terms. Chords in the study of music harmony are designated by capital and lowercase Roman numerals (often followed by small Arabic numbers). Most technical terms that include numbers, however, express them in Arabic form.

> blood-clotting factor VII
> quadrant III

the cranial nerves II and IX
HIV-III virus
Population II stars
type I error
vii$_6$ chord
> *but*
adenosine 3′,5′-monophosphate
cesium 137
PL/1 programming language

17. Miscellaneous uses of Roman numerals include the Articles, and often the Amendments, of the Constitution. Roman numerals are still sometimes used for references to the acts and scenes of plays and occasionally for volume numbers in bibliographic references.

> Article IX
> Act III, Scene ii   *or*   Act 3, Scene 2
> (III, ii)   *or*   (3, 2)
> Vol. XXIII, No. 4   *but usually*   Vol. 23, No. 4

Punctuation

These paragraphs provide general rules for the use of commas, hyphens, and en dashes with compound and large numbers. For specific categories of numbers, such as dates, money, and decimal fractions, see Specific Styling Conventions, beginning on page 217.

Commas in Large Numbers

1. In general writing, figures of four digits may be written with or without a comma; including the comma is more common. If the numerals form part of a tabulation, commas are necessary so that four-digit numerals can align with numerals of five or more digits.

> 2,000 cases   *or less commonly*   2000 cases

2. Whole numbers of five digits or more (but not decimal fractions) use a comma to separate three-digit groups, counting from the right.

> a fee of $12,500
> 15,000 units
> a population of 1,500,000

3. Certain types of numbers of four digits or more do not contain commas. These include decimal fractions and the numbers of policies and contracts, checks, street addresses, rooms and suites, telephones, pages, military hours, and years.

> 2.5544   Room 1206
> Policy 33442   page 145
> check 34567   1650 hours
> 12537 Wilshire Blvd.   in 1929

4. In technical writing, the comma is frequently replaced by a thin space in numerals of five or more digits. Digits to the right of the decimal point are also separated in this way, counting from the decimal point.

> 28 666 203
> 209.775 42

Hyphens

5. Hyphens are used with written-out numbers between 21 and 99.

> forty-one years old
> his forty-first birthday
> Four hundred twenty-two visitors were counted.

6. A hyphen is used in a written-out fraction employed as a modifier. A nonmodifying fraction consisting of two words only is usually left open, although it may also be hyphenated. (For details on fractions, see the section beginning on page 219.)

> a one-half share
> three fifths of her paycheck *or* three-fifths of her paycheck
> *but*
> four five-hundredths

7. Numbers that form the first part of a modifier expressing measurement are followed by a hyphen. (For units of measurement, see the section on page 221.)

> a 5-foot board
> a 28-mile trip
> an eight-pound baby
> *but*
> a $6 million profit

8. Serial numbers, Social Security numbers, telephone numbers, and extended zip codes often contain hyphens that make lengthy numerals more readable or separate coded information.

> 020-42-1691
> 413-734-3134 *or* (413) 734-3134
> 01102-2812

9. Numbers are almost never divided at the end of a line. If division is unavoidable, the break occurs only after a comma.

Inclusive Numbers

10. Inclusive numbers—those that express a range—are usually separated either by the word *to* or by a hyphen or en dash, meaning "(up) to and including."

> spanning the years 1915 to 1941
> the fiscal year 1994–95
> the decade 1920–1929
> pages 40 to 98
> pp. 40–98

Inclusive numbers separated by a hyphen or en dash are not used after the words *from* or *between*.

> from page 385 to page 419 *not* from page 385–419
> from 9:30 to 5:30 *not* from 9:30–5:30
> between 1997 and 2000 *not* between 1997–2000
> between 80 and 90 percent *not* between 80–90 percent

11. Inclusive page numbers and dates may be either written in full or elided (i.e., shortened) to save space or for ease of reading.

> pages 523–526 *or* pages 523–26
> 1955–1969 *or* 1955–69

However, inclusive dates that appear in titles and other headings are almost never elided. Dates that appear with era designations are also not elided.

> *England and the French Revolution 1789–1797*
> 1900–1901 *not* 1900–01 *and not* 1900–1
> 872–863 B.C. *not* 872–63 B.C.

12. The most common style for the elision of inclusive numbers is based on the following rules: Never elide inclusive numbers that have only two digits.

> 24–28 *not* 24–8
> 86–87 *not* 86–7

Never elide inclusive numbers when the first number ends in 00.

> 100–103 *not* 100–03 *and not* 100–3
> 300–329 *not* 300–29

In other numbers, do not omit the tens digit from the higher number. *Exception:* Where the tens digit of both numbers is zero, write only one digit for the higher number.

> 234–37 *not* 234–7
> 3,824–29 *not* 3,824–9
> 605–7 *not* 605–07

13. Units of measurement expressed in words or abbreviations are usually used only after the second element of an inclusive number. Symbols, however, are repeated.

> ten to fifteen dollars
> 30 to 35 degrees Celsius
> an increase in dosage from 200 to 500 mg
> *but*
> 45° to 48° F
> $50–$60 million
> *or* $50 million to $60 million

14. Numbers that are part of an inclusive set or range are usually styled alike: figures with figures, spelled-out words with other spelled-out words.

> from 8 to 108 absences
> five to twenty guests
> 300,000,000 to 305,000,000
> *not* 300 million to 305,000,000

Specific Styling Conventions

The following paragraphs, arranged alphabetically, describe styling practices commonly followed for specific situations involving numbers.

Addresses

1. Numerals are used for all building, house, apartment, room, and suite numbers except for *one,* which is usually written out.

> 6 Lincoln Road   Room 982
> 1436 Fremont Street   Suite 2000
> Apartment 609   One Bayside Drive

When the address of a building is used as its name, the number in the address is often written out.

> the sophisticated elegance of Ten Park Avenue

2. Numbered streets have their numbers written as ordinals. Street names from First through Tenth are usually written out, and numerals are used for all higher-numbered streets. Less commonly, all numbered street names up to and including One Hundredth are spelled out.

> 167 Second Avenue
> 19 South 22nd Street
>   *or less commonly* 19 South Twenty-second Street
> 145 East 145th Street
> in the 60s *or* in the Sixties [streets from 60th to 69th]
> in the 120s [streets from 120th to 129th]

When a house or building number immediately precedes the number of a street, a spaced hyphen may be inserted between the two numbers, or the street number may be written out, for the sake of clarity.

> 2018 - 14th Street
> 2018 Fourteenth Street

3. Arabic numerals are used to designate highways and, in some states, county roads.

> Interstate 90 *or* I-90
> U.S. Route 1 *or* U.S. 1
> Texas 23
> County 213

Dates

4. Year numbers are written as figures. If a year number begins a sentence, it may be left as a figure but more often is spelled out; the sentence may also be rewritten to avoid beginning it with a figure.

> the 1997 edition
> Nineteen thirty-seven marked the opening of the Golden
>   Gate Bridge.
>   *or* The year 1937 marked the opening of the Golden
>   Gate Bridge.
>   *or* The Golden Gate Bridge opened in 1937.

5. A year number may be abbreviated to its last two digits when an event is so well known that it needs no century designation. In these cases an apostrophe precedes the numerals.

> the blizzard of '88
> class of '91 *or* class of 1991
> the Spirit of '76

6. Full dates are traditionally written in the sequence month-day-year, with the year set off by commas that precede and follow it. An alternative style, used in the military and in U.S. government publications, is the inverted sequence day-month-year, which does not require commas.

> *traditional:* July 8, 1976, was a warm, sunny day in Philadel-
>   phia.
>   the explosion on July 16, 1945, at Alamogordo
> *military:* the explosion on 16 July 1945 at Alamogordo
>   the amendment ratified on 18 August 1920

7. Ordinal numbers are not used in full dates. Ordinals are sometimes used, however, for a date without an accom-

panying year, and they are always used when preceded in a date by the word *the.*

> December 4, 1829
> on December 4th *or* on December 4
> on the 4th of December

8. All-figure dating, such as 6-8-95 or 6/8/95, is usually avoided except in informal writing. For some readers, such dates are ambiguous; the examples above generally mean June 8, 1995, in the United States, but in almost all other countries mean August 6, 1995.

9. Commas are usually omitted from dates that include the month and year but not the day. The word *of* is sometimes inserted between the month and year.

> in October 1997
> back in January of 1981

10. References to specific centuries may be either written out or expressed in figures.

> in the nineteenth century *or* in the 19th century
> a sixteenth-century painting *or* a 16th-century painting

11. The name of a specific decade often takes a short form, usually with no apostrophe and uncapitalized. When the short form is part of a set phrase, it is capitalized.

> a song from the sixties
> *occasionally* a song from the 'sixties *or* a song from the
>   Sixties
> tunes of the Gay Nineties

The name of a decade is often expressed in numerals, in plural form. The figure may be shortened, with an apostrophe to indicate the missing numerals; however, apostrophes enclosing the figure are generally avoided. Any sequence of such numbers is generally styled consistently.

> the 1950s and 1960s *or* the '50s and '60s
>   *but not*
> the '50's and '60's
> the 1950s and '60s
> the 1950s and sixties

12. Era designations precede or follow words that specify centuries or numerals that specify years. Era designations are unspaced abbreviations, punctuated with periods. They are usually typed or keyboarded as regular capitals, and typeset in books as small capitals and in newspapers as full-size capitals. The abbreviation B.C. (before Christ) is placed after the date, while A.D. (*anno Domini,* "in the year of our Lord") is usually placed before the date but after a century designation. Any date given without an era designation or context is understood to mean A.D.

> 1792–1750 B.C.
> between 600 and 400 B.C.
> from the fifth or fourth millennium to c. 250 B.C.
> between 7 B.C. and A.D. 22
> c. A.D. 100 to 300
> the second century A.D.
> the 17th century

13. Less common era designations include A.H. (*anno Hegirae,* "in the year of [Muhammad's] Hegira," or *anno Hebraico,* "in the Hebrew year"); B.C.E. (before the com-

mon era; a synonym for B.C.); C.E. (of the common era; a synonym for A.D.); and B.P. (before the present; often used by geologists and archeologists, with or without the word *year*). The abbreviation A.H. is usually placed before a specific date but after a century designation, while B.C.E., C.E., and B.P., are placed after both a date and a century.

> the tenth of Muharram, A.H. 61 (October 10, A.D. 680)
> the first century A.H.
> from the 1st century B.C.E. to the 4th century C.E.
> 63 B.C.E.
> the year 200 C.E.
> 5,000 years B.P.
> two million years B.P.

Degrees of Temperature and Arc

14. In technical writing, a quantity expressed in degrees is generally written as a numeral followed by the degree symbol (°). In the Kelvin scale, neither the word *degree* nor the symbol is used with the figure.

> a 45° angle
> 6°40′10″N
> 32° F
> 0° C
> Absolute zero is zero kelvins or 0 K.

15. In general writing, the quantity expressed in degrees may or may not be written out. A figure may be followed by either the degree symbol or the word *degree;* a spelled-out number is always followed by the word *degree.*

> latitude 43°19″N
> latitude 43 degrees N
> a difference of 43 degrees latitude
> The temperature has risen about thirty degrees.

Fractions and Decimal Fractions

16. In nontechnical prose, fractions standing alone are usually written out. Common fractions used as nouns are usually unhyphenated, although the hyphenated form is also common. When fractions are used as modifiers, they are hyphenated.

> lost three quarters of its value   *or*   lost three-quarters of its value
> had a two-thirds chance of winning

Multiword numerators and denominators are usually hyphenated, or written as figures.

> one one-hundredth of an inch   *or*   1/100 of an inch

17. Mixed fractions (fractions with a whole number, such as 3½) and fractions that form part of a modifier are usually expressed in figures in running text.

> waiting 2½ hours
> a ⅞-mile course
> 2½-pound weights

Fractions that are not on the keyboard or available as special characters on a computer may be typed in full-sized digits; in mixed fractions, a space is left between the whole number and the fraction.

> a 7/8-mile course
> waiting 2 3/4 hours

18. Fractions used with units of measurement are usually expressed in figures, but common short words are often written out.

> ⅟₁₀ km   half a mile
> ⅓ oz.   a half-mile walk
> ⅞ inch   a sixteenth-inch gap

19. Decimal fractions are always set as figures. In technical writing, a zero is placed to the left of the decimal point when the fraction is less than a whole number; in general writing, the zero is usually omitted. Commas are not used in numbers following a decimal point.

> An example of a pure decimal fraction is 0.375, while 1.402 is classified as a mixed decimal fraction.
> a .22-caliber rifle
> 0.142857

20. Fractions and decimal fractions are usually not mixed in a text.

> weights of 5½ lbs., 3¼ lbs., and ½ oz.
> *or*   weights of 5.5 lbs., 3.25 lbs., and .5 oz.
> *not*   weights of 5.5 lbs., 3¼ lbs., and ½ oz.

Lists and Outlines

21. Both run-in and vertical lists are often numbered. In run-in numbered lists—that is, numbered lists that form part of a normal-looking sentence—each item is preceded by a number (or, less often, an italicized letter) enclosed in parentheses. The items are separated by commas if they are brief and unpunctuated; if they are complex or punctuated, they are separated by semicolons. The entire list is introduced by a colon if it is preceded by a full clause, and often when it is not.

> Among the fastest animals with measured maximum speeds are (1) the cheetah, clocked at 70 mph; (2) the pronghorn antelope, at 61 mph; (3) the lion, at 50 mph; (4) the quarter horse, at 47 mph; and (5) the elk, at 45 mph.
> The new medical dictionary has several special features: *(a)* common variant spellings; *(b)* examples of words used in context; *(c)* abbreviations, combining forms, prefixes, and suffixes; and *(d)* brand names for drugs and their generic equivalents.

22. In vertical lists, each number is followed by a period; the periods align vertically. Run-over lines usually align under the item's first word. Each item may be capitalized, especially if the items are syntactically independent of the words that introduce them.

> The English peerage consists of five ranks, listed here in descending order:
> 1. Duke (duchess)
> 2. Marquess (marchioness)
> 3. Earl (countess)
> 4. Viscount (viscountess)
> 5. Baron (baroness)

The listed items end with periods (or question marks) when they are complete sentences, and also often when they are not.

> We require answers to the following questions:
> 1. Does the club intend to engage heavy-metal bands to perform in the future?
> 2. Will any such bands be permitted to play past midnight on weekends?
> 3. Are there plans to install proper acoustic insulation?

Items that are syntactically dependent on the words that introduce them often begin with a lowercase letter and end with a comma or semicolon just as in a run-in series in an ordinary sentence.

> Among the courts that are limited to special kinds of cases are
>
> 1. probate courts, for the estates of deceased persons;
> 2. commercial courts, for business cases;
> 3. juvenile courts, for cases involving children under 18; and
> 4. traffic courts, for minor cases involving highway and motor vehicle violations.

A vertical list may also be unnumbered, or may use bullets (•) in place of numerals, especially where the order of the items is not important.

> Chief among the important advances in communication were these 19th-century inventions:
> Morse's telegraph
> Daguerre's camera
> Bell's telephone
> Edison's phonograph
> This book covers in detail:
> • Punctuation
> • Capitalization and italicization
> • Numbers
> • Abbreviations
> • Grammar and composition

23. Outlines standardly use Roman numerals, capitalized letters, Arabic numerals, and lowercase letters, in that order. Each numeral or letter is followed by a period, and each item is capitalized.

> III. The United States from 1816 to 1850
>   A. Era of mixed feelings
>   1. Effects of the War of 1812
>   2. National disunity
>   B. The economy
>   1. Transportation revolution
>   a. Waterways
>   b. Railroads
>   2. Beginnings of industrialization
> IV. The Civil War and Reconstruction, 1850–77

Money

24. A sum of money that can be expressed in one or two words is usually written out in running text, as is the unit of currency. But if several sums are mentioned in the sentence or paragraph, all are usually expressed as figures and are used with the unspaced currency symbol.

> The scalpers were asking eighty dollars.
> Grandfather remembered the days of the five-cent cigar.
> The shoes on sale are priced at $69 and $89.
> Jill wanted to sell the lemonade for 25¢, 35¢, and 45¢.

25. Monetary units of mixed dollars-and-cents amounts are expressed in figures.

> $16.75
> $307.02

26. Even-dollar amounts are often expressed in figures without a decimal point and zeros. But when even-dollar amounts appear near amounts that include cents, the decimal point and zeros are usually added for consis-

tency. The dollar sign is repeated before each amount in a series or inclusive range.

> They paid $500 for the watercolor.
> The price had risen from $8.00 to $9.95.
> bids of $80, $90, and $100
> in the $80–$100 range

27. Sums of money in the millions or above rounded to no more than one decimal place are usually expressed in a combination of figures and words.

> a $10-million building program
> $4.5 billion

28. In legal documents a sum of money is usually written out fully, often capitalized, with the corresponding figures in parentheses immediately following.

> Twenty-five Thousand Dollars ($25,000)

Organizations and Governmental Entities

29. Ordinal numbers in the names of religious organizations and churches are usually written out.

> Seventh-Day Adventists
> Third Congregational Church

30. Local branches of labor unions and fraternal organizations are generally identified by a numeral, usually placed after the name.

> Motion Picture Studio Mechanics Local 476
> Loyal Order of Moose No. 220
> Local 4277 Communications Workers of America

31. In names of governmental bodies and electoral, judicial, and military units, ordinal numbers of one hundred or below are usually written out but often not.

> Second Continental Congress
> Fifth Republic
> First Congressional District
> Court of Appeals for the Third Circuit
> U.S. Eighth Army
> Twelfth Precinct *or* 12th Precinct
> Ninety-eighth Congress *or* 98th Congress

Percentages

32. In technical writing, and often in business and financial writing, percentages are written as a figure followed by an unspaced % symbol. In general writing, the word *percent* normally replaces the symbol, and the number may either be written out (if it does not include a decimal) or expressed as a figure.

> *technical:* 15%
> 13.5%
> *general:* 15 percent
> 87.2 percent
> Fifteen percent of the applicants were accepted.
> a four percent increase *or* a 4% increase

33. In a series or range, the percent sign is usually included with all numbers, even if one of the numbers is zero.

> rates of 8.3%, 8.8%, and 9.1%
> a variation of 0% to 10% *or* a 0%–10% variation

Plurals

34. The plurals of written-out numbers, including fractions, are formed by adding *-s* or *-es*.

> at sixes and sevens
> divided into eighths
> ever since the thirties
> still in her thirties

35. The plurals of figures are formed by adding *-s* or less commonly *-'s*, especially where the apostrophe can prevent a confusing typographic appearance.

> in the '80s
> since the 1980s [*or less commonly* 1980's]
> temperatures in the 80s and 90s [*or* 80's and 90's]
> the *1*'s looked like *l*'s

Ratios

36. Ratios are generally expressed in figures, usually with the word *to;* in technical writing the figures may be joined by a colon or a slash instead. Ratios expressed in words use a hyphen (or en dash) or the word *to.*

> odds of 10 to 1
> a proportion of 1 to 4
> a 3:1 ratio
> 29 mi/gal
> a fifty-fifty chance
> a ratio of ten to four

Time of Day

37. In running text, the time of day is usually spelled out when expressed in even, half, or quarter hours or when it is followed by *o'clock.*

> around four-thirty
> arriving by ten
> planned to leave at half past five
> now almost a quarter to two
> arrived at nine o'clock

38. Figures are generally used when specifying a precise time.

> an appointment at 9:30 tomorrow morning
> buses at 8:42, 9:12, and 10:03 a.m.

39. Figures are also used when the time of day is followed by *a.m.* and *p.m.* These are usually written as punctuated lowercase letters, sometimes as small capital letters. They are not used with *o'clock* or with other words that specify the time of day.

> 8:30 a.m. *or* 8:30 A.M.
> 10:30 p.m. *or* 10:30 P.M.
> 8 a.m. *or* 8 A.M.
> home by nine o'clock
> 9:15 in the morning
> eleven in the evening

With *twelve o'clock* or 12:00, it is helpful to specify *midnight* or *noon* rather than the ambiguous *a.m.* or *p.m.*

> The third shift begins at 12:00 (midnight).

40. Even-hour times are generally written with a colon and two zeros when used in a series or pairing with any times not ending in two zeros.

> started at 9:15 a.m. and finished at 2:00 p.m.
> worked from 8:30 to 5:00

41. The 24-hour clock system—also called *military time*—uses no punctuation and omits *o'clock, a.m., p.m.,* or any other additional indication of the time of day. The word *hours* sometimes replaces them.

> from 0930 to 1100
> at 1600 hours

Units of Measurement

42. In technical writing, all numbers used with units of measurement are written as numerals. In nontechnical writing, such numbers often simply follow the basic conventions explained on page 215; alternatively, even in nontechnical contexts all such numbers often appear as numerals.

> In the control group, only 8 of the 90 plants were affected.
> picked nine quarts of berries
> chugging along at 9 [*or* nine] miles an hour
> a pumpkin 5 [*or* five] feet in diameter
> weighing 7 pounds 9 ounces
> a journey of 3 hours and 45 minutes

The singular form of units of measurement is used in a modifier before a noun, the plural form in a modifier that follows a noun.

> a 2- by 9-inch board *or* a two-inch by nine-inch board *or*
>   a two- by nine-inch board
> measured 2 inches by 9 inches *or* measured two inches by
>   nine inches
> a 6-foot 2-inch man
> is 6 feet 2 inches tall *or* is six feet two inches tall
> is six feet two *or* is 6 feet 2

43. When units of measurement are written as abbreviations or symbols, the adjacent numbers are always figures. (For abbreviations with numerals, see the section on page 214.)

> 6 cm   67.6 fl. oz.
> 1 mm   4'
> $4.25   98.6°

44. When two or more quantities are expressed, as in ranges or dimensions or series, an accompanying symbol is usually repeated with each figure.

> 4" × 6" cards
> temperatures of 30°, 55°, 43°, and 58°
> $450–$500 suits

Other Uses

45. Figures are generally used for precise ages in newspapers and magazines, and often in books as well.

> Taking the helm is Colin Corman, 51, a risk-taking high
>   roller.
> At 9 [*or* nine] she mastered the Mendelssohn Violin Concerto.
> the champion 3[*or* three]-year-old filly
> for anyone aged 62 and over

46. Figures are used to refer to parts of a book, such as volume, chapter, illustration, and table numbers.

vol. 5, p. 202
Chapter 8 *or* Chapter Eight
Fig. 4

47. Serial, policy, and contract numbers use figures. (For punctuation of these numbers, see paragraph 3 on page 216.)

Serial No. 5274
Permit No. 63709

48. Figures are used to express stock-market quotations, mathematical calculations, scores, and tabulations.

Industrials were up 4.23.
$3 \times 15 = 45$
a score of 8 to 2 *or* a score of 8–2
the tally: 322 ayes, 80 nays

6 Notes and Bibliographies

Writers and editors use various methods to indicate the source of a quotation or piece of information borrowed from another work.

In high-school papers and in popular writing, sources are usually identified only by casual mentions within the text itself.

In college term papers, in serious nonfiction books published for the general public, and traditionally in scholarly books and articles in the humanities, footnotes or endnotes are preferred. In this system, sequential numbers within the text refer the reader to notes at the bottom of the page or at the end of the article, chapter, or book; these notes contain full bibliographic information on the works cited.

In scholarly works in the natural sciences, and increasingly in the social sciences and humanities as well, parenthetical references within the text refer the reader to an alphabetically arranged list of references at the end of the article, chapter, or book.

The system of footnotes or endnotes is the more flexible, since it allows for commentary on the work or subject and can also be used for brief discussions not tied to any specific work. However, style manuals tend to encourage the use of parenthetical references in addition to or instead of footnotes or endnotes, since for most kinds of material they are efficient and convenient for both writer and reader.

In a carefully documented work, an alphabetically ordered bibliography or list of references normally follows the entire text (including any endnotes), regardless of which system is used.

Though different publishers and journals have adopted slightly varying styles, the following examples illustrate standard styles for footnotes and endnotes, parenthetical references, and bibliographic entries. For more extensive treatment than can be provided here, consult *Merriam-Webster's Standard American Style Manual; The Chicago Manual of Style; The MLA Handbook for Writers of Research Papers; A Manual for Writers of Term Papers, Theses and Dissertations;* or *Scientific Style and Format.*

Footnotes and Endnotes

Footnotes and endnotes are usually indicated by superscript numbers placed immediately after the material to be documented, whether it is an actual quotation or a paraphrase of the language used in the source. The number is placed at the end of a paragraph, sentence or clause, or at some other natural break in the sentence; it follows all marks of punctuation except the dash.

> As one observer noted, "There was, moreover, a degree of logic in the new LDP-SDPJ axis, in that the inner cores of both parties felt threatened by the recent electoral reform legislation,"[7] and . . .

The numbering is consecutive throughout a paper, article, or monograph; in a book, it usually starts over with each new chapter.

The note itself begins with the corresponding number. Footnotes appear at the bottom of the page; endnotes, which take exactly the same form as footnotes, are gathered at the end of the article, chapter, or book.

Endnotes are generally preferred over footnotes by writers and publishers because they are easier to handle when preparing both manuscript and printed pages, though they can be less convenient for the reader.

Both footnotes and endnotes provide full bibliographic information for a source the first time it is cited. In subsequent references, this information is shortened to the author's last name and the page number. If more than one book by an author is cited, a shortened form of the title is also included. The Latin abbreviation *ibid.* is sometimes used to refer to the book cited in the immediately preceding note.

The following examples describe specific elements of first references and reflect humanities citation style; notes 12–14 show examples of subsequent references. All of the cited works appear again in the Bibliographies and Lists of References section beginning on page 224.

Books

The basic elements for book citations are (1) the author's name; (2) the book's title; (3) the place of publication, publisher, and date of publication; and (4) the page(s) where the information appears.

One author:
1. Elizabeth Bishop, *The Complete Poems: 1927–1979* (New York: Farrar, Straus & Giroux, 1983), 46.

Two or three authors:
2. Bert Hölldobler and Edward O. Wilson, *The Ants* (Cambridge, Mass.: Belknap–Harvard Univ. Press, 1990), 119.

3. Charles T. Brusaw, Gerald J. Alred, and Walter E. Oliu, *The Business Writer's Handbook,* 4th rev. ed. (New York: St. Martin's, 1993), 182–84.

Four or more authors:
4. Randolph Quirk et al., *A Comprehensive Grammar of the English Language* (London: Longman, 1985), 135.

Corporate author:
5. Commission on the Humanities, *The Humanities in American Life* (Berkeley: Univ. of California Press, 1980), 58.

No author:
6. *Information Please Almanac: 1996* (Boston: Houghton Mifflin, 1995), 324.

Editor and/or translator:
7. Arthur S. Banks, ed., *Political Handbook of the World: 1994–1995* (Binghamton, N.Y.: CSA Publications, 1995), 293–95.

8. Simone de Beauvoir, *The Second Sex,* trans. and ed. H. M. Parshley (New York: Knopf, 1953; Vintage, 1989), 446.

Part of a book:
9. Ernst Mayr, "Processes of Speciation in Animals," *Mechanisms of Speciation,* ed. C. Barigozzi (New York: Alan R. Liss, 1982), 1–3.

Second or later edition:
10. Albert C. Baugh and Thomas Cable, *A History of the English Language,* 4th ed. (Englewood Cliffs, N.J.: Prentice Hall, 1992), 14.

Two or more volumes:
11. Ronald M. Nowak, *Walker's Mammals of the World,* 5th ed., 2 vols. (Baltimore: Johns Hopkins Univ. Press, 1991), 2: 661.

In subsequent references:
12. Nowak, 662.
13. Baugh and Cable, *History,* 18–19.
14. Ibid., 23.

Articles

The basic elements for citations of articles are (1) the author's name, (2) the article's title, (3) the name of the periodical, with information identifying the issue (following the form the periodical itself uses), and (4) the page(s) referred to.

Weekly magazine:
15. Richard Preston, "A Reporter at Large: Crisis in the Hot Zone," *New Yorker,* Oct. 26, 1992: 58.

Monthly magazine:
16. John Lukacs, "The End of the Twentieth Century," *Harper's,* Jan. 1993: 40.

Journal paginated by issue:
17. Roseann Duenas Gonzalez, "Teaching Mexican American Students to Write: Capitalizing on the Culture," *English Journal* 71, no. 7 (Nov. 1982): 22–24.

Journal paginated by volume:
18. Stephen Jay Gould and Niles Eldredge, "Punctuated Equilibria: The Tempo and Mode of Evolution Reconsidered," *Paleobiology* 3 (1977): 121.

Newspaper:
19. William J. Broad, "Big Science Squeezes Small-Scale Researchers," *New York Times,* Dec. 29, 1992: C1.

Signed review:
20. Gordon Craig, review of *The Wages of Guilt: Memories of War in Germany and Japan,* by Ian Buruma, *New York Review of Books,* July 14, 1994: 43–45.

In subsequent reference:
21. Gonzalez, 23.

Parenthetical References

Parenthetical references are highly abbreviated bibliographic citations that appear within the text itself, enclosed in parentheses. These direct the reader to a detailed bibliography or list of references at the end of the work, often removing the need for footnotes or endnotes.

A parenthetical reference, like a footnote or endnote number, is placed immediately after the quotation or piece of information whose source it refers to; punctuation not associated with a quotation follows the reference.

> As one observer noted, "There was, moreover, a degree of logic in the new LDP-SDPJ axis, in that the inner cores of both parties felt threatened by the recent electoral reform legislation" (Banks, 448), and . . .

Any element of a reference that is clear from the context of the running text may be omitted.

> As noted in Banks, "There was, moreover, a degree of logic in the new LDP-SDPJ axis, in that the inner cores of both parties felt threatened by the recent electoral reform legislation" (448), and . . .

Parenthetical references in the humanities usually include only the author's (or editor's) last name and a page reference (see extract above). This style is known as the *author-page system.*

In the sciences, the year of publication is included after the author's name with no intervening punctuation, and the page number is usually omitted. This scientific style is commonly called the *author-date system.*

> As some researchers noted, "New morphological, biochemical, and karyological studies suggest that *P. boylii* actually comprises several distinct species" (Nowak 1991), and . . .

To distinguish among cited works by the same author, the author's name may be followed by the specific work's title, which is usually shortened. (If the author-date system is being used, a lowercase letter can be added after the year—e.g., 1992a, 1992b—to distinguish between works published in the same year.)

Each of the following references is keyed to an entry in the bibliographic listings in the following section.

Humanities style:
(Banks, 448)
(Quirk et al., 135)
(Baugh and Cable, *History,* 14)
(Comm. on the Humanities, 58)

Sciences style:
(Gould and Eldredge 1977)
(Nowak 1991a)

Bibliographies and Lists of References

A *bibliography* lists all of the works that a writer has found relevant in writing the text. A *list of references* includes only works specifically mentioned in the text or from which a particular quotation or piece of information was taken. In all other respects, the two listings are identical.

Bibliographies and lists of references both differ from bibliographic endnotes in that their entries are unnumbered, are arranged in alphabetical order by author, and use different patterns of indention and punctuation. Entries for periodical articles also list their inclusive page numbers. The following lists illustrate standard styles employed in, respectively, the humanities and social sciences and the natural sciences.

The principal differences between the two styles are these: In the sciences, (1) an initial is generally used instead of the author's first name, (2) the date is placed directly after the author's name, (3) all words in titles are lowercased except the first word, the first word of any subtitle, and proper nouns and adjectives, and (4) article titles are not enclosed in quotation marks. Increasingly in scientific publications, (5) the author's first and middle initials are closed up without any punctuation, and (6) book and journal titles are not italicized. The following bibliographic lists include both books and periodical articles.

Humanities style

Banks, Arthur S., ed. *Political Handbook of the World: 1994–1995.* Binghamton, N.Y.: CSA Publications, 1995.

Baugh, Albert C., and Thomas Cable. *A History of the English Language.* 4th ed. Englewood Cliffs, N.J.: Prentice Hall, 1992.

Beauvoir, Simone de. *The Second Sex.* Trans. and ed. H. M. Parshley. New York: Alfred A. Knopf, 1953; Vintage, 1989.

Bishop, Elizabeth. *The Complete Poems: 1927–1979.* New York: Farrar, Straus & Giroux, 1983.

Brusaw, Charles T., Gerald J. Alred, and Walter E. Oliu. *The Business Writer's Handbook.* 4th rev. ed. New York: St. Martin's, 1993.

Commission on the Humanities. *The Humanities in American Life.* Berkeley: University of California Press, 1980.

Craig, Gordon. Review of *The Wages of Guilt: Memories of War in Germany and Japan,* by Ian Buruma. *New York Review of Books,* July 14, 1994: 43–45.

Gonzalez, Roseann Duenas. "Teaching Mexican American Students to Write: Capitalizing on the Culture." *English Journal* 71, no. 7 (November 1982): 22–24.

Information Please Almanac: 1996. Boston: Houghton Mifflin, 1995.

Lukacs, John. "The End of the Twentieth Century." *Harper's,* January 1993: 39–58.

Quirk, Randolph, Sidney Greenbaum, Geoffrey Leech, and Jan Svartvik. *A Comprehensive Grammar of the English Language.* London: Longman, 1985.

Sciences style

Broad, W. J. 1992. Big science squeezes small-scale researchers. *New York Times,* 29 Dec.:C1.

Gould, S. J., and N. Eldredge. 1977. Punctuated equilibria: The tempo and mode of evolution reconsidered. *Paleobiology* 3:115–51.

Hölldobler, B., and E. O. Wilson. 1990. *The ants.* Cambridge, Mass.: Belknap–Harvard Univ. Press.

Mayr, E. 1982. Processes of speciation in animals. *Mechanisms of speciation.* Ed. C. Barigozzi. New York: Alan R. Liss.

Nowak, R. M. 1991. *Walker's mammals of the world.* 5th ed. 2 vols. Baltimore: Johns Hopkins Univ. Press.

Preston, R. 1992. A reporter at large: Crisis in the hot zone. *New Yorker,* 26 Oct.:58–81.

Special Cases

Lists of references frequently contain items that do not fit neatly into any of the categories described above. Some are printed items such as government publications, others are nonprint items. These special references are styled in formats similar to those used for books and articles.

Television and radio programs

Burns, Ken. *Baseball.* PBS. WGBY-TV, Springfield, Mass. 28 Sept. 1994.

Computer software

World Atlas. CD-ROM. Novato, Calif.: Software Toolworks, 1990.

Microform

"Marine Mammals; Permit Modification: Naval Facilities Engineering Commission (P8D)." *Federal Register* 55.1:90. Washington: CIS, 1990. Microfiche.

Government publications

United States. Department of Labor. Employment and Training Administration. *Dictionary of Occupational Titles.* Rev. 4th ed. Washington: GPO, 1991.

U.S. Congress. Senate. Subcommittee on Administrative Law and Government Relations of the Committee on the Judiciary. *Hearings on Post-Employment Restrictions for Federal Officers and Employees.* 101st Cong., 1st sess. 27 Apr. 1989. H.R. 2267.

Congressional Record. 29 June 1993: S8269–70.

Personal interview

Norris, Nancy Preston. Conversation with author. Wilkes-Barre, Pa., 10 October 1995.

Christian, Dr. Lionel. Telephone conversation with author, 2 January 1996.

7. Editing and Proofreading

Basic editing, called *copyediting,* primarily requires checking a manuscript for grammar, spelling, punctuation, stylistic consistency, and factual accuracy, and may also involve editing or even rewriting entire sentences and paragraphs. The example on this page shows how a manuscript page is copyedited.

The term *proofreading* means literally the reading and checking of *proofs* (copies of newly typeset material—that is, material set in type by a typesetter or compositor) against the original manuscript. But *proofreading* is generally used today to mean the final checking of *any* written material.

The principal difference in marking between copyediting and proofreading is that in formal proofreading (that is, when checking typeset proofs) each error must be marked both where it occurs and in the margin immediately to the left or right. Whereas manuscript for copyediting is normally double-spaced, lines of typeset material are usually set close together, so only small marks can be made within the text. Thus, the margins provide room for larger marks and the insertion of omitted material; just as important, marginal notations make the corrections more visible so that the typesetter will not overlook them.

The table of proofreaders' marks and the example of a proofread page on the following pages illustrate the proofreading process. Most of the proofreaders' marks can be used equally for copyediting and for proofreading.

A Copyedited Page

A copyeditor must have an easy familiarity with the conventions of the English language, a fairly wide general knowledge, the ability to use reference books, and a knowledge of the basics of book production, including typography. Familiarity with house style is also required. In addition, the editor must be able to read extremely closely, noticing details, and remembering them so thoroughly that he or she will spot the smallest inconsistency. A copyeditor must also learn the conventional symbols used to mark up a manuscript, as able to write precise and unambiguous instructions to the compositor.

Copyediting involves not only reading the copy carefully and making needed revisions, but also making those revisions in such a way as to make them unambiguous to the typesetter. When revisions are required, the editor must be able to make them with an eye to how they fit with the rest of the copy.

Does the copyeditor rewrite copy? Not unless specifically instructed to do so. Senior editors, with authority from the publisher or author, often rewrite or reorganize the material to better achieve the author's purpose, or they suggest these revisions to the author. However, most copyeditors have to resist the temptation to rewrite a manuscript in their own style. Their first duty is to the author. Revisions are made only to correct factual or stylistic errors, to make the author's meaning clearer, or to make the material consistent.

Proofreaders' Marks

℞ or ߁ or ⌐ delete; take it out

⌒ close up; print as one word

⌒℞ delete and close up

∧ or ⟩ or ⅄ caret; insert here ⟨something⟩

insert a space

eq# space evenly where indicated

stet let marked text stand as set

tr transpose; change order the

⌐ ⌐ set farther to the left

⌐ set farther to the right

= straighten alignment

‖ ‖ straighten or align

✗ imperfect or broken character

□ indent or insert em quad space

¶ begin a new paragraph

⟨sp⟩ spell out ⟨set 5 lbs. as five pounds⟩

cap set in capitals ⟨CAPITALS⟩

sm cap or s.c. set in small capitals ⟨SMALL CAPITALS⟩

lc set in lowercase ⟨lowercase⟩

ital set in italic ⟨*italic*⟩

rom set in roman ⟨roman⟩

bf set in boldface ⟨**boldface**⟩

= or -/ or ⌣ or /H/ hyphen

$\frac{1}{N}$ or en or /N/ en dash ⟨1965–72⟩

$\frac{1}{M}$ or em or /M/ em — or long — dash

∨ superscript or superior ⟨as in πr^2⟩

∧ subscript or inferior ⟨as in H_2O⟩

∧ or ∨ centered ⟨for a centered dot in $p \cdot q$⟩

˅ comma   : or ⊙ colon

˅ apostrophe   ˅˅ or ˅˅ quotation marks

⊙ period   (/) parentheses

; or ;/ semicolon   [/] brackets

A Proofread Page

bf/ /cap
(stet)
special
(#)/^
s
c
o/(lc)
quickly
=

The Proofreaders task

The job of the proofreader is narrower but ~~even~~ more exacting then that
of the copyeditor.   It requires habits of mind, which can only be
acquired by concentration and practice. whereas normal readers tend
to read phrase by phrase, proofreaders must focus sharply on each
separate word and frequently on each separate character. In fact,
proofreaders must learn to read much the way a computer reads. They
must retrain any tendency to be lulled by the ~~the~~ rhythm of the prose
or to become involved in the subject matter. The proofreader who is
learning from the manuscript as he or she reads is probably not doing
a careful job. Proofreading may thus be even more of a strain on the
mind than on the eyes. Yet professional proofreaders can work for 8
hours a day without tiring or losing their concentration. Proofreading
cannot be done, except by unusually gifted people; as a result,
impatient personalities can find it frustrating and sometimes
maddening. But it remains an important in fact, essential duty. For
technical material it can be all important; for non technical material it
can mean the difference between a document that is sloppy and even
incomprehensible and one that is accurate and elegant.

a
(cap)
s
(sp)
1/m /1/m
2/ /t
(tr)